ABNORMAL PSYCHOLOGY

David L. Rosenhan
STANFORD UNIVERSITY

Martin E. P. Seligman
UNIVERSITY OF PENNSYLVANIA

ABNORMAL
PSYCHOLOGY

W. W. NORTON AND COMPANY
New York   London

Printed in the United States of America
Published simultaneously in Canada by George J. McLeod Limited, Toronto.
All rights reserved
First Edition

Library of Congress Cataloging in Publication Data

Rosenhan, David L.
  Abnormal psychology.

  Includes index.
  1. Psychology, Pathological.   2. Psychotherapy.
I. Seligman, Martin E. P.   II. Title.
RC454.R578   1984   616.89   83–25523
ISBN 0-393-95277-0

The text of this book is composed in Times Roman, with display type set in Times Roman.
Composition by New England Typographic Service, Inc.
Manufacturing by The Murray Printing Company.
Book design by Nancy Dale Muldoon.

Cover illustration: *The Anxious Journey,* by Giorgio di Chirico. Collection, The Museum of Modern Art, New York. Acquired through the Lillie P. Bliss bequest.

Acknowledgments and copyrights appear on pages 727–728, which constitute a continuation of the copyright page.

W. W. Norton & Company, Inc., 500 Fifth Avenue, New York, N.Y. 10110
W. W. Norton & Company Ltd., 37 Great Russell Street, London WC1B 3NU

1 2 3 4 5 6 7 8 9 0

For our children

Nina and Jack Rosenhan
Amy and David Seligman

Contents in Brief

Contents

PART II   Approaches to Abnormality

Preface

This book is written for the basic undergraduate course in abnormal psychology. But it was conceived in, of all places, a mental hospital. One of us, David Rosenhan, was engaged in a study in which a diverse group of "normal" people went into mental hospitals pretending to have a single symptom: they heard voices that said "empty," "meaningless," and "thud." From the start, these "pseudopatients" were labeled as "crazy" and treated as such. Martin Seligman had heard about the study and wrote Rosenhan to express his admiration for the courage it involved. To his surprise, Seligman received a phone call several days later inviting him to enter a hospital with Rosenhan. So it came about that in October 1973 both of us assumed false names and wound up in the locked men's ward of a state mental hospital.

There are few better places for two psychologists to become fast friends than in such trenches. In the hours and days that followed, discussions ranged over an enormous variety of topics: how we and our fellow patients were being treated; our personal and academic lives; and then such issues as the legal rights of mental patients, how to choose a therapist, the dehumanizing effects of labeling, the diagnosis of schizophrenia (more often, its misdiagnosis), depression and suicide, and finally teaching itself—how the experience of psychopathology, of hospitalization, of therapy, of diagnosis, and the range of psychological miseries, could be communicated to students. We left the hospital good friends, and with the hope that we might some day attempt to do something to improve the teaching of abnormal psychology.

This book is the result of more than ten years of collaboration, research, clinical experience, delving into a vast literature, writing—and teaching abnormal psychology to undergraduates.

In the last twenty years, the progress that has been made in understanding and treating psychological disorders has been simply extraordinary. Disorders that were once wholly mysterious and untreatable, like the schizophrenias, depression, the anxiety disorders, the sexual dysfunctions, can now be treated, often with considerable success. They are no longer shrouded in mystery. Our new text reflects this progress.

What is remarkable about the recent advances in the field is the variety of keys that unlock each of the disorders. For example, the greatest strides made in understanding schizophrenia have been biological and social. In contrast, the most important progress in the treatment and understanding of phobias and the sexual disorders have been behavioral. Similarly, depression has been treated most usefully by combining cognitive and pharmacological therapies. Hysteria, on the other hand, is still best understood by psychodynamic thinking. In order to make these advances clear, our text describes in detail and sympathetically the major modern approaches to psychopathology: biomedical, psychoanalytic, behavioral, cognitive, and humanistic. An entire chapter is devoted to each. In spite of the fact that each of these schools has attempted to explain virtually everything, none of the approaches works for everything, or even almost everything. Rather, each of the schools has a natural home in the one or two disorders that they illuminate and treat best.

Textbooks in abnormal psychology are of two varieties. One variety is *biased* toward a particular school of thought or model. In such books, disorders are uniformly presented from a behavioral, or from a psychodynamic framework. These textbooks lose the richness of understanding that comes from viewing etiology from a variety of promising perspectives. The other variety is the uncritical, encyclopedic textbook. These books present all models for all disorders. But they take no stand. The first kind of textbook says there is only one winner, and only one group shall have the prize; the second kind of textbook says everyone is a winner, and all shall have the prize, without ever questioning this obvious contradiction. In contrast, our text attempts to say which therapies and what schools of thought best fit each disorder, and why. We have tried to provide a new integrative view of the field which, without being superficial, is at once sympathetic and critical of each major school of thought. Moreover, we had the advantage of writing our text just as the Diagnostic and Statistical Manual of the American Psychiatric Association (DSM-III) was being revised. Our text reflects the changes and the new terminology in DSM-III. But here as well, we went beyond mere description of the DSM-III classifications. Since we believe that students should develop a critical perspective, our presentation of DSM-III is a critical one.

In writing *Abnormal Psychology,* we have tried to include the many new developments in the field. For example, we take up new material on the biological basis of phobias (Chapter 10); psychological states and physical illness (Chapter 12); attribution and depression (Chapter 13); a fully integrative approach to unipolar depression (Chapter 13); genetic, biochemical, and psychosocial insights into schizophrenia (Chapter 17); and the modern approach to organic disorders (Chapter 19); in addition, there are full chapters on abnormality and the law (Chapter 20) and on how to find psychological help (Chapter 21).

We have tried to keep in mind that this text is for undergraduates, not professionals. To facilitate understanding of each disorder, we present the symptoms of the disorder, its possible causes, and its preferred treatment in the particular chapter in which we discuss the disorder. Thus, we have avoided collecting all the therapies together and sticking them at the end of the text, apart from the disorders. Also, we have illustrated each of the major disorders with clinical cases. This has been done, not by tacking on a case at the end of the discussion of a disorder, but by integrating the clinical case with the presentation of the disorder itself so that students can see what does and does not illustrate a particular disorder. We have provided definitions for all terms, disorders, and therapies. There is a glossary of essential terms at the end of the text and review summaries at the end of all chapters. There are numerous photographs throughout the text. Our hope is that these photographs illustrate points made in the text, rather than presenting a fun-house of horrors at the expense of the individual sufferer.

This brings us to a final point. Some textbooks on psychopathology are committed to a single-minded and "scientific" approach: they present field research, epidemiological studies, outcome studies, and experiments that are relevant to each of the major disorders—but they overlook the human aspect of these disorders. Other textbooks present sensitive case histories, good therapeutic dialogues, and good portraits of real people. But too often, they fail to recognize the scientific advances in the psychopathologies they treat so humanely. In this book, we have attempted to blend the rigor of science and the warmth of the therapeutic endeavor. We hope we have succeeded.

THE PLAN OF THE BOOK

This book is designed to be used in a one-semester or one-quarter basic undergraduate course in abnormal psychology. The definitions, history, and major schools of thought of abnormality are presented first. Then, each of the major disorders—their description, their causes, and their treatments—is laid out in light of the competing schools of thought.

The book opens with two chapters on abnormality across time and place (Part I). In Chapter 1, the notion of abnormality is defined. We argue that there is no one element that all cases of abnormality have; rather several important elements combine to yield the judgment of abnormality. Chapter 2 examines how the view of madness had changed across history and across cultures. It emphasizes a notion that is now considered "common sense"—that the origins of madness may be either physical or psychological—a view that was not accepted until the twentieth century.

Part II describes the prominent schools of thought and their approaches to abnormality. Chapter 3, the biomedical model, looks at abnormality as a disease of the body. It examines the role of germs, of genes, and of biochemistry in the production of abnormality. Chapter 4 turns to the psychoanalytic model of abnormality, concentrating on the towering work of Sigmund Freud, as well as on more modern views of psychoanalysis. Chapter 5 examines the behavioral school of thought, emphasizing the role of classical conditioning and of instrumental learning as potential causes and treatments of abnormality. All of Chapter 6 is devoted to the newest school of thought on abnormality, the cognitive school, which holds that psychological abnormality is produced by disordered thinking, and that changing disordered thinking produces cure. Finally, Chapter 7 describes the humanistic approach to abnormality as an outcome of the failure to grow, the failure to find meaning, and the failure to be responsible for oneself and others.

Having outlined the major schools of thought of abnormality, Part III turns to how abnormality is investigated and how it is diagnosed. Chapter 8 investigates the role of different methods of assessment for illuminating the cause and cure of abnormality. Case histories, laboratory experiments, correlational studies, experiments of nature, and experimental models are all examined and compared. We conclude that each method contributes to our knowledge of abnormality, and we describe how they do so. This section ends with Chapter 9, which discusses the diagnosis and assessment of abnormality. DSM-III is fully described and evaluated, and part of it is reprinted as an appendix at the end of the book. Varieties of psychological tests, which help to diagnose abnormality, are examined.

In Part IV, which covers anxiety and the psychosomatic disorders, we provide a detailed examination of psychopathology. The three chapters on anxiety and psychosomatic disorders are organized around the degree to which anxiety is apparent in the disorder itself. Chapter 10 discusses those anxiety disorders in which the sufferer actually feels fear and anxiety: phobia, post-traumatic stress disorder, panic disorder, and generalized anxiety disorder. Chapter 11 turns to those disorders in which the existence of anxiety is inferred rather than apparent: obsessive-compulsive disorders, hysterical conversion (now called a somatoform disorder), dissociative disorders, and multiple personality. Chapter 12 looks at the psychosomatic disorders, those disorders in which physical illness is influenced, and in the strongest case, caused by psychological factors. We examine in detail psychosomatic principles and illustrate these principles through discussing the disorders of stomach ulcers, hypertension, and sudden death.

Part V turns to the major depressive disorders. Chapter 13 deals with depression and suicide. It describes the symptoms of depression, the distinguishing features of manic-depressive disorder and unipolar depression, and it provides a description of the four major competing theories and therapies of depression. We propose an integrative theory of depression, and then discuss the most tragic consequence of depression, suicide.

In Part VI, we look at social and interpersonal disorders. Chapter 14, on sexual disorders, begins with an examination of human sexuality. We first examine sexual function and dysfunction. We then look at sexual order and disorder, examining the paraphilias and then transsexuality. Finally, we present an integrative theory of the origin of sexual disorders. In Chapter 15, we examine drug use and abuse, and discuss the prevalence of drug use in the United States today, as well as the basic principles of pharmacology. We then look at each of the major classes of abused drugs, including cocaine and the amphetamines, the barbiturates, marijuana, the opiates, and alcohol. We conclude the chapter with an evaluation of the effectiveness of treatment programs for drug abuse. In Chapter 16, we discuss the personality disorders, that is, disorders in which a person's entire character structure presents a problem for the individual or for society. We focus particularly on the antisocial personality disorder.

Part VII is devoted to the psychoses. In Chapter 17, we describe schizophrenia and its symptoms, illustrating the disorder with rich case history material. We conclude the section with an evaluation of competing psychological, biochemical, and societal theories of schizophrenia and a discussion of the prospects for treatment and rehabilitation of people with this devastating disorder.

In Part VIII, we take up abnormality through the lifespan. In Chapter 18, we look at the disorders of childhood. In many respects, children and adults suffer similar problems: fears, phobias, eating disorders, and the like. But in Chapter 19, we concentrate on those disorders—especially the disorders of the nervous system—which tend to afflict older people. We differentiate here between psychological problems and neurological problems, and we describe assessment techniques by which neurological damage is detected. Finally, we examine the major disorders of the nervous system, including the aphasias, Alzheimer's disease (the disorder of senility), and amnesia.

The final section of the book—Part IX—considers the legal issues related to psychological abnormality, and the issues associated with choosing a psychotherapy. In Chapter 20, we look at society's institutionalized reaction to abnormality and our laws about commitment—voluntary versus involuntary commitment. We then examine the insanity defense and ask: When, if ever, is insanity an excuse for a criminal action? In the final chapter, Chapter 21, we ask, "How can one use the information in this book to best choose an appropriate psychotherapy?" We review the specificity of different schools of thought and their therapies for different disorders. We make suggestions about what therapies are apt to be most effective for what particular disorders. We then examine the general characteristics of psychotherapists and psychotherapy, which enable individuals to grow.

ACKNOWLEDGMENTS

Over the years of writing this textbook, we have accumulated intellectual and personal debts to many colleagues, students, friends, and family. Many have been more generous with time and criticism than we had a right to anticipate. Chief among these is Paul Rozin, Norton's editorial adviser and our colleague and friend. In addition to raising pointed questions in every draft of every chapter, he wrote for us the chapter on disorders of the nervous system. His contribution was augmented by other friends and colleagues, among others: Lyn Abramson, University of Wisconsin; Lauren Alloy, Northwestern University; Marianne Amarel, National Institute of Education; Paul Baltes, Max Planck Institut, Berlin; Aaron T. Beck, University of Pennsylvania; John Beletsis, private practice; Susan Beletsis, Stanford University School of Medicine; J. Paul Brady, University of Pennsylvania; Rogers Elliott, Dartmouth College; Norman Endler, York University; Henry Gleitman, University of Pennsylvania; David Goldberg, University of Manchester; Robert Howell, Brigham Young University; Seymour S. Kety, National Institute on Aging; Gardner Lindzey, Center for Advanced Study in the Behavioral Sciences; Dorothy Louise, writer and editor; Neil MacMillan, Brooklyn College; Isaac Marks, Maudsley Hospital, University of London; Jack Maser, National Institute of Mental Health; Suzanne Miller, Temple University; Mark Mills, University of California at Los Angeles; Morris Moscovitch, University of Toronto; Susan Nolen-Hoeksema, University of Pennsylvania; Jonathan Olson, Stanford University; Christopher Peterson, Virginia Polytechnic Institute and State University; Ed Pugh, University of Pennsylvania; S. J. Rachman, University of British Columbia; Leslie Rescorla, University of Pennsylvania; Jerome J. Rose, private practice; Peter Salovey, Yale University; Barry

Schwartz, Swarthmore College; Myrna Schwartz, University of Pennsylvania; James Stinnett, University of Pennsylvania; Albert Stunkard, University of Pennsylvania; Dennis Turk, Yale University; Niko Tinbergen, Oxford University; Bill Underwood, Southwestern Data Consultants; George Vaillant, Dartmouth College; Madelon Visintainer, Yale University; Iris Wildman, Stanford Law School; and Susan York, Pillsbury, Madison, and Sutro. We thank William Yule, Maudsley Hospital, University of London, who prepared early drafts for the chapter on childhood disorders; John Grabowski, National Institute on Drug Abuse, who prepared an early draft of the drug chapter; Oakley Ray, Vanderbilt University, for his assistance in the preparation of the drug chapter; and Reuben Gur, University of Pennsylvania, who prepared an early draft of the disorders of the nervous system chapter. Our special thanks go to Mollie Rosenhan, who brought the skills of an historian and editor to many of these chapters. And there's one institution that we would like to thank—the Center for Advanced Study in the Behavioral Sciences (NSF grant #BNS 76-22943-A02) where Martin Seligman spent 1978–1979. We gratefully acknowledge the help of the Center and its staff.

We also thank the following colleagues for their helpful reviews. Some read various parts of the manuscript; others, the entire manuscript.

Aaron T. Beck
University of Pennsylvania

Thomas F. Cash
Old Dominion University

Robert R. Dies
University of Maryland

Jay S. Efran
Temple University

Norman S. Endler
York University

Raymond E. Fancher
York University

Martha N. Gizynski
University of Michigan

Philip S. Holzman
Harvard University

Frederick Kanfer
University of Illinois

Alan E. Kazdin
Pennsylvania State University

Philip C. Kendall
University of Minnesota

John F. Kihlstrom
University of Wisconsin

Branch Koslett
Temple University

Neil MacMillan
Brooklyn College

William T. McReynolds
University of Missouri-
   Columbia

Donald Meichenbaum
University of Waterloo

Morris Moscovitch
University of Toronto

S. J. Rachman
University of British Columbia

Oakley S. Ray
Vanderbilt University

Lynn P. Rehm
University of Pittsburgh

Leslie Rescorla
University of Pennsylvania

Dennis C. Turk
Yale University

Warren W. Tyron
Fordham University

Bill Underwood
Southwestern Data
   Consultants

Arnold Witte
University of Pennsylvania

A book that is more than a decade in the making requires the administrative and supportive assistance of many people. In this, we are indebted to Elaine Andersen, Jutta Bischof, Camillo Castellon, Patricia Frederick, Greta Rathjen, Patricia Regon, Jack Rosenhan, Nina Rosenhan, and Teresa Vollmecke.

We also thank those who have written the ancillaries that accompany the text: Christopher Peterson, Virginia Polytechnic Institute and State University, who prepared the *Study Guide;* Joseph Lowman, University of North Carolina, who wrote the *Instructor's Manual;* and Elaine Vaughan, Stanford University, who prepared the *Test Item File.*

And finally, we extend our gratitude to those at Norton, with whom we have worked over the last seven years of this project. We want to thank especially our editor, Donald Fusting, who guided this book every step of the way and who criticized every chapter, offering conceptual as well as editorial suggestions. Next we thank Sandra Lifland, whose extraordinary and sustained efforts over the last year of production brought the book to its final polished form. We also thank an excellent production team—Ruth Mandel, Roy Tedoff, Ben Gamit, and Hugh O'Neill. Finally, we thank those who have lent their full support to the project—Donald S. Lamm, President of Norton; Edwin Barber, Director of the College Department; and his predecessor, Neil Patterson.

D.L.R.
M.E.P.S.
August, 1983

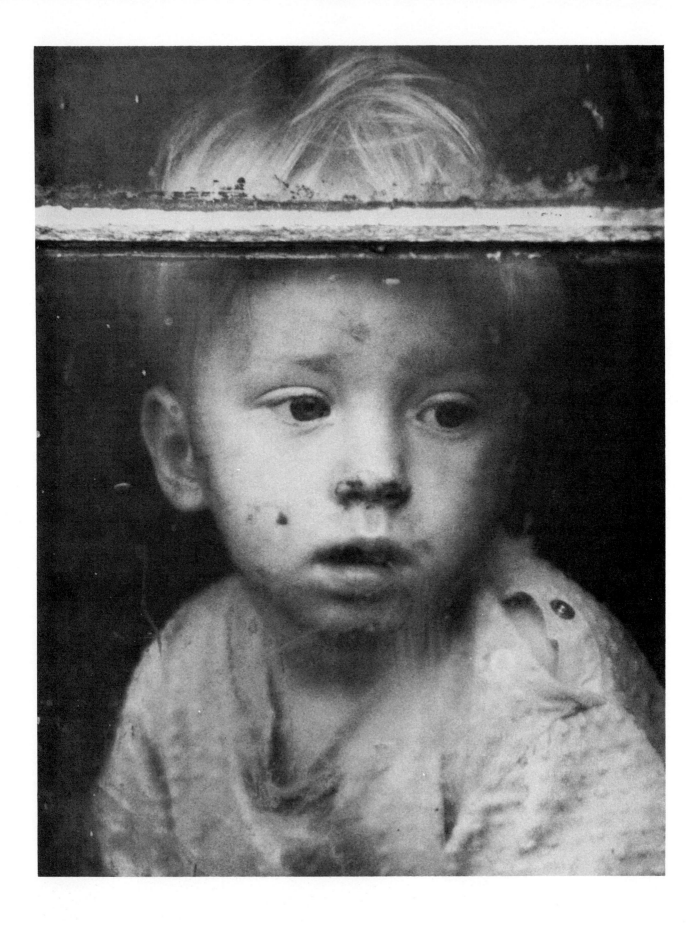

Part I

THE NATURE AND HISTORY OF ABNORMALITY

The Meanings of Abnormality

W HO is normal? Who is abnormal? And what do normality and abnormality mean?

These questions have no easy answers. There are no clear-cut definitions of abnormality, and no infallible way to recognize abnormality. Many of us will have suspected as much from our own experience. Recall your descent from innocence when, after periods of special distress, you asked yourself "Am I normal?" or "Is she normal?" Those were difficult questions whose answers were not immediately forthcoming. And they were often questions that were quickly abandoned, lest they lead to uncharted areas in ourselves or others that were more difficult and distressing than the behaviors we were trying to understand in the first place.

ABNORMALITY

If abnormality cannot be defined simply and clearly, does that mean that there is no such thing as abnormal behavior? Far from it. Abnormality is recognized everywhere, in every culture, by nearly everyone. Sometimes the impression of abnormality comes through clearly and unambiguously. At other times, reasonable people will disagree as to whether a particular person, action, or thought is or is not abnormal. The following clinical vignettes make this clear:

• Don is viewed by nearly everyone as a quiet mild-mannered executive. But one day, gripped by a sudden seizure in the temporal lobe of the brain, he picks up his sales manager, chair and all, and hurls her to death through the eleventh floor window of an office building.

• Vanessa, a teenage girl, eats nothing at all for several days, then gorges herself on eight hot-fudge sundaes within two hours, vomits explosively, and then eats nothing more for three days.

• Carla's religious principles forbid her from wearing makeup or drinking liquor. Her college friends do both. She is continually anxious when she is with them.

The sculptured figures above the gates to St. Mary's of Bethlehem Hospital (formerly referred to as "Bedlam") in London seem to epitomize abnormality. But as we will see, such clear-cut cases of abnormality are not typical. (Courtesy Victoria and Albert Museum)

Of these cases, two things can be said immediately. First, they involve very different behaviors, which arise from sources as diverse as brain pathology and religious beliefs. And second, while some people will be quite confident that all of these instances represent abnormality, not everyone will agree. Everyone will judge the first case abnormal. Nearly everyone will judge the second case abnormal. But there will be vigorous debate about the third.

WHY CAN'T ABNORMALITY BE EASILY DEFINED?

The act of defining the word "abnormal" suggests that there is some single property that these three cases of abnormality, and all others, must share. This shared property is called a *necessary* condition for abnormality. But there is no common element among these three cases, for what is it that temporal lobe seizures, gorging oneself on hot-fudge sundaes, and conflict between religious conviction and social acceptance have in common? Moreover, the definition of "abnormal" requires that there be at least one distinguishing element that only cases of abnormality share and that no cases of "normality" share. This is called a *sufficient* condition of abnormality. But is there any one feature that separates all cases of abnormality from all those that we would call normal? Not any that we can find. In fact, as we will shortly see, there is no single element shared by all cases of abnormality, and no single element that distinguishes abnormality from normality.

In short, the word "abnormal" cannot be defined precisely. Indeed, few of the words we commonly use, and especially those that are used socially, are precisely defined, for the use of language often depends on flexible meanings. But the fact that abnormality cannot be defined "tightly" does not mean that abnormality doesn't exist or that it can't be recognized at all. It does exist, and it is recognized in much the same way that families are recognized. How do we know, for example, that Ed Smith is the son of Bill and Jane Smith? Well, he *looks* like them. He has Bill's blue eyes and sandy hair, and Jane's upturned nose and easy smile. Even though Ed is six inches taller than his father and has a rounder face than his mother, we sense a ***family resemblance*** among them because they have many significant elements in common.

Abnormality is recognized in the same way, by determining whether the behavior, thought, or person bears a family resemblance to the behaviors, thoughts, and people we would all recognize as abnormal. That determination is made by spelling out the properties of abnormality, the various *elements* that count toward defining a behavior as abnormal. The more such elements there are and the more clearly each one is present, the more likely it is that the behavior, thought, or person will be judged abnormal. Let's examine those elements.

THE ELEMENTS OF ABNORMALITY

We will look at seven properties or elements that count toward deciding whether an action or a person is abnormal. Our analysis describes the way ordinary people and well-trained psychologists actually use the word. These elements or properties of abnormality are:

- Suffering
- Maladaptiveness
- Irrationality and incomprehensibility
- Unpredictability and loss of control
- Vividness and unconventionality
- Observer discomfort
- Violation of moral and ideal standards

The more of these elements that are present, and the more clearly they can be seen, the more certain we are that the behavior or person is abnormal. At least one of these elements *must* be present for abnormality to exist. But no one particular element must always be present, and only rarely will all of the elements be present. Let us examine these elements in greater detail.

SUFFERING

Abnormality hurts. A depressed housewife feels miserable. For her, the prospect of going through another day seems unbearable.

We are likely to call people abnormal if they are suffering psychologically, and the more they suffer, the more certain we are. But suffering is not a *necessary* condition of abnormality: it does not have to be present for us to label a behavior as abnormal. Someone who phones the President in the middle of the night, certain that the Chief Executive wants to hear all about his latest disarmament plan, can feel exuberant, cheerful, and full of hope. Nevertheless, such a person is viewed as abnormal, as the other elements of abnormality override the absence of suffering and convince us that his behavior is abnormal.

Suffering, moreover, is not a *sufficient* condition for abnormality because suffering is commonplace in the normal course of life. A child will grieve for a dead pet, for example, much as all of us mourn the loss of loved ones. If no

Suffering. The person in this painting is obviously suffering, but the decision about the abnormality of her suffering would depend on whether other elements of abnormality are present. (Painting by Edgar Degas, 1834–1917, Courtesy The Phillips Collection)

other elements of abnormality are present, however, grief and suffering will not be judged as abnormal.

Suffering, then, is an element that counts toward the perception of abnormality. But it is neither necessary nor sufficient. The context in which the suffering occurs counts heavily toward whether it is seen as abnormal.

MALADAPTIVENESS

Whether a behavior is functional and adaptive—how well it enables the individual to achieve certain goals—is a fundamental element in deciding whether the behavior is normal or abnormal. In biology, the fundamental scientific yardstick of adaptiveness is applied to the three important questions: Does it promote survival of the species? Does it promote the well-being of the individual? And does it promote the well-being of society? Psychologists tend most strongly to ask the last two questions: How well does the behavior foster individual well-being? And how well does it foster the well-being of society? Behaviors that strongly interfere with individual or social well-being are maladaptive and would count as factors in assessing abnormality.

By *individual well-being,* we mean the ability to work and the ability to conduct satisfying relations with other people. Depression and anxiety interfere with love and work and, almost always, with an individual's sense of well-being. A fear of going out (agoraphobia) can be so strong that it keeps the sufferer locked inside an apartment, unable to fulfill any of the individual's goals. Such a fear grossly interferes with the enjoyment of life, the ability to work, and relations with others. The more there is such interference, the clearer the abnormality.

It is abnormal to interfere strongly with the ***well-being of society.*** Murderers and arsonists are often called psychopaths, indicating society's judgment that their actions are abnormal. But are those actions truly abnormal? Are there enough elements of abnormality in these actions to make the family resemblance plausible? Or are these actions merely wrong or illegal? A "psychopathic" mobster may go about his work well, arranging theft and murder without the slightest pang of conscience. But he may also be an attentive husband, devoted father, and a lover of the good life. His behavior is maladaptive for the group, causing a negative social judgment of his behavior. But whether his behavior is ultimately held to be *abnormal* will depend on how many of the other elements of abnormality are present.

Irrationality and Incomprehensibility

When a person's behavior seems to have no rational meaning, we are inclined to call that behavior and that person abnormal. People who, like Vanessa, alternately gorge themselves and vomit, who speak earnest gibberish, who somehow ensure that they will be disliked by precisely those from whom they most desire affection—these people exhibit incomprehensible and irrational behaviors that are elements of abnormality.

One kind of incomprehensibility that counts very strongly for the designation of abnormality is ***thought disorder,*** a major symptom of schizophrenia. Beliefs that are patently absurd and bizarre, perceptions that have no basis in objective reality, and mental processes that ramble from one idea to another unrelated one constitute thought disorders. A memorable example of such thought disorganization occurred during a formal experiment. The patient's task consisted of sorting colored blocks of various shapes and colors into a number of groups. The patient was cooperative and earnest. But he also exhibited an irresistible tendency to sort objects on the desk and on the experimenter's person, as well as parts of the room, things he pulled from his pockets, and even the experimenter himself, whom the patient recommended be remade of wood and cut into blocks. Here is what he said:

> I've got to pick it out of the whole room. I can't confine myself to this game. . . . Three blues [test blocks] . . . now, how about that green blotter? Put it there too. Green peas you eat. You can't eat them unless you write on it (pointing to green blotter). Like that wristwatch (on the experimenter's wrist, a foot from the subject)—don't see three meals coming off that watch . . . To do this trick *you'd* have to be made of wood. You've got a white shirt on—and the white blocks. You have to have them cut out of *you!* You've got a white shirt on—this (white hexagonal block) will hold you and never let you go. I've got a blue shirt on, but it can't be a blue shirt and still go together. And the room's got to be the same . . . (Excerpted from Cameron, 1947, p. 59.)

Unpredictability and Loss of Control

We expect people to be consistent from time to time, predictable from one occasion to the next, and very much in control of themselves. To be loved one day and hated the next is troubling. One hardly knows how to respond or what to expect. Our need to control our environment (Rotter, 1966; Sel-

Maladaptiveness. Depression and anxiety interfere with love and work, and almost always with an individual's sense of well-being. (© Ira Berger 1982/Woodfin Camp)

igman, 1975; Rothbaum, Weisz, and Snyder, 1982) and to retain our own freedom (Brehm and Brehm, 1981) require that other people be predictable. In a predictable world, there is consistency and control. In an unpredictable one, we feel vulnerable and threatened. Don, the mild-mannered executive who hurled his sales manager out the window, is frightening in much the same way that Dr. Jekyll's alter ego, Mr. Hyde, is: both are unpredictable and out of control.

The judgment that behavior is out of control will be made under two conditions. The first occurs when the ordinary guides and inhibitors of behavior suddenly break down. Don exemplifies this judgment. The second condition occurs when we do not know what causes an action. Imagine coming upon someone who is angry—raging and screaming in the streets. There may be good and socially acceptable reasons for such an anger. But if we do not know those reasons and are unable to elicit them at the time, we are likely to consider that the person is out of control and to designate those actions as abnormal.

Not all instances of loss of control, however, are abnormal. *Flexible control,* the ability to retain control or give it up as the self and situation require, is a hallmark of good psychological functioning (London and Rosenhan, 1968). The inability to relinquish control during sexual intercourse, for example, is likely to breed problems rather than reflect them.

Vividness and Unconventionality

Generally, people recognize as acceptable and conventional those actions that they themselves are willing to do. Those who accede to a request to walk around campus wearing a sandwich board that reads "EAT AT JOE'S" are likely to estimate that a healthy majority of their peers would make the same choice. On the other hand, those who are unwilling to wear such a sign estimate that relatively *few* people would be willing. Thus, with the exception of behaviors that require great skill or daring, we tend to judge the abnormality of others' behavior by our own. If *we* do it, it's conventional and normal. If we don't, it stands out vividly as unconventional and abnormal (Ross, Greene, and House, 1977). The sound of a motorcycle in a quiet courtyard is vivid and irritating—unless of course, it's our motorcycle, in which case the sound is thrilling.

What is conventional and acceptable in any society is always changing. Those who are on the leading edge of that change are very visible compared to the rest of us (whose behavior is still conventional), and they run the risk of being labeled as deviants, and therefore as abnormal. Thirty years ago, for example, beards were rare. Those who wore them, stood out in the crowd and were perceived as deviant and abnormal. Today, of course, those same beards would hardly be noticed.

The element of vividness is affected by whether an action is rare. Behaviors that are rare *and* undesirable are very likely to seem quite vivid, and hence to be considered abnormal. It hardly matters whether the behavior actually *is* rare, so long as it is *perceived* to be rare. Thus, there are many varieties of sexual and aggressive fantasies that are quite common but that are perceived to be rare and therefore abnormal. Nor is rareness itself a neces-

Vividness. Who is abnormal and who is normal? Teenagers who are dressed in punk style might seem abnormal to some people. To others, they might appear to be quite conventional and normal. Just as styles of dress change over time, so do notions of abnormality. (Photograph by Alon Reininger/Leo de Wys, Inc.)

Observer discomfort. This man is dressed up as an alien from outer space. Those who pass him experience surprise and discomfort. Such observer discomfort is one element that contributes to the judgment of abnormality. (Photograph by Francene Keery/Leo de Wys, Inc.)

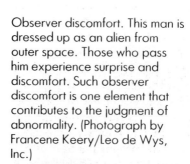

sary condition for abnormality. Depression is a common disorder, as are anxiety states, and both are considered to be abnormal. But behavior that is both rare and socially undesirable is seen as abnormal. A rare behavior that is socially desirable, would be considered a "gift" and only abnormal in the statistical sense. Genius is rare. So is high moral character. But if they are abnormal, they are abnormalities to which most of us aspire.

OBSERVER DISCOMFORT

People who are very dependent on others, or ingratiating, or hostile, create discomfort in observers. Their behaviors often enable them to feel more comfortable, but the psychological conflicts they create are painful for others. In some ways, they are like people who are becoming gradually deaf and who turn up the volume on their radio to compensate. Suddenly, they can hear perfectly well again, but the noise that is created is intolerable to others.

We are most likely to experience vague observer discomfort when someone violates unwritten or *residual rules* of behavior (Scheff, 1966). Residual rules are rules that no one ever teaches but that we nonetheless know intuitively and use to guide our behavior. Violation of those rules creates the kind of discomfort that leads to the designation "abnormal."

For example, in some cultures, there is an unwritten rule which states that, except when angry or making love, one's face should be at least ten inches away from that of one's partner. Should that invisible boundary be overstepped, a residual rule will be violated, and the partner will feel uncomfortable. Similarly, there are unwritten rules about speech fluency (that one ought not to stutter) and about clothing one's genital area which, when violated, contribute to the impression that the person is abnormal.

Violation of standards. At times, behavior is assessed against idealized norms about how people should properly behave. This woman is holding an open umbrella although it is not raining. She has all her life's possessions beside her on this sidewalk rather than in her home. Is she abnormal? (Photograph by Joan Roth)

VIOLATION OF MORAL AND IDEAL STANDARDS

There are times when behavior is assessed, not against our judgments of what is common and conventional, but against moral standards and idealized norms that are believed to characterize all right-thinking and right-acting people. This view starts with the notion that people *ought* to behave in a certain way, whether they really do or not, and it concludes with the view that it is normal to behave in the way one ought, and abnormal to fail to behave properly. Thus, it is normal to work, and abnormal not to do so (unless wealth, the unavailability of job openings, or illness exonerate one). It is normal to love, to be loyal, and to be supportive, and abnormal not to—regardless of the fact that evidence for these dispositions is not widely found in modern society. It is abnormal to be too aggressive or too restrained, too shy or too forward, too ambitious or not sufficiently ambitious. It is abnormal to believe in the devil and abnormal *not* to believe in a good supernatural being. As far as ideal standards are concerned, abnormality becomes another word for all manner of behaviors that range from that which is downright wicked to that which is best done without.

ABNORMALITY AS A SOCIAL JUDGMENT

Unlike the judgment of temperature, the judgment of abnormality is a social one. Look again at some of the elements: observer discomfort, vividness and unconventionality, and violation of moral and ideal standards. These all require the presence of other people, while the remaining elements of abnormality can also easily be interpreted socially. Social judgments can easily be abused, and because the judgment of abnormality is so heavily social, it is even more susceptible to social abuse. At times, those who have worked for social change, as well as political dissenters, have been labeled as abnormal. We might well wish that this were not the case and that abnormality were a more objective judgment. But our present wishes are beside the point, though eventually abnormality may be assessed with considerably greater objectivity. We are not endorsing the way abnormality is presently judged. Nor are we prescribing how the word "abnormal" should be used. Rather, we are merely describing how the word is actually used by laymen and professionals alike.

APPLYING THE ELEMENTS OF ABNORMALITY

Family members resemble each other across a fixed number of dimensions, such as height, hair and eye color, and shape of nose, mouth, and ears. Similarly, abnormality is assessed according to the match between an individual's characteristics and the seven elements of abnormality. Examine the following case study with a view toward determining the "family resemblance" between the individual and the elements of abnormality.

> Ralph, the seventeen-year-old son of a physician and a pharmacist, moved with his family from a small farming town to a large suburban community during the middle of his junior year in high school. The move was sudden: both his parents were offered jobs that were simply too good to turn down. The abruptness of the move generated no complaint from Ralph, nor did he acknowledge any difficulty. Nevertheless, he seemed to withdraw. At the outset, his family hardly noticed, but once the family settled down, his distant behavior became apparent. He made no friends in his new school, and when the summer came, he seemed to withdraw even further. He spent a good deal of the summer in his room, emerging only to take extended walks around the house. He often seemed preoccupied, and occasionally seemed to be listening to sounds that only he could hear.
>
> Autumn approached and with it the time for Ralph to return to his senior year of high school. Ralph became even more withdrawn. He had difficulty sleeping, and he paced inside and outside the house. Shortly after he returned to school, his behavior deteriorated further. Sometimes, he seemed not to hear when called upon in class, while at other times his answers bore no relation to the questions. Both behaviors generated a good deal of mocking laughter in his classes, and his classmates actively avoided him. One day, he marched into class, stood up, and began to speak absolute gibberish. School authorities notified his parents, who came immediately to pick him up. When he saw them, he grimaced and began to roll a lock of hair between his fingers. He said nothing as he was brought to a psychiatric clinic. (Adapted from DSM-III Training Guide, 1981.)

Is Ralph abnormal according to the preceding criteria? Even this brief vignette, which fails to describe fully the richness of Ralph's problem, leaves us convinced that Ralph is suffering some kind of psychological abnormality. Let us return to the elements of abnormality, and examine the extent to which Ralph's actions reflect those elements.

· *Suffering.* We have no information about whether, or to what degree, Ralph is suffering. His withdrawal from his family *might* reflect subjective distress. But then again, it might not.

· *Maladaptiveness.* Ralph's behavior is highly dysfunctional. Not only does he needlessly draw negative attention to himself, but he obviously fails to respond to the demands of school. Such behavior neither serves his own needs nor those of society.

· *Incomprehensibility and irrationality.* There can be little doubt that Ralph's behavior is incomprehensible to observers, and that his verbalizations seem irrational to them.

· *Unpredictability and loss of control.* There is little evidence for loss of control in the vignette, but Ralph's parents would presumably find his behavior unpredictable. So too might his schoolmates.

· *Vividness.* Ralph's behavior is quite vivid. His silent withdrawal stands out noticeably and his speeches in class make him the center of undesirable attention.

· *Observer discomfort.* It is not clear from the vignette whether *all* observers are made uncomfortable by Ralph's behavior, but it is a fair guess that his schoolmates are avoiding him because they feel uncomfortable.

· *Violation of moral and ideal standards.* There is no evidence that Ralph's behavior violates widely held moral standards.

In the main, then, Ralph's behavior is dysfunctional and incomprehensible. These elements alone would have qualified his behavior as abnormal in most people's judgment. Additionally, there is some evidence that his behavior is unpredictable, vivid, and creates discomfort in observers. These elements lend additional strength to the judgment that his behavior is abnormal.

What is the locus of Ralph's abnormality? His behavior is abnormal. His thought is abnormal. And because these problems of behavior and thought last for such a long time and occur across so many different situations, we come to call Ralph himself abnormal. This is the convention; it invites us to generalize from the actions and thoughts of an individual to the individual himself. This linguistic convention is not without costs, however, for we can easily be misled into believing that a particular pattern of behavior or thought is much more disabling and pervasive than it really is. It is tragic enough that Ralph had the problems he was afflicted with. But it adds considerably to his tragedy to somehow infer that Ralph himself is flawed, rather than merely realizing that *sometimes* and in *some* situations Ralph's *behaviors and thoughts* are abnormal.

ABNORMALITY AND PSYCHOLOGICAL DIAGNOSIS

Abnormality is a global term. It serves only to indicate that something is judged to be wrong psychologically with a person's behavior or personality. But once the judgment is made that a person's behavior is abnormal, the question arises: How is it abnormal?

DSM-III and Diagnosis

The specific ways in which people are judged to be abnormal are described in the *Diagnostic and Statistical Manual of Mental Disorders* (Third Edition), commonly called DSM-III, which was published by the American Psychiatric Association in 1980. This catalog of psychological distress is large and all-embracing, and we will describe it at some length in Chapter 9. For the present, however, it is important to know that arriving at a specific disorder or diagnosis in DSM-III itself amounts to using family resemblances. DSM-III describes the elements that are said to characterize a particular disorder. Moreover, it describes the criteria for recognizing whether a particular element is present. The better the match between an individual's behavior and the elements offered for the disorder, the more confident we can be of the diagnosis (Cantor, Smith, French, and Mezzich, 1980.)

"Family Resemblance" Approach and Its Hazards

The virtue of a family resemblance approach to abnormality arises from the fact that, much as there is no *single* way in which all sons resemble all fathers, neither is there a *single* way in which all abnormal behaviors resemble each other. The notion that all abnormality must involve psychological suffering, or vividness, or observer discomfort is simply false, as we have seen. No single element exists that binds the behaviors of, say, a person who is deeply depressed, a person who is afraid to be alone, and a person who gorges herself and then vomits. Yet, we regard each of these people to be suffering an abnormality because their behaviors are members of the family of characteristics that we have come to regard as abnormal.

But there are some hazards to the family resemblance approach to abnormality. Let's look at three of these hazards: society's error, disagreement between observers, and disagreement between actor and observer.

SOCIETY MAY ERR IN WHOM IT CALLS ABNORMAL. The notion of abnormality can easily and erroneously be applied to all manner of behavior that society presently finds objectionable. As we indicated earlier, those who wore beards thirty years ago, were seen as abnormal because they "stood out in the crowd." Their behavior matched one of the elements of abnormality, and they were, therefore, erroneously termed abnormal.

In the film *One Flew over the Cuckoo's Nest,* based on a novel by Ken Kesey, it is ambiguous whether the main character is abnormal or not. (Copyright © 1975, Fantasy Films and United Artists Corporation)

But it is not merely vivid behavior that can trigger allegations of abnormality. Behavior that creates discomfort in observers, for whatever reason, risks triggering those allegations. The student who refuses to haze when his fraternity brothers are doing so, or the person who, for deeply philosophic reasons, refuses to fight in any war, and therefore refuses to register for the draft—these people march to their own drummers, and they create discomfort in the observers who disagree with them. Similarly, those who violate the ideal standards of others in the course of maintaining their *own* ideal standards risk being termed abnormal.

OBSERVERS WILL DISAGREE ABOUT PARTICULAR BEHAVIORS OR INDIVIDUALS.   A family resemblance approach to abnormality is bound to generate some disagreements about whether or not a behavior qualifies as abnormal. Two observers might disagree that any given element was present. Moreover, they might disagree about whether enough elements were present, or whether they were present with sufficient intensity to constitute a clear case of abnormality.

In a study that will be more fully described in Chapter 9 (pp. 180–81), daily visitors came to large psychiatric hospitals to visit "pseudopatients," that is, people who were in the hospital to study it, not to be treated. These visitors quickly learned that they had to leave the hospital before the next staff shift came to work. Otherwise, they would be faced with the difficult task of proving that they, the visitors, were not patients. After all, they shared at least two visible elements with true patients: Like true patients, they had no keys! And like many of them, the visitors insisted that they did not belong there. That common family resemblance was occasionally strong enough to create some difficult moments for the visitors.

Such an approach generates disagreement for the further reason that the elements of abnormality are neither so precise nor so quantifiable that everyone will agree that a behavior or person fits the category. The more dramatic the behaviors and the longer they are sustained, the more agreement there will be among observers. The problem of observer disagreement is a serious one. As we shall see in Chapter 9, the problem is dealt with, to some extent, by stipulating as clearly as one can, the kinds of behaviors that are associated with each element of abnormality. When this is done, wider agreement occurs.

OBSERVERS AND ACTORS WILL OCCASIONALLY DISAGREE.   There will occasionally be different opinions as to whether a behavior or person should be judged as abnormal, according to who is doing the judging: the individuals who are generating the behaviors in question—we call them actors—or those who observe the behaviors. Generally, actors will be less inclined to judge their own behaviors as abnormal for three reasons: First, they have much more information available to them about their own behaviors than do observers. What seems unpredictable or incomprehensible to an observer may seem quite predictable and comprehensible to an actor, and what generates discomfort in an observer may, as we indicated, generate none in the actor. Second, people who are psychologically distressed are not

To many of his peers, this protester was behaving in accord with ideal standards. These soldiers and many other members of society, however, had a different view. (Photograph by Dennis Brack/Black Star)

distressed all the time. Distress comes and goes. People, therefore, may be "crazy" at one time, but not crazy at another. Actors are uniquely positioned to recognize changes in themselves. Observers, however, often assume a continuity of psychological state that does not exist. Third, people generally are inclined to see themselves in a more favorable light than observers see them. As a result, actors will tend to see themselves and their behaviors more favorably, and hence more normally, than observers.

NORMALITY

We have dealt at length with the meaning of abnormality and the elements that are associated with it, but it will not take us as long to define normality. *Normality is simply the absence of abnormality.* It means nothing beyond that. If abnormality is a matter of judgment and social perspective, so is normality. If abnormality is much more a matter of degree than of kind, so too is normality. And if there are enormous gray areas associated with the judgment of abnormality, such that we often don't really know whether a behavior or person is abnormal, those same gray areas will apply to the question of normality.

Positives and Negatives

Words can be stated in positive and negative forms. Usually, the positive form is well-defined, while the negative form is merely the opposite of the positive one. We know what "embarrassed" means, and it follows that "unembarrassed" means not embarrassed. The positive word is the primary member of the opposing pair and the "un" word gets its meaning only by negating the positive word. If we did not already know the meaning of the positive word, we would not understand its negation.

But this is not always the case. Sometimes the primary meaning resides in the *negative* case, and the positive word only makes sense as a negation of the negative word. The logic of "normal-abnormal" reflects the primacy of the negative case. Abnormal is the concept that makes primary sense. *Normal means nothing over and above "not abnormal."* To decide whether a person or an action is normal, we merely ask about the absence of the elements of abnormality. Are only a few of the elements of abnormality present, and those not intensely? Once we decide that actions or persons are *not* abnormal, we have simultaneously decided that they *are* normal. Normality has no meaning beyond the absence of abnormality.

We are occasionally uneasy about our own normality because of the logic of abnormality. Many things that we do have one or two elements of abnormality in them. While this is not enough for our actions to be termed abnormal, it is enough to make us uneasy about our own normality, particularly if we persist in the belief that normality is a state that has meaning beyond the absence of abnormality. Consider masturbation as a case in point. A fifteen-year-old boy who masturbates every day may wonder if he is normal. But if we examine that action against the elements of abnormality, we find very little to be concerned about. Is his masturbation *irrational?* Not at all. Is it *dysfunctional?* Not in any obvious way. Does he *suffer?* Quite the contrary (though worrying about it gives some pain). Does it produce *observer discomfort?* No, there are no observers. Is it *visible and unconventional?* No, over 90 percent of males acknowledge masturbation at one time or another, and adolescents who masturbate as often as three times a day are not uncommon. Is the behavior unacceptable because it *violates moral standards?* Marginally, with enormous variation from subculture to subculture. Overall, then, masturbation is somewhat unacceptable from some moral viewpoints, but it shares in no other element of abnormality. Why, then, would anyone be concerned about whether masturbation is normal? Because of that marginal unacceptability to some subcultures. The fact that it taps into one (and only one) element of abnormality is sufficient to make some people worry about its normality.

BEYOND NORMALITY: LIVING OPTIMALLY

To be normal is not necessarily to live well, for there is more to living than being normal and avoiding abnormality. There are pleasures, maturities, insights, achievements, and wisdoms—the joys of life. The strategies and criteria for living optimally are a constant preoccupation of humanistic psychology, which we take up in Chapter 7. They are mentioned here because without them, our conceptions of psychological life can become so oriented around abnormality that we fail to attend sufficiently to the positive aspects of living. These positive aspects constitute a good defense against abnormality itself (Rosenhan, 1969, 1970), if only because it is difficult for suffering and irrationality to exist simultaneously with joy and wisdom.

There is really no satisfactory psychological term to describe the positive side of life, nor any psychological theory to tell us how to achieve it. Some writers call it "self-actualization," a term, unfortunately, that describes a happy sadist and a happy homemaker equally well (Goldstein, 1939;

Rogers, 1961; Maslow, 1971). Others (Jahoda, 1958) call it "positive mental health," stressing its medical, and implicitly, its disease aspects. We call it **optimal living.**

SOME ELEMENTS OF OPTIMAL LIVING

Like abnormality, optimal living is more a matter of degree than of kind. One doesn't live optimally all the time, any more than one is abnormal all the time. Rather, optimality is a goal that, on some days and under some conditions we feel more of, and at other times and conditions, less. No one lives optimally all the time.

There are six areas in which optimality can be recognized (Jahoda, 1958). They are:

- Positive attitudes toward self
- Growth and development
- Autonomy
- Accurate perception of reality
- Environmental competence
- Positive interpersonal relations.

Positive Attitudes Toward Self

The phrase **self-acceptance** has many connotations, but generally it implies knowing ourselves, accepting rather than denying what we know, and feeling good about that knowledge. "Self-acceptance implies that a person has learned to live with himself, accepting both the limitations and possibilities he may find in himself" (Jahoda, 1958, p. 24). This does not mean we are thinking about ourselves all the time; rather, much of the time we take ourselves for granted. But when we do think about ourselves, we accept and like what we see.

Growth and Development

Living optimally involves a desire to utilize one's abilities instead of stagnating, to devote oneself to a mission or vocation, and to establish long-range goals (Maslow, 1954). At its best, this kind of growth involves a full investment in living, a capacity to get out of one's skin and to lose oneself in work, thought, sport, or other people (Allport, 1937).

Autonomy

Optimal living both requires and generates a degree of emotional freedom from the demands of the immediate social environment and greater responsiveness to one's own internal standards. Increasingly, *self*-regard—the approval of oneself by oneself—rather than the approval of others, becomes the mark of this kind of maturity. Often, it is the exercise of one's own standards that brings about such self-rewarded independence.

Eleanor Roosevelt devoted herself to human rights and to helping the poor, oppressed, and dispossessed. "The important thing," she said, just before she died, "was that you never let down doing the best that you were able to do . . ."

Accurate Perception of Reality

When we dislike someone, we prefer to believe that they are thoroughly unpleasant, rather than finding that in many ways they are really nice. If the latter perception is more accurate, however, it is also more constructive because it leads us to investigate the conditions that led to the difficulties in the first place. Is it possible that we misunderstood? Could her awful behavior have been accidental? In short, testing our perceptions against reality involves some risk that we may have been wrong, but also the greater gain that we can do something about it.

Closely related to that concern for accurately assessing reality is the ability to tolerate realities that are simply ambiguous without prematurely casting them into present molds. The ability to say "I don't know," to live with ignorance, to wait for information that is accurate—these abilities strongly influence our capacity to perceive reality accurately.

Environmental Competence

Being competent in life's tasks—in work, love, and play—contributes enormously to the sense of living optimally. The reasons for this are obvious: competence brings with it not only external gratifications but also internal ones. Coping with the requirements of one's environment and meeting one's own standards of performance contribute to one's sense of efficacy (Bandura, 1977a).

Positive Interpersonal Relations

The final area of optimal living involves positive interpersonal relations—the ability to enjoy the company of others, to empathize with them, to give and receive support, to respect others regardless of their status, and the capacity to love and be loved—all of these are implied in the notion of positive interpersonal relations. Some theorists believe that the absence of such relations is a major source of emotional misery, resulting in alienation, loss of sense of community, and finally fear of one another (May, 1953).

Positive interpersonal relations with family and friends help us avoid emotional misery, alienation, and serious psychological disorders. (*Left:* © 1982 Michael Hayman/Black Star. *Right:* Wide World Photos)

WARNING: IATROGENIC ILLNESSES

There is almost no one who has not harbored secret doubts about his or her normality. "Do I cry too easily?" "Am I too afraid of speaking up in class?" "Do other people occasionally have fantasies about their parents dying in violent accidents?"

There is a phenomenon called "interns' syndrome" or *iatrogenic illness* (meaning illness caused by a physician). In the course of early training, the fledgling medical student finds in himself symptoms of almost every disease he studies.

> I remember going to the British Museum one day to read up the treatment for some slight ailment of which I had a touch—hay fever, I fancy it was. I got down the book, and read all I came to read; and then, in an unthinking moment, I idly turned the leaves, and began to indolently study diseases, generally. I forgot which was the first distemper I plunged into—some fearful, devastating scourge, I know —and, before I had glanced half down the list of "premonitory symptoms," it was borne in upon me that I had fairly got it.
>
> I sat for a while frozen with horror; and then in the listlessness of dispair, I again turned over the pages. I came to typhoid fever—read the symptoms—discovered that I had typhoid fever, must have had it for months without knowing it—wondered what else I had got; turned up St. Vitus' Dance—found, as I expected, that I had that too—began to get interested in my case, and determined to sift it to the bottom, and so started alphabetically—looked up ague, and learnt that I was sickening for it, and that the acute stage would commence in about another fortnight. Bright's disease, I was relieved to find, I had only in a modified form, and, so far as that was concerned, I might live for years. Cholera I had, with severe complications; and diptheria I seemed to have been born with. I plodded conscientiously through the twenty-six letters, and the only malady I could conclude I had not got was housemaid's knee.
>
> I felt rather hurt about this at first; it seemed somehow to be a sort of slight. Why hadn't I got housemaid's knee? Why this invidious reservation? After a while, however, less grasping feelings prevailed. I reflected that I had every other known malady in the pharmacology, and I grew less selfish, and determined to do without housemaid's knee. Gout, in it's most malignant stage, it would appear, had seized me without my being aware of it; and zymosis I had evidently been suffering with from boyhood. There were no more diseases after zymosis, so I concluded there was nothing else the matter with me. . . . I had walked into that reading-room a happy healthy man. I crawled out a decrepit wreck." (Jerome, 1889)

As you read this book, you too will encounter symptoms in yourself that will make you think you have each disorder in turn. Be forewarned: It is a very unpleasant experience and one about which neither authors nor readers can really do much. In part, it arises from the privacy that surrounds our lives. Many of our thoughts, and some of our actions, strike us as private, if not secret—things about which no one should know. If they did know, people, even (perhaps particularly) friends, might think less of us, or be offended, or both. One consequence of this privacy is the development of an exaggerated sense of the uniqueness of our forbidden thoughts and behaviors. Seeing them suddenly alluded to on these pages and associated with certain syndromes (commonly in contexts that are quite different from the contexts of our own behaviors—but we don't notice that) makes us believe that we have fallen prey to that problem too.

There are two things that can be done to combat the distress you may experience from reading this book and going to lectures. First, read carefully. You may, for example, be concerned when you read about depression: "Yes, I'm blue. I cry now more than I used to." But as you inquire deeply into the symptoms of depression, you will find that the absence of suicidal thoughts, your continued interest in sex or sports, your optimism about the future, all count against the diagnosis of depression.

Second, talk with your friends. Sometimes, merely mentioning that "when I read Chapter so-and-so, I get the feeling they're talking about me. Do you ever get that feeling?" will bring forth a chorus of "you bets," and relief for all of you.

SUMMARY

1. There are no hard and fast definitions of normality and abnormality, for there is no single element that all instances of abnormality share, nor any single property that distinguishes normality from abnormality.

2. *Abnormality* is recognized the way members of a family are recognized: because they share a *family resemblance* in that they have many significant elements in common.

3. With regard to abnormality, there are seven properties or elements that count toward deciding whether a person or an action is abnormal: suffering, maladaptiveness, irrationality and incomprehensibility, unpredictability and loss of control, vividness and unconventionality, observer discomfort, and violation of moral and ideal standards. The more of these elements that are present, and the more visible each element is, the more likely are we to judge the person or the action as abnormal.

4. Because the judgment of abnormality is a *social judgment,* there is sometimes disagreement about who is abnormal, and about which thoughts and actions qualify as being considered abnormal. Society occasionally errs about whom it calls abnormal, as sometimes do observers, even those who are qualified diagnosticians. But the absence of complete agreement should not be taken to mean that abnormality is always or frequently a matter of dispute.

5. *Normality* is simply the absence of abnormality, nothing more. To be normal is to possess so few of the elements of abnormality, and those at such a minimal degree, that no qualified observer would make the judgment of abnormality. To be normal, however, is not necessarily to live happily or well.

6. *Optimal living* requires some quite positive capacities, among them: positive attitudes toward oneself, capacity for growth and development, autonomy, an accurate perception of reality, social and vocational competence, and positive interpersonal relationships.

CHAPTER
2

Abnormality across Time, Place, and Culture

OVER the thousands of years of Western history, there have been many different notions about what behaviors can be defined as madness. This is only to be expected, for as the elements of abnormality change over time, so must the notions of what is normal and abnormal. Behaviors that have been revered in one time or place may have been defined as clear examples of madness in others. The ancient Hebrews and the ancient Greeks held in awe those who claimed to be prophets and had "the gift of tongues." Yet in the modern world, those who claim to see into the future generate suspicion, and those who speak in unknown words and rhythms are often classified as schizophrenics.

So too have there been different and contradictory theories about the causes of abnormal behavior. Shakespeare portrayed Ophelia as driven "mad" by Hamlet's cruel rejection, implying to his Elizabethan audiences that Ophelia's withdrawal and eventual suicide were products of the social influences in her immediate environment. Yet, during the same period in history, other "mad" women were accused of having willfully made pacts with Satan. Clearly, a society's definitions of madness and perceptions of its causes have played significant roles in how the abnormal have been viewed: they have influenced whether the mad were revered, feared, pitied, or simply accepted. In turn, these perceptions have determined the ways in which the mad have been treated: whether they were honored for their unique powers or incarcerated, treated, or abandoned for their madness.*

The history of abnormality, like the history of most other human phenomena, is not linear and logical but meandering and inconsistent. In this chapter, we will examine two significant issues in the history of madness: (1)

---

* Curiously, even the forms of abnormal behavior have been different in different ages and cultures. For example, hysteria, identified for more than two thousand years as a discrete syndrome, was especially prevalent at certain times. It was rife in the nineteenth century, if the historian is to judge by the notebooks of physicians and the guest registries of hostels like those in Lourdes. Yet, hysteria seems to have all but disappeared in the present century.

theories of cause, and (2) methods of treatment and care. Of course, we must remember that notions of abnormality change when values change, for notions of normality and abnormality are guided by the predominant values of a culture. We take it for granted, for example, that wearing a bikini to the pool is acceptable behavior today. But we know it would have been scandalous a hundred years ago. Why? Because our view of what is modest and immodest has undergone enormous change during the past century. So, too, has our view of abnormality.

THE PERCEIVED CAUSES OF ABNORMAL BEHAVIOR

There is, unfortunately, very little about abnormality that tells what caused it or that provides clues about where to look for causes. Yet, because treatment and cure depend on perceived cause, people find it difficult to resist speculating about causality. Thus, there were times when abnormality was attributed to supernatural causes—from the wrath of the gods to possession by demons. At other times and in other places, earthquakes and tides, germs and illness, interpersonal conflict and bad blood were separately and together used to explain the origins of abnormality. When the world is perceived in supernatural terms, abnormality is likely to be viewed as a supernatural phenomenon. When people believe in and are threatened by witchcraft, then abnormal behavior may be attributed to a supernatural source. And when the dominant beliefs of a culture are scientific, abnormality will be interpreted in those terms. Although their precise articulation has been distinctly different in different epochs and cultures, we will present three general explanations of abnormality, discussing in turn supernatural causes, physical causes, and psychogenic origins.

SUPERNATURAL CAUSES

In a remote cave in the French Pyrenees, there is a twenty-thousand-year-old painting that portrays a dancer disguised as an animal with massive branching horns. The figure is thought to represent a sorcerer (Cohn, 1975). The belief that the natural world is inhabited by spirits and demons has pervaded history. With it, too, has come the conviction that such spirits and demons can be controlled through supernatural means. Such beliefs prevail today in many cultures.

In premodern societies, mental disturbance was often ascribed to **supernatural** causes. One of the most common explanations of madness was that evil spirits had taken **possession** of an individual and controlled that person's behavior. Much as a parasitic tapeworm lives in and weakens the body, so could a parasitic spirit inhabit and weaken the mind. Some skulls of Paleolithic cave dwellers have characteristic holes, called **trephines,** that appear to have been chipped out by stone instruments. It is thought that trephining was performed to provide an exit for demons or evil spirits trapped within the skull.

People could be possessed by many different kinds of spirits. The spirits of ancestors, animals, gods, and heroes, and of victims whose wrongs had not been redressed, were among those who could wreak madness. These spirits

This Paleolithic cave drawing portrays a dancer disguised as an animal, and is thought to represent a sorcerer.

Paleolithic cave dwellers are believed to have produced these holes in the skulls of those who were "possessed" by evil spirits. This method, which is called *trephining,* freed the possessed from the presence of evil spirits. (Courtesy University Museum, University of Pennsylvania)

could enter a person through their own cunning, through the work of an evildoer with magical powers, or through a lack of faith on the part of the possessed individual. Not surprisingly, because possession was a result of supernatural forces, freeing the possessed individual from these spirits required supernatural techniques. Across time and place, there has been the widespread belief in the power of some individuals to use magic both to induce evil and to expel it; shamans, witch doctors, sorcerers, and witches were all believed to be able to influence the supernatural (Douglas, 1970). In medieval Europe, for example, individuals from all levels of society resorted to sorcerers and witches for spells, potents, and prophecies. Although they were often feared, witches were generally left alone unless they were thought to have murdered or to have destroyed property. But even then, they were prosecuted by secular, not religious, authorities (Currie, 1968).

Much of what is presently understood as originating from psychological distress was earlier attributed to supernatural causes. Dancing *manias,* for example, often involved hundreds of people, who danced for days on end until they succumbed to exhaustion. These manias spread like an epidemic throughout much of Western Europe. *Tarantism,* a form of the dancing mania that occurred in Italy, was thought to have been brought on by the tarantula. Episodes of *lycanthropy,* in which groups of people believed they were wolves and acted accordingly, were common in rural areas. In these examples, *animal possession* was the dominant motif. In many other cases, individuals were thought to be possessed by evil spirits (Ellenberger, 1970).

By the middle of the fifteenth century, tolerance for bizarre behavior became strained. The perception of witches and the response to them changed radically, and for nearly three hundred years thereafter, Europe was caught up in a frenzied fear of witches—a fear that caused thousands to be led to their death. For modern students of abnormal psychology, these witch-hunts provide a fascinating look at how the supernatural was used to explain madness and why it was such a convincing theory at the time.

Great social and intellectual upheaval prevailed during the late fifteenth century and the sixteenth century (McFarlane, 1970). With the rise of capi-

The frontispiece of one of the many editions of the *Malleus Maleficarum*, by Heinrich Kraemer and Johann Sprenger. (Courtesy The New York Public Library, Astor, Lenox and Tilden Foundations)

talism, individual values were replacing communal ones, towns were replacing rural communities, and the structure of the medieval family and village was being disturbed (Midelfort, 1972). Traditional authority was weakening. The Church itself was rife with schism as the Protestant Reformation plunged much of Europe into religious civil wars that further upset social equilibrium (Trevor-Roper, 1970).

It was within this context of extensive social instability that a belief in witches flourished in Europe. Witches were those who made pacts with Satan and who took delight in harming others. A Biblical injunction, hardly used until that time, was recalled vividly and implemented:

> *Any man or woman among you who calls up ghosts or spirits*
> *shall be put to death.*

The Church had earlier considered witchcraft mere "illusion" to be dealt with by secular authorities. Now it was heresy, treason against God, to be suppressed by the Church of Rome through its investigative agency, the Holy Inquisition. Two Dominican monks, Heinrich Kraemer and Johann Sprenger, wrote the *Malleus Maleficarum*, or *The Witches' Hammer*, a 1486 manual for hunting and disposing of witches. Printed on the recently invented printing press, the *Malleus Maleficarum* was widely distributed. Its official stamp and easy availability made it enormously popular, and more than thirty editions were published in the next hundred years (Summers, 1971). But it was not the only such treatise. Scores of "handbooks" on detecting the presence of witches flooded Europe.

Who were the witches? Overwhelmingly, they were women. "All witchcraft comes from carnal lust," the *Malleus Maleficarum* states, "which is in women insatiable." The most heinous crimes of which witches were accused were linked to reproduction: robbing men of their sexual potency, murdering born and unborn babies, and wanton lust. Men were protected from this heinous crime because Jesus was a man. The *Malleus Maleficarum*, then, was a religious document that reflected a strong fear of women's sexuality. Profoundly misogynist, it legitimized the persecution, torture, and death of women.

Various methods were used to extract confessions from suspected witches, among them the strappado and the rack. (From M. Molinos, 1745)

This title page from a 1613 text on witches depicts another common test for witchcraft: throwing the suspect into water. If the woman floated, she was guilty; if she sank, innocent. (Copyright Bodleian Library, Oxford, U.K.)

The occurrence of inexplicable events led one to suspect witchcraft. When, for example, illness occurred without warning in an otherwise healthy person, and that illness seemed not to be of physical origin, then witchcraft was the suspected cause. In fact, some witches were believed to be skilled in confirming the presence of witches. After holding molten lead over a sick man, they would pour it into a bowl of water. If the lead condensed into an image, they would conclude that the sickness was due to witchcraft.

Confirming evidence regarding a suspected witch could be obtained in two ways: through body marks and confessions. Any birthmark, scar, or mole on the woman's body indicated that a pact had been formed between her and Satan. Confession was more ideal. "Common justice demands that a witch should not be condemned to death unless she is convicted of her own confession." The inquisitors were not especially enamored of what today is called "due process." Any means of extracting a confession was permissible and many methods were simply cruel.

> The courts were careful to preserve the records and testimonies of those accused of witchcraft. The court record of an Englishwoman named Margaret Moone depicts a fairly typical catalog of offenses. Moone had killed a number of cows and pigs belonging to other villagers; she had spoiled several brewings of beer and batches of bread; she had caused a dray horse to break its neck; she had caused the death of several children; she had caused a man "to be deprived of his senses" and a child to be taken "sick with strange fits and shriekings out." Moone confessed to all these crimes, acknowledged that she was a witch and had at her service twelve imps. (Manning, 1974, p. 164)

It was believed that there was no "cure" for witchcraft, except for the physical destruction of the witch. On the continent, the confessed witch was burned by the secular authorities. In England and the colonies, witches were hanged. Conservatively, between the middle of the fifteenth and seventeenth century, more than 100,000 people (mostly women) in Europe and in the American colonies died as a result of the witch trials (see Box 2-1) (Deutsch, 1949). Witch-hunting was not the monopoly of the Church of Rome. With the Reformation, many Protestant sects also mounted zealous campaigns against the lustful consorts of Satan. Not surprisingly, charges of witchcraft were often hurled at members of rival religions (Thomas, 1971).

PHYSICAL CAUSES

While beliefs in the supernatural served to explain psychological distress for centuries, an approach to abnormality that emphasizes *physical* causes can also be traced back to the ancient world. In fact, it is possible that the prehistoric peoples who practiced trephining were employing a primitive surgical technique to relieve the pain of severe headaches. One of the first psychological disorders that was thought to have arisen from physical causes was *hysteria.*

Papyri from early Egypt, as well as the writings of Greek physicians, record a remarkable disorder that was found mainly among women who were virgins or widows. Its symptoms included such complaints as epileptic-like fits, pains of all sorts in various parts of the body, aphonia (loss of voice), headaches, dizziness, paralysis, blindness, lameness, listlessness, and melancholia. The Greeks believed that all of these difficulties arose from a single source: a roaming uterus.

The Greeks believed that the uterus was an animated organ that had somehow dislodged itself from its normal place to rove around the body, perhaps in search of water and nourishment, but often enough, for no good reason. In the course of its wanderings, it would attach itself here or there and create havoc. If it attached itself to the liver, for instance, the person would lose her voice, grind her teeth, and her complexion would turn ashen. Lodged in the chest cavity, this roaming uterus would produce convulsions similar to epilepsy, and at the heart it would produce anxiety, oppression, and vomiting. The Greek word for uterus is *hystera,* and the Greeks believed so deeply that the uterus was responsible for these difficulties that they named the entire disorder after it—hysteria (Veith, 1965).

This view of hysteria prevailed until the second century A.D., when it was challenged by Soranus and Galen, physicians who recognized that the uterus was not a living animal. Soranus wrote, ". . . the uterus does not issue forth like a wild animal from the lair, delighted by fragrant odors and fleeing bad odors; rather it is drawn together because of stricture caused by inflammation" (Veith, 1965, pp. 30–31). This new view of hysteria led to entirely different views of its origins and treatment. Since the *hystera* was not a roaming animal but rather a malfunctioning sexual organ, might there be a similar organ in men which, when malfunctioning, could cause them to have similar symptoms? Galen believed there was. He had observed that both men and women suffer similar symptoms following periods of sexual abstinence. He, therefore, argued that hysteria has a sexual basis, a view that is widely accepted today.

Attributing psychological distress to physical causes took a peculiar twist hundreds of years later with the belief in *animalism.* This belief asserted that there were remarkable similarities between animals and mad people. Like animals, the mad could not control themselves and therefore needed to be severely controlled. Like animals, the insane were capable of violence, often suddenly and without provocation. Like animals, they could live without protest in miserable conditions, conditions under which normal people simply could not exist (see Box 2-2). One proponent of this view pointed to

The Greek physician Galen (circa 130–201 A.D.) was an early theorist who believed that some apparently physical disorders were psychological in origin. (Courtesy National Library of Medicine)

The ease with which certain of the insane of both sexes bear the most rigorous and prolonged cold. . . . On certain days when the thermometer indicated . . . as many as 16 degrees below freezing, a madman . . . could not endure his wool blanket, and remained sitting on the icy floor of his cell. In the morning, one no sooner opened his door than he ran in his shirt into the inner court, taking ice and snow by the fistful, applying it to his breast and letting it melt with a sort of delectation. (Foucault, 1965, pp. 74–75)

The relatively primitive notions of physical cause that are captured in the early Greek views of hysteria, or in animalism, gradually yielded to more sophisticated approaches. With the development of modern medicine, many physicians came to consider madness to be a form of illness amenable to the same kinds of treatment as physical illness. Purges, bleeding, and forced vomiting were choice medical remedies of the seventeenth and eighteenth centuries, and these were administered to the infirm and the insane alike. Gradually, these views and treatments yielded to the kinds of approaches that characterize present-day medicine, in particular, surgery and pharmacology (see Chapter 3).

PSYCHOGENIC ORIGINS

The quest for understanding psychological abnormality was pursued down still another path by the ancient Greeks and Romans, this time to its ***psychological*** origins. In addition to his observations about hysteria, Galen contributed important insights into the psychological causes of abnormality. In a particularly striking instance, Galen examined a woman who complained of sleeplessness, listlessness, and general malaise. He could find no direct evidence of physical illness and ultimately narrowed his inferences to two possibilities. Either she was suffering from melancholy, which was a physical disorder of one of the four body "humors," or fluids, "or else she was troubled about something she was unwilling to confess," a psychological explanation. He concluded:

> After I had diagnosed that there was no bodily trouble, and that the woman was suffering from some mental uneasiness, it happened that at the very time I was ex-

amining her, this was confirmed. Somebody came from the theatre and said he had seen Pylades dancing. Then both her expression and the colour of her face changed. Seeing this, I applied my hand to her wrist, and noticed that her pulse had suddenly become extremely irregular. This kind of pulse indicates that the mind is disturbed; thus it occurs also in people who are disputing over any subject. So on the next day I said to one of my followers that, when I paid my visit to the woman, he was to come a little later and announce to me, "Morphus is dancing today." When he said this, I found that the pulse was unaffected. Similarly also on the next day, when I had an announcement made about the third member of the troupe, the pulse remained unchanged as before. On the fourth evening I kept very careful watch when it was announced that Pylades was dancing, and I noticed that the pulse was very much disturbed. Thus I found out that the woman was in love with Pylades, and by careful watch on the succeeding days my discovery was confirmed. (Galen, cited in Veith, 1965, p. 36)

Galen's assessment of possible cause is the hallmark of the scientific method that was eventually to advance our understanding and treatment of psychological disorders. Rather than leaping to a conclusion, Galen tested two alternative hypotheses and decided which was correct according to the evidence. In this case, the evidence favored the hypothesis that stressed psychological experience rather than physiology.

Galen's observations on the psychological origins of abnormality were forgotten for centuries. Thus, until the middle of the eighteenth century, hysteria was believed to be a female neurological disorder that had its origins in genital illness. The recognition that mental disorders were psychological in origin and could be treated by psychological means did not arise again until the middle of the eighteenth century. To understand how this view arose, we first need to look at one of the most colorful people in the history of abnormal psychology, Franz Anton Mesmer (1734–1815).

Mesmerism and Hypnotism

Mesmer is not only one of the most colorful, but surely one of the most maligned characters in the history of abnormal psychology. Variously called a genius and a charlatan, he proposed that many diseases, from epilepsy to hysteria, develop from the obstruction of the flow of an invisible and impal-

Franz Anton Mesmer (1734–1815) and his patients around the *baquet*. The baquet was supposed to concentrate a patient's magnetic fluid and induce a crisis, which would eventually restore the body's equilibrium, and the patient's health. (Courtesy The Mansell Collection)

pable entity that he first called "universal magnetic fluid" and later *animal magnetism.* Very much a man of the Enlightenment, Mesmer was influenced by contemporary discoveries in electricity and proposed the existence of a physical magnetic fluid which, when unequally distributed, causes disease in the body. He theorized that magnetic fluid was influenced by the lunar cycle, the tides, the planets, and the stars. Mesmer believed that health could be restored by using certain techniques which induced "crises" in the body. These crises would be provoked again and again, but each time would be experienced as less severe by the patient, until they disappeared and the body was back in equilibrium.

Mesmer went to Paris from Vienna in 1778. He opened a clinic where patients suffering from the various symptoms of hysteria were seen in groups. In a heavily curtained room, patients were arranged around a large wooden tub, or *baquet,* which was filled with water and magnetized iron filings. Iron rods protruded from the tub and were pointed by the patients to their ailing parts. The baquet was supposed to concentrate the magnetic fluid and induce the patient's crisis. Mesmer, dressed in a lavender cape, would pass among the patients to the accompaniment of gentle music, fixing his eye on them, and touching each with his iron wand. One patient would experience strange sensations, including trembling and convulsions. After the first succumbed, others were not long in having similar experiences, though there were always a few who were unaffected (Pattie, 1967).

Mesmer had departed from Vienna under a cloud: he had been accused of charlatanry. And, despite his therapeutic successes, it was not long before similar accusations were leveled against him in Paris. So heated and acrimonious were the charges and countercharges, that in 1783, Louis XVI appointed a Royal Commission to investigate animal magnetism. Its eminent members included the chemist Lavoisier, the astronomer Bailly, and Benjamin Franklin, who was then serving as U.S. ambassador to France. The Commission heard evidence, deliberated for five months, and concluded that there was no such thing as animal magnetism. Interestingly, the Commission did not question Mesmer's success in curing patients of their ills; rather, it addressed his theory that the ills themselves were the result of the imbalance of magnetic fluid in the body. The Commission found that there was no physical proof for the existence of this fluid. Thus, they concluded that Mesmer's cures were entirely due to "imagination." Crushingly defeated, Mesmer, a proud man, vanished into obscurity. But the *reality* of his "cures" remained. People in distress continued to seek this kind of help, and to benefit from it, so much so that animal magnetism came to be called *mesmerism.*

The findings of the Royal Commission were deadly to the scientific theory of mesmerism, but the techniques themselves survived. Underground in France, but publicly in the United States and in Germany, mesmerism continued to be practiced and studied. (Indeed, one of the most famous patients to be treated by this method in America was Mary Baker Eddy, the founder of Christian Science.) While the quest for finding the elusive magnetic fluid led to a dead end and was finally abandoned, the cures that derived from mesmerism continued to excite interest. The process that had been called mesmerism underwent a name change and came to be known as *hypnotism.*

A major figure in the scientific study of hypnosis was Jean Martin Charcot

Jean Martin Charcot (1825–1893) demonstrating hypnosis to a class of medical students. (Courtesy National Library of Medicine)

(1825–1893), Medical Director of one of the largest sections at La Salpêtrière and Professor of Diseases of the Nervous System at the University of Paris. Charcot was widely regarded as a first-rate scientist, the most eminent neurologist of the nineteenth century, and an awesome and much-feared teacher. The latter characteristic, we shall see, was his scientific undoing.

While Charcot was at La Salpêtrière, one of the wards in his charge housed women patients who suffered from convulsions. Charcot sought to distinguish hysterical convulsions from those brought on by epilepsy. In order to distinguish hysteria from other neurological disorders, Charcot employed hypnosis. If, for example, a patient who suffered a paralyzed arm was able to move her arm under hypnosis, then the diagnosis of hysteria could be given; otherwise, the appropriate diagnosis was a neurological disorder. Charcot extended his study to male patients as well, demonstrating that the symptoms of traumatic paralysis in men were the same as those of hysterical paralysis (Ellenberger, 1970).

Hypnosis fascinated Charcot, and he quickly generated a neurological theory about it. His students, ever eager to please, tested his views and brought back confirmatory evidence. But Charcot himself never hypnotized his patients. Rather, his students "worked them up" and taught them how to perform, after which Charcot unwittingly used them as demonstration subjects. Other scientists, particularly Hyppolyte Bernheim in Nancy, were unable to replicate Charcot's findings, and quickly located the source of error. Once again, a theory of hypnosis fell into disrepute, though the fact that hypnosis could be used to cure was unquestioned.

Charcot trained a large number of neurologists and psychiatrists, among them Sigmund Freud, the father of psychoanalysis. Freud proposed psychogenic causes as the root of madness. His contribution to the psychological approach to abnormality is so great, however, that we will take it up separately in Chapter 4.

After studying with Charcot, Sigmund Freud (1856–1939) went on to articulate a theory whose influence continues to be felt in modern psychology and psychiatry. (Courtesy Austrian Information Service)

TREATMENT OF THE MENTALLY DISTRESSED

How a psychological disorder is treated depends heavily on how it is understood. When mental disturbance was deemed to be the result of supernatural causes, supernatural means were often needed to rid the individual of the distress. Similarly, when its origins were believed to be physical or psychological, treatment tended to rely on those means.

TREATING SUPERNATURAL POSSESSION

Possession by supernatural forces—demons, spirits, and the like—was most commonly treated by *exorcism,* a ceremonial ritual during which the demons were expelled from the victim's bodies. Exhausting and often time-consuming, exorcism rituals generally involved a cooperative relationship between the *shaman* or priest, and the afflicted. Together they tried to make the alien spirits identify themselves and then to cajole, threaten, and overwhelm the intruders so that they would leave the poor unfortunates. The belief that mental distress is the result of possession by evil spirits has been a persistent one. While they are rare and commonly frowned upon, exorcism rituals are performed even today in the United States.

When exorcism failed, *ostracism,* which is casting out the person as well as his or her demons, might be used. Ostracism was sometimes carried to extremes. In certain parts of Europe during the Middle Ages, there were *narrenschiffen,* literally ships full of "fools," quite possibly manned by madmen, which went from harbor to harbor, seeking but not finding safe port (Foucault, 1965).

This sixteenth century woodcut depicts a demon being exorcised from a woman. The exorcism is being performed by a bishop in front of the altar in a cathedral. (Courtesy National Library of Medicine)

A fifteenth century woodcut of a ship of "fools." (Courtesy National Library of Medicine)

TREATING PHYSICAL CAUSES

When hysteria was thought to result from a wandering uterus, there were a prodigious number of proposed cures. The Egyptians and Greeks based most of them on the pull-push principle: Draw the uterus back to its proper place with pleasant experiences and aromatic substances, and drive it away from its current attachment with fetid fumigations. Perfumes and gentle massage played a therapeutic role in pulling the uterus back to where it was supposed to be; garlic and burning dung were applied to the aching areas in order to drive the prodigal uterus away. Later, in the Middle Ages, human attempts to keep the uterus in its place appear to have been abandoned in favor of divine intercession, as the following excerpt from a tenth-century prayer indicates.

PRAYER FOR THE WANDERING WOMB

Lord, our God, who commands the host of angels that are standing before Him in trembling awe. Amen, amen, amen. O womb, womb, womb, cylindrical womb, red womb, white womb, fleshy womb, bleeding womb, large womb . . . O demoniacal one! . . .

I conjure thee, O womb. . . . not to harm that maid of God, N., not to occupy her head, throat, neck, chest, ears, teeth, eyes, nostrils, shoulder blades, arms, hands, heart, stomach, spleen, kidneys, back, sides, joints, navel, intestines, bladder, thighs, shins, heels, nails, but to lie down quietly in the place which God chose for thee, so that this maid of God, N., be restored to health. . . . (Excerpted from Zilboorg, 1941, pp. 131–32.)

THE RISE OF PSYCHOGENIC TREATMENTS

By the eighteenth century, the explanations that stressed supernatural causes, while never completely abandoned, no longer commanded respect among serious thinkers. Instead, emphasis turned to two other explanations, both of which, as we have seen, were first proposed in ancient times.

One, following notions of physical cause, defined psychological distress as fundamentally *illness,* not different in kind from other physical illnesses. The other held that psychological disorder was fundamentaly *psychological,* and *very* different in kind from physical illness. These theories continue to dominate our thinking today. Both views command considerable supportive evidence. We will examine the biological or medical view of psychological distress and its implications for treatment in the next chapter. Now, we focus on the treatments that grew out of psychogenic theories of madness.

Much of the excitement that was generated by the psychogenic viewpoint came about, as we have seen, through the study of hysteria. With its paralyses, anesthesias, and convulsions, its loss of voice, sight, or hearing, and occasional loss of consciousness, hysteria seemed patently a *physical* disorder. It was on the basis of his physical theory of animal magnetism that Mesmer developed the technique which came to be called hypnosis. Charcot, in his path-breaking work, was subsequently able to use hypnosis to distinguish between symptoms that had an organic cause and symptoms that were hysterical in nature. Subsequent theorists suggested that the therapeutic effects of hypnosis resulted from psychological suggestion (Bernheim, 1886, cited in Pattie, 1967). Thus, "psychotherapeutics" became an accepted treatment for the mentally disturbed.

By the end of the nineteenth century, hypnosis was widely used in Europe and in the United States for treating hysterical disorders. It formed the basis for the development of modern forms of psychotherapy, and it was a significant milestone in the psychogenic approach to mental disorders.

One of the people who used hypnosis in his treatment of patients was Josef Breuer (1842–1925), a distinguished Viennese internist whose practice included a large number of hysterical patients. Breuer's treatment often consisted of inducing these patients to talk about their problems and fantasies under hypnosis. Frequently patients would become emotional under hypnosis, reliving painful experiences, experiencing a deep **emotional catharsis,** and emerging from the hypnotic trance feeling much better. The patients, of course, were unaware of a relationship between what they discussed under hypnosis, how emotional they had become, and how they felt subsequently. But Breuer believed that because his patients had experienced a catharsis under hypnosis, their symptoms disappeared.

Just as Breuer was making these discoveries, Sigmund Freud, then a neurologist, returned to Vienna. Freud had just completed his studies with Charcot and began to work with Breuer. Together they utilized Breuer's "cathartic method," encouraging patients to report their experiences and fantasies under hypnosis. Freud, however, noticed that similar therapeutic effects could be obtained *without* hypnosis, so long as the patient reported everything that came to mind and experienced emotional catharsis. It was this discovery that led Freud to the theory and therapeutic technique called **psychoanalysis,** which is described in detail in Chapter 4.

Josef Breuer (1842–1925) collaborated with Sigmund Freud in writing *Studies in Hysteria* (1895). (Courtesy Ernest Freud)

THE RISE OF THE PSYCHIATRIC HOSPITAL

There is no precise date to mark the beginning of modern treatments for madness. In fact, beliefs in supernatural causes persisted into the twentieth century in some parts of the West. Nonetheless, most observers date the beginning of the modern psychological era with the establishment of the psychiatric hospital, an institution that itself has a rather special history.

The word "hospital" has only recently acquired its strong medical connotation. Even as late as the early twentieth century, it meant something quite different: an asylum for the underprivileged. Even today, Webster's primary definition of hospital is "a charitable institution for the needy, aged, infirm or young."

The medical hospital, and surely the psychiatric one, is a relatively modern invention. Both evolved in the seventeenth century from institutions that were created to house and confine the poor, the homeless, the unemployed, and among them, the insane. Throughout the sixteenth and seventeenth centuries, poverty was widespread. War and economic depression had dislocated large numbers of people and reduced them to begging and petty crime. In 1532, in Paris, these problems were so severe that beggars were arrested and forced to work in pairs in the city's sewers. Two years later, a new decree forced "poor scholars and indigents" to leave the city. All to no avail, for at the beginning of the seventeenth century, Paris, which had a population of fewer than 100,000 people, had more than 30,000 beggars! In 1606, it was decreed that beggars should be publicly whipped, branded, shorn, and driven from the city. And a year later, in 1607, an ordinance established companies of archers who were located at the gates of the city—their sole task to forbid the return of these indigents.

It was in this social and economic climate that, in 1656, the Hôpital Général of Paris was founded for the poor "of both sexes, of all ages, and from all localities, of whatever breeding and birth, in whatever state they may be, able-bodied or invalid, sick or convalescent, curable or incurable" (Edict of 1656, cited in Foucault, 1965, p. 39). From a strictly humane point of view, the Hôpital Général, which included La Salpêtrière, La Pitie, and La Bicêtre—institutions that later became famous in their own right—was surely an improvement over the conditions that preceded it. For the first time in France, the government took responsibility for feeding and housing its "undesirables." But in return, those undesirables—the poor, the homeless, the mad—yielded up the privilege of roaming the streets. Personal liberty was traded for room and board. It was not a voluntary trade; shortly after the decree was proclaimed, the militia scoured the city, hunting and herding beggars into the various buildings of the Hôpital. Within four years, the Hôpital housed 1 percent of Paris's population.

Paris was not alone in its concern to confine undesirables. During the same period, all over France and throughout Europe, similar institutions were being established. To the modern mind, it seems inconceivable that the poor, the mad, the aged, the infirm, and even the petty criminal could somehow be lumped together and signed over to the same institution. Yet, a compelling commonality bound these people together. *They were not gainfully employed.* Unemployment was viewed, not as the result of economic depression, technological change, or bad luck, but as a personal, indeed a moral, failure. Simple indolence was its accepted name. The task of the Hôpital Général was a moral one: to prevent "mendicancy and idleness as the source of all disorders" (Edict of 1656, cited in Foucault, 1965, p. 47). Whatever restrictions were imposed, whatever behaviors required, and whatever punishments meted out, all were justified by the moral mission of the Hô-pital Général.

The hospital was a place of confinement during periods of economic depression. But during economic growth, the hospital was easily and justifiably converted into a workhouse. It required that its residents work (but it paid them a mere fraction of what they would ordinarily make). With increasing industrialization in England, for example, many such workhouses were established in industrial centers, providing cheap, forced labor to growing industries.

SEGREGATING THE INSANE

While governments failed to distinguish the insane from the other unfortunates, within the hospital such distinctions were quickly made and were ultimately institutionalized. The insane were given much worse care than other residents of the hospital, and were subjected to brutal physical abuse. At the end of the eighteenth century, one visitor to La Bicêtre described the miserable condition in which he found one mad inmate:

> The unfortunate whose entire furniture consisted of this straw pallet, lying with his head, feet, and body pressed against the wall, could not enjoy sleep without being soaked by the water that trickled from that mass of stone. (Desportes, cited in Foucault, 1965, pp. 70–71)

The same reporter said of La Salpêtrière that what made the place more miserable, and often more fatal, was that in winter, "when the waters of the Seine rose, those cells situated at the level of the sewers became not only more unhealthy, but worse still, a refuge for a swarm of huge rats, which during the night attacked the unfortunates confined there and bit them wherever they could reach them; madwomen have been found with feet, hands, and face torn by bites which are often dangerous and from which several have died" (Desportes, cited in Foucault, 1965, pp. 70–71).

A day at the lunatic asylum was a popular excursion in the eighteenth century, much as a day at the zoo is today. To judge by the gate receipts, visits to La Salpetrière in Paris, Bedlam in London, and the Pennsylvania Hospital in Philadelphia were popular attractions. This engraving by the eighteenth century painter William Hogarth shows visitors touring Bedlam. (Courtesy National Library of Medicine)

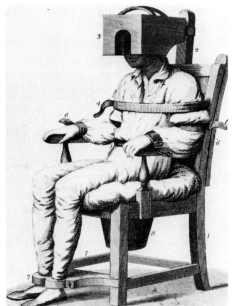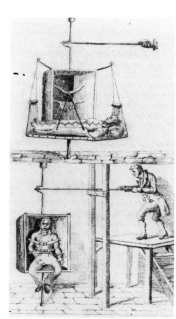

Chains and braces, the primitive ancestors of today's straitjackets, were used to control patients and enable them to overcome their "animality." The Industrial Revolution mechanized these instruments. Shown here are mechanisms that were used to treat patients in early American psychiatric hospitals. From left to right are: (a) patients who were hanged by their neck and arms, (b) the tranquilizing chair, which was used by Benjamin Rush, the father of American psychiatry, to treat patients, and (c) the circulating swing. (Courtesy National Library of Medicine and Culver Pictures)

Paris was not unique. In the London hospital, St. Mary's of Bethlehem (which soon became known as Bedlam), patients were chained to the walls or kept on long leashes. Nearby, in Bethnal Green, patients were bound hand and foot, and confined in filthy quarters.

The United States established its first hospital, the Pennsylvania Hospital, in 1756. At the urging of Benjamin Franklin, the government set aside a section for "lunatics." They were consigned to the cellar and

> Their scalps were shaved and blistered; they were bled to the point of syncope; purged until the alimentary canal failed to yield anything but mucus, and in the intervals, they were chained by the waist or the ankle to the cell wall . . . It was not considered unusual or improper for the keeper to carry a whip and use it freely. (Morton, 1897, cited in Deutsch, 1949, p. 600)

The Pennsylvania Hospital was then considered the most advanced and humane center for "lunatics" in America.

These practices, however cruel they seem, were neither instituted for nor guided by cruel reasons. Rather, they arose from the widely believed theory of madness, animalism. Even Philippe Pinel, who was concerned with the psychological well-being of those in institutions and who eventually revolutionized aspects of the care of the insane, believed that the afflicted did not have the physical sensitivities of human beings but rather were like animals in their lack of sensitivity to pain, to temperature, and to other external stimuli.

THE GROWTH OF HUMANE TREATMENT

By the end of the eighteenth century, the idea that the incarcerated insane should be treated as animals was under attack. No degree of intellectual or theological rationalization could conceal the torment that these punitive treatments imposed on patients. From a variety of respected sources, protest grew over the conditions of confinement, and especially over the shackles, the chains, the dungeons, and the whippings. Other models for treatment were sought. One was found at Gheel, a Belgian community that had been accepting the insane for quite some time. New ones were found through courageous experiments in Italy, France, England, and the United States.

Gheel

As the site of a religious shrine in Belgium, the small town of Gheel had been a recuperative center for the insane since the Middle Ages. There, consistent with a religious ethos, "cure" was achieved through prayer and in the "laying on of the hands." Those who prayed were treated in a special, and for the time, unusual way. The deeply troubled were shown habitual kindness, courtesy, and gentleness. The insane lived in the community and, apart from being forbidden alcohol, suffered few restrictions. They took rooms in people's homes, where they were treated as guests. Gheel's reputation grew, and so did the number of people who went there. It provided a model of treatment that stressed sympathy, respect, and concern.

Striking Patients' Chains

William Norris was erroneously confined for fourteen years in Bedlam before coming to the attention of members of Parliament. He had been confined by a "stout iron ring, rivotted round his neck," which was attached to a twelve-inch chain, which in turn was attached to the wall. He was therefore unable to move more than twelve inches from the wall and could not even turn over in his bed because of the shortness of the chain. (Courtesy Clements Fry Collection, Yale University)

Gheel was not a hospital, but rather a refuge for those who were fortunate enough to make their way there. Although some of the insane were tolerated within their own communities, most of them were impoverished, abandoned, or simply unlucky. They filled the public institutions, which were cruel beyond the telling. But late in the eighteenth century, things began to change. The first hospital to remove the chains from psychiatric patients was St. Boniface in Florence, Italy. There, in 1774, by allowing patients freedom of movement, Vincenzo Chiarugi introduced a radical reform in patient care. It took hold. Later, in 1787, Joseph Dacquin initiated similar reforms in the Insane Department of the hospital at Chambéry, France. And in 1792, during the French Revolution, Philippe Pinel, the newly appointed directory of La Bicêtre, unshackled the patients of the Hôpital Général of Paris. Pinel was not applying the dicta of liberty and equality to psychiatric patients. Indeed, he believed in the need for control and coercion in psychiatric care. But, he insisted that for coercion to be effective, it needed to be *psychological* rather than physical. The control exerted by shackles and chains would be ended just as soon as the patient was discharged. What was required was internalized control that would endure after the patient left the hospital grounds. Therefore, shortly after assuming the directorship of La Bicêtre, he "freed" its inmates from their chains, moved them from the cellar dungeons into sunny and airy rooms, and allowed them freedom of the hospital grounds.

His was not an easy decision. There was little public support for Pinel's views. Not only did the view that the insane were like animals linger on, but more important, the belief that they were "dangerous animals" also remained. Moreover, the political consequences of his decision were potentially disastrous. The function of La Bicêtre and its sister institutions was **confinement.** Most people believed that the hospitals existed in order to protect the civilized citizens of France from the dangerous and disturbing

The eighteenth century French reformer Philippe Pinel shown ordering the removal of chains from mental patients. (Courtesy National Library of Medicine)

excesses of madmen. "Liberty, equality, and fraternity" were not meant to apply to the mentally deranged! An' interchange between Pinel and Couthon, an aide to one of the Revolution's most radical leaders, reveals how foolhardy Pinel's reforms were thought to be. Couthon, after having been insulted and cursed by La Bicêtre's patient, had turned to Pinel and said:

"Now citizen, are you mad yourself to seek to unchain such beasts?"

Pinel replied calmly: "I am convinced that these madmen are so intractable only because they have been deprived of air and liberty."

"Well, do as you like with them, but I fear you may become the victim of your own presumption."

(Foucault, 1965, p. 242)

It is not difficult to apreciate Couthon's position in this debate. Abnormal behavior makes other people fearful and defensive. They worry much more about possible consequences than about causes. Couthon was concerned about what these people might do, and he failed to see, as both Pinel and James Carkesse (see Box 2-3) had seen, that violent behavior might, at least partially, be a *result* of the cruel confinement.

Religious Reforms in England

Reforms in France were undertaken by secular authorities, but those in England developed from religious concerns. In 1791, Hannah Mills, a Quaker, was admitted to the Lunatick Asylum at York, one of the two major institutions for the insane in England (the other being Bedlam in London). Mills's friends came to visit her but were denied entry on the grounds that she was in no condition to see visitors. A few weeks later, Mills was dead. Her friends suspected that the treatment she had received at York caused or at least contributed to her death. Their suspicions were not entirely groundless, for the conditions in England's institutions for the insane were widely known to be horrible, even by the standards of those days.

Among Mills's friends was William Tuke who, moved by her death, urged the Yorkshire Society of Friends to establish a humanitarian institution for the insane. Despite stiff opposition, similar to the opposition Pinel faced in France, the Retreat at York was established in 1796. It was called a retreat in order to avoid the stigma of such words as "madhouse," "insane asylum" and "lunatickhouse." The name conveyed "the idea of what such an institution should be, namely, a place in which the unhappy might obtain a refuge; a quiet haven in which the shattered bark might find the means of reparation and safety." The kind of treatment that had originated at Gheel —long established, successful, but ignored—was finally being implemented elsewhere (Hunt, 1932, cited in Deutsch, 1949, p. 93).

From the outset, the Retreat's approach to care was dramatically different from practices elsewhere in England. Patients were guests, not "prisoners," as they were called at both Bedlam and the Lunatick Asylum at York. The cornerstones of care were kindness, consideration, courtesy, and dignity. To the extent that treatment principles were defined at the Retreat, two dominated: the need for esteem and the value of work, especially physical work. This emphasis on the therapeutic value of work was unique to the Retreat. The moral virtue of work is deeply embedded in Quaker philosophy. It was consistent with the widely held work ethic of the day and its concomitant distaste for unemployment and the unemployed. The need for esteem was an even more highly valued principle. Treatment took the form of encouraging the insane to acquire social skills, to utilize them, and to gain rewards for meeting the requirements of everyday social interaction. Thus, in the manner of the English during those times, the staff of the Retreat would regularly invite the guests to tea (Foucault, 1965, p. 249).

The effects of the Retreat upon some of its guests were dramatic. Samuel Tuke, the founder's grandson, tells of a guest who was brought to the Retreat in such a violent condition that even though he was chained and shackled, his escorts were afraid of him. Immediately upon entering the Retreat, however, his chains were removed. He was invited to dine with the staff and then was courteously shown to his room. So long as he was considerate of the needs of others, he was told, there would be no need for restraint. (Restraint was not entirely abolished. In emergencies, patients at the Retreat were

A sketch of the English reformer William Tuke. (Courtesy The Warder Collection)

bound in broad leather belts which left the arms free. In extreme circumstances, straitjackets were used.) The patient promised to restrain himself. When, however, he became agitated, he was reminded of the agreements he had made on his first day. "He would listen with attention to the persuasions and arguments of his friendly visitor. After such conversations, the patient was generally better for some days or a week" (Tuke, 1813, cited in Foucault, 1965, p. 246). At the end of four months, he was able to leave the Retreat.

Moral Treatment in the United States

The ideas that led to the founding and success of Tuke's Retreat at York spread quickly to the United States. The essence of this form of treatment, called **moral treatment,** was enunciated by Dr. Romeyn Beck, of New York, in 1811. He wrote:

> . . . The rules most proper to be observed are the following: Convince the lunatics that the power of the physician and keeper is absolute; have humane attendants, who shall act as servants to them; never threaten but execute; offer no indignities to them, as they have a high sense of honour; punish disobedience pre-emptorily, in the presence of other maniacs; if unruly, forbid them the company of others, use the strait waistcoats, confine them in a dark and quiet room, order spare diet . . . ; tolerate noisy ejaculations; . . . Let their fears and resentments be soothed without unnecessary opposition; thus acting, the patient will "minister to himself." (Beck, 1811, cited in Deutsch, 1949, pp. 91–92)

In 1817, the Friends Asylum at Frankford, Pennsylvania, was established. Shortly thereafter, in 1821, the Bloomingdale Asylum was founded through the efforts of Thomas Eddy, a Quaker businessman who had been much influenced by Samuel Tuke. The Bloomingdale Asylum, located on the site of the present campus of Columbia University in New York City, stressed the

The hospital grounds of the Willard Asylum for the Insane in western New York State. Opened in 1869, it was one of the early American mental institutions and sheltered 1500 patients. (Courtesy Harvard University Library)

two features that were the hallmarks of humane care: kind treatment and the virtues of work. For the first time, moreover, records were kept of patients' progress in the hospital as well as of their condition before entering it. The efforts at the Bloomingdale Asylum served as the model for several later hospitals, including the Hartford Retreat and the McLean Hospital. Among patients treated in these centers, 70 percent of those who had been hospitalized for less than one year were discharged, having recovered or improved (Tourney, 1967; Rothman, 1971).

SUMMARY

1. The times and culture in which individuals live and the general way in which they perceive the world influence how abnormality is understood and treated.

2. When the world is perceived in supernatural terms, abnormality is likely to be viewed as a *supernatural* phenomenon. Prehistoric people attributed abnormality to possession by spirits trapped in the head and chipped *trephines* in the skull to let the spirits out.

3. Some Greeks and Romans attributed abnormality to *physical* causes. For example, they believed that *hysteria* was caused by a wandering uterus that created discomfort wherever it settled. They treated it by trying to draw the uterus back to its proper place. Galen challenged this idea and said that hysteria was caused by a malfunctioning sexual organ. Furthermore, Galen also contributed important insights into *psychological* causes of abnormality.

4. In medieval Europe, some behaviors that might seem bizarre today were esteemed as being evidence of piety and holiness. Other behaviors, equally bizarre from a modern perspective, were held to be the result of *possession.* Individuals so possessed were subjected to rites of exorcism and were sometimes ostracized from their communities entirely.

5. The late Middle Ages and Renaissance were especially bleak periods for those who were suffering from psychological distress. If not viewed as possessed themselves, they were often accused of practicing witchcraft and causing others to be possessed. Tens of thousands of people were accused of being witches and were hanged or burned during this period, as there was no known "cure" for witchcraft.

6. In the seventeenth century, hospitals grew out of institutions that were originally created to house and confine the poor, lame, dispossessed, and insane. The insane, however, were segregated from the other residents of the hospital and were subjected to brutal physical abuse. Treatment in the early insane asylum was predicated on the view that the insane displayed the characteristics of animals and could therefore be treated like animals.

7. In the middle of the eighteenth century, it gradually was recognized that mental disorders were *psychological* in origin and could be treated by psychological means. Mesmer tried to induce crises to restore the flow of *animal magnetism.* Charcot treated mental disorders by *hypnosis,* after distinguishing hysterical convulsions from symptoms with an organic cause. Both Breuer and Freud used hypnosis to induce *catharsis* in hysterical patients.

8. By the end of the eighteenth century, new and more humane treatments for the insane were found. The best hospitals began to stress the need for *moral treatment,* for patient dignity and work, and they began to keep records of patients' condition, both before they entered the hospital and while they were being treated.

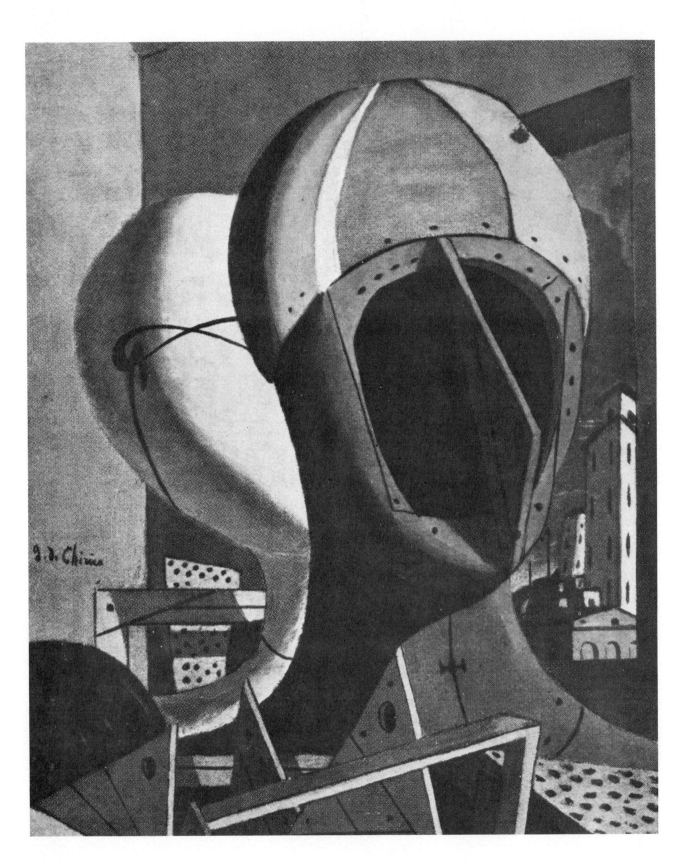

Part II

APPROACHES TO ABNORMALITY

The Biomedical Model

A s we saw in Chapter 1, defining abnormality is itself a major problem. At what point should a person be considered abnormal? How does one person's abnormality differ from another person's abnormality? The checkered history that we read about in Chapter 2 reflects society's attempts to cope with the elusive nature of abnormality. To us, many of the therapies of the past seem at best crude and at worst inhuman and cruel. Our ancestors' sometimes wayward approach to madness resulted in part from the basic problem of definition. But some order did come out of the apparent chaos of our predecessors' methods: abnormality seems to be a result of either some mental disorder or a physical malfunction. Thus, a person's thoughts, such as the memory of a childhood event, might be responsible for abnormal behavior. Or, a physical malfunctioning, some chemical or anatomical deficit, might be causing the madness.

As we saw in Chapter 2, Charcot demonstrated that hypnosis could both produce and relieve the symptoms of hysteria, thereby showing that psychological events could cause mental disorder. At the same time, a series of landmark experiments showed that physical illness could also cause psychopathology, making credible the view that some psychopathology had its origin in an organic disorder. This idea is the subject of this chapter.

MODELS OF ABNORMALITY

Before we review the landmark experiments that support the biomedical model of abnormality, we should say something about what a *model* is. As you saw in the last chapter, there have been, over the course of history, several ways of defining and approaching abnormality. Some approached it from the moral standpoint; others from a more supernatural one. Others, specifically Sigmund Freud, took a more psychological approach to abnormality. In effect, each of these approaches could be considered a model of abnormality.

To understand what a model of abnormality is, consider the example of an individual suffering from depression. He or she may have several symp-

Psychological disorders involve several levels of debilitation. Is this woman depressed because she believes her future is bleak, because her interpersonal relations no longer bring her satisfaction, because the chemistry of her brain has changed, because she feels sad and hopeless, or because her behavior is utterly passive? Any given model of depression will focus on only one level of symptoms. (© 1983 Stephen Shames/Black Star)

toms. Her emotional life is troubled: she feels sad and blue. Her thinking is distorted: she believes the future is bleaker than it really is. Her behavior has changed: she is more passive and lethargic than she used to be. Her interpersonal relations have withered: she becomes indifferent to people she once loved. Also her biology is altered: she is losing weight and sleeping too little, and the very chemistry of her brain is changing.

How does one go about the task of understanding depression, and then alleviating it? A scientist's particular approach or model will determine how to proceed. For example, someone who takes a biomedical view of the abnormality will concentrate on those symptoms of the depressive that are related to the depressive's biological processes. There is some accepted evidence that the chemistry of a depressive's brain changes when he is depressed. The biological scientist will experiment with these biochemical factors in order to see if they are the cause, or etiology, of the depression. Also, in an attempt to alleviate the disorder, the investigator will be more likely to develop therapies, in this case chemical therapies or drugs, that might counteract other biochemical factors. On the other hand, someone who follows a cognitive model might well emphasize the disordered thinking of the depressive as the cause and use therapies to change these cognitive distortions.

As you can see, following a particular model of abnormality is a matter of choice, and the choice always involves risk. For example, an investigator might believe that early childhood experiences are the primary influence on adult psychopathology. He could spend years studying his manic-depressive patient's past history and never cure him, for it might turn out that manic-depression is caused by a biological problem and cured by a chemical. His strict adherence to a particular model would have blinded him to this other possibility—in this case, a biological explanation of manic-depression. In sum, there is a danger inherent in following any particular model of abnormality. By concentrating on one level of evidence, we might neglect some of the other, more crucial evidence. The kinds of abnormality vary so much that it is unlikely that one particular model of abnormality will explain all mental disorders.

At present, there are five major models, sometimes complementary, often competing in their attempt to understand and cure abnormality. We begin with the *biomedical model,* which holds that abnormality is an illness of the body. We will then turn to the *psychodynamic model,* which holds that abnormality is driven by hidden conflicts within our personality. We will examine the *behavioral model,* which holds that we learn through conditioning to be abnormal, and that we can unlearn these maladaptive ways of behaving. We will discuss the most recent major model, the *cognitive model,* which holds that abnormality springs from disordered thinking about oneself and the world. Finally, we will examine the *existential-humanistic model,* which holds that disorder results when an individual fails to confront the basic questions of life successfully: What is the meaning of life? How can I live up to my fullest potential? How can I face death?

THE BIOMEDICAL MODEL

Those who advocate the biomedical model typically approach abnormality as medical researchers approach an illness: identifying a *syndrome* (diverse symptoms that tend to occur together), searching for the *etiology* (cause) of the syndrome, and deciding on a *treatment* for the illness. Having observed the symptoms of a syndrome, biomedical researchers will consider three possible causes for the illness: germs, genes, and biochemistry. Thus, they will first try to find whether a germ has invaded and disrupted the patient's biological system. Second, they will review the patient's relatives' records to find out if the illness is inherited. And third, they will examine the patient's biochemistry and anatomy for any possible irregularities, determining, for example, if the patient lacks an essential vitamin. Whatever they find to be the organic problem underlying the illness, they will use a biochemical treatment to counteract it, for example using a drug to fight off germs, or dosages of an essential vitamin to return the patient's biochemistry to normal.

Similarly, the psychologists and psychiatrists who adhere to the biomedical model will seek underlying organic factors in their search for the causes of psychological abnormality. They will group diverse, but co-occurring, symptoms together into a coherent syndrome. Then they will search for a *germ* causing the syndrome. They will study the patient's relatives to see if the person's *genes* might be causing the disorder. And they will examine the patient's *biochemistry* and anatomy, specifically the patient's brain, to see how they could be influencing the abnormality. Once an etiology has been discovered, some biological treatment, usually a drug, will be sought to alleviate the abnormality.

The idea that psychological disorders have physical etiologies is both ancient and venerable. We saw in the last chapter that the ancients believed that hysteria resulted from a wandering uterus. The Egyptians, Greeks, and Romans sought to cure this psychological abnormality by physical means: assaulting the body of the sufferer with a great variety of drugs, massages, fumigations, and so on. Behind all these treatments lay the belief that the cause of the psychological disorder was a physical disorder. It was not until the latter half of the nineteenth century, however, that anyone convincingly

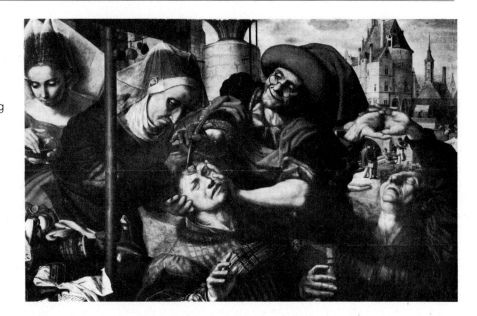

The view that mental illness was a disorder of the body reached its most concrete stage with the stone of Folly. Here in Jan Sanders van Hemessen's painting (c. 1530), early "physicians" attempt to remove one such stone from a bound patient possessed with madness. This appears crude in its execution, but we now have far more sophisticated methods for removing, not the stone of Folly, but rather tumors—growths in the brain that sometimes bring about abnormality. (Courtesy Museo del Prado, Madrid)

demonstrated that any form of psychological disorder was caused by organic illness. At that time, it was found that syphilis caused general paresis. This story illustrates how the isolation of a syndrome led to the discovery of an etiology, which in turn led to the discovery of a therapy. In addition, it illustrates how a mental disorder can be caused by a germ (one of the biomedical model's three possible causes of abnormality). This proved to be one of the great sagas in the history of biomedical science.

GERMS AS ETIOLOGY: SYPHILIS AND GENERAL PARESIS

There was an enormous upsurge in the incidence of a particular kind of mental illness during the sixteenth century, after Columbus discovered the New World. We have come to call this disorder *general paresis.* In the sixteenth century, its symptoms seemed to be mainly delusions of grandeur: the false notion that one is rather more important than the objective facts indicate. Such delusions presumably existed before the sixteenth century, and the newly deluded seemed no different, except in number, from those who had preceded them.

As early as 1672, Thomas Willis (1621–1675), an English anatomist, observed that some of these patients exhibited dullness of the mind and forgetfulness that seemed to develop into downright stupidity and foolishness. Later in life, these same people would fall into paralysis. This was not a precise observation. Rather, it served loosely to differentiate one group of madmen from others, based on signs of developing stupidity and paralysis. In 1805, the French physician, Jean Esquirol (1772–1840), added another significant observation: the mental deterioration and paralysis observed in this group of patients quickly culminated in the death of the patients.

There the matter stood until 1826, when Esquirol's student, A. L. J. Bayle, undertook the first major step necessary for a disorder to be understood as biomedical: organization of symptoms into a syndrome, which allowed precise description and diagnosis of the illness. He formalized the diagnosis by giving a complete and exact description of the physical and psychological symptoms, and arguing strongly that these constituted a separate disease, a different madness, if you will, from all others then known. He argued that mental deterioration, paralysis, and subsequent death, among others, were a group of symptoms that clustered together and formed the distinct syndrome of general paresis.

Bayle's rigorous definition of the disorder led to considerable speculation about its etiology. Quite early, there had been some suspicion that it was caused by syphilis. But at the time, Wilhelm Greisinger (1817–1868), an eminent psychiatric authority of physiological bent, had dismissed that view on the seemingly sound basis that paresis occurred among people in whom no trace of syphilitic infection could be found. Reports of cases in which paretics were known to have had syphilis were clearly not sufficient, since these were contradicted by the paretics who adamantly denied they had ever had syphilis and who showed no evidence of syphilis.

Despite Greisinger's opinion and the support of his colleagues, evidence gradually emerged that syphilis was somehow implicated in general paresis. But that evidence was difficult to accumulate for three reasons. First, and perhaps most important, syphilis precedes paresis by as many as thirty years. The connection between the one and the other was difficult to see. Second, syphilis was then, as now, a disease about which there was considerable shame. People were often unable to admit to themselves, and surely not to others, that they had contracted the disease. Third, the diagnosis of syphilis was itself not an exact science. In the early part of the nineteenth century, techniques were still not available for ascertaining that someone had syphilis, because the overt symptoms that occur immediately after contracting it soon disappear. Not until there were improvements in microscopy, was it ascertained that syphilitic organisms (spirochetes) remain in the body long after the overt symptoms vanish.

The evidence, then, accumulated slowly. By about 1860, it was possible to demonstrate that there was enormous destruction in the neural tissue of the brains of people who had died from general paresis. Later, in 1869, D. M. Argyll (1837–1909); a Scottish eye surgeon, demonstrated that the central nervous system was implicated in syphilis by showing that the eyes of syphilitics failed to show the standard pupillary reflex—the narrowing of the pupil to bright light. In 1884, Alfred Fournier (1832–1914), a French physician, provided highly suggestive *epidemiological* evidence (that is, evidence from many individuals) on the relation between syphilis and general paresis: some 65 percent of paretics had a demonstrable history of syphilis, compared to only 10 percent of nonparetics. That evidence, of course, was merely suggestive: it did not demonstrate cause since it did not show that 100 percent of paretics had prior histories of syphilis. But it added significantly to the mounting tide of data, turning belief away from Greisinger's view that strong spirits and cigars were the culprits, toward the syphilis-paresis link.

The overt symptoms of syphilis—the sores (chancres) on the genitals—may disappear in a few weeks, but the disease does not. It goes underground, attacking the central nervous system. Cures for syphilis were unknown then. Thus, not only was it true that if you had the disease you couldn't get rid of it, but it was equally true and also known that *like measles, if you contracted*

In this woodcut, syphilis patients are shown in various stages of deterioration. (Courtesy The Bettman Archive)

syphilis once, you couldn't get it again. More bluntly, if someone who has already become syphilitic (a paretic) comes in contact with another syphilitic germ, he will not develop sores on his genitals.

Consider the situation of those who believed that this psychological disorder (general paresis) was caused by the syphilitic germ. On the one hand, there was evidence that many paretics had syphilis. But some paretics claimed never to have contracted syphilis. The investigators had a hypothesis: perhaps those paretics who claimed not to have had syphilis actually had had the disease and did not know it or were too ashamed to admit it. If indeed these paretics were ignorant or not telling the truth, then the case for a biological cause of general paresis would be convincing. There was one means, but a risky one, of finding out by way of an experiment if these paretics had previously had syphilis. The investigators reasoned that if you inject these paretics with the syphilitic germ, one startling result would come about. The paretics would not contract the disease; since you cannot get syphilis twice. Betting on this outcome, the German neurologist Richard von Krafft-Ebing (1840–1902) performed this critical experiment. In 1897, he innoculated nine paretics who had denied ever having had syphilis, with material from syphilitic sores. None developed sores themselves, leading to the conclusion that they must have already been infected. The link between syphilis and general paresis was forged.

It is worth pondering for a moment whether you would have done that experiment, or permitted it to be done. Consider the facts. The year is 1897, nearly three-quarters of a century after Bayle defined the syndrome. General paresis is now a raging disorder, perhaps the most widespread of the psychoses, affecting the great (Henry VIII and Randolph Churchill, Winston's father, were probably both paretics) and the ordinary alike. There is no question that if a direct connection between paresis and syphilis can be demonstrated, there will be an enormous leap forward in the direction of understanding and therefore conquering the disease. But in 1897, the relationship between syphilis and paresis is still speculative: a good hunch, but only a hunch. What if the hunch is wrong? Syphilis is still uncurable. If the hunch is wrong, you will be taking people whose lives are already burdened by paresis and adding incurable syphilis to their misery. Can such an experiment be justified? Would you carry out such an experiment under such conditions?

We suspect that such an experiment could not be done in our society today. The risks are now deemed too large, regardless of the possibility that the gain may be overwhelming. But such a judgment is not an easy one to make. Many would argue that the benefits to each of us from huge advances in medicine are such that we are, each of us, obligated to contribute to those advances (Eisenberg, 1977).

Krafft-Ebing's was a crucial experiment, but had he not conducted it, a similar link might have been forged less dangerously within a decade. In 1906, a German physician and bacteriologist, August von Wassermann (1866–1925), developed a blood test for detecting the presence of syphilis. More than 90 percent of paretics responded positively to the test, again powerfully suggesting a link between syphilis and paresis. The causal connection between the syphilis germ and paresis, a mental disorder, was now understood.

Once the syndrome of paresis was isolated and its etiology understood, it

The German neurologist Richard von Krafft-Ebing (1840–1902), an unsung hero of the biomedical model, performed the crucial experiment that forged the link between syphilis and general paresis. (Courtesy National Library of Medicine)

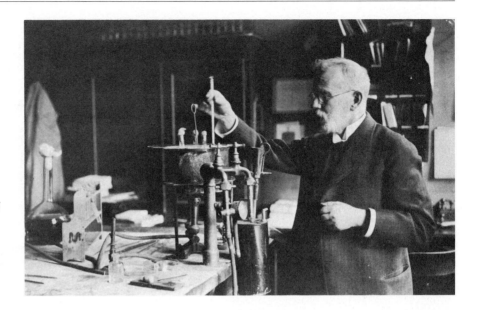

The German bacteriologist Paul Ehrlich (1854–1915), shown in his laboratory, discovered "606," an arsenic compound that was the first effective cure of syphilis. The compound was so named because it was discovered after 605 failures. (Courtesy The Bettman Archive)

was only a matter of time before investigators developed a treatment for general paresis. In 1909, a German bacteriologist, Paul Ehrlich (1854–1915), discovered "606," an arsenic compound that was given that name because it followed after 605 failures! Arsphenamine, the first effective cure of syphilis, acted by killing the syphilis germs in the bloodstream. By curing syphilis it prevented the occurrence of paresis. It was not until the 1940s that penicillin, a drug that arrests syphilis almost at any point in its development, replaced "606" as the preferred treatment.

Thus was general paresis, a psychological disorder characterized by stupidity and delusions of grandeur, understood and eradicated. These early advocates of the biomedical model found it to be caused by a germ in much the same way that germs cause pneumonia. Moreover, it was successfully treated in the way one might treat any physical illness. The magnitude of that success needs to be understood before the implications of the method can be appreciated. Paresis was perhaps the most widespread psychological disorder of that time. Yet today, it is common to meet psychologists and psychiatrists who have *never* seen a case of general paresis, so rare is the abnormality now. But a number of other mental disorders still exist today, and we will now see how the biomedical model is applied to a major disorder that continues to baffle scientists: schizophrenia.

GENETICS AS ETIOLOGY: TWINS AND SCHIZOPHRENIA

The conquest of paresis illustrates the first of the three biomedical etiologies of mental disorder: germs. Genetics is the second biomedical etiology that may lead researchers to consider a psychological disorder as being a physical illness.

Schizophrenia is a severe psychotic condition that strikes approximately 1 percent of the population the world over. Usually beginning in adolescence or early adulthood, it results in highly disordered thinking, perception, and language. Schizophrenic individuals function poorly in complex and primitive societies alike. What causes schizophrenia? One view has held

Genetic studies provide a means to study disorders. Shown here are the two kinds of twins: identical and fraternal. The two elderly women are identical twins and have the same genes. The girl and boy are fraternal and have only half of their genes in common. When identical twins have higher concordance for a disorder than fraternal twins, researchers infer that the disorder is at least partly heritable. (Wide World Photos)

that bad environmental conditions—bad mothering, early trauma, and the like—set it off, while another view, the biomedical model, has held that it is an illness passed on genetically. Investigators in this latter camp have approached schizophrenia by studying twins.

There are two kinds of twins: identical and fraternal. Identical twins have all the same genes, whereas fraternal twins have only half of their genes in common—exactly the same proportion of common genetic material as any two siblings share. Twins are an exquisite research tool for those who advocate the biomedical model because twins usually share very similar environments (same age, same social class, same food, similar social circles, etc.), while they differ systematically on how many genes they share.

If there are genes that determine whether one will be schizophrenic or not, and if one twin becomes schizophrenic, what is the probability that the other twin will also be schizophrenic? (Assume, for the sake of the argument, that diagnosis of schizophrenia is infallible and environment has no influence.) Since identical twins share all of their genes, if one identical twin is schizophrenic, then the other *must* also be schizophrenic. The same is not so with fraternal twins, since they share only half their genes. Depending on the nature of the alleged gene, the prediction would be 75 percent or 25 percent for fraternal twins. Those who hold the biomedical view use this method of observing identical and fraternal twins and recording their histories. If they find that one twin is schizophrenic, they will then find out if the other twin is also schizophrenic. When both twins are schizophrenic, they are called ***concordant*** for schizophrenia; when only one is schizophrenic, they are called ***discordant.***

About ten studies from Europe, Japan, and the U.S.A. have looked at about 400 pairs of twins in this way. Overall, identical twins have a concordance rate for schizophrenia of about 50 percent, while fraternal twins have a concordance of about 10 percent. Keep in mind that the rate of schizophrenia in the population as a whole is about 1 percent. So when one of the identical twins is schizophrenic, the other is five times more likely to be schizophrenic than the fraternal twin of a schizophrenic, who is in turn ten times more likely than the average to be schizophrenic. This suggests a causal influence of genes, but not genetic determination, since concordance for identical twins is only 50 percent, not 100 percent. And since the concordance for identical twins is less than 100 percent, genes cannot be the whole etiological story. Environment also must have an influence on the cause of schizophrenia. This issue, the inheritance of schizophrenia, remains hotly debated. We will take it up more fully in Chapter 17. In this section, however, we have emphasized how adherents of the biomedical model have approached this disorder.

BIOCHEMISTRY AS ETIOLOGY: DOPAMINE AND SCHIZOPHRENIA

As we mentioned earlier, those believing in the biomedical model may also look for the cause of a disorder in a third category: irregularities in an individual's biochemistry or anatomy. The genetic etiology is often, but not always, linked with this. For it could well be that the biochemical or anatomical irregularity is inherited, and is therefore a genetic disorder. One hypothesis about schizophrenia is that it is caused by an unbalanced biochemistry. The "dopamine hypothesis," as it is called, states that schizophrenic behavior is caused by too much dopamine in the brain. Dopamine is a chemical in the brain that allows "messages" to be relayed from one neuron to another. There is a considerable amount of evidence in favor of this hypothesis. But all of it is rather indirect, since it is still technically impossible to look into the brain of a living person and count how much of a given chemical is there. The most important evidence comes from the fact that drugs which usually relieve the symptoms of schizophrenia also lower the amount of usable dopamine in the brain. Such drugs do not completely cure schizophrenia, but they do reduce hallucinations and delusions, improve concentration, and make schizophrenic symptoms less bizarre. This action is called dopamine "blocking," and these drugs block dopamine by binding themselves to the nerve cells in the brain that receive dopamine, thus preventing naturally occurring dopamine from getting to these receptors. And the more dopamine that can be blocked by various drugs, the greater the ability of the drugs to relieve schizophrenic symptoms (Matthysse, 1973). Some investigators conclude that since these drugs decrease dopamine, an increase of dopamine causes schizophrenia.

Such evidence argues that the symptoms of schizophrenia are caused by too much dopamine in the brain. From the viewpoint of the biomedical school, evidence which shows that altering the biochemistry or anatomy of the brain alters the symptoms of a disorder (for better or worse), suggests that the disorder is an illness, just as does evidence that the disorder is caused by a germ and is relieved by killing that germ, or that a disorder can be transmitted genetically.

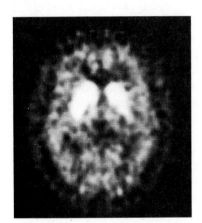

The "dopamine hypothesis" states that schizophrenia may be caused by excess dopamine in the brain. Here is a PET (positron emission tomography) scan of a human brain after it has been injected with a drug that enables researchers to visualize the distribution of dopamine receptors in the brain. (Courtesy Henry N. Wagner, Jr., M.D., Divisions of Nuclear Medicine and Radiation Health Sciences, The Johns Hopkins Medical Institutions)

EVALUATING THE BIOMEDICAL MODEL

STRENGTHS

The biomedical model is grounded in mature sciences. Its basic concepts, such as dopamine, heritability, and the central nervous system, seem measurable and objective. It has a well-defined sequence of methods: syndrome, etiology, and treatment. One hundred years of biomedical research, highlighted by such stunning successes as the eradication of smallpox and of general paresis, make it clear that its hypotheses are testable and, when correct, applicable. The pursuit of the biological bases of abnormality is so extensive that all of Chapter 19 is devoted to it. There, we take up in detail the boundary between neurologically based disorders and psychologically based ones.

WEAKNESSES

With all this, why don't we stop our search for models right here? Because the model also has several problems. First, psychological events sometimes cause psychopathology, and changing these events—without directly changing anything about the body—can indeed cure. As we shall see, eliminating a phobic's fear of cats by behavioral procedures and changing a depressive's belief that he is useless by cognitive means, can greatly help these patients. Second, biomedical treatments sometimes produce nasty side effects. Drugs that relieve the symptoms of schizophrenia can produce tardive dyskinesia, which is marked by a loss of muscular control. Because of such effects, many patients cannot tolerate biomedical treatments. Finally, some disorders may indeed be illnesses of the body, but others are ***problems in living*** (Szasz, 1961). General paresis is a disease, the consequence of syphilitic spirochetes. But marital discord, fear of public speaking, and depression following the death of one's child are not. These are psychological problems that can best be alleviated by psychological means. In the next several chapters, we will examine the four important psychological models of abnormality: the psychodynamic, the behavioral, the cognitive, and the humanistic.

SUMMARY

1. The *biomedical model* holds that psychological disorders are illnesses of the body.

2. The biomedical school of thought dictates an ideal procedure for isolating a psychological disorder as an illness: grouping the symptoms into a coherent *syndrome* that can be diagnosed reliably; searching for an *etiology,* or cause, of the syndrome; and finding a *treatment* and *prevention* that follow from knowing the cause.

3. Three sorts of evidence about etiology of a disorder point toward a psychological disorder being considered a physical illness: discovery of a *germ* causing the illness, *genetic transmission* of the disorder, and a disordered *biochemistry* or *anatomy of the brain* producing the disorder.

4. We discussed examples of each of these etiologies: the eradication of general paresis by the discovery that it was caused by the spirochete that caused syphilis exemplified the germ etiology; the evidence that schizophrenia is partly transmitted genetically exemplified the genetic etiology; and the relationship between the blocking of dopamine and the alleviation of schizophrenia exemplified the biochemical and anatomical etiology.

5. The main strengths of the biomedical model are that it is grounded in well-established biological sciences, and that physical treatments are often able to bring relief.

6. The main weaknesses of the biomedical model are that psychological treatments also are able to bring relief to individuals with psychological problems, that some psychopathological problems are *problems in living,* and that there are side effects to some biomedical treatments.

Psychodynamic Approaches

I N this chapter, we examine an influential set of theories that together are called psychodynamic theories. They are so named because they are concerned with the unconscious psychological forces that influence the mind and subsequent behavior. These inner forces—desires and motives—often conflict. When they do, people may experience anxiety and unhappiness, against which they may try to defend themselves.

We are all familiar with *conflict.* To study or ski, to satisfy self or parents, to go to one movie or the other, to heed conscience or desire—these are some of life's conflictual concerns. But we may be less familiar with the consequences of conflict: the discomforts that result from unresolved conflict as well as the growth that comes upon its successful resolution. Nor are we likely to be aware of how conflict has shaped personality, and how personality itself develops from successive resolutions of conflicts that begin to occur shortly after birth. It is on these matters that psychodynamic theories offer especially interesting and often very compelling insights.

Psychodynamic approaches to personality and abnormality begin with the work of a single towering genius—a Viennese physician named Sigmund Freud. Born in 1856, Freud produced some twenty-four volumes of theoretical observations and case histories before he died in 1939. His own methods of studying and changing personality are called *psychoanalysis.*

Throughout his life, Freud's consuming intellectual and clinical passion was with *psychic energy.* The natural scientists of his time were having a heyday with physical energy. Electricity had been harnessed during Freud's youth, and engines invented. In the spirit of the times, Freud turned his attention to the energies that fuel psychological life. People are endowed with a fixed amount of psychic energy, he assumed. Why is it, then, that sometimes people seem to be vigorous and full of life, while at others they seem listless? How is it that some people devote their energies to love and work, while others are largely concerned with their aches and pains? How is psychic energy used at the very beginnings of life, and how do those uses become transformed as a person matures?

We begin our examination of psychodynamic theories with the last question: How is psychic energy used very early in life, and how are its uses

Sigmund Freud (1856–1939) in 1909. (Courtesy National Library of Medicine)

Freud's consultation room in Vienna. (Courtesy Austrian Information Service)

changed as a result of maturation? Conflict, anxiety, and defense play large roles here, and not only negative ones, for these matters play constructive as well as destructive roles in psychological development.

THE DEVELOPMENT OF PERSONALITY

From birth to maturity, people go through five overlapping stages of psychosexual development: the oral, anal, phallic, latency, and genital stages. Psychoanalysts call this kind of maturation **psychosexual** because it underscores the relationship between mind and pleasure. Sexuality, in Freudian usage, is not restricted to sexual intercourse, or even to the fantasies and behaviors that precede it. Rather, sexual energy is one important form of pleasurable psychic energy. Long before sexuality takes its adult form, sexual energy exists as **libido** (from the Latin, meaning desire or lust). Libido, then, is psychic energy that can become associated with a host of pleasurable activities. Early in life, during the oral stage, for example, those pleasures are associated with the gratification of biological needs. Later on, libido becomes attached to social and psychological needs.

ORAL STAGE

The oral stage is the first psychosexual stage. Through nursing, this two-week-old infant is simultaneously satisfying his basic need for food and deriving pleasure. (Copyright John Blaustein 1982/Woodfin Camp)

The first psychosexual stage develops out of the central biological activity of very young infants: feeding. Their sucking response is instinctive, and it is through this behavior that a basic need is gratified. But Freud observed that, quite independent of this biological need, sucking provides pleasure of its own. The mouth, tongue, and sucking itself are early pleasure centers, or as Freud called them, **erogenous zones.**

Psychological development may be stimulated by not gratifying hungers immediately, as this will give infants the incentive to progress beyond the oral stage. If life were always cozy and comfortable, they might become **fix-**

ated at the oral stage, moving beyond it only with great difficulty. But if orality were not wholly comfortable, they might be encouraged, in some small measure, to move beyond the oral stage. This would prepare them for what is to come.

Fixation at this, or any subsequent stage, can occur because it is very gratifying. But fixation can also occur because the stage is not sufficiently gratifying. Infants whose needs have not been met properly or in sufficient time during the oral stage may show strong signs of that deprivation later. As adults, they may remain "oral" in the sense that, like infants, they are heavily dependent on others and are overwhelmingly disposed to receive rather than give. They may be, moreover, distrustful that others will fulfill their needs. Thus, fixation at the oral stage may breed *oral character traits* that are enduring dispositions to react in dependent and distrustful ways.

ANAL STAGE

As infants begin to overcome their dependence, and as they become more autonomous and exploratory, they are confronted with social control. Social control takes many familiar forms, nearly all of them preceded by "don't." "Don't throw your food," "Don't go into that closet," "Don't play in the street"—these are the parental dicta to children in the "terrible two's." But a particular kind of parental control has been of interest to psychoanalysts because it centers on the body and provides yet another outlet for pleasurable energy as well as opportunity for conflict and defense. This is the control involved in toilet training.

During the anal stage, toilet training provides an outlet for pleasurable energy as well as an area of potential conflict between parent and child. (Photograph by Suzanne Szasz)

From a parental perspective, toilet training is merely a way of controlling a child's mess. To the extent that parents speak of it at all, they speak of the gradual disappearance of diapers and the occasional occurrence of "accidents." From the infant's viewpoint, toilet training may be an opportunity to savor the joys of increasing self-control, to please parents, and to be lavished with praise. Or it may be an opportunity to rebel, to pit a growing will against that of adults. Because parents often check to see whether or not a child has eliminated, it may lead the child to believe that body wastes are valuable and that they should be "held in" and saved. But regardless of how the child views toilet training, one thing is certain from the psychoanalytic viewpoint: parental concern with toilet training makes the child attend to the anal area, to the sensations that arise there, and the body products that are eliminated. The anal region can now be stimulated through the voluntary retention and expulsion of feces as well as through manual stimulation. Thus, libido—pleasurable energy—is now associated with the anal area.

Opportunities for conflict and for fixation are rife in this stage. Early on, conflict may arise between infants' natural inclination to eliminate when and where they will, and parental insistence that elimination occur in a particular place, and often at a particular time. If that conflict is not resolved, children may later manifest the remnants of that experience in character traits of messiness, disorderliness, and even rebelliousness. But even greater opportunities for conflict come later in the anal stage, when children have already learned to control their bowel movement. Then, a particularly strict toilet training will render children especially careful, or orderly, about their wastes. Moreover, because parents applaud their timely eliminations, they may come to consider their body wastes as especially valuable, and they may resist giving them up. Fixation can therefore generate enduring **anal character traits** of orderliness, stinginess, and stubbornness—a triad of traits that will persist into later life.

By the time children are approximately three years old, they will have traversed the anal stage more or less successfully. Now relatively autonomous and exploratory, they are ready to discover the pleasures of the third stage of psychosexual development. These pleasures lie in the genital area.

PHALLIC STAGE

The phallic stage is different from the stages that precede it in one very important sense. In the oral stage, libido was associated with a biological process, feeding. In the anal stage, it was associated with social control. But phallic pleasures are self-initiated ones, arising from curiosity, first about one's own body and gradually from curiosity about other people's bodies. At first, the idea that children stimulate themselves genitally, that they masturbate, horrified Freud's Victorian contemporaries. Gradually, and with accumulating evidence, the notion took hold, such that it is now commonly accepted that young children, from the ages of about three through six or seven, engage in pleasurable genital stimulation that is the rudimentary form of adult sexuality.

The Oedipus Complex

Adult sexual adjustment is often crucially determined at this stage by the outcome of what Freud called the **Oedipus complex.** That conflict takes its name from a Greek legend that is now more than 2500 years old, in which Oedipus killed Laius the king of Thebes and married the queen, Jocasta, only later to find that the king was his father, and that he had therefore married his mother. Appalled by his unintentional crime, Oedipus gouged his eyes out. That legend symbolized for Freud the desire that all young children have: to do away with the parent of the same-sex, and take possession of the parent of the opposite sex. That desire is often captured in the commonplace remarks of little boys—"when I grow up I'm going to marry you, mommy"—as well as in their fantasies.

What prevents young children from acting vigorously on their desire to take the opposite-sex parent for themselves and to do away with the same-sex one? Fear. The very curiosity that guided their interest in the opposite-sex parent teaches them quickly that the same-sex parent is bigger and stronger than they, and that that parent will resist their attempted conquest. Boys, especially, are vulnerable to this fear. During their childish explorations, sooner or later they come to know that women do not have a penis. Assuming that women once had a penis like themselves, they infer that their penis must have been cut off. The fear that they, too, will be castrated by their father if they persist in such longings is sufficient to dampen those desires considerably. **Castration anxiety,** then, terminates incestuous desire in boys.

Psychoanalysts consider that, by identifying with the same-sex parent, the child is able to resolve the Oedipal conflict. (*Left:* Photograph by Suzanne Szasz. *Right:* Photograph by Hal Chase/Black Star)

For girls, the matter is more complicated and, in psychoanalytic theory, less well resolved. The young girl, too, sees the absence of a penis as a lack and may be angry with her mother for having created her incomplete and inferior. She continues to experience ***penis envy,*** which results in her further desire for her father, even in the desire to have a child by him and thereby to symbolically acquire a penis. Only the mother's greater strength, as well as her father's resistance to the idea, restrains the impulse to take him. These factors are less effective in terminating the Oedipal conflict in girls than is castration anxiety in boys.

The outcome of this intense conflict is not merely withdrawal. It is ***identification*** with the same-sex parent: becoming that person in a psychological sense, such that the adult's values, attitudes, standards, sexual orientation, and even mannerisms become the child's own. Identification resolves the Oedipal conflict because the child internalizes the very values that prohibit incest.

LATENCY STAGE

The Oedipal conflict is exhausting and frightening, and it is not surprising that by the age of six or seven when it is over, sexual interest declines. Sexuality is repressed, that is, deflected from consciousness. This decline of sexual interest marks the beginning of the latency period. During latency, the child is relatively asexual. Attention is directed toward mastering social and cognitive skills.

GENITAL STAGE

The final stage of psychosexual development comes with the onset of puberty. Sexual impulse reawakens, but now in a more mature and socialized form. Earlier sexuality was fundamentally narcissistic, concerned nearly entirely with self-gratification. The developing adolescent is much more socialized than the child was, and adolescent sexual energies are channeled to reflect that growth. In the heterosexual sphere, others now are valued in their own right, and not merely as adjuncts for self-gratification. Love becomes possible and pleasurable, and altruism—the concern for another's welfare, independent of one's own—becomes possible too. Additionally, some sexual energy is channeled into work. Competence and efficacy in the workplace become rewarding in themselves, independent of the riches they bring.

Full-fledged genitality involves the capacities to love and to work, the two capacities that Freud felt were most significant for maturity. Psychoanalysts use the term *sublimation* to denote the transfer of libidinal energies from relatively narcissistic gratifications to those—like love and work—that gratify others and are highly socialized.

PERSONALITY DYNAMICS

THE THREE PROCESSES OF PERSONALITY

According to Freud, human personality is composed of three kinds of forces: the id, ego, and superego. These are neither objects nor places in the mind. Rather, they are dynamic and interactive *processes,* with their own origins and specific roles. The word *id* originates from the German "das es," literally meaning "it," and connotes processes that seem to lie outside of an individual's control. *Ego,* in German, means "ich" or "I," and designates the self, while *superego* (in German "Uberich" or "over I") describes those processes that are "above the self"—conscience, ideals, and morals.

The Id

The id designates the mental representation of processes that are fundamentally biological in origin. In the newborn infant, nearly all psychic energy is devoted to such biological processes. And over the course of development, id processes continue to fuel personality, providing the energy for the diverse pursuits that are associated with biological survival.

Biological drives are raw and urgent. They create desires that clamor for immediate gratification, tensions that seek instantaneous relief. They are dominated by the *pleasure principle,* which demands immediate impulse gratification and tension reduction. The id is like a spoiled child. It wants what it wants when it wants it. When they seek external gratification, id drives know nothing of appropriateness, or even danger. Were people wholly dominated by id processes they would, like the spoiled child, eat any food when they were hungry, regardless of whether it was theirs, healthy, or even still alive.

The Ego

Whereas the id seeks pleasure, the ego seeks reality. One function of the ego is to express and gratify the desires of the id in accordance with the requirements of reality. While the id operates on the pleasure principle, the ego utilizes the *reality principle.* It tests reality to determine whether the expression of an impulse is safe or dangerous. It delays the impulses of the id until the time is right, and may even divert those impulses toward appropriate targets. Freud described the relations between ego and id this way:

> The ego's relation to the id might be compared with that of a rider to his horse. The horse supplies the locomotive energy, while the rider has the privilege of deciding on the goal and of guiding the powerful animal's movement. But only too often there arises between the ego and the id the not precisely ideal situation of the rider being obliged to guide the horse along the path by which it [the id] itself wants to go. (Freud, 1923/1976, p. 77)

The ego's success in enabling impulses to be realistically and safely gratified depends on its ability to use thought processes, like reasoning, remembering, evaluating, and planning. The ego is the executive of the personality, carrying out the demands of the id in such a way as to minimize negative consequences.

The Superego

Those processes of mind that comprise both conscience and idealistic striving are termed superego processes. Conscience is acquired through parents. It arises from the forceful resolution of the Oedipal conflict, and it results in the internalization of society's views of which thoughts, impulses, and behaviors are permissible and forbidden, as well as which goals and ideals should be pursued.

Superego processes are just as irrational as id processes; neither cares or knows much about reality. Conscience can also be overly harsh, suppressing not only permissible behaviors, but even the very thought of those behaviors. Whereas the person whose id processes are relatively uncontrolled seems impulse-ridden, the person who is overly dominated by his or her superego seems wooden and moralistic, unable to be comfortable with pleasure and overly sensitive to "Thou shalt not . . ."

The processes that regulate normal personality and development are identical to those that regulate abnormal personality. What distinguishes normal from abnormal personality is the manner in which psychic energy is distributed between the three components of personality. In normal personality, psychic energy is strongly invested in ego processes, as well as those of the id and superego. In abnormal personality, psychic energy is distributed improperly, with the result that either the id or the superego is too strong, and ego processes are unable to control desire or conscience.

Id, ego, and superego regularly interact and often conflict. Sexual desires that arise in a classroom, for example, may be delayed by ego processes until a more permissible place is found. But even in such a place, they may be blocked by superego processes which proclaim that sex is sinful, or that the time might better be spent studying. As the executive, the ego is supposed to mediate these conflicts. But how does the ego do this? And what happens to desires that are blocked? The answers to these questions become clear when we examine three additional ideas that have become central to psychodynamic thinking: unconscious ideas and impulses, anxiety, and defense.

Unconscious Ideas and Impulses

Freud (1923) proposed that there are three levels of consciousness. The first is ***perceptual consciousness.*** At this level are the very small number of mental events to which the individual is presently attending. Being aware of reading a book and of the meaning of a passage would exemplify this kind of consciousness.

The second level of consciousness is ***pre-conscious.*** It consists of information and impulses that are not at the center of attention but that can be retrieved more or less easily. Though not now part of one's central awareness, last night's dinner can be recalled with little difficulty.

The large mass of memory, experience, and impulse lies at the third level of consciousness: the ***unconscious.*** Two kinds of memories become unconscious: (1) those that are forgotten, and (2) those that, because of conflict are ***repressed,*** or actively barred from consciousness. Ordinary forgotten events, such as the cost of a loaf of bread last year, gradually decay and exert no subsequent influence on personality. But repressed events live on, and all the more vigorously, because they are not subject to rational control. They reveal their potent identities in normal fantasies and dreams, in slips of the

Dreams reveal unconscious impulses. Here the young mother hears the cries of her child, but she tries to go on sleeping, despite her awareness that he needs to urinate. As she resists awakening, she dreams that the child continues to urinate, and thereby floods the town, which turns into an ocean. Finally, she awakens. (Fidibusz, Budapest)

tongue and "motivated" forgetting, under hypnosis and in a variety of abnormal psychological conditions. By far, unconscious forces are the dominant ones in personality.

> Ann was in love with two men, Michael and Jules. Both wanted to marry her, and she could not decide between them. Finally, after more than six months, she decided for Michael. The next night, she had the following dream:
>
> "I was climbing the fire-escape outside my dormitory. It was a dark and rainy night, and I was carrying a big box under my raincoat. I came to the fifth floor, opened the door silently, and tiptoed quickly to my room. Once inside, I double-locked the door, and put this box—it's a treasure chest—on my bed. I opened it, and it was full of diamonds and rubies and emeralds."
>
> In Ann's dream, "diamonds and rubies and emeralds" = jewels = Jules. Her dream reveals her continuing attachment to her former lover, and quite possibly her desire to maintain the relationship secretly. The mind's extraordinary capacity to play on Jule's name and to transform it into visual symbols is revealed in this dream.

Certain personality processes operate more at the unconscious level than do others. Id impulses are entirely unconscious, as are many superego processes. In contrast, ego processes, because they must mediate between desire, conscience, and reality, are often preconscious or conscious.

ANXIETY

Conflicts among the various personality processes regularly give rise to a kind of psychic pain that Freud termed *anxiety.* Anxiety can be conscious or unconscious, and its presence is always a signal that conflict is at hand. When the conflict causes the person to feel overwhelmed, helpless, and unable to cope, anxiety arises. The degree of experienced anxiety depends on the anticipated consequences to self.

Psychoanalytic theorists distinguish three kinds of anxiety, each of which arises from a different source of perceived danger. *Realistic anxiety* arises from the expectation that real-world events may be harmful to the self. Ordinarily, this is what is meant by fear. A person who slips while crossing the street may experience realistic anxiety as moving traffic approaches. *Neurotic anxiety* arises from the possibility that one will be overwhelmed by one's impulses, especially unconscious sexual and aggressive ones. The unconscious desire to vanquish someone who controls an important destiny —say, a father, employer, or lover—may breed neurotic anxiety. Finally, *conscience* or *moral anxiety* arises when one anticipates that one's behavior will violate one's personal standards, or when that behavior has, in fact, violated those standards. The legend of Oedipus (described earlier) contains a classic instance of moral anxiety. Having learned that he has murdered his father and married his mother, Oedipus is overwhelmed with guilt, shame, and revulsion and, as a result, gouges out his eyes.

The experience of anxiety, even the anticipation of anxiety, is an uncomfortable experience that people try to relieve immediately. Humans are particularly well-endowed with strategies for alleviating anxiety. Beyond "overcoming fear" as we do when we learn to ride a bicycle, or "fleeing the field" when pursued by strong enemies, humans can, in their own minds, alter the very meaning and significance of troublesome drives and impulses. They perform these alterations by using coping strategies, or defenses.

THE COPING STRATEGIES OF EVERYDAY LIFE

"The mind is its own place," the poet John Milton tells us. "It can make a heaven of hell or a hell of heaven." This is especially the case when the mind is experiencing conflict and anxiety. Then, the mind becomes enormously creative, finding all sorts of ways to reduce anxiety. The ways in which the mind accomplishes this are often automatic and unconscious, occurring outside the willful control of the individual. Sometimes it can be achieved in a direct and conscious effort to mitigate conflict and minimize psychic pain. We call the ways in which the mind alters painful psychological events ***coping strategies*** or ***defense mechanisms.***

Repression

The most fundamental and widely used means for altering psychological realities is repression. In *Notes from Underground,* the Russian novelist Fyodor Dostoyevsky describes why repression is used and the role it plays. He writes:

> Every man has reminiscences which he would not tell to every one, but only to his friends. He has other matters in his mind which he would not reveal even to his friends, but only to himself, and that in secret. But there are other things which a man is afraid to tell even to himself, and every decent man has a number of such things stored away in his mind. The more decent he is, the greater the number of such things in his mind. (Dostoyevsky, 1864, pp. 57–59)

Repression is a defense by which the individual unconsciously forces unwanted thoughts or prohibited desires out of mind. Memories that evoke shame, guilt, humiliation, or self-deprecation are often repressed.

Not all painful memories are repressed nor, for that matter, are all repressed memories objectively painful. Whether repression occurs depends, at least partly, on the degree to which an experience or memory conflicts with self-image. People who think little of themselves and their abilities may well repress memories of the praise they received for a job well done. Such repression stabilizes their self-image and reduces anxiety that might arise from discrepant information.

Two processes facilitate repression: ***mental inhibition*** and ***attention withdrawal.*** Mental inhibition occurs when images or memories are blocked. Blocking can be either intentional and conscious (under which condition it is sometimes called suppression), or automatic and unconscious. Young children, for example, are frequently and uncomfortably concerned with dying. They may try to put those thoughts out of their mind. But putting thoughts out of mind is difficult. Because thinking about death is painful, the entire blocking process may become unconscious and automatic, relieving the child of the difficult burden of repressing consciously.

Repression can also occur through withdrawing attention and redirecting

Young children are frequently concerned with dying. In order to reduce the pain of thinking about death, they may engage in mental inhibition and ultimately repress these thoughts. (Photograph by Dorka Raynor/ Leo de Wys, Inc.)

it. If thinking about sex makes people feel guilty, for example, they can think about success and achievement instead, which makes them feel good. If repression is successful, each sexual impulse will be replaced by fantasies of fame and success. Repression can be nearly complete, or it can be partial. When an idea or memory is partially repressed, some aspects may be consciously available, while others are not. For example, a person who had had a difficult relationship with a parent, may recall crying at that parent's funeral but may not recall what he or she cried about or anything else about the event. The available evidence also suggests that it is *partially* repressed conflicts and memories that play a significant role in abnormal behavior (Perkins and Reyher, 1971; Reyher and Smith, 1971; Burns and Reyher, 1976; Silverman, 1976). In ***multiple personality,*** for example, an individual has two or more personalities that are alien to each other. When one personality is dominant, the others are repressed.

The capacity of the mind to be "its own place" is not limited merely to its ability to repress, to reject images and memories from consciousness, as important as that ability is. Rather, the mind is an editor, deleting whole chapters of experience and reorganizing others. Ordinarily, even in the absence of conflict, both perception and memory are reconstructive (Anderson and Bower, 1973). This is to say that minds take direct experience, edit, and make something "new" of it, by adding to, or subtracting from perception, by embellishing memory in ways that range from innocent decoration to filling memorial gaps with new "memories." It is no surprise, therefore, that these enlivening capacities of the mind should be used in the coping process, when anxiety is experienced or when conflict occurs between self-image and impulse or behavior. Here, sometimes consciously, but more often unconsciously, editing processes are invoked to enable the individual to cope by making perception and memory more pleasant.

© 1982 Jules Feiffer. Reprinted with permission of Universal Press Syndicate. All rights reserved.

The editing process itself is very flexible and very subtle. An "I" can be changed to a "you," a "he" to a "she." Some features of experience or perception can be edited, others substituted and, in the process, experience can be made more pleasant. Quite commonly, many editorial changes are taking place simultaneously, supplementing the fundamental ability of the mind to simply repress conflict. A description of some of the more significant coping strategies that rely heavily on editing follows.

Projection

Fundamentally, projection consists of attributing private understandings and meanings to others, of substituting "you" for "I." It is the bedrock upon which language comprehension rests. Consider the sentence "I love Mary." Anyone reading that sentence will have little difficulty comprehending it because she will ***project*** her own notion of love onto the speaker's phrase and mind. Generally, when someone says that "she hurt my feelings" or "I'm worried about that exam," we feel we understand what she is saying, even though in another context, we would readily grant that our own "hurt" might feel different from hers, and our "worry" different, too. We call this ***assimilative projection*** because it is an attribution to another of something that we are quite aware of feeling ourselves. It is part of the general process of quickly assigning meanings to events. Such attributions can be correct or incorrect, and they can obviously lead to a host of wrong predictions and misunderstandings (Nisbett and Ross, 1980).

Another kind of projection, called ***disowning projection,*** is more common in the coping process. It consists in attributing to others those feelings and experiences that we personally *deny* having and that we usually repress. Think of the preacher who sees and decries sin everywhere but denies having a sinful impulse himself. That's disowning projection. Robert R. Sears (1936), in the first experimental validation of disowning projection, asked students in a dormitory to rate themselves and their fraternity brothers on four traits: stinginess, obstinacy, disorderliness, and bashfulness. The extent to which individuals actually possessed each trait was estimated from the average of the ratings assigned to them by their fraternity brothers. When that average departed significantly from the rating the person gave himself, it was assumed that the person lacked self-awareness and, as a result, it was predicted that he would project more of that trait onto his fraternity brothers. And indeed he did, as Figure 4-1 indicates. Similarly, people who deny or repress their own sexual impulses have been shown to project them on others and to rate others as more lustful than in fact they are (Halpern, 1977).

Psychoanalytic thinkers point out that projection plays a double role in psychological distress. First, it reduces distress by allowing a person to attribute an anxiety-provoking impulse to another person, rather than the self. Thus, if anger makes us feel anxious, then the anxiety that anger creates can be reduced by attributing that anger to someone else. Second, projection allows us to do something about anger, for when someone is angry at us, are we not permitted to take aggressive or retaliative action in our own defense? Thus, projection can provide the rationale for engaging in the behavior that would have been forbidden in the first place.

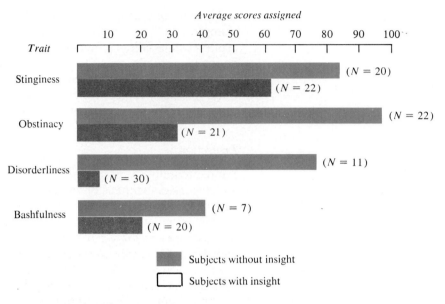

Average scores assigned

Figure 4-1
Average scores on four traits that were assigned to others by people who were themselves high scorers on those traits, and who either had or did not have insight into themselves on those dimensions. (Source: Based on data from R. Sears, 1936)

Reaction Formation

In the process of editing experience, we can delete a verb and substitute its opposite. Sometimes we say, "I hate her," when in fact we really mean "I love her." Such an editorial process is called ***reaction formation,*** because an opposite reaction is formed to the initial impulse.

Reaction formation, in fact, is a special case of a more generalized ***feeling substitution,*** which is easy to accomplish because feelings are often so ephemeral and difficult to label. For example, people in whom feelings of dependency are especially stressful may unwittingly experience and express anger each time they are in a situation that would ordinarily evoke dependency.

Reaction formation may be especially significant in ***mania.*** There, individuals behave as if they are full of joy and boundless energy, but one senses that their fundamental experience is one of sadness and depression, against which a reaction has been formed. Reaction formation is also seen in ***counterphobia,*** where individuals pursue precisely those activities that they deeply fear.

But if the mind can so easily revise experience and substitute a real feeling for its opposite, how can one tell the real feeling from its false opposite? When someone says "I love you!" how do we know he or she is not "really" feeling hatred? And conversely, if someone says "I can't stand you" should we not take that as a frank declaration of affection? Psychodynamic theorists offer two clues. First, because the conditions for experiencing and expressing the "real feeling" are not present in the reaction formation, the latter expressions of feeling tend to be thin, shallow, and seemingly wooden. Fabricated affections and genuine feelings are expressed in quite different ways. Second, the reaction formation is inflexible. Precisely because a stated fondness is formed, say, in reaction to hot anger, the anger must be avoided at all costs. Yet, anyone who has really liked someone knows that we are all occasionally annoyed or angry with people we truly care for. And we say so. Those who engage in reaction formation rarely are angry and rarely say so.

Displacement

When the strategy of ***displacement*** is used, the individual edits the target of his or her emotions by replacing the true object with one that is more innocent and less threatening. People who are angry and frustrated at work, but who cannot vent those feelings at work, are unconsciously using displacement strategies when they return home and vent their feelings on innocent spouses and children.

Identification

Identification describes the process by which the characteristics of others—their ideas, values, mannerisms, status, and power—are internalized in ourselves. Identification is the opposite of projection. It is a fairly common strategy for overcoming fear and inadequacy. Thus, some people are willing to spend considerably more money for a house in a "proper" neighborhood, than they would spend for the identical house at a less fashionable address, feeling that if their home is in a better neighborhood, they must perforce be better people. Similarly, people often rate themselves and each other by the college they attended, where they buy their clothes, or by the car they drive, even though we are, all of us, precisely what we are, no more and no less, regardless of the neighborhood we live in, the status of our college, where we buy our clothes, or the car we drive.

Identification relies heavily on people's sensitivity to context. Much as the perceived color of gray is changed according to whether it is seen against a black or white background, so are the perceived qualities of people altered by whether they are seen in an attractive or unattractive context.

There seems to be considerable clinical evidence for a special form of identification: identification with the aggressor. Bruno Bettelheim, a Jewish psychoanalyst who was interned at two notoriously cruel Nazi concentration camps during World War II, observed how people coped with concentration camp conditions. One of his most striking descriptions concerns how some of the old prisoners—those who had been in the camps more than three years—identified with their Nazi jailers. They used the language of the Gestapo, adopted its mannerisms and even its carriage. Occasionally, they wore scraps of discarded Nazi uniforms or altered their own clothing to resemble Nazi uniforms. At times, they appeared to use the same patterns of cruelty as the Gestapo used toward other prisoners. When it became necessary to kill another inmate, they would do so in a manner that was strikingly similar to that used by the Gestapo. Bettelheim sensed that the only way these prisoners could allay their own fears of the Gestapo was by identifying with the Gestapo and pretending to have its power (Bettelheim, 1943).

Identification is a particularly useful strategy for coping with fear. Anna Freud tells of a little girl who was afraid to cross the hall in the dark lest she meet a ghost. She handled this fear by making peculiar gestures as she crossed the hall. "There's no need to be afraid in the hall," she explained to her little brother, "you just have to pretend that you're the ghost who might meet you" (A. Freud, 1936, p. 119). Incidentally, this example points out what has been stressed previously: coping strategies need not be unconscious.

Identification plays an especially large role in psychodynamic views of depression. People who are depressed, as we shall see in Chapter 13, often suffer enormously from self-deprecation, feelings of worthlessness, and suicidal impulses. Such feelings arise from the combined action of mourning and identification. When people suffer a loss, either through death or rejection, they go through a period of mourning. That much is quite normal. Often, however, people identify with these lost objects, unwittingly merging these objects with themselves. Because they feel a good deal of unconscious anger toward these objects for having abandoned or rejected them, that anger now comes to be experienced toward the self, and they become depressed. An examination of their feelings of self-deprecation and worthlessness would reveal, in the psychoanalytic view, that these feelings are more properly directed toward those who have died or rejected them.

Denial

If repression obliterates inner facts, **denial** does away with distressing external ones. Denial commonly occurs when our sense of security and of being loved is threatened. The fact that people generally find it difficult to accurately perceive negative feelings directed toward themselves suggests that the denial process is widespread (Taguiri, Bruner, and Blake, 1958). Denial is often used when people are threatened by death. The parents of a fatally ill child, much as the fatally ill themselves, often deny that anything is wrong, even though they have the diagnosis and prognosis in hand.

Isolation

Whereas in repression and denial, both the affective and informational components of experience are deleted, in **isolation** only the affective ones (which, after all, are the sources of distress) are repressed, while information is retained. People who have suffered great brutality and humiliation, such as those in the German death camps during World War II, or those who have been raped, may utilize isolation. They may be able to recount their experience precisely and in copious detail but unable to recall the accompanying intense feelings. The very experiences that would ordinarily bring tears to a teller's eyes or make a listener wince in empathic pain, would be related blandly, suggesting that the feelings that were originally associated with the experience have been isolated.

Isolation can also be a constructive strategy. The parent who responsibly reprimands a child cannot be too sensitive to the hurt feelings the reprimand engenders, else the reprimand will fail. Neither can a surgeon allow herself to be overly sensitive to the fact that the tissue she is cutting is human flesh. Isolation constructively permits these emotional concerns to be withheld from consciousness.

Intellectualization

Related to denial and isolation, **intellectualization** consists of repressing the emotional component of experience, and restating the experience as an abstract intellectual analysis. Unable to deal with a particularly intense feeling, we sometimes seek to read all about it and to produce elaborate self-analyses that are all but devoid of feeling.

Rationalization

In recalling experiences and accounting for them, people commonly edit not only the facts of the experience, but the motives as well. The process of assigning to behavior socially desirable motives that an impartial analysis would not substantiate is called **rationalization.** Late to a party that they didn't want to attend in the first place, some people will offer socially desirable excuses: the car broke down, or their watch stopped. Those excuses are rationalizations.

The process of rationalization is beautifully illustrated in experiments involving posthypnotic suggestion (Hilgard, 1965). A person is hypnotized and told that upon awakening, he should attend carefully to the handkerchief in the hypnotist's pocket. When that handkerchief is removed, the subject is instructed to open the window. The subject is further given a posthypnotic amnesia, that is, he is instructed to forget that the hypnotist ever told him to open the window. He is then aroused from the hypnotic trance. He circulates among the people in the room, all the while keeping a careful eye on the hypnotist. The hypnotist removes his handkerchief. The subject hesitates: after all, one simply does not go around opening windows for no reason at all. "Isn't it a bit stuffy in here?," he finally asks—and then, having found a proper rationalization for his behavior, proceeds to raise the window.

Rationalization plays a dramatic role in the development of **hypochondriasis,** which is the conviction in the absence of medical evidence that one is ill or about to become ill. "I can't do the job, not because I fear failure or because I fear it won't be done as well as the next guy, but because I'm not feeling well." Because illness evokes concern from others, the seemingly ill are encouraged to abandon the job and given a good measure of comfort to boot. Thus, the tendency to rationalize is often supported by the positive reactions it evokes from others.

Sublimation

Sublimation is the process of rechanneling psychic energies from socially undesirable goals to constructive and socially desirable ones. As we have seen, capacities for love, work, altruism, and even humor involve such rechanneling of raw sexual and aggressive impulses. According to Freud, love is an especially powerful form of sublimation because it allows people also to achieve sexual gratification in a socially acceptable context. Simultaneously, however, loving leaves one vulnerable to rejection or the death of a loved one. Thus, the gratifications of loving and working are often matched by the anxieties to which they give rise. Sublimation, in Freud's view, is therefore as fragile as it is constructive.

THE ORGANIZATION OF COPING STRATEGIES

Everyone uses coping strategies. But are some strategies better—more effective, more adaptive, more useful—than others? Psychoanalysts believe that some defenses are primitive and immature in the sense that they distort reality; others do less violence to reality and are therefore more mature. These strategies can be classified into four levels of maturity. Level I is the least mature and involves strategies wherein the cloth of reality is either wholly invented or entirely discarded. Denial or outright distortion of external reality, as well as delusional projection is included here. Level II strategies include projection, as well as the strategies that result in hypochondriasis and passive-aggressive behavior. At Level III, one finds the mechanisms of intellectualization, isolation, repression, and displacement —strategies that are awfully common, although somewhat debilitating in all of us. The most mature strategies—Level IV—include sublimation and with it, altruism, humor, conscious suppression, and impulse delay (Vaillant, 1977).

Recently, evidence has emerged to support the view that there is a *maturational hierarchy* of coping strategies. A group of men who graduated Harvard College between 1939 and 1944 were studied then and for thirty years subsequently. Initially selected because they were quite independent, there was, even in this highly qualified group, considerable variability in the maturity of their coping strategies. Thirty years after they were first studied, the following question was asked: did differences in the way they coped as undergraduates result in differences in the quality of their lives some thirty years later?

Indeed they did, and dramatically so, as can be seen in Table 4-1. Not only does the maturity of coping strategies affect overall psychological and social adjustment subsequently, but even *medical* adjustment is dramatically affected. People whose coping strategies were relatively immature tended later to be objectively in poorer health and to feel worse than those who coped more maturely.

Carl Jung (1875–1961). (Courtesy The Bettmann Archive, Inc.)

THE NEO-FREUDIANS

Though they were rejected at first, Freud's ideas later came to attract a number of highly original thinkers who elaborated on his views and often disagreed with them. In some cases, the disagreements led to a break with Freud. Such was the case with Carl Jung (1875–1961) and Alfred Adler (1870–1937).

What were the differences between Freud and the other thinkers? First, some theorists differed with Freud regarding the origins of motivation. Granting that motivation was mainly unconscious, these thinkers believed that Freud held much too narrow a view of *what* was unconscious. For example, Jung felt that there was also a **collective unconscious,** consisting of the memory traces of the experience of past generations and not just memories of early childhood as Freud thought. In Jung's view, we are born wiser than we think, already afraid of darkness and fire because our ancestors were, and already knowing of death because past generations have died. Jung called these universal ideas with which we are born **archetypes.** For Jung, these archetypes form the basis of personality, accounting for why people are not merely driven by their past experiences but also strive to grow

Table 4-1 A Comparison between Men Who Used Mature Adaptive Mechanisms and Those Who Used Immature Adaptive Mechanisms

| | Adaptive Strategies | | |
	Mature n = 25	Imma- ture n = 31	Statistical Significance of Difference
Overall Adjustment			
1) Top third in adult adjustment	60%	0%	***
2) Bottom third in adult adjustment	4%	61%	***
3) "Happiness" (top third)	68%	16%	***
Career Adjustment			
1) Income over $20,000/year	88%	48%	**
2) Job meets ambition for self	92%	58%	***
3) Active public service outside job	56%	29%	*
Social Adjustment			
1) Rich friendship pattern	64%	6%	***
2) Marriage in least harmonious quartile or divorced	28%	61%	**
3) Barren friendship pattern	4%	52%	***
4) No competitive sports (age 40–50)	24%	77%	***
Psychological Adjustment			
1) 10 + psychiatric visits	0%	45%	**
2) Ever diagnosed mentally ill	0%	55%	***
3) Emotional problems in childhood	20%	45%	*
4) Worst childhood environment (bottom fourth)	12%	39%	*
5) Fails to take full vacation	28%	61%	*
6) Able to be aggressive with others (top fourth)	36%	6%	*
Medical Adjustment			
1) Four or more adult hospitalizations	8%	26%	
2) 5 + days sick leave/year	0%	23%	*
3) Recent health poor by objective exam	0%	36%	*
4) Subjective health consistently judged "excellent" since college	68%	48%	*

*** Very significant difference (p < .001—a difference that would occur by chance only one time in a thousand)
 ** Significant difference (p < .01)—a difference that would occur by chance one time in a hundred.
  * Probably significant difference (p < .05)
SOURCE: Adapted from Vaillant, 1977, p. 88.

Alfred Adler (1870–1937).
(Courtesy Alexandra Adler)

and become something better. In essence, Jung saw the self as striving for wholeness.

Freud's emphasis on biological urges—the id impulses—as determinants of behavior is the basis of a second major dispute, particularly with Alfred Adler. In Freud's view, human activity serves fundamental sexual and aggressive needs arising from the id and mediated by the ego. But according to Alfred Adler, the self serves a more meaningful purpose. The self enables us to fulfill our life style, to become more than the genes with which we are endowed and the environment that presses on us. The self creates something new, something unique, something that is not wholly determined by biological impulse or cultural press (Ansbacher and Rowena, 1956).

There is considerable difference in a third area, that of psycho*sexual*

Erik Erikson (1902–   ).
(Photograph by Jon Erikson)

Trust. (Copyright James R.
Holland/Black Star)

Box 4-1   ERIKSON'S STAGES OF MAN

Because he views people as fundamentally *social,* Erik H. Erikson's stages of human development reflect social learnings and social crisis. And in contrast to Freud's psychosexual stages of development which terminate in early adulthood, Erikson's eight stages continue throughout the life cycle, as seen below:

Stage I   *Basic Trust vs. Mistrust.* Infants are helpless and vulnerable. Whether they survive depends on whether their adult caretakers nourish them properly. From the infant's perspective, knowing that one will be fed lovingly, willingly, and comfortably generates a basic trust in others. Basic trust is essential for the development of a loving relationship, both in childhood and beyond. This developmental stage occurs at the same age as Freud's *oral* stage, but the psychosocial emphasis is quite different.

The absence of basic trust can express itself in a variety of ways. Manifestations of *mis*trust include the sense of being "no good," the fear of "being left empty" or of simply being abandoned by people about whom one cares, and the absence of self-confidence.

Stage II   *Autonomy vs. Shame and Doubt.* Erikson's second stage overlaps, both in time and in experience, with Freud's *anal stage.* At this stage, infants become more exploratory and autonomous. Their growing independence raises, for the first time, issues of *control.* Learning to respond properly to parental control and learning to control oneself are the crucial tasks of this stage.

Rarely is a wise mixture of firmness and understanding more required of parents than it is when they are teaching self-control during toilet training. When parental firmness is blended with patience, children gradually learn not only to control their own bodies but also to satisfy others, cooperate with them, and give and take pleasure in these abilities. All of this sets the stage for the socialized sense of initiative and exploration that follows.

But shame and self-doubt arise when parents have set too rigid or demanding a standard, and where they have failed to understand the occasional failures that accompany a ripening repertoire. Then, self-control brings none of the pleasure that is present in children who have been taught patiently. Children of whom too much has been demanded may approach autonomy as a chore, and decision making as a perpetual crisis.

Stage III   *Initiative vs. Guilt.* As they begin to trust their world and feel autonomous, it is natural for children to begin to *initiate* behaviors. They begin to explore themselves, discovering the genital area that is central to Freud's *phallic stage.* And they begin to explore the world, too, learning whether a behavior is safe or dangerous, acceptable or forbidden. One need only imagine the kinds of skills necessary for a safe climb to a cookie jar on the top shelf to appreciate its hazards.

In the process of exploration, children innocently trample the haloed beliefs and possessions of adults and are often surprised by the reaction of adults to their explorations. That climb to the cookie jar evokes parental fear and concern; exploring one's own or friends' genitals tests parental values, morality, and tolerance. If such explorations are greeted with rational understanding, children will gradually become moral masters of their impulses. If, on the other hand, those explorations are met with deprecation, guilt-ridden people will result, people who are moralistic (though not necessarily moral), lacking in spontaneous desire, and who quite commonly deny their own impulses and fantasies.

Industry. (Photograph by Suzanne Szasz)

Intimacy. (Copyright Jim Caster/Black Star)

Stage IV *Industry vs. Inferiority.* At about the age of five or six, when they enter Freud's *latency* stage, children begin to deal with the pleasures and problems of being industrious and productive.

Attention, learning, perseverance, and mastery are the experiences of this stage. A sense of one's efficacy—one's ability to do things—is the outcome. But a sense of personal inferiority can also arise at this stage. Not everyone can be a superb tennis player or chess master, and one learns soon enough from direct experience and from peer evaluation that one's talents here may be limited. *That* is merely reality. But there are societal practices that induce a needlessly severe sense of inferiority. Such practices include overly harsh criticism, competitive practices which necessitate that many must fail in order that a few succeed, and failure to reward competence promptly. A diminished sense of efficacy restricts the activities that one would engage in, which further restricts efficacy.

Stage V *Identity vs. Identify Diffusion.* By the time children enter adolescence, they have already traversed the early crises of trust, autonomy, initiative, and industry. They now arrive at the time when they must put all of this together, when they must establish *identity*. With the onset of adolescence, eyes turn outward and forward, away from family, and toward peers and the future. It is a time of physical maturation, changes in expectations, intense sexual preoccupations, and concerns with peers, cliques, vocation, and ''the future,'' as well as with changing relations to parents. It is a time of turmoil, one that itself creates a need to answer the question: ''Who am I?''

Identity describes one's sense of personal coherence and competence, and a sense that there is a place for oneself in society. The consolidation of identity prepares one for adulthood and particularly for the experiences of loving and intimacy. The relative failure to attain a consolidated identity results in identity diffusion.

Stage VI *Intimacy vs. Isolation.* When identity is strong and well-defined one can, with minimal threat to self, engage in *intimate* relations with others: form partnerships, marry, cooperate, and collaborate. When identity is diffused, however, collaboration is difficult because the potential threat to the self is too great. Interpersonal relationships are shallow. Isolation—*distantiation* is what Erikson calls it—affords protection against the anxiety of role confusion, as well as the threats to self-esteem that come from being suffused with self-doubt.

Stage VII *Generativity vs. Stagnation.* Much as the child depends on the adult, the mature adult depends on the child. Mature people in middle-adulthood need to be able to serve the present generations, as well as future ones. Erikson calls this need to be of service (particularly to forthcoming generations) *generativity,* by which he implies usefulness to others in the form of parenthood, creativity, or productivity. Failure to achieve generativity results in stagnated self-concern, self-indulgence, and invalidism.

Stage VIII *Integrity vs. Despair.* If the previous crises are more or less resolved satisfactorily, old age and the prospect of death bring a certain equanimity, an acceptance of the biological life cycle and a recognition that one is part of a larger biological process. One subscribes to the natural order and meaning of things. That order and meaning (as well as the death which is implied in it) fails to threaten. The integrity of self is maintained.

Despair is the opposite pole of integrity. It expresses the feeling that life was too short and that now there is too little of it left to try some other path. It is manifested in strong regrets about the conduct of one's life, and in fear of death.

versus psycho*social* development. Fundamentally, that difference reduces to whether people are fundamentally biological or social animals. For example, Karen Horney (1885–1952) saw basic anxiety as a social rather than simply a biological experience. For her, that basic anxiety consisted of "the feeling a child has of being isolated and helpless in a potentially hostile world" (Horney, 1945, p. 41). That anxiety may lead children to develop one of three modes of coping. They may become hostile, seeking revenge against those who rejected them. Or they may become submissive, hoping thereby to regain the lost love. Or they may simply withdraw, giving up the quest entirely. These three strategies—moving against, moving toward, and moving away—are social responses to a fundamentally social anxiety.

Similarly, Harry Stack Sullivan (1892–1949) held that the very notion of personality is itself an illusion that cannot be separated from the social context in which it is seen and operates. According to Sullivan, psychological problems do not merely originate in faulty social development, they *consist* of faulty social relationships and need to be examined and treated as such.

Erik Erikson (1902–   ) has provided a broader theory of development, one that stresses the psycho*social* nature of people and the interrelations between individuals and society. Unlike Freud, who believed that the foundations of personality were essentially completed in childhood, Erikson sees human personality as developing and changing throughout life, from infancy on through adulthood and old age. Moreover, Erikson's eight stages of man, even where they overlap with Freud's stages during early childhood, emphasize the social aspects of development (see Box 4-1).

Erich Fromm (1900–1980) saw personality as fundamentally social. At birth and with development, humans find themselves increasingly isolated from others. That isolation—the fundamental human condition—is painful, and however much people cherish their freedom, they also seek to terminate their isolation. They can do this either through love and shared work—a constructive mode—or through conformity and submission to authority, a very destructive mode.

Left: Karen Horney (1885–1952). (Courtesy National Library of Medicine) *Center:* Harry Stack Sullivan (1892–1949). *Right:* Erich Fromm (1900–1980). (Wide World Photos)

Freud's own views and those of his disciples and descendants find expression in the modes of treatment that they have generated. Here, theory and practice come together. For it was from the clinic that Freud's most interesting ideas developed. We therefore turn to psychodynamic treatment in order to examine those views in practice.

PSYCHODYNAMIC TREATMENT

Like psychodynamic theory, psychodynamic treatment focuses on conflict, anxiety, and defense. It seeks to alter thought and behavior by examining early conflicts and especially by making conscious that which is repressed through *free association* and discussing dreams and resistances. In so doing, psychic energy is freed for more constructive purposes, and the individual is able to find more constructive resolutions for conflict. Anxiety is reduced because impulses now find "safe" methods of expression. And coping strategies, where they are required, are now more mature. These matters become much clearer when we examine an actual case.

It has been more than two years since Patty had had a moment's peace. Her problems were in her head, quite literally. There, continually pounding headaches kept her in bed all day every day, unable to sleep, unable to rise, clawing at the sheets.

The headaches themselves were not unusual. What was unusual was the simultaneous presence of three of them, and their intensity. One was a drilling headache. "It's as if someone were drilling from the top of my head to the center of my brain." The second pulsed at the back of her head and felt as if someone were ripping the two lobes of her brain apart. And the third was a fairly common headache, one that felt as if there were a steel band around her head which was getting tighter and tighter.

Patty had sought help for these headaches for well over a year. She had had several medical and neurological work-ups. She had seen two allergists in the hope that they could find whether something she was ingesting was harmful to her. "In the hope . . ." is the appropriate phrase here, for, after searching for so long, anything that remotely promised an answer, however difficult, was more comforting than the perpetual pain.

She finally requested neurosurgery in the hope that the severing of nerve endings would alleviate the pain. Informed that nothing could be done surgically, she became exceedingly depressed. The situation by now seemed entirely hopeless to her. A burden to her husband, useless to her young children, there seemed little to do but end it all. It was then that she was referred for psychodynamic therapy.

The early part of her first meeting was spent describing the problem. With great pain, she described her headaches but quickly ran out of things to say. She didn't think that the problem was psychological, nor that anyone in their right mind would feel as she did under the circumstances. There being nothing more to say, she turned to the therapist and asked "What should I talk about now?"

Psychodynamically oriented psychotherapists seek to understand the present by reference to the past. Having acquired as full an account of the patient's current status as possible, they enquire about the past. Therefore, in response to Patty's question, the therapist said, "Tell me about your childhood."

She began slowly and then with growing animation to describe her father. (Indeed, during the remainder of that very long interview, Patty alluded to her mother only in passing.) Her father had come originally from a stretch of land that borders Greece and Turkey. He was a man of violent passions and frustrations, a man who had once angrily left his family for four years, only to return as suddenly as he had gone. In her earliest memory of him, he threatened to take a train to a far off place, never to return.

He was, in her description, a drunk, a womanizer, an erratic supporter of the family, a man who often beat her mother. Despite this, Patty retained a hidden fount of fondness for him, one that was particularly evident (so it seemed to her therapist) in her description of the times he used to take her with him to the neighborhood saloon. He would put her up on the bar, and she would dance while everyone else clapped. It was a particularly warm memory in an otherwise distressing relationship.

"Did you ever go to bed with your father?" The question came suddenly, without warning.* Patty paled. "How did you know?," she asked. And then, not waiting for the answer, she burst into tears.

"Yes, it was him. And I still hate him. He's an old man now. And I still hate him. On Sunday morning, my mother would clean the house. All of us, except my mother, slept late on Sunday. When she cleaned my room, I went into her bed. I would get under the covers, close my eyes, and go back to sleep. My father was there. He would touch me. . . rub . . . the rat. How could he do that to his own daughter?"

In anger, in sadness, and in shame, she cried. Her headaches receded momentarily into the background as she tore furiously into incidents that had occurred more than a quarter century ago, when she was eight years old.

Suddenly, she stopped crying, even talking. Then smiling in disbelief, she said "They're gone. The headaches are gone." She rose slowly and walked around the office, moving her head from side to side. For the first time in more than two years, she felt normal.

Before the session was over, those headaches would return again. But regardless, a connection had been made between her present suffering and her early memories of her father.

During subsequent sessions, Patty was able to retrieve from memory more experiences with her father. Her father, it appeared, had had another family, which he had left behind in Greece when he came to America and married her mother. Patty felt it was her responsibility to keep him in America by making him so happy that he would not want to return. The fear of abandonment ran deep in both Patty and her mother.

She could not recall what her father had done to her in bed, but she knew that it was bad and that even *he* must have thought so. Once, after an outing with a group of friends, her father spotted her on a subway platform. He pulled her roughly aside from her schoolmates, slapped her hard across the face, and called her "Whore."

Those recaptured events—relived, remembered, re-experienced during therapy—brought relief over longer and longer periods. But certain experiences and even thoughts brought on headaches suddenly and fiercely, as when:

· she was shopping for a brassiere;
· Phil, her husband, was bouncing their young daughters on his lap, and the three of them were laughing;
· friends suggested that they go to a movie;

---

* Such questions are not usually asked so directly or so early in psychodynamic treatment. In this case, however, Patty's depression seemed so overwhelming that the therapist felt he had to quicken the therapeutic pace.

> · she had gone with the family to a Greek wedding celebration, and all the young people were dancing; and
> · she was washing the children's laundry.
>
> All of these scenes vaguely connoted sexuality and therefore brought pain. Talking about them was difficult. There was a tension between exploring the psychodynamics of her situation and risking disturbing a trouble-free day. But she pushed on, pursuing her mental and emotional associations to early experiences and memories, not only about father and mother, but also about husband, children, friends, and later even about the therapist.

To a psychodynamic therapist, this search into Patty's past suggested that her headaches resulted from severe sexual conflicts that appeared to arise during the phallic stage. These conflicts paralyzed her, rendering her unable to even initiate caretaking activities on behalf of her husband, children, and increasingly, even herself. Thus, we see that Erikson's broader psychosocial stage of initiative vs. guilt was implicated here (see Box 4-1, Stage III).

The three headaches were themselves testimony to the fluidity of psychic energy and the power of coping strategies. Those headaches—the drilling one, the one that felt as if the lobes of her brain were being torn apart, and the steel band that somehow refused to yield—symbolically suggested a conflict about rape. But since the conflict was going on in Patty's own mind, it suggested, too, a conflict about her *own* sexual desires. By some process which is not yet understood, these conflictual desires were repressed and displaced, not outward to other people, but upward to her head.

Patty clearly projected much of this conflict onto her husband and even her children. Their horseplay was seen, not as an innocent rumpus, but as a highly sexualized event. Shopping for underclothes, weddings, Greek dancing, and the weekly laundry were all similarly sexualized. Ego processes that normally differentiate these events and allow people to share social perceptions of them were clearly defective here. The defects, psychoanalytic therapists hold, arose because of the intense and poorly contained pressure that was generated from Patty's own sexual conflicts.

It was *catharsis,* the uncovering and reliving of early traumatic conflicts, that mainly enabled Patty to rapidly remit her symptoms. But in psychodynamic theory, symptom remission is only part of the treatment, often the smallest part. Much more significant is the fact that enduring patterns of perceiving and reacting in adults are laid down in childhood and pervade all adult activities. They need to be altered because they are transferred from the people and impulses that originally stimulated the conflict to other significant people in one's life. Psychodynamic therapy seeks, therefore, not merely to relieve symptoms, but to alter personality—the very attitudes, perceptions, and behaviors that were misshaped by early experience.

How does psychodynamic treatment achieve personality changes? In practice, psychodynamic therapists must be nonreactive. They must listen calmly and intensely, but they must not be shocked by the clients' revelations, nor should they commonly offer opinions or judgments. They should act as blank screens, onto which clients can project their own expectations, imaginings, and attributions. Over time, therapists themselves become central in the lives of their clients. This centrality is of such therapeutic importance that it is given a technical name in psychodynamic theory:

transference. Transference describes the fact that during psychodynamic therapy, clients come to transfer emotions, conflicts, and expectations from the diverse sources from which they were acquired, onto their therapists. Therapists become mother, father, son, daughter, spouse, lover, and even employer or stranger, to their clients. In this emotional climate, clients are encouraged to speak frankly, to let their minds ramble, to freely associate to emotionally charged ideas, even if the resulting ideas seem silly, embarrassing, or meaningless. Under these conditions, what was formerly repressed and distorted becomes available to consciousness and therefore more controllable by ego processes, as can be seen from further examination of Patty's case.

In less than three months, Patty's symptoms had abated. Her attention turned away from her headaches to other matters. Her mother, for example, was a "pain." She had always been melancholy and merely obedient, surely no fun to live with. Patty quickly related the impression that "she was no fun to live with" to her own relationship with her father. He had already abandoned a family in Greece. Had she been trying to keep him in the family? Might he not abandon them? More important, could her own sexual involvement with her father have been little more than an attempt to keep him at home? That possibility cast her memories in a much more positive light, relieving her of the guilt that the memories evoked. Shortly thereafter, she could observe her husband and children playing together, without suffering from headaches and guilt.

Gradually, attention turned from her parents, even from her husband and children, to the therapist himself. His lack of reacting now provoked discomfort; his occasional lateness caused her to feel anxiety; and when her therapist took a week-long vacation, she experienced dread. In turn, these feelings led to long, blocked silences during the therapy sessions. What thoughts lay behind these silences? It was difficult for her to say, and nearly impossible for her to free associate. But finally, she was able to allude to the embarrassing sexual fantasies that attended these events, fantasies now about the therapist himself. This was transference, for it shortly became clear that she interpreted his silences, lateness, and absences as abandonment, and she was unconsciously motivated to do what she had wanted to do in the past to retain the affections of significant others. She was, of course, initially unaware of the unconscious connection between abandonment and sexuality, and she was therefore deeply embarrassed by the thoughts that assailed her. Once she understood the reasons for those thoughts, however, she was able to see her relationship to the therapist in more objective terms, to recognize that an occasional lateness or absence is not the same as abandonment, and to find less self-demeaning and guilt-provoking ways to express her affections.

At about this time, and seemingly for no good reason, Patty began to explore an entirely new matter: what to do with her life. Upon graduating high school, she had considered going to college, but had given up that idea as "simply ridiculous." She had also been attracted to dance, but had not acted on that interest either. Now both ideas returned, as well as the desire to take a job again, and she began to explore those ideas with great enthusiasm. In Freud's view, energies that had once been bound up in repression and other defensive maneuvers, were now freed for other activities. Erik Erikson would point out that having resolved many of the guilts that were associated with sexuality, she was now free to take initiatives on her own behalf, to do something with her life.

Ultimately, over a period of a year, many of Patty's conflicts were resolved. She no longer felt that she had to be different from her mother, more sexual, more "fun to live with." Nor did she continue to feel that sexual behaviors were the only ones that would make her attractive and enable her to retain prized relationships.

One result of these explorations was that her personal identity underwent considerable change. She had been an ineffectual, guilt-ridden person, dominated by forbidden impulses. She became an actively initiating and exploring person who trusted much more in others and took her own worth increasingly for granted.

Her stronger and more mature identity resulted from the greater understanding she had of herself and the greater control over impulses that this understanding brought. And it had one further result. The more Patty probed, the less clear it became that she had actually had a sexual relationship with her father. Eventually, that "memory" came to be seen as a false one, reflecting her own desire to retain his affections, rather than his actual behavior. In this, Patty repeated the experience of many of Freud's clients, for the mind, Freud observed, is a powerfully inventive place in which even "memories" can arise from desires, conflicts, and defenses.

EVALUATING PSYCHODYNAMIC THEORY

STRENGTHS OF PSYCHODYNAMIC THEORIES

Psychodynamic theory is nothing less than a comprehensive description of human personality. This theory describes personality's development, the way personality functions, and every aspect of human thought, emotion, experience, and judgment—from dreams through slips of the tongue to normal and abnormal behavior.

Because of this, Freud is considered, along with Marx and Darwin, one of the great geniuses of the century. Perhaps the most important of his ideas is the view that the psychological processes that underlie normal and abnormal behaviors are fundamentally the same. Neither conflict, nor anxiety, nor defense, nor unconscious processes are the sole property of abnormal people. Rather, the *outcome* of conflict and the *nature* of defense will determine whether behavior will be normal or abnormal.

In addition, Freud developed a method for investigating psychodynamic processes and treating psychological distress. This was important for several reasons. First, his methods of investigation shed light on abnormal processes and thus demystified them. By accounting for why they behaved as they did, Freud "rehumanized" the distressed, making their suffering more comprehensible to the rest of humankind. Second, by providing a method of treatment, Freud encouraged an optimism regarding psychological distress that had been sorely lacking before him.

SHORTCOMINGS OF PSYCHODYNAMIC THEORIES

Any theory that aspires to be as comprehensive as psychodynamic theory inevitably has faults, and Freud's theories and those of his successors have been no exception. We have already seen that not long after they were first enunciated, Freud's theories were attacked for several broad reasons. Over time, these deficiencies were remedied. But there are further criticisms of psychodynamic theory and therapy that have been more difficult to remedy: (1) the theory relies too heavily on observations of individual cases; (2) the theory is simply too difficult to prove or disprove; (3) when studies have been conducted, psychodynamic theories have often failed to be supported;

(4) in emphasizing the role of the person, these theories neglect the situation; and (5) psychodynamic therapies have not been proven notably effective. We will examine each of these criticisms in this section.

Reliance on Individual Cases

Freud's theories and those of his intellectual descendants were derived from carefully observing clients who had come for treatment. The virtue of those theories lay in the fact that they arose from the detailed examination of the personalities of clients. But that was also their liability, for Freud's clients were mainly Viennese women, in early and middle adulthood, who suffered a fairly restricted range of psychological symptoms. Yet, from experience with these people, Freud generalized to normal people, to adults as well as children, to people in the Viennese culture and throughout the rest of the world. Such restricted experience, it has often been said (Eysenck, 1961b; Mischel, 1968; Hall and Lindzey, 1970), is hardly the basis for such generalization. Many of these generalizations simply proved to be wrong.

The use of single clinical cases has another shortcoming as well: there is no control case with which to compare the clinical one. Consider the fact that most of Freud's clients were upper-middle-class women from Vienna. It was only natural for Freud to conclude that the repressed sexuality that seemed to generate their difficulties characterized *all* difficulties. But what if Freud had had an opportunity to compare these women with people who came from the lower classes of Vienna, or with Greek, Italian, or American women, or with men from the same culture or a different one? Would he necessarily have arrived at the same conclusion regarding the prominent influence of sexual desires?

Ultimately, of course, Freud's disciples *did* analyze people from other cultures and classes. And eventually, many men came into psychoanalysis. But by then, the impressions gleaned from upper-middle-class Viennese women were formalized into theory, becoming self-fulfilling prophecies about each new therapy client. In short, by then it may well have been too late.

Difficulties of Proof

A second criticism of psychodynamic theories is that it is quite difficult to either support or disprove them. Some of the difficulty arises because they take complex views of personality and behavior. Many behaviors are held to be **overdetermined,** that is, determined by more than one force and with more than the required psychic energy. Altering a particular psychological force—for example, by recovering a crucial early memory—may have no visible effect on a particular trait or behavior because the latter are supported and sustained by many interrelated psychological forces.

Nevertheless, problems of proof are serious. Only rarely is it possible to confirm, for example, that a particular unconscious motive is really operating. Precisely because the motive is unconscious, it is invisible to the client and only **inferred** by the therapist. Even in Patty's case, where seeming confirmation was obtained because the headaches gradually disappeared, can we be sure that these changes were due to her increasing awareness of sexual motives and fears of abandonment? Might not the cure have arisen, with equal plausibility, from the fact that she had finally found someone whom she trusted and in whom she could confide?

Lack of Scientific Evidence

Psychodynamic theories have been subjected to a variety of ingenious studies, many of which have failed to confirm the theories. Consider the Oedipus conflict, for example. The notion that boys desire to replace their fathers as their mothers' lovers has failed to find support in a variety of studies (Fisher and Greenberg, 1977). Similarly, the universality of castration anxiety remains to be demonstrated. Moreover, the idea that females, because they lack a penis, feel inferior to males has not been demonstrated either. Also, studies have not been able to prove Freud's notion that unresolved conflicts that occur during the oral stage of development are responsible for adult dependency. In short, many aspects of psychodynamic theories have yet to accrue sufficient scientific support to merit belief.

Person versus Situation

Psychodynamic theories overwhelmingly emphasize the impact of traits and dispositions, those stable constellations of attitude and experience that are held to influence behavior. But what of situations? Because psychodynamic theories are derived mainly from information conveyed by clients during treatment, and because clients are encouraged to talk about their own reactions rather than the situation in which they find themselves, psychoanalytic theory underestimates the role of situation and context. For example, it is much easier to infer that a person's continuing irritation with his employer results from unconscious and unresolved conflicts about authority when the employer's behavior has not been observed directly than when it has been. Similarly, it is easier to construe marriage conflicts in terms of the traits of the spouse who has sought consultation precisely because one has no first-hand experience with that spouse's marital situation.

Relative Inefficacy of Psychodynamic Treatments

On the whole and regardless of their popularity, psychoanalytic treatment and those treatments that are derived from it, have not proved particularly effective. Many studies indicate that overall, psychoanalytic treatment is no more effective than no treatment at all is (Eysenck, 1952a). Other studies demonstrate that treatments which are derived from cognitive and behavioral theories are considerably more effective (Bandura, 1969; Beck, 1976; Kazdin and Wilson, 1978; Wilson and Rachman, 1983). Moreover, there is reason to believe that broad-spectrum psychodynamic treatments (as opposed to narrowly based psychoanalytic ones) have considerable effectiveness (Smith, Glass, and Miller, 1980; Rosenthal, 1983; Shapiro and Shapiro, 1983). To some extent, the problem lies in the fact that orthodox psychoanalysts employ a single technique for treating a host of diverse problems. It is hard to believe that there might be a single prescription that could cure all human ills. Similarly, the notion that a single therapeutic technique could cure a diverse spectrum of psychological problems also strains the imagination.

By comparison to techniques derived from other theories, psychodynamic ones suffer a further deficiency, which is that it is difficult to find good criteria for "improvement" or "cure." We take this matter up in greater detail in Chapter 8, which deals with discovering the causes and cures of psychological distress. But for the moment, it should be noted that global measures of personality are simply insensitive to the kinds of changes that may be produced in psychodynamically oriented therapies.

Of all the criticisms of psychodynamic theories and therapies, three have been influential in spawning new approaches to abnormality. Humanistic approaches have grown, in part, from disenchantment with the deterministic emphasis in psychodynamic theories. Behavioral and cognitive approaches have been spurred on by two further criticisms: (1) the difficulty in obtaining verifiable proof of the assumptions and postulates of psychodynamic theories, and (2) the failure of psychodynamically oriented treatments to be as effective as had been hoped. We turn to the humanistic, behavioral, and cognitive approaches to abnormality in the succeeding chapters.

SUMMARY

1. Psychodynamic theories are centrally concerned with conflict, anxiety, and defense. *Conflict* arises when desires cannot find immediate gratification because such gratification is not permitted by reality or conscience. Conflict generates *anxiety,* a form of psychic pain that arises when individuals feel they cannot cope. Anxiety can be either conscious or unconscious and gives rise to *defense mechanisms,* which are the mind's flexible editing mechanisms that allow individuals to alter or entirely obliterate painful stimuli that arise from either desire or reality.

2. From birth to maturity, people move through five psychosexual stages, in which the use of *psychic energy* changes. The first is the *oral stage,* during which sensual pleasure is located around the mouth. Subsequently, they move through the *anal stage,* when pleasure is focused on the anus, and then the *phallic stage,* when pleasure is centered on the genitals. The *latency period* follows, during which time sexual instincts lie dormant. Individuals then emerge into the final stage of development, the *genital stage,* which marks the beginning of adult sexual functioning.

3. Adult sexual adjustment necessitates the child's resolution of the *Oedipal conflict.* Children desire to do away with the parent of the same sex and to take possession of the opposite-sex parent. *Castration anxiety* terminates the incestuous desire in boys. *Penis envy* is experienced by girls, who must also overcome their desire for the opposite-sex parent. *Identification* with the same-sex parent enables the child to resolve the Oedipus conflict.

4. Freud divided the personality into three kinds of processes: id, ego, and superego. The *id* is concerned with sexual and aggressive desires and is dominated by the *pleasure principle.* The *ego* is concerned with the individual's safety, allows desire to be expressed only when aversive consequences from other sources are minimal, and is dominated by the *reality principle.* The *superego* consists of the individual's conscience and ideals, and regardless of what reality permits, it either forbids individuals from expressing desires, or urges them toward the achievement of higher goals.

5. Freud proposed three levels of consciousness: perceptual consciousness, the pre-conscious, and the unconscious. The large mass of memory, experience, and impulse lies in the unconscious, which includes forgotten memories and repressed memories. Repressed memories live on because they are not subject to rational control; they are the dominant forces in personality.

6. There are three kinds of anxiety: realistic anxiety, neurotic anxiety, and moral anxiety. To relieve anxiety, individuals use such coping strategies as repression, projection, reaction formation, displacement, identification, denial, isolation, intellectualization, rationalization, and sublimation. Psychoanalysts believe that there is a maturational hierarchy of coping strategies and classify the strategies into four levels of maturity. Those that do less violence to reality are considered to be more mature strategies.

7. Jung asserted that the unconscious is not merely a concealed storehouse of sexual and aggressive desires, but that it contains a rich variety of attributes. Among these are the *collective unconscious,* which contains the memory traces of the experiences of past generations in the form of *archetypes,* or universal ideas.

8. Adler, Horney, Sullivan, Erikson, and Fromm stressed the impact of *social* relationships on psychological development, as well as the central role of ego processes in personality. According to these later theorists, ego processes have energies of their own which generate goals that are neither sexual nor aggressive.

9. Psychodynamic therapies seek to make conscious that which is unconscious through encouraging the client to *free associate* and to examine dreams, resistances, and the *transference* that occurs between the client and therapist. Psychodynamic treatment aims to enable the client to reduce the amount of psychic energy that is invested in defensive maneuvers, and to achieve greater control over impulse expression.

10. Psychodynamic theories have demystified psychological processes and have offered the possibility of overcoming psychological distress. But critics cite their tendency to overgeneralize from narrow samples, their indifference to the scientific method and scientific proof, their disregard of the situation, and their failure to be especially effective.

The Behavioral Model

The child's development is affected by the environment. If that environment changes, the whole course of the child's life may be changed. When applied to social sciences, behaviorism claims that crime, prejudice, and stupidity can be overcome respectively by spreading wealth, learning, and environmental enrichment. (Bill Strode/Black Star)

Is schizophrenia the result of conflicts over mother, or is it an inherited malady? Are phobias learned, or are they merely innate fears rekindled by environmental trauma? Is mental retardation acquired, or is it inherited from one's parents? Questions of this type bring to the forefront one of the major debates in psychology: the nature-nurture issue. Is our behavior determined by heredity or by our environment?

The seventeenth century French philosopher, René Descartes (1596–1650), founded a movement called rationalism. Its adherents believed that many of the basic ideas that human beings hold—the ideas of self, of God, of space, of time, of causality—are inborn. This was called the *doctrine of innate ideas.* In contrast, the British empiricists believed that all knowledge comes from the senses, that all that we know and all that we are result from our experiences. John Locke (1632–1704), one of the founders of empiricism, claimed that at birth the mind of the child is a *tabula rasa,* a blank slate, on which experience "writes." A child's development is determined by what gets "written." If a certain child had had a wholly different set of experiences, he would be a wholly different person. But how does this child learn about the world? The empiricists answer "through associations." Associations between ideas are the mental glue holding the future to the present. David Hume (1711–1776), the most influential of the empiricists, claimed that the connections we make between ideas reduce to two simple principles: resemblance and contiguity. Through **resemblance,** the idea of a portrait of any individual makes us think of the real individual. Through the principle of **contiguity,** or conjunction in time or place, imagining one part of a face will call up images of the rest of the face. For Hume, causality reduces to contiguity: we believe that A causes B, when each A is followed by a B. Since all knowledge consists only of ideas derived from the senses, and associations between ideas come only from our experience, it follows that we are creations of our environment, of our past. It was out of this empiricist tradition that behaviorism grew.

ASSUMPTIONS OF THE BEHAVIORAL VIEW

Behaviorism is not only a model for the study of abnormal behavior, it is a world view. Its first assumption is ***environmentalism,*** which states that all organisms, including humans, are shaped by the environment. We learn about the future through the associations of the past. This is why, for example, our behavior is subject to rewards and punishments. If our employers paid us twice as much per hour for working one Saturday, we would be more likely to work on future Saturdays. If a child were denied the evening T.V. hour for not eating her vegetables, her plate would be cleaned more often than not in the future.

The second assumption of behaviorism is ***experimentalism,*** which states that through an experiment, we can find out what aspect of the environment caused our behavior and how we can change it. What causes us to work on Saturdays? If the crucial element is withheld, the present characteristic will disappear. If the crucial element is reinstated, the characteristic will reappear. Remove double-time pay, and work on Saturday will stop. Reinstate double-time pay, and work on Saturday will resume. This is the heart of the experimental method. From the experimental method, we can determine what causes people, in general, to forget, to be anxious, to fight, and we can then apply these general laws to individual cases. This is in contrast to the clinical method, which pervades the psychodynamic and humanistic models. For these models, the individual case must first be understood, and general laws then extrapolated.

The third assumption of behaviorism is ***optimism*** concerning change. If an individual is a product of the environment and if those parts of the environment that have molded him can be known by experimentation, he will be changed when the environment is changed. It is more than coincidence that behaviorism flourishes most in two countries—the United States and Soviet Russia—where egalitarianism and the belief that people can be changed by changing the environment also flourish. When applied to social problems, behaviorism claims that crime is caused by poverty and other environmental circumstances and that it can be overcome by spreading wealth, that prejudice is caused by ignorance and can be overcome by learning, that stupidity is caused by deprivation and can be overcome by environmental enrichment, and so on.

These three assumptions of behaviorism apply directly to abnormal psychology. First, abnormal as well as normal behavior is learned from past experiences. Psychopathology consists of acquired habits that are maladaptive. Second, we can find out by experiment what aspects of the environment cause abnormal behavior. Third, if we change these aspects of the environment, the individual will unlearn his old, maladaptive habits and will learn new, adaptive habits. Herein lies behaviorism's method for the cure of abnormality.

But specifically how do we learn and what is it we learn? For the behavioral psychologist, two basic learning processes exist, and it is from these two that all behaviors, both normal and abnormal, derive. We can learn what goes with what through ***Pavlovian*** or ***classical conditioning.*** And we can learn what to do to obtain what we want and rid ourselves of what we do not want through ***instrumental*** or ***operant conditioning.***

Ivan Pavlov (1849–1936) discovered the conditional reflex, which has come to be called the conditional response. (Courtesy Sovfoto)

PAVLOVIAN CONDITIONING

Just after the turn of the century, the Russian physiologist, Ivan Pavlov (1849–1936), accidentally made a discovery that would change the nature of all his future research. But more importantly, it would form the basis of a school of thought that has had a major impact on psychology. Pavlov was studying the digestive system of dogs, specifically the salivary reflex. During his experiments, he would put food powder in the dog's mouth, and he would then measure the drops of saliva by way of a tube surgically inserted into the dog's mouth. But in the course of his work, Pavlov noticed that dogs began to salivate merely when he walked into the room. This salivation could not be a reflex since it did not occur the first few times Pavlov walked in; it only occurred once the dog had learned that Pavlov's appearance signaled food. That is, Pavlov's appearance became associated with a future event: food. He called this a psychic reflex, or a conditional reflex, since it was conditional upon past experience. It has come to be called, through mistranslation, a ***conditioned response,*** or ***CR.*** A typical Pavlovian conditioning experiment goes as follows: we know that food (unconditioned stimulus, US) produces salivation (unconditioned response, UR).

$$\text{US (food)} \longrightarrow \text{UR (salivation)}$$

We present a tone just prior to presenting the food. Because the tone itself does not produce salivation, it is a neutral stimulus. But after pairing the tone with the food several times, we discover that salivation will occur upon presentation of the tone. The tone can now be called a conditioned stimulus (CS) because it produces salivation, the conditioned response (CR). In short:

$$\text{CS (tone)} \longrightarrow \text{US (food)} \longrightarrow \text{UR (salivation)}$$

After several pairings of CS and US:

$$\text{CS (tone)} \longrightarrow \text{CR (salivation)}$$

This kind of experiment has been carried out using many species (Siamese fighting fish, rats, dogs, and humans), conditioned stimuli (tones, lights, tastes), and unconditioned responses (salivation, fear, nausea). It can be used in therapeutic situations to eliminate unsatisfactory behaviors. For example, Pavlovian conditioning may be used to cure alcoholism (Baker and Cannon, 1979). The following case illustrates how the conditioning would proceed when curing alcoholism.

> Steven drinks a quart of vodka daily and has done so for several months. His drunkenness interferes greatly with his work, his marriage is falling apart, and he has been arrested twice for drunken driving. He has sought out a dramatic form of therapy: Pavlovian aversion therapy.
>
> In the therapist's office, Steven gulps down a shot of his favorite vodka. He then drinks ipecac, a drug that causes him to become nauseated within a few minutes. He vomits. A week later, the same procedure is repeated. The taste of vodka (CS) is paired with the ipecac (the US). The ipecac produces nausea and vomiting (the UR). After several such sessions, a major change in Steven's preferences has occurred. Vodka now tastes terrible to him (CR). Merely thinking about alcohol makes him nauseous. And, most importantly, he no longer drinks liquor.

THE BASIC PAVLOVIAN PHENOMENA

There are two processes in Pavlovian conditioning that occur time and time again, regardless of what species, which kind of CS or US, or what kind of a response is tested. Pavlov discovered both: acquisition and extinction.

Acquisition is the learning of a response based on the pairings of a CS and US. Depending on the response to be learned, acquisition usually takes from three to fifteen pairings. *Extinction* is the loss of the CS's power to produce the formerly acquired response. This is brought about by presenting the CS, and no longer following it with the US. For example, it is possible to condition fear in humans. Fear can be measured by increased heart rate, perspiration, and muscle tension. When mild shocks (US) are given to humans, these measures become evident, that is, pain (UR) is produced. After several pairings of tone (CS) and shock (US), the tone (CS) alone begins to elicit fear (CR). That is what we call acquisition. But if we now repeatedly present the tone (CS) no longer followed with the shock (US), the individual no longer shows signs of fear. The tone (CS) no longer signals a shock (US). We call this process extinction.

PAVLOVIAN CONDITIONING, EMOTIONS, AND PSYCHOPATHOLOGY

There are situations in the world that arouse strong emotions in us. Some of these arouse the emotion *unconditionally,* or from our very first encounter with them: a loud clap of thunder startles us the very first time we hear it. Other objects acquire emotional significance: the face of a person we love produces a sense of well-being; seeing a stranger in a dark alleyway arouses dread. Pavlovian conditioning provides a powerful account of how objects take on emotional significance; it is this account that makes conditioning of great interest to the student of abnormality.

According to the behavioral account, the basic mechanism for all acquired emotional states is the pairing of a neutral object (CS) with an un-

Pavlovian conditioning provides a powerful account of how objects take on emotional significance. The sight of all dogs may produce dread in this child due to this early frightening encounter with a German shepherd. (Courtesy Leo de Wys, Inc.) Conversely, the sight of its mother's face will produce a sense of well-being in a baby due to the pairing of the mother's face with the baby's sense of contentment. (Photograph by Suzanne Szasz)

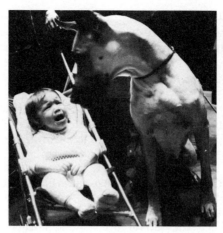 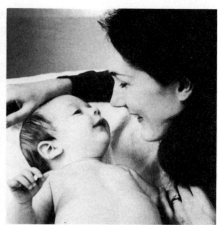

conditioned emotional state (US). With enough pairings, the neutral object will lose its neutrality, become a CS, and all by itself produce the emotional state (CR). Consider the case of a child who is continually beaten with a tan hairbrush by his father. Before the beatings, the child had no feelings about the brush whatsoever. But, after several beatings (US), the brush becomes a CS and merely seeing the tan brush produces fear (CR).

If normal emotions are acquired in this way, the same should be true of acquired emotional disorders. Several of the psychopathological disorders explored in the following chapters involve the acquisition of an exaggerated or unusual emotional state in regard to inappropriate objects. For example, phobias are said to be a result of Pavlovian conditioning. A **phobia** is a fear greatly out of proportion to how dangerous the phobic object actually is. For example, a cat phobic had a history of cats (CS) paired with painful events such as being scratched (US). As a result, cats become terrifying to the phobic individual, despite the fact that cats generally are not dangerous.

Here we can contrast the behavioral view of what causes emotional disorders with the biomedical model and the psychodynamic model. According to the behavioral view, the symptom of the disorder is the disorder. In the case above, the phobic individual's fear of cats is the disorder. There is no underlying pathological state that produces the symptoms. For the biomedical model, an underlying pathology such as a "virus," a disordered biochemistry, or a dysfunctional organ causes the symptoms. For the psychoanalytic view, an intrapsychic conflict, usually sexual or aggressive in nature and stemming from childhood fixations, causes the symptoms.

The therapeutic optimism of the behavioral view follows directly from this view of the cause of the disorder. If the disorders are the symptoms and do not reflect an underlying pathology, eliminating the symptoms will cure the disorder. Since the symptoms of emotional disorders are emotional responses acquired by Pavlovian conditioning, it follows that those techniques which have been found experimentally to extinguish conditioned emotional responses will cure emotional disorders. This contrasts with the biomedical and psychodynamic stance on therapy: for these models, getting rid of the symptoms is only cosmetic; cure consists of removing the underlying disorder. For example, treating the symptoms of general paresis instead of attacking the syphilitic spirochete would not help much, for the underlying pathological process would remain intact. A strong test, then, of the behavioral view as opposed to the medical and psychoanalytic views of emotional disorders would be whether the symptoms can be removed by extinction procedures, and whether other emotional problems will then occur, reflecting an uncured underlying pathology, after behavior therapy has removed one set of symptoms (see Chapter 10).

THE PAVLOVIAN THERAPIES

In the chapters on phobias and sexual dysfunction, we will look in detail at the therapies involving Pavlovian extinction of emotional disorders. But, some of the specific therapies should be briefly mentioned now.

Two Pavlovian therapies involving extinction have been applied to phobias and other anxiety disorders. The first, *systematic desensitization,* was developed by Joseph Wolpe, then a South African psychiatrist. Wolpe's (1969) therapy consists of having the phobic patient imagine a set of gradually more frightening scenes involving the phobic object at the same time as he is engaged in deep muscular relaxation. For example, the cat phobic will think about the fear-evoking object, the cat (CS), at the same time as he is making a response incompatible with fear. Pavlovian extinction will occur with this exposure to the CS (thoughts about and eventually the actual phobic object) without the US (original trauma) and the UR (terror). This is the critical, or one of the critical, aspects of the therapy. Another is the substitution of a pleasant response relaxation—for the unpleasant response of fear. Systematic desensitization has been demonstrated to be highly effective in curing phobias in a brief time, without the recurrence of other symptoms.

The second behavior therapy, also used with phobias, is *flooding.* In flooding, the phobic patient is immersed in the phobic situation (either real

In this mild form of flooding, a child who has acquired a fear of dogs is gently prodded toward one. Upon learning that the dog no longer presents danger, the child's fear of dogs disappears. (Photographs by Erika Stone)

Edward L. Thorndike
(1874–1949) studied animal
intelligence and formulated the
"law of effect." (Courtesy
National Library of Medicine)

B. F. Skinner (1904–   )
formulated the basic concepts of
operant conditioning.
(Photograph by Christopher S.
Johnson)

or imagined) for several consecutive hours. For example, a claustrophobic (who is terrified of being in small enclosed places) would be placed in a closet. After a while, the person no longer would be terrified of being enclosed (Marks, 1969). Flooding is a Pavlovian extinction procedure; the CS (phobic situation) is presented without the US (original trauma), and fear of the CS diminishes (Stampfl and Levis, 1967).

Pavlovian conditioning, then, provides a theory of how we normally learn to feel a given emotion toward a given object. By applying its basic phenomena to emotional disorders, we can arrive at a theory of how emotional disorders come about, and we can deduce a set of therapies that should undo abnormal emotional responses.

OPERANT CONDITIONING

At about the same time as Pavlov discovered an objective way of studying how we learn "what goes with what," Edward L. Thorndike (1874–1949) founded the objective study of how we learn "what to do to get what we want." Thorndike was studying animal intelligence. In one series of experiments he put hungry cats in puzzle boxes and observed how they learned to escape confinement and get food. He designed various boxes—some had levers to push, others had strings to pull, and some had shelves to jump on —and he left food—often fish—outside the box. The cat would have to make the correct response to escape from the puzzle box.

Thorndike's first major discovery was that learning what to do was gradual, not insightful. That is, the cat proceeded by trial and error. On the first few trials, the time to escape was very long; but with repeated success, the time gradually shortened to a few seconds. To explain his findings, Thorndike formulated the "law of effect." Still a major principle, this holds that when, in a given stimulus situation, a response is made and followed by positive consequences, the response will tend to be repeated; when followed by negative consequences, it will tend not to be repeated. Thorndike's work, like Pavlov's, provided an objective way of studying the properties of learning.

This tradition was refined, popularized, and applied to a range of real-life settings by B. F. Skinner (1904–   ), who worked largely with rats pressing levers for food and with pigeons pecking lighted discs for grain. It was Skinner who formulated the basic concepts of operant conditioning.

THE CONCEPTS OF OPERANT CONDITIONING

Through his basic concepts, Skinner defined the elements of the law of effect rigorously. His three basic concepts consist of the reinforcer (both positive and negative), the operant, and the discriminative stimulus.

A *positive reinforcer* is an event which increases the probability that a response preceding it will occur again. In effect, a positive reinforcer rewards behavior. A *negative reinforcer* is an event that decreases the probability of recurrence of a response that precedes it. We also call this punishment, or an aversive event. The omission of a negative reinforcer increases the probability of a response that precedes such an omission.

Winning at cards is a positive reinforcer for this little girl. She will probably play cards with the boys again in the future. (Photograph by R. E. Burdick/Leo de Wys, Inc.)

An *operant* is a response whose probability can either be increased by positive reinforcement or decreased by negative reinforcement. If a mother reinforces her twelve-month-old child with a hug every time he says "Daddy," the probability that he will say it again is increased. In this case, the operant is saying "Daddy." If the mother hugs the child for saying Daddy only when the child's father is in sight, and does not hug him for saying "Daddy" when the father is not around, she is teaching the child to respond to a discriminative stimulus. In this case, the father being in sight is the *discriminative stimulus,* a signal that means that reinforcement is available if the operant is made.

THE OPERANT PHENOMENA

Acquisition and Extinction

The phenomena of *acquisition* and *extinction* in the operant conditioning of voluntary responses parallel the Pavlovian conditioning of involuntary responses. Consider a typical operant paradigm. A hungry rat is placed inside an operant chamber. The desired operant is the pressing of a lever. Each time the rat presses a lever, food is delivered down a chute. During this acquisition procedure, learning to lever press proceeds gradually, as shown in Figure 5-1. It takes about ten sessions for the rat to learn to press at a high

Figure 5-1
Acquisition and extinction of lever pressing. This curve depicts the growth in the frequency of lever pressing over the course of a number of experimental sessions, followed by its extinction when reinforcement is discontinued. (Source: Schwartz, 1984)

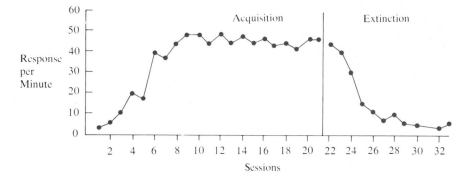

and constant rate. Extinction is then begun (in session 22), and the reinforcer (food) is no longer delivered when the rat presses the lever. As a result, responding gradually diminishes back to zero.

Partial Reinforcement and Schedules of Reinforcement

An operant experimenter can arrange a rich variety of relationships between the responses that his subjects make and the reinforcers they receive. In the simplest relationship, each and every time a subject makes a response a reinforcer is delivered. This is called **continuous reinforcement (CRF).** For example, every time the rat presses a lever, a food pellet arrives. In the real world, however, reinforcements do not usually come with such high consistency. More often, reinforcements only occur for some of the responses that are made, and many responses are in vain. To capture this, the experimenter arranges the relationships such that reinforcement is delivered for only some of the responses that the subject makes. This is called a **partial** or **intermittent reinforcement** schedule. So, for example, the rat might receive one food pellet only when he has pressed the bar fifty times, rather than for each press.

Partial reinforcement schedules make initial learning slower, but these schedules have two other properties that are important for engineering human behavior. In the first place, a great deal of work can be produced for very little payoff. So, for one small food pellet, a rat or a person can be made to emit hundreds of responses. The second property has to do with extinction and is called the **partial reinforcement extinction effect.** After a subject has been partially reinforced for a response, and extinction (consisting of no reinforcement at all) has begun, a surprisingly large number of responses will occur before the subject gives up. A rat who had responded on a partial reinforcement schedule in which it pressed the lever fifty times in order to get one reinforcement will respond hundreds of times during extinction before it quits. In contrast, a rat who has had continuous reinforcement and whose behavior is then extinguished will stop pressing after only five to ten attempts.

Maladaptive human behavior in the real world is often highly resistant to extinction in the same way that partially reinforced operant behavior is in the laboratory. For example, a compulsive "checker" who fears that she left the gas in the stove on may check the stove hundreds of times a day. She is reinforced very little; that is, she almost never checks and finds that the gas is on. Most of her responding is in vain. The operant explanation of her behavior is partial reinforcement. Because once every several hundred times she was reinforced by finding the gas on, she will now check thousands of times in order to get one reinforcer (Rachman and Hodgson, 1980).

THE OPERANT THERAPIES

The operant therapist uses these principles in asking three essential questions: (1) What undesirable behavior or maladaptive operants does the patient engage in? (2) What reinforcers maintain these maladaptive responses? (3) What environmental changes, usually reinforcement or discriminative stimulus changes, can be made to change the maladaptive behavior into adaptive behavior? (Ullmann and Krasner, 1965). A variety of operant

This child may be trying to manipulate her mother by crying because she has occasionally been reinforced for crying in the past by being held and attended to. It will be difficult to extinguish the child's crying because attention for crying was inconsistent in the past. This is an instance of the partial reinforcement extinction effect. (Courtesy Leo de Wys, Inc.)

Selective positive reinforcement. This autistic boy is being fed each time he hits the drum with his stick. Thus, one of his symptoms—lack of social interaction—is targeted for change into adaptive behavior through the reinforcement of being fed. (Photograph by Allan Brant)

therapies have been employed for a variety of forms of psychopathology. We will look at a selection of them now and others will be discussed in more detail in the chapters that involve the specific disorders that these therapies treat.

Selective Positive Reinforcement

In the technique of selective positive reinforcement, the therapist selects a **target behavior** or adaptive behavior that is to be increased in probability. By the systematic delivery of positive reinforcement contingent on the occurrence of the target behavior, this behavior becomes more frequent.

Anorexia nervosa is a life-threatening disorder that, for the most part, afflicts women in their teens and early twenties. They literally starve themselves to death. By engaging in bizarre eating habits, such as eating only three Cheerios a day, an anorexic will lose 25 to 30 percent of her body weight within a couple of months. When they are hospitalized, the first problem with these patients (who may weigh as little as seventy-five pounds) is not curing them, but just saving their lives. Such patients usually do not cooperate with regimes that attempt to force them to eat. One highly effective way of saving the life of an anorexic woman is to selectively reinforce her for eating by using a reinforcer that is more highly desired than is eating. But, if you ask her what would be a reward that would induce her to eat, she will probably not tell you. In such a situation, a therapist will look for a behavior that the patient engages in frequently and will only give her the opportunity to perform it if she first eats (Premack, 1959). If we observe and time what an anorexic does during the day, we might find, for example, that she watches television for an hour and a half, spends forty-five minutes talking with fellow patients, and spends an hour pacing the halls. An operant therapist would then set up a regime such that in order to be allowed to do any one of these three activities, the anorexic would have to first eat a fixed amount. For example, if she first ate a tablespoon of custard, she would then be allowed to watch television for ten minutes; if she ate all of her steak, she would then be allowed to pace the halls for twenty minutes (Stunkard, 1976).

Pop singer Karen Carpenter died of complications of anorexia nervosa. (Wide World Photos)

The use of selective positive reinforcement can also be seen in a type of interpersonal therapy called **behavioral contracting.** In this therapy, two people, usually a married couple, contract with each other to perform some behavior that one of them wants the other to do in exchange for the other engaging in behavior that the first wants. For example, a wife might not want her husband to stay out late at night several evenings a week drinking with his friends; a husband might not want his wife to return late from her class. The husband's drinking irks the wife, and the wife's failure to return from class irks the husband. In this situation, the wife will contract to come home earlier if the husband has stayed home the night before. Similarly, the husband will contract to stay home if the wife comes home earlier. Both members of the pair receive positive reinforcement contingent on their performing specific desired responses. Such marital contracting often removes sources of conflict in a disturbed marriage and in addition shows each spouse that they can affect the behavior of their mate (Stuart, 1969; Patterson, Weiss, and Hops, 1976).

During twenty years of research, selective positive reinforcement has been shown to be an effective technique across a very wide range of behavioral disorders. When a discrete and specifiable instrumental response is missing from the adaptive repertoire of an individual, application of selective positive reinforcement will generally produce and maintain that response.

Selective Punishment

In **selective punishment,** or selective negative reinforcement procedures, the therapist selects a target behavior that is maladaptive. By applying an aversive event when this target behavior occurs, the therapist causes its probability of occurrence to decrease.

Although we are not sure why, some autistic children engage in self-mutilation.* This maladaptive behavior is persistent, and most attempts at intervention on the part of a therapist will produce no or only temporary effects. In some of these cases, operant therapists have applied selective punishment. In one particular case, whenever the autistic child hit himself, a shock was delivered to him. The child soon learned that his behavior brought punishment, and he engaged less often in self-mutilation (Lovaas and Simmons, 1969; Dorsey, Iwata, Ong, and McSween, 1980). This procedure did not cure the child's autism, but it did stop his maladaptive behavior.

Extinction

Punishment involves imposing some noxious event on the patient such as a loud noise, an electric shock, or a nauseating drug. Even though such stimuli can be highly effective in removing unwanted behaviors, there are obvious undesirable aspects to such therapy. For example, patients may come to find the entire therapeutic setting aversive. Or many therapists, quite understandably, may feel uncomfortable with shocking, nauseating, and otherwise scaring fellow human beings, particularly those already burdened

---

* Autism, a psychotic disorder, is characterized by severe social withdrawal (see Chapter 18).

with psychological problems. Extinction is sometimes an alternative strategy: one can eliminate a behavior by merely omitting some highly desired event whenever the target behavior occurs. This procedure is sometimes called "time out from reinforcement" (Kazdin, 1980).

The most common use of extinction in behavior therapy is when the therapist suspects that some maladaptive target behavior is being performed in order to get some positive reinforcement. The therapist then arranges the contingencies so that this behavior no longer produces the reinforcement. If the behavior decreases in frequency, extinction has been successful. For example, there was a case of a female psychotic patient who would make numerous disruptive visits to the nurses' office on the ward. An operant therapist believed that the attention that the patient received from the nurses when she barged into their office was a positive reinforcer that maintained the disruptive behavior. So the therapist instructed the nurses to ignore the patient completely when the patient entered their office, thereby eliminating what was believed to be positive reinforcement. After seven weeks of treatment, the patient's visits dropped from an average of sixteen per day to two per day (Ayllon and Michel, 1959).

Biofeedback

The notion of the "operant response" captures in a rigorous way what we ordinarily mean by a "voluntary response." Operant or voluntary responses are those responses that can be modified by their consequent reward or punishment.

In contrast, there are some responses over which we clearly have no voluntary control. The pupils of the eye contract when exposed to light, and such contraction is not under operant control. If someone were to offer us a reward for not contracting the pupils in our eyes in the face of a bright light, we would fail despite our best effort. But there is a large middle ground between clearly voluntary and clearly involuntary responses. **Biofeedback** attempts to modify these marginally voluntary response systems by electronically detecting, amplifying, and feeding back to the individual the

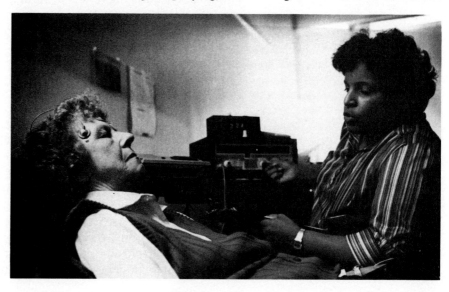

Biofeedback has been used to treat headaches. Here a woman is learning to reduce muscle tension, one cause of headache. (Photograph by Jeffrey Grosscup)

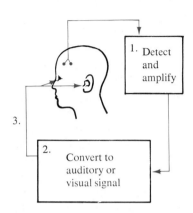

Figure 5-2
The steps of biofeedback. (1)
Bioelectric potentials are
detected and amplified, (2)
bioelectric signals are converted
to easy-to-process information,
(3) this information is fed back to
the patient, and with immediate
feedback, the patient learns
voluntary control response.
(Source: Blanchard and Epstein,
1978, p. 3)

information that the response has been made. Among the systems sensitive to operant relationships using biofeedback are heart rate, blood pressure, the movement of small muscles, stomach secretions, brain waves, and penile erection.

Biofeedback's application to abnormal psychology depends on technological advances in electronics, which permit the detection of minute electrical signals resulting from the beating of the heart, changes in blood pressure, and the movement of small muscles. Biofeedback consists of the three steps shown in Figure 5-2: (1) electrical signals from the target response system are electronically detected and amplified, (2) the signals are converted to a visual or auditory signal, and (3) the signal is fed back to the patient (Blanchard and Epstein, 1978). With the immediate feedback, the patient can learn voluntary control over the response system. The following case demonstrates the successful use of biofeedback in the modification of pain:

> Tom had had a splitting headache off and on for three and a half years. The headache seemed to be caused by a chronically high level of muscular tension in Tom's forehead and the back of his neck. Tom was unable to reduce this muscle tension voluntarily, and he could not tolerate the side effects of strong doses of muscle-relaxing drugs. He turned to biofeedback as an alternative treatment. Tom sat in a comfortable chair and electrodes were placed over the relevant muscle groups in his forehead and neck. Whenever muscle tension in these groups dropped below the desired level, a tone went on; whenever muscle tension went back above this level, the tone went off. After several sessions of relaxation training, Tom found that he was able to keep the tone on most of the time and, to his surprise, the headache disappeared. Home practice of relaxation plus occasional booster sessions have kept Tom headache-free for the last two years. (Budzynski, Stoyva, Adler, and Mullaney, 1973)

Therapy using biofeedback has expanded in the last five years. It has been applied with notable success to headaches and pain of muscular origin, and to the alleviation of paralysis following strokes. It has also been applied with somewhat encouraging results to cardiac arrhythmia, phobia, essential hypertension, migraine headache, spastic colon, peptic ulcer, asthma, and epilepsy. In Chapter 12, we will discuss in more detail the uses of biofeedback for psychosomatic disorders.

AVOIDANCE LEARNING

As we have seen, learning theorists regard human beings as capable of learning two sorts of relationships: the Pavlovian relationship—what goes with what—and the operant relationship—what to do in order to get what you want. There are many situations in which both sorts of learning go on at the same time. Prominent among such situations is learning to avoid aversive events. In an **avoidance situation,** two relationships have to be learned: (1) what predicts the aversive event, and (2) how to get away. The avoidance situation combines both a Pavlovian relationship and an operant relationship. To investigate avoidance, behavior theorists typically place a rat in a two-compartment chamber called a shuttlebox. After a while, a tone is turned on. Ten seconds after the tone has gone on, an electric shock is delivered through the floor of the apparatus. If the rat runs to the other side of the shuttlebox before the shock comes on, the tone terminates and the shock is prevented from occurring. Rats, dogs, and people usually learn to avoid shock altogether in these circumstances. In order to avoid the shock, the subject must learn two relationships (Mowrer, 1948; Rescorla and Solomon, 1967): (1) He must learn that the tone predicts shock, and he must become afraid of the tone. This is a Pavlovian relationship in which the CS is tone, the US is shock, and the CR is fear. (2) Having learned to fear the tone, he must learn what to do about it. He must learn that running to the other side of the shuttlebox terminates the fearful tone and prevents the shock from occurring. This is an operant relationship in which the discriminative stimulus is the tone, the operant is running to the other side of the shuttlebox, and the reinforcer is the termination of fear and the omission of shock.

An understanding of avoidance learning helps in the treatment of certain psychopathologies. The behavioral view of obsessive-compulsive disorders, for example, involves the concept of avoidance learning. According to this view, the obsessive-compulsion checker believes that by engaging in the compulsive behavior of checking the stove several hundred times a day, she can prevent disaster from befalling her family. In this case, the occurrence and persistence of the compulsion may be explained by avoidance learning.

Behavior therapists often use both operant and Pavlovian relationships. Recall Steven, the chronic alcoholic who came to hate the taste of vodka after he received vomit-inducing ipecac. Whenever Steven made the operant response of reaching for vodka, he felt queasy and withdrew his hand. By Pavlovian conditioning, the taste of bourbon had become nauseating. By operant conditioning, Steve had learned that withdrawing his hand from the bottle of vodka would reduce his queasiness.

SUMMARY

1. The behavioral school of abnormality grows out of British empiricism, the view that knowledge is caused by experience and that *resemblance* and *contiguity* between ideas are the two simple principles which are the mental glue of experience.

2. The behavioral model sees the cause of abnormality as the *learning of maladaptive habits.* It aims to discover, by laboratory experiment, what aspect of the environment produced this learning, and it sees successful therapy as learning new and more adaptive ways of behaving.

3. Two kinds of basic learning processes exist: *Pavlovian* and *operant conditioning.* These have each generated a set of behavior therapies.

4. Pavlovian therapies begin with the assumption that emotional habits have been acquired by the pairing of a *conditioned stimulus* with an *unconditioned stimulus.* The formerly neutral conditioned stimulus now produces a *conditioned response,* which is the acquired emotion. Two Pavlovian therapies, *systematic desensitization* and *flooding,* extinguish some maladaptive emotional habits quite successfully.

5. Operant conditioning is based on three concepts: reinforcer, operant, and discriminative stimulus. Operant therapies are based on the assumption that people acquire voluntary habits by positive reinforcement and punishment. Operant therapies provide new and more adaptive repertoires of voluntary responses and extinguish maladaptive voluntary responses. Among such therapies are *selective positive reinforcement, selective punishment, extinction,* and *biofeedback.* These have been applied with some success to such disorders as *anorexia nervosa, autism,* and chronic headache.

6. The understanding of *avoidance learning* combines operant and Pavlovian theory, and helps in the treatment of obsessive-compulsive disorders.

The Cognitive Model

"Men are not moved by things, but the views which they take of them"—
Epictetus (first century, A.D.).

THE cognitive school is a modern outgrowth from, and reaction to, the behavioral school. As we remember from the previous chapter, the basic premise of behavioral therapy is that behavior is determined by events in the environment: an individual's behavior is initially acquired either through Pavlovian or operant conditioning, and it changes according to these principles when the environment changes. Moreover, according to the behaviorists, abnormal behavior is a learned response to the environment, and when the therapist changes the environment, the client's behavior will change.

Implicit in the behavioral view is the assumption that the connection between the environment and behavior is direct. But since its beginnings, behaviorism has been challenged on this point. Others, specifically cognitive psychologists, hold that behavior is influenced by more than just this direct relation between environment and response. Rather, they contend that what a person thinks, believes, expects, attends to—in short, his or her mental life—influences how he or she behaves. Behaviorists, when pressed, frequently admit that mental life exists (Skinner, 1971). But they deny that such cognitions play a causal role in behavior. Rather, they dismiss cognitive processes, calling them *epiphenomena.* An epiphenomenon is a process that, while not causal, reflects the underlying process that is causal. A behaviorist who admits that mental processes exist likens them to the speedometer of an automobile. While a speedometer reflects how fast the automobile is going, it does not itself influence the speed.

ASSUMPTIONS OF THE COGNITIVE VIEW

The cognitive psychologist, as opposed to the behaviorist, believes that mental events are not mere epiphenomena, that cognitive processes influence behavior. Specifically, the cognitive psychologist contends that disordered cognitive processes cause some psychological disorders and that by changing these cognitions, the disorder can be alleviated and perhaps even cured.

An artist's depiction of the fear of speaking in public. (Drawing by John Vassos. Courtesy the Mayfield and George Arents Research Libraries, Syracuse University)

This elderly man sits by the telephone, waiting for someone to call. He becomes progressively sadder and more depressed as the phone remains silent and he thinks, "No one will call. No one loves me. I'm all alone in the world." These thoughts increase his depression. (Photograph by Jeffrey Grosscup)

The following case demonstrates the difference in emphasis between those holding the behavioral view and those holding the cognitive view:

> Two individuals have the same speaking skills, but one is very anxious when giving a public speech, and the other speaks with ease in public. On different occasions, each gives a public speech and, as is common during the course of almost any speech, a few members of the audience walk out of the room during each speech. When these two people record what they were thinking when a member of the audience walked out, a very different pattern emerges. The anxious individual thinks, "I must be boring. How much longer do I have to speak? This speech is going to be a failure." In contrast, the low-anxiety person says to herself, "The person walking out must have a class to make. Gee, that's too bad, he will miss the best part of my talk." The same environmental event—people walking out of the room during the speech—produces a very different set of thoughts: the high-anxiety individual has depressing and tension-inducing thoughts, whereas the low-anxiety individual does not. (Meichenbaum, 1977)

How do the behavioral and cognitive therapists look at this? On the one hand, the behaviorist will focus on the particular environmental event—people walking out during a speech—and how this affects behavior. In this example, however, the environmental event is the same, but the consequences are different. The cognitive therapist, on the other hand, will focus on the difference in the *thoughts* of the two speakers, on how he or she *interprets* the event. For the cognitive therapist, a person's thoughts are of primary importance.

COGNITIVE THERAPY

Underlying the cognitive model is the view that mental events—that is, expectations, beliefs, memories, and so on—can cause behavior. If these mental events are changed, behavior change will follow. Believing this, the cognitive therapist looks for the cause, or etiology, of psychological disorders in disordered mental events. For example, if someone is depressed, the cognitive therapist will look for the cause of the individual's depression in her beliefs or thoughts. Perhaps she believes that she has no control over the events of her life. Thinking that she has no control, the individual may well become passive, sad, and eventually clinically depressed. Successful therapy for such disorders will consist of changing these thoughts. In the case of the depressive, a cognitive therapist will draw out, analyze, and then change the individual's thoughts, hoping to discover, and then reverse the thoughts that caused the depressive's feeling of hopelessness.

To understand what a cognitive therapist does, let us return to the case study of the two speech givers. What if the high-anxiety speaker becomes increasingly depressed when he sees members of the audience walking out? He may label the speech, and himself, a failure. Perhaps he gets so depressed that he can no longer give a good speech, or worse, refuses to speak before an audience. Because of this problem, he may enter therapy. What will a cognitive therapist do?

Because a cognitive therapist is concerned primarily with what a person thinks and believes, he or she will inquire about the anxious speaker's thoughts. Upon finding out that the speaker thinks that he is boring his audience, the therapist will pursue two hypotheses. First, there is the hypothesis that the speaker in reality is boring. If, however, in the course of the therapy, the therapist learns that the person's speeches have in the past been received very well and that some have even been reprinted, the therapist will conclude that the first hypothesis is wrong.

After discarding the hypothesis that the speaker really is boring, the therapist will turn to the hypothesis that the speaker's thoughts are distorting reality. According to this hypothesis, the speaker is selecting negative evidence by focusing too narrowly on one event: he is thinking too much about those members of the audience who walked out. He believes that they think he is boring, that they dislike him, and so on. Here, the therapist gets the client to point out the contrary evidence. First, he has a fine speaking record. Second, only a very small number of people walked out; some probably had important appointments to catch and were glad to have heard at least part of the speech. Perhaps some of them were bored. But third, and most important, he minimized the fact that almost all of the audience remained, and he paid no attention to the fact that the audience applauded enthusiastically. The therapist's job is to draw out all of the distorted negative thoughts, to have the client confront the contrary evidence, and then to get the client to change these thoughts.

COGNITIVE PROCESSES

What kinds of mental events do cognitive therapists deal with? For the purposes of therapy, cognitive processes can be divided into short-term and long-term processes. The short-term processes are conscious. We are aware of them, or can become aware of them with practice. These include expectations, appraisals, and attributions. The long-term cognitive processes are not, generally speaking, available to consciousness. They are hypothetical constructs or dispositions that show themselves in the way they govern the short-term processes. One long-term process involves beliefs. We will discuss the short-term processes first.

Expectations

Expectations are cognitions that explicitly anticipate future events. The speech giver who, upon seeing a few people walk out, thought "this is going to be a failure" is reporting an expectation. He anticipates future consequences, in this case, bad ones.

In his seminal work, Albert Bandura analyzed the notion of expectation and helped to usher in the cognitive school of therapy. In his early work, Bandura showed that people learned not only by direct reinforcement but also by observing others being reinforced. He concluded that the behavioral principles of reinforcement were insufficient and that such "vicarious learning" must involve the learning of expectations (Rotter, 1954; Bandura and Walters, 1959; Bandura, 1977a, 1978). For Bandura, a person in therapy has two kinds of expectancies: an **outcome expectation** is a person's estimate that a given behavior will lead to a desired outcome, and an **efficacy expectation** is the belief that he can successfully execute the behavior that pro-

Albert Bandura analyzed the notion of expectation. (Courtesy of Dr. Albert Bandura)

The behavior of these twin girls reflects two different efficacy expectations. The twin on the left believes that she can execute the response that will solve the puzzle. The twin on the right believes she cannot execute the response, and therefore she gives up. (Photograph by Suzanne Szasz)

duces the desired outcome. Outcome and efficacy expectations are different because a person may be certain that a particular course of action will produce a given outcome, but he may doubt that he can perform this action. For example, he may realize that touching a snake will reduce his snake phobia, but he may still be unable to touch the snake. Bandura believes that the success of systematic desensitization and modeling therapies in curing phobias (Chapter 10) is attributable to changes in self-efficacy expectations. In both situations, the patient learns that he can make those responses—relaxation and approach—which will overcome the phobia. A "micro-analysis" of efficacy expectations and behavioral change in snake phobics has confirmed this speculation. Successful therapy created high efficacy expectations for approaching a boa constrictor. The higher the level of efficacy expectations at the end of treatment, the better was the approach behavior to the snake (Bandura, 1977, 1982; Bandura and Adams, 1978; Staats, 1978; Biran and Wilson, 1981).

Appraisals

We are constantly appraising and evaluating both what happens to us and what we do. These **appraisals** and evaluations are sometimes very obvious to us, but at other times we are unaware of them. For cognitive therapists, such automatic thoughts often precede and cause emotion (Beck, 1976). The speech giver becomes anxious and depressed once he thinks, "This is going to be a failure." He is not only expecting future consequences, he is also appraising his actions. He judges them to be failures, and this appraisal causes his negative emotions. This appraisal process is automatic. After a lifetime of practice, it occurs habitually and rapidly. The individual in therapy must be trained to slow down his thought process to become aware of such thoughts. Automatic thoughts are not vague and ill-formed, rather they are specific and discrete sentences. In addition, while they may seem implausible to the objective observer, they seem highly reasonable to the person who has them (see also Lazarus, 1976; Kanfer and Karoly, 1972; Mahoney and Thoresen, 1974; Rehm, 1978).

Test-anxious individuals are often found to make self-defeating appraisals. A student, for example, taking an examination may say to himself, "Look at that other student. She just left the room. She's much smarter than I am. My going so slowly means I will surely fail." In therapy, this person is taught to reappraise the situation: in short, to test his original appraisal of the event. "She left the room early because she didn't bother to check her answers. Chances are I probably won't fail. And even if I do people probably won't think I'm stupid. And even if they do that doesn't mean I *am* stupid." The goal of the therapist here is to get the client to catch hold of his self-defeating thoughts as they come about, criticize them, control them, and thereby avoid the occurrence of anxiety (Goldfried, Decenteceo, and Wineburg, 1964; Goldfried, Linehan, and Smith, 1978; see also Langer, Janis, and Wolfer, 1975; Meichenbaum, 1977).

A major proponent of cognitive therapy, A. T. Beck (1976) argues that specific emotions are *always* preceded by discrete thoughts. Sadness is preceded by the thought "something of value has been lost." Anxiety is preceded by the thought "a threat of harm exists," and anger is preceded by the thought "my personal domain is being trespassed against." This is a sweeping and simple formulation of emotional life: the essence of sadness, anxiety, and anger consists of appraisals of loss, threat, and trespass, respectively. Thus, for cognitive therapists, modifying those thoughts will alter the emotion.

Attributions

Another kind of short-term mental event that cognitive therapists try to modify is attribution. An **attribution** is an individual's conception of *why* an event has befallen him. When a student fails an examination, he asks himself, "Why did I fail?" Depending on the causal analysis he makes, different consequences ensue. The student might make an **external** or **internal attribution** (Rotter, 1966). He might believe that the examination was unfair, an external cause. Alternatively, he might believe that he is stupid, an internal cause. A second dimension along which attributions for failure are made is **stable** or **unstable** (Weiner, 1974). A stable cause is one that persists in time; an unstable cause is one that is transient. For example, the student might believe that he failed because he did not get a good night's sleep, an unstable cause (which is also internal). Alternatively, the student might believe that he has no mathematical ability, a stable cause (which is also internal). Finally, an attribution for failure can be **global** or **specific** (Abramson, Seligman, and Teasdale, 1978). An attribution to global factors means that failure must occur on many different tasks, and an attribution to specific factors means that failure must occur only on this task. For example, the student who fails might believe that he failed because he is stupid, a global cause (which is also stable and internal). Or he might believe that he failed because the form number of the test was 13, an unlucky number. This latter is a spe-

This boy believes that his team failed because he is a poor athlete. This attribution is internal, stable, and quite global. It will lead him to expect that in the future he will do poorly in sports, and this expectation will undermine his trying. (© Jon Laitise/Black Star)

Table 6-1 CHARACTERISTICS OF ATTRIBUTIONS OF STUDENTS WHO DO POORLY ON THE GRADUATE RECORD EXAMINATION

| | Internal | | External | |
	Stable	Unstable	Stable	Unstable
Global	Lack of intelligence	Exhaustion	ETS gives unfair tests.	Today is Friday the 13th.
	(Laziness)	(Having a cold makes me stupid.)	(People are usually unlucky on the GRE.)	(ETS gave experimental tests this time that were too hard for everyone.)
Specific	Lack of mathematical ability	Fed up with math problems	ETS gives unfair math tests.	The math test was form No. 13.
	(Math always bores me.)	(Having a cold ruins my arithmetic.)	(People are usually unlucky on math tests.)	(Everyone's copy of the math test was blurred.)

Note: ETS = Educational Testing Service, the maker of graduate record examinations (GRE)
SOURCE: Abramson, Seligman, and Teasdale, 1978.

cific attribution (which is also external and stable). Table 6-1 presents these alternative attributions (Heider, 1958; Kelley, 1967; Weiner, 1972).

Cognitive therapists try to change an individual's attributions. For example, women with low self-esteem usually make internal attributions when they fail. They believe that they have failed because they are stupid, incompetent, and unlovable. To deal with this attribution, each week, the therapist has them record five different bad events that have occurred during each week and then he has them write down *external* attributions for the events. For example, one woman might write, "my boyfriend criticized my behavior at a party last night, not because I am socially unskilled, but rather because he was in a bad mood." The goal is to get the woman to shift from internal to external what she believes to be the causes of bad events. After a few weeks, clients begin to see that there are alternative causes for their failures, and the low self-esteem and depression brought about by the internal attributions begin to lift (Ickes and Leyden, 1979; Beck et al., 1979).

Long-Term Cognitive Process: Beliefs

The short-term mental events that we have examined—expectations, appraisals, and attributions—are available to consciousness. Long-term cognitive processes are different. They are hypothetical constructs, inferred dispositions that govern the mental events now in consciousness. One of these long-term cognitive processes is **beliefs.**

Albert Ellis, the founder of rational-emotive therapy, argues that psychological disorder stems largely from irrational beliefs. Over the course of a

Albert Ellis, founder of rational-emotive therapy, argues that psychological disorder stems largely from irrational beliefs. (Courtesy Institute for Rational Living)

lifetime, a client had had a set of destructive beliefs instilled in him by his parents and by society. Among these are the ideas that: (1) it is a dire necessity for an adult human being to be loved or approved by virtually every significant other person in his community; (2) one should be thoroughly competent, adequate, and achieving in all possible respects in order to be worthwhile; (3) it is awful and catastrophic when things are not the way one would very much like them to be; (4) human unhappiness is externally caused, and we have little or no ability to control our own sorrows; (5) our past history is an all-important determinant of our present behavior; if something once strongly affected our life, it should always have a similar effect; and (6) there is invariably a right, precise, and perfect solution to human problems, and it is catastrophic if this perfect solution is not found (Ellis, 1962).

These irrational and illogical beliefs shape the short-term distorted expectations, appraisals, and attributions that produce psychological disorder. The client is afflicted with a "tyranny of should's," and the job of the therapist is to break the hold of these "should's." Once the patient abandons the above beliefs, it is impossible for him to remain disturbed. The job of the therapist is to rid the individual of these beliefs. The therapy is an aggressive one. It makes a concerted attack on the client's beliefs in two ways: (1) the therapist is a frank counter-propagandist who contradicts superstitions and self-defeating propaganda embodied in the irrational beliefs of the patient, and (2) the therapist encourages, persuades, cajoles, and occasionally insists that the patient engage in behavior that will itself be forceful counter-propaganda against the irrational beliefs (Ellis, 1962).

This particular brand of cognitive therapy is called rational-emotive therapy, and it is among the most active and aggressive of psychotherapeutic procedures. The following case illustrates the force of therapeutic persuasion:

During his therapy session, a twenty-three-year-old man said that he was very depressed and did not know why. A little questioning showed that this severely neurotic patient, whose main presenting problem was that he had been doing too much drinking during the last two years, had been putting off the inventory keeping he was required to do as part of his job as an apprentice glass-staining artist.

PATIENT: I know that I should do the inventory before it piles up to enormous proportions, but I just keep putting it off. To be honest, I guess it's because I resent doing it so much.

THERAPIST: But why do you resent it so much?

PATIENT: It's boring. I just don't like it.

THERAPIST: So it's boring. That's a good reason for disliking this work, but is it an equally good reason for resenting it?

PATIENT: Aren't the two the same thing?

THERAPIST: By no means. Dislike equals the sentence, "I don't enjoy doing this thing, and therefore I don't want to do it." And that's a perfectly sane sentence in most instances. But resentment is the sentence, "*Because* I dislike doing this thing, I shouldn't *have* to do it." And that's invariably a very crazy sentence.

PATIENT: Why is it so crazy to resent something that you don't like to do?

THERAPIST: There are several reasons. First of all, from a purely logical standpoint, it just makes no sense at all to say to yourself, "Because I dislike doing this thing, I shouldn't *have* to do it." The second part of this sentence just doesn't follow in any way from the first part. Your reasoning goes something like this: "Because *I* dislike doing this thing, *other people* and the *universe* should be so considerate of me that they should never make me do what I dislike." But, of course, this doesn't make any sense. Why *should* other people and the universe be that considerate of you? It might be nice if they were. But why the devil *should* they be? In order for your reasoning to be true, the entire universe, and all the people in it, would really have to revolve around and be uniquely considerate of you. (Ellis, 1962)

Here the therapist directly attacks the client's belief, arguing that it is irrational. This is an important distinction between cognitive therapists, on the one hand, and behavioral or dynamic therapists on the other. Behavioral and dynamic therapists point out that a client's actions and beliefs are maladaptive and self-defeating. Cognitive therapists emphasize that, in addition, the beliefs are irrational and illogical.

COGNITIVE-BEHAVIORAL THERAPY

Cognitive therapists, then, believe that distorted thinking causes disordered behavior and that correcting the distorted thinking will alleviate and even cure the disordered behavior. Behavior therapists, in contrast, view disordered behavior as learned from past experience, and they attempt to alleviate the disorders by training new, more adaptive habits. These two positions are not incompatible, and many therapists try both to correct distorted cognitions and to train new habits. When therapists combine both techniques, it is called cognitive-behavioral therapy (Ellis, 1962; Mahoney, 1974; Meichenbaum, 1977; Beck et al., 1979).

Arnold Lazarus is one of the therapists who integrates cognitive and behavioral techniques in therapy. Lazarus argues that disorder occurs in the same patient at seven different levels, and that there are levels of therapy appropriate to each level of disorder. The mnemonic device for these seven levels is BASIC ID, where B is behavior, A affect, S sensation, I imagery, C cognition, I interpersonal relations, D drugs. The job of the therapist using

Arnold Lazarus integrated cognitive and behavioral techniques in multi-modal therapy. (Photograph by Alex Webb/Magnum)

Table 6-2 BASIC ID TECHNIQUES

Modality	Problem	Proposed Treatment
Behavior	Inappropriate withdrawal responses	Assertiveness training
	Frequent crying	Nonreinforcement
	Excessive eating	Low-calorie regimen
Affect	Unable to express overt anger	Role playing
	Frequent anxiety	Relaxation training and reassurance
	Absence of enthusiasm and spontaneous joy	Positive imagery procedures
Sensation	Stomach spasms	Abdominal breathing and relaxing
	Out of touch with most sensual pleasures	Sensate focus method
	Tension in jaw and neck	Differential relaxation
Imagery	Distressing scenes of sister's funeral	Desensitization
	Recurring dreams about airplane bombings	Eidetic imagery invoking feelings of being safe
Cognition	Irrational self-talk: "I am evil." "I must suffer." "Sex is dirty." "I am inferior."	Deliberate rational disputation and corrective self-talk
	Syllogistic reasoning and overgeneralization	Parsing of irrational sentences
Interpersonal relationships	Childlike dependence	Specific self-sufficiency assignments
	Easily exploited and submissive	Assertiveness training
	Manipulative tendencies	Training in direct and confrontative behaviors
Drugs	Disordered biochemistry	Anti-psychotic drugs

SOURCE: Adapted from Lazarus, 1976.

such **multi-modal therapy** is to separate the disorder into its different levels and to choose appropriate techniques for each level. Lazarus is willing to use cognitive techniques, behavioral techniques, and even psychoanalytic procedures. Table 6-2 shows the variety of treatments used in the course of the thirteen-month therapy for Mary Ann, a twenty-four-year-old woman diagnosed as a chronic undifferentiated schizophrenic with a very poor prognosis. She was overweight, apathetic, and withdrawn. She had been heavily medicated but with little effect. But the end of thirteen months of the techniques shown in Table 6-2, she was functioning well and engaged to be married.

EVALUATING THE BEHAVIORAL AND COGNITIVE MODELS

There are several virtues of behavior therapy and cognitive therapy: they are effective in a number of discrete disorders; therapy is generally brief and inexpensive; they seem to be based on a science of behavioral and cognitive psychology; and their units of analysis, stimuli, responses, reinforcers, expectations, and attributions can be measured. Behavior and cognitive therapy, however, are not without problems. Perhaps the most serious allegation is that they are superficial.

Are humans more than just behavior and cognition? Are psychological disorders more than disordered action and disordered thinking? Must therapy, in order to be successful, do more than merely provide more adaptive actions and more rational ways of thinking? Because behavior therapists and cognitive therapists restrict themselves to an analysis of the discrete behaviors and cognitions of the human being, they miss the essence: that individuals are wholes, that individuals are free to choose. A phobic patient is more than a machine who happens to be afraid of cats. He is an individual whose symptoms are deeply rooted in his personality and psychodynamics. Alternatively, he is an individual who has made bad choices but who can still choose health. An autistic child who treats other human beings as if they were pieces of furniture may be taught by behaviorists to hug other people in order to receive food or to escape from shock. But in the end, all we have is an autistic child who hugs people. Merely changing how one behaves fails to change the underlying disorder.

Those who object to the behavioral and cognitive views feel that there are deeper disorders that produce symptoms. Because of this, seemingly superficial behavioral change may be short-lived, as in the case of what had been highly successful behavioral treatments of obesity. After one year and three years, obese individuals who had undergone behavior therapy had kept their weight down. But after five years, their weight returned (Stunkard and Penick, 1979). Although behavior therapy had led to change by removing the symptom of obesity, the underlying problem remained and ultimately sabotaged the therapy.

How might behavioral and cognitive therapists respond to these charges of superficiality? A militant response might be to deny the concept of the "whole person." To radical behaviorists such a concept is romantic; it makes sense in literature and in poetry, but not for human beings in distress and in need of relief. We would make a less militant reply. Removing symptoms—either behavioral or cognitive—at least helps. Symptom substitution has rarely, if ever, followed successful behavioral or cognitive therapy. Some disorders are highly specific, peripheral to the heart of an individual's being and amenable to behavioral and cognitive therapies. Phobias, obsessions, stuttering, and some sexual problems are such disorders. On the other hand, there may be deeper disorders left untouched by behavior and cognitive therapy: schizophrenia and psychopathy, perhaps. For these disorders, change of personality, uncovering dynamics, and drugs are probably necessary.

We believe that human misery, including problems of psychological disorder, is sometimes, but not always, produced by an unfortunate set of environmental circumstances or by distorted cognition. To counteract such circumstances by applying behavioral and cognitive laws does not diminish or devalue human wholeness or freedom, but rather enlarges it. An individual who is so crippled by a phobia of leaving his apartment that he cannot work or see those he loves, is not free. By applying behavioral and cognitive therapy to such an individual, one can remove this phobia. Such an individual will then be free to lead a rational life.

SUMMARY

1. The cognitive school is an outgrowth and reaction to the behavioral school.

2. In contrast to the behaviorists, the cognitive school holds that mental events are not *epiphenomena,* rather they cause behavior. More particularly, disordered cognitions cause disordered behavior, and changing these disordered cognitions will alleviate and sometimes cure psychopathology.

3. Cognitive therapy is carried out by attempting to change different sorts of mental events, which can be divided into short-term mental events and long-term mental events.

4. Short-term mental events consist of expectations, including *outcome and efficacy expectations, appraisals,* or mental evaluations of our experience, and *attributions,* the designation of causes concerning our experience.

5. Long-term mental events include *beliefs,* some of which are irrational and illogical. A prominent example is a set of beliefs called the "tyranny of should's," which has been viewed as a cause of depression.

6. Many therapists practice both cognitive and behavioral therapy and are called *cognitive-behavioral therapists. Multi-modal therapy* is an example of the use of cognitive and behavioral techniques along with techniques from the other models.

7. The cognitive and behavioral models have been seriously criticized. The most important criticisms argue that human beings are more than their behaviors and cognitions, and that it is superficial to treat only the symptoms rather than the whole person. The cognitive and behavioral schools reply by arguing that many times it is helpful to the client merely to remove the symptoms.

CHAPTER

7

Humanistic and Existential Approaches

Humanistic psychologies are often concerned with the positive aspects of living, more simply, one's passion for life.
(Photograph by Irene Gabriel/ Leo de Wys, Inc.)

THE humanistic and existential psychologies are a *third force* in psychology, a force that is concerned with the distinctly human elements of the human enterprise, a force in which there are powerful roles for will, responsibility, and reciprocal determinism. Humanistic psychologies are often concerned with the positive aspects of living, specifically self-actualization. They are easier to accept than either the psychodynamic or behavioral theories, which were each considered revolutionary in their time.

Psychoanalytic theory suggests that people are dominated by unconscious rather than conscious motives; that infantile experience shapes and colors adult thought and behavior; that sexuality, in both its narrow and larger senses, permeates seemingly nonsexual pursuits. When Sigmund Freud first enunciated them, these ideas encountered enormous resistance. Moreover, when the behaviorists first propounded their view that the rich spectrum of human activity is made up of a minutiae of conditioning and reinforcement, people also found it difficult to accept this theory.

The humanistic and existential approaches to abnormality will seem less radical to the reader because they are centrally concerned with conscious human experiences, experiences with which all of us are familiar. They are concerned with understanding experiences that are inherently human. Although they are mainly concerned with conscious experience, they do not neglect the role of unconscious processes, and while they are fundamentally interested in human psychology, they often examine animal studies in order to illuminate the human condition.

Beyond their concern with human experience, humanistic and existential psychologists are united in revolting against the narrow determinism that often characterizes earlier theories. The psychoanalytic notion that early feeding experiences during the oral stage, for example, forever stamp the maturing personality in oral ways is fundamentally abhorrent to humanists and existentialists alike. They believe that the determinants of personality are infinitely more complex and that people can exercise much greater freedom than was realized in earlier views.

We begin our exploration of humanistic and existential views of personality and abnormality by examining their common view of determinism and freedom. We then turn to a core of concepts that mark the humanistic emphasis: the notion of self, the significance of personal experience, and the organization of significant needs. We then examine some of the core notions of existentialists: fear of death, personal responsibility, and will.

FREEDOM AND DETERMINISM

Are people free to make what they will of their lives, or are their lives wholly determined? Those who model psychology on natural sciences such as physics argue that much as natural phenomena are all caused and determined, so are human behaviors. To a certain extent, Sigmund Freud held that view, as does B. F. Skinner. Others, such as the twentieth century philosopher Jean Paul Sartre (1905–1980) argue the opposite view—that what characterizes people most is their freedom to be, to become, and to make choices. People are what they choose to make of themselves. Indeed, they are condemned to freedom, and they suffer awful consequences when they attempt to escape it.

Humanistic and existential psychologists take a middle road in this debate. They acknowledge that some aspects of human experience are determined—by genetics and constitution, by age and gender, and by the very times in which people live. But that is not the whole of it, for those determinants lie outside of individual control. There are many situations in which people have control, or at least believe that they have control. Human beings can imagine, dream, engage in reflective thought, use symbols, and create and manipulate meanings. These abilities allow people to plan and choose among alternative courses of action, rather than simply performing rigidly prescribed actions, or suffering the consequences of thoughtless actions. Human experience, moreover, is characterized by ***reciprocal determinism*** (Bandura, 1978). That is, we interpret our environment and therefore control our responses to it. We affect the environment quite as much as it affects us.

THE ABSENCE OF FREEDOM

When people believe that they have no freedom, personal crises may ensue. Constraints on perceived freedom may first lead to ***psychological reactance*** (Brehm and Brehm, 1981), the tendency to react against those constraints rather than make free choice. But the implications of absence of freedom do not stop there. For example, when people believe that they cannot control their own futures, that nothing that they do will have any appreciable effect, they may become severely depressed (see Chapter 13, pp. 336–42). When they feel that all of their thoughts and behaviors are determined, they may become paranoid. And when they feel that they cannot be themselves and end up being what others want them to be, they become alienated from themselves, often unable to tell what they themselves feel and want. Whether one feels free to choose and control and how one uses that freedom play a significant and central role in humanistic and existential approaches to abnormality.

People have the freedom to make choices and to try to control their environment through their actions. These demonstrators believe that their actions may lead to an end to war. (Photograph by Claus Meyer/Black Star)

BASIC ASSUMPTIONS OF THE HUMANISTIC VIEWS

Humanistic psychologists have contributed enormously to our understanding of the nature of human needs, the notion of self, and the role of feelings and experiences in personal growth and understanding.

THE FEELING AND EXPERIENCING SELF

Humanistic psychologists are generally opposed to formal personality diagnosis. Many of the diagnostic categories, such as bipolar depression and schizophrenia, are alien to the humanistic spirit. Why should that be? Fundamentally, it is because humanistic psychologists believe that there is only one useful way of understanding human experience, and that it is from the inside. According to Carl Rogers (1902–   ), a leading humanistic thinker and therapist, each person lives in a "continually changing world of experience of which he is the center." No one can know a person's private world as well as that person does. If we wish to understand someone's personal world, we must understand that person's private experience, and we must take care not to confuse that experience with our own. Diagnostic categories are not created that way, nor are they intended to summarize private experience. Rather they are created from without, on the basis of observed behaviors and verbalizations, as well as the diagnostician's assumptions regarding how a mature person should function. Those perceptions and assumptions do not conform with humanistic notions.

The notion of the self is central to understanding the private world of experience. According to Rogers, the self is that aspect of personality that embodies a person's perceptions and values. There are two kinds of values: those that are acquired from experience and those that are introjected or acquired from others. Values that arise from experience are easily labeled by the individual and therefore they are easily accessible to the individual. They are the kinds of values that contribute to personal growth and self-knowledge. Values that are introjected, however, are confusing, for they often require that a person deny his or her own feelings in order to conform to the desires of another. When children are told that it is bad to be angry with a sibling, for example, they gradually come to avoid labeling their feelings toward siblings as anger in order to preserve parental affection. Their conscious self is not in tune with their true self, and that produces tension and conflict, particularly when they are with those siblings.

Humanistic psychologists place great emphasis on three features of the self: feelings, experience, and perceptions. When the self is integrated and not threatened, experience and feelings are deep and alive, and perceptions are accurate. Under such conditions, individuals are free to actualize themselves, to become what they want to be, to fulfill their potentials. But when the self is threatened or divided, experience becomes blunted and perception distorted (Laing, 1965). Personal growth is slowed, if not halted, and the possibilities for self-actualization are correspondingly diminished.

Proper psychological growth is fostered by unconditional love. (© Lisa Ebright 1978/Black Star)

SELF-ACTUALIZATION

Humanistic psychologists stress that people are naturally good. Given the kinds of psychological conditions that are necessary for psychological development, people will grow and fulfill themselves. In short, they will **self-actualize.** Think of a seed in this regard. It has the capacity to grow, but it will not do so until it gets the basics—sun, water, and nutrients—and in the right amounts, for it can as easily be ruined through over-attention as it can by neglect. So it is with people. Their natural destiny is to become everything they were created to be, to actualize all of their potentials. And they will do precisely that, provided that they are given adequate nourishment and are not thwarted by society. This notion differs from the psychodynamic view, which holds that people are essentially bad, that without such traumas as the Oedipal conflict, raw *id* would simply run rampant, gratifying one selfish desire after another, and that socialization consists of tempering these untrammeled impulses, channeling them, and making them more acceptable. Humanists instead believe that given a good psychological environment, without threats of dire punishment or withdrawal of love, humans will grow and self-actualize.

What conditions foster proper psychological growth? Carl Rogers suggests that early in their development, children develop a need for self-regard and for positive regard from others. These needs are gratified to the extent that children experience **unconditional love.** Given this, children feel free to be themselves. But unconditional love is a notion that many people find difficult to accept. Won't the child become spoiled if love is unconditionally given, without regard for the child's behavior? How does one offer unconditional love when a child is being willful or bratty? The following vignette may make the matter clear:

A two-year-old banged on his high chair while the rest of his family conversed during dinner. Subsequently, he began to throw his food, dishes, and utensils to the floor, one by one. Other parents might have punished this annoying behavior. His father, however, behaved differently. Instead of berating him, or even noticing what he was doing, his father attended to him, playing gently with him, and holding him while continuing conversation. The child stopped banging and throwing, and continued to eat like everyone else.

Within Rogers's framework, the principal causes of psychological disorder arise from the application of conditional love: love that is given only when the child behaves as his or her parents desire, and love that is withdrawn when he or she does not behave as they wish. Under such conditions, children become what their parents want them to be, not what they want themselves to become. They acquire parental values and attitudes and incorporate those values into their self-image, creating an ever-widening gap between their self-image and their true selves. Their own self-actualizing drives become thwarted as they continually implement others' desires in order to acquire their affection. Personality disturbance arises from people's attempts to become what others want them to be. Over time, many people lose track of who they are and end up living out their lives in unwilling accommodation to others.

Self-actualization, then, is a central notion in humanistic psychology. It is not to be equated with selfishness or self-centeredness, however, for the self-actualizing person is well socialized, cooperative with others, and altruistic precisely because he or she has high self-regard and is gratifying significant desires. Positive personal experiences quite naturally breed cooperation and altruism (Rosenhan, Moore, and Underwood, 1974; Rosenhan, Karylowski, Salovey, and Hargis, 1982).

THE ORGANIZATION OF NEEDS

Humanistic theories are concerned with defining the needs that are central to human functioning. Abraham Maslow (1908–1970), one of the early and influential humanistic thinkers, described human needs in terms of a pyramid (see Figure 7-1). At the bottom of the pyramid are the fundamentally physiological needs for food, air, water, and sex. Further up are needs for safety, love, esteem, and so on, up to self-actualization. Individuals organize their lives around these needs, trying to gratify the needs at each level. As each of the lower needs becomes gratified, more needs higher on the pyramid emerge and require fulfillment. If at any level, our needs are not gratified, conflict ensues. Until the conflict is resolved, we do not proceed to the next level. Moreover, if lower needs cease to be satisfied, regression to lower levels will occur until the lower needs are again being satisfied.

We first attempt to gratify our need for food. What we do in life is organized around ways to achieve this goal. Once achieved, we go on to the next need, the need for safety, and in doing so, we organize our life differently. Once safety needs are gratified, needs for love, affection, and belongingness emerge. Now the person feels keenly, as never before, the absence of friends, sweetheart, spouse, or children. These needs can be very intense and can dominate personality and motivation. The absence of love and affection is

Abraham Maslow (1908–1970) was one of the early humanistic thinkers. (Courtesy of Marcia Roltner. Reprinted with permission of Brooks/Cole Publishing Co.)

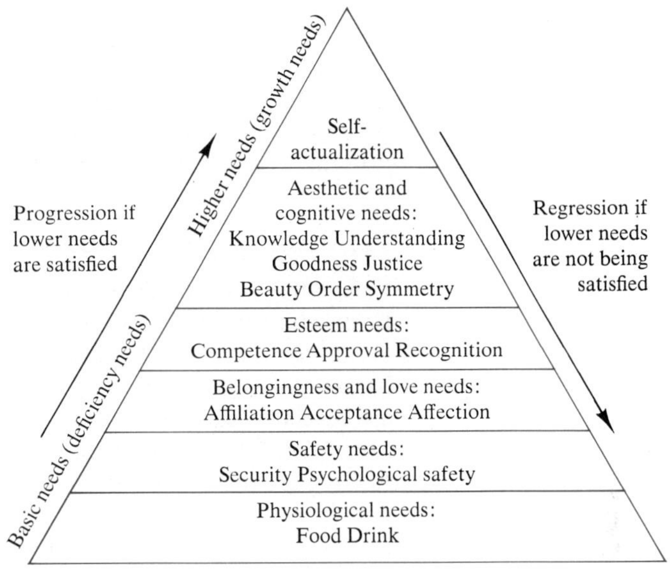

Figure 7-1
Maslow's hierarchy of needs.
This need hierarchy ranges from
basic biological needs to
self-actualization. As deficiency
needs become gratified, growth
needs emerge and require
fulfillment. (Source: Smith,
Sarason, and Sarason, 1982)

Higher needs (growth needs)

Basic needs (deficiency needs)

Progression if
lower needs
are satisfied

Regression if
lower needs
are not being
satisfied

Self-
actualization

Aesthetic and
cognitive needs:
Knowledge Understanding
Goodness Justice
Beauty Order Symmetry

Esteem needs:
Competence Approval Recognition

Belongingness and love needs:
Affiliation Acceptance Affection

Safety needs:
Security Psychological safety

Physiological needs:
Food Drink

seen as a major contributor to conflict and unhappiness. Until these needs are gratified, the individual cannot proceed to the next level: the need for esteem. Once the individual achieves competence, approval, and recognition, thereby satisfying the need for esteem, he will proceed on to the level of aesthetic and cognitive needs. These growth needs include the search for knowledge, understanding, justice, beauty, order, and symmetry. Finally, at the top level of the pyramid, the needs for self-fulfillment and self-actualization will emerge, the "desire to become more and more of what one is, to become everything that one is capable of becoming" (Maslow, 1968, p. 92).

Those at the top of the pyramid, self-actualizing people, tend to accept themselves and others. They have a nonhostile sense of humor and appreciate the novel and unexpected. They tend to be problem-centered rather than ego-centered, concerned with problems that exist outside of themselves. They have a mission in life. They like solitude more than most people, yet they experience deep feelings of empathy, affection, and identification with others. Because their fundamental needs have been gratified, they are growth- rather than deficiency-motivated, and they tend therefore to be relatively autonomous of their environment.

Self-actualizing people, however, are not without problems and conflicts. They experience anxiety, guilt, sadness, self-castigation, conflict, and so on. But for the most part, these experiences do not arise from deficiency-motivated sources. Rather, life itself is often difficult and sad, and that fact is reflected in the lives of self-actualizing people, as in the lives of all others.

Attention to self, to feeling and experiencing, and to the organization of needs is what centrally marks the thinking of humanistic psychologists. In fact, these concerns shade over imperceptibly to those of the existential psychologists. For that reason, humanistic and existential are often hyphenated. We turn now to the issues of concern to existential psychologists, bearing in mind that no sharp distinction exists between their views and those of the humanists.

THE BASIC ASSUMPTIONS OF THE EXISTENTIAL VIEWS

In seeking to define what is especially human and significant in human experience, the existential theorists find three issues that are particularly important: fear of dying, responsibility, and will.

THE FUNDAMENTAL ANXIETY: DEATH AND LIFE

Existential psychologists assert that the central human fear and the one from which most psychopathology develops is the *fear of dying*. Anxiety about death is most prominent in, and best recalled from childhood. Perhaps because children are vulnerable, and because their worst imaginings are barely informed by reality, their fears are stark, vivid, and memorable. For them, the idea of death does not involve mere biological process. It is terrifyingly full of awful meanings. Death means being forgotten, being left out. Death means helplessness, aloneness, finiteness. In short, the idea of death is so awful that children and adults nearly universally employ coping strategies for dealing with it.

How does one deal with the fear of nonbeing? Broadly speaking, there are two kinds of strategies: by coming to believe oneself special, and by fusion. (Yalom, 1980).

Specialness

One way through which some people protect themselves from death fears is by cultivating in themselves the notion that they are special. It is a peculiar notion in that it holds that the laws of nature apply to all mortals except oneself. The *notion of specialness* manifests itself in many ways. For example, the terminally ill simply cannot believe that it is they who are dying. They understand the laws of nature full and well, but they believe themselves somehow to be exempt from them. Similarly, people who smoke heavily, overeat, or fail to exercise sufficiently may also believe that somehow they are exempt from nature's laws.

People sometimes try to protect themselves from death by cultivating a notion of specialness. Motorcycle daredevil Evel Knievel may have attempted stunts like jumping over these fourteen cars because he believed that he was exempt from the laws of nature. (Wide World Photos)

People may attempt to protect themselves against nonbeing by fusing with others. These five people had plastic surgery so that they would look like famous rock stars (Jim Croce, Linda Ronstadt, Kenny Rogers, Elvis Presley, and Buddy Holly). By so doing, they merged their identities with those of their favorite stars. (Wide World Photos)

The notion of specialness underlies many valued character traits. Physical courage may result from the belief that one is inviolable. So too may ambition and striving, and especially striving for power and control. But at the extreme, the unconscious belief in one's specialness may also lead to a spectrum of behavior disorders. The workaholic who compulsively strives to achieve success and power may also harbor the delusion that achieving that one kind of specialness may confer the other, immortal kind. Narcissistic people who devote enormous attention to themselves and are correspondingly insensitive to the requirements of others may believe that only that kind of self-nourishment will protect them from death and its associated anxieties.

Fusion

Protection against the fear of death or nonbeing can also be achieved by fusing with others. **Fusion** is an especially useful strategy for those whose death fears take the form of loneliness. By attaching themselves to, and making themselves indistinguishable from others, they hope that their lot is cast with them. They believe that much as these others continue to live, so will they. They also develop a fear of standing apart, as they believe that if they do stand apart, they will no longer be protected from death.

The fear of standing apart has socially valuable features. Why else would we marry and have children if not to create fusions? Why else would we form clubs, communities, and organizations? Such attachments protect against loneliness, against being separated from the flow of life. At the extreme, however, fusion is responsible for much unhappiness. Children who have grown up in brutal homes may be unwilling to leave them, not because they have nowhere else to go, but because they have established a fusion with their powerful parents and are afraid to destroy it. Similarly, spouses whose marriages have long ceased providing them satisfaction often find it difficult to separate lest in their old age, they find themselves alone. One example of an individual's need for fusion in order to ward off his fears of death is as follows:

A well-trained, enormously presentable business executive had held seven positions in as many years, and he was now finding it difficult to gain employment. Each of his employers had been impressed both by his credentials and his industriousness. He was moved gradually into positions of greater responsibility. Oddly, however, just as he had begun to inspire faith in others, he would "foul up." His errors were as costly as they were inexcusable, and they led quickly to termination from the job. In the course of treatment with an existential therapist, it was found that success had a powerfully unconscious meaning for him. He feared success, for it meant isolation, standing apart from others. For him, success was analogous to death, in that it destroyed fusion. He unconsciously felt that it was better to be indistinguishable from the mass of people than to stand alone, even successfully.

Authenticity and Inauthenticity

The desire for either specialness or fusion can lead to **inauthentic,** or false, modes of behavior. These ways of acting are false in that they are designed to achieve unattainable goals. Consider someone who tries to avoid the fear of nonbeing by fusing with others. He may say things to others that he hopes will please them, but that he does not really mean. For example, he may conform his opinions to theirs, bend his behaviors to suit them, do the things they do, even though his mind and body would rather believe and do something else. Gradually, he comes to lose sight of what it is he wants to do, while finding his conformity to others' opinions and behaviors only a pale pleasure. He has paid for a tenuous security against the fear of death by sacrificing his own authenticity.

The fear of death, then, promotes a host of irrational behaviors, according to existential thinkers. But that is not the only source of human irrationality. Whether one believes that one is fully responsible for one's life plays an equal role in determining human happiness or misery.

RESPONSIBILITY

The assumption of personal **responsibility** is central to existential thinking, for responsibility means authorship. It says that we are responsible for the way we perceive the world and for the way we react to those perceptions. To be responsible "is to be aware that one has created one's own self, destiny,

Existentialists believe that we are responsible for the way we perceive the world and for the way we react to those perceptions. This includes taking responsibility for those who are close to us when they are too young or old to be able to help themselves. (*Left*: Photograph by Suzanne Szasz. *Right*: Photograph by Jay Hoops/Leo de Wys, Inc.)

life, predicament, feelings and, if such be the case, one's own suffering" (Yalom, 1980).

The degree to which we are responsible for our own feelings and behaviors, if at all, has been a matter of considerable theoretical dispute. Personal responsibility for experience and behavior plays only a minor role in psychodynamic theory. Psychoanalysts tend to hold the past more responsible for the present.

Radical behaviorists similarly minimize the role of personal responsibility. Although they are less inclined to view the past as the molder of current behavior and attitudes, they hold the present environment (rather than the individual) responsible. "A person does not act upon the world," B. F. Skinner writes, "the world acts upon him" (Skinner, 1971, p. 271).

Existential psychologists take strong exception to both the orthodox psychoanalytic views and the behavioral ones. They find a strong role for responsibility in both normal and abnormal personality.

Responsibility, Language, and Avoidance

Existential psychologists generally pay careful attention to language; they are especially sensitive to the use of such words as "can't" and "it." People often say, "I just can't study" or "I can't get up in the morning," implying that the behavior is somehow removed from their control. What they really mean is, "I won't do it." They bury an act over which they have control beneath the appearance of disability. Young children who break something are inclined to say, "it broke," not "I broke it." Similarly, for adults to say that "something happened" or "it happened" is to imply that one is passively influenced by a capricious world. In short, they do not want to be held responsible. Generally, the use of the passive rather than the active voice, the avoidance of first person pronouns, as well as the attributions of the causes of current events to historical sources (i.e., my upbringing, my parents, the things I did as a child), are seen as signs of responsibility avoidance.

Responsibility avoidance is occasionally achieved by losing control. More accurately, it is achieved by *appearing* to lose control, by *seeming* to go out of one's mind, by *making it appear* that forbidden actions were taken because one was drunk or crazy. But behavior that is "out of control" is never really so. Otherwise, it could hardly be so purposive. For what is remarkable about "crazy" anger is the accuracy with which it is targeted: the blows fall, not on any random person, but precisely on the person toward whom the anger was experienced.

> Robert, age twenty-two, had just had an enormous fight with his father, and he was still furious. He went to his room and drank heavily. Inflamed, he took his bottle and went out for a drive—not in his own car, but in his father's sports car. At the end of the driveway, he turned too hard and accidentally dented the car's fender on a large oak tree.

> Sara had been married for many years to a brutal and insensitive man who, without notice, one day asked for a divorce. She went "crazy." She followed him around town, repeatedly vandalized his apartment, and created wild scenes while he was dining with friends in a restaurant. Her crazy behavior defeated him. At first, he sought police protection, then he required emergency psychiatric hospitalization. Once he was hospitalized, she suddenly "regained her sanity." (Adapted from Yalom, 1980)

Because people can see themselves as responsible for their experiences and because they can plan for the future as well as live in the present, they are capable of *will,* which is a further theme in existential psychology.

WILLING

The capacity to will is as central a feature of existential views as are freedom and responsibility. Yet, despite its centrality, will is difficult to define unambiguously. Will is used psychologically in at least two senses. First, there is will as in willpower: the will of gritted teeth, clenched jaw, and tensed muscle. This is **exhortative will.** It can be useful at times, as when we force ourselves to work when we would rather play.

A second and more significant kind of will is associated with future goals. It is called **goal-directed will.** Much as memory is the organ of the past, goal-directed will has been called "the organ of the future" (Arendt, 1978). It is quite different from exhortative will, for it develops out of hope, expectation, and competence. Unlike exhortative will, it is not urged upon us but is rather a freely chosen arousal in the service of a future that is willingly embraced. This kind of will cannot be created: it can only be unleashed or disinhibited.

> Susan was bright enough to do well in college but nevertheless was having a struggle. It was difficult for her to get up in the morning, difficult to crack the books, and difficult to put away the temptations that deflected her from achievement. She had no sense of what she wanted to study in college and, therefore, little motivation to work in her courses. After her midyear grades were posted, she went to the counseling center to "try to get myself down to work." During several counseling sessions, she realized that although she had plenty of intelligence, she lacked confidence in her ability to do well in college and, as a result, found it difficult to commit herself to any career. She had had a difficult start in the primary grades, and those bruises had remained with her. During one significant counseling session, she realized that grade school was far behind her and that, moreover,

Goal-directed will develops out of hope, expectation, and competence. It is enabling this runner to push herself to her limits in order to win this race. (Photograph by Barton Silverman/Leo de Wys, Inc.)

she had achieved a good deal since those experiences. Nearly simultaneously, a long-buried desire surfaced: to be a doctor.

At the next session, she reported that "her life had come together during the past week." No longer did she find it difficult to get up in the morning or to resist going to the movies. It was easy to study now, and indeed, she bounded out of bed and headed for the books effortlessly. "Now that I know what I want to do, everything else has fallen into place. I no longer have to force myself."

WILLING AND WISHING

As seen in the above case, goal-directed will arises from the capacity to wish (May, 1969). Wishes are quite specific. We do not wish for a career, but rather we wish to be a doctor. Unless we are starving, we do not wish for food, but rather for a steak or a hamburger. Willing is nourished by wishing, and in turn will provide the motor power that may ultimately gratify the wish.

Disorders of will are found among people who know what they should do, what they ought to do, and what they must do, but who have no notion of what they want to do. Lacking that knowledge of what they *want,* their goals seem apparently lusterless, and movement toward them is correspondingly difficult. People may fail to know what they want for three reasons. First, they may simply fear wanting. Wanting makes them vulnerable to failure and hurt, and that is especially difficult for those who wish to appear strong. Second, they may fail to know what they want because they fear rejection. They long ago learned that if their wishes departed from those of their friends or family, their wishes would infuriate and drive others away. Finally, they may fail to know what they wish because they want others, magically, to discover their silent wishes and fulfill them.

Most graduate students complete a dissertation before receiving their doctoral degree, and the dissertation is often viewed by them as a significant hurdle in their graduate career. For some, however, that final hurdle is insurmountable. Such seemed to be the case for Cathy. She had done well until that point. Her course grades were excellent, and the research that she had completed while in graduate school had been quite interesting. But somehow she found it difficult to get down to the dissertation. In fact, she had begun three separate studies and had dropped each of them for no particular reason other than that she had lost interest. The fact of the matter was that she viewed the dissertation as a major undertaking, much bigger than anything she had undertaken before, and much beyond her abilities. Her fear of being criticized by her teachers or, worse, of failing her oral examination prevented her from finding a study that she really wanted to do.

For existential and humanistic psychologists, then, goal-directed willing is more than just forcing oneself to do something (exhortative will). Rather, it is going through the pain and risk of finding what one really wants and then doing it.

HUMANISTIC-EXISTENTIAL THERAPIES

Unlike the behavioral and psychodynamic treatments, no coherent set of procedures marks the humanistic-existential therapies. Rather, these therapies seem to be a loose federation of therapeutic styles that are united by three philosophical beliefs. First, they seek to explore inner experience with an emphasis on the here and now. In that exploration, they are concerned with examining experience solely from the client's perspective. Second, they emphasize personal responsibility, freedom, and will, both with regard to therapeutic change and, more generally, insofar as individuals conduct their lives. Third, humanistic-existential therapists participate actively in treatment. We will examine the techniques of three therapists, Carl Rogers, Frederick Perls, and Viktor Frankl, to illustrate the variety of approaches within the humanistic-existential camp.

CARL ROGERS AND CLIENT-CENTERED THERAPY

Perhaps the best-known and most widely practiced humanistic therapy, *client-centered therapy,* rests on two fundamental assumptions. The first is that therapy proceeds best when the client experiences the therapist's *unconditional positive regard.* That regard arises from the therapist's belief that people are fundamentally good even when they are doing "bad" things. Indeed, they do "bad" things precisely because they have not experienced such unconditional respect. Thus, clients who are rude, boorish, liars, thieves, and brutes are both entitled to and needy of such unconditional regard. Without it, all people simply become defensive and when they are defensive, the process of change is retarded.

The second hallmark of client-centered therapy resides in the therapist's attempt to achieve *empathy* with the client, to see the world as he or she does. Client-centered therapists listen carefully to what the client says and then reflect or mirror their understanding back to the client. This procedure enables clients to clarify and properly label their own experiences, and eventually to accept them.

> CLIENT: Well, I made a very remarkable discovery. I know it's—*(laughs)* I found out that you actually *care* how this thing goes. *(Both laugh.)* It gave me the feeling, it's sort of well—"maybe I'll let you get in the act," sort of thing. It's—again you see, on an examination sheet, I would have had the correct answer, I mean—but it suddenly dawned on me that in the—client-counselor kind of thing, you *actually care* what happens to this thing. And it was a revelation, a—not that . . . That doesn't describe it. It was a—well, the closest I can come to it is a kind of relaxation, a—not letting down, but a *(pause)* more of a straightening out without tension if that means anything. I don't know.
>
> THERAPIST: Sounds as though it isn't as though this was a new idea, but it was a new *experience* of really *feeling* that I did care and if I get the rest of that, sort of willingness on your part to let me care.
>
> CLIENT: Yes.

Because the client feels accepted and because he or she senses that the therapist is trying to understand, the client feels free to examine the host of feelings that lie just beneath surface behavior and that have been suppressed. That emphasis on feeling is, as we have seen, one of the significant features of these therapies.

> CLIENT: You know over in this area of, of sexual disturbance, I have a feeling that I'm beginning to discover that it's pretty bad, pretty bad. I'm finding out that, that I'm bitter, really. Damn bitter. I—and I'm not turning it back in, into myself.

. . . I think what I probably feel is a certain element of "I've been cheated." *(Her voice is very tight and her throat chokes up.)* And I've covered up very nicely, to the point of consciously not caring. But I'm, I'm sort of amazed to find that in this practice of, what shall I call it, a kind of sublimation that right under it—again words—there's a, a kind of passive force that's, it's pas—it's very passive, but at the same time it's just kind of *murderous.*

THERAPIST: So there's the feeling, "I've really been cheated. I've covered that up and seem not to care and yet underneath that there's a kind of a, a latent but very much present *bitterness* that is very, very strong."

CLIENT: It's very strong. I—that I know. It's terribly powerful.

THERAPIST: Almost a dominating kind of force.

CLIENT: Of which I am rarely conscious. Almost never. . . . Well, the only way I can describe it, it's a kind of murderous thing, but without violence. . . . It's more like a feeling of wanting to get even. . . . And of course, I won't pay back, but I'd like to. I really would like to.

In the above excerpt, the feelings of bitterness and the desire for revenge begin to surface as a result of the therapist's patient understanding and reflection. Client-centered techniques, however, are not the only ones available for reaching a patient's feelings. Gestalt therapists, to which we now turn, utilize a different approach to the same issue.

FREDERICK PERLS AND GESTALT THERAPY

Trained in Europe as a physician and psychoanalyst, Frederick (Fritz) Perls (1893–1970) repudiated large portions of psychoanalytic theory, while using some other aspects of that theory as part of his Gestalt therapy (1970). In common with other humanistic-existential therapists, Gestalt therapists have little interest in the past except as it impacts on the immediate present. When it does, then Gestalt therapists seize upon it, open it up, and make it extraordinarily vivid. If, for example, a young woman is still rankling over the way her mother treated her when she was eight, then a Gestalt therapist will take the mother's role and ask the client to act out the conflict. In this way, the vivid experience of those times will be re-experienced and confronted, perhaps even resolved. Gestalt clients are urged to re-experience these emotions as vividly and as violently as is necessary. They are encouraged to swear, kick, and scream, all in the service of teaching people that they can know, control, and be responsible for their feelings, rather than allowing their feelings to control them.

One of the techniques that Perls carried over from psychoanalysis to Gestalt therapy was dream analysis. But rather than have the therapist and client merely interpret dreams, Perls encouraged them to act out the dreams, as the following excerpt indicates:

In a large group therapy session, Jane has just described a dream in which she has returned to her parents' home. She opens the door to the large house, but the house is dark. She calls out to her mother and father, but there is no answer, and so she goes from room to room looking for them. Finally, "I get into the bedroom and my mother and father are in bed but they're, they're just, they're not my m— they're skeletons. They don't have any skin. They're not, they don't talk. . . they don't say anything. And I shake—This dream happens over and over and lately I've gotten brave enough to shake them." At one point during the analysis of this

Frederick (Fritz) Perls (1893–1970) developed Gestalt therapy. (Courtesy Mrs. Frederick Perls)

dream, Perls asked Jane to "resurrect" the skeletons, and to talk to them.

PERLS: Talk to them.
JANE: Wake up! (Perls: Again.)
JANE *(loudly):* Wake up! (Perls: Again.)
JANE *(loudly): Wake up!* (Perls: Again.)
JANE *(loudly): Wake up! (loudly, almost crying)* You can't hear me! Why can't you hear me? . . . *(sighs)* And they don't answer. They don't say anything.

The analysis of the dream continues, and Perls tells Jane to talk to her parents again.

PERLS: Tell them that you still need them.
JANE: I still need you.
PERLS: Tell them in more detail what you need.
JANE: I still need my mother to hold me.
PERLS: Tell this to her.
JANE: I still need you to hold me. *(crying)* I want to be a little girl, sometimes—forget the "sometimes."
PERLS: You're not talking to her yet.
JANE *(sobbing):* O.K. Mother, you think I'm very grown up. . . . And I think I'm very grow up. But there's a part of me that isn't away from you and I can't, I can't let go of.

Confronting feelings is the first step in accepting and taking responsibility for them. It is, moreover, a way of understanding how the emotional experiences of the past directly affect the present, the here and now.

VIKTOR FRANKL AND LOGOTHERAPY

Viktor Frankl (1905–   ) uses techniques of dereflection and paradoxical intention to communicate that individuals are free to control their lives and to endow them with meaning. (Copyright Ernst Kainerstorfer)

Learning about one's feelings and especially about personal values—the meaning that life has—is a central feature of existential therapies. Viktor Frankl (1905–   ), a leading existential analyst, was imprisoned in Nazi concentration camps during World War II. Even under those conditions of unbearable suffering, however, Frankl found that life can be made meaningful. For example, he found meaning by helping others rather than concentrating merely on self-preservation and his own personal suffering. Though physically imprisoned under harsh circumstances, he believed that people were still free to give meaning to their lives.

Logotherapists (and their existential counterparts) use a variety of techniques to communicate that individuals are free to control their lives and to endow them with meaning. Two techniques especially should be noted here. The first is **dereflection,** which involves turning clients' attention from their symptoms and pointing out how much they could be doing, becoming, and enjoying if they were not so preoccupied with themselves. The second is termed **paradoxical intention,** which encourages clients to indulge and even exaggerate their symptoms. Clients who claim that they cannot control their desires for, say, ice cream, are encouraged to eat it by the gallon, while those who need to wash their hands twenty times a day are told to double or triple their ablutions. In that way, clients quickly learn that they have considerable control over their symptoms and not vice versa. Moreover, they can then consider whether the values that are represented by, say, self-indulgence or excessive cleanliness are values that they would freely choose for themselves.

EVALUATING THE HUMANISTIC-EXISTENTIAL APPROACH

The humanistic-existential approach to personality and its disorders is very difficult to evaluate, in large measure because the approach is really a group of philosophical positions rather than a scientific theory. This especially applies to the existential components of that viewpoint, for who can prove whether people are really good rather than evil, free rather than bound by the past and present, capable of will or fully responsible for their acts? Fundamentally, these are matters of belief.

Among the very attractive features of these views is the degree to which they accord with everyday notions of personality. Most people believe that there is such a thing as the self, and they reflect that belief in their ordinary language when they say such things as "myself," "yourself," and "ourselves." Moreover, people behave as if they and others are responsible, as if they are free to do what they will, and as if their lives have meaning. Thus, the law, for example, holds people responsible for their behavior with fairly rare exceptions. It reflects the common belief that people act freely, for better or for worse, and that they should be held accountable for their actions. Rightly or wrongly, the humanistic-existential perspective reflects a good deal of common sense.

There are, however, two criticisms of the humanistic-existential approach that merit careful consideration. The first is that the approach spans such a diverse collection of views that even if it were possible to evaluate them, it would be hard to know how to begin. The approach seems a conglomeration of views that have little coherence and often bear little relation to each other. Moreover, what has been called humanistic at one time may not be termed humanistic at another (Wertheimer, 1978). Thus, it is sometimes difficult to know which views to include under this flag, and which to omit.

A second criticism is directed toward the treatments that have emerged from the humanistic-existential perspective. With only one notable exception, about which we will speak momentarily, those who have derived treatments from humanistic and existential issues have neglected to examine the effectiveness of those treatments. And when they have been examined, as we will see in Chapter 21, they have proved to be by and large ineffective. However, just why they are ineffective is not clear, for unlike behavioral, cognitive, and psychoanalytic therapists, humanistic-existential therapists have not been careful to stipulate their procedures such that they or others can determine precisely the causes of their ineffectiveness.

The one exception to the general failure of humanistic therapists to be concerned with evaluation is that of Carl Rogers and his students. Early on, Rogers insisted on evaluating the effectiveness of client-centered therapy. He invented techniques for assessing therapeutic techniques, and particularly a technique called the Q-sort, which enables researchers to examine the subjective world of the client (Rogers and Dymond, 1954). Rogers also was one of the first therapists to tape-record his counseling sessions, and thereby to open his therapeutic endeavors to the scrutiny of other scientists. Finally, Rogers and his students have conducted considerable research on the characteristics of good therapists, and they have by and large substantiated their

Humanistic psychologist Carl Rogers (1902–   ) developed a therapy based on unconditional positive regard and therapist empathy. Additionally, Rogers developed techniques to evaluate the effectiveness of client-centered therapy. (Photograph by Nozizwe S.)

view that therapist empathy and warmth are significant ingredients in the therapeutic process (Mitchell, Bozarth, and Krauft, 1977). One effect of Rogers's scientific efforts has been to open the entire field of psychotherapy to research, both with regard to process and to outcome (see Garfield and Bergin, 1978; Parloff, Waskow, and Wolfe, 1978). The results of these efforts appear to indicate that client-centered therapy is a moderately effective treatment with clients who are not psychotic.

SUMMARY

1. Both humanistic and existential psychologies assert the philosophical premise that people are fundamentally free or that, at the very least, they need to perceive themselves as being free. That freedom makes choice meaningful, and it enables them to be responsible for their choices, actions, and their futures.

2. Human experience is characterized by *reciprocal determinism.* People affect the environment as much as it affects them.

3. When there are constraints on perceived freedom, there may be *psychological reactance,* the tendency to react against the constraints rather than making free choices.

4. Humanists place heavy emphasis on the role of the *self* as the organizer of perception and behavior. They believe that the self provides a sense of wholeness and unity to the personality. Humanists believe that the self is naturally good and seeks fulfillment through *self-actualization,* which in turn develops best when individuals experience *unconditional love.*

5. Most humanists subscribe to Maslow's view that needs are organized *hierarchically.* The needs that must first be satisfied are those that keep the individual and species alive: food, air, water, and sex. Once those are gratified, needs for safety, love, and esteem emerge and clamor for gratification. And once those are satisfied, higher needs, such as self-actualization, emerge.

6. Existentialists believe that the fundamental anxiety is *fear of death.* Psychologically, death means nonbeing. Because the fear of death is so threatening, people attempt to endow themselves with immortality by becoming *special* or by *fusion* with others, which may lead to *inauthentic,* or false, modes of behavior.

7. Existential theorists hold that we are the authors of our experience. We determine what we perceive and what we experience; we are *responsible* for how we behave. Freedom and responsibility, however, may create anxiety. Responsibility avoidance is occasionally achieved through denying ownership of behavior and thought. In extreme form, that denial appears as "craziness" or drunkenness, which are purposeful behaviors designed to make it seem that we are not responsible.

8. Existentialists often posit two kinds of will: *exhortative will* forces us to do what we know we should do, and *goal-directed will* is unleashed when we have freely chosen our goals and want to pursue and achieve them.

9. Carl Rogers's *client-centered therapy* stresses the role of *unconditional positive regard* and therapist empathy and warmth in enabling people to overcome their defensiveness and to begin to self-actualize.

10. Fritz Perls's *Gestalt therapy* stresses conscious experience and feelings, dealing with the past only insofar as it has implications for the present. Gestalt therapists are particularly concerned to re-evoke and resolve conflictual feelings. Patients are encouraged to act out feelings, roles, dreams, and events.

11. *Logotherapists* like Victor Frankl stress the meanings that symptoms have for an individual's life, as well as the individual's freedom to alter those meanings. They use two techniques to do this: *dereflection* and *paradoxical intention.*

12. Much about the humanistic-existential approach cannot be evaluated, such as matters of belief and values. Other aspects of the approach require careful evaluation, particularly those that relate to treatment. With the exception of Rogers's client-centered therapy, however, humanistic and existential treatments have generally not undergone careful evaluation.

Part III

INVESTIGATING AND DIAGNOSING ABNORMALITY

CHAPTER

8

Investigating Abnormality

THE chapters later in this book describe many individuals' abnormal behaviors. Some people are terrified at the thought of entering an elevator; some seem to act in a way that seems totally inappropriate, like laughing at a close friend's funeral. Others complain of physical ailments that have no biological basis. Why do they act this way? What can one do to treat these individuals?

These two questions arise from the human fascination with scientific phenomena. We take notice of various phenomena, and then we seek understanding of them. We ask "Why?" What is the cause or *etiology* of the phenomena? When we find the etiology, we seek a way of applying our newly found knowledge. Physicists and engineers developed nuclear power plants after they studied the whys of the atom. Psychologists and psychiatrists developed therapies after studying abnormal (and sometimes, normal) behavior. This chapter is devoted to examining the ways, or methods, in which we investigate abnormality. We will look closely at the two principal methods: clinical case histories and experimental studies.

We will begin with *clinical case histories,* which provide the major source of hypotheses and intuitions about the causes and cures of abnormality. While case histories provide rich hypotheses, however, they cannot isolate the causal elements. *Experimental studies,* which manipulate possible causes in order to isolate the crucial elements, are our next concern. Often, however, for ethical or practical reasons, experiments cannot be carried out on people who have problems of psychopathology. Three alternate methods are therefore available to the scientist: *correlational studies, experiments of nature,* and *laboratory models of psychopathology.* It is most satisfying when several or all of the methods converge to form a woven fabric of evidence.

Before we begin our examination of method, a warning is in order. Sound method is a means, not an end. The end is becoming justifiably convinced that *A* is the cause of *B;* where *A* is a past event and *B* a form of abnormality, or where *A* is a therapy and *B* the relief of abnormality. Understanding can be arrived at by any of the methods discussed here; no one of them is the only road to truth. It is easy to become a slave to method, and to forget that the study of method describes how scientists or clinicians have attained understanding in the past. The study of method does not prescribe how this must be done in the future. Great thinkers have often developed (sometimes by accident) new methods at the same time as they discovered new truths.

THE CLINICAL CASE HISTORY

If we keep in mind that the end point of any method is the discovery of evidence about cause, we will see that each of the methods we examine can lead toward this end. The first, the ***clinical case history,*** is the record of part of the life of an individual as seen during therapy. In developing his theories of personality, Sigmund Freud made extensive use of clinical case histories. For example, much of what we know about hysteria today came out of Freud's hypotheses based on his patients' case histories. After seeing a number of patients with hysterical symptoms, Freud hypothesized that repressed wishes were the cause of their hysteria. The clinician who is observing and recording the case history can not only make hypotheses, but sometimes he or she can test them and discover compelling evidence as to whether he or she is right or wrong. The following case of hysterical "anniversary blindness" is such an instance.

A CLINICAL CASE HISTORY

At age fifty, Jack went completely blind. For three months, he had been unable even to distinguish light from dark. His symptoms had begun, rather suddenly, at Christmas time. An exhaustive series of eye tests revealed nothing wrong physically. A variety of medications and several types of psychotherapy had been tried, all to no avail.

Jack was conscious of no incident that might have precipitated the blindness, and nothing in Jack's narration of his life provided a clue. At this point, his therapist formulated an hypothesis: hysterical blindness. This was indicated by the total absence of physical cause plus the absence of psychological insight (almost to the point of indifference) concerning precipitating events. If this were classical hysteria, then some event, so traumatic that it had been driven out of the patient's consciousness and repressed, should be responsible. If this were so, Jack might have access to the event under hypnosis, and reliving the trauma might bring about a cure. The therapist therefore decided to hypnotize Jack. Under hypnosis, he instructed Jack to go back to any period of his life that he could not remember when he was awake. Jack then relived an astonishing event.

Twenty-five years ago, Jack had been deeply in love. Both he and an acquaintance, Ronald, were courting Sarah in open competition. One day—it was Christmas—she confronted Jack with bad news: she was in love with Ronald and would no longer see Jack. In a state of wild jealousy, he went to Ronald and told him a tragic lie: Sarah, Jack said, was not in love with either of them, but with a third party. Ronald became extremely upset, jumped into his car, and drove off at high speed. In a frenzy of rage, he tried to race a train to a crossing, but his car was hit, and he was killed. Sarah found out soon afterward that Ronald had been killed, and she suspected that Jack was involved. Sarah made Jack come with her to the scene of the accident, and as they arrived, the wreckage was being cleared and Ronald's mangled body was being taken away by ambulance. Sarah accused Jack of being directly responsible for Ronald's death. The whole incident was described under hypnosis with extreme emotion, and Jack climaxed the narrative by sobbing out, "She made me go up and *see* what I had done; that I had killed him!"

This was the buried trauma that the therapist had guessed was there. At this point, he reassured Jack that although he had some responsibility, he had not foreseen or intended Ronald's death, that it was an accident.

At this point yet another revelation occurred: every Christmas, Sarah, who had married someone else, called Jack to remind him of what he had done. This last Christmas had been the twenty-fifth anniversary and shortly after the call, the blindness had begun. The therapist inferred that Jack could no longer bear to *see* what he had done, and the memory of both the calls and the initial trauma had been repressed.

With the trauma relived under hypnosis, the therapist told Jack that upon waking, if he wanted to see, his sight would gradually return in the next few days, which, in fact, it did. (Stinnett, 1978)

Here then is an exemplary case history. A skilled therapist is presented with a syndrome: blindness with no physical cause. He then hypothesizes that it is hysterical blindness. Drawing on his knowledge of past case histories, theory, and therapeutic technique, he tests his hypothesis by finding under hypnosis a precipitating trauma of tragic proportions. Once the trauma is relived, the blindness disappears. Under hypnosis, two missing pieces—the accident and the anniversary phone calls—fall into place, and the etiology of the blindness becomes clear.

In a lifetime, a therapist may come across only a handful of such dramatic encounters in which the causal chain is so clear. No experiment and no personality test could bolster our certainty about the origin of Jack's blindness. Much more common, however, are those cases in which painstaking work on the part of the therapist and patient results in only gradual understanding of the complex network of cause and in only gradual symptom relief. But in all cases, whether they be dramatic or more commonplace, the method is the same: with the aid of a therapist, the patient comes to grips with past events and their influences on his present problems. Based on a patient's history, a therapist will hypothesize about possible causes and then help the patient overcome his past.

EVALUATING THE CLINICAL CASE HISTORY

As a method of inquiry, the study of the clinical case history has four advantages. First, it is not artificial. The investigation is working with an actual person who has an actual problem. The reader can easily empathize with a well-reported case and understand the connection between past events and present problems, and between therapeutic actions and the patient's improvement. As we will see later, methods involving laboratory experiments and statistical surveys are more artificial in nature.

Second, the clinical case history can document a phenomenon so rare or bizarre that it probably could not be explored by other standard forms of investigation. The origin of Jack's blindness is such a phenomenon.

Third, the clinical case history is a major source of hypotheses about the etiology and cure of abnormality. At the present state of knowledge, no other method equals it in the generation of ideas and insights that can then be tested in the laboratory and the clinic. Finally, a convincing clinical case history can provide disconfirming evidence against a generally accepted hypothesis.

But there are also four major disadvantages to clinical case histories: selectivity of memory, lack of repeatability, lack of generality, and insufficient evidence for causality.

Selectivity

The reported "evidence" may be distorted. Clinical reports are almost always *retrospective;* they deal with incidents in the past, often in the distant past. The patient may have an axe to grind; he may, for example, want to absolve himself of blame or, conversely, emphasize his guilt. To accomplish this, he may select the evidence that serves these purposes. While talking to his therapist, he may magnify trivial events and ignore important ones. Commonly, he has his own explanation about what happened, and he will remember and report the evidence that best fits this explanation.

Sometimes it is the therapist, not the patient, who has the axe to grind. A therapist might believe in a particular theory, which may influence what evidence she considers relevant and what evidence she ignores. If the therapist is an orthodox Freudian, she may seek and emphasize evidence about early life events, while ignoring evidence about present events. If the therapist is an orthodox behavior therapist, she may focus on ways to change the patient's present behavior, while neglecting childhood events. Although such selectivity does not invalidate the insights gained through the single case, we must keep in mind that this method is particularly susceptible to bias by patient and therapist.

Lack of Repeatability

Case histories, because they are part of the flow of real life, are not repeatable. If we could repeat an observation exactly, we could look carefully at the details, making certain that it happened the way it was reported to us. If an observation could be repeated, we would have a better chance of determining what caused it, for we could vary one and only one element and see if the observation changed. But this is not the case with clinical case histories; they each differ in one respect or another from one another.

Lack of Generality

Even a convincing case history, like Jack's, is specific to one person. Does *all* hysterical blindness begin with an unconscious wish not to see, and conversely, do *all* such wishes result in hysterical blindness? How many people have unconsciously not wanted to see something yet have not become hysterically blind? We simply do not know, and a single case history can, at best, tell us only that one such case of hysterical blindness began in this way. By studying several case histories of hysterical blindness, we might find that each individual had an unconscious motivation not to see; this would indicate that such a desire is general to hysterical blindness. But we would still be ignorant about whether individuals who are not hysterically blind lack such a desire. And this is just what is needed to infer cause.

Insufficient Evidence for Causality

Single clinical case histories only rarely convince us about etiology. In cases like Jack's, the cause was clear, but usually cause is more ambiguous. In most cases, there are several incidents, each of which might be the cause, or there is no obvious incident at all. This is the most serious problem with clinical case histories. In order to know that *A* causes *B*, we must at least know that every time *A* occurs, *B* follows. If we collect many cases of *B*, we could determine if, in general, *B*'s are preceded by *A*'s. But here the causal question is the converse: When *A* occurs, does *B* always follow? Are unconscious wishes not to see followed, in general, by hysterical blindness? To determine this, we would have to look at many cases of people who are not hysterically blind and find that they lack the unconscious wish. The case history method, however, investigates only people with the disorder, not those without the disorder, and therefore it usually cannot isolate the cause.

Clinical case histories provide the richest source of hypotheses about the cause and cure of abnormality. Usually case histories generate several possible causes that cannot be unraveled even by adding further similar cases. The search for the cause among several possible causes is the theme of this chapter. This search provides the central rationale for us to move from examining the clinical case to discussing the experiment.

SCIENTIFIC EXPERIMENTATION

The grand ambition of all scientific experiments is to provide understanding by answering the question of cause. The basic experimental method is simple: (1) you make a guess (hypothesis) at the cause of an event; (2) you remove the suspected cause, and see if the event fails to occur; (3) you put the suspected cause back in and see if the event now reoccurs.

An experiment, then, consists of a procedure in which the hypothesized cause is manipulated and the occurrence of the effect is measured. The hypothesized cause, which the experimenter manipulates, is called the ***independent variable.*** The effect, which the experimenter measures, is called the ***dependent variable,*** because its occurrence depends on whether the cause precedes it. Both independent and dependent variables are operationally defined. An ***operational definition*** is the set of observable and measurable conditions under which a phenomenon is said to occur. So, for example, obesity can be operationally defined as being 15 percent or more above the normal weights for a given height as given in a table of weights, or depression as having greater than a given score on a checklist of symptoms. When manipulating an independent variable produces changes in a dependent variable, an ***experimental effect*** has been obtained.

Clinical case histories, you will recall, usually cannot answer the causal question definitively. While multiple similar cases can establish that hysterical blindness is generally preceded by unconscious wishes, they cannot establish whether such wishes are generally followed by the symptom in question. In principle, a well-done experiment can answer this question by imposing the wish (independent variable) on individuals and see if hysterical blindness follows (dependent variable). There are a variety of ethical and practical reasons, however, why this experiment would never be done. We will now turn to an actual experiment designed to test the effectiveness of a novel therapy for depression.

An Experiment

Several clinical case histories about sleep deprivation recently came to the attention of researchers looking for cures of depression. It appeared that, in a few instances, depressed individuals who for one reason or another missed several whole nights of sleep surprisingly became less depressed. Putting this together with the fact that two antidepressant drugs, tricyclics and MAO-inhibitors, incidentally reduce the amount of dreaming, investigators hypothesized that dream deprivation itself might relieve depression (Vogel, 1975).

When we dream, our eyes move rapidly back and forth beneath our closed lids; the muscles from the neck down lose their tone; and in males, the penis becomes erect. Since we can monitor when an individual is dreaming, we can deprive him of dreams by waking him up every time these signs appear. Such dream deprivation, carried out in a sleep laboratory for several nights running, was the independent variable that was manipulated in this experiment. Individuals who had been hospitalized for depression were the subjects, and the dependent variables were changes in ratings of the severity of depression on a variety of symptoms. The investigators obtained the expected experimental effect: when the depressed people were deprived of dreaming over a period of three weeks, they became markedly less depressed. But not all the depressed people improved. Only the subgroup who suffered from a specific kind of depression (called endogenous depression, see Chapter 13) showed signs of improvement.

In the sleep laboratory, studies of dream deprivation are carried out by using electrical signals which detect rapid eye movements to turn on an alarm clock, waking up the subject. (Courtesy The Warder Collection)

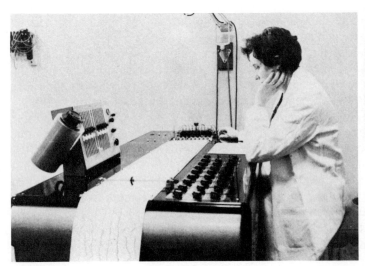
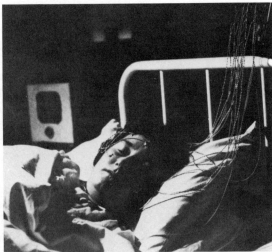

Can we now conclude that dream deprivation causes relief from depression? Not yet. Perhaps it was not the dream deprivation that was effective, but some other aspect of what was done to the depressed patients. For example, the patients had electrodes strapped on them, got less total sleep than normal, and slept in a laboratory. Any one of these might have been effective, rather than the specific manipulation of preventing them from dreaming.

Factors other than the independent variable that might produce an experimental effect, which occur along with the independent variable, are called **confounds.** In order to eliminate such confounds, experimenters use **control groups.** In principle, a control group is a group of subjects similar to those in the experimental group, who experience just the confounded factors that the experimental group had, but who do not experience the hypothesized cause. In contrast, the **experimental group** experiences both the confounds and the hypothesized cause. In general, whenever there is reason to suspect that some factor confounded with the independent variable might produce the effect, groups that control for that confounding factor must be run.

In this study, the investigators ran an appropriate control group, which controlled for a number of confounds. Other depressed patients were put through exactly the same procedure as above. They spent three weeks sleeping in the laboratory, electrodes were taped on them, and they were awakened the same number of times during each night as were those in the experimental group. But there was one crucial difference: the awakenings occurred, not when the patients were dreaming, but during non-dreaming phases of sleep. The patients in the control group did not become less depressed. This study is a good example of a **therapy outcome study,** in which the effects of a therapy are observed as it attempts to alleviate a disorder. Such experiments allow us to determine which therapies are effective. Here we can conclude that dream deprivation alleviates depression in endogenously depressed patients.

EXPERIMENTAL CONFOUNDS

A well-done experiment can allow us to determine whether *A* causes *B.* Experimenters, however, must be on their guard against a variety of subtle confounds, which might actually produce the experimental effect. Common among these are nonrandom assignment, experimenter bias, subject bias, and demand characteristics.

Nonrandom Assignment

In an experiment that includes an experimental group and a control group, it is important that subjects be assigned to groups on a random basis. Such **random assignment** means that each subject should have had an equal chance of being assigned to each group. If subjects are not assigned by random selection, disastrously mistaken inferences, like the following example, can occur.

Who gets more stomach ulcers, individuals with a great deal of responsibility or individuals who have little responsibility? To decide this, four "executive" monkeys learned to lever press in order to avoid shock both for

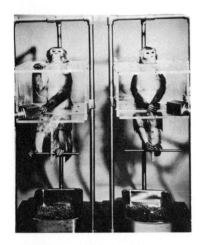

Executive monkeys learned to lever press to avoid shock for themselves and their yoked partners. Nonrandom assignment of subjects to the "executive group," however, may have confounded the results of this experiment and produced more ulcers in the executive group. (Courtesy Dr. James Brady)

The placebo effect. The mere belief that a treatment (here, a sugar pill) will help is often enough to bring about noticeable improvement. (Photograph by Jeffrey Grosscup)

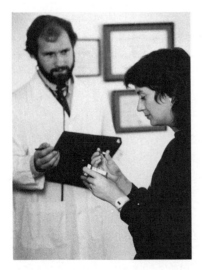

themselves and for their four yoked partners (Brady et al., 1958). In a *yoking* procedure, both experimental and control groups receive exactly the same physical events (shocks), but only the experimental group influences these events by its responses. In the case of the executive monkeys, those in the experimental group could avoid the shocks by pressing a level. The yoked control group, on the other hand, received exactly the same shock but had no responsibility for turning it off; they were helpless since no response they made enabled them to avoid shock. The study showed that the "executives" developed stomach ulcers and died, while their helpless partners remained healthy. Many readers drew the conclusion that executives run a higher risk of psychosomatic illness than more powerless individuals. Only years later did other scientists notice that the monkeys had not been randomly selected for the two groups. When the experiment began, all eight of the monkeys were shocked, and the first four to start pressing the lever were assigned to the "executive" group. We now realize that the more emotional the monkey was or the more the shock hurt him, the sooner he started banging at the lever. As it turned out, the four most emotionally reactive monkeys became the executives and the four most stolid became the yoked controls. Not surprisingly, the emotional "executives" died with ulcers, and the stolid but helpless monkeys stayed healthy. When the experiment was repeated thirteen years later, this time with randomly assigned subjects, the helpless animals developed more ulcers than the executives (Weiss, 1971).

Experimenter Bias

Another source of mistaken inference from experiments comes from *experimenter bias.* If an experimenter wants or expects a particular result, he can subtly influence his subjects to produce that result, sometimes without being aware of it. If the experimenter merely nods his head agreeably at the crucial time he might be able to produce the experimental result spuriously (Greenspoon, 1955). An even bigger problem than experimenter bias is *subject bias.* Human subjects routinely form beliefs about what they are expected to do. When someone believes that a drug that is actually useless is going to help him, he may still sometimes get better after taking the drug. For example, following major surgery, pain is frequent and severe. Yet, about 35 percent of patients report marked relief after taking a useless drug, or *placebo* (Beecher, 1959). Morphine, even in large doses, relieves pain only 75 percent of the time. We can conclude from this that suggestion probably provides much of the pain-killing benefits of morphine (Melzack, 1973). To deal with subject bias, investigators use an experimental group that receives a real drug and a control group that is given a placebo. Both groups are given identical instructions. The mere belief on the part of all subjects that any pill should work has powerful effects. For it to be considered effective, the investigators must then find the real drug to be more potent than the placebo alone.

If neither the experimenter nor the subject knows whether the subject is in the experimental or the placebo control group, the results cannot be affected by either experimenter or subject bias. This elegant design in which both subject and experimenter are "blind" as to which subjects have received a drug or placebo is called a *double-blind experiment.* An experiment in which only the subject does not know whether he is receiving a drug or placebo is called a ***single-blind experiment.*** The design in which only the experimenter is blind, and the subject is not is an ***experimenter-blind design.***

Demand Characteristics

Most subjects want to be good subjects and to confirm the experimenter's hypothesis. Frequently at the end of an experiment, subjects ask, "I hope I didn't ruin the experiment?" A few subjects want to be bad subjects and try to undermine the experiment. Both need, first, to figure out what the experimenter's hypothesis is and then to act accordingly. Campus scuttlebutt, the advertisement to get subjects, the personality of the experimenter, the explicit statement of the instructions, implicit suggestions in the instructions, and the setting of the laboratory all constitute a set of ***demand characteristics*** that may induce a subject to invent a hypothesis about how he should behave.

The demand characteristics can be powerful cues, which lead to grossly mistaken inferences. In the 1950s, the topic of sensory deprivation was fashionable. In studies of this phenomenon, college students were paid $20 for a twenty-four-hour day of lying on cots in darkened, sound-deadened rooms. They wore translucent goggles that made sight impossible, gloves and cuffs that made feeling impossible, and they listened to masking noise that blocked hearing (Bexton, Heron, and Scott, 1954). The investigators found that the subjects had hallucinations: first they saw simple patterns, later they saw complex, moving figures. They also felt highly stressed, nauseous, agitated, and fatigued. It was concluded that removing vision, touch, and hearing for normal human subjects produced stress-induced hallucinations.

But in reviewing these sensory deprivation experiments, Martin Orne and his associates noticed something fishy about their design. There seemed to be some powerful demand characteristics: subjects were first greeted by a doctor in a white coat; a sign "Sensory Deprivation Laboratory" was on the door; the subjects had to sign awesome release forms absolving the experimenter of responsibility should anything untoward happen; and they had a panic button that would release them from the experiment if "anything undesirable should happen." Could it be that these trappings communicated to the subject that he was expected to be stressed and perhaps to have hallucinations? This would mean that it was not the sensory deprivation but the demand characteristics that produced the experimental effect.

To test this, subjects were led into a room labeled "Memory Deprivation Laboratory," and they were greeted by a doctor in a white coat with a stethoscope. Awesome release forms were signed. Subjects were told that if the experiment proved to be too much for them, they could use the red panic button conspicuously installed in the wall of the experimental room. *No sensory deprivation whatsoever was imposed on the subjects.* Rather, they sat in a well-lighted room with two comfortable chairs, they were provided with ice water and sandwiches, and they were also given an optional task of adding numbers. In this situation, the subjects also reported stress-induced hallucinations, indicating that the demand characteristics and not the sensory deprivation may have caused the hallucinations (Orne, 1962).

Demand characteristics can provide powerful clues to how a subject should behave. Here, a subject is participating in a sensory deprivation experiment. Will he have stress-induced hallucinations during isolation because of the sensory deprivation or because he *believes* he should be having hallucinations during such an experience? (Photograph by Yale Joel, *Life Magazine* © 1958, Time Inc.)

STATISTICAL INFERENCE

Frequently there is room for doubt about whether an experimental manipulation really worked, even when experimental confounds have been ruled out. This is particularly true when there is an experimental and control group, each made up of several subjects. What happens when most, but not all subjects in the experimental group show an effect, and few, but not many subjects in the control group do not? How do we decide whether an effect is real, rather than due to chance?

Statistical inferences are the procedures we use to decide whether the *sample,* or particular observations we made, truly represents the *population,* or the entire set of potential observations we might have made.

Let us say we try out a new drug therapy on a sample of ten schizophrenics, and at the end of a year, six of them recover from schizophrenia. Did the drug cure the disorder? To begin with, we need to compare the drug therapy group to a control group of schizophrenics who were given placebos. Let's say we have an excellent control group: there is a control group consisting of 100 other wards in which each of the ten schizophrenic individuals is untreated, that is, merely given a placebo. On the average, for all of these wards, three out of ten schizophrenics have recovered by the end of the year. Is the difference between six out of ten recoveries with the drug and an average of three out of ten recoveries with the placebo, real? Or, could as many as six out of ten of the patients have recovered, untreated, by chance alone? If this were so, the new drug would be worthless. It is vital to decide this, for unless we can, we will not know if it is worthwhile to use the drug for the population of schizophrenics as a whole.

To decide if the difference between six out of ten and three out of ten could have occurred by chance, we need to know the *frequency distribution* of recoveries from ward to ward. A frequency distribution is the number of occurrences in each given class observed; in this case, the number of wards showing no recoveries, one recovery, two recoveries, and so on. This frequency distribution shows how different numbers of recoveries among the wards are distributed. We know that the *mean,* or total number of recoveries divided by the total number of schizophrenics, is three out of ten, but for how many of the other wards did six (or more) out of ten schizophrenics recover? With a mean of three out of ten, six could be a very infrequent occurrence. For example, if exactly three out of ten recovered in each and every ward, then six out of ten would be very unlikely to occur by chance. With a different distribution, it could be a very frequent occurrence, for example, if for 50 of the wards, six out of ten recovered, but for the other 50 wards, zero out of ten recovered. In the first case, we could be very confident that the drug produced a real effect; in the second case, we would have very little confidence that the drug worked, and we would assume that six out of ten recoveries was just a chance fluctuation in the recovery rate.

Let us say we know the distribution of recovery for the 100 placebo wards (see Figure 8-1). In only 5 wards (noted by shading) did six (or more) schizophrenics recover without treatment. This means that only 5 percent of the time (i.e., in 5 out of 100 placebo wards) will chance fluctuation produce recovery in as many as six out of ten cases. Scientists are generally quite conservative about making claims, and by convention, a real effect will be

Figure 8-1

Frequency distribution for spontaneous recovery of schizophrenics. The bar graph shows the number of schizophrenic patients recovering without drug treatment out of ten in a given ward. The bars in color show the wards in which six or more patients recovered without treatment.

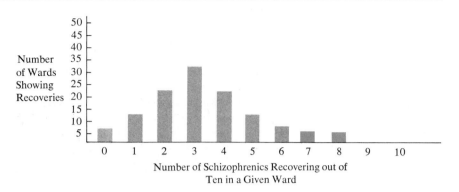

Number of Wards Showing Recoveries

Number of Schizophrenics Recovering out of
Ten in a Given Ward

claimed only with at least 95 percent confidence that chance did not produce the result. When effects exceed this conventional confidence level, they are called ***statistically significant.***

Making inferences in this way, however, can result in two kinds of mistakes: ***misses*** (saying x is false when it is true) and ***false alarms*** (saying x is true when it is false). A miss can occur when, for example, confidence does not reach the 5 percent level: say we are only confident at the 10 percent level that the number of drug recoveries was not due to chance and so we reject the hypothesis that the drug causes recovery, and yet the drug really does cure schizophrenia. We have missed a real cure by our conservative procedure. On the other hand, a false alarm can occur when confidence does reach the 5 percent level: say we accept the hypothesis that the drug causes recovery, but this turns out to be one of the 5 percent of the wards in which six people would have recovered without treatment and the drug really does nothing. Here not being conservative enough caused us to adopt a therapy which was really ineffective.

These two kinds of mistakes have both occurred many times in science; in fact, they are inversely related, they stand in a trade-off relationship to each other. The choice of a confidence level is always a difficult and sometimes a life or death decision. If we require a very conservative level of confidence before we accept a new therapy, say 1 percent, then we will have very few false alarms. As a consequence, we will incorrectly believe a therapy works when it does not, only 1 percent of the time. But the cost of this is that we will miss many therapies that really are effective. On the other hand, if we set a much less conservative level—say 20 percent—we will not miss many real therapies, but we will believe that certain therapies work quite often when they are actually ineffective.

Experiments with a Single Subject

Most experiments involve an experimental group and a control group, each with several subjects. Several subjects, as opposed to one, increase our confidence in the causal inference made in an experiment because of two factors: (1) ***repeatability***—the experimental manipulation is repeated and has its effect on several individuals; and (2) ***generality***—several randomly chosen individuals, not just one, are affected, and this increases our confidence that any new individual, randomly chosen, would also be so affected.

But useful experiments can be carried out with just one subject, and a *single-subject experiment,* well designed, can accomplish the goal of demonstrating repeatability. The demonstration of generality, however, always requires several subjects. An example of a single-subject experiment follows:

Walter was a retarded ten-year-old, whose outbursts in his special education class were contagious, and therefore particularly disruptive. His teacher, in conjunction with several experimental and clinical psychologists, hypothesized that his outbursts, or "talk outs" were maintained by the teacher's attention to him when she reprimanded him, and that by ignoring the talk outs and giving attention to him for more constructive actions, the talk outs would extinguish. They designed what is called an "A-B-A-B" experiment to test this. In such a design untreated, or baseline, behavior is measured (A_1), then treatment is instituted (B_1), then there is a return to no treatment (A_2), then treatment is reinstituted (B_2). (You may notice, incidentally, that a clinical case history, like the case of Jack in which a therapeutic procedure is tried, is an A-B design: A_1, untreated, followed by B_1, treatment.)

The experiment to change Walter's behavior was divided into four phases, during each of which the number of talk outs was counted. In the first five-day phase (A_1-untreated) the teacher handled the talk outs as she normally did, by reprimanding him. In the second five-day phase (B_1-treatment$_1$), the teacher ignored the talk outs and paid attention to Walter whenever he did anything constructive. The third phase (A_2-untreated$_2$) repeated the first phase: talk outs were again reprimanded. Finally, the fourth five-day phase (B_2-treatment$_2$) repeated the second phase: the talk outs were ignored, and the teacher only paid attention to him for constructive actions.

As you can see from Figure 8-2, the hypothesis proved correct. During A_1, there were about four outbursts in each session, but when contingent attention was instituted (B_1), Walter rapidly learned to produce no outbursts. The most important and convincing part of the experiments, however, were the repeated procedures, A_2 and B_2. These phases gave us evidence of repeatability. By reinstituting reprimands and showing that talk outs again increased, the experimenters showed that the decrease in talk outs during

Figure 8-2
A record of talking-out behavior of a retarded student. A_1 untreated—before experimental conditions. B_2 treatment— systematic ignoring of talking out and increased teacher attention to appropriate behavior. A_2 untreated—reinstatement of teacher attention to talking-out behavior. B_2 treatment—return to systematic ignoring of talking out and increased attention to appropriate behavior. (Source: Hall et al., 1971)

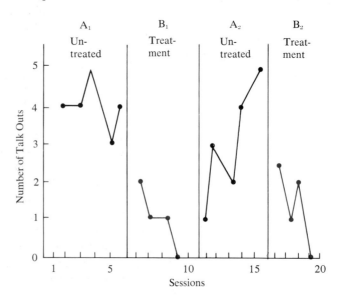

treatment was unlikely to have been caused by chance; rather the high rate of outbursts probably was caused by the reprimands. Then, by reinstituting treatment and showing fewer outbursts once again, we can infer that treatment probably caused his quieter behavior rather than chance. In addition, since the two conditions (each repeated) differed only in the direction of the teacher's attention—to bad behavior or to constructive behavior—cause is isolated in the same way that a control group isolates cause in a multi-subject experiment.

It could be, however, that only Walter in particular, rather than misbehaving, retarded boys in general, would improve with attention to constructive behavior. Only repeating the procedure with several subjects would show generality. When there is only one subject available, however, as in a rare disorder or unique therapy, single-subject designs are the only way of determining causality.

EVALUATION OF THE EXPERIMENTAL METHOD

The experimental method has three strengths and three weaknesses. The first strength is that it is the foremost method for isolating causal elements. Second, it is general to the population sampled, when group—as opposed to single-subject—experiments are done. Third, it is repeatable. The first weakness is that an experiment is artificial; it does not capture the full reality of a disorder. Second, inferences made are probabilistic, not certain. Finally, performing certain experiments sometimes may be unethical or impractical, we now turn to these difficulties.

Limits on Experimentation: Practical and Ethical

Often the road to experimental inquiry is completely blocked, and an alternate method must be used to attempt to investigate etiology. The reason an experiment cannot be done is often practical. It may be too expensive or time consuming. For example, will changing the child-rearing practices of schizophrenic parents lower the chances that their children will eventually become schizophrenic? An experiment may require more subjects than can be practically obtained. For example, "Will anti-anxiety drugs prevent hysterical blindness?" The right technology may not yet exist. For example, "Will stimulating single brain cells related to satiation reduce obesity in humans?"

Very often we do not experiment for ethical reasons. In 1920, an experiment was performed on a healthy nine-month-old infant, Little Albert (see Chapter 10). Investigators experimentally instilled in him a phobia of small animals by pairing a startling loud noise with his playing with a white rat (Watson and Rayner, 1920). But look at the experiment from Little Albert's point of view. An innocent and healthy child, with no say in the matter, was caused to be terrified of small, furry creatures. Should he have had to endure this suffering? Further, Albert was taken from his orphanage before curative procedures could be tried out, and he was never heard from again. Was he victimized by a lifelong phobia of rats? The moral climate has changed, and this is an experiment that could not be undertaken today.

But now look at the Little Albert experiment from a real phobic's point of view. Forget, for a moment, Albert's suffering and the possibility that he became a phobic. As we shall see in the fear and phobia chapter, as a direct result of the Little Albert experiment, curative procedures were tried out in fearful children, experimental models of phobias were developed and refined in animals and then applied to human adults, and a cure for many phobias is now known. Thousands of phobic individuals today are free to lead normal lives because of a line of experimentation that began with Little Albert's suffering. There is a clear conflict of interest here, and it is very difficult to decide whose rights are more important: one innocent Albert made phobic through no choice of his own versus thousands of phobics who have been cured.

Protection of the welfare of human (and animal) subjects is presently a value on the rise in our society. But deciding to increase such protection is not made without cost. There is an unavoidable consequence: some research that might have benefited troubled people is left undone. There is, however, one set of values that investigators of abnormality generally do agree on: the less drastic experiment is preferable to the more drastic, less shock to more shock, less deceptive experiments to more deceptive ones, using animals to using humans. But even here there are costs, since we must infer that the results found with less drastic conditions are valid for more drastic conditions, or that the finding is general beyond the species investigated.

There are a variety of ethical and practical reasons why the road to experimentation is often blocked in the study of abnormal psychology. The most frequent reason is that we value the right of the subjects in experiments to be treated humanely more than the right of humanity to possible experimental knowledge about cure and cause of abnormality. When the relevant experiment cannot be done, three other methods have been devised to provide information about etiology and cure: correlation, experiments of nature, and laboratory models.

CORRELATION

In an experiment, the experimenter manipulates the independent variable in order to discover cause. He or she imposes the independent variable on the subjects in the experimental group, but withholds it from subjects in the control group. If the experimental group but not the control group shows the effect, the experimenter infers causation. For ethical and practical reasons, such manipulation cannot be done in many settings of abnormality, so correlation is a widely used investigative technique. *Correlation* is pure observation, without manipulation. An observer performing a correlation measures two classes of events and records the relationship between them. There are three possible relationships: (1) As one increases, so does the other. This is called a *positive correlation.* Height, for example, correlates positively with weight, for the taller a person is, generally the more he weighs. This correlation is shown graphically in Figure 8-3A. (2) As one increases, the other decreases. This is called a *negative correlation.* Studying is, in general, negatively correlated with failure, for the more we study, the less

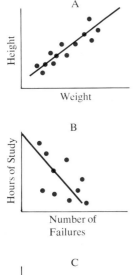

Figure 8-3
Correlations. Here are three scatterplots illustrating a positive correlation (A), a negative correlation (B), and a lack of correlation (C). The positive correlation indicates that taller individuals tend to weigh more. The negative correlation indicates that individuals who study less tend to fail more. The lack of correlation indicates no relationship between hair length and failure on algebra exams.

likely we are to fail (Figure 8-3B). (3) As one changes, the other does not change in any systematic way. Two such events are said to be **_uncorrelated._** Hair length is uncorrelated with failure on algebra exams, for how long our hair is, in general, makes no difference as to whether or not we fail (Figure 8-3C). The central point here is that in correlational studies, we are observers of the variables; we do not manipulate weight, height, hair length, studying, or failure. Instead, we look at the relationships among variables.

Let us now see how correlation can be applied to burning issues of abnormal psychology by working through an example of a negative correlation. One investigator proposed an elegantly simple theory of human depression: that depression is caused by having too few rewards in daily life (Lewinsohn, 1975). Experimentation on this is limited by ethical considerations; we cannot take nondepressed people and withhold rewards in their daily lives to see if depression results. But we can perform relevant correlations: Does depth of depression correlate with the number of pleasant activities that different individuals engage in? The experimenter predicted a negative correlation: as pleasant activities decrease, the degree of depression increases. Both variables can be operationally defined: degree of depression by a self-report test (Beck Depression Inventory), which totals up the number and severity of mood, cognitive, behavioral, and somatic symptoms that an individual reports; and a Pleasant Events Scale, which totals up the number of good events, such as going on a date, listening to music, watching TV, dancing, that the individual has recently engaged in. The predicted negative correlation has been found: the higher the degree of depression, the fewer pleasant events that have been engaged in.

Consider the following hypothetical, but representative data, showing a negative correlation between depression and pleasant events in ten individuals (Table 8-1). The data show a strong negative correlation between depression and pleasant activities. Adam, who is far and away the most depressed, engaged in only one pleasant activity in the past week: watching TV. Sarah and Amy, who are not at all depressed, did many enjoyable

Table 8-1 Negative Correlation between Depression and Number of Pleasant Activities

Name	Degree of Depression (the higher the score, the more depression)	Number of Pleasant Activities (in the past week)
Adam	30	1
Minerva	24	4
Davey	19	2
Elmo	11	4
John	7	7
Alphonso	6	9
Lynn	3	6
Lauren	2	11
Sarah	0	13
Amy	0	10

Figure 8-4
Graph of the negative correlation between depression and number of pleasant events documented in Table 8-1. As pleasant events increase, severity of depression decreases.

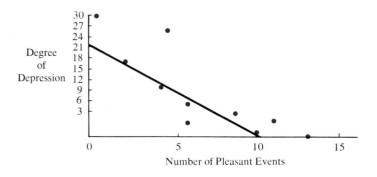

things. In general, among the other seven individuals, the more the depression, the fewer pleasant activities they engaged in. The correlation is strong, but less than a perfect negative correlation, since, for example, Minerva was considerably more depressed than Davey (24 vs. 19) but engaged in more pleasant activities (4 vs. 2), although both were near the low end of activity.

This negative correlation can be seen graphically in Figure 8-4. Each person is represented by a point. A straight line is "fitted" to the points and the negative correlation is indicated by the descending line: the more depression, the fewer activities. If the correlation had turned out positive (the more depression, the more activities), the best fitting line would have been ascending.

CORRELATION COEFFICIENTS

The strength of the relationship between two classes of events can be expressed by a ***correlation coefficient,*** the symbol for which is *r* (representing the Pearson Product Moment Correlation Coefficient, which is named after its inventor, Karl Pearson). The range for *r* is as follows: *r* can be as great as + 1.00, for a perfect positive correlation; it can vary through 0.00, meaning no relationship at all; and it can go down to − 1.00 for a perfect negative correlation. The *r* for our depression scores and pleasant activities turns out to be − .87, a strong negative correlation. The level of confidence that the relation did not occur by chance, or its ***statistical significance,*** can be determined for *r,* by using logic similar to that used for deciding whether or not two groups really differ. In general, the farther the correlation coefficient is from .00, in either the positive or negative direction, and the more observations there are that contribute to the correlation, the higher is our confidence that the relationship did not occur by chance. Conventionally, the 95 percent level of confidence is chosen as statistically significant.

CORRELATION AND CAUSALITY

Given the strong negative correlation in our example, can we conclude that a life with few rewards *causes* depression? The answer is no. And herein lies the main disadvantage of the correlational method compared to the experimental method. There are really three causal possibilities and not just one: (1) engaging in only a few pleasant activities might cause depression; (2) depression itself might cause people to engage in fewer pleasant activities; for example, perhaps depression blunts the desire to be social; and (3) both depression and lower activity could be caused by some unobserved third variable, such as some biochemical imbalance. In general, whether there is a correlation between X and Y, it can be either that X causes Y, that Y causes X, or that Z causes both X and Y.

Carrying out correlation studies, then, does not always lead us to discovering cause. But there are ways of narrowing down the possible causes. One way is to perform an experiment. For example, an experiment has actually been done to test causation for the depression example above. In this experiment, depressed students were induced to increase the number of pleasant events they engaged in each day. Depressed students who increased their activities did not become any less depressed than the control group of depressed students, who did not change their activity level; rather they became more depressed (Hammen and Glass, 1975). So the fact that activity and depression correlate negatively does not seem to reflect a causal relationship. Having few rewards probably does not cause depression, rather depression either causes individuals to engage in fewer rewarding activities, or both are caused by an unobserved third variable. We infer this because the number of pleasant activities has been experimentally manipulated, yet depression has not been alleviated.

Doing the relevant experiment is one way of determining the direction of causality that has been suggested, but not proven, by a correlation. A second way has to do with the order in which the variables occur in time. For example, positive correlations have been found between illness and the number of major life events, such as divorce and job loss, in the year preceding illness; the more life events before, the more illnesses after (Holmes and Rahe, 1967). Here, temporal sequence narrows the possibilities of cause from three to two: a hassled life could produce illness, or some third variable, like unstable personality, could produce both more illness and more life events, but the hypothesis that the illness causes the increases in life events is ruled out.

EVALUATION OF THE CORRELATIONAL MODEL

There are several advantages, and one major disadvantage, to correlational studies of abnormality. The use of correlations allows a quantitative and rigorous observation of relation between variables. Also, because the observations are on natural phenomenon, correlations do not have the artificiality of laboratory studies. Further, correlational studies are an option when performing an experiment is not a possibility, whether for practical or for ethical reasons. Lastly, correlations are repeatable. On the negative side, the major disadvantage in performing correlational studies is that the cause of a particular phenomenon usually cannot be isolated. One can move closer to discovering the cause, but other methods, such as experimental tests, are needed to determine causation more definitively.

EXPERIMENTS OF NATURE

Nature sometimes performs the experimental manipulation that scientists themselves could not do because of ethical or practical considerations.

Sometimes a striking event happens in the course of events that changes the lives of individuals. An alert investigator can take advantage of such accidents and use them to make inferences about what causes and cures abnormality. Because the accident is usually so striking, it is reasonable to suppose that *it,* and not some other extraneous event that happens to occur at the same time, is the cause. Such a strategy is an ***experiment of nature,*** in short, a study in which the experimenter observes the effects of an unusual natural event.

An act of nature may permit us to study the effects of trauma on human behavior. We can go into villages to find survivors of earthquakes, volcano eruptions and so on, and we can observe their behavior. Because of ethical reasons (if not practical ones), scientists do not intentionally subject humans to traumatic stress. But because knowledge about the effects of trauma is so important to the study of abnormality, scientists will occasionally visit the scenes of natural disasters to observe the effects of such experiments of nature. One such study was of the survivors of a flood in the Buffalo Creek area of Appalachia. For many months following the trauma, the survivors showed symptoms of terror, disturbed sleep, guilt over surviving, and reliving of the events (Erikson, 1976). These observations helped to give rise to a new category of anxiety disorder called "post-traumatic stress disorder" (see Chapter 10).

An experiment of nature is usually retrospective, with systematic observation beginning only after the precipitating event. In principle, experiments of nature can also be *prospective,* with observation beginning before the target event. So, for example, prospective studies are now underway with children deemed vulnerable to schizophrenia because one or both of their parents are schizophrenic. As some of these children will become schizophrenic in the natural course of their lives, and others will not, we may be able to determine what sorts of life stress will trigger schizophrenia in a genetically vulnerable population (Griffith, Mednick, Schulsinger, and Diderichsen, 1980).

Victims of disasters are often observed and studied by psychologists. One victim of the Buffalo Creek flood related, "I have good new neighbors, but it's not the same . . . The day the flood came, the people of Buffalo Creek started running, and they are still running inside their minds. They don't have time to stand and talk." (Wide World Photos)

EVALUATION OF EXPERIMENTS OF NATURE

Experiments of nature have three strengths as a method of inquiry: (1) like a case history, they document an actual happening and lack the artificiality of the laboratory experiment or the abstractness of a correlation; (2) no unethical manipulation is performed by the investigator since he merely observes an event produced by nature; and (3) the gross cause can be determined, in fact, the gross cause defines the investigation as an experiment of nature. However, the method also has three weaknesses: (1) we cannot isolate the elements in the gross cause that are active from those that are inactive, for example, we cannot know which aspects—the suddenness of the disaster or seeing others die or the uprooting of the community—of the Buffalo Creek Flood produced the stress disorder; (2) experiments of nature, as they are rare and conspicuous events, are not repeatable; and (3) like case histories, this method is also subject to retrospective bias by both victim and investigator.

THE LABORATORY MODEL

Correlations and experiments of nature are both used by investigators of abnormality when the road to experimentation is blocked. The final technique for getting around the impossibility of direct experimentation is the *laboratory model.* In the last decade, scientists have made considerable strides in understanding psychopathology by using such laboratory models.

A laboratory model is in essence the production, under controlled conditions, of phenomena analogous to naturally occurring mental disorders. That is, a particular symptom or constellation of symptoms is produced in miniature to test hypotheses about cause and cure. Confirmed hypotheses can then be further tested in situations outside the laboratory. Both human or animal subjects are utilized in laboratory models.

As an example, let us see how one goes about studying a biologically based animal model of human obesity. The theory states broadly that obesity is caused by a lesion in a part of the brain called the ventromedial hypothalamus (VMH). For ethical reasons, we obviously cannot destroy the VMH in human subjects to see if they become obese. But, we can in animals. In doing so, we construct an animal model of obesity. It turns out that when the VMH is destroyed in rats, they will almost double their weight in about three months, and then their weight will level off. It also turns out that these lesioned rats exhibit symptoms very similar to those in obese humans. For example, obese humans and VMH rats both:

- eat more food than nonobese rats and humans, when the food tastes good
- eat less food than the nonobese, when the food tastes bad (finickiness)
- eat somewhat more total food than the nonobese
- eat fewer meals per day than the nonobese
- eat considerably more per meal than the nonobese
- eat faster than the nonobese

For ethical reasons, animals are often used in laboratory experiments. Here a rat was used in a study on obesity. This rat became obese after a lesion to the ventromedial hypothalamus. But can experimenters generalize from models of animal obesity to actual human obesity? (Courtesy Neal E. Miller)

- are more emotionally excitable to external cues than the nonobese
- are more lethargic than the nonobese
- are less willing to expend energy to eat than the nonobese (Schachter, 1971)

All of this seems to offer convincing evidence that this animal model accurately mirrors the symptoms of human obesity. But, before an observer can extrapolate from the results of an animal model and apply them to a human situation, he or she must answer a few questions:

1. Is the similarity of symptoms between the model and naturally occurring abnormality convincingly demonstrated? That is, do both obese rats and obese people behave the same way?

2. Does the laboratory model describe only a subgroup of the naturally occurring abnormality? Are all groups of obese humans like obese rats, or only some?

3. Is the laboratory phenomenon a model of a specific disorder, or does it model general features of all disorders (Abramson and Seligman, 1977)? Do only obese humans have lesions in the VMH or do schizophrenic people have these lesions as well?

EVALUATION OF THE LABORATORY MODEL

Laboratory models have three strengths: (1) as experiments, they can isolate the cause of the disorder; (2) they are repeatable; (3) they minimize unethical manipulation. Like all other methods, they also have several weaknesses: (1) as laboratory creations, they are artificial; (2) they are *analogous* to but not identical with the real disorder itself. As similarity of symptoms, cause, physiology, cure, and prevention mount, however, we become more convinced that the model is the actual disorder; (3) since observers often use animal subjects in laboratory models, they must infer that humans and the species being investigated are similarly susceptible to the disorder. In later chapters, we will see examples of models that have given insight into the cause and cure of such disorders as depression, stomach ulcers, and phobias. Sophisticated laboratory modeling is a new development in the field of abnormality. The verdict is not entirely in on any one model, but the technique promises to add to our understanding of abnormality.

COMBINING SEVERAL METHODS: A WOVEN FABRIC

There is no single, most convincing, way to understand abnormality. Each method has strengths and weaknesses (Table 8-2). But clinical case histories, experimental studies, correlational studies, experiments of nature, and laboratory models all can provide some insight. Each by itself can, on occasion, provide conclusive understanding. But most of the time, each taken in isolation resembles blind men groping at an elephant: one has hold of the tail, another the trunk, another a foot. Each captures only one aspect of being an elephant, but none captures the whole thing. Similarly, the clinical case, well done, best conveys the reality of a disorder, but it usually fails to isolate the

Table 8-2 STRENGTHS AND WEAKNESSES OF VARIOUS METHODS

Method	Strengths	Weaknesses
Single Clinical Case	1. Is not artificial. 2. Documents rare events. 3. Generates causal hypotheses.	1. Is selective and susceptible to retrospective bias. 2. Is not repeatable. 3. Is not general. 4. Does not isolate causal elements.
Experiments	1. Isolate causal elements. 2. Are general to population sampled (not true of single-subject experiments). 3. Are repeatable.	1. Are artificial; don't capture full reality of the disorder. 2. Inferences are probabilistic or statistical, rather than certain. 3. It is unethical or impractical to manipulate many crucial variables.
Correlations	1. Quantify and observe relationships. 2. Are not artificial. 3. Are repeatable.	1. Do not isolate causal elements.
Experiments of Nature	1. Are not artificial. 2. There is no unethical manipulation. 3. Isolate gross cause.	1. Do not isolate active elements of the cause. 2. Are not repeatable. 3. Are susceptible to retrospective bias.
Experimental Models	1. Isolate causal elements. 2. Are repeatable. 3. Minimize unethical manipulation.	1. Are artificial. 2. Are analogous to but not identical with the real disorder. 3. Need cross-species inferences (with animal models).

cause. The experiment, well done, isolates the cause, but it remains artificial. The correlation, well done, picks out crucial relationships, but not necessarily causal ones. But when the methods together converge on a theory, a fabric of understanding is woven. In the particular disorders that we are close to understanding, case history evidence, experimental studies, correlations, experiments of nature, and laboratory models all play a role. A worthy scientific fabric of converging evidence has already been woven for phobias, for the genetics of schizophrenia, for depression, for certain kinds of brain damage, and for sexual identity. For some of the specific disorders that we will discuss in the ensuing chapters, the reader when done, will probably feel bewildered, at sea. For most others, the reader probably will feel that he or she understands it partially but that pieces of the puzzle are still missing. But for several others, the reader should feel the pleasure and excitement of discovery and understanding, because these are examples of the woven fabric.

SUMMARY

1. The *clinical case history* is the record of part of the life of an individual as seen during therapy. Based on the patient's case history, the therapist

will hypothesize about possible causes of a problem and then help the patient overcome his past.

2. A *scientific experiment* consists of a procedure in which the hypothesized cause *(the independent variable)* is manipulated and the occurrence of the effect *(the dependent variable)* is measured. Both independent and dependent variables are operationally defined. An *operational definition* is the set of observable and measurable conditions under which a phenomenon is said to occur. When manipulating an independent variable produces changes in a dependent variable, an *experimental effect* has been obtained.

3. *Confounds* are factors other than the independent variable that might produce an experimental effect. An *experimental group* experiences both the confounds and the hypothesized cause. The *control group* is similar to the experimental group, but the control group only experiences the confounds. Subtle confounds that might produce the experimental effect include nonrandom assignment, experimenter bias, subject bias, and demand characteristics.

4. *Statistical inferences* are the procedures used to determine whether the *sample* (the particular observations) truly represents the *population* (the entire set of potential observations). When effects exceed a conventional confidence level, they are called *statistically significant.*

5. If an hypothesis is rejected but it is really true, the mistake is called a *miss.* If an hypothesis is accepted but it is really false, the mistake is called a *false alarm.* Misses and false alarms stand in a trade-off relationship to each other; when there are many misses, there are few false alarms; when there are many false alarms, there are few misses.

6. *Correlation* is pure observation without manipulation. In a correlation, two classes of events are measured and the relationship between them is recorded. In a *positive correlation,* as one variable increases, the other does too. In a *negative correlation,* as one variable increases, the other decreases. Events are *uncorrelated* when, as one variable changes, the other does not change in any systematic way.

7. A relationship is *statistically significant* if it is unlikely to have occurred by chance. Generally, the farther the correlation is from .00 in either the positive or negative direction and the more observations that are made, the higher the level of confidence and the greater the likelihood that the relationship did not occur by chance.

8. *Experiments of nature* are studies in which the experimenter observes the effects of an unusual natural event.

9. In a *laboratory model,* investigators produce, under controlled conditions, phenomena that are analogous to naturally occurring mental disorders. This is done to test hypotheses about biological and psychological causes and cures of symptoms.

10. No one method alone will provide complete understanding of psychopathology. But each method may lead us to an understanding of various aspects of abnormality. When all these methods converge in confirmation of a theory, we can say that a fabric of understanding has been woven.

Psychological Assessment and Classification

PEOPLE differ. There are tall people and short ones, thin people and stout ones, redheads and brunettes. Such physical differences among people are obviously useful—they allow us to classify people according to their height or weight or hair color. But differences are useful in a more subtle way—they allow us to ask important questions about people. For example, we might want to know whether tall people are more successful than short ones, whether thin people live longer than fat ones, or whether redheads are more temperamental than brunettes. Being able to classify people according to certain physical characteristics may enable us to explore other significant questions.

People differ psychologically too. There are shy people and outgoing ones, industrious people and lazy ones, depressed people and happy ones. This observation too is a commonplace, but it leads to some very important ideas. Psychological classification permits us to group people according to their similarities, to ask how they came to be that way and how they can be changed. Without classification, there can be no science, no understanding of how things came to be and how they will evolve.

In this chapter, we take up the assessment and classification of abnormal psychological conditions. Because such classification often arises in a medical context and is modeled after medicine itself, it is often called psychological or psychiatric diagnosis. You know already from the biological approach to abnormality (Chapter 3) that psychological diagnosis has already been a beneficial enterprise, for without it medical research could not have erased a disorder called general paresis. Those useful insights occurred nearly a century ago, however; here we will concern ourselves with modern psychological assessment and diagnosis. What kinds of assessment techniques promise reliable understandings of human misery and lead to useful diagnosis? What diagnostic categories seem most promising for understanding and treating psychological distress? Indeed, how do we assess whether an assessment procedure or diagnostic category is useful or promising?

Psychologists seek to understand individuals through a variety of procedures. They talk to people, administer psychological tests, and assess their behavior in real life situations. The first theme of this chapter consists of the contribution of these assessment techniques to the process of classification. The second theme concerns diagnosis itself: the reliability and usefulness of current diagnostic schemes.

PSYCHOLOGICAL ASSESSMENT

Assessment is undertaken to achieve a deep understanding of the client. That understanding may result in a diagnosis, but it commonly also results in much more. Commonly, assessment yields a sense of a person's individuality, the forces that generate his or her uniqueness. Often, it will give a sense of why a person is in difficulty, and occasionally a clue as to how the difficulty can be resolved.

In order for an assessment device to generate meaningful understandings about people, it must possess two characteristics. First, it must be *reliable,* that is, it must generate the same findings on repeated use; it must be stable. Much as a rubber yardstick has limited utility for measuring a room, a psychological test that yields different findings on different occasions has limited usefulness for understanding people. Second, it must be *valid.* It must be useful for the purposes for which it is intended. Even a good thermometer is useless for measuring a room. Similarly, a psychological test can be useful for one purpose and thoroughly invalid for others. Before examining specific assessment techniques, it is particularly important to have a good grasp of what is meant by reliability. The discussion of validity will be delayed until we take up psychological classification.

RELIABILITY

Imagine a physical universe in which yardsticks are made of rubber. Each time you would measure something, you would come up with different answers simply because of the nature of the measuring instrument, for rubber stretches. Such an instrument would be *un*reliable, which is to say you could not depend on it to come up with the same measurement each time it was used. Though we don't often think about it, reliability is basic to all kinds of measurement, including the psychological measurement of people. In order to diagnose a problem, psychologists have developed certain measures, or tests, that aid in the assessment of people. The major challenge is to develop tests that are reliable. Do two psychologists arrive at the same impression on the basis of test or interview evidence? If they do, this is held to be evidence of *inter-judge reliability.* To what extent will a test administered today yield the same results when given a week or a month from now *(test-retest reliability* or *test stability)*? Reliability refers to the extent to which an instrument—be it a test or an observer—yields the same result in repeated trials or with different observers. When a group of psychologists examines a patient, and all arrive at the same conclusion, that conclusion is said to have *high reliability.* When, however, they cannot agree, each proffered viewpoint is considered to have *low reliability.* Figure 9-1 describes reliability graphi-

Figure 9-1
These diagrams depict various levels of reliability. Notice that even if reliability is relatively high, such as .67, there is considerable difference between say, the scores on Variable X and those on Variable Y that are supposed to measure the same thing.

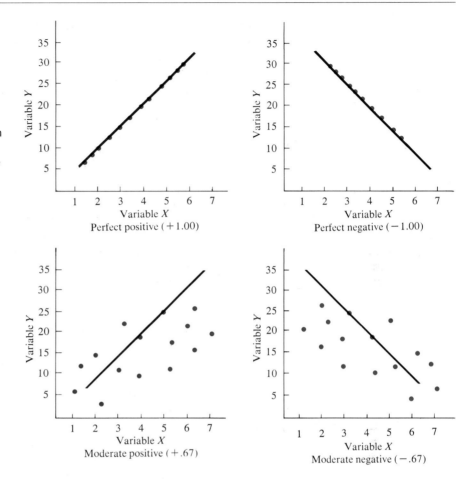

cally. When two observers or tests are in complete agreement, their reliability is said to be 1.00. When they arrive at diametrically opposite conclusions, reliability is said to be − 1.00. And when there seems to be no relationship between their conclusions, the reliability of those conclusions is 0.00.

As anyone who has tried to measure a floor knows, even using physical yardsticks, one rarely gets a reliability of 1.00. There are tiny measurement differences. Depending upon the purpose of the measurement, such differences may mean a great deal or nothing at all. A difference of an eighth of an inch means little to the height of an oak, but a lot to the diameter of a diamond. So it is with psychological measurement. How reliable an instrument needs to be depends upon many things, among them the purposes for which it is being used and the consequences of small and large errors (Cronbach et al., 1972). Generally, a high degree of reliability is required when individuals are being assessed, especially when the findings are to be used for individual care and treatment rather than, say, research. The human consequences of error in diagnosis and treatment are harsh: nothing less than individual well-being is at stake. Therefore, the reliability standards are stringent. A research diagnosis, however, is tentative until it is proven useful. Little harm is done with such diagnoses (Rosenhan, 1975). One cannot specify a degree of reliability that will be acceptable for all occasions of measurement and for all uses to which a measure will be put. But conservatively, a measure or observation whose reliability is below .80 should not be used for purposes of individual assessment or care, while one whose reliability descends below .60 is unreliable for research purposes.

THE CLINICAL INTERVIEW

Here a psychologist is conducting a clinical interview with a client. (Photograph by Lee Lockwood/ Black Star)

Assessment techniques are divided into three processes: interviewing, testing and observing. The first of these, the ***clinical interview,*** is the favorite instrument of clinical psychologists and psychiatrists, reflecting the widespread view that we don't know someone well until we've met and talked with him. Good interviewers get information, not only from what people say, but from how they say it: their manner, tone of voice, body postures, and degree of eye contact (Exline and Winters, 1965; Ellsworth and Carlsmith, 1968; Ekman, Friesen, and Ellsworth, 1972). Of course, in order to get this information, there must be a good rapport between the client and interviewer. One should not expect people to be honest if they feel that their statements are going to incriminate them or lead to aversive decisions about their future. For an interview to be maximally informative, the client needs to perceive the interviewer as being nonthreatening, supportive, and encouraging of self-disclosure (Jourard, 1974).

The clinical interview may range from an unstructured conversation to a quite structured encounter in which all of the interviewer's questions are prepared in an ***interview schedule*** and may, in fact, be read. Fundamentally, an ***unstructured interview*** allows the interviewer to take advantage of the exigencies of the moment. The client may want to talk about a particular problem, and right now, rather than later. The unstructured interview permits that. Similarly, the interviewer may want to inquire into a particular issue that might not be on a structured interview schedule. The unstructured interview, therefore, is very flexible, but it "pays a price" for that flexibility. Because they are unstructured, no two of these interviews are the same. They elicit different information and, therefore, the reliability and validity of the information that is elicited may be reduced (Fisher, Epstein, and Harris, 1967).

Although the unstructured interview may seem like a rambling event, it is not random. The kind of information interviewers attempt to elicit is heavily determined by their own orientation, by the theory that guides their own understanding of human behavior. For example, interviewers with a psychoanalytic orientation will often concentrate on early childhood experiences, sexual experiences, and dreams because such data enable them to form a psychoanalytic impression of personality. Behaviorists and humanists, on the other hand, tend to concentrate on current events, on behavior that is presently distressing and the events and experiences that surround it, again because those experiences are especially meaningful within their theoretical framework.

The fact that different interviewers pursue different issues and, therefore, often arrive at varying conclusions, has led increasingly to the use of ***structured interviews***. The questions that are asked in a structured interview depend on the purpose of the interview. Diagnostic interviews contain different questions than do those that assess the ability of a person to undergo a particular kind of therapy. For example, the Schedule for Affective Disorders and Schizophrenia (SADS) adds considerably to the reliability of the diagnostic interview (and the diagnoses that emerge from it) by providing a formal interview schedule (Endicott and Spitzer, 1978). If a therapist is using the SADS to assess if a patient is a schizophrenic, he will direct the questioning around the symptoms of schizophrenia. Since schizophrenics hallucinate and sometimes hear voices, the therapist will ask:

· Has there been anything unusual about the way things looked, or sounded, or smelled?

· Have you heard voices or other things that weren't there or that other people couldn't hear, or seen things that were not there?

· The (sounds, voices) that you said you heard, did you hear them outside your head, through your ears, or did they come from inside your head?

· Could you hear what the voice was saying?

· Did you hear anything else? What about noises?

PSYCHOLOGICAL TESTING

Additional psychological information about the nature of an individual's problems and disabilities comes from psychological testing. Personality assessment is a subject that fascinates many people, so much so that there are thousands of personality tests, and hundreds of books written about them. Some tests are focal, designed to illuminate a single personality attribute, such as anxiety or depression, or to uncover a particular kind of brain damage. Others are omnibus, seeking to describe a larger portion of personality and abnormality. Many tests are unstructured or projective, requiring the client to draw a person or persons or a series of designs, to determine abnormality through careful interviewing, while others aspire to the same goal through formal, structured examinations.

Most psychological testing procedures are relatively standardized. That important fact increases the likelihood that different examiners will obtain similar information from the client: that is, that the test will be reliable. If several examiners give the Wechsler Adult Intelligence Scale to the same client, for example, then the client's score should be approximately the same from one examination to the next.

Psychological tests fall into three categories: psychological inventories, "projective" tests, and intelligence tests.

Psychological Inventories

Nearly everyone has taken a ***psychological inventory*** at one time or another for vocational guidance, or personal counseling, or in connection with a job. These tests are highly structured and contain a variety of statements that can be answered "true" or "false." The client is asked to indicate whether or not each statement applies to her. Inventories have enormous advantages: they are commonly highly reliable; they can often be given to several people simultaneously and are therefore relatively inexpensive to administer and score; and by providing statistical norms, they allow comparative judgments to be made. The inventory that is used most widely is the Minnesota Multiphasic Personality Inventory. Less widely used, but very useful for certain purposes, are the Q-sort and the Rep Test.

Psychological testing may be projective, requiring the person to draw a series of designs or to put together a figure. (Photograph by Jeffrey Grosscup)

The Minnesota Multiphasic Personality Inventory (MMPI) is used to assess behaviors, thoughts, and feelings. (Sepp Seitz 1982/Woodfin Camp)

MINNESOTA MULTIPHASIC PERSONALITY INVENTORY (MMPI).   By far, the most widely used and studied personality inventory in clinical assessment is the *Minnesota Multiphasic Personality Inventory* or the *MMPI* (Hathaway and McKinley, 1943). The MMPI consists of 550 test items that inquire into a wide array of behaviors, thoughts, and feelings. Although each item can be administered separately to individual clients, the MMPI is most often administered to small groups of people. All respondents are usually given the same test items, but the meaning of those items may not be identical for each respondent. Thus, a college student who responds "yes" to the statement, "I usually feel fine," obviously means something quite different from the hospitalized person who responded "yes" without reading the statement. As a consequence, the meanings of the MMPI items are by no means self-evident, and they have had to be ascertained by empirical research. Scales have been constructed by examining the responses of people with known characteristics, such as depressed versus nondepressed persons, manic versus non-manic, introverted versus extraverted. All in all, the MMPI provides scores for the ten categories shown in Table 9-1. These categories have been validated against diagnostic judgments that arose from psychiatric interviews and other tests.

Any paper-and-pencil inventory is subject to a variety of distortions, and the MMPI is no exception. One can simply lie. One can be evasive. Or one can try to put oneself in the best possible social light. And one can do these things intentionally or unintentionally. However, the MMPI contains four "validity" scales that are designed to alert the diagnostician to such distortions. Thus, if a person were to respond "yes" to the following items: "I never tell lies," and "I read the newspaper editorials every day," it might be reasonable to surmise that the test-taker is trying to present herself as favorably as she can—since it is a rare person who never tells lies and who reads the editorials daily. Notice that these judgments about social desirability and lying are *not* absolutely foolproof. Rather they are "best guesses." Most

Table 9-1 PERSONALITY CHARACTERISTICS ASSOCIATED WITH ELEVATIONS ON THE BASIC MMPI SCALES

Scale	Characteristics
1 (Hs), Hypochondriasis	High scorers are described as cynical, defeatist, preoccupied with self, complaining, hostile, and presenting numerous physical problems.
2 (D), Depression	High scorers are described as moody, shy, despondent, pessimistic, and distressed. This scale is one of the most frequently elevated in clinical patients.
3 (Hy), Hysteria	High scorers tend to be repressed, dependent, naive, outgoing, and to have multiple physical complaints. Expression of psychological conflict through vague and unbased physical complaints.
4 (Pd), Psychopathic Deviate	High scorers often are rebellious, impulsive, hedonistic, and antisocial. They often have difficulty in marital or family relationships and trouble with the law or authority in general.
5 (MF), Masculinity-Femininity	High-scoring males are described as sensitive, aesthetic, passive, or feminine. High scoring females are described as aggressive, rebellious, and unrealistic.
6 (Pa), Paranoia	Elevations on this scale are often associated with being suspicious, aloof, shrewd, guarded, worrisome, and overly sensitive. High scorers may project or externalize blame.
7 (Pt), Psychasthenia	High scorers are tense, anxious, ruminative, preoccupied, obsessional, phobic, rigid. They frequently are self-condemning and feel inferior and inadequate.
8 (Sc), Schizophrenia	High scorers are often withdrawn, shy, unusual, or strange and have peculiar thoughts or ideas. They may have poor reality contact and in severe cases bizarre sensory experiences—delusions and hallucinations.
9 (Ma), Mania	High scorers are called sociable, outgoing, impulsive, overly energetic, optimistic, and in some cases amoral, flighty, confused, disoriented.
0 (Si), Social Introversion-Extraversion	High scorers tend to be modest, shy, withdrawn, self-effacing, inhibited. Low scorers are outgoing, spontaneous, sociable, confident.

SOURCE: Butcher, 1969.

(but not all) people who respond positively to the above items will be, willingly or unwittingly, trying to improve their image. For all we know, however, there may well be some people who read every editorial every day and who never tell lies (bless 'em!).

The results of the MMPI are recorded in the form of a profile (Figure 9-2). The profile tells a clinician more than the individual scores would. By utilizing an MMPI atlas (e.g., Gilberstadt and Duker, 1965), the profile of a particular person can be compared with similar profiles obtained from individuals about whom a great deal is known. The resulting personality assessment is more than the sum of the individual's MMPI scores. This larger assessment can then be examined against inferences from other sources of information that the clinician has obtained, with the goal of noting consistencies and reconciling inconsistencies (Korchin, 1976).

Figure 9-2
An example of Minnesota Multiphasic Personality Inventory (MMPI) profile with an "automated" interpretation provided by a computer. The computer prints out statements that have been found to have some validity for other individuals with similar profiles. (Source: Courtesy of NCS Interpretive Scoring Systems)

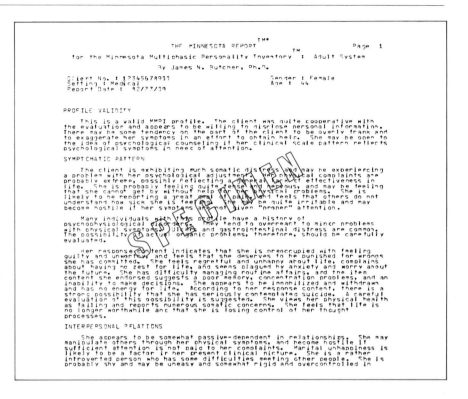

Q-SORT. Many psychologists, especially humanistically oriented and behavioral ones, are considerably less interested in diagnostic categories and personality traits than they are in the individual's subjective experience. They ask such questions as: How does this person perceive himself now? What kind of person would he like to become? Quite apart from predicting the individual's behavior or response to treatment, the answers to these questions are of intrinsic interest. They provide a basis for comparing the individual's *real* and *ideal* self, as well as the degree to which he is dissatisfied with himself. Data for these impressions arise from tests such as the Q-sort.

The **Q-sort** consists of a large number of cards, each of which contains a statement like "is an assertive person," "evades responsibility," or "is sensitive." The client is asked to place each statement in one of nine piles, according to whether the statement is more or less characteristic of him. Moreover, in order to forestall the possibility that clients would only use extreme or center categories in describing themselves, the number of items allowed in each of the nine categories is ranged in accord with the bell-shaped normal distribution. Fewer items are permitted at the extremes, and more in the center. (This enhances the Q-sort as a research instrument as well.) Clients may also be asked to rearrange these cards to reflect the kind of person they would like to be—their "ideal" selves. Humanistic therapists have demonstrated that, as treatment progresses, the discrepancy between the real and the ideal self described by the Q-sort test declines (Rogers, 1959).

ROLE CONSTRUCT REPERTORY TEST (REP TEST). Another psychological test that is favored by both humanistic and behavioral psychologists is the **Role Construct Repertory Test** or the **Rep Test,** as it is commonly called

(Kelly, 1955). This test proceeds from the assumption that all events are subject to varying interpretations or constructions. It attempts to elicit the particular constructs that each client uses in interpreting significant events. A construct is deduced by examining the ways in which two things are alike but different from a third. To begin with, the client lists the important people in his life, such as his mother, father, roommate(s), girlfriend, etc. When he has completed the list, he examines these people in groups of three, and he indicates the ways in which two of them are similar to each other and different from the third person. In this way, the subjective constructs an individual uses to determine similarity and difference emerge. For example, after examining all of the ways in which the client perceives two people to be similar to each other and different from a third, one might notice that the similar people are all perceived as angry, and they are seen as differing from the other people who are calm. "Angry vs. calm" would therefore be an underlying construct for this person, a primary way in which her psychological world is organized. Further examination of similarities and differences might reveal other significant constructs. Indeed, simply appraising the number of constructs that were used would suggest something about the richness and variety of her experiential life.

Projective Tests

For many psychologists, and especially those who are psychodynamically oriented, the focus of assessment is on unconscious conflicts, latent fears, sexual and aggressive impulses, and hidden anxieties. Structured inventories, because they inquire about *conscious* experience and feelings, obscure these deeper dynamics. But because ***projective tests*** utilize meaningless stimuli, such as inkblot forms, or very vague ones, they minimize reality constraints, encourage imaginative processes, and maximize the opportunity for conflictual or unconscious concerns to emerge (Murray, 1951). Two of the most widely used projective tests are the Roschach Test and the Thematic Apperception Test.

THE RORSCHACH TEST.   Invented by Hermann Rorschach (1884–1922), a Swiss psychiatrist, the ***Rorschach Test*** consists of ten bilaterally symmetrical "inkblots," some in color, some in black, grey, and white, and each on an individual card. The respondent is shown each card separately and asked to tell the examiner everything she sees on the card, that is, everything the inkblot could resemble. Figure 9-3 shows two such cards.

Here are the responses made by one person to the card on the left (Exner, 1978, p. 170):

Figure 9-3
Facsimiles of Rorschach Test cards. These projective instruments are composed of stimuli that seem like inkblots and that allow the respondent to project impressions of what those inkblots might be. (Source: Based on Gleitman, 1981, p. 635)

PATIENT: I think it could be a woman standing in the middle there . . . Should I try to find something else?

EXAMINER: Most people see more than one thing.

PATIENT: I suppose the entire thing could be a butterfly. . . . I don't see anything else.

Responses to these inkblots are scored in several ways. First, they are scored for the nature and quality of what has been seen. In this instance, the woman and the butterfly are well-formed percepts, indicative of someone whose view of the world is relatively clear. Second, whether the percept is commonly seen by others, or relatively rare (and if rare, whether creative or bizarre) is scored. Seeing a woman and a butterfly on this blot is a common occurrence. It suggests that this person is capable of seeing the world as others do. Additional scoring will examine whether the entire blot or only part of it was used, and whether color is used and integrated into the percept. These scores, as well as what is seen in the blot, are integrated to give an overall picture of the vitality of the respondent's inner life, his conflicts, the degree to which he can control sexual and aggressive urges, and the like.

Perusal of the inkblot on the left in Figure 9-3 will give some sense of the thinking that goes into Rorschach interpretation. Imagine someone who has responded to the bits of ink that surround the central percept, but who failed to respond to the main part of the blot. You might hypothesize (and it is *only* a hypothesis) that this individual has difficulty confronting "central" realities and perhaps, as a result, turns her attention to trivia, as if *they* were central. Using the responses to a single blot, of course, that would be merely one of any number of hypotheses you might entertain. There might, for example, be something about the central percept of this particular card that the respondent finds aversive. If so, the response would indicate little about generalized tendencies to avoid centralities. If, however, such responses were forthcoming on several cards—if on each of them the respondent "missed" the central percept and puttered about at the edges, an examiner might feel that the hunch was well-substantiated. This is the kind of thinking that is used to examine the use of color, of forms, of the popularity of the percept, and so on. A test record that reveals only commonly given percepts might be judged to be behaviorally conformist and cognitively banal, especially if all other indices were consistent with that view.

Interpreting the Rorschach requires enormous skill. It is a fascinating and complex process, whose full richness is not given by the above examples. But it is not without its hazards. Precisely because the interpretative logic is so compelling, there is a strong tendency to believe in it without validation, and to disregard contrary evidence. Indeed, the interpretation of Rorschach protocols turns out to be a place to examine the attributional errors that the intuitive mind makes (Ross, 1977; Nisbett and Ross, 1980). For example, clinicians might be asked to assess which of the following sets of responses given by a male respondent to the card on the right in Figure 9-3 indicates the presence of homosexual tendencies:

Protocol 1: The whole thing looks ominous. There are violent monsters here. You can see them clawing at each other. I don't know what kind they are, but they sure are scary. . . . In fact, the entire blot looks like an angry centaur, rearing on its hind legs. You can see the human face and the animal body, and the arms there, the horse here.

A clinician uses the Rorschach test to assess a client's feelings and conflicts. (Copyright Sepp Seitz 1982/Woodfin Camp)

Protocol 2: Well, these in the center seem like sex organs. Male sex organs. . . . And over here, this looks like a dress and a bra. Kind of a padded bra, it looks like. . . . Here's someone's butt. Kind of a child's butt—you can even see the err . . . uh, rectum I think. . . . And this is—what do you call them—someone who is part man and part woman. The bottom part looks like it's a man, but when you look up here, it's a woman.

Clinicians who examined many such protocols were emphatic in interpreting responses of the kind given in Protocol 2 as indicative of homosexuality, while responses like those in Protocol 1 were given much less weight (Chapman and Chapman, 1969). In fact, the responses shown in Protocol 2 are *entirely invalid* as indices of homosexual interest or behavior, having no research support whatsoever. Those in Protocol 1, however, though seemingly removed from homosexuality at the intuitive level, are moderately well-supported in validation studies as signs of homosexuality.

The conflict between intuition (or common sense) on the one hand and validated data on the other pervades assessment, as it pervades psychological judgment in general. Time and again, it will seem to clinicians that a certain sign makes sense as an indicator of a larger behavior, so much so that it hardly seems worth the effort to assess the validity of the sign empirically. And time and again, when that assessment *is* made, it will be found that the correlation between sign and indicator is *illusory* (Chapman and Chapman, 1969), being based merely on a commonly held view and not on reality.

As might be expected with an instrument that is so complex and that is predicated on ambiguity, neither the reliability nor the validity of the Rorschach have been high. Reliability of scoring is low despite the variety of manuals that are available to assist the clinician (e.g., Aronow and Reznikoff, 1976; Exner, 1974, 1978). One attempt to objectify and standardize scoring has resulted in a new set of inkblots (Holtzman, 1961; Hill, 1972), which mainly has been used in research rather than in clinical practice.

Tests that purport to reveal "underlying psychodynamics" are particularly difficult to validate because such dynamics are inferred. Technically, they are *hypothetical* constructs, assumed to be there for theoretical reasons since they cannot be directly examined nor directly verified. When, however, interpretations from the Rorschach have been susceptible to verification (as when the indices point to homosexuality or predict suicide),

Figure 9-4
Facsimile of a TAT picture. These pictures are designed to be sufficiently vague to allow respondents to project their own meaningful story onto them. (Source: Gleitman, 1981, p. 637)

validation studies have been conducted. And in those studies, the evidence in the main has gone against the Rorschach (Zubin, Eron, and Schumer, 1965; Mischel, 1968, 1976; Peterson, 1968).

THEMATIC APPERCEPTION TEST.   Another commonly used instrument is the *Thematic Apperception Test,* or the *TAT.* It consists of a series of pictures that are not as ambiguous as Rorschach cards, but not as clear as photographs either (see Figure 9-4). Respondents are asked to look at each picture and to make up a story about it. They are told to tell how the story began, what is happening now, and how it will end. As with the Rorschach, it is assumed that because the pictures are ambiguous, the stories will reflect the respondent's proclivity to see situations in a particular way. If a respondent repeatedly uses the same theme to describe several different pictures, this is considered especially indicative of underlying dynamics.

The TAT has been used extensively as a research instrument to explore a variety of motives, particularly the need for achievement (McClelland et al., 1953; Atkinson, 1958). Its use in that context has been fruitful and provocative. But its use as a clinical instrument for assessing individual personality is prey to the same problems that beset the Rorschach. Although reliability of scoring is adequate (Harrison, 1965), the interpretations of TAT protocols by different clinicians is quite diverse (Murstein, 1965).

Intelligence Tests

Perhaps the most reliable and, for many purposes, the most valid of all psychological tests are those that measure intelligence. Originally designed by Alfred Binet to differentiate bright school children from those who are less gifted, the test underwent many revisions, culminating in the Stanford-Binet Intelligence Test for Children. Somewhat later, David Wechsler standardized individually administered intelligence tests for both adults and children. These tests include the Wechsler Adult Intelligence Scale (WAIS), the Wechsler Intelligence Scale for Children (WISC), and the Wechsler Preschool and Primary Scale of Intelligence (WPPSI).

The Wechsler Scales provide a total IQ (Intelligence Quotient) which is composed of two subscores: Verbal IQ and Performance IQ. Verbal IQ comprises such matters as vocabulary, ability to comprehend verbal statements and problems, and general information. Performance IQ measures intelligence in ways that are less dependent upon verbal ability, such as the ability to copy designs and to associate symbols with numbers.

Intelligence tests play an important role in assessing mental retardation and brain damage. Moreover, they are the only psychological tests that are routinely administered to school children and that determine, in some measure, the kind of education that children will obtain. It is important, therefore, to understand what intelligence tests actually measure.

Intelligence itself is not directly knowable. It can only be inferred from behavior, and it is inferred best from behavior on standardized tasks. Intelligence tests sample certain behaviors, particularly those that predict success in school. Other behaviors, like the ability to make it "on the street" or the ability to appreciate classical music, are simply not measured. For that reason, intelligence has often been defined as what an intelligence test mea-

This client is being given an intelligence test by a psychologist. (Photograph by Constantine Manos/ © Magnum Photos, Inc.)

sures. That is not quite a satisfying definition, but it is accurate. If one's working definition of intelligence differs from the one that is implicit in a particular intelligence test, one should not be surprised that the test score fails to meet expectations. An intelligence test that measures verbal facility will not predict well ability on psychomotor tasks.

BEHAVIORAL ASSESSMENT

The assessment techniques reviewed so far—the interview, the standardized and projective tests, the intelligence test—have had one thing in common: all of them are verbal and all of them use words to portray psychological assets and liabilities. But words are often imprecise. Often they overstate the matter. Depressed people are wont to say that "My life is just miserable all the time," an expression that conveys the full sense of their feelings right now, but no sense at all of what the problem is, how often it occurs, and how to begin working on it. In marital conflict, for example, the following complaints are not uncommon:

HE: She never has a meal on the table on time.

SHE: He never takes me out.

Both clearly believe what they are saying and their beliefs amplify their anger with each other. The beliefs, however, are false. When they begin to take notice of actual behavior, rather than accusations, they find that most (but not all) of the meals are on the table on time, and they go out with some frequency (but not as often as she would like). Already the gap between them has narrowed, creating a smaller disagreement out of what seemed to be a major conflict.

More than a quarter century ago, Wendell Johnson (1946; cited in Goldfried and Davison, 1976) captured the significance of behavioral assessment for treatment:

To say that Henry is mean implies that he has some sort of inherent trait, but it tells us nothing about what Henry has done. Consequently, it fails to suggest any specific means of improving Henry. If, on the other hand, it is said that Henry snatched Billy's cap and threw it in the bonfire, the situation is rendered somewhat more clear and actually more hopeful. You might never eliminate "meanness," but there are fairly definite steps to be taken in order to remove Henry's incentives or opportunities for throwing caps in bonfires . . . (What needs to be done) . . . is to get the person to tell him not what he *is* or what he *has,* but what he *does,* and the conditions under which he does it.

Behavioral assessment is commonly used in conjunction with treatment itself: to define the problem, to narrow it, to provide a record of what needs to be changed, and subsequently, of what progress has been made. The assessment does not stand apart from the treatment, nor is it an evaluation of the client for the therapist's use only. It is rather, part and parcel of the treatment, a procedure of interest to both client and therapist, and one in which they fully share.

Behavioral assessment consists in keeping as accurate a record as possible of the behaviors and thoughts one wishes to change: when they occur (incidence), how long they last (duration), and where possible, how intense they are. When the assessment includes, not only the behaviors, but also the stimuli that are presumed either to increase or decrease the incidence of those behaviors, the assessment is called a *functional analysis.*

A person might report, for example, that she becomes nervous when she has to speak in public. If a fairly precise measure of how nervous she becomes were required, she could be asked to deliver a speech publicly (Paul, 1966). One could then record, in good detail, not only how anxious she was —in blocks of thirty seconds throughout her speech—but what forms the anxiety took, utilizing the assessment form shown in Figure 9-5. Moreover, the overall degree of anxiety could be assessed by summing the scores on each of the twenty variables.

Behavioral assessment can also be done by clients themselves. People who desire to give up smoking are commonly asked to begin by recording when and under what conditions they smoke each cigarette. People who desire to lose weight are asked to record when, where, how much, and under what conditions they eat. Assessments by clients are not only useful for overt behaviors, but for private thoughts as well. Mahoney (1971), for example, asked a client to record each time she had a self-critical thought. Her record became the basis for evaluating whether subsequent interventions had any effect.

Sometimes behavioral assessment reveals causes for distress of which the respondent was unaware and that were not elicited in the interview. Metcalfe (1956; cited in Mischel, 1976) asked a patient who was hospitalized for asthma, but free to take leave from the hospital, to keep a careful record of the incidence, duration, and the events surrounding her asthma attacks. Attacks occurred on fifteen of the eighty-five days during which records were kept. Nine of the attacks occurred after contact with her mother. Moreover, on 80 percent of the days in which she had no asthma attacks, she also had had no contact with her mother. But while "contact with mother" seemed to be a source of the attacks, attempts to induce an attack by *discussing* her mother during an interview, or by presenting the patient with mother-relevant TAT cards, were unsuccessful. Because words, as symbols of experience, sometimes do not elicit the behaviors that the direct experiences

Figure 9-5
Behavior assessment form. This behavior rating form permits assessment of speech anxiety. Each time period is thirty seconds long. Evidence of any of the twenty anxiety-relevant behaviors during each time period is indicated by a (✔) in the relevant boxes. (Source: Paul, 1966)

Behavior observed	Time period 1	2	3	4	5	6	7	8	Σ
1. Paces									
2. Sways									
3. Shuffles feet									
4. Knees tremble									
5. Extraneous arm and hand movement (swings, scratches, toys, etc.)									
6. Arms rigid									
7. Hands restrained (in pockets, behind back, clasped)									
8. Hand tremors									
9. No eye contact									
10. Face muscles tense (drawn, tics, grimaces)									
11. Face "deadpan"									
12. Face pale									
13. Face flushed (blushes)									
14. Moistens lips									
15. Swallows									
16. Clears throat									
17. Breathes heavily									
18. Perspires (face, hands, armpits)									
19. Voice quivers									
20. Speech blocks or stammers									

themselves produce, interviews that rely heavily on words often fail to be fully diagnostic.

While behavioral assessment has clear advantages, it cannot be used with every psychological problem. Sometimes, tracking behavior in the required detail is simply too costly or time-consuming. Often, when the tracking is done by the client alone, the assessment fails for lack of motivation or precision. Finally, there are situations in which behavioral assessment may not work well: covert behaviors such as thoughts and feelings are not as amenable to reliable assessments as are overt behaviors.

Psychophysiological Assessments

Some abnormal psychological states are reflected in physiological ones, while others grow directly out of physiological disorder. Careful diagnosis and treatment of abnormality therefore often requires psychophysiological assessment, which has become increasingly sophisticated during the past decade. The treatment of both physical tension and some sexual disorders has been enhanced by using psychophysiological assessment.

Anxiety, fear, and tension often have physiological correlates. When people are anxious, they may feel it in their muscles or in the way they breathe or perspire. Psychophysiological assessment, not only confirms whether there is a physiological component to the anxiety, but how intense that component is, and whether treatment affects it. Indeed, some treatments can actually be pegged to psychophysiological changes. Biofeedback proceeds by alerting the client to small psychophysiological changes, and to the psychological states that bring them about. Tension headaches often arise from contraction of frontalis muscles. Those contractions can be directly measured through the use of an *electromyagraph* (EMG) and communicated to the client. As the client is trained to relax, he can immediately see the effects of that relaxation on the EMG, and he can gradually eliminate muscle tension and headache by using the techniques he has learned (Budzinski, Stoyva, Adler, and Mullaney, 1973).

This client is being alerted to psychophysiological changes through the use of an electromyagraph. (Courtesy Dr. Steve Wolf, Emory University)

Physiological difficulties commonly accompany sexual disorders, too. Among men, the inability to become sexually aroused is often manifested in the failure of the penis to become engorged with blood and therefore to become erect. In women, absence of sexual excitement is evidenced in the failure of the vaginal walls to become engorged. In both men and women, these conditions can be measured with considerable precision with devices that are called *genital plethysmographs.* A penile plethysmograph consists of a thin circular tube that contains a small amount of mercury. The tube is placed around the penis. As the penis became engorged, the pressure on the tube increases. The vaginal plethysmograph is shaped like a tampon and has a light at the upper end. The light reflects from the vaginal walls and provides a measure of the degree to which the walls are engorged. Increases in sexual arousal due to treatment can easily be detected on these psychophysiological instruments.

DIAGNOSIS

The first hallmark of a good assessment instrument—whether it is a structured or unstructured interview, an objective or projective test, or a behavioral rating system—is its *reliability.* Will two skilled users obtain the same findings? And provided nothing changes, will the test impressions obtained at one time be similar to those obtained at a later date? These are the first issues with which one is concerned. But they are not the only issues. Equally important are the purposes for which the test is being used. The purpose of assessment is to understand people, and one form of understanding is categorization, or *diagnosis.* We turn now to an examination of the reasons for, and nature of, diagnosis.

REASONS FOR DIAGNOSIS

Properly executed, diagnosis is a long and complicated procedure. What does one gain from careful diagnosis? There are four important reasons to make a diagnosis: (1) diagnosis is a communication shorthand, (2) it tells something about treatment, (3) it may communicate etiology, and (4) it aids scientific investigations.

Communication Shorthand

As we will shortly see, troubled people often have a host of symptoms. They may, for example, have trouble keeping their thoughts straight, often feel that people are out to get them, be unable to go to work, feel tense all the time, and have visual hallucinations. And they may be troubled by each of these symptoms simultaneously. A single diagnosis, in this case paranoid schizophrenia, incorporates all of these symptoms. Rather than going down an endless list of troubles, the diagnostician can merely indicate the syndrome (that is, the collection of symptoms that run together) in the single phrase: paranoid schizophrenia.

Treatment Possibilities

There is an ever-increasing fund of treatments available for psychological distress, and most are specific to certain disorders. Diagnosis enables the clinician to concentrate on the handful of treatments that might be useful in particular situations. Paranoid schizophrenia, for example, does not yield readily to verbal psychotherapies, nor is it effectively treated by Valium. But paranoid schizophrenics often respond well to a drug called chlorpromazine. A good diagnosis, then, suggests a small number of treatments that might alleviate the symptoms.

Etiology

People's problems arise from an infinity of sources, but certain problems are more reliably associated with particular causes or etiologies. For example, psychodynamic theorists believe that an anxiety neurosis arises from the anxiety that is spawned by poorly repressed conflicts and wishes. Knowing the diagnosis may tell something about the underlying cause.

Aid to Scientific Investigations

Abnormal psychology and psychiatry are developing sciences that have yet to discover all the causes and cures of human misery. By collecting together people with like symptoms, diagnosis allows psychological investigators to learn what those symptoms have in common by way of etiology and treatment. Indeed, for a developing science, this may be the single most important function of diagnosis.

HISTORICAL ORIGINS

The psychological diagnosis of personality has a long and interesting history. The Greeks, for example, recognized such diagnoses as senility (a disorder of aging), alcoholism, mania, melancholia (or depression), and paranoia. Many of these early diagnoses are still used today. Later, during the Middle Ages, it was widely believed that psychological disorders were caused by demons, and many different demonic "diagnoses" were described in such books as *The Witches' Hammer* (see Chapter 2).

The formal classification of human abnormalities, modeled upon biological classification of plants and animals, began with Philippe Pinel (1745–1826), the psychiatric reformer. He divided psychological disorders into melancholia, mania with and without delirium, dementia, and idiotism—a classification system that was to undergo many revisions and refinements during the next two centuries.

The first comprehensive system of classification of psychological disorders was created in 1896 by Emil Kraepelin (1856–1926). He believed that mental disorders have the same basis as physical ones and that the same diagnostic criteria and procedures should be applied to them. Above all, he insisted that diagnosis of mental disorders ought to be based on *symptoms* in much the sense that diagnosis of physical disorders proceeds from a careful assessment of physical symptoms. He might have stressed alternative bases for diagnosis such as drives, social deviance, level of adjustment, or social efficacy. But those bases were either merely inferred or social rather than physical. Inspired by the notion that there was a purely *physical* basis to psychological disorder, he proceeded to give psychological diagnosis the flavor of medical diagnosis, a flavor it still retains today.

Kraepelin's was not the only diagnostic system used for mental disorders. Early in the twentieth century, other clinicians, among them Eugen Bleuler, Adolf Meyer, and Ernst Kretschmer suggested other systems. Each of these systems enjoyed some popularity, with the result that different languages of diagnosis were invented and often used simultaneously. But because one basic function of diagnosis is communication, it is important to have a single and widely accepted language. This need for communication led to the creation, in 1952, of the first *Diagnostic and Statistical Manual of Mental Disorders* (DSM). Approved by the American Psychiatric Association, it was refined and ultimately replaced by DSM-II in 1968. DSM-II, however, was plagued by low reliability. When asked to diagnose a troubled person, diagnosticians had great difficulty agreeing with each other, and often they agreed no more than they would have by chance (Beck et al., 1962; Rosenhan, 1975; Spitzer, 1975). Those problems alone dictated the need for a new diagnostic system, one that took quite a different approach to diagnosis than did the one that originated with Kraepelin. The results of this new approach were published in 1980, in what is called DSM-III (more formally, *Diagnostic and Statistical Manual of Mental Disorders,* Third Edition).

Emil Kraepelin (1856–1926) created the first comprehensive system of classification of psychological disorders. (Courtesy National Library of Medicine)

The Diagnostic and Statistical Manual (DSM-III)

A task force of eminent mental health professionals was appointed by the American Psychiatric Association to develop the DSM-III. Its members needed, first of all, to consider what is meant by a **mental disorder.** Understandably, there was considerable debate about this issue, and it took considerable time to arrive at a consensus. The view of the task force was that a mental disorder was a behavioral or psychological pattern that either *caused* the individual distress or *disabled* the individual in one or more significant areas of functioning. In addition, one had to be able to infer that there was a genuine **dysfunction,** and not merely a disturbance between the individual and society. The latter is social deviance, and social deviance is not a mental disorder. The full definition of mental disorder is given in Box 9-1.

Beyond defining mental disorder, DSM-III sought to provide specific and operational diagnostic criteria for each mental disorder. In large measure, the unreliability of previous diagnostic systems, especially DSM-II, arose from the fact that its definitions were vague and imprecise. For example, DSM-II described a depressive episode, but left it to the diagnostician to determine what precisely an "episode" consisted of. The definition left unresolved such practical questions as: Would a one-hour depressive experience qualify? Would depression that continued for a month be considered more than a single episode? DSM-III took much of the guesswork out of this by offering sharper definitions. With regard to a major depressive episode, for example, it states that, "Each of at least four of the following symptoms have been present nearly every day for a period of at least two weeks . . .," and it lists eight different symptoms. It was hoped that the use of functional definitions would contribute to the reliability of diagnosis.

In DSM-III, diagnosis is not a single classifying statement, but rather it consists of multidimensional diagnostic guides. All told, there are five dimensions or axes that should be used, not only to classify a disorder, but to help plan treatment and predict outcome (see Appendix for Axes I and II categories and codes). This is an advance over former diagnostic systems that were used merely to classify individuals. DSM-III provides useful information for functional diagnoses on the following axes:

• *Axis I—Clinical syndromes.* The florid and fairly traditional clinical labels are included here, among them such familiar diagnostic terms as paranoid schizophrenia, major depression, and the various anxiety disorders. Also included on this axis are conditions that are *not* mental disorders as defined in DSM-III but that may nevertheless require treatment. Among the latter are school, marital, and occupational problems that do not arise from psychological sources.

• *Axis II—Personality disorders and specific development disorders.* Here are included disorders that are not listed on Axis I but that often accompany Axis I disorders. Often, such disorders are overlooked by the diagnostician. Listing them as a separate axis ensures that they will be attended to. Axis I and II, then, comprise all of the psychological diagnoses.

• *Axis III—Physical disorders and conditions.* All medical problems that may be relevant to the psychological ones are listed here.

· *Axis IV—Psychosocial stressors.* Included here are sources of difficulty during the past year, or anticipated difficulties such as retirement, which may be contributing to the individual's present difficulties.

· *Axis V—Highest level of adaptive functioning during the past year.* The level of adaptive functioning in the recent past has powerful prognostic significance, since individuals commonly return to their highest level of functioning when their psychological difficulties become less intense. The assessment on Axis V considers three areas: social relations with family and friends, occupational functioning, and use of leisure time.

Information gathered along all five axes can yield greater understanding about a person's difficulty than can a simple descriptive diagnosis based on Axis I. Here is an example of the way a DSM-III diagnosis would look using the multiple axes approach (DSM-III, p. 30):

Axis I:	296.23	Major Depression, Single Episode, with Melancholia
	303.93	Alcohol Dependence, In Remission
Axis II:	301.60	Dependent Personality Disorder (Provisional, rule out Borderline Personality Disorder)
Axis III:	Alcoholic cirrhosis of liver	
Axis IV:	Psychosocial stressors: anticipated retirement and change in residence with loss of contact with friends	
	Severity: 4—Moderate	
Axis V:	Highest level of adaptive functioning past year: 3—Good	

Comparing DSM-II and DSM-III

The number of psychological diagnoses nearly doubled between the publication of DSM-II and DSM-III. To the outsider, it might appear that a vast number of mental disorders had been discovered in the twelve-year period between 1968, when DSM-II was published, and 1980, when DSM-III appeared. But this is not so. Much of the difference in the number of available diagnoses arises from the greater precision and detail in DSM-III. Where DSM-II was, in some cases, content with a single designation, DSM-III divided many disorders into several categories. In the following example, notice how *phobic neurosis* has been broken down into several discrete and more exact subgroups.

DSM-II		*DSM-III*
300.2 Phobic neurosis	300.21	Agoraphobia with panic attacks
	300.22	Agoraphobia without panic attacks
	300.23	Social phobia
	300.29	Simple phobia
	309.21	Separation anxiety disorder

But other DSM-III diagnoses reflect a *broadening* of the diagnostic umbrella, a tendency to include as psychological disorders a group of behaviors and difficulties that either escaped diagnostic attention earlier or were questionably diagnosed. Consider the following:

DSM-II	*DSM-III*
306.1 Specific learning disturbance	315.00 Developmental reading disorder
	315.10 Developmental arithmetic disorder
	315.31 Developmental language disorder
	315.39 Developmental articulation disorder
	315.50 Mixed specific developmental disorder

Here, one effect of expanding the DSM-II category was to include a host of problems—with reading, arithmetic, and speech—that were not previously thought of as mental disorders, and whose remediation was, indeed, in the province of schools rather than psychiatrists and psychologists (Garmezy, 1977a).

Finally, there were new diagnoses of behaviors that previously were not considered mental disorders but now clearly are considered as such: "305.1 Tobacco Dependence" is one such mental disorder. It was included in DSM-III for several reasons: tobacco has deleterious effects on physical health; many individuals are unable to control the habit; and suffering accompanies the withdrawal of tobacco. Another new diagnosis, "305.1 Phencyclidine Abuse," is included because of the rising popularity of this substance (PCP or "angel dust"). In 1968, its usage had been uncommon.

Generally, the greater number of diagnoses in DSM-III results from its greater specificity, an enlarged tendency to include ambiguous patterns of behavior as mental disorders, and the rise of a few new disorders during the period of time between 1968 and 1980.

The Reliability of DSM-III

DSM-II was badly flawed by problems of reliability. Experienced diagnosticians using DSM-II found they could not agree with each other. In some instances, interjudge reliability was so low as to make a diagnostic category functionally useless. Indeed, Spitzer and Fliess (1974), in a review of all of the reliability studies of DSM-II, found that only three broad categories were sufficiently reliable to be clinically useful: mental retardation, alcoholism, and organic brain syndrome. These are fairly broad categories, and when diagnosticians attempted to use finer categories—to distinguish the different kinds of alcoholism or brain damage, for example—the diagnostic reliability fell further.

The compilers of DSM-III hoped to change all that, as we have seen, by making the categories much more specific and precise, and by having criteria for both including and excluding behaviors and people. Even more important, however, was the intention of conducting reliability studies *before* DSM-III was issued (rather than afterwards, as was the case with DSM-II) in order to minimize reliability errors. Reliability studies were in fact conducted, but they did not turn out quite as well as one would have hoped. Practicing clinicians were asked to examine the same patients and to arrive at independent diagnoses. They were asked not to confer before arriving at a diagnosis and to submit their findings to the research committee even if they later learned that they had disagreed. Unfortunately, there was no mechanism to prevent collaborative discussions before the clinicians arrived at a diagnosis, nor was there any way to prevent discussion after they arrived at different diagnoses. In addition, it is impossible to know whether they sent in their discrepant diagnoses as consistently as their nondiscrepant ones. Thus, while the official reliabilities of DSM-III, as they emerged from these studies, are substantially higher than those of DSM-II, there is still some question about their acceptability. This is especially true of the diagnosis of children's disorders as well as of diagnoses in the narrower diagnostic categories.

The Validity of DSM-III

The validity of an instrument is a measure of its ultimate usefulness, whether it does what it is supposed to do. People who obtain high scores on a good test of clerical ability, for example, should perform better in clerical tasks than those who obtain low scores. With regard to systems of diagnosis such as DSM-III, we want to know whether the diagnostic categories satisfy the central functions of clinical diagnosis. Do they facilitate communication by describing patients, and particularly by differentiating patients in one category from those in another? This is called *descriptive validity.* Do diagnostic categories enable one to predict the course and especially the outcome of treatment? This is called *outcome* or *predictive validity* (Blashfield and Draguns, 1976).

DESCRIPTIVE VALIDITY.   To the extent that DSM-III resembles its forebears, DSM-I and DSM-II, its descriptive validity is problematic. Most clinicians, when told that a patient is schizophrenic, for example, do not seem to get a rich sense of how that person will think, feel, and act. This failure has less to do with their imaginativeness and much more to do with the way clinical categories are used. A study by Zigler and Phillips (1961) exemplifies this problem. They investigated the relationship between the symptoms that patients presented to diagnosticians and the diagnoses that were made. In all, 793 patients were diagnosed in four broad categories: neurotic, manic-depressive, character disorder, and schizophrenic. Then the symptoms that these patients experienced were examined. Table 9-2 shows the results. A person whose symptom was "depressed" was likely to be diagnosed "manic-depressive." But he or she was also just as likely to be diagnosed "neurotic." Even of those diagnosed schizophrenic, better than one-quarter were likely to be depressed. Thus, the evidence from this study strongly suggests that diagnosis does not convey the kind of information about symptoms that might allow one to differentiate one patient from the other, or to have a reliable sense of what symptoms that patient has.

Perhaps that is the way it should be. After all, diagnosis does not proceed by simply listing symptoms and hoping they will *add* up to a particular diagnosis. Rather, a diagnosis emerges from a *pattern* of symptoms and from the current state of scientific understanding of abnormality. In the realm of physical disorder, "fever" yields a different diagnosis according to

Table 9-2 PERCENTAGE OF INDIVIDUALS IN TOTAL SAMPLE AND IN EACH
DIAGNOSTIC CATEGORY MANIFESTING EACH SYMPTOM

Symptom	Total Hospital (N = 793)	Manic-Depressive (N = 75)	Psychoneurotic (N = 152)	Character Disorder (N = 279)	Schizophrenic (N = 287)
Depressed	38	64	58	31	28
Tense	37	32	46	33	36
Suspiciousness	35	25	16	17	65
Drinking	19	17	14	32	8
Hallucinations	19	11	4	12	35
Suicidal attempt	16	24	19	15	12
Suicidal ideas	15	29	23	15	8
Bodily complaints	15	21	21	5	19
Emotional outburst	14	17	12	18	9
Withdrawn	14	4	12	7	25
Perplexed	14	9	9	8	24
Assaultive	12	5	6	18	5
Self-depreciatory	12	16	16	8	13
Threatens assault	10	4	11	14	7
Sexual preoccupation	10	9	9	6	14
Maniacal outburst	9	11	6	7	12
Bizarre ideas	9	11	1	2	20
Robbery	8	0	3	18	3
Apathetic	8	8	8	4	11
Irresponsible behavior	7	3	7	9	7
Headaches	6	7	10	4	5
Perversions (except homosexuality)	5	0	5	10	2
Euphoria	5	17	2	2	5
Fears own hostile impulses	5	4	9	5	2
Mood swings	5	9	5	4	4
Insomnia	5	11	7	3	5
Psychosomatic disorders	4	7	6	3	5
Does not eat	4	9	4	2	4
Lying	3	0	1	7	0
Homosexuality	3	3	3	8	2
Rape	3	0	3	8	1
Obsessions	3	8	3	1	4
Depersonalization	3	4	1	0	6
Feels perverted	3	0	3	1	5
Phobias	2	4	5	0	2

SOURCE: Zigler and Phillips, 1961, p. 71.

whether it is accompanied by a stuffed nose, swollen glands, or acute stomach pains. Similarly, symptoms such as "depressed" and "tense" mean different things when they are accompanied by other symptoms and form different patterns. Of course, this view of the diagnostic process only underscores the fact that summary diagnoses, such as schizophrenia and personality disorder do not convey much information about a person.

OUTCOME VALIDITY. A diagnostic system with good outcome or predictive validity should tell something about the future course of the disorder, and about what gave rise to the disorder. Will the problem respond to particular kinds of treatment? Will the affected individual be violent or suicidal? What kinds of early childhood experiences are likely to bring about the disorder? These are the kinds of questions that can be answered if a diagnostic system has high outcome validity.

Outcome validity is many-faceted. The validity of a system depends on the questions that are asked. The predictive validity for "296.6 Bipolar Affective Disorder, Mixed" is quite high when the disorder is treated with a drug called lithium. Here, the diagnosis performs a fine predictive function, in that a specific treatment is mandated. So, too, does "302.7 Premature Ejaculation," in that the disorder responds well to specific behavioral and social learning treatments. In these instances, the diagnosis indicates a treatment that has a high probability of succeeding. Unfortunately, in most diagnostic situations merely having a diagnosis is of limited use. Often, the diagnosis does not dictate a particular course of treatment, nor can the outcome of particular treatments be predicted. Moreover, the diagnosis does not say much about the causes of the disorder. When much more is learned about the nature of particular forms of abnormality, we may be able to say that a particular diagnostic scheme is valid. But right now, the predictive validity of many diagnostic categories of the DSM-III and its predecessors is still an open question.

CONDITIONS THAT BIAS DIAGNOSES

Psychological diagnoses are not at all like medical diagnoses. In the latter, there are physical data to support the final judgment. These include fever, X-ray results, and palpation. Often surgery and laboratory reports back up the diagnosis. Psychological diagnosis is quite different. No evidence of psychological disorder can be found in feces, or blood, or on X rays. You cannot palpate psychological disorder or see its physical presence. The evidence for psychological disorder is always transient, and highly subject to a variety of social psychological considerations. Three of the most important influences on diagnoses are context, expectation, and source credibility.

Context

The context in which a behavior is observed can dramatically affect the meaning that is ascribed to it (Asch, 1951; Gergen, 1982). In one study, a group of people who were free from major psychological symptoms *simulated* a particularly idiosyncratic symptom to the admitting doctors at general psychiatric hospitals. The "patients" alleged that they heard a voice—nothing particularly idiosyncratic about that—and that the voice said "dull," "empty," and "thud." Now *those* particular verbalizations were quite idiosyncratic, but nothing else about these people was unusual. Indeed, they had been carefully instructed to behave as they commonly behave, and to give truthful answers to all questions, except those that dealt with their auditory hallucinations. Had they been outside of the hospital context, their simulation would have been detected, or at least suspected. Surely someone would have indicated that this single symptom with no accompanying symptoms was strange indeed. But that did not happen in the hospitals in which these patients sought admission. Rather, they were admitted mainly with the diagnosis of schizophrenia, and they were discharged with the diagnosis of schizophrenia in remission. The fact that most patients in hospitals who hallucinate are schizophrenics created a compelling context for these pseudopatients to be considered schizophrenics. Although their symptoms were not those of schizophrenia, the context of the symptoms mattered more in the diagnosis than did the symptoms themselves (Rosenhan, 1973).

Not only hospital settings, but the diagnoses themselves can constitute contexts that admit certain kinds of information and interpretations, bias other kinds, and disallow still others. For example, once the pseudopatients were admitted to the hospital, they of course began to observe their surroundings carefully and to take copious notes on their observations. Patients asked them what they were writing. Soon the patients concluded that the writers were not patients at all, but rather were journalists or college professors doing a study of the hospital. It was not an especially ingenious inference for the patients to make, since the pseudopatients did in fact behave quite differently than many of the real patients did. But the staff, on the other hand, made no such inference. They too noted that the pseudopatients often wrote. "Patient engages in writing behavior," the staff recorded about a particular patient. But they interpreted his writing within the context of the diagnosis itself, viewed the writing as yet another confirming bit of psychopathology, and closed off any explanation that lay outside of the diagnostic context.

Similar findings about the effects of contexts are demonstrated in a study in which clinicians were shown a videotape of a young man talking to an older, bearded man about his feelings and experiences in various jobs (Langer and Abelson, 1974). Some of the mental health professionals were told that the young man was a job applicant, while the others were told that he was a clinical patient. After seeing the videotape, all were asked for their observations about the young man. Those who saw the "job applicant" found him "attractive and conventional looking," "candid and innovative," an "upstanding middle-class citizen type." Those who saw the "patient" described him as a "tight, defensive person," "dependent, passive, aggressive," and "frightened of his own aggressive impulses."

In this study, the different labels—"job applicant" and "patient"—created not only a context for perceiving the person but also for explaining his behavior. The therapists were asked: "What do you think might explain Mr. Smith's outlook on life? Do you think he is realistic?" Those who saw the "patient" offered such observations as "Doesn't seem to be realistic because he seems to use denial (and rationalization and intellectualization) to center his problems in situations and other people," "seems afraid of his own drives, motives . . . outlook not based on realities of "objective world." But those who saw the "job applicant" explained the identical behavior in a quite different way. "His attitudes are consistent with a large subculture in the U.S. . . . the silent majority," "he seems fairly realistic, fairly reality oriented; recognizes injustices of large systems but doesn't seem to think that he can individually do anything to change them."

The descriptive comments that were made by the clinicians were subsequently quantified by raters who had no knowledge about either the experimental conditions (patient or job applicant) or the hypotheses that guided

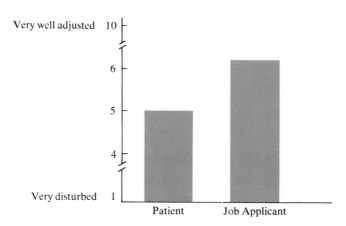

Figure 9-6
Overall adjustment ratings of "job applicant" and "patient"

this study. These raters were simply asked to score the comments on a scale that ranged from 1 (very disturbed) to 10 (very well adjusted). The data are provided in Figure 9-6. Context clearly affected the evaluations of adjustment, as well as the perception of the causes of the behavior.

Expectation

Whether a diagnostician is expecting to see a person in distress or a normal person may heavily influence diagnostic judgment. For example, one hospital administrator, having heard how easily the pseudopatients described earlier had been diagnosed as schizophrenic and had gained admission to a hospital, insisted that "it can't happen here." As a result, a simple study was devised (Rosenhan, 1973). The hospital was informed that sometime during the following three months, one or more pseudopatients would appear at the admissions office. During this period, each staff member—attendants, nurses, psychiatrists, and psychologists—was asked to rate each patient who sought admission or who was already on the ward, using a scale that indicated how likely it was that the patient was, in fact, a pseudopatient. More than 20 percent of the patients who were admitted for psychiatric treatment were judged, with high confidence, to be pseudopatients by at least one staff member, and nearly 10 percent were thought to be pseudopatients by two staff members. Set in the direction of finding a pseudopatient, they found many. In fact, not a single pseudopatient ever presented himself for admission—at least not from this study!

Source Credibility

Psychological diagnosis is particularly vulnerable to suggestions from "unimpeachable authorities." That vulnerability is demonstrated in a study in which groups of diagnosticians heard a taped interview of a man who seemed to be going through an especially happy and vigorous period in his life (Temerlin, 1970). His work was rewarding and going well, his relationships with others were cordial and gratifying, and he was happily married and enjoyed sexual relations. He was also entirely free of the symptoms that commonly generate a psychiatric diagnosis: depression, anxiety, psychosomatic symptoms, suspiciousness, hostility, and thought disturbance. After listening to the interview, one group of diagnosticians heard a respected au-

Table 9-3 EFFECTS OF "AUTHORITATIVE" SUGGESTIONS ON PERCEPTIONS OF MENTAL HEALTH

Suggestion	Percent indicating		
	Very disturbed	Somewhat distressed	Healthy
"Disturbed"			
Psychologically trained			
diagnosticians	29	53	8
Untrained diagnosticians	27	58	15
"Healthy"	0	0	100
"Job interview"	0	29	71
No suggestion	0	43	57

SOURCE: Temerlin, 1970.

thority say that the man seemed neurotic but was actually "quite psychotic." Other diagnosticians heard the same authority say that the person was quite healthy. Yet others heard someone on the tape say that it was an interview for a job. The results of this study, shown in Table 9-3, are quite dramatic. Psychologically trained diagnosticians—psychiatrists, psychologists, and clinical psychology graduate students—were highly influenced by the assertions that this man might be quite disturbed. Indeed, they were somewhat more influenced by that assertion than were untrained diagnosticians, including law students and undergraduates. Correspondingly, when a composite group of diagnosticians (including both trained and untrained ones) was told that the individual was "healthy," their diagnoses mentioned no evidence of disturbance.

EVALUATING PSYCHOLOGICAL DIAGNOSES

Patently, there is a good deal that needs to be improved about psychological diagnosis. It is often unreliable: equally expert diagnosticians arrive at different diagnoses of the same individual. This is, of course, a problem in medicine too, but it is much more prevalent in psychological diagnosis since, as we mentioned earlier, there are few physical guideposts to support the psychological diagnostic effort. Psychological diagnosis, moreover, is not always valid, for it often fails to suggest a clear-cut and useful treatment, and to communicate a known cause of the disorder. And, as we have said, psychological diagnosis is vulnerable to context, expectation, and source credibility effects.

But can we do without diagnosis? Absolutely not. In the first place, seeing itself involves categorization. As we read these words, we may be aware that we are reading words (a categorization) rather than merely black ink (a categorization) on white paper (another categorization). And diagnosis is just another word for categorization, one that arises from a medical model. Second, and more important, there can be no science and no advance in understanding abnormality, without somehow segregating one kind of abnormality from another. That you recall, is what initiated the understanding and, subsequently, the cure for general paresis (Chapter 3). Diagnosing general paresis as something quite different from other mental disorders ultimately made the treatment breakthrough possible. Without diagnosis, that advance would not have been possible.

We cannot live without diagnosis, but this does not mean that every diagnosis is accurate, or that every diagnostic term in DSM-III truly reflects illness or mental disorder. The accuracy and utility of any diagnosis needs to be demonstrated. Indeed, as scientific understanding progresses, we come to understand which diagnoses are useful and which are not. Some diagnoses already have proven usefulness and precision. They are already reliable and valid. Most, however, are promising at best. Eventually, they may shed light on the nature and treatment of particular kinds of psychological distress. Meanwhile, however, they are necessary if research is to proceed, with their utility mainly residing in their promise as **research diagnoses** (i.e., hunches that may prove useful in communicating about people and in treating them). The difference between a research and clinical diagnosis is very important; it rests on the reliability and validity of the diagnosis (Rosenhan, 1975). The remaining chapters of the book describe what is known about disorders for which we have fairly reliable diagnostic information.

SUMMARY

1. Personality assessment techniques may be divided into three processes: interviewing, testing, and observing. Assessment devices must be reliable and valid. *Reliability* refers to the stability of a measure, whether it yields the same findings with repeated use. *Validity* refers to how useful the device is, whether it can be used for the purposes for which it is intended.

2. When two psychologists arrive at the same assessment of a patient, there is said to be interjudge *reliability.*

3. The clinical interview may be structured and have questions prepared in an *interview schedule,* or it may be unstructured and therefore more flexible.

4. Psychological tests fall into three categories: *psychological inventories,* including the MMPI, the Q-sort, and the Rep Test; *projective tests,* including the Rorschach and the TAT; and *intelligence tests,* including the WAIS and the WISC. All of these are verbal tests and use words to portray psychological assets and liabilities.

5. *Behavioral assessment* is used in conjunction with treatment. It consists of a record of the patient's behavior and thoughts—their incidence, duration, and intensity. A *functional analysis* assesses the behavior and the stimuli affecting that behavior.

6. *Psychophysiological assessment* confirms whether there is a physiological component to abnormal psychological states—how intense it is and whether treatment affects it.

7. *Diagnosis* is the categorization of psychological disorders according to behavioral or psychological patterns. To be useful, or valid, the diagnosis should describe the patient's status, predict the course of the difficulty (with or without treatment), or aid in deepening our understanding of abnormality.

8. DSM-III is a multidimensional diagnostic guide. It seeks to provide specific and operational diagnostic criteria for each mental disorder. Within

DSM-III, there are five dimensions, or axes, to classify a disorder and to help plan treatment and predict outcome.

9. *Descriptive validity* refers to whether a diagnosis successfully differentiates patients in one category from those in another. *Outcome* or *predictive validity* refers to whether the diagnosis tells something about the future course of the disorder, what gave rise to the disorder, and whether the disorder will respond to treatment.

10. The accuracy and usefulness of a diagnosis may be compromised by the *context* in which it occurs and by the *expectations* and *credibility* of the diagnosticians and their informants.

11. Diagnosis and assessment are fundamental to treatment and necessary for scientific advancement. However, that does not mean that every assessment is useful or necessary.

Part IV

ANXIETY AND PSYCHOSOMATIC DISORDERS

CHAPTER 10

Fear and Phobia:
Anxiety Observed

WE now begin our discussion of the particular psychological disorders themselves. In this chapter and Chapter 11, we discuss the disorders that have been called "neuroses." In this chapter, we consider the disorders in which anxiety is actually felt by the victim. In Chapter 11, we will deal with the neuroses in which anxiety generally is not felt, although its existence can be inferred from the patient's symptoms. In Chapter 12, we will consider the psychosomatic disorders, in which an organic problem can be exacerbated or even started by anxiety and other psychological events.

NEUROSIS DEFINED

What is a neurosis? What are the neurotic disorders? What is neurotic behavior? The term "neurosis" was first used in the eighteenth century by William Cullen, a Scottish physician. Cullen's approach was biomedical; he guessed that the nervous system was the part of the body causing emotional disturbance. This belief prevailed until the twentieth century when Freud rejected it and claimed that neurosis resulted from anxiety. Freud believed that conflict between the ego and the id generated anxiety and that neurotic symptoms resulted from an attempt to harness this anxiety (Freud, 1924). In 1980, DSM-III redefined the term "neurosis." In contrast to Freud, DSM-III uses the term only to describe a class of disorders; it disregards the issue of whether the disorders are caused by anxiety.

NEUROSIS AND ANXIETY

Freud not only used the term "neurosis" to *describe* emotionally distressing symptoms in an individual whose reality testing was intact, but he also used the term to refer to the *process* of defending against anxiety. He thought that this underlying process in which an unconscious conflict produced anxiety, coped with by a malfunctioning defense mechanism, caused the neurotic symptom.

The distinction between description and process is a fundamental one. Consider the relation of a hard-boiled egg to an uncooked egg. We can *describe* how the symptoms of being a hard-boiled egg differ from the symptoms of being an uncooked egg: the white of the egg is actually white and not transparent; the yolk is solid and not liquid; the membrane of the egg can be peeled. Alternatively, we can talk about the *process* by which an uncooked egg becomes a hard-boiled egg: the uncooked egg is covered with water; heat is applied to the water until the water boils; the boiling water causes a chemical change in the white, the yolk, and the membrane of the egg. Similarly, in discussing a neurosis, *description* is a list of the symptoms of being neurotic, whereas *process* is the cause or etiology of becoming neurotic.

Freud saw two kinds of neurotics: (1) individuals with disorders in which anxiety was acutely felt, and (2) individuals with disorders in which no anxiety was felt, but in which anxiety was suspected as being the cause of the neurotic symptoms that were observed. Phobics, individuals who show irrational fear of specific objects, fall into the first category. When in the presence of the phobic object or when anticipating that he or she might be in its presence, the phobic is overcome with anxiety. On the other hand, conversion hysterics who lose the physical functioning of part of their body for psychological, rather than physical causes, are usually not anxious at all. Freud theorized that these individuals, although they could not be described by the presence of anxiety, showed the results of the neurotic process: their physical loss was a successful defense against underlying anxiety, and as such, anxiety was not seen.

Hans Eysenck, the British personality theorist, also views the neuroses as the result of anxiety. He argues that neuroticism is a major dimension of human personality and that varying degrees of neuroticism lie along a continuum—from normal to extremely neurotic. People at the end of this continuum have strong emotions that are easily aroused. They are moody, anxious, and restless. At the other end of this continuum are non-neurotic people. They are emotionally stable, calm, even-tempered, carefree, and reliable (Eysenck, 1952; Eysenck and Rachman, 1965). Eysenck claims that neuroticism can be genetically transmitted to one's offspring. Identical twins brought up either separately or together correspond more in their answers on questionnaires testing neuroticism than do fraternal twins (Shields, 1962).

In contrast to Freud and Eysenck, we will distinguish between neurosis when it is used as a description of symptoms, and when it is used to refer to a more speculative, causal process. Freud's distinction between neurotic disorders in which anxiety is felt versus neurotic disorders in which anxiety is inferred, however, is still very much with us. DSM-III calls both kinds of disorders "neurotic," retaining the term largely because it is already so widely used. DSM-III uses the term merely in its descriptive sense, without invoking a process or committing itself to any specific etiology for the disorder. Thus, as we shall see, it uses "neurosis" to describe symptoms that are distressing, recognized as unacceptable, with reality testing intact, and with symptoms that do not grossly violate social norms. Table 10-1 shows how Freud's categories relate to those of DSM-III.

Hans Eysenck (1916–   )
(Courtesy Dr. S. J. Rachman)

Table 10-1 NEUROSIS FOR FREUD AND DSM-III

Definition (Freud)	*Definition (DSM-III)*

Psychoneurosis
  descriptive
    1. distressing symptom
    2. intact reality testing
	Neurosis
	  descriptive
	    1. distressing and enduring symptom
	    2. symptom recognized as unacceptable
	    3. reality testing is intact
	    4. does not grossly violate social norms
	    5. not temporary reaction to stress
	    6. not organic

process
    1. unconscious conflict leads to
    2. anxiety leads to
    3. maladaptive defense mechanism
      leads to
    4. symptom
	process
	  none

Types (Freud)		*Types (DSM-III)*
Anxiety felt	Phobic Neurosis	Phobic Disorder
		Post-Traumatic Stress Disorder
	Anxiety Neurosis	Panic Disorder
		Generalized Anxiety Disorder
Anxiety inferred	Obsessive-Compulsive Neurosis	Obsessive-Compulsive Disorder

	Hysteria	The Somatoform Disorders
		  Conversion Disorder
		  Psychogenic Pain Disorder
		  Somatization Disorder
		The Dissociative Disorders
		  Amnesia
		  Fugue
		  Multiple Personality
		  Depersonalization Disorder

NEUROSIS VERSUS PSYCHOSIS

Neuroses, together with the psychoses, are the two overarching categories of abnormality. The most important use of the term "neurosis" is to mark off the class of disorders that are nonpsychotic. Thus, DSM-III uses "neurosis" to describe the emotionally painful disorders that leave thinking, perception, and reality testing intact, whereas it uses "psychosis" to denote the sweeping disturbances of perception, thinking, and reality testing.

Neurotic Disorders

An individual is considered to have a neurotic disorder if he (1) is emotionally distressed by enduring or recurrent symptoms, (2) finds the symptoms alien and wishes to be rid of them, (3) can test reality relatively well (unlike the psychotic), and (4) exhibits behavior that does not grossly violate social norms, although that behavior may be uncomfortable for others and extremely painful for the neurotic person. However, such a disorder is also distinguished by two features that it must *not* have: (1) it must not be a transient reaction to stress, and (2) it must not be the result of organic damage. The case of Phillipa provides a clear example of a neurosis:

> Phillipa was a twenty-eight-year-old graduate student who went into therapy to end a problem she called "noodging." She was intelligent, attractive, personable, and had no problem at all meeting men and beginning intimate relations with them. After knowing her for a few weeks or months, however, man after man fled. Her problem was sustaining love. Here was her pattern: as she and her latest friend spent more and more time together, she would one day fix on some small incident that she would interpret as a first sign of rejection. So, for example, Tim once failed to call her as he usually did during his lunch break. She panicked. When she saw Tim that evening, she noodged incessantly: "Do you love me, do you really love me? I love you so much I can't stand it when you don't call. Did you really not have a lunch break today, really?" She smothered him with her doubts and insecurities. This always began a cycle. The man would begin to back off. She would sense this rejection and noodge him even more. Within a few days of such escalation, the relationship would collapse.

Phillipa's problem has the four features of a neurosis: (1) it is a long-lasting problem that causes her great distress; (2) she is plagued by her thoughts of rejection and by her inability to stop noodging, and she has come to therapy to end them; (3) she is a clear-headed and intelligent individual who has no trouble at all with reality testing, except when it comes to rejection; (4) while her thoughts of rejection torment her and her noodging is self-destructive, noodging and insecurity do not violate social norms.

A hallmark of neurotic behavior is the discrepancy between how distressed an individual feels and his awareness that his distress is out of proportion to reality. The neurotic finds himself extremely anxious and cannot help it, although he knows the objective circumstances don't warrant such anxiety. He may find himself depressed, although he recognizes that objective circumstances are not enough to justify such sadness and pessimism. He knows he should act, but he finds himself paralyzed. Phillipa knows she should not noodge when she senses rejection, but she cannot help it.

Psychotic Disorders

In contrast with neurotics, psychotic individuals have disturbances of their higher mental processes—thinking, speaking, and testing reality—and their behavior violates social norms in a bizarre manner. Most prominent among the psychotic disorders is schizophrenia. Schizophrenia is characterized by an enduring and marked incoherence of thinking and speech, by global loss of contact with reality, by delusions, and by grossly disorganized behavior. These symptoms are accompanied by deterioration in working, in emotional relationships, and in taking care of self. Contrast Carl's problem (which we will discuss at length in Chapter 17) with Phillipa's problem.

> Carl was always an intensely shy, rather uncommunicative, and somewhat untidy young man. When he was twenty-seven, his roommate and only close friend, John, was killed in an automobile accident. Carl moved back into his parent's

home. He became more and more reclusive, exceedingly sloppy, and bizarre in his behavior. Finally, they took him to the hospital. In the hospital, Carl often showed inappropriate emotions. He smiled when he was uncomfortable, and he smiled even more when he was in pain. He cried during television comedies. He became frightened when people complimented him, and he roared with laughter on reading a story in which a young child burnt to death. He told his psychologist, "I am an unreal person. I am made of stone, or else I am made of glass. I am wired precisely wrong, precisely . . . . Never, ever, will you find the lever, the eternalever that will sever me forever with my real, seal, deal, heel."

In contrast with Phillipa's neurotic problem, Carl has a psychotic disorder in which his higher mental processes are grossly disturbed and in which his behavior grossly violates social norms.

FEAR AND ANXIETY

In Alfred Hitchcock's film *Psycho*, Vera Miles displayed the emergency reaction when she feared she would be killed. (Courtesy The Museum of Modern Art/Film Stills Archive)

There are four neurotic disorders in which fear and anxiety are actually felt by the individual, and these divide into two classes: the fear disorders and the anxiety disorders. Phobias and post-traumatic stress disorders constitute the fear disorders; in these disorders, a specific object causes the anxiety. In *phobic disorders*, the individual shows fear of an object (such as cats) which is out of all proportion to the reality of the danger that object presents. In *post-traumatic stress disorders*, the individual experiences anxiety, depression, numbing, and constant reliving of the trauma after experiencing some catastrophe beyond the normal range of human suffering. For example, an undergraduate who was raped in her dormitory may subsequently relive the trauma repeatedly in memory and in her dreams, becoming numb to the world around her and experiencing intense anxiety whenever she is alone with a man.

Panic disorder and generalized anxiety disorder are the anxiety disorders. In these two disorders, no specific danger or object threatens the individual, yet he or she still feels very anxious. In *panic disorder*, an individual is suddenly overwhelmed with brief attacks of anxiety, apprehension, and then terror. *Generalized anxiety disorder*, on the other hand, consists of chronic anxiety that can be more or less continually present for months on end.

All four of these disorders share in common an exaggerated version of the normal and adaptive fear that each of us has felt on many occasions. We begin our discussion of these disorders by examining what fear and anxiety are.

FEAR

All of us have experienced fear. The degree of danger we encounter has to do in large part with our job, where we live, and so on. Being a member of a team responsible for constructing an oil rig in the wintry North Sea opens one up to more danger than being an accountant. But an accountant living in New York City may experience more danger than one working in De Kalb, Illinois. When the oilman experiences fear, it is directly related to the danger of his situation; his reactions will be appropriate and normal. Similarly, the accountant's heart has every reason to beat rapidly upon hearing a

The degree of danger we encounter has to do in large part with the realities of our job. Construction workers of the sort shown here may experience considerable fear because the work is highly dangerous. (Photograph by Ray Skobe/Leo de Wys)

noise at the window at three o'clock in the morning. Normal fear and anxiety, unlike the disorders we will discuss in this chapter, are in keeping with the reality of the danger.

Elements of Fear

When we experience danger, we undergo the various somatic and emotional changes that make up the fear response. There are four elements to the fear response: (1) cognitive elements—expectations of impending harm; (2) somatic elements—the body's emergency reaction to danger, as well as changes in our appearance; (3) emotional elements—feelings of dread and terror and panic; and (4) behavioral elements—fleeing and fighting (Lang, 1967; Rachman, 1978). These four elements of the fear response are summarized in Table 10-2.

Fear may take several forms, and different elements may be involved. No two individuals need display the same elements of fear when they are afraid. Nor is there any particular element that must be present. Fear is diagnosed according to the following logic: (1) all of the elements need not be present; (2) some of the elements must be present, although there need not be the same combination every time; (3) no one element must be present; (4) the more intense any element and the more elements present, the more confident are we in labeling the state as "fear." What are each of these elements of fear?

The ***cognitive elements*** of fear are expectations of specific impending harm, usually in the immediate future. A large doberman growls menacingly at you. You think, "He's going to bite me," and you feel a surge of fear. On a dark and lonely street, you sense a sudden movement behind you. You think, "It's a mugger," and you freeze. You are unprepared at a recitation, and the teacher calls on you. You break into a cold sweat as you think, "I'm going to be humiliated."

Table 10-2 ELEMENTS OF FEAR

Cognitive
Thoughts of impending harm
Exaggerating the actual amount of danger

Somatic	
Paleness of skin	Bronchioles widen
Goosebumps	Pupils dilate
Tension of muscles	Sweat glands secrete
Face of fear	Coagulants and lymphocytes increase in blood
Heart rate increases	
Spleen contracts	Adrenaline is secreted from adrenal medulla
Respiration accelerates	
Respiration deepens	Stomach acid is inhibited
Peripheral vessels dilate	Loss of bladder and anal sphincter control
Liver releases carbohydrates	Salivation decreases

Emotional-Subjective	
Feelings of dread, terror, panic	Tight stomach
Queasiness and butterflies	Creeping sensations

Behavioral	
Appetitive responding decreases	Avoidance
Aversive responding increases	Freezing
Escape	Aggession

    Somatic or bodily reactions also occur when we are afraid. There are two classes of bodily changes: external changes and internal changes. Like the octopus, who changes from green to red when afraid, human appearance changes, often dramatically, when we are afraid. A keen observer will notice the changes in bodily surface: our skin becomes pale, goosebumps may form, beads of sweat appear on our forehead, the palms of our hands become clammy, our lips tremble and shiver, and our muscles tense. But, most salient of all, fear can be seen in our face (see Figure 10-1). In addition to the changes in appearance, there are internal changes within the body. In

Figure 10-1
The faces of fear. When individuals are afraid, their eyebrows are raised and drawn together, wrinkles appear in the center of their forehead, eyes are wide, and their mouth will open with the lips stretched and tense. (Source: Ekman and Friesen, 1975, p. 62)

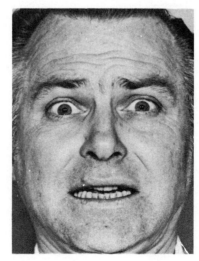
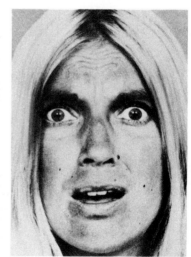

a matter of seconds after we perceive danger, our body's resources are mobilized in the *emergency reaction*; these internal changes are the physiological elements of fear (see Box 10-1).

Fear is also accompanied by the following strong *emotional elements*: dread, terror, queasiness, the chills, creeping sensations, a lump in the pit of

Box 10-1   THE CHAIN OF COMMAND OF THE
            EMERGENCY REACTION

When faced with a potential attacker, a person may have certain thoughts or cognitions about what is going to happen. Terror or other emotions may overcome him. He may react or behave in several ways: by running or by attacking the assailant. He may begin breathing heavily, his muscles may tense up, and any number of other somatic changes may occur.

The somatic changes that begin in a few seconds after a person perceives danger constitute the emergency reaction, in which the body mobilizes to maximize its chances for survival. These internal changes are directly caused by our **autonomic nervous system** and our **adrenal glands,** which are in turn controlled by our **central nervous system** (CNS).

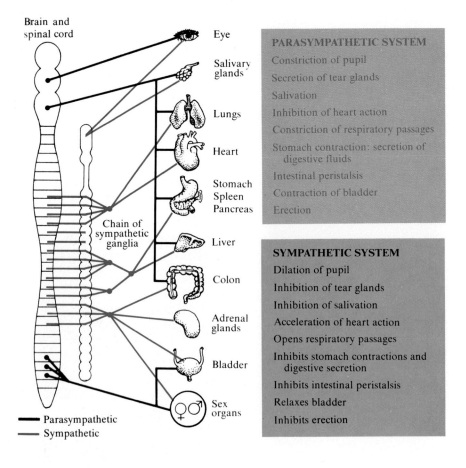

PARASYMPATHETIC SYSTEM
Constriction of pupil
Secretion of tear glands
Salivation
Inhibition of heart action
Constriction of respiratory passages
Stomach contraction: secretion of digestive fluids
Intestinal peristalsis
Contraction of bladder
Erection

SYMPATHETIC SYSTEM
Dilation of pupil
Inhibition of tear glands
Inhibition of salivation
Acceleration of heart action
Opens respiratory passages
Inhibits stomach contractions and digestive secretion
Inhibits intestinal peristalsis
Relaxes bladder
Inhibits erection

SOURCE: Gleitman, 1981, p. 66.

the stomach. These elements are familiar to us because we talk about them when describing our feelings of fear. We are also more conscious of the emotional elements, whereas we generally do not stop to reflect on our cognitions, nor are we particularly aware of the inner physiological workings set off by fear.

First, the danger registers, and this perception is transmitted from the sense organs and the higher centers of the brain (cortex) to the **hypothalamus** by wholly unknown processes. The hypothalamus is a brain structure about the size of a walnut, which lies under the cortex. (Roughly, if you follow the line of your nostrils up into your brain, you soon come to the hypothalamus.) The hypothalamus greatly influences eating, drinking, and sexual behavior, and is involved in regulating fundamental bodily processes, including metabolism and water balance. In times of emergency, it sends out messages of alarm.

The message from the hypothalamus activates the **sympathetic nervous system** (SNS) and, via this route, the **adrenal medulla,** the central part of the adrenal glands. These two systems then produce bodily changes by sending out adrenaline (epinephrine) and noradrenaline (norepinephrine) as their chemical messengers. The SNS releases norepinephrine from its neurons at the juncture with the neurons that excite the organ in question. The adrenal medulla amplifies the action of the SNS by releasing its chemical message into the blood, from where it diffuses into the organ tissues.

The chemicals released by the SNS and the adrenal medulla race throughout the body, producing the internal changes that constitute the emergency reaction. The heart beats faster and blood is pumped in greater volume. Peripheral blood vessels widen so that more oxygen will be pumped more rapidly around the body, and blood is redistributed from the skin and gut to the muscles and the brain. The spleen contracts, releasing stores of red blood cells to carry more oxygen. Breathing becomes deeper, and the air passages widen to take in more oxygen. The liver releases sugar for use by the muscles. Sweating increases to allow rapid cooling of the muscles and perhaps to increase tactile sensitivity. The content of the blood changes so that coagulation to seal possible wounds will occur more rapidly and lymphocyte cells that repair damage will increase in number.

The emergency reaction can be counteracted by the **parasympathetic nervous system** (PNS), which is responsible for producing a relaxation response. The PNS and the SNS generally oppose each other; together they make up the autonomic nervous system (ANS), which controls the organs that regulate the internal environment of the body, including the heart, stomach, adrenals, and intestines. Thus, when the PNS is excited, the heart slows down, whereas when the SNS is excited, the heart speeds up; while the PNS turns stomach acid secretions on, the SNS inhibits the secretion of acids. The SNS is an **adrenergic** system, using adrenaline and noradrenaline as the chemical messengers to produce an emergency reaction. The PNS is a **cholinergic** system, which uses the chemical transmitter acetylcholine to produce the relaxation reaction.

The completed mobilization of the body during the emergency reaction will increase the oxygen and energy resources that are available to the tissues, will increase circulation so that these resources can be moved through the body more quickly, will provide for waste product release, tactile sensitivity, surface protection, and quick repair of tissue damage. This will enable the individual to react to danger adaptively, so that he is able to run from an assailant or other fear-provoking situations. When the danger has passed, there will be a relaxation response, with a slowing down of the heart and breathing and a reduction in blood pressure.

Table 10-3 FEAR AND CLASSICAL CONDITIONING. FEAR IS CONDITIONED IN A CHILD WHEN A NEUTRAL STIMULUS, AN ALLEY, IS PAIRED WITH REPEATED UNPLEASANT ENCOUNTERS WITH BULLIES. AFTER A FEW PAIRINGS, THE ALLEY ITSELF ELICITS FEAR IN THE CHILD.

Neutral CS	Fear Conditioning Trial	Test
CS (alley) ↓ No CR (no fear response)	CS (alley) ↓ US (encounter with bullies) ↓ UR (Pain and fear reaction)	CS (alley) ↓ CR (fear reaction)

The ***behavior*** we engage in when afraid constitutes the fourth and final element of fear. There are two kinds of fear behavior: ***classically conditioned*** fear responses, which are involuntary reactions to being afraid, and ***instrumental*** responses, which are voluntary attempts to do something about the object we are afraid of.

In the world of elementary school children, bullies sometimes pick on a hapless child on his way home from school, perhaps in what was once a safe alley. After this occurs a few times, the youth will become afraid when approaching that alley. He will display a number of involuntary fear reactions, like sweating and faster heartbeat. This is an example of classical conditioning of fear. From Chapter 5, we know that classical fear conditioning takes place when a previously neutral signal is paired with a traumatic event. As a result of this pairing, the signal itself will cause fear reactions. In this case, the signal is the conditioned stimulus (CS), the trauma is the unconditioned stimulus (US), and fear is the conditioned response (CR) (see Table 10-3). Once conditioning has occurred, the signal alone causes the physiological emergency reaction to occur, profoundly changing other voluntary behavior. In our example, when the hapless youth sees the alley, he will stop munching on potato chips and will cease reading his comic book.

Fleeing and fighting are the main instrumental behaviors in response to fear. There are two types of flight responses: escape and avoidance. In ***escape***

Figure 10-2
Phobia versus normal fear. This figure gives us a schematic way of distinguishing normal fear from a phobia. It plots the degree of the reality of the danger (as measured by societal consensus) against the degree of accompanying fear (as measured by the strength of the emergency reaction). The 45 degree line indicates normal fear. The area in color shows the phobic range. *A* plots an accountant at work, *B* plots an oil rig construction worker in the wintry North Sea. He probably feels more fear, but the level of fear is in proportion to what he should feel compared to an accountant. *C*, however, plots a phobic, whose reaction to the feared object is far out of proportion to the real danger. *D* plots decorated bomb disposers, who when placed in laboratory fear tasks, show a lack of reaction (Cox, Hallam, O'Connor, and Rachman, 1982). Although these courageous individuals are in dangerous situations that would cause a high level of fear in most individuals, the bomb disposers display only a minimal emergency reaction.

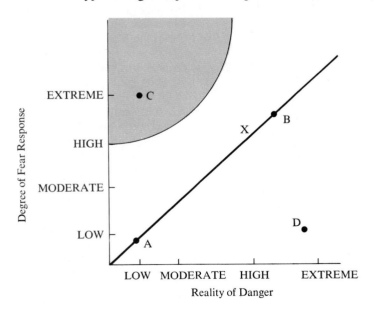

responding, the harmful event actually occurs and the subject runs out of it. For example, the child while being beaten up by his schoolmates will run out of the alley if given the chance. Similarly, a rat will jump across a hurdle to escape from and terminate an electric shock. In contrast, in **avoidance responding**, the subject will leave *before* the harmful event occurs. A signal will herald the bad event: the alley is a signal that some bullies might await the child, just as a tone might signal shock to a rat. The child will run out of the alley and take another route home, even if no bullies are beating him up. Responding to the tone, a rat will avoid the shock before it comes on, thereby preventing the shock from occurring at all. The signal, because of its previous pairing with shock (in early trials, in which the subject failed to make the avoidance response, shock occurred), produces fear, and the subject responds during the signal to remove itself from fear.

Degree of Fear

The degree of fear varies in different people and in different situations. Some people actually like to step inside a cage with a chair and whip to teach lions tricks. Lion tamers probably experience some fear, whereas most of us would be terrified. Hence, we do not go into cages. Instead, we go to the circus or the zoo. This is considered normal behavior.

There is a range of dangerous situations, as well as a range of fear responses. We accept our fear response when it is in proportion to the degree of danger in the situation. But when the fear response is out of proportion to the amount of danger, we label it abnormal, in short, a phobia. While fear is normal and a phobia is abnormal, they are both on the same continuum; they differ in degree, not in kind (see Figure 10-2).

ANXIETY

Anxiety has the same four components as fear but with one crucial difference: the cognitive component of fear is the expectation of a clear and specific danger, whereas the cognitive component of anxiety is the expectation

Pictured here are a person afraid of heights, a mountain climber, and a bomb disposer. Where on the graph of Figure 10-2 would we plot these individuals? (*Left:* Photograph by Jeffrey Grosscup. *Center:* © 1980 Robert McQuilkin/Black Star. *Right:* Wide World Photos)

of a much more diffuse danger. "Something terrible might happen!" is the essential thought in a panic disorder or generalized anxiety disorder, whereas in phobic and post-traumatic stress disorders the typical expectation might be,"A dog might bite me" or "There are clouds in the sky; it might flood again." The somatic component of anxiety is the same as that of fear: the elements of the emergency reaction. The emotional elements of anxiety are also the same as those of fear: dread, terror, apprehension, a lump in the pit of the stomach. Finally, the behavioral components of anxiety are also the same as those of fear: flight or fight is elicited. But the object that the afflicted individual should escape or avoid, or against which he should aggress, is shapeless.

We now turn to the specific disorders themselves. First, we will examine the two fear disorders: phobia and post-traumatic stress disorder. Then, we will discuss the two anxiety disorders: panic disorder and generalized anxiety disorder. We begin with the phobias.

PHOBIA

We single out phobia to begin our study of the "neuroses" for several reasons: (1) phobia is an unusually well-defined phenomenon, and when a diagnostician sees this phenomenon, there is little trouble diagnosing it correctly; and (2) it is a disorder about which much is known concerning its cause and cure. Until a few years ago, phobias were a mysterious disorder from which there was no escape—unless you were one of the lucky individuals whose phobia disappeared just as inexplicably as it arrived. Today, most phobias can be successfully treated, and of all psychological disorders, phobias are perhaps the best understood.

This section narrates the story of the conquest of phobia. We begin by defining phobia and then proceed to discuss what kinds of phobias exist. We discuss two rival theories of phobias: the psychoanalytic and the behavioral, and then we discuss the four therapies that seem to work on phobias. Finally, we present an integrated theory of phobia, which seems to account quite adequately for symptoms, cause, and treatment.

PHOBIA DEFINED

A *phobia* is a persistent fear reaction that is strongly out of proportion to the reality of the danger. For example, there are some people who, out of exaggerated fear, will not go to the circus or the zoo. In fact, such cat phobics cannot even be in the same room with a house cat because of their extreme fear of cats. Although we can repeatedly tell the cat phobic that house cats rarely attack humans, the fear will persist nonetheless.

A fear reaction may interfere with a phobic's entire life. Consider the following case in which fear is so great that the woman is even afraid to leave her home:

Anna was housebound. Six months ago, the house next door had become vacant and the grass had begun to grow long. Soon, the garden had become a rendezvous for the local cats. Now Anna was terrified that if she left her house, a cat would spring on her and attack her. Her fear of cats was of thirty years' status, having begun at age four when she remembered watching in horror as her father drowned a kitten. In spite of saying that she believed it was unlikely that her father actually did such a thing, she was haunted by the fear. At the sight of a cat, she would panic and sometimes be completely overwhelmed with terror. She could think of nothing else but her fear of cats. She interpreted any unexpected movement, shadow, or noise as a cat.

Anna is housebound because she is afraid that she might be attacked by a cat if she goes outside. Her fear is greatly out of proportion to the reality of the danger of actually being injured by a cat. The real danger is near zero, but her fear is extreme and irrational. Her problem is more than fear; it is a phobia. Very intense fear, however, does not constitute a phobia unless the actual danger is slight. For example, all of us would be housebound upon hearing about an approaching tornado. Here, the danger is great; the behavior is rational.

We must recognize that what we label a phobia is, by definition, partly a societal judgment. If the consensus of a society is that cats are extremely dangerous, it would not be considered a phobia to avoid them at all costs. Some superstitious societies attributed certain powers to animate and inanimate objects. Reacting to such objects with extreme fear would not constitute a phobia. For members of that society, such reactions made good rational sense.

There is no question that phobias cause one to suffer. They are maladaptive, since the individual's activities are greatly restricted; they are irrational, since the sense of danger is out of proportion to the reality of the danger. Phobics make others uncomfortable, and their behavior is considered socially unacceptable. Phobias are out of the individual's control, and phobics want to be rid of their fear. Thus, phobias are clearly abnormal.

An artist's conception of the fear of animals. Such a phobic could not even be in the same room as a house cat. (Drawing by John Vassos. Courtesy the Mayfield and George Arents Research Libraries, Syracuse University)

PREVALENCE OF PHOBIAS

The most recent estimate of the prevalence of phobias in the United States puts the rate at 7.7 percent of the population with mild phobias—stronger than intense fear, but not severely debilitating—and 0.22 percent of the population with severe phobias—phobias so strong that they might, for example, keep the phobic housebound (Agras, Sylvester, and Oliveau, 1969). *Prevalence* is defined as the percentage of population having a disorder at any given time and is contrasted with *incidence*, which is the rate of new cases of a disorder in a given time period. So mild phobias are a widespread disorder, although crippling phobias are uncommon.

In clinical practice, about 5 to 10 percent of all psychiatric patients have phobias. There is little trouble diagnosing a phobia when it is present, since its symptoms are unambiguous: (1) persistent fear of a specific situation out of proportion to the reality of the danger, (2) compelling desire to avoid and escape the situation, (3) recognition that the fear is unreasonably excessive, and (4) symptoms that are not due to another disorder, such as schizophrenia, depression, or obsessive-compulsive disorder. Finally, with the exception of agoraphobics (who fear crowds and open spaces), a phobic's psychological problems are quite isolated; typically, the only problem is the phobia itself, and phobics function well in most other areas of their life (Marks, 1969).

KINDS OF PHOBIAS

While there are reports of such unusual phobias as fear of flowers (anthophobia), the number 13 (triskaedekophobia), and snow (blanchophobia), these are very rare. The most common phobias in our society are fear of places of assembly and open spaces (agoraphobia), social phobias, and three classes of specific phobias: (1) fear of particular animals, usually cats, dogs, birds (most commonly pigeons), rats, snakes, and insects; (2) inanimate object phobias, including dirt, heights, closed places, darkness, and travel; and (3) fear of illness, injury, or death (see Table 10-4).

Agoraphobia

The most common phobia is **agoraphobia**, literally "fear of the marketplace." Approximately half of all phobics treated in clinics are agoraphobics, although only 10 percent of mild phobics are agoraphobic. Agoraphobia is not a particularly apt term, since these unfortunate individuals are beset not only with a terror of being in the marketplace, but also of open spaces, crowds, traveling, and streets. Typically, the agoraphobic believes that some disaster, most typically a panic attack, will befall her when she is away from the security of her home, and that no one will help her. She

Table 10-4 THE COMMON PHOBIAS

		Approximate Percent of All Phobias	Sex Difference	Typical Age of Onset
Agoraphobias (fear of places of assembly, crowds, open spaces)		10–50%	large majority are women	early adulthood
Social Phobias (fear of being observed doing something humiliating)		10%	majority are women	adolescence
The Specific Phobias *Animals*		5-15%	vast majority are women	childhood
Cats (ailurophobia)	Birds (avisophobia)			
Dogs (cynophobia)	Horses (equinophobia)			
Insects (insectophobia)	Snakes (ophidiophobia)			
Spiders (arachnophobia)	Rodents (rodentophobia)			
Inanimate Objects Phobias		20%	none	any age
Dirt (mysophobia)	Darkness (nyctophobia)			
Storms (brontophobia)	Closed spaces (claustrophobia)			
Heights (acrophobia)				
Illness–Injury (nosophobia)		15-25%	none	middle age
Death phobia (thanatophobia)				
Cancer (cancerophobia)				
Venereal disease (venerophobia)				

then goes to great lengths to avoid such places. Agoraphobia is the most crippling of the common phobias because many agoraphobics are unable to leave their home. Here is the account of an agoraphobic who experienced a phobic attack in the snows of Vermont:

> As a cold wind hit the hill, she stood holding her chin, looking back at the house in the distance. Her friends heard her mutter something—that she had snow in her boot, or needed the bathroom—some such lie. Then she began to run, looking down at the snow. She couldn't look at the house, it seemed too far away. She started to sweat and her legs went soft. She could not feel her feet, but they were running. Her heart was pounding, her face flushed. She began to pant. She felt as though she were coming apart, as if she had been running forever through the syrupy snow of a nightmare. Six Miltowns rattled against four Valiums in her pocket. The sweat on her body tripped triggers in her brain, the adrenaline signaled the nerves to further panic. "What if I die?" she thought. "Oh, my God, I'm going crazy." Then she was at the house, the "safe" place. But she had added more fears to an already long list. She was afraid of snow. She was afraid of hills. And, above all, she was afraid of ever again feeling the way she did running from that snowy hill in Vermont. (Baumgold, 1977)

Notice her fear of open spaces, and the panic that occurs when she fears that she may not easily reach the safety of a contained space—the house. Agoraphobics dread a variety of objects connected with open space: smooth bodies of water, bleak landscapes, the street, train travel on clear days. These objects are much less terrifying when the space is more comfortably circumscribed as by a snow-storm or trees, or when an enclosed space is easily within reach.

The majority of agoraphobics are women, and their phobia begins in early adulthood with a panic attack, as in the following typical onset:

> A girl of nineteen suddenly came home from her work as a shop assistant and screamed that she was going to die. While standing at her counter, she had experienced the worst sensations in her life. Her heart began to pound like a jackhammer, she could not catch her breath, she was gripped by panic and dread, she felt the ground underneath her was about to give way, and she was convinced she was having a stroke or heart attack. She spent the next two weeks in bed and, thereafter, she refused to walk beyond the front gate. She did not improve after four months as a psychiatric in-patient. After her discharge, she left her home only twice in the following seven years.

Agoraphobics are prone to panic attacks even when they are not in the agoraphobic situation. Moreover, they have more psychological problems —other than their phobia—than the other types of phobics. In addition to their phobic symptoms, these patients are often highly anxious and generally depressed. Obsessive-compulsive disorders occasionally accompany agoraphobia as well. Untreated, agoraphobia will sometimes remit spontaneously, and then return mysteriously, or it may be unabating (Marks, 1969; Zitrin, Klein, Woerner, and Ross, 1983).

Social Phobias

All of us are, at times, anxious in social situations. **Social phobias** are exaggerations of such fears. In the 4th century B.C., Hippocrates, the Greek physician, described a classic social phobic who

> . . . will not be seen abroad: loves darkness as life, and cannot endure the light, or to sit in lightsome places; his hat still in his eyes, he will neither see, nor be seen by his good will. He dare not come in company for fear he should be misused, disgraced, overshoot himself in gesture or speeches, or be sick, he thinks every man observes him. . . . (Burton, 1621, p. 272, quoted in Marks, 1969)

Social phobics fear being seen or observed. They are terrified of speaking, or eating and drinking in front of other people. They may be unable to eat in a restaurant for fear they will vomit and be humiliated. A student may stop writing during an exam when watched by a teacher for fear of shaking violently. A factory worker may stop going to work lest he be unable to tie packages when observed. An actor may be terrified that he will begin to stutter or forget his lines when on stage. The fears are almost always unrealistic: individuals who fear they *might* shake, do not shake, nor do those who fear vomiting in public actually vomit in public.

As in agoraphobia, social phobias also usually begin in adolescence, and only rarely in childhood. The disorder is distinguishable from agoraphobia, however. Both agoraphobics and social phobics are afraid of crowds, but for different reasons. The agoraphobic fears being crushed or suffocated by the mass, or he fears that no one will come to his aid if he is in need of help. The social phobic, on the other hand, fears that some individuals in the crowd will look at him and observe him doing something embarrassing. Social phobias usually begin gradually. For example, while brooding about whether the groom is really good enough for her, a bride may begin to fear that she will tremble when she walks down the aisle with her father and that the guests will see how nervous she is. Thereafter, being observed by others in public may become more and more frightening for her. In contrast, sometimes a particularly dramatic incident will cause a social phobia. For example, a young man may actually vomit at a dance before making it to the toilet. This may so greatly embarrass him that he will no longer interact socially.

These phobias make up about 10 percent of all phobic cases, and they are reported somewhat more frequently by women than by men. Unlike in agoraphobics, in social phobics the phobia itself is generally their only psychological problem.

The Specific Phobias

There are three classes of **specific phobias:** animal phobias, phobias of inanimate objects, and illness and injury phobias. The first of these, **animal phobias,** such as Anna's cat phobia, contrasts with agoraphobia. Animal phobias uniformly begin in early childhood, almost never beginning after puberty. While common in childhood, most animal phobias are outgrown by adulthood.

A specific childhood incident may set off a phobia. This child may grow up to be a dog phobic. (© Frostie 1978/ Woodfin Camp)

Animal phobias are highly focused: Anna may be terrified of cats, but she is rather fond of dogs and birds. Agoraphobic problems, in contrast, are diffuse, ranging over a great variety of situations. Untreated animal phobias can persist for decades with no period of remission, while untreated agoraphobia fluctuates from remissions to relapses.

Only about 5 percent of all crippling phobias and perhaps 15 percent of milder phobias are of specific animals. The vast majority (95 percent) of animal phobias are reported by women; unlike agoraphobics, they are rather healthy individuals and the phobia is apt to be their only psychological problem.

Animal phobics sometimes can describe a specific childhood incident that they believe set the phobia off. Anna seemed to recall that her father had drowned a kitten. Dog phobias may begin with a dog bite; a bird phobia may begin if a bird lands on a child's shoulder. Overall, about 60 percent of phobic patients can describe a clear precipitating trauma. But for the remaining 40 percent, no clear incident, only vague clues extracted from the mists of childhood memory can be isolated (Öst and Hugdahl, 1981). One child seemed to have developed a phobia by reading about a warrior dog in a fairy tale, and then hearing that a boy down the street had been bitten by a dog. Another child, already somewhat apprehensive about birds, was teased mercilessly with feathers by her playmates. In each case, there are a number of events, often several accumulating over time, that might contribute to the phobia. But uncovering the essential events, if such exist, can be enormously difficult. Usually animal phobias are outgrown, but for unknown reasons, a few remain robust and persist into adulthood.

Inanimate object phobias share many of the same characteristics as animal phobias. Heights, closed spaces, storms, dirt, darkness, running water, travel, and wind make up the majority of these phobias. As in animal phobias, the symptoms are focused on one object, and the individuals are otherwise psychologically normal. Onset is sometimes embedded in a traumatic incident. For example, a nineteen-year-old develops an airplane phobia after a plane he has just gotten off crashes at its next stop. An eight-year-old girl, who saw a boy hit by lightning and killed, develops a phobia of thunder and lightning. These phobias are somewhat more common than animal phobias, and they occur about equally in women and men. Unlike animal phobias, they can begin at any age.

Hilda's case illustrates how a traumatic incident can bring about a phobia. It is unusual in that the trauma occurred when she was eleven years old, but the phobia went underground for twenty years and then reemerged during an adult stress. The trauma, in reality, was life-threatening; the abnormal aspect was how widely her fear generalized, showing that even a very specific phobia can disrupt one's entire life.

Hilda, a thirty-two-year-old married woman, came into therapy because of an unusual type of phobia: a fear of snow.

This phobia was her major presenting feature and had become increasingly handicapping and troublesome. As one consequence of her husband's business success, they had moved to the suburbs, where there was likely to be even more snow than in the city. More travel was required—at times through snow during wintertime—to get to the store or to any other place; and in the last several winters, there had been a great deal of snow in her particular metropolitan area.

Claustrophobia is the fear of enclosed spaces. (Drawing by John Vassos. Courtesy the Mayfield and George Arents Research Libraries, Syracuse University)

It is hard to picture adequately the extent of fear: this woman's fear of snow petrified her. She could not stand to go out in it; she could not stand to see it; in winter she could not listen to weather reports because someone might make some reference to snow! Any reference to snow, or even subjective thoughts about it, would make her uncomfortable, frightened, and tense. The many, many ways in which this phobia could affect her day-to-day living were almost incredible. The effects were pervasive and thereby profound.

In this instance, we were most fortunate eventually to uncover what proved to have been the major precipitating event in the onset of the phobia. This was a traumatic experience dating from when the patient was eleven years old. This experience had lain completely out of sight, hidden in her unconscious, for twenty-one years—repressed, but hardly dormant.

In the winter of her eleventh year, she had accompanied an aunt and an uncle to a ski lodge in Vermont. One afternoon, she wandered off by herself, into a small ravine that lay parallel to, but considerably below an old logging road. She played and gradually waded her way through the snow for several hundred yards down the ravine. Looking up at this point, she could see some people on the road far above her. There was some banter exchanged between them. A few snowballs or stones were thrown in her direction. A large chunk of snow either came loose or was started toward her. To her intense horror, it quickly gathered speed and volume. Suddenly she found herself in the path of a miniature avalanche. She was helpless to move out of the way in time, and was engulfed. She was literally buried alive, and was unable to move or to extricate herself. Somehow, however, she managed to maintain, or was fortunate enough to have, a channel so that she could continue breathing. The people on the road above simply disappeared, either not knowing what had transpired, or perhaps in a guilty attempt to dissociate themselves from tragedy.

The little girl remained there, absolutely petrified with fear, for an indeterminate period of time, until discovered through most fortuitous circumstances by her worried uncle. It had seemed an eternity.

Her complete repression of this episode was caused by its unbearable horror, plus her certainty of death. This may have also been encouraged a bit by her fear of having her parents ever learn about the near tragedy. Each felt in some measure responsible and subject to censure. Any possibility of future excursions would, in addition, become extremely unlikely. (Adapted from Laughlin, 1967.)

Illness and injury phobias (nosophobias) are the final class of specific phobias. Phobias of illness, injury, and death make up between 15 percent and 25 percent of all phobias. A person with such a phobia fears having one specific illness, although the kind of illness feared has changed throughout the centuries. In the nineteenth century, nosophobics feared they had tuberculosis or perhaps syphilis and other venereal diseases. More recently, cancer, heart disease, and stroke have been the terrors.

A nosophobic is usually perfectly healthy, but he worries endlessly that he may have or will soon contract a particular disease. He searches his body for the slightest sign of the disease, and since fear itself produces symptoms like tightness in the chest and stomach pain, he interprets these symptoms as further evidence that the disease is upon him. And so it spirals to more stomach or chest pain and to more certainty that he has the dreaded disease.

There are no sex differences in overall reports of nosophobia, although cancer phobias tend to occur more in females and phobias of venereal disease almost always occur in males. Other psychological problems accompany the disorder frequently, and it usually arises in middle age. Nosophobics often know someone who has the feared disease.

Strangely enough, contracting the disease may cure the phobia. A man was admitted to a hospital, beside himself with syphilophobia. After discharge, he actually caught syphilis. The phobia disappeared at once, and the patient happily had his syphilis cured by medical treatment (Rogerson, 1951, cited in Marks, 1969).

Nosophobia is distinguished from *hypochondriasis.* Hypochondriacs are highly anxious and vigilant about a variety of illnesses in various parts of the body, unlike the phobic who is concerned with one specific illness in one organ. Today, hypochondriasis is not regarded as a phobia. Rather it seems to be a feature of many different disorders, although it was originally believed to be a discrete disorder of a nonexistent organ, the *hypochondria,* located in the abdomen.

We have now described the characteristics of the various kinds of phobias. How do phobias come about, and how can they be treated? There are two schools of thought that present comprehensive theories about phobias: the psychoanalytic and the behavioral.We now turn to these contrasting theories, and then to the therapies that work successfully on phobias.

THE PSYCHOANALYTIC ACCOUNT OF PHOBIAS

The psychoanalytic account of phobias was put forward in 1909 by Sigmund Freud in the famous Little Hans case. To this day, psychodynamic accounts of phobia rely heavily on the logic of this case (Odier, 1956; Arieti, 1979). Freud's interpretation of a phobia consists of several steps: (1) the phobic (if he is male) is in love with and wants to seduce his mother; (2) he jealously hates his father, and wishes to kill him (these first two steps constitute the Oedipus complex); (3) the phobic fears that, in retaliation, his father will castrate him; (4) this conflict produces enormous anxiety in the phobic; because the wishes are unacceptable to the conscious mind, the anxiety is displaced onto an innocent object (the phobic object), which symbolizes the conflict and is a more acceptable receptacle for fear; (5) the phobia is cured when the phobic gains insight into the nature of the underlying conflict.

The Little Hans Case

Hans was a five-year-old boy who developed a fear of horses intense enough to keep him indoors. When he was four, he saw a horse fall down in the street and then thrash his legs violently in an apparent attempt to get up. Hans was very upset by this and thereafter was reluctant to leave the house, lest he be bitten by a horse who had fallen in the street. After extensive conversation with his father who had been guided by Freud, Little Hans's phobia gradually weakened.

Freud weaves an enchanting story, and in the 150-page case history, marshals evidence for each of the five premises of phobic origin. Here is a sample of the evidence.

HANS'S DESIRE TO SEDUCE HIS MOTHER.   Hans had shown an active interest in widdlers (penises) from an early age, and was an affectionate and physical child toward his parents and playmates. When he was four-and-a-quarter years old, a scene of considerable sexual interest occurred. That morning, Hans was given his usual daily bath by his mother, and afterward, he was dried and powdered. As his mother was powdering around his penis and taking care not to touch it, Hans said, "Why don't you put your finger there?"

MOTHER: Because that'd be piggish.
HANS: What's that? Piggish? Why?
MOTHER: Because it's not proper.
HANS: (*laughing*) But it's great fun.

HANS'S HATE OF AND DESIRE TO KILL AND TO REPLACE HIS FATHER.   Hans had the following conversation with his father:

FATHER: Did you often get into bed with Mummy at Gmünden?
HANS: Yes.
FATHER: And you used to think to yourself you were Daddy?
HANS: Yes.
FATHER: And then you felt afraid of Daddy?
HANS: *You know everything; I didn't know anything.*
FATHER: When Fritzl fell down, you thought, "If only Daddy would fall down like that!" and when the lamb butted you, you thought, "If only it would butt Daddy!" Can you remember the funeral at Gmünden?
HANS: Yes. What about it?
FATHER: You thought then that, if only Daddy would die, you'd be Daddy.
HANS: Yes.

RESOLUTION OF THE PHOBIA WITH RECOGNITION OF THE OEDIPUS CONFLICT.   At the time the phobia was waning, Hans related the following fantasy to his father:

HANS: The plumber came; and first he took away my behind with a pair of pincers, and then gave me another, and then the same with my widdler. He [the plumber] said, "Let me see your widdler!"
FATHER: He gave you a *bigger* widdler and a *bigger* behind.
HANS: Yes.
FATHER: Like Daddy's, because you'd like to be like Daddy.

Freud interpreted all of this by saying the following:

We have already considered Hans's two concluding phantasies, with which his recovery was rounded off. One of them, that of the plumber giving him a new and, as his father guessed, a bigger widdler, was not merely a repetition of the earlier phantasy concerning the plumber and the bath. The new one was a triumphant, wishful phantasy, and with it he overcame his fear of castration. (Freud, 1909/1976)

Evaluation of the Psychoanalytic Account

The psychoanalytic account of phobias is not compelling. There are three grounds for skepticism: (1) the account is based almost entirely on case history material, and the theoretical inferences from this material are loose; (2) psychoanalytic therapy for phobias works only infrequently, and then only with years of therapy; (3) there exists a viable alternative account—the behavioral analysis—which is based on both experimental evidence and case histories and which is associated with therapies that treat most phobias successfully within a few months.

First, we will consider the looseness of inference from the case history evidence. Did Hans really secretly wish to seduce his mother? The only evidence for this is based on Hans's primitive attempt to get his mother to touch his penis. It is a large leap of inference from such a common expression of sexual interest to a desire to possess the mother and replace the father. At most, we have evidence of some sexual interest, not very well disguised at that.

Did Hans really wish to kill and to replace his father? Hans never expressed fear or hatred of his father. He was told by Freud—who saw Hans only once—that he hated his father. Later, he was asked by his father about this, in a series of leading questions. First, Hans denied that it was so, and eventually he answered with a single "yes."

FATHER: Are you fond of Daddy?
HANS: Oh yes.
FATHER: Or perhaps not. . . . You're a little vexed with Daddy because Mummy's fond of him.
HANS: No.
FATHER: Then why do you always cry whenever Mummy gives me a kiss? It's because you're jealous.
HANS: Jealous, yes.

Would any evidence "count" as a disconfirmation of the theory? Hans's denial that he is vexed with his father does not count—in fact, it can be construed as confirmatory, by showing that Hans is defending himself against realizing his unacceptable hatred of his father. The theory is built in such a way that both denying and accepting an interpretation confirm that theory. This makes the theory difficult to test.

Did Hans really lose his phobia when he resolved his Oedipal conflict? There is little evidence for such a conflict to begin with, but if we assume it, should we be convinced that it was resolved? The resolution comes, allegedly, in the plumber fantasy, which is as much about *losing* as gaining a widdler and a bottom. Hans's father seizes on the interpretation of gain, and Hans then agrees to it. Here, Hans has to be, in Freud's words, "told many things he could not say himself." Further, Hans's phobic improvement seems to be smooth and gradual through this period, not a sudden remission following his "insights." It has since been documented that children between the ages of two and six suddenly develop strong fears of animals, which decline gradually on their own with no therapy (Holmes, 1935; Mac-

Farland, Allen, and Honzik, 1954.) Hans is well within the age in which fear spontaneously declines; this speculation is more consistent with the gradual elimination of his phobia than with the interpretation that his Oedipal conflict was suddenly resolved.

The success of a therapy can sometimes be relevant evidence for the theory from which the therapy is derived. What is the psychoanalytic therapy for phobias, and how does it fare? The psychoanalytic therapy for phobia follows from the theory that phobic fear is the displacement of anxiety generated by unacceptable intrapsychic conflict onto some innocent object. The therapist must help the patient to bring the unconscious conflict to light, and to gain insight into the repressed traumatic incident that generated the phobia. In addition, some analysts recommend that the patient's attention should be focused away from the phobic object, but that as the patient comes to recognize the unconscious conflict, he should be encouraged to re-experience the phobic situation while learning that the fear is not intolerable. Psychoanalysts recognize that the prognosis for phobics under this regime is not good (Laughlin, 1967; Arieti, 1979).

> One must anticipate that many, many sessions will be required. A great deal of time and effort is generally required on the part of both doctor and patient alike.
> Further, no guarantee as to the results can be given. . . . It may be a strenuous job, taking hundreds of therapeutic sessions over some years. The end results can be worth far more than the considerable investment of time, effort and money required. (Laughlin, 1967, p. 601)

Overall, then, the Little Hans case history provides unsatisfactory evidence for the psychoanalytic view of phobias. The interpretations are large, uncompelling leaps. This alone would not necessarily be fatal to the theory if there existed experimental evidence to support the interpretation, or if psychoanalysis cured phobias. There is no such evidence, however, and psychoanalytic therapy is of doubtful value for overcoming phobias. Moreover, there exists an alternate account that is consistent with case history material and experimental evidence, and that is of considerable therapeutic value: the behavioral account.

THE BEHAVIORAL ACCOUNT OF PHOBIAS

The behavioral analysis of phobias begins by assuming that normal fear and phobia are learned in the same way. According to this view, both fear and phobia arise when a neutral signal happens to be around at the same time as a bad event. If the bad event is mild, the neutral signal becomes mildly fear provoking. If, however, the bad event is particularly traumatic, as when Anna watched in horror as her father drowned a kitten, the signal becomes terrifying, and the phobia develops. Phobic conditioning is simply an instance of classical fear being conditioned by a particularly traumatic unconditioned stimulus.

Classical Conditioning of Fear

Recall that classical conditioning consists of a procedure in which a conditioned stimulus (CS)—or signal—happens to occur at the same time as an

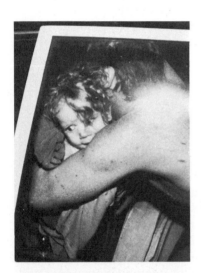

This frightened child was just saved from a burning building. The behavioral account of phobia claims that any future and exaggerated fear of fire would be a result of this early trauma. (Wide World Photos)

Table 10-5 THE BEHAVIORAL ACCOUNT OF PHOBIAS. WHEN THE SIGNAL (CS) IS PAIRED IN TIME WITH THE TRAUMATIC EVENT (US), THIS ELICITS A REACTION (UR). LATER WHEN THE CS AGAIN OCCURS, IT PRODUCES A PHOBIA (CR).

Case	Signal (CS)	Traumatic Event (US)	Reaction (UR)	Phobia (CR)
Little Hans	Horse	Sight of horse falling down, thrashing violently	Fright	Horse phobia
Anna	Kitten	Sight of kitten being drowned by father	Horror, fright	Cat phobia
Hilda	Snow	Being buried alive by avalanche	Fear of death, freezing, panic, helplessness	Snow phobia
Social Phobic	Party	Vomiting in public before reaching toilet	Humiliation	Phobia of social gatherings
Little Albert	Rat	Hearing a loud noise	Crying, being startled	Fear of rats, rabbits, fur

unconditioned stimulus (US)—or traumatic event in the case of fear conditioning—which evokes a strong unconditioned reaction (UR). Thereafter, the previously neutral CS produces a conditioned response (CR) that resembles the UR. The CR is the phobic response and the CS is the phobic object. Hans's experience fits this description. Hans himself asserted that his phobia began suddenly when he saw a horse fall down in the street and violently thrash its legs. This gave him an awful fright. The sight of a horse, once not fearful, is a neutral CS. As he looks at the horse, it falls down and thrashes about (US) which evokes fear (UR). Thereafter, the CS of seeing a horse produces a CR of fear. Hans has been classically conditioned to fear horses; we need not postulate deeper fears or lusts. According to this analysis, Hans was not afraid of castration by his father; he was afraid of horses (Wolpe and Rachman, 1960). The precipitating trauma, when it occurs in phobic cases, can be well described by classical fear conditioning. Table 10-5 details the classical fear conditioning analysis of several of our phobic case histories.

In addition to fitting many case histories, a substantial body of experimental evidence supports the hypothesis that pairing a neutral object with a frightening situation produces strong fear of the neutral object. In 1920, John B. Watson and Rosalie Rayner performed the first experiment on this topic. Little Albert B. was a normal, healthy eleven-month-old who, from birth, had been reared in the hospital in which his mother worked as a wet nurse. On the whole, he was big, stolid, and unemotional. One day, Albert was presented with a white rat, and he eagerly began to reach for it. Just as his hand touched the rat, the experimenters struck a metal bar suspended above Albert's head with a hammer. This produced such a loud and startling sound that Albert jerked violently, burying his head in the mattress, and whimpered. This pairing of the rat and the sound was repeated several

John B. Watson (1878–1958). (Courtesy The Bettman Archive)

times. When Albert was shown the rat later, he began to cry. He fell over on his side, and began to crawl away as rapidly as he could. A phobia had been conditioned.

This experiment was a primitive, but pioneering study. We will discuss in the critique of the behavioral account of phobias section below some of the flaws (Harris, 1979; Seligman, 1980). Nonetheless, since the Little Albert experiment, literally hundreds of studies of classically conditioned fear in animals and several in humans have been published. It is now well established that pairing a neutral CS with a traumatic US produces strong acquired fear to the CS. So classical conditioning of fear provides a potential experimental model of phobias because it fits many case histories and seems to be a sufficient condition for learning strong fear.

The Persistence of Phobias

Can the behavioral analysis also offer an account of persistence, a defining feature of phobias? After fear is classically conditioned in the laboratory by pairing a tone a few times with shock, extinction will occur rapidly when the tone is presented without the shock. Within ten or twenty presentations of the tone without shock, fear will always disappear. Even when shock is extremely painful, fear of the tone will extinguish in no more than forty trials (Annau and Kamin, 1961). Phobias, on the other hand, are very robust. They seem to resist extinction; some persist for a lifetime. How can a model based on an ephemeral phenomenon, classical fear conditioning, capture phobias that last and last?

An *extinction trial* in fear conditioning occurs when the fear-evoking signal is presented to the subject, but the traumatic event no longer follows. For example, a rat is put into the box in which it has received shocks. A fear-evoking tone that has been paired with shock comes on but no shock is presented. The rat can do nothing to escape the tone and is exposed to the fact that the tone no longer predicts shock. Because the rat cannot escape, it *reality tests* and finds out that the trauma no longer follows the signal. Under these conditions, fear extinguishes rapidly.

In contrast, phobics rarely test the reality of their fears. When the phobic object is around, they rarely sit there waiting to be passively exposed to an extinction trial. Rather, they run away as quickly as possible. For example, Anna would avoid cats as best she could, but if she did happen across a cat, she would flee as fast as she could. She would not reality test by staying in the presence of the cat and finding out what would happen.

Since phobias involve avoidance and escape from the phobic object, does fear of a signal that has been paired with trauma extinguish under the parallel laboratory conditions when the subject avoids the trauma by fleeing from the signal as soon as he is permitted to do so? Consider a rat in an avoidance procedure: a tone comes on, and at the end of ten seconds shock occurs. Remember that the tone equals the phobic object, and the shock equals the traumatic event that originally conditioned the phobia. If the rat jumps onto a platform before the ten seconds are up, the tone will go off and shock will not occur. Soon the rat learns to jump up, and does so in less that two seconds on every trial. When extinction begins, the shock is disconnected (the phobic object no longer signals trauma). Now the rat undergoes one hundred trials in which he jumps up after two seconds of tone, the tone goes off promptly, but shock never occurs. If the rat's fear of the two-second tone is measured behaviorally or physiologically, fear has extinguished. But is the rat still afraid of the longer ten-second tone? Remember that he has not reality tested: he has *not* remained on the grid floor for ten seconds and has not found out that shock is no longer delivered. When tested with the full ten-second tone, the rat shows great fear. Escaping the signal and avoiding the trauma has protected the fear of the signal from extinction (Baum, 1969; Seligman and Johnston, 1973).

Now consider the social phobic who no longer goes to parties because he was humiliated when he once vomited at a party. He avoids parties altogether, and if he must attend one, he escapes as quickly as he can. He is afraid that if the finds himself at a party (CS—the signal), he will again throw up (US—the trauma) and be publicly humiliated (UR—the reaction). His fear does not extinguish because he does not allow himself to be exposed to extinction trials—being at a party and finding out that he does not throw up and is not humiliated. He does not test the reality of the fact that parties (CS) no longer lead to vomiting (US) and humiliation (UR). The ability to avoid and escape the phobic object protects fear of the phobic object from being extinguished, just as allowing a rat to avoid reality testing protects fear from extinguishing.

The behavioral analysis can thus account for the persistence of phobias. Most importantly, it makes direct predictions about therapy; those procedures that extinguish fear conditioning in the laboratory should also cure phobias.

Therapies for Phobias

There are three therapies that have proven highly effective against phobias: systematic desensitization, flooding, and modeling. All three were developed within the framework of the behavioral analysis. Historically, the first is systematic desensitization.

Systematic Desensitization

In the 1950s, Joseph Wolpe, a South African psychiatrist, classically conditioned cats to fear a chamber in which they had been shocked. Using this animal model of phobias, Wolpe developed the therapy of **systematic desensitization**. First he cured his cats of their acquired fear, and then he successfully applied the therapy to human phobias.

Systematic desensitization is effective and brief, usually lasting at most a few months. It involves three phases: training in relaxation, hierarchy construction, and counterconditioning. First the therapist trains the phobic patient in deep muscle relaxation, a technique in which the subject sits or lies with eyes closed, with all his muscles completely relaxed. This state of relaxation will be used in the third phase to neutralize fear, since it is believed that individuals cannot be deeply relaxed and afraid at the same time (that is, fear and relaxation are incompatible responses). Second, with the aid of the therapist, the patient constructs a hierarchy of frightening situations, in which the most dreaded possible scene is on the highest rung and a scene

Psychiatrist Joseph Wolpe is conducting systematic desensitization with a patient. The patient is imagining a fear-evoking scene while engaged in deep muscle relaxation. If fear becomes unbearable, she will signal this by lifting her left forefinger. (Courtesy Dr. Joseph Wolpe)

evoking some, but minimal, fear is on the lowest rung. For example, a hierarchy constructed by a woman with a phobia of physical deformity (from Wolpe, 1969) might be as follows (from minimally feared situations to maximally feared situations):

1. Ambulances (minimally feared)
2. Hospitals
3. Wheelchairs
4. Nurses in uniform
5. Automobile accidents
6. The sight of somebody who is seriously ill
7. The sight of bleeding
8. Someone in pain
9. The sight of physical deformity (maximally feared)

The third phase removes the fear of the phobic object by gradual counterconditioning; that is, causing a response that is incompatible with fear to occur at the same time as the feared CS. The patient goes into deep relaxation, and simultaneously imagines the first, least-arousing scene in the hierarchy. This serves two purposes. First, it pairs the CS, ambulances, with the absence of the original traumatic US. (You will recall that presenting the CS, without the original US, is an extinction procedure that will weaken the fear response to the CS.) Second, a new response, relaxation, which neutralizes the old response of fear occurs in the presence of the CS. This is repeated until the patient can imagine scene 1 of the hierarchy without any fear at all. Then scene 2, which provokes a slightly greater fear than scene 1, is paired with relaxation. And so the patient progresses up the hierarchy by the graded extinction procedure until she reaches the most terrifying scene. Here the patient again relaxes and visualizes the final scene. When she can do this with no fear at all, the patient may be tested in real life by being confronted with an actual instance of something at the top of her hierarchy—in this case, with a real physical deformity. Therapy is considered successful when the patient can tolerate being in the actual presence of the most terrifying item on the hierarchy.

Eighty to ninety percent of specific phobias improve greatly with such treatment. These gains are usually maintained over follow-ups of a year or two. Follow-up studies universally report that new symptoms rarely, if ever, develop to replace the phobia. (For a sample of such studies, see Paul, 1967; Kazdin and Wilcoxon, 1976.) This absence of "symptom substitution" argues that Freud's theory of phobias, as anxiety displaced from deep intrapsychic conflict onto an innocent object, is mistaken: characteristically, the psychoanalytic view of phobias claims that the phobia is merely a superficial symptom of a deeper, unresolved conflict, which is the genuine disorder. The psychoanalytic view maintains that removing the symptoms by desensitizing the phobic object cannot resolve the underlying conflict, and that therefore a new phobia or some other disorder will arise to bind the anxiety that can now no longer be displaced onto the newly desensitized object. This has not been shown to be the case.

Flooding

Recall that behaviorists believe that phobias persist because phobics will avoid the phobic object if at all possible, and if forced into its presence, they will escape rapidly. This failure to find out that the phobic object no longer predicts the original traumatic event will protect the phobia from extinction.

What happens when a phobic is forced or volunteers to be in the presence of a phobic object? What happens when rats, who are avoiding shock by escaping the tone in two seconds, are forced to sit repeatedly through the ten-second tone and find out that shock no longer occurs? Such a *flooding* or reality-testing procedure in rats reliably brings reduced amount of fear and eliminates future avoidance (Baum, 1969; Tryon, 1976). The success of eliminating fear in animals by a flooding procedure encouraged behavior therapists to try, with caution, flooding in real phobic patients (Stampfl and Levis, 1967).

In a flooding procedure, the phobic patient agrees, usually with great apprehension, to imagine the phobic situation or to stay in its presence, without attempting to escape for a long period. For example, a claustrophobic will be put in a closet for four hours, or an agoraphobic will listen to a long and vivid tape recording that describes his going to a shopping center, falling down, being trampled by crowds, hearing them laugh as they observe him vomiting all over himself. Usually the phobic is terrified for the first hour or two of flooding, and then gradually the terror will subside. When he is then taken to a shopping center, he will usually be greatly improved, and the phobia may be gone.

In general, flooding has proven to be equal, and sometimes even superior, to systematic desensitization in its therapeutic effects. This has been particularly true of treatment for agoraphobia, which sometimes resists desensitization but is effectively treated by flooding. Treatment gains are maintained: four years after flooding, 75 percent of a group of seventy agoraphobics remained improved (Marks, Boulougoris, and Marset, 1971; Crowe, Marks, Agras, and Leitenberg, 1972; Emmelkamp and Kuipers, 1979). By forcing a patient to reality test and to stay in the phobic situation,

By watching others handle snakes, those formerly fearful of them learn to do so themselves, and by doing so, lose their fear of snakes. Such "modeling" is a form of therapy used to overcome phobias. (Photograph by Billy Grimes/Leo de Wys)

and thereby find out that catastrophe does not ensue, extinction of the phobia can usually be accomplished. This directly confirms the hypothesis that phobias are so persistent because the object is avoided in real life and therefore not extinguished by the discovery that they are harmless.

Modeling

The third effective therapy for phobias is modeling. In a typical modeling procedure, the phobic watches someone who is not phobic perform the behavior that the phobic is unable to do himself. For example, a snake phobic will repeatedly watch a nonfearful model approach, pick up, and fondle a real snake (Bandura, Adams, and Beyer, 1977). Seeing that the other person is not harmed, the phobic may become less fearful of the situation. However, if the phobic thinks that the model is endowed with special powers to deal with a snake, he may continue to fear the situation. In order to change this belief about the model, the therapist will attempt to find a model who resembles the phobic. Then, the therapist will gradually involve the phobic in the exercises. First, the phobic may be asked to describe aloud what he sees, then to approach the snake, and finally to touch it. The procedure will be repeated until the phobia diminishes.

Overall, modeling, when used in therapy, seems to work about as well as both desensitization and flooding in curing both mild and severe clinical phobias (Rachman, 1976). This therapy brings about cognitive change, as well as behavioral change. Once a patient has observed a model, the single best predictor of therapeutic progress is the extent to which he now expects that he will be able to perform the actions he formerly was unable to do (Bandura, Adams, and Beyer, 1977).

A single underlying process—extinction—seems to be the operative element in all three effective therapies for phobias. In all three treatments, the patient is exposed, repeatedly and enduringly, to the phobic object in the absence of the original traumatic event. Each technique keeps the phobic in the presence of the phobic object by a different tactic so that extinction can take place: desensitization by having the patient relax and imagine the object, flooding by forcibly keeping the phobic in the phobic situation, and modeling by encouraging the phobic to approach the phobic object as the model has done. The fact that each of these three therapies works and employs classical fear extinction supports the view that the phobia was originally acquired by classical fear conditioning.

Drugs

Antidepressant drugs, particularly imipramine and MAO-inhibitors (which we shall discuss in Chapter 13) may be very helpful in alleviating phobias, either alone or when given in concert with behavior therapy and supportive therapy (Tyrer, Candy, and Kelly, 1973; Zitrin, Klein, and Woerner, 1978; Klein and Davis, 1969; Marks, Gray, Cohen, Hill, Mawson, Ramm, and Stern, 1983; Zitrin, Klein, Woerner, and Ross, 1983). But there is an important distinction between the phobics who will benefit from antidepressant medication and those who will not. The distinction is between phobics who do and who do not have ***spontaneous panic attacks.*** As we mentioned earlier, agoraphobics typically have spontaneous panic attacks in which their heart pounds, they believe the ground is trembling beneath them, and they think they are going to die. In fact, agoraphobia often develops in early adulthood following such a panic attack. Specific phobics, on the other hand, are not as prone to spontaneous panic attacks. The antidepressant drugs seem particularly useful in quelling the agoraphobic's spontaneous panic attacks. Once the panic attack is so controlled, the agoraphobic need no longer fear going into the street, perhaps because the panic attack had been the traumatic event (the US) that he had feared and that he now knows will no longer occur. If this is so, the effectiveness of the antidepressants in curing agoraphobia may also provide us with a fourth type of therapy that works because fear of the CS—fear of the phobic object—is extinguished by learning that the dreaded US will not occur.

EVALUATION OF THE BEHAVIORAL ACCOUNT

The behavioral model of phobias appears to be adequate—in fact, it is as good a model of a form of abnormality as any we know. It is consistent with case history material; it has generated three effective therapies based on classical fear extinction; and it is supported by a good deal of laboratory evidence. However, there are three main problems with this account: selectivity, irrationality, and lack of traumatic conditioning. We will now examine these three problems and will look at the theory that has been used to account for them: prepared classical conditioning.

Selectivity of Phobias

Phobias occur almost entirely to a highly restricted set of objects, whereas ordinary classical conditioning of fear occurs to any object that happens to be around at the same time as trauma. Why are phobias of the dark so common but phobias of pillows are nonexistent, although both are paired with nighttime trauma? Why are phobias of knives so rare even though knives are often paired with injury? Why have we never heard of a phobia of electric outlets? Why are there rat, horse, dog, and spider phobias, but not lamb or kitten phobias?

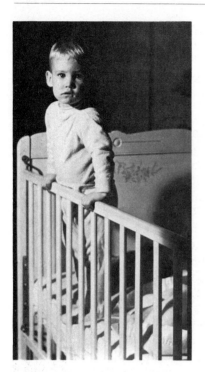

Phobias of the dark are very common, but phobias of pajamas do not exist. This may be due to prepared classical conditioning. (Photograph by Suzanne Szasz)

Although Watson and Raynor had found it simple to condition Little Albert to fear rats, E. L. Thorndike (1874–1949), the American learning theorist, had difficulty trying to train his children to stay away from sharp objects and to stay out of the street, even though such trespasses were paired with spankings. In consequence, Thorndike decided to study this phenomenon experimentally. He brought young children to his laboratory and presented them with objects like curtains and wooden ducks which, unlike rats, do not contort and move themselves. These objects were paired with traumatic noise. No fear conditioning resulted, even after many pairings (Valentine, 1930; Bregman, 1934). Phobic conditioning, both in and out of the laboratory, is highly selective. Can the behavioral analysis accommodate this observation?

Yes, with some modification of its basic principles (Seligman, 1970; Eysenck, 1979). Although ordinarily laboratory conditioning may be nonselective (as Pavlov claimed), there is a kind of classical conditioning that is highly selective: *prepared classical conditioning*, such as the conditioning of taste aversions. In an experiment by John Garcia, rats received sweet-tasting water at the same time as being subjected to light and noise, all signaling radiation sickness. They learned to hate the sweet taste in one trial, but the light and noise did not become at all aversive. Rats who received the same compound signals paired several times with shock, rather than stomach illness learned to fear the light and noise, but they continued to love the sweet taste (Garcia and Koelling, 1966). Evolution seems to have selected rats who learn aversions very readily when taste is paired with stomach illness, and who do not learn to fear noise and light when they become sick.

The great majority of common phobias are of objects that were once actually dangerous to pre-technological man (De Silva, Rachman, and Seligman, 1977). Natural selection probably favored those of our ancestors who, once they had minimal exposure to trauma paired with such signals, were highly prepared to learn that strangers, crowds, heights, insects, large animals, and dirt were dangerous. Such primates would have had a clear reproductive and survival edge over others who learned only gradually about such real dangers. Thus, evolution seems to have selected a certain set of objects, all once dangerous to man, that are readily conditionable to trauma, and it seems to have left out other objects that are much more difficult to condition to fear (such as lambs, electric outlets, knives), either because they were never dangerous or because their origin is too recent to have been subject to natural selection.

In an important series of experiments, Arne Öhman, Kenneth Hugdahl, and their collaborators at the University of Uppsala in Sweden, created what appears to be a close laboratory model of phobias (Öhman, Fredrikson, Hugdahl, and Rimmo, 1976). Fear was conditioned in student volunteers using a variety of prepared—once dangerous to Homo sapiens—or unprepared fear CSs: pictures of snakes or spiders (prepared) versus pictures of houses, faces, or flowers (unprepared). In a typical experiment, in the "prepared" group, the pictures of snakes signaled that brief, painful electric shock would occur ten seconds later. In the "unprepared" group, pictures of houses signaled shock. Fear conditioning, as measured by galvanic skin response (akin to sweating), occurred much more rapidly to prepared signals than to unprepared ones when each was paired with shock. In fact, conditioning took place in one pairing with snakes or spiders, but it took four or five pairings with shock for fear of unprepared signals to be conditioned.

This study demonstrates that humans seem more prepared to learn to be afraid of certain objects than of others. Consider guns, therefore, as a potentially phobic object. Guns are too recent to have been prepared for fear conditioning by evolution, but guns have had voluminous cultural preparation: stories, TV shows, parental warnings. Does the fear conditioned to pictures of guns have the properties of snakes and spiders, or of houses and flowers? Guns turn out to resemble houses and flowers, not spiders and snakes in their conditioning properties. This indicates that the preparedness of spiders and snakes is biological, not cultural.

The behavioral reply to the selectivity of phobias is to assert that phobias are not instances of ordinary classical conditioning, but rather they are instances of ***prepared classical conditioning***: certain evolutionarily dangerous objects are prepared to become phobic objects when paired with trauma, but others are not and require much more extensive and traumatic conditioning to become phobic objects. Phobias to snow, knives, lambs, and the like may be conditioned, but more trials and more intense trauma must occur. Thus, such unprepared phobias are very rare.

One researcher tells the story of a four-year-old girl who saw a snake while walking through a park in England. She found the snake interesting, but she was not greatly frightened by it. A short time later, she returned to the family car, and her hand was smashed in the car door. She developed a lifelong phobia, not of cars or doors but of snakes (Marks, 1977). So we see that phobias are selective, both in the laboratory and in real life.

Irrationality of Phobias

Laboratory fear conditioning seems very rational. When a signal predicts shock, the subject learns to expect shock and fear develops. When the signal predicts no shock (extinction or "inhibition"), the subject gradually learns to expect no shock, and fear accordingly is eliminated. When a signal is redundant and tells the subject no more than she already knows about when the shock will occur, no learning occurs (Rescorla and Wagner, 1972). Phobias, in contrast, are not so rational. The elevator phobic, when far away from the elevator, may believe that the probability of the cable snapping is negligible. But, as she approaches and gets on, in her mind the probability grows to 1/100, then to 1/2, then to certainty and panic sets in.

This irrationality is at the heart of what has been called "the neurotic paradox" (Mowrer, 1950; Eysenck, 1979). This paradox characterizes not only phobias but all the neurotic conditions. Neurotic behavior is self-perpetuating and self-defeating. How can theories like the behavioral theory of fear conditioning, calling on the rationality of human beings, explain it? Put another way, "Common sense holds that a normal, sensible man, or even a beast to the limits of his intelligence, will weigh and balance the consequences of his acts: if a net effect is favorable, the action producing it will be perpetuated; if a net effect is unfavorable, the action producing it will be inhibited, abandoned. In neurosis, however, one sees actions that have predominantly unfavorable consequences, yet they persist over a period of months, years, or a lifetime" (Mowrer, 1950). A phobic's life may be so impoverished by avoiding the phobic object that she cannot even leave her house. Why doesn't she merely give up the avoidance behavior and change her beliefs so that they match the realities of the danger? Any considerations that will help us out of the neurotic paradox in the case of phobias will also help us out of the neurotic paradox for all the other neuroses; we present one such consideration now.

Unprepared classical conditioning may be rational, but prepared classical conditioning is not. Taste aversions do not seem to be phenomena that accurately reflect the actual probability of danger. Once an aversion to Sauce Bernaise is learned—based on vomiting after eating the sauce—merely knowing that a stomach virus rather than the Sauce Bearnaise caused the vomiting will not change the acquired distaste for Sauce Bearnaise. Instead, taste aversions are better seen as examples of blind, irrational conditioning (Garcia and Koelling, 1966; Rozin and Kalat, 1971; Seligman and Hager, 1972). If prepared conditioning is more like phobic fear than is unprepared fear conditioning, phobias should be irrational.

Kenneth Hugdahl and Arne Öhman (1977) have provided the relevant evidence for this conclusion. Swedish students were conditioned to fear either snakes and spiders or houses and faces by pairing each CS with shock. At the end of the conditioning, the electrodes were removed, and the subjects were told that shock would not be delivered anymore. Fear extinguished immediately to houses and faces, but remained full-blown to snakes and spiders. Similarly, it is utterly futile to try to convince a cat phobic by arguing that cats aren't dangerous, while it is quite easy to convince the very same phobic that the building he works in has been effectively fireproofed. In general, the irrationality of neurotic behavior may be due to the fact that it is prepared, rather than unprepared, learning (Eysenck, 1979).

Non-traumatic Phobias

Classical fear conditioning requires an explicit pairing of the CS with a traumatic event. Sometimes phobias have such a history (e.g., Hilda's snow phobia), but frequently they do not (Lazarus, 1971). For example, a phobia may develop gradually with minor impetus: the phobic's mother was always afraid of birds, when the patient was a child she saw a film in which people were attacked by flocks of birds, and she came to develop a phobia to birds. Can the behavioral analysis based on traumatic conditioning also account for non-traumatically induced phobias? It turns out that prepared fear conditioning, unlike unprepared, can occur with minimal relations between CS and US. In fact, this is the definition of prepared conditioning. Even if six-hour delays occur between taste and illness, the taste aversion will still form (Garcia, Ervin, and Koelling, 1967).

Arne Öhman and his collaborators have also provided the direct evidence that prepared fear conditioning can occur without the experience of trauma paired with the signal. Verbal threat of shock alone produced robust fear conditioning following prepared signals, but fear conditioning did not follow unprepared signals (Hygge and Öhman, 1978). In addition, social modeling alone (without threat of shock) was more effective in producing robust fear conditioning to pictures of snakes and spiders than to flowers, mushrooms, and berries (Bandura, 1969; Hygge and Öhman, 1978).

Susceptibility to Phobias

One large mystery remains to be solved: who becomes a phobic and who doesn't? Many people are exposed as children and young adults to potentially phobic signals paired with traumatic or subtraumatic events: they are bitten by large dogs, are involved in auto accidents, throw up in public. But only a few develop phobias. Most show a transient disturbance that dissipates in time. The behavioral account does not now provide us with a way of telling in advance if a disturbance will become a phobia. A complete explanation of phobias will need to account for such individual differences as preparedness and proneness to spontaneous panic attacks.

POST-TRAUMATIC STRESS DISORDER

Phobia, as we saw, is a disorder in which fear is triggered by a specific object. There is a second emotional disorder that is also precipitated by a specific event: ***post-traumatic stress disorder***. In phobia, the objects or events that set off the phobia are quite commonplace, for example, crowds, embarrassment, cats, and illness. But the precipitant of a post-traumatic stress disorder, in contrast, is a catastrophic event beyond the normal range of human suffering, for example, an earthquake, a rape, combat, or imprisonment in a concentration camp. Three symptoms that result from the catastrophe define the disorder: (1) the person becomes *numb* to the world; (2) the person *relives* the trauma over and over in memory and in dreams; and (3) the person experiences symptoms of *anxiety*. The anxiety symptoms include excessive arousal, over-alertness, trouble concentrating, memory impairment, and phobic avoidance of situations that are reminders of the trauma. In addition, the individual may be wracked with guilt about surviving the catastrophe when others did not.

NATURALLY OCCURRING DISASTERS

The Buffalo Creek Flood of 1972 produced devastation and death in a small West Virginia Community, setting off many cases of post-traumatic stress

Following a fire or a flood, survivors may be beset by post-traumatic stress disorder. The photo on the left shows survivors of a fire. (Wide World Photos) The photo on the right shows victims of the Buffalo Creek flood. Survivors lived in tent cities and lined up for food, injections, and medicine, as shown here. One reason the Buffalo Creek disaster had such lasting effects was that the social organization of Buffalo Creek was swept away by the flood. (Photograph courtesy of Southern West Virginia Regional Health Council, Inc.)

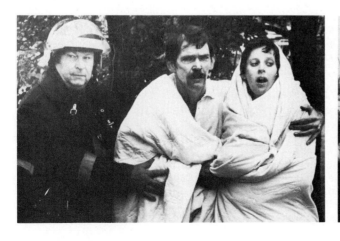

disorder among its survivors (Erikson, 1976). In the early morning of February 26, 1972, the dam on Buffalo Creek in the coal region of West Virginia collapsed, and within a few seconds, 132 million gallons of the sludge-filled black water roared down upon the residents of the mountain hollows below. Wilbur, his wife Deborah, and their four children managed to survive. What happened to them is described below.

> For some reason, I opened the inside door and looked up the road—and there it came. Just a big black cloud. It looked like 12 or 15 foot of water . . .
>
> Well, my neighbor's house was coming right up to where we live, coming down the creek . . . It was coming slow, but my wife was still asleep with the baby—she was about seven years old at the time—and the other kids were still asleep upstairs. I screamed for my wife in a bad tone of voice so I could get her attention real quick . . . I don't know how she got the girls downstairs so fast, but she run up there in her sliptail and she got the children out of bed and downstairs . . .
>
> We headed up the road . . . My wife and some of the children went up between the gons [railway gondonas]; me and my baby went under them because we didn't have much time . . . I looked around and our house was done gone. It didn't wash plumb away. It washed down about four or five house lots from where it was setting, tore all to pieces.

Two years after the disaster, Wilbur and Deborah describe their psychological scars, the defining symptoms of a post-traumatic stress disorder. First, Wilbur experiences symptoms of *anxiety*, including hyper-alertness and phobic reactions to events that remind him of the flood, such as rain and impending bad weather:

> . . . I listen to the news, and if there is a storm warning out, why I don't go to bed that night. I sit up. I tell my wife, "Don't undress our little girls; just let them lay down like they are and go to bed and go to sleep and then if I see anything going to happen, I'll wake you in plenty of time to get you out of the house." I don't go to bed. I stay up.
>
> My nerves is a problem. Every time it rains, every time it storms, I just can't take it. I walk the floor. I get so nervous I break out in a rash. I am taking shots for it now . . .

Second, Wilbur *relives* the trauma repeatedly in his dreams:

> What I went through on Buffalo Creek is the cause of my problem. The whole thing happens over to me even in my dreams, when I retire for the night. In my dreams, I run from water all the time, all the time. The whole thing just happens over and over in my dreams . . .

Third, Wilbur and Deborah have become *numb* psychologically. Affect is blunted and they are emotionally anesthetized to the sorrows and joys of the world around them. Wilbur says:

> I didn't even go to the cemetary when my father died (about a year after the flood). It didn't dawn on me that he was gone forever. And those people that dies around me now, it don't bother me like it did before the disaster . . . It just didn't bother me that my dad was dead and never would be back. I don't have the feeling I used to have about something like death. It just don't affect me like it used to.

And Deborah says:

I am neglecting my children. I just simply quit cooking. I don't do no housework. I just won't do nothing. Can't sleep. Can't eat. Just want to take me a lot of pills and just go to bed and go to sleep and not wake up. I enjoyed my home and my family, but outside of them to me, everything else in life that I had any interest in is destroyed. I loved to cook. I loved to sew. I loved to keep house. I was all the time working in making improvements in my home. But now I just got to the point where it don't mean a thing in the world to me. I haven't cooked a hot meal and put it on the table for my children in almost three weeks.

Wilbur also suffers from *survival guilt:*

At that time, why, I heard somebody holler at me, and I looked around and saw Mrs. Constable. She had a little baby in her arms and she was hollering, "Hey, Wilbur, come and help me; if you can't help me, come get my baby." But I didn't give it a thought to go back and help her. I blame myself a whole lot for that yet. She had her baby in her arms and looked as though she were going to throw it to me. Well, I never thought to go help that lady. I was thinking about my own family. They all six got drowned in that house. She was standing in water up to her waist, and they all got drowned.

MANMADE CATASTROPHES

The catastrophe that brings about a post-traumatic stress reaction need not be a naturally occurring one like the Buffalo Creek Flood. Human beings have made a hell of the lives of other human beings since time immemorial; concentration camps, war, and torture ruin the lives of their victims long after the victims have ceased to experience the original trauma. Unfortunately, the disorders following these catastrophes may be even more severe and long-lasting than those following natural disasters; it may be easier for us to deal with the "acts of God" than with the acts of men.

The survivors of the Nazi concentration camps illustrate how long-lasting and severe the post-traumatic stress reaction can be. In a study of 149 camp survivors, 142 (or 97 percent) were still troubled with anxiety twenty years

These Jews in the Warsaw Ghetto are being rounded up by German soldiers who will send them to concentration camps. Many survivors of the concentration camps still suffer the psychological effects of one of the most deliberately evil acts of this century. (Courtesy The Warder Collection)

after they were freed from the camps (Krystal, 1968). Phobic symptoms were marked: 31 percent were troubled with fears that something terrible would happen to their mates or their children whenever they were out of sight. Many of them were phobic about certain people whose appearance or behavior reminded them of their jailors; for example, the sight of a uniformed policeman or the inquisitive behavior of a doctor might be enough to set off panic. Seven percent had such severe panic attacks that the individual became confused and disoriented, entering a dreamlike state in which he believed himself to be back in the concentration camp.

The survivors relived the trauma in dreams for twenty years; 71 percent of these patients had anxiety dreams and nightmares, with 41 percent having severe ones. These nightmares were usually reruns of their persecution. Particularly terrifying were dreams in which only one detail was changed from the reality; for example, dreaming that their children who had not yet been born at the time of the camps, had been imprisoned with them in the camps.

Eighty percent of the patients suffered survivor guilt, depression, and crying spells. Survival guilt was especially strong when the patient's children had been killed; those who were the most severely depressed had lost an only child or had lost all of their children, with no children being born since. Ninety-two percent expressed self-reproach for failing to save their relatives, and 14 percent wished they had been killed instead of their relatives (Krystal, 1968).

RAPE TRAUMA SYNDROME

The catastrophe that brings about a post-traumatic stress disorder need not be experienced en masse, as in flood, war, and concentration camp; it can be solitary. Rape is, perhaps, the most common such catastrophe in modern American society. A woman's reaction to rape looks very much like the post-traumatic stress syndrome and has been called the *rape trauma syndrome* (Burgess and Holmstrom, 1979).

The reactions can be divided into two phases: the acute (disorganization) and the long-term (reorganization). In one study, researchers found that immediately following rape, a roughly equal number of women exhibited one of two emotional styles; expressive—showing fear, anger, anxiety, crying, sobbing, and tenseness, or controlled—masking feelings and showing a calm exterior. There soon followed symptoms that strongly resemble reactions to floods, combat, and concentration camps, particularly anxiety and reliving of the rape. Physical symptoms also appeared: sleep disturbances with inability to get to sleep or sudden awakening, stomach pains, genitourinary disturbances, and tension headache. Women who had been suddenly awakened by the rapist found that they would awake each night, at about the same time the attack had occurred, screaming from rape nightmares. Dreams and nightmares of the rape continued for a long time, with one-third of the victims reporting terrifying rape dreams.

Like flood victims, they startled easily in response to even minor episodes, such as being alone. In addition, fear, depression, humiliation, embarrassment, anger, and self-blame became dominant emotions, particularly fear of violence and death. Like the victims of flood and concentration camps, these women sometimes developed phobias. Women who had been at-

After being raped, a woman may experience symptoms of the rape trauma syndrome. (Photograph by Jeffrey Grosscup)

tacked indoors developed phobias of the indoors, and women who had been attacked outdoors developed phobias of the outdoors. Sexual fears were fairly common after rape, and some women were unable to resume normal sexual activity. Five months after being raped, a woman said, "There are times I get hysterical with my boyfriend. I don't want him near me; I get panicked. Sex is okay, but I still feel like screaming." According to another study, depressive symptoms seemed to disappear in most rape victims within about four months (Resick and Ellis, 1982).

In the long-term process of reorganization, most women took action to ensure safety. Many changed their telephone numbers, and half of the women made special trips home to seek support from family members. Half of the victims moved. One victim who couldn't afford to move first stayed with relatives, and then she rearranged her home. The rape had occurred in her bedroom, and here is what she did: "Wouldn't sleep in my own bed. Stayed with friends for a while. Changed my bedroom around, and got a new bedroom set." Many of the victims began to read about rape and to write about their experience. Some became active in rape crisis centers and assisted other victims, and of these, 70 percent recovered in a few months. When contacted four to six years after the rape, three-quarters of the victims felt that they had recovered, half of these within a few months and the other half within several years. One-quarter of the women, however, felt that they still had not recovered (Burgess and Holmstrom, 1979).

COURSE OF POST-TRAUMATIC STRESS DISORDER

Not much is known about the specific course of the post-traumatic stress disorder. Sometimes the symptoms disappear within a few months, resembling recovery from a depressive disorder (see Chapter 13). But overall, the prognosis is probably bleak, particularly for the victims of very severe trauma. As we saw, a high percentage of concentration camp victims are still troubled with anxiety and guilt twenty years later. This also seems to be true of some veterans of combat. Sixty-two veterans of World War II who suffered chronic "combat fatigue," with symptoms of exaggerated jumpiness, recurrent nightmares, and irritability, were examined twenty years later. Irritability, depression, restlessness, difficulties in concentration and memory, blackouts, wakefulness, fatigability, and jumpiness persisted for twenty years. These symptoms were more prominent in the veterans suffering from combat fatigue than in noncombat patients or in healthy combat veterans. Combat fatigue victims still jumped when they heard noises of jets and firecrackers. Three-quarters of these men reported that their symptoms interfered with providing for their family. Half reported their sex lives were unsatisfactory, and that they were unduly irritable with their children. A third of the men were unemployed. Figure 10-3 presents the incidence of symptoms of World War II combat fatigue victims compared to control groups twenty years later (Archibald and Tuddenham, 1965).

TREATMENT AND PREVENTION

In spite of the fact that so many of our fellow human beings are victims of extraordinary traumas, almost nothing is known about how to alleviate or

Veterans of combat may suffer symptoms of chronic "combat fatigue," which may last for years following their combat experiences. (Photograph by David Sherman, *Life Magazine*, © 1945 Time Inc.)

Figure 10-3
Post-traumatic stress disorder in veterans. The bars indicate the percentage of incidence of symptoms twenty years after World War II in veterans who suffered combat fatigue in comparison to healthy combat veterans and noncombat patients. (Source: Archibald and Tuddenham, 1965, p. 478)

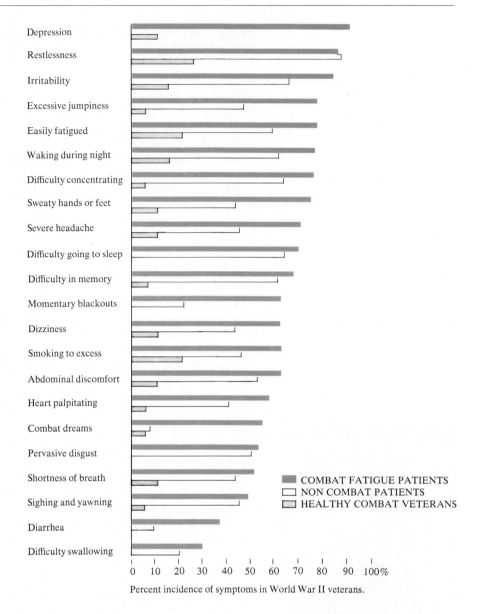

Percent incidence of symptoms in World War II veterans.

prevent post-traumatic stress reactions. Relatives, friends, and therapists are inclined to tell the victims of catastrophe to try to "forget it," but it should be apparent that such painful memories cannot be easily blotted out. Only small improvement has been reported by either drug therapy or psychotherapy among victims of trauma. Two important caveats are in order, however. First, it is difficult to find out what the individuals who suffer stress reactions to trauma were like before. It is possible that those individuals whose symptoms persist for years and years also had poor adjustment before the trauma, whereas those individuals who were in good psychological shape before the trauma were less hurt by it and therefore didn't show up for long-term follow-up. We cannot tell if the trauma itself, or the combination of trauma and a vulnerable individual, produces the reactions that are so devastating and often permanent. Second, there is the problem of *secondary gain:* victims occasionally have some incentive for staying ill for a long time. The Buffalo Creek victims, for example, were in the process of suing the Pittston Company (the owner of the dam that collapsed) for millions of dollars. Only careful longitudinal work will tell us who is most vulnerable to post-traumatic stress reactions, how long such reactions last, and what therapy can work. These studies have not yet been done (Chodoff, 1963; Leopold and Dillon, 1963; Archibald and Tuddenham, 1965; Merbaum, 1971).

Although we know almost nothing about how to treat post-traumatic stress disorder once it has set in, some steps have been taken to prevent the reaction once a trauma has been experienced. When a tornado strikes a town or when soldiers return from combat, therapists have an excellent opportunity to use preventative procedures. Thus, therapists can try to prevent a stress reaction from occurring in victims of a trauma. They can try to prevent the onset of three symptoms—anxiety, numbness, and reliving—in the victims, or the therapists can attempt to minimize the symptoms before they take hold. Such an attempt was made by therapists who worked with the victims of the takeover of the B'nai B'rith national headquarters in Washington, D.C., after the victims had been freed by their terrorist captors.

From March 9 to March 11, 1977, more than one hundred persons had been held hostage by members of the Hanafi Muslim sect in a B'nai B'rith headquarters. During the thirty-nine hours of their captivity, they had been exposed to physical violence, verbal abuse, threats, severe physical restraints, hunger, humiliation, and the continual threat of imminent death. What happened to Shirley is shown in the following case:

Here one of the hostages of the Hanafi Muslims' takeover of B'nai B'rith headquarters recounts how gunmen broke into her office. Psychologists may attempt to prevent post-traumatic stress disorder by intervening just after the trauma. (Wide World Photos)

Shirley is a forty-two-year-old white, married, Jewish female who was working as an administrative assistant for the B'nai B'rith on March 9, 1977. She was at her desk when several Hanafis burst into her work area. She was herded together with all her colleagues on the floor, and was pushed into the stairwell to be marched up to the eighth floor conference room that was to serve as their prison for thirty terror-filled hours. Shirley did not see the actual stabbing of another employee, but she did hear the screams and did see the bloodied machete of her Hanafi captor. She remembers her body aching from the damp cold of the concrete floor and her head aching from repeated crying spells. She recalls vividly the men being separated from the women and being roughly bound. She also remembers the humiliation heaped on several of the men because one wept, another wet himself, and still another behaved too effeminately.

She remembers many moments of overwhelming fear—the worst seemed to coincide with appearances of Khaalis, the Hanafi leader, who repeatedly threatened grisly death to specific individuals and then the entire group. She recalls images of bodies pressed against each other for comfort and protection and her annoyance at the petty grumbling about the sharing of food and floor space for sleeping. . . .

Shirley's ordeal was not over, however, once she was released by the Hanafis. For several months she experienced a number of symptoms related to the extreme stress she had undergone while held prisoner. Shirley had great difficulty returning to work; she found herself crying without explanation and intolerant of others. She felt considerable anxiety and mild, persistent depression. She associated this emotional state with a sense of being exhausted much of the time, as if she "had mononucleosis." Shirley slept poorly at first, reliving scenes of the building takeover, bloodied faces and clothes. (Sank, 1982)

The Health Maintenance Organization of Washington decided to seek the victims out and offer care immediately, rather than wait for calls for help from the victims well after their release. The idea was to *prevent* post-traumatic stress disorder which, as we have seen, frequently occurs in the weeks and months following extraordinary stress. The treatment format was short term and was derived from the multimodel behavior therapy of Lazarus (1976; see pp. 108–10). You will recall that this therapy uses a variety of techniques, both behavioral and cognitive, to treat neurotic problems. Therapy sessions were held in the building that had served as the work site of the victims and as their prison, and approximately half of the B'nai B'rith hostages came to therapy. Systematic desensitization was used to curb phobic reactions; group sharing of the experience was used to counteract numbness. Substituting calming imagery for fantasies of the takeover was used to prevent and counteract reliving the trauma repeatedly. Table 10-6 shows the different forms of behavioral and cognitive therapy for dealing with the symptoms that the victims already had or for symptoms that the therapists believed would arise in the victims in the future.

No systematic follow-up of the victims was carried out, but a few anecdotal reports show that some were doing quite well in 1982, but others still had trauma-related problems (Sank, 1982). Without such follow-up, we cannot know if this treatment prevented post-traumatic stress reactions, but it is a unique and exemplary use of preventative procedures for fear disorders.

PANIC DISORDER AND GENERALIZED ANXIETY DISORDER

In our discussion so far, we have focused on phobia and post-traumatic stress disorders, which we consider *fear disorders.* Both are problems in which anxiety is felt. Also, the individual afflicted by either of them experiences the four elements of fear: expectations of danger (the cognitive element); the emergency reaction (the somatic element); feelings of terror, apprehension, and dread (the emotional element); and avoidance and escape (the behavioral element). Phobia and post-traumatic stress disorder are similar in that they both stem from dread of a specific object; the phobic object (cat, etc.) in the case of phobias, and the precipitating situation (flood, etc.) in the cases of post-traumatic stress disorder. In contrast, in the *anxiety disorders,* panic disorder and generalized anxiety disorder, although anxiety is also felt, there is no specific object that is feared. In these disorders, the anxiety felt by the individual is not focused on a clear and specific object. We will now consider the two anxiety disorders. Panic attacks are acute experiences of anxiety, whereas generalized anxiety disorder is the chronic experience of anxiety.

PANIC DISORDER

How many of us have at some time been suddenly overwhelmed by intense apprehension? Physically, we feel jumpy and tense. Cognitively, we expect that something bad—we don't know what—is going to happen. Such an attack comes out of nowhere; no specific object or event sets it off, and the at-

Table 10-6 HOSTAGES' MULTIMODAL PROFILE

Modality of Therapy	Problem	Treatment
Behavior	Avoidance (of stairwells, taxis, elevators, being alone, the work site)	*In vivo* and systematic desensitization
	Crying	Deep Muscle Relaxation (DMR)
	Fear of isolation	Writing and sharing experience with others
Affect	Numbness	Group sharing of the experience and writing about feelings
	Mild Depression	Planning rewarding activities and reassurance
	Anxiety attacks	DMR, coping imagery, assertiveness training
	Anger	Assertiveness training
Sensation	Sleep disturbance	DMR, scheduling relaxing activities, exercise, coping imagery
	Headaches	DMR with concentration on muscles of the face, neck, and shoulders
Imagery	Reliving of takeover and holocaust fantasies	Substituting calming imagery
	Being vulnerable in all life situations	Assertiveness imagery
Cognitions	"I'll never get over this." "The Hanafis know my name and address and will come to kill me later." "No place is safe anymore."	Rational-Emotive Therapy (RET; see pp. 108-10)
	Isolation	Group sharing, therapists providing information about the human reactions to stress
Interpersonal	Suspicious of strangers	Take more realistic precautions (lock car and home, etc.), *in vivo* desensitization
Drugs	Increased used of tranquilizers, sleeping medications, alcohol	Substitution of DMR, exercise, coping imagery, limited use of drugs
	Somatic disturbances	Medical check after release and before rejoining families, medical follow-ups of new complaints or old ones exacerbated by stress

SOURCE: Adapted from Sank, 1979, pp. 334–38.

Many of us have felt at times a sudden and overwhelming sense of apprehension or anxiety. Those who have frequent and severe attacks of anxiety are said to suffer from panic disorder. (Photograph by Rocky Weldon/Leo de Wys)

tack gradually subsides. But some people have more severe attacks, and have them frequently. These people suffer from ***panic disorder.*** Panic disorder consists of recurrent panic attacks.

A panic attack consists of the four elements of fear, with the emotional and physical elements most salient.

Emotionally the individual is overwhelmed with intense apprehension, dread, or terror.

> It was just like I was petrified with fear. If I were to meet a lion face to face, I couldn't be more scared. Everything got black, and I felt I would faint; but I didn't. I thought I won't be able to hold on". . . (Laughlin, 1967 p. 92)

Physically, a panic attack consists of an acute emergency reaction.

> My heart was beating so hard and fast it would jump out and hit my hand. I felt like I couldn't stand up—that my legs wouldn't support me. My hands got icy and my feet stung. There were horrible shooting pains in my forehead. My head felt tight, like someone had pulled the skin down too tight and I wanted to pull it away. . .
> I couldn't breathe. I was short of breath. I literally got out of breath and panted like I had run up and down the stairs. I felt like I had run an eight-mile race. I couldn't do anything. I felt all in; weak, no strength. I can't even dial a telephone. . . . (Laughlin, 1967, p. 92)

Cognitively, the individual thinks he might die, go crazy, or blow out of control.

> Even then I can't be still when I am like this. I am restless and I pace up and down. I feel like I am just not responsible. I don't know what I'll do. These things are terrible. I can go along real calmly for awhile. Then, without any warning, this happens. I just blow my top. (Laughlin, 1967, p. 92)

Such an attack usually lasts for a matter of minutes, subsiding rather gradually. What distinguishes a panic attack from a phobic disorder is that a panic attack comes out of nowhere, rather than in response to a specific threatening situation. As we mentioned earlier, some phobics, particularly agoraphobics, are subject to panic attacks before their phobic disorder develops, and the agoraphobia may in fact begin with a panic attack. There is no definitive data on the frequency of panic attacks, although they are quite common. Clinical experience indicates that they occur more frequently in women than in men.

Generalized Anxiety Disorder

In contrast to a panic attack, which is sudden and acute, generalized anxiety is chronic, and may last for months on end, with the elements of anxiety more or less continually present (see Box 10-2). Emotionally, the individual feels jittery and tense, vigilant, and constantly on edge.

> I feel tense and fearful much of the time. I don't know what it is. I can't put my finger on it. . . . I just get all nervous inside. . . . I act like I'm scared to death of something. I guess maybe I am. (Laughlin, 1967, p.107)

Cognitively, as in panic attacks, the individual expects something awful, but doesn't know what.

Anxious individuals may attempt to flee shapeless dangers. (Painting by Juan Genoves. Courtesy Marlborough Fine Art, Ltd.)

Box 10-2   **ANXIETY: STATE VERSUS TRAIT**

As we have seen, some individuals have acute attacks of anxiety and do not have them again for some time (panic disorder); others seem to feel anxious all of the time (generalized anxiety disorder). Some have suggested that there is a **state** versus **trait** distinction that may explain this observation. That is, many of us at one time or another may feel panic whether or not we understand what it was in the situation that brought it on. In short, we fall into a state of anxiety. But the others, those who feel anxious all of the time, may have a predisposition to anxiety. They are always ready to feel anxiety; they are chronically anxious. We say that they have a trait of anxiety.

Various paper and pencil tests have been designed to determine whether one is in a state of anxiety, whether one has a trait for anxiety, or if neither measure applies. Among the most widely used are Janet Taylor Spence's Manifest Anxiety Scale (Taylor, 1951, 1953), Marvin Zuckerman's Affect Adjective Checklist (Zuckerman and Lubin, 1965), and Charles Spielberger's State-Trait Anxiety Inventory (Spielberger, Gorsuch, and Lushene, 1970). These questionnaires ask about the four elements of anxiety.

An anxiety *state* questionnaire asks how the individual feels right now, whereas an anxiety *trait* questionnaire focuses on an individual's dispositions to display the elements of anxiety across time and across different situations. For example, the following questions might be asked: ''Are you a steady person?'' ''Do unimportant thoughts run through your mind and bother you?'' ''Do you worry too much over something that really doesn't matter?'' Affirmative answers to such questions point toward a trait of anxiety-proneness. Some sample items that seek to find state anxiety are shown on p. 233. This questionnaire was developed by Norman Endler and his colleagues at York University (Endler, Magnusson, Ekehammar, and Okada, 1975). The questions ask how the individual feels at the time that he or she is taking the test.

I am frightened, but don't know what I fear. I keep expecting something bad to happen. . . . I have thought I could tie it to definite things, but this isn't true. It varies, and is unpredictable. I can't tell when it will come on. If I could just put my finger on what it is. . . (Laughlin, 1967, p.107)

Physically, the individual experiences a mild chronic emergency reaction: he sweats, his heart races, his stomach is usually upset, he feels cold, light-headed, and his hands usually feel clammy.

Behaviorally, he is always ready to run away, flee, or hide.

For the past week or so I don't want to get away from the house. I fear I might go all to pieces, maybe become hysterical. . .

Sometimes I get fearful and tense when I am talking to people and I just want to run away. (Laughlin, 1967, p.107)

Please circle a number from 1 to 5 for each of the items in response to the question: "HOW DO YOU FEEL AT THIS PARTICULAR MOMENT?"

		Very Much				Not at All
Cognitive	1. Self-Confident	1	2	3	4	5
		Able to Focus				Unable to Focus
	2. Able to focus my thoughts	1	2	3	4	5
		Very Calm				Not at All
Emotional	3. Calm	1	2	3	4	5
		Not at All				Very Nervous
	4. Nervous	1	2	3	4	5
		Not at All				Very Uneasy
	5. Uneasy	1	2	3	4	5
		Not at All				Very Moist
Somatic	6. Hands Moist	1	2	3	4	5
		Not at All				Very Irregular
	7. Breathing is irregular	1	2	3	4	5
		Not at All				Very Tense
	8. Tense in my stomach	1	2	3	4	5
		Not at All				Very Much
Behavioral	9. Want to avoid this situation	1	2	3	4	5

SOURCE: Adapted from Endler, Magnusson, Ekehammar, and Okoda, 1975.

While the symptoms of panic disorder and generalized anxiety disorder are quite clear, their causes remain mysterious (Wolpe and Lazarus, 1969; Klein, 1980). Unfortunately little is known about how to treat them, although drug therapy, particularly with tranquilizers, sometimes helps.

SUMMARY

1. Freud used the term "neurosis" to *describe* the symptoms that are distressing to an individual in whom reality testing is intact. He also used the term to refer to the causal *process* of defending against anxiety. Eysenck also believed that neuroses result from anxiety.

2. DSM-III merely *describes* neurosis without invoking a process or etiology for the disorder. It considers an individual to have a neurotic disorder if

he has emotionally distressing symptoms that he wishes to be rid of, if he can test reality relatively well, and if he exhibits behavior that does not grossly violate social norms.

3. Psychotic disorders differ from neurotic disorders in that psychotic disorders are sweeping disturbances of perception, thinking, language, and reality testing. Unlike neurotic behavior, psychotic behavior grossly violates social norms.

4. Prominent among the emotionally distressing symptoms of neurotic disorders are the states of fear and anxiety. Phobias and post-traumatic stress disorder are both fear disorders in that specific objects or events set them off. Panic disorder and generalized anxiety disorder are both anxiety disorders in that the individual feels very anxious although no specific danger is anticipated.

5. The state of fear consists of four elements: *cognitively*, the individual expects danger; *somatically*, the individual experiences the emergency reaction; *emotionally*, the individual feels apprehension, terror, or dread; and *behaviorally*, the individual tries to flee the feared situation. The elements of anxiety are identical to those of fear except for the cognitive element; the anxious individual does not expect a specific danger but simply that *something* bad will happen.

6. A *phobia* is a persistent fear of a specific object in which the fear is greatly out of proportion to the amount of danger actually present. There are five types of phobias: agoraphobia (fear of the marketplace), social phobias, phobias of animals and insects, phobias of specific inanimate objects, and phobias of illness and injury (nosophobia).

7. The psychoanalytic school holds that phobias occur when anxiety stemming from an intrapsychic conflict is displaced onto an innocent object.

8. The behavioral school holds that phobias are merely instances of the normal classical conditioning of fear to an innocent object that happened to be around when a traumatic event occurred. The behavioral model is consistent with case histories and laboratory evidence, and it has generated three effective therapies based on classical fear extinction: systematic desensitization, flooding, and modeling. Moreover, there is reason to believe that antidepressant drugs may be helpful in treating agoraphobia because these drugs prevent the spontaneous panic attacks that agoraphobics often have.

9. The three problems with the behavioral model—selectivity of phobias, irrationality of phobias, and non-traumatic phobias—can be accounted for by the theory of *prepared classical conditioning*, which states that humans seem more prepared to learn to be afraid of certain objects than of others.

10. *Post-traumatic stress disorder* is a fear disorder that resembles phobias in that it is set off by a specific event. In this case, the specific event is a catastrophic happening beyond the normal range of human suffering. Natural disasters, rape, combat, and imprisonment in a concentration camp may all set off post-traumatic stress disorder. Following the event, symptoms of fear, reliving the event in dreams and waking, and numbness toward the external world may develop. Also, the individual may experience survivor guilt. The symptoms may last a lifetime; very little is known about how to cure or prevent them.

11. *Panic attacks* come out of the blue, with no specific event or object setting them off. They last for only a few minutes and consist of the four elements of the anxiety reaction. *Panic disorder* consists of recurrent panic attacks.

12. *Generalized anxiety disorder* is similar to panic disorder in that there is no specific event that sets it off. However, in generalized anxiety disorder, the anxiety is milder and is chronic, with the elements of anxiety more or less continually present for weeks or months on end.

11

Obsession, Hysteria, and Dissociation: Anxiety Inferred

WE have divided neurotic disorders into two classes: those in which anxiety is actually experienced by the sufferer, and those in which anxiety is not experienced but is inferred to explain the neurotic symptoms. In the last chapter, we discussed those disorders in which anxiety is manifest: phobia, traumatic stress disorder, panic disorder, and generalized anxiety disorder. In this chapter, we will discuss those neurotic disorders in which underlying anxiety has often been inferred to be the cause of the symptoms.

We will discuss three types of disorders. First are the *obsessive-compulsive disorders* in which the individual is plagued with uncontrollable, repulsive thoughts and engages in seemingly senseless rituals. An obsessive-compulsive may think that he left the gas stove on and get out of bed to check it twenty times during the night, or he may have continual thoughts of killing his children and keep all knives and sharp objects out of his own reach. The second disorder is the somatoform disorder that is sometimes called *hysterical conversion.* This disorder is characterized by a loss of physical functioning not due to any physical disorder but apparently resulting from psychological conflict. An individual may, for no biological reason, suddenly become blind, deaf, paralyzed, or suffer excruciating pain as a result of psychological stress. The third kind of disorder consists of the *dissociative disorders,* in which the individual's very identity is fragmented. Among these are *amnesia,* in which an individual suddenly loses the memory of who he is and *multiple personality,* in which more than one personality exists in the same individual, each with a relatively rich and stable life of its own.

In contrast to the disorders in the last chapter, anxiety is not usually felt by the victims of these three types of disorders. Obsessive-compulsives sometimes feel anxiety, but if their compulsion is frequent and fast enough they can ward off anxiety altogether. Individuals with somatoform and dissociative disorders usually feel little anxiety. In fact, they may be surprisingly indifferent to their symptoms. But when psychoanalytic clinicians and researchers look at the conflicts that precede these disorders, they often infer that the symptoms are an attempt to harness underlying anxiety that otherwise threatens to overwhelm the individual. For example, a man who believes he caused the paralysis of his friend may himself unconsciously assume the symptoms of paralysis; or a teenager who is plagued with unresolvable troubles at home and in school may forget who he is, wander to a new city, and assume a new identity. We begin our discussion of these disorders with obsessions and compulsions.

OBSESSIONS AND COMPULSIONS

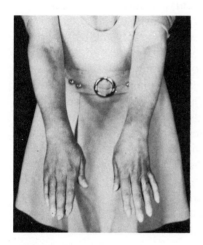

The discolored and scarred hands of a forty-two-year-old woman who had been washing compulsively for more than ten years. Each day she spent between three and five hours washing her hands and arms in an attempt to obtain relief from the anxiety that some contaminating dirt might have adhered to her. (Courtesy S. J. Rachman)

All of us at least occasionally have distasteful and unacceptable thoughts. Most people at one time or another have had the following thoughts: "Might I do violence to someone I love?" "Am I absolutely sure that I've locked all the doors and windows?" "Have I left the gas in the stove on?" Most of us pay little attention to these thoughts when they occur or if we do, we soon dismiss them. Such is not the case in individuals with obsessive-compulsive disorders. An example of such an individual follows:

A thirty-eight-year-old mother of one child had been obsessed by fears of contamination during her entire adult life. Literally hundreds of times a day, thoughts of being infected by germs would occur to her. Once she began to think that either she or her child might become infected, she could not dismiss the thought. This constant concern about infection resulted in a series of washing and cleaning rituals that took up most of her day. Her child was confined to one room only, which the woman tried to keep entirely free of germs by scrubbing it—floor to ceiling—several times a day. Moreover, she opened and closed all doors with her feet, in order to avoid contaminating her own hands. (Rachman and Hodgson, 1980)

Obsessive-compulsive disorder consists of the two components from which we derive its name: obsessions and compulsions. **Obsessions** are repetitive thoughts, images, or impulses that invade consciousness, are often abhorrent, and are very difficult to dismiss or control. In the case above, the mother is occupied with repulsive thoughts and images of disease and infection, which she cannot turn off. **Compulsions** are the behavioral responses to obsessive thoughts. A compulsion is a repetitive, stereotyped, and unwanted action that can be resisted only with difficulty. The mother above reacts to her thoughts of germs by compulsively scrubbing her child's room. Generally, individuals who are afflicted with obsessions also suffer from compulsions (Rachman, 1978; Rachman and Hodgson, 1980). Because obsessions and compulsions are usually found together, some writers use the terms "obsessive" and "compulsive" interchangeably, but essentially they refer to two distinct events: obsessions are thoughts, compulsions are actions.

What distinguishes obsessions of clinical proportions from more harmless recurring thoughts? There are three hallmarks: (1) obsessions are *unwelcome* and *intrude* on consciousness; an obsessive complains, "The thought that I might strangle a child keeps returning and prevents me from concentrating on my work," whereas mere recurring thoughts do not interfere with work; (2) obsessions arise *from within*, not from an external situation; and (3) obsessions are very *difficult to control*. Someone with merely recurring thoughts can readily distract himself and think of something else; obsessives, in contrast, complain, "I can't help myself—I keep saying the numbers over and over again."

OBSESSIONS AND THE SOCIAL CONTEXT

The content of obsessions changes over time. In past centuries in the Western world, obsessions were often religious and sexual. John Bunyan, seventeenth century author of *A Pilgrim's Progress*, was "fiercely assaulted" with the wicked suggestion to "sell Christ" running in his mind. " 'Sell him, sell him, sell him, sell him,' as fast as a man could speak. Against which also in my mind I answered, 'No, no, not for thousands, thousands, thousands,' at least twenty times together." Other famous religious personalities believed they suffered from "pollution of the mind" with "naughty and blasphemous thoughts" of committing sexual sins "revolving in a restless circle." Today, obsessions about religion and sex have become somewhat rarer; obsessions about dirt and contamination, violence, and orderliness are more common (Hunter and MacAlpine, 1963; Akhtar, Wig, Varma, Pershard, and Verma, 1975; Rachman, 1978; Rachman and Hodgson, 1980). One patient embodied this historical trend in the course of her thirty-five-year-long disorder. For the first ten years, she was obsessed with contracting syphilis. She repeatedly scrubbed and disinfected herself, and took extraordinary care to avoid walking on used condoms in public places. The syphilis fear disappeared and gave way to obsessions about being infected with cancer, and she continued to wash and disinfect herself many times. Obsessions about contamination are perhaps the most common kind of obsession today. Here is a description of a striking case:

Pictured here is Howard Hughes, who in the last half of his life, was afflicted with a severe obsessive-compulsive disorder about germs. (Wide World Photos)

> Howard Hughes was one of America's richest and most colorful tycoons. During at least the last half of his life, Hughes was apparently afflicted with a severe obsessive-compulsive disorder about infection. He lived as a recluse, but unlike most obsessives, he was rich enough to be able to hire a retinue of servants to carry out his rituals for him, rather than doing them himself. Hughes's fear of germs and contamination dominated his life. He wrote numerous memos in which he explained in detail what he wanted done to prevent the "back transmission" of germs to him. For example, in a three-page memo, he explained how he wanted a can of fruit opened to prevent "fallout" of germs. He required that special equipment be used to open the can, writing, "The equipment used in connection with this operation will consist of the following items: 1 unopened newspaper, 1 sterile can opener; 1 large sterile plate; 1 sterile fork; 1 sterile spoon; 2 sterile brushes; 2 bars of soap; sterile paper towels." The ritual he devised for opening the can had nine steps: "preparing a table, procuring of fruit can, washing of can, drying the can, processing the hands, opening the can, removing fruit from can, fallout rules while around can, and conclusion of operation." He worked out complicated procedures for each step of the operation; for example, to wash the can, he wrote:
>
>> The man in charge then turns the valve in the bathtub on, using his bare hands to do so. He also adjusts the water temperature so that it is not too hot nor too cold. He then takes one of the brushes, and, using one of the bars of soap, creates a good lather, and then scrubs the can from a point two inches below the top of the can. He should first soak and remove the label, and then

brush the cylindrical part of the can over and over until all particles of dust, pieces of paper label, and, in general, all sources of contamination have been removed. Holding the can in the center at all times, he then processes the bottom of the can in the same manner, being very sure that all the bristles of the brush have thoroughly cleaned all the small indentations on the perimeter of the bottom of the can. He then rinses the soap from the cylindrical sides and the bottom of the can. (Bartlett and Steele, 1979, p. 233)

Hughes's persistent fear of contamination led to a series of compulsive rituals that increasingly dominated his daily life. He eventually became a prisoner of his obsessions, confined to his "sterile" rooms, and seeing only his selected servants. Hughes's compulsive rituals bore a rational relationship to the obsession—if there really was rampant danger of infection from germs around food, the compulsion might have cut down the risk—but it was his obsession that germs were rampant that was irrational. The ritual to control contamination need not be so rational, as this next case illustrates.

A twenty-seven-year-old veterinarian described his severe compulsive ritual. His compulsion required him to flush the toilet a multiple of three times whenever he entered a bathroom. Sometimes he was "satisfied" with three times only; but on other occasions, nine, twenty-seven, or even more were needed. He was at a loss to control his compulsive ritual which had sometimes embarrassed him socially and was professionally handicapping. (Laughlin, 1967, p. 351)

ANXIETY, DEPRESSION, AND OBSESSIONS

What motivates an obsessive-compulsive to perform such strange actions as flushing a toilet in multiples of three? How does he feel when he has obsessive thoughts and performs his compulsive rituals? The thoughts (the obsessive component) are very disturbing. Typically, the individual suffers considerable internal distress. A mild emergency reaction of the type described in the previous chapter is often present; he feels foreboding and dread. If the ritual is performed frequently and fast enough in response to the thoughts, he can reduce or even ward off the ensuing anxiety. This is why obsession-compulsion is put in the anxiety-inferred category. The obsessive finds ways of dealing with the anxiety—by acting out his compulsions. But if his compulsive ritual is prevented, he will first feel tension similar to what we would feel if someone prevented us from answering a ringing telephone. If the barrier persists, intense distress will sweep over the patient. Here, of course, the anxiety will be felt. The individual's distress then can only be alleviated by carrying out the compulsion, thereby neutralizing the anxiety evoked by the obsessive thoughts and images. The next case illustrates this.

A middle-aged woman complained of an obsession concerning colors and heat,"The main problem is colors. I cannot look at any of the colors that are in the fire, red, orange or pink."
She believed the colors blue, geeen, brown, white, and gray were neutral, and she used these colors to "neutralize" the fiery colors. "If I happen to see a fire color, I've got to immediately look at some other color to cancel it out. I've got to look at a tree or flowers out on the grounds, something brown or white, to neutralize it." She used to walk around with a small piece of green carpet in order to neutralize the effects of any orange colors she might happen upon and see or imagine.

She described the traumatic feelings that images of colored stimuli (or hot stimuli) evoked:

> It starts in my mind, and when I look at the color, I start to tremble, and I go hot all over, just as though I'm on fire. I cannot stand up; I've got to sit down or else I'll fall. I feel sick, and all I can say is that it is a traumatic feeling, that's the only word I can think of to describe it. If it is the last color I look at before I get into bed, I just won't sleep all night. . . .
>
> I try to fight it, and get into bed and tell myself it is ridiculous. I know it can't hurt me physically, although it does harm me mentally. I lie there and this hot feeling comes over me, and I start to tremble. If that happens, I have to get up, put all my clothes on again and start once more, as though I am getting into bed. Sometimes I have to do this four or five times before finally getting to sleep. (Rachman and Hodgson, 1980)

Anxiety is in some way always there. And it is not the only negative affect associated with obsessions. Depression bears an intimate relationship as well. Obsessions and clinical depression appear frequently together; in fact, from 10 to 35 percent of depressed patients may have obsessions as well (Gittleson, 1966; Sakai, 1967; Beech and Vaughan, 1979). During their periods of depression, the incidence of obsessions triples over the rate before and after the depression (Videnbech, 1975). Not only do depressed patients tend to develop obsessions, but obsessional patients are prone to develop depression (Wilner, Reich, Robins, Fishman, and Van Doren, 1976; Teasdale and Rezin, 1978).

VULNERABILITY TO OBSESSIVE-COMPULSIVE DISORDERS

Obsessive-compulsive disorders are not common. Depending upon era and culture, only between 0.3 and 0.6 percent of psychiatric outpatients are diagnosed as obsessive-compulsive (Black, 1974). Men and women seem equally vulnerable. The disorder usually comes on gradually beginning in adolescence or early adulthood. Our patient with color obsession describes the typically vague and gradual onset of her disorder:

> It is hard to say exactly when the obsession started. It was gradual. My obsession about colors must have been coming on for a couple of years very, very gradually. I only noticed it fully during the past twelve years when it got worse and worse. I can't look at certain colors, can't bathe, can't do any cooking, have to repeat many activities over and over again. . . .
>
> I think it all began some years ago when I had a sort of nervous breakdown. At the onset, I went very hot; it seemed to happen overnight somehow. I was in bed, and woke up feeling very hot. It was connected with an obsession that I had about my ailing mother at the time. I feared for her safety, and when I got a horrible thought that she might have an accident or a serious illness, this horrible hot feeling came over me. (Rachman and Hodgson, 1980)

Is there a specific type of personality that is vulnerable to an obsessive-compulsive disorder? Based on case histories, psychodynamic theorists focus on the *obsessive personality,* and this notion has crept into ordinary language. The person with an obsessive personality is methodical and leads a very well-ordered life. He is always on time. He is meticulous in how he dresses and what he says. He pays exasperatingly close attention to detail,

Felix Ungar in the *Odd Couple* was an obsessive personality. He was methodical, paid close attention to detail, and disliked dirt. He did not, however, have an obsessive-compulsive disorder, as he was proud of his meticulousness and love of detail. (Courtesy The Museum of Modern Art/Film Stills Archive)

This man has collected twine and rolled it into a ball for thirty years. His ball of twine is now 310,037 miles long. Obsessive-compulsives also sometimes collect large quantities of objects as part of their rituals. (Copyright Bernsen's International Press Service Ltd.)

and he strongly dislikes dirt. He may have a distinct cognitive style, showing intellectual rigidity and focusing on details. He is deliberate in thought and action, and highly moralistic about himself and others (Sandler and Hazari, 1960; Shapiro, 1965; Pollack, 1979).

What is the relationship between having an obsessive-compulsive *personality* and having an obsessive-compulsive *disorder*? One hypothesis is that when an individual with an obsessive personality is under stress, he reacts by developing an obsessive-compulsive disorder (Shapiro, 1965). This is an important hypothesis, because if true, it would give us a way of predicting in advance who might be especially at risk for this disorder. Unfortunately, the evidence for this hypothesis is unconvincing. The crucial difference between having an obsessive personality and having an obsessive disorder has to do with how much the person *likes* having the symptoms. An obsessive person views his meticulousness and love of detail with pride and self-esteem. For an individual with an obsessional disorder, however, these characteristics are abhorrent, unwanted, and tormenting. They are "ego-alien."

When one actually looks at the personality of individuals with obsessive-compulsive disorders, little evidence emerges showing that they also have an obsessive personality. To test this, S. J. Rachman and Ray Hodgson of the Maudsley Hospital in London developed a questionnaire that distinguishes between patients with obsessive-compulsive disorders and patients with other neurotic disorders. Table 11-1 presents some of the questions from the Maudsley Obsessive-Compulsive Disorder Inventory. The questionnaire isolates three major components of obsessive-compulsive disorders: cleaning, checking, and doubting. Patients who had either an obsessive-compulsive disorder or some other neurotic disorder took both this inventory and an inventory that measured obsessive personality by focusing on orderliness, perseverance, and rigidity. While there were extreme differences between patients with obsessive-compulsive disorders and those with other neurotic disorders on the Obsessive-Compulsive Disorder Inventory, there were no differences between these two groups on obsessive personality measures. These results suggest that the obsessive personality is not a precursor of obsessive-compulsive disorders, and that individuals who are meticulous and lead a well-ordered life are no more likely to develop an

Table 11-1 SAMPLE QUESTIONS FROM THE MAUDSLEY OBSESSIVE-COMPULSIVE DISORDER INVENTORY

Components of Obsessive-Compulsive Disorder	*Obsessive-Compulsive Disorder Answer*
Cleaning	
1. I am not excessively concerned about cleanliness.	False
2. I avoid using public telephones because of possible contamination.	True
3. I can use well-kept toilets without any hesitation.	False
4. I take a rather long time to complete my washing in the morning.	True
Checking	
1. I frequently have to check things (gas or water taps, doors) more than once.	True
2. I do not check letters over and over again before mailing them.	False
3. I frequently get nasty thoughts and have difficulty getting rid of them.	True
Doubting-Conscience	
1. I have a very strict conscience.	True
2. I usually have serious doubts about the simple everyday things I do.	True
3. Neither of my parents was very strict during my childhood.	False

SOURCE: Rachman and Hodgson, 1980.

obsessive-compulsive disorder than any other individuals (Sandler and Hazari, 1960; Shapiro, 1965; Rosenberg, 1967; Rack, 1977; Pollack, 1979; Rachman and Hodgson, 1980).

THEORIES OF OBSESSIVE-COMPULSIVE DISORDER

What causes an obsessive-compulsive disorder? There are two major theoretical views: cognitive-behavioral and psychoanalytic. Their strengths complement each other well. The psychoanalytic view wrestles with the question of the genesis of the obsession—who gets it and why it takes a particular form—but is less illuminating about why it persists for years once it has started. The cognitive-behavioral view illuminates its persistence, but leaves us in the dark as to who gets it and what its content will be.

Cognitive-Behavioral View of Obsessive-Compulsive Disorders

S. J. Rachman and Ray Hodgson have formulated the most comprehensive cognitive-behavioral theory of obsessions (Rachman, 1978; Rachman and Hodgson, 1980). The theory begins with the assumption that we all experience obsessional thoughts occasionally. The thought "Step on a crack and you'll break your mother's back" followed by an avoidance of sidewalk cracks is a common obsessive-compulsive ritual in children. For others, memories of radio jingles often intrude, unbidden, into consciousness. But most of us outgrow the sidewalk ritual, and we easily are able to distract ourselves from and habituate to the radio jingles. We can also dismiss the more abhorrent thoughts that occasionally run through our heads. Individuals with obsessive-compulsive disorders, however, differ from the rest of us in that they are unable to habituate, dismiss, and distract themselves from abhorrent thoughts.

S. J. Rachman has formulated a comprehensive cognitive-behavioral theory of obsessions. (Courtesy S. J. Rachman)

The more anxiety-provoking and depressing the content of the obsession, the more difficult it is for anyone— obsessive or non-obsessive—to dismiss the thought or distract himself from it. When normal individuals are shown a brief but stressful film, most of them have intrusive and repetitive thoughts. For example, a stressful film depicting a gruesome woodshop accident brought about anxiety and repetitive thoughts about the accident. The more emotionally upset an individual was made by the film, the more intrusive and repetitive the thoughts (Horowitz, 1975). This supports two of the assumptions of the cognitive-behavioral view of obsessions: (1) we all have unwanted and repetitive thoughts; and (2) the more stressed we are, the more frequent and intense are these thoughts.

Recall now the link between depression and obsession. To the extent that an individual is depressed beforehand, obsessive thoughts will be more disturbing and therefore more difficult to dismiss. In addition, as we will see in Chapter 13, depressed individuals display more helplessness (Seligman, 1975). This means that they are less able to initiate voluntary responses to relieve their own distress. The act of distracting oneself is a voluntary cognitive response, and like other such responses, it will be weakened by depression. A background of depression is therefore fertile soil for an obsessive disorder.

Here, then, is the chain of events that distinguishes an obsessive from a non–obsessive, according to the cognitive-behavioral view. For a non-obsessive, some initiating event, either internal or external, leads to a disturbing image or thought. A non-obsessive person may find this thought unacceptable but will not be made anxious by it. If he is not in a state of depression, he will easily dismiss the thought or distract himself from it. In contrast, the obsessive will be made anxious by the thought, and the anxiety will reduce his ability to dismiss it. The thought will persist, and the obsessive's inability to turn the thought off will lead to further anxiety, helplessness, and depression, which will increase his susceptibility to the intrusive thought.

The cognitive-behavioral view also attempts to explain compulsive rit-

Drawing by W. Miller
© 1982 The New Yorker Magazine, Inc.

uals. The rituals are reinforced by the temporary relief from anxiety that they bring. Since the obsessive cannot remove the thoughts by the distraction and dismissal techniques that the rest of us readily use, he resorts to other tactics. He attempts to neutralize the bad thought, often by substituting a good thought. The fiery color obsessive neutralized the color orange by looking at a swatch of green carpet. Alternatively, he attempts to neutralize the bad thoughts by an action that ensures safety. So, in an attempt to allay his fear of germs, the late millionaire Howard Hughes, saw to it that his servants did not cough on the fruit he ate. Individuals who are obsessively afraid that their doors are not locked check them dozens of times a night. These compulsive rituals produce temporary relief, but they also produce a stronger tendency to check, wash, or seek reassurance, since they are followed by anxiety reduction and therefore strengthened. But the rituals can only be cosmetic, and the relief they provide is temporary. They leave the obsessions intact; they continue to return with frequency and intensity. Each time a thought recurs, the ritual must be performed in order to produce any relief.

The strength of the cognitive-behavioral view is that it provides an account of why obsessions and compulsions, once started, might be maintained. But what are their origins? There are two questions about their origins that the cognitive-behavioral account leaves unanswered. The first has to do with the *content* of the obsessive thought and the compulsive act. Why this particular thought and this particular ritual? The second has to do with *individual susceptibility.* Since we all have intrusive thoughts, why are so few people afflicted with obsessive-compulsive disorders? Why are particular individuals deficient in their ability to dismiss, distract, and habituate to abhorrent thoughts? Complementing the cognitive-behavioral view of obsessive-compulsive disorders, the psychoanalytic view focuses on these questions.

The Psychodynamics of Obsessive-Compulsive Disorders

The questions "Who will get an obsessive disorder?" and "What form will it take?" lie at the heart of the psychoanalytic view of obsessive thoughts. According to this view, an obsessive thought is seen as a *defense* against an even more unwelcome and unconscious thought. This defensive process involves *displacement* and *substitution* (see Chapter 4). What happens is that an unconscious dangerous thought, such as "my mother might die of a fever," threatens to break into the individual's consciousness. This arouses anxiety. To defend against this anxiety, the individual unconsciously displaces this anxiety from the original terrifying thought onto a less unwelcome substitute, like hot and fiery colors. The defense has a powerful internal logic, and the thoughts that are substituted for the underlying thought are not arbitrary. Fiery and hot colors symbolize the fever that her ailing mother might die of.

Freud's original case of obsessional neurosis, the "Rat Man," illustrates the logic of obsessional defenses (Freud, 1909/1976):

> The Rat Man, whose name derives from his obsessional images of rats chewing their way into anuses, was plagued with a host of other obsessional thoughts, often of a violent nature. While a young man, the Rat Man lost some weeks of study,

because he was distressed about his girlfriend's absence. She had left him to nurse her seriously ill grandmother. While trying to study, an obsessional thought intruded—"If you were commanded to cut your throat with a razor, what then?" Freud interpreted this as caused by an unconscious rage that was even more threatening and more unacceptable: "I should like to go and kill that old woman for robbing me of my love!" The moral and high-minded Rat Man, with this horrendous thought knocking on the doors of consciousness, substitutes a more acceptable command "Kill yourself" and this is a fitting punishment for his savage and murderous passion. (Freud, 1909/1976, pp. 187-98)

Psychoanalytic theory explains *who* will develop an obsession in response to underlying conflict-arousing anxiety, and *what form* the obsession will take on to symbolize the underlying conflict. The following case of obsession about infanticide illustrates why the particular individual would be susceptible to the particular form of obsession she developed:

A thirty-two-year-old mother of two had obsessional thoughts of injuring and murdering her children and more infrequently, her husband. These thoughts were almost as threatening and as guilt-provoking as the very act itself. Therapy uncovered even more threatening impulses from her childhood which had been displaced onto her children. She had been the eldest of three siblings and while very young had been given undue responsibility for their care. She felt deprived of affection from her parents and was greatly resentful of her younger sister and brother. She entertained murderous fantasies about them, which were accompanied by tremendous guilt and anxiety. As a result, these fantasies had been completely driven from consciousness. When she became an adult, her children symbolically stood for her siblings, whose destruction would make her the sole object of parental love and relieve her of her childhood burden. Her own mother's occasional visits triggered the obsessions. She was particularly susceptible because she had unresolved and anxiety-provoking resentment against her own parents and siblings. Her obsession had the content of death as it symbolized the death of her siblings, which would have solved her childhood problem. (Adapted from Laughlin, 1967, pp. 324–26.)

Thus, the psychodynamic view of obsessions claims that powerful, abhorrent wishes and conflicts that have been repressed and threaten to break into consciousness put an individual at risk for obsessions, and that adopting the defense of displacement and substitution provides the immediate mechanism for relief. In addition, the particular content of the obsessions these individuals acquire will be a symbol for the underlying conflict.

TREATMENT FOR OBSESSIVE-COMPULSIVE DISORDER

The prognosis of obsessive-compulsive disorders, either untreated or treated with the therapies (other than behavior therapy) used over the last forty years is not particularly promising. Electroconvulsive shock, antidepressant drugs, supportive psychotherapy, and surgical removal of part of the brain (lobotomy) have all been tried frequently. Overall, five years after treatment, roughly half of obsessive-compulsives are unchanged or worse, with only 20 to 40 percent markedly improved. Roughly the same outcome is found ten years after treatment (Pollitt, 1960; Grimshaw, 1964; Kringlen, 1965). Are there any therapies that can improve on this prognosis? How do the psychoanalytic and behavior therapies fare?

In psychoanalytic therapy for obsessions, the central issue is to enable the patient to recognize the underlying conflict by undoing repression of this unconscious conflict. The mother with thoughts of infanticide must gain insight into her impulses to do away with her siblings during childhood and understand the connection of this conflict to her present problems. The psychodynamic treatment of the obsessive patient involves a thorough analysis of the obsessive's defenses and can be expected to take several years (Fenichel, 1945; Laughlin, 1967). Because there has been no controlled study of psychoanalytic treatment of obsessive-compulsive disorders, we can conclude little about its effectiveness.

In contrast, behavior therapies for obsessive-compulsive disorders have been explored in several controlled studies (Marks and Rachman, 1978). The results have been promising but are not conclusive. A combination of the three basic techniques of behavior therapy—response prevention, flooding, and modeling—are used in treating obsessive-compulsive disorders. These three procedures all encourage and persuade but do not force the patient to endure the disturbing situations that set off obsessions, without engaging in compulsive rituals to undo the thoughts. For example, one patient had obsessive thoughts that he might be contaminated with germs. He spent four hours a day washing himself. In therapy, he first watched the therapist contaminate herself with dirt (modeling). He then was urged to rub dirt and dust all over himself (flooding) and endure it without washing it off (response prevention). After about a dozen sessions of covering himself with dirt and just sitting there without washing it off, the thoughts of contamination diminished and the washing rituals no longer occurred in his daily life.

In this case, flooding the patient and preventing him from washing off the dirt cured the compulsion. In addition to such case histories, there have been six controlled studies of response prevention, flooding, and modeling in obsession. These indicate marked improvement in about two-thirds of the patients; follow-up for as long as two years indicates that improvement is maintained (Rachman, Hodgson, and Marks, 1971; Hodgson, Rachman, and Marks, 1972; Rachman, Marks, and Hodgson, 1973; Roper, Rachman, and Marks, 1975; Marks and Rachman, 1978; Salzman and Thaler, 1981). The behavior therapies are specific in their effects: obsessive thoughts, compulsive rituals, and anxiety all decrease, but depression, sexual adjustment, and family harmony are not clearly helped. These results are not conclusive, however, since very few patients lose all their symptoms completely or are functioning well in all areas of life at follow-up. In addition, roughly 20 to 30 percent fail to improve at all (Meyer, 1966; Hackmann and McLean, 1975; Rabavilos, Boulougouris, and Stefanis, 1976; Beech and Vaughan, 1978; Rachman, Cobb, Grey, MacDonald, Mauson, Sartory, and Stern, 1979).

Why do flooding, response prevention, and modeling work, and what are their critical elements? Recall that in the laboratory, flooding and response prevention reliably extinguish avoidance responding. If a rat is prevented from making his habitual avoidance responses by a barrier interposed between him and safety (response prevention), while sitting and hearing a signal that used to predict shock (flooding), avoidance behavior extinguishes. On future trials, even when the animal is free to flee, he will sit still during the signal. Response prevention has forcibly exposed the rat to the fact that the signal is no longer followed by shock and that he does not have to make the response in order to be safe (Seligman and Johnston, 1973).

Reconsider the man who washed himself for four hours a day. He had the obsession that some terrible illness would strike him if he did not wash. When he was persuaded to endure being dirty without washing, his obsessive thoughts of illness waned, and his compulsive rituals of washing vanished. What had he learned during flooding and response prevention? By covering himself with dirt and then not washing, his fear that dirt would lead to illness extinguished. The CS was the dirt, and the anticipated US was illness. He received stark exposure to being dirty without getting sick, and Pavlovian extinction occurred. In addition, he learned that illness did not happen even though he did not wash. This was an instrumental extinction procedure for the compulsive ritual of washing. So flooding and response prevention may work for two reasons: (1) by showing the patient that the dreaded event does not occur in the feared situation (Pavlovian extinction), and (2) by showing the patient that no dreaded event occurs even though the compulsive ritual is not performed (instrumental extinction of the compulsion).

OBSESSIVE-COMPULSIVE DISORDER: ANXIETY REVISITED

This chapter deals with those disorders in which anxiety is not directly felt by the afflicted individual. But we have assumed that anxiety underlies these disorders, specifically the obsessive-compulsive disorder. What is the evidence for this? There are four clues that anxiety underlies obsessive-compulsive disorder. First of all, the fact that flooding and response prevention seem to work suggest that obsessive-compulsive disorders are basically anxiety disorders. Since it is known from the laboratory that flooding and response prevention are techniques that produce extinction of conditioned fear and anxiety, we infer from the fact that they work that the obsessive suffered anxiety that is then extinguished in therapy.

The second clue relates to the integral relationship between the obsessive thought and the compulsive act. An obsessive who continually thinks that he left the gas on will compulsively check the kitchen stove. In observing him we probably would not see him as particularly anxious. But what if we do not allow him to perform his checking ritual? In this case, the obsessive may be overcome with anxiety, and think that his house will blow up as a result of the gas leak. This suggests that the function of the ritual is to ward off underlying anxiety. In short, when the compulsive symptoms are successful, they prevent anxiety from being experienced.

The third clue is that some obsessives actually do experience some anxiety during the obsession but lose it when the compulsion is performed. The color obsessive felt traumatized when she saw the color orange, and felt her anxiety turn off when she looked at the swatch of green carpet.

The fourth clue is the most intriguing of all. The content of the obsession can often be seen as a symbol of an underlying, unresolved conflict which when recognized provokes great anxiety. The mother with the infanticide obsession may have displaced her anxiety and guilt over wanting to murder her siblings onto a less unwelcome thought. During therapy, when she realized that she had done that even unconsciously, she felt very anxious.

Overall then there is reason to suspect that anxiety underlies obsessive-compulsive disorders. Sometimes the anxiety can actually be observed, as it is in phobias and panic attacks; but at most other times, the role of anxiety is inferred from clues about the patient's past, or by arranging special conditions such as response blocking to bring anxiety to the surface. In the next section, we will examine a set of disorders in which anxiety is almost never observed. In fact, it is the absence of anxiety that is often remarkable. These are the somatoform disorders, in which psychological factors cause the loss of some bodily function. We will look principally at hysterical conversions.

SOMATOFORM DISORDERS

The French neurologist Jean Martin Charcot (1825–1893) believed the symptoms of hysterical conversions were produced by psychological events.

As we learned in Chapter 2, Professor Jean Martin Charcot (1825-1893), a great French neurologist in Paris working at La Salpêtrière, saw a large number of female patients who had such symptoms as convulsive fits and muscular paralysis, although he could not find any clear organic basis for them. These symptoms characterized disorders that were called *hysterical conversions,* and Charcot believed that they were produced by psychological events. To show this, he hypnotized normal women and, by suggestion, produced in them symptoms identical to hysterical paralysis and hysterical convulsions. In addition, he hypnotized patients who had these symptoms and, by hypnotic suggestion, was able to remove the symptoms. Charcot's demonstration that hysterical conversion, a somatoform disorder, could be induced and removed merely by influencing the mind formed the basis of the theories of neurosis put forth by Pierre Janet (1859-1947), Josef Breuer (1842-1925), and most importantly, by Sigmund Freud himself (1856-1939).

THE TYPES OF SOMATOFORM DISORDERS

What is a somatoform disorder? There are five factors to consider. First, there is lost or altered physical functioning. One may, for example, become deaf or paralyzed. Second, the symptom cannot be explained by a known physical condition. There is no evidence of neurological damage to produce the deafness or the paralysis. Third, there is positive evidence that psychological factors have caused the symptom. Fourth, the patient is often, but not always, indifferent to the physical loss. More specifically, he or she does not feel anxiety. Finally, the symptoms are not under voluntary control. Conversion, Briquet's syndrome, and psychalgia are all considered somatoform disorders by DSM-III.

Conversion

Before DSM-III, *conversion* was called "hysterical conversion." It was renamed by DSM-III to remove the suggestion that it affects only women. "Hysteria," is derived from the Greek word *hystera,* which means womb, implying that the disorder is confined to women only. We now know this to be false, as men also suffer from the somatoform disorders (Veith, 1965; Chodoff, 1974, 1982). The case below illustrates a conversion disorder, where psychological stress has been converted into physical symptoms:

Bear was a burly twenty-five-year-old construction worker who was paralyzed from the waist down—totally without movement or feeling—and had been so for three weeks. What's more, he was not particularly upset by his paralysis; that is, he was a bit concerned that he could not walk, but he was not emotional nor excessively anxious.

After three days of tests that failed to show anything, the neurologist examining Bear had decided that there was nothing wrong with him physically and had sent him to Psychiatry.

In Psychiatry, there was the same frustration as that experienced by the neurologist. Bear's recent life seemed uneventful to him, and he recalled no precipitating incident. He had used drugs occasionally, and he drank a bit, but he had no previous psychiatric history. Mystified, groping for any lead, one of the residents asked him if he knew anybody else who was paralyzed. At first, Bear couldn't think of anyone, but after a minute or so, he mumbled, without any show of emotion:

"Yeah, come to think of it, Tom, a good friend of mine, is paralyzed from the waist down. Broke his neck."

"How did that happen?"

"It was really sad, and, you know, I guess it was pretty much my fault. Tom's a virgin, like in every way possible. Doesn't even drink or smoke. Well, we were together at a party about a month ago, and I was riding him. I thought he should live a little, try some LSD. I guess he couldn't take it, so he gave in.

"Well, we downed a couple of tabs, and within a few minutes he was flying. Seeing all sorts of weird things. He ran out of the apartment, and I followed, a little afraid for him. God, it was awful! He was running away from something in his head. Next thing I knew, he jumped off the bridge. You know, the one over the tracks at 30th Street Station. He was still alive when the rescue squad got him down from the high tension lines. They say he'll never walk, or anything, again."

"Bear, tell me again when your problem started."

"Out of nowhere. About three weeks ago. I was at work, driving my forklift down at the station. As I crossed over the tracks under the high tension lines, suddenly I was all dead down there. I shouted for help, and my buddies took me off to. . . . Oh, my God! Don't you see what I've done!"

And within a few days, Bear walked home. (Stinnett, 1978)

Bear's paralysis has the five symptoms of somatoform disorder. First, he has lost physical functioning: he is paralyzed. Second, physical damage cannot explain the paralysis, since he is neurologically sound, and the paralysis is not under voluntary control. Third, Bear seems remarkably indifferent to his paralysis. Fourth, he feels no anxiety. And fifth, there is good evidence that psychological factors caused the symptoms: (1) he has a friend with paralysis caused partly by his actions; (2) the paralysis began at the same site that his friend's paralysis occurred; (3) Bear did not easily remember the incident when his friend was paralyzed, nor did he relate it to his own paralysis; and (4) Bear could not control his paralysis, but when he gained insight into this, his paralysis remitted.

Briquet's Syndrome

In **Briquet's syndrome,** the individual will have a dramatic and complicated medical history for most of her adult life (Mai and Mersky, 1980). She will receive extensive medical care from a variety of physicians for multiple and recurrent bodily complaints in many organs, although these are not physically caused. The symptoms may include headaches, fatigue, fainting, nausea, vomiting, stomach pains, allergies, menstrual and sexual difficulties, as well as one or more specific conversion symptoms. Unnecessary surgery, addiction to prescription medicines, depression, and attempted suicide are common complications of Briquet's syndrome. The fundamental difference between Briquet's syndrome and conversion is that the Briquet's syndrome individual will suffer from many physical problems; the conversion patient generally has only one complaint.

Psychalgia

Psychalgia is pain that is not attributed to physical cause; statistically, it may be the most frequent of the somatoform disorders today (Watson and Buranen, 1979; Drossman, 1982). The following case illustrates an individual suffering from psychalgia:

> Harry, a forty-one-year-old man, suffered a sudden onset of severe abdominal pain. Emergency surgery was about to be performed, but there was no elevated white cell count, and other physical symptoms were normal. In addition, Harry seemed emotionally indifferent to the pain and the fact of impending surgery. He was obviously in pain, but not anxious about it.
>
> Upon consultation, it was decided to abandon urgent preparations for surgery, and to explore for a possible psychological basis. It emerged that Harry had had a childhood that predisposed him to psychalgia. His parents had been materially wealthy, but they had given him very little love and affection. The one break in this emotional barrenness in his childhood had been his appendectomy. The love he had received during this period was meaningful, real, and what he had "always longed for."
>
> The present abdominal pain was set off by an incident of domestic deceit. His wife had become infatuated with another man and had threatened to go off with him. At this very point, the abdominal pain had begun. (Adapted from Laughlin, 1967, pp. 667-68.)

The hypothesis in Harry's case is that whenever he is under serious stress, Harry will suffer pain in his abdomen. This pain becomes a somatic excuse for not suffering the anxiety brought on by the stressful events.

DIAGNOSING SOMATOFORM DISORDER

A somatoform disorder is one of the most difficult disorders to diagnose correctly. In the case study discussed earlier, how can we tell if Bear was faking paralysis or if he had some obscure physical illness that was as yet undiagnosed?

In an attempt to make diagnosis more clear, DSM-III distinguishes somatoform disorders from four other disorders with which it can be confused, sometimes tragically. These disorders are malingering, psychosomatic disorders, factitious disorders, and undiagnosed physical illness. In principle, there are two differences between **malingering** (faking) and an authentic somatoform disorder—neither of which is easy to pin down in practice. First, the symptoms of a malingerer are under his volun-

tary control, whereas they are not under the voluntary control of an individual with a somatoform disorder. A malingerer can turn the paralysis on and off, although it may be difficult indeed to induce him to display his voluntary control for you. The individual suffering conversion cannot. For example, even if we had offered Bear an irresistibly large amount of money to get up out of his wheelchair and walk away, he would not have been able to do so. Second, the malingerer acquires an obvious environmental goal as a result of his symptom (e.g., getting out of the army by feigning paralysis), whereas an individual with a conversion disorder does not necessarily achieve anything obvious by his symptom.

Malingering itself should be distinguished from **secondary gain.** Secondary gain consists of deriving benefits from one's environment as a consequence of having abnormal symptoms. Individuals with somatoform disorders frequently get secondary gains. So, for example, a person with psychalgia may get more love and attention from his family when he is in pain. The use of secondary gain seems to be part of the universal human trait of making the best of a bad situation. A person with a somatoform disorder, who derives secondary gain, differs from a malingerer. The malingerer is faking the initial symptoms and then may, in addition, use them to benefit. The individual with the somatoform disorder, in contrast, is not faking the symptoms but may well derive benefit from having them.

The second disorder that resembles somatoform disorders are **psychosomatic disorders,** which are the subject of the next chapter. What distinguishes psychosomatic disorders from somatoform disorders is the existence of a physical basis that can explain the symptom. Although some individuals who have a peptic ulcer or high blood pressure may have these conditions exaggerated or even initiated by psychological factors, the ulcers and hypertension are actually being caused by specific known physical mechanisms. In contrast, **glove anesthesia,** a conversion symptom in which nothing can be felt in the hand and fingers, but in which sensation is intact from the wrist up, cannot be induced by any known pattern of damage to the nerves innervating the hand.

The third disorder from which somatoform disorder must be distinguished is **factitious disorder,** also called "Münchhausen syndrome." This disorder is characterized by multiple hospitalizations and operations in which the individual voluntarily produces the signs of illness, not through underlying anxiety, but by physiological tampering (Pope, Jonas, and Jones, 1982). He might, for example, take anticoagulent drugs, then seek treatment for his bleeding. There was one documented case of a thirty-four-year-old man who, over a decade, had made 200 visits to physicians under dozens of aliases at more than sixty-eight hospitals and who had cost Britain's health service $2,000,000. In contrast to malingering, a factitious disorder has no obvious goal other than gaining medical attention. It is crucially different from somatoform disorders because the symptoms are voluntarily produced by the person who has them and they are physically based.

Finally, a somatoform disorder may be misdiagnosed and actually result from an **undiagnosed physical illness.** The diagnosis of a somatoform disorder is for many people degrading, as the patient and his family are told that the disease is in his mind, not in his body. Current medical diagnosis is far from perfect, and occasionally an individual who has been labeled "hysteric" will eventually develop a full-blown physical disease, such as multiple sclerosis, which in fact had caused the earlier "hysterical" symptoms. This is one reason the diagnosis must be made with caution.

Table 11-2 summarizes the distinctions among conversion, malingering, psychosomatic disorders, factitious disorders, and undiagnosed physical illness.

Table 11-2 CRITERIA FOR DIFFERENTIAL DIAGNOSIS OF SYMPTOMS SUGGESTING PHYSICAL ILLNESS

Classification	Can a known physical mechanism explain the symptom?	Are the symptoms linked to psychological causes?	Is the symptom under voluntary control?	Is there an obvious goal?
Conversion	Never	Always	Never	Sometimes
Malingering	Sometimes	Sometimes	Always	Always
Psychosomatic Disorders	Always	Always	Never	Sometimes
Factitious Disorders	Sometimes	Always	Always	Never (other than medical attention)
Undiagnosed Physical Illness	Sometimes	Sometimes	Never	Never

SOURCE: Based on DSM-III and Hyler and Spitzer, 1978.

VULNERABILITY TO SOMATOFORM DISORDERS

Conversion disorders are not particularly common. Estimates vary widely, but probably not more than 5 percent of all nonpsychotic patients (or much less than 1 percent of the entire American population) have conversions (Laughlin, 1967; Woodruff, Clayton, and Guze, 1971). Initially, conversions symptoms usually are displayed from late adolescence to middle adulthood; they are rare in children and old people. Because conversion disorders were long regarded as hysteria, and hysteria (a wandering womb) was by definition a disorder of women, conversion disorders in men were somehow overlooked. This is the basis of the most common myth about conversion: that it afflicts only women. On the contrary, contemporary studies indicate that between 20 and 40 percent of conversion disorders occur in men (Ziegler, Imboden, and Meyer, 1960; Chodoff, 1974).

Briquet's syndrome (the somatoform disorder in which the patient has a complicated medical history before the age of thirty-five, with a large number of symptoms ranging across many organ systems, and with no known medical explanations) is more common. As many as 2 percent of all adult women may display this disorder, and it is rarely diagnosed in men (Woodruff, Clayton, and Guze, 1971).

While there is no evidence that conversion disorders run in families, Briquet's syndrome probably does. The sisters, mothers, and daughters of women with this disorder are ten times more likely to develop it than women in the general population (Woodruff, Clayton, and Guze, 1971). Nothing is presently known about family patterns of psychalgia.

COURSE OF SOMATOFORM DISORDERS

What is the course of these disorders once they appear? Surprisingly, there has not been a single useful longitudinal study of conversion disorders, and our knowledge is based only on clinical impressions. Conversion disorders come on suddenly, and they remit suddenly and spontaneously. They probably do not last very long, and it has been estimated that 50 percent spontaneously disappear within two years (Rachman and Wilson, 1979). Briquet's syndrome is much more insidious. Seventy percent of women who develop Briquet's syndrome probably will still have it fifteen years later, and as many as one-third of them will then be diagnosed as psychotic (Ziegler and Paul, 1954; Perley and Guze, 1962; Woodruff, Clayton and Guze, 1971; Coryell and Norten, 1981).

THE ETIOLOGY OF SOMATOFORM DISORDERS

What causes the loss of the function of a bodily organ in the absence of any underlying physiological basis? This remains one of the great questions of psychopathology.

The Psychoanalytic View

The psychoanalytic view was put forth by Sigmund Freud in 1894. Freud believed that the physical symptom was a defense that absorbed and neutralized the anxiety generated by an unacceptable unconscious conflict.

(Freud, 1894/1976, p. 63). Today, the psychodynamic explanation of conversion still revolves around this notion, and postulates three distinct processes: First, the individual is made anxious by some unacceptable idea, and the conversion is a defense against this anxiety. Second, psychic energy is transmuted into a somatic loss. The anxiety is detached from the idea, rendering it neutral. Because anxiety is psychic energy it must go some place, and in this case it is used to debilitate a physical organ. Third, the particular somatic loss symbolizes the underlying conflict. For Bear, the three processes seem to play a role: Bear is unconsciously anxious and guilty about causing Tom's paralysis and he walls off these feelings from consciousness by transmuting the guilt and anxiety into his own paralysis. The particular symptom—paralysis—obviously symbolizes the real paralysis suffered by his friend.

This theory is just about the only idea that can explain one of the strangest symptoms of conversion: "la belle indifference." Unlike patients with actual physical loss due to injury, conversion patients are often strangely indifferent to their physical symptoms. For example, a patient with conversion paralysis may show much more concern over a minor skin irritation on his legs than with the fact that he cannot move them (Laughlin, 1967, pp. 673-74). In the psychoanalytic view, a conversion symptom may absorb anxiety so well by transmuting it into a physical loss that the patient can actually be calm about being crippled, blind, deaf, or insensate.

While no complete behavioral view of somatoform disorders has been put forward, the psychoanalytic view gives a hint of what the behavioral view might look like. If conversion symptoms do, in fact, absorb anxiety, anxiety reduction reinforces the patient for having a symptom.

The concept of anxiety has exerted a mighty hold on theories about psychopathology for the last hundred years. For Freud and for the diagnostic systems prior to DSM-III, anxiety was the most important emotion we experienced. *All* of the *neuroses* were said to be caused by the process of defending against anxiety. In neuroses like phobias and panic attacks, in which anxiety was observed, the patient felt dread and displayed an emergency reaction; so its role could not be denied. But in others, such as conversion, in which anxiety was not observed, its existence was inferred to explain the symptom.

Why did anxiety play such a central role in psychoanalytic theory? Part of the answer might have to do with the circumstances of Sigmund Freud's life. Freud grew up in Vienna in the declining days of the Hapsburg empire, in the last half of the nineteenth century, and much of his theorizing took place while his society was collapsing around him. The dissolution of the fixed order, with the attendant uncertainty about the future and about values, may have made anxiety a dominant emotion among the patients that Freud saw. The turn of the century in Vienna may truly have been the "age of anxiety."

The Communicative View

There are negative emotions other than anxiety that theorists might focus on as central to the neuroses; sadness, anger, guilt, awe, bewilderment, and shame are all elements of the human experience. Phobics and obsessives experience these emotions as well as anxiety, particularly sadness and anger.

Moreover, patients with conversions—if they are defending at all—might not be defending against anxiety but against depression, guilt, or anger. This possibility has spawned another theory of conversion, which emphasizes the *communicative,* rather than the defensive, function of the symptom. The communicative model claims that the patient uses the disorder to deal with a variety of distressing emotions—not only anxiety—and to negotiate difficult interpersonal transactions. He expresses his underlying distress to himself in terms of physical illness, thereby distracting himself from his distress. He then communicates the fact that he is distressed to others with his physical loss. He unconsciously chooses his symptoms according to his own conception of a physical illness—which will derive in part from the illnesses that important people in his life have had—and according to what in his time does and doesn't count as an illness. His particular symptoms will then simulate physical illness either expertly or crudely, depending on how much he knows (Ziegler and Imboden, 1962).

The communicative model views the case study of Bear in the following way: Bear is depressed, anxious, and guilty over his role in paralyzing his friend. In addition, he cannot *talk* about his distress because he is not verbal about his troubles. By paralyzing himself he is able to distract himself from these emotions, so he *shows* his distress to others by his paralysis. Bear's particular symptom derives directly from identification with his friend's paralysis.

The communicative model explains the odd fact that the kinds of physical losses produced by conversion have changed over the last hundred years, and that they vary with education. For Charcot in Paris in the 1880s, convulsions with frenzied, uncoordinated movements were the most common hysterical conversion. By the turn of the century in Vienna, Freud and his contemporaries saw in their upper-middle-class patients fewer convulsions and more paralysis, "glove" anesthesia, "stocking" anesthesia, blindness, and deafness. At the time of World War I, *clavus*—the painful sensation of a nail being driven into the head—and a severe low back pain producing a forwardly bent back were common. Today in urban America, pain, dizziness, headache, loss of sensation, and weakness are the most common conversion reactions; whereas in backwoods America, conversion reactions of the type Freud saw still predominate (Laughlin, 1967; Watson and Buranen, 1979; Chodoff, 1974; Woodruff, Goodwin, and Guze, 1974).

The communicative model holds that conversion reactions "talk." They are a cry for help, particularly among individuals who are reluctant or unable to *talk* about their emotional distress. Such people may be forced to rely on physical symptoms to tell the people they love and their physicians that all is not well in their emotional lives. The physical losses that such individuals generate will correspond to what they know about illness. Once an age or a social class discovers that glove anesthesia is physically impossible, it is no longer a "plausible" symptom to communicate with. Pain, paralysis, and deafness are still plausible somatic symptoms in sophisticated, urban America, and so they are still seen as symptoms in conversion disorders.

The Percept Blocking View

There is a third view of somatoform disorders compatible with either the psychoanalytic or communicative views. It focuses on how a perception can be blocked from conscious experience. This view is best illustrated by hysterical blindness, a conversion disorder in which blindness is the physical loss. Surprisingly, in spite of the claim that he is aware of no visual input at all, the behavior of a hysterically blind person is often controlled by visual input. Such individuals usually avoid walking in front of cars and tripping over furniture, even though they report no awareness of actually seeing anything. In the laboratory, they also give evidence that some visual material is getting through. When given discrimination tasks that can only be solved by visual cues, such as "pick the side—left or right—that has the square, as opposed to the circle, on it," they perform significantly *below* chance. They do worse than if they were guessing at random, and they systematically pick the side that has the circle. In order to be so wrong, the patient must be right— the square of which he is not aware must register at some level of his mind, and then be reacted to by choosing the circle (Theodor and Mandelcorn, 1973; see also Brady and Lind, 1961; Gross and Zimmerman, 1965).

What are we to make of this? If we assume that the hysterically blind individual is not lying when he says he is not aware of anything visual, then we are led to the following model: visual input can register in the sensory system and directly affect behavior (hence the avoidance of furniture and below-chance performance), while being blocked from conscious awareness (hence the report "I see nothing"). The conversion process consists in the blocking of the percept from awareness (Hilgard, 1977; Sackeim, Nordlie, and Gur, 1979). This is compatible with both the psychoanalytic and communicative models since it makes no claims about what motivations can cause blocking—a need to defend against anxiety or a desire to distract oneself from inner distress. This model is also physiologically possible. When some parts of the brain that control vision are destroyed, individuals report that they can see nothing at all in specific regions of their visual field. But in spite of consistent reports of blindness, such patients perform above chance on visual discrimination problems. When confronted with this fact, the patients, like the hysterically blind, insist they saw nothing at all and were merely guessing (Weiskrantz, Warrington, Sanders, and Marshall, 1974). So we conclude that the mechanism of hysterical blindness may be the blocking of a visual percept from awareness. The blockade could be motivated either by anxiety (as Freud held), by a need to communicate distress, or it might be reinforced by anxiety reduction (as a behaviorist would hold).

TREATMENT OF SOMATOFORM DISORDER

There is an ancient Persian legend about a physician named Rhazes who was called into the palace for the purpose of diagnosing and treating a young prince. Apparently, the prince could not walk. After the usual examination of the day, Rhazes determined that there was nothing wrong with the prince's legs, at least not physically. With little more than a hunch, Rhazes set out to treat what may be the first recorded case of conversion. In doing so, he took a risk: Rhazes unexpectedly walked into the prince's bathroom brandishing a dagger and threatened to kill him. Upon seeing him, "the startled prince abruptly fled, leaving his clothes, his dignity, his symptom, and undoubtedly part of his self-esteem behind" (Laughlin, 1967, p. 678).

Modern clinicians tend to approach their "princes" brandishing a less drastic technology. They will sometimes confront a conversion patient and try to force him out of his symptom. For example, therapists may tell hysterically blind patients that they are performing significantly below or above chance on visual tasks in spite of seeing nothing, which may cause visual awareness to gradually return in the patient (Brady and Lind, 1961; but see also Gross and Zimmerman, 1965). But these recoveries are usually temporary, and they may produce conflict and loss of self-esteem in the patient. They also may make the patient feel that the therapist is unsympathetic, and so they may ultimately undermine therapy.

Suggestion

Simple suggestion, merely telling a patient in a convincing manner that the symptoms will go away, may fare somewhat better than confrontation does. Conversion patients are particularly suggestible, and certain therapists have found improvement by directly telling the patient, in an authoritative sounding way, that the symptom will go away. In an account of 100 cases of patients with conversion symptoms, one investigator found that following strong suggestion 75 percent of the patients were either symptom-free or much improved four to six years later (Carter, 1949). But since there was no comparison group that might have controlled for the spontaneous disappearance of conversion without suggestion, we cannot be sure that suggestion had any real effect (Bird, 1979).

Insight

Insight, or coming to recognize the underlying conflict producing the physical loss, is the therapy of choice for conversion disorders among psychoanalysts. According to these therapists, when the patient comes to see, and emotionally appreciate, that there is an underlying conflict that is producing a conversion disorder, the symptom should disappear. A number of dramatic case histories confirm this. For example, when Bear realized that his paralysis expressed his guilt over his friend's paralysis, the symptom remitted. Unfortunately, there does not exist a well-controlled study that tests whether psychoanalytic insight has any effect over and above suggestion, confrontation, spontaneous remission, or the mere formation of a therapeutic alliance.

Somatoform disorders still remain a great challenge for students of abnormality. These disorders are a real phenomenon—hysterically blind or paralyzed individuals are not feigning their symptoms. When Charcot showed that the symptoms could be produced by hypnotic suggestion and removed by hypnosis, he convinced most of the world that conversion disorders were psychological in origin. Thereupon Freud proposed that the symptoms defended against anxiety. More recent theorists have proposed that the symptoms are meant to communicate more global distress by individuals who find it impossible to talk about their problems. But we have not come much farther since Charcot. The theories of somatoform disorders have yet to be tested in a definitive way, and their cure remains a mystery.

In Alfred Hitchcock's film *Spellbound*, Gregory Peck plays an amnesic in the fugue state. He lost memory of his identity as a defense against unbearable guilt and anxiety. (Courtesy The Museum of Modern Art/Film Stills Archive)

DISSOCIATIVE DISORDERS

All of us have at one time or another awakened in the middle of the night and being somewhat befuddled, wondered, "Where am I?" Sometimes the disorientation is more profound. "Who is the person sleeping next to me?" "Who am I, anyway?" When such *depersonalization* happens—most commonly following fatigue, travel, or drinking—it usually wears off in a few seconds or minutes, and knowledge of our identity returns. But for others it is different. Such a loss of memory about identity sometimes occurs in people who have suffered a strong psychological trauma. It is then more profound, extends over a longer time, and is at the heart of the ***dissociative disorders.*** They are called "dissociative" because some area of memory is split off or dissociated from conscious awareness.

The dissociative disorders have much in common with our last topic, the somatoform disorders, particularly conversion. In conversion disorders, anxiety is not experienced by the victim; in fact, complete indifference is common. Rather, the symptom can be seen as a way to prevent underlying anxiety from surfacing. So it is with dissociative disorders. For example, when an individual suddenly loses his memory following an unbearable trauma, he is not necessarily overtly anxious. Rather, theorists infer that the loss of memory allows him to escape from intolerable anxiety brought on by the trauma.

We will discuss two dissociative disorders: ***psychogenic amnesia,*** a sudden loss of memory caused by severe trauma, such as the death of a child or the dashing of a career; and ***multiple personality,*** in which two or more distinct personalities exist within the same individual and each leads a rather full life.

PSYCHOGENIC AMNESIA

Timmy was fifteen years old and attending high school in upstate New York. He was teased mercilessly by his fellow students and was doing poorly in his schoolwork. In addition, he fought constantly with his parents. He was very upset about his problems, and it seemed to him that they had become absolutely insoluble. One spring afternoon, he went home from school extremely distressed and threw his books down on the porch in disgust.

At that moment, Timmy became a victim of amnesia. This was his last memory for a year, and we will never know exactly what happened next. The next thing we know with certainty is that a year later, a young soldier was admitted to an army hospital after a year of military service. He had severe stomach cramps and convulsions of no apparent physical origin. The following morning, he was better, calm and mentally clear. Astonishingly, he was at a total loss to explain where he was or how he got there. He asked how he came to be in the hospital, what town he was in, and who the people around him were. He was Timmy, all right, awake and in a military hospital with his last memory that of throwing his books down on the porch in disgust. Timmy's father was phoned, and he corroborated the story. At his father's request, Timmy was discharged from the service as underage. (Adapted from Laughlin, 1967, pp. 862-63.)

Timmy was the victim of amnesia (the loss of memory of one's identity). As in many cases of amnesia, Timmy wandered and took up a new life by joining the army. Such unexpected travel away from home during amnesia is called a ***fugue state,*** from the Latin *fuga,* meaning flight. Timmy's loss of memory and fugue are understandable as a flight from intolerable anxiety caused by his problems at home and at school. Timmy adopted the most extreme defense against a painful situation: he became amnesic, not only for the situation, but for his very identity, and he took up a new identity. By becoming amnesic, he was able to escape from his anxiety. During his army life he remembered nothing about his previous painful life and following recovery of his earlier memories, he was totally amnesic for his year in the army.

Kinds of Psychogenic Amnesia

What happened to Timmy was a ***global*** or ***generalized amnesia:*** all the details of his personal life had vanished when he joined the army. Amnesia can be less global than this. ***Retrograde amnesia*** is a more localized amnesia, in which all events immediately before some trauma are forgotten. For example, an uninjured survivor of an automobile accident may be unable to recall anything that happened during the twenty-four hours up to and including the accident that killed the rest of her family. Somewhat rarer is ***anterograde amnesia,*** in which all events *after* the trauma are forgotten. Finally, there exists ***selective*** or ***categorical amnesia,*** in which only events related to a particular theme vanish (Hirst, 1982).

Psychogenic Versus Organic Amnesia

Amnesia can also be caused by physical trauma, such as a blow to the head or a gunshot wound to the brain, alcoholism, and stroke (see Chapter 19). Such organically caused amnesia should be distinguished from psychogenic amnesia. Aside from its physical basis, organic amnesia differs from psychogenic amnesia in several ways. First, a psychogenic amnesic is usually sorely troubled by marital, financial, or career stress before the amnesia, whereas an individual who suffers organic amnesia need not be. Second, psychogenic amnesia resembles glove anesthesia—it does not result from any known neural damage.

A psychogenic amnesic shows a four-fold pattern of memory loss that no organic amnesic has ever shown. First, a psychogenic amnesic loses his past, both recent and remote—he cannot remember how many brothers and sisters he has; he cannot remember a well-learned fact from the distant past, nor can he remember the recent episode of what he had for breakfast right before the amnesia started. Organic amnesics, on the other hand, remember the distant past well—after a blow on the head, they can tell you perfectly well who taught them Sunday school when they were six years old, or the starting lineup of the 1948 Dodgers—but they remember the recent past poorly. Second, an individual with psychogenic amnesia loses his personal identity—name, address, occupation, and the like—but his store of general knowledge remains intact. He still remembers who the President is, what the date is, and what the capital of Saskatchewan is (Regina). Organic amnesics, in contrast, tend to lose both personal and general knowledge.

Third, psychogenic amnesics have no anterograde loss; they remember well events that happen after the moment amnesia starts. In contrast, organic amnesics have severe anterograde amnesia; they remember very little about episodes that happen after the organic damage (like the name of the doctor treating them for the blow on the head). Finally, psychogenic amnesia often reverses abruptly. Psychogenic amnesia often ends within a few hours or days, and within twenty-four hours of the return of his memory the individual may even recall the traumatic episode that set off the memory loss. In organic amnesia, memory only gradually returns, following organic treatment, and memory of trauma is never revived (Suarez and Pittluck, 1976).

Vulnerability and Causes of Psychogenic Amnesia

Only a few other facts about psychogenic amnesia are known, and they tell us a bit more about vulnerability to this disorder. Psychogenic amnesia and fugue states are rare disorders in peacetime, but in times of war and natural disaster they are much more common. They apparently occur in men more than in women and in younger people more than in old people.

The cause of psychogenic amnesia is a mystery, more shrouded even than the causes of the somatoform disorders, which it resembles. We can speculate on how it might be caused, however. If we take the symptoms of conversion at face value, we assume that the mind sometimes can deal with emotionally distressing conflicts by producing physical losses. So, Bear, anxious and guilty about causing his friend's paralysis, converts his distress into his own paralysis. We do not know the mechanism of this conversion, but whatever it is, it might also be working in the amnesic. What happens when a vulnerable individual faces an even more traumatic conflict, such as occurs during war? What happens when one's physical existence is suddenly threatened, or when one's entire life plans are shattered? Enormous anxiety should be generated. Perhaps we have one ultimate psychological escape hatch—to forget who we are and thereby neutralize our anxiety about our death, our shattered future, or our insoluble problems. Both the psychoanalytic model and behavioral model are compatible with this explanation. For the psychoanalyst, the painful memory of who we are is repressed, and this defends successfully against anxiety. For the behaviorist, anxiety reduction reinforces the symptom of taking on a new identity. In short, amnesia may be the most global of defenses against anxiety produced by very traumatic and unacceptable circumstances.

We will now take up the final disorder in this chapter, multiple personality, in which amnesia plays a major role. Here it will be quite clear that the multiple personalities and their attendant amnesia for each other function to minimize unbearable anxiety.

MULTIPLE PERSONALITY

Multiple personality is defined as the occurrence of two or more personalities in the same individual, each of which is sufficiently integrated to have a relatively rich and stable life of its own (Taylor and Martin, 1944). It is as astonishing a form of psychopathology as exists. Multiple personality used to be thought of as a very rare disorder—only 200 cases had been reported, but now that clinicians are looking for it, much more of it seems to be around. One researcher, Eugene Bliss, has seen 14 cases of it in the recent past, just in Utah (Bliss, 1980).

Bliss's first introduction to multiple personality occurred in 1978 when he received a call from a distressed supervisor of nurses at a Salt Lake City hospital. The supervisor suspected that one of her nurses had been secretly injecting herself with Demerol. The supervisor and Bliss called the nurse into the office and accused her of improper conduct. They asked the nurse to roll up her sleeves because they wanted to examine her arms for needlemarks. The nurse complied, and the telltale marks were there. But in the process of complying, the nurse underwent a remarkable transformation. Her facial expression, her manner, and her voice all changed, claiming that she was not Lois, the demure nurse, but Lucy, the brazen drug addict. Almost everyone has heard of other famous multiple personalities, as in "The Three Faces of Eve" (Thigpen and Cleckley, 1954), Sybil (Schreiber, 1974), or Dr. Jekyll and Mr. Hyde. Among the more recent cases is that of Julie-Jenny-Jerrie (Davis and Osherson, 1977):

> Julie came to therapy through her son, Adam, age nine, who had been referred for counseling because of very poor school performance, poor relations with peers, and aggressive behavior at home. Eventually it was decided to see his thirty-six-year-old mother, Julie, in hope that she could help in the therapeutic process.
>
> Julie was highly cooperative, sophisticated, and concerned about Adam. She seemed to have a good understanding of herself, and her general style of solving interpersonal problems was discussion and compromise. She felt that she had trouble setting limits for her son, and she worried that she sometimes behaved too rigidly toward him.
>
> During a session in the sixth week of discussions with Julie, she suddenly announced that she wanted to introduce someone to the therapist. The therapist assumed there was someone out in the waiting room, but to his astonishment he witnessed the following: Julie closed her eyes for a few seconds, frowned, and then raised her eyelids slowly. Putting out her cigarette, she said, "I wish Julie would stop smoking. I hate the taste of tobacco." She introduced herself as Jerrie, and later in the hour and in the same way, she introduced Jenny, yet a third personality.

Chris Sizemore, on whose life the film *The Three Faces of Eve* is based, is a well-known multiple personality. Here the real Chris Sizemore is shown next to her own painting that shows the coexistence of her three personalities. (Staff photo by Gerald Martineau, The Washington Post)

Jenny revealed that she was the original personality and said that she created Jerrie at age three and subsequently created Julie at age eight. Both times Jenny created the new personalities to cope with her disturbed family life. Jerrie emerged as the outer personality when Jenny was recovering from a severe case of measles, and Jerrie became a buffer who allowed Jenny to keep her distance from seven rejecting siblings and two frightening parents. Jenny said that observing Jerrie was like observing a character in a play.

Between the ages of three and eight, Jenny remembers that her physical welfare was neglected, that she was sexually molested by a neighbor, and was given away for permanent adoption at age eight, with her parents telling her she was "incorrigible." At this time, Jenny created Julie, a gentle personality who was better able to cope with rejection and not as vulnerable to cruelty as either Jerrie or Jenny. Remarkably, while Julie was allowed to know about Jenny, the original personality, Julie was kept unaware of the existence of Jerrie. Julie did not find out about Jerrie until age thirty-four, two years before therapy began.

At age eighteen, Julie-Jenny-Jerrie left home for good. Jerrie and Julie by this time were always the alternating outer personalities, and Jenny was always inside. In fact, Jenny had been "out" only twice since age seven. At age twenty-six, Jerrie married, and the couple adopted Adam, who was the husband's son by a woman with whom he was having an affair while he and Jerrie were married. Jerrie soon divorced him, but she kept Adam.

The three personalities were strikingly different. Jenny—the original—was a frightened person, very shy and vulnerable. She was the most insecure and childlike of the three and felt "exposed" whenever she was out. Jenny felt she had created two Frankensteins who were now out of her control. She liked Julie better, but she was put off by Julie's stubbornness and strong individuality. She felt Jerrie was tougher than Julie and better able to cope with the world, but she didn't like her as well. Jenny's main hope in therapy was that Julie and Jerrie would come to get along better with each other and therefore be better mothers to Adam.

Julie seemed to be the most integrated of the three personalities. Julie was heterosexual, and emotionally invested in being a good mother—this in spite of the fact that it was Jerrie who had adopted Adam.

Jerrie was the opposite of Julie. Jerrie was homosexual, dressed in masculine fashion, sophisticated, and sure of herself. She was accomplished and proficient in the business world, and she enjoyed it. Jerrie didn't smoke, whereas Julie was a heavy smoker, and Jerrie's blood pressure was a consistent twenty points higher than Julie's.

Jerrie had known about Julie since Julie was "born" at age eight, but she had been in touch with her only in the past two years. She wanted to have nothing to do with Julie because she was afraid Julie would have a mental breakdown. Julie and Jerrie did not get along. When one of them was out and having a good time, she would resist relinquishing her position. But when a crisis was at hand, the personality who was out would duck in, leaving the inner personality to face the problem. For example, Julie took LSD and then let Jerrie out so that Jerrie would be the victim of the hallucinations.

Ultimately Jerrie was able to tell Adam that there were two personalities who had been contributing to his misery, and Adam's immediate response was amusement and curiosity. He was able to accept the explanation that "Mother is two people who keep going in and out, but both of them love me." Adam appeared relieved rather than disturbed. Soon thereafter, Jerrie terminated therapy. Julie, in a suicidal depression, had gotten herself admitted to a state hospital against Jerrie's will, but Jerrie had gained control and talked her way out of the hospital. Julie wrote the therapist that she wanted to come to therapy, but Jerrie would not allow it and refused to come anymore. And this was the last that was seen of Julie-Jenny-Jerrie. (Adapted from Davis and Osherson, 1977.)

This fascinating case exemplifies much of what is known about multiple personality. Amnesia of some kind or other almost always exists. It is common for one of the personalities to be aware of the experience of the other personalities (Jenny knew of both Julie and Jerrie, and Jerrie knew of Julie), and for one of the personalities to be amnesic about the others (Julie did not know of Jerrie). The presence of unexplained amnesia—hours or days each week that are missing—is a clue to the undetected presence of multiple personality.

> There is a personality who says, "I just have fun. I go out with the kids and drink beer." The patient, who had been instructed to listen, comments, "So that is the reason why I wake up drunk in the morning with terrible headaches." (Bliss, 1980)

In the history of multiple personalities, the several personalities within an individual—like Julie-Jenny-Jerrie—differ along many dimensions. Not only do they differ in their memories, but also in their wishes, attitudes, interests, learning ability, knowledge, morals, sexual orientation, age, rate of speech, personality test scores, and physiological indices such as heart rate, blood pressure, and EEG (Lester, 1977). Remarkably, women with multiple personality report that they menstruate much of the month because each personality has her own cycle (Jens and Evans, 1983). For unknown reasons, most cases of multiple personality are women.

The personalities also differ in psychological health. Often, the dominant personality is the healthier personality. One patient, a proper Southern lady, was publicly accused of wanton sexuality, including sexual intercourse with strangers. She made a clumsy attempt at a self-induced abortion, but she could not remember it. Her submerged personality said, "I did it because I suspected a pregnancy. I took a sharp stick and shoved it inside, then I started to bleed badly" (Bliss, 1980). The dominant personality, however, is not always the healthiest, and the submerged personality may actually sympathize with the unhealthy dominant personality and try to help. In one case, the submerged personality wrote to the dominant personality giving her helpful information to try to make her healthier (Taylor and Martin, 1944).

Multiple Personality and Schizophrenia

Multiple personality is commonly confused with schizophrenia by the layperson. This is because "schizophrenia" is mistakenly thought to refer to a "split personality." Schizophrenia actually refers to one mental process, such as emotion, being split off from another, such as judgment, rather than to the splitting of one entire personality from another. Schizophrenia, as we will see in Chapter 17, is characterized by incoherence of speech and thought, hallucinations, delusions, and blunted or inappropriate emotion, along with deterioration in work, social relationships, and self-care. The individual with multiple personalities on the other hand, may show none of these symptoms. Multiple personality is diagnosed merely by the existence of two or more coherent and well-developed personalities in the same person. While some schizophrenics may have multiple personalities as well, and some individuals with multiple personality may be schizophrenic, the two disorders are distinct.

The Etiology of Multiple Personality

Where does multiple personality come from? The fourteen cases of multiple personality, all seen by Bliss, share some important common features, and provide us with some clues as to how multiple personality begins and how it develops. Bliss's hypothesis about how multiple personality proceeds has three steps. First, an individual between ages four and six confronts a serious emotional problem, which she copes with by creating another personality to take the brunt of the problem. Second, the individual is particularly vulnerable because she is highly susceptible to self-hypnosis, a process by which one is able to put oneself at will into trance states that have the properties of formal hypnotic inductions. Third, the individual finds out that creating another personality by self-hypnosis relieves her of her emotional burden, so that, in the future, when she confronts other emotional problems, she creates new personalities to take the brunt.

There is some evidence for each of these three steps. First, all fourteen of the patients that Bliss saw did, in fact, create their first alternative personality between the ages of four and six, and each seemed to be created in order to cope with very difficult emotional circumstances. Roberta, for example, created the first of her eighteen personalities when her mother held her under water and tried to drown her. This personality had the purpose of controlling and feeling Roberta's anger and of handling Roberta's homicidal rage without Roberta's having to do so. Another patient was molested at age four by an adult man; she created her first alternative personality in order to handle the molestation and thereafter used this personality to handle all sexual encounters.

Dear Others,

I would like all of you to sign your name and state your purpose in my life. What exactly do you do for me.

Debbie — I give you happiness.
Elizabeth — you can't cry so I do it for you.
Margo — speak the way you can't
Julie — Sex Sex Sex Sex Sex!!!!!
Brenda — Knowledge, the ability to talk to people intellectually.
Chiara — I am gay (lesbian)
Laurie — When a stranger talks to you I come around because I'm not afraid of people I don't know.
Kristine — I express deep feelings.
Bobby — Fighting physically.
Deanne — the only thing I know how to do is run away.
Mellissa — I'm scared.
Valerie — Free Spirits.
Cynthia — I'm the comedian.
Bethanne — love all people and talk to as many as I can.
Monica — Partying is my game.
Sarah — I play games. You always worry that you're going to win but I don't.

A sample of the handwriting of a patient with multiple personality. When one of the person's personalities dominates the individual's consciousness, the handwriting changes. Here each of seventeen personalities, as identified by their names, has written a message in a different handwriting. (Courtesy Dr. Eugene L. Bliss)

Second, there is evidence that these patients are extraordinarily good at self-hypnosis. All fourteen of Bliss's patients were excellent hypnotic subjects. When Bliss hypnotized them, they went rapidly into trance on the first induction. During the hypnosis, when he instructed them to have amnesia for what happened during hypnosis, they did this as well. In addition, when these patients reported the way in which they created the personalities, they described a process that sounds like hypnotic induction. One of the personalities of a patient said, "She creates personalities by blocking everything from her head, mentally relaxes, concentrates very hard and wishes." Another said, "She lies down, but can do it sitting up, concentrates very hard, clears her mind, blocks everything out and then wishes for the person, but she isn't aware of what she is doing." Once these patients were introduced to formal hypnosis in therapy, most reported that this experience was identical to experiences they had had dating back to their childhood, and that an inordinate amount of their lives had been spent in this altered state of consciousness. One patient said, "I spent an awful lot of time in hypnosis when I was young. I'd wish for music, and then hear it. I've always lived in a dream world. Now that I know what hypnosis is, I can say that I was in a trance often. There was a little place where I could sit, close my eyes and imagine, until I felt very relaxed, just like hypnosis—and it could be very deep."

Third, patients used new personalities to defend against distress later in life. Jenny, you will recall, created Julie, a gentle personality, to cope with her parents' putting her up for adoption at age eight. Most of the patients reported instances in which they created new personalities to cope with new stresses even when they were adults.

In short, multiple personality may come about in the following way: An individual, who is particularly good at self-hypnosis, confronts a serious trauma while a young child. She copes with this by producing a second personality to endure the trauma, rather than enduring it herself. She finds out that this tactic relieves her of emotional stress and, in the future, when she confronts new problems, she creates new personalities to bear them.

Psychotherapy for Multiple Personality

As in the case of Julie-Jenny-Jerrie, the treatment of patients with multiple personalities is difficult and frustrating. The first step is to make the patient aware of the problem. Although she may have lived in this strange state for many years, had amnesias, and been told by others about her bizarre behavior, she may not yet have confronted the fact of other personalities.

Under hypnosis, the therapist calls up the alter-egos and allows them to speak freely. In addition, the patient herself is asked to listen and then is introduced to some of these personalities. She is told to remember the experience when she emerges from hypnosis. Enormous distress and turmoil often follow this discovery, but it is important for her to keep hold of the facts of many personalities. At this point, she may display one of the most troublesome problems for therapy—dodging back into a self-hypnotic state and so avoiding the unpleasant reality. The therapist may then try to enlist the aid of various personalities. Bliss reports that "a perceptive, cooperative alter-ego can be a remarkable guide, keeping the therapist current while alerting him to resistances or unfinished business."

After the patient is made fully aware of her many personalities, the therapist explains to her that they are products of self-hypnosis induced at an early age and without any conscious or malicious intent. The patient is told that now she is an adult, strong and capable, and that if she has the courage, she can flush these specters out and defeat them. The other personalities may object, or want to continue their own life, but she is the only real person here. There is only one body and one head, and the other personalities are her creations. She will have the privilege of deciding what aspects of the personalities she will retain. Because there are so few cases treated this way, we do not yet know how often such therapy will work.

Overall, then, multiple personality, like somatoform disorders and amnesia, can be seen as an attempt to defend against intolerable emotional distress. A child of four to six who is unusually capable of self-hypnosis creates a new personality—an imaginary companion and ally—to help her deal with the anxiety generated by a traumatic experience. This innocent, childhood ploy inadvertently becomes an adult disaster as the patient repeatedly uses this technique to cope with the new stresses as she grows up.

DSM-III AND THE NEUROSES

In this chapter and Chapter 10, we have examined disorders that appear, on the surface, to be quite varied: phobia, post-traumatic stress disorder, panic disorder, generalized anxiety disorder, obsessions, somatoform disorders, amnesia, and multiple personality. In the past, these disorders looked more like a coherent whole than they do today. Historically, they were all viewed as "neuroses," and all were thought to involve anxiety as the central process. In the case of phobia and post-traumatic stress disorder, fear is on the surface; in panic disorder and generalized anxiety disorder, anxiety (fear without a specific object) is also on the surface. The individual with one of these problems feels anxiety, apprehension, fear, terror, and dread in his daily life. In obsessive-compulsive disorders, on the other hand, anxiety is sometimes felt, but not if the compulsion is frequent and effective. In contrast, in the somatoform disorders and the dissociative disorders, anxiety is not usually observed. But in order to explain the bizarre symptoms of these disorders, theorists have inferred that, with his symptoms, the individual is defending against underlying anxiety. To the extent that the defense is successful, the symptoms will appear, and anxiety will not be felt.

The last fifteen years have witnessed a sea change in the field of psychopathology: our categories have become more descriptive and less theoretical. DSM-III uses the term "neurotic" to describe common symptoms, but it disavows a common process—defending against anxiety—as the mechanism of the neuroses. The dissociative disorders and conversion disorders no longer fall under the larger class "Anxiety Disorders" in DSM-III, which includes as anxiety disorders only those disorders in which anxiety is observed: phobia, panic disorder, generalized anxiety disorder, post-traumatic stress disorder, and obsessions. We see this move as a healthy one, but we are not complacent about it.

Descriptively it makes good sense to segregate those disorders in which anxiety is observed from those in which anxiety is only inferred by a theory. But at a theoretical level, we are not content. For phobia and post-traumatic stress disorder, theories that come out of behavioral models seem appropriate, as in both of these disorders we can postulate a trauma that imbued parts of the environment with terror, and the symptoms, the course, and the therapies roughly follow known behavioral laws. The obsessive disorders are not as easy to handle in this way. How obsessions stay around once they have been acquired fits reasonably well within behavioral views, as do therapies that alleviate obsessions. But this is only part of the story. The questions of who is vulnerable to obsessions and what content obsessions will take are not answered by the behavioral school, nor is there even a useful theory from this tradition. These questions may be best viewed within a psychodynamic tradition, in which emotional distress lurks beneath the surface. Finally, we have somatoform disorders, psychogenic amnesia, and multiple personality. Here theories of surface anxiety are useless, and there exists no adequate behavioral theory of these three disorders. Anxiety, or some other dysphoric emotion that lies beneath the surface and is being defended against, seems to make more sense of the symptoms of these disorders, but the details of their etiology and which therapy is best for them remain a mystery.

Overall, then, we find that when fear and anxiety are on the surface, behavioral models serve us well. As fear and anxiety tend to disappear from the surface, however, we find ourselves in need of models to attempt to explain what we do observe. It seems likely that for the present we still need, at least for disorders like conversion, amnesia, and multiple personality, theories such as the psychodynamic model, which postulates deep, unobserved emotional conflict and psychological defenses that are so rich as to still inspire awe in those who study these disorders closely.

SUMMARY

1. This chapter examined the neurotic disorders in which anxiety is inferred to exist as opposed to being observed. Three kinds of anxiety disorders were considered: obsessive-compulsive disorders, somatoform disorders, and dissociative disorders.

2. *Obsessive-compulsive disorders* consist of *obsessions,* which are repetitive thoughts, images, or impulses that invade consciousness, are often abhorrent, and are very difficult to dismiss or control. In addition, most obsessions are associated with *compulsions,* which are repetitive, stereotyped, and unwanted actions to undo the obsession. Compulsions can be resisted only with difficulty.

3. The content of obsessions has changed over history. In past centuries, they were mostly religious and sexual; now they are concerned mostly with dirt and contamination, violence, and orderliness.

4. An obsessive-compulsive individual displays anxiety when his or her rituals are blocked. In addition, depression is associated with this disorder. When such an individual is depressed, obsessions occur much more frequently. Moreover, such individuals are more prone to depression than the normal population. There is no personality type that seems predisposed to obsessive-compulsive disorders. Individuals who are obsessive in their daily life and concerned with order are not more vulnerable to the obsessive-compulsive disorder. What distinguishes these individuals from individuals with the disorder is that individuals with the obsessive personality are proud of their meticulousness and love of detail, whereas individuals who have the disorder are tormented by their symptoms.

5. Cognitive-behavioral theory explains why the disorder and its rituals are maintained. The theory claims that individuals with the disorder are unable to habituate, dismiss, and distract themselves from disturbing thoughts. Behavior therapies for obsessive-compulsive disorders include *flooding,* forcing the patient to endure the aversive situation, *response blocking,* preventing the individual from engaging in the ritual, and *modeling,* watching another person refrain from the ritual. These therapies bring about marked improvement in about two-thirds of the patients with obsessive-compulsive disorders.

6. Psychoanalytic theory explains who is vulnerable to the disorder and why it has the particular content it does. It claims that the obsessive thought is a *defense* against an even more unwelcome unconscious thought. The anxiety the unconscious thought arouses is displaced onto a less unwelcome substitute, which symbolically stands for the underlying conflict.

7. The *somatoform disorders* have five symptoms: (1) lost or altered physical functioning, (2) the absence of a known physical cause, (3) positive evidence that psychological factors have caused the symptom, (4) indifference to the physical loss, and (5) the absence of voluntary control over the symptom.

8. The three kinds of somatoform disorders are (1) *hysterical conversion,* in which one physical function is lost or altered, (2) *Briquet's syndrome,* in which there is a dramatic and complicated medical history for multiple and recurrent bodily complaints in many organs, although the symptoms are not physically caused, and (3) *psychalgia,* which is pain not attributed to physical cause, and which is the most common somatoform disorder today. Somatoform disorders should be distinguished from malingering, secondary gain, psychosomatic disorders, and undiagnosed physical illness.

9. Psychoanalytic theory holds that somatoform disorders are a defense against anxiety, that psychic energy is transmuted into somatic loss, and that the particular somatic loss symbolizes the underlying conflict.

10. The *dissociative disorders* involve the symptoms of *depersonalization* and a *loss of memory* about identity. In these disorders, some area of memory is split off or dissociated from conscious awareness.

11. *Psychogenic amnesia* is a sudden loss of memory caused by unbearable trauma and can either be general or highly specific. *Retrograde amnesia* is a specific amnesia in which events immediately *before* some trauma are forgotten. *Anterograde amnesia* is an amnesia in which events *after* a trauma are forgotten.

12. *Multiple personality* is the existence of two or more personalities in the same individual, each personality being sufficiently integrated to have a relatively rich and stable life of its own. This disorder is more frequent than previously believed and seems to involve individuals who are highly susceptible to self-hypnosis, who experience a serious emotional problem between ages four and six, and who use the creation of alternative personalities to bear this trauma, which they are unable to cope with in any other way.

12

Psychosomatic Disorders and Behavioral Medicine

DOES what we think and what we feel change our physical well-being? We have learned from our discussion of emotion in the last two chapters that our thoughts and emotions can modify how our body reacts. One of our bodily reactions is, of course, disease, and we do not usually think of physical disease—stomach ulcers, high blood pressure, cancer, tuberculosis, asthma—as reactions that can be influenced by thoughts and feelings. But there is a good deal of evidence that the course, and perhaps the very occurrence, of such illnesses can be influenced by the psychological states of their victims. Such a disorder is called a ***psychosomatic disorder*** and is defined as a disorder of the body (the soma) that is influenced by, or in the strongest case, caused by the mind (the psyche). The field that deals with these disorders stands at the border of psychology and medicine, and is now called ***behavioral medicine*** (Blanchard, 1982).

We will present an overview of psychosomatic, or ***psychophysiological disorders,*** followed by a close look at three such disorders: peptic ulcers, high blood pressure, and sudden death. We will then distill the principles used to analyze these three examples by discussing various theoretical approaches to psychosomatics. We begin with a striking example of a psychosomatic phenomenon on the skin: stigmata.

STIGMATA

One of the most dramatic examples of psychosomatic disorder is the rare phenomenon of ***stigmata.*** Stigmata are marks on the skin—usually bleeding or bruises—often of high religious or personal significance, brought on by an emotional state. About 300 instances of stigmata, many of them called miracles, have been reported in the last 2,000 years. Most are found in religious histories, but only a handful of these are documented well enough to take seriously scientifically. But this handful provides the quintessential demonstration of a psychosomatic phenomenon: a mental state causing the body to react in a way usually thought of as being purely physical. Consider the following case history:

Bandages cover the stigmata on this priest's hands. In some religious beliefs, such stigmata are held to be an impression of the wounds of Christ, and appear only in a rare few controversial cases. (Courtesy Religious News Service)

> Since childhood, Steven had suffered from nightmares and sleepwalking. His sleepwalking became a particular problem when, in 1935, he was hospitalized because of an infection. To prevent him from sleepwalking about the ward in the middle of the night, he was restrained physically while he slept; his hands were tightly bound behind his back when he went to sleep. On one such occasion he awoke, and in a half-conscious state, found himself tied down. Although he could not untie his hands, he was still able to evade his bodyguard and escape into the surrounding countryside, from which he returned a few hours later.
>
> Some ten years later, at age thirty-five, Steven was again admitted to a hospital —this time in an attempt to cure his recurrent sleepwalking. One evening at about midnight the nurse saw him struggling violently on his bed, apparently having a nightmare. He was holding his hands behind his back and seemed to be trying to free them from some imaginary bond. After carrying on in this way for about an hour, he crept out of bed still holding his hands behind his back, and disappeared into the hospital grounds. He returned twenty minutes later in a state of normal consciousness. As the nurse put him into bed, she noted deep weals like rope marks on each arm, but until then Steven seemed unaware of their presence. The next day the marks were still visible and were observed by the hospital staff. Three nights later the marks had disappeared.
>
> His physician believed that the marks were stigmata caused by reliving the traumatic event of a decade earlier. To test this, he caused Steven to relive the experience of ten years before under a hypnotic drug. While reliving the experience, Steven writhed violently on the couch for about three-quarters of an hour. After a few minutes weals appeared on both forearms. Gradually these became deeply indented and finally blood appeared along their course. Next morning the marks were still clearly visible (see Figure 12-1). (Moody, 1946)

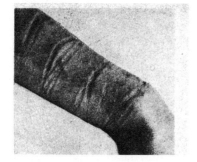

Figure 12-1
Steven's right forearm shows indented weals, resembling rope marks. They appeared in the course of reliving an earlier traumatic experience, which occurred while Steven was under an hypnotic drug. (Source: Moody, 1946)

Here is a clear example of an essentially psychosomatic phenomenon. A process that we usually believe to be strictly physical—the appearance of rope marks and bleeding—is induced by the mental state of recalling a traumatic incident with high emotion. The patient was carefully observed during the development of the rope marks, and there is no ready explanation other than an emotional state influencing a physical state.

AN OVERVIEW OF PSYCHOSOMATIC DISORDERS

It is already clear that psychosomatic illness may take a bizarre form. In the case of Steven, there is little doubt of the existence of a psychosomatic disorder. But what about those cases where there is less dramatic evidence? Many believe that some ulcers, high blood pressure, and other physical problems are partly caused by an adverse psychological state. But how does a clinician know this, and when there is evidence, how does he or she classify it?

The diagnosis of psychosomatic disorder is made if (1) there is a disorder of known physical pathology present, *and* (2) psychologically meaningful events preceded and are judged to contribute to the onset or worsening of the disorder. This diagnosis is contained in DSM-III's apt name for these disorders "psychological factors affecting physical condition."

Environmental stressors, such as overwork, may influence the development of peptic ulcers. (© Leonard Freed/Magnum)

The first criterion distinguishes psychosomatic disorders from somatoform disorders. Conversion, psychogenic amnesia, and the like have no known physical basis, whereas psychosomatic disorders do. Bear's paralysis was not accompanied by any physical damage to his nerves or spinal cord, whereas an individual whose peptic ulcer flares up every time he is criticized by his boss (which meets the second criterion) has actual physical damage to the lining of his gastrointestinal system. By these criteria, Steven's forearm weals are a clear case of psychosomatic disorder, since symptoms of known physical pathology are present—rope marks and bleeding—and a psychologically traumatic incident—being bound while asleep—preceded and was demonstrated by the hypnotic reliving to have contributed to the weals and bleeding.

These two defining criteria of psychosomatic disorder have been incorporated into a particular model: *the diathesis-stress model.* "Diathesis" refers to the constitutional weakness that underlies the physical pathology, and "stress" to the psychological reaction to meaningful events. According to this model, an individual develops a psychosomatic disorder when he both has some physical vulnerability (diathesis) and experiences psychological disturbance (stress). If an individual is extremely weak constitutionally, very little stress will be needed to trigger the illness; if, on the other hand, extreme stress occurs, even individuals who are constitutionally strong may fall ill. In effect, the model suggests that individuals who develop peptic ulcers are both constitutionally vulnerable to gastrointestinal problems and experience sufficient stress to trigger the pathology.

Psychological factors can affect many physical conditions in a large number of organ systems: the skin, the skeletal-musculature, the respiratory, the cardiovascular, the blood and lymphatic, the gastrointestinal, the genitourinary, the endocrine systems, or the sense organs (Looney, Lipp, and Spitzer, 1978). There is no evidence, however, that the process causing psychosomatic effects is different for different organs, although any given individual may be especially vulnerable to psychosomatic influence in only one organ system. Some of us react to stress with the stomach, others by sweating, some by muscle tension, and still others with a racing heart.

Figure 12-2
A human stomach ulcer. The esophagus enters at the top center, and the exit to the small intestine lies between the top dotted line *a* and the bottom dotted line *b*. The ulcer lies at the border of the exit (pyloric sphincter) and the duodenum. (Source: Oi, Oshiba, and Sugimura, 1959)

PEPTIC ULCERS

A *peptic ulcer* is a circumscribed erosion of the mucous membrane of the stomach or of the duodenum, the upper portion of the small intestine (see Figure 12-2). Such ulcers are called "peptic" because it is commonly thought that they are at least partially caused by pepsin, which is contained in the acidic juices normally secreted by the stomach. There are two sorts of peptic ulcers named by their location: a stomach (gastric) ulcer and a duodenal ulcer.

Roughly two million people in the United States today have a peptic ulcer, and about five thousand people die of peptic ulcer each year in the United States (Center for Disease Control, 1982). We begin our discussion of psychosomatic disorders with the peptic ulcers because they are so widespread and because much is known, both about the physical pathology underlying ulcers and about psychological influence on their development and course. Carlos's gastrointestinal problems illustrate the ways in which environmental stress influences peptic ulcers.

> Carlos has had an ulcer for the last seventeen years. Until recently he had it under control; for whenever he experienced gastric pain, drinking a quart of milk or eating eggs would relieve it. Three years ago he was promoted to manager of a major department store and moved from his home town to a distant city. Since he took on this increased responsibility, he has experienced severe ulcer pain.
>
> He had been born and raised in a small New England town. His father was wealthy and the head of a chain of department stores. Although his father was in general dominating and intolerant (and also had an ulcer), he was kind and generous to Carlos. After graduation from college Carlos entered the department store business and even now, at age forty-one, he feels incapable of holding a job without his father's intervention, influence, and support.
>
> As soon as Carlos took over the management of the store, he became tense and anxious and began to brood over trivial details. He was afraid the store would catch fire; he was afraid that there would be bookkeeping errors that he might not catch; he was afraid the store would not make a big profit. Convinced he was a complete failure, and plagued with severe pains from his duodenal ulcer, he entered psychotherapy. During these sessions, Carlos and his therapist learned how much the psychological factors in his life contributed to the worsening of the ulcer. The following three incidents particularly illustrate this.
>
> First, on a day when the store was full of people a large ventilating fan broke. The store began to shake as the customers rushed to the street, and Carlos went into a panic. As soon as the excitement subsided and his panic diminished, severe ulcer pains started.
>
> Second, Carlos's mother had for many years complained of a "heart condition." While his mother's physician had never isolated a physical cause, Carlos nevertheless worried about it. One day Carlos saw a hearse pass in front of the store. Immediately he thought that his mother had died and in panic ran several miles to her home finding her quite alive. As he started to run the stomach pains broke out, and these pains remained until he saw his mother was not ill.
>
> Third, one night Carlos's store burned to the ground. He was highly anxious that he would be found negligent during the ensuing insurance investigation. As he awaited the results of the inquiry, his wife called and told him that his daughter had broken a leg. He ran home and found his wife in tears, and he immediately developed severe stomach pains.
>
> Before he had become manager of the store he had occasionally had stomach pains while on the job, but he had found a technique for reliably and immediately alleviating them: he would go to an older person for comfort. Upon being reassured by an authority figure, his ulcer pain would disappear. In his new job, however, he was the authority figure, there was no one to turn to, and his ulcer pains persisted, unrelieved. (Adapted from Weisman, 1956.)

For some, increased responsibility may be a source of psychosomatic problems. (Photograph by David Burnett/ Black Star)

SYMPTOMS OF PEPTIC ULCER

Carlos suffered the main symptom of peptic ulcer: abdominal pain. Such abdominal pain can vary from mild discomfort to severe and penetrating, extreme pain. Pain may be steady, aching, and gnawing, or it may be sharp and cramp-like. Pain is usually not present before breakfast; it generally starts from one to four hours after meals. Bland foods and antacids usually alleviate the pain and peppery food, alcohol, and aspirin usually intensify it (Lachman, 1972; Weiner, 1977). Peptic ulcers that become very serious sometimes perforate or bleed. Without well-timed surgery, a perforated ulcer can lead to death from internal bleeding.

PHYSIOLOGICAL DEVELOPMENT OF AN ULCER

In order to understand how these symptoms come to be, we must first take a brief look at the actions of the digestive system. Digestion breaks down food in the stomach so that when the food passes through the intestines, the appropriate materials can be absorbed for use by the body. In order to digest food, the stomach secretes two highly corrosive juices: hydrochloric acid, which breaks food down, and pepsin, which decomposes protein. Why, you might wonder, does the stomach not digest itself? Fortunately, the stomach and the small intestine are lined with a mucous membrane that protects them from corrosion by the hydrochloric acid they secrete. In addition, gastric juices are normally secreted only when there is food in the stomach to absorb most of the corrosive acid. But sometimes the system develops a problem. A break may occur in the mucous coating of the stomach or duodenum. Such a break may occur when some of the thin lining is worn away in the normal course of digestion. It may also occur when an overdose of aspirin, particularly in combination with alcohol, is ingested, or when naturally secreted bile attacks the membrane. If a break occurs in the absence of too much gastric juice, it will repair itself and no ulcer will form, since cell growth completely renews the stomach lining every three days (Davenport, 1972). If an excess of hydrochloric acid or pepsin is around, however, particularly when food is not in the stomach, the abrasion will worsen and an ulcer will form (see Figure 12-2).

WHO IS SUSCEPTIBLE TO ULCERS?

The way an ulcer develops gives us clues about what diathesis, or constitutional weakness, makes ulcers more likely. Individuals who secrete excess hydrochloric acid or pepsin, individuals with an especially weak mucous defense against acid, and individuals whose stomach lining regenerates slowly may generally be more susceptible to ulcers. This condition may be genetically inherited.

The prevalence of peptic ulcer varies widely from country to country, and from decade to decade. Today, approximately 1 percent of the adult American population has an ulcer, and almost four hundred thousand Americans are hospitalized yearly for peptic ulcers. The frequency of peptic ulcers has, for unexplained reasons, declined by about 25 percent over the last decade in the U.S. and Europe (McConnell, 1966; Lachman, 1972; Weiner, 1977; Elashoff and Grossman, 1980).

The susceptibility of women versus men seems to have undergone a major change over the past 100 years. Before 1900, peptic ulcers occurred more frequently in women than in men, but in the beginning of the twentieth century a shift occurred, with men becoming considerably more ulcer prone. By the late 1950s, men had 3.5 times as many duodenal ulcers as women (Watkins, 1960). In recent years the male/female ratio has been changing (Elashoff and Grossman, 1980). By 1978, men had only 1.2 times as many peptic ulcers as women in America, as ulcers in men had become less frequent and ulcers in women had either stayed the same or slightly increased.

Social class does not strongly influence the incidence of ulcers. For a time it was commonly believed that highly pressured, upwardly mobile and professionally successful individuals develop the most ulcers. But in fact many patients with peptic ulcer are poor and wholly unsuccessful (Rennie and Srole, 1956).

Age also does not make much of a difference beyond the age of twenty, although children probably have ulcers less frequently than adults. Among children, girls have peptic ulcers about twice as frequently as boys (Christodoulou, Gergoulas, Paploukas, Marinopoulou, and Sideris, 1977; Medley, 1978).

Ulcers clearly run in families. The relatives of patients with duodenal and gastric ulcers are about three times as likely to have an ulcer as those in the general population (McConnell, 1966). Further, healthy individuals who have relatives with peptic ulcers secrete more gastric juice than individuals without relatives with ulcers (Fodor, Vestea, and Urcan, 1968). This increased susceptibility in families could either be genetic or environmental, since family members share many of the same stresses, as well as genes. But twin data suggest it is genetic. If one of two identical twins has a peptic ulcer, the chances are 54 out of 100 that the co-twin will also have a peptic ulcer; whereas if one of two fraternal twins has a peptic ulcer, there is only a 17 percent chance that the co-twin will also have peptic ulcer (Eberhard, 1968).

Here then is the foundation of the diathesis, in the diathesis-stress model of peptic ulcers. How much acid and pepsin the stomach secretes contributes to the formation of an ulcer. High acid and pepsin secretion runs in families and may be the constitutional weakness that makes individuals more susceptible to ulcers (Mirsky, 1958).

Psychological Factors Influencing Peptic Ulcers

To what extent does stress influence the development or worsening of peptic ulcers? When individuals who have a constitutional weakness of the intestinal system—such as hereditary oversecretion of acid—encounter certain kinds of stress, peptic ulcers may result. By "stress" researchers refer to the reaction of an individual to disturbing events in the environment. A stress

Tension and anxiety may cause individuals with a constitutional weakness of the intestinal system to develop ulcers. (Photograph by Ann Chwatsky/Leo de Wys)

reaction can either be a short-term emotional reaction induced by a specific situation, or it can be a long-term pattern of such emotional reactions, adding up to an ulcer-prone personality. We turn first to the evidence that emotional states influence peptic ulcer, and then we examine the possibility that individuals who have a certain personality pattern of reacting to stress are ulcer prone.

Gastric Secretion, Peptic Ulcer, and Emotional States

Let us now take a look at the evidence that emotional states affect gastric secretion. Two researchers were afforded a rare opportunity to study directly the effects of anxiety and depression on digestion when they discovered a man who, because of a childhood experience, was forced to feed himself through a hole in his stomach.

> Tom was a fifty-seven-year-old workman who at age seven swallowed some very hot soup, which so burnt his esophagus that it had to be surgically sealed off. After many unsuccessful attempts at corrective surgery, Tom had to resort to feeding himself by chewing his food (to satisfy his taste) and then depositing the food directly into his stomach using a funnel and a rubber tube. He was secretive about this for many years, but when he was in his fifties, Tom allowed himself to be experimented upon. Investigators directly examined his gastric secretions under different emotional conditions. When Tom was anxious, angry, or resentful, gastric secretions increased. When he was sad, his gastric secretions decreased (Wolff, 1965).

In another study, thirteen patients with ulcers and thirteen normal subjects were interviewed under emotion-provoking conditions. The patients with ulcers showed a greater secretion of hydrochloric acid in the stomach and more stomach motility than the patients without ulcers (Mittelmann, Wolff, and Scharf, 1942). Findings with normal individuals under hypnosis also confirmed that gastric secretions are influenced by emotion. Hypnotically induced thoughts of anger and anxiety produced high gastric secretion, while thoughts of depression, helplessness, and hopelessness produced low secretion (Kehoe and Ironside, 1963).

High rates of peptic ulcer were also found in people in occupations that produce high anxiety. For example, air traffic controllers have twice the ulcer rate of matched control groups, and those controllers who work at towers with much traffic have twice the ulcer rate of those who work at towers with less traffic (Cobb and Rose, 1973). We must be cautious, however, about this correlation between occupation and ulcers. It could be that ulcer-prone individuals, for some reason, choose anxiety-provoking jobs. If this is the case, it need not be the anxiety of the job that causes the ulcer.

The evidence presented above does suggest that emotional states like anxiety and anger cause excess stomach acid; this in turn, contributes to the development of peptic ulcers. Also, certain anxiety-producing occupations may lead to more employees with stomach ulcers. Here again, greater anxiety produces excess acid in the stomach. This latter point fits in with Carlos's story narrated earlier. Like many individuals with ulcers, Carlos's ulcer worsened and caused more pain after emotional crises. When he was anxious, needed reassurance, and felt excessive demands for responsibility, his

Air traffic controllers have a high incidence of peptic ulcers. (Photograph by Erich Hartmann/ © 1968 Magnum Photos)

ulcer flared up. When he allowed himself to be dependent, his ulcer was inactive.

Animal Models of Peptic Ulcer

Some investigators have shed light on the relation between emotional states and ulcers by studying animals. In doing so, they have put animals in conditions that change the emotional state of the animal. We will look at three such situations: conflict, unpredictability, and uncontrollability. All of these factors increase anxiety.

CONFLICT. Can "conflict" be aroused in a rat in order to find out whether or not conflict produces ulcers? One way to bring about conflict is to make a hungry rat run through shock in order to get food. This is called an "avoidance-approach" conflict. In one experiment, one group of rats was required to cross a shock grid in order to obtain food and water for forty-seven out of forty-eight hour cycles. During one hour, the grid was not electrified so that the animals could have sufficient water and food. Six of nine rats in this group developed ulcers, whereas none of the comparison group rats did. Control groups with shock alone, food and water alone, or nothing got fewer ulcers. So avoidance-approach conflict is more likely to produce stomach ulcers than is electric shock, hunger, or thirst without conflict (Sawrey, Conger, and Turrell, 1956; Sawrey and Weiss, 1956). Therefore conflict, a psychological state that produces anxiety, can engender ulcers in rats.

UNPREDICTABILITY. When noxious events are experienced by an individual, they can either be signaled, and therefore predictable, or unsignaled, and therefore unpredictable. For example, the rockets that fell on London in World War II were signaled by an air raid siren. But when a concentration camp guard arbitrarily singled out a prisoner for a beating, this was entirely unsignaled. There is considerable evidence, both in rats and humans, that when noxious events are signaled, individuals are terrified during the signal. But they also learn that when the signal is not on, the noxious event does not occur, so they are safe and can relax. Also if something can be done, a signal allows a person to prepare for the bad event. In contrast, when the identical noxious event occurs without a signal, individuals are afraid all the time because they have no signal of safety that tells them they can relax (Seligman and Binik, 1977). Since oversecretion of gastric juices occurs during anxiety and more anxiety occurs with unpredictability, we might expect that more ulcers would occur as well. It has been found that they do.

In one study, investigators took two groups of rats and deprived them of food. Each group received occasional brief electric shocks. For one group, the shocks were predictable: each shock was preceded by a tone or a light. Another group of rats received exactly the same shocks and at the same times, but they had no signal to tell them when shock would occur and therefore no absence of signal to tell them when they were safe. More of the rats who received unpredictable shock formed ulcers, and the ulcers they formed were larger than those in the predictable shock group. Being in the presence of chronic anxiety—as produced by unpredictable shock—causes ulcers in rats (Seligman, 1968; Weiss, 1968).

Uncontrollable life events like losing one's job can be a factor in the development of psychosomatic problems. During the recent recession, a large number of automobile workers lost their jobs through no fault of their own. (© 1981 Andy Sacks/Black Star)

UNCONTROLLABILITY. When noxious events occur, sometimes you can do something about them, but at other times you are helpless. So, for example, being a victim of lung cancer is at least partly controllable; you can take action to avoid lung cancer by not smoking cigarettes. Losing your job during a national depression, however, is quite uncontrollable. There is very little you can do to protect your job once economic panic has set in and most of your colleagues are being fired. More precisely, an event is *uncontrollable* when no response an individual can make will change the probability of the event. An event is *controllable* when at least one response the individual has in his repertoire can change the probability of the event. Which produces more ulcers, controllable or uncontrollable dangers? This question has an intriguing twenty-year history, and it has only recently been resolved.

In 1958, a study, now known as the "executive monkey" study was performed. Eight monkeys were given occasional electric shocks. Four of them could avoid the shocks by pressing a lever. The other four received exactly the same shocks as their four executive partners, but they were helpless; no response that they made would affect whether or not they were shocked; only their executive partners' actions made any difference. The monkeys could not see or hear each other. The executives in each of the four pairs developed duodenal ulcers and died; their helpless partners remained healthy (Brady, 1958). The conclusion from this study was that having control over threat would cause ulcers. The moral was that executives, or others in a position of great responsibility, would be more prone to ulcers than their employees.

This study was widely publicized, and for years many believed it was valid. It is, however, an artifact. When experimenters in the 1960s had trouble replicating it, the details of the procedure were scrutinized. As it turned out, the eight monkeys had not been randomly assigned to the executive group. The four monkeys who probably had been the most emotionally reactive had become the executives and had developed the ulcers; but it probably had been their preexisting high emotionality (which was indicated by their readiness to lever press when shocked) and not the fact of having to execute a controlling response, which had produced the ulcers.

In another study, the methodological problems of the executive monkey study were avoided and the opposite results were obtained. Rats were divided into six groups. Two of the groups received escapable shock, shock they could turn off by rotating a wheel in front of them. Two of the groups were "yoked." They received exactly the same pattern of shock, but it was inescapable—no response they made affected the shock; it went on and off for them at the same time as for their "executive" partners in the "escapable" group. Two of the groups received no shock. Within each of these groups, shock was either signaled or unsignaled. In this experiment, then, both the controllability and predictability of the shock were varied. The rats were assigned to these six groups randomly, thereby distributing any preexisting emotionality equally among the groups (Weiss, 1971).

As can be seen from Table 12-1, two basic findings emerged. First, unpredictability leads to ulcers—the rats developed more ulcers when they were subjected to unsignaled than to signaled shock, whether or not they could escape it. Second, uncontrollability leads to ulcers—rats who received ines-

Table 12-1 MEDIAN NUMBER OF ULCERS AND WHEEL TURNS

	Ulcers	Wheel Turns
Escape Groups		
Signaled	2.0	3,717
Unsignaled	3.5	13,992
Yoked, Inescapable Groups		
Signaled	3.5	1,404
Unsignaled	6.0	4,357
No Shock Groups		
Signaled	1.0	60
Unsignaled	1.0	51

SOURCE: Adapted from Weiss, 1971.

capable shock developed more ulcers than rats who could escape shock, whether or not the shock was signaled.

What are we to conclude from this and other animal studies? First of all, it seems clear that the "executives" were actually less likely to develop ulcers. Second, this and other studies set up three conditions—conflict, unpredictability, and uncontrollability—that produce anxiety, and eventually a greater number of ulcers. Research on how humans react in parallel situations continues. Indeed our environment may well be constructed in a way to produce ulcers in some individuals. Other researchers, however, have looked elsewhere for the cause of ulcers. Specifically, they have looked into the dynamics of personality.

Personality and Susceptibility to Peptic Ulcer

Dr. Franz Alexander postulated that an unconscious conflict of dependence versus independence predisposes an individual to ulcers. (United Press International Photo)

In 1950, the psychoanalyst Franz Alexander formulated the most influential statement of the ulcer-prone personality (Alexander, 1950). Based on his observations of his ulcer patients, mostly men from upper-middle-class backgrounds, Alexander postulated that an unconscious conflict of dependence versus independence predisposes an individual to ulcers. He claimed that the ulcer patient has a deep-seated wish to be loved and nurtured like an infant. But at the same time, these motives give rise to shame and guilt and are rejected by the adult ego. To avoid displaying the oral motives of an infant, which he considers shameful, the ulcer-prone person puts on a mask of exaggerated self-sufficiency and "pseudoindependence." He is characterized by driving ambition and inappropriate displays of strength. When his dependency wishes are rearoused, the conflict is intensified with gastric hypersecretion worsening the symptoms. For example, Alexander would consider Carlos, from our earlier case study, as having an ulcer-prone personality, for when the fire breaks out in Carlos's store, his need for nurturance by his father is evoked and his ulcer pain is exacerbated.

Alexander's formulation contains three parts: (1) the predisposition—pseudoindependent defenses against the need to be dependent, (2) the conditions for exacerbation—the rearousal of the oral-dependency conflict, and (3) a physiological mechanism—gastric hypersecretion brought on by this conflict (Alexander, 1950; Weiner, 1977).

This formulation has received some experimental support. A group of specialists in internal medicine and a group of psychoanalysts were asked to diagnose which psychosomatic illnesses were suffered by a group of patients. The judges had to do this on the basis only of edited interviews that omitted all reference to the patients' psychosomatic symptoms. Each of the eighty-three patients had one of the seven "classic" psychosomatic illnesses (arthritis, ulcer, high blood pressure, dermatitis, ulcerative colitis, asthma, and thyroid oversecretion). The judges were asked to pick out which ones had the ulcers using Alexander's characterization of the ulcer-prone personality. Eighteen of the patients actually had ulcers. The group of psychoanalysts correctly picked out 50 percent of the men but only 16 percent of the women who had ulcers. The group specializing in internal medicine made a successful diagnosis of 40 percent of the men and 10 percent of the women. Chance guessing would have gotten 14 percent (one out of seven) right. This indicates that Alexander's formulations may separate the ulcer-prone man from men who have other psychosomatic disorders but that his theory does not work for women (Alexander, French, and Pollack, 1968). So far, these remain tentative findings, for more studies are needed to clarify exactly what might be an ulcer-prone personality.

TREATMENT OF PEPTIC ULCERS

In times past, peptic ulcers were treated primarily by giving patients antacid drugs in an attempt to lower stomach acidity. In addition, bland diets that restricted intake of foods that stimulate hydrochloric acid secretion were recommended to patients. Smoking, drinking alcohol, and drinking coffee or tea were also restricted. About half of the ulcers usually healed under such a regimen. In the late 1970s, a new drug—cimetidine—came into use. Cimetidine reduces stomach acid by about two-thirds, and it produces healing in 70 to 95 percent of patients with peptic ulcers in a few months. It is now clearly the treatment of choice for peptic ulcer (Bardhan, 1980).

Psychological treatments of ulcers are less well charted. Rest, relaxation, anxiety management, and removal from the external sources of psychological stress are often prescribed for ulcer patients, and there is at least strong clinical evidence that these are effective. Psychoanalytic therapy has been reported to be effective with ulcer patients, but the appropriate controlled studies have yet to be done (Orgel, 1958). Finally, some individuals without ulcers can learn to control their level of gastric acid secretion voluntarily by using biofeedback about their gastric acid secretion (Welgan, 1974). But it has yet to be demonstrated that patients who actually have ulcers can learn voluntary control over gastric acid secretion or that this will alleviate their peptic ulcers.

To summarize, peptic ulcers are best viewed within a diathesis-stress model. A peptic ulcer is caused when gastric juice that is naturally secreted in the stomach eats a hole into the protective mucous membrane of the stomach or the duodenum. This erosion is the ulcer. Three kinds of constitutional weaknesses or "diatheses," can make an individual prone to ulcers: (1) an oversecretion of gastric juices, and there is evidence that this can be genetically inherited; (2) a weak mucous membrane, and (3) a stomach lining that regenerates slowly. Psychological factors can also influence the formation of a peptic ulcer in individuals who have such a diathesis. There is evidence that emotional states, particularly anxiety, cause oversecretion of acid in the stomach. In addition, there is further experimental evidence that rats who experience anxiety when placed in conflict, in the presence of unpredictable stressors, or in the presence of uncontrollable stressors develop peptic ulcers. This suggests that chronic or frequent anxiety may cause oversecretion of stomach acid which, in turn, may produce ulcers in individuals whose gastrointestinal system is genetically vulnerable.

HIGH BLOOD PRESSURE

Hypertension, the technical name for high blood pressure, is the most serious of the physical disorders that are clearly influenced by psychological factors. When hypertension becomes chronic, it can lead to heart disease, stroke, or kidney failure. High blood pressure is widely used by insurance companies as a major predictor of life expectancy, for untreated, it leads to a mean life expectancy of roughly twenty years following its onset and the average age of death of untreated individuals is about fifty-five years old (Lyght, 1966). In the U.S., half of all the deaths of individuals over forty-five are caused by some form of cardiovascular disease, and hypertension is a major contributor (Lachman, 1972; Weiner, 1977). In its early stages, hypertension seems to be symptomless. Roughly 10 percent of American college students have high blood pressure—most without knowing they have it. As a person grows older, the risk increases markedly.

The development, the course, and the consequence of high blood pressure can be influenced by psychological factors. But as we saw with ulcer victims, these factors act on physically vulnerable individuals. We will first look at the diathesis underlying hypertension, and then at the role of psychological stress.

Defining High Blood Pressure

When the blood pressure of an individual at rest is more than 140/90, he is said to have **borderline hypertension,** and when more than 160/95 *definite*

Drawing by Cheney
© 1983 The New Yorker Magazine, Inc.

hypertension. * Such individuals are at risk for developing much higher blood pressure later in life. Roughly 10 percent of high blood pressure is caused by known kidney and endocrine diseases. The other 90 percent is called "essential" hypertension, meaning that its causes, physical and psychological, are unknown.

In hypertension, the small arteries resist the flow of blood, and this resistance causes the heart to pump the blood through the blood vessels under higher pressure. In its early stages, no other symptoms may occur, but later, top-of-the-head headaches, dizziness, ringing in the ears, and irritability are sometimes experienced. As the disease progresses, the individual becomes more prone to heart attack and stroke.

SUSCEPTIBILITY TO HIGH BLOOD PRESSURE

Hypertension hits some populations harder than others. Individuals from the lower classes are more likely to develop it than are those from the middle or upper classes. Men have more hypertension than women, blacks more than whites, city dwellers more than those who live in the country. In general, cross-cultural studies indicate that between 5 and 25 percent of adults have high blood pressure. But some cultures have more of it than others. For example, among the Zulu of South Africa, 20 percent of men under age forty-five and an astonishing 58 percent of older men have high blood pressure (Scotch, 1961).

The older one is, the more likely it is that he or she will contract essential hypertension. About 10 percent of twenty-year-olds are hypertensive, but by age sixty a full 40 percent are. Among some groups, such as southern black Americans, the rise is steep and begins early in life, but among other groups, such as Navajo Indians on reservations and among some rural Africans and Asians, no increase with age occurs. Young women seem to show less high blood pressure than young men, but by middle age women may show more high blood pressure than do middle-aged men (Henry and Cassel, 1969; Aleksandrou, 1967).

High blood pressure runs in families. If one parent has high blood pressure, the chances are roughly one in four that the child will have high blood pressure. If both parents have high blood pressure, the chances are roughly one in three. If a sibling has high blood pressure, the chances are close to one in two that the other sibling will also have high blood pressure.

But does high blood pressure run in families for genetic reasons or because families share similar environments? There is strong evidence that predisposition to high blood pressure can be inherited. The blood pressure of identical twins is much more alike than the blood pressure of fraternal twins (Hines, McIlhaney, and Gage, 1957; Mathers, Osborne, and De-George, 1961). This suggests an inherited diathesis for hypertension.

There is also evidence in the family studies, that personality and environment influence high blood pressure as well. A fascinating result has emerged from the study of identical twins in which only one of the twins has high

---

* These two numbers refer to how high the blood pressure can raise a column of mercury. The first number is systolic and the second number diastolic blood pressure. Systolic blood pressure is the arterial pressure when the heart is pumping, and diastolic pressure is the arterial pressure when the heart is at rest.

blood pressure. The twin who has the high blood pressure tends to be more obedient, quiet, reserved, submissive, insecure, and withdrawn than the twin without high blood pressure (Torgersen and Kringlen, 1971). Further, spouses (who of course are not related except by marriage), tend to have similar blood pressure for as long as they stay married. This indicates that part of the reason that blood pressure runs in families is because they share the same hypertension-inducing environments (Winkelstein, Kantor, Ibrahim, and Sackett, 1966).

PSYCHOLOGICAL INFLUENCES ON HIGH BLOOD PRESSURE

If an individual has the diathesis for hypertension, psychological factors may come into play. As with peptic ulcers, there is evidence for two sorts of emotional influence: (1) emotional states of hostility and threat produced by stressful environments may raise blood pressure, and (2) having a time-urgent, competitive, and hostile personality contributes to chronic high blood pressure. Nigel's history illustrates both types of psychological influence, as shown below:

Constant pressure from business affairs may cause anger and anxiety, and ultimately high blood pressure. (Painting by Francis Bacon. Courtesy Hamburger Kunsthalle)

> Nigel was a thirty-nine-year-old businessman. He felt constant pressure from his business affairs and experienced friction with his business partners. For years Nigel had always set deadlines for himself and had competed with his business rivals. He now sensed that he could no longer live up to his standards, and he felt failure closing in. He could not stop brooding about these problems and took his troubles home with him. He lay awake at nights alternately angry and anxious, fretting and expecting financial disaster. The worst did not occur in his business affairs, but he developed high blood pressure. Psychotherapy, rather than drug treatment, was recommended. As a consequence of therapeutic advice, he changed his way of life. He sold his part of his company and used the proceeds to buy into a business with little pressure. He learned to lower his reaction toward daily frustrations. He found new outlets for his energy in social and recreational pursuits. His blood pressure dropped into the normal range within six months. (Adapted from Lachman, 1972.)

Both Nigel's personality traits—hard driving, competitive, and time urgent—and his emotional reaction to daily stresses—anxiety and hostility—contributed to his high blood pressure. We will first look at the evidence that emotional states raise blood pressure and then at the evidence that certain personality traits are associated with high blood pressure and cardiovascular disease.

Emotional States and Blood Pressure

Blood pressure normally increases when individuals experience threat. Workers who are threatened with job loss and unemployment show high blood pressure which drops when they find a new job (Kasl and Cobb, 1970). Similarly, those who feel threatened by death or injury also often have high blood pressure. For example, following an explosion in 1947 in Texas City, residents had elevated blood pressure for one to two weeks (Ruskin, Beard, and Schaffer, 1948). How do we react emotionally to such threats to well-being and security? Two common emotional reactions are anxiety and hostility, and there is evidence that each of these emotional states can raise blood pressure.

When individuals with high blood pressure keep a record every thirty minutes of what is happening, what mood they are in, and what their blood pressure is, a fascinating correlation emerges: high blood pressure occurs most frequently when the individual is anxious, alert, and under time pressure (Sokolow, Werdegar, Perloff, Cowan, and Bienenstuhl, 1970). This finding is supported by studies of animals and hypertension.

Rhesus monkeys who learn to avoid shock in a test cage by pressing a lever on a complex and difficult schedule not only show high blood pressure while they are being tested, but if the schedule is difficult enough, blood pressure remains high back in the home cage (Forsyth, 1968). In addition, there are several ways of producing chronic high blood pressure in mice: (1) by mixing together male mice who are strangers, (2) by forced crowding, and (3) by exposing mice to a cat for six to twelve months (Henry, Mehan, and Stephens, 1967). Situations such as avoiding shock, defending against strangers, intruders, and predators, all call for a *continual emergency reaction.* That is, the animal or human is in a constant state of anxiety and readiness for danger, with high blood pressure being part of this emergency reaction to danger (see Chapter 10). So we have evidence that an anxiety response to danger raises blood pressure.

Threats of the sort mentioned above not only produce anxiety, but other emotions as well. Among these emotional reactions is hostility, and there is evidence that hostility also raises blood pressure. In one experiment, subjects were brought to anger by being insulted by a stooge. These subjects, who were already hypertensive, responded to this added stress by an increase in blood pressure (Schachter, 1957).

The elevated blood pressure response of hypertensives may be related to threat in general and anger toward the threat in particular. When individuals with high blood pressure were interviewed, blood pressure changes were related to the emotional tone of the interview. Although the hypertensive individuals were usually friendly to the interviewer, during the interview their blood pressure rose more than did the blood pressure of individuals without hypertension. When the dominant mood was either hostility or anxiety, the hypertensive's blood pressure rose. When it was despair, their blood pressure fell (Wolf, Cardon, Shepard, and Wolff, 1955). The more hostile the content of the speech of individuals with high blood pressure, the more their blood pressure went up (Kaplan, Gottschalk, Magliocco, Rohobit, and Ross, 1960). These findings suggest that hypertensives are particularly sensitive to hostility and respond with blood pressure elevation.

Our day-to-day lives often require a certain level of diplomatic competence. This can result in our not expressing the hostility we may feel, let's say about a particular situation at work. The studies reported above suggest that hostility can raise blood pressure. But is there a difference in the blood pressure of those who feel hostility and do not express it, and those who feel and express it? To investigate this, researchers first demonstrated that when normal individuals who have to count back from ninety-nine by two's are harassed by a stooge, their blood pressure goes up. Later, half of the subjects are given an opportunity to retaliate and aggress against the stooge, but half are not. The opportunity to aggress consists in allowing the subject to choose

Hostility and experienced threat may raise blood pressure. Conversely, the opportunity to take action that copes with the threat or that vents hostility may reduce blood pressure. (Courtesy Leo de Wys)

whether or not he wishes to punish or reward the stooge. As it turned out, the opportunity to aggress caused the elevated blood pressure to subside. But for those who had no opportunity to retaliate, blood pressure subsided more slowly (Hokanson, 1961; Hokanson and Burgess, 1962; Hokanson, Willers, and Koropsak, 1968). It seems likely that the opportunity to vent hostility lowers blood pressure, and the failure to release hostility may keep blood pressure high. Our alternate, less specific view of this data, however, holds that the emergency reaction—be it elicited by hostility, fear, or pain—raises blood pressure, and the opportunity to take any action that copes with the threat reduces blood pressure.

As we have shown, clinical and experimental data indicate that blood pressure normally goes up when individuals are in the emotional state of anxiety or of hostility. This makes reasonable biological sense, since the sorts of threats that elicit anxiety and hostility also elicit the emergency reaction. An increase in blood pressure is part of the emergency reaction, which serves an adaptive function when it occurs in response to an occasional threat. If an individual feels *constantly* threatened, however, his blood pressure may become chronically high. This could happen if an individual were in a chronically stressful job, such as being an air controller in towers with high density traffic (Cobb and Rose, 1973; Karasek, Baker, Marxer, Ahlbom, and Theorell, 1981), or it might happen if an individual habitually viewed the world as a threatening place and was constantly engaged in vigilance and defense against threat. Such a habitual pattern is an example of a personality trait that would produce hypertension, and we now turn to the evidence that such a personality type exists.

Personality and Hypertension

The major theme that runs through psychodynamic theories about the hypertensive personality is dammed-up hostility. Franz Alexander theorized that individuals with high blood pressure were struggling against their own aggressive impulses. As young children, hypertensives have tantrums of rage, but as they mature they learn to control them because they are afraid of losing the affections of others. As a consequence, they become unusually compliant and unassertive. When promoted to executive responsibility, they are poor at asserting themselves appropriately and making others follow their orders (Alexander, French, and Pollack, 1968). Clinical observation bears out the role of hostility in patients with high blood pressure (Dunbar, 1943; Wolf, Cardon, Shepard, and Wolff, 1955). Some patients with high blood pressure tend to perceive others as dangerous and untrustworthy and because of this perception, maintain distant relationships. Paradoxically, this provokes and angers others—the very reactions the hypertensive fears most and is trying to avoid (Weiner, 1977).

Based only on psychological history and excerpts from interviews, nine judges attempted to sort out patients with high blood pressure from patients with the six other psychosomatic disorders. For male patients, the judges were correctly able to pick out 42 percent of the hypertensives, well above the chance level of 14 percent (one out of seven). Women with high blood pressure were not reliably sorted out.

A more recent study offers further evidence that personality affects high blood pressure. Seventy-eight Harvard juniors were tested in the late 1930s and early 1940s for high blood pressure and various personality characteristics. Ten years later, these individuals were given a projective test in which they told stories about five pictures from the TAT (see Chapter 9). The themes of the stories they told were used as indications of what their personality was like. Twenty years later, in the early 1970s, these men were tested for high blood pressure. The findings are remarkable.

The expression of need for "power" and need for "affiliation" was judged from their TAT stories. A person was scored as having a high need for power if his story contained a reference to having an impact on others by aggression, persuasion, and prestige. A person was scored as having a high need for affiliation if his story included being friendly with other people. Finally, a person was judged for the amount of "inhibition of the need for power" by the number of times the word "not" appeared in his stories. Those of particular theoretical interest were the men who had a high need for power (which was greater than their need for affiliation), but who showed high inhibition in their stories. Twenty-three of the men fell into this group at approximately age thirty. By the time these men were in their fifties, 61 percent had shown definite signs of hypertensive pathology, whereas only 23 percent of the remaining forty-seven men showed hypertensive pathology. These findings become even more remarkable when we realize that they are unrelated to the blood pressure of these men when they were in their thirties. In other words, the need for power combined with its inhibition at age thirty predicted that individuals would be at risk for severe high blood pressure at age fifty, irrespective of what their blood pressure was when they were thirty years old (McClelland, 1979).

The likelihood of the existence of such a high-blood-pressure-prone personality is greatly strengthened by the research on the Type A personality carried out over the last decade.

THE TYPE A BEHAVIOR PATTERN. *Type A personality* was said to have been discovered by an upholsterer. When he came to reupholster the chairs

Figure 12-3
The Type A logo. A clenched fist holding a stopwatch indicates the Type A's exaggerated sense of time urgency.

in the office of a physician who specialized in seeing patients who had had heart attacks, he noticed that the chairs were worn in the front of the seat, not the back. Coronary-prone individuals, Type A's, sit on the edge of their chair (see Figure 12-3). They are defined by (1) an exaggerated sense of time urgency—deadlines are always with them, (2) competitiveness and ambition, and (3) aggressiveness and hostility, particularly when things get in their way. They contrast to *Type B persons,* who are relaxed, serene, and have no sense of time urgency. When Type A's miss a bus, they become upset. When Type B's miss a bus, they say to themselves, "Why worry? There will always be another bus coming along." Both the Type A and the hypertensive personality discussed above probably see the environment as threatening, and both seem to be engaged in prolonged emergency reactions.

Classifying individuals into Type A's and Type B's is done either by a standard stress interview or by a self-administered questionnaire. Typical questions are:

1. "Has your spouse or friend ever told you that you eat too fast?" Type A's say, "yes, often." Type B's say, "yes, once or twice" or "no."

2. "How would your spouse (or best friend) rate your general level of activity?" Type A's say, "too active, need to slow down." Type B's say, "too slow, should be more active."

3. "Do you ever set deadlines or quotas for yourself at work or at home?" Type A's say, "yes, once a week or more often." Type B's say, "no" or "only occasionally." (Jenkins, Rosenman, and Friedman, 1967; Glass, 1977).

Type A's are more at risk for heart attack than Type B's. In the most comprehensive prospective study of coronary disease, 3,000 normal men living in California were followed for eight-and-a-half years. Half of the men were Type A's, half of them Type B's. Type A's had more than twice as many heart attacks as Type B's. After the first heart attack, Type A's were five times as likely to have a second heart attack. Even when the traditional risk factors for heart attacks, such as cigarette smoking, high blood pressure, and cholesterol level were held constant, Type A's still had twice the risk of heart attacks as Type B's. Being a Type A may be the strongest single predictor of recurrent heart disease, a better predictor than cholesterol and cigarette smoking (Rosenman, Brand, Jenkins, Friedman, Straus, and Wurm, 1975; Jenkins, Zyzanski, and Rosenman, 1976).

Type A women, like Type A men, are also more vulnerable to coronary disease. Nine hundred fifty women, aged forty-five to sixty-four, were given extensive psychological tests in 1965-1967 in Framingham, Massachusetts. They were then observed for the next eight years. Type A's had two to three times as many heart attacks as Type B's. Both working women and housewives showed this effect and were at similar risk for heart attacks (Haynes, Feinleib, and Kannel, 1980).

Type A individuals seem to be engaged in a lifelong struggle to control a world they see as threatening. David Glass suggests that it is this struggle for control that crucially distinguishes a Type A from a Type B personality. Glass postulates that a cycle of desperate efforts to control the environment, alternating with giving up when the environment proves uncontrollable, is repeated over and over again during the lifetime of the Type A individual.

Type A's make desperate attempts to control their environment. This man may have an exaggerated sense of time urgency that upsets him in this traffic jam. (Photograph by Henri Cartier-Bresson/Magnum)

This struggle may result in high blood pressure and other physiological changes that in turn cause heart attacks.

Glass has demonstrated that Type A's and Type B's show a different reaction to helplessness and that it is this reaction that may predispose them to coronary disease (see Chapter 13). Both Type A and Type B subjects are presented with cognitive problems that are unsolvable, and failure is made highly salient. Type A's response to this uncontrollable and highly stressful situation is twofold: (1) they respond to salient and stressful threats to their sense of control with desperate efforts to keep control, and (2) when they are forced into the recognition that they are helpless, their giving up is profound and they fail to solve cognitive problems given later in the experiment. Type B individuals do not give up in such a profound way, and they end up solving more easily the solvable problems given later. This confirms Glass's suggestion that a life of attempting to control, then giving up, then trying all over again, may characterize Type A individuals and predispose them to coronary heart disease.

In the last century, Sir William Osler (1849-1919), a famous Canadian physician, prefigured what was to be learned in our century about personality and heart attacks:

> A man who has early risen and late taken rest, who has eaten the bread of carefulness, striving for success in commercial, professional, or political life, after twenty-five or thirty years of incessant toil, reaches the point where he can say, perhaps with just satisfaction, "Soul, thou has much goods laid up for many years; take thine ease," all unconscious that the fell sergeant has already issued the warrant. (Osler, 1897)

Thus, psychological factors as well as biological factors influence hypertension and coronary heart disease. Threatening life events—like loss of work—particularly when responded to with anxiety and anger, may bring on high blood pressure or worsen it in individuals who already have high blood pressure. Individuals who see the world as threatening and are engaged in a struggle for control may find themselves in a chronic state of readiness for emergency. Hostility, aggressiveness, and time urgency may be the psychological components of this emergency reaction, and high blood pressure the relevant biological component.

TREATMENT OF HIGH BLOOD PRESSURE

High blood pressure can be treated either by drugs or by a variety of forms of psychological therapy. For severe high blood pressure, anti-hypertensive medication is the treatment of choice. In a well-controlled study of anti-hypertensive drugs, only two of seventy-three medicated patients had heart attacks, strokes, and other severe complications over one-and-a-half years of observation, as opposed to twenty-seven of seventy patients who were treated with only a placebo. The estimated risk of developing a severe complication over a five-year period was reduced from 55 percent to 18 percent by drugs (Veterans Administration Cooperative Study Group, 1972). Over the last decade, the incidence of strokes in the United States declined 42 percent, possibly due to the widespread use of medication to control hypertension (Kolata, 1983)—cheering news indeed!

One method of treatment for high blood pressure is a stress reduction class. (Photograph by Jeffrey Grosscup)

With such good drug results, we might wonder why psychotherapy should be used at all. There are three basic reasons: First, drug therapy does not seem to be too effective in patients with mild hypertension; they have heart attacks and strokes just as frequently as unmedicated controls. Second, the side effects of anti-hypertensive drugs are highly noxious for some people, producing depression, sedation, or sexual dysfunction, and a substantial number of patients stop taking the drugs because of their side effects. Third, drugs treat the symptoms, but not the cause of hypertension. So there exists a clear need for alternate treatments, particularly for patients with borderline high blood pressure (Smith, 1977; Agras and Jacob, 1979).

In the last ten years, three specific psychotherapeutic procedures have become popular in treating high blood pressure: relaxation, biofeedback, and transcendental meditation (TM). All of them seem to have a significant effect in lowering high blood pressure. In relaxation, the patient learns to relax his entire skeletal musculature (Benson, 1975; Fine and Turner, 1982; Suedfeld, Roy, and Landon, 1982). In biofeedback, the patient learns to voluntarily lower blood pressure using the visual or auditory feedback from a blood pressure meter (see Box 12-1). In transcendental meditation the patient sits in a comfortable position twice a day for twenty minutes with his eyes closed and repeats silently a one-syllable "mantra" (Sanskrit for "a

Box 12-1 LEARNING TO CONTROL YOUR BLOOD PRESSURE

In July 1972, Al Fogle, a thirty-six-year-old man, went to visit his sister on Long Island. As he approached her house, a huge man came racing toward him. Chasing him was a smaller man waving a revolver. The shorter man shouted, "Kill the bastard!" and a shot rang out. The bullet hit Fogle in the chest and severed his spinal cord.

After eight months of rehabilitation, Fogle learned to use his arms, sit up, and walk on crutches. But a serious problem occurred whenever he elevated himself. He would faint. The reason for his fainting was purely physical. When a normal individual is lying down and starts to stand up, his brain transmits the message "constrict the blood vessels in the arms and legs" to the sympathetic nervous system, resulting in extra blood being pumped to the head. If it did not do this, gravity would prevent enough blood from flowing to the head. But when the spine is cut, although the brain still sends its message, the message cannot be delivered to the blood vessels in the arms and legs to cause them to constrict, since the message must go through an intact spinal cord.

Through biofeedback treatment, Fogle learned to raise his blood pressure before elevating himself. At New York's Goldwater Memorial Hospital, he was treated by a young psychologist, Bernard Brucker, using the theory and findings of Neal Miller about biofeedback in rats. Fogle was first taught to raise or lower his blood pressure upon command. Feedback was given to him by telling him the number of millimeters his blood had been raised or lowered. He succeeded and eventually was able to increase his blood pressure by as many as twenty millimeters. In addition, he learned to distinguish changes of a few millimeters. He says he uses mental imagery to accomplish this: he imagines the terrifying moment in which he was shot.

Regardless of how he does it, Fogle no longer faints. Before he raises his body, he voluntarily raises his blood pressure to a point sufficient for the heart to pump the needed blood to his brain. (Adapted from Kobler, 1978.)

Box 12-2   **CHANGING TYPE A BEHAVIOR**

If present health trends continue, the chances are one in two that you will die of heart attack or a stroke. Many people who are now college students will die from such diseases long before their time. What is known about susceptibility of college students to subsequent cardiovascular disease? Students who have high blood pressure, who smoke cigarettes, who are overweight, who are short, whose parents die prematurely, who do not exercise, and who are anxious and irritable are more prone to later cardiovascular disease (Paffenbarger, Wolf, Notkin and Thorne, 1966).

There have been substantial developments in the understanding and treatment of cardiovascular diseases in the last twenty years: open heart surgery, heart transplants, anti-hypertensive drugs, and the like. But it is possible that scientific technology has reached an upper limit on what it can do to save our lives once we have developed coronary disease. Even if no further technological breakthroughs occur, vastly better health is still possible. We may be able to reduce our chances of dying from heart attack and stroke by making certain choices about how we live our lives.

Our present life style may be leading us into serious risk of cardiovascular disease. The elements of a life style that does this are known, even though the mechanism of their deadly action is not fully understood. If we smoke cigarettes and if we fail to exercise regularly, we substantially increase our risk of premature death.

We have discussed another risk factor for cardiovascular disease: the Type A personality. If a person has a Type A personality—if he or she is usually time urgent, hard driving, ambitious, competitive, and striving for control—he or she may be engaged in a way of life even more deadly than smoking and lack of exercise.

Can the Type A personality be changed? And if it is changed, will this lower the person's risk of heart disease? The answer to the first question is Yes—a person can exert voluntary control over Type A behavior. The answer to the second question is at present unknown. All we have at the moment is a correlation, not a causal link, between being a Type A and having heart attacks. It is possible that some third factor causes both Type A behavior and susceptibility to heart disease. If this is so, unless the person also changes this unknown causal factor, changing his Type A behavior will have no effect on his risk of heart disease.

Should a person try to change his Type A behavior? It is likely that Type A behavior has benefits, as well as costs. Being time urgent, competitive and ambitious may well produce professional success in our society, and changing may produce better health but less success. But if being Type A causes coronary disease, then changing a person's Type A life style may lower his risk of heart attack.

How can we liberate ourselves from a Type A life style? Meyer Friedman and

word whose sonic properties are known"). Positive results have been reported for all three procedures in controlled studies, but TM and relaxation may have a slight edge over biofeedback, although all of them are usually found to be superior to placebo controls. These results have not been uniform, however, and all three treatments have, under some circumstances, also failed to produce large enough decreases in blood pressure to be clinically helpful (e.g., Frankel, Patel, Horwitz, Friedewalt, and Gaarder, 1978; Agras and Jacob, 1979).

Counseling that often accompanies drug therapy for high blood pressure emphasizes three general goals: (1) the therapist tries to get the patient to recognize that the environment is not necessarily hostile, (2) he also will encourage the patient to respond to the environment by trying to change it

Ray Rosenman, two of the cardiologists who discovered the Type A proneness to heart attacks, offer a set of drills against "hurry sickness"—drills that allow us to re-engineer our life:

1. Each morning, noon, and evening remind yourself that *life is always an "un-finishedness."* Begin to accept your life as a mélange of activities in which only some manage to get finished. You are only finished when you are dead.

2. Practice listening quietly to the conversation of others without interrupting or hurrying them.

3. If you see someone doing a job slower than you know you can do it, don't interfere.

4. When you are in doubt as to whether you should say something, don't say it unless it is really important.

5. Whenever possible, shy away from making appointments at definite times.

6. Purposely frequent restaurants and theaters where you know you will have to wait. Drive at the minimum speed limit. Learn that even if you have to wait and you go slowly, things will come out all right—you get fed, you see the play, you catch the plane, anyway.

7. Whenever you catch yourself speeding up your car to get through a yellow light, penalize yourself by immediately turning right at the next corner and circling the block to approach the same intersection. Then go through the signal light again when it is green.

8. Read books that demand your entire attention and a good deal of patience.

9. Find periods each day in which you purposely seek total body relaxation and empty your mind. Seek out lonely periods. (Friedman and Rosenman, 1974).

We do not yet have definitive evidence that changing from a Type A to a Type B lowers heart attack risk, but several studies are suggestive. For example, forty-four patients who survived their first heart attack were given group psychotherapy. Group therapy emphasized education about heart attacks, and some attempt was made to modify coronary-prone behavior. These patients experienced less coronary illness and death over the following three years, and they succeeded in reducing their time urgency and overwork more than control heart attack patients without psychotherapy. One patient who owned several wristwatches in order to be sure he would always have one working, threw them all away after the group discussed time urgency. (Roskies, Spevack, Surkis, Cohen, and Gilman, 1978; Suinn and Bloom, 1978; Jenni and Wollersheim, 1979; Levenkron, Cohen, Mueller, and Fisher, 1983)

more effectively, and (3) the therapist will encourage the patient to release hostility in a constructive way (Schwartz, 1977). In contrast to biofeedback, relaxation, and TM, there has not been a controlled study of the effectiveness of this general counseling approach.

Overall, then, anti-hypertensive drugs are the treatment of choice for severe hypertension. For mild hypertension, systematic training in either relaxation, transcendental meditation, or biofeedback will produce some smaller lowering of blood pressure. These methods can also be used as an adjunct to drug treatment for severe hypertension. No one of the three techniques has proven itself clearly superior to the others (Agras and Jacob, 1979). (See Box 12-2 for another method of treating people at risk for heart disease.)

To summarize, hypertension, like ulcers, can be viewed within a diathesis-stress model. The diathesis, or constitutional factors, that produce hypertension can be genetically inherited, since identical twins show more similar blood pressures than do fraternal twins. When an individual has such a diathesis, psychological factors may act to produce a condition of chronic high blood pressure. The emotional states of anxiety and hostility both produce increases in blood pressure. Anxiety and hostility are caused by threatening situations, and these situations produce increases in blood pressure. This sequence makes sense biologically, since the emergency reaction consists, in part, of the perception of threat, followed by the experience of anxiety and hostility, and is accompanied by an increase in blood pressure. This is an adaptive response to an occasional threat, but if an individual engages in an emergency reaction for a large portion of his life, dangerous chronic hypertension may result. Jobs that produce anxiety or hostility may also produce hypertension. And personality types who chronically view the world as a dangerous place may also suffer from high blood pressure. The Type A personality may be such a type: these individuals are time urgent, competitive, ambitious, and they become hostile when they are thwarted. Such individuals not only have higher blood pressure but they are at substantially greater risk for heart attacks than are Type B individuals. Severe high blood pressure is best treated by medication, but mild hypertension can be helped by relaxation, biofeedback, and transcendental meditation.

SUDDEN DEATH

A prolonged emergency reaction set up by continued mobilization against a threatening environment can cause high blood pressure, and an individual with high blood pressure may be more susceptible in the long run to death from heart attack or stroke. What happens when a person perceives the environment as threatening, but rather than mobilizing against the danger, gives up? Under some circumstances, the most catastrophic of all psychosomatic phenomena can occur, *sudden death.*

> In 1967 a distraught woman, pleading for help, entered the Baltimore City Hospital a few days before her 23rd birthday. She and two other girls, had been born of different mothers assisted by the same midwife in the Okefenokee Swamp on a Friday the 13th. The midwife cursed all three babies, saying one would die before her 16th birthday, another before her 21st birthday, and the third before her 23rd birthday. The first had died in a car crash during her 15th year; the second was accidentally shot to death in a nightclub fight on the evening of her 21st birthday. Now she, the third, waited in terror for her own death. The hospital somewhat skeptically admitted her for observation. The next morning two days before her 23rd birthday, she was found dead in her hospital bed—physical cause unknown. (Seligman, 1975, p. 5)

THE PROCESS OF SUDDEN DEATH

One sequence of events that could produce sudden death seems to be the following: (1) perceiving a strong threat to life followed by giving up and ac-

This is the apparatus used by Curt Richter in his experiments on the phenomenon of sudden death. Richter found that the rats drowned within a few minutes of being placed in this apparatus, apparently of "hopelessness." (Source: Richter, 1957)

cepting one's fate, (2) a depressed, quiescent state; and (3) death. This phenomenon has been explored in animals by the American physiologist Curt Richter. Richter found that, on occasion, when he held a wild rat tightly it would die—right there, in his hand (Richter, 1957). He hypothesized that when animals gave up in the face of threat and entered a state of hopelessness, they would die. To test this, he took wild rats and held them in his (chain-mailed) gloved hand until they stopped struggling. Then he put them in a vat of water three feet deep with a jet of water playing down on them to stop them from floating. The rats would swim for three to five minutes, then dive to the bottom and drown. In contrast, wild rats who had not been restrained in the experimenter's hand until they gave up would swim from sixty to eighty hours—vigorously trying to survive.

There were two findings that led Richter to believe that these were deaths from hopelessness. The first was that if he took the rat and held it in his hand until it stopped struggling, then released the rat "showing the rat there was hope," held the rat in his hand again, released it, then held it until it stopped struggling, and finally put it in the vat, the rat would swim for between sixty and eighty hours. Second, if he restrained the rat in his hand until it gave up, then put the rat in the water and waited three to five minutes until the rat started to go down, plucked it out, released it—again "showing it there was hope"—and then repeated the process several times, when the rat was finally placed in the water it would swim for sixty to eighty hours.

Richter believed that this phenomenon was related to "Voodoo Death." The American physiologist W. B. Cannon (1871-1945) had been the first scientist to describe "Hex Death," or "Voodoo Death." Cannon had reviewed many reports of such deaths across a variety of cultures and wrote:

> A Brazilian Indian, condemned and sentenced by a so-called medicine man, is helpless against his own emotional response to this pronouncement—and dies within hours. In Africa a young negro unknowingly eats the inviolably-banned wild hen. On discovery of this "crime" he trembles, is overcome by fear, and dies within 24 hours. In New Zealand, a Maori woman eats fruit that she only later learns has come from a tabooed place. Her chief has been profaned. By noon of the next day she is dead. In Australia a witch doctor points a bone at a man. Believing that nothing can save him, the man rapidly sinks in spirit and prepares to die. He is saved only at the last moment when the witch doctor is forced to remove the charm. The man who discovers that he is being boned by an enemy is, indeed, a pitiable sight. He stands aghast with his eyes staring at the treacherous pointer, with his hands lifted to ward off a lethal medium, which he imagines is pouring into his body. His cheeks blanch, and his eyes become glassy, the expression of his face becomes horribly distorted. He attempts to shriek but usually the sound chokes in his throat, and all that one might see is froth at his mouth. His body begins to tremble and his muscles twitch involuntarily. He sways backward and falls to the ground, and after a short time appears to be in a swoon. He finally composes himself, goes to his hut, and there frets to death. (Cannon, 1942, pp. 169-70)

LOSS AND SUSCEPTIBILITY TO ILLNESS AND DEATH

There is more than anecdotal evidence of this sort for sudden death following giving up in man. Loss of one's spouse by death can be an experience of profound helplessness. Following the death of their wives, 4,500 British wid-

Individuals who lose what is most important to them may experience feelings of hopelessness and depression that may make them more susceptible to illnesses or environmental pathogens. (Photograph by Dan McCoy/ Black Star)

owers fifty-five years or older were identified from British records. During the first six months of their bereavement, 213 of them died. This is 40 percent more than the expected mortality for men of this age. Susceptibility to death during bereavement seems to be concentrated in the first six months, since the death rate returns to normal thereafter. Most of these men died from cardiac problems (Parkes, Benjamin, and Fitzgerald, 1969).

These findings cause us to hypothesize that individuals who lose what is most important to them seem more susceptible to death from a variety of causes. The most typical sequence is this: the individual perceives a threat; he struggles against it but gives up, becoming hopeless, depressed, and passive; and he thereupon becomes susceptible to any of a variety of illnesses, dangers, or pathogens in his environment, which he would normally resist but which are now deadly to him.

There are two prospective studies that indicate such susceptibility to pathogens following experiences of hopelessness and depression. Six months before an influenza epidemic swept an Army base, 600 employees had been given a battery of personality inventories. Twenty-six individuals came down with the flu during the epidemic; of these, 12 still had the flu three weeks later. These 12 individuals had been significantly more depressed six months earlier than the rest of the population, and as we shall see in Chapter 13, depression is intimately related to helplessness induced by giving up.

One of the most insidious of all illnesses influenced by psychological factors is cancer. There is mounting evidence that hopelessness may play a role in susceptibility to cancer. Fifty-one women who entered a Rochester, New York, clinic for a cancer test were interviewed upon arriving. Each of these women had previously shown suspicious cells in her cervix which might indicate cancer, but which could not definitely be diagnosed as cancer without further testing. The investigators found that eighteen of these fifty-one women had experienced significant losses in the last six months to which they reacted with feelings of hopelessness and helplessness. The others had experienced no such life event. Of the eighteen who had experienced hopelessness, eleven were found to have cancer. Of the other thirty-three, only eight had cancer. The difference between the two groups was statistically significant (Schmale and Iker, 1966). Similarly, lack of meaning in one's life, job instability, and no plans for the future predict who has lung cancer better than does the amount of smoking (Horne and Picard, 1979).

ANIMAL MODELS OF HELPLESSNESS AND ILLNESS

This evidence suggests that experience with helplessness and hopelessness may weaken the immune system, making it less able to fight off illnesses successfully. Animal models of helplessness and hopelessness may allow us to investigate the way in which these experiences make us more susceptible to illness. Rats were injected with tumors, and on the following day, they were divided into three groups. One group was given escapable shock— electric shock that the rats could turn off by bar pressing. A second group received exactly the same pattern of electric shock, but it went on and off independently of all the rats' actions; those in this group were helpless to turn off the shock. The third group was not shocked at all. How did such experience with helplessness affect the rejection of tumors? Fifty-five percent of the animals who were not shocked rejected the tumor, and 65 percent of the animals that received experience mastering electric shock rejected the tumor. Only 27 percent of the animals who received helplessness experience, however, rejected the tumor. Investigators are presently looking at how the immune system changes in response to helplessness and hopelessness in rats and in humans. Natural killer cells and T-Lymphocytes, cells in the immune system that fight off foreign invaders, seem to be suppressed following helplessness. This may provide us with some clues about how to intervene to prevent the psychological experiences of hopelessness from making people more susceptible to viral illness (Sklar and Anisman, 1979; Visintainer, Volpicelli, and Seligman, 1982; Maier, 1983; Rodin, 1983).

LACK OF CONTROL IN NURSING HOMES

While giving up is a profoundly lonely and individual experience, it may be that the structure of some institutions promotes it on a massive scale. Consider patient care in nursing homes. When we arrange care for the elderly, there is sometimes a tendency to try to do everything for them. On the one hand, this seems benevolent, but on the other hand, we end up taking all of their control away. By treating them as total patients, we undermine self-care (Bandura, 1982).

When we remove the last vestiges of control over the environment from human beings already weakened by age, we put them in a helpless situation, one without purpose. Some give up and die. Conversely, if we bring choice and control into geriatric wards, we may be able to prolong life. Ellen Langer and Judith Rodin divided nursing home residents of equal health into two groups. One group was given enhanced choice and control over small things at the nursing home. They were encouraged to decide how they would spend their own time, they were given the choice of what night to attend a movie, and they were given the opportunity to select a plant for their room and to take care of it themselves. Those in the comparison group were told about all the good things that were available to them, they were told on what day they would see a movie, and they were given a plant (no choice) and told that the nurse would care for it. The comparison group was treated very much like ordinary geriatric patients. Although they experienced some positive events, they exerted little or no control over their life. Eighteen months later, 30 percent of the comparison group (thirteen out of forty-four patients) had died, while only 15 percent (seven of forty-four patients) of the group that had control and responsibility had died. These differences were statistically significant (Langer and Rodin, 1976; Rodin and Langer, 1977).

Patient care in nursing homes may promote giving up when everything is done for the patient. (Photograph by Jeffrey Grosscup)

In conclusion, how much control one exerts over the important things in one's life may affect one's susceptibility to illness and even death itself. We have much more to learn in this area, but it does seem that when an individual perceives a major threat, tries to control it, and fails, he or she will become hopeless, depressed, and passive. Thereupon any of a variety of pathogens in the environment that are normally resisted may become life threatening.

THEORIES OF PSYCHOSOMATIC ILLNESS

We have now had a detailed look at three physical problems that are influenced by psychological factors: stomach ulcers, high blood pressure, and sudden death. In addition to these three, many other diseases are often thought to have psychosomatic components: migraine headaches, arthritis, chronic pain, and asthma, among others (see Box 12-3).

Let us now look at the different principles that recur through explanations of the cause and the alleviation of these psychosomatic disorders. There are four theories, and they correspond to four of the schools of abnormality: biomedical, psychodynamic, behavioral, and cognitive. All are compatible with the diathesis-stress perspective.

Box 12-3 ASTHMA IN CHILDREN AND FAMILY SEPARATION

Asthma is a condition in which the air passages of the bronchia narrow, swell, and secrete excess fluid to a variety of stimuli. This results in wheezing, which in its worst form can be severe and can produce a convulsive struggle for breath. Asthma can be caused by infection, by allergy, or by psychological factors. It has been estimated that each of these plays the dominant role in about a third of the cases (Weiner, 1977). Put differently, asthma stems from psychological sources in only a minority of cases. In this minority, the personal relations between parents and the asthmatic child have long been suspected to be the major source of psychological disturbance.

Anecdotes indicated that when European children with asthma were sent off by their parents to spas "to take the waters" they cheerfully ignored their parents' long lists of instructions, showed few signs of asthma, and seemed to be psychologically improved as well. To test the possibility that separation from parents might alleviate asthma, Dennis Purcell and his colleagues chose twenty-five chronically asthmatic school children who lived with their families (Purcell, Brady, Chai, Muser, Molk, Gordon, and Means, 1969). They divided these children into two groups—those in whom emotional factors had usually preceded past attacks of asthma at home, and those in whom emotional factors seemed irrelevant to the onset of past attacks. The first group was expected to benefit from separation, but not the second.

The parents and siblings were removed from the home and sent to a motel for two weeks, while the child continued to live in his home environment. A surrogate parent was provided, and the child continued normal attendance at school and normal play activities. After two weeks of not seeing their child, the parents returned to the home and life went on as usual.

As predicted, the effects were beneficial for the group suspected of emotionally induced asthma. Their medication during separation was reduced by half during daily physician checks, and on top of this the number of asthma attacks and amount of wheezing was reduced by half as well. When the parents returned, wheezing, number of attacks, and amount of necessary medication all increased. Beneficial effects of separation on asthma did not appear for the group in which emotional factors had been judged unimportant.

So, for some children, emotional factors are probably irrelevant to asthma. For others, however, family stresses may set off or worsen asthmatic attacks. In these cases, if the family members learn more effective and less stressful ways of dealing with each other, the child's asthma may get better.

THE BIOMEDICAL MODEL OF PSYCHOSOMATIC DISORDERS

The biomedical model emphasizes the diathesis underlying psychosomatic illness. There are four components that fall under the biomedical view: genetic, specific organ vulnerability, evolutionary selection, and the general adaptation syndrome. These components do not all exclude one another, and most biomedical theorists emphasize more than one of them when explaining psychosomatic disorders.

Genetic

Is the predisposition to psychosomatic disorders genetically inherited? We have seen evidence that this is so for both hypertension and ulcers. If one identical twin has ulcers or hypertension, then his co-twin is more likely to have ulcers or hypertension than is the case between fraternal twins. All the genes of two identical twins are the same, but only half the genes of fraternal twins are the same. The higher concordance of identical twins is most likely explained by genetics, since the environment fraternal twins share is probably almost as similar as that of identical twins. In the case of peptic ulcer, similar oversecretion of gastric juices or weakness of the mucous membrane of the stomach, each producing similar vulnerability to ulcers, is probably what is inherited. It is unknown what is inherited in the case of high blood pressure.

Specific Organ Vulnerability

A variant of the genetic view holds that it is weakness in a specific organ that is inherited. That is, when an individual is stressed, the weakest link in his bodily chain snaps. The hypothesis that oversecretion of stomach acid is an inherited cause of ulcers is an instance of the specific organ vulnerability hypothesis. Organ specificity is confirmed by the fact that individuals tend to react to stress with one characteristic part of the body. Some of us usually react to stress with a queasy stomach, others with headache, others with sweating, and still others with a racing heart. Patients with hypertension tend to react to threatening stimuli with an increase in blood pressure, patients with ulcers react with gastric secretion, and patients with recurrent headaches tend to react with increased muscle tension (Malmo and Shagass, 1949; Lacey, 1950).

Evolution

Evolution may have actually favored the development of certain psychosomatic disorders. Consider the emergency reaction for which evolution has clearly selected. In a generally threatening environment, individuals who tended to perceive the world as hostile and responded crisply with elevation of blood pressure, muscle tension, and the like would be those most likely to survive and reproduce. Only under modern conditions, in which the level of physical threat has been reduced from the days of the cave and the jungle, is hypertension considered a disorder rather than a strength. Notice that hypertension does not kill young persons; it is deadly to individuals who are

Canadian researcher Hans Selye believed that when a person or animal is stressed, the general adaptation syndrome will ensue. (Courtesy Public Archives Canada)

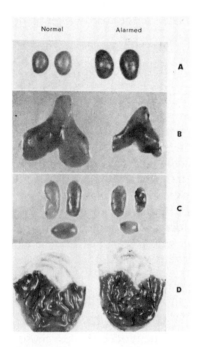

Figure 12-4
Characteristic symptoms of the general adaptation syndrome. Note the enlarged adrenals (A), the involuted thymus (B) and lymph nodes (C), and the ulcerated stomach wall (D). (Source: Selye, 1956)

many years past the prime age of reproduction. This seems to suggest that tendencies to various psychosomatic disorders are inherited because at one time in history these "diseases" actually favored survival and reproduction.

Stress and the General Adaptation Syndrome

Hans Selye (1907–1983) integrated the emergency reaction of the sympathetic nervous system into the major theory of reaction to stress. He emphasized the stress side of the diathesis-stress model. Selye believed that the general adaptation syndrome is nonspecific, that one and the same stress reaction will occur to the whole gamut of disturbing events. He held that when a human being or an animal is stressed, a sequence of three stages called the **general adaptation syndrome** ensues. The first stage is the *alarm reaction.* After an initial phase of lowered resistance, the system goes into *counter shock*—the pituitary gland releases ACTH (adrenocorticotrophic hormone) into the blood stream, which stimulates the adrenal cortex. This throws the organism into the emergency reaction. If the alarm reaction stage is successful, it restores bodily balance. The alarm reaction is followed by a second stage—the stage of *resistance,* in which defense and adaptation are sustained and optimal. If the stressor persists, the final stage, *exhaustion,* ensues, and adaptive responding ceases. Illness and, in some cases, death may follow (Selye, 1956).

The reaction of rats to long-term cold stress illustrates the general adaptation syndrome. Rats were placed in a refrigerated room where the temperature was near freezing. During the first forty-eight hours, the rats showed the alarm reaction. They developed stomach ulcers, had swollen adrenals, and showed the changes of the thymus gland illustrated in Figure 12-4. The rats continued to live in this environment for many weeks. After five weeks, they had apparently entered the stage of resistance, for when these animals were placed in a still colder chamber they survived temperatures that animals who had not become adapted could not withstand. Finally, the stage of exhaustion was demonstrated. After several months in the cold room, these rats could not survive a change to cold temperature that normal rats could survive.

From the point of view of this theory, symptoms such as high blood pressure and stomach ulcer may indicate that the individual is in an alarm reaction to stress. The theory postulates that psychosomatic symptoms are general stress reactions underlying the general adaptation syndrome (Selye, 1975; but see Mason, 1971, 1975a, 1975b).

THE PSYCHODYNAMIC MODEL

Diathesis and other biological considerations play a large role in the predisposition to psychosomatic disorders, but there is also evidence that personality and psychodynamics play a role as well These factors contribute to the stress side of the diathesis-stress model.

Franz Alexander (1950, 1968) is the most influential psychoanalytic theorist of psychosomatic disorders. His view integrates genetic organ vulnerability, personality factors, and life stress. A person who is genetically vulnerable in a specific organ and has specific psychodynamic conflicts will develop disease of that organ when the stress of living arouses his psychodynamic conflicts and he is no longer able to defend against them. All three factors—a vulnerable organ system, an underlying dynamic conflict, and a precipitating life situation—interact to produce the disorder. As we saw earlier, the essence of the personality constellation for an individual who will develop peptic ulcer is conflict over dependent needs versus independent self-assertion, and the hypertensive conflict involves the damming up of anger toward others. Alexander postulates other conflicts for asthma, arthritis, and skin disorders.

As we have seen, some evidence supports this theory: from the psychological profile alone, researchers have been able to pick out which male patients have hypertension and ulcer well beyond the level of chance. Further, both gastric secretion and blood pressure elevation occur when the relevant emotions are aroused in individuals who have ulcers and hypertension.

BEHAVIORAL AND COGNITIVE MODELS

Theories that stem from behavioral and cognitive views hold that learning or cognition produces psychosomatic disorders, and they emphasize the stress side of diathesis-stress. The stress can be produced by conditioning, cognitions, or by life events.

Conditioning

The conditioning view of psychosomatic disorders maintains that the symptoms are a conditioned response acquired when a neutral stimulus was paired with an unconditioned stimulus that produced the disorder. For example, asthma has been conditioned in the laboratory:

> A thirty-seven-year-old shop assistant suffered from severe bronchial asthma that could be reliably set off by house dust. In the laboratory, she was sprayed with an aerosol having a neutral solvent; the aerosol was to be the conditioned stimulus. Following being sprayed with the aerosol, she inhaled housedust (unconditioned stimulus), and an asthma attack (unconditioned response) followed. Thereafter, upon inhaling from the aerosol, asthma attacks ensued. (Dekker, Pelse, and Groen, 1957)

Since individuals who suffer from asthma sometimes have attacks following exposure to highly specific events, such as experiencing a family argument or other emotional conflicts, this is an appealing model of psychosomatic illness (see again Box 12-3). It has, however, only been demonstrated under limited laboratory conditions and only some patients can be so conditioned.

Cognitions and Psychosomatic Disorders

Could it be that specific thoughts set off physical symptoms? William Grace and David Graham argue that an individual's perception of the world and what he thinks about threat predicts what psychosomatic disorder will develop. This argument antedates, but is wholly compatible with the cognitive model of abnormality. Grace and Graham interviewed 128 patients with a variety of diseases to find out what situations immediately preceded the onset of the symptoms and how the individual perceived what was happening to him. They found specific thoughts associated with specific illnesses. For example, individuals with high blood pressure were in a state of constant preparation to meet all threats, and when confronted with threat they thought, "Nobody is ever going to beat me. I'm ready for everything." Table 12-2 lists other illnesses that have specific thoughts associated with them (Grace and Graham, 1952).

Table 12-2 COGNITIONS AND PSYCHOSOMATIC DISORDERS

Illness	Cognition	Examples of thoughts during illness-producing event
1. Hives	Perception of mistreatment.	"My fiance knocked me down and walked all over me, but what could I do?"
2. Eczema	Being prevented from doing something and helpless to deal with the frustration.	"I want to make my mother understand but I can't."
3. Asthma	Wishing the situation would go away or someone else would take over the responsibility for it.	"I just couldn't face it."
4. Diarrhea	Wishing to be done with the situation and have it over with.	"If the war was only over with."
5. Constipation	Grim determination to carry on even faced with an unsolvable problem.	"This marriage is never going to be any better but I won't quit."
6. Ulcer	Revenge seeking.	"He hurt me, so I wanted to hurt him."
7. Migraine headache	Engaged in an intense effort to carry out a definite plan.	"I had a million things to do before lunch."

SOURCE: Based on Grace and Graham, 1952.

The modern cognitive school has yet to put forward a more articulate, research-supported view, but we expect to see such a view within this decade.

Life Events

The final behavioral theory of psychological influence on illness involves life stressors. It holds that stressful life events set off disease. If our reaction to stress makes us susceptible to physical disease, then frequent stressful life events should correlate with frequent disease. In the early pioneering research on this question, Thomas Holmes and Richard Rahe devised a life events scale, the Social Readjustment Rating Scale, by having individuals rank the amount of stress different life events would cause them. Based on these rankings, Holmes and Rahe assigned a number to each stressful event (see Table 12-3). Death of a spouse was the most stressful life event; divorce and separation were near the top; taking a new job in the middle; holidays,

Table 12-3 SOCIAL READJUSTMENT RATING SCALE

Rank	Life event	Mean value
1	Death of spouse	100
2	Divorce	73
3	Marital separation	65
4	Jail term	63
5	Death of close family member	63
6	Personal injury or illness	53
7	Marriage	50
8	Fired at work	47
9	Marital reconciliation	45
10	Retirement	45
11	Change in health of family member	44
12	Pregnancy	40
13	Sex difficulties	39
14	Gain of new family member	39
15	Business readjustment	39
16	Change in financial state	38
17	Death of close friend	37
18	Change to different line of work	36
19	Change in number of arguments with spouse	35
20	Mortgage over $10,000	31
21	Foreclosure of mortgage or loan	30
22	Change in responsibilities at work	29
23	Son or daughter leaving home	29
24	Trouble with in-laws	29
25	Outstanding personal achievement	28
26	Wife begins or stops work	26
27	Begin or end school	26
28	Change in living conditions	25
29	Revision of personal habits	24
30	Trouble with boss	23
31	Change in work hours or conditions	20
32	Change in residence	20
33	Change in schools	20
34	Change in recreation	19
35	Change in church activities	19
36	Change in social activities	18
37	Mortgage or loan less than $10,000	17
38	Change in sleeping habits	16
39	Change in number of family get-togethers	15
40	Change in eating habits	15
41	Vacation	13
42	Christmas	12
43	Minor violations of the law	11

SOURCE: Holmes and Rahe, 1967.

vacations, and minor violations of the law were considered the least stressful.

The more life events an individual experiences, the more likely is he or she to get sick from a variety of disorders. For example, individuals who had heart attacks had more total significant life events in the six months prior to their heart attack than in the year before. Similarly, individuals who became depressed had a larger number of life events, particularly losses, than those

Stressful life events may make us susceptible to physical disease. The death of a close relative, losing a job or a move or eviction all constitute stressful life events. (*Top:* Josef Koudelka/ Magnum). *Center:* © 1981 Andy Sacks/Black Star. (*Bottom:* © 1978 Thom O'Connor/Black Star)

who did not (Holmes and Rahe, 1967; Paykel, Meyers, Dienelt, Klerman, Lindenthal, and Peffer, 1969; Theorell and Rahe, 1971).

Since the construction of the Social Readjustment Rating Scale, investigators have taken a closer look at the nature of the life events themselves. First of all, some of the life events listed by Holmes and Rahe could themselves reflect the fact of ongoing illness. For example, an individual might be forced to retire (item 10) because he had high blood pressure, as opposed to getting high blood pressure as a consequence of retiring. Modern investigations of life events now distinguish between events that are confounded with illness and those that might contribute to it (Dohrenwend and Dohrenwend, 1974).

Second, some of the life events are positive *entrances,* such as item 25, outstanding personal achievement, while others are negative *exits,* like item 1, the death of a spouse. Losses or exits seem to produce more problems than do entrances (Paykel, 1974).

Third, the repetitive, daily hassles of life may be better predictors of illness than the major life events in Table 12-3. Losing your wallet, a price rise in the weekly food bill, and the breaking of a window may ultimately push health around more than deaths, divorces, and pregnancies (Kanner, Coyne, Schaefer, and Lazarus, 1981). That is, it may be the gradual chipping away at an individual by stresses that wear him or her down to a point where susceptibility to illness jumps dramatically.

CONTROLLABLE VERSUS UNCONTROLLABLE LIFE EVENTS.   Another development in life events research concerns control over one's life. Recall that David Glass argued that a Type A's vigorous struggle to control threat followed by profound helplessness in the face of an uncontrollable event predisposes him to coronary disease. Glass predicts that it is not life events in themselves but ***uncontrollable life events*** that precede heart attacks, especially among Type A's. Thus, he differentiates between uncontrollable and controllable life events. For example, he categorized death of a close family member, death of a best friend, and being laid off from work as uncontrollable losses, but divorce, separation, and changes in eating habits as controllable life events (Dohrenwend and Martin, 1978).

Three groups of patients answered a life events questionnaire based on the Social Readjustment Rating Scale. One group was in the coronary care unit following heart attack, a second group was in the general medical and psychiatric ward for non-coronary illnesses, and a third group was healthy. As expected, the patients hospitalized for heart attacks tended to be Type A's, whereas the patients hospitalized for non-coronary illnesses tended to be Type B's. The three groups did not differ on *total number* of life events in the preceding year. What distinguished the hospitalized groups from the non-hospitalized group, however, was the number of *uncontrollable* life events. Both the individuals who had had heart attacks and the indivduals who had been hospitalized for other illnesses experienced more helplessness-inducing life events than did the healthy controls. Taken together, these results indicate that a combination of being a Type A and experiencing uncontrollable life events—as opposed to a large number of life events per se—may be a formula for heart attack (Glass, 1977).

SUMMARY

1. Psychological factors can influence the course, and even the beginning, of a physical illness. *Psychosomatic disorders* are defined as physical illnesses whose course or onset can be influenced by such psychological factors.

2. Psychosomatic disorders can best be viewed within a *diathesis-stress model*. In this view, psychosomatic disorder occurs when an individual is both constitutionally vulnerable to a particular physical problem and experiences life stress.

3. *Peptic ulcers* occur when the naturally secreted hydrochloric acid of the stomach erodes the protective mucous membrane of the stomach or duodenum. Emotional states, particularly anxiety, can cause an oversecretion of hydrochloric acid in the stomach.

4. Conflict, unpredictable bad events, and uncontrollable bad events all produce anxiety and may all contribute to the formation of peptic ulcers.

5. *Hypertension,* or high blood pressure, like ulcers, is produced both by constitutional, genetically inherited tendencies to high blood pressure, and by psychological factors.

6. The emotional states of anxiety and hostility both produce increases in blood pressure in the laboratory and in real life. Such an increase in blood pressure is part of the adaptive emergency reaction to threat. If an individual engages in it for a large proportion of his or her life, chronic and dangerous hypertension will result.

7. Individuals who hold jobs that require constant vigilance and personality types who chronically view the world as hostile and threatening (Type A) may be prone to high blood pressure and be at greater risk for heart attack.

8. Severe high blood pressure should be treated by anti-hypertensive medication, but *biofeedback, transcendental meditation,* and *relaxation* can all reduce mild hypertension.

9. When a person perceives the environment as threatening, but rather than mobilizing against the danger, gives up, **sudden death** may occur.

10. Biomedical, psychodynamic, behavioral, and cognitive models have all shed light on the causes and treatment of psychosomatic disorder. All are compatible with the diathesis-stress perspective.

11. The biomedical view emphasizes the "diathesis" of the diathesis-stress model, and it argues that genetic inheritance and vulnerability in a specific organ contribute to psychosomatic disorders.

12. The psychodynamic view emphasizes the personality types in whom underlying dynamic conflicts, a vulnerable organ system, and a precipitating life situation interact to produce psychosomatic disorders.

13. The behavioral and cognitive views emphasize the "stress" of the diathesis-stress model. They hold that the way individuals learn to cope with threat, think about threat, and the actual stressful and uncontrollable life events that they experience play the major role in the way psychological factors cause and aggravate physical illness.

Part V

MAJOR DEPRESSIVE DISORDERS

CHAPTER

13

Depression and Suicide

DEPRESSION is the most widespread psychological disorder. It is the common cold of mental illness. Almost everyone has felt depression, at least in its mild forms. Feeling blue, low, sad, downhearted, discouraged, and unhappy are all common depressive experiences. But familiarity does not produce understanding; for it is only in the last two decades that major advances have been made. Today the great majority of individuals suffering from severe depressions can be helped. We also now know some of its causes.

NORMAL VERSUS CLINICAL DEPRESSION

Loss and pain are inevitable parts of growing up and growing older. Sometimes people we care for reject us, we write bad papers, our stocks go down, we fail to get the job we want, people we love die. When these losses occur we go into mourning, and then emerge, our lives poorer, but with hope for the future. Almost everyone reacts to loss with some of the symptoms of depression. We become sad and discouraged, apathetic and passive, the future looks bleak, some of the zest goes out of living. Such a reaction is normal—and we have repeatedly found that at any given moment 25 to 30 percent of college undergraduates will have such symptoms, at least to some extent (Seligman, unpublished). Nancy's depression is mild and within the normal range of reaction to loss.

Within a two-day period, Nancy got a C on her Abnormal Psychology midterm and found out that the boy she had loved in her home town during high school had become engaged. The week that followed was awful: her future looked empty since she believed she would now not get into graduate school in clinical psychology and that she would never find anyone she could deeply love again. She blamed herself for these failures in the two most important arenas of her life. For the first few days she had trouble getting out of bed to go to class. She burst into tears over dinner one evening and had to leave the table. Missing dinner didn't much matter anyway since she wasn't hungry. After one week, the world started to look better. The instructor said that because the grades were so low on the midterm, everyone

Sorrow by Vincent Van Gogh (Courtesy Rijksmuseum Vincent Van Gogh)

had the option of writing a paper to cancel out their midterm grade, and Nancy found herself looking forward to a blind date that her roommate had arranged for the weekend. Her usual bounce and enthusiasm for life began to return, and with it her appetite. She thought, "It will be an uphill battle, but I'm basically O.K. and I think I may find love and success."

How does such "normal" depression relate to the more serious depressive disorders? There are two kinds of depressive disorders, **unipolar depression** in which the individual suffers only depressive symptoms without ever experiencing mania, and **bipolar depression** (or **manic-depression**) in which both depression and mania occur. **Mania** is defined by excessive elation, expansiveness, irritability, talkativeness, inflated self-esteem, and flight of ideas. The existence of two mood disorders, which go in apparently opposite directions, has given rise to the name **affective disorders** to embrace unipolar depression, bipolar depression, and mania. Normal depression differs in degree from unipolar depression; both have the same kinds of symptoms, but the unipolar depressive has more symptoms, more severely, more frequently, and for a longer time. The line between a "normal" depressive disturbance and a clinically significant depressive disorder is blurry.

Bipolar depressions, on the other hand, are clearly distinguishable from normal and unipolar depressions. They involve swings between episodes of mania and episodes of depression, and as we shall see, they probably have a genetic component. Bipolar depression develops at a younger age, and is often more crippling to the individual. Fortunately, a specific drug, lithium carbonate, seems to help considerably.

For many years, all depression was viewed as part of manic-depression. In the last decade, it has become clear that the large majority of depressions are unipolar and unrelated to manic-depression. Depression usually occurs in people who have never had mania, and mania may occur in people who have never been depressed. For this reason, we shall first discuss unipolar depression. We will then take up bipolar depression (manic-depression). We conclude by examining the most catastrophic outcome of both unipolar and bipolar depression: suicide.

UNIPOLAR DEPRESSION

SYMPTOMS OF UNIPOLAR DEPRESSION

Depression is widely regarded as a disorder of mood, but this is an oversimplification. There are actually four sets of symptoms in depression. In addition to mood symptoms, there are thought symptoms, motivational symptoms, and physical symptoms. An individual does not have to have all these symptoms to be correctly diagnosed "depressed," but the more symptoms he has and the more intense is each set, the more confident we can be that the individual is suffering from depression.

Mood or Emotional Symptoms

When a depressed patient is asked how she feels, the most common adjectives she uses are: "sad, blue, miserable, helpless, hopeless, lonely, unhappy, downhearted, worthless, humiliated, ashamed, worried, useless, guilty."

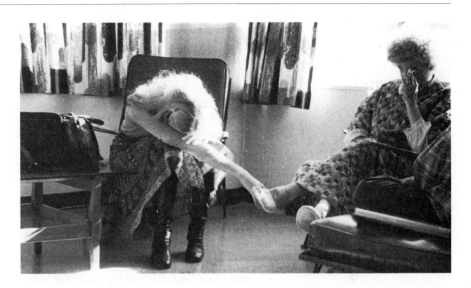

Sadness is the most salient emotional symptom in depression. A depressive may be so sad that she cries continuously during the day. (Copyright Christina Thomson 1982/Woodfin Camp)

Sadness is the most salient and widespread emotional symptom in depression. One person's life was so dominated by sadness that she cried during almost all her waking hours. She was unable to carry on a social conversation because of excessive crying. This occurred even in therapy to such an extent that almost no therapy was taking place (Beck et al., 1979). This melancholic mood varies with time of day. Most commonly, depressed people feel worse in the morning, and the mood seems to lighten a bit as the day goes on. Along with feelings of sadness, feelings of anxiety are very often present in depression (Gersh and Fowles, 1979).

Almost as pervasive as sadness in depression is loss of gratification, the numbing of the joy of living. Activities that used to bring satisfaction feel dull and flat. Loss of interest usually starts in only a few activities, such as work. But as depression increases in severity, it spreads through practically everything the individual does. The pleasure derived from hobbies, recreation, and family diminishes. Gregarious individuals who used to enjoy partygoing avoid social gatherings. Finally, even biological functions, such as eating and sex, lose their appeal. Ninety-two percent of depressed patients no longer derive gratification from some major interests in their life, and 64 percent of depressed patients lose their feeling for other people (Beck, 1967).

Thought Symptoms

A depressed person thinks of himself in a very negative light. He has low self-esteem and views the future as being hopeless.

NEGATIVE VIEW OF THE SELF. A depressed individual often has low self-esteem. He believes he has failed and that he is the cause of his own failures. He believes he is inferior, inadequate, and incompetent. He believes that he lacks the qualities necessary to succeed in those areas of his life that are important to him, be they intelligence, attractiveness, wealth, health, or talent (see Box 13-1). These views of failure and incompetence are often distortions.

One patient managed to wallpaper a kitchen although very depressed. Here is how he distorted this achievement into a failure:

Box 13-1 DEPRESSION AND THE PERCEPTION OF REALITY

Depressed people clearly have more negative beliefs about themselves and their future than nondepressed people. But who is accurate? Sometimes the distortion from reality is in the mind of the depressive as in the example of the man who believed his wallpaper job was a failure because a couple of the panels weren't perfect. But is it possible that depressed individuals are sometimes more in touch with reality about their abilities than are nondepressed individuals? Perhaps it is nondepressed individuals who are making optimistic distortions? Lauren Alloy and Lyn Abramson (1979) conducted a study in which depressed and nondepressed college students performed a task where they pushed a button on some trials and refrained from button pushing on other trials. When the button was pushed, a green light sometimes went on. They were asked to judge how much control they had. For one group (75–0), the green light went on 75 percent of the time they pressed the button, and never went on when they didn't press the button. Their actual control was 75. For another group (75–50), the green light went on 75 percent of the time they pressed the button, but also went on 50 percent of the time when they didn't press the button, resulting in actual control of 25. In the most interesting group (75–75), the green light went on 75 percent of the time, whether or not they pressed the button. In this condition, actual control was zero since the green light went on regardless of whether they pressed the button.

The figure below shows the surprising results. Depressed people accurately judge how much control they have. When they exert control, they judge the contingency correctly. When they do not have control, they say that they do not. There *is* a net difference between depressed and nondepressed individuals, but the distortion resides in nondepressed individuals who believe they have control even when they do not. Alloy and Abramson speculated that depressed people are sadder, but wiser. What needs explaining on this account is not why people are sometimes depressed, but how nondepressed people successfully defend themselves from a grim reality (Alloy and Abramson, 1979).

This conclusion has been borne out in studies of perception of social ability. Depressed patients' assessment of their own social skills is closer to the assessment

THERAPIST: Why didn't you rate wallpapering the kitchen as a mastery experience?

PATIENT: Because the flowers didn't line up.

THERAPIST: You did in fact complete the job?

PATIENT: Yes.

THERAPIST: Your kitchen?

PATIENT: No. I helped a neighbor do his kitchen.

THERAPIST: Did he do most of the work?

PATIENT: No, I really did almost all of it. He hadn't wallpapered before.

THERAPIST: Did anything else go wrong? Did you spill the paste all over? Ruin a lot of wallpaper? Leave a big mess?

PATIENT: No, no, the only problem was that the flowers did not line up.

THERAPIST: So, since it was not perfect, you get no credit at all.

PATIENT: Well . . . yes.

THERAPIST: Just how far off was the alignment of the flowers?

PATIENT: (holds out fingers about 1/8 of an inch apart) About that much.

THERAPIST: On each strip of paper?

PATIENT: No . . . on two or three pieces.

THERAPIST: Out of how many?

of their skills by a panel of judges than is the assessment of nondepressed patients to the assessment of the judges. The nondepressed patients tend to believe that they are more socially skilled than the judges believe they are (Lewinsohn, Mischel, Chaplin, and Barton, 1980). Depressed people have low self-esteem, but this low self-evaluation may not always be a distortion; sometimes it may be merely a sober and accurate assessment of reality, which contrasts to that of others who may overinflate their view of themselves.

Judgment of control in depressed and nondepressed students. Depressed students accurately judge that they exert control over a green light when they in fact have control (75–0, 75–50), and they are also accurate in judging that they do not have control when the light comes on 75 percent of the time, whether or not they button press (75–75). Nondepressed students judge that they exert control even when they do not. (Source: Alloy and Abramson, 1979)

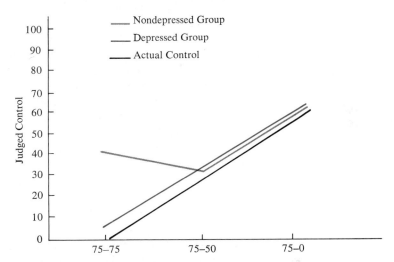

The probability of the green light going on when a response is made versus the probability of the green light going on when a response is not made. At point 75–75, the green light goes on 75% of the time whether or not a response is made. At point 75–50, the green light goes on 75% of the time when a response is made, but only 50% of the time when a response is not made. At 75–0, the green light goes on 75% of the time when a response is made, but never comes on when a response is not made.

PATIENT: About 20–25.
THERAPIST: Did anyone else notice it?
PATIENT: No. In fact, my neighbor thought it was great.
THERAPIST: Did your wife see it?
PATIENT: Yeah, she admired the job.
THERAPIST: Could you see the defect when you stood back and looked at the whole wall?
PATIENT: Well . . . not really.
THERAPIST: So you've selectively attended to a real but very small flaw in your effort to wallpaper. Is it logical that such a small defect should entirely cancel the credit you deserve?
PATIENT: Well, it wasn't as good as it should have been.
THERAPIST: If your neighbor had done the same quality job in your kitchen, what would you say?
PATIENT: . . . . pretty good job!
(Beck et al., 1979)

Depressed people not only have low self-esteem, but they blame themselves and feel guilty for the troubles that afflict them. When failure occurs, depressed individuals tend to take the responsibility on themselves.

When failure has not yet occurred, they imagine that it will soon and that it will be caused by them. Those who are the most severely depressed may even believe that they are responsible for the violence and suffering of the world and that they should be greatly punished for their sins.

BELIEF IN A HOPELESS FUTURE.   In addition to negative beliefs and guilt about the self, the depressed individual almost always views the future with great pessimism and hopelessness. A depressed individual believes that his actions, even if he could undertake them, are doomed. For example, when a middle-aged, depressed woman was told by her therapist that it would be a good idea for her to get a job, she replied, "I just couldn't possibly do it. How would I find the number of an employment agency? Even if I found the phone number, no one would want to hire me because I'm unqualified." Upon being reminded that she held a Ph.D. she replied, "Well, they might hire me, but they will surely fire me because I'm incompetent; and even if they kept me on it wouldn't be because of competence, but only because I'm so pathetic" (Seligman, unpublished). The depressed individual is equipped with a host of reasons for future failure, and no reasons at all for why success might occur.

Small obstacles in the path of a depressive seem insuperable barriers. One patient wanted to go swimming but was overwhelmed by the difficulties she saw in her way:

> PATIENT: There is nowhere I could go swimming.
> THERAPIST: How could you find a place?
> PATIENT: There is a YWCA if I could get there. . . . I'd get my hair wet and get a cold.
> THERAPIST: How could you get there?
> PATIENT: My husband would take me.
> THERAPIST: How about your wet hair?
> PATIENT: I couldn't take a hair dryer; someone would steal it.
> THERAPIST: Could you do something about that?
> PATIENT: They don't have lockers.
> THERAPIST: How do you know?
> PATIENT: I just don't think they do.
> (Beck et al., 1979)

The depressive's belief that future action will be ineffective has been demonstrated experimentally. Hospitalized depressives worked on a task of skill and a task of chance. When they succeeded at the task of skill, their expectancies for future success did not go up, and when they failed, their expectancies that they would succeed did not go down. Unlike nondepressed individuals and unlike schizophrenics (either depressed or nondepressed), whose expectancies rise when they succeed and lower when they fail, depressed patients did not seem to believe that their responses could make any difference to future success (Abramson, Garber, Edwards, and Seligman, 1978).

Motivational Symptoms

People vary as to how motivated they are. Most of us, however, are able to get up in the morning, go to work, find ways of entertaining ourselves and others, and so on. But depressed individuals have great trouble getting

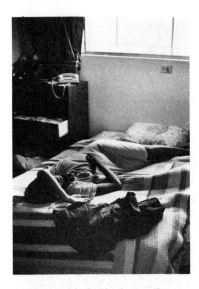

Depressed individuals may have trouble motivating themselves to get up in the morning to go to work or study. Depressive problems are usually worse in the morning. (Photograph by Arthur Tress)

started. This passivity or lack of response initiation undermines working and loving. An advertising executive loses his initiative in planning a major sales campaign; a college professor cannot bring herself to prepare her lectures; a student loses the desire to study.

One depressed man who was hospitalized after a suicide attempt merely sat motionless day after day in the lounge. His therapist decided to prepare a schedule of activities to get the patient engaged:

> THERAPIST: I understand that you spend most of your day in the lounge. Is that true?
> PATIENT: Yes, being quiet gives me the peace of mind I need.
> THERAPIST: When you sit here, how's your mood?
> PATIENT: I feel awful all the time. I just wish I could fall in a hole somewhere and die.
> THERAPIST: Do you feel better after sitting for two or three hours?
> PATIENT: No, the same.
> THERAPIST: So you're sitting in the hope that you'll find peace of mind, but it doesn't sound like your depression improves.
> PATIENT: I get so bored.
> THERAPIST: Would you consider being more active? There are a number of reasons why I think increasing your activity level might help.
> PATIENT: There's nothing to do around here.
> THERAPIST: Would you consider trying some activities if I could come up with a list?
> PATIENT: If you think it will help, but I think you're wasting your time. I don't have any interests.
> (Beck et al., 1979)

In extreme form, lack of response initiation is "paralysis of the will." Such a patient cannot bring himself to do even those things that are necessary to life. He has to be pushed and prodded out of bed, clothed, and fed. In severe depression, there may be *psychomotor retardation* in which movements slow down and the patient walks and talks excruciatingly slowly.

Lack of response initiation in depression has been seen clearly in the laboratory. Depressed college students fail to escape loud noise when performing tasks in which all that is required to turn off the noise is moving the hand two feet. This lack of response initiation occurs not only in instrumental motor behavior but also in cognitive tasks as well. Depressed students and depressed patients fail to solve anagrams that nondepressed individuals solve readily. The more depressed an individual is, the more severe are these deficits (Miller and Seligman, 1975, 1976; Price, Tryon, and Raps, 1978).

Difficulty in making a decision also seems to be a common symptom of depression (Hammen and Padesky, 1977). The following case illustrates how indecisiveness can overwhelm a depressed individual:

> Sylvia is a very bright college student whose life is being ruined by her depression. She finds it increasingly difficult to get on with routine studying because she can't take the initial steps. Now a major life decision has paralyzed her for the last three weeks. She has been accepted to two good graduate schools and has to make up her mind which to accept. One school offers a large scholarship, the other is more prestigious. She constantly ruminates over being selfish if she chooses the prestigious one without money, versus the cowardliness of giving in to her parents by choosing the other. Sylvia has managed to turn a can't-lose situation into a can't-win situation. (After Beck et al., 1979.)

For a depressed individual, making a decision may be overwhelming and frightening. Every decision seems momentous, of make or break significance, and the fear of the wrong decision can be paralyzing.

Physical Symptoms

Perhaps the most insidious set of symptoms in depression are the physical changes. As depression worsens, every biological and psychological joy that makes life worth living is eroded.

Thought D (Failure)	0	I do not feel like a failure.
	1	I feel I have failed more than the average person.
	2	I feel I have accomplished very little that is worthwhile or that means anything.
	3	I feel I am a complete failure as a person (parent, husband, wife).
Motivation E (Work initiation)	0	I can work about as well as before.
	1a	It takes extra effort to get started at doing something.
	1b	I don't work as well as I used to.
	2	I have to push myself very hard to do anything.
	3	I can't do any work at all.
Motivation F (Suicide)	0	I don't have any thoughts of harming myself.
	1	I have thoughts of harming myself but I would not carry them out.
	2a	I feel I would be better off dead.
	2b	I feel my family would be better off if I were dead.
	3a	I have definite plans about committing suicide.
	3b	I would kill myself if I could.
Physical G (Appetite)	0	My appetite is no worse than usual.
	1	My appetite is not as good as it used to be.
	2	My appetite is much worse now.
	3	I have no appetite at all any more.
Physical H (Sleep loss)	0	I can sleep as well as usual.
	1	I wake up more tired in the morning than I used to.
	2	I wake up 1–2 hours earlier than usual and find it hard to get back to sleep.
	3	I wake up early every day and can't get more than 5 hours sleep.

SOURCE: Beck, 1967.

Loss of appetite is common. A gourmet finds that food does not taste good to her anymore. Weight loss occurs in moderate and severe depression, although in mild depression weight gain sometimes occurs. Sleep disturbance occurs as well. Depressed individuals may experience trouble getting to sleep at night, or they may experience early morning awakening, with great difficulty getting back to sleep for the rest of the night. Sleep disturbance and weight loss both lead to weakness and fatigue. A depressed individual also may lose interest in sex. Erectile difficulties in men and lack of arousal in women are common side effects of depression.

A depressed individual is often self-absorbed and focused on the present. His body absorbs his attention, and increased worry about aches and pains can occur. In addition to more worrying about health, depressed individuals may, in fact, be more susceptible to physical illness, since depression, as it becomes severe, may erode basic biological drives. For example, when a flu swept through an army base, those individuals who had been depressed took significantly longer to recover (Imboden, Cantor, and Cluff, 1961).

CLASSIFYING DEPRESSION

Depression of all kinds produces mood, thought, motivational, and physical deficits. What kinds of depression exist? DSM-III has adopted the most reliable and basic distinction in depression: the unipolar-bipolar distinction, which we defined above. In addition to the bipolar-unipolar distinction, however, DSM-III also distinguishes between *episodic* and *chronic* depressions. In a chronic depression, the individual has been depressed for at least two solid years without having had a remission to normality of at least two months in duration. An episodic depression, which is much more common, is of less than two years' duration and has a clear onset which distinguishes it from previous nondepressed functioning.

Endogenous vs. Exogenous Depression

The endogenous vs. exogenous distinction in depression, called by DSM-III depression with melancholia vs. depression without melancholia, is an attempt to separate biologically based from psychologically based depressions. The word *endogenous* (biological—with melancholia) means "coming from within the body," and *exogenous* (psychological—without melancholia) means "coming from outside the body"; the implication of these terms is that an exogenous depression is precipitated by a life stressor, while an endogenous depression arises from a disordered biology. This distinction is associated with two fairly reliable symptom clusters: endogenous depressions involve psychomotor retardation, more severe symptoms, the lack of reaction to environmental changes during the depression, loss of interest in life, and somatic symptoms, while exogenous depressions show fewer of these characteristics. In addition, early morning awakening, guilt, and suicidal behavior may be more associated with endogenous than exogenous depressions (Mendels and Cochran, 1968).

The usefulness of the endogenous-exogenous distinction is compromised, however, by a lack of difference in precipitating events. Endogenous depressions have been found to have no fewer precipitating events than exogenous depressions (Paykel, Meyers, Dienelt, Klerman, Lindenthal, and Pfeffer, 1969; Leff, Roach, and Bunney, 1970). But while there is no difference in precipitating events, there may be different treatment implications: endogenous depressions, identified by the endogenous symptom cluster may respond better to antidepressant drugs and electroconvulsive shock, while exogenous depressions may fare better with psychotherapy alone. The results of differential treatment studies have not been uniform, however, and the distinction must be viewed with caution (Fowles and Gersh, 1979).

Finally, there is also a good possibility that the distinction between mild and severe may be the basis of the endogenous-exogenous continuum, with the endogenous depressions merely being more severe. This would mean that there is only one type of unipolar depression but that there are important differences in intensity.

We will distinguish below only between unipolar and bipolar depression. We now turn to the question of who is particularly vulnerable to unipolar depression.

VULNERABILITY TO DEPRESSION

How specific can we be about this "common cold of mental illness"? At the very moment about one out of fifteen Americans is moderately or severely depressed, and chances are one in three of having a depressive episode of clinical proportions at least once in your lifetime (Weissman and Myers, 1978). Depression has always been with us. Early Greek and Roman tracts describe the disorder in terms that still ring true. The Roman historian Plutarch in the second century, A.D., described melancholia as follows:

> He looks on himself as a man whom the gods hate and pursue with their anger. A far worse lot is before him; he does not employ any means of averting or of remedying the evil, lest he be found fighting against the gods. The physician, the consoling friend, are driven away. "Leave me," says the wretched man. "Me, the impious, the accursed, hated of the gods, to suffer my punishment." He sits out of doors wrapped in sackcloth or in filthy rags. Ever and alone, he rolls himself, naked, in the dirt confessing about this and that sin. (Zilboorg, 1941)

Who is vulnerable to depression? Everyone. No group—not blacks or whites, not women or men, not young or old, not rich or poor—is wholly spared. While depression is found among all segments of mankind, some groups, however, are more susceptible than others.

Sex Differences in Depression

Women seem to be rather more vulnerable to depression than men. About twice as many women as men are treated for depression. Moreover, a similar ratio is found when door-to-door surveys are taken of men and women in urban communities, indicating that the ratio is not a result of women's greater willingness than men's to seek treatment. The 2–1 ratio applies across cultures, holding both in Europe and the United States, as well as in two small villages in Uganda (Orley and Wing, 1979). When an investigator matched large numbers of women and men for such influences as income, employment, age, marital status, head of household, and others, she found that in every category save two, greater numbers of women reported more depression than men. For example, among women and men earning the same amount of money, depression was more frequent in women. Only among single heads of household and among groups of those over sixty-five was the frequency of depression the same for men and women (Radloff and Rae, 1979).

Several hypotheses have been advanced to account for the sex difference in depression. First, women may be more willing to express depressive symptoms than men are in our society. When they confront loss, women are more reinforced for passivity and crying, while men are more reinforced for anger or indifference (Weissman and Paykel, 1974). Second, biological hypotheses suggest that chemical enzyme activity, genetic proneness, and a monthly bout of premenstrual depression influence vulnerability in women. Also there is the possibility that female carriers of a depressive gene become depressed, whereas male carriers of the same gene become alcoholic (Robinson, Davis, Nies, Ravaris, and Sylvester, 1971; Winokur, 1972.) A third hypothesis grows out of the learned helplessness theory of depression (see pp. 336–39). If depression is related to helplessness, then to the extent that women learn to be more helpless than men, depression will appear more frequently in women than in men. A society that rewards women for becoming passive in the face of loss while rewarding men for active coping attempts may pay a heavy price in later female depression (Radloff, 1975).

Age and Depression

No age group is exempt from depression, although the older one is the greater the risk for depression. Comparison of the frequency of depression across age is controversial since depression may have different manifestations at different times of life.

The earliest psychological state that may be related to depression was described by the American psychiatrist Rene Spitz in 1946 and was called **anaclitic depression.** Spitz observed that when infants between the ages of six and eighteen months were separated from their mothers for prolonged periods of time, a state of unresponsive apathy, listlessness, weight loss, increased susceptibility to serious childhood illness, and even death occurred. The mothers' return, or the substitution of a different, permanent mother, reversed these effects (Spitz, 1946). Similar effects have been observed when infant rhesus monkeys are separated from their mothers. A regular sequence of the reaction to the separation—first protest, then despair, then reattachment— has been documented (Bowlby, 1960; Kaufman and Rosenblum, 1967; McKinney, Suomi, and Harlow, 1972).

Childhood depression is a controversial issue (Schulterbrand and Raven, 1977). Until recently, it was alleged that depression in childhood with the core symptoms of passivity, negative cognitions, resigned behavior, sadness, and inhibition in working and loving, was relatively rare. Instead, reaction to loss was thought to take other forms, such as hyperactivity, aggression, and delinquency (Cytryn and McKnew, 1972). More sensitive tests of depression in childhood have recently been developed and have revealed as high a rate of depressive symptoms in children as among adults, along with accompanying intellectual deficits (Kovacs and Beck, 1977; Kaslow, Tanenbaum, Abramson, Peterson, and Seligman, 1983).

The loss of a parent by divorce may precipitate depression among children, as illustrated by the following case:

Infants between the ages of six and eighteen months who are separated from their mothers for prolonged periods may develop symptoms of anaclitic depression. (Photograph by Gary Renaud/Magnum)

> Peter, age nine, had not seen his father, who lived nearby, more than once every two to three months. We expected that he would be troubled, but we were entirely unprepared for the extent of this child's misery. The interviewer observed: "I asked Peter when he had last seen his dad. The child looked at me blankly and his

Women may become depressed between the ages of forty-five and sixty because they lose the nurturant role when their children leave home. (Photograph by Steve Schapiro/Black Star)

thinking became confused, his speech halting. Just then, a police car went by with its siren screaming. The child stared into space and seemed lost in reverie. As this continued for a few minutes, I gently suggested that the police car had reminded him of his father, a police officer. Peter began to cry and sobbed without stopping for 35 minutes. (Wallerstein and Kelly, 1980)

In adolescents, depression has all the symptoms that we saw for depression in adults. In addition to the core symptoms of depression, depressed adolescents, particularly boys, are commonly negativistic and even antisocial. Restlessness, grouchiness, aggression, and strong desire to leave home are also common symptoms; and sulkiness, uncooperativeness in family activities, school difficulties, alcohol and drug abuse can also be symptoms of adolescent depression.

Depression among adults seems to increase somewhat in frequency and in severity with age. So prevalent is depression between the ages of forty-five and sixty, particularly among women, that the category of ***involutional melancholia*** was widely used in diagnosis for the last twenty-five years. This category was associated with the endocrine changes of menopause, the loss of role with children grown up, doubts about sexual attractiveness, and a taking stock of life as death approached. This category has now been abandoned since therapy and prognosis is similar in this group to therapy and prognosis for the other unipolar depressions. Finally, in old age, depression is compounded by the helplessness induced by increasing physical and mental incapacities. Depression is widespread among the aged; a visit to any old-age home will dramatically confirm this.

Race and Social Class

There are no strong or consistent differences in the incidence of depression according to race or social class. For many years, depression was thought to be uncommon among North American blacks, but recent research does not bear this out. In the largest study to date, race and social class made little difference in incidence of depression among 159 black and 555 white patients. There was a tendency for the blacks to be more negativistic, more angry, and to make more suicidal attempts that the whites. In addition, the blacks were younger and had more rapid onset of symptoms (Raskin, Crook, and Herman, 1975). Caution should be used, however, in interpreting any study of cross-racial, cross-age, cross-sex, or cross-cultural psychological disorders. Since diagnosis is, for the most part, made by middle-class white psychiatrists and psychologists, insensitivity to symptoms of depression within another culture or elicitation of greater hostility among the patients may easily contaminate the results (Tonks, Paykel, and Klerman, 1970).

No strong differences occur in depression among social classes. Unlike schizophrenia, which is less frequent in middle and upper classes, depression is democratic. Again, however, it is possible that depression may have different manifestations according to the patient's social class: lower-class patients may show more feelings of powerlessness and hopelessness, middle-class patients stronger feelings of loneliness and rejection, and upper-class patients greater pessimism and social withdrawal (Schwab, Bialow, Holzer, Brown, and Stevenson, 1967). At any rate, the similarities in the occurrence of depression between black people and white people and between rich people and poor people, far outweigh the differences.

Effects of Life Events

Are the lives of depressed people, before the onset of their depression, different from the lives of people who do not become depressed? Depressed individuals have experienced more early childhood losses than nondepressed individuals and more frequent stressful losses within a year or two before the onset of the depression. Yet, many individuals suffer both early childhood loss and recent loss without becoming depressed, and a substantial number of depressed individuals do not suffer early childhood loss or recent loss. So we are far from saying that such life events *cause* depression, but some events do seem to increase the risk of depression.

EARLY CHILDHOOD LOSS.   The death of a person's mother before the child is eleven years old may predispose an individual to depression in adulthood. In a study of depression in its natural setting, the English sociologists George W. Brown and Tirril Harris interviewed women door-to-door in the working class borough of Camberwell in London. They found that an alarmingly high percentage—15 to 20 percent—were moderately to severely depressed and that these women were not receiving treatment for their depression. The rate of depression was almost three times higher among women who, before age eleven, had lost their mother and who also had experienced a severe recent loss than among women who before age eleven, had not lost their mother but who had experienced a similar recent loss. Death of the mother after the child reached age eleven, or of the father at any time, had no effect on risk for depression according to this study (Brown and Harris, 1978).

RECENT LOSS.   Most depressions are preceded by a recent stressful loss. Failure at work, marital separation, failure at school, loss of a job, rejection by a loved one, illness of a family member, and physical illness are common

Children who suffer early childhood loss may be at risk for depression in adulthood. (Photograph by Arthur Tress)

precipitants of depression. Individuals who become depressed show more such losses preceding their depression than matched controls (Leff, Roatch and Bunney, 1970; Paykel, 1973; Brown and Harris, 1978).

But such losses do not always bring on depressions, by any means. Only about 10 percent of those persons who experience losses equivalent in severity to those of an average depressed person, themselves become depressed. Why is it that the other 90 percent do *not* become depressed? Brown and Harris proposed that there are four invulnerability factors that can help prevent depression from occurring, even in the presence of the predisposing factors and recent loss. Only half the women who, before age eleven, had lost their mother and who also had suffered a recent loss became depressed. What about the other half? The invulnerable women had either (1) an intimate relationship with a spouse or a lover, or (2) a part-time or full-time job away from home, or (3) fewer than three children still at home, or (4) a serious religious commitment. So intimacy, employment, a life not overburdened by child care, and strong religious belief may protect against depression. Perhaps what these four invulnerability factors have in common is that they contribute self-esteem and a sense of mastery, while undercutting the formation of an outlook pervaded by hopelessness. All of these, in effect, help to ward off depression.

THE COURSE OF DEPRESSION

When a vulnerable individual becomes depressed, what is likely to happen if the individual fails to seek out treatment? If anything good about depression can be said, it is that it usually dissipates in time. After the initial attack, which comes on suddenly about three-quarters of the time, depression seems to last an average of about three months in outpatients. Among inpatients, who are usually more severely depressed, it lasts about six months on the average. At first, the depression gets progressively worse, eventually reaching the bottom, but then the depressed individual begins to recover gradually to the state that existed before the onset (Beck, 1967; Robins and Guze, 1972). What our grandmothers told us about our own personal tragedies—time heals all wounds—is certainly true for depression. The mind, or the body, seems incapable of sustaining a dark mood forever, and unknown homeostatic mechanisms take over and, in time, correct the disorder.

The time that a depressive episode lasts, however, is painfully long, and to an individual suffering from it, it seems like forever. For this reason, a therapist will always emphasize that the depressive episode will go away in time. Without minimizing the suffering the patient is feeling now, the therapist should tell the patient that complete recovery from the episode occurs in 70 to 95 percent of the cases. For some, this ray of hope may speed the time when the depression will lift.

Once a depressive episode has occurred, one of three patterns may develop. The first is *recovery without recurrence.* About half the patients who have had a depressive episode will not have another one, at least during the following ten years. Generally, the more stable a person is before the episode, the less likely depression will recur. On the other hand, half of depressed individuals will show the second pattern: *recovery with recurrence.*

The second depressive episode, if it occurs, will tend to be of about the same duration as the first attack. On the average, however, most individuals who have recurrent episodes of depression can expect an average symptom-free interval of more than three years before the next episode, and the interval between episodes in recurrent depression tends to become shorter over the years. For some individuals, the third pattern will develop: *chronic depression.* Roughly 10 percent of those individuals who have a major depressive episode will not recover and will remain chronically depressed (Perris, 1968; Kerr, Roth, Schapira, and Gurney, 1972; Schuyler, 1974). Therapy for depression usually attempts to make the current episode shorter or to postpone the time at which another episode might strike. The therapies for depression derive from four different theories, and it is to these theories and therapies we now turn.

THEORIES AND THERAPIES OF UNIPOLAR DEPRESSION

What causes depression, and how is depression most effectively treated? In the last fifteen years, we have moved out of the dark ages in our understanding of depression. Substantial strides have been made in the understanding and treatment of the disorder. Between 80 and 90 percent of severe depressions can now be markedly alleviated with a brief course of therapy. Although several theories, with substantial research support, have emerged to explain the origins of depression, we still cannot say with certainty what the cause of depression is or how it can best be treated. We can, however, make highly educated guesses. There are four main theories and therapies for depression: the biological model, the psychodynamic model, the behavioral model, and the cognitive model. These theories overlap, and there is also a good deal of overlap in the therapies each recommends, but each tends to focus on one aspect of depression. At the end of this section, we will attempt a synthesis of these models.

THE BIOLOGICAL MODEL OF DEPRESSION

According to the biological model, depression is a disorder of the body. While in principle, depression could be caused by a problem in any bodily organ—the liver, the blood, the stomach—speculation has centered almost entirely on the brain, and in particular on depletion of those substances (biogenic amines) that help transmit nerve impulses across the gaps (synapses) between nerve cells (neurons). There are four clues that the body is intimately involved in depression (Schuyler, 1974). First of all, depression occurs with some frequency following periods of natural physiological change in women: after giving birth to a child, at menopause, and just before menstruation. Second, there is considerable similarity of symptoms across cultures, sexes, ages, and races, indicating an underlying biological process. Third, somatic therapies, in particular drugs like tricyclic antidepressants and MAO inhibitors, and electroconvulsive shock, are effective treatments of depression. Fourth, depression is occasionally induced in normal individuals as a side effect of medications; in particular depression may be induced by reserpine, a high-blood-pressure reducing drug (Schuyler, 1974). These clues have fueled the search for a biological basis of depression.

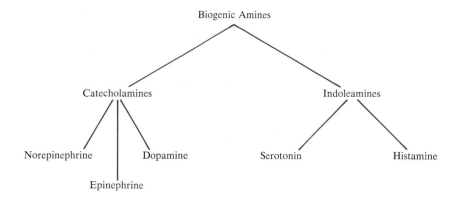

Figure 13-1
The biogenic amines.

The Neurochemical Basis of Depression

The biological model holds that depression is a disorder of motivation caused by insufficiencies of the biogenic amines. The **biogenic amines** are neurochemicals that facilitate neural transmission. They divide into two groups with different chemical structures: the **catecholamines,** which include norepinephrine, epinephrine,and dopamine; and the **indoleamines,** which include serotonin and histamine (see Figure 13-1).

The biogenic amines play significant roles in neural transmission in the medial forebrain bundle (MFB) and the periventricular system (PVS). The MFB and PVS are two major pathways that run through lower centers of the brain. Research with animals indicates that the MFB and PVS may be the neuroanatomical basis of reward and punishment respectively (Stein, 1968). Electrical stimulation of the MFB is highly reinforcing to rats, and electrical stimulation of the periventricular system is very punishing. The MFB may function as a "go" system that facilitates active behavior, whereas the PVS may act as a "stop" system. When the biogenic amines are depleted, the functioning of these systems is reduced and depression, with its loss of motivation, may ensue. Speculation about the neurochemical basis of depression has centered primarily around decreased availability of one of the catecholamines, **norepinephrine (NE)** (Schildkraut, 1965).

Figure 13-2 depicts the hypothesized mode of action of norepinephrine in transmission of a nerve impulse from one neuron across the synapse to a

Figure 13-2
Schematized action of norepinephrine (NE) in neural transmission. NE produced in nerve cell 1 is discharged into the synapse, where it stimulates nerve cell 2 to fire. In order to stop the NE from stimulating nerve cell 2, NE can be inactivated either by being reabsorbed back into nerve cell 1 (reuptake) or by being broken down and excreted out of the synapse (breakdown). Antidepressant drugs keep NE available in the synapse by blocking its reuptake (tricyclics) or slowing its breakdown (MAO inhibitors).

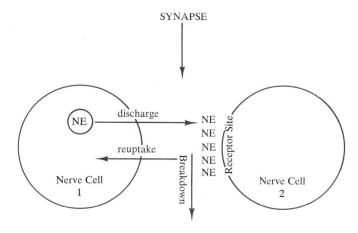

second neuron in the brain. When a nerve impulse occurs in neuron 1, norepinephrine is discharged into the synapse (the gap between neuron 1 and neuron 2). This stimulates neuron 2 to fire when the NE makes contact with the receptors on the membrane of neuron 2. Norepinephrine is now sitting in the synapse and on the membrane of neuron 2. Neuron 2 will continue to fire until the NE is inactivated. There are two relevant ways that norepinephrine can now be inactivated. The first way is by *reuptake*, in which neuron 1 reabsorbs norepinephrine, thereby decreasing the amount of norepinephrine at the receptors. The second is by *breakdown.* This is facilitated by the enzyme, monoamine oxidase (MAO), among others. This enzyme breaks down the norepinephrine chemically and renders it inactive. As we said above, norepinephrine is a catecholamine, which is one of two classes of biogenic amines. The biogenic amines affect our motivation. And when we decrease the amount of biogenic amines (in this case, norepinephrine), we will have less motivation. The catecholamine hypothesis claims that when reuptake and/or breakdown are doing their job too well, our norepinephrine level drops too low, and we become highly unmotivated, in short, depressed.

Two groups of drugs are used to treat depression: tricyclic antidepressants and MAO inhibitors. Each affects the availability of NE in the brain. It was a serendipitous finding that led to their use as antidepressants. Individuals with tuberculosis, who are frequently depressed, were tested with a new drug, iproniazid. It turned out that the drug didn't help cure their tuberculosis, but it did produce a much brighter mood in the patients, and they became less depressed. Why did this happen? The drug, iproniazid, is an MAO inhibitor. As we have seen, the enzyme MAO facilitates breakdown, thereby making less norepinephrine available for neural transmission. So this drug, iproniazid, inhibited the enzyme MAO in the patients with tuberculosis, and in part prevented breakdown of NE. The catecholamine hypothesis claims that, as a result, more norepinephrine was available, and with more NE available, the tuberculosis patients became less depressed. Since then, MAO inhibitors have been successfully used in treating depression, thereby rendering support for the biological model, specifically the catecholamine hypothesis.

Also discovered by accident, the tricyclic antidepressants affect the availability of NE. These drugs block the process of reuptake. As we saw above, reuptake occurs when the neuron that released NE absorbs it back. If reuptake is blocked, then less NE is absorbed, and more will be available. As a result of more NE, the patient will become less depressed. This provides further evidence for the catecholamine hypothesis.

Further evidence for this hypothesis has come from reserpine-induced depression. Reserpine is a powerful sedative given to high blood pressure patients. Physicians discovered that it produces an unwanted side effect, depression with suicidal tendencies, in about 15 percent of the people who take it. It turns out that reserpine, among other actions, depletes norepinephrine. With less NE, these high blood pressure patients became depressed.

Despite the favorable evidence supporting the catecholamine hypothesis based on the action of these drugs, advocates of the hypothesis are appropriately cautious. The reason is that reserpine, the tricyclics, and the MAO inhibitors all have a large number of effects other than their effect on norepinephrine. Because of this, it is very possible that their effects might be due to some other properties of the drugs and not necessarily to their effect on norepinephrine.

Somatic Therapies for Depression

Advocates of the biological model approach the treatment of unipolar depression, particularly when it is severe, in two ways. The first is to treat the patient with drugs like the tricyclics and the MAO inhibitors. The second approach is to administer electroconvulsive shock.

DRUG TREATMENT.   Tricyclic antidepressants, you will recall, block the reuptake of norepinephrine. As a result, less NE is absorbed, more NE is available, and the patient becomes less depressed. In the United States, the brand name of the most popular tricyclics are Tofranil (imipramine), Elavil (amitriptyline), and Sinequan (doxepin). On the average, between 63 and 75 percent of depressed patients given tricyclics show significant clinical improvement (Beck, 1973). Further, maintaining a patient who is susceptible to recurrent depressions on tricyclics between attacks reduces the probability of recurrence (Gelenberg and Klerman, 1978).

The MAO inhibitors prevent the breakdown of norepinephrine by inhibiting the enzyme MAO. With more NE available, the patient becomes less depressed. But MAO inhibitors are now prescribed much less often than tricyclic antidepressants, largely because the MAO inhibitors can have lethal side effects. When combined with cheese, alcohol, pickled herring, narcotics, or high blood-pressure-reducing drugs, MAO inhibitors can be fatal. Most studies show MAO inhibitors to be superior to placebos in alleviating depression, however, and if tricyclics fail, the MAO inhibitors should be tried.

ELECTROCONVULSIVE SHOCK (ECT).   Electroconvulsive shock is, to the layman, the scariest of the antidepressant treatments. In the two decades following ECT's discovery as a psychotherapeutic treatment in 1938, enthusiasm was high, and it was promiscuously prescribed for a very broad range of disorders. The treatment, particularly in its less refined forms, can have very serious side effects, however, and it has come to be regarded by the general public as "barbaric" and "punitive." But strong evidence exists that ECT, when given to severely depressed unipolar depressive patients, is a highly effective antidepressant therapy. Modern techniques have greatly reduced the common and severe side effects of yesteryear (Fink, 1979).

Typically, ECT is administered by a medical team consisting of a psychiatrist, anesthesiologist, and a nurse. Metal electrodes are taped to either side of the patient's forehead, and the patient is anesthetized. The patient is given drugs to induce muscular relaxation in order to prevent the breaking of bones during the convulsion. A high current is then passed through the brain for approximately a half second. This is followed by convulsions that last for almost one minute. As the anesthetic wears off, the patient wakens and will not remember the period of treatment. Within twenty minutes, the patient is functioning reasonably well and has little, if any, physical discomfort. A course of ECT usually consists of a half dozen treatments, one every other day (Schuyler, 1974).

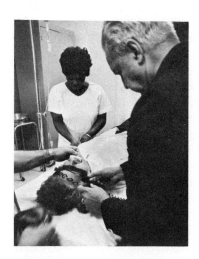

Metal electrodes are being taped to the patient's forehead before electroconvulsive shock therapy is administered to him. (Photograph by Paul Fusco/ Magnum)

Electroconvulsive shock is today often administered unilaterally, that is, to only half of the brain. Producing the convulsion on the side of the brain that does not contain the speech centers (in the nondominant hemisphere, see Chapter 19) greatly reduces the possibility of the side effect of impaired speech following ECT. Unilateral ECT is an effective antidepressant, but it probably is not as effective as bilateral ECT (Scovern and Killman, 1980; Abrams, Taylor, Faber, Ts'o, Williams, and Almy, 1983).

How ECT works to break up depression is unclear. It probably increases available norepinephrine and other biogenic amines, but it is such a gross technique—shocking the entire brain—and has so many other effects, including memory loss and motivational changes, that isolation of the effective ingredient in ECT is quite difficult.

THE PSYCHODYNAMIC MODEL OF DEPRESSION

Psychodynamic theorists have stressed three causes of depression: anger turned against the self, excessive dependence on others for self-esteem, and helplessness at achieving one's goals.

Anger Turned upon the Self

The first contributions of the psychodynamic model to the understanding of depression came from the early psychoanalysts. Karl Abraham (1911) and Sigmund Freud (1917) in his classic paper, "Mourning and Melancholia," both stressed the importance of anger turned inward upon the self in producing depression.

On the surface, depressed individuals often seem drained of anger, and this leads to the suspicion that their anger may be bound up inside them. For Freud, the main clue to their inner state came from the difference between normal bereavement (mourning) and depression (melancholia). The normal individual and the depressive have two strikingly different reactions to the loss of a person they love. For the mourner, the world now seems empty, but his self-esteem is not threatened. The mourner will survive the loss. In contrast, according to Freud, the depressive will begin to feel a powerful sense of worthlessness and self-blame. He will feel rotten and guilty; he will accuse himself of being a failure. This self-reproach is usually moral, grossly unjustified, and most remarkable, publicly and shamelessly declared. It provides the clue that anger turned against the self is actively motivated and generates the low self-esteem of depression.

On the surface, depressed individuals may seem drained of anger, but their anger may be bound up inside them. (Copyright by Harry Bleyenberg/Freelance Photographer's Guild)

How could it come about that some individuals react to loss or rejection by turning their fury against themselves? For Freud, such a motivation for self-punishment follows from events in the depressive's childhood. During childhood, the future depressive forms an intense love that is undermined by disappointment with the other person. The depressive feels rage at having been disappointed. The libidinal energy underlying love is freed, but it does not become attached to any other person. Instead, the ego identifies with or "incorporates" the lost person, and the released libido attaches to this part of the ego. The rage originally felt for the person now is directed against the self.

Subsequent losses and rejection reactivate the primal loss and cause the depressive's rage to be turned again toward the original traitorous person, who has now been fused with the depressive's own ego. Such turning of anger in upon the self is the crucial step in producing the symptoms of low self-esteem, public accusation, the need for punishment, and in the most extreme cases, suicide. Depression ends either when the rage has spent itself or when the new loss is devalued—ends, that is, until a new loss starts the depressive sequence yet again.

The incorporation of a lost love object and anger turned inward upon the self producing depression is well illustrated by the following case:

> Debby was a nineteen-year-old who was hospitalized because of strong suicidal impulses. During her hospitalization, she made a number of unsuccessful suicide attempts, and in addition, she engaged in a bizarre form of self-mutilation: clawing terribly at a particular spot on her left arm. These actions and impulses frightened her because she experienced them as originating outside of herself. On the other hand, however, she saw them as justified because she wanted to atone for her own worthlessness and promiscuity.
>
> Debby's depression seemed to be closely related to her feelings about her mother, who had died a few years earlier under compromising circumstances; she had been murdered by a soldier with whom she had been spending the night. The body was so badly battered that it was identified only by a large distinctive birthmark on the left arm.
>
> After her mother's death, Debby felt more warmth toward her mother than ever before. She became her mother's staunchest defender. When her mother was accused of ruining the family's reputation, Debby maintained that her mother had been badly misunderstood and ill treated by the family, and that this had caused her to carry on with other men. At the same time, however, Debby began to drop her former friends and to take up new friendships with people who had "bad reputations." She began to think of herself as a "bad person." As if to satisfy her new self-image, she began for the first time to behave promiscuously.
>
> Debby's promiscuity seemed to result from identification with her mother, for this new part of herself provided the perfect target for the rage that her mother's death provoked. Debby's genuine feelings were mixed: both love and anger. We do not easily condemn the dead in our society, so instead Debby vented her anger by hating the part of herself that had become her mother. This was expressed most concretely through her self-mutilation. The specific part of her arm that she scratched so terribly was the exact location of her mother's birthmark. By mutilating herself, she was simultaneously able to *identify* with her mother by creating an ugly disfigurement on her left arm and to express her anger toward her mother.
>
> Once Debby began to acknowledge her feelings of anger toward her mother consciously during therapy, her depression began to lift. The crisis and resolution came violently, when Debby smashed every pane of glass in a door with her fist. During this experience she believed she was hitting not a door but an image of her mother. The conscious acknowledgment of this rage removed the need for indirect and symbolic expression, and Debby's feelings of worthlessness and self-hatred began to disappear. (Adapted from Fancher, 1973.)

The Depressive Personality

Psychodynamic theorists since Freud have emphasized a personality style that may make individuals especially vulnerable to depression: the depressive depends excessively on others for his self-esteem. The depressive desperately needs to be showered with love and admiration. He goes through the world in a state of perpetual greediness for love, and when his need for love is not satisfied, his self-esteem plummets. When he is disappointed he has difficulty tolerating frustration, and even trivial losses upset his self-regard and result in immediate and frantic efforts to relieve discomfort. So depressives are seen as love addicts, who have become exquisitely skilled at producing demonstrations of love from others and who insist on a constant flow of love. Beyond receiving such love, however, the depressive cares little for the actual personality of the person he loves (Rado, 1928; Fenichel, 1945; Arieti and Bemporad, 1978).

Helplessness at Achieving One's Goals

The third major strand in psychodynamic theorizing about depression comes from the psychoanalyst Edward Bibring's (1953) claim that depression results when the ego feels helpless before its aspirations. Perceived helplessness at achieving the ego's high goals produces loss of self-esteem, the central feature in depression. The depression-prone individual has extremely high standards, and this increases his vulnerability to feeling helpless in the face of his goals. The combination of strongly held goals to be worthy, to be strong, and to be good, along with the ego's acute awareness of its helplessness and incapacity to live up to these goals, is for Bibring the mechanism of all depression.

Psychodynamic Therapy for Depression

In general, psychodynamic theory emphasizes the long-term predisposition to depression, rather than the losses that happen to set it off in the short-term. Psychodynamic therapies similarly are directed toward long-term change, rather than short-term alleviation of depression. Several therapeutic strategies follow from the three strands of psychodynamic theorizing about depression. First, psychodynamic therapists inclined toward the anger-turned-inward theory of depression will (as in Debby's case) attempt to make the patient conscious of his misdirected anger and the early conflicts that produced it. Learning to come to terms with the anger that loss and rejection produce and to direct it toward more appropriate objects should prevent and relieve depression. Second, psychodynamic therapists who deal with the depressive's strong dependence on others for self-esteem will attempt to get the patient to discover and then resolve the conflicts that make him perpetually greedy for love and esteem from others. Such a patient must learn that true self-esteem comes only from within. And third, therapists who work within Bibring's helplessness approach try to end the patient's depression by getting him to again perceive his goals as being within reach, to modify his goals so that they can now be realized, or to give up these goals altogether.

BEHAVIORAL MODELS OF DEPRESSION

The behavioral models of depression concentrate on the most obvious behavioral symptom of depression: the reduction in active behavior, which we called the ***motivational deficit.*** They approach the question of depression by asking why the depressed person does so little, and what the contingencies of

Depressed individuals fail to stay in effective contact with the rewards of their environment. This may either be because pleasant events do not occur to them very much, or because they actively withdraw from encounters with positive reinforcers. (Photograph by Arthur Tress)

reinforcement are that cause depressed patients to be passive. All of the behavioral models explain the reduction in active responding as a deficiency in operant behavior and claim that therapies which increase operant behavior will reverse depression.

How do operant theorists explain the reduction in active behavior in depression? Psychologist Peter Lewinsohn suggests that these behaviors have been extinguished by a low rate of response-contingent positive reinforcement; that is, depressed individuals cannot cause good events to happen to them at a rate that is frequent enough to motivate active behavior. The patient who sits day after day immobile in the lounge and believes that there is no point in being active fits the operant analysis of depression well. Lewinsohn emphasizes that the cause of depression is not simply too few pleasant events but also a lack of control over reinforcement. Passively experiencing rewards will not be enough to counteract depression, rather these events must be brought about by the individual's own actions.

Lewinsohn and his colleagues developed a pleasant events scale and found that depressed patients do engage in fewer pleasant events, finding these events less enjoyable than nondepressed patients (Lewinsohn, 1974, 1977; MacPhillany and Lewinsohn, 1974). One major reason for this is that depressives often lack social skills. An individual who complains, is passive, withdrawn, and who does not become vigorously engaged with other people, will not get much social reinforcement. Compounding the disadvantages of lack of social skills, the depressive symptoms themselves will repel others. Individuals who display depressive symptoms are less desired as companions than those who do not. Depressive behaviors may be initially maintained by the solicitous concern they produce in others, but eventually these depressive symptoms will drive others away and result in an ultimate, substantial loss of social reinforcement (Coyne, 1976). Misery may love company, but company does not love misery.

Psychologist Charles Ferster views the reduction in instrumental behaviors as the main symptom of depression. Depressed individuals fail to stay in effective contact with the rewards of their environment and fail to avoid its aversive aspects. Ferster points to several environmental conditions that would reduce instrumental behavior, for example, living by too lean a schedule of reinforcement. Some people organize their lives in a way in which too much work is required to gain too infrequent reinforcement. Students, professors, and housewives, by the nature of their jobs, may be victims of such lean schedules.

Behavior Therapy for Depression

Behavioral theories of depression see the reduced frequency of operant behavior and the low rate of rewards as the key symptoms of depression. Because of this, behavior therapies are designed to obtain rewards.

Here is a case in which Peter Lewinsohn raised the frequency of rewards for a woman suffering depression in a marriage in which her reward schedule was leaner than her husband's:

Mary K. was an attractive, twenty-four-year-old female who was referred to a psychologist because she had been depressed for several months. She had been married to Bill for three years, and both had been employed as teachers since their graduation from college. During the preceding spring, however, Mary had resigned from her job—"because the pressure was too much," and she had obtained employment as a retail clerk. Bill had begun taking graduate courses and was preparing for a new teaching position. The therapist went into the K.'s home and observed their conversations closely. A striking regularity revealed itself: much more time was spent discussing topics of interest to him than to her. In addition, she "dispensed" a great number of positive reactions to his conversation, but he "dispensed" few positive reactions to her remarks. Therapy then centered around teaching the couple to spend more time on topics of interest to Mary and to increase the amount of positive reaction from Bill. Once this was achieved, Mary became less depressed and the K.'s reported that things were definitely better between them. They agreed that most of their problems had lain in the interactions between them and that they had now been able to break the pattern. (Adapted from Lewinsohn and Shaw, 1969.)

A variety of other behavior therapies are also directed toward increasing social reinforcers for the depressed individual. Behavior therapists recognize that one of the most impoverished aspects of the depressive's life is his inability to bring about the love, affection, admiration, and esteem of others by his own actions. Social skills training and assertiveness training are two techniques used to increase the personal effectiveness of depressed individuals. With these techniques, the patients explore the social consequences of their actions, behavioral goals are established, and social reinforcement is used to increase active and assertive behaviors, and to extinguish depressive behavior (Lewinsohn, Weinstein, and Shaw, 1968; Lewinsohn, Weinstein, and Alper, 1970; Liberman, 1970; Liberman and Raskin, 1971; Seligman, Klein, and Miller, 1976).

Graded task assignment is another technique used to raise the activity level of depressed individuals and bring them into contact with more rewards. The logic of graded task assignments is to increase the depressive's actions by reinforcing her for taking one small step at a time, rather than allowing her to become discouraged at the prospect of too overwhelming a task. For example, shy people may become depressed. They are often afraid of speaking in front of others. To treat such a person, the therapist will first assign a very simple task to perform, such as reading a paragraph aloud. When she completes this, she will go on to a more difficult task, reading a paragraph and interpreting it in her own words. The culmination of such a hierarchy is giving an extemporaneous speech on a topic of her own choosing. A substantially lighter mood follows successful completion of graded task assignments (Burgess, 1968; Beck et al., 1974; Seligman, Klein, and Miller, 1976).

COGNITIVE MODELS OF DEPRESSION

The two cognitive models of depression view particular thoughts as the crucial cause of depressive symptoms. The first, developed by Aaron T. Beck, derives mainly from extensive therapeutic experience with depressed patients, and it views depression as caused by negative thoughts about the self, about ongoing experience, and about the future. The second, developed by Martin E.P. Seligman, derives mainly from experiments with dogs, rats, and mildly depressed people, and it views depression as caused by the expectation of future helplessness. A depressed person expects bad events to occur and believes that there is nothing he can do to prevent them from occurring.

Aaron T. Beck has devised cognitive treatments for depression.

Beck's Cognitive Theory of Depression

Aaron T. Beck (along with Albert Ellis) founded a new type of therapy, called cognitive therapy, which we reviewed in Chapter 6. For Beck, two mechanisms, the **cognitive triad** and **errors in logic,** produce depression.

THE COGNITIVE TRIAD. The cognitive triad consists of negative thoughts about the self, about ongoing experience, and about the future. The negative thoughts about the self consist of the depressive's belief that he is defective, worthless, and inadequate. The symptom of low self-esteem derives from his belief that he is defective. When he has unpleasant experiences, he attributes them to personal unworthiness. Since he believes he is defective, he believes that he will never attain happiness.

The depressive's negative thoughts about experience consist in his interpretation that what happens to him is bad. He misinterprets neutral interaction with people around him as meaning defeat. He misinterprets small obstacles as impassable barriers. Even when there are more plausible positive views of his experience, he is drawn to the most negative possible interpretation of what has happened to him. Finally, the depressive's negative view of the future is one of hopelessness. When he thinks of the future, he believes that the negative things that are happening to him now will continue unabated because of his personal defects. The following case illustrates how a depressive person may negatively interpret her experiences:

> Stella, a thirty-six-year-old depressed woman, had withdrawn from the tennis games she had previously enjoyed. Instead, her daily behavior pattern consisted of "sleeping and trying to do the housework I've neglected." Stella firmly believed that she was unable to engage in activities as "strenuous" as tennis and that she had become so poor at tennis that no one would ever want to play with her. Her husband arranged for a private tennis lesson in an attempt to help his wife overcome her depression. She reluctantly attended the lesson and appeared to be "a different person" in the eyes of her husband. She stroked the ball well and was agile in following instructions. Despite her good performance during the lesson, Stella concluded that her skills had "deteriorated" beyond the point at which lessons would do any good. She misinterpreted her husband's positive response to her lesson as an indication of how bad her game had become because in her view, "He thinks I'm so hopeless that the only time I can hit the ball is when I'm taking a lesson." She rejected the obvious reason for her husband's enthusiasm in favor of an explanation derived from her negative image of herself. She also stated that she didn't enjoy the tennis session because she wasn't "deserving" of any recreation time. (Adapted from Beck et al., 1979.)

Stella's depression exemplifies the negative triad: (1) She believed that her tennis abilities had deteriorated (negative view of self), (2) she misinterpreted her husband's praise as indication of how poor her game was (negative view of experience), and (3) she believed that no one would ever want to play with her again (negative view of the future). Her motivational and cognitive symptoms stemmed from her negative cognitive triad. Her passivity (giving up tennis for sleeping and housework) resulted from her hopelessness about her abilities. Her cognitive symptoms were the direct expressions of her negative views of herself, her experience, and her future. Beck also claims that the other two classes of depressive symptoms—emotional and physical—result from the depressive's belief that he is doomed to failure.

ERRORS IN LOGIC. Systematic errors in logic are Beck's second mechanism of depression. According to Beck, the depressive makes five different logical errors in thinking, and each of these darkens his experiences: arbitrary inference, selective abstraction, overgeneralization, magnification and minimization, and personalization.

Arbitrary inference refers to drawing a conclusion when there is little or no evidence to support it. For example, an intern became discouraged when she received an announcement which said that in the future all patients worked on by interns would be reexamined by residents. She thought, incorrectly, "The chief doesn't have any faith in my work." *Selective abstraction* consists of focusing on one insignificant detail while ignoring the more important features of a situation. In one case, an employer praised an employee at length about his secretarial work. Midway through the conversation, the boss suggested that he need not make extra carbon copies of her letters anymore. The employee's selective abstraction was, "The boss is dissatisfied with my work." In spite of all the good things said, only this was remembered.

Overgeneralization refers to drawing global conclusions about worth, ability, or performance on the basis of a single fact. Consider a man who fails to fix a leaky faucet in his house. Most husbands would call a plumber and then forget it. But the depressive will overgeneralize and may go so far as to believe that he is a poor husband. *Magnification and minimization* are gross errors of evaluation, in which small bad events are magnified and large good events are minimized. The inability to find the right color shirt is considered a disaster, but a large raise and praise for his good work are considered trivial. And lastly, *personalization* refers to incorrectly taking responsibility for bad events in the world. A neighbor slips and falls on her own icy walk, but the depressed next-door neighbor blames himself unremittingly for not having alerted her to her icy walk and for not insisting that she shovel it.

Cognitive Therapy

Beck's cognitive theory of depression considers that depression is caused by negative thoughts of self, ongoing experience, and future, and by errors in logic. Cognitive therapy for depression attempts to counter these cognitions (Beck, 1967; Beck, Rush, Shaw, and Emery, 1979). Its aim is to identify and correct the distorted thinking and dysfunctional assumptions underlying depression (Rehm, 1977; Beck et al., 1979). In addition, the patient is taught to conquer problems and master situations that he previously believed were insuperable. Cognitive therapy differs from most other forms of psychotherapy. In contrast to the psychoanalyst, the cognitive therapist is continually active in order to guide the patient into reorganizing his thinking and his actions (see Box 13-3). The cognitive therapist talks a lot and is directive. She argues with the patient. She persuades; she cajoles; she leads. Beck claims that nondirective classical psychoanalytic techniques, such as free association, cause depressives to "dissolve in the morass of their negative thinking." Cognitive therapy also contrasts with psychoanalysis by being centered in the present. Childhood problems are rarely discussed, rather the major focus is the patient's current thoughts and feelings.

Cognitive therapy uses such behavioral therapy techniques as activity raising, graded task assignment, and assertiveness training against depressive symptoms. But in cognitive therapy, these techniques for changing behavioral symptoms are just tools for changing thoughts and assumptions that are seen as the underlying causes of depressed behavior. So, for example, the cognitive therapist believes that teaching a depressive to behave assertively works, only insofar as it changes what the depressive believes about his own abilities and his future.

There are five specific cognitive therapy techniques: detecting automatic thoughts, reality testing automatic thoughts, training in reattribution, searching for alternatives, and changing depressogenic assumptions.

DETECTION OF AUTOMATIC THOUGHTS.   Beck argues that there are discrete, negative sentences that depressed patients say to themselves quickly and habitually. These automatic thoughts maintain depression. Cognitive therapy helps patients to identify such automatic thoughts. Here is a case in which the patient had been unaware of her automatic thoughts:

A mother of three found that her depression was at its worst from seven to nine in the morning when she prepared breakfast for her children. She was unable to explain this until she was taught to record her thoughts in writing as they occurred. "As a result, she discovered she consistently compared herself with her mother, whom she remembered as irritable and argumentative in the morning. When her children misbehaved or made unreasonable requests, the patient often thought, 'Don't get angry, or they'll resent you,' with the result that she typically ignored them. With increasing frequency, however, she 'exploded' at the children and then thought, 'I'm worse than my mother ever was. I'm not fit to care for my children. They'd be better off if I were dead.' " (Beck et al., 1979)

REALITY TESTING AUTOMATIC THOUGHTS. Once the patient has learned to identify such thoughts, the cognitive therapist engages in a dialogue with the patient in which evidence for and against the thoughts is scrutinized. This is not an attempt to induce spurious optimism, rather to encourage the patient to use the reasonable standards of self-evaluation that nondepressed people use. The mother who thought she was unfit would be encouraged to remember that her children were flourishing in school, partly as a result of her tutoring them. Similarly a young student despondent over the belief that she would not get into a particular college was taught to criticize her automatic negative thoughts.

THERAPIST: Why do you think you won't be able to get into the university of your choice?
PATIENT: Because my grades were really not so hot.
THERAPIST: Well, what was your grade average?
PATIENT: Well, pretty good up until the last semester in high school.
THERAPIST: What was your grade average in general?
PATIENT: A's and B's.
THERAPIST: Well, how many of each?
PATIENT: Well, I guess almost all of my grades were A's, but I got terrible grades in my last semester.
THERAPIST: What were your grades then?
PATIENT: I got two A's and two B's.
THERAPIST: So your grade average would seem to me to come to almost all A's, why don't you think you'll be able to get into the university?
PATIENT: Because of competition being so tough.
THERAPIST: Have you found out what the average grades are for admission to the college?
PATIENT: Well, somebody told me that a B +average should suffice.
THERAPIST: Isn't your average better than that?
PATIENT: I guess so.
(Beck et al., 1979)

By learning to scrutinize and criticize her automatic thoughts and marshaling evidence against them, the patient undermines her negative automatic thoughts, and they wane.

REATTRIBUTION TRAINING. Depressed patients tend to blame themselves for bad events for which they are not, in fact, responsible. To counteract such irrational blame, the therapist and the patient review the events, applying the standards of nondepressed individuals in order to come up with an assignment of blame. The point here is not to absolve the patient of blame, but rather to let him see that there may be other factors besides his own incompetence that contribute to a bad event.

> A fifty-one-year-old bank manager in a state of deep depression believed he was ineffective in his job. His therapy session proceeded as follows:
>
> PATIENT: I can't tell you how much of a mess I've made of things. I made another major error in judgment which should cost me my job.
> THERAPIST: Tell me what the error in judgment was.
> PATIENT: I approved a loan which fell through completely. I made a very poor decision.
> THERAPIST: Can you recall the specifics about the decision?
> PATIENT: Yes. I remember it looked good on paper, good collateral, good credit rating, but I should have known that there was going to be a problem.
> THERAPIST: Did you have all the pertinent information at the time of your decision?
> PATIENT: Not at the time, but I sure found out six weeks later. I'm paid to make profitable decisions, not to give the bank's money away.
> THERAPIST: I understand your position. But I'd like to review the information which you had at the time your decision was required, not six weeks after the decision had been made.
>
> When the patient and the therapist reviewed this information, they concluded that the patient had made his judgment on sound banking principles. He recalled that he had even made an intensive check into the client's financial background, which he had forgotten (Beck et al., 1979).

Such reattribution training enables patients to find sources of blame other than themselves, and it thereby raises their low self-esteem.

THE SEARCH FOR ALTERNATIVES.   A fourth technique of cognitive therapy attacks the patient's closed system in which all problems are seen as unsolvable. Alternative solutions to the problems are explored and a course of action set.

> A twenty-two-year-old graduate student had been given a C on his paper by his English professor and was convinced that he was "a reject." The therapist offered alternative interpretations for the C, other than this being proof that "he couldn't make it in school." Each alternative was rated by the patient.
> The rating simply consisted of proportions of 100 percent that would represent the degree of "believability" of each explanation. The listing in decreasing order of believability went as follows:
>
> 1. "I'm a reject who doesn't have any ability in English." 95%
> 2. "The grade was not very different from that of other students." 3%
> 3. "The professor provided the comments to help with future essays and therefore thinks I have some ability." 2%
>
> Fortunately, the therapist convinced the patient to get some more information before he withdrew from the course. He encouraged the patient to call his professor from his office. On the telephone, the patient found out that (1) the average class grade was a C, and (2) the professor thought that although the style of the essay was "wanting," the content was "promising." The professor suggested that they have a further discussion to explain his criticisms. As a result of this new information, the patient became more animated and cheerful. Instead of viewing himself as a "reject," he readily agreed that he required concrete instruction in

writing style. He decided to get some tutoring and to complete the term rather than withdraw from the course. (Adapted from Beck et al., 1979.)

The patient believed that getting a C meant he was incompetent. Alternative explanations were not credible to him and he was prepared to act based on his most catastrophic interpretation of the situation. Once alternatives were furnished and the patient gained realistic information, both the depressed mood and the self-destructive actions of the patient were reversed.

CHANGING DEPRESSOGENIC ASSUMPTIONS.   The final technique of cognitive therapy is the explicit change of depressogenic assumptions (Ellis, 1962). Beck outlines six assumptions that depressed individuals base their life upon, thereby predisposing themselves to sadness, despair, and disappointment: (1) in order to be happy, I have to be successful in whatever I undertake; (2) to be happy, I must be accepted by all people at all times; (3) if I make a mistake, it means I am inept; (4) I can't live without love; (5) if somebody disagrees with me, it means he doesn't like me; and (6) my value as a person depends on what others think of me. When the patient and therapist identify one of these assumptions, it is vigorously attacked. The validity of the assumption is examined, counterarguments are marshaled, plausible alternative assumptions are presented, and the disastrous consequences of holding the assumptions are exposed.

The Learned Helplessness Model of Depression

The second cognitive model of depression is the **_learned helplessness model._** It is cognitive because it holds that the basic cause of depression is an expectation: the individual expects that bad events will occur to him and that there is nothing he can do to prevent their occurrence. We will discuss the phenomenon and theory of learned helplessness, and then we will discuss the relationship between learned helplessness and depression.

EXPERIMENTAL DISCOVERY OF LEARNED HELPLESSNESS.   Learned helplessness was discovered quite by accident. In the course of experiments on the effects of prior Pavlovian conditioning on later instrumental learning, Steven Maier, Bruce Overmier, and Martin Seligman found that dogs first given Pavlovian conditioning with inescapable shock became profoundly passive later on when they were given escapable shock. In the latter condition, although they had the opportunity to flee the shock, they _did not_ even attempt to escape.

Here is the basic phenomenon: a dog is strapped into a hammock and given between sixty and eighty five-second inescapable shocks. The shocks are moderately painful, but not physically damaging. The shock is uncontrollable: no response the dog makes during this session will affect the shock, since the shock is programmed to go on and off at a particular moment, independently of all responses. Twenty-four hours later, this dog is placed in a two-compartment shuttlebox from which it is possible to escape shock. When shock is turned on, the dog engages in about thirty seconds of frantic activity, but then it lies down during the shock and does not move, not even

Figure 13-3
The effects of matched escapable and inescapable shocks on later escape learning. This figure shows the escape latencies in the shuttle box for three groups of dogs: (a) those given escape training in the shuttle box as naive subjects, (b) those given prior escape training in a different situation, and (c) those given prior inescapable shocks, but matched in duration and temporal distribution to the shocks for the escape-training group (Maier, Seligman, and Solomon, 1969).

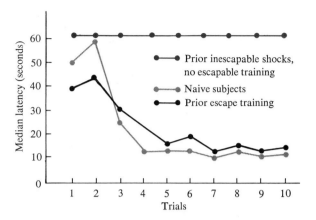

attempting to escape shock. This passivity continues trial after trial. This is the basic motivational deficit in learned helplessness: a failure to initiate voluntary responses to escape following a previous experience with uncontrollable events. This behavior is in marked contrast to the behavior of two other groups of dogs who first received escapable shock or who received no shock when strapped into the hammock. These dogs respond readily later on in the shuttlebox, jumping back and forth across the barrier, and learning to escape and avoid shock. This use of these three groups (the triadic design) tells us it is not shock *per se*, but the uncontrollability of the shock that produces the motivational deficits (see Figure 13-3).

There is another basic deficit of learned helplessness found in dogs, rats, and people. This is the failure to learn that responding can be successful, even once a response is made and it succeeds in controlling the outcome. Dogs and rats, who first had inescapable shock, when later placed in the shuttlebox, often sit for three or four trials and fail to escape shock. On the fifth trial, the animal may stand up, cross the barrier, and successfully terminate shock. Such an animal, surprisingly, often does not catch on: during later trials it will revert to sitting and taking the shock, even though it has made a successful response. This is, again, in marked contrast to other animals that have had prior escapable shock or no shock. Once these other animals make a response that works, they catch on (Overmier and Seligman, 1967; Maier and Seligman, 1976).

LEARNED HELPLESSNESS IN HUMANS. Following the exploration of learned helplessness in animals, it became important for investigators to find out whether or not learned helplessness occurred in normal human beings. It does. In the basic procedure that produces learned helplessness in humans, the triadic design is used with nondepressed volunteers who receive loud noise delivered through earphones. For the first group, the noise is *inescapable;* it is preprogrammed to go on and off independently of what they do. The second group can *escape* noise by pressing a series of buttons in front of them. The third group receives *no noise*. Then all three groups are taken to a human shuttlebox, and noise goes on. If they move their hand from one side of the shuttlebox to the other, the noise goes off. The results parallel those in animals. Individuals who have received inescapable noise sit there passively and fail to escape. Those other groups who first learned to escape noise by button pressing or had no noise at all, escape noise readily in the shuttlebox (Hiroto, 1974).

The deficits produced by learned helplessness in humans are quite general. Experience with inescapable noise produces deficits at later noise escape, deficits in cognitive tasks such as the solution of anagrams, deficits in seeing patterns in anagrams, and lowered expectancy change following success and failure in skilled tasks. The inducing events for helplessness in man need not be aversive. Not only do inescapable noise and shock produce the phenomenon, but also unsolvable cognitive problems produce it.

Learned helplessness theory argues that the basic cause of all the deficits observed in helpless animals and humans after uncontrollable events occur is the expectation of future noncontingency between responding and outcomes. This expectation that future responding will be futile causes the two helplessness deficits: (1) it produces deficits in responding by undermining the motivation to respond, and (2) it produces later difficulty in seeing that outcomes are contingent upon responding when they are. The three-group design is the basic evidence for this hypothesis. Recall that just the experience of shock, noise, or problems in themselves does not produce the motivational and cognitive deficits, only *uncontrollable* shock, noise, and problems produce these deficits. This strongly suggests that both animals and humans learn during uncontrollable events that their responding is futile and come to expect this in future situations.

ATTRIBUTIONS IN HUMAN HELPLESSNESS. When a human being experiences inescapable noise or unsolvable problems and perceives that his responding is ineffective, he goes on to ask an important question: What causes my present helplessness? The causal attribution that a person makes is a crucial determinant of when and where expectancies for future failure will recur. There are three attributional dimensions that govern when and where future helplessness deficits will be displayed (Abramson, Seligman, and Teasdale, 1978).

The first dimension is the ***internal-external dimension.*** Consider an individual who has received unsolvable problems in an experiment. When he discovers that responding is ineffective, he can either decide that he is stupid but the problem is solvable, or that the problems are rigged to be unsolvable and he is not stupid. The first attribution for his failure is internal (stupidity) and the second is external (unsolvable problem). Evidence suggests that when individuals fail at important tasks and make internal attributions for their failure, passivity appears and self-esteem drops markedly. When individuals make external attributions for failure, passivity ensues but self-esteem stays high (Abramson, 1978).

In addition to deciding whether or not the cause of failure is internal or external, an individual who has failed also scans the dimension of ***stability***: "Is the cause of my failure something permanent or transient?" An individual who has failed may decide that the cause of the failure is stable and that it will persist into the future. Examples of such stable factors are stupidity (which is internal as well as stable), or the difficulty of the task (which is stable but external). In contrast, an individual may decide that the cause of his failure is unstable. An individual who has failed an exam can believe that the cause was his bad night's sleep the night before, an unstable cause that is

If an individual believes that her failure is stable and will persist into the future, long-lasting feelings of helplessness and depression may result. (© Joel Gordon 1981)

internal. Alternatively, he might decide that he failed because it was an unlucky day, an unstable cause that is external. The attributional theory of helplessness postulates that when the cause of failure is attributed to a stable factor, the helplessness deficits will persist in time. Conversely, if the individual believes that the cause of his failure is unstable, he will not necessarily fail again when he encounters the task months hence. According to the attributional model of learned helplessness, stable attributions lead to permanent deficits, and unstable attributions to transient deficits.

The third and final dimension is **global-specific**. When an individual finds that he has failed, he must ask himself whether or not the cause of his failure is global—a factor that will produce failure in a wide variety of circumstances—or specific—a factor that will produce failure only in similar circumstances. For example, an individual who has failed to solve a laboratory problem may decide that he is unskilled at solving laboratory problems and probably unskilled at other tasks as well. In this instance, being unskilled is global and the expectation of futility will recur in a wide variety of other situations. It is also a stable and internal factor. Alternatively, he might decide that these particular laboratory problems are too hard. The difficulty of laboratory problems is a specific factor, since it will only produce the expectation that future responding will be ineffective in other laboratory problems and not in real life. This factor, aside from being specific, is stable and external. The attributional model of helplessness holds that when individuals make global attributions for their failure, helplessness deficits will occur in a wide variety of situations. When individuals believe that specific factors cause their failures, the expectation of response ineffectiveness will be narrow, and only a narrow band of situations will produce helplessness deficits.

Parallels between Depression and Learned Helplessness

We have now examined the basic learned helplessness phenomena in animals and humans and the theory behind it. Learned helplessness has been suggested as a model for depression. Table 13-1 outlines the similarity in symptoms, cause, cure, prevention, and predisposition between learned helplessness in the laboratory and unipolar depression as it occurs in real life.

SYMPTOMS.   The failure to escape noise and to solve problems after experience with uncontrollable events is the basic *passivity deficit* of learned helplessness. This passivity seems similar to the motivational deficits of depression. Failure to initiate responses by depressed individuals has been systematically demonstrated in the laboratory: depressed students and patients fail to escape noise and fail to solve anagrams. The more depressed they are, the more severe is this deficit (Miller and Seligman, 1975, 1976; Price, Tryon, and Raps, 1978).

Nondepressed individuals given inescapable noise or unsolvable problems show the *cognitive deficit* of learned helplessness: they have difficulty learning that responding is successful, even when it is. Depressed individuals show exactly the same deficit. Nondepressed human beings made helpless fail to see patterns in anagrams and fail to change expectancy for future

Table 13-1 SIMILARITY OF LEARNED HELPLESSNESS AND DEPRESSION

	Learned Helplessness	*Depression*
Symptoms	Passivity	Passivity
	Cognitive deficits	Negative cognitive triad
	Self-esteem deficits	Low self-esteem
	Sadness, hostility, anxiety	Sadness, hostility, anxiety
	Loss of appetite	Loss of appetite
	Loss of aggression	Loss of aggression
	Norepinephrine depletion	NE depletion
Cause	Learned belief that responding is independent of important outcomes (plus attributions to internal, global, and stable factors)	Generalized belief that responding will be ineffective
Therapy	Change belief in response futility to belief in response effectiveness	Cognitive and behavioral antidepressnt therapy
	ECT, MAO-I, Tricyclics	ECT, MAO-I, Tricyclics
	REM deprivation	REM deprivation
	Time	Time
Prevention	Immunization	Invulnerability factors
Predisposition	Insidious attributional style	Insidious attributional style

success when they succeed and fail in skill tasks. Depressed students and patients show these same deficits in the laboratory (Miller and Seligman, 1975, 1976; Abramson, Garber, Edwards, and Seligman, 1978). These results suggest that the cognitive deficit both in learned helplessness and depression may be produced by the expectation that future responding will be ineffective, and this expectation seems central to the negative beliefs about self, ongoing experience, and about the future, which cognitive therapists like Beck postulate as the central cause of depression.

When individuals are made helpless by inescapable noise and attribute their failure to their own shortcomings as opposed to external causes, not only are the motivational and cognitive deficits of helplessness and depression observed, but *self-esteem* drops as well. In contrast, when helpless subjects are led to make external attributions and blame the task difficulty for their failure, the motivational and cognitive deficits are observed but self-esteem deficits are not. This parallels the low self-esteem that occurs in depressives, particularly among individuals who blame themselves for their troubles (Abramson, 1978).

Parallel *mood changes* occur both in learned helplessness and depression. When nondepressed subjects are made helpless by inescapable noise or unsolvable problems, they become sadder, more hostile, and more anxious. These reports parallel the emotional changes in depression: more sadness, anxiety, and perhaps more hostility.

In the laboratory, rats who receive inescapable shock eat less food, lose more weight, aggress less against other rats, and lose out in competition for food with rats who had received either escapable shock or no shock. This *loss of appetite* and *loss of aggression* produced by helplessness in the laboratory parallels the somatic symptoms of depressives: they lose weight, eat less, their social desires and status drop, and they become less aggressive.

Finally, learned helplessness in the rat is accompanied by *norepinephrine depletion.* In an exciting series of studies over the last decade, Jay Weiss at Rockefeller University has demonstrated that the brains of rats who have received inescapable shock have less available norepinephrine than the brains of animals who receive no shock or escapable shock. Weiss argues that it is the norepinephrine depletion and not the expectation of response-outcome independence that causes learned helplessness. While the evidence is not yet in on whether it is the norepinephrine depletion, the expectancies of response-outcome independence, or both that are fundamental in learned helplessness, it is important that norepinephrine depletion is probably a correlate of depression in humans (Weiss, Glazer, and Pohoresky, 1976).

In summary, there are several parallel symptoms in laboratory-created learned helplessness and depression as found in nature. In both conditions, the four basic symptoms of depression are displayed: motivational deficits, thought deficits, mood changes, and physical deficits. Since these four deficits were created in the laboratory by a known factor—by imposing the expectation that future responses and important outcomes will be independent—could it be that when we observe the same four symptoms in nature and call the condition depression, that the same cause—a belief in the futility of responding—is at work?

CAUSE. The learned helplessness hypothesis says that depressive deficits, which parallel the learned helplessness deficits, are produced when an individual expects that bad events may occur and that they will be independent of his responding. When this is attributed to internal factors, self-esteem will drop; to stable factors, the depression will be long-lived; and to global factors, the depression will be general. Recent evidence confirms this. This attributional style has been found in depressed students, children, and patients. Depressed patients, moreover, believe that the important goals in their life are less under their control than do other psychiatric patients (Seligman, et al., 1979; Eidelson, 1977; Raps and Seligman, 1980). Most important, individuals who have this attributional style but are not depressed, become depressed when they later encounter bad events (Peterson and Seligman, 1984).

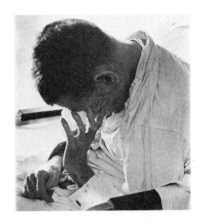

Depressed patients have a particular attributional style. They tend to believe that bad events are caused by internal factors (it's me), by stable factors (it's going to last forever), and by global factors (it's going to undermine everything I do). (Copyright Bill Strode 1980/ Woodfin Camp)

THERAPY. Since the cause of learned helplessness and depression is hypothesized to be the expectation that responding will be ineffective in controlling future events, the basic therapeutic theme should be to change this belief to one in which the individual believes that responding will be effective and anticipated bad events will be avoided. The attributional theory of learned helplessness suggests some basic strategies for doing this. So, for example, learned helplessness theory suggests that therapies such as teaching social skills and assertiveness training should be antidepressive because they teach the individual that he can control affection and the esteem of other people by his own actions. Further tactics such as criticizing automatic thoughts (it's not that I'm an unfit mother, rather I'm grouchy at 7 A.M.) help alleviate depression because they change attributions for failure from internal, stable, and global (unfit mother) to external, unstable, and specific (7 A.M.). Notice how similar these stategies are to the techniques of cognitive and behavioral therapies that we have just reviewed.

In addition to cognitive and behavior therapy parallels, there are *somatic therapy* parallels as well. Four kinds of somatic therapy appear to break up learned helplessness in animals: electroconvulsive shock, MAO inhibitors, tricyclics, and dream deprivation (Dorworth, 1971; Porsolt, et al., 1978; Brett, Burling, and Pavlik, 1981). These are the four somatic therapies that also can break up unipolar depression. In summary, there is reason to believe that the somatic, the cognitive, and the behavioral therapies that reverse learned helplessness also reverse depression.

PREVENTION AND PREDISPOSITION.   Learned helplessness in animals is prevented by prior experience with mastery and immunization. If an animal first controls important events, such as shock and food, then later helplessness never occurs. In effect, it is prevented. Such immunization seems to be lifelong: rats who learn to escape shock as weanlings do not become helpless when as adults they are given inescapable shock. Conversely, lifelong vulnerability to helplessness is produced by early experience with inescapable shock: rats who receive inescapable shock as weanlings become helpless adults (Hannum, Rosellini, and Seligman, 1976). This parallels the data on the prevention of and vulnerability to depression. Individuals whose mother dies before the child is eleven years old are more vulnerable to depression than those whose mother does not. There are, however, invulnerability factors that prevent depression from occurring in such individuals: a job, an intimate relationship with a spouse or lover, not having life burdened with child care, and religious belief (Brown and Harris, 1978). These invulnerability factors may all increase the expectation of future control, and vitiate the expectations of future helplessness.

The final parallel in the predisposition to helplessness and depression is that depressed individuals have an insidious attributional style: when they fail, they tend to attribute their failure to internal, global, and stable factors; but when they succeed, they attribute their success to external, unstable, and specific factors (Seligman, Abramson, Semmel, and von Baeyer, 1979). This is a style that maximizes the expectation that responding will be ineffective in the future. The helplessness model suggests that it is this attributional style that predisposes an individual to depression, and recent evidence confirms this.

Two groups of equally nondepressed students with the opposite attributional styles for failure—one internal, stable, and global, the other external, unstable, and specific—were followed for one semester. Those students with the insidious attributional style became more depressed when confronted with later failure (i.e., disappointing mid-term grades) than those students with the opposite attributional style. This suggests that it is a catastrophizing attributional style that is common in depression—it's me, it's going to last forever, and it's going to affect everything I do— that predisposes an individual to depression and that the opposite attributional style may prevent depression when bad events occur (Peterson and Seligman, 1984).

Problems of the Cognitive Model of Depression

The cognitive model of depression has three main problems. First, it is vague on what kind of depression is modeled (Depue and Monroe, 1978). It is probably not an especially good model of the subclasses of unipolar depression that are "biological" and "endogenous." Biological depressions may be better treated by somatic therapy than cognitive-behavioral therapies, although this has yet to be tested. Second, cognitive theory is weak in accounting for the physical symptoms of depression; these seem better explained by the biological model. Similarly, although the cognitive model does not predict that somatic therapy would be effective, the effective somatic therapies do succeed in breaking up learned helplessness in animals, as well as depression in humans.

Finally, experimental controversy still rages over many of the major points of the learned helplessness model of depression. Some critics doubt whether learned helplessness in animals is produced by an expectation, believing it to be either learned inactivity or norepinephrine depletion (Glazer and Weiss, 1976; Weiss, Glazer, and Pohoresky, 1976, Anisman, 1978). Others have argued that the learned helplessness deficits seen in human beings do not follow closely from the theory (Buchwald, Coyne, and Cole, 1978; Costello, 1978). There also has been difficulty in replicating some of the basic human phenomena (McNitt and Thornton, 1978; Willis and Blaney, 1978). Further, the learned helplessness model has been tested more often in mildly depressed students than it has been tested in clinically depressed patients. It is still controversial whether the relationship between mild depression and severe depression is continuous or discontinuous (Abramson, Garber, Edwards, and Seligman, 1978; O'Leary, Donovan, Krueger, and Cysewski, 1978; Price, Tryon, and Raps, 1978; Smolen, 1978).

INTEGRATION OF THEORIES AND THERAPIES FOR UNIPOLAR DEPRESSION

No one theory of depression—not the biological, not the psychodynamic, not the behavioral, and not the cognitive—explain all the phenomena of depression. But each of them seems to have a piece of the truth and most important of all, the theories are not, by and large, incompatible. Depression is, in fact, a disorder that occurs on at least four levels. There are clear thought deficits—hopelessness and worthlessness being the most prominent; there are clear behavioral deficits—passivity being the most prominent; there are clear biological deficits—the somatic symptoms and their biogenic amine correlates; and there may well be psychodynamic predispositions—the dependent and helpless personality style. Cognitive, behavioral, biological, and psychodynamic factors all may play a role in accounting for the predisposition, the symptoms, the causal mediation, and in producing success in therapy (Akiskal and McKinney, 1973, 1975).

Predisposition

Predisposition to become depressed and invulnerability from depression may have determinants at all levels of analysis. Biological evidence suggests that individuals who are predisposed to alterations in functional level of biogenic amines may be more vulnerable to depression. At the psychodynamic level, individuals who are heavily dependent on other people and who set such high standards that they frequently find themselves helpless before these standards may also be more vulnerable. At the cognitive and behavioral levels, individuals who have had early experience with loss and who have developed an attributional style in which loss is construed as internal, global, and stable may be more vulnerable to depression.

Precipitating Incidents

Cognitive theory explains precipitating incidents well: the expectation of loss or threat of loss seems to set off most depressions, at least those in which precipitants can be identified. In addition, biogenic amine changes, as postulated by the biomedical model, may explain why depression begins when no obvious loss has occurred.

Symptoms

The symptoms of depression can be described at the cognitive, behavioral, and biological levels of analysis. Thought symptoms, motivational symptoms, mood symptoms, and physical symptoms all make up depression. The duration and generality of these symptoms may be governed by the attributions an individual makes about loss, with those losses that stem from internal, stable, and global causes producing the most sweeping and long-lasting symptoms.

Mediation

There seem to be two likely candidates for the internal state that immediately sets off depression. The first is at the cognitive level and is the expectation of future uncontrollable bad outcomes. The second is at the biological level and may be a depletion of biogenic amines, specifically, norepinephrine. The evidence is not in about which of these causes is primary, but we suspect that neither is the sole cause and that either taken alone will produce many of the symptoms of depression. There is one fact about depression that none of the four theories has yet adequately accounted for; the episodic rather than permanent nature of depression. Any complete theory of causal mediation must tell us not only how depression starts but also why it will, in and of itself, usually stop.

Therapy

All four levels of analysis have contributed insights into therapy for depression. An episode of depression, even severe depression, is no longer cause for despair. A combination of the biological treatments and the cognitive-behavioral treatments of depression can probably alleviate severe depression roughly 90 percent of the time. In addition, to the extent that there is a depressive personality, dependent and inclined to helplessness, psychodynamic therapies may help to prevent the recurrence of depression.

Thus, biological, psychodynamic, behavioral, and cognitive views can all be usefully brought to bear on depression. By taking the best from each, a woven fabric may be created in which the predisposition, the symptoms, the mediation, the precipitating incidents, and the symptoms may be understandable. Most important of all, depression can now be effectively treated.

BIPOLAR DEPRESSION (MANIC-DEPRESSION)

We have now explored the great majority of depressions: 90 to 95 percent of depressions are unipolar and occur without mania. This leaves between 5 and 10 percent of depressions that occur as part of *manic-depression.* These are called *bipolar depressions.*

We classify bipolar depressions in the following way. Given the presence of manic symptoms, an individual is judged to be manic-depressive if he has had one or more depressive episodes in the past. On the other hand, he is diagnosed as having experienced only a *manic episode* if he has never had a depressive episode. Mania itself can occur without depression, although this is very rare. Usually, a depressive episode will occur eventually, once a manic episode has happened. Finally, a chronic form of mania is called *chronic hypomanic disorder* or *hypomanic personality.* This diagnosis is made when an individual has experienced an unbroken two-year-long manic state.

Since the depressive component of manic-depression is highly similar to what we have described for unipolar depression, we need only describe mania here in order to have a clear picture of bipolar depression. Here is what it feels like to be in the manic state of a manic-depressive disorder:

> When I start going into a high, I no longer feel like an ordinary housewife. Instead, I feel organized and accomplished, and I begin to feel I am my most creative self. I can write poetry easily. I can compose melodies without effort. I can paint. My mind feels facile and absorbs everything. I have countless ideas about improving the conditions of mentally retarded children, how a hospital for these children should be run, what they should have around them to keep them happy and calm and unafraid. I see myself as being able to accomplish a great deal for the good of people. I have countless ideas about how the environmental problem could inspire a crusade for the health and betterment of everyone. I feel able to accomplish a great deal for the good of my family and others. I feel pleasure; a sense of euphoria or elation. I want it to last forever. I don't seem to need much sleep. I've lost weight and feel healthy, and I like myself. I've just bought six new dresses, in fact, and they look quite good on me. I feel sexy and men stare at me. Maybe I'll have an affair, or perhaps several. I feel capable of speaking and doing good in politics. I would like to help people with problems similar to mine so they won't feel hopeless. (Fieve, 1975, p. 17)

Symptoms of Mania

The onset of a manic episode usually occurs fairly suddenly, and the euphoric mood, racing thoughts, frenetic acts, and the resulting insomnia stand in marked contrast to the person's usual functioning. Mania presents four sets of symptoms: mood, thought, motivational, and physical symptoms.

Mood or Emotional Symptoms

The mood of an individual in a manic state is euphoric, expansive, and elevated. A highly successful manic artist describes his mood:

> I feel no sense of restriction or censorship whatsoever. I'm afraid of nothing and no one. During this elated state, when no inhibition is present, I feel I can race a

car with my foot on the floorboard, fly a plane when I have never flown a plane before, and speak languages I hardly know. Above all, as an artist, I feel I can write poems and paint paintings that I could never dream of when just my normal self. I don't want others to restrict me during this period of complete and utter freedom. (Fieve, 1975)

Grandiose euphoria is not universal in mania, however. Often the dominant mood is irritability, and this is particularly so when a manic individual is thwarted in his ambitions. Manics, even when high, are peculiarly close to tears, and when frustrated may burst out crying. This is one reason to believe that mania is not wholly the opposite state of depression, but that a strong depressive element coexists with it.

Thought Symptoms

The manic cognitions are appropriate to the mood. They are grandiose. The manic does not believe in limits to his ability, and worse he does not recognize the painful consequences that will ensue when he carries out his plans. A manic who spends $50,000 buying three automobiles in a week does not recognize that he will have a great deal of trouble trying to pay for them over the coming years; a manic who calls the President in the middle of the night to tell him about her latest disarmament proposal does not recognize that this call may bring the police down on her; the manic who enters one sexual affair after another does not realize the permanent damage to his reputation that may ensue.

A manic may have thoughts or ideas racing through his mind faster than he can write them down or say them. This *flight of ideas* easily becomes derailed because the manic is highly distractible. In some extreme cases, the manic has delusional ideas about himself: he may believe that he is a special messenger of God; he may believe that he is an intimate friend of famous political and show business figures. The manic's thinking about other people is black and white: the individuals he knows are either all good or all bad; they are his best friends or his sworn enemies.

Motivational Symptoms

Manic behavior is hyperactive. The manic engages in frenetic activity, be it in his occupation, in political or religious circles, in sexual relationships, or elsewhere. Describing the mania of a woman, one author wrote:

Her friends noticed that she was going out every night, dating many new men, attending church meetings, language classes, and dances, and showing a rather frenetic emotional state. Her seductiveness at the office resulted in her going to bed with two of the available married men, who didn't realize that she was ill. She burst into tears on several occasions without provocation and told risqué jokes that were quite out of character. She became more talkative and restless, stopped eating and didn't seem to need any sleep. She began to talk with religious feeling about being in contact with God and insisted that several things were now necessary to carry out God's wishes. This included giving herself sexually to all who needed her. When she was admitted to the hospital, she asked the resident psychiatrist on call to kiss her. Because he refused to do so, she became suddenly silent. Later, she talked incessantly, accusing the doctor of trying to seduce her and began to talk about how God knew every sexual thought that she or the doctor might have. (Fieve, 1975, pp. 22–23)

The activity of the manic has an intrusive, demanding, and domineering quality to it. Manics sometimes make us uncomfortable because of this. It is difficult to spend much time with an individual who delivers a rapid succession of thoughts and who behaves in a frenetic way almost in disregard of those around him. Other behaviors that commonly occur during mania are compulsive gambling, reckless driving, poor financial investments, and flamboyant dress and makeup.

Physical Symptoms

With all this flurry of activity comes a greatly lessened need for sleep. Such hyposomnia virtually always occurs during mania. After a couple of days of this, exhaustion inevitably sets in and the mania slows down.

COURSE AND CHARACTERISTICS OF MANIC-DEPRESSION

Between .4 and 1.2 percent of the population of the United States will have manic-depression in their lifetime (Weissman and Myers, 1978). Unlike unipolar depression, which affects more women than men, manic-depression affects both sexes equally. The onset of manic-depression is sudden, usually a matter of hours or days, and typically no precipitating event is obvious. The first episode is usually manic, not depressive, and it generally appears between the ages of twenty and thirty. This first attack occurs somewhat earlier than a first attack in unipolar depression. Ninety percent of manic-depressives will have had their first attack before they are fifty years old. Manic-depressive illness tends to recur, and each episode lasts from several days to several months. Over the first ten years of the disorder, the frequency and intensity of the episodes tends to worsen. Surprisingly, however, not many episodes occur twenty years after the initial onset. Both manic and depressive episodes occur in the disorder, but regular cycling (e.g., three months manic, followed by three months depressive, and so on) is rare. The depressive component of manic-depressive illness is similar in kind to that of unipolar depression, but it is often more severe (Angst, Baastrup, Grof, Hippius, Poldinger, and Weiss, 1973; Loranger and Levine, 1978; Depue and Monroe, 1979).

Manic-depressive illness is not a benign, remitting disorder. For some, extreme manic episodes may bring about much hardship. Their hyperactivity and bizarre behavior may be self-defeating. Employers may become annoyed at their behavior, and some manic-depressives may then find themselves without a job. For others, entire careers may be lost. In addition, manic-depressives' social relationships also tend to break down. The manic person is hard to deal with. A much higher percentage of married manic-depressives divorce, than do married unipolar depressives. Alcohol abuse, either in attempted self-medication or due to poor judgment and impulsiveness, is very high in manic-depression. The more severe the mania, the more frequent the alcoholism. In all, between 20 and 50 percent of manic-depressives suffer chronic social and occupational impairment. In most extreme cases, hospitalization is required. And for a few, suicide is a constant threat. The rate of attempted and successful suicides is also higher in bipolar than in unipolar depressions. As many as 15 percent of manic-depressives may end their life by suicide (Brodie and Leff, 1971; Carlson, Kotin, Daven-

Theodore Roosevelt is said to have been a manic-depressive. (*Left:* Collections of the Library of Congress. *Right:* The National Archives)

port, and Adland, 1974; Reich, Davies, and Himmelhoch, 1974; Dunner, Gershom, and Goodwin, 1976).

When the mania is more moderate and the depressions are not too debilitating, however, the manic-depressive's ambition, hyperactivity, talkativeness, and grandiosity may lead to great achievements. This behavior is conducive to success in our society. It is no surprise that many creative people, leaders of industry, entertainment, politics, and religion may have been able to use and control their manic-depression. For example, Abraham Lincoln, Winston Churchill, and Theodore Roosevelt probably all were manic-depressives. They may have benefited from a condition that produces so much distress and even ruin in others.

CAUSE OF MANIC-DEPRESSION

The cause of manic-depressive illness is unknown. On the surface, with its euphoria and hyperactivity, it looks like the opposite state of depression. But as we have seen, feelings of depression are close at hand during the mania. The bipolar individual, when manic, is close to tears; he voices more hopelessness and has more suicidal thoughts than normal individuals. This has led some theorists to believe that mania is a defense against an underlying depression, with a brittle euphoria warding off more fundamental sadness.

Other theorists believe that manic-depression results from homeostatic biological processes that have become ungoverned. When a normal individual becomes depressed, the depression is allegedly ended by switching in an opposite, euphoric state that cancels it out. Conversely, when a normal individual becomes euphoric, this state is kept from spiraling out of bounds by switching in a depressive state that neutralizes the euphoria. A disturbance in the balance of these opposing processes, with the reaction to depression or mania overshooting its mark, may be responsible for the manic-depressive disorder. Investigations of the biochemistry of the switching process from mania to depression may illuminate the biological underpinnings of the disorder in the future (Bunney, Murphy, Goodwin, and Borge, 1972; Solomon and Corbit, 1974).

Individuals may be genetically vulnerable to manic-depressive illness. Manic-depressive individuals are more often found in families in which successive generations have experienced depression or manic-depression. Unipolar depressives are more usually found in families with no history of manic or depressive disorders (Winokur and Clayton, 1976). A disorder can run in families either because it is inherited or because family members share a similar environment. Twin data can help decide between these alternatives (Chapters 3 and 8), since identical twins share all their genes, but fraternal twins share only half their genes. When an identical twin is manic-depressive, the probability that his co-twin will also be manic-depressive is higher than it is for fraternal twins (Allen, 1976). This suggests that the disorder is partially inherited. The mechanism of such genetic transmission and the existence of stressors that set off manic-depression when combined with genetic vulnerability are still matters of speculation and controversy.

TREATMENT

By and large, manic-depressive illness can be successfully contained by lithium salts. Lithium was originally used as a table salt substitute. In 1949, John Cade, an Australian physician, having found that lithium made guinea pigs lethargic, tried it to dampen mania in humans and found that lithium ended severe manic attacks. Since that time, lithium carbonate has been used extensively with manic-depression. Over the last thirty years, lithium has been shown to be an effective treatment both for mania and for the depressive aspects of manic-depression. Approximately 80 percent of manic-depressives will show a full or partial alleviation of symptoms during lithium administration. It is also clear, however, that the other 20 percent of bipolar depressives do not respond (Depue, 1979). Lithium has also been used as a preventative treatment for manic-depression, and repeated dosage with lithium in a vulnerable individual may prevent manic-depressive relapses (Depue, 1979). While lithium can be viewed as a miracle drug for manic-depression, its side effects, particularly its cardiovascular, digestive, and central nervous system effects can be quite serious. Close medical supervision should always accompany the administration of lithium. Both the evidence on the effectiveness of lithium and the evidence on genetic vulnerability suggest that manic-depression is best understood within the framework of the biological model.

SUICIDE

Suicide is the most disastrous consequence of depression, bipolar or unipolar. Depression is the precursor of a vast majority of suicides. Death only rarely results directly from other psychological disorders: the anorexic patient who refuses food; the hallucinating schizophrenic, who believing he is Christ, attempts to walk on water; the heroin addict who administers an overdose. But it is depression that most frequently results in irreversible harm: death by suicide.

Suicide is the second most frequent cause of death among college students. Further, it is on the rise in this age group. The death of a young person, because of all his unfulfilled promise, is a keenly felt tragedy. As a

Depression is the precursor of a vast majority of suicides. Police reach out to grab this suicidal man. (Wide World Photos)

young man before composing his second symphony, Beethoven almost took his own life. What held him back was the thought that he had not yet produced the best that might be inside him.

Suicide is an act that most societies forbid. Many religions regard it as a sin; and it is, astonishingly, a crime in several states. No act leaves such a bitter and lasting legacy among friends and relatives. It leaves in its wake bewilderment, guilt, shame, and stigma that relatives may carry to their own graves.

Suicide is occasionally an act of high rationality. Seneca, the first century Roman stoic, said:

> Living is not good, but living well. The wise man, therefore, lives as well as he should, not as long as he can . . . He will always think of life in terms of quality, not quantity . . . Dying early or late is of no relevance, dying well or ill is. . . Even if it is true that while there is life, there is hope, life is not to be bought at any cost. (Seneca Epistle #70)

More often, however, even though the decision seems rational to the individual who takes his life, he is usually strongly ambivalent about the decision. One vote can tip the balance, as in a declaration of war (see Table 13-2). For example, when a physician canceled an appointment with a pa-

Table 13-2 FABLES AND FACTS ABOUT SUICIDE

Fable	Fact
Individuals who talk about killing themselves do not kill themselves.	Of every ten persons who have killed themselves, eight gave definite warnings of their intentions.
Suicidal individuals have made a clear decision to die.	Most are undecided about living or dying. They often gamble with death, leaving it to others to save them.
Once an individual is suicidal, he is forever suicidal.	Usually individuals who wish to kill themselves are suicidal only for a limited period. Suicidal wishes are often locked to depression, and depression usually dissipates in time.
The suicidal risk is over when improvement occurs following a suicidal crisis.	Most suicides occur while the individual is still depressed, but within about three months after the beginning of "improvement." It is at that time that the individual has better access to weapons and more energy to put his suicidal plans into effect than when he is in the hospital or at the nadir of his depression.
Suicide occurs more often among the rich.	Suicide is equally frequent at all levels of society.
The suicidal act is the act of a sick person.	While the suicidal person is almost always extremely unhappy, he is not necessarily "mentally ill." Suicide can be a rational act.

SOURCE: Adapted from Schneidman, 1976.

tient, this last straw in a series of disappointments tipped the balance toward suicidal death.

The ethical quandaries of suicide are immensely difficult. Does an individual have a right to take his own life, not interfered with by others, just as he has a right to dispose, unimpeded, of his own property? (Szasz, 1974).

WHO IS AT RISK FOR SUICIDE?

The list of famous suicides is very long: Marilyn Monroe, Samson, Ernest Hemingway, Cleopatra, Sid Vicious, Virginia Woolf, Jack London, Modigliani, Adolph Hitler, Jim Jones and his People's Temple victims, to name a very few. At the very least, 25,000 people end their lives by suicide every year in the United States. There are also estimated to be at least ten times as many suicide attempts as successful suicides, and it has been estimated that in the United States today, five million people are alive who have attempted suicide.

The estimate of 25,000 suicidal deaths per year in the United States is highly conservative, and the real number is probably between 50,000 and 100,000. There are several reasons for the underreporting of suicide. Such stigma attaches to the act that the influential can often get coroners to label a relative's death as an accident rather than a suicide , and there is often family pressure on physicians not to report deaths as suicides. Many one-car accidents on clear roads are suicides, but they are usually labeled accidental death. Those individuals who flirt with death by high-risk hobbies or occupations, by adopting lethal habits such as heavy smoking, drinking, and drugs, as well as the physically ill who terminate their own life by discontinuing medication are not counted as suicidal deaths. In subcultures in which suicide is seen as feminine and passive, but murder is seen as active and masculine, "victim-induced homicide"—for example, an adolescent provoking a policeman to kill him—is not counted as a suicide (Schyler, 1974; Diggory, 1976; Linden and Breed, 1976).

Jim Jones and his People's Temple followers committed mass suicide in Guyana by drinking poisoned fruit juice after Congressman Leo Ryan was killed. (United Press International photo)

Depression and Suicide

Depressed individuals are the single group most at risk for suicide. While suicide occasionally occurs in the absence of depression and the large majority of depressed people do not commit suicide, depression is a strong predisposing factor to suicide. An estimated 80 percent of suicidal patients are significantly depressed. Depressed patients ultimately commit suicide at a rate that is at least twenty-five times as high as control populations (Pokorny, 1964; Flood and Seager, 1968; Robins and Guze, 1972).

Sex Differences and Suicide

Women make roughly three times as many suicide attempts as men, but men actually succeed in killing themselves three times more often than women. These discrepancies seem to have diminished a bit over the last few years. The greater rate of suicide attempts in women is probably related to the fact that more depression occurs in women, whereas the greater completed suicide rate in men probably has to do with choice of methods:

women tend to choose less lethal means, such as cutting their wrists and overdosing on sleeping pills; whereas men tend to shoot themselves and jump off buildings. The suicide rate for both men and women is higher among individuals who have been divorced and widowed; loneliness as well as a sense of failure in interpersonal affairs surely contributes to this statistic. Men who kill themselves tend to be motivated by failure at work, and women who kill themselves tend to be motivated by failure at love (Mendels, 1970; Linden and Breed, 1976; Schneidman, 1976). As one female patient who tried to find surcease in suicide after being rejected by her lover said, "There's no sense in living. There's nothing here for me. I need love and I don't have it anymore. I can't be happy without love—only miserable. It will just be the same misery, day in and day out. It's senseless to go on" (Beck, 1976).

Cultural Differences and Suicide

Race, religion, and nationality contribute somewhat to vulnerability to suicide. The suicide rate of young black and white men is approximately the same (Hendin, 1969; Linden and Breed, 1976), but black women and older black men probably kill themselves less often than whites (Swanson and Breed, 1976). There is some evidence that American Indians may have a higher suicide rate than the rest of the population (Frederick, 1978). Religion, at least in the United States, does not offer any protection against suicide in spite of varyingly strong strictures against it. Also, the rate of suicide is roughly the same whether the individual is nonreligious, or Catholic, Protestant, or Jewish.

Suicide occurs in all cultures, even primitive ones, but it seems to be more common in industrialized countries. At the present time, the countries of central Europe seem to have the highest suicide rate, with Hungary, Austria, and Czechoslovakia ranking respectively first, third, and fourth. Ireland and Egypt have very low suicide rates, perhaps because suicide is considered a mortal sin in these cultures. West Berlin has the highest suicide rate in the world, more than twice that of West Germany as a whole. The United States has, on the world scale, an average suicide rate. Sweden has a middling high rate of suicide. Some have blamed this on the lack of incentive provided by its social welfare system, but its suicide rate has remained the same since about 1910, before the introduction of social welfare (Schneidman, 1976).

Age and Suicide

One is more likely to commit suicide when one is older. In children, suicide is rare, with probably fewer than 200 suicides committed in a year in the United States by children who are under the age of fourteen (see Figure 13-4). Discussing her wish to die, Michelle, age nine, talks with Joaquim Puig-Antich, a leading expert on childhood depression:

> JOAQUIM PUIG-ANTICH: Do you feel you should be punished?
> MICHELLE: Yes.
> JPA: Why?
> M: I don't know.
> JPA: Have you ever had the thought that you might want to hurt yourself?

A depressed child may consider committing suicide. (© Joel Gordon 1983)

Figure 13-4
The ''will'' of a suicidal 8-year-old girl (name blocked out) was found by her parents, who subsequently arranged to have the child receive psychiatric care. (Source: McKnew, Cytryn, and Yahraes, 1983)

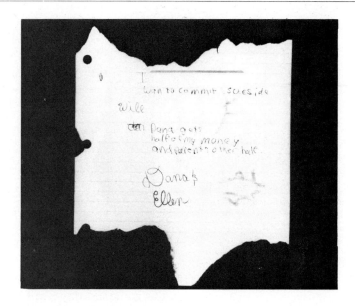

M: Yes.
JPA: How would you hurt yourself?
M: By drinking a lot of alcohol, or jumping off the balcony.
JPA: Have you ever tried to jump?
M: I once stood on the edge of the terrace and put one leg over the railing, but my mother caught me.
JPA: Did you really want to jump?
M: Yes.
JPA: What would have happened if you had jumped?
M: I would have killed myself.
JPA: Did you want to get killed?
M: Uh-huh.
JPA: Why?
M: Because I don't like the life I live.
JPA: What kind of life do you live?
M: A sad and miserable life.
(Jerome, 1979)

Suicide rate rises dramatically through middle age and into old age. Increasing depression, loneliness, moving to a strange setting, loss of a meaningful role in family and society, and loss of people they love all surely contribute to the high rate of suicide among old people. In cultures and communities in which the aged are revered and remain important in the life of the family, suicide is infrequent.

Within two years of the death of her beloved husband with whom she had spent fifty joyous years, Mrs. K. committed suicide. "Alan," she told her son a few days before, "I wasn't made to sleep alone." Percy Bridgman, Nobel Prize winner in physics and famous American positivist, shot himself at age eighty. He had cancer and was in great pain. The day before he killed himself, he mailed the index for his collected works to the Harvard University Press. He had repeatedly asked for euthanasia and had been, of course, refused. His suicide note was published in the *Bulletin of the Atomic Scientists*

Novelist Arthur Koestler with his wife Cynthia were found dead at their London home after an apparent suicide pact. The terminally ill Koestler preferred to die rather than live in great pain. (United Press International photo)

(1962): "It is indecent for Society to make a man do this thing himself. Probably this is the last day I will be able to do it myself. PWB" (Schneidman, 1976).

THE MOTIVATION FOR SUICIDE

In the first major modern study of suicide, the French sociologist Émile Durkheim (1858–1917) distinguished three motivations for suicide, all of them intimately related to the way an individual sees his place in society. He called these motives anomic, egoistic, and altruistic. *Anomic suicide* is precipitated by a shattering break in an individual's relationship to his society: the loss of a job, economic depression, even sudden wealth. *Egoistic suicide* occurs when the individual has too few ties to his fellow humans. Societal demands, principal among them the demand to live, do not reach the egoistic individual. Finally, *altruistic suicide* is required by the society. The individual takes his own life in order to benefit his community. Hara-kiri is an altruistic suicide. The Buddhist monks who burned themselves to death to protest the injustices of the Vietnam War are recent reminders of individuals who committed altruistic suicide.

Buddhist monks in Vietnam burned themselves to death in order to protest the injustices of their government. (United Press International photo)

Modern thinkers see two more fundamental motivations for suicide: *surcease* and *manipulation.* Those who wish surcease have simply given up. Their emotional distress is intolerable, and they see no alternative solution. In death, they see an end to their problems, sleep, or nothingness. Fifty-six percent of the suicide attempts observed in a systematic study were classified as individuals trying to achieve surcease. These suicide attempts involved more depression, more hopelessness, and they tended to be more lethal than the remaining suicide attempts (Beck et al., 1976).

The other motivation for suicide is the wish to manipulate other people by a suicide attempt. Some wish to manipulate the world that remains by dying: to have the final word in an argument, revenge on a rejecting lover, to ruin the life of another person. More commonly in manipulative suicide, the individual intends to remain alive, but by showing the seriousness of his dilemma, he is crying for help from those who are important to him. Trying to prevent a lover from leaving, getting into the hospital and having a temporary respite from problems, and being taken seriously are all manipulative motives for suicide with intent to live.

Thirteen percent of suicide attempts were found to be manipulative; these involved less depression, less hopelessness, and less lethal means than did the surcease attempts (Beck, 1976). Those suicides that are manipulative are clearly cries for help, but it shoud be apparent that all suicides are not cries for help (see Box 13-4). The individual who wishes to escape because life is

---

Box 13-4   SUICIDE NOTES

About one-sixth of those individuals who die by their own hand leave suicide notes. A romantic view would lead us to expect that these final words, like those that are supposed to be uttered on the deathbed, would be masterful summaries of a life that preceded them and of the reasons for dying. Only occasionally are they:

"There should be little sadness, and no searching for who is at fault; for the act and result are not sad, and no one is at fault.

"My only sorrow is for my parents who will not easily be able to accept that this is so much better for me. Please, folks, it's all right, really it is.

"I wanted to be too many things, and greatness besides—it was a hopeless task. I never managed to really love another person—only to make the sounds of it. I never could believe what my society taught me to believe, yet I could never manage to quite find the truth.

"Two-fifteen p.m.—I'm about to will myself to stop my heartbeat and respiration. This is a very mystical experience. I have no fear. That surprises me. I thought I would be terrified. Soon I will know what death is like—how many people out there can say that?"

But much more often the notes are commonplace. Creative, unique, and expansive pieces of writing are rare in suicide notes. The individual is usually constricted, his field of consciousness has narrowed, and he is in despair. This is not a state conducive to creativity.

"Dearest darling I want you to know that you are the only one in my life I love you so much I could not do without you please forgive me I drove myself sick honey please believe me I love you you again and the baby honey don't be mean with me please I've lived 50 years since I met you, I love you—I love you. Dearest darling I love you, I love you. Please don't discriminate me darling I know that I will die don't be mean with me please I love you more than you will ever know. Darling please and honey, Tom, I don't tell Tom why his daddy said goodbye honey. Can't stand it anymore. Darling I love you. Darling I love you."

A good number of suicide notes merely contain instructions and directions:

"Dear Mary. I am writing you, as our divorce is not final, and will not be til next month, so the way things stand now you are still my wife, which makes you entitled to the things which belong to me, and I want you to have them. Don't let anyone take them from you as they are yours. Please see a lawyer and get them as soon as you can. I am listing some of the things, they are: a blue davenport and chair, a Magic Chef Stove, a large mattress, and electrolux cleaner, a 9 x 12 rug, reddish flower design and pad. All the things listed above are almost new. Then there is my 30-30 rifle, books, typewriter, tools and a hand contract for a house in Chicago, a savings account in Boston, Massachusetts. Your husband."

And some are simple and starkly practical. A workman before hanging himself in an abandoned house chalked his suicide note on the wall outside.

"Sorry about this. There's a corpse in here. Inform police."

Source. Adapted from Schneidman, 1976.

not worth living is not crying out for help, but for an end to his troubles. The remaining 31 percent of suicide attempts combine surcease and manipulative motivation. Here the individual is not at all sure whether he wishes to live or die, whether he wishes surcease or a change in the world. In this undecided group, the more hopeless and the more depressed the individual is, the stronger are the surcease reasons for the suicide attempt (Beck, Rush, Shaw, and Emery, 1979).

PREVENTION OF SUICIDE AND TREATMENT OF THE SUICIDAL PERSON

In the initial therapeutic interview with a depressed individual, suicide is the overriding question in the back of the therapist's mind. If clear suicidal intent and hopelessness are pervading themes, crisis intervention, close observation, and hospitalization will probably ensue. If they are not, therapy will proceed at a somewhat more leisurely pace, directed toward careful understanding of the other depressive problems.

In the late 1960s, a network of more than 300 suicide prevention centers was established in the United States to deal with suicidal crises. In addition, hospitals and outpatient units set up hot-lines to deal with the crises of acutely suicidal individuals. It was believed that if someone was available for the suicidal individual to talk to, the suicide could be prevented.

In terms of prevention of suicide, once the suicidal person makes contact with a telephone hot-line volunteer, a psychologist, a psychiatrist, a family physician, a pastor, or emergency room doctor, evaluation of the suicidal risk takes first priority. Does the individual have a clear plan? Does he have access to the weapon? Does he have a past history of suicidal acts? Does he live alone? Once suicidal risk in a crisis is assessed, a treatment decision must be hastily made: home visit, hospitalization, medication, the police, or outpatient psychotherapy. In some cases, merely holding the person on the phone may be appropriate action. Long-term follow-up and after-care must then occur.

Success of the suicide prevention centers is uncertain. Whereas the suicide rate seems to have dropped in Britain in the areas in which centers exist, no differences in suicide rate have yet been reported in the United States in cities with or without prevention centers (Weiner, 1969, Schuyler, 1974; Fox, 1976).

In addition to suicide prevention, psychological intervention in the lives of the surviving relatives is also important. As we have seen, the survivors are themselves more vulnerable to later depression and suicide. They are faced with shame, guilt, bewilderment, and stigma. This is a group that has been neglected and that might benefit greatly from systematic care.

SUMMARY

1. The *affective disorders* consist of three types: unipolar depression, bipolar depression, and mania.

2. *Unipolar depression* consists of depressive symptoms only and involves no symptoms of mania. It is by far the most common of the depressive disorders.

3. *Bipolar depression* occurs in individuals who have both periods of depression and periods of mania as well.

4. *Mania* consists of four sets of symptoms: euphoric mood, grandiose thoughts, overactivity, and lack of sleep.

5. There are four basic symptoms of unipolar depression: emotional symptoms, largely sadness; motivational symptoms, largely passivity; cognitive symptoms, largely hopelessness and pessimism; and bodily symptoms, including loss of weight and loss of appetite. Untreated, these symptoms will usually dissipate within about three months.

6. Women are more at risk than men for depression. Depression becomes slightly more common as an individual grows older.

7. Four theories—biological, psychodynamic, behavioral, and cognitive—have all shed light on unipolar depression.

8. Biological models have generated three effective therapies; *tricyclic antidepressant drugs, MAO inhibitors,* and *electroconvulsive therapy* (ECT). The biomedical school holds that depression is due to depletions in certain central nervous system neurotransmitters, most usually *norepinephrine.*

9. Psychodynamic theories concentrate on the personality that predisposes one to depression. These theories hold that depression stems from *anger turned upon the self,* and that individuals who are predisposed to depression are overdependent on other people for their self-esteem.

10. The behavioral model holds that depression is caused by the reduction of active responding and by insufficient amounts of *response-contingent positive reinforcement.* Behavioral models have generated therapies that teach depressives how to control the important goals in their lives.

11. Cognitive models concentrate on particular ways of thinking and how these cause and sustain depression. There are two prominent cognitive models: the view of Aaron Beck, which holds that depression stems from a *negative cognitive triad,* and the *learned helplessness model* of depression.

12. Unipolar depression can now be effectively treated: nine out of ten people who suffer a severe unipolar depressive episode can be markedly helped either by drugs, ECT, or by cognitive therapy.

13. Bipolar depression, or *manic-depressive illness,* is the most crippling of the affective disorders. It results in ruined marriages, irreparable damage to reputation, and not uncommonly suicide. Eighty percent of bipolar depressions can now be greatly helped by *lithium.* This disorder is best viewed within the biomedical model.

14. *Suicide* is the most disastrous consequence of bipolar and unipolar depression. It is the second most frequent cause of death among college students. Women make more suicide attempts than men, but men actually succeed in killing themselves more often than women. There are two fundamental motivations for suicide: *surcease,* or desire to end it all, and *manipulation,* or desire to change the world or other individuals by a suicide attempt.

Part VI

SOCIAL AND INTERPERSONAL DISORDERS

Sexual Behavior, Dysfunction, and Disorder

Notions of what is sexually normal and what is sexually abnormal have changed with time and place. What one society has labeled as deviant may well be labeled as normal by another. Although in the past, premarital sex, masturbation, oral sex, and homosexuality were all condemned by our Puritan society, today most people consider these sexual behaviors to be quite normal.

In the past, what constituted "normal sexual order" and "normal sexual function" was clearer than it is today. Ordinary sexual practices among men and women in our society seem to be more diverse today than they were in the past. And so, our concept of what sexual order is has broadened and our concept of what sexual disorder and dysfunction are has narrowed. We now believe there are three basic classes of sexual problems: sexual dysfunctions, the paraphilias, and transsexuality.

In this chapter, we will discuss the scientific study of sexual behavior. We will explain what has been learned about normal sexual functioning—the sexual response of arousal, excitement, and orgasm. Then we will discuss sexual problems. Despite changing attitudes and more permissiveness in our society, we still find many instances of sexual problems, both in the form of sexual dysfunction and sexual disorder. The sexual dysfunctions are problems of low desire, low arousal, or orgasm. The sexual disorders are problems of sexual object choice and sexual identity. Disordered sexual object choice manifests itself through sexual arousal to the unusual or bizarre, such as fetishes for panties, masochism, and exhibitionism. These are the paraphilias. Disorders of sexual identity can be seen in transsexuality, in which a man believes he is a woman trapped in the body of a man, or a woman believes she is a man trapped in the body of a woman. Both the sexual dysfunctions and the sexual disorders grossly impair affectionate, erotic relations between human beings, and as such, are considered abnormal.*

* There have been long-standing controversies about what to call these sexual behaviors. Some prefer to call them "variations"; others label them "deviations," or even "diseases." We will adopt the term "dysfunction" to refer to the first class of problems, the sexual inabilities. We will adopt the term "disorder" to refer to the second and third problems, the paraphilias and transsexuality.

We begin our discussion of human sexuality with material on the scientific study of sexual behavior. The data from these studies have helped us to learn about normal sexual function and normal sexual order. This in turn has enabled us, by contrast, to identify sexual dysfunction and sexual disorder.

THE SCIENTIFIC STUDY OF SEXUAL BEHAVIOR

The first major contribution to the scientific understanding of human sexual behavior came from the work of Alfred Kinsey and his colleagues (Kinsey et al., 1948, 1953). Acting in the face of societal taboos, they interviewed over 20,000 adult men and women, asking them explicit questions about their sexual practices. They gathered data on sexual intercourse in marriage, homosexuality, masturbation, premarital intercourse, oral sex, and other sexual activities. They looked at patterns of sex at different times of life, and broke these down by gender, education, religion, and other sociological factors. For example, Kinsey found that masturbation to orgasm was almost universal among men, becoming less frequent with age. He found that women, on the other hand, masturbate less often than men, but that as they become older, they masturbate more frequently than when they were younger.

Kinsey gave us a glimpse into American sexuality. In 1951, Clellan Ford, an anthropologist, and Frank Beach, a psychologist, broadened our knowledge by comparing the sexual behavior of some 190 cultures spread across the world. In addition, they compared cross-cultural human sexual practices to sexual behavior in animals, looking for what was universal and what was specific to a particular culture or species. So, for example, foreplay before intercourse occurs in all cultures and all mammals, but what kind— kissing, fondling, oral caresses—varies from culture to culture and species to species (Ford and Beach, 1951).

More recent data on sexual practices and attitudes among Americans have come from a variety of surveys, similar to those pioneered by Kinsey. Among these are Morton Hunt's (1974) study of 2,000 sexually liberal and sexually active American men and women, and Paul Rozin's (1978, 1981) surveys of sexual practices of several hundred University of Pennsylvania introductory psychology students over several years in the early 1970s.

Although all of these studies have told us much about what people do and how people feel about what they do, they all share some basic problems. First, consider the nature of the subject. One's sexual behavior is usually a very private matter. Many individuals are unwilling to participate in studies of sexual attitudes and behavior. Because of this, we only know about those who are willing to talk openly. In effect, therefore, these studies were not based on a random sample. Second, the results of these surveys are based on self-reporting about a topic that for some people is private, but for others, offers an opportunity for boasting. Many individuals will be candid about their sexuality; others may distort, suppress, or even lie outright about their sexual behavior. As a result, we only know from these surveys what a selected sample of people are willing to say about their sexual practices and attitudes.

Dr. Alfred Kinsey interviewing a woman about her sexual practices. (Photograph by Wallace Kirkland. *Life Magazine* © 1948 Time Inc.)

William Masters and Virginia Johnson brought the study of sexual behavior into the laboratory. (Photograph by Scott F. Johnson)

While others were collecting data by way of surveys, two researchers, William Masters and Virginia Johnson (1970), were taking a different tack. They brought the study of sexual behavior into the laboratory just as one might study other aspects of behavior. In their work, they observed and recorded at least 15,000 sexual acts. They observed sexual acts under a wide variety of conditions: between married couples, between strangers, between couples with a variety of sexual and interpersonal problems, and under self-stimulation. A rather complete picture of the physiology of human sexual response has emerged from their observations. In addition, Masters and Johnson have spent much of their efforts discovering both the nature of sexual dysfunction and its possible treatment. As was the case with the surveys, however, these data come from a selected group of volunteer subjects who allowed themselves to be watched. We can be quite certain that Masters and Johnson's physiological findings are general to human adults, but we cannot always be certain that either their therapeutic outcomes or the subjective reports are general to the entire population of adult men and women. Even so, the scientific study of sexual behavior has brought us much closer today to understanding the nature of sexual behavior, its physiology, and its frequency than was possible in the past.

SEXUAL FUNCTION

To label an individual's sexual practice as a "dysfunction" implies that we know something about what normal sexual functioning is, or should be. In this section, we will discuss the physiology of the normal human sexual response, and then we will discuss sexual dysfunction—what it is, what causes it, and how it can be treated.

THE PHYSIOLOGY OF THE HUMAN SEXUAL RESPONSE

In both men and women, the sexual response consists of three phases: the first is *erotic arousal,* in which a variety of stimuli—tactile, visual, and more subtle ones such as fantasy—produce arousal. The second phase, ***physical*** *excitement,* consists of penile erection in the male and of vaginal lubrication and swelling in the genital area of the female. The third phase is *orgasm.* We shall review these phases in some detail because sexual dysfunction can disrupt any of them.

In men, erotic arousal results from a wide variety of events. Being touched on the genitals or looking at and touching a sexually responsive partner are probably the most compelling stimuli. In addition, visual stimuli, smells, a seductive voice, and erotic fantasies, among many others, all produce arousal.

The second phase of excitement is intertwined with the first phase of erotic arousal. In the male, it consists of penile erection. Sexual excitement stimulates parasympathetic nerves in the spinal cord, and these nerves control the blood vessels of the penis. These vessels widen dramatically and blood streams in, producing erection. The blood is prevented from leaving by a system of valves in the veins. When these parasympathetic fibers are inhibited, the vessels empty, and rapid loss of erection occurs.

Orgasm in men consists of two stages that follow each other very rapidly —emission and ejaculation. Unlike arousal and erection, orgasm is controlled by the sympathetic nervous system, as opposed to the parasympathetic nervous system. When sufficient rhythmic pressure on the head and shaft of the penis occur, the stage of orgasmic inevitability is reached and orgasm arrives. Orgasm is engineered to deposit sperm deep into the vagina near the head of the uterus, maximizing the possibility of fertilization. Emission occurs when the reproductive organs all contract. This is followed very rapidly by ejaculation, in which powerful muscles at the base of the penis contract vigorously, ejecting sperm from the penis. During ejaculation, these muscles contract by reflex at intervals of 0.8 seconds. This phase of orgasm is accompanied by intense pleasure. After orgasm has occurred, a man unlike a woman, is "refractory," or unresponsive to further sexual stimulation for some interval. This interval varies from a few minutes to a few hours, and it lengthens as the man gets older.

The sexual response of a woman transforms the normally tight and dry vagina into a lubricated, perfectly fitting receptacle for the erect penis. The

Erotic arousal results from touching a sexually responsive partner. (Photograph by Catherine Ursillo/Leo de Wys)

Auguste Rodin's *Eternal Spring.* (Courtesy The Rodin Museum: Gift of Jules E. Mastbaum. Photographed by Philadelphia Museum of Art)

stimuli that produce arousal in women are similar to those that produce arousal in men. Kissing and caressing, visual stimuli, and a whole host of subtle cues are usually effective as sexually arousing stimuli. In our culture, at least, there appear to be some gender differences in what is arousing, with subtle stimuli and gentle touch more initially arousing to women than direct stimulation.

With arousal, the excitement or "lubrication-swelling" phase begins in the woman. When at rest, the vagina is collapsed, pale in color, and rather dry. When arousal occurs, the vagina balloons exactly enough to "glove" an erect penis, regardless of its size. At the same time, the clitoris swells and lubrication occurs on the walls of the vagina, making penile insertion easier. As excitement continues, the walls of the uterus fill with blood, and the uterus enlarges. This engorgement of blood and swelling greatly add to erotic pleasure and set the stage for orgasm.

Orgasm in women consists of a series of reflexive contractions of the muscles surrounding the vagina. These contract rhythmically at 0.8 second intervals against the engorged tissue around the vagina, producing the ecstatic sensation of orgasm. Both the clitoris, a small knob of tissue located forward of the vagina, and the vagina itself play a role: orgasm is triggered by stimulation of the clitoris, and then expressed by contraction of the vagina.

Thus, the sexual response of both men and women is quite similar. Similar stimuli produce erotic arousal in both sexes. Blood flow under the control of the parasympathetic nervous system produces physical excitement, both penile erection and the lubrication and swelling phases of the vagina. Orgasm consists of powerful muscular contractions at 0.8 interval seconds, produced by rhythmic pressure on the head and shaft of the penis in the man and of the clitoris of the woman. These parallels are lovely and deep. Before they were known, it was easy to fall prey to the belief that chasms separated the experience of sex between men and women. To learn that one's partner is probably experiencing the same kind of joys that you are is powerful and binding knowledge.

SEXUAL DYSFUNCTION: THE SEXUAL INABILITIES

In order to function normally, an individual must be capable of sexual desire, sexual arousal, and orgasm. When the mechanism of desire, arousal, or orgasm goes awry, we say an individual suffers a sexual dysfunction. Dysfunction can occur in any or all of these three areas of sexual response: (1) fantasies about and interest in sexual activity may be low or nonexistent, and thus erotic arousal may be dysfunctional; (2) when in an appropriate sexual situation, failure to have or maintain an erection in men and lack of vaginal lubrication and genital swelling in women may occur; (3) orgasm may be disrupted; in women, orgasm may fail to occur altogether; in men, ejaculation may be premature, occurring within the first few seconds of intercourse, or retarded, occurring only after a half hour of intercourse, if at all.

Impairment may occur in only one of these three areas of sexuality, or in all three in the same individual. The impairment may be lifelong or acquired, it may be limited to only one situation or occur in all situations, and it may occur infrequently or all the time. For example, the failure to maintain an erection can develop after years of satisfactory intercourse, or it can occur from the very first attempt at sexual intercourse. It can occur only with one partner or with all women. It can occur only once in a while or it can occur every time the individual tries to have intercourse.

THE IMPAIRMENT OF EROTIC AROUSAL AND EXCITEMENT

Because erotic arousal and physical excitement are so intertwined, we will treat them together. In women, lack of sexual desire and impairment of physical excitement in appropriate situations is called *sexual unresponsiveness* (formerly "frigidity"). Some of the symptoms are subjective: the woman may not have sexual fantasies, she may not enjoy sexual intercourse or stimulation, and she may consider sex an ordeal. Other symptoms are physiological: when she is sexually stimulated, her vagina does not lubricate, her clitoris does not enlarge, her uterus does not swell, and her nipples do not become erect. Frequently, she becomes a spectator rather than losing herself in the erotic act. When she finds herself unstimulated, she begins to worry about her own sexual adequacy and what her partner is thinking about her. She thinks, "He must think I'm frigid." "Is he getting pleasure?" "Will I climax?" She remains outside the act, observing and studying how she and her partner are reacting. Fear of failure, scanning for cues of failure, and presiding as a judge at one's lovemaking can diminish pleasurable sex and worsen the problems of arousal and of orgasm. The woman may be unresponsive in all situations or only in specific ones. For example, if the problem is situational, she may be enraged or nauseated by the sexual advances of her husband, but she may feel instantly aroused and may lubricate when an attractive, unavailable man touches her hand. Such a woman may have problems with orgasm as well, but it is not uncommon for a "sexually unresponsive" woman—whose arousal and excitement are impaired—to have orgasm easily once intercourse takes place.

Women's reaction to this problem varies. Some patiently endure nonexciting sexual intercourse, using their bodies mechanically and hoping that their partner will ejaculate quickly. But this is often a formula for resentment. Watching her husband derive great pleasure from sex over and over, while she feels little pleasure may be frustrating and alienating for the woman. And eventually some women will attempt to avoid sex, pleading illness or deliberately provoking a quarrel before bedtime (Kaplan, 1974).

The partner's reaction to the woman's sexual unresponsiveness also varies. Some men accept it and indeed may expect it, based on a false belief that women don't or aren't supposed to enjoy sex. Other men attribute their mate's lack of arousal to inadequate performance on their part and feel that they are poor lovers. Still others will pressure their wife to perform anyway and this, of course, only makes her more unresponsive. Many other couples seem to have good marriages in spite of this and spend a lifetime together without the woman ever responding to her husband sexually.

In men, the most common dysfunction of arousal and excitement is called *erectile dysfunction* (formerly "impotence"). It is defined as a recurrent inability to have or maintain an erection for intercourse. This condition can be humiliating, frustrating, and devastating since male self-esteem across most cultures involves good sexual performance. When erection fails, feelings of worthlessness and depression often ensue.

Here, as with the other sexual dysfunctions, the man becomes a spectator during sex. He mentally steps back and thinks, "Will I fail to get an erection this time too?" "She probably thinks I'm not really a man." "Is she really getting pleasure or just pretending?" These fears make it even more difficult for him to maintain an erection.

Like sexual unresponsiveness in females, erectile dysfunction in the male can be either primary or secondary, situation specific or global. Men who have had *primary erectile dysfunction* have never been able to achieve or maintain an erection sufficient for intercourse; whereas men who have *secondary erectile dysfunction* have lost this ability. When the dysfunction is *situation specific,* a man may be able to maintain an erection with one partner, but not with another. Some men can become erect during foreplay, but not during intercourse. When the dysfunction is *global,* a man cannot achieve an erection with any partner under any circumstances. It is important and reassuring for a man to know that a single failure in no way implies "erectile dysfunction," which is by definition, recurrent. Virtually every man on one occasion or another—particularly when upset or fatigued—cannot get an erection or keep it long enough for intercourse.

Here is a case of primary impotence that begins, typically, with a particularly sordid circumstance surrounding the man's first attempt at intercourse:

> Sheldon was nineteen when his teammates from the freshman football team dragged him along to visit a prostitute. The prostitute's bedroom was squalid; she seemed to be in her mid-fifties, had an unattractive face and a fat body, and foul-smelling breath. He was to be the last of a group of five friends scheduled to perform with her. Sheldon had never had intercourse before and had been anxious to begin with. His anxiety increased as his teammates returned one by one to describe in detail their heroic successes. When his turn arrived, the other four decided to watch and cheer him on, and Sheldon could not get an erection. His teammates shouted that he should hurry up and the prostitute was obviously impatient. He was pressured beyond any ability to perform and ran out of the room.
>
> After this incident, he avoided all erotic contact with women for five years, fearing that he would fail again. At age twenty-four, when his fiancée pressured him to have sex, he was overwhelmed with fears that he would fail, remembering his humiliating failure with the prostitute. In fact, he failed again. This brought Sheldon into therapy for primary erectile dysfunction. (Adapted from Masters and Johnson, 1970.)

ORGASMIC DYSFUNCTION

Some women and some men do not achieve the third phase of sexual response: orgasm. How easily different women can achieve orgasm lies on a continuum. At one extreme are the rare women who can have an orgasm merely by having an intense erotic fantasy, without any physical stimulation at all. Then there are women who climax merely from intense foreplay, women who have orgasm during intercourse, and women who need long and intense clitoral stimulation in order to climax. At the other extreme are approximately 10 percent of adult women who have never had an orgasm in spite of having been exposed to a reasonable amount of stimulation.

Nonorgasmic women frequently have a strong sexual drive. They may enjoy foreplay, lubricate copiously, and love the sensation of phallic penetration. But as they approach climax, they lose psychologically what they are prepared for physiologically. The woman may become self-conscious; she may stand apart and judge herself. She may ask herself, "I wonder if I'll climax." "This is taking too long; he's getting sick of it." Frustration, resentment, and the persistent erosion of a couple's erotic and affectionate relationship bring nonorgasmic women into therapy (Kaplan, 1974; McCary, 1978).

Failure to have an orgasm may be primary, with orgasm never having occurred, or secondary, with loss of orgasm. It may be situation specific, with orgasm occurring, for example, in masturbation when alone but not in intercourse, or it may be global.

In men, there are two kinds of orgasmic difficulties and they are opposite problems: premature ejaculation and retarded ejaculation.

Premature Ejaculation

Most men have ejaculated occasionally more quickly than their partner would like, but this is not equivalent to premature ejaculation. Premature ejaculation is the recurrent inability to exert any control over ejaculation, such that once sexually aroused, the man reaches orgasm very quickly. This is probably the most common of male sexual problems.

Premature ejaculation can wreak havoc with a couple's sex life. A man who is worried that if he becomes aroused he will ejaculate right away cannot be a sensitive and responsive lover. His partner expects him to be better. Not being so, he becomes more self-conscious, and she commonly feels rejected, sometimes perceiving him as cold and insensitive. Not uncommonly, secondary erectile dysfunction follows untreated premature ejaculation.

Retarded Ejaculation

Retarded ejaculation, which is less common than premature ejaculation, is defined by great difficulty reaching orgasm during sexual intercourse. Frequently, the man may be able to ejaculate easily during masturbation or foreplay, but intercourse may last for an hour or more with no ejaculation. Contrary to myth, the staying power of the retarded ejaculator does not place him in an enviable sexual position. His partner may feel rejected and unskilled, he may feign orgasm, and he may have high anxiety accompanied by self-conscious thoughts like, "She must think something is wrong with me." Secondary erectile dysfunction sometimes follows.

It is dangerous to attach time numbers to both retarded ejaculation and premature ejaculation, saying, for example, that premature ejaculation occurs whenever ejaculation persistently takes less than thirty seconds and retarded ejaculation occurs whenever ejaculation persistently takes more than half an hour. This misses the important point that the definition of the sexual problem, both orgasmic and arousal, is always relative to one's partner's expectations. Many couples are able to work out quite satisfactory erotic relationships even when one partner climaxes very quickly or very slowly, and it would be inappropriate to label these individuals as having a sexual dysfunction.

The Causes of Sexual Dysfunction

Physical Causes

The physical causes of sexual dysfunction probably account for a very minor fraction of the problems. Injuries, physical anomalies of the genitals, hormonal imbalances, neurological disorders, inflammations, drugs and alcohol, and the aging process itself can all interfere with a woman's capacity for sexual arousal (Kaplan, 1974; McCary, 1978).

As for male sexual dysfunctions, perhaps 15 percent are physical, caused by excessive alcohol or drugs, circulatory problems, aging, exhaustion, or anatomical defect. There is a useful way of distinguishing between which men are physically and which men are psychologically unable to get erections. All of us dream approximately 100 minutes a night, and in the male dreaming is almost invariably accompanied by an erection (in the female by vaginal lubrication). We are not certain why this occurs, but it does tell us if a man is physically capable of erection. If a man who is otherwise "impotent" gets erections during dreaming or has an erection upon waking in the morning, the problem is of psychological, not physical, origin.

Psychological Causes

Psychological problems probably cause the great majority of the sexual dysfunctions. There is general clinical agreement that negative emotional states impair sexual responsiveness. Earlier, we spoke of the sensitive interplay of physiological and psychological factors. The physiological part of the sexual response is autonomic and visceral; essentially it is produced by increased blood flow to the genitals under the control of the autonomic nervous system. Certain autonomic responses, sexual arousal among them, are inhibited by negative emotions. If a woman is frightened or angry during sex, visceral responding will be impaired. Similarly if a man is frightened or feeling pressured during sex, there may not be sufficient blood flow to cause erection.

What are the sources of the anxiety and anger that women feel which might cause sexual unresponsiveness? From a psychoanalytic point of view, one cause may be unresolved unconscious conflict: a woman unconsciously hostile toward her husband might express her hostility by withholding her sexual response, just as a consciously hostile woman would.

Psychoanalysts also express a view about male sexual dysfunctions. They claim that erectile dysfunction is a defense against castration anxiety. According to Freud, a boy between the ages of three and five wishes to possess his mother and, in his own mind, becomes a hated rival to his father. He fears that his father will castrate him in retaliation. When this Oedipal conflict is unresolved, erectile dysfunction may later ensue. By failing to have an erection, he wards off the anxiety of castration. That is, he will not commit the act with his "mother" and thereby not be castrated by his "father."

These psychoanalytic formulations have not been tested in the laboratory and indeed are quite difficult to test. But in cases of erectile dysfunction, clinical experience suggests substantial unresolved conflicts over the man's mother and father (Masters and Johnson, 1970; Kaplan, 1974). Alternatively, erectile dysfunction can be understood dynamically not as a defense to ward off anxiety but as a physiological response to anxiety that may be coming from any source. When an individual's defenses fail to prevent anxiety, erection will not occur.

There are other, less complex sources of anxiety and anger, all of which interfere with sexual arousal in men and women. A woman may fear that she will not reach orgasm. A woman may feel helpless or exploited. Some men and women may feel shame and guilt, or they may believe that sex is a sin; they may have grown up in situations where sex was seen as dirty and bad, and they may have trouble ridding themselves of feelings of shame and guilt even in the shelter of marriage. Some women may expect physical pain in intercourse and therefore dread it. Many men fear rejection and become self-conscious, thereby inhibiting an otherwise normal physiological potential. And often there is the fear of pregnancy.

Negative emotions arising in relationships must not be overlooked either. Relationships do not always progress well. People change, sometimes developing different living habits and preferences. Their partner may not change accordingly, and conflict may then ensue, bringing about negative feelings between the couple. Understandably, it is often difficult to discard these feelings when the couple enters the bedroom. In such cases, one or both partners might develop a sexual dysfunction, probably specific in nature.

The behavioral school offers an explanation of the causes of sexual dysfunction based on learning theory. For men, erectile dysfunction may result from an early sexual experience. A particularly traumatic first sexual experience will condition strong fear to sexual encounters. Recall Sheldon's first and formative sexual encounter. Heterosexual activity was the conditioned stimulus (CS), which resulted in a humiliating, public failure to have an erection (US) and an unconditioned response (UR) of ensuing shame and anxiety. Future exposures to the CS of sexual encounters produced the conditioned response (CR) of anxiety, which in turn blocked erection. This formulation fits many of the instances in which there is an early traumatic experience, and it also fits the success of direct sexual therapy with erectile dysfunction. It fails to account for those cases in which no traumatic experience can be discovered, and it also does not account for why certain individuals are more susceptible to sexual traumatic experiences than others. For every individual who undergoes an initial sexual experience that is a failure (such as Sheldon's) and develops erectile dysfunctions, there are many who encounter similar initial failures but do not.

In addition to psychodynamic and behavioral accounts of sexual dysfunctions, the cognitive view suggests other important considerations as well. We saw that for both the orgasmic and the arousal dysfunctions, what an individual thinks can greatly interfere with performance. Men and women with orgasm difficulties become "orgasm watchers." They may say to themselves, "I wonder if I'll climax this time." "This is taking much too long; he must think I'm frigid." Men and women who have arousal dysfunctions may say to themselves, "If I don't get an erection, she'll laugh at me." "I'm not going to get aroused this time either." These thoughts produce anxiety, which in turn blocks the parasympathetic responding that is the basis of the human sexual response. Such thoughts get in the way of abandoning oneself to erotic feelings. Complete therapy for the sexual dysfunctions must deal with problems at four levels: physical, behavioral, psychodynamic, and cognitive, for difficulties at any of these levels can produce human sexual dysfunction.

TREATMENT OF SEXUAL DYSFUNCTIONS

It has been estimated that half of American marriages are flawed by some kind of sexual problem (Lehrman, 1970; Masters and Johnson, 1970). Sexual problems usually occur in the whole context of a relationship between two human beings. When sex goes badly, many other aspects of the relationship may go badly, and vice versa. Sex—often, but not always—mirrors the way two people feel about and act toward each other overall. Sex therapists often find that underneath the sexual problem are more basic problems of a relationship—love, tenderness, respect, honesty—and that when these are overcome, a fuller sexual relationship may follow.

In the last fifteen years, substantial progress has been made in treating those problems of arousal and orgasm which stem from psychological causes. Overall, only about 25 percent of individuals with these problems fail to improve with a brief course of therapy. Let's look closely at one case:

> When they came to therapy, Carol, age twenty-nine, and Ed, age thirty-eight, had been married for three-and-a-half years and had one child. When they were first married, Carol had achieved orgasm almost every time they made love, but now orgasm was rare for her. She was feeling more and more reluctant to have intercourse with Ed. Ed had a strong sex drive and wanted to have intercourse every day. But Carol had made rules about sex, stating what Ed could and could not do.
>
> As time went on, Carol found it more and more difficult to keep her part of the bargain. Carol's headaches, fatigue, and quarrels deterred Ed's effective initiation of lovemaking. When he did make love to her, Carol would complain about his lovemaking technique. This effectively ended the encounter.
>
> When they first sought out sexual therapy, they were having intercourse once every two weeks, but Carol was becoming progressively more reluctant and intercourse was becoming even more of a dreaded ordeal for her. (Adapted from Kaplan, 1974, case 22.)

Masters and Johnson led us out of a period in which sexual dysfunction could not, by and large, be alleviated by therapy. Following their pioneering work on the anatomy and physiology of the human sexual response, they founded "direct sexual therapy" with sexually dysfunctional patients like Ed and Carol.

Direct sexual therapy differed in three important ways from previous sexual therapy. First, it defined the problem differently: sexual problems were not labeled as "neuroses" or "diseases" but rather as "limited dysfunctions." A woman like Carol was not labeled "hysterical," defending against deep intrapsychic conflicts by "freezing" her sexual response, as psychodynamic therapies claimed. Rather, she was said to suffer from "inhibition of arousal." Second, and most dramatic, through direct sexual therapy, the clients explicitly practiced sexual behavior with the systematic guidance of the therapists. A couple like Carol and Ed would first receive education and instruction about their problem, then an authoritative prescription from Masters and Johnson about how to solve it, and most importantly, accompanying sexual practice sessions together. Their third major departure was that people were treated not as individual patients but as couples. In treating individuals, Masters and Johnson had often found that sexual problems do not reside in one individual but in the interaction of the couple. Carol's lack of interest in sex was not only her problem. Her husband's increasing demands, rage, and frustration contributed to her waning interest in sex. By treating the couple together, Ed and Carol's deteriorating sexual interaction could be reversed.

Sensate focus is the major strategy of direct sexual therapy for impaired excitement in females and erectile dysfunction in males. The basic premise of sensate focus is that anxiety occurring during intercourse blocks sexual excitement and pleasure. In the female, anxiety blocks the lubrication and swelling phase; in the male, it blocks erection. The overriding objectives of treatment are to reduce this anxiety and to restore confidence. The immediate goal is to bring about one successful experience with intercourse. This is accomplished, however, in a way in which the demands associated with arousal and orgasm are minimized. Sensate focus has three phases: "pleasuring," genital stimulation, and nondemand intercourse (Masters and Johnson, 1970; Kaplan, 1974). Let us look at the sensate focus treatment for Carol and Ed.

In the "pleasuring" phase, Carol and Ed were instructed not to have sexual intercourse and not to have orgasm during these exercises. Erotic activity was limited to gently touching and caressing each other's body. Carol was instructed to caress Ed first, and then the roles were to be reversed and Ed was to stroke Carol. This was done to permit Carol to concentrate on the sensations later evoked by Ed's caresses without being distracted by guilt over her own selfishness. It also allowed her to relax knowing that intercourse was not going to be demanded of her.

After three sessions of pleasuring, Carol's response was quite dramatic. She felt freed from pressure to have an orgasm and to serve her husband, and she experienced deeply erotic sensations for the first time in her life. Further, she felt that she had taken responsibility for her own pleasure, and she discovered that she was not rejected by her husband when she asserted herself. They then went on to phase two of sensate focus—"genital stimulation." In this phase, light and teasing genital play is added to pleasuring, but the husband is cautioned not to make orgasm-oriented caresses. Orgasm and intercourse are still forbidden. The woman sets the pace of the exercises and directs the husband both verbally and nonverbally, and then the roles are reversed.

The couple's response was also very positive here. Both felt deep pleasure and were aroused and eager to go on to the next step, "nondemand intercourse." In this final phase, after Carol had reached high arousal through pleasuring and genital stimulation, she was instructed to initiate intercourse. Ed and Carol were further instructed that there was to be no pressure for Carol to have an orgasm.

In spite of—or because of—the instruction, Carol had her first orgasm in months. At this point, Ed and Carol were able to work out a mutually arousing and satisfactory style of lovemaking. Carol and Ed's improvement was typical: only about 25 percent of patients fail to improve with sensate focus for female sexual unresponsiveness or for male erectile dysfunction (Masters and Johnson, 1970; Kaplan, 1974; and McCary, 1978).

EVALUATION OF DIRECT SEXUAL THERAPY

Direct sexual therapy seems to be quite effective in alleviating the dysfunctions of arousal and orgasm in both men and women (Marks, 1981; Heiman and LoPiccolo, 1983). In addition to good success with erectile dysfunction and female unresponsiveness, failure to improve occurs only in 2 percent of cases of premature ejaculation, and in 20 percent of the remaining orgasmic disorders. Moreover, systematic desensitization may also be effective in enhancing desire and orgasm, particularly in women with sexual anxiety (Andersen, 1983). Caution is required in two respects, however. First, the Masters and Johnson reports of success are not as well documented as many would like. Masters and Johnson do not report percentages of *successes,* but rather they report percentages of *failures.* So, for example, they report that only 24 percent of females "failed to improve" following sensate focus training for arousal dysfunction. This is not equivalent to a 75 percent *cure* rate. What "failure to improve" means is not well defined. Moreover, the percentage of patients showing only mild improvement, great improvement, or complete cure is not reported. While direct sex therapy techniques are far superior to what preceded them, well-controlled replications with explicit criteria for sampling and for improvement will be needed before they can be considered definitive (Zilbergeld and Evans, 1980).

The second caution is that while the therapeutic techniques seem effective, the reasons for their good effects are not wholly clear. As has often been the case in psychology and in medicine, effective cure often precedes understanding, and this seems to be the case for sexual dysfunctions as well.

We now turn from the sexual dysfunctions, in which arousal and orgasm are inadequate, to those sexual problems in which arousal and orgasm are adequate, but in which they occur to unusual and bizarre objects. These are the sexual disorders.

SEXUAL ORDER AND DISORDER

Sexual order is largely determined by one's biology and by society's attitudes toward sexuality. Sexual disorder is what society considers to be abnormal sexual identity, behavior, and object choices. What is considered normal sexual behavior has undergone sweeping changes as society has changed.

ATTITUDES TOWARD HUMAN SEXUALITY

Attitudes toward sexuality have changed with time. Surveys have found that sexual behavior is by no means restricted to intercourse during marriage (Kinsey et al., 1948, 1953; Hunt, 1974; Rozin, 1978). Sexual behavior in general has increased, in part probably due to the birth control pill, but also due to society's greater permissiveness. Particular sexual practices have become more frequent, mostly as a result of society's attitudes toward these practices. Moreover, a greater variety of sexual behaviors are considered normal today, including masturbation, premarital sex, oral sex, homosexuality, and bisexuality. Society's attitudes also have a profound influence on the frequency of sexual behavior and on kinds of sexual behavior engaged in, or at least on how an individual may feel about his or her behavior. Let us consider a few of these formerly forbidden sexual practices.

C H A P. I.

Of the Heinous Sin of Self-Pollution.

ELf-Pollution is that unnatural Practice, by which Persons of either Sex may defile their own Bodies, without the Assistance of others, whilst yielding to filthy Imaginations, they endeavour to imitate and procure to themselves that Sensation, which God has ordered to attend the carnal Commerce of the two Sexes for the Continuance of our Species.

It is almost impossible to treat of this Subject, so as to be understood by the meanest Capacities, without trespassing at the same time against the Rules of Decency, and making Use of Words and Expressions which Modesty forbids us to utter. But as my great Aim is to promote Virtue and Christian Purity, and to discourage Vice and Uncleanness, without giving Offence to any, I shall chuse rather to be less intelligible to some, and leave several things

B   to

In the past, masturbation was condemned by society. Pictured here is an early tract against "self-pollution," or masturbation. (ONANIA: Or The Heinous Sin of Self-Pollution and Its Frightful Consequences in Both Sexes, . . . By N. Cronch, London [1725?])

Masturbation

Depending on age, subculture, religion, and so on, about 95 percent of males and from 50 to 90 percent of females masturbate, or stimulate their own genitals, to orgasm. Indeed, roughly two-thirds of boys have their first orgasm while masturbating (Kinsey et al., 1948; McCary, 1978). In the 1980s, we accept this data without question. But our attitude toward masturbation is very different from attitudes in years past. This practice was long regarded as a disorder by psychiatrists. At the turn of the century, one might well have found himself hospitalized as a mental patient for frequent masturbation. Various religions have also condemned the practice. Whether these negative attitudes resulted in much less frequent masturbation in years past is not clearly known, but they probably brought about much more anxiety and guilt in those who engaged in the practice or who considered doing so.

Premarital Intercourse

More than 75 percent of college students believe that virginity is unimportant in the person they marry, and more than three-fifths of Americans believe that premarital intercourse is acceptable if the couple is sufficiently involved emotionally (Gallup Poll, 1970; Hunt, 1974; McCary, 1978; Rozin, 1978). Even being cautious about the findings of the surveys, we can see that there is a high frequency of sexual intercourse prior to marriage. But years ago, attitudes were different. Our grandfathers warned our fathers against premarital intercourse, usually for three reasons: (1) there was the possibility of contracting venereal disease (VD)—syphilis or gonorrhea; (2) there was a greater risk of pregnancy, and the possibility of being forced to marry; and (3) many worried that their children would get involved with someone from a different social sphere. But a combination of technology and social opportunity in our culture has caused all three of these barriers to become less formidable, and premarital intercourse has increased. In the 1940s, penicillin was introduced to cure syphilis; in the 1960s, the birth control pill promised fewer unwanted pregnancies; and the greater social mobility of the 1950s and 1960s weakened social stratification.

Looking at other cultures, anthropologists have found that when one or more of these barriers are eliminated, more premarital intercourse is likely to occur. For example, in some cultures VD is rare and as a result we find more premarital intercourse. But society can make the barrier even stronger, as in cultures where who marries whom is of the utmost importance. In such tightly stratified societies, there is less premarital intercourse (Ford and Beach, 1951; Whiting and Whiting, 1974).

Homosexuality and Bisexuality

More than one-third of all men and one-fifth of all women have had at least one orgasm with a member of the same sex. Figures are lower in the college population, with about 15 percent of men and fewer than 10 percent of women having been involved in at least one homosexual act. Among Rozin's introductory psychology students (1978), almost none of the women reported homosexual experience.

The Embrace by Auguste Rodin pictures a lesbian couple. (Courtesy The Metropolitan Museum of Art. Kennedy Fund, 1910)

A single homosexual act is far more common and should be distinguished from ***exclusive homosexuality,*** which is an enduring pattern of sexual acts and fantasies involving only members of one's own sex. About 4 percent of men in the United States are exclusively homosexual and about 4 percent are mostly homosexual (Kinsey et al., 1948, 1953; Gagnon, 1977; Bell and Weinberg, 1978; McCary, 1978; Rozin, 1978).

Homosexuality has usually been deplored in our society. It is a crime in some states, and in past psychiatric classifications, it has been called a "disorder." American attitudes toward homosexuality are shifting, however. Around 50 percent of Americans believe homosexuality should not be a crime, with white-collar workers more approving than blue-collar workers, and younger people more approving than older people. More than 60 percent of introductory college students approved of homosexual activity (Rozin, 1978). DSM-III has eliminated the classification of homosexuality as a disorder. Only ***ego-dystonic homosexuality,*** or homosexuality in which the sexual preference is unwanted and a source of strong distress, has been classified as a sexual "disorder" by DSM-III.

Individuals who are neither exclusively heterosexual nor exclusively homosexual are called ***bisexual.*** The number of American bisexuals is large: about 15 percent of men and 10 percent of women. Among bisexuals, the preference for partners of their own sex varies in all possible ways. Some bisexuals have sex with members of their own sex about as often as with members of the opposite sex, others have relations with members of their own sex the vast majority of the time, but the majority have sex with members of their own sex only a small percentage of the time (McCary, 1978).

Masturbation and premarital intercourse, as well as oral sex and extramarital intercourse, are common practices in our society. Homosexuality, while not nearly as common, is widespread, and the absolute number of homosexuals is large indeed. One major criterion for calling a practice "abnormal" is rarity, and none of these forms of sexuality is rare today. What seems to have made these sexual behaviors unacceptable in the past was society's attitude about them, and not any physiological or psychological anomaly.

Sexual Identity

The rearing of a child includes the passing on to the child of a sense of sexual identity and a notion of what is acceptable sexual behavior in today's world. Sexual identity has three aspects: object choice, gender identity, and gender role. ***Gender identity*** is the awareness of being male or female. ***Gender role*** is the public expression of gender identity, what an individual says or does to indicate that he is a man or she is a woman. ***Sexual object choice*** consists of the types of persons, parts of the body, and situations that are the objects of sexual fantasies, arousal, and sexual preferences.

How does *gender role* come about? By age two, children are able to distinguish between males and females. By three, they can identify gender differences, and they understand that certain behaviors are appropriate to their gender role. By school age, they understand that a person's gender will not change, even if aspects of the person's appearance or behavior do change.

Because parents and others in society respond differently to girls and boys from birth onward, taking on a gender role begins immediately.

The process of taking on a *gender identity*—feeling like a boy or a girl—is more mysterious than the process of taking on a gender role. Identification and internalization and imitation of parents each probably play some role. Fear of the same-sex parent or desire for the parent's resources or emotional bonding with the same-sex parent all lead to identification with the same-sex parent, and they lead the young child to imitate the parent's behavior and attitudes, including the parent's sexual behavior and attitudes. The child will then internalize these behaviors and attitudes. Biological processes are important as well; for example, the balance of hormones the fetus is bathed with *in utero* contribute to sexual identity (Money and Ehrhardt, 1972). However it is accomplished, the process of taking on a gender identity is complete by age two, at which time the child feels like a male or female; this identity will never change (see pp. 61–62).

Sometime in the first fifteen years of life, individuals acquire their *sexual object choices,* and this preference is likely to stay with them for the rest of their life. For most men, the objects of sexual choice are women; for most women, the objects of sexual choice are men. There is a very large range of situations that men and women find sexually arousing: holding a member of the opposite sex in their arms, dancing, seductive conversation, being caressed by a member of the opposite sex, seeing a member of the opposite sex naked, and the like. Being aroused in real life and in fantasy by these sexual object choices facilitates affectionate sexual activity between human beings.

SEXUAL DISORDERS: THE PARAPHILIAS

When sexual object choice is so disordered that it impairs the capacity for affectionate erotic relations between human beings, the sexual object is called a **paraphilia** (from the Greek "love of [philia] what is beyond [para]"). The paraphilias comprise an array of unusual objects and situations that are sexually arousing to some individuals. Among the more common paraphilias are female underwear, shoes, inflicting or receiving pain, and "peeping." Among the more bizarre paraphilias are human feces, dead bodies, and amputated limbs.

Types of Paraphilias

The paraphilias divide into three categories: (1) sexual arousal and preference for nonhuman objects, including fetishes and transvestism; (2) sexual arousal and preference for situations that involve suffering and humiliation, including sadism and masochism; and (3) sexual arousal and preference for nonconsenting partners, including exhibitionism, voyeurism, and child molesting.

Fetishes

To have a **fetish** is to be sexually aroused by a nonliving object. In many cases, it may be harmless. For example, women's panties are sexually arousing to many men. When a man fantasizes and talks erotically about panties during sexual intercourse with a mutually consenting partner, the paraphilia may be playful and lead to heightened arousal. More typically, however, his partner feels excluded; when the underwear a woman wears displaces the woman, and her partner cannot be sexually aroused unless she is wearing it, the object is no longer a means to arousal but the end of arousal. And when it becomes the preferred or exclusive mode of sexual arousal it becomes pathological. At this point it is of clinical interest. The most common fetishes are for female underwear, shoes, boots, various textures such as rubber, fur, silk, and velvet, parts of the female body such as feet, hair, ears, and eyes. Rarer fetishes include human feces (coprophilia), human urine (urophilia), dirt (mysophilia), animals (zoophilia) and even dead bodies (necrophilia). Here is an example of a fetish, specifically a foot fetish:

> At the age of seven Leo was taught to masturbate by his older half sister. In the course of the lesson she accidentally touched his penis with her slipper. From that time on, the mere sight of a woman's shoe was enough to induce sexual excitement and erection. Now twenty-four, virtually all his masturbation occurred while looking at women's shoes or fantasizing about them. When he was at school he was unable to keep himself from grasping his teacher's shoes and in spite of punishment continued to attack her shoes. He found an acceptable way of adapting his life to his fetish. When he was eighteen, he took a job in a shop which sold ladies' shoes and was excited sexually by fitting shoes onto his customers. He was absolutely unable to have intercourse with his pretty wife unless he was looking at, touching, or thinking about her shoes at the same time. (Krafft-Ebing, 1931, case 114)

It is typical that a fetish is acquired during childhood. The object that will become the fetish accompanies early erotic play. The fetish grows in strength when it is repeatedly fantasized about and rehearsed, especially during masturbation. A fetish may reveal itself when adult interpersonal relationships are unsatisfactory. At this point, one's childhood experience may take over and the fetishist may seek comfort in the simpler sexual pleasures of childhood instead of dealing with the complexity of another human being.

Interestingly, virtually all cases of fetishes and the vast majority of all paraphilias occur among men. Such a man is usually full of shame and guilt about his fetish, which isolates him from sexual activity with other people. Erectile dysfunction is the regular consequence of fetishism when the fetish is absent. Depression, anxiety, and loneliness often accompany the fetish. In addition to such individual problems, fetishists are occasionally in trouble with the law. They may steal objects of the fetish, lunge for the objects in public, and they may masturbate on the objects. Some will frequently acquire a collection of the objects. One young shoe fetishist was discovered with a collection of 15,000 to 20,000 pictures of shoes.

Transvestism

Transvestism occurs when a man persistently dresses in the clothes of a woman in order to achieve sexual arousal. It is usually carried on in secret, although a transvestite's wife may share the secret and cooperate by having

This painting is of Edward Hyde, Lord Cornbury, governor of the colonies of New York and New Jersey. Hyde, a man, is shown here dressed as a woman. (Courtesy of the New York Historical Society, New York City)

intercourse with him when he is dressed as a woman. The secrecy of the act makes its prevalence difficult to estimate, but it is probably rare—occurring in fewer than one percent of adult men. There have been virtually no reports of transvestism in women.

Transvestism usually begins with cross-dressing in childhood, as shown in the following case of Sam:

> At about the age of fourteen, I discovered in my dad's photo album a photo he had taken of me at five-and-a-half just before having my long (bobbed) hair cut off. My mother had dressed me in girls' clothes to see what I would have looked like if I had been a daughter, which is what she had wanted first. When I saw the photo I recalled the incident clearly and the sight of the photo thoroughly "shook" me, for it appeared to be a rather pretty young girl.
>
> The emotional result was twofold. It aroused my first interest in girls and also an interest in girls' clothes. I found myself compelled to go back to look at the photos again and again.
>
> One winter my wife and I were living alone. Our marital relations were good. We were spending New Year's Eve entirely alone and for some reason my wife, not knowing of my mere leanings (at the time) toward transvestism (a word I did not know then), decided to put one of her dresses on me and make up my face just as a sort of New Year's Eve prank. When she finished we sat around for a while and she asked me how I liked it. When I answered in the affirmative she became resentful and very anxious for me to take off the clothes she had put on me voluntarily. (From Stoller, 1969, subject 3.)

When cross-dressing begins, only one or two items of clothing, such as panties, may be used. This item of clothing may become a fetish habitually used in masturbation and in intercourse with a cooperating partner. Such a man may wear these panties under his daily masculine garb. Cross-dressing usually progresses from a single item to a total costume. When dressed as a woman, the transvestite feels considerable pleasure and relaxation; he is intensely frustrated if circumstances block his cross-dressing. A transvestite may believe he has two personalities: one male, which dominates his daily life, and the other female, which comes out when he is dressed up. In other respects, the transvestite is unremarkably masculine in appearance and conventional in his behavior.

Transvestism is often mistakenly confused with homosexuality on the one hand and with transsexuality on the other. Transvestites are decidedly not homosexual: almost three-quarters of them are married and have children, and on the average they have had less homosexual experience than the average American man (Benjamin, 1966; McCary, 1978). Further, a transvestite is aroused by his fetish, whereas a homosexual is obviously aroused by another person. While a male homosexual will occasionally dress in female clothes in order to attract another man, a homosexual, unlike a transvestite, is not sexually aroused by the fact that he is in "drag."

Since most transvestites merely want to be left alone in order to pursue their habit secretly, we must ask why it is considered a problem. Depression, anxiety, shame, and guilt often occur in transvestites; and while sexual arousal is intense during cross-dressing, affectionate sexuality is often impaired by transvestism. A transvestite will commonly be impotent unless he is wearing some female clothing, and this is often not possible when his partner objects.

Sadomasochism is the subject of Luis Buñuel's film *Belle de Jour*. (Courtesy Museum of Modern Art/Film Stills Archive)

Sadomasochism

The second class of paraphilias involves inflicting or receiving suffering as a means to sexual excitement, and it consists of two distinct disorders that complement each other. In **sadism** the individual becomes sexually aroused by inflicting physical and psychological suffering or humiliation on another human being, while in **masochism** the individual becomes sexually aroused by having suffering or humiliation inflicted on him. These terms are greatly overused in ordinary language. We often hear individuals who cheerfully put up with suffering or hardship called masochists, and individuals who are aggressive and domineering called sadists. Much more than this is required for sadism or masochism. A sadist *repeatedly* and *intentionally* inflicts suffering on his partner, sometimes a nonconsenting partner, in order to produce sexual excitement. And a masochist repeatedly and intentionally participates in activity in which he is physically harmed, his life is threatened, or he is otherwise made to suffer in order to feel sexual excitement. Not uncommonly, the masochist and sadist will seek each other out and marry, in order to engage in mutually desirable sadomasochism. Both disorders are accompanied by persistent and insistent fantasies in which torture, beating, binding, and raping are common themes producing high sexual arousal.

Many individuals who are neither sadists nor masochists have occasional sexual fantasies about humiliation and suffering. Kinsey found that about 20 percent of men and 12 percent of women reported sexual arousal when they were told stories about rape, bondage, chains, whips, and discipline. But such fantasies are hardly necessary for sexual arousal or orgasm in the great majority of individuals, and this differentiates them from sadomasochists (Gagnon, 1977; McCary, 1978). In addition to fantasies, overt acts involving suffering and humiliation in order to produce arousal must occur for sadism or masochism to be diagnosed. Nor are all overt acts that produce pain during sex play considered sadomasochistic: lightly biting a partner's earlobe, leaving scratch marks on a partner's back, or bruises whose origin is unknown are common elements of sex play. The true sadist or masochist both has the relevant fantasies and engages in acts that sexually arouse him, causing more than minimal pain. Biting, whipping, pinching, and slapping are typical physical acts of the sadist; bullying, threatening, using sarcasm, and belittling are common psychological acts.

Sadism takes its name from the Marquis de Sade (1740–1814), whose descriptions of sadomasochism in his novels are among the most vivid in the literature.

> He has harshly ordered me to be silent. I strive to melt him . . . but in vain, he strikes out savagely at my now unprotected bosom: terrible bruises are immediately writ out in black and blue; blood appears as his battering continues, my suffering wrings tears from me, they fall upon the vestiges left by the monster's rage, and render, says he, yet a thousand times more interesting . . . He kisses those marks, he devours them and now and again returns to my mouth, to my eyes whose tears he licks up with lewd delight. (Sade, 1791/1965, pp. 597–98)

Masochism derives its name from Leopold Sacher-Masoch (1836–1895), a very popular German novelist of the nineteenth century, whose male characters were often sexually degraded by women. Below is a description of a typical sadomasochistic interaction:

> Thomas, a masochist, and his wife enact a periodic sadomasochistic ritual, in which about once every six weeks Thomas has himself beaten by his wife. She punishes him for his "weak" and "feminine" behavior. In his daily life he is an aggressive and controlling executive, but underneath he deeply longs to be controlled. He feels he should be punished because it is wrong for him to have feelings of needing to be dominated, and so he has his wife tie him to a rack in their cellar and beat him. (Adapted from Gagnon, 1977.)

Severe cases of sadism and masochism are rare, although mild forms of it occur rather frequently. About 5 percent of the men and 2 percent of the women in one survey of liberal and sexually active individuals at one time or another had gotten sexual pleasure from inflicting pain (Hunt, 1974). The incidence was greater among younger people than older people, and much greater among single men than married men. The great majority of sadists and, contrary to popular belief, masochists as well, are men; but both phenomena appear in women as well.

Exhibitionism, Voyeurism, and Pedophilia

The final category of paraphilias involves sexual arousal with nonconsenting partners. Unlike the foregoing, all of these paraphilias are crimes in our society. The criminal aspect derives from the fact that they violate the freedom of others to make unconstrained sexual decisions. *Exhibitionism* involves exposing the genitals to unwitting, and usually unwilling, strangers. *Voyeurism* involves observing the naked body, the disrobing, or the sexual activity of an unsuspecting victim, and *pedophilia* involves sexual relations with children below the age at which we consider it reasonable for them to give mature consent. Beyond these, *rape*—the sexual violation of one person by another—is the most heinous instance of sex involving nonconsenting partners. We shall not discuss rape in this section for two reasons: First, it is not clearly a paraphilia. To be a paraphilia, the act must be the individual's exclusive, or vastly preferred, mode of sexual release. The shoe fetishist does not become erect or have an orgasm unless he is fantasizing about, seeing, or touching shoes. In contrast, the vast majority of rapists, most of the time, can and do become sexually aroused and achieve sexual release in activities other than rape. While fetishism and sadism may play some role in rape, the coercive violence involved is not usually necessary for sexual arousal by the rapist. Second, rape is a major crime, an act for which it is imperative that society hold the individual responsible, punishing him accordingly. If we were to include rape as a *disorder* in the nosology of paraphilias, there would be some tendency to excuse the act and lighten the burden of the rapist's individual responsibility—even if there was not a shred of evidence other than the rape itself that indicated psychological abnormality. The acts of murder, assault, and theft are not automatically thought of as psychological disorders unless there is additional evidence of abnormality, and we believe rape should be thought of in the same way. The expression "Only a sick man could have done that," when applied to rape or murder seems to us deeply and insidiously confused.

EXHIBITIONISM. *Exhibitionism* consists of exposing the genitals to an unwitting stranger, on repeated occasions, in order to produce sexual excitement. The exposure itself is the final sexual act, and the exhibitionist does not go on to attempt sexual relations with his victim after exhibiting himself. A "flasher," or "flagwaver" as they are called in prison slang, typically approaches a woman with his genitals exposed. He usually has an erection, but sometimes he is flaccid. Sometimes he will ejaculate while exhibiting himself or more commonly, he will masturbate when he is alone afterwards (Katchadourian and Lunde, 1972).

Exhibitionism is the most common sexual crime in the United States, with roughly one-third of sexual offenders arrested for it. Surprisingly enough, exhibitionism is very rare outside the United States and Europe and nonexistent in cultures such as India and Burma. Almost half of convicted exhibitionists have had four or more prior convictions for this offense (Gebhard, Gagnon, Pomeroy, and Christenson, 1965).

Exhibiting one's genitals or naked body in a public place is viewed quite differently by our society, depending on whether it is done by a man or by a woman. When a man undresses before a female stranger, he is the exhibitionist and she is the victim. When a woman undresses before a male stranger, he is the voyeur and she is again the victim. As Katchadourian and Lunde (1972) put it, "However badly females fare in other areas of sexual behavior, when it comes to voyeurism and exhibitionism the law is on their side." For this reason, exhibitionism and voyeurism are disorders mostly of men.

The exhibitionist has a favorite type of victim and will expose himself exclusively to female adults or exclusively to children. He wishes to shock and horrify his victim, and this is essential for the act to be gratifying. A woman who acts calmly when confronted with an exhibitionist and placidly suggests to him that he needs psychological help will usually foil the act.

Exhibitionists are usually not dangerous. The act usually takes place six to sixty feet away from the victim; very rarely is the victim touched or molested. The exhibitionist is more of a nuisance than a menace, and it is much more common for child molesters to become exhibitionists than for exhibitionists to become child molesters (Gagnon, 1977; McCary, 1978).

The settings in which exhibitionists perform vary. The most common are in front of girls schools or churches, in crowds, and in parks; and in these settings, the exhibitionist may pretend he is urinating. Among the more imaginative scenarios are wearing only a raincoat in a department store, taking out a whistle and blowing it, and as the female shoppers look in the direction of the whistler, opening the raincoat; rapping on the window of a house with one's erect penis; sitting down near women in darkened movie theaters and masturbating. All these situations have one important element in common: they are public and it is very unlikely that sexual intercourse could possibly take place. These points provide clues to the dynamics of an exhibitionist. The exhibitionist needs to display his masculinity without the threat of having to perform in an adequate sexual role (Kaplan, 1974).

What is the personality of the typical exhibitionist like? He is a quiet and timid man with feelings of inadequacy and insecurity. Most exhibitionists are married, but there is conflicting evidence about whether or not their sexual relationships with their wives are poor or good (Maletzky, 1974; Rooth and Marks, 1974; McCary, 1978). He is usually between the ages of thirteen and forty, with the peak being about twenty-five. Exhibitionism may begin any time from preadolescence to about age forty. When an onset occurs after age forty, it is usually associated with another more severe condition like senility. Exhibitionism may be an impulsive response to a transitory stress like being slighted by a woman, or it may be compulsive, insistent, and ritualistic. Overall, however, the one word that best characterizes exhibitionists is "immature."

VOYEURISM.   In the eleventh century Leofric, the Lord of Coventry, agreed to lower taxes if his wife, Lady Godiva, would ride unclothed on a white horse through the town. As a friend of the poor, Lady Godiva consented, and everyone in town shuttered their windows and hid their eyes out of respect and gratitude. Only Tom, the tailor, peeked; and he went blind, becoming our legendary peeping Tom, the "original" voyeur.

Voyeurs are individuals who repeatedly seek out situations in which they can look at unsuspecting women who are either naked, disrobing, or engaged in sexual activity. The acts of a peeping Tom are secret. The voyeur will masturbate during these acts and while fantasizing about the memory of these encounters. Watching an unsuspecting stranger is the final act, and the voyeur almost never approaches his victim for sexual contact. Visual stimulation is commonly erotic both to men and women, but merely being aroused by seeing a naked woman or a sexual act is not equivalent to voyeurism. In normal individuals, visual stimulation is usually a prelude to further sexual activity. In contrast to voyeurs, normal men do not need to watch an unsuspecting stranger in order to become aroused.

Almost all information about voyeurs comes from those cases in which they are caught. The act is a crime, and many of the problems—such as shame and danger to reputation—that it produces come only in the aftermath of the arrest and exposure. In addition to shame, voyeurs sometimes fall off window ledges, are shot as burglars, and are assaulted by couples who catch them peeping.

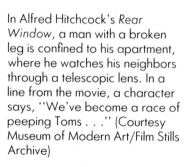

In Alfred Hitchcock's *Rear Window*, a man with a broken leg is confined to his apartment, where he watches his neighbors through a telescopic lens. In a line from the movie, a character says, "We've become a race of peeping Toms . . ." (Courtesy Museum of Modern Art/Film Stills Archive)

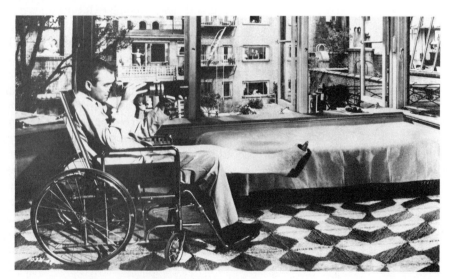

What is the personality of the typical voyeur? The data on this must be viewed with caution, since we know only a selected sample—those who have been caught and convicted by the court. These data may reflect the difference between the caught and the uncaught as much as the difference between voyeurs and nonvoyeurs. (The same caveat holds for exhibitionists and pedophiles as well.) Typically the voyeur is a man, although recent FBI reports indicate that one out of nine individuals arrested for voyeurism are women (McCary, 1978). He is usually the youngest child or an only child, and only rarely does he come from an all-female home. Through adolescence, he had fewer girlfriends and was slower to begin premarital intercourse than his peers. He is shy, and voyeurism enables him to receive gratification and feel sexual power without having to go through the task of approaching and getting to know a woman and thereby risking rejection. Between one-third and one-half of voyeurs are married, and the quality of their marriages does not differ strikingly from the quality of the marriages of the rest of the male population. Finally, 30 percent of convicted voyeurs had also been convicted as juveniles of a variety of nonsexual minor offenses, more than any other group of sexual offenders (Gebhard, Gagnon, Pomeroy, and Christenson, 1965).

PEDOPHILIA. The **pedophile,** sometimes called the child molester, prefers sexual activity with prepubertal children and acts out his preference repeatedly. Society feels a special sense of horror and reserves special fury for the child molester. Pedophilia is the most heavily punished crime of the paraphilias. About 30 percent of all convictions for sex offenses are for child molesting, but it is probably even more common than generally supposed. Between one-quarter and one-third of all adults report that when they were children they had been approached sexually by an adult (Kinsey et al., 1948; McConaghy, 1969; McCary, 1978). There are probably two reasons society consigns pedophiles to a special hell. First, we do not consider a child capable of consenting to sexual activity in the same way a mature adult can, and so the child's freedom is seen as being grossly violated in such circumstances. Second, there is a common belief in sexual imprinting; the child's attitude toward future sexuality may be warped by these early sexual contacts.

In spite of the fact that the child molester is so despised, physical violence probably occurs in no more than 3 percent of all cases of child molesting, and in only about 15 percent of all cases does threat or coercion occur. Provocation and active participation by the victim may occur in about 10 percent of the cases (Swanson, 1968; McCary, 1978).

The molested child is twice as likely to be a girl as a boy. Typically the pedophile exposes himself to the child, or he has the child sit on his lap and he manipulates her genitals. Penetration probably occurs in only about 10 percent of the cases of child molestation. Generally, after being molested, the child is emotionally upset and frightened but usually less so than are her parents. The intense reaction of parents and other adults to the incident may even amplify the trauma of the molested child.

Society's image of the child molester as a dirty stranger lurking in the shadows is far from the truth. Most acts of convicted pedophiles take place between the child and a family acquaintance, neighbor, or relative. The acts usually occur in the child's own home or during a voluntary visit of the child

Peter Lorre plays a pedophile in Fritz Lang's film M. (Courtesy Museum of Modern Art/Film Stills Archive)

to the home of the pedophile. The relationship is not usually particularly intimate, nor is it prolonged: it typically ends when the child begins to protest or reports it to the parents. As with exhibitionism and voyeurism, however, our picture of the pedophile comes from those who have been caught and convicted, and therefore it may not accurately represent those who have successfully evaded capture.

While some convicted molesters are mentally retarded, senile, or schizophrenic, the vast majority are not. The convicted molester is typically older than those in any other class of sex offenders, with the average age being thirty-seven. The majority of those convicted are married. Older offenders seek out younger children in the eight- to ten-year-old age range whereas younger offenders seek out preadolescents of ten to twelve years old. Convicted pedophiles are highly Victorian and rigid in their own sexual attitudes. They generally believe in the double standard and, quite surprisingly, are often highly religious. They see themselves as devout, they read the Bible regularly, and they pray often for cure of their pedophilia. They are often beset with conflicts about religious piety versus sexuality, are guilt-ridden, and feel doomed. They are usually uneasy in adult social and sexual relations and feel more comfortable with children than adults. Occasionally an isolated act of pedophilia will be precipitated by a stressor, most commonly finding out that one's wife or girlfriend has been unfaithful. In other cases, child molesters may be substituting child contact for adult contact that they have been unable to get (Gagnon, 1977).

THE CAUSES OF PARAPHILIA

There are some objects that we treat as means to certain ends that merely symbolize other more important objects. Money, for example, stands for the things it can buy and the pleasures it can bring. Similarly, some of our acquaintances are merely contacts we value not for themselves but because of what they do for us. Other objects serve no other master and become an end in themselves: stamps for the stamp collector, work for a "workaholic," power for some politicians. Above all, the objects of sexual choice become ends in themselves: women for most men, shoes for a shoe fetishist, inflicting suffering for a sadist, shocking an unsuspecting woman for the exhibitionist. This is the stuff out of which human passion is made. Where does it begin and how do these processes go awry to produce the paraphilias? Two schools of thought, the psychodynamic and the behavioral, have wrestled with the problem of the origin of paraphilias. While neither has been completely successful, both have contributed to our understanding.

The Psychodynamic View of Paraphilias

According to Freud, the concepts of "fixation," "object-cathexis," and "sexual object choice" are attempts to describe and explain how certain objects become imbued with erotic attraction for certain individuals as they grow up. *Cathexis* refers to the charging of a neutral object with psychical energy, either positive or negative. In the case of a "positive cathexis" the libido, or the sexual drive, attaches to the object, and it becomes loved. In the case of a "negative cathexis," the object becomes feared.

Freud described the case of the typical foot fetishist who recalled that when he was six, his governess, wearing a velvet slipper, stretched her foot out on a cushion. Although it was decently concealed, this kind of foot, thin and scraggy as it was, thereafter became his only sexual interest (Freud, 1920/1976, p. 348). The fetishist had cathected onto this kind of foot. Freud considered this cathexis to be a concentration of very high psychical energy, bounded and protected by a shield of dead layers. This protection against external stimuli allowed the cathected object to retain its erotic power through life, and only traumatic experiences could breach the protective gates.

Cathected paraphilias have the same three properties as other objects of sexual interest: (1) they have their beginnings in childhood experience; (2) they resist change, particularly rational change; and (3) they last and last—usually remaining for a lifetime. Thus, for example, a foot fetish begins in childhood; telling a foot fetishist that feet don't ordinarily signal sexual pleasure does not diminish their attractiveness; and generally a foot fetish will endure for a lifetime.

While the concept of cathexis is useful descriptively, it is not a satisfactory explanation, for as Freud acknowledged, it is unknown why it strikes one individual rather than another. And this is the main question that concerns us here. The psychodynamic view is content to *describe* the origins of passion for the fetishist, the transvestite, the sadist, the masochist, the exhibitionist, the voyeur, and the pedophilic as an acquired cathexis. But it only describes the fact that for all of these individuals their sexual object choice is not a means to an end but an end in itself, that it is persistent, and that it does not yield to reason. Cathexis does not explain how this happens.

The Behavioral View of Paraphilias

The learning theorists, too, have wrestled with the problem of erotic attachment. The most common account is Pavlovian. Recall the case of Leo, whose foot fetish began when, as a seven-year-old, his half sister's slipper touched his penis. The conditioned stimulus (CS) here is the sight of the slipper. It is paired with the unconditioned stimulus (US) of genital stimulation and the unconditioned response (UR) of sexual pleasure. As a result, future slippers come to produce the conditioned response (CR) of sexual arousal. Such an account explains how cathexis might occur to odd objects in childhood, and it supplements the Freudian account by providing a mechanism.

But this account leaves unanswered the question: Why do paraphilias persist? Recall that the Pavlovian account of phobias had the same problem (see Chapter 10, pp. 212–13). Once a conditioned stimulus has been paired with an unconditioned stimulus, it usually extinguishes readily when it occurs without the original unconditioned stimulus. When the shoe no longer signals that his sister will touch his penis, Leo should once again come to find shoes uninteresting—just as the dog, who used to have the clicking sound paired with food but who no longer experiences food following the clicking, will stop salivating to the click. To explain the persistence of phobias, we could make the following argument: once the phobic object became fearful, it was avoided so completely that the phobic never found out that the phobic object was no longer paired with the original trauma. The phobic object remained frightening because it was untested behind its protective wall. But the paraphilic does not avoid the newly erotic object. On the contrary, he continues to seek it, embraces it, fantasizes about it, *and he masturbates to it.*

This latter fact explains the persistence of the paraphilia, once conditioned. Once the fetishistic object has been paired with erotic stimulation and the paraphilic masturbates in the presence of the fantasy of the object or in the presence of the very object itself, he may provide himself with additional Pavlovian conditioning trials, thereby greatly strengthening the connection between the object and the unconditioned response of sexual pleasure. So an adolescent who experienced the sight of panties originally paired with sexual teasing by the girl next door may greatly strengthen his attachment to panties when he masturbates to orgasm while fantasizing about panties (McGuire, Carlisle, and Young, 1965; Storms, 1981).

There is a bit of laboratory evidence to supplement the case histories, which suggests that Pavlovian conditioning may be at the origin of paraphilias. S. J. Rachman and Ray Hodgson of Maudsley Hospital, University of London, attempted to condition a fetish. Pictures of boots (CS) were paired in time with pictures of naked women (US)—the latter causing their male subjects to have erections (UR). After several dozen pairings, the pictures of the boots (CS) themselves caused erections (CR). So a previously neutral object became erotic following Pavlovian sexual conditioning. But the erotic arousal to boots quickly extinguished when boots were no longer followed by the pornographic pictures—in all but one of the six subjects. Perhaps if the subjects had repeatedly masturbated to boots in fantasy the fetish might have resisted extinction (Rachman and Hodgson, 1968).

There is another factor, **preparedness**, which was brought up in explaining phobias and which might also help to account for the irrationality and resistance to extinction of fetishes. Phobias are not arbitrary—only several dozen human phobias exist (see Chapter 10). There are no lamb phobias, no tree phobias. Evolution seems to have allowed only a certain class of objects that were actually dangerous at one time or another in evolutionary history to become potentially phobic. A parallel argument may hold for fetishes. There are a limited set of objects that actually become paraphilic. Why are fetishes about parts of the body and about dominance and submission common, but fetishes about windows, pillows, or yellow walls nonexistent despite the fact that such objects are often paired with sexual stimulation in childhood? If there are a special class of objects that are *prepared* to take on an erotic character once they have been paired with unconditioned sexual stimuli—then the other properties of preparedness should follow. Such objects, once conditioned, should be irrational, robust, and learned about readily. These facts describe both the paraphilias and phobias.

Thus, both psychodynamic thinking and learning theory may contribute to the explanation of paraphilias. Pairing of certain objects with actual sexual stimulation in childhood eroticizes these objects. They can be described as "cathected" because they are irrational and they resist extinction. The process by which they become cathected may be explained by Pavlovian conditioning, in which a prepared object is paired with an erotic object. Paraphilias and normal sexual object choices will resist extinction because fantasies (CS) about them are paired repeatedly with sexual arousal and or-

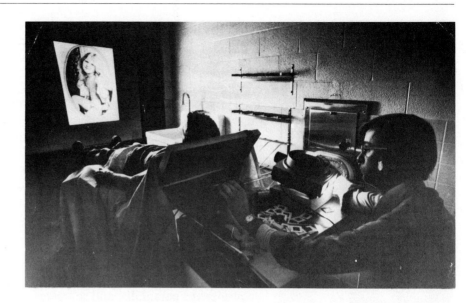

Behavioral therapy for a pedophile. The patient views slides of children, and when he becomes aroused, he receives an electric shock. This helps to extinguish his paraphilia. (Photograph by Ernie Hearion/ The New York Times)

gasm (US) produced by masturbation and by wet dreams. Such an account of cathexis is compatible with the undoing—or therapy—for the paraphilias, to which we now turn.

THE TREATMENT OF THE PARAPHILIAS

Behavior therapists have reported some favorable results in changing the paraphilias, but the success rate is far from perfect (Maletzky, 1974; Rooth and Marks, 1974; Blair and Lanyon, 1981). If paraphilias arise by conditioning during fantasy and masturbation, it might be sufficient for aversion therapy to concentrate on fantasy. For example, the following regime should be effective in changing paraphilias (McGuire et al., 1965). During voluntary therapy, a paraphilic is instructed to imagine a highly sexually stimulating fantasy involving his paraphilia. While engaged in this fantasy, an aversive stimulus, such as a strong electric shock or a nausea-inducing agent, is presented. When the aversive event goes off and relief is experienced, he is told to imagine conventional heterosexual fantasies. This procedure should produce conditioned aversion to the paraphilic fantasy and conditioned excitement to the nonparaphilic fantasy. Behavior therapists also use desensitization and reconditioning to appropriate sexual stimuli, social skills training, and imagery stopping techniques to modify paraphilias. Although some success has been reported using these techniques with exhibitionists (Maletsky, 1974), these procedures have also been known to fail (McConaghy, 1969).

EGO-DYSTONIC HOMOSEXUALITY

Up to only a few years ago, the topic of *homosexuality* was listed in textbooks as a paraphilia or a "sexual deviation." We now believe that there is good reason for homosexuality not to be classified as a disorder. Sexual disorders used to be defined as conditions that grossly impaired affectionate sexual relations between a man and a woman, and homosexuality qualified

Ego-syntonic homosexuality is not a source of distress to a homosexual and is not accompanied by the desire to change sexual preference. (Photograph by John Robaton/ Leo de Wys)

as such a disorder. But DSM-III defines sexual disorders as "conditions which grossly impair affectionate sexual relations between two *human beings.*" Homosexuality, while it may impair such relations between men and women, does not, of course, impair them between a man and a man, or a woman and a woman.

The underlying justification for excluding homosexuality as a disorder distinguishes between ego-syntonic and ego-dystonic homosexuality. *Ego-dystonic homosexuality* is defined as a sustained pattern of homosexuality which is a source of distress and which is accompanied by the desire to acquire or increase heterosexuality. *Ego-syntonic homosexuality*, in contrast, is not a source of distress and is *not* marked by a desire to change sexual preference. When we compare ego-dystonic homosexuality to ego-syntonic homosexuality, we see that the former involves suffering and a desire to change, while the latter does not. Since these two elements count strongly toward calling a behavior disordered, we believe that ego-syntonic homosexuality is legitimately excluded from the catalogue of psychological disorders. In contrast, we believe that ego-dystonic homosexuality could be considered a paraphilia, and so treated.

The crux of the matter is that a significant proportion of homosexuals are satisfied with their sexual orientation, do not show signs of psychopathology, and function quite effectively at love and at work. Ego-dystonic homosexuals, on the other hand, are dissatisfied and distressed by their sexual orientation. They are depressed, anxious, ashamed, guilty, and lonely. They are also manifestly impaired in their capacity to love. On the one hand, they feel ashamed of their attraction to members of their own sex, but on the other, they are not sexually aroused by members of the opposite sex.

Because ego-dystonic homosexuality is a new category, not much is known about its prevalence, its male to female ratio, its predisposing factors, and its course. Typically, an ego-dystonic homosexual will have attempted heterosexual relations unsuccessfully. But merely knowing that he was unaroused by females, or she by males, may have prevented heterosexual attempts altogether. Because there is a highly supportive homosexual subculture in many parts of the United States today, some ego-dystonic homosexuals accept their sexual orientation and give up the yearning to become heterosexual. Spontaneous occurrences of satisfactory heterosexual relations in individuals who have been exclusively homosexual are rare.

The Etiology of Ego-Dystonic Homosexuality

There are two different questions about the causes of ego-dystonic homosexuality: Where does one's dissatisfaction with one's homosexuality come from and where does one's sexual preference, one's homosexuality, come from?

Part of the dissatisfaction or dystonicity stems from the desire to have children and a conventional family life. Another source of dissatisfaction comes from pressures that our society puts on individuals to conform to its sexual norms. Even though American attitudes are changing toward homosexuality, 70 percent of Americans still believe that homosexuals are "sexually abnormal," 50 percent believe they are "perverted," and 40 percent believe they are "mentally ill" (Weinberg and Williams, 1974). Against this sort of disapproval, it would be difficult to retain one's equanimity day in and day out. Also, a major source of the distress felt by ego-dystonic homosexuals stems from rejection and disapproval by their families, their acquaintances, their co-workers, and their own images of "normality."

Some writers believe that the suffering that society's oppression inflicts on homosexuals raises serious ethical questions about whether a therapist should ever consent to treat homosexuality. When an ego-dystonic homosexual comes into therapy with a request that the therapist help him to change his sexual orientation, these writers believe that the therapist should refuse. They believe that because the self-loathing and the desire to become heterosexual are products of the oppression of homosexuals by society, the desire of the ego-dystonic homosexual to change his orientation has been coerced and is not "voluntary," and so should be disregarded (Davison, 1976, 1978). Others disagree. They believe that individual suffering is often the product of societal disapproval and rejection. Exactly how the suffering comes about is theoretical and speculative, but what is not speculative is that another human being comes into the therapist's office and voices a desire to change. The expressed desire to change is, for some, the bottom line of therapeutic decision. The therapist is first and foremost an agent of the patient. When a patient, in obvious distress, asks for help, the patient has called on the therapist's primary duties. The bottom line of interaction between patient and therapist, just as between any two human beings, is that the expression of desires are taken seriously and, if possible, acted upon.

Locating the cause of the distress is a simpler question than discovering the cause of the homosexuality. Many of the same considerations that apply to sexual learning in both normal heterosexuality and in the paraphilias, also apply to homosexuality. Prepared Pavlovian conditioning, masturbatory fantasies, nocturnal emission leading to cathexis, all probably play a role in the acquisition of a homosexual orientation. One recent theory proposes that the timing of the maturation of sex drive is critical. If most of your social group are the same sex as you when sex drive matures, you will tend to become homosexual. If opposite sexed, you will tend toward heterosexuality. This theory predicts that early maturing males and individuals with same-sex siblings will have a higher rate of homosexuality, and this may be so (Storms, 1981). In addition, homosexuality may be partially determined by hormones, by heredity, or by how a child is treated by his mother and father.

The Treatment of Ego-Dystonic Homosexuality

Since this is a new category, little is known about its treatment. There are two aspects, either of which might be treated: the ego-dystonicity and or the homosexuality. The anxiety, depression, guilt, shame, and loneliness that make up the ego-dystonicity may be amenable to the treatments for anxiety and depression outlined in the anxiety and depression chapters. Cognitive therapy, assumption challenging, and progressive relaxation (see Chapters 5 and 6) should each allay the sadness and fears that make up the distress.

Homosexuality itself may be changeable if the individual strongly wants to change it. Traditional psychotherapy does not seem to hold much promise for changes of sexual orientation, but behavior therapy may help. In two controlled studies involving seventy-one male homosexuals, a group of British behavior therapists found that sexual orientation could be changed in nearly 60 percent of the cases by using aversion therapy of the sort described for the paraphilias. They defined "change" as the absence of homosexual behavior, plus only occasional homosexual fantasy, plus strong heterosexual fantasy, and some overt heterosexual behavior one year after treatment. Individuals who had had some heterosexual experience before therapy showed more change than primary homosexuals who had had no prior pleasurable heterosexual history (Feldman and MacCulloch, 1971).

SEXUAL DISORDERS: TRANSSEXUALITY

There are different levels of depth of psychological disorder, and each level may have a level of therapy appropriate to it. Some problems are relatively superficial, such as simple cases of impotence. In order to cure—in the full sense of cure—such a problem, only the behavior needs to be changed. The backup machinery is all there: desire and sexual identity are intact; all that is missing is working peripheral machinery, and behavior therapy works well to cure this problem. Other disorders are at a moderate level of depth, such as sadism. Here the peripheral machinery is working, but what is disordered is the desire. A sadist is passionate only when inflicting suffering on another human being; his cognitions and cathexes are disordered. On the other hand, the sadist's sexual identity is still ordered, for the sadist knows he is a man, or she a woman. Any cure of sadism would not simply be a matter of getting peripheral machinery to work, but it would consist of a radical change in what the sadist is passionate about. Deepest of all disorders are the disorders of sexual identity. Few things are more basic to what we are than our sense of what sex we are, and it is this sense that has gone awry in transsexuality. The therapy for most sexual disorders is psychologically based, but the therapy for transsexuality does not consist of changing the psychosexual identity. Here it is a matter of actually changing the body to conform to the otherwise unchangeable psychosexual identity.

Dr. Richard Raskin *(left)* in a tennis match before the transsexual operation that enabled him to become a woman. His name is now Renee Richards *(right)*. (Wide World Photos)

A transsexual is a man who feels as if he is a woman trapped in a man's body, wants to be rid of his genitals, and wants to live as a woman; or a transsexual is a woman who feels that she is a man trapped in a woman's body, wants to acquire male genitals, and wants to live as a man. Transsexuals feel, from early in life, that by some cosmic mistake they were given the wrong kind of body. This body often disgusts them and the prospect of having to remain in it all their days makes them hopeless, depressed, and sometimes suicidal. By their early twenties, many transsexuals will masquerade in the clothes of the opposite sex. Formerly, many male transsexuals would have become secretaries; female transsexuals, truck drivers. In effect, transsexuals often do everything they can to pass for members of the opposite sex. Unlike transvestites, such actions, particularly the cross-dressing, are not sexually exciting to them but are the means of leading the life compatible with what they perceive to be their sexual identity. Transvestites are decidedly not transsexual and would be horrified at the idea of having a sex-change operation.

Before this century, transsexuals were doomed to live out their lives in a body that repelled them. In the last twenty-five years, medical procedures have developed—although they have not been perfected—which allow transsexuals to acquire the anatomy they desire. The case of Allen-Allison shows the transsexual's problems with sexual identity:

> For the last four years, Allen has been passing by all who know him, as a female, but he is in reality an anatomically normal twenty-three-year-old male. Six months ago, he had his first operation: plastic surgery to enlarge his breasts. He takes female hormones, has had his facial and chest hair removed, and expects in the next two years to undergo the surgery to remove his penis and replace it by a vagina.
>
> Allen says that "As early as I can recall I never had any normal interests and wanted to become a girl and change my name to Allison." He loved to dress in his mother's clothes and always preferred to play with "feminine" things. On one occasion, when he was given a fire engine, he threw a tantrum insisting that he wanted a doll. From about kindergarten on, he demanded acceptance from his parents as a girl and this made for constant conflict. Finally in the fourth grade, he persuaded his parents to allow him to "be" a girl at home, except that he had to wear boys' clothes to school. For the next few years he led a double life, attending school dressed as a boy and then returning home to dress and live as a girl. By eighth grade, he began to feel very uncomfortable around people. The boys teased him mercilessly for being effeminate and the girls would not accept him. He began to avoid school and spent a great deal of time alone.
>
> At fifteen, both school life and family life had become unbearable, and he ran away to San Francisco, where he experimented with homosexuality. He found he could not tolerate homosexual males and left after only a month. While he was attracted to men as sexual partners, only those normal heterosexual men who had accepted him as a female aroused him sexually. Soon, thereafter, he began the odyssey of physical transformation: Allen is now becoming Allison. (Adapted from Pauly, 1969)

Allen-Allison's history is typical of the adult male transsexual. By age three or four his identity as a female is well on its way to being fixed. Before puberty, most transsexual boys will play almost exclusively with girls, will act like girls, prefer to play with dolls, sew and embroider, and help their

This transsexual couple married and had a child. However, both felt that they were born with ''wrong bodies.'' Subsequently, each had an operation to change their gender. (Photograph by Chris Steel Perkins/Magnum)

mothers with housework. They refuse to climb trees, play cowboys and Indians, or roughhouse. By puberty, they feel completely like females, they want to be accepted by society as females, and when they come to know sex-change operations exist they desperately want one. This desire is so intense that in some cases, male transsexuals actually try to cut their own genitals off (Walinder, 1967; Pauly, 1969; Stoller, 1969; Money and Ehrhardt, 1972).

Male transsexuals have three kinds of sexual histories: homosexual, heterosexual, and asexual. The *homosexual transsexual* is aroused by other males, but denies that this is "homosexual" since he feels like a woman. In other words, he wants what he considers "heterosexual" contact only, since his identity is female. In a study of seventy-two transsexuals seen at the University Clinic in Manchester, England, three-quarters had exclusively homosexual fantasies and roughly one-third of them engaged in homosexual behavior (Hoenig and Kenna, 1974). In this study, 15 percent of the sample were *heterosexual transsexuals*. Their sexual fantasies were exclusively about women. Finally, *asexual transsexuals* denied ever having any strong sexual desires, and were preoccupied merely with the desire to live as a woman and to get rid of their male genitals. They had had little or no sexual experience.

Transsexualism is chronic. Once it has developed, there is not a single case on record in which it has spontaneously disappeared. A man who feels like a woman trapped in a man's body, or a woman who feels like a man trapped in a woman's body, will retain this belief for the rest of his or her life.

Transsexuality is rare. The most recent estimate is that about 1 in 100,000 people is transsexual (Walinder, 1967; Pauly, 1974). There are probably more male transsexuals than female transsexuals, and the best estimate of the ratio seems to be about 1.5 or 2 to 1 (Pauly, 1974). The life history of the typical female transsexual parallels that of the typical male transsexual.

THE ETIOLOGY OF TRANSSEXUALITY

Where does such a deep disorder come from? What sorts of events must conspire in order for a physically normal girl to be convinced that she is really a boy or a boy to feel that he is a girl? The answers are very speculative but there are two sets of factors that might disrupt sexual identity, and both of these occur very early in life.

Fetal Hormones

In the course of a normal pregnancy, the fetus is bathed in a variety of hormones. These hormones modulate physical growth, bodily differentiation, and psychological growth as well. Fetal hormones may influence the way we think and act, and evidence for this comes from the rare, but theoretically important, phenomenon of hermaphroditism.

Hermaphrodites who are chromosomally female (46XX), if hormonally masculinized as a fetus, are born with ambiguous-looking genitals. Either because of genetic defect or because of drugs taken by the mother during pregnancy, some fetuses receive too much **androgen** while they are in the uterus. Hormonal androgenization is principally responsible for the masculinized development of the external genitals in the male. When a female is fetally androgenized, upon birth her clitoris is enlarged and penis-like, and her vagina may be partially sealed off. When the diagnosis is promptly made, the vaginal opening is brought to the exterior, and the clitoris is surgically feminized in early infancy. Such females are raised as girls. If the external masculinization is complete, with a penis in an empty scrotum, such a baby may be raised as a boy. Subsequently, circumstances may conspire, and such a child may, on rare occasions, request sex reassignment. Figure 14-1 shows a desperate note from a twelve-year-old child to his doctor expressing the realization of a need for a sex reassignment.

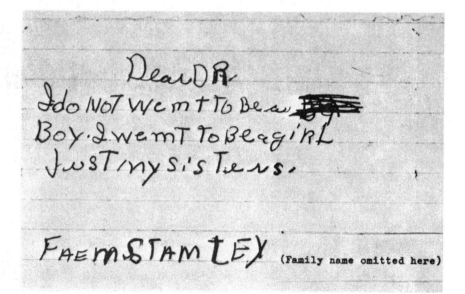

Figure 14-1
The note written by a twelve-year-old boy who wished to have a sex change. (Money and Ehrhardt, 1972)

John Money, one of America's leading sex researchers, intensively studied thirty fetally androgenized hermaphrodites, raised in the female role, as children and as adolescents. He found that when compared to girls matched for IQ, race, and class, these girls differed psychologically along several stereotyped dimensions of masculinity and femininity. They expressed more dissatisfaction with the female sex role, they had more athletic interest and skills, they preferred male companions, and they wore slacks, rather than dresses, more often than the controls. These findings lead us to conclude that some stereotyped sex-role behavior may be determined in the uterus by fetal hormones (Money and Ehrhardt, 1972; Money, Schwartz, and Lewis, 1983). None of these girls believed they were boys, but some researchers have speculated that in the prenatal history of transsexuals a hormonal or related biochemical error affecting sexual pathways in the brain must have occurred. But no proof has yet been forthcoming.

Rearing Practices

How parents treat a young child affects the sexual identity of the child. What would happen to a male child who was given a girl's name, dressed as a girl, and introduced to friends, relatives, and other children as a girl? Parents of a pre-transsexual child are usually ambivalent about what to do. They put off decisions and ultimately panic when the gender disorder doesn't go away. But whether this is a cause or a consequence of the child's transsexuality is unknown. The accidental loss of a penis by one of two identical twins in early childhood provides some evidence that how a child is raised by his or her parents may influence sexual identity. The rearing of this child is described below:

A terrible accident took place in the life of one of two identical twins when he was seven months old. As he was being circumcised, his entire penis was burned off by a faulty electrical device. After medical and psychological advice, the parents decided to rear the child as a girl, starting at seventeen months of age. But would his sexual identity change? Would he, in spite of his male internal organs, male hormones *in utero*, and seventeen months of being treated as a boy, ever come to feel, act, and have the sexual desires of a girl? At twenty-one months, plastic surgery was undertaken and the appearance of a vagina constructed. The parents, in consultation with the surgeon and psychiatrists, decided to rear the child in the most female-stereotyped way: clothes and hairdo were feminized, and the child was given pink shirts, frilly blouses, bracelets, and hair ribbons. Within a year the little child clearly preferred dresses over slacks, and was proud of her long hair. She became much neater and daintier than her twin brother. Her mother taught her to squat while urinating, unlike her brother who stood. For the next few years, the mother began to prepare the child to become a wife and housekeeper, and the child began to imitate her mother in the housekeeping role. The little girl now preferred dolls and mother roles in play, while her male identical twin preferred toy cars and father roles in play.

By the time the twins were almost six, they had a different vision of their future. "I found that my son chose very masculine things, like a fireman or policeman, or something like that. He wanted to do what Daddy does, work where Daddy does, and carry a lunch kit, and drive a car. And she didn't want any of those things. I asked her, and she said she wanted to be a doctor or a teacher. And I asked her, 'Well, did she have any plans that maybe someday she'd get married, like Mommy?' She'll get married someday—she wasn't too worried about that. She didn't think about that too much but she wants to be a doctor. But none of the things that she ever wanted to be were like a policeman or a fireman, and that sort of thing never appealed to her." (Money and Ehrhardt, 1972)

The twins are now in adolescence and the indications are that the female twin, in spite of being genetically a male—but having been reared as a female—shows some, but not all, the aspects of female role and identity. (Williams and Smith, 1979)

It is possible that rearing conditions, particularly while the child is very young, and in individuals who are predisposed—perhaps by fetal hormones—may influence sexual identity decisively. The future may hold a way of identifying hormonally vulnerable children and then paying special attention to appropriate rearing conditions. Since we know that transsexuality, once acquired, is very difficult to reverse, the need for a preventative technique of this sort is acute.

THERAPY OF TRANSSEXUALISM: SEX-CHANGE OPERATIONS

Transsexualism does not spontaneously change in the lifetime of the transsexual. Also conventional therapies have only very rarely been able to reverse it (see Barlow, Abel, and Blanchard, 1979, for the single report of reversal of transsexuality—by exorcism). In spite of this, there is some hope for transsexuals today. Sex-change operations, while still imperfect, allow transsexuals to get the genitals they desire and to marry. As we have seen, normal sexual identity is shaped both by biological conditions, such as what hormones we are exposed to in the womb, and by environmental conditions, such as people reacting to us as male or female. Therapy for transsexuals consists of changing the external reproductive organs by surgery; in addition, this change is supported by social, vocational, domestic, and bodily changes in an attempt to shore up the new gender status.

Therapists treating a transsexual who is a candidate for sex-change surgery often require that the person first live for two years in the new gender role. If after two years of passing for and being treated as a female or male, the individual still wants surgery, the psychological hazards of the surgery are probably lessened. Those who are schizophrenic, delusional, or otherwise emotionally disordered should probably not undertake it (Money and Ambinder, 1978).

Bodily changes are prerequisite to sex-change surgery. In male-to-female sex changes, there is a combination of hormonal treatment to make the breasts grow and make facial hair disappear, and surgery to remove the penis and transform it into a vagina. Because the skin of the penis is used to line the vagina, sexual intercourse—when the surgery is successful—is erotically pleasurable. Orgasm is a warm, sometimes spasmodic, glow through the body.

In female-to-male sex-change operations, the surgery is much more complicated and extensive. It involves multiple operations that take place over several years. First, hormonal treatment suppresses menstruation, deepens the voice, and causes growth of facial and body hair. Then surgery is performed to remove the breasts, the ovaries, and rarely to construct a penis. The capacity for orgasm is always retained, but such a penis cannot become erect, and a prosthetic device has to be used for sexual intercourse.

There has not been a massive and well-controlled follow-up of patients who have undergone sex-change operations. In one eight-year follow-up of seventeen male transsexuals after sex-change surgery, modest gains in working and interpersonal relationships occurred, as well as larger gains in sexual satisfaction. Level of psychological disturbance did not change, however (Hunt and Hampson, 1980).

Some clinicians claim that when the two-year trial period in the role of the desired sex precedes the operations, patients always benefit from the surgery, both in their sense of well-being and in their ability to love. Job status improves, sexual relationships tend to be more stable, and patients indicate that if they had to do it over again—even though the surgical outcome may have been disappointing—they would do so (Money and Ambinder, 1978).

But there is disagreement about this. In a follow-up of fourteen patients operated on at UCLA, almost all of the patients had had surgical complications. Urination was frequently difficult and sexual intercourse often proved impossible. One patient committed suicide after surgery, and some of the others became depressed and apathetic (Stoller, 1978).

On balance, sex-change operations seem to provide the best—indeed the only—hope, at present, for transsexuals. As surgical techniques improve, the operation is apt to become more satisfactory, although even then the transsexual must cope with other problems of adjustment. But because there seems to be no alternative but despair, sex-change operations seem to be the therapy of choice.

SUMMARY

1. There are three basic classes of sexual problems: the *sexual dysfunctions*, the *paraphilias*, and *transsexuality.*

2. The scientific study of sexual behavior has illuminated both how the body works during sexual arousal and what the frequency of a variety of sexual acts is.

3. The human sexual response is similar in both men and women and consists of three phases: *erotic arousal, excitement*, which consists of penile erection or vaginal lubrication, and *orgasm.* Any or all of these three phases of sexual response can be disordered.

4. The *sexual dysfunctions* consist of impairment of desire, excitement, or orgasm. In women, these are manifested by insufficient arousal, lack of excitement in sexual intercourse, and infrequent or absent orgasm. In men, there is lack of erection, *premature ejaculation,* and *retarded ejaculation.*

5. There is hope for all these conditions, and the work of Masters and Johnson, using *direct sexual therapy* and *sensate focus*, suggests that many, if not most of these sexual dysfunctions, may be curable or greatly improved in a short period of time.

6. The *paraphilias* consist of sexual desires for unusual and bizarre objects. They include sexual arousal to nonhuman objects, most commonly *fetishes,* and *transvestism.* They also include *sadomasochism*—sexual arousal in situations that produce suffering and humiliation—and *exhibi-*

tionism, voyeurism, and *child molesting*—sexual arousal with nonconsenting partners.

7. The paraphilias are often lifelong, and they may have their origin in *cathexes,* or emotional binding, which is then reinforced and potentiated by masturbatory fantasies about the object.

8. It is difficult to change the paraphilias in therapy, but recent behavior therapy techniques have had some success.

9. *Transsexuality* is a disorder of men who believe they are really women trapped in men's bodies and of women who feel that they are really men trapped in women's bodies. These individuals want to get rid of their genitals and live in the opposite sex role. Sex-change operations provide some relief for this most distressing condition.

Drug Use and Abuse

W HEREAS other chapters have described changes in behavior, in mood, in perceptions, in feelings resulting from disease or illness, in this chapter we will discuss the same kinds of changes but as they result from the voluntary use of drugs. In fact, drug-induced changes in behavior and feeling and perception are many times more common than any of the changes discussed in other chapters.

We differentiate between *use* and *abuse* of drugs. Use of drugs has become more common in our society. The questions are: When does use turn into abuse? Who is most likely to abuse drugs? What kinds of treatments can be used to help drug abusers?

In this chapter, we will examine both drug use and abuse. We will discuss society's attitudes toward drugs and why individuals use drugs. We will then discuss drug abuse, examining how DSM-III diagnoses substance abuse, and we will also discuss who is likely to become a drug abuser. We will then focus on the use and effects of some of the major classes of psychoactive drugs: stimulants, including caffeine, cocaine, and amphetamines; hallucinogens, including LSD and PCP; narcotics, including opium, morphine, heroin, and methadone; marijuana; and alcohol. We will comment briefly on such depressants as the barbiturates and methaqualone. Finally, we will discuss treatment methods for individuals with alcohol or drug problems. The difficulties, the failures, and the successes of the different treatment programs are included, as well as some insights into the treatment of substance abusers.

DRUG USE

Humans have always used chemicals to alter their states of consciousness and to change their behavior. In primitive societies, drugs and chemicals were unknown, but plants that influenced perceptions and consciousness were eaten, smoked, or snorted. These plants were not used casually for recreational purposes, rather they were taken into the body so the user could acquire the spirit that clearly lived in each psychoactive plant. Using psy-

Drug use, particularly marijuana among high school and college students, increased during the 1970s, as did the need for drug counseling centers (*Left:* © 1979 Richard Stark/Black Star. *Right:* Photograph by Jeffrey Grosscup).

choactive plants for these religious and personal reasons made good sense to these individuals surrounded by an unknown, bewildering, and dangerous world. The same basic rule holds true today—to the user, drug use makes sense, it has a purpose. To drug users, taking certain chemicals into their body has meaning, value, importance. To the extent that the community and society support these values, drug use will spread.

THE DRUG-USING SOCIETY

It's difficult for some of us today to appreciate the great changes that have occurred in patterns of drug-taking behavior over only the last ten, twenty, or thirty years. In the 1950s, except for very low levels of marijuana use in some of the larger cities in the East and on the Gulf Coast, and some heroin use in the inner cities, there was very little drug use by young people, other than—of course—cigarette smoking and the use of alcoholic beverages. Since the 1950s, however, we have moved from a predominantly drug-free society into a drug-using society. There is still debate over why this occurred, but the major themes seem clear. We will try to identify the social-historical trends that have brought us to where we are in the use of drugs so that we can glimpse some of the future directions of drug use.

In many ways, the change in drug use has been due to the major changes in the way the general population thinks about drugs. In the 1930s and 1940s, antibiotics, penicillin, and sulfa drugs were introduced, and people came to realize that these drugs could be used to help diseased bodies return to their normal, healthy state. In the 1950s, the major and minor tranquilizers were first widely used for the treatment of emotional problems and mental illness. People learned that drugs could help a diseased mind return to normal—just as the other drugs had helped diseased bodies. In 1960, there was another significant event—oral contraceptives first appeared in the marketplace. Healthy women took these powerful drugs (hormones) to change their body chemistry in order to enhance their life, to make their life better—in brief, to take some of the hassle out of living! As many as 9 million American women a year legally used powerful drugs—not because they were sick, but just to improve the quality of their life. And Americans began to change their attitudes about drugs: drugs began to be an option that was available to solve problems—problems other than illness.

In the 1960s and 1970s, Americans explored new life styles and followed the opportunities provided by easier transportation and expanding job markets. We reached out, wondering what else we could try. One of the newly available options was drugs (Ray, 1983). Thus, recreational drug use increased as Americans looked for more and different ways to use their leisure time.

Among students, in particular, drug use increased through 1979. Up to 1979, increasing percentages of students tried such drugs as marijuana, the hallucinogens, stimulants, and sedatives (see Table 15-1). But in 1980, some downward trends appeared, which have continued. Just as the many changes in society led to increases in drug use over the last thirty years, many social changes have contributed to the decline in drug use: the increased emphasis on natural health among young people; a backing-off from the expansionistic, liberal economic and social beliefs that were previously dominant; the aging of the baby-boom generation; and the decline in the size and importance of the youth culture. Some drug use has continued to increase into the 1980s, however, particularly use of the stimulants: amphetamine and cocaine. It is probably not just by chance that these drugs, more than the others, provide their pleasurable effects very directly. They don't expand your horizons or open new worlds—they just make you feel good.

All of the foregoing provide a reasonable basis for understanding the ebb and flow of drug use in society as a whole. The social changes just mentioned, however, were more apparent in large than small cities, in urban than rural areas, in males than in females, in the Northeast and the West Coast than in the Plains States or the South. And in every case—where the social change was greatest, so was the increase in recreational drug use.

Table 15-1 PERCENTAGES OF EVER USED[a]/CURRENT[b] DRUG USERS IN HIGH SCHOOL SENIORS IN THE SPRING OF EACH YEAR

Drug Class (only non-medical drug use reported)	Class of						
	1975	1976	1977	1978	1979	1980	1981
Marijuana-Hashish	47/27	53/32	56/35	59/37	60/37	60/34	60/32
Hallucinogens	16/5	15/3	14/4	14/4	19/6[c]	16/4[c]	16/3[c]
Cocaine	9/2	10/2	11/3	13/4	15/6	16/5	17/6
Heroin	2/0	2/0	2/0	2/0	1/0	1/0	1/0
Other Opiates	9/2	10/2	10/3	10/2	10/2	10/2	10/2
Stimulants	22/9	23/8	23/9	23/9	24/10	26/12	32/16
Sedatives	18/5	18/5	17/5	16/4	15/4	15/5	15/5
Tranquilizers	17/4	17/4	18/5	17/3	16/4	15/3	15/3
Inhalants	–	10/1	11/1	12/2	19/3[d]	18/3[d]	18/2[d]
Alcohol	90/68	92/68	93/71	93/72	93/72	93/72	93/71
Cigarettes	74/37	75/39	76/38	75/37	74/34	71/31	71/29

[a] Percentages rounded; 0 to 0.4 shown as 0
[b] Current users are those who used in the month preceding the survey
[c] Includes PCP
[d] Includes amyl and butylnitrites
SOURCE: U.S. Department of Health and Human Services, NIDA, 1982.

Our next focus is on the individual: Why do some individuals use drugs, while others don't? Why do some misuse and abuse drugs, while others don't? We now focus on the personal and individual antecedents to drug use, but remember that all of the foregoing social and historical trends touch on the individual.

THE INDIVIDUAL DRUG USER

Before we get involved in specific studies and discuss specific predictions, consider one general rule: drug-taking behavior is like all other behaviors; it is not unique; drug-taking follows the same rules as other behaviors. People do drugs for the same reasons they do other things. Sometimes the reasons are smart, sometimes dumb; sometimes the reasons are good, sometimes bad. Similarly, the particular drugs that an individual selects to use are determined in the same way the individual selects sports and other activities: availability, personality, peer group pressure, role modeling by parents, social trends, and social acceptance.

Some people avoid drugs because they are dangerous. Some, however, take drugs because the danger is a challenge. They hear about the bad experiences of their peers, but they believe that "it won't happen to me." They think they are smarter, or more careful. There are a number of reports that for some individuals in some situations, it is the risk that attracts them to the drug. Interviews with heavy PCP users showed that they all knew its reputation as a drug that produced bad trips and knew that using it too frequently meant the possibility of permanently losing normal behavior and intelligence (U.S. Department of Health and Human Services, 1980). But knowing the risk made no difference—part of the challenge was "beating the drug." That shouldn't really surprise anyone—many of us engage in activities in which part of the attraction is the danger—the risks involved.

In the early and mid-1960s, a college student who used marijuana frequently was a very unusual person. He really stood out in the crowd—it was a rare behavior, something like driving a sports car—not very many people did it. There were big differences between the drug user and the nondrug user (as between sports car drivers and family car drivers). In the mid-1950s, a major textbook in pharmacology described marijuana users as frequently being homosexual. But times have changed. Today, the use of illegal drugs at the college level does not identify a clearly unique group of people. In fact, some people claim that marijuana use has become normal behavior in most colleges.

A report that compared drug-using and nondrug-using college students in the late 1970s found essentially *no* differences in their grades, career plans, participation in athletics, political alienation, or involvement in extracurricular school activities. Only two differences—other than the drug use—were found: drug-using students engaged in more sexual behavior, and they visited psychiatrists more often than nondrug-using students (Pope et al., 1981). But drug use was not the reason for the increased visits or sexual activity, rather it was a matter of values and attitudes toward self. Similar comparisons have not been made of all of younger drug users, but the available data are fairly clear: as the age of the drug user (and the matched nondrug user) decreases, there are increasingly large differences between the two groups. Greater alienation, anti-establishment attitudes, lower grades in school, and more dating characterize the twelve- to fourteen-year-old drug user.

Sociological characteristics, not psychological ones, best distinguish the young drug user from the young nondrug user. Some researchers have referred to a pattern of **social deviance** as a description of the young (i.e., junior high school) drug user. The use of marijuana or alcohol by the young often stems from socially deviant behavior, as does increased sexual behavior and some criminal delinquency. This is the pattern seen primarily in young white adolescents. Thus, there is less likelihood of drug use in individuals at high school age and below if the home environment is stable, religious, and has traditional values, and where the parents have clear sex roles, the rules of behavior are clear, and discipline is firm and consistent (Gray, 1980).

Finally, the basic rule is that people seem to use drugs because the drugs meet unfilled needs. That doesn't mean drugs are bad, or a crutch, or are different from most other things in life. Perhaps the one way in which the use of drugs *is* different from some of the other ways in which we meet our needs is that drugs are easier to use and have faster effects. If an individual feels uncomfortable, anxious, or insecure in social situations he can—as most of us have done—tough it out and learn the social skills that are necessary to feel comfortable. But it's much easier and quicker and—over the short term—more effective to smoke marijuana before or during the anxiety-arousing situations. The concern that many people have about drug use is not that it is *one* of the ways that society allows individuals to solve problems but rather that drug use may become the *primary* way in which people deal with problems, and that individuals may avoid learning the real-life skills needed to deal with their problems in the long run.

DRUG ABUSE

DIAGNOSING SUBSTANCE ABUSE

Diagnosing substance abuse became much easier in 1980 with DSM-III's introduction of clear and objective guidelines. These guidelines primarily deal with three questions: (1) Is this an acute, probably transient, disorder (i.e., just an episode of substance intoxication)? (2) Is the individual a user or an abuser? (3) Is the individual dependent (addicted) or not? Answers to these questions have great importance in determining the type, duration, and probable success of treatment. Diagnosing intoxication will vary with each substance, but the overriding principles are that there are clear physical signs, psychological symptoms, impaired functioning—and that they all have occurred within a short time of use of the drug.

Substance-using individuals are labeled *abusers* only if they meet three criteria: (1) a pattern of pathological use; (2) impairment in social or occupational functioning because of use; and (3) at least one month's duration of the disturbance. The pattern of pathological use is, of course, different for each substance, but there are two characteristics common to all: inability to decrease or stop use, and intoxication all day long. Impairment of function is pretty straightforward—if one repeatedly loses jobs and friends, misses work or school, or gets in trouble with the law because of substance use, that's impairment. If any of the above have existed for at least one month —the third criterion is obviously met.

Diagnosing dependency (addiction) to a drug is also straightforward. If the individual shows either tolerance to the effects of the drug *or* withdrawal signs when drug use stops, then a diagnosis of dependence is made.

THE INDIVIDUAL DRUG ABUSER

There seems to be a different etiology for those who are drug abusers than for those who are simply drug users. Those who engage in drug-taking to the point where it can be called ***drug*** or ***substance abuse***, frequently have some psychiatric or emotional problems—and the problems most often come *before* the drug abuse. Sometimes these people use drugs as self-medication—to reduce their distress. Drug use becomes drug abuse when the drug-taking behavior disrupts the relationship between the individual and his job, school, friends, or family. Thus, most people who *use* drugs are not emotionally disturbed, but many who *abuse* drugs do so as a result of emotional problems.

The heroin user (© Ian Berry/ Magnum).

When an individual engages in behavior that is very different from the behavior of others like him, there is a high probability of a psychological problem. Thus, there is a greater likelihood of psychopathology in drug abusers who use a drug that is uncommon in their demographic group. For example, white heroin addicts and female alcoholics are statistically rarer than black heroin addicts and male alcoholics. In a study of heroin addicts in treatment, it was found that, given the same general background, black addicts were psychologically much more like black nonaddicts than white addicts were like white nonaddicts, and that white addicts had more psychopathology than black addicts. Similarly, female alcoholics are much more likely to have psychological problems compared to matched nonalcoholic females, than are male alcoholics compared to similar nonalcoholic males.

The type of drug abused is related to personality and to psychopathology. In a group hospitalized for psychiatric treatment, abuse of amphetamines or hallucinogens was associated with a high proportion of paranoid schizophrenia and a low incidence of depression. On the other hand, barbiturate abuse was associated with a high proportion of depression and a low proportion of schizophrenia (McLellan and Druley, 1977, p. 182). Another study showed the relationship between specific drug use, hallucinogen and stimulant abuse, depressant abuse, narcotic (mostly heroin) abuse, and the development six years later of specific forms of psychopathology. At the beginning of the six-year period, none of the individuals had a psychiatric diagnosis, and all had low symptom levels. After six more years of on-and-off drug abuse, over half of the hallucinogen/stimulant users were diagnosed as schizophrenic (and most were hospitalized for treatment); one-third of the depressant abusers had attempted suicide, and although most showed high levels of depression and anxiety, there was virtually no evidence of psychiatric symptoms in the narcotic abusers. Over the six years, the narcotic group showed very little psychological change and generally low levels of psychological symptoms with little evidence of psychosis or organic illness (McLellan et al., 1979, pp. 1312–13). This absence of a relationship between narcotic use and the development of a major psychiatric syndrome not only fits with what is known from other studies and treatment programs but makes sense clinically. Narcotic drugs function to medicate the individual, reducing symptoms of anxiety, depression, and paranoia; they do not have the same extreme effect on thinking processes or level of arousal as do the hallucinogens, stimulants, and depressants.

Thus, drug abuse has some relationship to personality and psychiatric diagnosis. Drug abuse will often be a response to deep-rooted emotional distress. We now turn to a discussion of the basic mechanisms of action and effects of drugs. We will then discuss the particular patterns of use and effects of specific psychoactive drugs.

THE BASIC EFFECTS OF DRUGS

In discussing specific effects of selected drugs, it is well to remember that there are no ghosts. Even when the mechanism of action of a drug is completely unknown—as in the case with the active chemical in marijuana, tetrahydrocannabinol (THC), and with phencyclidine (PCP)—researchers and clinicians assume that these drugs affect behavior, consciousness, and mood because they act in specific biochemical ways on the brain. Whenever possible we will mention the mechanisms of action of a drug. The brain is a complex, interrelated set of systems in which information flow proceeds through a sequence of electrochemical and biochemical operations. All psychoactive drugs alter these normal operations in one of three ways: a drug can increase, decrease, or interfere with the ongoing action in one or more of the systems in the brain.

The effects of a drug are superimposed on what is already going on, or already stored in memory, in the brain. This is why the effect obtained with a drug depends in part on the personality and mood of the particular person using the drug. Drugs do not have effects in a vacuum—they have effects in a specific person in a specific situation. Change either the person or the situation, and the drug effect changes. This is also why anyone can have a bad drug experience.

But now let's look at some general principles. ***Pharmacology*** is the science that works specifically with drugs, their actions, and their effects; it studies how chemicals (drugs) interact with cells and chemicals in the body. ***Psychopharmacology*** is that part of pharmacology that studies drug actions affecting consciousness, mood, and behavior (i.e., drugs that affect the psyche). Drugs with these effects are called ***psychoactive drugs.***

Drug Effectiveness and Potency

For a drug to have a psychoactive effect, it must either enter the brain, or in some other way bring about changes in the brain. Not every drug can get into the brain. Because of the sensitivity of the neurons in the brain to disruption, and their importance in maintaining the individual in a stable way, the brain has a special protective device that other organs don't have. This device is called the ***blood-brain barrier.*** It is not well understood, but it works to keep some chemicals in the blood as they pass through the brain, while allowing other chemicals to leave the blood, enter the brain, and have an effect on the nerve cells there. The more easily a drug passes through the

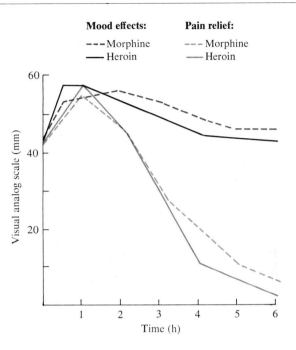

Mood effects: Pain relief:

---- Morphine   --- Morphine
—— Heroin   —— Heroin

Figure 15-1
Comparison of effects of morphine and heroin. Twice the amount of morphine (10 mg) was needed to achieve the same effects as heroin (4.8 mg). (Source: Kaiko et al., 1981, p. 1501)

·The visual-analog scale (VAS) consisted of a 10-mm line on which the patient marked the point between extremes in effect. The extremes for relief were "no relief of pain" on the left and "complete relief of pain" on the right, and those for mood were "worst I could feel" and "best I could feel." The distance from the extreme left to the mark was the VAS score.

blood-brain barrier, the less drug is needed and the more rapidly it will affect the brain. One example is the difference between two narcotics, heroin and morphine. Both drugs have the same effect because heroin is changed into morphine in the brain. When heroin or morphine is injected into the bloodstream, as an addict might do, one-half to one-third as much heroin as morphine is needed to get the same effects—more heroin than morphine passes through the blood-brain barrier. So the heroin enters the brain more rapidly, and thus has an effect sooner than does morphine. Narcotic addicts prefer heroin to morphine for both reasons: the effect is faster with heroin; less heroin is needed than morphine. Figure 15-1 compares heroin and morphine effects on both pain and mood, showing that there are no major differences, except that the effects of heroin occur sooner (Kaiko et al., 1981).

Comparing heroin and morphine effects introduces another concept: **drug potency.** The potency of a drug refers only to how much drug is needed to get a particular effect. It took double the amount of morphine (10 mg) compared to heroin (4.8 mg) to get the same effect shown in Figure 15-1. Heroin is therefore about twice as potent as morphine. That just means you use less heroin than morphine to get the same effect—it does *not* mean heroin is twice as effective, rather both are equally effective.

Another concept is the **dose-response relationship.** At very low drug levels, there will be no response. As the amount of the drug in the brain increases, so will the response, i.e., the effect of the drug will increase. But at some level of the drug, the response is as great as it can be. Adding more drug will not increase the response any more. Two aspirin are better than one, which may be better than none, in reducing certain kinds of pain. In some cases, three aspirin may be better than two. Taking six aspirin is not generally better than taking two or three. Two or three aspirin give the maximum response of pain reduction—more drug does not necessarily give more response. And more drug than is necessary may result in toxic effects.

The more drug in the blood, the more drug in the brain. It follows that one of the concerns of a drug user (or of a physician prescribing a drug) is how best to get the drug into the blood. The least efficient, and least effective, way to get a drug into the blood is also the most common: taking a drug orally. This is because (1) when a drug is taken into the stomach, there are many factors that may interfere with the absorption of the drug into the blood; and (2) blood from the gut goes first to the liver, and one of the primary functions of the liver is to deactivate drugs (i.e., make drugs less capable of entering and acting on the brain).

One way to overcome both those problems is to inject the drug directly into the bloodstream; addicts call this **mainlining.** Repeated punctures of a vein with a hypodermic needle, however, can result in the vein collapsing and failing to function. Another method of getting the drug into the blood is to inject it under the skin (subcutaneously); addicts call this **skinpopping.** Using this method, the drug is usually fairly rapidly absorbed into the blood.

The two most rapid and effective ways of getting certain drugs into the blood are inhalation and snorting. Drugs that are volatile (such as inhalants) or drugs that can be vaporized without being destroyed by the heat (such as nicotine) are easily absorbed in the lungs, are carried readily in the blood to the brain, and thus have a rapid effect. Snorting—sharp, hard sniffing—that carries a drug to the remote parts of the nasal cavities, where the drug is absorbed through the olfactory tissue, also results in a rapid onset of drug effects.

How long a drug will continue to act on brain tissue depends mostly on two factors. One is the rate of deactivation—how rapidly the drug is changed so that it can no longer affect the brain. Pharmacologists use the term **half-life** to compare duration of action of different drugs—the length of time it takes for the level of drug in the blood to be decreased by 50 percent. One narcotic, methadone, is effectively used in some treatment programs for addicts of another narcotic, heroin, because the half-life of methadone is such that it can be taken once a day. The half-life of heroin is so short that it must be used four to six times a day to prevent the discomfort of withdrawal.

The second major factor that determines how long a drug will continue to act in the body is whether the drug gets stored in a way that keeps it active as long as it is stored. When a drug user takes a large amount of a drug, only some of it will be absorbed into the brain and blood. The rest will be stored in the body and released only when the drug already in the brain and blood has been deactivated. In this way, a drug can be taken only once, and still have effects lasting far beyond the time when normally all the drug would be deactivated. Such storage usually occurs only with fat-soluble drugs—the barbiturates and marijuana are good examples. THC (the active drug in marijuana) is stored in fat cells and slowly released so that it can still be in the body thirty days after a one-time, heavy marijuana use. The amount being released in this case seems not to be enough to cause any behavioral effects.

TOLERANCE, WITHDRAWAL, AND ADDICTION

Duration of action, as well as storage and gradual release are not the only drug effects that are time related. Two other pharmacological concepts are important here: tolerance and withdrawal.

Tolerance occurs with many psychoactive drugs, including narcotics, hallucinogens, barbiturates, stimulants. Tolerance to a drug occurs when there is less response to a specific dose of a drug with repeated use; "smoking more now and enjoying it less." For example, there is tolerance when the response to the twentieth use of a drug is less than the response to the tenth use, which was less than the response to the first use of the drug—even though the same amount of the same drug was used each time. The converse is also true: if tolerance occurs with repeated drug use, we need to use more of a drug each time to get the same response each time. When scientists talk of tolerance, the time periods involved are usually weeks or months. Tolerance can also occur across drugs. Tolerance to alcohol, for example, results in tolerance (called *cross tolerance*) to both the barbiturates (depressant drugs) and to the benzodiazepines (minor tranquilizers, such as Valium and Librium). Cross tolerance means, for example, that if we have developed a tolerance to alcohol then we also have a tolerance to Valium—even though we have never taken Valium!

Withdrawal is another pharmacological concept that occurs over time. But first we must explain *addiction*—or, as some prefer to call it, dependence. When some classes of drugs are taken regularly—perhaps two to four or more times a day—for a period of time, the physiology of the body changes in specific ways, so that the individual is said to be addicted to (or dependent on) the drug being used. For some drugs, such as heroin, addiction may occur after one or two weeks of regular use. For other drugs, alcohol for example, it will take longer.

There are six basic facts about addiction and withdrawal. One is that as regular use of the drug occurs, the body continually adjusts itself so that, after a time, it functions normally only when the drug is in the body. Second, most drugs that depress the activity of the brain are addicting, but addiction does not occur to all drugs. Third, any drug that addicts is also a drug that causes tolerance. Not all drugs that cause tolerance, however, cause addiction. Fourth, when drug use is stopped suddenly in an addicted person certain physiological and psychological changes occur, these changes are called withdrawal. It is not the absence of the drug that gives rise to the symptoms, but rather a lower-than-normal level of the drug. Fifth, the physiological and psychological symptoms that occur in withdrawal are almost the opposite of the acute responses that occurred when the drug was being used. For example, withdrawal from drugs that depress the nervous system and slow behavior results in stimulation and hyperactivity during withdrawal. Finally, the severity and the rate at which withdrawal occurs depend on the dose to which the body has become accustomed, the duration of drug use at that dose, and the rate at which the drug level decreases. The higher the intake, the longer the use, and the faster the drop, the more severe the effects of withdrawal.

PSYCHOLOGICAL DEPENDENCE ON DRUGS

In contrast to addiction, *psychological dependence* refers to a situation in which the use of a drug has become very important in an individual's life. It becomes so important that the individual plans much of his or her activity around ensuring a supply and using the drug—even when the drug is *not* addicting. Psychological dependence to drugs occurs, and it's important to recognize this when a drug abuser enters treatment. A problem with the term is that it suggests that drug use is different from other behaviors. And it's not. Drug taking behavior follows the same rules as other behaviors. Many of us are psychologically dependent on various behaviors, for example, listening to music. That's very similar to what happens with someone who is psychologically dependent on drugs. Use the term psychological dependence if you wish, just make sure you remember that drug use is not a unique type of behavior.

Drugs disrupt behavior according to the complexity of the behavior, how well learned the behavior is, and the dosage of the drug. Better-learned and better-motivated behavior is more difficult for drugs to disrupt than poorly learned or poorly motivated behavior; simple behaviors are harder for drugs to disrupt than complex behaviors. So, abstract thought, complex behavior, and poorly learned behaviors will be disrupted at lower dose levels than simple, concrete, well-learned behaviors.

Another psychological principle is that an individual's thoughts and behaviors are influenced by the setting in which they occur. Part of the setting for each of us is the world we live in: our society. Other parts of our setting are the beliefs, attitudes, and information we learn as we grow up. As we become more mature, more stable, more emotionally secure about who we are, we become more resistant to influence by the storms of life that go on around us. We also become less susceptible to disruption by the actions of drugs. For this reason, most bad drug trips occur in younger people, and in those who are less mature emotionally. They are less stable, and it's easier to upset their emotional applecart.

A final psychological principle is that behaviors and thoughts persist—that is, get repeated—if they make the individual feel good, or less miserable. When an individual's drug use persists, the drug is probably making the person feel better. And drug taking will generally persist as long as the positive effects outweigh the negative consequences.

Most drugs decrease or impair performance and thought. Only in a very few instances does drug use produce clearer thinking or improved performance. When there is improved performance—as there might be with stimulant effects on a behavior requiring a high level of alertness—the improved performance following drug use can usually be produced only by a very narrow dose range. Even in a task requiring high levels of alertness, it is possible to be *too* alert, too aroused, to be able to perform well.

Summarizing all of the above, the basic rule in psychopharmacology is that to understand and predict the effect of a drug you need to know the drug, the individual, and the setting.

THE PSYCHOACTIVE DRUGS

The major classes of drugs include the stimulants, the hallucinogens, the narcotics, marijuana, and alcohol. In this section, we will examine the use and effects of these drugs, and when their use turns to abuse.

STIMULANTS

The **stimulants** are the only class of drugs whose use has continued to grow during the early 1980s. Stimulants include a wide-ranging collection of chemicals—from the caffeine in most cola soft drinks and coffee, to phenyl-propanolamine (a nonprescription appetite suppressant), to the amphetamines, to cocaine, which is at the most potent end of the continuum. These stimulants vary greatly in their potency and abuse potential, and to some degree in their mechanisms of action. We will focus on the amphetamines and cocaine, but we will make passing mention of phenylpropanolamine because of the unique drug crises associated with its use, and we will briefly discuss caffeine because of its widespread and generally accepted use.

Caffeine

Caffeine is the psychoactive drug in coffee and many soft drinks. It is rapidly absorbed after oral intake and some of its effects begin in thirty minutes, although maximum effects usually aren't reached until two hours after use. Caffeine primarily stimulates the central nervous system and the skeletal muscles. About 200 mg—the amount in two or three cups of coffee, or six or seven soft drinks—activates the brain, alerts and arouses the individual, lengthens the time it takes to fall asleep, decreases fatigue, and lengthens the time the individual can do exhausting work. Over-the-counter drugs sold to reduce fatigue and increase alertness usually contain 100 or 200 mg of caffeine.

Tolerance develops to caffeine, and some withdrawal signs (usually a throbbing headache) may develop after eighteen hours of abstinence, in a daily user of five or more cups of coffee. Much more common than withdrawal is a syndrome that develops from a high intake of caffeine. Some call it *caffeinism,* and its symptoms are difficult to distinguish from those of a panic attack (see Chapter 10). Nervousness, irritability, and insomnia are the more common symptoms of caffeinism.

Cocaine

Cocaine is one of the oldest stimulants known to man and is the psychoactive agent in the coca plant. Coca (do not confuse this with cocoa—the chocolate drink) has been cultivated in Peru and Bolivia for hundreds, perhaps thousands, of years. The leaves of the coca bush are chewed by the natives in the rural areas as a mild behavioral and psychological stimulant and as an anti-appetite agent. Similar to amphetamine, cocaine increases energy and the ability to work; it combats both fatigue and boredom. It is also a euphoriant, enhancing the individual's response to things going on around him, as well as increasing the positive feelings the individual experiences. At low doses of both amphetamine and cocaine, the world and the individual's experiences just plain look better.

In the second half of the nineteenth century, cocaine hydrochloride was isolated from coca leaves. Various individuals became cocaine users, including two world famous personages: Sherlock Holmes and Sigmund Freud. The fictional person, Sherlock Holmes, explained to Dr. Watson why he (Sherlock) used cocaine intravenously:

> My mind . . . rebels at stagnation. Give me problems, give me work, give me the most abstruse cryptogram, or the most intricate analysis, and I am in my own proper atmosphere, I can dispense then with artificial stimulants. But I abhor the dull routine of existence. I crave for mental exaltation. (Doyle, 1938, pp. 91–92)

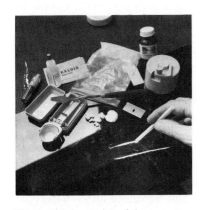

The paraphernalia of the cocaine user. (Photograph by Arthur Tress)

The real person, Sigmund Freud, also experimented with cocaine, extolling it as a safe exhilarant. Freud called it " . . . a magical drug . . . I take very small doses of it regularly against depression and against indigestion, and with the most brilliant success." (Freud, 1884, in Taylor, 1949, p.17).

When the truth is known, cocaine is all of these things, but it is also not safe and the letdown after its use can be very difficult. Conan Doyle never clarified whether Sherlock Holmes ever stopped using cocaine. We do know that one of Freud's friends developed a cocaine psychosis and that with difficulty Freud was able to help his friend stop using cocaine. This turned Freud very much against the use of all drugs.

We now jump across almost a century of time and various patterns of cocaine use to our world today. In the interim, cocaine found its way into, and out of, Coca-Cola; into, and out of, the Cole Porter song "I Get a Kick Out of You"; and it ended up as the *in* drug of the 1980s. The mechanisms of action that underlie the psychoactive effects of cocaine and amphetamine (below) are about the same, and are fairly well established. One of the differences between these two drugs is that amphetamine has a longer duration of action. For now, it is enough to know that these drugs are **sympathomimetic agents,** that is, the use of cocaine or amphetamines mimics the physiological, behavioral, and psychological effects that develop when the sympathetic nervous system is activated. (You will recall from Chapter 10 that the sympathetic system is that part of the autonomic nervous system that causes the emergency reaction, through which the body's resources are mobilized for fight or flight, including faster heart beat, increased pumping of blood and oxygen, and increased amount of lymphocyte cells available for repair of tissue damage.)

Many intertwined effects are involved with the sympathetic nervous system and its neurotransmitter, noradrenaline. Both cocaine and amphetamine mimic the action of noradrenaline, as well as causing it to have more effect when it is released naturally. The reticular activating system—a system of nerves that alerts the brain—becomes more aroused, and we become more responsive to all the stimuli that we hear and see. We become more active; more blood flows to our muscles, and fatigue drains away. That part of the brain having to do with pleasure becomes more active, and we feel better. As the activation of this system increases, we go from feeling better, to experiencing real pleasure, to euphoria—exaltation. Our behavioral arousal parallels physiological and psychological arousal. At low dose levels, there is a simple increase in activity and energy level; as the dose increases, there is activity, the inability to sit quietly or calmly, the expectation that everything should be done *now,* and that we can do it, and the belief that everything is possible. Before further elaborating on the cocaine experience, we will take a quick look at the ways in which this drug is used today.

FORMS OF COCAINE USE, MISUSE, AND ABUSE.   Cocaine is one of the few drugs that you can use by sucking, swallowing, shooting, snorting, or smoking. These uses for cocaine will be briefly mentioned before discussing the pattern that sends users to hospital emergency rooms.

As we said earlier, cocaine has been used for centuries in Peru and Bolivia, where the natives usually chew or suck on coca leaves. This allows in a low dose by slow absorption of the drug. A hundred or so years ago in Europe, cocaine lozenges were regularly sold. Toward the end of the nineteenth century, cocaine was not only used in a large number of patent medicines, but it also found its way into a French wine. Today, about the only oral use of cocaine in modern society is in elixirs such as the Brompton Mixture. This is a combination of cocaine, heroin, and other drugs, which has found widespread use in England and Europe in hospices—places where the terminally ill are maintained in comfort and in supportive surroundings until their death. The heroin combats the pain and the cocaine lifts their spirits.

Cocaine is now typically used by either injecting it into a vein, or by snorting it—inhaling it high into the nasal cavity. When the cocaine is snorted, it is absorbed via the nasal mucosa, which gives it a direct and rapid route into the brain. Snorting the cocaine is the more frequent form of use as many people have a hard time inserting a needle into themselves and fear the danger of infection and scars from the needle marks. The process of preparing the cocaine for snorting, however, can also be dangerous, as the cocaine base that is smoked may explode.

If we survive its production, we can smoke the cocaine base. The production and the use of cocaine base are called free-basing. The effects are the same, or greater, than using cocaine hydrochloride by injection:

> . . . tachycardia, increased blood pressure and respiration rate are the autonomic effects. The "rush" is sudden and intense. Feelings of energy, power and competency are described. The euphoric high subsides after a few minutes into a restless irritability . . . Sleep is impossible during a free base binge, but exhaustion eventually supervenes. Enormous weight loss takes place in heavy users due to the anorexic action of cocaine. Manic, paranoid or depressive psychoses have been seen. Overdoses can cause death due to cardiorespiratory arrest. (Cohen, 1980)

The head of the Haight-Ashbury Free Clinic in San Francisco describes cocaine users as follows: "heavy cocaine users exhibit symptoms similar to those of the 'speed freak.' Continued high doses result in irritability, suspicion, paranoia, nervousness and unrelieved fatigue, lapses in attention, inability to concentrate, and hallucinations" (Physicians Washington Report, 1980).

What used to be called the "post-cocaine blues," the depressed mood that comes after a period of snorting or free-basing turns out to be the "post-cocaine anguish." The down is as bad as the up was good. To reduce the anguish, more cocaine is used—until there is no more.

Heavy cocaine users (those who use frequent and/or high doses) experience several symptoms that are clearly abnormal. Similar effects can, and sometimes do, occur with high-level amphetamine users. One of the effects of cocaine is to cause some sensory neurons to fire spontaneously. When sensory nerves are activated in the absence of a stimulus in the real world, hallucinations result: the individual reports sensory stimulation in the absence of sensory input. A common hallucination in heavy cocaine users (or snow birds) is the visual "snow lights"—flashes or moving "lights" (bright spots). Sometimes they are labeled and identified by the person experiencing them—an attempt to bring some order and meaning into a strange experience.

Much less common but more disruptive is the appearance of "cocaine bugs"—the technical name is *formication.* The individual feels bugs crawling under his skin—he can feel them move but can't see them so they must be under his skin. Sometimes the hallucination is so severe that the individual will use a knife to try to cut out the bugs. More common though are open sores where the person has been scratching and picking at his "bugs." Again, it's the result of cocaine-induced spontaneous firing of neurons—but it feels real. All of us have had a miniature version of this: when we feel an "itch" and there's no obvious reason why that place should itch, one or more neurons has fired spontaneously.

Amphetamines

Let's now take a look at another stimulant—amphetamines. As with others, this stimulant is used to get a sense of euphoria. All of the sympathomimetic effects characteristic of cocaine are true of amphetamines. That is, the sympathetic nervous system becomes overly aroused. Tolerance to an amphetamine tends to develop fast. Most individuals using an amphetamine for its euphoric effect will start a pattern of oral use—maybe 20 to 30 mg—and as tolerance develops, the dose will be increased and the method of administration will shift to intravenous; this may be the injection of 100 mg every two to three hours. These extended periods of amphetamine use may last three to four days, until the individual either collapses from the lack of sleep and fatigue, or the amphetamine runs out.

The effects of the acute use of amphetamine and cocaine are difficult to distinguish. From the user's perspective, the amphetamine high may be somewhat harsher than that induced by cocaine. But from the outside looking in, except for the longer duration of the amphetamine effect, there are no significant differences. Friends or family may bring the acute amphetamine user to the emergency room because he is "so different." The difference usually is that under the influence of an amphetamine, the individual is hyper in *all* respects: he is particularly talkative, feels self-important and confident, euphoric, shows behavioral activation, agitation, and sleeplessness. These effects may cause friends and family some distress. Particularly disturbing to them will be the user's report that he feels fine—never better in fact—and his insistence that he doesn't want, and certainly doesn't need, to go to a hospital or to talk to anyone. This individual might be given a diagnosis of amphetamine intoxication.

Amphetamine intoxication is used as a diagnosis when the following five criteria are met: (1) recent use of an amphetamine; (2) within one hour of use, the occurrence of at least two of the following symptoms: psychomotor agitation, elation, grandiosity, excessive talking, or hypervigilance; (3) within one hour of use, occurrence of at least two of the following symptoms: very rapid heart rate, dilation of the pupils, high blood pressure, perspiration or chill, or nausea or vomiting; (4) maladaptive behavioral effects such as fighting, impaired judgment, and so on; and (5) no other basis for the syndrome.

There is a particular problem with amphetamine users. With the intravenous use of an amphetamine, the moderate to high level user will frequently become very suspicious and hostile. This combination of a suspicious, hostile person with high activity and a sense of power, along with nervousness and anxiety, and a heightened startle response, can be very dangerous. Thus, unlike some other heavy drug users, the heavy stimulant user may become dangerous.

Because of increased abuse of prescription drugs, particularly amphetamines, the Federal Drug Administration (FDA) restricted the freedom with which physicians can prescribe them. (Photograph by Arthur Tress)

EVERY MORNING BEFORE LARRY COULD SEE ME DEAD AND BLOWSY I DRAGGED OUT OF BED AND TOOK 100 MG. OF SPEMOCLAGULATE–
WHICH GAVE ME ENERGY THROUGH BREAKFAST–
WHEN I FELL INTO A SUICIDAL DEPRESSION, TAKING FOR IT 250 MG. OF PHENOAPTHAMINE–
SO I'D BE CHEERFUL WHEN LARRY MADE HIS LATE AFTERNOON PHONE CALL–
AFTER WHICH I FELL INTO A SUICIDAL DEPRESSION UNTIL JUST BEFORE DINNER TIME–
WHEN I HAD TWO MARTINIS IN ORDER TO BE VIVACIOUS WHEN LARRY GOT HOME FROM WORK–
AFTER WHICH I HID IN THE KITCHEN WITH A SUICIDAL DEPRESSION UNTIL 10:30–
WHEN I TOOK 500 MG. OF DIPHETOCAINE WHICH MADE ME ALERT AT BEDTIME WHEN LARRY DISCUSSED HIS DAY AT THE OFFICE–
AFTER WHICH I TOOK 750 MG. OF OSCULAVENOL AND SLEPT SOUNDLY THROUGH THE NIGHT.
THIS MORNING I WOKE UP DRAGGED MYSELF TO THE BATHROOM–
AND FOUND THAT I WAS ALL OUT OF EVERYTHING.
WHEN LARRY CAME DOWN FOR BREAKFAST HE SCREAMED: "WHO ARE YOU AND WHAT HAVE YOU DONE WITH DOROTHY?"

There is another kind of problem associated with amphetamines. Not long ago, drug companies started marketing a nonprescription anti-appetite drug called phenylpropanolamine (PPA). The problem developed when some manufacturers started producing this legal, mild, anorectic stimulant in the same shape, color, and markings as the much more potent prescription drug, amphetamine. The problem came when an abuser of PPA bought pills on the street. It takes a lot of PPA pills to become high. If the user believed that the pills were PPA, and thus took a lot of them—and they were really an amphetamine that looked like PPA, the person was in real danger of a drug overdose crisis, usually including high body temperature, convulsions, and cardiovascular shock. Several people died in this way since a lethal dose of amphetamines is less than 100 mg in a nontolerant person.

Chronic amphetamine use is almost always intravenous, and at high dose levels it results in a syndrome indistinguishable from paranoid schizophrenia (see Chapter 17). About the only way to tell it's an amphetamine reaction and not paranoia is by the history of amphetamine use—or the disappearance of the syndrome after three to four days of hospitalization. The similarities are marked: delusions of persecution, ideas of being talked about ("reference"), visual and auditory hallucinations. All of this occurs in what is called an "unclouded sensorium." This just means that the individual maintains a relatively clear awareness of his environment and that there is no thought disorder. He knows where he is, and when it is, and who he is. The suspiciousness, however, "requires" the individual to put new meanings on familiar situations, objects, or activities. For example, one patient was convinced that he knew important military secrets and that he was being followed by an agent of a foreign government. It made sense to him. He had noticed on the bus he took to work that every time he glanced at one person, that person was looking at him. Why? There must be some reason. Since the patient had received a "secret" clearance when in the army, he must know secrets. It all made sense to the patient. We've all had the experience of thinking someone was looking at us—the more we looked at him, the more he looked at us. It's the additional, unsupported inferences that make it a delusion, and that make it pathological.

The delusions that occur have been called *primary delusions* since they develop without any distortion of perception or impairment in general intellectual ability. For many years, there was debate over whether the amphetamine did anything more than uncover a personality predisposed to paranoid schizophrenia. Today, however, it is believed that a paranoid schizophrenia-like response can occur in almost anyone by continued, three to four days' use of high doses of amphetamine or cocaine. But in most situations that develop in the real world, this response seems to be an interaction of predisposition and amphetamine. Those who develop the amphetamine-cocaine psychosis usually already have personalities that include suspiciousness and feelings of low self-worth.

HALLUCINOGENS

Chemicals that cause large perceptual changes have been used in religious ceremonies for thousands of years. It is only since 1960 that there has been a great increase in the secular use of these hallucinogenic drugs. The two most known *hallucinogens* are lysergic acid diethylamide (LSD) and phencyclidine (PCP).

Lysergic acid diethylamide (LSD)

In 1945, a Swiss biochemist and researcher, Albert Hofmann, accidentally ingested a chemical that had been synthesized about seven years earlier. That chemical was LSD. His report of that accident was not released until sometime later. Below follow some excerpts from the report:

> I had great difficulty in speaking coherently, my field of vision swayed before me, and objects appeared distorted like images in curved mirrors. I had the impression of being unable to move from the spot, although my assistant told me afterwards that we had cycled at a good pace. . . .
> By the time the doctor arrived, the peak of the crisis had already passed. As far as I remember, the following were the most outstanding symptoms: vertigo, visual

Many users of hallucinogens realized profound differences in their effects (*Left:* Photograph by A. Maine/Magnum. *Right:* Photograph by Wayne Miller/ Magnum).

disturbances; the faces of those around me appeared as grotesque, colored masks; marked motor unrest, alternating with paresis; an intermittent heavy feeling in the head, limbs and the entire body, as if they were filled with metal; cramps in the legs, coldness and loss of feeling in the hands; a metallic taste on the tongue; dry, constricted sensation in the throat; feeling of choking; confusion alternating between clear recognition of my condition, in which state I sometimes observed, in the manner of an independent, neutral observer, that I shouted half insanely or babbled incoherent words. Occasionally I felt as if I were out of my body.

The doctor found a rather weak pulse but an otherwise normal circulation.

Six hours after ingestion of the LSD-25 my condition had already improved considerably. Only the visual disturbances were still pronounced. Everything seemed to sway and the proportions were distorted like the reflections in the surface of moving water. Moreover, all objects appeared in unpleasant, constantly changing colors, the predominant shades being sickly green and blue. When I closed my eyes, an unending series of colorful, very realistic and fantastic images surged in upon me. A remarkable feature was the manner in which all acoustic perceptions (e.g., the noise of a passing car) were transformed into optical effects, every sound causing a corresponding colored hallucination constantly changing in shape and color like pictures in a kaleidoscope. At about 1 o'clock I fell asleep and awakened next morning somewhat tired but otherwise feeling perfectly well. (Hofmann, 1968, pp. 185–86)

The one fact that made this report of great importance was *not* the fact that ingesting a chemical could cause psychotic-like symptoms. That had been known for years. Mescaline, one of the active ingredients in the Peyote cactus, produced similar effects, which had been studied during the nineteenth century. The crucial fact was the amount of LSD-25 that could induce a psychotic-like state: as little as 50 gamma/kilogram of body weight. In a 165-pound person, that works out to .0013 of an ounce. When that small amount of a drug can cause the great and dramatic cognitive, perceptual, and emotional changes that occur with LSD, it becomes entirely feasible that an endogenous biochemical manufactured by the body could cause schizophrenia, or other psychoses. That research still continues (see Chapter 17).

LSD in millionth of a gram (gamma) doses causes changes in body sensations, perception, emotion, and cognitive processes. LSD sometimes produces psychotic symptoms that seem to resemble schizophrenia, but on close and extensive study it has become clear that the LSD experience really wasn't parallel to schizophrenia (see Table 15-2).

Table 15-2 SOME DIFFERENCES IN BEHAVIOR BETWEEN THE SCHIZOPHRENIC PERSON AND THE LSD-USER

	Schizophrenic	*LSD-user*
1. Interpersonal contacts	Withdrawal	Withdrawal is unusual
2. Communication ability	Poor	Poor
3. Concern over inability to communicate	Little or none	Very high
4. Predominant hallucinations	Auditory and threatening	Visual and pleasant or neutral
5. Suggestibility	Very low	Very high

The somatic symptoms of an LSD experience include dizziness, weakness, tremors, and nausea. Perceptual symptoms range from the simple alteration of shapes and colors, to visual hallucinations and a distorted time sense. Affective and cognitive symptoms include depersonalization, difficulty in thinking, as well as large and rapid mood changes (Ray, 1983). The perceptual changes are the most prominent—and usually the primary reason for taking LSD. One of the more interesting aspects of this experience —and of other hallucinogenic drug experiences—is the individual's ability to observe himself, as he experiences the effect. Except at very high (and not usually taken) doses, LSD users usually contemplate the drug experience they are having as if they were both experiencing and monitoring the experience. Although this is a positive experience for many people, for some it is disastrous. Under the influence of LSD, one woman got up out of her chair, walked away, then turned and looked back. She was startled to see herself still sitting in the chair and carrying on the previous conversation. For some people, the reaction might be, "Neat, I can now see myself as others always see me." Others might also feel that this was a great experience and say "Watch me sit in my own lap and become one person, then get up and leave and become two people again." This woman did neither. She saw herself still sitting in the chair and became very anxious about even being able to re-enter her body. Her panic was so great that she required long hospitalization.

That example introduces us to one of the dangers of the use of hallucinogens. With the stimulants, and most drugs, the intensity of the experience grows with the amount of drug in the brain. When the drug is metabolized, deactivated, and excreted, the drug experience diminishes and goes away. But with the hallucinogens, especially LSD, there are occasional disruptions of the individual's psychological stability that last long beyond the disappearance of the drug from the body. These are drug-precipitated psychoses, which usually require extended hospitalization. They have not been well studied, but they seem to occur primarily in individuals who had poor personality organization even before taking the drug.

When an individual has a marginal hold on reality, multiple anxieties, doubts about his identity and self-worth, poor techniques for coping with the slings and arrows of the world, is something of a social isolate with a poor social support system, then you have a person at risk for an extended psychosis following the use of potent hallucinogens. We use the term *ego strength* to describe the capability of individuals to maintain their identity under stress, and to manipulate and modify the environment to meet their needs. Individuals with good ego strength are able to absorb and deal with the very great disruptions of the world around them (in times of disaster and stress, they are the "pillars of strength"). Those with little ego strength are fragile and have little resiliency—they have no resources and no reserves, so that when the slightest change occurs in their world they "fall apart." Individuals with little ego strength are unable to handle "mind wrenching" effects of an LSD experience, as they have depended on a stable world to maintain their own stability. The stability of their world is disrupted when it looks, sounds, and feels different, and when *they* feel different, with new sensations coming from their body, such as, "I feel as if my left big toe is going to vomit." When they can't organize their thoughts, or understand their feelings, these people are unable to put everything back together when the drug wears off. They stay in a confused, psychotic state, and usually require hospitalization and treatment (Bowers, 1977). The following case history is an example of this unfortunate situation:

> A twenty-three-year-old man was admitted to the hospital after he stood uncertain whether to plunge an upraised knife into his friend's back. His wife, an intelligent, nonpsychotic but masochistic woman, reported that he had been acting strangely since taking LSD approximately three weeks before admission. He was indecisive and often mute and shunned physical contact with her. On admission he was catatonic and mute. He appeared to be preoccupied with auditory hallucinations of God's voice and thought he had achieved a condition of "all mind." On transfer to another hospital one month after admission, there was minimal improvement. During his adolescence the patient had alternated between acceptance of and rebellion against his mother's religiosity and warnings of the perils of sex and immorality. He had left college during his first year after excessive use of amphetamines. He attended, but did not complete, art school. His marriage of three years had been marked by conflict and concern about his masculinity. Increasing puzzlement about the meaning of life, his role in the universe and other cosmic problems led to his ingestion of LSD. Shortly after ingestion he was ecstatic and wrote to a friend, "We have found the peace, which is life's river which flows into the sea of Eternity." Soon afterward, in a brief essay, he showed some awareness of his developing psychosis, writing, "I am misunderstood, I cried, and was handed a complete list of my personality traits, habits, goals, and ideals, etc. I know myself now, I said in relief, and spent the rest of my life in happy cares asylum. AMEN." (Frosch, Robbins, and Stern, 1965)

Prolonged psychosis precipitated by hallucinogen use is usually accompanied by overwhelming fear, and often by paranoid symptoms. Almost half of the individuals with a drug-precipitated psychosis have had some type of psychiatric treatment in their history. Over one-third of the psychotic episodes occur in individuals following their very first dose of LSD. But when the psychosis required the drug experience to precipitate it, and when these individuals had relatively stable personalities beforehand, the prognosis for complete recovery is very good. Compared to other individuals hospitalized for an acute psychotic reaction, almost two-thirds of those hospitalized for a drug induced psychotic episode clear in one week and no longer require hospitalization or treatment.

A different, but fairly common, reaction that sends hallucinogen users to the hospital is the panic reaction. The person may be having "a good trip" but some part of the experience—or more accurately, a response to part of the experience—may induce a great state of fearfulness and anxiety. The typical situation is one in which individuals react to the drug experience with a fear that they "are going crazy." This can occur even when the individuals are aware that the effects come from the drug—the experiences are so strong that they begin to doubt that they will ever return to normal. With distorted perceptions and diminished cognitive ability, they are unable to reduce the fear and anxiety over not getting back to normal, which spirals into a full-blown panic. The panic here is not to the drug experience per se but to their reaction to the drug experience—regardless of the source, it still sends many people to emergency rooms. Continual reassurance—that the effects will go away as the drug disappears from the body—and perhaps a low dose of one of the anti-anxiety drug (such as Valium) is usually enough treatment to bring the individual back to his pre-drug state.

Less common than panic reactions, but more frequent than the need for prolonged hospitalization for hallucinogen-induced psychoses, are the very unsettling experiences of ***flashbacks.*** Flashbacks have been reported with both LSD and marijuana and refer to a situation in which the individual, not under the drug, re-experiences some of an earlier, usually bad, drug experience. The phenomenon is not well understood. It is known that it is *not* due to any residual physiological or biochemical changes, or to low amounts of the drug retained in the body. Since flashbacks seem to occur mostly in individuals who have marginal stability even under monotonous conditions, the flashbacks may be most similar to dissociative or fugue states (see Chapter 11). They occur less frequently as the bad drug experience becomes more remote in time. The following case history is typical:

> A man in his late twenties came to the admitting office in a state of panic. Although he had not taken any drug in approximately two months he was beginning to re-experience some of the illusory phenomena, perceptual distortions and the feeling of union with things around him that had previously occurred only under the influence of LSD. In addition, his wife had told him that he was beginning to "talk crazy," and he had become frightened. Despite a somewhat disturbed childhood and an interrupted college career he had carefully controlled his anxiety by a rigid obsessive-compulsive character structure, which had permitted him to work with reasonable success as a junior executive. Although for six years before admission he had felt the urge to seek help and self-understanding, he had never sought psychiatric care. He had tried marijuana, peyote and finally ground morning-glory seeds. Most of his fifteen experiences with LSD had been pleasurable although he also had had two panic reactions, neither of which had led to hospital admission. On these occasions he thought that he was losing control and that his whole body was disappearing. At the time of admission he was concerned lest LSD have some permanent effect upon him. He wished reassurance so that he could take it again. His symptoms have subsided but tended to reappear in anxiety-provoking situations. (Frosch, Robbins, and Stern, 1968)

The three types of situations presented here—flashback, prolonged psychosis, and panic—along with the report of Hofmann's LSD experience pretty much cover the major kinds of reactions to LSD-like drugs. As mentioned earlier, the reactions to these drugs are different in different people at different times. In fact, one of the reasons why these drugs are attractive to some people is that they yield different effects in the same person when used repeatedly.

Phencyclidine (PCP)

PCP differs from LSD in that the effects of PCP seem to be less dependent on the characteristics of the user and the specific setting in which the use occurs. PCP was developed as an anesthetic agent, but it was never marketed for human use because many volunteers coming out of its anesthesia experienced hallucinations and confusion.

PCP has multiple effects, and none are really understood. It induces changes primarily in the body sensory systems but also sensitizes the user to any sensory input; it also leads to feelings of depersonalization. The changes in the body sensory systems result in changes in body image—sometimes gross distortions, e.g., "my arms feel like a twenty-mile pole with a pen at the end." The sensitizing of all sensory input fits in with the finding that in-

To contain a PCP user, police often resort to shark nets. (Courtesy Sygma)

creased sensory stimulation increases the PCP delirium, and with the fact that you do not try to talk down the person having a PCP experience; it only makes things worse. The less stimulating the environment is for someone on a PCP trip, the sooner he will return to normal.

Hallucinations are generally absent in the PCP state. The individual does not have the ability to observe his drug-induced state—as do most LSD users. Another contrast to the LSD experience is that there is at least partial amnesia for the PCP episode, and frequently there is no memory or recall for the entire experience. PCP elicits an experience that seems very similar to a state of delirium: diminished awareness of self and environment, disorientation in time and space, muddled thinking, impaired attention and memory. It's hard to understand why anyone would seek out this experience, although it's very easy to understand why many PCP users end up in emergency rooms. At low doses, the experience is more like a moderate drunk: confusion, loss of inhibitions, poor psychomotor coordination. Contrary to their image, few chronic users of PCP are violent. What seems to happen is that the police, or others, get involved because the person looks drunk. The increased stimulation of being picked up or arrested, and especially of being grabbed, increases PCP user's arousal. In the flailing around to get away—even from friends trying to restrain the person—people may get hurt. Another contributing factor to the popular belief that the PCP user is a violent person is the fact that the PCP is an analgesic agent that reduces the response to pain and injury—so the activity may continue when it might stop in someone not on PCP.

There are now many studies that confirm the early reports: there are no significant differences between emergency-room cases of PCP users and those undergoing an acute psychotic response. The PCP condition usually goes away faster, however. As the 1980s continue, there are sure to be more and more complete reports about the long-term use of PCP. At this time there are only hints, but regular—daily—use of PCP seems to cause a permanent decrease in thinking and memory, as well as resulting in a flattening of emotion (U.S. Department of Health and Human Services, 1980).

NARCOTICS

Narcotics have been used therapeutically against pain for several thousand years—and for most of that period, they were about the only effective drug that doctors had. Narcotics reduce pain without producing a loss of consciousness (as would an anesthetic). Researchers have recently discovered that the brain is actually capable of producing a molecule similar in size and shape to that of the narcotic morphine and that this chemical (called an *endorphin*—an endogenous morphine) acts in ways similar to a narcotic. Narcotics do not reduce pain by blocking the pain impulses—instead, they block the emotional response to the pain. You know you are feeling pain, but you don't care.

We will begin by discussing the different kinds of narcotics. Opium is the chemically active substance in the opium poppy. There are reports of opium cakes being sold widely in the days of the Roman Empire. Opium reduces cares and anxiety and produces a pleasurable reverie. In 1806, morphine, which has about 10 percent of the bulk of an equally potent amount of opium, was extracted from opium. By the late 1800s, a minor chemical modification was performed on morphine, transforming it into heroin, which is about two to four times as potent as an equal bulk of morphine. Methadone is a completely synthetic chemical that is not derived from organic matter (e.g., a plant), but that has the same effects as opium, morphine, and heroin. All of the narcotics have similar physiological effects, although the drugs differ in potency and duration of action. Moreover, tolerance develops to the use of narcotics, and addiction can occur.

There are probably more false beliefs about narcotics than about any other class of drugs. For example, it was believed that snorting heroin would not lead to addiction. In fact, tolerance and addiction occur with regular use of a narcotic, no matter how it is ingested. In Southeast Asia during the Vietnam War, American GIs snorted 95 percent pure heroin, believing erroneously that addiction occurred only if the heroin was injected. Many GIs learned the hard way that it is the drug that produces addiction, not the mode of administration.

Another false belief is that mainlining heroin always initially results in an ecstatic experience—a full-blown, long-lasting orgastic experience. It does that for some people. One addict described the effect of mainlining heroin by saying, "Imagine every cell in your body had a tongue—and they were all licking honey!" Others reported that following the injection they became nauseous and vomited—and then had the euphoric experience. In some individuals, the nausea overshadowed the pleasurable experience, and they were unwilling to use heroin again.

Heroin Users

One hundred years ago, the typical narcotic addict was white, female, middle-aged, and Southern. She primarily used morphine, took it orally, probably never had a narcotic high, did not see herself as an addict, was a "solid" citizen, and if she lived on a farm she may have ordered her morphine from mail-order stores.

In the mid-1980s, the typical narcotic addict is black, male, less than thirty years old, and lives in the inner city. He primarily uses heroin, mainlines it, tries to achieve a high as often as possible, knows he is addicted (and may be proud of it), and lives outside the law—both in the activities designed to generate use and in the purchase of heroin. Every year, however, the typical heroin user is less black and less male. In the early 1970s, black inner city heroin users were better educated and were at a higher socioeconomic level than the average black, inner-city nonaddict. These addicts supported their drug use in many ways, especially with crime—usually crimes against property. In the 1980s, the characteristics of the black heroin user are less clear.

Narcotic Intoxication and Withdrawal

The effects of the use of narcotics and the effect of stopping use are not as dramatic as the effects of other classes of drugs discussed in this chapter. Nor are the effects of narcotics of great interest psychologically; there are no hallucinations or delusions, no high excitability. Other depressant drugs—the barbiturates and especially alcohol—cause more anguishing symptoms, particularly in withdrawal. It may be that narcotics have milder effects because they act at very specific locations, and in the same way as a naturally occurring substance—the endorphins. This may also be the reason why the course of narcotic withdrawal is less life threatening than withdrawal from alcohol and barbiturates.

Narcotic intoxication is diagnosed if there is recent use of a narcotic, no other basis for the symptoms, and all of the following: (1) pupillary constriction (or pupillary dilation due to lack of oxygen from severe overdose); (2) at least one of the following—euphoria, dysphoria, apathy, psychomotor retardation; (3) at least one of the following—drowsiness, slurred speech, impairment in attention or memory; and (4) maladaptive behavior, such as impaired judgment. Several points need comment. Constriction of the pupils is the typical response to narcotics. But in an overdose, respiration is seriously depressed (even to the point of death), and the low oxygen supply to the brain results in dilation of the pupils—which overrides the usual constriction. Narcotics are depressant drugs; they slow the central nervous system. It is not surprising that slurred speech and drowsiness accompany the post-high period. The user drifts in and out of a sleep-like state—but the user is easily aroused, and it is not a deep sleep. Addicts talk of being "on the nod."

Narcotic withdrawal is diagnosed when (1) there is no other basis for the symptoms; and (2) there is a history of prolonged, heavy use of a narcotic; and (3) at least four of the following occur due to reducing or stopping narcotic use—tearing, runny nose, pupil dilation, goose bumps, sweating, diarrhea, yawning, slight increase in blood pressure, fast heart rate, fever, insomnia. Notice that all of the withdrawal symptoms are physiological, not psychological, with the possible exception of insomnia.

Marijuana

Marijuana is a plant of the species cannabis that contains at least one psychoactive drug: tetrahydrocannabinol (THC). THC is a very interesting chemical for several reasons. First, depending on dose, it has effects that range from a very mild euphoria at low doses, to true LSD-like hallucinations at much higher doses. Few drugs do that. Second, THC is rapidly metabolized in the body and is picked up and stored in fatty tissue. As a result, THC is released only very slowly. After one dose of THC (one or two joints of marijuana), 25 percent to 30 percent of it may still be in the body after one week, and it may take a month before it is completely gone. This storage and slow release is unlike any of the drugs discussed in this chapter. And the big problem is that no one knows for sure what effect this slow release will have on those who ingest it.

THC at low doses produces dose-related impairment of function. THC decreases attentiveness and vigilance; that is, impairment of the ability to focus on a task (like driving an automobile) over an extended period. THC use also leads to an intrusion of extraneous ideas, so that not only is the task at hand not continually attended to, but irrelevant inputs are added to the situation. Last, but far from least, at the doses of THC reached with social use of marijuana, there is impairment of the ability to engage in sequential thinking.

Two different problems account for most of the concern about psychopathology and marijuana use. The first problem is by far the most frequent —the panic reaction that occurs in some marijuana users. The second issue is whether marijuana can cause a "marijuana psychosis" (just as an amphetamine can cause an amphetamine psychosis) or whether the psychosis that occasionally accompanies marijuana use is a nonspecific psychosis. The debate has gone on for over a century, and it is most likely that there is not a specific psychotic syndrome elicited by marijuana. The final answer probably will not be reached until sometime after there is more known about the mechanism of action of THC. The symptoms that occur in the rare marijuana-induced psychosis seem to fit well into the general category of toxic hallucinatory state, including clouding of consciousness, disorientation, and some delusions and paranoia (but not well organized). In almost every case in the clinical literature, the marijuana psychosis clears within a few days.

If heavy, chronic use of marijuana/THC (cannabis) increases in frequency in the United States, the following will be important:

> The only cannabis-induced psychosis picture which is supported by sufficient evidence at this moment is a short-lasting condition—from a few days to four weeks —with symptoms of mental confusion, memory impairment, regressive and impulsive behavior, delusional formations, and sensory-perceptive distortions. The frequency of occurrence in Western societies is quite low, and it seems to affect mainly very heavy users. A commonly found predisposing factor is a high degree of premorbid personality disturbance. (National Academy of Sciences, 1982)

The most frequently occurring negative response to marijuana/THC use is panic reaction. Some studies found that as many as "33 percent of regular users reported that while intoxicated they occasionally experienced such symptoms as acute panic, paranoid reaction, hallucinations, and unpleasant distortions in body image" (Addiction Research Foundation, 1981, p. 121). Inexperienced (first time) users are more likely to report this; the effects are more likely to occur in a setting that the user sees as threatening (i.e., where the user might be busted!). Because it is impossible to separate the effect of the drug from the effect of doing an illegal thing that might be discovered, a better index of the anxiety-panic response to marijuana/THC use comes from laboratory studies. Those studies have shown that the probability of a panic reaction increases with dose level, it can occur after a single dose, and the effects rarely last more than two to four hours.

There is one final psychological response to THC. When THC has been used therapeutically—as it was in the beginning of the twentieth century and then again more recently—it is not uncommon for older patients to show "severe dysphoric reactions characterized by disorientation, catatonic-like immobility, acute panic, and heavy sedation . . . " (Addiction Research Foundation, 1981, p. 122). But the basis for the response is *not* the dose level, since those used were only moderate. It is more the situation: the older person is usually in a hospital (isolated and restricted environment) and medically ill (particularly vulnerable and insecure). Therefore, an older person experiencing the new and strange perceptual and body sensations induced by THC would be more understandably anxious and uncomfortable.

What can we say about the diagnosis of cannabis intoxication, its abuse, and dependence on it? Much like other substances, cannabis abuse is diagnosed when: (1) an individual uses cannabis almost every day for at least a month, and is high throughout the day; *and* (2) the individual also has impaired social or occupational functioning because of cannabis use. Cannabis dependence is diagnosed when either of the above factors is present, *and also* when tolerance has developed to cannabis. Tolerance to cannabis is not common nor has it been well studied, but it does occur. The fact that THC is stored in the fat cells of the body might even suggest the development of *reverse tolerance,* in which less drug is needed to get the same effect with further use. There is some clinical and research evidence, as well as many anecdotal reports, to support the concept of reverse tolerance.

Most of the individuals who appear in emergency rooms as a result of cannabis use are given a diagnosis of cannabis intoxication. That diagnosis is made using the following criteria, all five of which must be present: (1) recent use of cannabis; (2) fast heart rate; (3) at least one of the following within two hours of use: euphoria, sensation of slowed time, apathy, the experiencing of intensified perceptions; (4) at least one of the following within two hours of use: increased appetite, dry mouth, reddening of eyes; and (5) maladaptive behavioral effects such as suspiciousness, excessive anxiety, impaired judgment, and so on.

The diagnosis of cannabis intoxication is used more and more frequently because there is an increase in the number of individuals going to emergency rooms as a result of cannabis use. Between 1970 and 1980, there was about a 400 percent increase in cannabis-based visits to emergency rooms. Most of these visits were due to anxiety attacks and panic reactions.

In addition to the increase in the total number of marijuana users, a probable reason for the increase in adverse reactions was the increase in the THC level in marijuana. In 1970, marijuana averaged about a 1 percent THC content. That gradually increased—particularly in the late 1970s—to about 5 or 6 percent in the early 1980s. For a premium price, one could buy sinsemilla (specially cultivated marijuana from Northern California) or Hawaiian marijuana; both had a 6 to 12 percent THC content. If someone has been accustomed to low THC marijuana and then intentionally or, worse, unintentionally uses something five to ten times as potent, it is not surprising that the individual believes he or she is falling apart and panics. Imagine drinking a glass of vodka thinking it was beer. As more potent marijuana becomes more readily available, it is likely that the incidence of adverse reactions will continue to increase.

ALCOHOL

In many respects, **alcohol** is by far the number one drug used in this country. More people have used, do use, and do abuse alcohol than any other drug. In spite of years of research, there is no evidence that there is an alcohol-prone personality or that the factors leading to alcohol abuse are any different from those leading to the abuse of other substances.

About two-thirds of the adults in this country report that they use alcohol. At least 10 percent of them have some social, psychological, or medical

Adolescents, as well as adults, use and abuse alcohol. (Photograph by Charles Gatewood)

problems resulting from alcohol use. Probably half of that 10 percent are addicted to alcohol. Adolescents also use and abuse alcohol.

Table 15-1 (page 400) shows the data for U.S. high school seniors—nine of ten have tried alcohol, seven of ten used it in the month preceding the survey.

More people get into trouble as a result of alcohol use than due to the use of any other drug. Over 50 percent of automobile fatalities involve drivers who have alcohol in their blood. The trouble may be a psychological or medical emergency—alcohol use has contributed to the medical problems of at least 25 percent of the individuals hospitalized in this country. The single most common thing that brings individuals to hospital emergency rooms is alcohol overdose—including intoxication. This occurs so often that most emergency rooms do not record the frequency of visits caused only by alcohol. They do record those visits that involve alcohol in combination with another drug, and they are far more frequent than visits involving any other drug (except alcohol alone). In 1980, alcohol in combination with another drug was responsible for 14 percent of all recorded drug-related visits to emergency rooms. These findings were taken from a national survey, and there had been a 25 percent increase in these alcohol-in-combination visits just from 1978 and 1980. Clearly, alcohol is this country's number one drug problem.

Research seems to indicate that the problem of alcohol abuse will probably worsen. One study shows that the incidence of alcohol abuse is most closely tied to the number of individuals using alcohol and that the number of users is closely related to the availability of places where alcohol can be purchased (Frankel and Whitehead, 1981). These results also show that, so far, all of the programs designed to teach "responsible drinking" have not been effective in reducing alcohol abuse. In short, as alcohol becomes more available, more people will use it, and more people will abuse it. That was certainly reflected when the legal drinking age was lowered in many states from twenty-one to eighteen years of age. Traffic accidents and fatalities of eighteen- and nineteen-year-olds increased 20 to 50 percent, and alcohol was

Alcohol is by far the most heavily used drug in our society. (Photograph by Leonard Freed/ Magnum)

the primary factor implicated. Some states have since raised their minimum drinking age—and in those states there has been a significant drop (up to 20 percent) in traffic accidents in the age group involved.

There seems to be some truth to the phrase that surfaced in the late 1960s, in the early days of increased marijuana use: marijuana is a mind drug, alcohol is a body drug. As of the mid-1980s, it is true that the negative effects of alcohol on the body are much greater than the negative effects of marijuana. Regular use of substantial amounts of alcohol is associated with the following: hypertension, strokes, heart muscle failure, cancer of the mouth and throat, decrease in testosterone level, apparent decrease in brain tissue, and cirrhosis of the liver. Also, alcoholics have a mortality rate that is two-and-a-half times that of nonalcoholics. There is no evidence, however, that one to three drinks a day has any significant negative physiological effect on adult males and nonpregnant females.

Alcohol is the one drug for which there are good dose-response data— partly because of the importance alcohol use has had in our society, but primarily because it is easy to measure alcohol level in the blood. Measuring the amount of alcohol in the air we breathe out (as in a breathalyzer) gives a reliable measure of the alcohol in the blood. The amount of alcohol in the blood is highly related to the alcohol in the brain (alcohol easily goes through the blood-brain barrier), and it is the alcohol in the brain that causes the impairment of behavior and of many psychological functions. Table 15-3 gives a good approximation of the relationship between alcohol intake and blood alcohol levels for men and women. Table 15-4 shows how increasing blood alcohol levels impairs function.

Table 15–3 RELATIONSHIPS AMONG SEX, WEIGHT, ORAL ALCOHOL CONSUMPTION, AND BLOOD ALCOHOL LEVEL

Absolute alcohol (ounces)	Beverage intake*	Blood alcohol levels (mg/100 ml)					
		Female (100 lb)	Male (100 lb)	Female (150 lb)	Male (150 lb)	Female (200 lb)	Male (200 lb)
1/2	1 oz spirits† 1 glass wine 1 can beer	0.045	0.037	0.03	0.025	0.022	0.019
1	2 oz spirits 2 glasses wine 2 cans beer	0.090	0.075	0.06	0.050	0.045	0.037
2	4 oz spirits 4 glasses wine 4 cans beer	0.180	0.150	0.12	0.100	0.090	0.070
3	6 oz spirits 6 glasses wine 6 cans beer	0.270	0.220	0.18	0.150	0.130	0.110
4	8 oz spirits 8 glasses wine 8 cans beer	0.360	0.300	0.24	0.200	0.180	0.150
5	10 oz spirits 10 glasses wine 10 cans beer	0.450	0.370	0.30	0.250	0.220	0.180

*In 1 hour.   SOURCE: Ray, 1983, p. 168.
†100-proof spirits.

Table 15–4 BLOOD ALCOHOL LEVEL AND BEHAVIORAL EFFECTS

Percent blood alcohol level	*Behavioral effects*
0.05	Lowered alertness, usually good feeling, release of inhibitions, impaired judgment
0.10	Slowed reaction times and impaired motor function, less caution
0.15	Large, consistent increases in reaction time
0.20	Marked depression in sensory and motor capability, decidedly intoxicated
0.25	Severe motor disturbance, staggering, sensory perceptions greatly impaired, smashed!
0.30	Stuporous but conscious—no comprehension of the world around them
0.35	Surgical anesthesia; about LD 1 (lethal dose 1%), minimal level causing death
0.40	About LD 50 (lethal dose 50%)

SOURCE: Ray, 1983, p. 166.

Although a specific blood alcohol level, at least 0.1 percent, is used in most states to determine legal intoxication, there are different criteria for a DSM-III diagnosis of alcohol intoxication. For this diagnosis, all of the following five criteria must be present: (1) recent ingestion of alcohol; (2) maladaptive behavioral effects—such as fighting, poor judgment, etc.; (3) at least one of the following— slurred speech, uncoordination, unsteady gait, nystagmus (rapid involuntary movements of the eye), flushed face; (4) at least one of the following—mood changes, irritability, excessive talking, impaired attention; and (5) none of the effects being due to any other disorder. Most of us have probably seen, or been with, individuals who would meet all of these criteria for the diagnosis of alcohol intoxication.

Even though alcohol is our most abused drug and there has been much research, time, and money invested in studying it, we are still not sure how it acts in the brain. There is not even complete agreement on many of its general effects on brain systems. We do know many things, however: (1) it is primarily a depressant drug (the increased activity sometimes seen for a period after its use is due to the fact that inhibitions are depressed first, at low dose levels); (2) tolerance develops to the effects of alcohol; (3) after prolonged use of moderate to high levels of alcohol, addiction occurs (instead of talking about an alcohol addict we call the individual an alcoholic, but essentially, they are the same thing); (4) a sudden decrease in alcohol intake in an alcoholic will result in a dangerous withdrawal syndrome called *delirium tremens*—DT's (this is medically more dangerous than withdrawal from any narcotic).

In addition to intoxication, alcohol abuse can lead to other alcohol-induced states that frequently appear in emergency rooms: alcohol hallucinosis and the above-mentioned delirium tremens. The diagnosis of *alcohol hallucinosis* is not easy. The individual will have hallucinations of some type, will have appropriate reaction to the hallucinations (i.e., be afraid if the hallucinations are fear provoking), have no delirium or confusion, and have no easily identifiable signs of heavy alcohol use. In some cases, the individual is misdiagnosed as schizophrenic—particularly if alcohol abuse is denied, and there is no friend or family member to set the record straight. Alcohol hallucinosis occurs in some long-term, heavy-drinking alcoholics who have stopped drinking or reduced considerably their alcohol intake in the previous forty-eight hours. There are no significant differences in the type of hallucinations or other symptoms between the schizophrenic and the alcoholic with hallucinosis: the only clear distinguishing characteristic is the history. This is a good example of a toxic psychosis having features that are identical to a functional psychosis.

The other alcohol-induced state, delirium tremens, is relatively easy to identify. The DT's are a sequence of symptoms resulting from a continuing decrease in alcohol levels in an alcoholic.

Two case histories below will provide a good overview of the syndrome. One is the classic description by Huckleberry Finn of his Pap, the other is a contemporary history of a recent patient.

Pap took the jug, and said he had enough whisky there for two drunks and one delirium tremens. . . . He drank and drank . . . .I don't know how long I was asleep, but . . .there was an awful scream and I was up. There was a pap looking wild, and skipping around every which way and yelling about snakes. He said they was crawling up on his legs; and then he would give a jump and scream, and say one had bit him on the cheek—but I couldn't see no snakes. He started and run around . . . hollering "Take him off! he's biting me on the neck!" I never see a man look so wild in the eyes. Pretty soon he was all fagged out, and fell down panting; then he rolled over . . . kicking things every which way, and striking and grabbing at the air with his hands, and screaming . . . there was devils a-hold of him. He wore out by and by . . . He says . . . "Tramp-tramp-tramp; that's the dead; tramp-tramp-tramp; they're coming after me; but I won't go. Oh, they're here; don't touch me—don't! hands off—they're cold; let go . . . "

Then he went down on all fours and crawled off, begging them to let him alone . . .

By and by he . . . jumped up on his feet looking wild . . . and went for me. He chased me round and round the place with a claspknife, calling me the Angel of Death, and saying he would kill me, and then I wouldn't come for him no more. . . . Pretty soon he was all tired out . . . and said he would rest for a minute and then kill me . . .

"Git it up! . . . "

I opened my eyes and look around. . . . Pap was standing over me looking sour—and sick, too. He says:

"What you doin' . . . ?"

I judge he didn't know nothing about what he had been doing. . . . (Twain, 1884/1983)

This forty-five-year-old white male had eight years of education and two years in the army. He started drinking at eighteen and, although he was court martialed three times and spent six months in the stockade for alcohol-related offenses, he says his drinking has been a problem only for the last ten years.

His drinking sprees now last three to four weeks and occur about six times a year. During these sprees he reports consuming at least a quart of whisky, a gallon of wine, and one to three six-packs of beer every day. He has had blackouts, extreme shakes, and hallucinations on a "few" occasions. He has had more arrests for public drunkenness than he can remember.

On his first admission to the hospital five years ago he said he only drank a few beers a day, but his wife brought him to the hospital because he was talking to the TV, hearing strange music, and seeing bugs and snakes. On his next admission two years later, he said he was ready for treatment but managed to miss all of his scheduled appointments. When confronted, he dressed and left the hospital. (Ray, 1983, p. 174)

Alcoholics' Anonymous (AA) is one of several successful treatments for those whose lives are severely affected by this drug (Photography by Jeffrey Grosscup).

There are four stages of symptoms in delirium tremens. Stage 1 begins the psychomotor agitation and hyperactivity of the autonomic nervous system that continues throughout all four stages. The shakes and anxiety may begin within two or three hours of no alcohol. The shakes (most noticeably tremors of the hands) get progressively more intense and disruptive—to the point where the individual may not even be able to feed himself. This initial stage is also characterized by a very rapid heart rate, heavy sweating, high blood pressure, insomnia, and loss of appetite. In the absence of treatment, or the drinking of more alcohol, these signs and symptoms increase continually. It may be four, six, or eight hours after the last drink, but the appearance of hallucinations will mark the beginning of stage 2. These hallucinations may occur in any sensory system—visual, auditory, tactile, etc.—and are similar to those that occur in alcohol hallucinosis. The differential diagnosis is easy, however; none of the stage 1 symptoms are present in alcohol hallucinosis.

As stage 3 delirium develops and delusions appear—intermittently at first and then for increasing durations—followed by amnesia for the episode. Disorientation to time and place is common. All of the foregoing stages may develop in the first twenty-four hours after the last drink—or it may take ninety-six hours for the stage to appear. The time course of the DT's depends on the rate at which the alcohol levels decrease. Finally, stage 4 is marked by convulsions. These are major, grand mal convulsions that may occur frequently, and sometimes cause death. The four stages overlap, merge, and are sometimes missed entirely, however, so the clinical situation is never quite like the prototype described here. In actual practice in a hospital setting, an individual clearly "going into" the DT's would be hospitalized—on a medical ward usually since the medical problems are more critical than the psychiatric problems—and treated with a long-lasting benzodiazepine, usually Librium. The benzodiazepine has cross tolerance with alcohol and will substitute for the alcohol—and thus stop withdrawal (the DT's). The amount of benzodiazepine is gradually reduced to zero over four to seven days, and at that point the individual has been "withdrawn" from addiction to alcohol.

The DT's and alcohol hallucinosis are of interest because they re-emphasize an important point made earlier in this chapter: anything that disrupts the normal functioning of the brain may give rise to mild, moderate, or severe psychological symptoms. In the case of addiction, however, the normal state of the brain is such that it contains a high level of the involved drug. Disruption means a decrease in drug level—not an increase, as with many examples of other drugs discussed in this chapter.

DEPRESSANTS

For the first fifty years of the twentieth century, **barbiturates** were important drugs in the physician's black bag and they were widely used. They were also abused. Because of their potential for abuse, very close control was placed on their manufacture, distribution, and prescription in the mid-1970s. The controls worked. Both the medical and recreational use decreased rapidly into the 1980s. Whether the future will see a resurgence of barbiturate use is difficult to predict. Whatever the cause, their potential for abuse is very great.

Barbiturates are a large group (now over 2500) of synthetic drugs developed from barbituric acid. Most of the barbiturates in common use have been available for years: phenobarbital (1912); amobarbital (1923); pentobarbital and secobarbital (1930). They are all superb depressants ("downers") of the central nervous system and vary primarily in potency and duration of action. In both therapeutic and recreational use tolerance develops, and addiction is always a risk.

At low doses, the barbiturates decrease anxiety and blunt sensitivity to the world around the user. At these low dose levels, barbiturates are prescribed and used as sedatives. At higher dose levels, the barbiturates are called hypnotics and are prescribed as sleeping pills. Both of these uses have decreased rapidly since the late 1970s. Their therapeutic use has been replaced primarily by the minor tranquilizers—especially by the benzodiazepines (such as Valium, for anxiety, and Dalmane, for sleep).

The transition from the barbiturates to the minor tranquilizers was not just a tribute to modern advertising, for there are some real advantages to the benzodiazepines. Although tolerance develops to both the barbiturates and the benzodiazepines, and addiction can occur to both classes of drugs, tolerance develops more slowly and addiction is less likely with the benzodiazepines. Most important, while it is quite easy to commit suicide with barbiturates, it is almost impossible with the benzodiazepines. (Until the mid-1970s, the barbiturates were the primary class of drugs used in both successful and attempted suicides.)

Use and Abuse of Barbiturates

One frequent type of barbiturate abuse occurred in the middle aged, especially in women. They never saw themselves as addicts, but sometimes they were. The sleep-inducing dose of a barbiturate is about one-third to one-half that necessary for addiction. As tolerance developed, the user would increase the dose more rapidly than necessary, and addiction would occur.

These individuals usually obtain their supply of barbiturates from physicians rather than from "street dealers." They visit many different physicians with the same complaint, usually difficulty in sleeping, in order to obtain several prescriptions for barbiturates. Sometimes it is also possible to refill the prescriptions without the physician's knowledge.

Confusion, decreased ability to work and episodes of acute intoxication with slurred speech and staggering finally draws attention to their addiction. Intentional (suicide attempt) . . . unintentional (due to confusion) overdose and accidents are the major medical hazard in this type of abuse pattern. (Wesson and Smith, 1971)

The barbiturates reduce REM sleep, depress and inhibit neural activity, affect the body's chemical balance, and decrease the functioning of some of the body's organs. In high doses, they cause such a depression of the central nervous system that breathing stops. At lower doses, they have effects that are almost identical to the effects of alcohol. Used recreationally, barbiturates provide an alcohol-like experience, without the alcohol taste or breath or expense. A report to the U.S. Senate investigating committee said:

For the youngster barbiturates are a more reliable "high" and less detectable than "pot." They are less strenuous than LSD, less "freaky" than amphetamines, and less expensive than heroin. A school boy can "drop a red" and spend the day in a dreamy, floating state of awayness untroubled by reality. It is drunkenness without the odor of alcohol. It is escape for the price of one's lunch money. (Cohen, 1971)

Recreational use of the downers has decreased, but the barbiturates of choice are still secobarbital or pentobarbital— both of which have a three- to six-hour duration of action. Barbiturate intoxication is " . . .marked by confusion, intellectual impairment, personality change, emotional lability, motor incoordination, staggering gait, slurred speech and nystagmus." The withdrawal effects from the barbiturates are similar to, as medically dangerous, and as psychologically anguishing as withdrawal from alcohol addiction.

Methaqualone

Methaqualone (Quaalude) is a nonbarbiturate, depressant drug that should never have been marketed. Even before it was sold in the United States, its recreational use had been associated with overdose deaths in several countries in Europe. It has no unique depressant, sedative, or hypnotic characteristics, and tolerance and addiction develop to it. It is of interest here for only two reasons. One is its street reputation as "heroin for lovers"—an aphrodisiac. There is *no* basis for that belief. The other reason is that an increasing number of individuals have been turning up in emergency rooms as a result of methaqualone use. From 1978 to 1980, there was an increase of almost 140 percent. In 1980, methaqualone was the fifth most frequently mentioned drug sending individuals to emergency rooms. And it looks as if the trend is still continuing toward more use. In short, it is a very dangerous drug.

TREATMENT AND REHABILITATION

Half-way houses provide one way for the chemically dependent to re-enter society (Photograph by Jeffrey Grosscup).

It is obvious that there is very great need for treatment programs. The drug problem is so large. And as with other problems, it makes more sense to try to prevent substance abuse than to treat it after it occurs. Alcohol and drug education programs are now everywhere. The effects of most of them are not all that clear: few have studied their results. But we do know a few things: when substance abuse programs in public school systems have been studied, the results are clear. Substance abuse education programs increase the general level of drug use, but they decrease the incidence of drug crises. Much could be said about these results, but they seem to suggest primarily that drug use or non-use reflects a life style and a set of values more than the presence of specific information. The results also suggest that we are going to need treatment programs for a long time, unless there is a breakthrough in ways to prevent substance abuse.

The substance abuse treatment industry is very large. At any one time in state, federal, local, and private programs, there may be 500,000 individuals in treatment for alcohol or drug abuse. In the late 1970s, the federal government alone spent over half a billion dollars a year on substance abuse treatment. Trends in treatment follow trends in use—when use of a drug increases, so does the number of abusers, and so does the number of individuals entering treatment because of that drug.

No specific programs for the treatment of alcohol or drug abuse will be mentioned here. The reason for this is that when evidence is studied, there are no miracles. It seems clear "that the person being treated brings his probability of recovery with him. There's very little affected by what goes on in treatment . . . variability in outcome is attributed more to subject variability . . . than it is to any variation in treatment or goals." (Rittenhouse, 1976, p.10). This shouldn't be too surprising considering the social and personal antecedents to substance use and abuse. They are not single, isolated factors. Rather they are pervasive and multiple, and they surround and envelop the individual as he or she grows up. As with weight-reduction and stop-smoking programs, and in prison rehabilitation programs and reformatories, the significance and the impact of twenty to thirty years of life is not to be offset or overcome by a brief interlude in a treatment or rehabilitation program (McLellan et al., 1982). But some lessons have been learned, and treatment programs do have some impact. Only by continued efforts can the rate of success be improved.

Treatment and rehabilitation of a substance abuser presents special problems. We have repeatedly said that drug use occurs because it meets some unfilled need in the individual. Because of this, it is very difficult to talk a drug abuser into entering treatment when he doesn't want to go into treatment. Treatment-rehabilitation centers report that a big problem with new workers is that they spend much of their time trying to talk a drug abuser into giving up drugs and entering a treatment program. That's like asking someone to stop seeing a close friend because "sooner-or-later" he'll get you into trouble. Most people won't give up their close friend—and most people won't enter treatment—just because things may get bad in the future.

A second major problem in the treatment of drug abusers is that of finding an acceptable substitute for drug use. If drug use satisfied some needs, how will those needs be met without drugs? It is difficult for many people to appreciate the magnitude of this problem. Most of us have many sources of satisfaction and different ways to meet our needs: work, home, school, family, friends, church, organizations, and so on. We have the necessary social and occupational skills so that we can give up one source of satisfaction, knowing that we still have another source of satisfaction to move on to . But what would we do if we had no occupational skills and a nonexistent or poor work history, and if the few sources of satisfaction we had were related to drug use and would be taken away by the treatment program? Most likely, we would stay away from treatment programs.

Getting individuals into a drug treatment program is difficult. Finding an alternative for alcohol or drug use, or for friends in that culture, is very difficult. If a substitute life style cannot be developed, the treatment program will probably not have a lasting impact, and drug use will resume. Much of the effectiveness of most programs rests on the ability of the staff to find jobs and a place for their clients to live.

Drug abusers generally enter treatment programs for one of two reasons: in about one in four cases the law enforcement system insists on it ("it's your choice, jail or treatment"), or their use of drugs is causing more problems than it's solving. To give up drug use before this point, would be to give up something that's apparently solving more problems than it's causing.

Knowing all of the above, we can make some good predictions about the type of individual who would most likely succeed in stopping the abuse of drugs, and staying stopped. If the individual had a satisfying life before the period of drug abuse, successful treatment would be more likely. That would also be true of a job to go to, a marketable skill, a spouse or family that would stay with the individual after treatment. In brief, the individual who had some good things in his life and then lost them as a result of drug abuse, would be much more likely to succeed in giving up drugs than would be the individual who had little or nothing going for him before his drug abuse.

There are also some general characteristics of treatment programs that are associated with success. Three seem to be important—no matter which drug has been abused. Residential programs (where those in treatment live together in a hospital or other facility) are more successful than nonresidential programs (in which those in treatment live in the community and travel every day to a facility to participate in the treatment program). Residential programs are also four to twelve times more expensive than nonresidential programs. Structured, active programs are more successful than loose, nondirective programs. At least one reason for this is that individuals who have just stopped using a drug will be anxious and uncomfortable—at loose ends—and the busier they are and more predictable their surroundings, the easier it is for them to learn to control their own behavior. Last, and possibly most important, programs with extended follow-up care (e.g., weekly therapy sessions or rap groups) are more successful than those without aftercare programs. This is because an intensive treatment program can do no more than start the process of learning about and living a new life; to maintain the new life for an extended period requires that the ex-drug abuser has continuing help.

Treatment outcome statistics are not plentiful. The best data come from alcohol treatment programs. One year after completing a one- to two-month residential treatment program, alcoholics can be put in three main groups. About 20 percent of these individuals still don't use alcohol. Another 20 percent are abusing alcohol just as they were before they entered the program. The remaining 60 percent still drink and still abuse alcohol, but they do it less often, or with less serious consequences. It doesn't much matter what philosophy or beliefs underlie the treatment program, the results are the same: 20 percent much improved, 20 percent not improved, 60 percent improved to some extent. In short, this means that alcohol treatment programs have positive effects on four out of five who complete the program.

Of the heroin treatment programs that are available, the best kind and the best-known type is the methadone maintenance program. Methadone programs may be residential or nonresidential in the early stage of treatment, but they all end up as nonresidential. Residential programs are more successful because they are able to keep a much higher percentage of addicts in treatment than can the nonresidential programs. Keeping addicts in treatment is good at least from society's point of view. While in treatment, the criminal activity of the addicts goes down almost to zero.

Methadone maintenance is based on the principle of drug substitution. One of the reasons a heroin addict continues using heroin is fear of the withdrawal effects. That fear is eliminated when the heroin addict is switched to methadone, which is given orally once a day. Methadone is a narcotic with an eighteen- to twenty-hour half-life ; it can be given once a day without the individual suffering from withdrawal.

The advantages of methadone are clear: it's inexpensive; it's oral; it's given once a day; the slow deactivation of methadone allows the individual to function normally without the highs and the lows that follow each of the three to six heroin injections a day; there's no risk to health. There are some disadvantages: the individuals are still addicted to a narcotic; they may have to take methadone for the rest of their life. Most programs, however, do try to reduce the addiction to methadone so that the individual can eventually

Group discussion in a methadone maintenance center (Wide World Photos).

lead a drug-free life. Another disadvantage is that the individual in a methadone maintenance program has to return each day to the clinic to get the methadone. Since methadone has considerable street value, it is unwise to give a supply of the drug to the addict.

The success of a methadone program—or any other substance abuse program—does not rest primarily on how well the reduction in drug use is carried out, or how well withdrawal symptoms are avoided. They are necessary components in a good program, but they are not sufficient. A treatment program will be successful only if it is able to provide its clients with a satisfying life that is not centered on alcohol or drug abuse. That's the hard part; it's also the exciting challenge. At this point in time, only minor advances have been made, but research goes on.

SOME CONCLUSIONS

We have covered much ground so far. We have discussed a little about the psychoactive drugs; about who takes what and why; about the types of reactions that drugs induce and how they are related to the functional disorders discussed elsewhere; how the similarities among treatment programs for abusers of different drugs are more important than their differences. In addition to those specific concepts, there are some basic ideas that stand out and have great generality.

None of the drugs produces states of consciousness or symptoms that are uniquely different from those that we can experience in the absence of drugs. This fact reinforces the idea that there are not a great many different effects (i.e., outputs), no matter how many different ways you disrupt the functioning of the brain.

The presence of the entire pattern of withdrawal-produced hallucinations—both with and without delirium—adds to the weight of evidence regarding the adaptability of the brain. That the brain can function normally in the presence of high levels of any of the addicting drugs is a monument to the brain's capability. Upsetting the balance is what leads to symptoms here, as is also true in those cases where the addition of a drug results in symptoms.

The fact that some drugs—particularly the stimulants—produce syndromes that are identical to a naturally occurring syndrome makes it more likely that we will be able to untangle the complicated web of brain systems, neurotransmitters, and biochemical changes that underlie other psychotic syndromes.

Do these psychoactive drugs have a relationship to the functional disorders discussed in our other chapters? Will a better understanding of drug-induced and drug-precipitated syndromes help us understand and then treat the endogenously produced disorders? We are confident that the answers to these questions are yes. Drugs that act on the brain can and should be used to help us better understand how the brain functions, and how the brain dysfunctions. Such an understanding can only be for the betterment of all of us.

Finally, a remark about treatment and an unfashionable concept—willpower. Our data on rehabilitation from alcohol and drug abuse come from a somewhat atypical sample: those individuals who could not give up the drug on their own. By the time an alcoholic or a heroin addict comes into treatment, he or she has usually tried—and failed—several times to give up the habit. In contrast, most individuals who become addicted to alcohol or narcotics or smoking or overeating probably give it up on their own without formal treatment (Schachter, 1982). This means that if you find yourself dependent on a drug, and your life is starting to suffer for it, the chances are very good that you will be able to stop— by the exercise of will. If you are one of the minority who cannot bring yourself to stop, the chances are still good that treatment will help.

SUMMARY

1. The United States became a *drug-using culture* sometime after 1950. The widespread use of tranquilizers and of oral contraceptives seems to have paved the way, with individuals using these drugs not to cure diseases but to improve the quality of life. By 1983, 60 percent of high school students had tried marijuana, and 93 percent had tried alcohol.

2. *Drug users* do not differ from the rest of the population in psychological characteristics, but *drug abusers* typically have personality and psychopathology problems.

3. The diagnosis of *drug abuse* occurs when three criteria are met: a pattern of pathological use; impairment in social and work functioning because of the use; and at least one month's duration of the disturbance.

4. A special protective device, called the *blood-brain barrier*, protects the brain from many substances in the blood. In order for a drug to work, it has to get past this barrier.

5. The *dose-response relationship* describes the fact that at very low levels of dose, there will be little or no response. As the amount of the drug increases, however, the response will increase, but at very high levels of the drug, the effect will not increase.

6. *Tolerance* to a drug occurs when there is less response to a specific dose of the drug after repeated use than there was initially.

7. *Addiction* does not occur to all drugs, but often, after regular use of a drug, the body will function normally only when the accustomed amount of drug is in the body. Drugs that produce addiction also cause tolerance.

8. When drug use is suddenly stopped in an addicted individual, there are a set of physiological and psychological changes. These changes are called *withdrawal.* Withdrawal responses are generally opposite the responses that occurred when the drug was being taken.

9. *Stimulants* are drugs that stimulate the central nervous system. They include caffeine, amphetamines, and cocaine. These drugs stimulate the reticular activating system and produce more alertness and response to all stimuli. Amphetamine produces such arousal and is associated with *amphetamine psychosis,* with delusions of persecution, ideas of reference, and visual and auditory hallucinations. The condition is very similar to paranoid schizophrenic psychosis.

10. *Hallucinogens* are chemicals that cause large perceptual changes, most importantly, visual hallucinations. The most common are lysergic

acid diethylamide (LSD) and phencyclidine (PCP). Minute doses of these drugs produce dramatic perceptual, cognitive, and emotional changes. These hallucinations are distinguishable from the hallucinations that occur in schizophrenia.

11. Opium is the most prominent of the *narcotics*, and is the active substance in the opium poppy. Morphine is a chemically active extraction of opium. Heroin is a chemical transformation of morphine, which makes it more potent, and methadone, is a completely synthetic chemical that has the same effects as the opiates. Tolerance and addiction develop to these drugs, and when they are withdrawn, withdrawal symptoms occur.

12. Tetrahydrocannabinol (THC) is the active ingredient in marijuana, which is a plant of the species cannabis. At low doses, it produces decrease in attentiveness and vigilance, impairment of the ability to focus on a task or to engage in sequential reasoning, and mild euphoria. THC is stored in the body's fatty tissue, and 25 to 30 percent of it may still be in the body after one week. THC does not produce addiction or tolerance. But a *panic reaction* is not an uncommon consequence of marijuana use.

13. *Alcohol* is the most widely used drug in the United States. It is responsible for a large number of medical complications and lethal accidents. *Alcohol intoxication* produces poor judgment, slurred speech, uncoordination, unsteady gait, flushing of the face, mood changes, irritability, talkativeness, and impaired attention. In higher doses, it may produce death. *Delirium tremens* (the DT's) and *alcohol hallucinosis* are consequences of alcohol addiction.

14. *Barbiturates* are the major example of *depressant* drugs. At low doses, they decrease anxiety and blunt sensitivity. At higher doses, they are called *hypnotics* and produce sleep. They may lead to tolerance and withdrawal symptoms that are among the most excruciating of any drug.

15. The *treatment* of chronic drug use is difficult. It often requires undoing twenty to thirty years of habits. Programs that do best are those that find jobs, new places to live, a new life style, and an acceptable substitute of the drug for the abuser. Treatments also do better if they are residential, and if they involve aftercare programs. The most typical result of treatment programs is that 20 percent of people are greatly improved, 60 percent are somewhat improved, and 20 percent are not improved at all.

CHAPTER

16

Personality Disorders

How does one describe people who cheat needlessly and lie without reason in all kinds of contexts? Or people who are always suspicious of others' intentions? Or people who respond passively to all provocations? Such people are hardly psychotic, for they often have a good grip on reality. Nor are they necessarily dominated by unwarranted fears (see Chapter 10), sexual difficulties, addictions, and the like. Nevertheless, their behaviors strike observers as odd, as deviant, or as abnormal. Theirs seem to be a disorder of personality. Their characteristic ways of perceiving and thinking about themselves and their environment are inflexible, and a source of social and occupational maladjustment. In addition, their behaviors may well be a source of distress for themselves and others. Their disorders are called *personality disorders.*

Consider a young employee who is up for promotion. She knows she has done a good job, and that she probably deserves appropriate credit. But, she feels anxious, thinking perhaps that one of her colleagues is trying to undercut her achievements. Learning of her fears, her friends call her "paranoid," pointing out that she is probably imagining the situation. Reassured, she is able to go about her business. Most of us have had similar concerns. Our worries are ones that grow out of specific situations. They are time-limited and easily dispelled. But some people's worries are not so easily relieved. Indeed, they spend much of their lives scanning the environment for cues that validate their paranoid feelings. Unlike the employee who has a few "paranoid" moments, individuals with the *paranoid personality disorder* are always suspicious of others' motives. While they are able to function and are not psychotic, they are continually troubled by deep distrust.

The personality disorders have provided a fascinating source of psychological study across the decades because they ascribe a stability and sturdiness to personality and behavior that extends across time and context. The personality disorders are fundamentally disorders of *traits*, that is, disorders that are reflected in the individual's tendency to perceive and respond to the environment in broad and maladaptive ways. Perhaps the most fascinating of these disorders is the *antisocial personality disorder*. Known also as *sociopathy* and *psychopathy*, this disorder has been studied extensively and is the best understood of the personality disorders.

THE ANTISOCIAL PERSONALITY DISORDER

People who suffer from the psychological disorders that were examined in earlier chapters create distress for their families and friends, but mainly they themselves are the ones who suffer. In contrast, the suffering in an individual with the antisocial personality disorder is muted. The hallmark of the disorder is a rapacious attitude toward others, a chronic insensitivity and indifference to the rights of other people that is marked by lying, stealing, cheating, and worse. Whereas those who suffer other psychological difficulties may be unpleasant, contact with antisocial personalities may be downright dangerous, for many of them are outright criminals. Because their numbers are not small, they constitute a major social and legal problem, as well as a psychological one. According to DSM-III, a little under 1 percent of women and about 3 percent of men suffer the disorder.

DISORDERS OF WILL

It is not only individuals with the antisocial personality disorder who steal and cheat. "Normal" people filch, forge, and embezzle too. When normal people steal and cheat, however, we call them criminals and their acts, crime. Why should those who suffer the antisocial personality disorder be regarded any differently?

The fact is that for the longest time antisocial personalities were *not* thought about in psychological terms. Throughout most of history, criminals were criminals and the only distinctions that were made had to do with the severity of their crimes. But in the nineteenth century especially, the idea developed that certain kinds of criminal behavior might arise from conditions over which the individual had no control—that is, from social, psychological, or biological sources. Their crimes then were not acts of will, but rather the result of circumstances beyond their control. Much as noncriminal but clearly dysfunctional behaviors might be caused by psychological experiences over which the individual had little control, so too might criminal, antisocial ones.

In the nineteenth century, such antisocial people were said to be afflicted by *moral insanity.* This disorder was distinguished from other psychological disorders by the English psychiatrist J.C. Prichard (1837). Among the morally insane, Prichard wrote:

> Intellectual faculties appear to have sustained little or no injury, while the disorder is manifest principally or alone, in the state of the feelings, temper, or habits . . . the moral and active principles of the mind are strangely perverted and depraved; the power of self-government is lost or greatly impaired; and the individual is found to be incapable, not of talking or reasoning upon any subject proposed to him, for this he will often do with great shrewdness and volubility, but of conducting himself with decency and propriety in the business of life." (Prichard, 1837, p. 15)

Moral insanity then, was viewed as a disorder of the *will.* Although the term moral insanity has been displaced by "antisocial personality disorder" today, it continues to be viewed as a disorder of will. Whether for biological, social, or psychological reasons, these people are found "to be incapable . . . of conducting [themselves] with decency and propriety in the business of life." Where people are *capable* of exercising will and of conducting themselves properly, but simply *choose* not to do so, they continue to be called criminals.

There is often debate about whether or not a person is actually suffering a personality disorder, and that debate arises from the very nature of the disorder itself. The antisocial personality disorder is a disorder of will, and will is not an all-or-nothing matter. One does not either have or not have will. Rather, like most other psychological functions, will exists on a continuum: normal people have more or less of it, but those who suffer this disorder have even less. The line that divides those who suffer disorders from the rest of us is arbitrary. Because of this, we diagnose this disorder with caution.

Also, like anxiety, will is *inferred.* One does not see will. Rather, its presence is inferred from behaviors that are believed to reflect it. Unless one examines those specific behaviors, judging whether someone does or does not suffer a personality disorder can be hazardous. For that reason, DSM-III offers behavioral diagnostic criteria for the antisocial personality disorder.

CHARACTERIZING THE ANTISOCIAL PERSONALITY DISORDER

Antisocial behavior alone is not sufficient for the diagnosis of antisocial personality disorder. Such behavior would merely qualify as "adult antisocial behavior," which in DSM-III is ruled out as a mental disorder. In order to qualify as a personality disorder, the antisocial behaviors must meet three criteria. First, the behavior has to be longstanding. There should be no period of more than five years in which antisocial behavior has not occurred. Second, current diagnostic criteria require substantial evidence of antisociality before the age of fifteen. Such evidence can include habitual lying, early and aggressive sexual behavior, excessive drinking, theft, vandalism, and chronic rule violation at home and at school. Third, the present antisocial behavior must be manifested in at least four classes of behavior, among which are: inconsistent work performance; irresponsible parenting; unlawful behaviors such as theft, pimping, prostitution, dealing drugs, or other felony convictions; inability to sustain a relationship with a sexual partner; repeated aggressiveness; recklessness that endangers others; repeated lying; and failure to honor financial obligations. The antisocial personality disorder then is defined by sustained antisocial behaviors that, having begun by adolescence, continue in a variety of areas during adulthood.

These behavioral criteria make clear who can be diagnosed as having an antisocial personality disorder and who cannot. What personality characteristics are reflected in such behaviors? Hervey Cleckley, a lifelong student of these behaviors and people, described some of their characteristics in *The Mask of Sanity* (1964). Cleckley lists sixteen features of the sociopath's personality. These sixteen characteristics can be reduced to three broad categories: inadequately motivated antisocial behavior, the absence of a conscience and sense of responsibility to others, and emotional poverty.

Inadequately Motivated Antisocial Behavior

Crime "makes sense" for normal criminals. We understand what they are doing and why, and so do they. They want to get rich—quick—and they may want status. These are motivations we can understand, however much we disapprove of the behaviors. But the crimes of sociopaths often seem aimless, random, and impulsive. We do not understand why they did what they did, and neither do they understand it. They seem not to be motivated by any rational purpose, but rather seem perversely impulsive.

On October 7, 1976, Gary Gilmore was sentenced to death by a Utah court after a seemingly purposeless crime spree, and on January 7, 1977, he became the first person to be executed in the United States since 1966. During a psychological evaluation to determine whether Gilmore was competent to stand trial, it was determined that he suffered an antisocial personality disorder. Gilmore's activities provide an interesting example of crime without understandable motives.

Gilmore had been released from prison only six months earlier, after serving time for armed robbery. He promptly violated parole by leaving the state. His probation officer gave him another chance. But shortly thereafter, following a heated argument with his girlfriend, Gilmore stole a stereo. Once again, he persuaded the police not to bring charges. Gilmore himself described the next events: "I pulled up near a gas station. I told the service station guy to give me all of his money. I then took him to the bathroom and told him to kneel down and then I shot him in the head twice. The guy didn't give me any trouble but I just felt like I had to do it."

The very next morning, Gilmore left his car at another service station for minor repairs and walked to a motel. "I went in and told the guy to give me the money. I told him to lay on the floor and then I shot him. I then walked out and was carrying the cash drawer with me. I took the money and threw the cash drawer in a bush and I tried to push the gun in the bush too. But as I was pushing it in the bush, it went off and that's how come I was shot in the arm. It seems like things have always gone bad for me. It seems like I've always done dumb things that just caused trouble for me."

Absence of a Conscience and a Sense of Responsibility to Others

The absence of shame or remorse for past misdeeds, of any sense of humiliation for egregious ones, is one of the most common characteristics of sociopaths. They lack conscience, and with it, any deep capacity to care about other people. Their relationships, therefore, tend to be quite shallow and exploitative. They lack a capacity for love and sustained attachment and are unresponsive to trust, kindness, or affection. They lie shamelessly and can mercilessly abuse those who have trusted them. Gary Gilmore did not have a serious relationship until several weeks before he committed the two murders. He was then thirty-six years old. Describing the affair, he said that it was "probably the first close relationship that I ever had with anyone. I just didn't know how to respond to her for any length of time. I was very insensitive to her . . . I was thoughtless in the way I treated her. . . . [H]er two children bugged me and sometimes I would get angry at them and slap them because they were so noisy."

Emotional Poverty

One of the major differences between the normal person who is a criminal and the sociopath lies in the depth of experienced emotion. Ordinary criminals presumably experience the same emotions as other normal people. But

If DSM-III had been available, convicted killer Gary Gilmore would have been diagnosed as having an antisocial personality disorder. (Courtesy *The Salt Lake Tribune*)

sociopaths experience very shallow emotions. They seem to lack the capacity for sustained love, anger, grief, joy, or despair. During a psychiatric interview, Gilmore observed that "I don't remember any real emotional event in all my life. . . . When you're in the joint, you stay pretty even all the time . . .I'm not really excitable you know. I don't get emotional." Indeed, their incapacity to experience emotion may be significantly related to their lack of conscience and to the ease with which they violate the expectations of others.

THE SOURCES OF SOCIOPATHY

Personality disorders are long-lived. The antisocial personality disorder originates in childhood or early adolescence as a conduct disorder (see Chapter 18), and then continues into adulthood. Once again, Gary Gilmore is a case in point. Examining his childhood, we find that he had been suspended from school on several occasions for truancy and for alleged thefts from his classmates. When he was fourteen, he was sent to a correctional youth facility for auto theft. By the time of his last arrest, Gilmore had spent fifteen of his sixteen adult years behind bars.

What factors give rise to such continuously antisocial behavior? Four potential sources have been given considerable attention: (1) the family and social context, (2) defects in learning, (3) genetics, and (4) physiological dysfunctions in the central nervous system.

The Family and Social Context

Because the sociopath seems not to have internalized the moral standards of the larger society, it is natural to examine the agents of socialization, particularly the family and social context, for clues about sociopathy. There is evidence, for example, that sociopaths who grew up in the lower social classes experienced more difficult childhoods than other people from those same social strata. A number of studies indicate that losing a parent through desertion, divorce, or separation (rather than through death or chronic hospitalization) is highly correlated with the later development of sociopathic behavior (Gregory, 1958; Greer, 1964; Oltman and Friedman, 1967). Moreover, the more severe the sociopathic behavior, the more likely it is that the sociopath experienced parental deprivation. Most writers believe, however, that it is not the parental deprivation per se that promotes sociopathy— otherwise the findings would include deprivation through death and hospitalization. Rather it is the emotional climate that precedes the divorce—the arguments and violent fights, the blatant promiscuity, alcoholism, parental instability, the neglectful father—which is implicated in socialization for sociopathy (Smith, 1978).

Similar, but substantially enlarged, findings emerged from a study of a large group of people who had been seen at a child guidance clinic between 1924 and 1929 (Robins, 1966). Fortunately, the clinic had maintained careful psychological and sociological records on the presenting problems and family circumstances of its clients. When these children grew up, they were carefully interviewed, along with a control group that had never been seen at the clinic. About 22 percent of the clinic referrals qualified for the adult diagnosis of sociopathic personality, while only 2 percent of the control group received that diagnosis.

What early experiences were correlated with the diagnosis of antisocial personality disorder in adulthood? First, as children, these sociopaths had been referred to that child guidance clinic for antisocial behaviors: theft, truancy, and school discipline problems dot their clinic records. Second, they tended more often than the control group to come from impoverished homes and from homes that were broken by divorce or separation. Their fathers themselves were often antisocial persons who may well have served as sociopathic models for their children (Bandura and Walters, 1963), while simultaneously creating the marital discord that may spawn sociopathic development (Robins, 1966). Again taking Gary Gilmore's life as an example, we find that although Gilmore's parents were never formally separated, his father spent so much of his time away from home that Gilmore considered himself to have been raised by "a single parent." During some of that time, his father was in prison, serving eighteen months on a bad check charge. His mother was simultaneously overindulgent and neglectful: Gilmore was often left to fend for himself. Reflecting on his family, he described it as "typical" and noted that "there wasn't much closeness in it."

The children who later became sociopaths were referred to juvenile court and were subsequently sent to correctional institutions much more often than other children. In such institutions, they very likely picked up some of the habits of their antisocial peers. These findings, however, should not be interpreted to mean that *all* punishment for juvenile offenses is necessarily harmful to the child. Indeed, one study revealed that children who were apprehended and *moderately* punished for juvenile crimes have a lower recidivism rate than those who were apprehended and released without punishment (McCord, 1980). In order for children to be deterred from further crime, they must be given a clear message that what they did was wrong. The message is clearest when it comes as punishment. *Too* clear a message —one that results in sending children to penal institutions—may teach that crime is wrong, but it may also put them in an environment where they can learn from their peers how to pursue a criminal career successfully.

Other longitudinal studies underscore the relationship of the home environment and subsequent criminality in delinquent boys. Once again, whether the father was absent or present was not a key determinant of subsequent criminality. The factors that did influence whether delinquent boys became criminal adults were maternal affection and self-esteem, parental supervision, harmony within the household, and the father's deviance. Indeed, separation and divorce do not lead to criminal behavior so long as the mother is affectionate and self-confident, the child is supervised, the level of discord between the parents is minimal, and the father is nondeviant (McCord, 1979).

Defects in Learning

Many clinicians have been struck by the seeming inability of the sociopath to learn from experience. Prichard (1837) called them "moral imbeciles." Cleckley (1964) observed that they failed especially to learn from punishing experiences, and as a result, had poor judgment. But sociopaths are often "savvy" and intelligent. If they suffer a defect in learning, it must be a fairly subtle one. What form might such a defect take?

DEFICIENCIES IN AVOIDANCE LEARNING. Cleckley's observations, in particular, suggested that sociopaths were especially deficient in *avoidance* learning. Ordinary people rapidly learn to anticipate and avoid punitive situations. But sociopaths, perhaps because they are under-aroused and under-anxious, fail to do so. To examine this possibility, sociopaths and normal people were taken into the laboratory to test their ability to master a certain task (Lykken, 1957). The task involved learning to press a "correct" lever, but the idea was to find out which group learned to avoid punishment.

Participants sat in front of a panel that had four levers. Immediately above each lever was a red light and a green light (see Figure 16-1). The subject's task was to find and press the lever that turned on the green light on each of a series of twenty trials. Since the correct lever changed on each trial, the subjects had to remember their sequence of responses, from the first trial to the one they were now working on. A certain pattern had to be learned, and it was quite a complicated task, a veritable mental maze.

On each trial, the subject had four choices, only one of which turned on the green light. Two of the levers turned on a red light—clearly a wrong response—while the third delivered electric shock. Having two kinds of wrong responses, one that simply says "wrong" and the other that delivers physical punishment, enabled the investigator to answer a telling question. Is it that sociopaths cannot learn from negative experience, or are there particular negative experiences, namely *avoidance* experiences, from which they cannot learn?

As expected, there were no differences in the total number of mistakes made by sociopaths and nonsociopaths. But whereas nonsociopaths quickly learned to avoid the electrified levers, the sociopaths made the most errors that led to shock, suggesting that their particular learning defect was an inability to learn from painful experiences (Lykken, 1957). In effect, punishment or threat of punishment does not seem to influence a sociopath's behavior.

Why should sociopaths be deficient in avoidance learning? One possibility is that sociopaths do not avoid shock because they do not find shock as noxious as do normal people, and they do not find shock as noxious because

Figure 16-1
Apparatus for Lykken's (1957) study of avoidance learning in sociopaths. On any given trial, only one of the four levers is correct, and the correct lever changes from trial to trial. Subjects must learn a pattern of twenty correct lever-presses. A correct lever-press turns on a green light. Of the remaining three levers (each of which is wrong), two turn on red lights, while the third delivers electric shock.

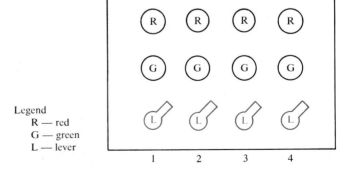

Legend
R — red
G — green
L — lever

they are chronically *under-aroused.* Put differently, sociopaths may actually seek stimulation in order to elevate arousal to an optimal level. Indeed, it has often seemed to clinical observers that that is the case (Cleckley, 1964). Gary Gilmore, the sociopath who was described earlier, may well have experienced under-arousal and the need for stimulation as a child. Gilmore said, "I remember when I was a boy I would feel like I had to do things like sit on a railroad track until just before the train came and then I would dash off. Or I would put my finger over the end of a BB gun and pull the trigger to see if a BB was really in it. Sometimes I would stick my finger in water and then put my finger in a light socket to see if it would really shock me."

To examine the sociopath's possible need for stimulation, sociopathic and normal subjects were injected either with adrenaline, which heightens arousal, or with a placebo and tested on the "mental maze" described above. Once again, in both the adrenaline and placebo conditions, sociopaths made no more errors than normals. But sociopaths who received the placebo failed to learn to avoid shock. Only when they were given adrenaline was their characteristic under-arousal overcome. Being already aroused by the adrenaline, the sociopaths avoided the shocked lever just as the normals did in the placebo condition (Schachter and Latane, 1964).

Cleckley's observation that sociopaths are emotionally flat was confirmed in this experiment. Because they are under-aroused in general, the emotions that ordinarily inhibit criminal behavior are not sufficiently aroused in sociopaths. At the same time, the emotions that propel people into crimes of passion are also absent. Sociopaths are mainly responsible for "cool" crimes such as burglary, forgery, and con games. When they are involved in violence, as Gilmore was, it tends to be impulsive and irrational violence, and perverse because it so lacks in feeling.

There are several kinds of punishment. There is *physical* punishment to which sociopaths do not respond as the above experiments suggest. But there is also *tangible* punishment such as the loss of money, and *social* punishment such as disapproval. Are sociopaths as unresponsive to the latter kinds of punishment as they are to physical punishment? The same "mental maze" was used to examine this question. But this time, if one of the wrong levers was pressed, the subject lost a quarter. If another was pressed, the subject received social disapproval, and the third wrong lever brought electric shock. Once again, sociopaths learned the task as quickly as nonsociopaths. And again, they were considerably less responsive to physical punishment than were normals. They were also less responsive to social disapproval. But they quickly learned to avoid the lever that would cost them a quarter. Indeed, they avoided this lever somewhat more than normals, indicating that sociopaths can learn to avoid punishment provided that the punishment is noxious to *them* (Schmauk, 1970).

THE IMMEDIACY OF CONSEQUENCES. The greater the interval between the time a behavior occurs and its consequences, the more difficult it is to learn the relationship between that behavior and its consequences. Some people generally have greater difficulty seeing a relationship between two events across time than do others. And it may well be that sociopaths have greater difficulty than most people. If this is the case, it would explain why sociopaths are not deterred from crime by the anticipation of punishment, since the punishment usually occurs long after the crime has been committed.

An experiment was devised to determine whether individuals with antisocial personality disorders anticipated punishment in different ways than did normals. In this experiment, three groups of subjects were used: (1) criminals who had been diagnosed as sociopaths; (2) criminals who had been diagnosed as nonsociopaths; and (3) noncriminals. These subjects were presented with the numbers "1" through "12," one at a time and consecutively. They were told that they would receive an electric shock when the number "8" appeared. In order to determine the level of anxiety experienced, the galvanic skin response (GSR), which is one measure of experienced anxiety, was assessed for each subject throughout the experiment. Both normals and nonsociopathic criminals displayed fear of the anticipated electric shock from the start. Moreover, their anxiety, as measured by the GSR, mounted markedly as the number "8" drew closer, and it plummeted afterwards. In contrast, sociopathic subjects exhibited dramatically lower anxiety levels throughout the experiment, and their measured fear did not increase as the number "8" approached. Even when the shock was administered, their arousal and GSR activity levels were far lower than those in the other two groups (Hare, 1965).

When the data on avoidance learning are combined with those on family and social antecedents of sociopathy, an interesting picture emerges. The antisocial personality disorder does not arise simply from harsh circumstances. Nor is its development deterred by physical punishment or even by imprisonment. Neither poverty nor parental deprivation necessarily led to sociopathy. But affectionate parents and parental supervision can inhibit the development of sociopathy. So, too, can punishment when it is *felt* to be painful and abhorrent, rather than when it is merely automatically applied.

Genetics and Criminality

The possibility that sociopathy has a genetic basis has long been attractive. In the popular imagination, sociopathy and antisocial behavior have long been associated with the "bad seed," and particularly the bad seed that came from a family of bad seeds. That view, however, is hard to assess. The problems of sorting environmental from genetic influences are as difficult here as elsewhere. But the task here is further compounded by the fact that it is *criminals*—those who have been apprehended and convicted of a crime—who come to our attention, not those who have eluded apprehension. Not all criminals are sociopaths, of course, nor are all sociopaths criminals.

The data on the biology of sociopathy are fascinating for, though they are complex, they appear to indicate that both genetics, and environment play strong roles in the development of sociopathy. We begin by considering twin and adoption studies, and then examine studies of men with an extra Y chromosome. But before doing so, one thing should be made clear. Most of these studies are concerned with the relations between biology and *criminality*. Criminality, as we indicated earlier, is not synonymous with sociopathy. Where the studies permit, we will distinguish between the two.

TWIN STUDIES.   One way to examine the relative influence of genetic and environmental factors in sociopathy is to study the concordance of sociopathic behavior in twins. Recall again that monozygotic or identical (MZ) twins each have exactly the same genetic heritage, while dizygotic (DZ) or fraternal twins are as genetically dissimilar as ordinary siblings (see Chapter 3). The environments of MZ and DZ twins are *nearly* the same. (These environments are nearly the same, rather than downright identical, because individuals contribute to their environments, and no two contributions are exactly the same.) This allows us to look at the other variable, genetics. If concordance for sociopathy or criminality is higher for MZ than for DZ twins, one can infer that genetic factors play a role.

According to the series of studies that examine the rates of criminality among MZ and DZ twins, there is a strong relationship between zygosity and criminality. In a total of 216 MZ pairs and 214 same-sex DZ pairs, 69 percent of the MZ but only 33 percent of the DZ pairs were concordant for criminality (Christiansen, 1977). By themselves, these studies would strongly suggest that genetic influences are powerful in criminality.

There are two sources of evidence that suggest that such a conclusion would be premature. First, such high concordance for criminality among MZ twins was only marginally higher than for DZ twins (Dalgard and Kringlen, 1976). The latter finding can be explained by the fact that MZ twins share a more similar environment than DZ twins. Monozygotic twins, being identical, are more likely to be treated the same by parents and others than are dizygotic twins. Indeed, they are often confused for each other. Second, and even more interesting, are the data regarding *opposite-sex* DZ pairs. Opposite-sex twins are no different genetically than same-sex DZ twins, though patently they share different environment. If criminality is determined by heredity and heredity alone, the data for opposite-sex twins should be identical to the data for same-sex DZ twins. But they are not. The concordance for criminality among opposite-sex twins is only 16 percent, less than half of what it is for same-sex twins. The difference in concordance rates between same-sex and opposite-sex twins underscores the environmental influences on criminality.

ADOPTION STUDIES.   When children are raised by their natural parents, it is impossible to separate the effects of genetics from those of environment on their development. But studies of children who have been adopted at an early age allow these influences to be separated. These studies also provide evidence for the influence of heredity in both criminality and sociopathy. One study examined the criminal records of adopted persons in Denmark (Hutchings and Mednick, 1977). Their names were drawn from the Danish Population Register, which records the names of both the adoptive and the biological parents of these adoptees. Thus, it is possible to compare the criminal records of the adopted children with those of both sets of parents. These comparative data are shown in Table 16-1. The incidence of crime among these offspring was lowest when neither the biological nor the adoptive father had been convicted of a criminal offense. Nearly indistinguishable from that low rate was the rate among adoptees whose adoptive fathers had been convicted, but whose biological fathers were "clean." The incidence of criminal conviction among adoptees jumped dramatically, however, when the natural father had a criminal record, but the adoptive father

Table 16-1 CRIMINALITY OF ADOPTED SONS ACCORDING TO THE CRIMINALITY OF THEIR ADOPTIVE AND BIOLOGICAL FATHERS

Father		*Percentage of sons who are criminal offenders*	*Number*
Biological	*Adoptive*		
No registered offense	No registered offense	10.5	333
No registered offense	Criminal offense	11.5	52
Criminal offense	No registered offense	22.0	219
Criminal offense	Criminal offense	36.2	58
Total			662

SOURCE: Modified from Hutchings and Mednick, 1977, p. 132.

had none, providing clear support for the view that the tendency to engage in criminal acts is hereditary. But highest of all was the incidence of criminality among adoptees when both their natural *and* adoptive fathers had criminal records, underscoring again the combined influence of heredity and environment on criminality. These individuals probably inherited a tendency toward criminality from their biological fathers and learned criminal behavior from their adoptive fathers. As we mentioned, however, criminality is not identical with sociopathy. But when a measure of sociopathy rather than criminality was used, similar findings were obtained (Schulsinger, 1972, 1977).

XYY: AN EXTRA CHROMOSOME? A person's sex is determined by a pair of chromosomes. Women have two X chromosomes (XX). Men have a single X and a single Y chromosome (XY). But some men have an extra Y chromosome (XYY). Since it is the Y chromosome that defines the male, the XYY (which is also called the Klinefelter syndrome) is sometimes considered a "supermale." Such a person, for example, is especially tall—much taller than the ordinary male. It is also widely believed that the XYY is especially violent and often prone toward criminal behavior.

These beliefs are difficult to verify. Not all tall men are XYY's. Nor, of course, are all criminals XYY's. Indeed, not more than 1.5 percent of criminals and delinquents who have been tested have this additional chromosome (Rosenthal, 1970). Some of the studies take their evidence from a few or even single cases, and they often fail to include normal control groups. Until recently, a definite relationship between the XYY syndrome and violence could neither be demonstrated nor disconfirmed.

A recent study examined the criminal records of all men who were born in Copenhagen between 1944 and 1947 (Witkin et al., 1976). Once again, the Danish Population Register provides very complete data on Danish citizens, and therefore permits this kind of thorough study. The investigators began with a group of 31,436 men, of whom 4,591 were at least six feet tall. Since XYY's are tall, the latter group promised to produce the maximum number of XYY's. In that group, twelve XYY's were discovered, yielding a prevalence of 2.9 XYY's per thousand population. Of those twelve, five or 42 percent had been convicted of one or more criminal offenses, as against 9.3 percent or ordinary XY males who were six feet tall or more. While the data support the view that XYY men are more likely to be convicted of a crime, they do not confirm the view that XYY's engage in *violent* crime.

A karyotype of an XYY—a man with an extra chromosome. Generally, a man will have one X chromosome and one Y chromosome. An XYY may be prone to violent behavior. (Courtesy Dr. Kurt Hirschhorn)

Only one of the five committed an act of violence against another person, and that act was relatively mild. Otherwise, nearly all of the crimes involved property. Indeed, of the 149 offenses for which the five XYY's were convicted, fully 145 were against property—usually crimes of theft.

But while XYY's are not more violent, the evidence from this study indicates that they are convicted of crime much more frequently than are "normal" male criminals. Why should that be? One interesting bit of information that emerged from the above study is that, compared to XY criminals, XYY's have markedly lower intelligence. Conceivably, lower intelligence itself leads to criminal activity, perhaps because the less intelligent find it more difficult to get jobs or to resist temptations. Alternately, these findings may not reflect differences in the incidence of crime, but merely differences in *apprehension* and *conviction.* With lower intelligence, XYY's may stand a greater chance of being apprehended, convicted, and sentenced.

Physiological Dysfunctions

To whatever extent genetics is related to criminality and sociopathy, the relationship is not likely a direct one. One does not directly acquire from genes the skills and disposition to engage in crime. What then is it that *is* acquired genetically? What is passed down through the genes that makes one more likely to engage in sociopathic activities?

A number of investigators have sought to discover physiological differences between sociopaths and normal people. And a good number of such differences have been discovered. For example, a substantial proportion of sociopaths have abnormal electroencephalograms (EEG's). This is especially true of the most violent and aggressive sociopaths. The abnormalities are of two kinds. First, sociopaths show the slow brain waves that are characteristic of children and that suggest brain immaturity. Second, a sizable proportion of sociopaths show positive spiking in their brain waves. Positive spikes are sudden and brief bursts of brain wave activity. These spikes occur in the EEG's of 40 to 45 percent of sociopaths as compared to about 1 to 2 percent of the general population (Kurland, Yeager, and Arthur, 1963). Positive spiking is itself associated with impulsive, aggressive behavior. Most individuals who commit aggressive acts and who also manifest positive spiking report no guilt or anxiety about their actions.

These findings are of interest for several reasons. First, the possibility that sociopaths suffer cortical immaturity (Hare, 1978) suggests that as they get older (and their cortexes become more mature) sociopaths should engage in less antisocial behavior. That is precisely what has been found. Particularly between the ages of thirty and forty, a substantial proportion of sociopaths show marked behavioral improvements (Robins, 1966).

Second, those positive spikes—the sudden and brief bursts of brain wave activity—appear to reflect a dysfunction in the brain's limbic system, precisely the system that controls emotion and motivation. And what emotion might be affected by this physiological dysfunction? Some theorists speculate that it is *fear,* the very emotion that is thought to be implicated in the phenomena of socialization and self-control (Cleckley, 1976). The sociopath's inability to inhibit behaviors and delay gratifications is generally thought to be similar to that of animals who have suffered lesions in the brain's septal region (Gorenstein and Newman, 1980). Thus, the sociopath's failure to learn from punishing experiences may be the product of faulty physiology. Biology, rather than malice, may be the wellspring of the antisocial personality disorder.

THE ANTISOCIAL PERSONALITY DISORDER: AN OVERVIEW

The sociopath has been given many different names over the decades, but the symptoms remain remarkably the same. Sociopathy originates in childhood, where it is characterized by such things as truancy, persistent lying, theft, and vandalism. Similar behaviors persist into adulthood, taking the forms of assaults against persons and property, defaulting on major debts and financial responsibilities, and involvement in the underworld. Sociopaths share a group of personality traits, which include the absence of a sense of shame or remorse, failure to learn from past experience, and impoverished emotions.

Thus, we come full circle. Clinical observations lead us to believe that sociopaths are deficient in the ability to experience emotion and in the degree to which conscience controls their behavior. These clinical observations are confirmed by laboratory studies, which indicate that physical punishment is particularly ineffective with sociopaths. Further studies suggest that physical punishment may be ineffective because sociopaths are under-aroused, a condition that may be due to aberrant limbic function. While the effects of environment are clearly evident in the development of sociopathy, there is evidence that genetics, too, plays a role. And speculation that genetic factors influence brain function, especially limbic function, is consistent with data that indicate that sociopaths are under-aroused.

OTHER PERSONALITY DISORDERS

The antisocial personality disorder is the best known and best studied of the personality disorders, but it is not the only one. People who are characteristically suspicious and distrustful, or passive, or inappropriately emotional, or overly dependent upon others, or enormously compulsive and orderly, such people, too, may be suffering from a personality disorder.

PARANOID PERSONALITY DISORDER

After his wife died, Seymour moved to a retirement community in Florida. Healthy and attractive, he immediately joined a folk dancing group, a current events discussion group, and a ceramics class. Within six weeks, however, he had dropped out of all the programs, complaining to his children that other residents were talking about him behind his back, that he was unable to find a dancing partner, ignored in the current events group, and given improper instruction in ceramics.

Before his retirement, Seymour had been a physicist. He had always been closed-mouthed about his work. His home study had always been locked. He had not permitted anyone to clean it, and he had become angry if anyone entered it without his permission. His son reported that his parents had been extremely close and affectionate, but that his father had had few other friends. He had been wary of new faces and concerned about the motives of strangers.

A hard worker throughout his life, he was now gripped by fear. He spent much of his time overseeing his investments, fearful that his broker would give him poor advice, or neglect to tell him when to buy and when to sell.

The prominent characteristics of the *paranoid personality disorder* are a pervasive and long-standing distrust and suspiciousness of others; hypersensitivity to slight; and a tendency to scan the environment for, and to perceive selectively, cues that validate prejudicial ideas and attitudes. Those who suffer from the paranoid personality disorder are often argumentative, tense, and humorless. They seem ready to attack. They tend to exaggerate, to make mountains out of molehills, and to find hidden motives and special meanings in the innocuous behavior of others. They tend to blame others for whatever difficulties they experience, and they cannot themselves accept any blame or responsibility for failure.

Because such people tend to externalize blame and guilt, they are rarely seen in clinics or psychiatric hospitals. Thus, it is difficult to estimate how prevalent this problem is. Generally, however, it is felt to be a problem that tends to afflict men more than women (Kass, Spitzer, and Williams, 1983). As might be expected from their tendency to externalize, the prognosis for this disorder is guarded indeed.

HISTRIONIC PERSONALITY DISORDER

People who have long histories of drawing attention to themselves and of engaging in excited emotional displays that are caused by insignificant events are captured in the diagnosis of *histrionic personality disorder.* Such people are apt to be superficially charming, warm, and gregarious, but they are often viewed by others as insincere and shallow. They seem to be seeking admiration by playing continually to unknown audiences. Once they form relationships, they become demanding and inconsiderate, egocentric, and self-absorbed. They can be enormously flirtatious or coquettish, yet their sexual adjustment is as often naive or frigid, suggesting that their flirtatious behavior serves the ends of attention-getting much more than those of sexuality. This disorder occurs more commonly among women (Kass, Spitzer, and Williams, 1983) but, as the following case indicates, it is also seen among men.

In *Sunset Boulevard,* Gloria Swanson plays a faded movie star with a histrionic personality. She is self-absorbed and demanding, living amidst her old photographs and viewing her old films. (Courtesy Museum of Modern Art/Film Stills Archive)

At forty-two, Michael entered therapy after his second marriage failed. He strikes you as every bit the college professor: pipe-smoking, tweedy, facile with words, and somewhat theatrical. His difficulties are gripping, and they extend beyond his marriage. He has been the victim of muggings and robberies, of badly diagnosed ailments, and wrongly prescribed drugs. His scholarly papers are often rejected by journal editors, and his colleagues seem not to appreciate his genius. For all of this, he seems clearly a charming man, though one who is more interested in the therapist's reactions than in understanding his own plight.

Michael reports that he has an interesting social life, though he complains in passing that people often do not invite him to dinner a second time. Nor do they lend him money or allow him to borrow their car. Some probing reveals that Michael has frequently failed to repay loans, and that he has often been involved in accidents with other people's cars ("well, they're insured . . ."). He is prone to cancel social engagements at the last minute if something more interesting comes up. Indeed, he calls often to change his scheduled therapy sessions and is upset when those changes cannot be arranged.

Narcissistic Personality Disorder

The central feature of the *narcissistic personality disorder* is an outlandish sense of self-importance. It is characterized by continuous self-absorption, by fantasies of unlimited success, power and/or beauty, and by exhibitionistic needs for constant admiration. Criticism, the indifference of others, and threats to esteem characteristically receive exaggerated responses of rage, shame, humiliation, or emptiness. Of course, the near-total preoccupation with self massively disturbs interpersonal relationships in a variety of ways. Such people may simply lack the ability to recognize how others feel. They may have an exaggerated sense of "entitlement," expecting that the world owes them a living without assuming reciprocal responsibilities. They may simply be exploitative, taking advantage of others to indulge their own desires. When they are able to establish a relationship, they may vacillate between the extremes of overidealization and enormous devaluation of the other person.

A narcissistic personality is characterized by self-absorption, fantasies of unlimited success and beauty, exhibitionism, and a need for constant admiration. (Photograph by Yemima Rabin)

> Marion is a bit player who, at twenty-four, has not had a major theatrical role since her high school play. She has just been turned down for the lead in a new musical. Plagued with self-doubt, she is simultaneously furious with the casting director, a man with whom she has studied acting for the past three years. In her view, she should have gotten the part—both because she was every bit as good as the young women who ultimately did get it, and because she was owed the support of the director who encouraged her and took her money for years. Marion is certain that the other actress got the part because she slept with the director. But her own time will come, Marion believes, and when it does, her own name will be displayed on the theater marquee.
>
> Beyond her vocational difficulties, Marion also has difficulty in establishing and maintaining friendships. Slender, beautifully dressed, and seemingly self-assured, she has no trouble attracting men. At first, she enthusiastically envisions great times with them. But shortly thereafter she drops them, terming them "duds," "sexually unexciting," or "just plain boring." Women seem to fare no better. Marion gave a friend a ticket to see her in a play. Instead, her friend visited a hospitalized aunt. Marion fumed and viewed her friend's absence as a "betrayal."

Avoidant Personality Disorder

The heart of the *avoidant personality disorder* consists of social withdrawal that combines a hypersensitivity to rejection and a desire for acceptance and affection. Individuals who experience this disorder want very much to enter into social relationships, but they may find themselves unwilling to do so unless they are given strong guarantees of uncritical acceptance. They are shy (Zimbardo, 1977). The slightest hint of disapproval by others leads them to withdraw, and they may interpret even apparently innocuous events as ridicule. People suffering from this disorder are likely to be distressed by their relative inability to relate comfortably to others, which adds to their low self-esteem, which in turn makes them even more sensitive to criticism and humiliation—an especially vicious cycle.

This disorder is thought to be quite common. It restricts social relations, and it may also affect occupational functioning, especially where interaction with others is required.

Elaine became quite distraught when her co-worker and close friend left to train as a nurse-practitioner. Her replacement was "nice enough," but Elaine feared the new woman would find her boring. At twenty-one, Elaine has only one other friend, her married sister. But her sister is "too busy with her family right now," and so Elaine spends very little time with her. Her social life in high school was quite restricted, and at present, she has no social life at all. At work, she eats lunch alone and is viewed by other workers as unfriendly.

DEPENDENT PERSONALITY DISORDER

Deference and fearfulness are characteristics of the dependent personality disorder. (Courtesy Mrs. James Thurber)

The central characteristic of the ***dependent personality disorder*** involves allowing others to make the major decisions, to initiate the important actions, and to assume responsibility for significant areas of one's life. People with this disorder often defer to spouse, parent, or friend regarding where they should live, the kind of job they should have, and who their friends should be. They subordinate their own needs to the needs of the people upon whom they are dependent, feeling that any assertion of their own needs may jeopardize the relationship. Such people will often tolerate enormous physical and/or psychological abuse for fear that they will be abandoned. Correspondingly, when they are alone even for brief periods of time, they may experience intense discomfort and helplessness. Thus, they often seek companionship at great cost. They lack self-confidence and self-esteem, and they often refer to themselves as stupid or helpless. The dependent personality disorder occurs more frequently among women than among men (Kass, Spitzer, and Williams, 1983).

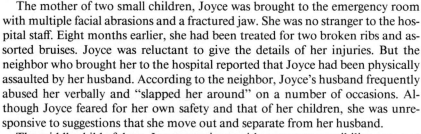

The mother of two small children, Joyce was brought to the emergency room with multiple facial abrasions and a fractured jaw. She was no stranger to the hospital staff. Eight months earlier, she had been treated for two broken ribs and assorted bruises. Joyce was reluctant to give the details of her injuries. But the neighbor who brought her to the hospital reported that Joyce had been physically assaulted by her husband. According to the neighbor, Joyce's husband frequently abused her verbally and "slapped her around" on a number of occasions. Although Joyce feared for her own safety and that of her children, she was unresponsive to suggestions that she move out and separate from her husband.

The middle child of three, Joyce was given neither great responsibility nor great attention during her childhood. Her father was a man of strong opinions and made all the decisions in the family. He believed adamantly that women belonged at home, and joked often and coarsely about "buns in the oven and bums in bed." He controlled the family finances, and delegated no responsibility in that area.

Apart from a course in typing, Joyce learned no vocational skills in high school, and dropped out to get married. Indeed, other than baby-sitting and summer jobs as a mother's helper, Joyce had no work experience at all.

During the five years of her marriage, Joyce left all decisions to her husband, even to the point of agreeing to the purchase of a sofa that she really disliked. Her husband was intensely jealous of her friendships, and she therefore abandoned all of them. Indeed, except for visits to her mother who lived in the neighborhood, she went nowhere without her husband.

This disorder is common, especially in women. It impairs occupational functioning if the nature of the job requires independent decision making. And social relations may be restricted to the few people upon whom the person is dependent.

COMPULSIVE PERSONALITY DISORDER

The *compulsive personality disorder* is characterized by the long-term inability to express warm emotions combined with an inappropriate preoccupation with trivial rules and details. The two facets of the disorder are related. The inability to express tender emotions lends a formal and conventional quality to the relationships of compulsive personalities. Lacking sensitivity to the affective nuances of relationships, people with the disorder tend to impose rules and regulations and to lose sight of the overall picture in favor of orderly and scheduled ways of doing things. As might be expected, such people are terribly work-oriented. Fun plays a minimal role in their lives; and vacations, even when they are considered, tend to be postponed endlessly.

This disorder marks people who are not only stingy with their emotions, but often also with their resources. While they themselves may be sensitive to unwarranted intrusions on their time and possessions, they can thoughtlessly intrude on the time of others, especially spouses and subordinates. Finally, such people tend to avoid making decisions, lest they make an error. As a result, they spend much of their time doing trivial tasks, leaving the important ones to the last moment. They work hard, but they work inefficiently. They spend their time organizing work priorities, rather than getting the work done. As might be expected, such a disorder can have incapacitating effects on occupational functioning.

Laura and Steve began to see a marriage counselor because Steve insisted on it. He had become extremely distressed by Laura's unavailability and perfectionism. At thirty-seven, Laura was a partner in one of the nation's largest accounting firms. She worked long hours at the office, brought work home, was unwilling to go out more than once a week, and resisted taking vacations. At home, she snapped out orders to the children about housework and schoolwork. She could not tolerate an unwashed dish or a jacket on the sofa. She was critical and demanding of household help, and the cleaning staff changed frequently. Much of the time, Steve found her sexually unresponsive.

Laura did not believe she had a "marriage problem," though she freely acknowledged feeling harassed at work and at home. She attributed her long hours at work to the demands of her profession. Snapping at the children and nit-picking about domestic order were, she insisted, the result of being the person who had to clean up after everyone else. Laura did not consider herself sexually unresponsive, but she did think she was often tense and fatigued. The only child of upwardly striving immigrant parents, Laura had been encouraged to excel. She was valedictorian of her high school class and among the top ten of her college graduating class. The social milieu in which she grew up put great stress on the value of close family relationships. Laura never doubted that she would be a wife and mother, and she married soon after graduating college.

PASSIVE-AGGRESSIVE PERSONALITY DISORDER

The essential feature of the *passive-aggressive personality disorder* consists of a special kind of resistance to social and occupational performance demands. The resistance is not expressed directly or overtly, but rather emerges in the form of procrastination, dawdling, stubbornness, inefficiency, and forgetfulness that seems to border on the intentional. For example, when given an assignment by his boss, a worker will not directly express his unwillingness or inability to do the work by saying such things as "I'm really overloaded right now," "I have no skills in that area," or "That's really Bill's job, not mine." Rather he may simply misplace the work order, or delay doing the job because a hundred more important things suddenly need to be done, or forget the instruction altogether. Such indirect sabotage is called passive-aggressive because it is assumed that covert hostility is being expressed. As might be expected, both the passive resistance and the ways in which it is expressed, lead to long-standing social and occupational ineffectiveness.

> Jeff, a thirty-year-old city planner, entered therapy when he learned that his contract would not be renewed. The city manager pointed to his chronic tardiness, his failure to keep up-to-date records, and his tendency to forget committee meetings and report deadlines. Jeff was very upset. He believed that he had performed quite well—better in fact, than might be expected, considering that budget cuts had eliminated a secretary and that his boss was carping and demanding. At the same time, Jeff recognized that this was a familiar scenario that had occurred often in the past with his bosses and teachers.
>
> Jeff had been a "difficult" child. As a youngster, he had temper tantrums. Later, he would sulk or leave if other children played a game that he did not choose. His college record was spotty—very good grades mixed with awful ones in no apparent pattern. In one seminar, for example, he failed to prepare the oral report he was scheduled to present. Yet, he insisted that he had been treated unjustly when an excellent term paper did not suffice to yield the "A" he thought he deserved.
>
> During the past three years, he has been living with Jennifer, but that relationship, too, is difficult. He is often sociable and fun to be with, but he is just as often uncooperative. He leaves the domestic work to Jennifer and neglects to do even the few tasks he has voluntarily accepted. When she makes her resentments known, he insists that she is nagging. They also seem unable to collaborate about how to use their free time. If Jennifer is firm about her preferences, Steve often simply refuses to join her. And when he does acquiesce, he makes his displeasure known through sullen silences and general lack of enthusiasm.

SCHIZOID PERSONALITY DISORDER

The central feature of the ***schizoid personality disorder*** is a defect in the capacity to form social relationships, as reflected in the absence of desire for social involvements, indifference to both praise and criticism, insensitivity to the feelings of others, and/or lack of social skills. Such people have few, if any, close friends. They are withdrawn, reserved, and seclusive. Others see them as "in a fog" and absent-minded. In short, they are extreme introverts. Their feelings tend to be bland and constricted; they seem to lack warm feelings or the capacity for emotional display and are therefore perceived as cold, aloof, or distant. Sometimes, and especially in jobs that require a good deal of social isolation, these characteristics can be assets. But more often, the very poverty of social skills restricts occupational and social success.

> A thirty-eight-year-old chemical engineer, Homer was forced into marriage counseling by his wife who complained of his failure to join in family activities or to take an interest in the children, his general lack of affection and responsiveness, and his disinterest in sex. His failure to relate socially to others extended also to his job, where colleagues characterized him as either shy and reticent, or as cold and aloof.

Homer's history revealed long-standing social indifference and little emotional responsiveness. He recalled that he was indifferent to the idea of marrying, but did so to please his parents. His wife tried repeatedly to arrange social situations that might be of interest to him, but to no avail.

SCHIZOTYPAL PERSONALITY DISORDER

The **schizotypal personality disorder** is described mainly by long-standing oddities in thinking, perceiving, communicating, and behaving—oddities that are severe enough to be noticed, but not serious enough to warrant the more serious diagnosis of schizophrenia. Odd thinking can be manifest in extreme superstitiousness, or in the sense that one is especially noticed by others. The latter sense, which is technically called an **idea of reference,** can also be a fertile breeding ground for suspiciousness and paranoia. Depersonalization—a sense of estrangement from oneself and from one's environment—may be present. Communication may be odd, but not downright peculiar. It may be tangential, digressive, vague, or overly elaborate, but it is not loose or incoherent. Finally, people suffering from this disorder may also experience constricted or inappropriate feelings, with the result that they are unable to maintain rapport in face-to-face interactions.

The schizotypal personality disorder seems genetically related to schizophrenia (Kety, 1974). Indeed, many of the disturbances described here are similar to those seen among chronic schizophrenics, but here the disturbances appear in milder forms. It is an error, however, to identify this disorder wholly with the schizophrenias because differences of degree are very important differences as far as psychological distress is concerned. Much as we do not confuse the poor and the rich, even though both have some money, so must the schizotypal personality disorder be distinguished from its more intense relatives, the schizophrenias.

At twenty-one, Mark complains that he feels "spaced out" and "creepy" much of the time. Unemployed, he lives with his parents and spends much of his time watching television or staring into space. He says that he often feels as if he is outside himself, watching himself through a TV screen, or running through a script that someone else has written. Mark has had several jobs, but none has lasted more than a month. He was fired from his last position as a toy salesman after several customers had complained that he had talked to them in vague terms about irrelevant things.

Mark is convinced that people do not like him, but he does not understand why. He is certain that people change their seats on buses to avoid sitting next to him. He is unhappy about his loneliness and isolation, but he has made no attempt to re-establish old relationships.

Several months ago, Mark learned that one of his parents' friends planned to open a chain of athletic shoe discount stores. Although he has no experience or training in business, Mark is "waiting" for an offer to manage one of these stores.

BORDERLINE PERSONALITY DISORDER

Borderline personality disorder is a very broad category whose essential feature is *instability* in a variety of personality areas, including interpersonal relationships, behavior, mood, and self-image. These areas are not necessarily related and, indeed, are themselves so broad that people with quite different problems are likely to be considered for this diagnosis.

Clearly, any diagnosis that is so broad and potentially inclusive runs the risk of becoming a "kitchen sink" diagnosis. In order to increase the validity of the borderline diagnosis, as well as limit its use to a restricted range of people, DSM-III requires that evidence for at least five of the following problems be present before the diagnosis can be made:

· Impulsivity or unpredictability in at least two potentially self-damaging areas, such as sex, gambling, drug or alcohol use, shoplifting, overeating, and physical self-damage.

· A pattern of unstable and intense interpersonal relationships marked by shifts of attitude, idealization, devaluation, or manipulation of others for one's own ends.

· Lack of control over anger.

· Identity problems, denoted by uncertainty about such matters as self-image, gender identity, long-term goals or career choice, friendship patterns, values, and loyalties.

· Affective instability, which involves marked shifts from normal mood to depression, irritability, or anxiety.

· Difficulty being alone, including frantic efforts to avoid being alone.

· Physically self-damaging acts, including suicidal gestures, self-mutilation, recurrent "accidents," or physical fights.

· Chronic feelings of emptiness and boredom.

There is no information about the prevalence of the disorder, nor about the factors that predispose one to it. However, even with the qualifying requirements that were indicated above, one senses that it is probably a relatively widely used diagnosis. A sense of how it might be applied is given in the following case:

Thomas Wolfe (1900–1938).

Thomas Wolfe was a writer whose first work was published in 1929 and who died less than ten years later, before he was forty. In that brief decade, he was a literary sensation, hailed by the greatest novelists of his time. He was enormously productive and driven. And he was painfully unhappy. Wolfe was described as nervous, surly, suspicious, given to brooding, to drinking, to violent outbursts, and sometimes even to fears that he was going mad. He was rude and dislikable. He said of himself that he was afraid of people and that he sometimes concealed his fear by being arrogant and by sneering magnificently.

It was hard for him to begin writing on any particular day, but once he began it was harder still for him to stop. The words would simply pour out of him. He would sleep late, gulp down cup after cup of black coffee, smoke innumerable cigarettes, pace up and down—and write endlessly. He would scrawl down the words on sheet after sheet of yellow paper, so hastily and hugely that the pages often contained only twenty words apiece, and those in abbreviated scrawl. At night, he would prowl the streets, drinking heavily, or spending hours in a phone booth, calling friends, and accusing them of having betrayed him. The next day, overcome with remorse, he would call again and apologize.

For all his writing, he had difficulty putting together a second book after *Look Homeward Angel.* Although he had written a million words, ten times that of an average novel, it still was not a book. He was fortunate to have as his editor Maxwell Perkins, who had discovered his talent and who cared to nurture it. Wolfe wrote: "I was sustained by one piece of inestimable good fortune. I had for a friend a man of immense wisdom and a gentle but unyielding fortitude. I think that if I was not destroyed at this time by the sense of hopelessness . . . it was largely because of . . . Perkins. . . . I did not give in because he would not let me give in." Perkins recognized that Wolfe was a driven man, and feared that he would suffer either a psychological or physical breakdown, or both. He proposed to Wolfe that, having written a million words, his work was finished: it only remained for both of them to sit down and make a book out of his effort.

That collaboration was difficult. A million words do not automatically make a book. Wolfe was reluctant to cut. Most of the editing, therefore, fell to Perkins. And as Perkins slowly made a book out of Wolfe's words, Wolfe's resentment of Perkins increased. The work was not perfect, Wolfe felt. And it upset him to bring forth a book that did not meet his standards.

Until the book was published, Wolfe believed it would be a colossal failure. The reviews were magnificent, however. But although Wolfe was at first heartened by the reviews, he gradually began to feel again that the book was less than perfect, a matter for which he held Perkins responsible. His relationship with Perkins deteriorated. He became suspicious, even paranoid. Yet, apart from Perkins, he had no close friends. He became increasingly unpredictable, yielding easily to incensed anger, unable to control it. Ultimately, he broke with Perkins. Rosenthal (1979) has suggested that Wolfe's emotional liability, his inability to control his anger, the difficulties he had in being alone, his many self-damaging acts, as well as his identity problems point to the diagnosis of a borderline personality disorder. At the same time, Wolfe also had personality features that were consistent with the schizotypal personality disorder, especially his ideas of reference that made him so suspicious and paranoid.

THE PERSONALITY DISORDERS: AN EVALUATION

Laboratory experiments, naturalistic studies, and longitudinal surveys all converge to support the existence of the antisocial personality disorder. On a variety of specific criteria, individuals with the disorder are demonstrably different from normal people. However, the legitimacy of the other personality disorders is far more problematic. No matter how convincing the descriptions of these disorders seem to be, the documentation for their existence as reliable and valid syndromes is, at bottom, anecdotal. It has grown out of clinical lore, and while it is not to be lightly dismissed for that reason, neither can it be easily accepted. For despite the effort that has gone into tightening the various categories of personality disorders they are still particularly prone to a variety of errors that easily erode their usefulness.

Alternative Views of the Personality Disorders

Because personality disorders are characterized by the presence of enduring *traits* that often originate in childhood or early adolescence, evidence for their existence needs to be accumulated across a considerable period of time. As a result, distortions of memory and failure to obtain and properly assess facts are powerful potential sources of error for these diagnoses. Consider Seymour who was held to be suffering from a paranoid personality disorder (page 449). The behavioral facts relating to his difficulties were quite accurate. But subsequently, a careful investigation of the sources of his difficulties yielded a quite different picture. It turned out that Seymour had been experiencing a marked hearing loss. He had not mentioned it during his early interviews both because he underestimated its extent and because he dreaded wearing a hearing aid. He had difficulty getting dancing partners because, while he heard the music, he often missed the instructor's calls and was commonly out-of-step. In the discussion group, he often repeated comments that had already been made by others or, worse, misheard others' comments, such that his own were inappropriate and disruptive. Similar difficulties pervaded his experience in the ceramics class. Moreover, his seeming distrust of others, which had been manifested in the locking of his study and in not talking about his work, takes on a somewhat different meaning when one learns that as a physicist, he had spent his entire career working on classified military problems. In addition, like many professionals of the 1950s and 1960s, Seymour had moved a great deal. Making new friends in each new location required a heavy expenditure of time and energy. Precisely because he had a close relationship with his wife and be-. cause he was deeply involved in his work, Seymour was simply unwilling to invest himself in new, but transient, relationships.

Thus, the potential for misinterpreting lifelong behaviors is a potentially dangerous one because the contexts in which those behaviors developed may not be readily retrievable now. But even when considerable information *is* available, therapists of different theoretical persuasions may arrive at different diagnostic conclusions as far as the personality disorders are concerned. Consider Laura (page 453) who appeared to have all of the characteristics of a compulsive personality disorder. Might not a feminist therapist who is sensitive to the conflicts that arise from the competing demands of gender and work roles, see the case differently? Laura, who was traditional in her attitudes toward family and home, was simultaneously ambitious in her professional life. In attempting to fulfill both roles with excellence, she unwittingly aspired to the impossible: to be a "superwoman." She wanted her house neat, her children at the top of their class, and herself at the top of her male-dominated profession. Her carping and her insistence that the house be spotless reflected this competition between roles, for if the house was not spotless, to whom would it fall to clean it up? Similarly, in her refusal to take holidays and her long working hours, she was behaving like the ambitious men in her profession.

In much the same way, it is possible to view Joyce's behavior (page 452) as the result of economic and social factors, rather than as evidence of a dependent personality disorder. With two small children and no marketable skills, it was extremely difficult for her to extract herself from an abusive situation. Her father's strict notions about a woman's place prevented her from returning home, while her husband's jealousy prevented her from developing a network of reliable friends who might extricate her from her present difficulties. Poverty, isolation, and despair provide explanations for the dependent behavior of abused women, which may be more cogent than the explanations that arise from the personality disorder diagnoses.

Finally, there are theorists who question whether the traits that presumably underlie the personality disorders really exist and, therefore, whether the personality disorders themselves are real (Mischel, 1973; Mischel and Peake, 1982). Although the notion that traits exist is nearly as old as the notion of personality itself, it has proved quite difficult to obtain evidence that people are consistent in their dispositions and perceptions across different situations. To say that someone suffers a dependent personality disorder, for example, is to say that they manifest the traits of passivity and dependence in a variety of different contexts. Evidence for that assertion is, in fact, very hard to find. Nearly all studies that have attempted to verify the cross-situational assumptions behind the notion of traits have failed. If the notion of traits has little merit, then the personality disorders that are built upon them have shaky foundations indeed. It is no wonder then that, with the exception of the antisocial personality disorder whose coefficient of reliability (see Chapter 8) ranges between .65 and .87, interjudge reliability of the remaining personality disorders is uncertain, often plummeting as low as .26.

SUMMARY

1. The personality disorders are fundamentally disorders of *traits,* that is, disorders that are reflected in the individual's tendency to perceive and respond to the environment in broad and maladaptive ways. The notion of a personality disorder assumes that people respond consistently across different kinds of situations.

2. Of all of the personality disorders, the *antisocial personality disorder* is the most widely studied. It is a disorder that is characterized clinically by inadequately motivated antisocial behavior, emotional poverty, and the apparent lack of conscience or shame.

3. The antisocial personality disorder originates in childhood or early adolescence, where it takes the form of truancy, petty thievery, and other rule-violating behavior. As children, those who suffer the disorder often come from emotionally deprived backgrounds and marginal economic circumstances. Moreover, there is evidence that their antisocial behaviors have a genetic basis that may be manifested in a constitutional brain defect. This defect makes them under-aroused emotionally, and therefore less able to learn from punishment or to control their impulses.

4. While severe punishment in childhood, such as sending a boy to a penal institution, increases the likelihood that the boy will subsequently engage in criminal activities, so too does no punishment at all. Moderate punishment—enough to make the boy take the consequences seriously, but not so much as to send him to places where he can learn to be a criminal—has a genuine deterrent effect.

5. The remaining personality disorders each center on a striking personality trait. *Paranoia, dependency, introversion, passive-aggressiveness,* and *compulsiveness* are traits that have become so dominant that they merit the personality disorder designation. In addition, some personality disorders, such as *schizotypal,* reflect many of the symptoms that are found in the corresponding Axis I disorder, but in lesser degree and without the florid thought disorder.

6. With the exception of the antisocial personality disorder, there is genuine disagreement regarding whether the personality disorders truly and reliably exist. To some extent, the disagreement arises from the low reliability of the personality disorder diagnoses. But to a larger degree, the disagreement is rooted in the scientific debate about the existence of personality traits. If traits play a relatively minor role in personality organization, then the personality disorders cannot play a large role in abnormal psychology, for they are based on the notion of traits.

Part VII

THE PSYCHOSES

The Schizophrenias

SCHIZOPHRENIA is the most puzzling and profound of the psychological disorders. Many theories try to account for it, but a complete understanding of this complex disorder continues to elude us. Briefly, *schizophrenia* is a disorder of thinking from which flows troubled behavior and troubled mood. This thought disorder is manifested by difficulties in maintaining and focusing attention and in forming concepts. It can result in false perceptions and expectations, in enormous difficulties in understanding reality, and in corresponding difficulties with language and expression.

"Schizophrenia" is a term that is used for a group of psychoses. As such, we often refer to these disorders as "the schizophrenias." We will try to understand the schizophrenic disorders by examining the symptoms that are part of them, and the psychological and biological determinants that promote them. Then we will examine the various treatments that are available for the schizophrenias. But before doing any of this, it is important to dispel the myths associated with these disorders, and to sketch out a general picture of the history, prevalence, and dimensions of the schizophrenias.

HISTORY AND BACKGROUND

MYTHS ABOUT SCHIZOPHRENIA

Schizophrenics have been called lunatics, madmen, raving maniacs, unhinged, deranged, demented. These words suggest that schizophrenics are dangerous, unpredictable, impossible to understand, and completely out of control. These notions, however, say more about non-schizophrenics' fear and ignorance than they do about the nature of schizophrenia itself.

Are Schizophrenics Dangerous?

Rather than being raving maniacs on the rampage, schizophrenics are often withdrawn and preoccupied with their own problems. Sometimes they yell and scream, and occasionally they strike someone. But it is by no means clear whether these behaviors arise from the actual disorder, or from the way schizophrenics are treated. Like others, schizophrenics often mirror their treatment. When the treatment is civilized, so are the patients. The mistaken notion that criminals are less dangerous than schizophrenics, and that one would be better off living near a prison than near a hospital, rests squarely on ignorance and fear.

Do Schizophrenics Have Split Personalities?

Eugen Bleuler (1857–1939). (Courtesy National Library of Medicine)

Another common misconception about schizophrenia is that it involves a split personality of the Dr. Jekyll and Mr. Hyde sort, with its attendant unpredictability and potential for violence. This error arises from the origins of the word schizophrenia: *schizo* = split, *phreno* = mind. When the Swiss psychiatrist Eugen Bleuler (1857–1939) coined the term in 1911, he intended to suggest that certain psychological *functions*, ordinarily joined in normal people, are somehow divided in schizophrenics. Consider thought and emotion, for example. When non-schizophrenics perceive, say, a horrifying incident, they immediately have an emotional reaction that corresponds to their perception. But according to Bleuler, this did not happen to schizophrenics for whom thought and emotion were split. Bleuler never meant to imply that there were two or more alternating personalities residing in the schizophrenic. And although Bleuler's view is no longer as widely believed now as it was in 1911, the misconception that arose from his view continues to exist.

Once a Schizophrenic, Always a Schizophrenic?

The schizophrenic disorders are not necessarily durable, and surely not life-long for all schizophrenics. Often, a single episode will occur and then disappear, never to recur. Sometimes, after a long period in which the individual has been symptom-free, another episode may occur. Much as one may suffer several colds during a lifetime and yet not always have a runny nose, so too can a person suffer several schizophrenic episodes during a lifetime, and be quite sane in between. Many people who have suffered a schizophrenic disorder engage in athletics, read newspapers and novels, watch television, eat their meals, and relate to their friends and families in much the same way that others do. Long stretches of time can pass without evidence of their distress. We do not know why a schizophrenic episode occurs any more than we understand why we come down with a cold. As when the symptoms of a cold are absent and the individual is considered healthy, so when the symptoms of schizophrenia are absent the individual is considered sane. Finally, it goes without saying that schizophrenics are as human as the rest of us.

EVOLVING VIEWS OF SCHIZOPHRENIA

Until about 1880, little progress was made in differentiating one form of disorder from another. There was a *sense* that there were different kinds of madness, but no shared view of what those differences might be. The first widely accepted classificatory system for severe psychological disorders was advanced by the German psychiatrist, Emil Kraepelin (1856–1926). One of the disorders he described in 1896 was ***dementia praecox***, literally, early or premature deterioration.

For Kraepelin, the diagnosis of *dementia praecox* was indicated when individuals displayed certain unusual symptoms. Included among these were inappropriate emotional responses, such as laughter at a funeral or crying at a joke; stereotyped motor behavior, such as bowing repeatedly before entering a room, or clapping five times before putting head to pillow; attentional difficulties, such as being unable to get to work on time because of distractions en route, or being unable to read because of shifting shadows; sensory experiences in the absence of appropriate stimuli, such as seeing people when none are present, or smelling sulphur in a jasmine garden; and beliefs sustained in spite of overwhelming contrary evidence, such as insisting that one is an historical personage like Napoleon, or that one is held together by wire. *Dementia praecox*, Kraepelin suggested, was primarily a biological disorder that began in adolescence and was incurable. Kraepelin was wrong about onset and wrong about prognosis, even in light of his own data (cited in Zilboorg and Henry, 1941). Nonetheless, his views powerfully influenced succeeding generations of psychiatrists, and are important historically for distinguishing and classifying the various forms of madness.

As we mentioned earlier, the term "schizophrenia" was coined by Eugen Bleuler. Like Kraepelin, Bleuler believed that the disorder was part of one's biological makeup and was likely to recur. He felt, however, that schizophrenia could first occur at any time during a person's life, not only during adolescence. That view is widely shared today. Moreover, he disagreed with Kraepelin regarding the prognosis of the disorder. While he recognized that schizophrenia was undoubtedly serious, and in many cases chronic, Bleuler asserted that recovery was possible.

Even Eugen Bleuler may have overestimated the chronic nature of the disorder because he saw patients only when they were troubled. In 1974, his son Manfred, also a psychiatrist, wrote of his father's patients:

> When they left the clinic, they were . . . out of sight and lost to him, and this was the case with most psychiatrists of his generation. For this reason, an unfavourable picture of the course of illness had to be inferred: the improved and healed patients disappeared beyond the horizon of the clinic, and he saw above all those who were unimproved or relapsed. (Bleuler, 1974, p. 92)

In contrast, Manfred Bleuler has followed many of his schizophrenic patients through their lifetimes, and not just those who remained troubled. He found that no more than 10 percent of his patients showed the lifelong chronicity that his father and Kraepelin wrote about.

Both Kraepelin and Bleuler were convinced that the causes of schizophrenia were biological and that the ultimate cure would be biomedical. Kraepelin hypothesized that a chemical imbalance was produced by malfunctioning sex glands and somehow interfered with the nervous system. Bleuler was convinced that brain disease caused schizophrenia, and he continually resorted to hypothetical brain pathology to account for schizophrenic symptoms. The search for a biological basis for schizophrenia was begun by these two pioneering scientists. But then, as now, careful examina-

Adolf Meyer (1866–1950). (Courtesy National Library of Medicine)

tions of the brain tissue and biochemical products of schizophrenics revealed no differences between them and normal people.

A completely different approach to understanding the origins and cure of schizophrenia was propounded by a contemporary of Kraepelin and Bleuler, Adolf Meyer (1866–1950). Meyer, an American brain pathologist, later became recognized as the dean of American psychiatry. He maintained that there were no fundamental biological differences between schizophrenics and normals, and that there were not any fundamental differences in their respective psychological processes. Rather, he believed that the cognitive and behavioral disorganization that was associated with schizophrenia arose from inadequate early learning, and reflected "adjustive insufficiency" and habit deterioration, and that individual maladjustment rather than biological malfunction lay at the root of the disorder. Meyer's approach mandated research in a wholly different area than did Bleuler's or Kraepelin's. While Bleuler and Kraepelin strengthened the biological tradition of research in schizophrenia, Meyer gave impetus to a tradition that focused on learning and biosocial processes. Let us consider some of the modern views of this disorder.

INCIDENCE AND PREVALENCE OF SCHIZOPHRENIA

Schizophrenia is the most prevalent of the severe psychological disorders. The various types are conservatively estimated to occur in less than 1 percent of the U.S. population (Dohrenwend and Dohrenwend, 1974; DSM-III, 1980), although some national estimates run as high as 3 or 4 percent (Heston, 1970). Moreover, among certain populations, such as college students, some estimates go as high as 18 percent (Koh and Peterson, 1974). These latter estimates are probably exaggerated, but even the conservative estimates mark the schizophrenias as a distressingly prevalent disorder.

The first occurrence of schizophrenia occurs mainly among people who are under forty-five. There are substantial sex differences in the time it occurs: men are at risk for schizophrenia before age twenty-five, while women are at risk after age twenty-five (Lewine, 1981; Zigler and Levine, 1981). It afflicts the poor, especially the urban poor. The overall incidence of the schizophrenias (the rate at which new cases develop) is about 150 per 100,000 population (Crocetti and Lemkau, 1967). But compared to incidence among the wealthy, the incidence of the schizophrenias among the poor is three times greater, while its prevalence (the proportion of schizophrenics in the population at any one time) is eight times as high.

At the time of admission to a hospital or day treatment center, the typical schizophrenic is relatively young and relatively poor. Occasionally, schizophrenics come for treatment on their own, but more commonly their family or the police bring them to a treatment center. Often a disturbing incident triggers painful behavioral anomalies that are stressful for family and friends, and that leads to the decision to seek treatment.

SCHIZOPHRENIA DEFINED

The definition of schizophrenia, as well as who is and who is not schizophrenic has generated heated debate ever since Kraepelin described the symptoms of *dementia praecox* in his *Psychiatrie* in 1896. The most recent definition was offered in 1980 in DSM-III. In order to be diagnosed as a schizophrenic now, the onset of the disorder must occur before age forty-five, the symptoms must last for at least six months, and those symptoms must have induced a marked deterioration from the individual's previous level of functioning. Those are the *temporal* criteria.

There are also two *substantive* criteria for the diagnosis: (1) There must be a gross impairment of reality testing, that is, the individual must evaluate the accuracy of his or her thoughts incorrectly and, as a consequence, must make grossly incorrect inferences about reality. Such an impairment in reality testing is called a **psychosis**. Psychoses reflect major disruptions of reality testing. Minor impairments, such as a tendency to undervalue one's abilities or attractiveness, do not qualify. (2) The disturbance typically must affect several psychological processes, including thought, perception, emotion, communication, and psychomotor behavior. Disturbances of thought characteristically take the form of delusions and hallucinations.

Delusions are false beliefs that resist all argument and are sustained in the face of evidence that normally would be sufficient to destroy them. An individual who believes that he has drunk of the Fountain of Youth and is therefore immortal suffers a delusion. And the individual who believes that he not only has knowledge of these legendary waters but also that others are conspiring to pry his secret knowledge from him, is probably suffering from several delusions.

Hallucinations are false sensory perceptions that have a compelling sense of reality, even in the absence of stimuli that ordinarily provoke such perceptions. In schizophrenia, hallucinations are commonly auditory. But they can also be visual or implicate other sense organs, such as taste and smell. An individual who is convinced that she has seen, shook hands with, and had dinner with a minotaur has had an hallucination.

The examples of delusion and hallucination that were just given have their roots in colorful myths. But when real, these disturbances and others that we will examine later are considerably more painful, as the following case (first discussed in Chapter 10) illustrates:

> Carl was twenty-seven years old when he was first admitted to a psychiatric facility. Gangling and intensely shy, he was so incommunicative at the outset that his family had to supply initial information about him. They, it seemed, had been unhappy and uncomfortable with him for quite some time. His father dated the trouble from "sometime in high school." He reported, "Carl turned inward, spent a lot of time alone, had no friends and did no schoolwork." His mother was especially troubled about his untidiness. "He was really an embarrassment to us then, and things haven't improved since. You could never take him anywhere without an argument about washing up. And once he was there, he wouldn't say anything to anyone." His twin sisters, six years younger than Carl, said very little during the family interview, but rather passively agreed with their parents.
>
> One would hardly have guessed from their report that Carl graduated high school in the upper quarter of his class, and had gone on to college where he studied engineering for three years. Though he had always been shy, he had had one close friend, John Winters, throughout high school and college. John had been killed in a car accident a year earlier. (Asked about Winters, his father said, "Oh, him. We don't consider him much of anything at all. He didn't go to church either. And he didn't do any schoolwork.")

Carl and John were unusually close. They went through high school together, served in the army at the same time and when discharged, began college together and roomed in the same house. Both left college before graduating, much to the chagrin of Carl's parents, took jobs as machinists in the same firm, and moved into a nearby apartment.

They lived together for three years until John was killed. Two months later the company for which they worked went out of business. John's death left Carl enormously distraught. When the company closed, he found himself without the energy and motivation to look for a job. He moved back home. Disagreements between Carl and his family became more frequent and intense. He became more reclusive, as well as sloppy and bizarre; they, more irritable and isolating. Finally they could bear his behavior no longer and took him to the hospital. He went without any resistance.

After ten days in the hospital, Carl told the psychologist who was working with him: "I am an unreal person. I am made of stone, or else I am made of glass. I am wired precisely wrong, precisely. But you will not find my key. I have tried to lose the key to me. You can look at me closely if you wish, but you see more from far away."

Shortly thereafter, the psychologist noted that Carl ". . . . smiles when he is uncomfortable, and smiles more when in pain. He cries during television comedies. He seems angry when justice is done, frightened when someone compliments him, and roars with laughter on reading that a young child was burned in a tragic fire. He grimaces often. He eats very little but always carries food away."

After two weeks, the psychologist said to him: "You hide a lot. As you say, you are wired precisely wrong. But why won't you let me see the diagram?"

Carl answered: "Never, ever will you find the lever, the eternalever that will sever me forever with my real, seal, deal, heel. It is not on my shoe, not even on the sole. It walks away."

"I am an unreal person. I am made of stone . . ." Painting by Magritte entitled, *The Song of the Violet.* (Private Collection)

TYPES OF SCHIZOPHRENIA

Although we speak of schizophrenia and schizophrenics as if this is a unitary disorder, the differences between the various types of schizophrenia overwhelm their similarities. So much is this the case, that (as we have seen) it is increasingly common to speak of "the schizophrenias" in order to underscore that diversity. We will focus on four subtypes of schizophrenia: paranoid, disorganized, catatonic, and undifferentiated (see Table 17-1).

PARANOID SCHIZOPHRENIA

The presence of systematized delusions marks this subtype. The ***paranoid schizophrenic*** suffers delusions of persecution or grandeur which are remarkably systematized and complex, often like the plots of dark mysteries.

Table 17-1 THE SCHIZOPHRENIC DISORDERS

	Type	*Major Symptoms*
295.1	Disorganized Schizophrenia	inappropriate behavior, incoherence
295.2	Catatonic Schizophrenia	frozen or excitable motor behaviors
295.3	Paranoid Schizophrenia	delusions of persecution or grandeur
295.9	Undifferentiated Schizophrenia	generally disturbing thought disorder

SOURCE: DSM-III, 1980.

This complexity renders his experiences comprehensible to the schizophrenic—a matter of no small importance to which we will return—while simultaneously making it impenetrable to the outsider.

Beyond experiencing delusions of persecution and/or grandeur, paranoid schizophrenics may also experience delusional jealousy, the deep belief that their sexual partner is unfaithful. But despite the intensity of their feelings, paranoid schizophrenics rarely display severely disorganized behavior. Rather, their demeanor tends to be extremely formal or quite intense.

DISORGANIZED SCHIZOPHRENIA

Formerly called hebephrenic schizophrenia, the most striking behavioral characteristic of *disorganized schizophrenics* is apparent silliness and incoherence. They burst into laughter, grimaces, or giggles without an appropriate stimulus. Their behavior is jovial, but quite bizarre and absurd, suggesting extreme sensitivity to internal cues and extreme insensitivity to external ones. Correspondingly, they are voluble, bursting into meaningless conversation for long periods of time.

Disorganized schizophrenics may experience delusions and hallucinations, but not systematized ones. Rather, theirs tend to be more disorganized and diffused than those experienced by paranoid schizophrenics, and they often center on their own bodies. For example, disorganized schizophrenics may complain that their intestines are congealed or that their brains have been removed. Sometimes the delusions may be quite pleasant and contribute to the silliness of their behavior.

Disorganized schizophrenics often disregard bathing and grooming. They may not only become incontinent but also frequently eat their own body products, as well as other dirt. Again, a marked insensitivity is found here, similar to their insensitivity to social surroundings.

CATATONIC SCHIZOPHRENIA

The salient feature of *catatonic schizophrenia* is motor behavior that is either enormously excited or strikingly frozen, and that may occasionally alternate between the two states. The onset of the disorder is sudden. When behavior is excited, the individual may seem quite agitated, even wild, vigorously resisting all attempts at control. Affect is quite inappropriate, while agitation is enormously energetic and surprisingly prolonged, commonly yielding only to strong sedation.

Stuporous or frozen behavior is also quite striking in this subtype of schizophrenia. Individuals may be entirely immobile, often adopting quite uncomfortable postures and maintaining them for long periods. If someone moves them, they will freeze in a new position. A kind of statuesque "waxy flexibility" is characteristic. After emerging from such a stuporous episode, patients sometimes report that they had been experiencing hallucinations or delusions. These sometimes center on death and destruction, conveying the sense that any movement will provoke an enormous catastrophe.

Some theorists find evidence of negativism among catatonic schizophrenics, so much so that, in addition to the excited and stuporous behaviors, they take negativism to define the category (Maher, 1966). Forbidden

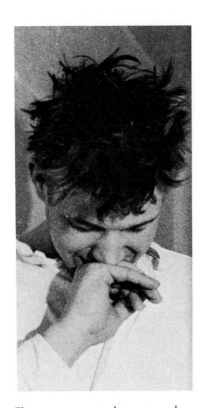

This man seems to be extremely sensitive to internal cues. He appears to be laughing without an appropriate stimulus causing the laughter. He may be suffering from disorganized, or hebephrenic, schizophrenia. (Photograph by Benyas-Kaufman/Black Star)

to sit, the catatonic will sit. Told to sit, the catatonic will insist on standing. Today this subtype is becoming rare, possibly because the behavior is being controlled with anti-psychotic drugs.

UNDIFFERENTIATED SCHIZOPHRENIA

Along with paranoid schizophrenia, this is a widely applied designation, used to categorize individuals who do not otherwise fit neatly into other classifications. It is a less specific diagnosis for disturbed individuals who present evidence of thought disorder, as well as behavioral and affective anomalies, but who are not classifiable under the other subtypes.

THE DIMENSIONS OF SCHIZOPHRENIA

Schizophrenics of all types differ in their behavior, life history, and prognosis. Many of these differences are quite useful in understanding the condition, communicating about schizophrenia, and in treating it. Among the most useful research dimensions in schizophrenia are: chronic versus acute and process versus reactive.

ACUTE AND CHRONIC

The most common distinction within schizophrenia differentiates acute from chronic conditions. The distinction is based on how quickly the symptoms have developed and how long they have been present. *Acute schizophrenics* are characterized by rapid and sudden onset of very florid symptoms. Quite frequently, one can point to a specific precipitating incident that led to the difficulties. In contrast, *chronic schizophrenics* seem to manifest a rather prolonged history of withdrawal. Symptoms tend to develop gradually over a long period of time. No precipitating incidents can be pinpointed.

In practice, however, the acute-chronic distinction rests on how many episodes a person has had and how long she has been hospitalized. First episodes that result in hospitalization for less than a year or several episodes that lead to a series of very brief hospitalizations qualify a person for an acute designation. Hospitalization that extends for more than two years invariably results in a chronic classification. When a person has been hospitalized from roughly eighteen to twenty-eight months, it is difficult to distinguish between acute and chronic conditions. That fact alone largely accounts for the low reliability of the classification.

PROCESS AND REACTIVE

There are substantial differences in the histories of schizophrenics that seem related to their symptoms. At one extreme, schizophrenia is *reactive*: it is precipitated by a severe social or emotional crisis, often a crisis from which the individual perceives no escape (Zigler and Phillips, 1961; Arieti, 1974). For some schizophrenics, that crisis may involve leaving home, leaving school for a job, their first sexual experience, the loss of a parent or sibling,

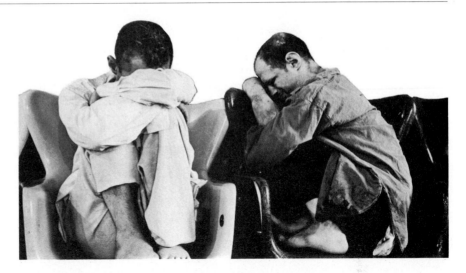

Process schizophrenia develops gradually, with no single crisis triggering the disorder. Process schizophrenics are less attuned to the social environment than are reactive schizophrenics. And they spend more time in psychiatric hospitals than do reactive schizophrenics. (Copyright Bill Stanton/Magnum)

or marriage. Prior to that crisis, their history seems well within normal bounds. Relations with parents and siblings, school adjustment, interest in friends of the same and opposite sex, physical health—all of these indices seem normal. Reactive schizophrenia commonly occurs in late adolescence or early adulthood. Onset of symptoms and response to treatment are both quite rapid.

Process schizophrenia lies at the other extreme. No single crisis or identifiable stresses trigger the disorder. Rather, it seems to develop gradually. Early history gives evidence of familial and peer rejection. School and social adjustment are inferior. Intense shyness and social withdrawal are also fairly common in the developmental history, with the result that peer relationships are impaired over a long period of time.

There are no purely reactive or process schizophrenics. These terms do not denote types, but rather dimensions (Garmezy and Rodnick, 1959). Schizophrenia rarely develops suddenly or in response to a single crisis. Nor does it develop without any precipitants. The terms "process" and "reactive" are anchor points on a dimension in which the visibility of precipitants and prior adjustment are pivotal. Moreover, while familial rejection and poor social competence characterize the process end of this continuum, they do not necessarily cause schizophrenia. There are "process normals," that is, people who have never had a schizophrenic episode, although their history is characterized by familial rejection and poor social competence (Wagener and Hartsough, 1974).

The symptoms associated with reactive schizophrenia are less severe than those of process schizophrenia. Those on the reactive side of the dimension, therefore, appear to have a better prognosis. They seem better able to deal with abstract tasks (Watson, C.G., 1973); their general level of thinking and perceiving is more integrated (Kilburg and Siegel, 1973; Watson, C.G., 1973); and their attentional capacities are less impaired (Nideffer, Neale, Kopfstein, and Cromwell, 1971; Bellisimo and Steffy, 1972; Neuchterlein, 1977). They seem more attuned to the social environment and more responsive to threat (Sappington, 1975). Finally, reactives spend much less time in psychiatric hospitals (Phillips, 1953; Depue and Dubkicki, 1974), which, of course, contributes to their designation as reactive.

THE SYMPTOMS OF SCHIZOPHRENIA

In the case history presented earlier, Carl exhibited many of the characteristics associated with schizophrenia: lack of interest in life, withdrawal from social activity, seemingly bizarre behavior, incomprehensible communications, and increasing preoccupation with private matters. These symptoms, like many of the others that are common in schizophrenia, involve three areas of psychological functioning: perception, thought, and emotion.

PERCEPTUAL DIFFICULTIES

Perceptual anomalies often accompany schizophrenia. Patients sometimes report spatial distortions, such that a room may seem much smaller and more constricting than it really is, or objects may seem farther away. Controlled laboratory studies indicate that compared to non-schizophrenics, schizophrenics are less able to estimate sizes accurately (Strauss, Foureman, and Parwatikar, 1974) and less able to judge the passage of time (Petzel and Johnson, 1972). Generally, upon admission to a hospital, schizophrenics report a great number of perceptual difficulties, such as difficulties in understanding others' speech or identifying them, or overly acute auditory perception. These perceptual difficulties may provide a fertile soil for hallucinations, which are discussed below. Other people, as well as the self, may be described and apparently experienced as hollow, flat, or two-dimensional. Carl, for example, feels that he is made of steel or of glass.

Hallucinations

As we noted earlier, hallucinations are false sensory experiences that have a compelling sense of reality. Hallucinations are often gripping. Sometimes terrifying. Nearly everyone has had a few visual hallucinatory experiences.

Auditory hallucinations are the most common hallucinations in schizophrenia (Malitz, Wilkens, and Escover, 1962). One finds their origins in ordinary thought, where it is common enough to conduct a private dialogue by imagining oneself talking to others and others talking back. And it is quite common for people to actually talk to themselves, or to talk with deities whose earful presence can only be presumed. (The psychiatrist Thomas Szasz [1970] observes that it is quite normal to talk with God, but only when God responds is it called an hallucination.) Of course, the non-schizophrenic has considerably greater control over the internal dialogue than does the schizophrenic. The latter, when experiencing an auditory hallucination, does not believe that the voices originate within the self, or that she has the ability to begin or end the talk. The inability to distinguish between external and internal, real and imagined, controllable and imposed, is central to the schizophrenic experience.

Some schizophrenics hallucinate, while others do not. Why? One possibility is that hallucinators have vivid imaginations. In an experiment that was designed to shed light on this problem, three groups of patients—hallucinating schizophrenics, non-hallucinating schizophrenics, and hospitalized but non-psychotic controls— were brought to a sound-deadened room and given the following instructions:

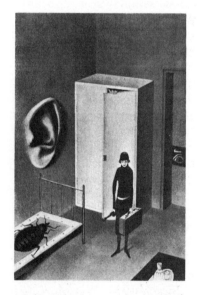

A schizophrenic may have visual and auditory hallucinations that have a compelling sense of reality. (*Das Hotelzimmer* by Anton Machet, from *Jugend*, Munich)

Table 17-2 THE VIVIDNESS OF AUDITORY IMAGERY AMONG HALLUCINATING
AND NON-HALLUCINATING SCHIZOPHRENICS AND AMONG CONTROLS

Vividness of Imagery	Hallucinating Schizophrenics	Non-hallucinating Schizophrenics	Hospitalized Non-psychotic Controls
High			
A. "I heard a phonograph record of 'White Chrismas' clearly and believed that the record was actually playing."	2	0	0
B. "I heard the phonograph record of 'White Christmas' clearly but knew there was no record actually playing."	15	1	8
Low			
C. "I had a vague impression of hearing the record playing 'White Christmas.'"	2	9	7
D. "I did not hear the record."	1	10	5

SOURCE: Adapted from Mintz and Albert, 1972.

> This is a test of the vividness of your imagination. I want you to close your eyes and imagine hearing a phonograph record with words and music playing "White Christmas" until I ask you to stop.

After twenty seconds in the sound-attenuated room, subjects were asked to indicate whether they had heard the record. The findings are quite remarkable and are shown in Table 17-2. Hallucinating schizophrenics experienced vivid imagery and overwhelmingly indicated that they heard "White Christmas" clearly. Non-hallucinators, on the other hand, experienced low vividness, many of them being unable to imagine they even heard the record. Indeed, of the three hallucinating schizophrenics whose vividness was low, two were the least frequent hallucinators in the group, while the third complained that his own private voices were so loud that he couldn't concentrate on hearing "White Christmas"! This evidence, then, points toward hallucinating schizophrenics as having vivid imaginations.

There is additional evidence from the same experiment to indicate that hallucinating schizophrenics are particularly unable to distinguish the internal from the external, and real from imagined events. Subjects in the same experiment listened to tape-recorded sentences through earphones. Some of the sentences were quite audible. Subjects were asked to tell what they heard. If the sentence was unclear, they were instructed to guess. And they were asked to indicate how confident they were that they had heard the sentence correctly. Their responses were scored for accuracy, and correlations were computed between their accuracy and the degree of confidence they expressed. Now, among people who are able to test reality, one expects the correlation between the accuracy of and confidence in their reports to be quite high. The correlations were indeed high for control subjects: .92. And they were nearly as high for non-hallucinating schizophrenics: .84. But for hallucinating schizophrenics the accuracy-confidence correlation declined to .54, suggesting a tenuous relationship between accuracy and confidence.

Examination of these data makes clear how tenuous that relationship is. The phrase "The water is too cold" was presented at a low intelligibility level to an hallucinating schizophrenic, who reported that he heard "Remember me please" and indicated that he was "positive that I received the message *correctly*." A control subject reported that he heard "Nobody likes me"—clearly an error. But he indicated that he was positive that he had received the message *incorrectly*. Thus, hallucinating schizophrenics, in addition to having vivid imaginations, also seem unable to test reality (Mintz and Albert, 1972).

THOUGHT DISORDERS

Insofar as schizophrenics' speech reflects their thought, schizophrenics' thought can be disordered in a variety of ways. Sometimes the *process* of thinking is disordered, and sometimes it is the *content* of thought that is peculiar.

The Disordered Process of Thought

When the process of thinking is disturbed, the train of thought seems moved by the *sound* of words rather than by their meaning. ***Clang associations***, that is, associations produced by the rhyme of words, such as " . . . my real, seal, deal, heel," abound. Schizophrenics like Carl may also come up with ***neologisms***, new words like "eternalever" that have only private meaning. Some of the most interesting evidence about schizophrenic thought arises from studies of attention and distractibility.

ATTENTIONAL DEFICITS.   Everyone at one time or another has had trouble paying attention or concentrating, in spite of trying hard to do both. Tired or upset, we find our attention roaming, and we cannot direct it. What we have experienced briefly and in microcosm, acute schizophrenics experience profoundly. One patient explains his problem with attention in this way:

> I can't concentrate. It's diversion of attention that troubles me . . . The sounds are coming through to me, but I feel my mind cannot cope with everything. It's difficult to concentrate on any one sound. It's like trying to do two or three different things at one time. (McGhie and Chapman, 1961, p. 104)

Consider for a moment what normal attention involves. We are continuously bombarded by an enormous number of stimuli, many more than our limited channel capacity can absorb. So we need some mechanism for sorting out stimuli to determine which ones will be admitted and which ones barred. That mechanism has been referred to metaphorically as a ***cognitive*** or ***selective filter*** (Broadbent, 1958). Normally, that filter is flexible, sensitive, and sturdy. Sometimes it permits several different stimuli to enter simultaneously, and other times it bars some of those same stimuli. When you drive a car on a clear road, for example, you usually can conduct a conversation with a passenger, often while listening to background music. But when the roads are treacherous, and below you is a several hundred foot drop, attention narrows: it now becomes impossible to conduct a conversation and what was formerly soothing music in now quite an irritant. All of the mind's energy, as it were, is directed to one thing and one thing only: driving safely. Everything else is filtered out.

Among schizophrenics, something seems wrong with the attentional filter, so wrong, in fact, that attentional deficits have long been thought to be at the heart of the thought disorder that characterizes schizophrenia (Kraepelin, 1919; Bleuler, 1924; Chapman and Chapman, 1973; Garmezy, 1977; Place and Gilmore, 1980). The sense that there is a breakdown of the filter, that the world's hodgepodge has simply invaded the mind, that one cannot control one's attention and therefore one's thoughts or speech, that it is difficult to focus the mind or sustain that focus once it is achieved—all of these experiences are said to be central to schizophrenia. A former patient puts it well:

> Each of us is capable of coping with a large number of stimuli, invading our being through any one of the senses. We could hear every sound within earshot and see every object, line and colour within the field of vision, and so on. It's obvious that we would be incapable of carrying on any of our daily activities if even one-hundredth of all these available stimuli invade us at once. So the mind must have a filter which functions without our conscious thought, sorting stimuli and allowing only those which are relevant to the situation in hand to disturb consciousness. And this filter must be working at maximum efficiency at all times, particularly when a high degree of concentration is required. What happened to me . . . was a breakdown in the filter, and a hodge-podge of unrelated stimuli were distracting me from things which should have had my undivided attention. (MacDonald, 1960, p. 218)

Some schizophrenics seem to suffer generalized attentional deficits; they seem not to be attending to anything at all. Others pay too much attention to some stimuli, and not enough to others. For example, someone who is experiencing hallucinations is likely to be hyper-attentive to the hallucinations and correspondingly insensitive to external social stimuli.

These subjective reports, as well as the observations of acute observers, find interesting confirmation in experimental studies of attention with schizophrenics. We cannot yet measure attention directly in humans. But we can infer attentional difficulties from performance on reaction time tasks. In the standard reaction time (RT) study, people are told to hold their finger on a button and to release that button as soon as a light appears or a buzzer is heard. They are given a "get ready" signal. The interval between that signal and the stimulus presentation, which is called the *preparatory interval*, can be constant or varied. When attention is wandering or is being insufficiently deployed, reaction time to the light or buzzer signal should be greatly slowed. Moreover, as the preparatory interval is lengthened, thereby allowing the attention to wander, RT should be retarded.

Chronic schizophrenics, whose condition is often characterized by withdrawal and apathy, consistently manifest slower RT's than either normals or acute schizophrenics (Huston, Shakow, and Riggs, 1937; Rodnick and Shakow, 1940; Tizard and Venables, 1956; Shakow, 1963). Moreover, when the preparatory interval exceeds eight seconds or is irregular, chronic schizophrenics again show retarded reaction times. The comparative performance deficits are substantial, as shown in Figure 17-1.

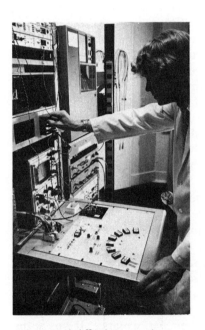

Attentional difficulties can be inferred from performance on reaction time tests, for which the monitoring equipment is shown here. The subject is in a separate, darkened room where he is presented with stimuli. The subject must try to respond to these stimuli as quickly as he can. (Photograph by Van Bucher/Photo Researchers)

Figure 17-1
Mean reaction times of 25
schizophrenic subjects and 10
normal subjects. (Source: Based
on Rodnick and Shakow, 1940)

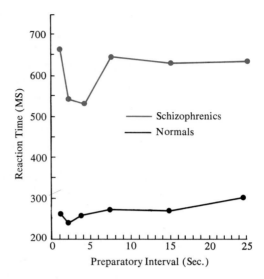

MOTIVATIONAL DIFFICULTIES. The slower reaction times of schizophrenics may arise from motivational difficulties. Two quite different kinds of motivational difficulties could account for their poor performance. The first is that, relative to normals, schizophrenics suffer a motivational deficit. When normal people participate in an experiment, they are usually motivated to perform well, to please the experimenter, to keep their side of the bargain. Schizophrenics, however, may not feel that way. They may be deficient in social cooperativeness (Shakow, 1962), or they may experience **anhedonia**, the inability to feel pleasure (Meehl, 1962), including perhaps the social pleasure that comes from being helpful in an experiment. Some theorists claim that both of these prevent schizophrenics from doing well on reaction time tests.

Another motivational explanation of schizophrenics' poor performance on reaction time tasks suggests an opposite hypothesis: rather than experiencing a motivational deficit, schizophrenics may be overmotivated, and especially sensitive to situations that might lead to criticism or disapproval (Garmezy, 1966). In fact, the RT task does not evoke either approval or disapproval from an experimenter. But precisely because the quality of their performance is left ambiguous, schizophrenics may become upset. Expectations of disapproval, where disapproval *might* be forthcoming, may be sufficient to disorganize them and retard their performance. If this is the case, then understandably their performance outside of the laboratory—on the job and at home—would very likely deteriorate, since in most real-life situations how and whether one will be evaluated is often vague and unpredictable.

OVERINCLUSIVENESS. Another possibility, which has received strong support from a variety of studies, is that schizophrenic thinking generally tends to be overinclusive (Cameron, 1938, 1947; Chapman and Taylor, 1957, Payne, 1966; Yates, 1966). **Overinclusiveness** refers to the tendency to form concepts from both relevant and irrelevant information. This thought defect arises from an impaired capacity to resist distracting information, and it strongly suggests a defect in cognitive filtering. The simple reaction time task may well be converted into a highly complicated one by schizophrenics. If they consider, not only the light or buzzer as the stimulus to be processed and responded to, but also the preparatory interval, the inter-trial interval and perhaps the entire experimental context, then no wonder their RT's are much longer than those of normals. They are processing much more information by virtue of their overinclusiveness. This explanation seems to be a promising one for accounting for schizophrenic attentional and cognitive deficits.

COGNITIVE DISTRACTIBILITY.   The notion of a defective filter that gives rise to overinclusiveness in schizophrenic thinking merits further examination. Are there rules that determine what is relevant information and what irrelevant? Of course not. Very likely all of us differ with regard to the kind of information that we attend to and exclude, even on so simple a task as the reaction time task. In what ways, then, may the thought and attentional processes of schizophrenics be different from normals?

The difference between schizophrenic and normal thinking is unlikely to be a qualitative one, since all of us have associations to a stimulus which may or may not prove to be relevant. The difference lies in the number of associative intrusions, the context in which they arise, and in how they are integrated conceptually. Imagine yourself writing a New Year's greeting to a friend. You wish her a happy and healthy year and then refer to the pleasures and sadnesses of the previous year. Compare your greeting to that written by one of Eugen Bleuler's patients:

> I wish you then a good, happy, joyful, healthy, blessed and fruitful year, and many good wine-years to come, as well as a healthy and good apple-year, and sauerkraut and cabbage and squash and seed year. (Bleuler, 1950, cited in Martin, 1977)

Here, there are many more associations than are found in normal greetings. These associations, moreover, arise in chains that appear to be generated by specific words that seem to distract the patient from his ultimate goal and impair the overall meaning of the greeting. The word fruitful seems to evoke associations to wine, apple, sauerkraut, cabbage, squash, and the like. Moreover, in this context, wine and sauerkraut are not normally the dominant associations of the word fruitful: abundance is. But the patient seems to have centered on "fruit" and to have generated associations that are appropriate for that word but not for "fruitfulness."

Many words have a variety of meanings, connotations, and associations. And all of us, schizophrenics and normals alike, are sensitive to those meanings and associations. But schizophrenics seem especially sensitive to the dominant associations of words, and are less influenced by the contexts in which they are used. In the following test item:

Pool means the same as

      1. puddle

      2. notebook

      3. swim

      4. none of the above.

The correct answer is "puddle." Many schizophrenics as well as some normals, however, will err and offer "swim" as the correct answer. The difference between normal and schizophrenic thought processes in items of this sort is a quantitative rather than a qualitative one (Chapman and Chapman, 1973; Rattan and Chapman, 1973).

The Disordered Content of Thought

Evidence for disordered thought is as commonly found in the content as the process of thinking. Sometimes the schizophrenic person develops the belief that certain events and people have special significance for him—that television newscasters are speaking to him, for example, or that strangers in the street are looking at him. These beliefs are called *ideas of reference.* When such beliefs become organized into a larger and coherent framework, they are called delusions.

KINDS OF DELUSIONS. Earlier we noted that a *delusion* is a private theory, deeply held, that often persists despite sound contradictory evidence, and that often does not fit with the individual's level of knowledge or cultural group. These beliefs are so deeply held that psychological lore tells of a delusional patient who was once wired to a lie detector and asked if she were the Virgin Mary. "No," she replied. But the detector indicated that she was lying!

There are four prominent kinds of delusions: delusions of grandeur, delusions of control, delusions of persecution, and delusions of reference. *Delusions of grandeur* refer to convictions that one is especially important. The belief that one is John Lennon, Jesus Christ, or fourth in line to the throne of Denmark, would indicate a delusion of grandeur.

Delusions of control are characterized by beliefs that one's thoughts or behaviors are being controlled from without. The patient attributes the source of angry, sexual, or otherwise sinful thoughts to external agents. For example, someone who believes that beings from another universe are giving him instructions is suffering from a delusion of control.

Delusions of persecution consist of fears that individuals, groups, or the government have malevolent intentions and are "out to get me." The focus of the delusion may be quite specific: a neighbor, one's boss, the FBI, or a rather vague "they." When these delusions combine with hallucinations so that the subject "sees" and "hears" evidence of a plot, they can induce continual panic. Confirmation for these imaginings can often be found in misinterpretations of everyday experience, as shown in the following case:

This hospitalized woman may have delusions of persecution. (Photograph by John Launuis/ Black Star)

Arthur, who had been insecure and shy for as long as he could remember, took a job in a large office. Unsure of his clerical abilities, he worked long and hard at his job, rejecting invitations to have lunch or coffee with his colleagues. Gradually they stopped inviting him, going off merrily by themselves, and returning full of laughter and cheer.

One day Arthur's supervisor found a substantial error in his work. Although it was his first error and the supervisor would easily have forgiven it, Arthur simply could not forget it. It seemed to underscore his own perception of his abilities, a perception that he was quite anxious to conceal. He came to believe that his supervisor knew of other mistakes he had made, and that his colleagues and supervisor were collaboratively examining his work daily. He "knew" that they were excluding him and talking about him, and that their lunchtime laughter was entirely at his expense. Moreover, he felt that their interest in his performance gradually overflowed into an interest in his personal life. When he encountered his co-workers after hours or on the weekend he felt certain that they were following him.

Six weeks after his error had been discovered, he began to "sense" that people had been through his drawers, both at home and in the office. Moreover, certain papers that were necessary for his work were missing, leading him to believe that others were now actively plotting his vocational downfall. Their failure to invite him to lunch was taken as further evidence of the plot.

He became very fearful and disorganized. Continually preoccupied with his troubles, he found it difficult to sleep, eat, or concentrate. His work deteriorated both in quality and in output. When his supervisor finally asked him what was wrong, he blurted out, "You know what's wrong. You and they have made it wrong ever since I came here." He then ran out of the office, never to return. Within the year, Arthur's behavior had so deteriorated that he was hospitalized with the diagnosis of paranoid schizophrenia.

Arthur's sense that others were actively seeking his errors and taking his papers constituted a delusion of persecution. But the continual misinterpretation of others' laughter, as well as their failure to invite him to lunch, constituted the fourth kind of delusion: a ***delusion of reference***. Such delusions rest on the incorrect assumption that the casual remarks or behaviors of others apply to oneself, and can extend to how others act in the street or subway, as well as to the behavior of actors on television. Depending on what they refer to, referential delusions can make a person miserably unhappy, as in the above instance, or quite joyful.

The sense of being under the influence of external forces is experienced in delusions of control. (Photograph by Yemima Rabin)

DELUSIONS: A NORMAL COGNITIVE ACTIVITY? Delusions are among the most striking symptoms of schizophrenia. To the observer, the content of a delusion seems so bizarre that it automatically suggests the thought disorder that is characteristic of schizophrenia. How else does one explain the feeling that one is being intensely persecuted, or that one is infinitely superior to ordinary mortals, all in the absence of confirming evidence? Indeed, it is the flowering of a delusion in the absence of confirmation, and its resistance to ordinary persuasion, that leads us to believe that the thought processes that are implicated in delusional activity are different from our own.

Before we consider the delusions from the schizophrenic's own vantage point, we might first look for analogies to delusional activity. These, of course, are only analogies, and likely rude analogies at that, but they give us some basis for understanding schizophrenic delusions.

Imagine that you have experienced a partial loss of hearing, and that you are unaware of that loss. You are with two other people who are talking, laughing, making funny faces, and looking at you. All three of you have to work together, but it seems that those two are doing a better job of it than you are. What are you likely to think? Remember that you can't *hear* what's going on very well, so you don't really *know* why they are laughing and looking at you. But that doesn't stop you from trying to make sense of the peculiar situation. One very real possibility is that you will infer that they are talking about *you* and laughing at *you*.

Such an experiment was in fact conducted among normal people who were highly hypnotizable and in whom partial deafness was induced. Subjects who were unaware that they were deaf were rated by judges (who had no knowledge of the subjects' hearing status) as being more agitated, irritated, hostile, and confused than either nondeaf subjects or subjects who were aware of the source of their deafness. Moreover, the experimental subjects rated themselves in very much the same way. Finally, formal measures of psychopathology, such as the Minnesota Multiphasic Personality Inventory (MMPI) and the Thematic Apperception Test (TAT), revealed much higher paranoia scores among subjects who were deaf and unaware of it (Zimbardo, Andersen, and Kabat, 1981).

While the sources of our feelings and perceptions are not always available to us, we do, in fact, develop theories to account for our experiences. These theories arise from the causal attributions we make about our experiences (Nisbett and Ross, 1980). In this sense, we behave like ordinary scientists: given a set of facts or experiences, we seek to explain them (Maher, 1974).

A similar process may occur with schizophrenics. Like the normal person, the schizophrenic asks: What is happening? How is it happening? And why is it happening to me and not to others? Because their attention is overinclusive, schizophrenics will frequently "see" aspects of their environment that they are at a loss to explain, and be inundated by stimuli that they cannot control (Venables, 1964). Moreover, there is growing evidence that schizophrenics actually suffer impairments of a physical sort. The sensory quality of their perceptual experience may be more vivid, intense, or defective than in normals (Cooper, Garside, and Kay, 1976; Cooper and Porter, 1976). Much as it is common for older people whose hearing is fading to believe that people are whispering about them, so it may be that schizophrenics' delusions derive from actual perceptual deficits. Such deficits and the experiences to which they give rise are genuine. But they lead schizophrenics to experience their world differently than the rest of us do.

Schizophrenics know that their own experiences are *real*. When others deny the reality of those experiences, schizophrenics have two alternative explanations: either the others are lying, or they are telling the truth. If schizophrenics decide that the others are lying, they feel victimized, and they suffer delusions of persecution. If schizophrenics decide that the others are telling the truth, then they feel privileged because of their special ability to perceive "realities" that are unavailable to others, and they suffer delusions of grandiosity.

"But why me and not others?," the schizophrenic asks. It is in explaining his special fate that the personal history of the schizophrenic may become relevant. If, for example, he harbors a guilty secret in his past, he may conclude that this is why he is being so terribly punished now. If he has done something that he views as especially praiseworthy, he may now see himself as anointed from above. The variety of possible explanations is limited only by the variety of life histories that exist among schizophrenics, while the regularity with which certain explanations occur derives from the common life experiences that a culture provides.

Finally, it is schizophrenics' persistence in maintaining their delusions despite contrary evidence that requires explanation. Reality is not a solid, concrete thing. It can and has been used by normal people to arrive at conclusions that other normals find tenuous. All theories about how the world operates, including scientific ones, are overthrown only when a more satisfactory theory can be found to replace it. Because schizophrenics' theories often rest on invisible agencies, what seems ridiculous to the observer provides schizophrenics with a cohesive and satisfactory account of their situation. On those occasions when it is contradicted by particular kinds of data, the theory (i.e., the delusion) becomes more elaborate and comprehensive to account for the seeming contradiction, much as scientific theories do when they must account for anomalies. For example, if a schizophrenic believes that he is being poisoned and he encounters a nurse who seems particularly kind, he may expand his delusion to include people who seem kind, but who are really poisoners. This occurs not because the schizophrenic fails to test reality, but because he has no more satisfactory theory to explain his present condition.

AFFECTIVE DISTURBANCES

Emotions, or affects, are jointly a function of perception, cognition, and physiological arousal. *Perceiving* a mad dog quickly generates some worrisome *cognitions* (or thoughts) that in turn generate an *emotion*, fear. Because schizophrenia arises from disorders of perception and cognition, it follows that there should be affective disturbances also.

For some schizophrenics, affect is characteristically flat or bland. They seem entirely unresponsive emotionally. So much is this the case that flat or restricted affect is still considered a diagnostic hallmark of the schizophrenic disturbance (Carpenter, Strauss, and Bartko, 1974). The apparent inability of some schizophrenics to display affect should not, however, be mistaken for absence of *any* affective experience. Schizophrenics are deeply emotional and deeply responsive to cognitions (Arieti, 1974). But the cognitions that affect them are not the ones that are evocative for most of us, and vice versa. In one respect, the schizophrenic experience is like our own when we visit unfamiliar places. For example, American guests at a Thai wedding, not knowing what all of the symbols mean, would hardly know how to act or what to feel. Shared symbolic meanings allow feelings to arise, be expressed, and be understood by others. Because schizophrenics have lost contact with

Some schizophrenic patients may suffer from flat or bland affect. They may seem entirely unresponsive emotionally. (*Left:* Photograph by Chris Maynard/ Magnum. *Right:* Photograph by Inge Morath/Magnum)

the socially shared domain of symbols and meanings, their affective responses to those stimuli are likely to be blunted.

Sometimes, schizophrenic affect is best characterized as inappropriate. Carl's affect seemed to take that form:

> He smiles when he is uncomfortable, and smiles more when in pain. He cries during television comedies. He seems angry when justice is done . . . and roars with laughter on reading that a young child was burned in a tragic fire.

Affective disturbance can take yet another form: intense ambivalence. A person or situation may arouse opposite feelings simultaneously. Such ambivalence may lead to behavioral paralysis, or to seemingly bizarre attempts to resolve the situation by expressing one affect overwhelmingly and suppressing the other entirely.

MEANING IN SCHIZOPHRENIA

Most people who read Carl's words are struck and upset by their incomprehensibility. "I am made of stone," he says, "or else I am made of glass. I am wired precisely wrong, precisely . . ." Neurotic communications evoke understanding. If you are told "I'm afraid to go outside" or "I can't stop daydreaming," you have little difficulty comprehending the communication, even empathizing with the speaker. But schizophrenic communications often seem to be gibberish; they seem to result in word salads and syllabic stews. Ideas are not transmitted. Unable to understand, people often turn away from schizophrenics, treating what schizophrenics say as part of the symptomatology of the disorder, and not as communication.

Do schizophrenics attempt to communicate? Is what they say gibberish? Was Carl saying anything that was meaningful? It appears that he was. But from the listener's viewpoint, it was difficult to find the communication in the thicket of strange verbalization.

> I am an unreal person . . . . I am wired precisely wrong, precisely. But you will not find my key . . . . You can look at me closely if you wish, but you see more from far away.

Carl is hiding. That is, he is trying "precisely" to mislead his observers. When angry, he pretends friendship; when sad, happiness. He wants to maintain privacy, and he may also feel in danger of being exposed. He is, therefore, all the more in need of concealment. When hiding by means of transparent opposites fails—as when he is asked an intrusive question—he hides more energetically, and in more bizarre ways: by generating neologisms, by using clang associations to speak—in short, by talking a lot and saying little, by conveying his need to hide in his talk.

The divided self is a self that operates at two levels (Laing, 1965). On one level, there is the silent self—clearly active but vulnerable and afraid to emerge. There is also a smoke-screen self, a mask, a disguise, designed to conceal and protect that silent self. There is no strong evidence for this two-self view, but many psychologists and psychiatrists who have worked with schizophrenics find merit in it. For example, later in his treatment, when his need to hide had abated, Carl had this to say of himself:

When it's all over, it's hard to remember what you said and how you said it. I wouldn't want to talk that way now even if I could. I was putting people off almost consciously by talking that way. It would have been impossible for me to let on how I really felt. It's still hard . . . But at the same time, while I was putting you off, I really wanted you to know. But I couldn't come out with it— that was too risky. Sometimes I would say things in a special way, hoping you'd take special notice. When I said I'm not angry . . . I wagged my hand back and forth, making a "no" sign—telling but not saying that I'm angry. I don't know why I wanted someone to know. After all, I was hiding. But it was a prison I had made for myself. I didn't know how to get out myself. So I kept throwing out little keys, hoping someone would get at the lock.

THE CAUSES OF THE SCHIZOPHRENIAS

While the schizophrenias have been studied for more than a century, progress in understanding them has been painfully slow. We know less about the origins and treatment of the schizophrenias than we do about some other disorders. In the following sections, we will outline the dominant approaches currently used in the search for the causes and treatment of the schizophrenias.

Knowledge about the origins of schizophrenia is concentrated in four major areas: genetics, the role of the family, neurochemistry, and the role of society. Research on the schizophrenias, like that on other psychological questions, is two-pronged, involving both biological and social questions. Some consider schizophrenia to be rooted in nature; others say that it is the product of social experience. Still others are convinced that nature-nurture interactions are involved, and that these interactions of genetic, biochemical, familial, and social factors predispose a person to schizophrenia (Zubin and Spring, 1977).

THE GENETICS OF SCHIZOPHRENIA

Various researchers have examined the notion of a genetic vulnerability to schizophrenia. Both twin studies and family studies have demonstrated a strong basis for the genetic component in schizophrenia.

Concordance for Schizophrenia in Twins

DZ AND MZ TWINS.   We can best understand human genetics by examining the similarities and differences between twins. As we discussed in Chapter 3, twins are of two kinds: identical and fraternal. Both kinds descend from the zygote, the fertilized egg from which all life begins. Identical twins are *monozygotic* (MZ), which means that both individuals developed from a single fertilized egg, which divided and produced two individuals. Because all of the cells of these two individuals derived from a single egg, the genes and chromosomes—in short, the heredity—of these individuals is identical. They will, of course, have the identical physical makeup: genes, blood type, eye color, and fingerprints will be the same. There may be differences between them, but such differences will be entirely attributable to different life experiences: one may be thinner because of nutritional differences, or the other may limp because of an accident.

Fraternal, or *dizygotic* (DZ) twins develop from two different eggs. Except for the fact that they are born at the same time, DZ twins are like ordinary siblings. Their hereditary makeup is quite different. They may be of different gender; they may have different eye color. They have different fingerprints. They can be accurately distinguished from MZ twins on the basis of these characteristics alone, and certainty can be increased by examining blood type.

The logic of a genetic study is really quite simple: if all other things are equal, the more similar people are in their genetic makeup, the more traits they will have in common if those traits are genetically influenced. MZ twins should resemble each other more than DZ twins or ordinary siblings. And DZ twins and siblings should have more in common than unrelated individuals. If both members of a twin set have a trait in common, we say that that twin set is *concordant* for that particular trait. If, however, one member has the trait and one does not, we call the twin set *discordant* for the trait.

MZ twins are wholly identical in their genes and chromosomes. If the traits that subsequently develop are entirely determined by their genetic makeup, there should be 100 percent concordance. If one twin has the trait, the other should have it too. Anything less than 100 percent concordance (but more than the percentage found in DZ twins) will suggest that heredity *influences*, but does not actually determine, the presence of the trait. What is more, that influence depends on the assumption that all other possible influences, such as nutrition, physical health, and psychosocial environment, are themselves about the same. If one twin's physical and social environment differs from the other's, that difference could explain any difference between the pair.

LINKING GENETICS AND SCHIZOPHRENIA.   Although genetic studies of schizophrenia have been conducted for over fifty years, Irving Gottesman and James Shields (1972) conducted one of the very few studies that were planned in advance. From 1948 through 1964, every patient admitted for treatment to the psychiatric unit at the Maudsley and Bethlem Royal Hospital in London was routinely asked if he or she was a twin. Over these sixteen years, the investigators located 57 patients (out of more than 45,000 admitted) who were twins and whose twin could be located and would cooperate in the study. For analytic purposes, the twin who was first seen at the psychiatric clinic is called the *index case* or *proband.* The other twin, who will be examined for the presence or absence of schizophrenia, is called the *co-twin*.

Of these fifty-seven sets of twins, it was determined that twenty-four were MZ twins and thirty-three were DZ twins. The twins ranged in age from nineteen to sixty-four, with a median age of thirty-seven. Concordance for schizophrenia, where it was already present in the co-twin at the time the proband was admitted to the hospital, could, of course, be determined immediately. Discordant pairs were followed for at least three and as long as sixteen years to determine if schizophrenia subsequently developed in the co-twin.

Such a lengthy study examines more than simple diagnosis. In analyzing an enormous variety of psychological, medical, and social data for each twin pair, Gottesman and Shields observed two findings of special relevance to our own investigation into the genetic causes of schizophrenia. First, they found strict concordance when the proband's co-twin had been hospitalized and diagnosed schizophrenic: 42 percent of MZ twins and 9 percent of DZ twins were concordant for schizophrenia, a ratio of roughly 4:1. Despite the small sample, this is a very significant finding, one consistent with other genetic studies of schizophrenia.

Second, using length of hospitalization to indicate severity of schizophrenia, Gottesman and Shields found substantial concordance differences between MZ twins whose probands had been hospitalized for more than two years and those whose probands had been hospitalized for less than two years. Hospitalization for more than two years is critical to a diagnosis of chronic schizophrenia, and it is also highly correlated with a diagnosis of process schizophrenia. It is therefore of enormous interest that concordance rates rose to 77 percent in this sample. For those who were hospitalized less than two years (very likely the acute, reactive schizophrenias), the concordance rate was only 27 percent (Gottesman and Shields, 1972).

The evidence from the many studies summarized in Table 17-3 is strong: concordance rates for MZ twins are higher than they are for DZ twins; con-

Table 17-3 CONCORDANCE RATES FOR SCHIZOPHRENIA IN STUDIES OF TWINS

	Number of Pairs		Concordance Percentages	
	MZ	*DZ*	*MZ*	*DZ*
Luxenburger (1929), Germany	19	13	58	0
Rosanoff et al. (1934), United States and Canada	41	53	61	13
Essen-Moller (1941), Sweden	11	27	64	15
Kallmann (1953), New York State	174	517	69	10
Slater (1953), England	37	58	65	14
Inouye (1961), Japan	55	11	60	18
Kringlen (1967), Norway	55	90	25	4
Pollin, Allen, Hoffer, and Stubeneau (1969), United States	95	125	14	4
Tienari (1971), Finland	19	20	16	5
Gottesman and Shields (1972), England	24	33	42	9
Fischer (1973), Denmark	21	41	24	10

SOURCE: Adapted and modified from Rosenthal, 1970b.

cordance rates for DZ twins are, with one exception, higher than the rate for unrelated persons in the general population (about 1 percent). Concordance, however, is never 100 percent because the genetic component of schizophrenia does not guarantee occurrence. Genetics only makes one vulnerable to schizophrenia: it does not guarantee that schizophrenia will occur.

Concordance for Schizophrenia in Families

Family studies begin from the same premise as twin studies: individuals who have a similar heredity are more likely to both possess a particular trait than are those who are unrelated. Parents and siblings of a schizophrenic proband should be more likely to be or become schizophrenic than remote relatives, who in turn are more prone to schizophrenia than are those who are not related. The data from more than a dozen studies support this conclusion (Rosenthal, 1970a). As can be seen in Table 17-4, the likelihood that siblings of a proband will also be schizophrenic ranges from 3.3 percent to 14.3 percent—much higher than the 1 percent one finds among the general population. The likelihood of a parent of a proband being schizophrenic is a bit lower, ranging from 0.2 percent to 12 percent. Moreover, the child of two schizophrenic parents has about a 35 percent chance of becoming

Table 17-4 RISK ESTIMATES FOR SCHIZOPHRENICS IN PARENTS AND SIBLINGS OF SCHIZOPHRENIC PROBANDS

Study	*Estimated Morbidity Risk*		
	Parents of Schizophrenics	*Siblings of Schizophrenics*	*General Population*
Brugger (1928)*	4.3	10.3	1.53
M. Bleuler (1930)**	2.0	4.9	
Schulz (1932)*	2.6	6.7	0.76
Luxenburger (1936)*	11.7	7.6	0.85
Smith (1936)*	1.2	3.3	
Galatschjan (1937)*	4.9	14.0	
Stömgren (1938)**	0.7	6.7	0.48
Kallmann (1938)***	2.7	7.5	0.35
M. Bleuler (1941)*	5.6	10.4	1.53
Kallmann (1946)***	9.2	14.3	
Böök (1953)****	12.0	9.7	2.85
Slater (1953)*	4.1	5.4	
Hallgren and Sjögren (1959)**	0.2	5.7	0.83
Garrone (1962)*****	7.0	8.6	2.40

AGE OF RISK: *15–40   ****15–50
          **20–40   *****15–70
          ***15–45

SOURCE: Adapted from Rosenthal, 1971, p. 65.

schizophrenic (Rosenthal, 1970b). Although the data vary, the evidence clearly supports genetic determination.

But Is It Really Genetic?

We began this discussion of genetics and schizophrenia with the critical assumption that if all other things were equal, the more similar people were in their genetic makeup, the more traits they would have in common if those traits were genetically influenced. But are all other things equal? Consider the finding that children of two schizophrenic parents stand a 35 percent chance of becoming schizophrenic themselves. Is that because they share a common gene pool, or is it because schizophrenic parents may be terrible parents, fully capable of inducing schizophrenia in their children, regardless of their common gene pool? Or consider again the twin studies. We know that MZ twins share a unique environment with each other. They tend to mature and to develop language more slowly than other children. They tend to be mistaken for one another and therefore to suffer identity problems of indeterminate magnitude. Could not these environmental problems, rather than genetics, be a major factor in their eventual schizophrenia?

Behavior geneticists have responded to these questions in three ways. First, they have tried to locate probands and co-siblings who have been reared apart. Studies of this kind are called ***adoption studies.*** Second, they have conducted studies of people who are presumed to be at risk for schizophrenia because other members of their families are schizophrenic. These high-risk studies seek to map the development of behavior before schizophrenia occurs, in the hope of relating causative, correlative, and especially preventive factors. Finally, there are studies of non-schizophrenic twins which bear on this question.

ADOPTION STUDIES. Leonard Heston (1966) studied forty-seven children of schizophrenic mothers who had been placed in adoptive or foster homes less than one month after birth. He compared them to fifty control offspring who had been reared in the same foster homes as the children of schizophrenic mothers. Thus, the environments for both groups were the same, and they were not environments produced by the schizophrenic mothers. All forty-seven children took intelligence tests and psychological tests. Each was interviewed by a psychiatrist. Then two other psychiatrists not previously involved in the experiment came in to evaluate the children's dossiers and, if necessary, to diagnose the children. Neither psychiatrist knew the children's origins, or the nature of the mothers' illness. Even so, the two evaluating psychiatrists diagnosed five of the children of schizophrenic mothers as schizophrenic. None of the children from the control group were so diagnosed. Moreover, thirty-seven of the forty-seven children of schizophrenic mothers were given some kind of psychiatric diagnosis, as compared with nine of the fifty children from the control group. Considering that the environments were identical for both groups and the very early age at which the children were placed, the much higher incidence of disordered behavior among the children of schizophrenic mothers points to a strong genetic component in the origins of schizophrenia.

Seymour Kety, David Rosenthal, Paul Wender, and Fini Schulsinger (1968) examined the records of all children born between 1924 and 1947 in Copenhagen, Denmark, who were adopted when quite young. From this large group, they selected those adoptees who were subsequently admitted to a psychiatric hospital and diagnosed schizophrenic. Thirty-three such probands were compared to a control group drawn from the same population but lacking any psychiatric history, The family histories of biological (but not adoptive) relatives of the schizophrenic index cases revealed a higher incidence of disturbance (which included schizophrenia, uncertain schizophrenia, and inadequate personality) than did those of the controls (8.7 percent to 1.9 percent), providing further evidence for a genetic vulnerability to schizophrenia.

Because these two studies have measured the separate influences of genetics and of environment, and because both have documented the persistence of the genetic link, their combined impact is clear. When environmental and genetic factors are compared for their effect on rates of schizophrenia in relatives of probands, heredity has more influence than does environment. It is important, however, to state this case precisely, and not to overstate it. Genes contribute to vulnerability to schizophrenia, but they do not in themselves completely explain its presence.

CHILDREN AT RISK FOR SCHIZOPHRENIA. At-risk studies are important because they can identify those children who are most likely to develop schizophrenia, and the investigators can then observe the effects of specific influences on such children in order to reduce the incidence of schizophrenia. At-risk children are more vulnerable to schizophrenia than are other children. Their vulnerability may derive from several factors. Often, at-risk children are defined as those whose parents or siblings are schizophrenic. As we will see later, other factors also make children vulnerable; these are factors that relate to environment and to social class: poverty, broken homes, families where the *double-bind* reigns. (This latter concept, formulated by Gregory Bateson, refers to two mutually exclusive messages from one person, which can neither be satisfied nor avoided.) All of these sources contribute to a child's vulnerability, or high risk for schizophrenia, and all can be studied in an at-risk program.

Perhaps the most extensive high-risk study of schizophrenia was a Danish study undertaken in 1962 by Sarnoff Mednick and Fini Schulsinger. These investigators isolated 207 subjects who were at significant risk for schizophrenia, and 104 low-risk people who were matched on such variables as age, gender, years of education, father's occupation, and place of residence. When the study began, the average age of the subjects was about fifteen years, and none of them were schizophrenic. Ten years later, 17 of the high-risk (and only 1 of the low-risk) people were diagnosed schizophrenic. The mothers of these schizophrenics were distinguished from the rest of the sample on a variety of characteristics. Most striking among these were the facts that the mothers' own psychotic episodes were precipitated by the childbirth, and that more generally, the mothers were unstable in their relations with men, and were not emotionally attached to the father when pregnancy occurred. Moreover, the fathers themselves were unstable at work and often addicted to drugs or alcohol (Talovic, Mednick, Schulsinger, and Falloon,

1980). The mothers of these disturbed offspring, moreover, were quite temperamental and tended to direct their emotions outwards in highly aggressive forms (Mednick, 1973).

Although at-risk studies may confirm the genetic hypothesis (many of the high-risk subjects in the Mednick-Schulsinger study were offspring of schizophrenic mothers), their primary importance rests in increasing understanding of the effects of nutrition, psychophysiology, family, social and academic history, skills, and liabilities on the development of schizophrenia. Ultimately, at-risk studies suggest intervention to break the chain that leads to schizophrenia, and thus to reduce its incidence.

NON-SCHIZOPHRENIC TWINS.   MZ twins grow up sharing a common environment that often treats them as if they were a single person. They are often dressed alike, confused for one another, compared to one another, and generally scrutinized more closely than are DZ twins or mere siblings. These experiences collectively create a distinct environment for MZ twins in addition to their identical genetic makeup. Could that environment account for the greater probability of schizophrenia in the co-twin when the proband is schizophrenic? Probably not. If the special environmental and psychological factors common to MZ twins were the factors that produced schizophrenia, then the rate of schizophrenia among MZ twins would be higher than that of the general population. But that is not the case. MZ twins are no more likely to become schizophrenic than are non-twins. A co-twin is more likely to become schizophrenic if, and only if, the proband is schizophrenic, and not otherwise (Rosenthal, 1970b). Thus, the identical environment in which MZ twins develop has no bearing on whether the twins become schizophrenic.

Representations of irrationality.
(*Top:* Plate from *Urizen* by William Blake, Courtesy Lessing J. Rosenwald, Library of Congress, Washington, D.C. *Bottom: Bacchanalian Scene* by Richard Dadd, Courtesy Sotheby Parke Bernet)

Another Side of Schizophrenia: Creativity

Any comprehensive treatment of the role of genetics in schizophrenia must take into account the possible relationship between schizophrenia and creativity. Being related to a schizophrenic may not be all bad. In fact, it may have some distinct advantages. Reporting on a follow-up study of children born to schizophrenic mothers and placed in adoptive or foster homes shortly after birth, Leonard Heston and Duane Denney note that the children who did not become schizophrenic, were more "spontaneous," "had more colorful life histories," "held more creative jobs," and "followed the more imaginative hobbies . . . ." than normals (Heston and Denney, 1968, p. 371). Indeed, one study reports that non-paranoid schizophrenics score higher on a test of creativity than either paranoid schizophrenics or non-paranoid controls (Keefe and Magaro, 1980; Magaro, 1981).

A study of genetics and schizophrenia in Iceland by Karlsson (1972) further supports the connection between creativity and schizophrenia. Karlsson observes that the "genetic carriers" of schizophrenia often exhibit "unusual ability" and display "a superior capacity for associative thinking" (Karlsson, 1972, p. 61). Fascinated by this finding, Karlsson proposes that society may even depend upon "persons with a schizophrenic constitution" for its social and scientific progress. He remarks that a disproportionate number of the most creative people in philosophy, physics, music, litera-

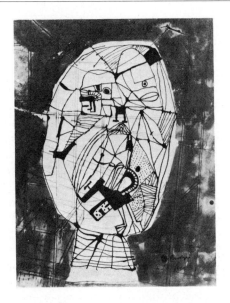 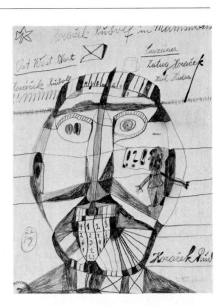

The painting on the left is by Eduardo Paolozzi and is entitled *Head I*. Note the similarities to Paolozzi's painting of the drawing on the right, which was done by a schizophrenic patient. (*Left:* Courtesy of the artist. *Right:* The Warder Collection)

ture, mathematics, and the fine arts often developed psychiatric disorders. *Superphrenic* is Karlsson's term for these people who are both related to schizophrenics and recognizably outstanding in politics, science, and the arts.

From this discussion of the genetic connection in schizophrenia, it is clear that a link exists. Although it does not embrace every important influence leading to schizophrenia, it does constitute one such influence. As David Rosenthal observed (1970b), "genetic factors do contribute appreciably and beyond a reasonable doubt" to the development of schizophrenia. Having described this, we turn to another strong influence on the development of schizophrenia, the schizophrenogenic (one which gives rise to schizophrenia) family.

THE SCHIZOPHRENOGENIC FAMILY

The above evidence convinces us that heredity plays a role in the development of schizophrenia. But heredity does not entirely dominate the stage, not by any means. Other factors—family, biochemistry, and society—contribute in as yet unknown ways and proportions to one's vulnerability to schizophrenia. Heredity tells us about a biological component of schizophrenia. It can suggest, perhaps, that an individual will be prone to attentional difficulties, to overinclusive thinking, to delusions, and to hallucinations. But heredity does not assure that a propensity will become a certainty. Nor does heredity specify the content of disordered thought and the social reaction it will elicit. In all likelihood, the family plays some role in the development of schizophrenia, although establishing the nature of its contribution with precision is difficult. Families that seem to foster the emergence of schizophrenia in one or more family members are called *schizophrenogenic families.* Such families may themselves be disordered in the way they communicate and in the family structure itself.

Communication within the Family

Since schizophrenia is centrally marked by a thought disorder and since we are examining the families from which schizophrenics come, it follows that we should look at communication within the family as a correlate or cause of such thought disorder. Many researchers believe that the parents of schizophrenics distort their children's perceptions in two principal ways: by encouraging them to doubt their own feelings, perceptions, and experiences (a process that is called **mystification**), and by catching them in double-binds (Bateson, Jackson, Haley, and Weakland, 1956; Laing and Esterson, 1964). Whatever one calls it, this "effort to drive the other person crazy" (Searles, 1959) involves distorting the child's reality both verbally and non-verbally.

Three processes occurring within the families of schizophrenics seem to influence thought disorders: injection of meaning, concealment of meaning, and denial of meaning. Although all three are clearly connected, each has particular manifestations (Wynne, Singer, Bartko, and Toohey, 1977).

Injection of meaning involves denying the clear meaning of another's message and substituting another meaning. The person who sent the original message can, with a persistent injector around, be left with two different meanings rather than one, with confusion rather than clarity, and with considerable self-doubt about perceiving reality accurately. An incident that occurred during a counseling session illustrates how the injection of meaning can easily lead to confusion.

> Mr. A entered the room quietly and sat down with a benign, attentive expression and posture directed toward his wife. Mrs. A was sputtering with rage: "I'm so furious I can't stand it." She then let loose with a stream of invectives at her husband and concluded with a threat of murdering him. After a few minutes, the husband leaned toward her, patted her arm and said, "You're not angry. You're feeling hurt. I'd like to help you with your pain." With that, the wife screamed: "I don't feel in pain. I feel like killing you." Then to the therapist: "In eight years of marriage that son of a bitch has never once believed that I could really be mad at him." Mrs. A. went on to assert that behind her husband's virtuous facade, he was sadistic and murderous. She claimed that on the way to this therapy session, he had deliberately driven carelessly, endangering both their lives, but with the knowledge that she was much more nervous than he about automobile accidents. He stoutly denied that he had had any feeling of maliciousness and said that he had been simply inattentive and preoccupied with other matters. He added that her accusation was part of her "paranoia" and the mental illness for which she needed help. At this point she collapsed in confusion and tears. When he again solicitously "comforted" her, she now no longer protested and by then her experience seemed to fit the "pain" that he had attributed to her— or, as I would say, had injected into her. (Wynne, 1972, p. 436)

Clearly, the husband first denies his wife's anger and its cause. He patiently, virtuously insists on his own explanation and holds his ground. When his wife explains her anger by detailing its causes, the husband only intensifies his denial. By now, the wife is uncertain. Confused, she breaks down, acting hurt, showing that she needs help. In fact, her behavior suggests that the injected meaning has become the reality, at least for the moment. She is still angry, however, and eventually she will experience that anger again, only to be met with another denial, another substitution.

Concealing clear meaning is another form of communication distortion within the schizophrenic family. A person may hide information when it is clear that the information exists. Or the person may simply remain silent, failing to acknowledge a patent fact or sending blurred vague or fragmented messages. These tactics serve to conceal meanings and distort facts.

Denial of meaning takes several forms (Laing and Esterson, 1964; Lidz, 1975). The denial can be a deliberate lie, consciously told. Or it can involve some automatic denial, automatically presented. Or it can be the result of a thought disorder in the parents themselves, one that is so encompassing that they do not even realize that they are denying anything. One patient, for example, felt that his parents were "somehow talking" about him. They denied it. Yet, when the entire family gathered together, it was clear that the parents surreptitiously nodded and winked to one another, as if they could not be seen. They were oblivious to the fact that their communication was visible. More important, they were oblivious to the fact that their winking and nodding was a form of "talking." They denied its reality.

Injecting, concealing, and denying all serve to either block access to consensual reality, or to distort it. Worse, they insidiously undermine the individual's faith in her own capacity to perceive reality. Thus, all of these tactics relate directly to the essential characteristics of schizophrenia: misperceived reality and disordered thought.

Family Structure

An extensive study of schizophrenogenic family structure isolated two types: the schismatic and the skewed (Lidz, 1975). In the **schismatic** or **divided family**, each parent is caught up in private personal problems that the marriage aggravates, and each treats the other parent with contempt. Predictably, the children are the pawns in this impossible game. Each parent tries to win the children's support and tries to get the gratification from them that the other spouse denies.

Although the **skewed family** displays less open discord, it also exacts a higher price than does the schismatic family. Rather than battle for power, the skewed family pits a dominant parent against a passive parent. Invariably deeply disturbed, often a non-hospitalized schizophrenic, the dominant parent imposes his or her view and treats the entire family as if it is his or her possession. The schizophrenic parent ignores the children's needs, yet intrudes in the children's lives. In order to keep the family intact, its members accept the views of the dominant parent. And since these views are irrational, they enter into a tacit contract to think irrationally. Lidz, who developed these views, calls it a *folie en famille,* or family madness.

> Illustrative of the . . . *folie en famille* group, the Dolfuss family lived like European gentry in a New England suburb, isolated from their neighbors. The family life was centered in the needs and opinions of Mr. Dolfuss, a successful but paranoically grandiose inventor. The children were raised by a seductive nursemaid of whom the cold and distant mother was intensely jealous. However, Mrs. Dolfuss devoted her life to her husband, catering to his whims and keeping the children

out of his way. Mr. Dolfuss's major interest was an Oriental religious sect. He believed that he and a friend were among the few select souls who would achieve a particular type of salvation. Both Mrs. Dolfuss and the nursemaid virtually deified him. They and the children shared his beliefs, as well as his grandiose notion of himself, living in what we termed a folie en famille. Here, the children were largely excluded from the lives of the parents, the model of the father was an unrealistic one for the sons, and the intellectual and emotional environment was estranged from that of the larger culture into which they had to emerge.

The children grew up to be disturbed. (Lidz, Fleck, and Cornelison, 1965, p. 144.)

Although this description is enormously compelling, it should be approached with caution. However intensely he has studied these families, Lidz provides no controls of normal families or families from which disturbed but non-schizophrenic offspring have emerged. Moreover, in these complex matters it is very difficult to separate cause from effect, and cause from correlation (Mischler and Waxler, 1968). Disturbed parents, in fact, may not automatically produce schizophrenia in offspring. Their disturbance may only correlate with their child's. And when the family of a schizophrenic is interviewed, how can we be sure that the family's present difficulties *caused* the offspring's schizophrenia and are not the result of it? The resolution of these vexing issues continues to elude us.

THE NEUROCHEMISTRY OF SCHIZOPHRENIA: THE DOPAMINE HYPOTHESIS

The idea that there may be biochemical antecedents to schizophrenia is not new. Researchers have frequently tried to find the biochemical differences between schizophrenics and normals, but with little luck. Reports of vast differences in the chemistry of blood or urine of normals as opposed to hospitalized schizophrenics have turned out merely to reflect differences in the diets of hospitalized and non-hospitalized people, or bad lab technique, or the absence of control groups, or experimenter bias.

More recently, the strategy has shifted. Instead of looking for biochemical substances that differentiate schizophrenics from normals, scientists are now searching for abnormalities in neurophysiological functioning. Specifically, they are looking at special chemicals in the brain, called **neurotransmitters.** The way these chemicals function, and how increases or decreases in the available quantities of neurotransmitters affect behavior and perhaps influence the development of schizophrenia—these are presently the dominant research concerns. By focusing on these chemicals and by drawing connections between schizophrenia, the amphetamine psychosis, and Parkinson's disease, scientists have constructed what is now called the **dopamine hypothesis** (as we first mentioned in Chapter 3).

First, consider the similarities between the symptoms of schizophrenia and the effects of the amphetamines, or "speed." Large doses of amphetamines can create a psychosis with symptoms indistinguishable from those of acute paranoid schizophrenia. Patients suffering amphetamine psychosis have, in fact, been wrongly diagnosed as schizophrenics (Snyder, 1974b) (see Chapter 15). What is more, a very low dose of a drug related to the amphetamines, methylphenidate, will exacerbate a schizophrenic's symptoms almost immediately: paranoid schizophrenics, for example, become increasingly paranoid. Finally, the drugs most helpful in treating the symptoms of schizophrenia—the neuroleptics (the phenothiazines and butyrophenones)—are also the best antidotes for amphetamine psychosis and for the exacerbated schizophrenic symptoms induced by amphetamines (Snyder et al., 1974).

These neuroleptics produce varying effects on schizophrenia. One class of neuroleptic, the phenothiazines, blocks the brain's receptors for a neurotransmitter called dopamine. Neurotransmitters are chemicals that facilitate the transmission of electrical impulses between the brain's nerve endings. There are perhaps twenty different neurotransmitters, of which dopamine is particularly important. Since the phenothiazines both decrease the amount of available dopamine and also relieve the symptoms of schizophrenia, it seems to follow that schizophrenia results from excess dopamine. These findings opened the door for the dopamine hypothesis, and the connection between Parkinson's disease and dopamine offers more support for the hypothesis.

Characterized by growing stiffness in the arms and legs, Parkinson's disease is particularly noticeable because it renders facial expressions flat and dull, and causes tremors, especially in the hands. It happens that the main pathway in the brain for dopamine is the corpus striatum—an area that helps co-ordinate motor activity. This pathway deteriorates in Parkinson's disease, thus explaining the patient's inability to move and tendency to shake. When victims of Parkinson's disease are treated with L-DOPA, a drug that increases the amount of dopamine available in the brain, their symptoms are relieved. Curiously, when individuals suffering from schizophrenia are treated with heavy doses of phenothiazines for a prolonged period of time, they display symptoms very much like those associated with Parkinson's disease. They, too, develop motor difficulties: they have tremors in their extremities and problems in controlling their body movements in general. While there is no direct proof of a connection, is it possible that the neurotransmitter, dopamine, is involved in schizophrenia? In Parkinson's disease, L-DOPA is given to overcome the insufficiency of dopamine. In schizophrenia, the phenothiazines seem to calm disordered behavior by reducing the amount of dopamine available in the brain. Over time, however, they seem to cause an insufficiency of dopamine, and bring about symptoms of Parkinson's disease. Perhaps an excess of dopamine is one of the roots of schizophrenia.

Let us summarize the evidence that supports the dopamine hypothesis thus far. First, the symptoms of acute paranoid schizophrenia and of amphetamine psychosis are nearly indistinguishable. Amphetamine psychosis seems to result from an overproduction of dopamine. Is it not reasonable to assume a similar mechanism for schizophrenia (Snyder, 1981)?

Further evidence comes from animal research, where it has been shown that the phenothiazines block dopamine receptors specifically, and not other neurotransmitters. In addition, the more potent the phenothiazine, the more powerfully it blocks dopamine receptors in animals.

The combined evidence suggests that dopamine overload, that is, excess dopamine at the synapse (see Figure 17-2), produces many of the symptoms

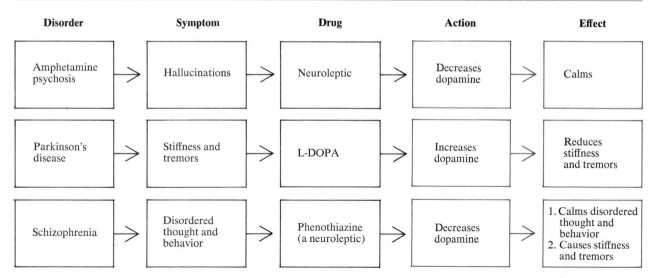

Disorder	Symptom	Drug	Action	Effect
Amphetamine psychosis	Hallucinations	Neuroleptic	Decreases dopamine	Calms
Parkinson's disease	Stiffness and tremors	L-DOPA	Increases dopamine	Reduces stiffness and tremors
Schizophrenia	Disordered thought and behavior	Phenothiazine (a neuroleptic)	Decreases dopamine	1. Calms disordered thought and behavior 2. Causes stiffness and tremors

Figure 17-2
Evidence for the dopamine hypothesis. This analysis of the effects of increasing or decreasing the availability of dopamine offers some support for the dopamine hypothesis.

of acute schizophrenia. Consider the attentional difficulties that are so characteristic of schizophrenia. When the **substantia nigra**, a bundle of nerves that go from the brain stem to the **corpus striatum** (an area of high dopamine concentration), is destroyed on one side of the brain, rats stop attending to stimulation on the other side of their bodies (Understedt, 1971). (The left brain controls the right side of the body; the right brain, the left.) It is not that the rats lose their sensory perception. It seems rather that they fail to attend. Phenothiazines may have a similar effect: by blocking dopamine receptors, attention may be diminished.

The dopamine hypothesis is still only that: an interesting hypothesis. We are some way from fully substantiating it, and further yet from seeing how dopamine production relates to other biological and environmental factors that contribute to schizophrenia.

SOCIETY AND SCHIZOPHRENIA

Whether we are schizophrenic or non-schizophrenic, we are all members of a society that, in many ways, exerts its influence upon us. In approaching any mental disorder, scientists will take society into account.

Schizophrenia and Social Class

It happens that, particularly in large urban areas, rates of mental disturbance, and especially of schizophrenia, are significantly and inversely related to social class: the lower the class, the higher the rate of schizophrenia (see Figure 17-3). The highest rates of schizophrenia occur in the centers of cities that, in turn, are inhabited by people of lower socioeconomic status (Faris and Dunham, 1939; Hollingshead and Redlich, 1958; Srole, Langner, Michael, Opler, and Rennie, 1962). Similar findings relate to occupation: rates of schizophrenia are highest in the lowest status occupations (Clark, 1948). The larger the city, the more powerful the relationship; in small cities, the relationship between schizophrenia and social class disappears (Clausen and Kohn, 1959).

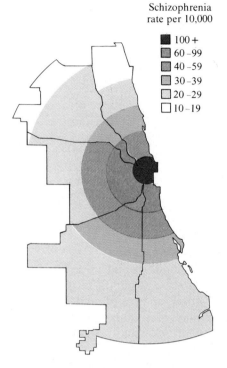

Schizophrenia
rate per 10,000

■ 100+
▨ 60–99
▨ 40–59
▨ 30–39
□ 20–29
□ 10–19

Figure 17-3
The prevalence of schizophrenia in a city. In this map of Chicago in 1934, the center zone is the business and amusement section, which is uninhabited, except for transients and vagabonds. Surrounding the center, there is a slum area, largely made up of unskilled workers of low socioeconomic status, and having the highest rate of schizophrenia. The next circle is occupied by skilled workers and has a lower rate of schizophrenia than the slum. The next zone is inhabited by middle-class and upper-middle-class people. The last circle is populated by upper-middle-class commuters and shows the lowest rate of schizophrenia. (Adapted from Faris and Dunham, 1939)

The problem of sorting out the relationship of class and schizophrenia is similar to the problem encountered in trying to understand the relationship between the family and schizophrenia. Are people who are already members of the lower class likely to become schizophrenics? Or is it more accurate, and more revealing, to say that some people who are schizophrenics find themselves drifting into the lower class? The resolution of this problem is no mere academic matter, because the rate of schizophrenia is eight times as high in the lower class as it is in the middle or upper social classes.

One logical way to resolve the question would be to examine the occupational status of the fathers of schizophrenics. If schizophrenics' fathers were at the lowest occupational rung, it would be likely that the schizophrenic was born into the lower class, and that class therefore preceded psychosis. Such a finding would strengthen the view that social class produces schizophrenia. If on the other hand, schizophrenics' fathers had higher occupational status, it would be likely that the schizophrenics were not born into the lower class, and that psychosis therefore precedes social class. This discovery would clearly support the view that schizophrenics drift into the lower class.

A survey of an entire county in New York State found support for both positions. The incidence of treatment for schizophrenia was remarkably high for people in the lowest occupational group, confirming the relationship between social class and schizophrenia. But the data regarding fathers' occupation was ambiguous, in that it was equally high for those whose fathers were in the lowest occupational group as it was for those whose fathers were employed in the highest occupational group. Although those schizophrenics whose fathers had been in the lowest occupational group had risen above their fathers' occupational level, they and the high occupational group stood at occupational levels lower than those of the general population (Turner and Wagenfeld, 1967).

Membership in the lower class carries with it a host of psychological as well as economic disadvantages that may well increase an individual's vulnerability to schizophrenia. For example, one researcher observed that lower-class people attach greater value to conformity to authority than do members of the middle class (Kohn, 1973). When such lower-class people find themselves confronted with personal crises, they are less able to cope than are people who have been more self-directed and less conforming. Solving personal problems has more to do with confronting internal pressures than it has to do with conforming to external demands. What makes the situation worse is that the defensive posture of the conforming person often invites attack. Thus, the habit of conformity does little to alleviate tension. With stress unabated, the conforming person may also be more vulnerable to schizophrenia.

The Stresses of Modern Living

Society's values are often contradictory and many people find those contradictions difficult, even impossible, to live with. Searching for some meaningful purpose in life, people are often confronted with meaninglessness on every level, from the personal to the global. They find themselves running in place so as not to fall behind, working at unfulfilling jobs, often for minimal pay, simply to keep up with the body's demands for food, clothing, and shelter. Even as astrophysicists meet the challenges of space travel, earthbound political leaders draw up moon treaties and calculate military capabilities in space. A rich nation is riddled with unemployment, inflation, and other economic ills. Many are precluded from enjoying material comforts, yet materialist dreams are instilled in all.

Some theorists argue that those who are well-integrated into such an insane society are truly mad, while those who remain alienated are the most sane. Many cope with social contradictions by adjusting to them and accepting them. Others, however, may be too sensitive to the pressures and contradictions of society to cope with them at all. These people may be especially vulnerable to the meaninglessness that pervades our world. Many of them, it has been hypothesized, become schizophrenics.

The hypothesis that schizophrenia is a response to a stressful environment has been expounded by numerous theorists, and is particularly central to the thinking of the Scottish psychiatrist, R. D. Laing (1927–   ). Laing's argument is more speculative than other analyses of schizophrenia. He maintains that the schizophrenic experience arises from a person's sense that the situation can neither be lived with nor evaded. The only way to escape the contradictions and impossibilities of reality is to withdraw from the world and take refuge in schizophrenia. The schizophrenic experience, Laing argues, is potentially beneficial to those who undergo it. He writes:

> Perhaps we will learn to accord to so-called schizophrenics who have come back to us, perhaps after years, no less respect than the often no-less-lost explorers of the Renaissance. If the human race survives, future men will, I suspect, look back on our enlightened epoch as a veritable Age of Darkness. They will presumably be able to savor the irony of this situation with more amusement than we can extract from it. The laugh's on us. They will see that what we call "schizophrenia" was one of the forms in which, often through quite ordinary people, the light began to break through the cracks in our all-too-closed minds. (Laing, 1967, p. 129)

All of the theories about the causes of schizophrenia that we have surveyed are fascinating but unsatisfactory in that they provide only part of the explanation for the emergence of schizophrenia in any one individual. Studies of twins lend credence to a fundamental *genetic* propensity to schizophrenia. But since perfect concordance does not exist even among MZ twins, it is likely that additional variables, particularly overproduction of neurotransmitters like *dopamine*, play a role in vulnerability to schizophrenia. Moreover, an individual's vulnerability to schizophrenia may be heightened by social and environmental factors. While schizophrenia may "run in the family" because of a common genetic background, some families (called schizophrenogenic families) may also create a stressful and disordered environment that may induce schizophrenia among the vulnerable (Lewis, Rodnick, and Goldstein, 1981; Roff and Knight, 1981). Similarly, very poor people whose lives are filled with the stress of maintaining a marginal subsistence and who live in the impersonal squalor of the inner cities may be particularly vulnerable to schizophrenia.

THE TREATMENT OF SCHIZOPHRENIA

Until the mid-1950s, treatment of schizophrenia was primarily custodial. Patients were warehoused for long periods of time in environments that were both boring and hopeless. Often their disorder and the hospital environment interacted to bring about behavior that required physical restraint. In 1952, however, a lucky accident changed this bleak situation, and led to a revolution in the treatment of schizophrenia.

DRUG THERAPY

While synthesizing new drugs called **antihistamines** that benefit asthmatics and those with allergies, researchers noticed the strong calming effects of these drugs. In fact, one of the drugs, promethazine, was so tranquilizing that the French surgeon Henri Laborit gave it to his patients as a prelude to anesthesia. Using a close relative of promethazine with even stronger sedative effects, French psychiatrists Jean Delay and Pierre Deniker treated various mentally disordered patients with varying results. Those who improved had a common diagnosis: schizophrenia. The drug they took was chlorpromazine. Now a prominent member of a class of drugs variously called **neuroleptics, psychotropics,** or **tranquilizing agents,** chlorpromazine revolutionized the treatment schizophrenia. In 1955, there were about 560,000 patients in American psychiatric hospitals. One out of every two hospital beds was devoted to psychiatric care. It was then estimated that by 1971, 750,000 beds would be required to care for growing psychiatric populations. In fact, there were only 308,000 patients in psychiatric hospitals in 1971, less than half the projected estimate, and about 40 percent fewer than were hospitalized in 1955. And by 1977, the patient census had declined to less than 160,000 (Witkin, 1981). Such is the power of the major tranquilizers (see Figure 17-4).

Anti-Psychotic Effects of Drug Therapy

Of the major tranquilizers, Thorazine and Haldol, whose generic names are respectively chlorpromazine and haloperidol, are two of the most commonly used. Their most striking effect is the degree to which they "tranquilize," make peaceful, even sedate. Could it be that these phenothiazines are no different from barbiturates, whose sedative action produces no greater improvements for schizophrenics than placebos? Some evidence suggests that this is not the case (Klein and Davis, 1969). The phenothiazines seem to have specific ameliorating effects on schizophrenic symptoms, beyond their sedative effects and even beyond their impact on anxiety (see Table 17-5). Thought disorder, hallucinations, affect, and withdrawal, all these are affected by the phenothiazines. Equally important, these drugs have virtually no effect on psychiatric symptoms that are not associated with schizophrenia (Casey, Bennett, Lindley, Hollister, Gordon, and Springer, 1960; Klein and Davis, 1969). Subjective emotional experiences, such as guilt and depression, continue unabated despite a course of drug treatment.

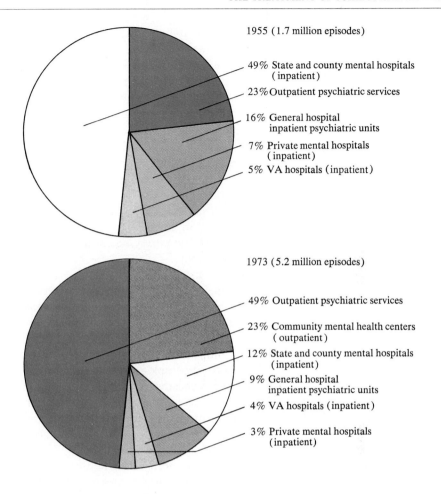

Figure 17-4
Distribution of inpatient and outpatient care in mental health facilities, by type of facility: United States, 1955 and 1973. Note the enormous shift from inpatient to outpatient facilities. (Source: Modified from Keith et al., 1976, p. 571)

1955 (1.7 million episodes)

49% State and county mental hospitals (inpatient)

23% Outpatient psychiatric services

16% General hospital inpatient psychiatric units

7% Private mental hospitals (inpatient)

5% VA hospitals (inpatient)

1973 (5.2 million episodes)

49% Outpatient psychiatric services

23% Community mental health centers (outpatient)

12% State and county mental hospitals (inpatient)

9% General hospital inpatient psychiatric units

4% VA hospitals (inpatient)

3% Private mental hospitals (inpatient)

Table 17-5 ANALYSIS OF SYMPTOM SENSITIVITY TO PHENOTHIAZINES

Symptom	Response to Treatment
Fundamental Symptoms	
Thought disorder	+ + +
Blunted affect-indifference	+ +
Withdrawal-retardation	+ +
Autistic behavior-mannerisms	+ +
Accessory Symptoms	
Hallucinations	+ +
Paranoid ideation	+
Grandiosity	+
Hostility-belligerence	+
Resistiveness-uncooperativeness	+
Non-schizophrenic Symptoms	
Anxiety-tension-agitation	0
Guilt-depression	0
Disorientation	0
Somatization	0

SOURCE: Snyder, 1974b, p. 28.

Just how the phenothiazines achieve their effects on schizophrenic symptoms is not yet clear. Regardless, the average hospital stay for a schizophrenic patient has declined to fewer than thirteen days, when formerly it was months, years, even a lifetime. Phenothiazines have, nearly alone, been responsible for a revolution in psychiatric care.

Side Effects of Drug Therapy

The antipsychotic drugs have a variety of unpleasant side effects that often lead patients to discontinue using them. Side effects of chlorpromazine (Thorazine), for example, frequently include dryness of mouth and throat, drowsiness, visual disturbances, weight gain or loss, menstrual disturbances, constipation, and depression. For most patients, these are relatively minor problems, but annoying enough to induce them to discontinue medications on discharge.

One class of more serious side effects, called extra-pyramidal or Parkinson-like effects, appears to arise because, as we have seen, anti-psychotic medications affect the dopamine receptors, which are in turn implicated in Parkinson's disease. These drugs do not cause Parkinson's disease, but they do induce analogous symptoms. These symptoms include stiffness of muscles and difficulty in moving, freezing of facial muscles which results in a glum or sour look as well as an inability to smile, tremors at the extremities as well as spasms of limbs and body, and *akathesia*—a peculiar "itchiness" in the muscles which results in an inability to sit still, and an urge to pace the halls continuously and energetically (Snyder, 1974a). Other drugs can control these side effects, but interestingly, no phenothiazine has yet been produced which avoids them.

Even more serious is a neurological disorder called *tardive dyskinesia.* Its symptoms consist of sucking, lip-smacking, and tongue movements that seem like fly-catching. Tardive dyskinesia is not reversible. Conservatively, it affects 18 percent of hospitalized schizophrenics, a figure that rises with the patients' age and length of time they have been on anti-psychotic medication (Klein and Davis, 1969).

The Revolving Door Phenomenon

The widespread use of psychotropic drugs promised a virtual revolution in the treatment of schizophrenia. Even if the disorder could not be cured, it seemed certain that it could be contained. No longer would thousands spend their lives in back wards. No longer would families and society be deprived of their contribution. And no longer would massive economic resources be wasted on custodial care. But the pharmaceutical revolution fell short of its promise. For, while the hospital population of schizophrenics has declined radically since 1955, the readmission rates for schizophrenics have soared. In 1972, for example, 72 percent of the schizophrenics admitted to hospitals had been there before (Taube, 1976). It is estimated that between 40 percent and 60 percent of schizophrenic patients will be rehospitalized within two years of discharge (Mosher, Feinsilver, Katz, and Wienckowski, 1971); 65 percent to 75 percent by the end of five years (Anthony, Buell, Sharratt, and Althoff, 1972). One likely reason for rehospitalization is that

Many of those released into the community from mental hospitals are unable to work or care for themselves. Were these "bag ladies" formerly mental patients? Will they be rehospitalized as a result of the "revolving door phenomenon"? (Photograph by Eugene Gordon)

only 15 to 40 percent of them are able to work or care for themselves (Keith, Gunderson, Reifman, Buchsbaum, and Mosher, 1976). Another is that they return to aversive environments (Leff, 1976), and to communities that are less than welcoming. Third, they lack work skills (Gunderson and Mosher, 1975) and social skills. Finally, they often stop taking medications on discharge because of the drugs' aversive side effects.

One can interpret this "revolving-door" aspect of psychiatric hospitals both negatively and positively. On the negative side, the readmission rates are discouraging; they suggest that the attempt to treat schizophrenics is futile. But on the positive side, is it not better for a patient to be readmitted, than never to have been discharged at all? This latter situation characterized the plight of many patients before the advent of the phenothiazines.

Even if one opts for the more positive response to the high readmission rate, the task of understanding its cause and of eventually reducing it remains. One thing is clear: anti-psychotic drugs help ameliorate the symptoms of schizophrenia, but the symptoms of schizophrenia are by no means the entire problem. Indeed, the very fact that these drugs alter symptoms and only symptoms raises profound questions about what is meant by treatment, recovery, and cure.

FULL TREATMENT: MILIEU AND THERAPEUTIC COMMUNITIES

Because schizophrenia appears between the ages of eighteen and thirty-five, it disrupts educational and vocational training, social skills, friendships, and marriages. In addition, because the seeds of the disorder are sown before the disorder appears, both in the individual and in the family, it is a safe bet that there are problems in communication and self-esteem—in short, *psychological problems*—that the anti-psychotic drugs simply do not touch. Given that these psychological problems exist and that drugs do not alleviate them, what, other than drugs, can help the schizophrenic live in the outside world? Part of the answer may lie in milieu therapy, which creates a supportive environment, and in the therapeutic communities, which illustrate milieu therapy's principles.

A study of readmission rates underscores the continued importance of considering psychological problems when treating schizophrenic disorders.

Patients who relapsed did not differ on their discharge examination from those who did not relapse. Apart from whether they continued their medications, two additional factors featured strongly in determining relapse rates: the emotional quality of the home, and how much time the patient spent there (Leff, 1976).

In this study, four considerations went into rating the emotional quality of the home environment: the family's hostility, over-involvement with the patient, comments that were critical of the patient, and the family's wealth. Patients who came from families that had highly charged emotional environments had a 51 percent relapse rate. Those whose family environment was relatively uncharged had a dramatically lower relapse rate—13 percent. Moreover, for the patients from highly charged environments, the relapse rate was affected by how much time they were spending at home. Those who spent less than thirty-five hours at home—which is to say, those who had jobs or went to a day center—were much less likely to relapse than those who were at home more of the time (see Figure 17-5).

What can be done to reduce the relapse rate? For one thing, hospitals have been undergoing enormous changes: from being merely custodial warehouses to becoming centers with a variety of programs designed to increase social skills. Under the broad label of ***milieu therapy***, patients are provided with training in social communication, in work, and in recreation. Hospi-

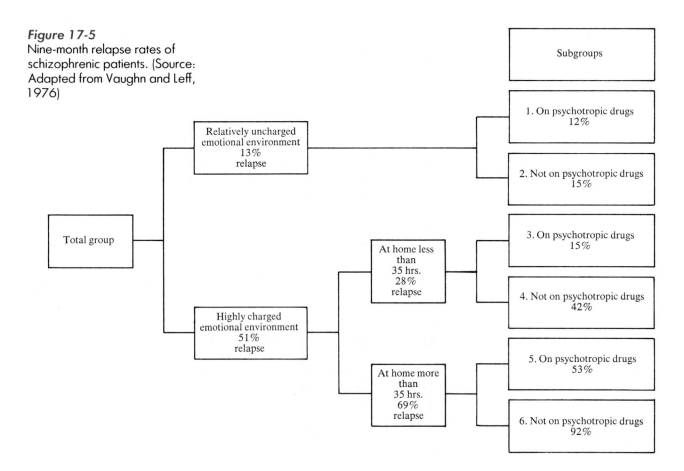

Figure 17-5
Nine-month relapse rates of schizophrenic patients. (Source: Adapted from Vaughn and Leff, 1976)

tals that have incorporated milieu therapy have successfully decreased their relapse rate.

In the late sixties and the seventies, several promising methods were developed for treating schizophrenia. One was organized by George Fairweather and his colleagues (1969). The project began after Fairweather noticed that chronically hospitalized patients who were organized into groups and given tasks to perform were discharged from the hospital much more quickly than patients who did not participate in task-oriented groups. But once discharged, many of these patients relapsed. Since they had improved in the hospital, Fairweather concluded that something must be wrong outside the hospital, that something being the lack of opportunity for task-oriented group experience. Fairweather and his colleagues established the Lodge, a special residence for newly discharged patients. The Lodge's residents had major responsibilities in running the household, shopping, and finding employment for each other. Over time, more and more responsibility was given to patients until finally the Lodge was taken over entirely by former patients. The effectiveness of this program was evaluated. The seventy-five patients who volunteered for it were compared to a matched group who did not volunteer and who received the hospital's routine discharge (which included patient psychotherapy, community assistance, and foster-home placement). After six months, some 65 percent of the Lodge members, but only 27 percent of the comparison group, remained outside the hospital. Fifty percent of the Lodge's members and only 3 percent of the controls were employed full time during this period. These findings held up over the next three and a half years. Clearly, the Lodge experience was a beneficial one for those involved.

Some programs seek alternatives to hospitalization altogether. They may use nonprofessionals to treat patients, rather than doctors, nurses, and psychologists (Kiesler, 1980). Soteria House is one of these **_therapeutic communities_** (Mosher, Menn, and Matthews, 1975). A community-based residential treatment center, it provides a home for people who are diagnosed as schizophrenics. The staff are selected for their ability to accept and relate to people undergoing an acute schizophrenic crisis. Schizophrenic episodes are viewed as valid, if often terrifying, experiences that have strong potential for individual growth and integration. This attitude is similar to that expressed by R. D. Laing. Anti-psychotic drugs are not provided at Soteria House, except in emergencies. But Soteria House does provide acceptance, understanding, and guidance through the painful journey.

In a study comparing hospitalized patients and patients living in Soteria House, there were no differences between those who were assigned to Soteria House and the controls who had been assigned to a good psychiatric hospital. Residents lived at Soteria House an average of five to six months, while controls remained hospitalized for less than two months. Despite the near-absence of anti-psychotic medications in the Soteria sample, both groups manifested the same degree of symptom remission. The intense interpersonal milieu at Soteria House effectively reduced the need for medications. Finally, six months after discharge, 60 percent of Soteria House's residents were able to live independently, while only 4 percent of the controls could live apart from their families.

How does one integrate the remarkable nondrug outcomes from such places as Fairweather's Lodge and Soteria House with the equally remarkable evidence from hospitals that *do* employ drugs? On the one hand, drugs have shortened the length of stay in psychiatric hospitals and have reduced the number of beds that are required for treatment. Yet, on the other hand, they seem responsible for the "revolving-door" phenomenon. It seems clear now that drugs alone cannot provide a full treatment for schizophrenia. The ideal treatment for schizophrenia involves carefully monitored psychopharmacological interventions that are combined with psychological ones.

SUMMARY

1. *Schizophrenia* is a thought disorder that is often combined with affective and behavioral anomalies. There are four subtypes of schizophrenia: *paranoid, disorganized, catatonic,* and *undifferentiated.* Schizophrenics are differentiated according to whether their condition is *acute* or *chronic,* and based on whether they suffer from *reactive schizophrenia* or *process schizophrenia.*

2. The schizophrenic's subjective experience is often one of being invaded by the world's stimuli, crowded by them, and unable to process them. We find this experience rooted in what appears to be a defective *cognitive filter,* itself related to serious *attentional difficulties.* The incapacity to focus attention, as well as the sense that too many stimuli are invading and capturing attention, is characteristic of many schizophrenics' experience.

3. In the cognitive domain, schizophrenics make the same errors of association that normals make, but they make many more of them. They seem especially attracted to the *dominant associations* or connotations of words, regardless of the context in which they are found. Often, their attentional difficulties seem to distract them from the ultimate goal of thought and speech. Thinking may therefore be *overinclusive,* and speech dotted with *clang associations* and *neologisms.*

4. Many schizophrenics appear to experience flattened or restricted emotion, which may make it difficult for them to meaningfully experience reality.

5. Schizophrenics seem to experience perceptual intensities or deficits that lead them to experience the world differently from others. Delusional, hallucinatory, or other cognitive experiences often bring grief or a sense of uniqueness, which they attempt to account for by constructing theories which, in form, are no different from the theories normals construct about their experiences.

6. Vulnerability to schizophrenia is a highly individual matter, but there seem to be four significant factors that promote it. First, there seems little doubt that the schizophrenias are in part a *genetic* disorder. The schizophrenias occur much more often among MZ than DZ twins, and among natural than adoptive families. Second, there is reason to believe that the schizophrenias are a disorder of the *neurotransmitters,* especially of *dopamine.* Third, faulty communications within the *family* may well promote the development of schizophrenia. Finally, schizophrenia is a disorder that afflicts the *poor* more than the rich, and it may be associated with the stresses of society.

7. Treatment of the schizophrenias has been revolutionized by the invention of strong *tranquilizers* that seem to work directly on symptoms of schizophrenia. Hospitalization has become briefer, and there is a greater probability that the schizophrenic person will return to society. The effectiveness of the anti-psychotic drugs, however, is limited.

8. Because schizophrenia is a psychological, as well as a biological, disorder there have been increasing attempts to discover nondrug methods for treating the schizophrenias. Among these are *therapeutic communities* that emphasize the positive aspects of the schizophrenic experience and that attempt to directly train the schizophrenic for social living.

Part VIII

ABNORMALITY ACROSS THE LIFESPAN

Childhood Disorders and Mental Retardation

I N this chapter, we turn to the problems of children and adolescents—
problems that, in many ways, are more difficult to capture than those of
adults. They are more difficult for reasons that arise from: (1) the nature of
psychological development, (2) parental agency, and (3) the situational-
specificity of children's problems.

Children's problems occur in the context of growing up, of psychological
development. But normal psychological development has a ragged edge.
Some aspects of development proceed vigorously; others lag behind. As a
result, it is often difficult to distinguish a genuine psychological problem
that requires attention from one that merely reflects a developmental lag.
For example, most children are toilet-trained by the time they are three
years old. Of those who are not, some are merely developmental "laggards,"
while for others, continued bed-wetting reflects deeper emotional insecurities. Distinguishing problems that reflect the unevenness of psychological
development from those that suggest deep emotional difficulties is an issue
one faces with children that is entirely absent among adults.

Second, very young children cannot communicate verbally, and older
children, who can speak, are required to speak through their parents first.
Thus, the problems of childhood are often filtered through the observations
of parents. The latter may mislabel a child's behavior as a "psychological
problem" when it is merely something the child will grow out of. Parents
may see it as a problem in growing up, when in fact it should not be ignored.
As a result of parental agency, we often know less about children's problems
than we do about adult difficulties.

Finally, children's problems are often quite specific to particular situations and contexts. Children may be aggressive at home, but not at school.
Even overactivity—a common complaint of teachers—depends on the circumstances and situations. One study found that 75 percent of children who
were allegedly overactive in school were not overactive at home or in the
clinic (Klein, 1975).

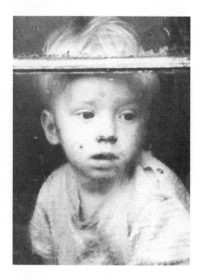

A child's problem may be characterized as a psychological disorder if it is persistent and severe and if it impairs the child or his relationships with others. (Photograph by Arthur Tress)

We will examine several kinds of children's problems. Some are relatively minor and transient; others are quite serious. All are psychological disorders, not only because the child deviates from what is expected of a particular age and sociocultural context, but also for two other reasons: (1) the problem is persistent and severe, and (2) it impairs the child or others. Either the child must be suffering, as when a child with an animal phobia is paralyzed with fear, or the child is making others suffer, as when the child's aggression is turned on schoolmates or pets.

Problem behaviors are very common in childhood. One study of children aged six to twelve years old, found that no fewer than 43 percent of them were reported by their mothers to have a staggering *seven* or more fears. Eighty percent of the children lost their tempers at least once a month, and 28 percent had nightmares (LaPouse and Monk, 1959). Other epidemiological studies—that is, studies of the prevalence of emotional disorders in total communities—suggest that by the time children are ten years old, some 25 percent of them have psychological problems, and 17 percent have problems that are severe enough to interfere with their school achievement (Werner, Bierman, and French, 1971; Werner and Smith, 1977). From study to study, estimates of disturbance vary, but the best single estimate of psychological disturbance among children is that put forth by the President's Commission on Mental Health (Snapper and Ohms, 1977). That figure—15 percent—indicates how serious these problems can be. Most of these problems are dealt with by parents, teachers, and family physicians, without recourse to the specialized help of psychologists and psychiatrists. While these problems bring varying degrees of suffering to the child, in the main they are simply a part of growing up. They are normal for a particular developmental stage.

What distinguishes a childhood disorder from normal variation of development is often only a matter of degree. With few exceptions, these disorders are not qualitatively different from normal, and minor variations of these problems can be found in many essentially normal children (Rutter, 1975). Thus, the temper tantrums that occur in most children once a month would hardly be labeled a psychological disorder. But if the tantrums were much more frequent, or it they occurred in peculiar circumstances or for a very long time, then the behavior might be considered abnormal.

CLASSIFYING CHILDREN'S DISORDERS

In the area of childhood disorders, there are several different diagnostic systems, many more in fact than there are diagnostic systems for adult disorders. In part, these different systems address different problems and purposes. Educational diagnostic systems, for example, are concerned with the various kinds of problems that affect school performance. But in larger measure, the different systems reflect different approaches to childhood disorders, and different views about how they can best be categorized.

In this chapter, we will use a broad system of classification that differentiates five major clusters of disorder: behavioral, emotional, physical, intellectual, and developmental. *Behavioral* disorders are those in which something behavioral, rather than emotional, seems amiss. They include hyperactivity and attentional problems, as well as the aggressive, destruc-

Educational diagnostic systems are concerned with the various kinds of problems that affect school performance. These nursery school children are being tested for perceptual difficulties. (Photograph by Burt Glinn/Magnum)

tive, and dishonest behaviors that both precede and constitute juvenile delinquency. *Emotional* disorders are those in which symptoms of fear, anxiety, inhibition, shyness, and overattachment predominate. School phobias and separation anxieties are examples of emotional disorders. *Habit* disorders are those in which the prominent symptoms are strikingly habitual and physical. They include a cluster of difficulties associated with eating (over- and under-eating, binge eating, and eating nonnutritive substances); a group of movement disorders or tics; and a diverse group of disorders with physical manifestations, such as bed-wetting, stuttering, sleepwalking, and epilepsy. *Intellectual* disorders are comprised of the various levels of mental retardation. *Developmental* disorders consist of serious deficits in language comprehension, speech, and responsiveness to others that may add up to a very serious disorder called infantile autism. In addition, the developmental disorders include severe educational difficulties. Table 18-1 shows the kinds of disorders that might be included in this broad diagnostic scheme.

Of course, there is bound to be some overlap between these categories and clusters. Aggressive behaviors, which are called behavioral disorders, have a strong emotional component, while emotional disorders nearly always manifest themselves behaviorally. But on the whole, the distinction between these categories, and particularly between the behavioral and emotional disorders, makes sense. For example, more boys than girls are found to have behavioral disorders. Moreover, the emotional disorders respond much more readily to treatment than do behavioral disorders. Finally, the long-term outlook for emotional and behavioral disorders is quite different. As can be seen in Box 18-1, an extensive follow-up of children who experienced psychological problems revealed that those who had *emotional* problems by and large grew up to be normal adults, no better or worse than their contemporaries. In sharp contrast, children who had suffered *conduct* disorders were poorly adjusted as adults: a high proportion had criminal records; many had marital problems; only one in six was completely free of psychiatric disorder in adulthood. Thus, the crude distinction drawn between emotional and behavioral disorders has powerful predictive value.

Table 18-1 MAJOR CLUSTERS OF CHILDHOOD DISORDERS

Behavioral	Attention disorders
	Hyperactivity
	Aggressive and destructive behaviors
	Juvenile delinquency
Emotional	School phobias
	Shyness
	Childhood depression
	Overattachment
Habit	Bed-wetting
	Stuttering
	Overeating
	Anorexia nervosa
	Bulimarexia
Intellectual	Mental retardation
Developmental	Reading disorders
	Infantile autism

**WHAT HAPPENS TO CHILDREN WITH
EMOTIONAL AND CONDUCT PROBLEMS?**

The St. Louis Municipal Psychiatric Clinic was one of the earliest Child Guidance Clinics set up as a demonstration project by the Commonwealth Fund in April 1922. Patients were treated there until it closed in 1944. Ten years later, its records were about to be destroyed when Dr. Patricia O'Neal of Washington University Medical School asked if they could be used for research purposes.

Dr. O'Neal and Dr. Lee Robins carefully examined all the records and realized they had a wealth of material to study the natural history of childhood disorders. They selected 524 children seen between 1924 and 1929 when they were under eighteen years old. The children were white offspring of mainly American-born Protestant parents of low income; 403 had been referred because of antisocial behavior and 118 for other reasons. Marital disruption and unemployment were high in the families at the time of referral.

Eighty-eight percent of these children were traced by the researchers and agreed to be interviewed at least thirty years later, when they were, on the average, forty-three years old. In addition, O'Neal and Robins traced 100 children from the same school system who had not been seen at the child guidance clinic. Ninety-eight of these agreed to be interviewed. The results were staggering, as can be seen in the table below. It is depressingly clear that youngsters who are diagnosed as having an antisocial or conduct disorder before the age of eighteen are many times more likely than others to have criminal careers, to experience poor marriages, and to be hospitalized for psychiatric problems.

Outcome Measure	Males (%)			Females (%)		
	Antisocial	Emotional	Controls	Antisocial	Emotional	Controls
Crime						
Any non-traffic crime	71	30	22	40	10	0
Major crime	44	12	3	8	0	0
Ever imprisoned	43	13	0	12	0	0

BEHAVIORAL DISORDERS

The **behavioral disorders** embrace two large categories of disturbed behavior: conduct disorders and attention disorders. **Conduct disorders** consist mainly of aggressive and rule-breaking behaviors. Ultimately, persistence in these behaviors may lead to careers in delinquency and to trouble with the law. The **attention disorders** are often accompanied by and made noticeable because of hyperactivity. Both kinds of disorders create considerable disturbance at home and in school, as well as among friends and age-mates.

Outcome Measure	Males (%)			Females (%)		
	Antisocial	Emotional	Controls	Antisocial	Emotional	Controls
Marital Disharmony						
Divorced	51	30	16	70	31	42
Children placed away from home	19	9	0	36	22	11
History of heavy use of alcohol	53	38	29	33	13	14
Ever hospitalized for psychiatric disorder	17	9	1	14	5	0

Robins writes:

We had expected that children referred for antisocial disorder would provide a high rate of antisocial adults, but we had not anticipated finding differences invading so many areas of their lives. Not only were antisocial children more often arrested and imprisoned as adults, as expected, but they were more mobile geographically, had more marital difficulties, poorer occupational and economic histories, impoverished social and organizational relationships, poor Armed Service records, excessive use of alcohol, and to some extent, even poorer physical health. The control subjects consistently had the most favorable outcomes, and those referred for reasons other than antisocial behavior tended to fall between the two. . . . It would follow from these findings that the children currently being referred to clinics for antisocial behavior are the group for whom successful intervention is the more urgently needed, to prevent personal misery for them as adults, for their spouses and children, and for the persons whom they will rob or swindle (Robins, 1966).

It is thus very clear that children with antisocial disorders have a very poor outcome, while children with emotional disorders have a better outcome in adult life.

The behavioral disorders occur more frequently in boys than in girls. In the case of juvenile delinquency, for example, for every girl so labeled there are ten boys. The ratio is three boys for every girl in the case of non-delinquent aggression. Overall, the prognosis for these children is poor: in the St. Louis study (Box 18-1), only one in six of these children was completely free of psychological disturbance when they became adults.

Conduct Disorders

A survey of 1425 British boys aged thirteen to sixteen years, from all socioeconomic groupings, found that 98 percent of them admitted to keeping

The extension of stealing into later childhood and adolescence is characterized as a conduct disorder. (Copyright Sepp Seitz 1982/Woodfin Camp)

something that did not belong to them (Belson, 1975). In only 40 percent of the instances were the goods worth more than two dollars, but even so the rate of childish dishonesty is quite high. Similar results are reported from other countries. In Norway and Sweden, 89 percent of children aged nine to fourteen confessed to petty illegal offenses (Elmhorn, 1965). In Poland, 63 percent of children aged twelve and thirteen confessed to having stolen property (Malewsha and Muszynski, 1970). For better or worse, it seems that stealing is a part of almost every child's development. Such stealing is of a minor sort. Most of it goes undetected and most children do not continue the practice. Some, however, do. It is the extension of this generally normal practice into later childhood and adolescence that constitutes a conduct disorder and may lead to juvenile delinquency.

Juvenile Delinquency

Alan is the sort of teenager who makes all caring professionals despair. He has been in and out of trouble since he was six years old. At that early age, he truanted from school, and by the time he was twelve Alan had been excluded from ordinary schools and had been brought into juvenile court for persistent stealing. Within his neighborhood gang, he was popular with both boys and girls, and he was sexually active before he was fourteen. But he was quick to pick fights with boys who did not belong to his gang.

At fourteen his criminal career seemed set. He had been sentenced several times for stealing cars, and no end of this activity was in sight. His probation officer had the sense of standing by impotently until either maturation or a heavy prison sentence altered Alan's behavior.

Alan seemed to have all the cards stacked against him. He was the youngest of a large family. His father had himself been in and out of prison before finally deserting his mother when Alan was four. The mother struggled to keep the family together, but she frequently became depressed, during which times Alan spent long periods in foster homes. School was no refuge from these difficulties. Despite being of near-average ability, Alan had experienced considerable difficulty learning to read and spell. At fourteen, he could scarcely write a letter home.

Alan belonged to a gang, and some if not all of his delinquent activity may have arisen because he conformed to the norms of his gang. Such delinquents are termed **socialized** in DSM-III, and contrast with unsocialized, aggressive delinquents who are "loners," acting out their own personal problems. This contrast between socialized and unsocialized delinquency is widely used, but may be an oversimplification. Some youths in gangs may indeed respond to the social standards of that subculture, but others in the same gangs may have failed entirely to internalize a consistent set of standards. In either case, the role of social factors in determining the development of this kind of behavioral disorder is overwhelming.

Possible Origins of Juvenile Delinquency

What is called juvenile delinquency during adolescence often evolves into adult behavior that is diagnosed as an antisocial personality disorder. In Chapter 16, we found that this kind of personality disorder often arises from genetic sources. An inherited biological disability interferes with learning to inhibit aggressive behaviors and may well be associated with deficits in autonomic arousal (Mednick, 1978). We take up the genetic influences momentarily. But before doing so, let us examine some possible social influences.

SOCIAL SOURCES OF DELINQUENCY.   Children with aggressive disorders often come from social environments that are unpleasant. Like Alan's family, their families tend to be those in which affection is lacking, and discord rampant; where discipline is either inconsistent, or extremely severe or lax; where the family has parted through divorce or separation; or where the children have been placed outside the home during times of family crisis (Rutter, 1975; Farrington, 1978; Hetherington and Martin, 1979). Often these children come from large families where there may be insufficient amounts of attention and affection to go around. And quite commonly, they are doing poorly in school, rendering them not only restless in the classroom during the long school day but also unavailable to the kinds of self-esteem socialization and feelings of competence that proper school performance engenders.

Family difficulties are augmented by poverty. Delinquency is particularly prevalent within inner cities. And even there, different schools, different housing areas, or different parts of town are associated with enormous variation in rates of conviction. Areas of high delinquency are characterized by high unemployment, poor housing, and poor schooling. Moreover, delinquency is highly related to indices of social pathology, such as illegitimate births, drug dependence, and venereal disease (West, 1976).

Delinquency in adolescence can be reliably predicted from the age of eight to ten years. In one study (Yule, 1978), boys were followed closely from age eight to seventeen years. Troublesome behavior at the age of eight, such as disobedience, truancy, and quarrelsomeness, differentiated boys who were later to be delinquent from their non-delinquent classmates. Five factors distinguished delinquent from non-delinquent boys: low family income, large family size, parental criminality, low intelligence, and poor child-rearing practices. Fifteen percent of the boys had three or more of these adverse factors, and those who did were *six times* more likely than the others to become juvenile recidivists, that is to appear before the court not once, but many times.

GENETIC INFLUENCES ON THE DEVELOPMENT OF JUVENILE DELINQUENCY.   While family and social factors strongly influence the development of aggressive patterns in children, they are not wholly responsible. There seem to be genetic factors that play a role in determining which children become delinquent and which do not. Clinically, it has often been observed that children who subsequently become delinquent are more difficult to raise than others. They seem *temperamentally* more difficult than other children. And because temperament is an inherited characteristic, those observations have suggested broad studies of the effects of genetics on criminality. These studies are similar in design to the genetic studies of schizophrenia that were described in Chapter 17. In this instance, they compare the criminal records (rather than the clinical diagnoses) of adopted children with those of their natural and adoptive fathers. If the incidence of criminality in the children is similar to that of the adoptive fathers, that would suggest that criminal habits are socially acquired. But if the off-springs' criminality resembles that of the biological parents, such data would strongly support a genetic influence. Recent studies (Mednick, 1978) have in fact demonstrated that the criminal records of adopted sons bear stronger resemblance to those of their biological fathers, with whom they never lived, than to the records of their adoptive fathers.

Such evidence cannot be ignored, for it strongly suggests that biological endowment plays a part in determining who becomes delinquent. But how might that come about? Surely one does not inherit criminal *behaviors*, for those must be *learned*. What then is inherited?

What may be inherited and what may influence subsequent criminality is the failure to experience high emotional arousal (see Chapter 16). Because of such failure, boys with conduct disorders are less responsive than others to praise and encouragement (Patterson, 1975). Psychophysiologically they manifest low arousal and show a learning deficit in fear avoidance situations (Davies and Maliphant, 1971; Trasler, 1973)—precisely those situations that encourage socialization and that discourage social rule violation. It is this inability to become emotionally aroused that is inherited and that interferes with the ability to respond to the praises and punishments that encourage socialization. Conversely, genetic inheritance may account for the fact that some children from very difficult circumstances fail to become delinquents. Because they have inherited the capacity to be aroused by social stimuli, they avoid delinquency by becoming socialized.

Treating the Conduct Disorders

Historically, the conduct disorders have been difficult to treat; the success rate has been low. But the recent situation is somewhat more optimistic. Heavy reliance is now being placed on treatments that are derived from social learning theory. For example, where the conduct disorder appears to arise from communication difficulties within the family, the treatment attempts to restore communication and thereby eliminate the child's need to act out, as the following case illustrates:

> John was fourteen when he was referred to a treatment center because he had been stealing from his mother. He frequently stole large sums of money, often in excess of twenty dollars. His mother, however, knew precisely how much money she had, and there was no way in which John could pretend that his stealing would go unnoticed.
>
> Interestingly, during early discussions with the therapist, it became clear that John respected his parents, and that they loved him. The problem was that they could no longer discuss things together. John's stealing had driven a wedge of distrust between them, such that his parents could think of nothing else, yet John resented not being trusted.
>
> In fact, stealing was simply the most irritating of a group of problems that typically arise during adolescence and that neither John nor his parents knew how to discuss and resolve. Among these problems were conflicts over curfew, neatness, personal cleanliness, and table manners.
>
> Recognizing that these conflicts were by no means trivial irritants, the therapist arranged a series of contracts between John and his parents, whereby the rewards and penalties for meeting or violating explicit agreements were clear to both sides.

In these contracts, John acknowledged that his lateness might be a source of great concern to his parents, while they recognized that his room was his own "space" which, subject only to fundamental rules of sanitation, was his to do with as he pleased. At the same time, the therapist encouraged John and his father to role-play how they might settle differences of opinion at home. After the first meeting, stealing was never discussed nor was it targeted as an area for contract or discussion. Nevertheless, it stopped altogether and long before the eight-week treatment terminated.

Where the fundamental problem seems not to be one of communication but rather of socialization, as is often the case among juvenile delinquents, the kind of treatment that is offered in such places as Achievement Place is quite promising. At Achievement Place, which began at the University of Kansas and is now in several locations around the country, two professionally trained "teaching parents" live together in a family-style arrangement with six to eight delinquent adolescent boys who have been sent to Achievement Place by the local court. Often their homes are in the same community, and they can continue to attend their regular school and visit in their own homes.

The aim of Achievement Place is to teach prosocial behaviors. The teaching parents develop a mutually reinforcing relationship with their charges and model, role-play, and reinforce the kinds of social skills they want the boys to acquire. They emphasize skills such as responding appropriately to criticism, as well as the academic skills that are necessary to make school interesting and to obtain employment afterwards. Moreover, Achievement Place emphasizes self-government, whereby the boys take increasing responsibility for their own behavior and for helping their housemates (Wolf, Phillips, and Fixsen, 1975; Kirigin, Wolf, Braukmann, Fixsen, and Phillips, 1979).

While all of the data are not yet in, there is reason to believe that the techniques used by Achievement Place are quite promising. In a comparison of children who were assigned to Achievement Place with those who were treated in an ordinary institution, 47 percent of the latter were institutionalized in the following two years, as against 22 percent of those who had resided in Achievement Place (Kirigin, Wolf, Braukmann, Fixsen, and Phillips, 1979). Moreover, keeping a boy at Achievement Place cost barely a third of what it would cost to send such a child to a state institution. Generally, then, both the efficacy and relative cost of behavioral resocialization programs generate optimism regarding the prognosis for delinquents.

DISORDERS OF ATTENTION AND HYPERACTIVITY

Parents and teachers often complain that children are overactive and restless, that they won't sit still and cannot concentrate for long. What they usually mean is that the children won't concentrate for as long as the *adults* would like, forgetting that attention span and concentration increase with age. But there are cases in which children do show gross overactivity, both at home and at school, and these children can truly be regarded as **hyperactive.** Their behavior is marked by developmentally inappropriate inattention, impulsiveness, and motor hyperactivity. In the classroom, their attentional difficulties are manifested in their inability to stay with a specific task. They have difficulty organizing and completing work. They often give the impression that they are not listening or that they have not heard what they have been told, and they seem unable to sit still. Similarly, at home they are described as failing to follow through on parental requests and instructions and failing to sustain activities, including play, for periods of time that are appropriate for their age. A good example of attentional deficit with hyperactivity is provided in the following case:

> James was seven years old when he was first admitted to a children's psychiatric ward as a day patient. Ever since infancy he had made life difficult for his elderly parents. As soon as he could crawl, he got into everything. He had no sense of danger. He slept very little at night and was difficult to pacify when upset. It was only because he was their only child and they could devote all of their time to him, that his parents managed to maintain him at home.
>
> His problems were noticed by others just as soon as James began school at age five. He made no friends among the other children. Every interaction ended in trouble. He rushed around all day, and could not even sit still at story time. His flitting from one activity to another completely exhausted his teachers. After some eighteen months of trying, his teachers suggested that he be referred to the hospital for assessment and treatment.
>
> On examination, no gross physical damage could be found in his central nervous system. Psychological examinations revealed that James had a nearly average intelligence. In the hospital, he was just as hyperactive as he had been in school and at home. He climbed dangerously to the top of the outdoor swings. He ran from one plaything to another and showed no consideration for other children who were using them. Left to his own devices, he was constantly on the move, tearing up paper, messing with paints—all in a nonconstructive manner.
>
> James was placed in a highly structured classroom, with two teachers and five other children. There his behavior was gradually brought under control. He was given small tasks that were well within his academic ability, and he was carefully shown how to perform them. His successes were met with lavish praise. Moreover, patience and reward gradually increased the length of time he would spend seated at the table.
>
> Ultimately, James was placed in a small, structured, residential school. By age sixteen, he had settled down a great deal. He was no longer physically overactive, but his conversation still flitted from one subject to another. He had no friends among his peers although he could relate reasonably well to adults. He showed little initiative in matters concerning his own life, and his prospects for gaining employment were not good.

Hyperactivity is usually evident by the time a child is three or four years old. Although the blatant presenting problem is overactivity, the underlying problem is inability to focus attention voluntarily (Ross, 1976). Because these children experience attentional difficulties, they seem impulsive and excitable, and this alienates them from their peers. By the end of the primary school years, they often manifest antisocial behaviors, particularly aggression. Not surprisingly, they also suffer severe learning problems.

Treatment

For the most part, the motor overactivity that hyperactive children display usually settles down during adolescence, but the teenagers remain awkward socially. Often, they continue to be socially isolated and, having mastered few skills at school, their prognosis is not very good. Such children, when very young, are very difficult to deal with. They quickly exhaust their teachers and parents, and often they cannot be taught in ordinary school classes. Psychotherapy promises little help for them. The two main therapeutic approaches are drug therapy and behavior management.

DRUG THERAPY. Paradoxically, hyperactive children are made worse by tranquilizers. Instead, their behavior calms down when they are given *stimulant* drugs, the commonest being an amphetamine called methylphenidate (whose trade name is Ritalin). This drug can have very quick and dramatic effects when the dosage is correct and carefully monitored. It is widely, and often unnecessarily, used in schools to control children's hyperactivity and to make the classroom more manageable. But unfortunately, there are dosage difficulties.

Let us return a moment to the profile of the hyperactive child. There are two major problems: (1) brief attention span, and (2) motor overactivity. It turns out that the attention problem is improved with relatively low dosages of Ritalin. Physical overactivity, however, is not reduced unless higher dosages are used. But with these higher dosages, the optimum conditions for learning are sacrificed (Sprague and Sleator, 1973, Sprague and Berger, 1980). Thus, it is quite difficult to control both the cognitive-attentional aspects of the disorder and the motor behaviors with the same drug regimen. Moreover, such gains that are achieved seem very short term. In the long run, children who receive these medications may be no better off than those who don't (Whalen and Henker, 1976). For these reasons, and because one should hesitate to medicate children when less risky treatment alternatives exist, clinicians have been increasingly advocating behavioral management methods.

BEHAVIOR MANAGEMENT. Operant conditioning programs have been relatively effective in treating overactivity and its associated attentional deficits, particularly in the short run. Several investigators have used these techniques to extinguish the hyperactive child's problem behaviors—for example, distracting others—while simultaneously extending the amount of time the child attends. In one case, for example, after carefully establishing how overactive a nine-year-old boy was—that is, his base rate of overactive behavior—the boy was rewarded for sitting still. For every ten seconds that he sat quietly, he earned a penny. The first experimental session lasted only five minutes. But by the eighth session, the boy's overactivity had virtually ceased and, at follow-up four months later, his teacher reported that not only was he much quieter but he was also progressing in reading and making friends. Thus, the straightforward use of attention and tangible reinforcers can produce significant and rapid changes when they are systematically applied (Patterson, 1965; see also Ayllon and Rosenbaum, 1977).

These single case reports, while awfully interesting, are not especially convincing in the long run, because there have been no studies of the long-term effects of behavioral treatments on hyperactive children. Moreover, even comparisons between drug and behavioral treatments are hard to come by. Some researchers (Gittelman-Klein, Klein, Abikoff, Katz, Gloisten, and Kates, 1976) find that drugs are more effective than behavioral treatments. Others (Wolraich, Drummond, Salomon, O'Brien, and Sivage, 1978; Kauffman and Hallahan, 1979) find that drugs and behavioral treatments are both effective, although only behavioral treatments affected children's academic performance. In any event, the studies that bear on the issue of comparative effectiveness are short-term studies, and these tell us nothing about the comparative effectiveness of the two treatments over longer durations. Drug treatments, however, may have serious side effects on children, such as weight loss, insomnia, and high blood pressure (Safer and Allen, 1976). Because behavioral treatments are less risky, they should always be tried before drug treatments are applied (Heads, 1978).

EMOTIONAL DISORDERS

Chronic sadness in a child may be symptomatic of an emotional disorder. (Photograph by Rhoda Sidney/Leo de Wys)

The rubric, *emotional disorders*, loosely describes those emotional abnormalities that are not accompanied by a loss in the sense of reality. Their symptomatology is frequently similar to that seen in adult neuroses (see Chapters 10, 11, and 12)—feelings of inferiority, self-consciousness, social withdrawal, shyness, fear, overattachment, chronic sadness, and the like. These complaints result in diagnoses that include anxiety states, depressive disorders, obsessive-compulsive conditions, phobias, and hypochondriasis (Hersov, 1976).

But there are several important differences between childhood emotional disorders and adult neuroses. First, adult neuroses are more common among women, while childhood emotional disorders occur equally among boys and girls and only begin to be more common among girls with the onset of adolescence. Second, many childhood emotional disorders are age-specific, that is, they occur or terminate at particular ages. Animal phobias, for example, always begin in early childhood, while agoraphobia is rarely experienced before adulthood. Finally, children with emotional disorders do not necessarily grow up to be neurotic adults. Untreated, many of the emotional disorders of childhood simply disappear by adulthood.

Because the emotional disorders of childhood do bear a strong resemblance to those of adulthood, we do not review all of the emotional disorders here. Rather, we shall examine one problem that afflicted all of us in childhood: fear. And we will look at the kinds of troubles that fear can create when it gets quite out of hand.

Phobic Behavior

Fears are very common throughout childhood, much more so than adults realize or remember from their own early years. Recall that 43 percent of children aged six to twelve years old have at least *seven* fears or worries at any one time (Lapouse and Monk, 1959). The nature of those fears, as we indicated earlier, often varies with age. Preschool children tend to be afraid of tangible objects, such as animals and insects. For example, Little Hans, you may recall from Chapter 10, developed his fear of horses at about age five. Tangible fears can continue throughout childhood and into adulthood, but they rarely begin after age five. As children grow older, so grow their

The explorations of childhood often lead to encounters that are troubling and that may cause fear in a child. (Photograph by Yemima Rabin)

fears of imaginary creatures, of disastrous events, and of the dark. Ghosts, murderers, and hidden dangers populate their imaginations. School-connected fears begin at age five or six when children are first enrolled in school, and they increase markedly between the ages of nine and twelve. From about age twelve and on through adolescence, children's fears begin to resemble those of adults, including fears about social relationships and anxieties about identity.

Fears become phobias when, as we saw in Chapter 10, the fear is out of proportion to the reality of the danger that an object presents (p. 200). The following case demonstrates the transition of fear to phobia:

Sometimes children's phobias develop in complex and unpredictable ways. Sara was referred for treatment of her phobias when she was thirteen, The referring physician indicated that the girl was afraid of airplanes and bees, but Sara, like so many such children, found it hard to put in words just what she was scared of. She acknowledged that, beyond airplanes and bees, she was also afraid of elevators, but nothing more. Yet, after she came to know and trust her therapist, it emerged that there was a fear that underlay and linked all the others: that was a fear of anesthesia. The link between airplanes, elevators, bees, and anesthesia was not immediately obvious, and it took some care to piece the following history together.

A number of years earlier, Sara had to have a tooth extracted. The dentist used a general anesthetic. As she "went under," everything went black, but Sara could still hear voices and rushing noises. (In fact, this is an almost universal experience since, physiologically, the nerves controlling vision are affected seconds before the nerves controlling hearing.) Sara was not prepared for these sensations, and they terrified her. Ever since, she has studiously avoided putting herself in a situation where she *might* be injured and therefore might be rushed to a hospital, where she *might* be given an anesthetic. Airplanes crash. So do elevators. Bees sting. Any one of these might land her in the hospital.

Like everyone else, Sara's parents did not understand the connection between her phobias and what gave rise to them. Rather, they tended to see her globally, simply as a fearful child. The therapist explained that what Sara had originally experienced, though unexpected and unpleasant, was hardly incomprehensible and very treatable. He then trained Sara in relaxation techniques that could be used in situations of high anxiety. By focusing on her fears of elevators, the therapist demonstrated to Sara that she could conquer one fear and could go on and conquer the others by herself. Within three months, Sara reported no more difficulties.

Sara's shifting fears were complicated, but not unusual. In her case, a plausible traumatic event was easily identified. In others, the cause is often uncertain. Regardless, phobias in children, like those in adults, respond best to behavioral treatments, though not all of these treatments can be adapted for children, and the efficacy of many of them for children's disorders remains to be demonstrated (Graziano, DeGiovanni, and Garcia, 1979). But one such behavioral treatment—modeling—has been found to be vastly effective with children's phobias (Bandura, 1969a; Gelfand, 1978; Rosenthal and Bandura, 1979). In these treatments, children are exposed to, and encouraged to imitate, models who are both attractive and relatively fearless. The use of such models enables children to quickly overcome their fear.

School phobia may develop in a child due to anxiety about self-esteem and an unrealistically high level of aspiration. (© Erika Stone 1983)

School Phobias

A common childhood disorder that creates significant distress in both children and their parents is **school phobia** or **school refusal**. Not very long ago, it was assumed that all children who were absent from school, except those who were physically ill and could prove it, were playing hooky and were therefore, truants. Yet, there seemed to be a subgroup of such absentees who differed markedly from the "real" truants who tended to be antisocial, underachieving children. In contrast, the subgroup tended to be children who were achieving very well at school, who said that they wanted to return to school, but who described all manner of anxiety symptoms whenever they set out to attend school. For example, they needed to go to the toilet frequently and they often felt sick and sweated profusely when the topic of school was brought up. Unlike the truants whose parents were often unaware that their offspring were not at school, these children stayed at home during their prolonged absences, and their parents knew exactly where they were. Consider the following case:

> Richard was a twelve-year-old who had been out of school almost continuously for five months. The previous summer he had won a scholarship to a well-known private school. He did exceedingly well in his first term. Then, just after the beginning of the second term, he contracted severe influenza which left him feeling very weak. He was worried that he would lose ground academically, and his anxious parents shared that concern. He tried to go back to school, but once in the classroom, he had a panic attack and ran home. Thereafter, he worried increasingly about what to say to the other boys and how to explain his flight and long absence. He was brought to a therapist for help in overcoming his fear.
>
> Richard was given some training in relaxation and was accompanied to his school in graded stages during the summer vacation. He and his therapist rehearsed what he would say to his friends when he returned in the fall. The therapist accompanied him to school for the first three mornings, but thereafter, he was on his own. Follow-up during the next two years revealed no further difficulty. (Yule, Hersov, and Treseder, 1980)

School phobia presents a serious challenge because it is so puzzling to teachers, to parents, and to the child who suffers from it. The situation is made more tragic by the fact that the child previously was a good attender and was doing well in school when, suddenly and for no apparent reason, he stopped going to school. Careful investigation often reveals many reasons for school refusal. In Richard's case and in most others, threats to self-esteem and an unrealistically high level of aspiration play significant roles in refusal. To a child who regularly receives straight A's, the threat of even a "B" can be highly aversive and anxiety-producing.

School refusal occurs at three points in children's school careers: at five to seven years, when children are first registered in school and the anxiety associated with leaving parents and home (called separation anxiety) is likely to be quite intense; at eleven to twelve years old, when children change schools and are fearful about their social or academic status; and at fourteen years old or older. In this oldest group, nonattendance may be the first sign of a more serious difficulty, such as adolescent depression or, more rarely, the early onset of schizophrenia. Whenever it occurs, school phobia requires careful attention, lest it fester into a more serious disorder (Yule, Hersov, and Treseder, 1980).

HABIT DISORDERS

The **habit disorders** comprise a group of diagnoses that are united by a single fact: the troublesome behavior has a habitual physical component. They include such problems as the inability to control bowel or bladder, eating too much or too little, and stammering or stuttering. While the causes of these disorders are not entirely clear, their psychological consequences are dramatic. To be a bed wetter or much overweight in Western society is to be stigmatized and to have to deal regularly with the taunts of others and assaults on one's self-esteem.

ENURESIS

Enuresis is arbitrarily defined as involuntary voiding of urine at least twice a month for children between five and six, and once a month for those who are older. Most children gain bladder control between eighteen months and four years of age. Thereafter, the proportion of children who have difficulty containing urine, either during the day or while in bed, drops markedly. At age five, 7 percent of boys and 3 percent of girls are enuretic; at age ten, 3 percent of boys and 2 percent of girls are still having difficulty with continence. At age eighteen, 1 percent of boys continue to be enuretic, and the disorder is nearly nonexistent for girls (DSM-III, 1980).

As with the other physical disorders, the problems of the enuretic are compounded by the social consequences of the disorder. Parents object to soiled clothes and bedding and commonly stigmatize the enuretic as immature. Schoolmates and friends are likely to tease the child who has an occasional "accident," the more so when those accidents are regular occurrences. Enuretics find it nearly impossible to accept overnight invitations from friends or to go to camp. These social consequences may create a fertile ground for other more serious psychological problems.

Causes of Enuresis

The social consequences of enuresis are especially unfortunate because little is known about its causes. Lay persons often think of it as a disorder of learning or as flawed self-control. But the weight of evidence suggests a strong *biological* component to the disorder. Approximately 75 percent of enuretic children have first-degree relatives who are or were enuretic, and the concordance for enuresis is higher in identical (MZ) than in fraternal (DZ) twins. That is, the more similar a person's genetic blueprint is to an enuretic's, the more likely the individual will also be enuretic.

Treatment

Some drugs, such as the amphetamines or imipramine, suppress bed-wetting temporarily. How these drugs work is not understood, and usually children begin to bed wet again once the drug is stopped. Even so, a few dry nights can be an enormous morale-booster to an enuretic child, particularly if it allows the child to visit friends overnight or go to camp without fear of embarrassment. Bear in mind, however, that these drugs may have significant side effects that outweigh their usefulness. Imipramine, for example, has induced occasional toxic death in children (Rohner and Sanford, 1975).

There are two treatments in particular that have been quite successful with enuresis, far more successful than drug treatment. Both treatments are fundamentally behavioral. The first is a procedure that was first described nearly fifty years ago (Mowrer and Mowrer, 1938). The child sleeps in his or her own bed. Beneath the sheets is a special pad which, when moistened by urine, completes a harmless electric circuit that sounds a bell and awakens the child, who then goes to the toilet. A number of studies have shown that approximately 90 percent of children treated by the "bell and pad" method gain bladder control during the two-week treatment period. There is a relapse rate of up to 35 percent, but that can be reduced by giving a longer treatment period or by offering an additional "booster" dose of treatment (Lovibond and Coote, 1970; Shaffer, 1976; Doleys, 1979).

A more intense procedure amplifies this approach (Azrin, Sneed, and Foxx, 1974). About an hour before bedtime, a "trainer" tells the child and his or her parents about the "dry-bed" procedure. At this time, the child drinks a favorite beverage. Then, the trainer attempts to develop in the child the habit of rousing and urinating. With the lights out, the child lies on the bed and counts to fifty. Then, he or she rises slowly, heads for the bathroom and attempts to urinate. This procedure is repeated many times over the course of that night's treatment. Subsequently, the child is given more to drink, reminded of these procedures, and told that he or she will be awakened each hour to practice going to the toilet. If there is an "accident," the child will have to change the bedsheets and practice using the toilet several times. And, of course, if there is no accident during the hour, the child will be praised for that continence. This procedure is rather more intensive than the bell and pad treatment, and it is even more effective. After four nights of such treatment, all of the children were continent throughout the six-month follow-up period.

STUTTERING

Stuttering or stammering is a marked disorder in speech rhythm. While most children go through transient periods of hesitating over particular words, the dysrhythmia is both more pronounced and more prolonged in those who are regarded as stutterers. Often, it is the initial consonants in certain words, particularly explosive sounds, that cause real problems. "I d-d-d . . . don't know what to d-d-d-do!" is a typically problematic sentence that is often accompanied by a flushed and pained face.

About 1 percent of all children are stutterers, and another 4 to 5 percent experience transient stuttering for a period of up to six months. For unknown reasons, boys outnumber girls as stutterers by four to one.

The causes of stuttering are still unclear, but as in other physical disorders, the consequences are enormous. Stutterers tax the patience of other children and teachers. They are often taunted and ostracized by peers. Teachers may avoid calling on them in class, with the result that their academic interest and performance may flag.

Treatment

By the time a stutterer seeks help, he or she is likely experiencing considerable tension that both results from the speech problem and magnifies it. Consequently, most treatments of stuttering combine psychotherapeutic counseling with specific reeducational techniques. The latter serve to distract the stutterer from his own speech while training him to speak fluently.

Three techniques seem particularly promising. The first is called ***delayed auditory feedback*** and involves hearing one's own speech played back over earphones at about a .1 second delay. When fluent speakers hear their own speech delayed in this manner, they stutter enormously. But when stutterers receive delayed auditory feedback, they become nearly fluent. These paradoxical findings suggest that feedback from their own speech is what maintains stuttering, and that any interference in that feedback will reduce it. The problem, of course, is affecting feedback outside of the treatment situation. Delayed auditory feedback works quite well in the clinic but transfers hardly at all outside of the clinic.

Shadowing is a variant of the delayed auditory feedback technique. Here, the therapist reads from a book, and the stutterer repeats the therapist's words shortly after the latter has spoken them (and without reading the words). This requires the stutterer to concentrate carefully on what the therapist is saying, and in the process, to ignore his own stuttering. Several studies indicate that shadowing may be useful in alleviating stuttering (Cherry and Sayers, 1956; Kondas, 1967).

A third method, called ***syllable-timed speech***, requires stutterers to speak in time to a metronome or bleeper that sounds in an earpiece. This procedure, too, may have the effect of distracting the stutterer from his own stuttering. Combined with a system of rewards for maintaining non-stuttering, this procedure has been found relatively effective in reducing stuttering (Meyer and Mair, 1963; Ingham, Andrews, and Winkler, 1972). None of these three techniques, however, can be described as more than "promising" for the treatment of stuttering.

ANOREXIA NERVOSA

The main symptoms of ***anorexia nervosa*** are substantial loss of body weight and deliberate restriction of calory intake. It is therefore sometimes called the "slimmer's disorder." The diagnosis is not accorded unless the individual has lost 25 percent of normal body weight (or, if the person is under eighteen, the actual weight loss and the weight that would have been gained as a result of ordinary maturation combine to meet the 25 percent criterion).

The central feature of anorexia nervosa is an intense preoccupation with body size and image. Even when they are emaciated, individuals with this disorder feel fat. About 95 percent of those suffering from the disorder are women. Moreover, its prevalence appears to be rising (Bruch, 1978; Yule, 1980), such that as many as 1 in 200 females between the ages of twelve and

Anorexics are preoccupied with body size and image. An anorexic suffers substantial loss of body weight due to a deliberately restricted calorie intake. This is a painting made by an anorectic during the severest stage of her illness. (© 1982 Susan Rosenberg/Photo Researchers, Inc.)

eighteen succumb (Crisp, Palmer, and Kalucy, 1976). Often, the disorder is accompanied by a variety of other physical changes. *Amenorrhea*—that is, loss of the menstrual period—is a common occurrence in women anorexics. Blood pressure may be lowered; sleep patterns may be disturbed, with early morning insomnia common; there may be noticeable hyperactivity and a general loss of interest in sex. The salient symptom, however, remains the persistent determination not to eat, a determination that is so powerful that, in nearly a fifth of the cases, it results in death. The following case illustrates this disorder.

Frieda had always been a shy, sensitive girl who gave little cause for concern at home or in school. She was bright and did well academically, although she had few friends. In early adolescence, she had been somewhat overweight and had been teased by her family that she would never get a boyfriend unless she lost some weight. She reacted to this teasing by withdrawing and becoming very touchy. Her parents had to be careful about what they said. If offended, Frieda would throw a tantrum and march off to her room— hardly the behavior they expected from their bright and sensitive fifteen-year-old.

Frieda began dieting. Initially, her family was pleased, but gradually her parents sensed that all was not well. Mealtimes became battletimes. Frieda hardly ate at all. Under pressure, she would take her meals to her room and later, having said that she had eaten everything, her mother would find food hidden away untouched. When her mother caught her deliberately inducing vomiting after a meal, she insisted they go to the family physician. He found that Frieda had stopped menstruating a few months earlier. Not fooled by the loose, floppy clothes that Frieda was wearing, he insisted on carrying out a full physical examination. Her emaciated body told him as much as he needed to know, and he arranged for Frieda's immediate hospitalization.

Theories of Anorexia Nervosa

Anorexia nervosa is a bizarre and worrisome condition. Why should any young woman starve herself to death? And what is the source of these strong fears of obesity that support an iron-willed determination to eat as little as possible? Unfortunately, there are many suggested explanations, but too little confirmatory evidence (Van Buskirk, 1977).

Psychoanalytic theory offers two views on anorexia. In one, eating is equated with sexual instinct and social role. Women who cannot face up to the demands of a full adult social and sexual role, starve themselves. In so doing, they avoid menstruation and the possibility of becoming pregnant. A second view holds that such patients often have fantasies of oral impregnation. Confusing fatness with pregnancy, they unconsciously believe that eating may result in pregnancy, and therefore they starve themselves. These hypotheses are difficult to confirm. The fact that amenorrhea precedes rather than follows weight loss seriously damages the first view. The second view may well be weakened by the fact that fantasies of oral impregnation are common in women of this age, but most of these women do not become anorexics.

Anorexia nervosa may result from faulty communication within the family. In Frieda's case, for example, anorexia seemed related to the way her family dealt with what was already a sensitive issue: the fact that she was slightly overweight. In turn, the daughter recognized how she could solve her weight problem and simultaneously retaliate against her family—for nothing mobilizes greater despair within a family than a child who is wasting away. The intense struggle between parents and child that subsequently took place maintained the anorexia. Recent efforts have aimed at reducing the family conflict by opening new avenues and styles of communication (Liebman, Minuchin, and Baker, 1974).

But anorexia nervosa is such a powerful disorder, one that results in death in 15 to 21 percent of the cases (Halmi, 1978), that we are inevitably led to suspect that there is more than faulty communication or misguided sexual identity at work here. Some suggest that there is a fundamental disorder in the hormonal and/or endocrine systems. Others postulate hypothalamic malfunctioning (Gelfand, Jenson, and Drew, 1982). Yet others believe that anorexics have not learned to label the hunger sensation and, as a result, simply do not eat (Agras, Barlow, Chapin, Abel, and Leitenberg, 1974).

Treatment

Quite often, hospitalization of the anorexic is recommended because the patient is dangerously ill and can be carefully monitored in the hospital. Even at the point where hospitalization is required, however, some anorexics will protest that they have no problem, that they are not ill, and therefore that they do not require treatment. As a result, they are often difficult patients. The more successful hospital treatment regimens combine sympathetic counseling with contingency management, which makes various privileges contingent on positive changes in eating habits and on weight gain (Bemis, 1978; Yule, 1979; Palmer, 1980).

BULIMAREXIA: THE GORGE/PURGE CYCLE

Bulimarexia is another increasingly common eating disorder, in which people alternately gorge themselves with enormous quantities of food, and then purge themselves of that food by vomiting, or by using laxatives or diuretics. Like anorexia, bulimarexia afflicts young women mainly. And like anorexics, bulimarexics are inordinately concerned with body image and attractiveness. But bulimarexics are obsessed by and drawn to food like moths to fire. Eating dominates their lives: the struggle to resist gorging themselves that alternates with "caving in" to the impulse and then purging the intake is a daily drama that generates shame, distress, and a sense of being dominated by forces outside their own control.

Bulimarexics begin to binge and purge mainly as a way of dealing with the stresses that arise from failures, anticipated or real, in their academic or social lives, in order to avoid sex, or to get back at others. Gradually, however, the habit becomes entrenched and responds to a spectrum of stimulus conditions: happiness, sadness, stress, or excitement all come to elicit binging and purging.

Anorexics often reject femininity, but bulimarexics embrace it. During early adolescence, bulimarexics seem particularly concerned with having boyfriends, more concerned than is usual for that age. That early concern develops into a relentless desire to please men, to be perfect in their eyes, and especially, to be attractive. That desire fuels the binging/purging cycle (Boskind-White and White, 1983).

Treatment

Bulimarexics are quite secretive about their eating behaviors, frequently feeling that they alone behave so shamefully. One result of this dishonest life style is that bulimarexics tend not to have friends who could support their resolve to break their cyclical habit. Because group treatment enables bulimarexics to overcome their shame and to develop supportive relationships with other women, it has generally been more successful than individual treatment. Treatment emphasizes that the disorder is learned, and therefore can be unlearned; that the payoffs for such behavior are few indeed; and that there are more constructive ways of handling stress. Finally, such treatment attempts to redefine femininity in more realistic and authentic directions. Indeed, as treatment progresses, women often find that they have been dominated by their *own* beliefs about what men find attractive, rather than being genuinely responsive to men's feelings and desires (Boskind-White and White, 1983).

OBESITY

Strictly speaking, obesity is not a psychological disorder. It is not included in DSM-III, nor was it included in its predecessors. Yet, obesity afflicts such a large number of children, has such dire consequences on their social and physical lives, and has such grave psychological effects that it is difficult to discuss the problems of childhood and adolescence without mentioning obesity.

Obesity is defined as excess fat on the body. But among *growing* children and adolescents, it is often difficult to know what is *excess* fat. A fairly strict standard defines a child as obese if his or her weight is more than 40 percent higher than the median weight for children of the same height (Rodin, 1977). Given this definition of obesity, there are between 5 and 8 million obese children in the United States alone.

Obesity restricts the range of physical, and especially athletic, activities in which children can participate, but this is not its central liability. Rather, the major problem for obese children lies in others' reactions to them. Obese children are taunted, scorned, and rejected by others. For example, a variety of drawings of children were shown to groups of school children, who were asked to select the ones they liked best. The drawings included normal boys and girls, as well as children who were obese, children who had facial deformities, children who had had limb amputations, and the like. Consistently, obese children were least liked. This rejection is the major psychological consequence of obesity (Richardson, 1970).

People become obese for constitutional and hereditary reasons, as well as for psychological ones. These children are exercising during a meeting of the Child Weight Control Program, a program aimed at curbing childhood obesity. (Wide World Photos)

Causes of Obesity

People become obese for constitutional and hereditary reasons, as well as for psychological ones. On the constitutional side, there appear to be vast differences in the size and number of fat cells that obese and normal children have. *Hyperplastic obesity* results from having many more fat cells than is normal. Normal people have around three billion fat cells, while obese people may have nearly twice that number. This kind of obesity appears to develop during childhood and is likely to remain throughout a person's life. ***Hypertrophic obesity*** develops in late adolescence and in adulthood, and results from having enlarged fat cells rather than too many such cells (Winick, 1975).

Eating, however, serves such significant psychological and social functions in most societies that it is difficult to overlook the habit component of this problem. Many families socially reinforce children for eating by reminding them of the importance of cleaning one's plate ("waste not, want not") or by tying eating to guilt and affection ("don't you like what daddy made for you?").

Treatment

Obesity in children as in adults is difficult to eliminate. A staggering variety of treatments have been tried over the years, with reasonable initial success that fades over the long term. The more promising treatments have emphasized the acquisition of self-control and *de-emphasized* weight loss per se as a goal of treatment (Jeffery, 1977; Stunkard, 1972, 1979). Overweight is merely considered the *outcome* of bad eating habits. These programs therefore concentrate on the eating habits themselves, and they encourage children to do such things as eating only at mealtimes, eating slowly, and expending more energy through exercise.

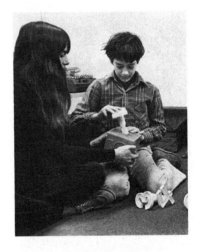

Mental retardation is the one and only childhood intellectual disorder listed by DSM-III. Mildly and moderately mentally retarded children can be taught numbers and eye-hand coordination. (Photograph by Alan Carey/The Image Works)

INTELLECTUAL DISORDERS: MENTAL RETARDATION

In DSM-III, there is one and only one childhood ***intellectual disorder*** listed, and that disorder is ***mental retardation***. It is a disorder that afflicts three out of every hundred children, two-thirds of them boys. Thus, it is a widely prevalent disorder, often heartbreaking in its emotional costs to families and in the lifelong economic burdens it imposes on them and on society. For all of its prevalence, however, and despite the fact that everyone feels they know what mental retardation is, it is a difficult disorder to define precisely and to diagnose accurately. In part, the difficulty arises from the stereotypes that people have about mental retardation. But in larger measure, the difficulty occurs because the notion of intelligence is at the heart of mental retardation, and intelligence is very difficult to define (Kamin, 1974; Gould, 1981).

The most comprehensive and detailed definition of mental retardation has been put forth by the American Association on Mental Deficiency: "Mental retardation refers to significantly subaverage general intellectual functioning existing concurrently with deficits in adaptive behavior, and manifested during the developmental period" (Grossman, 1973). "Subaverage intellectual functioning" refers to performance on individually administered intelligence tests that is minimally two standard deviations below the mean for that test. "Adaptive behavior" refers to the standards of personal independence and social responsibility expected for the person's age and cultural group. Finally, the "developmental period" is the period of time between birth and the eighteenth birthday.

Table 18–2 SEVERITY LEVELS OF MENTAL RETARDATION

Level	Percent of Retarded People	Weschler IQ
Mild	75.0	55–69
Moderate	20.0	40–54
Severe	3.5	25–39
Profound	1.5	below 25

LEVELS OF RETARDATION

The various levels of mental retardation and their associated IQ scores on a standard test of intelligence are shown in Table 18-2. What do these levels of retardation mean?

Mild Mental Retardation

The largest group of retarded children, about 75 percent of them, fall into this category. These children develop social and communication skills just like all others and at quite the same times. In fact, their retardation is often not noticed until they are in the third or fourth grade, when they begin to have academic difficulties. Without help, they can acquire academic skills through the sixth grade; with help, they can go beyond that level. In all other respects, their needs and abilities are indistinguishable from those of other children. Special education programs often enable these children to acquire the vocational skills that are necessary for minimal self-support. When under social or economic stress, they may need guidance and supervision, but otherwise they are able to function quite adequately in unskilled and semiskilled jobs.

Moderate Mental Retardation

Children in this category make up 20 percent of the mentally retarded. Like other children, they learn to talk and communicate during the preschool period. But unlike other children, the moderately retarded have difficulty learning social conventions. During the school-age period, they can profit from training in social and occupational skills, but they are unlikely to go beyond the second-grade level in academic subjects. Physically, they may be clumsy and occasionally they may suffer from poor motor coordination. They may learn to travel alone in familiar places and can often contribute to their own support by working at semiskilled or unskilled tasks in protected settings.

Severe Mental Retardation

Before they are five, the severely retarded provide considerable evidence of poor motor development, and they develop little or no communicative speech. At special schools, they may learn to talk and can be trained in elementary hygiene. Generally, they are unable to profit from vocational training, though as adults, they may be able to perform simple and unskilled job tasks under supervision.

Some mentally retarded children can be trained to participate in competitive games. (Photograph by Alan Carey/The Image Works)

Profound Mental Retardation

Children in this category are severely handicapped in adaptive behavior and are unable to master any but the simplest motor tasks during the preschool years. During the school years, some development in motor skills may occur, and the child may respond in a limited way to training in self-care. Severe physical deformity, central nervous system difficulties, and retarded growth are not uncommon. Health and resistance to disease are poor, and life expectancy is shorter than normal. These children require custodial care.

CAUSES OF MENTAL RETARDATION

There are two sources of mental retardation. The first is called ***cultural-familial retardation***, and it arises from genetic and environmental influences. Most mental retardates are from this group. The second source is associated with ***pathological physical conditions***. In this type, mental retardation arises as a secondary consequence of injury and disease.

Cultural-Familial Retardation

About 75 percent of all retardates fall into this class. Mainly these children are *mildly* and *moderately* retarded, and they often have siblings who are similarly retarded. Frequently, they come from poverty-stricken backgrounds and from broken families. Indeed, the association between this kind of retardation and simple poverty has been repeatedly demonstrated. While less than 3 percent of the general population is retarded, between 10 and 30 percent of the poor are retarded (Cytryn and Lourie, 1967).

The available data indicate that two factors give rise to retardation. The first is genetic. Retardation runs in families and is, to some extent, passed on through the genes. Identical (MZ) twins reared apart are more similar on tests of intelligence than fraternal (DZ) twins reared together (Scarr, 1975), and the IQs of adopted children correlate more powerfully with the IQs of their biological (.48) than their adoptive (.19) parents (Munzinger, 1975).

The second major contributor to this kind of retardation is the environment in which these children live and develop. Wealth and social class powerfully determine the kind of stimulation children get. Middle-class mothers, for example, tend to give children more verbal explanations of problem solutions, and more praise when the children have solved the problems, than do lower-class mothers. These explanations increase their children's verbal facility, while the praise augments their interest in such problems and their self-confidence in solving them. Lower-class mothers, on the other hand, tend to be more critical of a child's task performance, and they tend also to be nonverbally intrusive (Hess and Shipman, 1965; Bee, Van Egern, Streissguth, Nyman, and Leckie, 1969).

TREATMENT.   Mentally retarded children often have defects in language skills that manifest themselves even before the child enters school. Training in language necessitates that the required sounds be demonstrated, and that the child be rewarded for closer and closer approximations to normal speech. Such training, whether conducted by professionals (Baer and Guess, 1971; Garcia, Guess, and Brynes, 1973), or by parents who have been trained to do such teaching (Cheseldine and McConkey, 1977), can be very useful in helping the child communicate more effectively.

As we indicated earlier, many children, particularly those who are mildly handicapped, are not identified as requiring assistance until they enter school. There is considerable continuing controversy about the kind of remedial help they need once they are in school. One view holds that they should be educated with other school children, in the same classes and with the same teachers, since after all, the vast majority of them will ultimately live with their "normal" peers. Another view holds that the needs of the retarded are so different that they need to be educated separately, with separate teaching methods and different schedules and curricula. According to this view, the education of mentally retarded children proceeds best when they are segregated in different institutions, or at least in separate classes. The fact is that neither *mainstreaming*, as integrated education programs are called, or segregation has proven particularly effective in training mentally retarded children (Cegelka and Tyler, 1970; MacMillan and Semmel, 1977). Segregation to special institutions, however, has other deleterious effects that arise from conditions within institutions for the retarded, and from the educational deficits that develop there and that prevent the children from living effectively outside the institution (Ohwaki and Stayton, 1978; Birenbaum and Rei, 1979; Chinn, Drew, and Logan, 1979). Generally, then, the issue of how the mentally retarded are best educated is unresolved. Many educators feel that until it becomes absolutely clear that the child cannot function in the normal classroom, she should remain there for humanistic as well as educational reasons.

Retardation Associated with Illness and Disease

While the largest proportion of mental retardation is due to the natural interplay between normal genetic variation and sociocultural conditions, some retardation arises from organic causes, such as illness, disease, and chromosomal abnormality. Two common forms of this kind of retardation are Down's syndrome and phenylketonuria.

DOWN'S SYNDROME.   About 1 in every 600 children born in the United States suffers from *Down's syndrome*, a form of moderate-to-severe mental retardation that is named after Langdon Down, who recognized it in 1886. Down's childrens' eyes are almond-shaped and slanted, and their round faces have an Oriental cast, so much so that this syndrome is often called *mongolism*, and the children mongoloids. (The similarity between these features and true Oriental ones is superficial at best. The condition is as easily recognizable among Oriental as Caucasian children.) Children suffering from this disorder also suffer from numerous physical anomalies, among them heart lesions and gastrointestinal difficulties. About one-fourth of these children do not survive the first few years of life. And because they are uncommonly friendly, cooperative, and cheerful, their early death touches parents and siblings very deeply.

Down's syndrome is a form of moderate to severe mental retardation. (*Left:* Photograph by Nancy Kaye/Leo de Wys. *Right:* Photograph by Alan Carey/The Image Works)

Down's syndrome arises because there are forty-seven chromosomes, rather than the usual forty-six, in the cells of these children. The disorder itself does not seem to be inherited, but the reason for this chromosomal abnormality is not presently known. Interestingly, while the risk for the disorder is about 1 in 1500 for children born to mothers in their twenties, it increases to 1 in 40 when the mother is over the age of forty. It is now possible to detect a Down's syndrome fetus through *amniocentesis,* a painless test that is administered to the mother after the thirteenth week of pregnancy. In this procedure, a small amount of amniotic fluid (the fluid that surrounds the fetus) is drawn off and examined for the presence of the extra chromosome. When it is found, mothers have the option of continuing the pregnancy or undergoing an abortion.

PHENYLKETONURIA (PKU).   A rare metabolic disease that occurs in roughly 1 out of 20,000 births, *phenylketonuria (PKU)* results from the action of a recessive gene that is inherited from each parent. The infant's metabolism cannot digest an essential element of protein food called *phenylalanine.* As a result, phenylalanine and its derivative, phenyl pyruvic acid, build up in the body and rapidly poison the central nervous system, causing irreversible brain damage. About a third of such children cannot walk; nearly two-thirds never learn to talk; and more than half have IQs that are below 20.

At present, carriers of the recessive gene cannot be identified. But affected babies can be identified by a simple test of their urine about three weeks after birth. Provided they are kept on a diet that controls the level of phenylalanine in their system until age six, when the brain is nearly fully developed, their chances of surviving with good health and intelligence are fairly high.

DEVELOPMENTAL DISORDERS

The final group of childhood difficulties that we take up in this chapter are the *developmental disorders,* difficulties that reflect enormous developmental tardiness or gross developmental failure. *Tardy* development mainly affects the development of language and academic skills. Such difficulties are called **specific developmental problems.** They occur frequently in combination with other difficulties, and in fact, may spawn them. Problems that reflect *failure* to develop, especially the failure to develop the many fundamental psychological capacities that are necessary for maturation and normal functioning are called **pervasive developmental difficulties.** These difficulties are often all-embracing, such as the inability to relate to other people, or to communicate fundamental needs. They are unlikely to be accompanied by other problems, and if they are, they will very likely overshadow them.

SPECIFIC DEVELOPMENTAL DIFFICULTIES

To survive in adult life, people must be able to learn a language, to learn to read, and to do simple arithmetic. Because of this, most modern industrial societies make education compulsory for about ten years of a child's life. As in most developmental matters, children progress in their education at different speeds. A certain amount of lagging behind is to be expected of some children some of the time. But when a child is significantly below the expected level, as indexed by the child's schooling, age, and IQ, then the matter is viewed as a psychological problem. For children between the ages of eight and thirteen—the critical ages for the acquisition and implementation of academic skills—a significant problem may exist if a child is more than two years behind his or her age level.

Reading Difficulties

Of all the specific developmental disorders, reading difficulties have been studied most. As a group, poor readers are late in acquiring language, and they have more of a history of reading difficulty in their families. More than three times as many boys as girls suffer serious reading difficulties. Children with severe reading difficulties at age ten have an increased risk of other psychological disorders, particularly behavior disorders. Generally, the prognosis for reading disorders is not good. Four to five years after the disorder has been diagnosed, very few of the children will have made any significant progress in reading. If anything, they will have fallen further behind normal peers (Yule, 1973).

The social implications of serious reading problems are alarming. Poor readers who are of average intelligence rarely read books or newspapers. They aspire to little that involves reading and, therefore, they often fail to graduate high school. Retarded readers emerge from the school system handicapped educationally, socially, and economically, in the sense that their employment opportunities have been significantly constricted (Yule and Rutter, 1976).

An Educational or Psychological Disorder?

The specific developmental disorders are often correlated with, or give rise to, a host of distinctly psychological symptoms. It is mainly for this reason that these developmental disorders are considered *psychological*, rather than educational. But fundamentally, these are skills disabilities; they are in the domain of education rather than psychology and psychiatry. And many believe that they should continue to be viewed that way (cf. Garmezy, 1977a).

The argument is not without merit. There is no evidence, for example, that psychological treatment or drugs have any positive effect on say, the developmental reading disorder. Yet, calling the difficulty a *psychological* disorder may lead teachers to believe that reading disability is outside of their sphere, leaving the child helped neither by the teacher nor by the psychologist. Moreover, terming reading retardation a psychological disorder may stigmatize the child without contributing a solution to the problem. Indeed, it may simply compound the difficulties. Consider the case of Nelson Rockefeller, former governor of New York and Vice President of the United States. Rockefeller had a severe reading difficulty that handicapped him from childhood through adulthood. Even as an undergraduate, friends and others had to read his textbooks to him. Throughout his career, he much preferred oral communications to written ones. His problems were difficult enough to deal with. Would his life have been made any easier if those difficulties had been described as a severe psychological disorder of childhood? Indeed, could he have been elected to high office if he had been so diagnosed?

PERVASIVE DEVELOPMENTAL DISORDERS: INFANTILE AUTISM

There may be some question about whether the specific developmental disorders are psychological disorders at all, but no such question attaches to these disorders when they are pervasive developmental disorders. For the latter are all-encompassing, involving difficulties of such magnitude and across so many modalities—language, attention, responsiveness, perception, motor development—that little doubt remains about the psychological devastation they create. A sense of the massiveness of these disorders can be obtained from examining one of them closely: infantile autism.

The essential feature of ***infantile autism*** is that the child's ability to respond to others does not develop within the first thirty months of life. That lack of responsiveness is called ***autism***. Even at that early age, gross impairment of communicative skills is already quite noticeable, as are the bizarre responses these children make to their environments. They lack interest in, and responsiveness to, people and they fail to develop normal attachments. In infancy, these characteristics are manifested by their failure to cuddle, by lack of eye contact, or downright aversion to physical contact and affection. These children may fail entirely to develop language, and if language is acquired, often it will be characterized by ***echolalia***—the tendency to repeat or echo immediately or after a brief period precisely what one has just heard— or ***pronominal reversals***—the tendency to use "I" where "you" is meant, and vice-versa. Such children also react very poorly to change, either in their routines or in their environments. These symptoms will be taken up at greater length momentarily. But first, some of the difficulties created by infantile autism can be seen in the following case:

An autistic boy. (Photograph by Alan Carey/The Image Works)

Looking at family photographs of John, one sees a good-looking, well-built, sandy-haired ten-year-old. He looks like thousands of other ten-year-olds—but he's not. If one saw a movie of John it would be immediately obvious that his *behavior* is far from normal. His social relationships seem peculiar. He seems distant, aloof. He seldom makes eye contact. He rarely plays with other children, and when he does, he plays like a three-year-old, not like someone who is ten.

Some things fascinate him, and his most recent fascination has been with shiny leather belts. He carries one around with him nearly always and at times, whirls it furiously, becoming more and more excited in the process. At the height of his excitement, he lets out high-pitched, bird-like noises, jumps up and down on the spot, and flaps his hands at eye level. At other times, John appears to be living in a world of his own, entirely impervious to what is happening around him. A car can backfire near him, but he doesn't flinch. He stares into space, gazing at nothing in particular, occasionally flicking his fingers at something in the periphery of his vision.

In addition to the peculiar squeaks, John's speech is most unusual. He can follow a few simple instructions, but only if he is in familiar surroundings. He will say, "Do you want a drink?," and his parents will know that he means *he* wants a drink. Often, he will repeat complex phrases that he has heard a few days before; television commercials particularly feature in this sort of meaningless speech. At other times, he will echo back large chunks of his parents' speech, but they have realized that this is a signal that he has failed to understand them. He can ask for some things, but even simple requests come out muddled. When he fails to get his meaning across—and this can be several times a day—he will fly into temper tantrums that can become quite wild.

John's parents are both intelligent, articulate, professional people who, right from the early months after John was born, were convinced that something was wrong with him. But since John was their first child, they shrugged off their worries and attributed them to inexperience. So, too, did their family physician. But gradually, no amount of bland reassurance that John would soon "grow out of it" gave any comfort. John was still too good, too quiet, yet too little interested in them as people, and entirely unwilling to be cuddled.

Worried still, they brought John to child specialists. Again the opinions were reassuring. But as John approached age two and was not yet speaking, the experts' views began to change. Words like "slow," "backward," and "retarded" began to be used more frequently. Finally, John was formally tested by a psychologist, and a surprising fact emerged. Although he was grossly retarded in language development, he was advanced for his age on nonverbal puzzles. Difficulties with hearing were ruled out, and it was during these investigations that infantile autism was first suggested.

Oddly, merely knowing that what was wrong with John had a name, provided his parents with some relief. but it was only momentary, for as they read popular accounts of infantile autism, they found that many experts blamed the parents for the child's bizarre problems. Damning accounts of obsessional, emotionally remote parents—dramatized as "refrigerated mothers"— soon had them questioning whether they were fit parents. Their relationship to each other, as well as to John, was undermined.

John's parents managed to get him into a small class in a school for children with learning handicaps. The teacher took a special interest in John and, encouraged by his parents, she adopted a firm, structured approach to teaching him. To everyone's surprise, he took to some aspects of schoolwork readily. He loved counting things and could add, subtract, multiply, and divide by the time he was seven. Moreover, he learned to read fluently—except that he could not understand a single word of what he read. This was brought home to his parents when he picked up a foreign language journal of his father's and read a whole page in phonic French— without, of course, understanding a word! At about this time, he began talking. He referred to himself as "John," got his personal pronouns in a dreadful muddle, and learned to say "no." He used telegraphic sentences of a sort more appropriate to a boy many years younger than he, but at least he was beginning to make himself understood.

He seemed to cherish all kinds of monotonous routines. His diet consisted of a very restricted selection of foods, and he could not be induced to try new foods. He went to school by a prescribed and invariable route, watched television from the same armchair, and strenuously resisted change. Taking him outside was a nightmare, for there was no anticipating when he might throw an embarrassing tantrum. Try as she might, his mother could not help but be hurt by the glares and comments from passersby as she struggled to get John out of the supermarket or into their car. "If only he looked *abnormal*," she often said, "people would be more understanding."

Symptoms of Infantile Autism

The central feature of infantile autism, according to Leo Kanner, a child psychiatrist who was the first to recognize this disorder as a distinct syndrome, is the "inability to relate . . . in the ordinary way to people and situations . . . an *extreme autistic aloneness* that, whenever possible, disregards, ignores, shuts out anything that comes to the child from outside" (Kanner, 1943). This striking aloneness takes a variety of forms in the areas of language, behavior, intellectual and cognitive development, and in social relationships.

LANGUAGE DEVELOPMENT.   One of the striking features of autistic children is how poorly their understanding and use of spoken language develops. Most parents report that the language of autistic children is delayed and deviant right from the beginning. Toward the end of the second year, when normal children are babbling in a characteristically varied way, autistic children frequently show decidedly abnormal and idiosyncratic patterns. For example, they show little skill in such simple social imitations as "waving bye-bye." Later, their use of small toys in imaginative play is severely

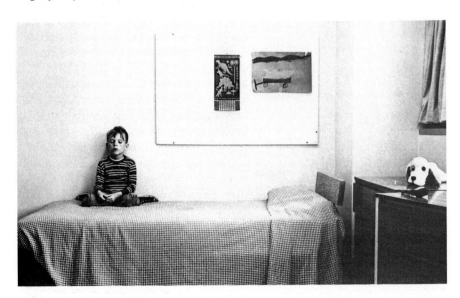

Autistic children shut out everything outside of themselves. They are thus characterized by extreme autistic aloneness. (Photograph by Allan Grant)

limited if, indeed, it ever develops. Because both imitation and imaginative play are both crucial for early language development, speech falters badly in these children. Unlike deaf children, who understand the idea of communication and who have developed nonverbal skills for communicating, autistic children do not use gestures and mime to make their needs known. They may point to objects they need, but if the object is not immediately present, their ability to communicate about it is very much restricted.

It is in their very peculiar use of sounds and words that autistic children's difficulties are most noticeable. About half of the autistic children never learn to use even simple words. Those who do, show many characteristic abnormalities. In the early stages, the child often uses a high-pitched, bird-like squeaking voice, as John did. Again, like John, both immediate and delayed echolalia occur for long periods after speech develops. The child latches on to a phrase from, say, a television commercial, and echoes it for weeks on end.

When speech does develop, autistic children show many of the same sorts of grammatical errors that normal children do. But with autistic children, these errors are more long-lasting and peculiar. We will look at two of these errors; pronoun reversal and the misuse of the rule for adding *-ing.*

Autistic children tend to reverse the pronouns *I* and *you.* For example, when the child wants a candy, he may say "Do *you* want a candy?" instead of "*I* want a candy." Why is this pronominal reversal so typical in autistic children? Two suggestions have been offered. Psychoanalysts have interpreted this reversal as either an unawareness or a denial of personal identity. The child refuses to say *I* because unconsciously he does not accept his own existence (Creak, 1961; Bettelheim, 1967). Others suggest a more parsimonious explanation that rests on the high correlation between echoing and pronominal reversal. Since personal pronouns occur more frequently at the beginning of sentences, and since autistic children have difficulty processing long sentences, they tend to echo the last few words only. When they are given artificial sentences with "I" and "me" placed at the end (for example, "give candy to me"), they do not reverse pronouns (Bartak and Rutter, 1974). Thus, pronominal reversal can be understood as an integral part of a more general language disorder, rather than as a symptom of emotional problems in identity formation.

While both normal and autistic children misuse the *-ing* rule, autistic children are older when the errors arise and the errors persist long after the age when normal children learn the rule. One nine-year-old autistic girl described a man smoking a pipe as "Daddy piping," while a boy blowing bubbles was "boy bubbling" (Wing, 1976). Autistic children also often identify objects by their use, such as "make-a-cup-of-tea" for kettle, and "sweep-the-floor" for broom.

These are but two of the kinds of language errors made by autistic children. For many of these children, language development proceeds no further. Even the small proportion of autistic children who do learn to talk, continue to use language in a noticeably peculiar way. Often it is *too perfect, too* grammatical, rather like a person using a foreign language learned artificially. There is a lack of colloquialism. Conversation is stilted. These children can maintain a concrete question-and-answer interchange, but the subtleties of emotional tone are lost on them. They seem to know the formal

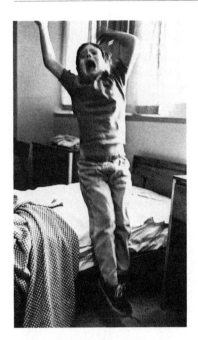

Autistic children often have severe temper tantrums, particularly when their environment changes suddenly. (Photograph by Allan Grant)

rules of language, but they do not comprehend the idea of communication. This defect extends to the nonverbal aspects of communication as well.

INSISTENCE ON SAMENESS.   Many normal children react badly to changes in their environment, particularly if those changes are sudden. But for reasons that are not at all clear, autistic children show this trait in greatly exaggerated form. For example, some autistic children will have severe temper tantrums if the furniture in the house is moved around. Others insist on being driven to school over the same route every day. Parents find that what begins as a harmless routine becomes so rigid that it seriously interferes with everyday life.

Insistence on sameness is seen in other ways. Autistic children frequently use toys and other objects to make long lines or complex patterns. They seem more interested in the pattern than in the functional or imaginative play qualities of the objects. Frequently, these children become intensely attached to one or more objects. John, you recall, carried around a long belt and gyrated it. Other children may refuse to part from a grubby piece of toweling. These intense attachments interfere with normal development and everyday living in a number of ways. If the object is lost, life is made unbearable for the child and the rest of the family. If it is a large object, it prevents hand-eye coordination since the child's hands are not free to play with other objects. As can be seen in Box 18-2, however, it is possible to reduce these abnormal attachments and promote normal development (Marchant, Howlin, Yule, and Rutter, 1974).

SOCIAL DEVELOPMENT.   One of the striking characteristics of the autistic child is aloofness, a physical and emotional distance from others that is especially troublesome to parents and quite noticeable by others. John was clearly aloof, and his mother particularly was troubled by it. This aloofness reflects a fundamental failure to develop social attachments. This is shown by the fact that when autistic children can choose where to spend their time, they will spend more time near a nonreacting adult than near an empty chair (Hermelin and O'Connor, 1970). Thus, active avoidance (which would have been shown by choosing to be near the empty chair) is not the case for autistic children.

Autistic children gradually improve in their social relationships beginning at about age five, provided that they have not been institutionalized in unstimulating surroundings. Ultimately, however, the relationships these children establish are difficult at best. Their social skills deficits show themselves in their lack of cooperative group play with other children, their failure to make personal friendships, and in the enormous difficulty they have in recognizing and responding appropriately to other people's feelings.

INTELLECTUAL DEVELOPMENT.   While autistic children do poorly on tests that require verbal ability, they may perform far above average on tests that involve rote memory or spatial tasks. Moreover, they may be quite talented in music or drawing. But despite evidence of islands of intelligence, autistic children function quite poorly in the cognitive domain. Only about one-quarter to one-third of them have IQ scores above 70, and those scores appear to be quite stable over a ten-year period. In fact, the child's measured

Box 18-2 TREATING INSISTENCE ON SAMENESS

One of the less obvious consequences of many autistic children's insistence on sameness is the direct interference with their already limited cognitive development. Many children become compulsively attached to unusual objects. Some carry small stones clenched tightly in their fists; one child refused to be parted from a metal wire filing basket; and others carry discs they can spin. Any attempt by their parents or teachers to remove these objects is met with an immediate and violent temper tantrum. In these circumstances, adults often give in to the child's wishes. The result can be that the child wanders aimlessly around with his hands fully occupied by the object. In turn, this means that his hands are not free to pick up other things and generally to interact with his physical environment so as to allow hand-eye coordination to develop. Missing out on this stage of normal development may interfere with the development of later, more complex cognitive skills.

Some professionals have advised parents not to interfere with their child's unusual object attachment, in the belief that the object somehow represents the parent and that to intervene will mean damaging an already precarious relationship. In contrast, Marchant and her colleagues argue that these objects fulfill different functions from other attachment objects and that intervention is desirable to promote cognitive growth.

Marchant reports on the case of a five-year-old non-speaking autistic boy who constantly carried around a large (2 foot by 2 foot) blanket. This effectively meant that he had only one arm free for all activities. His mother attempted to prevent him from carrying the blanket everywhere, but to no avail.

It was decided to use a graded-change approach. His mother was asked to cut a small piece off the blanket each night and to increase the amount cut off. The blanket was quickly reduced from 4 square feet to a small bundle of five threads. At this point, the boy was able to abandon for awhile what was left of the blanket. Soon the boy took to carrying other objects. Where these were deemed inappropriate, they were dealt with in the same way. In fact, he appeared to enjoy watching them being cut up! Within four months, he carried a wider range of objects and his interest in any one of them was short-lived. Objects that were of play value were not destroyed, rather he was praised for playing with them appropriately. A year later, he spontaneously abandoned objects for long periods of time and, by then, his comprehension skills as well as his social behavior were improving markedly.

This case illustrates that a direct behavioral approach can be helpful in dealing with one of the major behavioral problems presented by many autistic children. (Based on Marchant, Howlin, Yule, and Rutter, 1974.)

IQ is one of the best predictors of later progress: those with higher IQ scores do better in a variety of educational and remedial settings (Mittler, Gillies, and Jukes, 1966; Gittleman and Birch, 1967; Lockyer and Rutter, 1969; DeMeyer, Barton, Alpern, Kimberlin, Allen, Yang, and Steel, 1974).

Prevalence of Infantile Autism

Fortunately, the severe disorders of childhood are rare. Yet, the total number of children suffering from infantile autism is considerable. It occurs in about 2 to 4 cases per 10,000, about as frequently as deafness occurs among children, and twice as commonly as blindness (Lotter, 1966; Brask,

1967; Treffert, 1970). With regard to sex differences, boys outnumber girls by about three to one. The disorder is more common among children from the upper socioeconomic classes, although the reason for that is entirely unclear.

Causes of Infantile Autism

The sorts of behavior associated with infantile autism are so far removed from people's expectations of normal development that most now believe that there must be some obscure form or forms of biological abnormality underlying the syndrome. The professional climate has not always been so biologically oriented, however. Those who first studied the disorder tended to focus on the parents and *their* abnormal traits (Kanner, 1943). By examining these traits, they hoped to come up with possible psychological causes of autism. Since the evidence on parental traits is now fairly clear, let us examine this first.

PSYCHOGENIC THEORIES. To Kanner and others, the parents of autistic children seemed to be introverted, distant, intellectual, and meticulous. These children seemed to be reared under conditions of "emotional refrigeration." The introvertedness of the parents was reflected in their offspring: parental distance was seen in the child's aloofness, while parental meticulousness was mirrored in the child's repetitive behaviors. Even if one accepts the evidence, however, to conclude that the parents' behavior *caused* the child's disorder is not logical. It is equally plausible that, faced with such an unusual child, parental attitudes and behaviors became unusual. This alternative hypothesis was overlooked in the rush to demonstrate parental culpability.

The psychoanalyst Bruno Bettelheim (1967) offered a similar indictment of parents and family environments. He argued that, in their hopelessness and apathy, autistic children resemble inmates of concentration camps. In his view, the autistic child is one who actively withdraws from an increasingly hostile world, the hostility being relayed through his mother's insensitive handling. But there is little evidence to suggest that the parents of autistic children do behave very differently than the parents of normal children behave toward them. No confirmation of extremely damaging parental behavior exists. Few autistic children actually come from broken homes, and most have not experienced early family stresses. Their parents turn out not to be overly introverted or obsessional, nor do they show any excess of thought disorder. Most autistic children experience the normal range of parental attitudes and child-rearing practices (Cantwell, Baker, and Rutter, 1978).

BEHAVIORAL THEORIES. Behavioral and particularly social learning views of infantile autism are strikingly similar to the psychodynamic views that were just described. These behavioral theories suggest that the way parents interact with their infants interferes with the parents becoming strong reinforcing agents for the infants. That is, the parent does not attend to the infant and does not relate to the infant in the manner that normal parents do. In turn, this results in parents being much less influential in the developing child's behavior (Ferster, 1961).

EEG studies reveal that autistic children have a higher rate of abnormal brain waves than do normal children. This suggests a biological component to infantile autism. (Photograph by Allan Grant)

BIOLOGICAL THEORIES. Because psychogenic theories have not been substantiated (Ornitz, 1978), and because many autistic children appear to also suffer from a variety of physiological deficits, increasing attention has been directed to the possible biological origins of autism. During adolescence, nearly 30 percent of autistic children develop epileptic seizures (which are altered states of consciousness that are accompanied by abnormalities in the brain's electrical activity), even though they had shown no clear evidence of neurological disorder when they were younger. Furthermore, electroencephalographic (EEG) studies —that is, studies that examine the electrical activity of the brain—reveal that autistic children have a higher rate of abnormal brain waves than do normal children. The types of abnormalities found so far, however, do not suggest any specific form of central nervous system dysfunction. Nevertheless, both kinds of data suggest biological involvement. Biological studies of infantile autism have focused mainly on two areas: neurotransmission and genetics.

When neurotransmission is faulty, the brain is unable to pass messages efficiently from one neuron to another. As a result, both perception and learning are interfered with, and patchy cognitive development results. A variety of neurotransmitters could be at fault here, but the most promising leads concern the metabolism of a particular neurotransmitter called **serotonin** (Ritvo, Rabin, Yuwiler, Freeman, and Geller, 1978). Serotonin is involved in both perception and memory, and there seems to be evidence that this neurotransmitter is deficient in autistic children. Unfortunately, these findings are still quite tentative for a number of reasons, the most important being that children's body chemistry is much more labile than adults, which makes stable measurement difficult (Rodnight, 1978).

Because infantile autism is a relatively rare condition, it is difficult to gather extensive data on the genetics of the disorder. Available data indicate that the problem is fairly complex. In a study that compared eleven identical (MZ) twins and ten fraternal (DZ) twins, concordance was found for four of the MZ sets. But when the criterion was expanded to include not only autism but such separate symptoms as cognitive impairment or language delay, concordance was found in nine of the eleven MZ pairs and only one of the ten DZ pairs (Folstein and Rutter, 1978). That is, the separate symptoms of autism that together form the diagnostic entity are themselves inherited. Similar findings regarding the genetic transmission of the symptoms have been reported by Rimland (1964). Conservatively, the studies suggest that infantile autism itself is weakly transmitted genetically, but that many of the separate and serious symptoms of the disorder are strongly transmitted.

Treating Infantile Autism

Insight-oriented treatments that are derived from psychodynamic views of infantile autism have not proven to be particularly effective (Rutter, 1968). Instead, current treatment efforts arise mainly from behavioral sources that focus on the specific deficits that are engendered by infantile autism. Considerable effort, for example, has focused on language development, on the grounds that the inability to communicate properly is so central to this disorder. In these treatments, children's vocalizations are reinforced by the

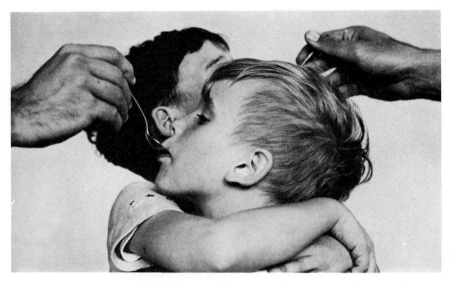

Behavioral techniques are used to treat specific deficits caused by infantile autism. Here, these autistic children are being positively reinforced for hugging each other. (Photograph by Allan Grant)

therapist until they occur very frequently. Next, the children are rewarded for imitating the sounds produced by the therapist, and simultaneously punished for producing meaningless sounds. When imitation is established, children are taught to label everyday objects. And finally, the same techniques are used to teach them to ask questions (Lovaas, 1966; Risley and Wolf, 1967). Early studies of the effectiveness of these methods engendered considerable optimism that these behavioral techniques might enable children to overcome the deficits associated with autism. But this optimism was tempered somewhat by the complexities that were revealed in later follow-up investigations. For instance, the language that was learned so laboriously in the clinic was often lost when the children returned to institutional care (Lovaas, 1973). When parents participate in treatment programs, however, both their behaviors and those of the children undergo change. And the more the parents are involved in the treatment program, the more likely are the language gains to be maintained (Hemsley, Howlin, Berger, Hersov, Holbrook, Rutter, and Yule, 1978).

Quite apart from behavioral approaches, direct *structured* educational approaches have proven beneficial to autistic children. These approaches zero in on the specific cognitive, motor, and perceptual handicaps of these children. A carefully designed educational program minimizes the kinds of distractions that accompany ordinary teaching, making it possible for these children to concentrate. For example, when normal children are taught to read, some texts and teaching materials print vowels in one color and consonants in another. While this helps normal children differentiate between vowels and consonants, it confuses children with pervasive developmental difficulties (Schreibman, 1975). Generally, structured education aimed at overcoming the specific handicaps of the disorder seems to be the best method presently available for helping these children.

Prognosis

Long-term follow-up studies of autistic children indicate that the prognosis for them is not favorable. Close to 60 percent will be unable to lead an independent life as adults. Only one in six will make a good enough adjustment to hold down a job, and even those will still be socially handicapped and will continue to be considered odd in their interpersonal behavior (Lotter, 1978).

The IQ score turns out to be one of the most sensitive early indices of later outcome. In the main, the higher the autistic child's IQ, the better his prognosis. Another good prognostic indicator is the presence of some useful spoken language before the age of five. While the outlook for such children is slowly improving as treatment slowly improves, most autistic adolescents and young adults will still need access to residential facilities.

SUMMARY

1. Children's psychological disorders are often difficult to distinguish from the relatively common problems of growing up because they occur in a developmental context, because children do not speak for themselves, and because children's problems are often specific to particular situations and contexts.

2. On the whole, children's problems can be divided into five areas: behavioral, emotional, physical, intellectual, and developmental.

3. The behavioral and emotional problems are quite similar to those that adults have. They include such difficulties as fears of all kinds (including school phobias), obsessions, anxiety attacks, behavioral acting-out, attentional problems, and the like.

4. The physical problems include those psychological problems that have visible physical manifestations, such as obesity, stuttering, anorexia nervosa, or bed-wetting.

5. Intellectual disorders comprise the various levels of mental retardation, whether they arise from illness or genetic anomalies (such as *Down's syndrome* or *phenylketonuria*) or from cultural-familial sources.

6. There are two kinds of developmental disorders. The first consists of skills deficiencies, particularly in the academic and communication areas. While it can be argued that these are educational, rather than psychological deficiencies, they so often result in psychological hardship that they are included here. The second kind consists of childhood psychoses, of which *infantile autism* is the most dramatic and painful example.

7. There is still much to be learned about the disorders of childhood, and especially about their treatment. The emotional disorders tend mainly to "go away by themselves." They create distress for the child, but they do not commonly result in impairment at adulthood. That, however, cannot be said for the other types of disorder—the behavioral, intellectual, and developmental disorders. These render childhood unhappy and adulthood unfit. There is, therefore, a great need for effective treatment techniques.

8. Increasingly, sustained behavioral treatments seem to be effective both for the behavioral disorders and for the physical disorders. Intensive reeducation for parents, as well as for children, which changes the environment in which a child grows up, can reverse the predicted tide of mental retardation. Even infantile autism yields somewhat to structured education, although the outcome of that disorder is not yet optimistic.

CHAPTER 19

Disorders of the Nervous System

by Paul Rozin

T<small>HE</small> brain is the "organ" of the mind. Most scientists believe that all of the phenomena of behavior and the mind have a basis in the activities of the nervous system. If this is so, then the same must hold true for all of psychopathology. But this leads to a puzzle. Why is the study of diseases of the nervous system ("organic syndromes")* only a small part of abnormal psychology? What does it mean that some disorders are "functional," that is, not organic? Modern medicine recognizes this organic-functional distinction in the establishment of two separate disciplines: neurology and psychiatry. If the domain of neurologists is diseases of the nervous system, what is left for psychiatrists or psychologists?

There must be different senses in which we make the claim that there is a neural basis for all behaviors and mental events. In practice, a case of abnormal behavior falls in the domain of neurology (and hence, would be classified as an organic syndrome) to the extent it can be explained by *known* pathology in the *structure* or *function* of the nervous system. Otherwise, it falls into the domain of psychiatry or psychology (as a functional syndrome).

The organic-functional distinction is like the distinction between hardware and software in computers. Hardware (corresponding to the structure and function of the nervous system) refers to the fixed, factory-produced components and wiring of the computer. Software is information (programs) fed into the system. The performance of the computer is the result of the interaction of software and hardware. The software is physically real, resides in some electrical form in the hardware, and yet is quite distinct from the hardware. The software can be modified from the outside by loading a

---

* The term "organic" actually refers to pathology in some organ system as a cause for disease. Though most organic bases for psychopathology occur in the nervous system, some occur in the endocrine system (e.g., over- or under-activity of the thyroid gland).

new program, whereas modification or repair of the hardware requires dealing directly with the components inside the computer. The people who design, improve, or "debug" software, that is, computer programmers, do not usually design or repair hardware. Roughly, those who deal with software are the psychologists or psychiatrists, and those who deal with the hardware are the neurologists.

In this chapter, we will begin by explaining why neurology is important in understanding psychopathology. We will then explore the different ways in which disorders of the nervous system may be reflected in mind and behavior, and we will illustrate how basic principles of nervous system function help us to understand psychopathology. We will briefly discuss the varieties and causes of diseases of the nervous system, and we will demonstrate how neurologists diagnose abnormality. We will consider language, movement, and memory disorders in light of the organic-functional distinction and the basic principles of function of the nervous system. Then, after a brief discussion of the treatment of diseases of the nervous system, we will return to the organic-functional distinction, discussing the relations among nervous system function, individual experience, and culture in the understanding of psychopathology.

WHY STUDY NEUROLOGY?

The human brain is the most complex biological structure on earth. We may know more about the human brain, its anatomy and physiology, than about any other biological structure. But that is partly because there is so much to know. It is also true that there is more that we *don't* know about the human brain than about any other biological structure (Figure 19-1).

Understanding of almost any type of abnormal behavior is aided by studying neurology. The relevance of neurology to abnormal psychology is that the clinical phenomena dealt with by psychologists and neurologists overlap substantially. This overlap occurs for three reasons. First, one might think that one could divide syndromes in terms of the extent to which they involve "mental" symptoms: neurology would handle the lower-level, be-

Figure 19-1
Anatomy of the human brain. (A) Photograph of the left hemisphere, showing the major lobes of the cerebral cortex. The front of the brain is at the left. (B) Diagram of the human brain cut on the mid-line (dividing the brain into equal left and right halves). (*Left:* Courtesy The American Museum of Natural History. *Right:* Modified from Keeton, 1980)

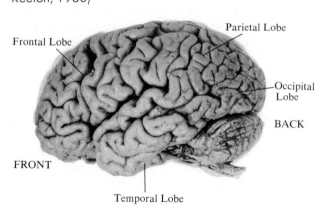

FRONT

Frontal Lobe

Parietal Lobe

Occipital Lobe

BACK

Temporal Lobe

A

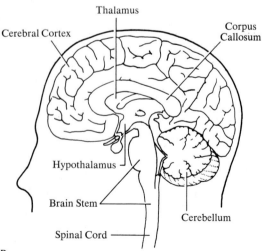

Thalamus

Cerebral Cortex

Corpus Callosum

Hypothalamus

Brain Stem

Cerebellum

Spinal Cord

B

havioral, nonmental problems like paralysis and loss of sensation, while psychology and psychiatry would deal with mental phenomena like emotions and memories. But this division is false on both sides. Apparently low-level symptoms that could be caused by damage to nerves or the spinal cord may in fact have no known neural basis. Clinicians have a general bias to accept a neurological explanation if one is available. If a patient is blind, and one can detect defects in the retina or optic nerve, one is inclined to rest with this explanation. But sometimes it is not possible to detect any damage in people who claim to be blind or in those who report pain in a particular limb or organ. On the other hand, definitely "mental" or psychological symptoms such as periodic aggressive behavior are occasionally caused by seizures or tumors in the brain, and serious acquired disorders in the use of language are usually the result of brain lesions (the word "lesion" refers to a localized pathological change).

A second overlap stems from the fact that we have so much to learn about the nervous system. A particular disorder now classified as functional may have a pathological basis in the nervous system that has not yet been discovered. This was certainly true for general paresis (neurosyphilis), discussed in Chapter 3. This disease has a variety of symptoms, developing over years, including paralysis and delusions. We now know that these symptoms are caused by the action of a micro-organism on the nervous system and that the disease is appropriately treated with penicillin rather than psychotherapy. In previous chapters, we have discussed the possibility that other syndromes, including depression and schizophrenia, may also have a neurological basis.

A third overlap occurs because some syndromes may result from an interaction of known pathology in the nervous system and psychological or cultural (software) factors. For example, loss of the ability to read can result from brain lesions. This is not considered pathology, however, unless it occurs in a literate society in which ability to read is considered normal.

In short, the line between known pathology of the nervous system and its absence is fuzzy. Clinicians are often forced, however, to make a determination of organic (neurological) or functional (psychological) disorder. This decision will have broad implications. It will determine the type of medical-psychological care one will get, as well as the insurance coverage. Most critically, it will affect the way the patient views himself and the way others view him. If episodes of uncontrollable anger are diagnosed as resulting from seizures in a part of the brain, we are inclined to sympathize with the person, and tolerate the behavior. This is less true if the anger is perceived as an aspect of the individual's "personality."

RELATIONS BETWEEN PSYCHOPATHOLOGY AND THE NERVOUS SYSTEM

On the basis of what we have said, one might conclude that psychology and psychiatry exist as disciplines simply because of our current ignorance of the neurological basis of some disorders and that further advances in the neurosciences would ultimately move all the phenomena of abnormal psychology into the domain of neurology. This is not the case, just as all problems of computers cannot be traced to defects in the hardware. One can arrange disorders of behavior and the mind in terms of the extent to which they can be explained as diseases of the nervous system. At one extreme are diseases that are totally accounted for in terms of pathology of structure and function. For example, because of the very orderly way in which nerve fibers going from each point in the retina arrange themselves in the brain, small lesions in the back of the cerebral cortex produce specific "blind spots." More general disorders can also be explained in terms of specific pathologies. For example, low levels of calcium in the body, perhaps produced by a disorder of the parathyroid gland, lower the sensitivity of nerves and muscles, and cause widespread cramps.

In most cases that come to the attention of neurologists, the linkage between pathology of the nervous system and the disorder is weaker. That is, we know of the relation between damage to a certain part of the brain and a symptom, but we don't understand why this particular lesion causes these symptoms. Accurate diagnosis of the site of the lesion can be made, but understanding is minimal. For example, brain damage (usually to the right parietal area, see Figure 19-1) sometimes leads to the phenomenon of unilateral (one-sided) neglect (Mesulam, 1981). Patients with such brain damage neglect the half of their body and the space in front of them that are on the opposite side from the site of brain damage. When dressing, they fail to put the hand from the neglected side into its shirt sleeve, or the leg into the pants. When writing, they may only use one side of the page, and when copying a figure, they may omit the part on the neglected side (Figure 19-2). Though there is a reasonably well-established anatomical relation between damage and symptoms, we do not fully understand why this brain damage produces these symptoms (Mesulam, 1981).

Moving further from clear nervous system–disease linkages, we come to psychopathological syndromes where there are suggestions of a biological explanation, and where a well-articulated neurological explanation may be developed in the future. For example, some investigators have proposed that schizophrenia results from abnormal levels of the neurotransmitter dopamine in parts of the brain (see Chapter 17).

Were we to stop here, we would confirm the view that all disorders would ultimately fall into the domain of the neurologist. But many psychological disorders are not diseases of the nervous system; rather they result from experience, the interaction of individual and culture. A horse phobia, though represented in the nervous system (perhaps as a pattern of connections in some neural circuits) should not be called a pathology of the nervous system. It is a record of experience (software) in the nervous system, and it qualifies as pathology only because fear of horses (as opposed to snakes) is considered bizarre in our culture.

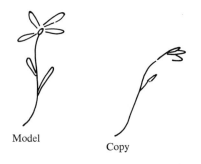

Model   Copy

Figure 19-2
Brain damage leading to unilateral neglect. These are copies of two drawings made by a patient with damage to the right hemisphere of the brain, showing the symptoms of neglect of the left side of space. (Source: Hecaen and Albert, 1978, p. 219)

THE ORGANIZATION OF THE NERVOUS SYSTEM AND PSYCHOPATHOLOGY

In this section, we will show how some basic principles of the structure and function of the nervous system can account for a variety of disorders of mind and behavior. We will illustrate each principle with an example from psychopathology, using this term loosely to mean any disorder of mind or behavior (see Luria, 1973; Gardner, 1975; Kolb and Whishaw, 1978; Adams and Victor, 1981; Kandel and Schwartz, 1981, for a more detailed treatment).

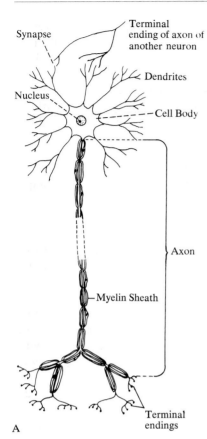

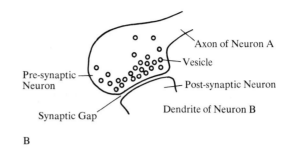

B

Figure 19-3

(A) Schematic diagram of the principal parts of a neuron. Neurons vary in form. The neuron pictured is a motor neuron from the spinal cord. The terminal endings of another pre-synaptic neuron are shown at the top, to illustrate synaptic endings. (Source: Modified from Katz, 1952) (B) Schematic diagram of a synapse. Neurotransmitters made in the pre-synaptic neuron are stored in vesicles in the ending of the pre-synaptic neuron. When a nerve impulse reaches the synaptic ending of the pre-synaptic cell, it causes release of the neurotransmitter into the synaptic gap. It diffuses across the gap, attaches to receptors on the membrane of the post-synaptic neuron, and produces electrical changes (excitation or inhibition) in the post-synaptic neuron. (Source: Modified from Gardner, 1975, p. 47)

NEURONS, SYNAPSES, AND NEUROTRANSMITTERS

Neurons are the "units" of the nervous system (see Figure 19-3A). Neurons communicate with one another by releasing neurotransmitter substances into the *synapse*, the gap separating one neuron from another (see Figure 19-3B). These transmitters either increase (excite) or decrease (inhibit) the activity of the other neurons. A simple example of synaptic function is strychnine poisoning. Strychnine is a highly toxic substance sometimes used in rat poison. It is, on rare occasions, eaten by children. Strychnine prevents inhibition at synapses. As a result, the delicate balance between excitation and inhibition in the nervous system is disturbed. The result is uncontrolled activity of the nervous system, manifested by a progression from irritability, to twitching, to seizures, to death due to spasm of the muscles responsible for breathing. Defects in the basic structure and function of synapses have been suggested as causes of some of the major mental illnesses. You will recall the catecholamine theory of depression (Chapter 13), which holds that a deficiency in the neurotransmitter norepinephrine in certain parts of the brain is the cause of depression.

SUPPORTIVE TISSUE AND STRUCTURES IN THE BRAIN

Although there are billions of neurons in the brain, most of the volume of the brain is made up of *supportive tissue and structures*. These include cells (glia cells) mixed in among the neurons (see Figure 19-4) and is responsible for the maintenance of neurons, blood vessels, and the protective mem-

Figure 19-4
Photomicrograph (magnified about 60X) of motor neurons of the spinal cord. The numerous small dots are nuclei of glial cells, indicating the large number of glia with respect to neurons. (Source: Carolina Biological Supply)

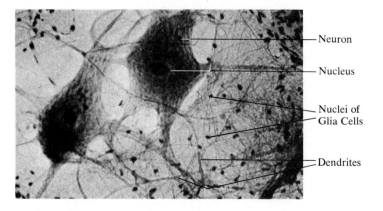

Neuron

Nucleus

Nuclei of Glia Cells

Dendrites

branes (meninges) covering the brain. Much brain pathology originates in the supportive tissue, and not in the neurons themselves. More than 50 percent of the tumors (growths produced by an abnormal, uncontrolled multiplication of cells) originating in the brain involve the glia, and 15 percent involve the meninges. These tumors produce symptoms by destroying neighboring neural tissue, displacing it, or causing increased pressure in the skull, which interferes with circulation in the brain. Multiple sclerosis is a disorder of the glial cells which manufacture and maintain the myelin sheath that surrounds the axons of many neurons in the central nervous system (Figure 19-3A). Some researchers believe that multiple sclerosis is caused by a virus that specifically attacks the myelin-producing glia. The destruction of myelin leads to failure to conduct nerve impulses in the afflicted axons. The pathology tends to appear in neighboring axons, the result being a characteristic "plaque" (mass of scar tissue around the damaged axons). The symptoms of this usually progressive disease vary with the particular sites that are affected: weakness or loss of sensation in arms or legs are common, as are disorders in eye movement.

Infections of the supportive tissue can produce pathological symptoms. And, of course, blood clots in the arteries feeding the brain can deny oxygen and nutrients to the part of the brain served by the artery in question, causing a stroke (damage to the affected area). Damage can also be produced by rupture of a blood vessel in the brain (hemorrhage). Finally, the brain and spinal cord have their own special circulatory system, which if damaged can result in pathological symptoms. This circulatory system is filled with a clear fluid (cerebrospinal fluid) that is secreted by cells in the brain and that eventually re-enters the blood supply. This system is of particular importance in neuropathology because tumors and other types of damage may obstruct the circulation of this fluid and cause a build-up of pressure in the skull. Headache, drowsiness, or loss of consciousness are common consequences of such a build-up in pressure.

SPATIAL ORGANIZATION OF THE BRAIN

The brain is spatially organized. That is, neurons very close to one another in the brain are likely to perform the same functions. This spatial organization of the nervous system allows a neurologist to determine the location of damage in the nervous system by just examining symptoms. Most damage to the nervous system affects a moderately well-defined area, as would clearly be the case for strokes, bullet wounds, or tumors. In general, both the brain and spinal cord are organized so that motor functions are in the front, and sensory functions in the back. Therefore, the damage involved in most sensory disorders occurs further back in the nervous system than that involved in motor disorders.

The nervous system contains areas in which nerve cell bodies are concentrated, called *gray matter,* and areas in which axons are concentrated into tracts, called *white matter,* because of the white myelin surrounding many axons. Tissue damage can occur in either or both regions. Functionally, we can think of the areas of gray matter as processing centers where neurons interact, and the tracts as the connections among the gray areas. Cell bodies of neurons are larger in diameter than their axons, and they tend to be spread further apart. A nerve tract, on the other hand, is a highly concentrated group of axons, usually serving one or a few functions. This has an important consequence for pathology. Since many forms of injury to the nervous system (e.g., small strokes) cause small, spatially well-defined lesions, they are more likely to totally interrupt a fiber tract than to totally destroy an area of gray matter that performs a specific function. Put simply, some disorders can be accounted for in terms of severing the "wires" connecting two areas. These disorders have been called *disconnection syndromes* (Geschwind, 1965).

LATERAL (HORIZONTAL) ORGANIZATION OF THE BRAIN

The human brain, more than the brain of any other species, is differentiated on a left-right basis. Among all vertebrates, the left half of the brain receives most of the input from the right side of the body, and the left half controls action primarily on the right side. This "contralateral" projection is of powerful diagnostic value. In almost all cases, if weakness, paralysis, or loss of sensation on one side of the body results from damage to the brain, the damage is on the side of the brain opposite to the afflicted body part.

There is a qualitative difference in the functioning of the two human cerebral hemispheres. The full significance of this difference is best illustrated by a very special man-made pathology, the split-brain syndrome. (For the rest of this chapter, assume that all statements refer to right-handers, unless otherwise indicated, for left-handers are much less consistent than right-handers in hemispheric organization.)

A surgical procedure has been found to reduce certain uncontrollable and very frequent brain seizures (a particularly severe form of epilepsy). In these cases, the seizure activity goes back and forth from one side of the brain to the other. The treatment, pioneered by Joseph Bogen, separates the two cerebral hemispheres by cutting the *corpus callosum* (Figures 19-1 and 19-5) and a few other structures that serve as the main connections between the two hemispheres. (This, of course, produces a massive disconnection syndrome.) Bogen's patients were carefully studied by Roger Sperry and his students (Gazzaniga, 1970; Levy, 1972; Sperry, 1974). In brief, the results

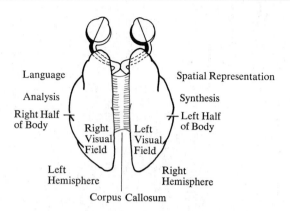

Figure 19-5
Schematic diagram of the human brain, as seen from above, to illustrate the corpus callosum and the specialized functions of each hemisphere. (Source: Modified from Levy, 1972, p. 163)

were striking: the patients appeared to have two consciousnesses in one head. The left brain was the only half that could speak, and it had a much more sophisticated understanding of language. The right brain was superior to the left brain in tasks involving spatial abilities and the recognition of complex forms that are difficult to describe in words. (e.g., faces) (Levy, 1972, 1980).

The differences between the hemispheres are well illustrated by the performance of the right hand (left hemisphere) and left hand (right hemisphere) in copying simple figures (Figure 19-6). The drawings of the right hand suggest a general deficit in the organization of the spatial world. The three-dimensional aspect of the figures is lost, whereas it is preserved in the

Figure 19-6
Split-brain patients were asked to make copies of various examples—one copy was made by the left hand (right hemisphere); the other by the right hand (left hemisphere). These results illustrate the superior spatial orientation capacity of the right hemisphere. Patients with damage to the right parietal lobe show, with either hand, the type of deficit seen in the right-hand drawings. (Source, Gazzaniga, 1970, p. 99)

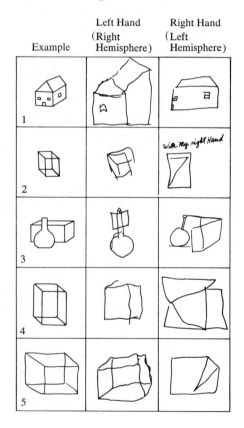

drawings by the left hand. One way to summarize the hemispheric differences is to say that the left hemisphere is better at analyzing inputs and breaking inputs or outputs into sequences over time, while the right hemisphere is better at synthesizing components into wholes and making spatial representations.

These differences have many implications for psychopathology. Language disorders are much more common with left hemisphere damage (for right-handers), while disorders in getting around in space or recognizing faces and other complex configurations occur much more frequently with right hemisphere damage.

BIOCHEMICAL ORGANIZATION OF THE BRAIN

Neurons have specific biochemical identities. They can be differentiated according to which chemicals are in their cell membranes and which neurotransmitters they produce. Neurons with similar biochemical properties tend to be located near one another, or in identifiable sequences of neurons running through the nervous system. We saw in Chapter 10 that the main transmitter of the sympathetic nervous system is norepinephrine, and the main transmitter of the parasympathetic system is acetylcholine. The importance of this for pathology is that some pathological agents (e.g., toxins) work because they specifically damage a particular neurotransmitter system. For example, curare, a poison used on arrow tips by South American Indians, causes complete paralysis and death by interfering with the action of acetylcholine at the junction between nerve and muscle. Similarly, depression is believed to be caused, in some cases, by deficits in neurons producing norepinephrine.

Neurons serving the same function have certain biochemical similarities in their membranes. Because of this, toxins, certain infectious agents (e.g., viruses), or other influences may specifically affect particular types of neurons. For example, in amyotrophic lateral sclerosis (Lou Gehrig's disease), there is selective degeneration of motor neurons, with progressive loss of movement in limbs, body, and head. The cause of this disease is unknown. However, since the damage is specific to motor neurons, there must be some specific and unique property of these cells that makes them more susceptible to a pathological agent.

HIERARCHICAL (VERTICAL) ORGANIZATION OF THE NERVOUS SYSTEM

The brain is organized vertically in a hierarchical structure. The idea of *hierarchy* is absolutely fundamental to the understanding of the nervous system in health and disease. Particular functions (e.g., control of movement) are carried out at a number of different levels in the nervous system, from spinal cord to cerebral cortex. The higher levels are generally more abstract, cognitive, and voluntary. This basic idea was expressed forcefully and eloquently by the nineteenth century British neurologist, John Hughlings Jackson (1884, in Taylor, 1958). The higher levels build on or modulate the lower levels, which represent the contact with the outside world, at the receptors or the action of the muscles. Jackson points out that the higher levels of the hierarchy appear later in evolution and in development. The highest levels, located in the cerebral cortex, include consciousness and the voluntary control and planning of action (which we shall discuss later in some detail). Jackson also claimed that the higher levels are more vulnerable than the lower levels, and more often than not are the first systems to malfunction in general diseases of the whole nervous system. This is illustrated by a common sequence of symptoms seen in some old adults as senility progresses: first there is a loss of ability to deal with new situations, then difficulty in chronological ordering of events, then loss of powers of narration with patchy memory, then loss of personal skills and abilities (e.g., knitting) and social habits, and eventually failures in ability to perform basic bodily functions (modified from Barbizet, 1970). A similar sequence is sometimes seen in gradually increasing intoxication with alcohol.

Because of the neural hierarchy, damage at any number of levels can compromise function. This damage can cause similar, but not identical symptoms, depending on what level has been damaged. The quality of the symptoms will pinpoint what level has been affected. The best example of this involves the control of action, and we shall consider it later in some detail.

BALANCE OF EXCITATION AND INHIBITION

Normal neural function involves a delicate balance between different centers and levels of function, mediated by a balance of **inhibition** and **excitation**. The normal brain is never either silent or in uncontrollable seizure activity. It remains in a dynamic equilibrium of controlled activity, with trillions of nerve impulses coursing through the brain every second. What keeps the brain from slipping into chaos, into massive seizures? The answer is inhibition, working within the high degree of structure of the nervous system. A carefully orchestrated interplay of inhibition and excitation keeps the system active and responsive, but not overactive. The powerful role of inhibition is revealed by the devastating convulsions produced by the drug, strychnine, which you will remember blocks inhibitory processes.

Think of two "centers" (brain areas with specific functions), such that center A inhibits center B. What will happen if A is damaged or destroyed? There will be less inhibition on B, so B will show increased activity. This is called a **release** from inhibition, or **disinhibition**. Release phenomena are seen clinically in the *increased* intensity or frequency of some behavior after damage to some parts of the brain (Teitelbaum, 1967).

A particularly clear example of release is the **Babinski sign,** a reflex normally shown only by infants. When the bottom of the foot is irritated, the toes fan out (Figure 19-7). This reflex disappears early in life. The circuits that mediate it remain intact, however, inhibited by higher centers. Severe damage to higher motor centers releases this reflex; this is one of the cardinal signs of damage to the higher parts of the motor system.

REDUNDANCY IN THE NERVOUS SYSTEM

Redundancy and the existence of alternative pathways are common in the nervous system. Redundancy, or overdetermination, occurs throughout

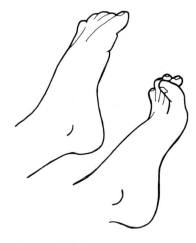

Figure 19-7
On the upper left is the normal response to scratching on the sole of the foot. On the lower right is the pathological Babinski response to this same stimulation. The Babinski response results from release of inhibition caused by damage to higher levels of the motor system. (Source: Gardner, 1975)

vital biological systems. Humans can function well with only one kidney, one eye, or without a majority of their liver cells. The brain is no exception.

The simplest form of redundancy is involvement of more neurons in a particular function than is absolutely necessary. As a result, destruction of some of the cells, or moderate damage to all of them—as might happen with small wounds produced by bullets, or small strokes— may not produce any observable symptoms. For example, even though there is a steady degeneration (without replacement) of the cells that respond to odors, most people in their seventies, although many of their original receptor cells are gone, are still able to detect and identify odors fairly well, and some remain professional wine tasters or perfumers. All systems do not show this type of redundancy, however, as small lesions sometimes do produce clear symptoms—depending on the amount of redundancy and the precise location of the lesion.

Another type of redundancy is produced by the presence of alternative pathways that can accomplish the same end. Thus, although movement of the right side of the body is primarily handled by neurons originating in the left brain, there is a smaller pathway leading from the right brain that allows people with split brains, or people with left hemisphere damage, to exert some control over most of the right side of their body (but not fine finger movements). Also, some functions (such as the control of eating or other basic bodily responses) are represented in equivalent form on both sides of the brain, so that damage to one side may not have a substantial effect.

The availability of alternative strategies also has the effect of reducing the symptoms resulting from tissue damage. For example, a person who has damage to the right hemisphere which affects his ability to recognize faces, might be able to recognize faces by relying more on explicit, verbally described features of the face (such as wears glasses, has thin lips), rather than the more holistic representation that one normally gets from the right hemisphere. Alternative strategies can also be facilitated by cultural inventions. For a person who is unable to walk, crutches make the arms into organs of locomotion.

Finally, because of redundancy, it is common to see normal function in partially damaged systems when conditions are optimal. But as the environmental challenges become greater (e.g., under stress), or as the person becomes fatigued, performance falls apart. Fatigue often brings on latent symptoms of diseases as varied as multiple sclerosis and senile dementia. Similarly, demented people often function better intellectually in the morning than later in the day.

RECOVERY OF FUNCTION

New neurons are rarely, if ever, made after infancy, yet there is typically recovery of function after damage to the nervous system. This is because neurons damaged (but not killed) by such factors as too little oxygen, toxins, or pressure can recover. Sudden damage to the nervous system, caused by trauma (bangs on the head), bullets, or strokes, usually produces a set of acute symptoms, many of which disappear over time. For example, after severe head trauma, a common sequence of recovery is: (1) return of simple reflex activity, (2) return of restless and purposeless movements, (3) more purposeful movements, but still no speech or understanding, (4) restless movements and the return of a few words or phrases, which are often explosive, (5) return of uninhibited speech and action, but disorientation and amnesia for current events, as well as many fabrications about the injury, and (6) return of orientation, social decorum, and behavior (Russell, 1959, p. 51). Some of these stages are illustrated in the following case:

> R.D., a shepherd, aged twenty-seven, was admitted to the hospital on May 3, 1931, having been thrown from his motorcycle . . . He made no attempt to speak and was in a deeply stuporous condition. . . . *May 5.* Today he was fighting hard against the straps that held him down, and calling out loudly without using any definite words. . . . *May 9.* He greeted me cheerfully with "Good morning, sir," and shook hands. Much of what he said was meaningless, but a few sentences were intelligible. He gave his name correctly, but in reply to a question, said "I've been here two years." *May 19.* He talked incessantly and repeated his arguments over and over again. . . . He paid little or no attention to what was said to him. He had no knowledge of where he was and absolutely no insight into his condition. *May 25.* He was quite changed. He remembered being troublesome in the ward and was now very apologetic. . . . He knew where he was and why he was there, and had a normal understanding of his environment. (Russell, 1959, pp. 52–53)

Recovery of function often proceeds in an orderly way, as is indicated in the case of head trauma that we just presented. Sometimes, the sequence of recovery progresses from lower level to higher level functions. In some cases, the sequence of recovery is like the sequence of development: those abilities that appear earlier in development tend to recover first. Conversely, in cases of gradual degeneration, those functions that drop out first are the same ones that recover and develop last. The sequence of events we described in the progression of senility (from initial drop out of higher mental functions to loss of control of basic bodily functions) is roughly reversed in development and recovery. In short, there are parallels among development, recovery, and dissolution of function in the nervous system (Jackson, 1884; Teitelbaum, 1967, 1977).

Recovery occurs for a number of reasons. Some of the cells affected are traumatized, but not killed. With time, they recover. Acute effects, such as swelling of the brain, recede, reducing the stress on neurons. Furthermore, the body has an impressive ability to repair itself. Damage to blood vessels can be healed, for example.

Neurons in the central nervous system show two forms of compensation or repair. When there is a notable drop over some period of time in the amount of input a healthy neuron receives from neurotransmitters, the neuron responds by increasing its sensitivity to the neurotransmitter. This ability probably accounts for the fact that only severe depletions in neurotransmitter levels produce observable symptoms. Another form of compensation is that healthy neurons may make additional connections (by small amounts of growth in their dendrites or axons) in response to the loss of innervation in neighboring neurons.

The young nervous system is more capable of "reorganizing" than the mature nervous system. Given the same brain damage, the prognosis for children below their teens is much better than for older children or adults. For example, although the left brain is the locus for most language function, and the exclusive locus for speech (in almost all right-handers), this arrangement can change in early childhood (Lenneberg, 1967). Thus, damage to the left brain of children leads to symptoms of language disorder in many cases, but recovery is extensive, while in adults, there is less recovery. In children, the right brain seems to have the capability of assuming many language functions in the face of damage to the left brain.

Finally, there is recovery of function because patients discover or are taught alternative strategies so that they can rely on intact systems, as we discussed above.

VULNERABLE SYSTEMS

Some functions or areas of the brain are more vulnerable to damage than others. All parts of the body or brain are not equally resilient. The lower back is a weak spot in the human skeleton, causing more than its share of misery. The stomach and cardiovascular system both seem particularly susceptible to stress-related problems and psychosomatic effects (see Chapter 12). Similarly, there are vulnerable parts of the brain. A consequence of this is that general damage to the nervous system (e.g., vitamin deficiencies, blows to the head, toxins) can produce surprisingly specific symptoms. It is as if you have a transistor radio with one vacuum tube in it. If you drop the radio—a general trauma—it is the vacuum tube that is likely to break.

A group of neurons may be more vulnerable because it has a relatively poor blood supply, for all parts of the brain are not equal in terms of blood supply (see an example in the section on language disorders). Some neurons, because they are especially large or active, have higher requirements for oxygen or nutrients (see the example of peripheral neuropathy in the section on lower motor neurons) or are located in a place where a stroke is more likely to occur. As we point out in the section on amnesia, the system that forms long-term memories is particularly vulnerable, and it is often selectively damaged by general trauma, such as blows to the head, or vitamin B1 deficiency. The cause of this vulnerability is unknown.

The principles of vulnerability and hierarchy combine to account for a basic general principle of neural organization that we have already referred to in our discussion of hierarchy and recovery. The basic idea is that the abilities high in the hierarchy are more vulnerable and those low in the hierarchy are less vulnerable. A clear example of this is that well-practiced (automated) skills, which require no attention to perform and are probably handled at lower levels of the nervous system, are less vulnerable. Habitual acts are among the few remaining capacities in the terminal stages of senile dementia.

GENERAL ASPECTS OF DISEASES OF THE NERVOUS SYSTEM

In our consideration of principles of structure and function in the nervous system, we have laid the groundwork for the study of diseases of the nervous system. In this section, we will discuss the causes of damage to the nervous system, the way that damage expresses itself as a symptom, the broad range of diseases of the nervous system, and the neurological diagnosis.

AGENTS OF DAMAGE TO THE NERVOUS SYSTEM

The agents of damage to the nervous system may produce acute or chronic symptoms. They may act locally, or throughout the body and nervous system. They may produce behavioral symptoms suddenly or gradually. We briefly review here the agents of disease.

Widespread disorders often result from deficiencies in nutrients (minerals like calcium, vitamins, amino acids) or oxygen (e.g., resulting from reduced blood supply caused by narrowing of the arteries, or atherosclerosis), ingested toxins, infections, trauma to the head, and general degeneration of neurons. In all of these cases, the agent of disease may pervade the nervous system. Because of differing vulnerabilities, however, symptoms may appear only, or at first, in specific systems. Many general disorders of this type affect level of consciousness and memory. A clearly localized site of damage may also produce widespread symptoms. For example, a tumor may cause a build-up in pressure of cerebrospinal fluid, thus affecting the whole brain and causing symptoms like headache and drowsiness.

More localized symptoms are often produced by tumors, disorders in blood supply (produced by either *stroke* [occlusion of blood vessels] or *hemorrhage* [ruptured arteries that leak blood]), localized infections, specific genetic malformations, or degeneration of cells in a specific area.

THE EXPRESSION OF DAMAGE IN THE NERVOUS SYSTEM

The kinds of symptoms that may appear after nervous system damage can be positive or negative. Common sense suggests that damage should result in negative symptoms—loss or deficiency in the function that the damaged area serves. This is true much, but not all of the time. Sometimes, there are "positive" symptoms, which may occur for two reasons. First, damage can cause irritation and can increase the activity of neurons in the injured area. Second, if damage decreases the activity of an area that inhibits another area, there will be an increase of activity due to release from inhibition in the inhibited area. In either case, the symptoms are positive in the sense that there is more activity in the nervous system and more behavior in the organism.

Epilepsy is the best example of a disorder whose primary symptoms are "positive." Epilepsy is a common disorder that affects over one million Americans. Damage to neural tissue produced by any of a number of different agents of disease may leave the tissue irritable and may lead to increased activity, because of damage to inhibitory systems or because the residue of the damage (e.g., scar tissue) excites neighboring neurons. The excessive activity (seizures) that is produced leads to an exaggerated (rather than deficient) expression of the function of the area. Seizures occur intermittently, with sudden discharge of neurons. These may be widespread, leading to muscle contraction throughout the body and loss of consciousness, or they may be much more localized. The part of the brain or type of mental event that appears first in the seizure is an indicator of the location of the primary damage in the brain. Depending on the location of the irritable tissue, the primary symptom may be sensory (e.g., an hallucination), motor (e.g., twitches or larger muscle contractions), or emotional (e.g., fear or laughing). Sometimes, the initial events of the seizure produce mild symptoms (an aura) related to the site of damage (e.g., unusual sensations or feelings). Some seizures spread progressively from the original site to other parts of the brain. Epilepsy can be treated by controlling the agent of disease that caused it, or by use of drugs that reduce the irritability of neurons (Adams and Victor, 1981).

Disorders of feeding illustrate the relations between neural damage and symptoms. In animals and humans, the lateral (side), as opposed to the medial (midline), part of the hypothalamus (Figure 19-1) produces eating when activated. Damage to this area may lead to the negative symptoms of cessation of eating and loss of appetite (Teitelbaum, 1967). The positive symptom of increased eating can occur for two reasons. One, as we have discussed, is that damage can cause irritation and increased activity in the injured area. There is some evidence that damage to the lateral hypothalamic area can produce occasional seizures, and that these seizures produce periods of excessive (binge) eating (Green and Rau, 1974). (Only a very small minority of "binge eaters," however, are suspected to have such seizures.) A second source of increased eating is release from inhibition. Damage to a part of the brain (the medial hypothalamus) that inhibits the lateral hypothalamus, releases the lateral hypothalamus from inhibition. The result is increased eating and obesity in animals and humans (Teitelbaum, 1967).

THE RANGE OF NEUROLOGICAL DISEASES

Since all perceptions, feelings, memories, ideas, and actions are represented in the nervous system, disorders of that system can produce pathology in all domains of human action and experience. Before considering a few disorders of the nervous system in detail, we will take an overview, and consider the range of diseases of the nervous system.

Alexander Luria (1973), the distinguished Russian neuropsychologist, divided the "higher" functions of the human brain into three broad domains: arousal, information processing, and planning-verification-action. Diseases of the nervous system can be assigned to one or more of these categories.

The arousal system is located primarily in the **brain stem** and the core of the cerebral hemispheres (Figure 19-1), and it is responsible for maintaining a state of appropriate arousal in the organism. The integrity and activity of this system determine the range of states from alertness through fatigue, drowsiness, sleep, and coma. This system is often affected in neurological diseases, either because the disease process directly damages it, or because of increased pressure in the brain resulting from swelling or a tumor in some other part of the brain. The usual result is extreme drowsiness or loss of consciousness.

The information-processing system handles the representation of the inputs from each of the senses and the integration of information from the senses, in the service of building a useful representation of the world. It includes the parts of the brain that receive inputs from the skin, ears, eyes, nose, and mouth in the midbrain and the forebrain (the primary projection areas), as well as the parietal and temporal lobes, which are heavily involved in both processing and integrating this information. In keeping with the general plan of the nervous system, these areas are toward the back of the brain. Damage to some areas tends to produce disorders in sensation or perception, while damage to others (especially the **parietal lobes,** see Figure 19-1) tends to produce higher-order disorders, including poor representations of space (see Figures 19-2 and 19-6), inability to recognize meaningful objects such as combs or hammers (agnosia), or inability to name objects (anomia).

The planning-verification-action system is primarily involved in acting upon the world. It plans and executes action, and it verifies the outcome of the action. Its primary neurological location is the frontal lobes. We discuss symptoms that result from damage to this system in the section on disorders of movement. Of course, most human activities involve activity of all three systems.

There is one class of symptoms that does not easily fall within any of the categories described by Luria. These are changes in emotional response or personality that may occur after brain damage. One problem is to determine whether the personality changes are direct effects of the damage, or if they result from the patient's reaction to the other effects of brain damage, such as loss of ability to speak. The case of Phineas Gage, presented below, is a particularly striking instance of personality change resulting from brain damage.

Phineas Gage was the twenty-five-year-old foreman of a group of men working on railroad track in Vermont in 1848. An explosion caused an iron bar, over an inch in diameter, to pass through the front of his skull, damaging a large part of the frontal area of his brain (see Figure 19-8). Miraculously, Gage survived, with no more than a few moments of loss of consciousness. After recovery, he reapplied for his job as foreman.

Figure 19-8
Skull of Phineas Gage, the patient described by Harlow (1868), showing the hole in the frontal bone made by the iron rod blown through his head. The bar entered below the left eye and passed through the skull. (Source: Harlow, 1868)

His contractors, who regarded him as the most efficient and capable foreman in their employ previous to his injury considered the change in his mind so marked that they could not give him his place again. The equilibrium or balance, so to speak, between his intellectual faculties and animal propensities, seems to have been destroyed. He is fitful, irreverent, indulging at times in the grossest profanity (which was not previously his custom), manifesting but little deference for his fellows, impatient of restraint or advice when it conflicts with his desires, at times perniciously obstinate, yet capricious and vacillating, devising many plans of future operations, which are no sooner arranged than they are abandoned in turn for others. . . . his mind is radically changed, so decidedly that his friends and acquaintances said he was "no longer Gage." (Harlow, 1868, pp. 339–40)

We cannot explain the relation between Gage's brain damage and the personality change, but it highlights a possible role for hardware in personality and emotion.

The Neurological Diagnosis

Before discussing specific diseases, we will briefly describe how the neurological diagnosis is made. Because of extensive knowledge of the structure and function of the nervous system, and because it is possible to objectively verify diagnoses with sophisticated measurements of the living brain, or at autopsy, diagnosis is more advanced in neurology than psychology. There is a "Sherlock Holmes" detective aspect to the logical analysis of symptoms leading to a diagnosis. The complexities and uncertainties about the operation of the nervous system, however, are such that great experience and skill are essential. It is both a science and an art.

The first task of the neurologist is to determine whether the patient is indeed suffering from a disease of the nervous system. This may be extremely difficult. One alternative is disease of some other system. For example defective vision could be caused by a cataract (a clouding over of the pupil) or a rigidity in the lens that prevented sharp focusing. Another type of alternative is that the symptoms result from a "software" disorder and should be treated by a psychologist or psychiatrist or not treated at all. Having some reason to believe that the symptoms are caused by a disease of the nervous system, the neurologist assumes that *one* disease process and/or *one* lesion can account for all of the symptoms. His problem is to determine what agent of disease, acting in what location, could produce the full pattern of symptoms, and *no other* symptoms. Thus, if a patient is paralyzed on the left side of the body, it is necessary to acount both for this paralysis and the lack of any paralysis or other symptoms on the right side of the body.

The neurologist has three sources of information: the history of the symptoms as described by the patient and her family, the neurological examination (interview and observation of the patient), and the use of special diagnostic techniques to gain direct information about events in the nervous system. The history and neurological examination may be sufficient to make a diagnosis; the special diagnostic tools may serve to confirm an almost certain diagnosis, or they may be of essential importance in determining the nature of the disease.

Our ability to find out what is going on inside the bony skull without going inside is quite remarkable. We briefly review some of these techniques here because they are clever and impressive and because they often play a central role in the determination of whether symptoms point to a neurological (hardware) or psychological (software) disturbance. Absence of evidence of damage to the nervous system makes it more likely that the symptoms have a psychological origin.

Samples of cerebrospinal fluid, taken from the base of the spine, can reveal evidence for internal bleeding, infection, and other sources of disease. Abnormal pressure of the fluid is suggestive of tumors or other obstructions. A whole family of techniques, including a dazzling array of computer hardware, allows visualization of what is going on in the living brain, from the outside. These techniques depend on the fact that abnormal brain tissue (e.g., a tumor, damaged or dead neurons or scar tissue) is different from normal tissue. Electrical differences are detected by the *electroencephalogram (EEG)*, which records electrical events occurring in the brain from wires taped to the surface of the head and scalp. This technique can often record the electrical changes that occur in particular parts of the brain during epileptic seizures, as well as other electrical changes in abnormal tissue.

Since abnormal tissue absorbs X rays to a different degree than bone or normal brain tissue, X rays are also used to detect abnormality. From a series of X rays of the brain taken at different angles, a three-dimensional representation of the brain can be constructed and abnormal tissue within the brain can be located. This technique is known as *computer-assisted tomography*, or the *CAT scan.*

More recently, techniques have been developed to measure, from the outside, the rate of metabolism of different parts of the brain. Abnormal tissue is usually abnormal in rate of metabolism. In one procedure, a radioactive substance is injected, and the rate at which it is taken up by neurons in different areas is measured by sensitive devices surrounding the head. With the aid of computers, a three-dimensional representation of the metabolic rate in different parts of the brain is produced (the *PET scan*). These and other techniques are becoming much more sophisticated, making it more and more likely that damage can be located and assessed.

It is not always possible to assess the precise location and nature of damage, and hence to determine the most appropriate treatment. In such cases, it may be necessary, if the costs of inaction are serious enough, to examine the brain directly. Exploratory neurosurgery, often leading directly into explicit surgical intervention to deal with the problem, is then called for. We will discuss this issue when we consider treatment later in this chapter.

We illustrate the process of neurological diagnosis with one case history:

> This fifty-five-year-old, right-handed . . . housewife . . . while working in her garden at 10:00 A.M. on the day of admission suddenly developed a weakness of her right side and was unable to speak. Apparently, the right-sided weakness mainly affected her face and arm since she was still able to walk. Neurological examination revealed the following: The patient was alert. She had no spontaneous speech and could not use speech to answer questions and could not even use yes or no answers. She could not repeat words. The patient was, however, able to indicate answers to questions by nodding or shaking her head if questions were posed in a multiple-choice situation. In this manner, it was possible to determine that she was grossly oriented for time, place and person. The patient was able to carry

out spoken commands and simple written commands . . . Strength of voluntary movement: there was a marked deficit in the right upper extremity (arm). There was a minor degree of weakness involving the right lower extremity (leg). Sensation appeared normal. Brain X rays and EEGs showed no abnormality. [This was in 1969, when the more modern, computer-enhanced techniques were not generally available.] The patient showed recovery over the following days. A significant amount of strength returned to the right hand within twenty-four hours, and by forty-eight hours, she could speak single words, but there was still no spontaneous speech. Some weeks later, she still had an expressive problem: her speech was slow and labored. (Curtis, Jacobson, and Marcus, 1972, p. 526–28)

The above pattern of symptoms clearly suggests damage to the left hemisphere, since this is the hemisphere that contains speech centers in almost all right-handers. The weakness of the right side of the body suggests left-hemisphere damage, because of contralateral contol. The greater weakness in the arm than the leg makes sense, because the areas innervating the arm are closer to the areas controlling speech than are the areas controlling the leg. The fact that all of the symptoms are in action (as opposed to sensation) suggests a forward location of the lesion, as does the fact that the language problem is in expression, rather than in comprehension of speech. Since the most striking and long-lasting symptom is the speech disturbance, it is reasonable to presume that the focus of damage is Broca's area in the left frontal lobe, since this is the center for speech production. The patient has an expressive (Broca's) aphasia (see next section), unconfirmed in this case by direct measurements on the nervous system. The source of the damage, given the sudden onset, is almost certainly a blockage of a blood vessel feeding this area, that is, a stroke.

SOME SELECTED DISEASES OF THE NERVOUS SYSTEM

We turn now to a consideration of three different groups of diseases of the nervous system: disorders of language, movement, and memory. We have selected them because they are relatively common, they differ markedly from one another, and they illustrate many of the principles we have discussed. Many of the symptoms we will discuss can result from software, as well as hardware disorders; we will illustrate ways in which this distinction can be made.

DISORDERS OF LANGUAGE: THE APHASIAS

Language is a uniquely human activity, and of vital importance to thought, communication, and social life. Hence, disturbances in language are particularly upsetting. Most major disorders of language have a well-defined neurological basis, and are called *aphasias.*

Aphasias illustrate particularly well the principles of spatial and left-right organization (see Geschwind, 1972; Marin, Saffran, and Schwartz, 1976; Adams and Victor, 1981, for general discussions of aphasia). We have already pointed out that most language functions are localized in the left hemisphere of right-handers; hence, aphasias in right-handers are almost always the result of damage to the left hemisphere. Speech is controlled pri-

Figure 19-9
Schematic side view of the left hemisphere of the human brain, showing parts of the brain concerned with language. The tract connecting Wernicke's area to Broca's area is labeled *A*. When this tract is destroyed (as at *A*), the result is conduction aphasia. (Source: Modified from Geschwind, 1975, p. 189)

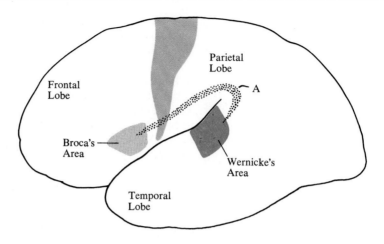

marily by neurons located in the part of the frontal lobe designated Broca's area, in honor of the nineteenth century neurologist, Paul Broca, who first described this syndrome (Figure 19-9). Damage in this area leads to difficulties in expression, as indicated in the case history in the last section. Perception and comprehension of language are often more or less intact, but speech is halting and labored, and many of the common small words are omitted. This pattern of symptoms is described as an ***expressive aphasia.***

The perception of speech is accomplished primarily in a part of the left temporal lobe called Wernicke's area (Figure 19-9). Damage to this area results in a ***receptive aphasia,*** often without any loss in ability to hear nonspeech sounds. The patient has difficulties in perceiving and/or comprehending speech, and so has difficulty following instructions. Speech is more fluent, however, than in expressive aphasia, and it may be more or less normal. Note that in accord with the motor-front, sensory-back principle, the speech production area is in front of the speech reception area.

Both Broca's and Wernicke's areas are connected to other parts of the brain that allow for the extraction of the meaning of language. There is also, however, a direct connection from Broca's area to Wernicke's area (Figure 19-9). Damage to this nerve tract, a classic example of a ***disconnection syndrome*** leaves speech production, speech perception, and the comprehension of language more or less intact. But in the absence of the direct connection from speech perception to speech production, these patients cannot repeat, verbatim, a sentence that they hear, a condition called ***conduction aphasia*** (Geschwind, 1965). They are still able, however, to extract the meaning of the sentence, and thus they can follow verbal instructions (e.g., "put your hands on your head").

There is another striking but rare aphasia that is just the opposite of conduction aphasia. In this disorder, Broca's area, Wernicke's area, and the connection between them are intact, but the speech perception and production unit that they make up is cut off from connection with the rest of the brain, due to extensive brain damage. This damage occurs because the "ring" of brain tissue surrounding Broca's area, Wernicke's area, and their connection is relatively far from the main artery that supplies blood to it. This "ring" is therefore more vulnerable to the effects of low levels of oxygen or other nutrients which result from exposure to some toxins, lung disease, and other causes. These areas cannot survive on the more limited rations of oxygen and nutrients, and permanent damage results. The following case illustrates the symptoms that result in a person whose speech perception and production "unit" is isolated from most of the rest of her brain.

> As a result of carbon monoxide poisoning, a twenty-two-year-old woman sustained the pattern of brain damage we have described. The result was an isolated speech system that functioned relatively well, in the absence of any ability to comprehend or spontaneously produce language. The patient could repeat sentences spoken to her, verbatim. But she could not understand anything that was said to her, and her very minimal spontaneous speech was of inappropriate and stereotyped expression (e.g., "Hi, daddy"). In short, she was much more compromised in language function than the conduction aphasic, because she could not really use language, although she could do the one thing conduction aphasics fail to do: repeat sentences verbatim. (Geschwind, Quadfasel, and Segarra, 1968)

We have described only a few of the many disorders of language, illustrating particularly clear-cut cases. Most cases of disordered language involve combinations of the deficits we have discussed, with one particular set of symptoms being more prominent than the others. Furthermore, most aphasias are accompanied by disorders outside of the area of language, such as weakness or paralysis on the right side, resulting from brain damage to areas near those that serve language.

Disorders of Movement of the Left Hand

Disorders of movement offer particularly good illustrations of the nervous system principles we have discussed, and ideal examples of the neurological approach. In addition, paralysis, one symptom of damage to motor system hardware, is one of the more common symptoms of software malfunction, in hysteria. You will remember the case of lower body paralysis in Bear (Chapter 11) following a traumatic event. This was a clear case of a conversion reaction, that is, a software problem. Knowledge of the nervous system is very helpful in differentiating hardware and software problems, that is, those that are primarily organic in origin from those psychological in origin.

We have selected one set of symptoms, disorders of movement of the left hand of a right-handed person, to accomplish this end. Our approach will be to move from the most peripheral disorders (e.g., damage to the nerves innervating the hand), through higher and higher levels of the nervous system. We will see that, in general, the more peripheral the neural damage, the more precisely we can relate structure and function of the nervous system to the disorder. As we move up the neural hierarchy, however, we will note that our understanding of the ways in which specific neurological damage produces symptoms becomes less satisfactory. Eventually, we will deal with symptoms that seem neurological but are in fact attributed to psychological factors: the phenomena of hysteria and malingering. We will emphasize the logic of neurological diagnosis, focusing on the determination of the site of the lesion (as opposed to the agent of disease), based primarily on the symptoms the patient presents.

By disorders of movement in the left hand, we refer to any abnormality, from paralysis or weakness, to clumsiness or inability to perform complex sequences. A patient would qualify if he had such symptoms, whatever other symptoms were exhibited in other parts of the body. From hundreds of disorders of the left hand, we have selected a few on the grounds that they are caused by neural damage (as opposed to arthritis and broken bones) and because they illustrate the themes of this section.

The Basic Structure of the Control of Movement

At the lowest level of organization, movement is controlled by the motor neurons (called *lower motor neurons*) with cell bodies in the spinal cord, and with axons running out to the muscles in peripheral nerves (Figure 19-10). The axons of the lower motor neurons are called the final common path, because all muscle movements in the body are produced ultimately by activity in these neurons. In the spinal cord, these neurons can be excited or inhibited by input from receptors in the muscles, skin, and joints. These connections form the reflex arcs. A second level of organization has to do with the linkages between the brain and the lower motor neurons: the *upper motor neurons* form these connections. Some of the upper motor neurons that control the hand originate in the motor area of the cortex (Figure 19-10), cross to the opposite side at the base of the brain, and descend in the spinal cord to form synapses with the lower motor neurons. This pathway from cortex to spinal cord is appropriately called the *corticospinal tract.* It allows for particularly fine and rapid movements (because there are no intervening synapses between the cortex and the lower motor neuron), and it is the dominant form of control for the fine movements of the hand, especially finger movements.

Figure 19-10
Diagram of the motor system of humans, showing peripheral nerves, spinal cord, and brain. Nerve fibers from the motor and sensory roots of a few spinal segments come together in the neck and sort out into different peripheral nerves. The lower motor neurons that innervate the muscles are influenced by upper motor neurons coming down from the motor cortex in the corticospinal tracts. The left part of the body is projected onto the right motor cortex. One nerve fiber originating in the left-hand portion of the motor cortex is diagrammed. Capital letters mark sites of damage referred to in the text and Table 19-1. (Source: Modified from Gardner, 1975, p. 217)

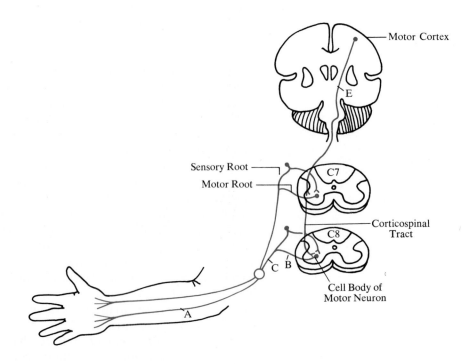

Finally, at the highest level of organization, the frontal and parietal lobes are involved in the planning and sequencing of movements. They influence the upper motor neurons. As we ascend from lower motor neurons to the frontal and parietal lobes, the unit of action becomes larger. For the lower motor neuron, it is parts of muscles. For the upper motor neuron, it is groups of lower motor neurons, and hence a more substantial and meaningful movement. At the level of the frontal and parietal lobes, it is groups of upper motor neurons activated in a pattern over a period of time, and thus meaningful coordinated movements, like striking a match.

With this general scheme in mind, we can discuss four potential areas of pathology: (1) the spinal cord and peripheral nerves, that is, the level of lower motor neurons; (2) the upper motor neurons in the corticospinal tract; (3) the frontal and parietal lobes; and (4) the software, that is, the particular brain circuits whose specific connections are the result of individual experience.

The nature and pattern of symptoms suggest which of these domains is the primary site of disease. We will examine each in turn, and we will show how damage to different parts within each domain causes distinctive symptoms. Symptoms that are particularly valuable in making the diagnosis are:

1. *The quality of the deficit.* The simpler the defect (e.g., weakness, reflex defects, paralysis), the more likely it involves the lower or upper motor neurons. The more complex the disorder (e.g., inability to follow commands with normal strength and reflexes), the more likely the damage is in higher systems. This distinction does not hold, however, for the disorders of psychological origin (software), which often have features that do not make sense in terms of the structure of the nervous system.

2. *The specificity of the defect.* The extent of the defect (e.g., only in the fingers, in the whole left arm, in the left and right hands) indicates the site of damage. The damage must be at a place where all of the affected areas are represented in the nervous system.

3. *The presence of sensory defects.* Sensory defects can in themselves lead to disorders of movement. For example, a hand without sensory innervation would not show reflex withdrawal to painful stimulation. Sometimes, there is a combination of sensory and motor deficits. In these cases, the pathology must be at a site where both the sensory and motor innervation of the areas affected are close together.

4. *Compromise in voluntary or involuntary movement.* Disorders of voluntary movement, with involuntary movement (e.g., reflexes) intact suggest disease above the level of the lower motor neurons. On the other hand, the higher levels depend on the integrity of the lower motor neurons, since these represent the final common path for action. Therefore, disorders in involuntary movement will usually be accompanied by disorders in voluntary movement, and they are likely to originate at the level of the lower motor neuron.

We will now consider disorders that occur with damage at different levels of the system for the control of action.

Disorders Caused by Damage at the Level of the Lower Motor Neuron

The disorders we discuss first are furthest from the brain, and from what might be of concern to psychologists. Nonetheless, we include them because they illustrate the best mapping between anatomy and behavior, and because many psychological (software) symptoms look like some of these peripheral damage syndromes. Damage to lower motor neurons leads to weakness, or if the damage is extreme, to paralysis in the affected muscles. Muscles lose their normal "tone" and become flaccid (limp). Since this is the final common path, damage to lower motor neurons affects both reflexive and voluntary movement. Damage to sensory fibers (axons) in the peripheral nerve or spinal cord will, of course, interfere with elicitation of reflexes, and lead to a loss in sensation from the afflicted area. With these general principles in mind, we must examine the anatomy in more detail, in order to understand the precise mapping between site of damage and symptom (Gray, 1973; Gardner, 1975; Kolb and Whishaw, 1980; Adams and Victor, 1981; Rowland, 1981).

Several spinal segments send axons to or receive sensory input from the hand area (we have shown some of these connections in Figure 19-10). The motor and sensory fibers from each spinal segment (each level of the spinal cord) leave the spinal cord separately (Figure 19-10) and then join together, forming the spinal root for each segment. The roots from different segments come together in the neck, where their fibers reassort themselves into different peripheral nerves. Two of these nerves, containing sensory and motor fibers from a number of different segments, innervate the hand (Figure 19-10).

For example, damage to the ulnar nerve (A in Table 19-1 and Figure 19-10), one of the two nerves that innervates the hand, causes impairment of sensation in the pinky and the pinky side of the fourth finger (Figure 19-11). The motor loss caused by this damage involves certain specific movements of all of the fingers except the thumb, which remains unaffected. The symp-

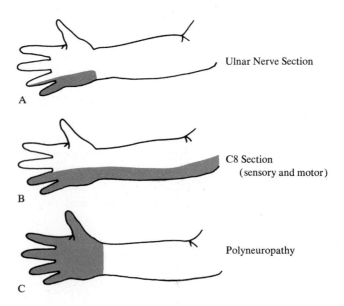

Ulnar Nerve Section

C8 Section
(sensory and motor)

Polyneuropathy

Figure 19-11
Sensory loss on front of left hand resulting from (A) section of the ulnar nerve, (B) section of cervical root 8, and (C) polyneuropathy (or hysterical anesthesia). (Source: Modified from *Gray's Anatomy,* 1973)

toms would be weakness or paralysis, depending on the extent of damage.

The ulnar nerve passes near the surface of the body at the elbow, and it is responsible for the symptoms resulting from leaning on the elbow, or being hit in the "funny bone." The result is sometimes tingling and some temporary loss of sensation, as mentioned, in the pinky and the pinky side of the fourth finger, caused by temporary pressure damage to the nerve. Here we see a little bit of neurology in everyday life.

In contrast to damage of the ulnar nerve, damage to the motor neurons in cervical root 8 (B in Table 19-1 and Figure 19-10) causes weakness or paralysis of the thumb and the muscles that cause the other fingers to spread apart and come together. There would be no sensory loss. Damage to both the sensory and motor axons in cervical root 8 (C in Figure 19-10 and Table 19-1) would, of course, produce the same motor loss. But in this case, there would also be an impairment of sensation in the fourth and fifth fingers (Figure 19-10). Note the type of subtle but reliable distinction that allows for precise diagnosis. While most sensory axons going into cervical 8 come in from the ulnar nerve, those from the thumb side of the fourth finger enter from a different nerve. One can distinguish whether there is loss of sensation only on the pinky side of the fourth finger or on both sides.

These and many other sites of damage to the nerves and different spinal roots produce specific and characteristic patterns of motor and sensory loss, limited to the left hand and arm. But in none of these lesions would the whole left hand be paralyzed or anesthetized, though this is the typical pattern in hysterical paralysis or anesthesia.

There are, however, a few neurological syndromes in which the whole hand might be weakened or paralyzed. One is peripheral neuropathy, a perfect example of the principle of vulnerability (D in Table 19-1).

Table 19-1 HAND SYMPTOMS FOR DIFFERENT DISORDERS

Disorder	Weakness or Paralysis	Reflexes Weak	Tone	Voluntary Paralysis	Sensory Loss	Distribution of loss	
						Sensory	Motor
A. Ulnar nerve	Yes	Yes	Flaccid	Yes	Yes	Pinky side of L hand up to pinky side of 4th finger.	Some movement loss in 2nd to 5th fingers
B. C8 motor	Yes	Yes	Flaccid	Yes	No	None	Thumb, spread apart and come together movements of 2nd to 5th fingers
C. C8 sensory and motor	Yes	Yes	Flaccid	Yes	Yes	Some loss in 4th & 5th fingers	
D. Peripheral neuro-pathy	Yes	Yes	Flaccid	Yes	Yes	Feet & hands, both sides glove pattern	
E. Upper motor neuron	No	No	Spastic	Yes	No	Depends on location	
F. Hysterical	No	No	Variable	Yes	No	Glove-like pattern one hand	

Peripheral neuropathy can result from infections, vitamin B1 deficiency, and from other sources; it compromises the function of nerves. Neurons with longer axons are more vulnerable to this disorder because they require more metabolic support than other neurons. Since the neurons that innervate the hands and feet have the longest axons, symptoms of sensory loss (a negative symptom), pain or tingling (positive symptoms), and muscular weakness tend to occur first in the extremities. The syndrome is distinct from all cases of lesions in particular nerves, the spinal cord, or brain, because, in peripheral neuropathy, the pattern of loss usually involves all four extremities (both hands and both feet). Since the vulnerability is related to axon length, and not the particular peripheral nerve, the intial areas affected are a glove-like area of the hand, and a stocking-like area of the foot (see Figure 19-11C). This pattern of "glove" paralysis or anesthesia does resemble hysterical disorders. Hysterical disorders, however, usually involve one hand (or foot), while peripheral neuropathy affects all four extremities.

The important things to note from this discussion are: (1) even without a history of the disorder or direct measurements on the nervous system, a precise diagnosis can be made; (2) this diagnosis is based on an understanding of the anatomy; and (3) understanding of the anatomy allows us to distinguish hardware from software disorders.

Upper Motor Neuron Lesions: The Corticospinal System

As we have said, the major pathway for voluntary control of the hand originates with the upper motor neurons in the motor cortex, most of which descend in the corticospinal tract on the opposite side, to synapse on lower motor neurons in the spinal cord (Figure 19-10). Lesions in the corticospinal system cause loss or weakness in *voluntary* movement. Since the sensory and lower motor neurons' innervation of the muscle is intact, reflexes are intact, and there is no weakness of the muscle (Table 19-1 E; E in Figure 19-10) (Gardner, 1975; Adams and Victor, 1981; Ghez, 1981). Many upper motor neurons inhibit more than excite lower motor neurons. Therefore, when the upper motor neurons are damaged, there is a release of inhibition on the lower motor neurons, so that many increase firing. The result is that muscles of the hand are rather tense and active (spastic), with very brisk reflexes (Table 19-1). Upper motor neuron damage also tends to produce inability to perform particular types of movement, rather than the defect in the ability to contract particular muscles that is observed with lower motor neuron lesions. Finally, since the axons in the corticospinal tract cross over at the base of the brain, damage to this system in the brain will produce a loss of voluntary movement on the opposite side, while damage to the same system in the spinal cord will cause defects on the same side. The extent of the loss depends on the degree of damage. A small lesion might affect voluntary movement of only part of the hand, while a larger lesion might affect the whole arm.

At both the lower and upper motor neuron levels, there is a clear-cut relation between anatomy and function and symptoms. As a result, we can accurately diagnose the illness and relate it to the damage (Table 19-1). Although we understand less about the function of the parts of the motor system that we will discuss in the next section, there will be no doubt that the syndromes we discuss are caused by diseases of the nervous system.

Damage to the Frontal and Parietal Lobes: Apraxia and Related Disorders

We now move to the highest levels of organization of action: disorders of movement that result from damage to the frontal or parietal lobes. The result is abnormalities in the planning or sequencing of movements, or defects in the linkage of movements with thought and language (Luria, 1973; Geschwind, 1975; Kolb and Whishaw, 1978; Heilman, 1979; Adams and Victor, 1981; Roy, 1982). When the basic disorder is in movement itself, in the absence of muscle weakness, sensory loss, or any damage to the systems we have already discussed, it is called an *apraxia*. In the following case, we illustrate one type of apraxia involving movement of the hand.

> Before the onset of her disorder, a woman had worked for years as a fish-filleter. When the symptoms of damage to both parietal lobes appeared, she began to experience difficulty in doing her job. "She did not seem to know what to do with her knife. She would stick the point in the head of a fish, start the first stroke, then come to a stop. In her own mind, she knew how to fillet fish, but yet she could not execute the maneuver. The foreman accused her of being drunk and sent her home for mutilating fish." (Critchley, 1966, pp. 158-159)

Apraxias are clearly diseases of the nervous system because they are associated with specific, localizable damage, usually to the frontal or parietal lobes (Figure 19-1). Indeed, the site of damage can be diagnosed by the symptoms in many cases. But we still do not understand these disorders well, for we have neither a satisfactory theory of the organization of action sequences nor of how the brain carries them out.

Two basic aspects of brain organization that we have considered are very relevant to our discussion. One is the left-right distinction, or lateralization of function. The other is the principle that motor functions are represented more in the front of the brain, and perceptual functions in the back. The two principles together account for the site of damage for a number of different movement disorders.

We act upon the world, and the planning and sequencing of action must be done in terms of our representation of the world. Hence, it is impossible to separate completely disorders of representation of the world (sensory, perceptual, or conceptual) from disorders of action. We will first consider a group of disorders in which the primary problem is perception, or representation of the world. These disorders usually result from damage toward the back of the brain, in the parietal or temporal lobes.

Damage to the right parietal area (the side more specialized for spatial or holistic processing) leads to inability to represent the basic shape of common objects that are drawn or copied by either hand. Damage to the left parietal area does not severely affect the drawing of basic shapes, but it leads to the absence of specific details. (These differences in copying ability are illustrated in Figure 19-6, which shows the results of copying of common objects by the hands of a split-brain patient. The left hand, connected only to the right parietal lobe, illustrates the deficit associated with damage to the left parietal lobe.) These two disorders of "hand movement" (drawing) illustrate the left-right specialization of the cerebral cortex.

Disorders in language can also lead to disorders in action. Patients with receptive aphasias are unable to make movements on verbal command, because they do not understand the commands, though their motor system may be perfectly normal. Furthermore, there are occasional cases of disconnection of the language centers in the left hemisphere from the motor centers in the right hemisphere. The result is that the left hand (controlled by the right hemisphere) cannot respond to commands, while the right hand can.

You will note that in discussing the lower levels of motor organization, the important aspect of left-right organization was opposite side control (right motor cortex controlling the left hand, etc.). At the level of the frontal and parietal lobes, however, we shift to a left-right distinction based on different modes of processing (analytic-verbal versus spatial-holistic). As a result, left-hand functions are controlled in both hemispheres at this more abstract level (as well they should be, since the two hands normally work together, moving about in the same world). Thus, lesions on one side frequently produce disorders of movement in both hands.

Damage to the left parietal or frontal areas is more likely to disturb the performance of highly skilled movements with either hand, than is corresponding damage to the right hemisphere. These skill disturbances are true apraxias, since the disorder is primarily in the movement systems. These skill deficits are often (but not always) associated with aphasia. It may be that it is no accident that skilled action and language are specialized in the same hemisphere; both language and motor skills involve a precise ordering of events (speech sounds or words, movements) in time.

As expected, given the forward location of the frontal lobes, apraxias resulting from frontal damage are directly related to the organization of action. Again, the hand disorders are often bilateral. The most characteristic feature of frontal damage is *perseveration*, a difficulty in making transitions between one action and the next, often expressed as an inability to terminate a particular action. Hence, we infer that the frontal lobes are critically involved in allowing the transitions from one sequence of action to another. Perseveration appears at many levels of function. Frontal patients have a tendency to grasp objects and then to be unable to let go. Similarly, they may repeat an action over and over, and have great difficulty in alternating two actions. This problem can be graphically illustrated by looking at what these patients do when told to draw a sequence of alternating figures. Typically, they continue to draw the original figure, and cannot shift (Figure 19-12). This perseverative tendency is also manifested at higher levels, in the planning and execution of strategies. Thus, frontal patients are particularly poor at abandoning a strategy they have learned, even after it ceases to work. Tasks in which a subject must change set (strategies) in order to succeed are particularly difficult for these patients (Milner, 1965). This "fixedness" or "inflexibility" in behavior has a clear neurological origin in damage to the frontal lobes. We can only wonder whether other examples of inflexibility, such as excessively repeated obsessional behavior, might share a common pathology, or at least, a common site of action.

We have reviewed a number of the many manifestations of apraxia, to show what disorders in higher levels of motor organization are like and to illustrate that while there is a solid link to nervous system pathology, the pattern of symptoms and damage makes much less sense, in detail, than one would like. As a final approach to understanding higher-level disorders of

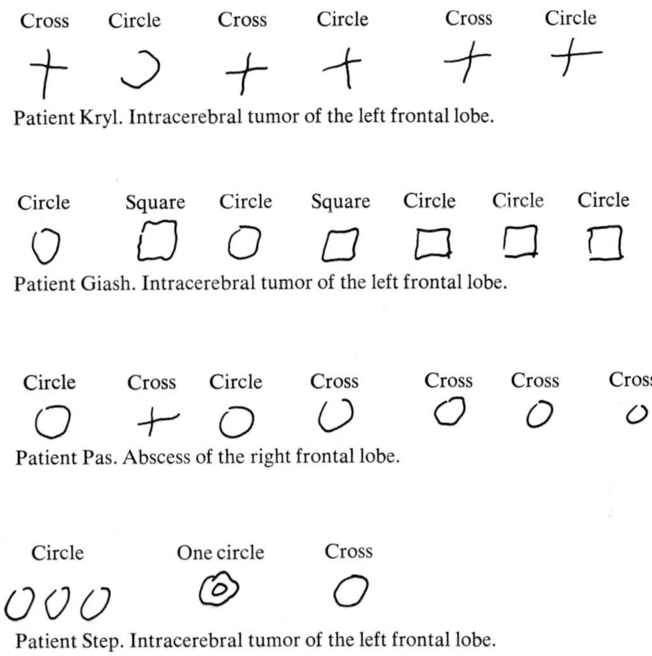

Figure 19-12
Drawings made by four patients with damage to the frontal lobes, in response to the instruction printed above each drawing. Each row represents the sequence of requests made to one patient. The tendency to repeat the previous response is called perseveration. (Source: Luria, 1970, p. 239)

Cross   Circle   Cross   Circle   Cross   Circle

Patient Kryl. Intracerebral tumor of the left frontal lobe.

Circle   Square   Circle   Square   Circle   Circle   Circle

Patient Giash. Intracerebral tumor of the left frontal lobe.

Circle   Cross   Circle   Cross   Cross   Cross   Cross

Patient Pas. Abscess of the right frontal lobe.

Circle   One circle   Cross

Patient Step. Intracerebral tumor of the left frontal lobe.

action, let us briefly consider the ways in which idea and action can come apart in the apraxias (Roy, 1982). At the level closest to movement, there is a disorder in the sequencing of action. Individual acts are performed well, but chains of acts are not. So, an apractic patient is asked to light up a cigarette. He reaches in his pocket, pulls out a match, pulls out a cigarette, and puts the match in his mouth. Or, he pulls out the match, puts it back in his pocket, takes it out again, etc. At a higher level, the sequencing of action is intact, but the patient cannot perform a series of actions unless the context supports his action. Thus, in the presence of a hammer, he can hammer in a nail. But if asked to pretend he is using a hammer (that is, to make a representation of the situation, and plan his action accordingly), he cannot do it. There seems to be some disconnection between idea and action. Another manifestation of this sort of split occurs when apractic patients claim they know how to do a task but can't execute the motions, as if there is a defect between the planning and execution stages. Then, we have patients whose action is totally intact, who can pretend actions, but whose action system is isolated from linguistic input: they cannot perform to command, although they can perform these actions as imitations, or when the context calls for them. These different pathologies suggest that apraxias and related disorders in general involve either the ordering of the execution of action, or the linkages between ideas, plans, and perception with action.

Disorders in the Software: Hysteria and Malingering

As we moved from lower motor neuron disorders to apraxias, the linkage between pathology and symptoms became weaker and weaker, but there was no question that we were dealing with diseases of the nervous system.

We now come full circle, and examine symptoms much like those produced by lower and upper motor neuron damage, but for which there is no known nervous system pathology. Surprisingly, these disorders of the hand usually resemble the simpler (upper motor neuron, paralytic) symptoms, rather than those of apraxia. One might have expected that a syndrome such as failure to make a fist on command, but ability to do so spontaneously (as in apraxia), would be the type that would result from software problems, but this is not the case.

The distinction between these disorders of software and the hardware disorders we have already discussed is not easy to make, especially in the case of neurological diseases that do not result from trauma, or that are in an early stage of pathology where direct measurements of the nervous system may not reveal any damage. In a puzzling case, say of weakness or paralysis of the left hand, the neurologist is faced with three options: (1) there is a neurological disease that is either atypical or too early in its development for accurate diagnosis; (2) the symptoms result from a software problem, but the patient has no control over the symptoms and is unaware of their origin (hysteria); or (3) The patient is faking symptoms (malingering) (see Brain and Walton, 1969; Hyler and Spitzer, 1978).

Hysteria, the somatoform disorder, as you will recall from Chapter 11, was a phenomenon of fundamental importance in stimulating Freud in his development of psychoanalysis. In psychoanalytic theory, it is conceived as an unconscious defense against anxiety (a conversion symptom). In one case (Brain and Walton, 1969), a young woman was compelled to give up her work to look after her invalid mother. She developed hysterical paralysis of one hand. This had the consequence of preventing her from doing housework.

The critical features of hysterical paralysis are: the paralysis symptom, no known physical explanation, anomalous characteristics of the paralysis which make it unlikely that it is caused by neurological damage, positive evidence that the defect is caused by psychological conflict, and absence of voluntary control of the symptom (Table 19-2). Unfortunately, direct evidence of the psychological factors that have produced the symptoms is often impossible to get.

Since hysterical symptoms result from action in the brain, they would have to resemble upper rather than lower motor neuron lesions. This is because upper motor neurons are the link between the brain and the lower

Table 19-2 COMPARISON OF NEUROLOGICAL ILLNESS, HYSTERIA, AND MALINGERING

	Physical Explanation	Voluntary Control	Obvious Goal	Makes Neurological Sense
Hysteria	No	No	Sometimes	Usually no
Malingering	No	Yes	Always	Usually no
Neurological Illness	Yes	No	Never	Yes

SOURCE: Adapted from Hyler and Spitzer, 1978.

motor neurons. Therefore, a hysterical paralysis of the left hand would involve a loss of voluntary movement (Table 19-2), but with the lower motor neurons and the rest of the spinal cord intact, there would be normal reflexes and no weakness in the muscle.

There are a number of features of hysterical paralysis that "violate" basic neurological principles. For example, paralysis of the hand, or hysterical anesthesia of the hand, tends to include the whole hand, in a glove-like pattern. Neither the peripheral nerves nor the spinal roots show this distribution of innervation to the hand (Table 19-1). (This pattern could be produced by a peripheral neuropathy, but one would then see the symptoms in the feet and other hand, and could measure the neuropathy in terms of nerve conduction time.) A glove-like pattern would be exceedingly unlikely with upper motor neuron lesions. Also, in hysterical paralysis there is usually a sharp boundary between the affected area and the normal neighboring parts. In neurological damage, the border is not as well defined. In spite of these differences, the diagnosis can be difficult, especially because one often cannot find a psychological (software) process that can account for the presence of hysterical symptoms of any sort.

Malingering is like hysteria, in that it is a psychological (software) disorder, with symptoms that are anomalous with respect to neurological principles. The differences are that in malingering, the symptoms are under voluntary control, and there is always some personal goal that the symptoms serve (Table 19-2). The same problems arise as with differentiating hysteria from neurological disease. However, there is a better chance of uncovering a self-serving, conscious motive, than of uncovering the deeper and less-understood motivations underlying hysteria. Thus, if the patient is involved in a suit for damages following an automobile accident, or attempting to get early retirement, the possibility for malingering is more likely.

However difficult the diagnosis, the importance of malingering in the general understanding of abnormal psychology is that, although it overlaps in symptoms with neurological disease, it is clearly a disorder of software. It is obvious that the malingerer does not have a malformed or diseased brain. We simply have a case where a person justifies fabrication of symptoms in terms of the rewards it may bring him. He may justify it more elaborately, saying, "Everybody gets ripped off by the insurance companies, and this is my chance to get back at them. I *did* hurt my hand in the accident, and it was almost paralyzed." Clearly, the explanation of malingering is in the personal history, experiences, values, and attitudes of the patient. It will never have a meaningful neurological explanation, although, of course, the personal history is represented in the nervous system.

A DISORDER OF MEMORY: THE AMNESIC SYNDROME

We have considered the varieties of pathology that can cause disorders in language or movement of the left hand. We now turn to one specific and common disorder: the amnesic syndrome.

We are now at what will be, in but a moment, a memory. It is the continuity of our experience of our past, the idea that it is "me" who has passed through all of these experiences, the yesterdays and years ago, that is what we are. Amnesia strikes at this junction between the present and the past (see Talland, 1965; Barbizet, 1970; Rozin, 1976; Squire, 1982, for more detailed reviews of amnesia).

The Syndrome

The great nineteenth century psychologist William James divided memory into two components: primary and secondary. He said that an object in primary memory "never was lost; its date was never cut off in consciousness from that of the immediately present moment. In fact it comes to us as belonging to the rearward portion of the present space of time, and not the genuine past." From what we can tell, primary memory (which we now call short-term memory) is quite normal in amnesia. James continues: "Memory proper or secondary memory as it might be styled, is the knowledge of a former state of mind after it has already once dropped from consciousness; or rather it is the knowledge of an event, or fact, of which meantime we have not been thinking, with the additional consciousness that we have thought or experienced it before" (James, 1890, p. 648). This capacity is severely compromised in the amnesic syndrome, with respect to events that have occurred since the onset of the illness. Sergei Korsakoff (1889), one of the pioneers in the study of the pathology of memory, described the amnesic syndrome in terms of two deficits: (1) the failure to recall events of the recent past, despite a more or less normal short-term (primary) memory, and (2) the loss of a feeling of familiarity or self-reference with respect to recent experiences that are either re-presented or happen to be recalled (as they occasionally are). To convey the character of this syndrome, we will describe two case histories. The first, H.M., is probably the most studied neurological case in history and is an example of as "pure" an amnesic syndrome as has ever been described. The second case is more representative.

H.M. was a blue-collar worker suffering from severe epileptic seizures. They became progressively worse, and by age twenty-seven, he was unable to work. Neurosurgeons removed parts of both temporal lobes (the source of the seizures) to control the seizures in 1953 (Scoville and Milner, 1957). H.M. was carefully evaluated prior to the operation, and had a normal memory and an I.Q. of 112. On the return of consciousness following surgery, he could no longer recognize the hospital staff, apart from Dr. Scoville, whom he had known for many years. He could not remember or learn his way around the hospital. He could not remember important events that occurred in the few years before the surgery, such as the death of his uncle, but his early memories appeared clear and vivid. His short-term (primary) memory appeared normal, and he could carry on a normal conversation. However, he could not remember any events that occurred after his operation, once they had passed out of his direct attention (short-term memory). He did the same puzzles day after day and reread the same newspapers and magazines. Each time he learned of the death of his uncle, he became very moved, treating it as a new occurrence. H.M. is still alive. His epilepsy is under control, but he still shows the same amnesic syndrome. He is dimly aware of his father's death, which occurred some years ago. He has aged normally in appearance, but he is surprised whenever he sees himself in a mirror, since he remembers himself as he was at twenty-seven (he is now about sixty). Remarkably, H.M.'s "intelligence" remained intact; over many years his IQ did not decrease. He has some realization that he has a memory deficit. He says: "Every day is alone in itself, whatever enjoyment I've had, and whatever sorrow I've had. . . . Right now, I'm wondering, have I done or said anything amiss? You see, at this moment everything looks clear to me, but what happened just before? That's what worries me. It's like waking from a dream. I just don't remember." As you might expect, H.M. is able to remember something if he can keep it "in mind." He can retain a number, say 584, by constantly repeating it to himself, or repeatedly adding up the three digits. After being interrupted with another task for less than a minute, however, he is unable to recall either the number or the fact that he had been rehearsing it for some minutes. (Adapted from Milner, 1970.)

The second case illustrates a common type of amnesia, Korsakoff's syndrome, that results from chronic alcoholism.

> The patient, aged sixty, was admitted to the hospital with a history of excessive alcohol consumption for many years. His memory had been deteriorating, and on admission, he was amnesic and disoriented. Even though it was 1963, he said the year was 1956, and his age was fifty-two. He gave his present home address as one from which he had in fact moved five years previously. He retained practically nothing of his current experience, but otherwise (e.g., in conversation) behaved as a person of about average intelligence. He showed no appreciation of the fact that he had a memory deficit, and this deficit never improved. (Adapted from Zangwill, 1966.)

The syndrome is an extreme form of what we normally call a "bad memory," an inability to retain information: to recognize people whom one has met, to remember definitions for multiple-choice tests, to remember appointments, and the like.

Memory and Aging: Alzheimer's Disease

For the moment, let us characterize the amnesic syndrome as a failure to store experiences in memory, that is, a failure to enter the items from short-term into long-term (secondary) memory. The forgetfulness of old age is typically an inability to remember recent events. Short-term memory and memories of the distance past are relatively intact.

Although in normal aging the symptoms do not develop into a full amnesic syndrome, the most common cause of the amnesic syndrome is probably *dementia,* a progressive loss of higher mental functions, usually in old age. Whether or not dementia should be viewed as accelerated or pathological aging, it is a disease of major proportions. About 15 percent of adults over sixty-four years of age suffer from this disorder, and about one-third of these people are severely handicapped (Terry and Davies, 1980). The beginning of this decline is sometimes seen in people in their fifties. About half of all people diagnosed as demented are considered to have *Alzheimer's disease.* Here is a case of Alzheimer's disease with early onset:

> A fifty-two-year old taxi driver is admitted to the hospital because of progressive failing memory. He has been a taxi driver in Philadelphia for the past twenty years. Approximately nine months ago, he first noted some difficulty in remembering certain street names and localities. . . . Three months ago, he was unable to find his way to the airport. . . . The patient has also become easily confused in giving change to customers and in remembering routine tasks such as maintenance of his automobile. Occasionally, he becomes withdrawn and seems depressed. He

shows less concern for his personal grooming and belongings. For the past two weeks, he has been unable to drive his taxi and remains home sitting in a chair. . . . The family has brought him to the hospital because they can no longer handle him.

In the hospital, he speaks only when spoken to and answers in single words or simple sentences. . . . The patient's attention span is very short, and he cannot recall three simple objects that are described to him after five minutes. (University of Pennsylvania Case Study, 1976)

Alzheimer's disease has a gradual onset, with loss of initiative and forgetfulness often the initial symptoms. Different symptoms predominate in different patients. In many patients, an amnesic syndrome will be the prominent symptom; in other patients, language disorders are the primary symptom (Schwartz, 1983). The disease progressively worsens, producing more and more severe deficits in more and more systems. Over a period that ranges from a few years to ten years, severe deterioration of intellectual and basic maintenance functions, and death, will result. Recently, a distinctive brain pathology has been identified in Alzheimer patients: malformations of neurons and loss of cells in a number of areas of the nervous system (Figure 19-13). A biochemical deficit has also been identified: an abnormality in the level of an enzyme that is critical in the synthesis of acetylcholine, a major brain neurotransmitter (Coyle, Price, and DeLong, 1983). The number of malformed neurons and the degree of the neurotransmitter deficit are related to the degree of dementia. Neural malformations are particularly common in the hippocampus, an area that we know is involved in memory formation. Furthermore, studies on both animals and humans have shown that brain deficits in acetylcholine are related to defective memory.

Precipitating Events: A Vulnerable System

The memory "systems" whose damage causes the amnesic syndrome are *the* prime example of vulnerable systems. The range of pathological agents that can produce the syndrome is astounding. In addition to the usual causes of specific neurological syndromes (strokes, tumors, etc.), a variety of

Figure 19-13

Photomicrograph of brain tissue from the cortex of a normal patient (A), and a patient with Alzheimer's disease (B). Note the small number of senile plaques (the darker areas) in the normal patient, and the larger number of plaques in the Alzheimer patient. (Source: Blessed, Tomlinsun, and Roth, 1968)

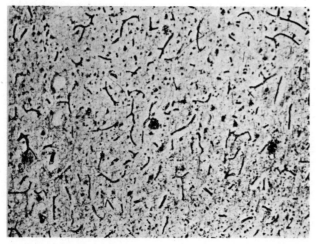

A

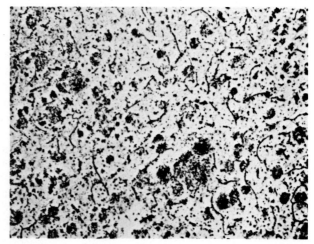

B

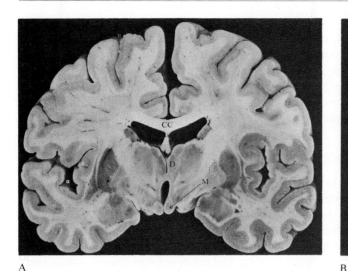

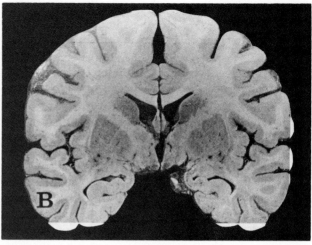

A   B

Figure 19-14
Normal brain compared to Korsakoff brain. The brain sections are made in a plane that would separate the body into the front and back. (A) A section from a normal brain. Arrows indicate the mammillary bodies *(M)* and also indicate the location of the dorsomedial nucleus of the thalamus *(D)*, a structure frequently damaged in Korsakoff's psychosis. For purposes of orientation, the corpus callosum is also labeled *(CC)*. (Source: Ghuhbegovic and Williams, 1980) *(B)* A section from a Korsakoff brain. Notice the damage to the mammillary bodies of the thalamus in this patient with Korsakoff's psychosis. (Source: Victor, Adams, and Collins, 1971)

generally harmful agents can cause amnesia. For example, infections can produce amnesia: when the herpes simplex virus attacks the nervous system, it seems to have a predilection for a few structures, including the hippocampus. Toxins and nutritional deficiencies can also cause amnesia. The Korsakoff syndrome, probably the second most common cause of amnesia (after Alzheimer's disease), is a result of chronic alcoholism. Many researchers believe that the damage to the brain in this case is caused by a nutritional deficiency. Chronic alcoholics get a good portion of their calories from alcohol, an essentially vitamin-free food source. They sometimes develop a deficiency in vitamin B1 (thiamine), a critical component of metabolic processes in all cells of the body. It is believed that, for some reason, a few groups of cells in the memory system are particularly vulnerable to this deficiency, and they are the first to be destroyed (Figure 19-14). Note that the vulnerability of this system to specific viruses, toxins, and deficiencies argues for specific biochemical properties of the cells in this system.

A concussion or other severe damage to the skull, as often happens in automobile accidents, and occasionally in sports and other activities, not infrequently produces a (usually transient) amnesic syndrome. Amnesia rarely occurs unless there was loss of consciousness. In some of the cases where consciousness is lost, the patient, on awakening, shows a full-blown amnesic syndrome, with no other symptoms. In almost all cases, there is a loss of memory for the accident, as well as a loss of memory for the period of seconds to minutes prior to the accident. There is also an inability to remember events after the accident. This may continue for minutes to years. In most cases, the patient recovers completely, and remains amnesic for only a short period of seconds or minutes before the accident, and for a longer period after the event (Russell, 1958; Barbizet, 1970). A similar, though usually shorter-lasting syndrome is observed in the clinic in patients given electroconvulsive therapy (electric current passed across their skull, throwing their brain into a temporary convulsion), as a treatment for depression (Cohen and Squire, 1981; see Chapter 13).

The fact that head trauma and electric shocks to the head often produce an acute and fairly pure amnesia suggests extreme vulnerability. The most delicate system is what breaks when a piece of complicated equipment or a brain is jarred. We do not know the source of this vulnerability. It could be that memory "formation" is vulnerable because it requires rapid protein synthesis. Animal memory formation is specifically disrupted by drugs that interfere with protein synthesis in *all* cells. Perhaps there is a "weak link" in the system, a place where everything comes together in the brain and that is poorly located in terms of blood supply or that is subject to compression when the skull is struck.

The Anatomy of the Amnesic Syndrome

Although we don't understand the process of memory formation, there are clear relations between a set of interconnected brain structures and amnesic syndromes (Victor, Adams, and Collins, 1971). In most cases of the Korsakoff syndrome, there is bilateral (both sides) damage to the mammillary bodies and the dorsomedial nucleus of the thalamus (Figure 19-14). In cases resulting from surgery, viral attacks, and other sources, there is often bilateral damage to the hippocampus, in the temporal lobe. Most critically, in cases of damage to the temporal lobes in which memory is spared, there is not bilateral damage to the hippocampus (Milner, 1972).

The fact that bilateral damage must occur to produce the full syndrome explains why the syndrome is more common after general insults to the brain, toxins, deficiencies, infections, or degenerative processes. All of these agents either operate on the brain as a whole, or they would attack both sides of the brain simultaneously. In contrast, tumors, strokes, and externally induced wounds almost always occur in one continuous spatial location, and hence they are not likely to produce corresponding damage on both sides.

Careful analysis of patients with damage to the critical structures on only one side (usually, people with damage to one hippocampus) reveals a more limited memory deficit, of just the type one would predict given the specialized functions of the two hemispheres. Left temporal damage (in right-handers, of course) leads to an amnesic type of syndrome primarily for verbal materials, and right temporal damage leads to deficits in memory for visual and other forms of "nonverbal" memory (Milner, 1972).

Description of the Memory Deficit

The nature of the memory defect in the amnesic syndrome has been explored in great detail because the issue of whether short- and long-term memory are separate entities is of central importance in the psychology of memory. The basic features of the syndrome are:

1. More or less normal short-term memory. This is often measured as "digit span," the number of digits a person can remember immediately after he hears them.

2. Severe deficits in recall of items from recent experience since the onset of disease (called **anterograde amnesia**). This faulty recall occurs even for material that was just mastered if the patient is briefly occupied with another task for less than a minute. (This presumably clears the first task out of short-term memory.)

3. Lack of a sense of familiarity ("I've seen it before") when re-presented with recently experienced events.

4. Loss of recall and a sense of familiarity often occurs for a period prior to the onset of disease. This is called a ***retrograde amnesia***. When someone has a slow onset disease (e.g., senile dementia), it is impossible to determine whether their amnesia is truly retrograde. In cases of amnesia produced by head trauma or surgery, however, there is no question about the onset of the memory defect, and there is often a retrograde amnesia. The retrograde amnesia typically runs back in time from the onset of the illness, and it covers recent events (days, months, years), but not early events of life. This is crudely assessed by asking a patient who the President is; sometimes he will give a name a few Presidents back in time, and he will know all the Presidents up to that President, but no further. Football players, after concussion injury on the field, sometimes show temporary retrograde amnesia for the prior events in the game, or in some cases, longer periods. One professional quarterback, following a head injury on the field, returned to the huddle and called plays that came from his previous team; he showed temporary retrograde amnesia for the period in which he had learned his new team's plays.

5. A severely amnesic patient has no recall of events that occurred even a few minutes ago, but he often has some type of memory of them. Some ten years ago, for example the author discussed baseball in the 1950s at some length with a Korsakoff patient. The patient had no recall of baseball players of the last five years or so, but he could list the line-up for the Brooklyn Dodgers in the early 1950s. After discussing each player with him for a while, in a conversation lasting some ten minutes, the author changed the subject for about thirty seconds. He then asked the patient what had just been discussed. The patient had no idea, and he recalled nothing. The author then suggested that it was baseball, and he suggested that the patient name some of the players that were being discussed. The patient claimed to have no idea of what had been discussed. When encouraged to guess, however, he came up with the very names of the players under discussion (e.g., Jackie Robinson, Pee Wee Reese). This is a commonly observed phenomenon in amnesics. There is also laboratory evidence for a record of events in the recent past. For example, when asked to remember a series of words, like *metal* or *carpet,* after a brief delay, amnesics failed miserably. But when prompted with partial cues (e.g., *met-* or *car-*) they guessed the words quite accurately, although they claimed no sense of familiarity with the words they uttered (Warrington and Weiskrantz, 1973). These findings suggest that although recall is severely impaired in amnesics, with certain kinds of prompts ("cued" recall), they can perform rather well.

6. Some types of learning and memory are preserved in amnesics. Acquired skills are an example. Amnesics do not show retrograde amnesia for even recently acquired skills like typing, and they can be taught new skills, such as making drawings while looking in a mirror (Milner, 1972). There is also some evidence that they can remember the emotional component of an experience. In the classic case, an amnesic was pricked by a pin while shaking hands with her doctor (Claparède, 1911). On their subsequent meeting, the amnesic withdrew her hand when the doctor offered to shake it. The patient could not explain why she did this, but she felt a negative emotion. It has not been possible to neatly describe those types of memory that are spared nor why they are spared. Perhaps skills and emotional memories are laid down at lower levels in the brain, and hence they are less vulnerable.

Table 19–3 ASPECTS OF AMNESIA EXPLAINED BY TWO THEORIES OF AMNESIA

Aspects of Amnesia	Consolidation Block	Retrieval Defect
1. Normal short-term memory	Yes	Yes
2. Anterograde amnesia	Yes	Yes
3. Lack of sense of familiarity	Yes	No
4. Retrograde amnesia	No*	No*
5. Cued recall of "lost" memories	No	Yes
6. Preserved perceptuomotor and other memories	Yes**	Yes**

*Consolidation block would predict no retrograde amnesia (loss of memories from before illness), while retrieval would predict retrograde amnesia for all memories. However, retrograde amnesia usually occurs only for memories in the period seconds to years prior to illness.

**Both theories hold that this type of learning (memory) is not affected by the proposed defective process.

Theories of Amnesia

There are a number of theories that attempt to explain the amnesic symptoms mentioned above. The most straightforward theory is **consolidation block** (Milner, 1972). This holds that the basic deficit is in the formation (consolidation) of new long-term memories. Thus, the process that permanently stores short-term memories is defective. This view clearly captures the salient symptoms of amnesia: poor recall and lack of a sense of familiarity. It also explains anterograde amnesia (see Table 19-3). But it has trouble explaining retrograde amnesia; after all, these memories were already in long-term memory before the illness. Why can't they be recalled? It also cannot explain cued recall; if no recent memories are formed, how can a cue word cause the subject to guess the right word?

An alternative theory holds that the disorder is not in storing memories, but in retrieving them (Warrington and Weiskrantz, 1973). **Retrieval failure** clearly explains poor recent memory (Table 19-3), and it explains the cued recall effect that puzzles adherents of consolidation theory. Cues are aids to retrieval; the memory is there, but it is hard to extract; the cue narrows down the field. Retrieval theory, however, has difficulty explaining the lack of a sense of familiarity. Once an item is retrieved, why should it lose its sense of being part of the subject's past? And although retrieval theory can explain retrograde amnesia (as consolidation cannot), it cannot explain a basic feature of retrograde amnesia. A retrieval deficit view would hold that all memories would be hard to recover. And yet, retrograde amnesia occurs very little, if at all, in some cases of severe anterograde amnesia. When it does occur, it usually covers only the previous minutes to years. Why should the old memories be intact if there is a retrieval deficit?

It is possible that both types of deficits are present, but that neither storage nor retrieval is completely destroyed. We should also note that a partial consolidation deficit would produce a problem in retrieval. If one stored a very impoverished version of an event, there would be fewer cues for retrieval. If a poor consolidation mechanism can only store frequently repeated events, it would not be able to record the time of occurrence of the daily flow of experience, because these occurrences are unique. The amnesic brain might have some dim record of a particular face seen over and over again, but it certainly would not record that this was the face seen two minutes ago, since that happened only once. It is possible to explain more of the symptoms with this assumption (Rozin, 1976). Only retrograde amnesia poses a problem for this view.

The Treatment of Amnesia

The amnesias produced by head trauma typically recover completely, and the main function of medical treatment is to keep the patient alive during the acute phase of the illness. Occasional cases caused by tumors or infections may be treated surgically or with drugs, with possible alleviation of some symptoms. At this time, however, there is no treatment that will arrest or slow down the degeneration of neurons that causes the senile amnesias.

Memory disorders can be treated as problems in living. Family members can accommodate to and compensate for some of the problems. Adjustments in living and working conditions can be made. Sometimes, memory tricks or simply writing notes on a pad can help. We must remember, there is a little amnesia in all of us. As we grow older, it becomes more severe in most people. Intelligent people compensate in their life style and in the memory supports or crutches they develop for themselves. This is graphically illustrated by a study that compared memory in sixty- to seventy-year-old University of Toronto alumni and current University of Toronto students (Moscovitch, 1982). Subjects from each age group were told they were participating in a study of memory, and that the task was simply to remember to call a particular phone number on a particular day and at a particular time (some weeks ahead), simply leaving their name. All agreed to do it. About half of the students failed to call, whereas almost all of the older group remembered to call. It appears that at least part of the result is due to different approaches to remembering. The students (subjects were interviewed after the study) were confident they would remember the task, and they made no special effort to remind themselves. The older people thought they would forget, and they wrote the date down in their date books, put notes by the phone, and so on. Old age would be a lot less tolerable if these compensations did not occur.

Amnesia: Hardware and Software

There are also amnesias that originate in the software: these are the hysterical or dissociative amnesias, including multiple personalities. In these cases, there is often a history of psychological disturbance, along with an absence in the history or clinical examination of any signs of neurological damage. In both hardware and software amnesias, learned skills tend to remain intact, and personal memories are most affected. The retrograde amnesia in functional amnesias, however, tends to extend back into childhood, whereas people with the neurologically based amnesic syndrome rarely forget their childhood or their name unless they are at the end of a long period of senile degeneration and have lost the ability for intelligent performance on any task.

The organically based amnesic syndrome has illustrated many basic principles of the function of the nervous system: specificity in anatomy and biochemistry, vulnerability, hierarchy (in the sparing of perceptuomotor learning), the left-right distinction in the verbal versus spatial and visual memory deficits after damage to one side of the brain. The syndrome is organic because clear brain damage has been demonstrated in amnesia resulting from most agents, and it is presumed to have occurred in other cases (e.g., after head trauma). Like many other hardware disorders of the nervous system, however, we know a great deal about the amnesic syndrome, but we have no effective way of treating it.

THE TREATMENT OF DISEASES OF THE NERVOUS SYSTEM

The prognosis and treatment of diseases of the nervous system are determined in large part by some of the basic principles we stated at the beginning of this chapter: the inability to make new neurons, the possibility for damaged neurons to recover, the principle of redundancy. The course and effectiveness of treatment depend on the nature of the disease process, the spatial extent of the pathology (generalized or highly localized), and the specific location of the pathology (whether it is accessible to surgery, for example) (Adams and Victor, 1981).

Many neurological symptoms are produced by damage to, but not destruction of neurons. Such reversible damage can be produced by lowered oxygen and nutrient supply (resulting from atherosclerosis or lung disease), acute pressure (produced by swelling of the brain after head trauma, infection, or a tumor that impedes circulation of cerebrospinal fluid). Since damaged or nutrient-deprived neurons can recover, intervention can produce a cure. This would be the case for infections, which can be treated with antibiotics, for acute cases of high intracranial pressure, which can be relieved by draining some of the fluid, or for certain tumors, which can be removed. Since the nervous system has some ability to repair itself, a large part of the treatment of some acute disorders is simply keeping the patient alive, to allow his nervous system to recover from the shock of trauma. Partial recovery from strokes occurs for this reason. However, for most of the degenerative diseases, as well as many of the cases of stroke or hemorrhage, there is little that can be done that would constitute a cure.

A second line of treatment, when cure is impossible, is to take medical measures to contain the problem or to treat the symptoms. The use of L-DOPA to replace the deficit in the amount of neurotransmitter in the basal ganglia in Parkinson's disease is an example of this. The drug does not cure the disease, but it reduces symptoms such as tremor.

The situation of many people with neurological damage can be improved by restructuring their patterns of living, usually with the help of their family or those who care for them. Because of the redundancy principle, it is sometimes possible to teach them ways around their deficit: Braille for the blind, memo pads for those with bad memories, etc. Family members can compensate for deficits by taking over or assisting in those functions that are compromised. And, more and more, specific devices, from wheelchairs to minicomputers, are becoming available that compensate for deficits.

When a patient is referred to a neurologist, he is often anxious, because he doesn't want to have a disease of the nervous system (a "psychological" disorder is preferable, to most people). In fact, much of what neurologists do is to discover that common neurological symptoms (e.g., tingling of the fingers, muscle twitches, headaches) are *not* indicative of diseases of the nervous system. Although the symptoms may be early signs of neurological disease, they are often either software problems, or minor disorders of unknown origin that will neither progress nor seriously compromise the life of the patient. In other words, some patients leave the care of the neurologist cured, some leave improved, some cannot be helped, and quite a few leave with the confidence that there is really nothing serious that is wrong with them.

For the moment, the triumph of neurology is in diagnosis, which is a precise science and a high art. It is a frustration to the neurologist that she can understand many disease processes, but she cannot cure them. It is much more common to have understanding without successful treatment in neurology than psychology. But although we know more about the hardware, we still have only limited abilities to repair it, and none to replace it. Thus, the ultimate prospects for repairing disorders in the software (clinical psychology and psychiatry) are probably better than those for repairing the hardware. Therefore, from the point of view of treatment, it is neither good nor bad that a particular disorder, like schizophrenia or depression, is found to have a biological basis. Sometimes this opens up the use of a wide range of therapeutic approaches such as drugs, but often the neurologist is helpless in the face of known pathology of the nervous system.

Because of rapid advances in neuroscience, the prospects for successful treatment of more diseases of the nervous system are very good. The steady stream of important findings on neurotransmitters and on the operation of the immune system, as well as surgical innovations, have already made some impact on neurology. And at this time, the most dramatic cures of disorders of behavior and the mind come from the neurologist and neurosurgeon, not from the psychologists and psychiatrists.

HARDWARE AND SOFTWARE: THE NERVOUS SYSTEM AND SOCIETY

Throughout this book, we have struggled with the concept of mental illness. The biomedical model offered a solution, in part by harnessing the greater knowledge and success of the more developed branches of medicine. The isolation of clear pathology in the nervous system underlying psychopathology makes us more comfortable about using the term "illness." Turning back to our computer metaphor, it is easier to use the term "illness," or "broken," when there is a problem in the hardware. But, although there are clear-cut cases of brain pathology in which basic human abilities are compromised, the borderline between normal variation in neural function and pathology is as elusive as the borderline between abnormal and normal behaviors.

Consider left-handedness. It has a clear biological basis, since it is an inherited characteristic. Left-handers as a group show different patterns of brain lateralization than right-handers (Levy, 1980). The verbal hemisphere of left-handers cannot be accurately predicted from their handedness; for about half, the more verbal hemisphere is on the right. Furthermore, left-handers as a group show less differentiation in the capacities of their two hemispheres; one result of this is that they suffer less damage to language function after strokes affecting one of their hemispheres.

Left-handers are a minority group, living in world designed for right-handers. Though there are some situations (e.g., baseball) where left-handedness is an advantage, it is fair to describe left-handedness as an inconvenience in our society, but hardly an illness. And yet, just two generations ago, left-handedness was considered a really undesirable feature, both because it was deviant and because it was thought to be related to cognitive and personality defects. (The technical word for left-hander, *sinistral*, comes from the same root as the word sinister; the word for right-hander, *dextral*, comes from the same root as dextrous, that is, well coordinated.) At one time, in schools and homes all over the country, genetically left-handed children were forced to favor their right hand in sports, writing, and other daily activities. We are not certain whether this had any negative effects on the developing cerebral organization of the left-handers of these generations, but it certainly must have made their lives much more difficult. Moreover, at that time, since left-handedness was considered socially undesirable, and hence maladaptive, and since it had a definite neurological basis, it was hard to resist labeling it as a neurological disease.

The changing view of left-handedness shows that whether or not a software or hardware difference straddles the line between normal and abnormal depends on cultural values. This point is so basic, that we will consider another example. Many neurological disorders result in an inability to read, called *alexia*. This symptom, in our literate society, can be crippling. Today, reading ability is almost a prerequisite to success. One hundred years ago, however, literacy was a capacity pretty much reserved to an economically and culturally privileged few. At that time, society was not built around the assumption of literacy, as ours is today (with its street signs, bus destination signs, and so on). Thus, an alexic would not be considered "sick" in such a system, or even in a contemporary culture that had widespread illiteracy. Furthermore, different writing systems, produced by different cultures, make different cognitive demands on the reader, and hence engage different brain mechanisms. The English alphabet is a writing system built on the sounds of speech, while the Chinese writing system is not. As a result, there is relatively more reliance on left hemisphere speech mechanisms in reading English than in reading Chinese. Thus, there is generally a more severe compromise of reading ability due to left hemisphere lesions in readers of

English. The point again is that cultural institutions increase the importance of certain skills, and decrease the importance of others. Reading disability is crippling in our society, and physical weakness is not. The reverse is true in hunting societies.

People don't like complexity; they like simple explanations. But biology, culture, and individual experience operate together to make us what we are, whether normal or abnormal. We can't avoid this fact, and therefore we must try to make sense of the interaction of these various parts of the whole. We must recognize that there are fundamental differences between hardware (organic) and software (functional) disorders, and yet that there are many pathologies that are difficult to classify in one or the other category. We must recognize that whether deviance in hardware or software is considered an illness depends to a significant degree on cultural values. And in the context of the study of abnormal psychology, we must appreciate the importance of organic factors, as background for the expression of functional disorders, as a cause of psychopathology, and as represented in the very sophisticated medical discipline of neurology.

SUMMARY

1. Although all mental illnesses are in some sense represented in the nervous system, one group of these illnesses can be traced to specific defects in the structure or function of the nervous system. This group, which can be thought of as organic disorders (involving "hardware"), falls in the domain of neurologists, while the remaining functional disorders (involving "software") fall in the domain of psychologists and psychiatrists.

2. Basic principles of the structure and function of the nervous system can account for many organic syndromes.

3. Principles of synaptic physiology and the action of neurotransmitters account for a number of disorders, including some types of depression.

4. Disorders in the supportive tissue of the brain account for many disorders, including multiple sclerosis.

5. The spatial and biochemical organization of the nervous system accounts for the fact that damage at specific sites or by specific toxins produces specific and distinctive symptoms.

6. The lateral organization of the brain explains why damage to the left hemisphere often produces verbal deficits, while damage to the right hemisphere often leads to disorders in spatial representation.

7. The hierarchical organization of the nervous system explains how similar symptoms can be produced by damage at different levels of the nervous system.

8. The fact that balance among various centers in the nervous system is produced by inhibition explains the appearance of symptoms by release of inhibition from a damaged area.

9. The principle of redundancy and the fact that damaged neurons can recover account for the fact that there is often some recovery from damage to the nervous system.

10. Some parts of the nervous system, such as parts involved in the formation of memories, are particularly vulnerable to damage. As a result, specific symptoms may result from general trauma to the nervous system, as in exposure to toxins or blows to the head.

11. The principles of vulnerability and hierarchy explain why higher functions are more susceptible to damage, and why, in senile dementia, there is progressive deterioration moving from higher functions like thinking to lower functions, like habitual acts.

12. There are many causes of diseases of the nervous system, including nutrient deficiencies, strokes, degenerative diseases, and head trauma. The symptoms of damage can be negative (a deficit) or positive (an increase in activity, resulting from irritability or release of inhibition).

13. The diagnosis of damage to the nervous system is a well-developed science and art, based on history of the disorder, current symptoms, and highly sophisticated techniques that allow direct measurement of events going on inside the brain.

14. Disorders of language can be subdivided in terms of whether reception, comprehension, or production of language is primarily affected. They illustrate two principles of spatial organization of the brain: (1) left-right specialization (language functions on the left), and (2) the control of motor functions in the front of the brain, and perceptual functions in the back of the brain, since *receptive aphasias* result from lesions near the back of the brain and *expressive aphasias* result from lesions near the front.

15. Disorders of action illustrate the principle of hierarchy, and the fact that our understanding of the mapping of the nervous structure onto behavior is much more precise for the lower parts of the nervous system. Damage to peripheral nerves, the spinal cord, or the motor cortex produces specific and distinctive patterns of movement deficit. Damage to the frontal or parietal lobes produces disorders (apraxias) in the organization of movements, with no disturbance in the action of individual muscles. The higher the damage in the hierarchy of control, the more the damage affects movements or their sequences, rather than specific muscles.

16. Hysterical disorders of movement usually take the form of hysterical paralysis, and they resemble the symptoms of lower levels of damage more than the apraxias. Software disorders, either hysterical or malingering, can usually be distinguished from cases of organic damage, in part because the former do not show a pattern of deficit that makes sense in terms of the structure of the nervous system.

17. The most common disorder of memory, the amnesic syndrome, most frequently results from aging (senile dementia, such as *Alzheimer's disease*) or chronic alcoholism *(Korsakoff's psychosis)*. The major feature of the amnesic syndrome is the inability to recall recent events. This defect seems to be caused by some combination of a defect in storing and retrieving new memories. The symptoms result from damage to a few particularly vulnerable areas of the brain, on both sides.

18. Because new neurons rarely, if ever, arise in adult humans, the prospects for treatment of neurological illness are limited. However, recovery occurs because damaged neurons can recover. In addition, symptoms can be treated by drugs and by teaching the patient strategies that help him to

minimize deficits. These strategies often involve enlisting the help of friends or family, and/or special devices such as wheelchairs.

19. Although there is a fundamental distinction between organic and functional disorders, the line between them is often hazy. Furthermore, functional problems interact with organic problems, and culture often determines whether a particular neurological abnormality should be considered a disease.

Part IX

ABNORMALITY, THE LAW, AND CHOOSING A PSYCHOTHERAPIST

CHAPTER

20

The Law and Politics of Abnormality

UNTIL now, we have examined psychological distress from the vantage point of researchers and clinicians, concentrating on the causes of, and remedies for, individual psychological suffering. In this chapter, we shift our focus to society and examine how society reacts to the psychological suffering of its members. We will concentrate on the mechanisms society uses to protect its members from psychological suffering and its consequences, mechanisms that find expression in the laws regarding involuntary and criminal commitment. In exercising these legal powers, society has to make difficult and often painful choices between its own needs, and the rights and freedom of its individual members. Those choices concern us here.

In addition to the issues associated with involuntary and criminal commitment, we will discuss two kinds of abuse of abnormal psychology. First, we will look at how a state or government abuses what we know about psychology and psychiatry by removing dissident (but sane) individuals or groups from society, or controlling their behavior. Second, we will look at a more general problem: the stigma that is cast over an individual when that individual is labeled "mentally ill." In any profession, there are often conflicts between the requirements of practice and those of society. The practice of psychology and psychiatry is no exception.

INVOLUNTARY COMMITMENT

No societal response to psychological suffering has received more attention during the past decade than has *involuntary commitment,* the process whereby the state hospitalizes people for their own good, and even over their vigorous protest. In effect, the state acts as parent to those who have "lost their senses," doing for them what they might do for themselves if they had their wits about them. Consider the following situations in which the state might seek to involuntarily commit an individual, and in which most people would agree that the state is right in doing so:

· As the result of a toxic psychosis, a young man wants to throw himself from the roof of a tall building. In twenty-four hours, both the impulse and the psychosis will have passed—if he is restrained now.

· A young man is despondent over the termination of his first love. To him, there is currently no alternative to suicide. A month from now, even sooner, he may think differently.

· An attorney is overcome by irrational guilt. She calls two of her clients and informs them that she has not handled their cases properly, and that she has stolen from them. Of course, this is untrue. She would have called the rest of her clients had the state, through her family, not intervened and hospitalized her against her will.

· Following the birth of two previous children, a woman suffered a post-partum depression, and attempted to murder the infants. She is about to give birth again, and is experiencing the same impulse. To protect those young lives, the state hospitalizes the mother involuntarily.

For most people, these cases are compelling arguments for involuntary hospitalization. Where there is clear-cut danger to self or to others, most people agree that some kind of intervention is necessary. But most cases are not nearly so clear-cut as these. Indeed, many cases test the very meanings of normality and abnormality that were discussed in Chapter 1. Abnormal by whose standard? Recall that some people believe themselves depressed for good reason, but "society" finds them "mentally ill" and in need of treatment. Others enjoy the relaxation and "highs" conferred by recreational drugs, yet society views them as addicts who require psychiatric attention. Still others radically alter their life styles on discovering a "true religion," but society may designate that discovery as psychotic and commit the discoverer to a psychiatric facility. *Mayock* v. *Martin** illustrated this issue well:

Mr. Mayock was hospitalized in July, 1944, after he had removed his right eye. He was subsequently diagnosed paranoid schizophrenic, eventually released on probation, and finally discharged three years later. Three days after discharge, Mayock removed his right hand, and was committed once again to the state hospital. At the time of trial, some twenty years later, Mayock was still confined involuntarily to the state hospital with the diagnosis of paranoid schizophrenia.

At his trial, Mayock insisted that there was nothing mysterious or crazy about his self-maimings. Rather, he is a deeply religious man who believes that society's attempts to establish peace by force are entirely misguided. God's way, he says, is to encourage peace through love. If society continues on its present path, many lives will be lost through war. Mayock believes that one man has been chosen to make a peace offering to God; that he, Mayock, is that man; and that it is better for one person to accept a message from God to sacrifice an eye or a hand than it is for society to suffer a great loss of human life.

During the twenty years that he had been hospitalized, Mayock had had complete freedom of the hospital grounds: He had not once maimed himself. Yet, he acknowledged that he would gladly do so again either as a significant freewill offering or in response to divine revelation.

Beyond this single symptom, there was no further evidence that Mayock was disturbed. He had risen to a position of considerable responsibility in the hospital,

* Mayock v. Martin, 157 Conn, 56, 245 A.2d 574 (1968).

running the recreation center for parole-privileged patients, as well as the hospital news stand. There was ample evidence that he could handle financial matters and take care of himself in all other respects.

Psychiatrists at the hospital contended that his prophetic view of himself was "grandiose," that his religious beliefs were "grossly false," and that the diagnosis of paranoid schizophrenic was entirely warranted by the facts. Mayock contended that he is religious, not mentally ill, and that his First Amendment constitutional rights ("Congress shall make no law respecting an establishment of religion or prohibiting the free exercise thereof . . .") had been violated.

Mayock lost. Some will feel that he should have lost, for only the truly mad would gouge out their eyes and chop off their arms. Others will feel that Mayock's loss is tragic, for he was acting with courage upon deeply held religious beliefs and harming no one but himself. Perhaps the tragedy lies in that ambiguity, for Mayock can be seen as quite abnormal by some standards, and not abnormal at all by others. Given a large area of doubt, how did it happen that he was involuntarily hospitalized, and for so long? In order to understand Mayock's case, as well as literally thousands of other commitments that occur involuntarily, we need to know something about the laws that regulate commitment procedures. Our focus will be on laws in the United States.

PROCEDURES TO COMMIT

Commitment Requirements

States differ enormously in the procedures that are used to commit people, and in the safeguards those procedures provide. All states require that the individual be suffering from a ***psychological disability,*** variously termed "mental illness," "mental disease," or "mental disability." But often these phrases are not specifically defined, leaving unclear which disabilities qualify and which do not.

In addition to psychological disability, all states stipulate that the individual must meet additional requirements. While these requirements vary from state to state, they require that one or more of the following "incapacitating conditions" must arise from the psychological disability: impaired judgments, need for treatment, behavioral disability, dangerousness, and danger to self. We will examine each in turn.

IMPAIRED JUDGMENT.   The person is so distressed that he does not recognize the need for hospitalization. Mayock could well have qualified for commitment under such a requirement since in the view of his psychiatrists, he was blind to his need for hospitalization.

NEED FOR TREATMENT.   The need for treatment often serves to qualify what is meant by mental disability. Thus, the state of Virginia defines a commitable person as one who is "afflicted with mental disease to an extent that . . . he requires care and treatment.*

But however humane the "need for treatment" statute may seem, experi-

In the movie *Frances*, Jessica Lange depicts Frances Farmer, whose involuntary commitment was based on "impaired judgment." Here Frances is being left in the sanitarium by her mother who has just committed her. (Courtesy The Museum of Modern Art/Film Stills Archive)

* Va. Code Ann. SS37. 1–67, 37.1.1 (Supp. 1973).

ence with it has demonstrated that this approach can have some surprisingly untoward consequences, as the case of Emily Bronson reveals.

> Emily Bronson, a widow, suffered two delusions: The first, that the restaurant at which she frequently ate, poisoned her food; and the second, that men were constantly planning sexual assaults upon her. These delusions were mild and harmless, and she continued to eat at the same restaurant, and her behavior with men seemed unaffected by these concerns. Her friends knew of her delusions, but they seemed to cause them or her no difficulty.
>
> One day Mrs. Bronson fell and injured her hip. She was brought to the emergency ward of a nearby hospital where she remained for several days during which time she spoke of her delusions. In this wholly fortuitous manner she was perceived as a paranoid schizophrenic who needed treatment and was transferred to a psychiatric hospital just as soon as her hip improved. Subsequently, she was involuntarily committed to a county facility where she remained for five years before she saw an attorney. During that time, the hospital ordered her estate to pay for her psychiatric hospitalization. (Brooks, 1974, p. 655)

BEHAVIORAL DISABILITY.   An increasing number of states require evidence that the individual's psychological disability results in serious behavioral disability. California, for example, defines such disability as "a condition in which a person, as a result of a mental disorder, is unable to provide for his basic personal needs for food, clothing or shelter."*

DANGEROUSNESS TO OTHERS.   Many states require that there be some evidence that the individual is dangerous, either to himself or to others. And indeed, more involuntary hospitalizations are justified on these grounds than on any others. In some state statutes, the definition of dangerousness is vague. Florida, for example, provides for commitment when the person is "likely to injure himself or others if not hospitalized."† Illinois, on the other hand, is much more explicit: a psychologically disordered person can be hospitalized if he "is reasonably expected at the time the determination is being made or within a reasonable time thereafter to intentionally physically injure himself or other persons . . .' "‡

But regardless of how carefully or vaguely it is defined, two serious problems arise from the notion of dangerousness, one legal and the other scientific. The legal problem is straightforward. Incarcerating people because they are *predicted* to be dangerous creates a dilemma because Western legal traditions generally mandate the deprivation of liberty only *after* a crime has been committed, not before. The mere fact that someone is expected to violate law is not sufficient reason for incarceration.

This legal problem has painful ramifications, for involuntary commitments are not entirely unlike imprisonment insofar as deprivation of liberty is concerned. Yet, few of the procedures that protect an alleged criminal defendant are available to the psychologically distressed who have been predicted to be violent. The latter can be involuntarily hospitalized on an emergency basis for as little as twenty-four hours (in Georgia) to as long as thirty days (in Oklahoma), entirely without a trial or judge, and often on the

Many involuntary hospitalizations occur when an individual is judged to be dangerous to himself or others. Would this man be a candidate for involuntary commitment? (Photograph by Charles Gatewood)

* California Welfare and Institutions Code Sec. 5008.
† Florida Stat. Ann. Sec. 394.367 (1973).
‡ Ill. Ann. Stat. Ch. 91 1/2, Sec. 1–11, 8–1 (Supp. 1973–74).

allegation of a spouse or friend. In some jurisdictions, hospitalization can be extended indefinitely, simply on the word of a physician who deems the individual in need of further observation or treatment. And even when the matter is subjected to judicial review, the courts often rubber-stamp the physician's view, on the grounds that the hospitalization is being undertaken with the patient's best interests in mind. Thus, at many such judicial reviews, the patient need not be present, and commonly is not afforded an attorney. Many writers, and especially psychiatrist Thomas Szasz (1963), see in the involuntary commitment process an enormous and needless abuse of constitutional protection. Yet, no "plot" to deprive the patients of their rights to due process is intended in these procedures. Rather, because patients are held to be "sick," and because they are being sent to a hospital, the ordinary protections of criminal law are deemed unnecessary.

The scientific problems inherent in the prediction of dangerousness are as difficult as the legal problems. There is reason to doubt whether dangerousness can ever be predicted so precisely that only the dangerous will be hospitalized, while the not dangerous will not be. Psychological tests are just not as reliable as we would like. A variety of studies indicate that psychiatrists and psychologists are simply unable to predict dangerousness (Diamond, 1974; Ennis and Litwack, 1974; Stone, 1975; Monahan, 1976). One of the most interesting of these studies (Steadman and Keveles, 1972, 1978) arose out of the case of *Baxtrom* v. *Herold*.*

> After serving more than two years for second-degree assault, Johnnie K. Baxtrom was certified as insane by a prison physician and transferred to a prison-hospital. Baxtrom's sentence was about to end, however, but because he was still in need of psychiatric care, the director of the prison-hospital petitioned that Baxtrom be committed involuntarily to an ordinary psychiatric hospital. That petition was denied for administrative reasons. Baxtrom, therefore, was forced to remain where he was.
>
> Baxtrom went to court with the following contention: If he was sane, he deserved to be discharged as soon as he completed his sentence. And if he was not sane, he should be transferred to an ordinary psychiatric hospital. Thus, he argued, his constitutional rights were being violated insofar as he was required to remain in prison beyond the termination of his sentence.

The United States Supreme Court agreed. And as a result, "Operation Baxtrom," which was designed to effect the rapid release of 967 similarly confined patients from New York State's prison-hospitals, was launched. These people were not merely predicted to be dangerous to others on the basis of their "insanity." They were also considered to be ***criminally insane,*** held to be violent now and in the future because they had been violent in the past and because, additionally, they were psychologically distressed. Would those predictions hold up?

Operation Baxtrom afforded Henry Steadman and his colleagues an excellent opportunity to follow up on these patients and examine how accurate psychiatric predictions about dangerousness are. Precisely because most of these patients had been convicted of a dangerous act, one would expect predictions about their dangerousness to be quite accurate, since the

* Baxtrom v. Herold, 383 U.S. 107 (1966).

past is the best predictor of the future. But that was not the case. After four years, Steadman and Keveles (1972) reported that only 2.7 percent of these released patients had behaved dangerously and were either in a correctional facility or back in a hospital for the criminally insane. Careful examination of those who were dangerous revealed no "set of factors that could have selected these returnees from all the Baxtrom patients without a very large number of false positives—i.e., patients with the same characteristics who did not act out violently" (Steadman, 1973, p. 318).

DANGEROUSNESS TO SELF.   Still another criterion for involuntary commitment is dangerousness to self. The kinds of behaviors that are held to be dangerous are defined by informal social convention. Suicidal impulses qualify, but cigarette-smoking and drunk-driving do not.

In general, the use of involuntary hospitalization for people who are believed to be dangerous to themselves ought to be guided by the "thank you" test (Stone, 1975). This test asks: Will the person, once recovered, be grateful for that hospitalization, however much it was protested? That test would likely be passed by the people you read about earlier on page 594, and by others who are severely depressed and suicidal and who, once the depression has lifted, are simply grateful to be alive.

But the informal social conventions that regulate who should and who should not be hospitalized because they are dangerous to themselves are sometimes inconsistent and ambiguous. People who seem to be experiencing similar degrees of danger to themselves may be seen as good candidates for commitment in one case but not in another, as the following two cases demonstrate:

Case 1: Emma Lake. At sixty, Emma Lake was involuntarily committed to St. Elizabeth's Hospital after she was found wandering the streets of Washington, D.C. At the commitment hearing, two psychiatrists testified that she was unable to care adequately for herself. At a subsequent hearing, she was held to be suffering from "chronic brain syndrome with arteriosclerosis (hardening of the arteries) . . ." She was prone to "wandering away and being out exposed at night or any time that she is out." On one occasion, it was related, Mrs. Lake left the hospital and was missing for about thirty-two hours. She was brought back after midnight by a policeman who found her wandering the streets. She thought she had only been gone for a few hours, could not tell where she had been, and suffered a minor injury, that she attributed to having been chased by boys.

Mrs. Lake acknowledged that there were times when she lost track of things. Nevertheless, she felt able to be at liberty and willing to run the requisite risks. Her husband and sister were eager for her release and willing to provide a home for her. Moreover, she was willing to endure some form of confinement at home rather than the total confinement of a psychiatric hospital.

Ultimately the court concurred with her psychiatrists and required that she be hospitalized. She spent the last five years of her life in a psychiatric hospital, during the last year of which she received no visitors (Chambers, 1972). Often, families that would willingly provide a home for a patient are unable or unwilling to visit a psychiatric hospital regularly.

Case 2: Robert Jackson. At the age of sixty-two, Justice Robert Jackson suffered a severe heart attack while serving on the United States Supreme Court. The Court's work is arduous and taxing. His doctors gave him the choice between years of comparative (though not, by any means, total) inactivity off the Court, and the risk of death at any time by continuing his work on the Court. Jackson chose to remain on the Court. He suffered a fatal heart attack shortly thereafter.

No court interfered with the Justice's decision, nor was it ever suggested that he was dangerous to himself and therefore in need of psychiatric care. Quite the contrary: his decision to continue the work of the Court was widely praised. Many people would choose to do the same: take their chances with the things they enjoy doing rather than be cooped up, inactively, for the rest of their lives.

What distinguishes Mrs. Lake's case from Justice Jackson's? For both, the choices jeopardized their lives, Jackson's even more than Lake's. Why was Lake involuntarily committed and Jackson never questioned? The major difference between Mrs. Lake's case and Justice Jackson's is that Mrs. Lake's request to live out her years at home, and with people who loved her, was "psychiatrized." That is, her choice was believed to arise from mental illness ("chronic brain syndrome"), while Justice Jackson's was not. The fact that she suffered "chronic brain syndrome" obscured the similarities between her choice and that of others. Now, it is clearly the case that some psychologically distressed persons suffer thought disorders of such magnitude that they are rarely, if ever, lucid. But that was not the case with Mrs. Lake, nor is it the case for most psychiatric patients, all of whom enjoy long periods of clarity during which they are as capable as others of making significant choices between the risks of liberty and the security of incarceration (Dershowitz, 1968).

Due Process of Law

If Mrs. Lake's case serves to teach anything, it is that once behavior is described or "explained" in terms of psychological abnormality, it encourages people to think of a different set of "solutions" than they would if it had been explained as the normal product of rational decision making. And because, as we have said, nothing less than deprivation of liberty is involved in involuntary commitment, it seems only reasonable to provide the psychologically distressed with the same privileges that are afforded to anyone whose liberty is threatened by state action—to criminal defendants, for example. These rights and privileges are collectively called "due process of law" and include:

- The right to be notified of trial in a timely manner
- The right to trial by jury
- The right to be present at one's own trial
- The right to legal counsel and the appointment of counsel in a timely manner
- The right to exclude unreliable evidence, such as hearsay evidence, from the testimony
- The right to challenge witnesses
- The privilege against self-incrimination
- The right to counsel at all interviews, including psychiatric interviews
- The right to know, with considerable precision, which laws one has violated and under which laws one stands accused.

In one case, *Lessard* v. *Schmidt,* Alberta Lessard complained that these very rights and privileges had been violated in her own involuntary commitment. Moreover, she argued that she had been detained without benefit of a hearing for better than three weeks, and could have been detained for as long as 145 days. The court held that Ms. Lessard's rights had been grossly violated and that all of her complaints were justified.* Commitment to a psychiatric hospital, the court held, may involve a serious restriction of individual rights. Those adjudged to be mentally ill, for example, like convicted felons, are unable to vote and may not serve on a jury. They may not drive a car. Their right to practice certain professions is restricted, as are their rights to make contracts, to sue, and to be sued. Those restrictions distinguish psychiatric from other kinds of medical care, and require that special attention be paid to due process issues.

In further support of its view that the psychologically distressed are entitled to due process, in the *Lessard* case, the court pointed out that psychiatric hospitalization may not be an entirely therapeutic experience.

Perhaps the most serious possible effect of a decision to commit an individual lies in the statistics which indicate that an individual committed to a mental institution has a much greater chance of dying than if he were left at large. Data compiled in 1966 indicate that while the death rate per 1000 persons in the general population in the United States each year is only 9.5, the rate among resident mental patients is 91.8. . . . Figures for Wisconsin are similar. [One] study showed a death rate for the Wisconsin populace in general of 9.7 per 1000 population per year (or less than one per cent) and a death rate in Wisconsin mental institutions of 85.1 per thousand (or 8.51 per cent).

Although part of this difference may be accounted for by a large number of older persons in mental institutions, studies indicate that other factors also are involved. One factor is the smaller number of physicians per patient in public mental institutions in comparison to the ratio of doctors to individuals in the general population. . . . The damage done is not confined to a small number among the population. In 1963, 679,000 persons were confined in mental institutions in the United States; only 250,000 persons were incarcerated in all prisons administered by the states and federal government. . . . It would thus appear that the interests in avoiding civil commitments are at least as high as those of persons accused of criminal offenses.†

Standard of Proof

Throughout this section, we have emphasized that involuntary hospitalization involves a significant deprivation of liberty. The degree of deprivation may vary: some patients are permitted freedom on the hospital grounds, while others are locked into the ward, day and night. But even those in the former group experience a restriction on their liberty, in that they must be in the hospital rather than elsewhere. In order to so restrict a person's freedom one must prove that, in accord with the law, they belong in a psychiatric hospital. Mere allegation is insufficient. What standard of proof should be required? Generally speaking, three standards of proof are available in law: preponderance of evidence, beyond a reasonable doubt, and clear and convincing proof.

---

* Lessard v. Schmidt, 349 F. Supp. 1078 (E.D. Wis. 1972). The Wisconsin court's judgment was vacated by the U.S. Supreme Court in 1974, on procedural rather than substantive grounds.
† Ibid, p. 1089.

Often called the 51 percent standard, *the preponderance of evidence* standard requires just enough proof to shift the weight of evidence to one side. This is the standard used in civil cases, where penalties are often monetary and do not involve deprivation of liberty.

Beyond a reasonable doubt is the most severe standard of proof and requires that the evidence be so compelling as to convince a reasonable listener beyond a reasonable doubt. This standard is used in criminal law, where the presumption of a defendant's innocence is very strong, and the costs of wrongful incarceration of an innocent person high indeed. It is often termed the 90 percent or 99 percent standard, implying that the weight of evidence must be such that people would be willing to stake high odds on the guilt of the defendant.

Clear and convincing proof is an intermediate standard that is not quite so severe as that requiring proof beyond a reasonable doubt, but not as lenient as the 51 percent standard that requires the mere preponderance of evidence. Consider it the 75 percent standard.

Recalling what you have read here regarding the validity of predictions of dangerousness, and what you have learned in Chapter 9 on the reliability and validity of psychiatric diagnoses generally, what standard of proof should be invoked in order to commit a person involuntarily? In 1979, the matter was taken up by the Supreme Court in *Addington* v. *Texas*.*

> Frank O'Neal Addington had been hospitalized seven times between 1967 and 1975. His mother now petitioned the court to have him involuntarily committed because he was both dangerous to himself and dangerous to others. In accord with Texas law, a jury trial was held to determine if he required hospitalization. The judge instructed the jury to determine whether there was "clear, unequivocal and convincing evidence"—the 75 percent standard—that Addington was mentally ill and required hospitalization for his protection and for the safety of others. The jury so found, but Addington appealed the decision to the U.S. Supreme Court on the grounds that the appropriate standard of proof should have been a tougher one—beyond a reasonable doubt—the 90 percent standard.
>
> The Supreme Court held that the 90 percent standard was simply too severe. Given the uncertainties of psychiatric diagnosis and prediction, requiring proof beyond a reasonable doubt would render the state unable to commit many truly distressed people who were much in need of treatment. The preponderance of evidence standard, on the other hand, was much too lenient. If the state wanted to deprive a person of liberty, it needed to bear a greater burden of proof than that implied in the 51 percent standard. The Supreme Court therefore upheld the original decision, maintaining that the presentation of clear and convincing evidence —roughly 75 percent certainty—is the minimum standard for involuntary commitment and that states may not commit below this minimum standard (though they are free to fix standards that are higher than this required minimum).

TREATMENT

The Right to Treatment

The *Lessard* and *Addington* cases dealt with the rights people can exercise and the standard of proof that is required before they can be involuntarily committed. What about after they have been committed? Is there a "right to

* Addington v. Texas, 99 S. Ct. 1804 (1979).

treatment" for those who have been deprived of their liberty, presumably because they required psychiatric treatment? Oddly, and with few exceptions, the courts have been very cautious on this matter. They are understandably reluctant to invent new "rights." Yet, deprivation of liberty is a serious matter in a democratic society, and the courts have occasionally been responsive to cases in which hospitalization has occurred without the person receiving adequate treatment. Thus, in *Rouse* v. *Cameron,** Judge David Bazelon clearly enunciated a right to treatment that was rooted in federal statute. He wrote:

> The purpose of involuntary hospitalization is treatment, not punishment . . . absent treatment, the hospital is transform[ed] . . . into a penitentiary where one could be held indefinitely for no convicted offense. (*Rouse* v. *Cameron,* 1966, p. 453)

Not all "treatments" count as treatment, however. Bazelon said:

> The hospital need not show that the treatment will cure or improve him but only that there is a bona fide effort to do so. This requires the hospital to show that initial and periodic inquiries are made into the needs and conditions of the patient with a view to providing suitable treatment for him. . . . Treatment that has therapeutic value for some may not have such value for others. For example, it may not be assumed that confinement in a hospital is beneficial "environment therapy" for all. (*Rouse* v. *Cameron,* 1966, p. 456)

In *Wyatt* v. *Stickney,*† Judge Frank Johnson insisted that the constitutional right to treatment is accorded to every person who has been involuntarily hospitalized. In his opinion, Johnson wrote:

> To deprive any citizen of his or her liberty upon the altruistic theory that the confinement is for humane therapeutic reasons and then fail to provide adequate treatment violates the very fundamentals of due process.

In a later opinion,‡ Judge Johnson recognized that the absence of therapeutic regimens in the Alabama state hospitals was less a matter of simple neglect than it was one of personnel and facilities. He therefore stipulated minimal objective standards of care, standards, by the way, that were far below those recommended by the American Psychiatric Association. Thus, he required that for every 250 patients, there should be at least two psychiatrists, three additional physicians, twelve registered nurses, ninety attendants, four psychologists, and seven social workers. While these may seem a large number of personnel for every 250 patients, remember that patients are in the hospital twenty-four hours a day, seven days a week, and that personnel are needed to take care of them on a continuous basis.

In that same opinion, Judge Johnson made clear that patients have a right to privacy and dignity, to the least restrictive regimen necessary to achieve the purposes of commitment, and to freedom from unnecessary or excessive

Conditions such as the starkness of this environment caused the courts to stipulate minimal objective standards of care in psychiatric hospitals. (Photograph by Raymond Depardon/Magnum)

* Rouse v. Cameron, 373 F. 2d 451 (D. C. Cir. 1966).
† Wyatt v. Stickney, 325 F. Supp. 781 (M.D. Ala. 1971).
‡ Wyatt v. Stickney, 344 F. Supp. 343 (M.D. Ala. 1972).

medication. He affirmed their right to send sealed mail and to use the telephone—privileges that are often denied patients on the grounds that they might say things that they would later have cause to regret. Finally, Johnson said that each patient was entitled to an individual treatment plan, and to periodic review of his or her plan and progress.

Judge Bazelon's and Judge Johnson's opinions have been hailed by civil libertarians and mental health professionals alike as major steps forward in the treatment of the psychologically distressed. Although other courts have not concurred that there is a right to treatment, these opinions have had far-reaching effects (see Box 20-1).

Releasing Mental Patients

Former mental patients who have been released from psychiatric hospitals often may end up walking the streets. (Photograph by Michael O'Brien)

Opinions written in such cases as *Rouse* v. *Cameron* and *Wyatt* v. *Stickney* have alerted people to the plight of psychiatric patients, and promise to improve their fate. But unfortunately, they have also had a major unintended consequence. Faced with the prospect of pouring more money into psychiatric care, many states have taken the least expensive route and have simply discharged patients from psychiatric hospitals, and closed the hospitals. During the seventies, for example, California closed a majority of its psychiatric hospitals and cut back severely on funding of mental health programs. Other states followed suit. As a result, thousands of people who were formerly housed in psychiatric hospitals have been shunted to "board and care" homes in local communities. Living conditions there are sometimes substandard. Treatment is minimal, and former patients have little to do but lie in bed or walk the streets. The new visibility of these people has frequently created a harsh and angry community reaction. The powerful stigma associated with those labeled mentally ill, and particularly the violence and unpredictability that is erroneously attributed to mental patients, creates enormous community fear and backlash.

Are patients better off in board and care facilities than in psychiatric hospitals? We don't yet know. Informal conversations with these patients strongly indicate that they prefer being in the community to being warehoused in psychiatric hospitals, and there is evidence that they are no worse off in the community than in hospitals (Lamb, 1979). But neither are they as well off as they would like to be or should be. Many find employment difficult to procure, and social relationships difficult to establish. They react strongly to community stereotypes about them.

The situation is not hopeless, however, by any means. In many communities, former psychiatric patients have established self-help organizations which, in addition to providing social networks and employment opportunities, also serve to give them a political base. These organizations, because they bring former patients assertively into contact with community agencies, have therapeutic as well as substantive value.

ABOLISH INVOLUNTARY HOSPITALIZATION?

Involuntary commitment gives rise to serious problems. Coerced hospitalization and coercive treatment please no one and require that one ask whether involuntary hospitalization should be abolished altogether. The

KENNETH DONALDSON'S SAGA

Perhaps Kenneth Donaldson needed treatment. But did he get it?

Kenneth Donaldson was already forty-eight years old when his parents, themselves in their seventies, petitioned for his commitment to Florida State Hospital at Chattahoochee. His life had not been an easy one until then, Donaldson frankly points out in his book, *Insanity Inside Out* (1976). He had had one psychiatric hospitalization of three-months' duration, some thirteen years earlier. It was a hospitalization that followed him, and marred his life subsequently. Afterwards, his marriage had failed, his relationship with his children had cooled, he had had difficulty holding a job, and sometimes he had felt that people were out to get him. But he was not dangerous to himself, had never been dangerous to others (although his father had alleged he was in order to get him committed), and he emphatically did not want to be committed to Chattahoochee. One hospitalization was more than enough.

The judge who committed Donaldson told him that he would be in the hospital for "a few weeks." A progress note written less than three months after he was admitted indicated that he appeared to be in remission. And because his first hospitalization had been brief, there was every reason to expect this one to be brief too. Nevertheless, Donaldson remained in Florida State Hospital for fourteen-and-a-half years.

Donaldson is a Christian Scientist. Medication and electric shock treatments were both offered to him, but he refused them on religious grounds. What care and treatment did he get then? None. He rarely saw Drs. O'Connor or Gumanis, his physicians, and then only briefly. Grounds privileges and occupational therapy were denied him during the first ten years of his hospitalization. Some six years after he had been hospitalized, Helping Hands, Inc., a reputable organization that operates halfway houses for mental patients, offered to care for Donaldson. But his psychiatrist, Dr. O'Connor, refused to release him to anyone but his parents. By this time, his parents were too old and infirm to accept that responsibility, and presumably Dr. O'Connor knew that. Finally, a college friend made four separate attempts to have Donaldson released in his custody. His requests were either refused outright or frustrated.

During this period, Donaldson smuggled letters out of the hospital to anyone who might help. Often, however, mail sent through hospital channels would be opened or simply thrown out. Donaldson's teenage daughter wrote "Daddy, I know you are not sick. But why don't you write?" "I was writing," Donaldson says.

"ayes" have had their vigorous spokesmen, from the English philosopher John Stuart Mill of the last century to psychiatrist Thomas S. Szasz today. In *On Liberty* (1859), Mill wrote:

> The only freedom which deserves the name is that of pursuing our own good in our own way, so long as we do not attempt to deprive others of theirs, or impede their efforts to obtain it. Each is the proper guardian of his own health, whether bodily, or mental and spiritual. Mankind are greater gainers by suffering each other to live as seems good to themselves, than by compelling each to live as seems good to the rest. (Mill, 1859, p. 18)

Thomas Szasz is one of the most critical analysts of the nature of psychiatry and its role in society today. Szasz points out that mental illness is different from physical illness. There are no clear or generally accepted criteria of mental illness. "[L]ooking for evidence of such illness is like searching for evidence of heresy: Once the investigator gets into the proper frame of mind,

Kenneth Donaldson is pictured here after the Supreme Court ruled in his favor. (Wide World Photos)

"Then her letters stopped." (Donaldson, 1976, p. 84). As a result, he acquired a reputation for being a difficult person. But he had much to be difficult about. Day after day was spent in a locked, crowded room with sixty other people, nearly one-third of whom had undergone criminal commitments. At night, some of the patients would have fits. It was frightening. Some of the beds in this crowded room were so close together that they touched. Donaldson lived in constant fear that someone would jump him during the night.

Donaldson sought the help of the Mental Health Law Project, a Washington, D.C., group of lawyers who serve the legal needs of the mentally distressed. And, finally, in 1971, Donaldson sued for his release and for damages from Drs. O'Connor and Gumanis, alleging "intentional, malicious, and reckless disregard of Donaldson's constitutional rights." The jury awarded Donaldson compensatory and punitive damages from both physicians. The physicians appealed, and the case went up to the Supreme Court, where many of the justices were simply outraged over Donaldson's incarceration (Woodward and Armstrong, 1979). On January 26, 1975, the Court unanimously wrote in *O'Connor v. Donaldson:*[*]

A state cannot constitutionally confine . . . a nondangerous individual who is capable of surviving safely in freedom by himself or with the help of willing and responsible family members or friends.

[*] O'Connor v. Donaldson, 422 U.S. 563, 95 S.Ct 2486 (1975).

anything may seem to him to be a symptom of mental illness" (Szasz, 1963, p. 225). As a result, Szasz believes that psychiatry has a great potential for social abuse, particularly as it lends itself, through involuntary commitment, to ridding society of all manner of deviants and eccentrics, all in the name of treating mental illness. Szasz is not opposed to voluntary hospitalization, provided patients are frankly told whether or not they will receive the best treatment. But he believes involuntary hospitalization should be abolished because adequate treatment is often absent.

CRIMINAL COMMITMENT

Involuntary commitment is sometimes called *civil commitment,* the process used to hospitalize people who have committed no crime. *Criminal commitment,* on the other hand, refers to the coerced psychiatric hospitalization

John Hinckley, Jr., successfully used the insanity defense when he was tried for the attempted assassination of President Ronald Reagan. (Wide World Photos)

of people who have acted harmfully but are not legally responsible because they lack a "guilty mind" or *mens rea.* "Where there is no *mens* (i.e., mind) there can be no *mens rea*" the legal maxim goes (Fingarette and Hasse, 1979, p. 200). In the eyes of the law, such people are insane, and the legal defense used in their cases is called the ***insanity defense.***

THE INSANITY DEFENSE

The insanity defense requires that the defendant was wholly or partially irrational *when the crime took place,* and that this irrationality affected his or her behavior. The psychologist or psychiatrist who serves as an expert witness in this matter is required to reconstruct the defendant's state of mind as it was before and during the crime. This is not a simple task. If diagnostic opinions are often unreliable for *present* behavior, as we saw in Chapter 9, how much more unreliable are they for speculative reconstructions of the past? No wonder, then, that experts for the defense are often contradicted by equally capable experts for the prosecution. And no wonder, too, that judges and jurors will disagree on the defendant's state of mind when he committed the crime.

Use of the Insanity Defense

Contrary to popular belief, the insanity defense is not widely used. It is invoked in fewer than 3 percent of all homicide cases that come to trial (Lunde, 1975), and not often with success. It is used far less often in nonhomicide trials. Even when successful, the defense usually leads to longterm incarceration in an institution for the criminally insane, a fate sometimes worse than incarceration in prison (see Box 20-2). Nevertheless the role and meaning of the insanity defense is one of the most hotly debated issues in criminal law. Why should that be?

While the insanity defense is something of a bother in the criminal law, "we must put up with [it] . . . because to exclude it is to deprive the criminal law of its chief paradigm of free will" (Packer, 1968). Thus, the insanity defense is the exception that proves the rule: the notion that each of us is responsible for his or her behavior is strengthened by the recognition that some of us patently are not (Stone, 1975; Rosenhan, 1983).

Tests for Determining the Insanity Defense

But what determines if the insanity defense can be used? When is a person considered to be so insane in the eyes of the law that the ordinary cannons of criminal law do not apply? Because the answer to these questions is crucial to the very meaning of criminal law, the questions themselves have generated hot dispute. Historically, there have been three views of the insanity defense. But before discussing these views, we will examine the three cases below (adapted from Livermore and Meehl, 1967). Is there *mens rea* in each of these defendants?*

> **Case 1: The Pigtail Snipper.** Victor Weiner, a hair fetishist, was charged with assault for snipping off a girl's pigtail while standing on a crowded bus. His experi-

* 51 Minn L. Rev. 789, 833–55 (1967).

ence before cutting off the pigtail (which was corroborated by psychiatric testimony and by an acquaintance with whom he had discussed this problem several days earlier) was one of mounting tension, accompanied by a feeling that was close to anxiety and erotic excitement. He made various efforts to distract himself and place himself in situations where he would be safe from performing this act, but finally he gave in to the impulse and boarded the bus with a pair of scissors in his pocket. Victor was diagnosed "sociopathic personality disturbance, sexual deviation, fetishism."

Case 2: The Axe-handle Murderer. Arthur Wolff, a fifteen-year-old, was charged with murdering his mother.* During the year preceding the crime, Wolff "spent a lot of time thinking about sex." He made a list of the names and addresses of seven girls in his community whom he planned to anesthetize and then either rape or photograph nude. One night, about three weeks before the murder, he took a container of ether and attempted to enter the house of one of these girls through the chimney. But he became wedged in and had to be rescued. In the ensuing weeks, Wolff apparently decided that he would have to bring the girls to his house to achieve his sexual purposes, and that it would therefore be necessary to get his mother (and possibly his brother) out of the way first.

On the Friday or Saturday before he murdered his mother, Wolff obtained an axe handle from the family garage and hid it under the mattress of his bed. On Sunday, he took the axe handle from its hiding place and approached his mother from behind, raising the weapon to strike her. She sensed his presence and asked him what he was doing; he answered that it was "nothing," and returned to his room and hid the axe handle under his mattress again. The following morning, Wolff ate the breakfast that his mother had prepared, went to his room, and took the axe handle from its hiding place. He returned to the kitchen, approached his mother from behind, and struck her on the back of the head. She turned around screaming. He hit her several more times, and they fell to the floor fighting. He got up to turn off the water running in the sink, and she fled through the dining room. He gave chase, caught her in the front room, and choked her to death with his hands.

Wolff then took off his shirt and hung it by the fire, washed the blood off his face and hands, read a few lines from the Bible or prayer book lying upon the dining room table, and walked down to the police station to turn himself in. He told the desk officer, "I have something I wish to report . . . I just killed my mother with an axe handle." The officer testified that Wolff spoke in a quiet voice and that "his conversation was quite coherent in what he was saying and he answered everything I asked him right to a T."

At his trial, four expert witnesses testified that Arthur Wolff had been suffering from schizophrenia when he murdered his mother.

Case 3: The Delusional Informer. Calvin Ellery was a paranoid schizophrenic who experienced delusions and hallucinations, and who believed that the Masons were plotting to take over the government. He believed, moreover, that the Masons had learned that he was aware of their intentions, and that because he was a potential informer, the Masons had determined to do away with him.

As a result of delusional misinterpretation of certain things he had heard on a news broadcast, Ellery believed that "today is the day for his execution." When a salesman with a Masonic button on his lapel came to the front door, he was sure that the salesman had been sent to kill him. When the salesman reached into his pocket for his business card, Ellery was convinced that he was reaching for a revolver. Ellery drew his own weapon and shot first in self-defense.

---

* People v. Wolff, 61 Cal. 2d 795, 800.

M'NAGHTEN: THE "RIGHT-WRONG" TEST. In 1843, Daniel M'Nagh-ten, after whom the "right-wrong" test was named, murdered Drummond, the secretary to the British Prime Minister, Sir Robert Peel. Drummond,

Box 20-2   IS A HOSPITAL FOR THE CRIMINALLY INSANE WORSE THAN A PRISON?

The word "hospital" and the phrase "treatment center" have such over-whelming kind and curative connotations that it is difficult to believe, as the text points out, that many people would prefer prison to these places. Yet, that is the case. Patients often resist being transferred to treatment centers because they re-strict individual rights and are more punitive. Documentary filmmaker, Frederick Wiseman, in *Titticut Follies*, depicted life at Bridgewater, Massachusetts, Treat-ment Center. And a former inmate there, Donald McEwan, compared Bridgewater with the nearby state prison in the following brief which was an appendix to *United States ex rel. Schuster v. Herold** (cited in Brooks, 1974, p. 423):

COMPARISON OF PUNITIVE MEASURES

Item	Treatment Center	State Prison at Walpole
Personal clothing	Limited to 3 pairs white underwear, 6 pairs white or gray socks, 1 pair shoes without steel shank. May be ordered only at specified times.	Allowed any color underwear, socks, sweatshirts, bathrobe, pajamas, slippers, shoes without regard to shank, black or blue sweater. No limit, many items available in canteen.
Institutional clothing	Always wrinkled, usually ill-fitted, frequently worn out. All marked by messy stencil with "T.C." and name. Can change only at specified times and places. Cannot have institutional underwear if have personal.	One pair pressed each week; proper size, replaced when worn-out. Shirt only marked, neatly, with name. Change as required in own cell. Underwear issued to everyone.
Punishment (lock-up)	No semblance of trial. Any guard may order.	Only disciplinary board (composed of deputy supt., a guard, and a civilian employee).
Rules and procedures	Different from night and day.	Same all the time.
Free time	Required to be either in yard or rec. room (no choice) or locked in cell.	Choice of yard, TV rooms, gym, chapel, own cell (which is open), other cell-block rec. areas.
Library	Cannot browse; no catalog available.	Open daily for browsing; catalog available.

* United States ex rel. Schuster v. Herold, 410 F2d 1071 (2d Cir. 1969).

however, was not M'Naghten's intended victim: Peel was. A "voice of God" had instructed M'Naghten to kill the Prime Minister. Unfortunately for Drummond, Peel had been invited to travel in Queen Victoria's carriage.

Visiting	1 hour once a week across table with wire fence underneath.	All morning or afternoon (2½ hours) twice a week, in chairs side by side.
Lawyer visit	In presence of guard.	Private.
State job	Assigned arbitrarily; just work under threat; little variety.	Inmate's preference consulted in assignment and job changes. Greater variety of jobs.
Pay	More than 50% make lowest wages. Little opportunity for increase.	Only 25% lowest wage. Easy to move to better paying job.
Entertainments	Sometimes forced to attend.	Always optional.
Food and menu	Frequently insipid and unimaginative.	Good quality, good preparation and imagination.
Silverware	Frequently only a spoon. Always counted.	Always have appropriate utensils. Not counted.
Cells	No lockers; no control of light from inside; no lamps allowed. No smoking. Arrangements of furniture, blankets, etc. specified in detail. No glass objects or food allowed.	Wall locker provided; light switch inside; lamps allowed. Smoking allowed. No specification on arrangements. Glass objects and food allowed.
Sleep at night	Frequently disturbed by guards.	Rarely disturbed.
Personal safety razor	Not allowed.	Issued by institution and available in canteen.
Personal appearance	Told when to get haircut, shave. No beards allowed.	Left to individual. Beards allowed.
Sanitary facilities	Primitive, no running water in cell; showers available only at specified times; frequently only 1 toilet to entire population (100 +).	Modern toilet and basin in cell; showers available any free time.
Mail	Frequently delayed by being passed to various persons. Outgoing certified mail may take weeks. Supt. includes apology in all mail to public officials. Censor stamp used on all mail.	Prompt delivery both incoming and outgoing. No unauthorized missives enclosed. Censor stamp not ordinarily used.

Drummond, his secretary, rode in the vehicle that normally would have been reserved for the Prime Minister, and was mistaken for him by M'Naghten.

The trial was remarkable in that M'Naghten's defense counsel relied heavily on *Medical Jurisprudence of Insanity* (1838), a recently published work by Dr. Isaac Ray. M'Naghten, the defense counsel argued, was clearly deranged, in that he suffered delusions of persecution (and, in modern terms, command hallucinations). It was one of the first times that psychiatric testimony had been permitted in a murder trial, and the judges were so impressed that the Lord Chief Justice practically directed a verdict for M'Naghten. Subsequently, the judges enunciated the **M'Naghten rule,** which holds that:

> It must be clearly proved that, at the time of the committing of the act, the party accused was laboring under such a defect of reason, from disease of the mind, as not to know the nature and quality of the act he was doing; or, if he did know it, that he did not know he was doing what was wrong.

The M'Naghten test is widely used in the United States. Nearly half of the states use it alone as the yardstick for insanity, while other states use the M'Naghten rule in conjunction with other rules. It is a relatively narrow test, which relies merely on what the accused knew and whether he knew it was wrong.

Under the M'Naghten rule, only Calvin Ellery, the delusional informer, would be acquitted, for only he clearly did not "know the nature and quality of the act he was doing," believing that he was acting in justifiable self-defense. The axe-handle murderer's behavior was clearly bizarre, yet because there was no evidence that he failed to distinguish right from wrong, he could not be acquitted according to the M'Naghten rule. Similarly, Weiner, the pigtail snipper, though clearly disturbed and seemingly caught up in an impulse that ultimately overcame his best efforts at suppression, could not be acquitted under the M'Naghten rule. He, too, knew right from wrong.

DURHAM: "THE PRODUCT OF MENTAL DISEASE." In *Durham* v. *United States,** Judge David Bazelon broadened the insanity defense to state that "an accused is not criminally responsible if his unlawful act was the product of mental disease or mental defect." Notice the difference between the Durham "mental disease" and the M'Naghten "right-wrong" test. In the **Durham test,** incapacitating conditions, such as the inability to tell right from wrong are not specified. One goes directly from "mental disease" to the act (Brooks, 1974), leaving it to advanced knowledge in psychiatry and psychology to determine whether the act was or was not a product of mental disease or mental defect. Under the Durham rule, the axe-handle murderer would probably have been acquitted on the grounds that, absent his schizophrenic conditions, he would not have murdered his mother. Likewise, defining fetishism as a "mental disease," the pigtail snipper, too, would have been acquitted on the grounds that were he not a fetishist, he would not have had such a prurient interest in little girls' pigtails. And of course, Calvin Ellery, the delusional informer, would also have been acquitted under the "mental

---

* Durham v. United States, 214 F. 2d 862 (D. C. Cir. 1954).

Box 20-3 EXPERIMENTING WITH THE INSANITY DEFENSE

The M'Naghten test had several flaws. Its chief deficiency was that it was limited to whether the defendant knew right from wrong. Many felt that the right-wrong test was simply too narrow, that simple justice required that other people who were deeply troubled, such as Victor Weiner (the Pigtail Snipper) and Arthur Wolff (the Axe-handle Murderer), be permitted to enter an insanity plea, regardless of whether they knew right from wrong. It was in this context that David Bazelon, then Chief Judge of the U.S. Court of Appeals, enunciated the Durham rule in 1954. In 1971, shortly before the rule was withdrawn, Judge Bazelon had this to say about it:

> Durham was frankly an experiment—and we embarked on that experiment knowing full well that experience might later lead us to refine or abandon the rule. Putting the merits of the rule aside for the moment, I have always been particularly proud of the court in those days for that willingness to experiment. For it was clear to almost all of us that the old test for responsibility was inadequate. And yet we could not with confidence announce the perfect alternative. In those circumstances, surely it is wrong to continue with a bad rule merely for want of one guaranteed to be better. . . .
>
> The immediate impact of our Durham experiment was to open the courthouse door to a wide range of information bearing on the question of criminal responsibility. With a broader legal test, more information became relevant to the question. We soon found, however, that, by casting the test wholly in terms of mental illness, we had unwittingly turned the question of responsibility over to the psychiatric profession; for mental illness is a very loose term with different meanings for different psychiatrists. When the only expert witnesses at trial testified that the defendant was mentally ill, according to their own unstated definitions of that term, the court felt strong pressure to direct a verdict of not guilty by reason of insanity. And when the only witnesses at trial had a narrow notion of mental illness and testified that the defendant was not mentally ill, the court had no basis for rejecting that conclusion either. When the experts disagreed, the court was left to choose between them without any standard for evaluating their testimony. As the Durham years progressed, it became increasingly apparent that the insanity defense was entirely in the hands of the experts involved in a particular case. That state of affairs pleased no one. . . .
>
> In some seventeen years of experimentation with the insanity defense, we've been unable to devise a simple scientific test that can be mechanically applied. Many of us have been forced to conclude that criminal responsibility, like negligence, is at bottom a concept that can only be determined by reference to prevailing community standards. (Bazelon, 1971, pp. 653, 658–60)

disease" test (he was paranoid schizophrenic), as well as under the M'Naghten "right-wrong" test.

As Justice Bazelon maintained (see Box 20-3), the Durham rule was an experiment, one that extended for some eighteen years, from 1954 until 1972, and during which time, a view of criminal responsibility and nonresponsibility was developed. Fundamentally, the Durham rule was withdrawn for two reasons: (1) it relied too heavily on the expert testimony of psychiatrists, rendering judge and jury wholly dependent upon psychiatric testimony for the determination of criminal responsibility, and (2) it was as difficult then as it is now to know and attain agreement about what constituted a "mental disease." The metaphor itself left much to be desired, implying a distinct and verifiable organic state. Moreover, one could never be sure which of the disorders listed in the *Diagnostic and Statistical Manual of Mental Disorders* qualified. Should stuttering, tobacco dependence, and sociopathy all be considered mental diseases that can produce unlawful acts? The seeming breadth of the Durham rule created problems that were difficult to adjudicate and that ultimately, led to its demise.

THE AMERICAN LAW INSTITUTE (ALI) RULE: "APPRECIATE AND CONFORM." In *United States* v. *Brawner,** some eighteen years after the *Durham* case, the Durham mental disease test was succeeded by a modification of the insanity defense that had earlier been propounded by the American Law Institute. That rule is considerably more specific than the Durham rule, and yet not so narrow as the M'Naghten rule. It states:

1. A person is not responsible for criminal conduct if, at the time of such conduct, as a result of mental disease or defect, he lacks substantial capacity either to appreciate the criminality (wrongfulness) of his conduct or to conform his conduct to the requirements of law.
2. As used in the Article, the terms "mental disease or defect" do not include an abnormality manifested only by repeated criminal or otherwise antisocial conduct. (American Law Institute, 1962, p. 66)

In the *Brawner* case, the court tried to further narrow the meaning of "mental disease." Citing an earlier case,[†] it wrote:

[A] mental disease or defect includes any abnormal condition of the mind which substantially affects mental or emotional processes and substantially impairs behavior controls.

The ***ALI rule,*** as modified in the *Brawner* case, has been adopted by thirty state courts and is the standard in all federal courts of appeal. Under that standard, Calvin Ellery would, of course, be acquitted. Convinced that the Masons were both plotting to take over the government and assassinate him, Ellery clearly lacked "substantial capacity . . . to appreciate the criminality (wrongfulness) of his conduct." The verdict with regard to Victor Weiner, the pigtail snipper, would depend on whether the court was willing and able to assess the strength of Weiner's desire and, therefore, his ability "to conform his conduct to the requirements of law."

The outcome of the case of Arthur Wolff, who murdered his mother because she seemed in the way of his sexual schemes, depends wholly on how a jury would interpret the word *appreciate* in the section of the ALI rule that says ". . . he lacks substantial capacity . . . to appreciate the criminality (wrongfulness) of his conduct. . . ." Wolf "knew" he did wrong in killing his mother, for he confessed immediately at the police station. But did he really

* United States v. Brawner, 471 F. 2d 969 (D. C. Dir. 1972).
† McDonald v. United States, 312 F. 3d 847 (D. C. Cir. 1962).

Table 20-1 Acquittal under the Various Insanity Defenses

Case	Diagnosis	M'Naghten "right-wrong" test	Durham "product of mental disease" test	American Law Institute (ALI) "appreciate and conform" test
Victor Weiner, Pigtail snipper	Fetishist	Guilty—he knew it was wrong	Not guilty—fetishism is a mental disease according to DSM-III	Maybe—depends on court's assessment of his ability to conform his conduct to law.
Arthur Wolff, Axe-handle murderer	Schizophrenic	Guilty—he knew it was wrong.	Probably acquitted— if he were not schizophrenic, he probably would not have murdered.	Probably guilty if *affectively,* he knew murder was wrong.
Calvin Ellery, Delusional informer	Paranoid schizophrenic	Not guilty—he thought he was shooting in self-defense.	Not guilty—the killing was clearly the product of his delusions.	Not guilty—he couldn't appreciate the criminality of his conduct.

appreciate that this was wrong? Did he "feel it in his heart" affectively, or did he merely "know" cognitively? If the latter, he would be acquitted under the ALI rule. If the former, he would be convicted of murdering his mother. (See Table 20-1 for a summary of how the various insanity defenses can be applied to each of these cases.)

COMPETENCE TO STAND TRIAL

For every defendant found not guilty by reason of insanity, at least a hundred defendants are found incompetent to stand trial and are sent to institutions for the criminally insane until they are able to be tried (Bacon, 1969). Being incompetent to stand trial augurs a long incarceration: the average confinement of people committed as incompetent was sixty-one months, and the average for those civilly committed (in Massachusetts at the time of the study) was fourteen months (McGarry and Bendt, 1969). It is not uncommon for people alleged to be incompetent to stand trial to be remanded to institutions for the criminally insane for decades, and simply forgotten. At one such institution, three people among those who were now fully able to stand trial but who had been "overlooked" had been incarcerated for forty-two, thirty-nine, and seventeen years respectively—this, before any determination of their guilt had been made! (McGarry and Bendt, 1969).

What does "incompetent to stand trial" mean? Most statutory definitions are similar to New York's, which defines an "incompetent person" as one "who as a result of mental disease or defect lacks capacity to understand the proceedings against him or to assist in his own defense."* The intent of the

* New York Criminal Code S730.10(1).

statute is noble, growing out of the English common law tradition that forbids a trial in absentia. While the defendant may be physically present, when he is judged incompetent to stand trial, he is believed to be ***psychologically absent,*** and the trial is delayed until he can participate in his own defense.

Until recently, there were no limits on *how long* people could be committed until judged competent to stand trial. What if they would *never* be competent to stand trial? Such a dilemma arose tragically in *Jackson* v. *Indiana.**

> Theon Jackson was a mentally defective deaf-mute. He could not read, write, or otherwise communicate except through limited sign language. In May, 1968, at the age of twenty-seven, Jackson was charged with separate robberies of two women, both of which robberies were alleged to have occurred in the previous July. The first robbery involved a purse and its contents; the total value was four dollars. The second concerned five dollars in cash. Jackson entered a plea of not guilty through his attorney.
>
> Had he been convicted, Jackson would likely have received a sentence of sixty days. But he could not be tried because, in accord with Indiana law, Jackson was examined by two psychiatrists who found that he lacked the intellectual and communicative skills to participate in his own defense, and that the prognosis for acquiring them was dim indeed. Moreover, Jackson's interpreter testified that Indiana had no facilities that could help someone as badly off as Jackson to learn minimal communication skills. The trial court, therefore, found that Jackson "lack[ed] comprehension sufficient to make his defense," and ordered him committed until the Indiana Department of Mental Health certified that the "defendant is sane."
>
> Jackson's attorney filed for a new trial, contending that Jackson was not insane, but that because his mental retardation was so severe, he could never attain competence to stand trial. Jackson's commitment under these circumstances amounted to a life sentence without his ever having been convicted of a crime! By the time the case reached the U.S. Supreme Court, Jackson had already been "hospitalized" for three and a half years. Justice Blackmun, writing for a unanimous court, concurred with Jackson's attorney that Indiana's rule was unconstitutional. Jackson was freed.

Theon Jackson's case resolved one issue—that a person who would never be competent to stand trial could not be detained indefinitely. Many others are still unresolved. What of a person who might some day be competent to stand trial? How long may he or she be held? Some states set no limits. Others, like New York, limit incarceration, depending upon the charge. Federal courts require release after eighteen months. But do even those limited periods violate a person's right to bail and to a speedy trial? And should they count against time served if convicted? Can a person be required to take medications against his or her will in order to be competent to stand trial? Practices in these matters vary enormously across states and are unlikely to be systematically resolved in the near future because such defendants, by definition, often lack the resources to press their claims vigorously.

As a result, some have urged that the notion of incompetence to stand trial be abolished on the grounds that even if impaired, the defendant is bet-

* Jackson v. Indiana, 406 U.S. 715 (1972).

ter off tried. "Withholding trial often results in an endless prolongation of the incompetent defendant's accused status, and his virtually automatic civil commitment. This is a cruelly ironic way by which to ensure that the permanently incompetent defendant is fairly treated" (Burt and Morris 1972, p. 75). This view, however, violates the Supreme Court's dictum in *Pate* v. *Robinson* that "the conviction of an accused person while he is legally incompetent violated due process . . ."*

THE SOCIAL AND POLITICAL ABUSE OF ABNORMAL PSYCHOLOGY

The ideal underlying clinical psychology and psychiatry is to help humankind, but in various societies at various times, these professions have been used toward political ends. In order to confine or control individuals holding dissident views, some political leaders have sanctioned abuses of personal liberties in the name of psychiatry. In large part, the potential for abuse arises from the very definition of abnormality that was discussed in Chapter 1. There we suggested that whether or not people are seen as abnormal depends on whether they possess a "family resemblance" to other abnormal people. There need not be an identity, or perfect match, between the behaviors of those people and the behaviors of abnormal people: so as long as *some* elements are similar, individuals might be considered abnormal by society. Among the behaviors or elements of abnormality are: whether the person produces discomfort in others, the degree to which his or her behavior is unconventional, and the degree to which the behavior violates idealized standards. If an individual's behavior triggers these criteria, he or she may be labeled abnormal, even though other criteria of abnormality, such as intense suffering, are absent. People who hold different views from those of a society's leaders might be seen (or made to be seen) as unconventional, or in violation of idealized standards. It is therefore easy to consider them abnormal and to overlook the fact that they fail to meet any of the other criteria for abnormality.

Beyond the political abuse that relies on the definitional ambiguities of abnormality, the potential for abuse arises from the fact that the meanings of abnormality change dramatically over time. For example, in DSM-II, which was approved by the American Psychiatric Association in 1968, homosexuality was listed as a mental disorder. But new information revealed that as many as 10 percent of the adult population practice homosexuality. The behavior, therefore, was no longer as unconventional as it had seemed, nor did it violate community standards as intensely as it had earlier. Consequently, in 1976, by a vote of its membership, the association decided that homosexuality was no longer a mental disorder. Similarly, in 1966, the American Association for Mental Deficiency reduced the IQ required for designating a person "mentally retarded" from 80 to 70, thereby releasing more than a million people from the retarded category (Bryan and Bryan, 1975). Attitudes toward work, sexuality, manners, the opposite sex, marriage, clothing—indeed, toward most of the significant aspects of social life

* Pate v. Robinson, 383 U.S. 375, 378 (1966).

—have changed over the decades and will continue to change. Canons of appropriate behavior and attitude are fundamental to judgments of normality and abnormality. As these canons change, so will change our notions of what is normal, and what is abnormal.

Potential for abuse arises also from the fact that society endows psychologists and psychiatrists with enormous power. Perry London (1964) says they constitute a "secular priesthood"; Thomas Szasz (1963) sees (and decries) the rise of the "therapeutic state." But any general reservations we might have about psychiatry and psychology often dissolve when our own lives are touched by psychological distress. We tend to accept the views of "experts." Our personal reliance on a practitioner, and our vulnerability to the practitioner's judgments and recommendations, make all clients of psychiatry and psychology particularly vulnerable to abuse. In the next section, we will distinguish broadly between two kinds of potential abuse: abuse by state and abuse by society.

ABUSE BY STATE

Psychiatric diagnosis and subsequent involuntary hospitalization have been used to stifle political dissent. Particularly during the past decade, it has been revealed that such political psychiatry is heavily relied upon in the Soviet Union. At least 210 cases of *sane* people who were interned in Soviet prison-hospitals for political reasons have been reported (Block and Reddaway, 1977). Others claim even higher figures (see Podrabenek, in Fireside, 1979).

How is this done? And how especially in the Soviet Union, where the legal safeguards against abuse of involuntary commitment procedures are clearly stronger than they are in many other countries? The Soviet code, for example, allows the individual's family to nominate one or more psychiatrists to the examining commission; it requires that the family be notified of the results of the examination; and it states that an individual cannot be held for more than three days. Nevertheless, considerable potential for abuse exists, as the experience of the Russian scientist Zhores A. Medvedev indicates.

The Soviet prison-hospital at Oryol, southwest of Moscow. (© Peter Reddaway)

Left: Pyotr Grigorenko. *Right:* Zhores Medvedev. (*Left:* Courtesy The Warder Collection. *Right:* © M. J. Tatham, National Institute for Medical Research, London)

Medvedev is a talented biologist whose interests run from gerontology (the science of aging), to the sociology and history of science. One of his manuscripts was confiscated by the Soviet secret police during a search of a colleague's apartment. There was nothing illegal about the manuscript, but it had been found amid a group of "samizdat," or underground publications. Medvedev, moreover, was known to be an outspoken scientist, who had been in "trouble" before. In fact, he had been unemployed for more than a year, having been relieved of his post in the Institute of Medical Radiology.

Medvedev was first tricked into a psychiatric interview, which was conducted under the guise of discussing his son. Subsequently, two psychiatrists, as well as several police, arrived at his home. Medvedev was interviewed under quite strained conditions and then forcibly removed to the local psychiatric hospital. He was seen subsequently by several other psychiatrists. He must have appeared generally quite robust to them, for the best they could say was that he had a "psychopathic personality" (the Soviet term for neurotic), "an exaggerated opinion of himself" and that he was "poorly adapted to his social environment." They noted that his writing in recent years was weaker than his earlier work, and observed as a further symptom that Medvedev had shown " 'excessively scrupulous' attention to detail in his general writings" (Medvedev and Medvedev, 1971).

Medvedev was held for nineteen days, a relatively brief period for these proceedings, and then released. Pyotr Grigorenko suffered a worse fate. Grigorenko was a distinguished general who had served in the Red Army for thirty-five years. At the age of fifty-four, he began to question the policies of the Communist Party of which he was a member. Ultimately, he was remanded for psychiatric examination at Moscow's Serbsky Institute, where his diagnosis read, "Paranoid development of the personality, with reformist ideas arising in the personality, with psychopathic features of the character and the presence of symptoms of arteriosclerosis of the brain." Shortly thereafter, he underwent an examination by a second group of psychiatrists who found him admirably sane and vigorous. But a third commission overruled the second. Grigorenko spent six years in three of the most difficult Soviet "psychoprisons" before he was permitted to emigrate to the United States. (Fireside, 1979)

While some of the psychiatrists who examined Medvedev and Grigorenko may well have subverted scientific knowledge to political expediency, many probably did not. Rather, they were well-known and highly regarded psychiatrists, both within and outside of the Soviet Union who truly believed that these people were ill. These psychiatrists would point out that

Left: Ezra Pound was confined in St. Elizabeth's Hospital after being judged incompetent to stand trial for treason. *Right:* This is the section of St. Elizabeth's Hospital where Pound was confined. (United Press International Photos)

one symptom of their "illness"—and not, by any means, the only one—was their unconventionality, which consisted in their open questioning and occasional defiance of the "system."

The unwitting use of psychology and psychiatry for political ends is not a practice that is confined to the Soviet Union. For example, they have also been so used in the United States, as shown below:

> When the Second World War was over, Ezra Pound, the eminent poet, was taken into custody by the American troops in Italy, returned to the United States, and charged with treason. Pound had lived in fascist Italy during the war and had supported Mussolini. It was alleged that the broadcasts that Pound made from Rome were treasonous. Pound denied the charge, but he never came to trial. Instead, the government and his attorneys agreed that he was incompetent to stand trial. He was therefore remanded to St. Elizabeth's Hospital in Washington, D.C., and effectively imprisoned without trial. Thirteen years later, in 1958, he was still considered "insane," incurably so, but not dangerous to others. He was therefore released.

All his life, Pound had been an eccentric: enormously conceited, flamboyant, sometimes downright outrageous. But he had never had a brush with the law, nor had he been remanded for psychiatric care. But because his politics were aversive, his eccentricities were invoked to indicate that he was not of sane mind and therefore that he could not stand trial (Torrey, 1983). As you saw in Chapter 9, relatively innocent behaviors change meaning drastically when observed in a diagnostic context. In Pound's case, conceit and flamboyance became "grandiosity of ideas and beliefs," contributing to the psychiatric impression that he was of unsound mind.

Abuse of psychology and psychiatry by the state occurs when the state is threatened by the actions of the individual. Fear underlies the state's abuse. It also underlies abuse by society, to which we now turn.

ABUSE BY SOCIETY

During the 1972 presidential campaign, George McGovern, the front-running Democratic nominee, proposed Senator Thomas Eagleton as his vice-presidential running mate. Eagleton apparently neglected to tell McGovern that he had been treated for depression, either because he viewed that as a private matter or because the stigma of such treatment might deprive him of the candidacy. In the latter, he was right: the press soon learned that Eagleton had undergone treatment and made a national story of it. After much pressure, McGovern took Eagleton off the ticket. There was no question of Eagleton's effectiveness: he had served splendidly as a senator from Missouri. Rather, there was considerable fear that he would weaken the ticket. He was, after all, stigmatized.

Society stigmatizes ordinary people who have sought psychiatric care, often to the disadvantage of both the individual and society, as the following case indicates:

> Myra Grossman had had a difficult childhood and adolescence. Yet she managed to survive well enough to graduate high school, enter college, and be at the very top of her class during her first two years. Conflicts with her parents, however, and a nagging depression continued unabated and, during her third year, she left school to seek treatment. She began seeing a psychotherapist and subsequently entered a private psychiatric hospital. During that year, Myra developed considerable ability to deal with her own distress and her family conflicts. She returned to college, continued to major in both chemistry and psychology, earned her Phi Beta Kappa in her junior year, and graduated magna cum laude.
>
> During her senior year, she applied to medical school. Her Medical College Aptitude Test (MCAT) scores were extraordinarily high, and she had won a New York State Regent's Medical Scholarship. But she was rejected by all thirteen schools to which she had applied.
>
> She consulted an attorney, and they jointly decided to concentrate on the "easiest" school that had rejected her. During the trial, it became known that fewer than 8 percent of those admitted to this school had won the Regent's Medical Scholarship, that none had been admitted to Phi Beta Kappa, and that she possibly had the highest MCAT scores of any applicant. She was an attractive person, obviously well motivated, clearly bright. Why then had she been rejected? Clearly, it was because of her prior psychiatric hospitalization.
>
> Ms. Grossman and her attorney marshaled clear evidence that she was quite well integrated psychologically. Five psychiatrists and a psychologist testified in effect that she was the better for her prior troubles, and that they had no doubt that she could successfully complete medical school and become a first-rate doctor. She and her attorney successfully demolished the contention that she might still suffer from her prior "illness." But still, the judge ruled against her. Ms. Grossman might have appealed that decision, and might well have won her appeal had not a far better medical school admitted her when the ruling came down. (Ennis, 1972)

SUMMARY

1. The constitutional privileges that are available to ordinary citizens are not extended to the severely distressed, who can be deprived of liberty through *involuntary commitment*, often without trial.

2. Depending on the state in which they reside, individuals who are psychologically disabled can be hospitalized involuntarily, provided they either experience impaired judgment, are in need of treatment, are suffering a behavioral disability, or are dangerous to themselves or others. The notion of dangerousness, especially, is rife with scientific, legal, and moral problems.

3. Involuntary commitment deprives a person of liberty. Before it occurs, *clear and convincing* evidence must be marshaled that indicates that the person requires hospitalization.

4. Several significant court decisions have held that those committed to psychiatric hospitals have a *right to treatment* that includes individual diagnosis and the preparation of a treatment plan that is periodically reviewed. One negative consequence of right-to-treatment decisions has been the decline in support for mental health programs, as the states often prefer to cut back their support for these programs rather than incurring the additional costs of implementing proper treatment.

5. *Criminal commitment* can occur either because a person was "insane" at the time of the crime, or because he or she is presently psychologically incompetent to stand trial.

6. The *insanity defense* requires that the defendant was wholly or partially irrational when the crime took place, and that this irrationality affected his or her behavior. While the insanity defense seemingly protects those who commit crimes while distressed, the fact is that such people are commonly sent to prison-hospitals, where care is worse than in prisons themselves, and incarceration longer. Because being indefinitely committed to a psychiatric hospital is often worse than going to prison, the insanity defense is rarely used.

7. Historically, there have been three views of the insanity defense: the M'Naghten "right-wrong" test, the Durham "product of mental disease test, and the American Law Institute (ALI) "appreciate and conform" rule. Today, there is no uniform insanity defense in Western countries, although in the United States an increasing number of states, as well as the federal courts, favor the American Law Institute formulation.

8. The notion of *competence to stand trial* is rooted in the right of every person to defend himself against accusations. A person judged incompetent to stand trial is sent to an institution for the criminally insane until he is able to be tried, which often means a long incarceration. The courts have recently decided that people who can never become competent to stand trial need not be "hospitalized" forever. But there is still no uniform practice regarding how long those who are treatably incompetent may be committed, and whether the time spent in such commitment is later to be subtracted from the defendant's sentence.

9. Psychiatry and psychology are particularly prone to social and political abuses. Both in the United States and in the Soviet Union, people who should have been given their day in court have been summarily committed to psychiatric hospitals, there to languish, often for many years.

10. Considerable stigma attaches to seeking or requiring psychological care. That stigma may continue long after the psychological problem has been solved.

A Consumer's Guide to Psychological Treatment

I T happens—more often than we would wish—that people have psychological problems. A century ago, these people might have been sent off to a good friend, a relative, or perhaps a priest who would have offered them sympathy, wisdom, and prayer. But today, as one writer observes, we have a "secular priesthood," a panoply of professional and nonprofessional counselors and therapists, all of whom stand ready to deal with the psychological troubles that were once the province of family and Church (London, 1964). One in five people will seek the advice of these therapists sometime during their lives, fully half of them for problems that are quite serious and painful. How should they go about it? From the many available therapists and therapies, how should they choose the ones that are most likely to help, and help quickly.

In this chapter, we bring together a group of issues associated with treatment, often issues that have been remarked upon earlier. First, we describe those who treat psychological difficulties. We then consider the ingredients that all good therapies have in common, regardless of whether they are biological, psychodynamic, cognitive, behavioral, or humanistic, and regardless of whether they are practiced by highly trained professionals or by nonprofessionals. Understanding these ingredients should enable anyone to make a better choice of a therapist, and also to avoid the pitfalls of poorly practiced treatments (which are also described in this chapter). Subsequently, we recommend the best treatments for certain kinds of problems. Our recommendations are based on good evidence where that exists and on clinical wisdom where it does not. Finally, we discuss community psychological approaches that are concerned with prevention as much as treatment, and with social and economic remedies as much as psychological ones.

© 1966 United Feature Syndicate, Inc.

WHO TREATS?

A large number of people and disciplines are concerned with treating psychological difficulties, and it is sometimes hard to distinguish among them. Some professional training takes many years to acquire, while other skills may require just a few months. Some therapists are certified and licensed in the states in which they reside. Others are not. A potential client is always entitled to inquire carefully about the training, licenses, certificates, and experience of anyone he or she consults. Do not be embarrassed to do this. It is equivalent to looking carefully at all the rooms in a house before purchasing or renting it. Professionals and nonprofessionals alike respect these questions; they spare all concerned from making costly mistakes.

Psychologists who offer psychological assessment and therapeutic services have obtained advanced graduate training in clinical, counseling, or school psychology. Usually, but not invariably, they hold a Ph.D. (Doctor of Philosophy) or a Psy.D. (Doctor of Psychology) degree. The former degree emphasizes training in both research and therapeutic techniques, while the latter emphasizes only therapeutic training. Training in these areas requires four or five years *after* the bachelor's degree, and it is usually followed by an extensive internship. Additionally, nearly all states require psychologists to pass a licensing or certification examination.

Not all psychologists are qualified to assess and treat. Only those trained in clinical, counseling, or school psychology should be consulted. *Clinical psychologists* work mainly with people who suffer psychological difficulties, *counseling psychologists* deal with vocational problems as well, while *school psychologists* focus on academic difficulties, mainly with children.

Psychiatrists are physicians who, after completing college, have earned a medical degree, and have completed a three-year residency in a mental health facility. Subsequently, many but not all psychiatrists take an examination in psychiatry and become board-certified. Psychiatrists are the only psychological professionals who can prescribe medications and administer such treatments as electroshock. Of course, psychiatrists often make use of psychological treatments as well.

Psychiatric social workers have completed a two-year postgraduate program in individual and group social work techniques, which includes extensive training in interviewing and in treatment.

Psychiatric nurses are centrally concerned with the care of hospitalized psychiatric patients. Beyond their basic courses in nursing, they receive training in psychiatry and psychology, as well as supervised experience on a psychiatric unit. On any psychiatric ward, the nurse is usually the person in charge of ward management, housekeeping, and recreation, as well as the one who administers medication.

Psychoanalysts are fully trained mental health professionals—psychiatrists mainly, but also psychologists, social workers, and sometimes clergy —who have undertaken further training in a specific treatment method: psychoanalysis. Such training is offered in psychoanalytic training institutes, and requires several years to complete. Psychoanalysts-in-training must undergo their own personal psychoanalysis, as well as treat several clients psychoanalytically, before they are considered fully accredited.

The *clergy,* that is, ministers, rabbis, and priests, are increasingly being trained to do personal counseling, not only with problems of a distinctly religious nature, but often with problems that go quite beyond those. While the quality of training in pastoral counseling, as it is sometimes called, is highly variable, many clergy augment their seminary training in graduate departments of psychology or social work, and in postgraduate institutes.

Psychiatric attendants or *aides* are paraprofessionals who work exclusively in psychiatric hospitals. Their training can vary widely. Some are high school graduates. Others have attended community colleges, many of which

Here a marriage counselor is treating a couple for problems in their relationship. (Photograph by Ann Chwatsky/Leo de Wys)

train mental health paraprofessionals to work on psychiatric wards. Most attendants receive brief on-the-job training to work with the severely disturbed. From the viewpoint of hospitalized patients, the attendants are the most important people in their day-to-day lives. It is the attendants with whom they interact most, and who determine whether their experience in the hospital will be pleasant or unpleasant.

Skills therapists also work in psychiatric hospitals and have special abilities in the work-related, recreational, or artistic realms. These include occupational, art, and educational therapists, music and dance therapists, as well as recreational therapists of all kinds. These therapists enable patients to pass time pleasantly and constructively. They also provide a setting for developing psychosocial skills and for expressing personal problems. A dance therapist, for example, may enable a person to express feelings through dance that cannot otherwise be expressed verbally.

Marriage and family counselors deal with relationship problems that arise within the family. These therapists usually have postgraduate training, but commonly they do not possess doctoral degrees. They are licensed to treat family problems.

The provision of therapeutic services has become a big business that has spawned a host of nonprofessional therapists during the past decade or two. Massage therapists, hypnotherapists, primal therapists, Zen therapists, and bioenergetic therapists, are among those who, for want of a better term, we call *miscellaneous therapists.* Becoming one or another of these therapists may require little or much training. But it is not formal training at a recognized academic or medical institution. Commonly, the government neither licenses these therapists nor certifies their skills, nor are there professional organizations that control their activities. Finally, by and large what they offer has not been evaluated for therapeutic effectiveness. As a result, *caveat emptor*—client, beware!

A young man had been "tight and tense" for more than two years when he began to experience paranoid delusions and hallucinations. He was referred by a friend to a massage therapist, who treated the client with deep massage while encouraging him to recall "the memories that are stored in your muscles and bones." This treatment continued for eighteen months. The man's condition deteriorated until finally he became so discouraged and disordered that he required hospitalization. Had he been seen earlier by a trained therapist, there seems little doubt that a combination of drugs and counseling would have brought about improvement in short order.

Several nonprofessional peer self-help groups exist to help overcome specific problems, and these groups appear to be quite effective. Alcoholics Anonymous (AA) is one such group; Weight Watchers and TOPS (Take Off Pounds Sensibly) are others. Similar problem-oriented groups, such as Daytop Village and Phoenix House, exist for drug addicts.

One type of self-help group deserves special note, and that is the consciousness raising (CR) or "rap" group. This form of self-help grew originally out of the political needs of minority groups, and it now extends to women, the elderly (e.g., The Gray Panthers), homosexuals (e.g., Gay Liberation), and a variety of mental patient groups. Fundamentally, such groups are political and intellectual. Through the common exploration of "personal" problems, group members come to understand that their difficulties are often shared by others. The recognition that painful individual problems are neither unique nor idiosyncratic encourages members to seek larger solutions to these problems, often through social and political action.

Jane Williams experienced enormous discomfort at her office. Her boss continually put his arm around her and frequently suggested that they see each other after work. At first, Jane felt that she had somehow provoked his interest. Resolving to put an end to his advances, she dressed conservatively for work and kept a professional distance. To no avail. Finally, with great embarrassment, she mentioned the problem at a meeting of a women's group to which she belonged, and she was surprised to find that many of her friends had had the same experience. The fact that the problem was not idiosyncratic gave her considerable comfort, and subsequently, a diplomatic visit to the personnel office brought about a much-hoped-for transfer to another department.

THE COMMON INGREDIENTS OF THERAPY

Psychological therapy consists of a systematic series of interactions between a trained therapist who has been authorized by society to minister to psychological problems, and one or more clients who are troubled, or troubling others, because of such problems. The goal of psychological therapy is to produce cognitive, emotional, and behavioral changes that will alleviate those problems. While professional therapists are trained for the job, and paid as well, that should not blind us to the fact that there are strong similarities between the ways they function and the manner in which friends, relatives, and clergy dealt with those problems in earlier times and continue to deal with them today.

In fact, it would be a serious mistake to identify treatment wholly with the training of the therapist and the nature of the treatment he or she dispenses, for there is much more to treatment than that. In order for treatment to be maximally effective, a therapeutic relationship needs to be established, one that is voluntary and cooperative and that maximally fulfills the expectations of each participant. For only rarely do clients enter treatment suddenly or lightly. The decision to seek professional help is commonly preceded by agonizing conflict, conflict that may last for months or years. To begin with, most people try to solve their problems by themselves. Then, they may seek out parents, teachers, ministers, and friends. But it is only when all else fails that they seek professional treatment. And then, they come with a headful of hopes, expectations, and information; some of it accurate, some inaccurate, and much of it likely to affect the course of treatment.

Unlike many other transactions, the effectiveness of the therapeutic relationship depends heavily for its success on the free choices, hopes, expectations, and relationships of the participants. You can have your shoes redone by the neighborhood cobbler and neither your personal view of him nor his of you matters for the success of that venture; only his cobbling skill counts. Not so in psychological treatment. There, a host of "common treatment factors" play a large role in determining outcome (Kazdin, 1979). The success of highly skilled therapists is augmented massively, or greatly reduced, by the interplay of such common treatment factors as the free choices of the client, his or her hopes and expectations, the personal qualities of the therapist, and the match between those qualities and the needs of the client. We begin with the matter of free choice because choice affects the therapeutic relationship from the very outset.

Free Choice and Treatment

You can bring a horse to water, the saying goes, but you can't make it drink. That adage holds for psychological treatment, too. Clinical experience strongly suggests that children who are dragged unwillingly into treatment, spouses who enter marriage therapy under threat of divorce, and patients who are involuntarily committed to psychiatric hospitals, all suffer substantial deficits in motivation and understanding that make treatment less effective. The best way to enter treatment is willingly and fully informed; any other way substantially diminishes the likelihood of successful outcome, regardless of the kind of therapy.

The role of choice and volition in therapeutic outcome was splendidly demonstrated by Devine and Fernald (1973). Clients who suffered snake phobias were shown films of four possible treatments. Some clients were permitted to choose the treatment they preferred; others were randomly assigned to treatment; and yet a third group was required to undergo a nonpreferred treatment. Those who received the treatment they preferred had the more successful therapeutic experience. Of course, each of the treatments was known to be useful with phobias of this sort. What would have happened if the clients chose a treatment that was inappropriate for the disorder? We do not presently know, nor for obvious ethical reasons can we find out directly. But quite probably, even clients who choose an inappropriate treatment will fare better than clients who are compelled to undertake that treatment.

Clients who are forced into treatment likely will view it as a mere exercise in compliance, or a punishment. Unless time and effort are taken to convince them otherwise, treatment will fail. Conversely, those who enter treatment of their own free choice are more likely to benefit from it. Their hopes and expectations are themselves curative, greatly augmenting the effectiveness of any treatment. We therefore turn to the nature of hopes and expectations in therapy.

HOPES AND EXPECTATIONS

A unique characteristic of humans is that their expectations about the future powerfully affect their experiences and behaviors in the present (Frank, 1978). The hope of eventual salvation has sustained countless people, enabling them to endure lifetimes of misery. For others, as we saw in Chapter 13, the belief that the future is hopeless has intensified their depression. In similar fashion, expectations strongly affect psychological treatment. "Expectation . . . coloured by hope and faith," Freud wrote, "is an effective force with which we have to reckon . . . in *all* our attempts at treatment and cure" (Freud, 1905/1976, p. 289).

Molding Client Expectations

Clients and therapists often have distorted expectations of each other that may impede therapeutic progress. Insight therapists, for example, expect clients to talk about their feelings, experiences, and often, their dreams. But clients, especially those from lower-class backgrounds, tend to talk about their psychological symptoms precisely as they might describe a sore throat to a physician. Their expectations about how therapists behave are frustrated when they are asked about feelings and dreams. Conversely, therapists gain the impression that clients will not profit from treatment when the clients persist in merely describing their ailments and when they continue to be reluctant to discuss feelings and dreams. One result of these jointly disappointed expectations is that lower-class clients drop out of insight therapy at a considerably higher rate than middle- and upper-class clients.

To deal with this problem, Jerome Frank and his colleagues devised a Role Induction Interview, during which clients' expectations about treatment could be molded (Hoehn-Saric, Frank, Imber, Nash, Stone, and Battle, 1964; Nash, Hoehn-Saric, Battle, Stone, Imber, and Frank, 1965; Orne and Wender, 1968). In a controlled study, lower-class clients were interviewed briefly before entering treatment and told what they could expect. Psychotherapy, they were told, is a way of learning to deal more effectively with life's problems, but it takes time and practice to implement what is learned. They were told that four months would be needed before improvement was seen, and even then, that they would still have problems, though they would be coping more effectively. Further, they were told that the therapist would talk very little, but would listen carefully and try to understand the problems. They were advised that they were to talk freely, describe fantasies and daydreams, express feelings, and especially, feelings toward the therapist. The concept of resistance was explained in everyday language and was described to them as evidence that the client was approaching and dealing with issues that were both significant for progress and difficult to face. Such difficulties were to be viewed as a positive sign of progress. A second group of clients was given no information on what they might expect during treatment.

The therapeutic results for clients who participated in the brief interview were remarkable. First, their drop-out rate declined precipitously. Therapists were behaving the way they were supposed to behave, so clients experienced less need to terminate. Second, therapist ratings of clients' improvement were considerably higher for these clients than for the control group that had not gone through the Role Induction Interview. Finally, clients rated themselves as considerably more improved on their target complaints if they had experienced the Role Induction Interview, than if they had not.

The Role Induction Interview may have brought client expectations in line with their therapists' expectations, led clients to behave in ways that increased therapist optimism about, and liking for, them. These considerations correlate highly with clients' tendency to remain in therapy (Rosenzweig and Forman, 1974; Shapiro, 1974), and with therapist ratings of client improvement (Shapiro, Struening, Shapiro, and Barten, 1976).

Anticipatory socialization of the sort that is conveyed in such interviews has been found to affect clients and therapists in a wide variety of settings. Hospitalized lower-class patients benefit from it (Heitler, 1973), as do clients in group therapy (Yalom, Houts, Newell, and Rand, 1967). Moreover, films that portray therapy sessions, and even tape recordings of therapy sessions, work as well as informative interviews to prepare clients for treatment (Truax, Shapiro, and Wargo, 1968; Strupp and Bloxom, 1973). In short, any information that enables clients to develop reasonable expectations about treatment facilitates treatment.

While shared expectations of clients and therapists regarding the process of treatment clearly affect its outcome, so too do expectations regarding the outcome itself. Indeed, the belief that treatment will be effective is itself such a powerful treatment that the mere anticipation of cure often brings at least momentary relief and, not uncommonly, permanent gains. Such cures are termed "placebo effects."

The Placebo Effect

A placebo is a pharmacologically inert substance, and the **placebo effect** describes positive treatment outcomes that result from the administration of such substances. Placebo effects, as we have seen in Chapter 8, occur with surprising regularity in a variety of settings. Beecher (1961) reported that about 40 percent of patients who were suffering from a painful heart disease called angina pectoris experienced marked relief from their symptoms after merely undergoing a mock operation! In a late study, Ross found that 60 percent of patients who had undergone surgery to improve their blood circulation showed clinical improvement, even though the surgery may have left the blood supply to the heart unchanged and, in fact, may have reduced it (Ross, 1976, cited in Frank, 1978).

Placebos are often as effective as psychotropic medications in treating psychological disorders, and their dosage curves show similar characteristics. In the first part of a double-blind study, about 35 percent of patients who were given either drugs or placebos at a particular dosage level improved. Subsequently, the dosages of drugs and placebos were doubled in the second part of the study, and improvement rates jumped to 66 percent for patients on active drugs, and 76 percent for those on placebos (Lowinger and Dobie, 1969).

What is it that makes the placebo, a mere inert substance, so powerful? The power of the placebo resides in the expectation that positive results will accrue from a particular treatment (Cousins, 1979). So long as the client believes that the treatment works, it will likely have some positive effect. In no way are these effects shams or fakes, or merely the results of the gullibility of impressionable clients. Rather, they appear to be powerful treatments in themselves for reasons that are not yet fully understood. Current speculation suggests that the effects of placebos are mediated through a group of enzymes called endorphins. Endorphins have been called "the brain's opiates." They affect how individuals subjectively experience pain and mood, and they may be produced when one expects to become well and able to cope.

Free choice, rational expectations, and effective hope are crucial for therapeutic success. But they are not sufficient. The therapist's personal characteristics, and how those characteristics fulfill the needs and expectations of the clients, are necessary ingredients for successful therapy. Not all characteristics play a central role in treatment, but some, such as empathy, warmth, and genuineness seem absolutely necessary. We turn to those characteristics now.

CHARACTERISTICS OF THE THERAPIST

Therapist Empathy, Warmth, and Genuineness

Humanistic therapists in particular have stressed the role of therapist empathy, warmth, and personal genuineness in facilitating the therapeutic relationship and, presumably, in increasing the likelihood of a positive outcome. **Empathy** describes the "ability of the therapist accurately and sensitively to understand experiences and feelings and their meaning to the client during the moment-to-moment encounter of psychotherapy" (Rogers and Truax, 1967, p. 104). **Warmth** is manifest in the therapeutic relationship when "the therapist communicates to his client a deep and genuine caring for him as a person with human potentialities, a caring uncontaminated by evaluations of his thoughts, feelings, or behaviors" (Rogers and Truax, 1967, p. 102). Therapist **genuineness** means precisely that: the therapist avoids communicating in a phony, "professional," or defensive manner. He is "freely and deeply himself" (Truax and Carkhuff, 1967). Obviously, a therapist can neither be empathic nor warm if he or she is not being genuine. Obviously, too, when shopping for a therapist, genuineness may be one of the first things to look for.

It is generally believed that warmth, empathy, and genuineness are necessary preconditions for successful therapy, though they do not guarantee it (Gurman, 1977; Mitchell, Bozarth, and Krauft, 1977). These characteristics would seem to apply to all kinds of therapists, regardless of their orientation. For example, with regard to behavior therapy (which concentrates on changing immediate behavior rather than the exploration of feelings), Marks and Gelder (1966) have argued that the single most important ingredient in determining outcome is the relationship between client and therapist. Moreover, Morris and Suckerman (1974a, 1974b) have shown that "warm" therapists are far more effective than "cold" ones in utilizing the behavioral techniques of desensitization for snake phobias.

Therapist Experience

Beyond warmth, empathy, and genuineness, are there other therapist characteristics that facilitate treatment? There probably are, but their meaning is not entirely clear. Consider the matter of experience. Some studies find that experienced therapists promote greater improvement among their clients than do inexperienced ones (Myers and Auld, 1955; Katz, Lorr, and Rubinstein, 1958; Cartwright and Vogel, 1960; Barrett-Lennard, 1962; Strupp, Wallach, and Wogan, 1964; Scher, 1975). To the extent that empathy and genuineness are requisites for therapeutic progress, they are likely to be found in greater quantity among experienced therapists, if only because experience makes one more comfortable and competent in that role. Nonetheless, other studies have found no relationship between therapist experience and client outcome (Fiske, Cartwright, and Kirtner, 1964; Fiske and Goodman, 1965; Strupp, Fox, and Lessler, 1969; Auerbach and Johnson, 1977). Relatively inexperienced therapists may bring enormous enthusiasm to treatment, thereby compensating for the fact that they are relatively "green." Conversely, experienced therapists may become tired and less empathic with time. Experience, then, is no uniform guarantor of excellence in therapy, although there are no studies in which inexperienced therapists were more successful than experienced ones.

Other Concerns

Other factors that might possibly influence therapeutic outcome, such as gender, race, social class, sexual preference, religious involvement, and marital status, have not been fully investigated yet. Some studies have found that opposite-sex dyads communicate more effectively with each other (Cartwright and Lerner, 1963; Brooks, 1974), others (e.g., Mendelsohn and Geller, 1963) have suggested that this is not the case. These are matters where good sense is more important than research findings. A woman whose problems touch on matters of feminism, for example, may want to see a female therapist. But because all female therapists are not feminists nor even sympathetic to feminist concerns, a sensitive male therapist may be as effective (Rawlings and Carter, 1977). Gender alone is no certain guide to insight and understanding.

During the first sessions, clients will do well to explore the concerns that lead them to prefer a particular type (i.e., female, religious) of therapist. A good therapist may well be sensitive to, and understanding of, a wide variety of concerns and issues that reach beyond the therapist's own gender, sexual orientation, religious preference, and the like. But the sad fact is that in therapy, as in other matters, one does not always get what one desires. Consider: about seven out of ten therapists are male, but the majority of clients are female. Therapists come mainly from the upper middle class, clients from all classes. Nearly all therapists are white, but clients come in all colors. In a very large city, a black woman who wants to consult a black feminist therapist may be lucky enough to find one. But people in small cities and towns, where few qualified therapists practice, are not likely to be lucky enough to find therapists with all the desired characteristics, as the following case demonstrates:

She is the intelligent, well-educated mother of two small children, wife of a popular internist in a small, remote town. Increasingly, she finds herself depressed. Worse, she finds herself jealous of her husband, who gets all of the community rewards ("Oh, Dr. Barker—isn't he just wonderful . . . ") while she gets the diapers. The very intensity of her feelings troubles her. With the passage of time, she hurts more and more and understands less and less. She tries to talk to her husband— really, her best friend—but he reacts guiltily and defensively. He really does love his work and finds it hard to understand that his pleasure and success should cause her such pain.

What to do? Somehow, she feels this is a "woman's problem" and would prefer to see a woman. In fact, she would prefer to see a woman who is a feminist, one who understands something of the social and political aspects of womanhood, in addition to the psychological ones. Most of all, she wants someone to reassure her that though she is quite upset, she is not crazy, and that her feelings have some basis in reality.

There are two therapists in her town, both men, both colleagues of her husband. One of them is "fresh out" of his residency. She finds him too young. The other is well into his seventies. He seems too old. She has other concerns about these therapists as well, but already her dilemma is clear. There are no nonprofessional alternatives in town: no women's groups in which these matters could be discussed, no sympathetic clergy. What should she do?

Perhaps you can find a solution to her dilemma. We cannot. Some problems simply do not lend themselves to easy solutions, and this is one of them. She might try one of the psychiatrists in town, and begin by discussing her reservations and discomforts about working with him. He *might* be able to get her over these hurdles, but then again he might not. Psychotherapists, like the rest of us, are merely human. Alternately, she might wait until spring thawed the mountain snow, and travel some three hours to a larger city. Even then, there is no guarantee that the help she wants would be found. For some problems there are no easy solutions.

Avoiding the "Psychonoxious" Therapist

Most therapists are professionals in whom one can trust. A few, however, are not. Whether from defects of training, character, or personality, they are unlikely to help and more likely to harm. In addition, there are therapists who, while useful to some, are harmful to others. Below follow some ways in which to detect such therapists (Haley, 1969; Segal, 1968).

NEVER WORK WITH A THERAPIST WHOSE PERSONALITY IS DISTASTEFUL. If you find the therapist is aggressive, frequently angry or sadistic, impatient, challenging, or nasty, find another! Such therapists, regardless of their reputation, are unlikely to be able to do any good, and can often do considerable harm, as in the following case:

One therapist spent two years mocking a client's passivity, appearing to retch every time she said something sweet. It was his conviction that this client needed to know how others felt about her, and he feigned retching in order to demonstrate. But the effects on the client were simply disastrous. Intimidated by him as she was by others, she became all the more sweetly passive, hoping thereby to avert yet another disaster. Only the insistence of friends made her terminate the treatment. While one ought not to expect a therapist to be constantly agreeable and protective, a therapist should appear to respect the client and to care for his or her well-being.

BEWARE OF SEXUAL EXPLOITATION.   A substantial minority of psychologists and psychiatrists acknowledge having had a sexual relationship with one or more clients (Keith-Spiegel, 1977). Occasionally, such relationships are rationalized by the therapists on the grounds that they teach clients to enjoy "intimacy" or simply to make love. Oddly and overwhelmingly, however, these clients are women, while the therapists are male. (Women therapists rarely find male clients in need of such instruction!) These practices have more to do with the needs of the therapists and their own psychological immaturity than any treatment goal. There is no evidence that physical intimacy with one's therapist works for the client's benefit. When intimacy is suggested, the client should terminate treatment.

AVOID SUSPICIOUSLY HIGH FEES.   One of the most self-serving myths among psychologists and psychiatrists is that the more the client pays, the more progress he or she makes in treatment. Pure nonsense! Some of the finest clinicians work in colleges and community clinics where fees are low or nonexistent. It you feel you are being overcharged, discuss the matter with your therapist. If you can't reach a comfortable understanding, seek help elsewhere.

KNOW YOUR MEDICINES.   If a psychiatrist has prescribed psychoactive drugs (and only a physician can prescribe such drugs), you deserve to know the names of the drugs that are being prescribed, what symptoms they are supposed to treat, how long it will be before effects are seen, how long you will have to take them, and what the short-term and long-term side effects of these drugs are. Anything less than a frank and open response to your inquiries violates the requirements of effective treatment that were discussed earlier, and may be dangerous to your health besides.

BE FREE TO QUESTION.   Sometimes treatment bogs down. Clients, and often therapists, feel that insufficient progress is being made. If you feel that way, raise the matter openly with the therapist. Often progress is blocked because the client has hit a *resistance*: a transient inability to deal with a significant issue. Such resistances may seem insurmountable, but they are commonly signs that progress is about to be made. Talking about feelings openly often helps to overcome resistances.

But sometimes progress is blocked, not by resistance, but by the therapist's lack of skill. Not all therapists can help all clients all the time. A therapist may occasionally lack the ability to help the client surmount particular kinds of difficulties. Again, open discussion of the stalemate can yield insight and resolution. If it does not, ask for a consultation with another professional. An objective third party can frequently shed light on the causes of stalemate, enabling client and therapist to continue their progress.

If the therapist refuses a consultation, however, seek help elsewhere. And surely if, at any time during treatment, the therapist forbids discussing treatment with anyone else, question the therapist carrefully. Such admonitions, often given on the grounds that therapy is a private matter, are equally often self-serving. They may be designed to protect the therapist, not you.

SPECIFY TREATMENT GOALS.   The goals of treatment should be specified early in the treatment process. Otherwise, the treatment risks floundering. Many therapists arrive at an agreement with clients, not only regarding goals of treatment, but also how long treatment will last. That agreement is put in the form of a contract that serves to remind each party of their aims and obligations. Though not universal by any means, such contracts appear to hasten progress in treatment, especially when time seems to be running out. Then, clients really bend their energies toward getting the most out of what time is left. When a therapist cannot specify the goals of treatment fairly concretely, or when client and therapist do not share a common understanding of these matters, it may be wiser to seek help elsewhere.

Avoiding the wrong therapist reduces the probability of dissatisfaction and harm. And finding the right therapist, one who gratifies expectations and promotes effective hope, goes a long way toward ensuring therapeutic progress. But it does not guarantee such progress by any means. Beyond the personal qualities of the therapist are the techniques that he or she employs. Some of these techniques are highly effective for certain kinds of problems. Others are less effective.

THERAPEUTIC EFFECTIVENESS

Broadly speaking, there are three ways in which one can assess the effectiveness of therapy. First, one can collect opinions regarding satisfaction with treatment from the client, as well as from his or her family, friends, and employers. Second, one can examine changes on a variety of personality measures, some of which were discussed in Chapter 9. Third, one can look at target behaviors—the behaviors that brought the client into treatment and that treatment is supposed to change. In a proper evaluation study, several measures of each of these types will be used. But some of these measures seem weaker than others.

Personal Satisfaction

Consider satisfaction. The fact of the matter is that most clients express considerable satisfaction with treatment. Indeed, it is rare to encounter someone who says that his therapy did him or her no good. Yet, client satisfaction, while important, cannot be a significant criterion of effectiveness. People can be satisfied for a variety of reasons having little or nothing to do with whether they were changed in significant ways. They may be inclined to indicate that they were satisfied merely because they had spent a good deal of time and money on treatment. It would make them quite uncomfortable to believe that it had all been for nought. Because their investment is so large, they may be motivated to seek genuine reasons for satisfaction, such as "I learned a lot about myself," even though those reasons are unrelated to the ones that brought them into treatment in the first place.

Personality Change

Global assessments of personality change are a second index of the effectiveness of treatment. Such measures are taken at the outset of therapy, often during therapy, and surely at the end of it, with "improvement" (or "deterioration") being attributed to the effects of the treatment.

This criterion of effectiveness is fraught with two kinds of hazards, the first commercial, the second scientific. The commercial one is straightforward: people rarely enter treatment to have their personalities changed (London, 1964). Rather, they seek help because they suffer a particular problem: they find it difficult to find and hold a job, hard to sustain a loving relationship, uncomfortable to be in school. They present *problems*, and it is those problems that they want to eliminate. Were it demonstrable that their problems arose from underlying personality difficulties, much as fever arises from an underlying virus, one would have little to complain about. But the relationship between presenting problems and the global personality characteristics that are said to underlie them has yet to be demonstrated. Thus, the client came to purchase one kind of help, but is sold another. That may simply be unfair from a business point of view.

Using personality change as a criterion for effectiveness encounters analogous scientific hazards, for until we truly know that a troublesome behavior is caused by an underlying personality trait, the law of parsimony suggests that therapy should attend to the client's desire that the behavior be changed. In fact, when a troublesome symptom is treated successfully, one often sees personality change. Thus, a person who is unassertive may also experience low self-esteem. Merely training him or her to be more assertive may have dramatically positive effects on self-esteem. But one ought to treat the symptoms first, on the grounds that behaviors clearly affect personality, while the reverse is not always so obvious.

Behaviors

Examining the impact of treatment on target behaviors is one of the most effective ways to assess treatment outcome. This criterion involves a careful, behavioral assessment of the problems the client presents at the outset of treatment, with further similar assessments during and at the end of treatment. These assessments may be conducted jointly by client and therapist, and they may also be conducted by outside "blind" evaluators. Their hall-

---

Box 21-1   AN FDA FOR PSYCHOLOGICAL TREATMENTS?

Before a drug can be marketed, it must undergo extensive testing and finally receive approval from the Food and Drug Administration (FDA), which ascertains that it is safe, beneficial, and effective. And from time to time, we hear that substances such as saccharin, which we had hitherto thought to be safe, may be dangerous and quite possibly should be taken off the market. Should there not be such an FDA for psychological treatment? There are estimated to be some 130 different "brands" of psychological treatment available (Parloff, 1976), and the number grows annually. Not all of these are beneficial; some may be harmful to some people or have negative side effects. Should there not be systematic evaluation of these treatments before they are made available to the public?

Gerald Klerman, the former chief of the Alcohol, Drug Abuse, and Mental Health Administration (ADAMHA) argues that such systematic evaluation must take place if only because the consumer movement and the pending National Health Insurance require it. Klerman points to the need to circumscribe legitimate mental health activity. He says:

We can attack the problem of defining boundaries in part by returning to the practical problem that many therapeutic methods are well-intended, but poorly established in terms of safety, efficacy and economy. One cannot demonstrate

mark, however, is that they are precise and replicable, and they stay quite close to the client's initial complaints.

These kinds of assessments are the benchmark of the action therapies; they have been very useful in demonstrating the effectiveness of these kinds of treatments. Indeed, they are largely responsible for the growing popularity of the action therapies, among both clients and therapists. But they are not entirely without hazards. Some behaviors are elusive and difficult to measure with precision and reliability. Problems of meaning are among these. Some complaints, moreover, are very complex and intertwined. The presence of multiple phobias, for example, which extend over a range of environments and stimuli, makes assessment complex and difficult. In the main, however, behavioral change, where it can be assessed, is the "kingpin" of measures of therapeutic effectiveness.

THE VARIETY OF TREATMENT

It has recently been estimated that clients can choose from among 130 different "brands" of therapy (Parloff, 1976). Each year the number of therapies grows. And, of course, each "therapy" has its loyal adherents who confidently proclaim its efficacy for a host of problems. Behavior modification, Rolfing, insight therapy, rebirthing, cognitive therapy, lithium, flooding, these and dozens more are possible choices. Unfortunately, it is extremely difficult to make informed choices. While claims for success are broad, the evidence is slim. Only a few controlled tests have been conducted to assess the effectiveness of particular therapies, and even fewer tests have been done to compare the relative efficacy of various treatments. Equally important, little is known about the possible harmful effects a therapy might have. There is no protection for the consumer of therapy analogous to the protection afforded the consumer of drugs (see Box 21-1). The Federal Drug

the efficacy of a therapy in terms of the intentions of its proponents. . . . Neither can a therapy be considered routine and acceptable on the basis of the testimony of authorities—that is, because outstanding members of the profession are of the opinion that it is useful, safe and effective. I believe that only evidence as to outcomes will suffice in the rigorous climate of consumerism and health insurance coverage. (A.P.A. Monitor, 1979, p. 9)

The argument for evaluating therapies before they are available in the marketplace is perfectly straightforward, but deceptively simple. Nicholas Cummings, former president of the American Psychological Association and a longtime student of psychotherapy, points out that a proper evaluation of the available therapies might take as long as twenty years (Marshall, 1980). What are we to do in the meantime? Simply let people suffer?

A more fundamental issue, however, arises from the nature of psychological treatment itself. Does psychological treatment come in the same kinds of measurable doses as, say, saccharin or red dye #2? Clearly not, for we have already seen that the nonspecific effects of psychotherapy are quite different from the very specific effects of saccharin. For saccharin's effects will occur irrespective of the circumstances under which it is taken, while psychotherapy's effects depend on the circumstances—the individuals under treatment, their hopes and expectations, the characteristics of the therapist, and other hard-to-measure variables.

Administration imposes stringent testing procedures on all new drugs *before* they can be marketed: they must be effective; they must be relatively harmless; side effects must be clearly stated. No governmental agency acts as watchdog in the case of psychotherapy. Claims can be made with no concern for evidence. Psychoanalysis, it will be recalled, was practiced for more than a half century before its claim that it was an effective treatment was scrutinized.

Nonetheless, choices have to be made. In the following section, we discuss some of the more prevalent forms of psychotherapy. After a description of the unique goals and methods of particular therapies, we turn to an examination of the kinds of problems that are best solved by one or another treatment. Although not an encyclopedic guide to all existing therapies, this overview will provide familiarity with the issues to consider when a choice must be made.

SPECIFIC VS. GLOBAL THERAPIES

It is rare that clients enter psychotherapy solely to explore themselves. More likely, clients are brought to treatment by one or more painful problems with which they are unable to cope. Loneliness, anxiety, vague or specific fears, addictions, consuming anger, these and other problems drive people to seek therapeutic help. *All* therapies share the goal of ridding the client of distress. But all therapies do *not* share the belief that ridding the client of immediate distress is the exclusive, or even primary, goal of treatment.

Therapies may be divided into two broad categories: those that are designed to treat specific problems and those that seek to encourage personal insight. **Specific therapies** attempt to resolve psychological problems without altering underlying personality problems. **Insight therapies** are quite different. They treat presenting problems as the symptoms of underlying personality distress and therefore seek to change those deeper personality patterns. Obviously, there is often overlap between these approaches. The insight therapist who ignores the concrete problems that brought the client into therapy is likely to fail because the client will be impatient and dissatisfied (Haley, 1969). Similarly, the behavioral or cognitive therapist who ignores an underlying problem that spawns a host of behavioral difficulties reduces his or her chances of therapeutic success.

We have discussed the details of many global and specific therapies in earlier chapters. But in order to make our therapeutic recommendations clear and meaningful, it is useful to review the kinds of treatment that are available and useful. We will not describe *all* of the treatments that are presently offered; that would require a book in itself. Rather, we will restrict ourselves to those that have proven useful or are very popular.

SPECIFIC THERAPIES

Specific therapies deal with specific problems. Those problems can often be defined quite narrowly and precisely, such as a fear of heights. Or the specific problem may be a broad one, such as depression which, as discussed in Chapter 13, encompasses a heterogeneous group of symptoms, among them fatigue, loss of appetite, somatic concerns, and the like. The important thing about specific therapies is that they take one or more target problems and seek to resolve them without going deeply into other aspects of personality or unconscious processes.

There are two classes of specific therapies: biological treatments and specific psychological therapies. We examine these in turn.

Biological Therapies

Among the biological therapies, drug treatments are by far the most popular. Psychoactive drugs are more often prescribed than others; among these, Valium is the second most commonly prescribed drug in the United States. Drug therapies have been successful with a variety of common disorders, including anxiety, unipolar and bipolar depression, and schizophrenia. They can often have quite specific effects. For example, certain drugs may affect schizophrenic thought, while others may influence schizophrenic emotion.

Another form of biological therapy is ***electroconvulsive shock therapy***, or ***ECT***. It consists of sending a pulse of electricity through the brain, thereby producing a minor convulsion. The treatment may be repeated six to ten times. As mentioned in Chapter 13, ECT is a fast and effective treatment for unipolar depression but it can have serious side effects.

Like all therapies, biological treatments are most effective with willing and cooperative clients. But unlike psychological treatments, many biological ones can be administered against the client's will and still have moderate effects. One of the major sources of failure in drug treatment, however, resides in the client's failure or refusal to take the prescribed medications. That failure often arises from the fact that the client is unwilling to take the treatment, fails to understand how it will help, or has not developed the cooperative relationship with the therapist that is necessary for successful treatment.

Biological therapies are designed to provide immediate relief for immediate problems. They cannot teach clients to alter their behaviors, to avoid stressful difficulties, or to cope better in the future. Nor do they try to bring about greater insight or understanding into the causes of personal difficulties. They affect biology, not learning. But in so doing, their effects are not at all trivial, for problems tend to breed further problems. In reducing current anxiety or depression, biological treatments prevent additional troubles from arising.

Specific Psychological Therapies

Like biological therapies, the specific psychological therapies seek specific solutions to specifiable problems. These therapies, too, fall into two classes: behavioral treatment and cognitive restructuring.

BEHAVIORAL TREATMENT.   The behavioral treatments see the roots of clients' distress, not in physiological processes gone awry, but in behavior itself (see Chapter 5). Distressing behavior is learned, and what is learned can be unlearned and replaced by more constructive modes of coping and adaptation. Behavior therapists therefore deal directly with the problem

Table 21-1 STRATEGIES OF BEHAVIOR THERAPY

Technique	Outcome
Contingency management	Altering the consequences of a behavior in order to change the frequency of the behavior.
Contingency contracting	Increasing desired behaviors, and decreasing undesired ones, by drawing up a contract that stipulates rewards and punishments for the relevant behaviors.
Stimulus control	Increasing the likelihood of a behavior by magnifying the stimuli that promote the desired behavior and eliminating the stimuli that undercut it.
Systematic desensitization	Training a person to engage in behavior that makes the unwanted behavior difficult or impossible to perform. Systematic desensitization eliminates anxiety, as it is difficult to experience anxiety during a state of relaxation.
Implosion	Extinguishing anxiety by inducing the client to imagine intensely anxiety-provoking scenes that, because they produce no harmful consequences, lose their power to induce fear.
Flooding	Extinguishing anxiety by exposing the client to actual fear-producing situations that, because they produce no harmful consequences, lose their power to produce fear.
Modeling	Exposing clients to desired behavior that is modeled by another person, and rewarding the client for imitating that behavior.
Aversion therapy	Eliminating an unwanted behavior by pairing it with powerfully aversive consequences.
Covert sensitization	Inducing an aversion for an unwanted behavior by pairing that behavior with vividly imagined aversive consequences.
Time out	Suppressing an unwanted response by removing the client to a "neutral" environment when that response is manifested.

that the client is experiencing, and seek to resolve that specific difficulty (see Table 21-1).

Although behavioral treatments have become popular only in the past quarter century, many of them have their roots in an ageless folk wisdom. Consider the child who fears darkness. At first, parents will naturally accede to the child's demand that the bedroom remain lit. Over time, however, the overhead light will be replaced by a low-wattage night-light. And finally, that too will be extinguished. Used therapeutically, that process is one form of in vivo *systematic desensitization* (see Chapters 5 and 10). Introduced by Joseph Wolpe in 1958, it is used primarily to treat phobias and specific anxieties. The client is first reassured and relaxed, and then exposed to stimuli that are minimally anxiety producing. Because one cannot be relaxed and tense simultaneously, the anxiety dissipates, and gradually, the client is trained to remain relaxed in the presence of stimuli that were formerly associated with increasing anxiety. Over time and training, stimuli that formerly induced panic are now greeted with calm.

Flooding treats anxiety in quite the opposite manner (see Chapters 5 and 10). Instead of gradually approaching the anxiety-provoking stimulus, clients are encouraged to experience the full force of the anxiety storm. Because by definition phobias are irrational fears, they are unlikely to elicit re-inforcement. Consequently, like any unreinforced behavior, they will extinguish. Someone who is agoraphobic and afraid to leave home, for example, would be encouraged to spend an hour in the park, and thus be flooded with anxiety. Gradually, through the process of extinction, that anxiety would abate.

Modeling is yet another form of behavioral treatment that has helped clients to overcome fears and acquire new standards for their behaviors (see Chapters 5 and 10). Here, for example, a client who is painfully shy might observe and gradually imitate the behavior of a model who both enjoys being outgoing and is rewarded for it. Combined with graded rehearsal and practice, modeling treatments are quite effective in overcoming fears and inhibitions (Bandura, 1969a).

Aversion therapy aims to rid a client of undesired behavior by pairing that behavior with aversive consequences (see Chapters 5 and 15). If alcohol is paired with a nausea-inducing drug, or a sexually deviant impulse is paired with electric shock, the expected result is that the client will avoid the undesired behavior.

Behavioral treatments often can be very effective in speedily eliminating sources of distress. As we will shortly see, they have been used quite successfully for a variety of psychological troubles. But their virtues are also their limitations, for they often fail to deal with the thoughts and feelings that promote irrational behaviors in the first place. For these thoughts and feelings, cognitive therapies are quite useful.

COGNITIVE RESTRUCTURING. Treatments that involve cognitive restructuring are predicated on the assumption that irrational thoughts breed irrational behaviors. Such thoughts are by no means rare, for they commonly arise from the fundamental attribution errors that people make about their own behaviors (Nisbett and Ross, 1980). Consider the person who says "I have no friends because I am boring." That would be an irrational thought on the part of a young man newly arrived at a college campus, irrational because insufficient time had passed for him to meet people and test that belief. It would also be an irrational thought, but a different sort, by a rude and critical member of a typing pool. Cognitive therapies seek to illuminate these thoughts, to make clear their irrational basis, and thereby, to change them.

Rational-emotive therapy is one of the more effective and popular cognitive therapies (see Chapter 6). Developed by Albert Ellis (1962), it attacks the faulty philosophical assumptions that are made by individuals and that generate irrational behaviors. The notion, for example, that it is absolutely necessary for an adult to be loved by each and every significant person in his or her community, is a widely held irrational assumption. So, too, is the assumption that in order to consider oneself worthwhile, one needs to be thoroughly competent, adequate, and fully achieving in all possible respects. These and other assumptions are vigorously challenged and attacked in rational-emotive therapy, with the aim of laying bare and ultimately changing these cognitions and the behaviors they promote.

Cognitive therapy is quite similar to rational-emotive therapy and is used primarily in the treatment of depression (Beck, 1976). Beck emphasizes such negative cognitions as self-devaluation, a negative view of life experience, and a pessimistic view of the future as leading to depression (see Chapter 13). He gently encourages clients to examine these views and change them. As will shortly be seen, this approach has been very successful in treating depression.

Acquiring and maintaining realistic cognitions is no easy task. Cognitive restructuring therapies use graded tasks, often done as "homework" outside of the therapy session, to yield a succession of mastery and success experiences. Like biological and behavioral therapies, cognitive therapies seek to eliminate a specific problem, and to eliminate it quickly. They differ from those treatments, however, in the requirement that, in order to alleviate a particular problem, one needs to understand and change the thoughts that promote it. And they differ from the global therapies, to which we now turn, both in their insistence on staying "close" to the client's presenting problem, and because they find it unnecessary to explore why the relevant cognitions were distorted in the first place.

GLOBAL THERAPIES

Cognitive and behavioral therapies are specific treatments for quite specific problems. Those therapies assume that the presenting problem *is* the problem that required treatment, and that nothing else requires treatment. Global therapies, on the other hand, all assume that the presenting problem is merely the symptom of some larger, underlying disorder. Much as fever is not itself the entire illness but rather a symptom of a deeper malaise, so are psychological symptoms merely the outcropping of underlying conflicts and erroneous perceptions. It is the latter that require treatment because they tend to radiate a host of cognitive and behavioral difficulties.

Global therapies are mainly those that are derived from the psychodynamic approaches, as well as humanistic and existential approaches. Each of these therapies assumes that psychological distress arises because something is *fundamentally* wrong with the client's personality. They differ, as we will shortly see, in their view of precisely what is wrong and how it can best be remedied.

Classical Psychoanalysis

As we saw in Chapter 4, the heartland of psychological distress in the psychoanalytic view lies in the anxiety and self-defeating postures that are generated by unacceptable impulses. These impulses are repressed and otherwise restrained from consciousness by the host of coping mechanisms that can be generated by an enormously creative and flexible mind. But ultimately, these defenses are costly, for they sap the strength of the ego and continue to leave residual anxieties that render individuals miserable. The solution for Freud, and for those who followed his tradition, was to make conscious the unconscious impulses so that acceptable means of gratifying them could be found.

With the help of the therapist, the client seeks to define his or her unconscious motivations. Classical psychoanalysts require their clients to lie on a couch in order to minimize their attention to the therapist, relax them, and enable them to engage in ***free association.*** Clients are instructed to say whatever comes to mind, regardless of how ridiculous or embarrassing it is, and without attempting to censor. The rationale behind this procedure is that the unconscious has a logic of its own that is manifested in these seemingly disconnected and meaningless associations. If the client associates freely, the unconscious motives and conflicts will reveal themselves through these disconnected verbal threads. The analysis of dreams proceeds in the same manner. There, the client associates to the content and theme of the dream and, in the process, uncovers its unconscious meaning.

Unconscious impulses and conflicts do not yield easily or readily to this form of exploration. As the client begins to confront a conflict, he or she is likely to resist going further. Such resistance can take many forms, such as changing the subject, starting an argument with the therapist, coming late, and even missing appointments. Trained not to take these matters personally, the therapist patiently interprets the resistance just as any other symptoms might be interpreted. These interpretations bring the client back to the "work of analysis."

As a psychoanalysis progresses, clients find themselves revealing things to their therapists that they had never revealed to anyone before, not even to themselves. Understandably, the relationship to the therapist becomes richly emotional and complex. And although the therapist remains impassive, clients react to him or her with intense love, dependency, biting anger, or rebellion, and often all at once. As we saw in Chapter 4, psychoanalysts view this behavior as the ***transference*** of conflicts and frustrations that were experienced with parents during early childhood, onto the therapist. The analysis of transference, because it is immediate and real, is a major opportunity for self-understanding and growth during psychoanalysis.

Psychodynamic Variants

Psychoanalysis is a time-consuming, costly, and cumbersome method of treatment. Moreover, as discussed in Chapter 4, not all therapists believe in all of its basic assumptions. As a result, a variety of psychodynamically oriented therapies have been developed. All of them retain the notion that unconscious impulses and conflicts spawn anxiety and other forms of human misery, and that insight into those conflicts is the goal of treatment. But the kinds of impulses that are examined, and the ways in which they can be made conscious, vary enormously from therapist to therapist. In general, modern psychodynamic therapies differ from classical psychoanalysis in three ways. First, the therapist is much more active, not merely in interpreting unconscious material, but also in offering advice and suggesting constructive options. Second, these therapies are more efficient and less time consuming. Whereas classical psychoanalysis required the client to lie on the couch five times a week for several years, modern psychodynamic therapies are conducted face-to-face, commonly no more than once or twice a week, and for a briefer duration. Third, perhaps because they are briefer, the newer psychodynamic therapies concentrate on the present rather than the past, and emphasize current social relationships rather than earlier ones.

The very content of these therapies may differ widely, according to the orientation of the therapist. Whereas classical psychoanalysis is concerned mainly with the dynamics of sexual and aggressive impulses, Jungian therapists take a larger view of the psyche and may, as we saw in Chapter 4, allude to a variety of archetypes, unconscious materials, and dynamics. Adlerian therapists stress the will to superiority, and Sullivanian therapists examine current social relationships. Many psychodynamic therapists are eclectic, meaning that they use insights from each school of treatment in accord with the needs of individual cases. These newer and briefer forms of treatment are among the most widely practiced and available today (Parloff, 1976).

Humanistic and Existential Treatments

The treatments that derive from humanistic and existential theories of personality rely less on illuminating unconscious processes, and considerably more on "being oneself." Rogerian therapy, as discussed in Chapter 7, starts with the assumption that humans are innately good and motivated to actualize their various potentials. The social environments (especially their families) in which they live, however, do not often recognize that innate goodness, and they commonly lay down unrealistic standards regarding performance and achievement that must be met before individuals are loved. Because people want to be loved, these "conditions of worth" are internalized and propel them to become something other than what they truly are. Large portions of desire and experience are blunted and suppressed in order for them to meet these conditions, with the result that they are aware of doing what they don't really want to do, not knowing what it is they really want to do, and they are generally miserable.

Rogerian or client-centered therapists offer clients total acceptance of themselves without conditions of worth (Rogers, 1951). Such unconditional positive regard is accompanied by the therapist's attempt to see the world through the client's eyes, thus encouraging clients to view their own experience as something of value. Client-centered therapists neither interpret nor advise. Rather, they reflect or mirror what clients are experiencing without evaluation, in order to enable clients both to clarify their experience and to accept their feelings. As clients come to know and approve of their true thoughts and feelings, they are more able to make free and genuinely constructive decisions.

For existential therapists, self-acceptance alone is no guarantor of either freedom or free choice, nor is the potential for self-actualization biologically endowed. Rather, these are gradually acquired through the individual's struggles with responsibility. Existential therapists, as seen in Chapter 7, encourage clients to view their psychological problems as being of their own making: individuals themselves are the sources of their own difficulties. Viktor Frankl (1975) first described two techniques that are now increasingly used by existential therapists and that underscore individual responsibility. The first is ***paradoxical intention,*** wherein the therapist encourages clients to indulge in and even exaggerate their symptoms. For example, someone who "just can't resist ice cream" will be encouraged to eat massive amounts of it in order to be convinced that he really does control his intake. Similarly, ***dereflection*** involves directing the client's attention away from his symptoms and pointing out how much he could be doing and enjoying if he were not so preoccupied with his troubles. As a result of taking responsibility for themselves, clients become more aware of their choices and values, and their lives and interpersonal relations become more open, honest, and meaningful.

Gestalt therapy similarly underscores taking responsibility for one's life by living in the "here and now." Fritz Perls, the founder of Gestalt therapy, felt that the single aim of this form of treatment was "to impart a fraction of the meaning of the word, now. To me, nothing exists except the now" (Perls, 1970, p. 4). While Gestalt therapists may examine their clients' past, they do so entirely with reference to the present, and in order to enable clients to experience the present more fully and openly. Exercises are devised that enable clients to experience themselves with greater immediacy and to take responsibility for their feelings and behaviors. Thus, clients are encouraged to communicate in the present tense, and to avoid the past and future tenses. They are instructed to use "I" language, rather than "it" language, which further underscores their own responsibility for their experiences. And they are encouraged to speak *to* each other, rather than at each other. These techniques and others heighten the sense of immediacy—of "nowness"—that clients experience, enabling them to capture their true feelings and take responsibility for both feelings and actions. Confronting their experience in this manner allows them to feel "whole" rather than fragmented, and frees energy that would otherwise be used for self-fragmentation.

Other humanistic and existential therapies, such as encounter therapies, borrow heavily on these techniques and use them in an eclectic manner. The latter therapies, however, are characterized by their intensity over a brief period of time. Encounter groups, for example, often meet on a weekend and provide very intense experiences that are directed toward heightening feelings and examining attitudes and beliefs. But because these and other "mod" therapies have undergone little evaluation, their overall effectiveness is yet unknown and, regardless of their popularity, we have nothing more to say about them.

With this brief overview of treatment modalities behind us, we now turn to the treatments that are especially useful for particular kinds of psychological problems.

THE CHOICE OF TREATMENT

Some problems lend themselves easily to relatively clear definition. Fear of public speaking is one such problem. Compulsions are another. Although there are important exceptions, the more specific the problem, the greater the likelihood that it can be treated successfully. It is common, therefore, for therapists to encourage clients to define their problems as carefully as possible. Such definition unfortunately does not guarantee therapeutic success, but it surely increases the likelihood that the outcome of treatment will be positive.

SPECIFIC TREATMENTS

Once a problem is defined, it may become especially amenable to treatment by the specific behavioral and cognitive therapies, as well as biological ones.

These therapies address symptoms primarily. But this is surely no short-coming, for as we have seen earlier in this chapter, the symptoms often *are* the problem and, in any event, they are fully capable of breeding more intense and intractable problems. Symptoms treatments are, therefore, significant treatments, made all the more so by their comparative likelihood of succeeding. We turn to these first.

Treatments for Fears, Phobias, and Anxieties

There are three psychological treatments that are enormously effective in reducing fears and anxieties (see Chapter 10). Perhaps the oldest, and surely the most researched of these, is systematic desensitization, which is useful not only for simple animal phobias, but also for the more complex social anxieties, as well as for agoraphobias and even insomnia (Steinmark and Borkevic, 1974). It is, in fact, so successful that it has become the yardstick against which the effectiveness of new treatment techniques is measured (Kazdin and Wilson, 1978).

A second psychological treatment consists of flooding and reinforced practice. As discussed earlier and in Chapter 10, flooding consists of encouraging the client to remain in the pesence of the feared object (Crowe, Marks, Agras, and Leitenberg, 1972; Leitenberg and Callahan, 1973). A variant of flooding, called **implosion,** requires clients to imagine fearful scenes (Stampfl and Levis, 1967; Levis and Carrera, 1967). Gradually, the terror that is induced by the feared stimulus will diminish. Flooding and implosion are particularly effective with agoraphobia, which sometimes is resistant to systematic desensitization.

The third psychological treatment that seems particularly effective with phobias is modeling, which consists in observing a nonfearful model perform the task that generates fear in the client (Bandura, Blanchard, and Ritter, 1969; Bandura, 1977b). Modeling appears to work as well as do desensitization and flooding in alleviating both mild and severe phobias (Rachman, 1978).

Biological treatments, such as the administration of Valium and Miltown, are often useful for alleviating anxiety, especially anxiety that is manifest in body tensions. Untreated, such body tensions tend to accumulate and mount, rendering a person continually anxious. Unlike psychological treatments, however, these biological treatments do not teach people to *cope* with anxiety; they merely alleviate the symptoms that present circumstances have generated. If active coping techniques are not learned, new troubling circumstances will probably bring further anxiety symptoms and require further treatment. Biological treatments, therefore, are relatively transient and passive treatments that minimize present symptoms and prevent new ones from developing during a particular crisis.

Treatments for Compulsions and Obsessions

Until recently, compulsions and obsessions were refractory to every form of psychological and psychopharmacological treatment. Neither systematic desensitization, the various insight therapies, nor chemotherapy appeared to have much effect. Recently, however, new techniques based on client-directed in vivo flooding and participant modeling have shown enormous promise in alleviating compulsions. As discussed in Chapter 11, when a client interrupts his own compulsive rituals after watching a model demonstrate the technique, there is a marked decline in the incidence of that symptom (Marks, Rachman, and Hodgson, 1975; Roper, Rachman, and Marks, 1975). Using self-interruption to alleviate *obsessions,* however, has not worked as dramatically as the technique has worked to relieve the compulsions. Thus, powerful techniques for dealing with the problem of obsessions have yet to be devised (Rachman and Hodgson, 1980).

Treatments for Depression

As described in Chapter 13, there are several powerful techniques for treating depression. Cognitive therapy is an especially useful treatment in unipolar depression, as are three biological treatments: tricyclic antidepressants, monoamine oxidase inhibitors, and electroconvulsive shock therapy. In addition, lithium is an excellent treatment of bipolar or manic-depression.

C nitive therapy encourages clients to identify those thoughts that are inaccurate, distorted, and that produce depression. These are replaced by objectively more accurate cognitions in a context where the therapist provides feedback and reinforcement for both cognitive and behavioral change. It takes two weeks or so before its effects are seen, but in spite of the delay, cognitive therapy appears to be a quite powerful treatment, more so than even the tricyclic antidepressants, which are the most commonly used treatments against depression (Rush, Beck, Kovacs, and Hollan, 1977; Beck, Rush, Shaw, and Emery, 1979).

Cognitive therapy is not yet widely practiced, and those who seek psychological treatment for depression may need to consider alternatives. Rational-emotive therapy is similar in structure and orientation to cognitive therapy and can be expected to have similar results. Behavior modification techniques, which involve behavior rehearsal and therapist-directed activity (Lewinsohn, 1974), appear less effective than cognitive therapy (Shaw, 1977), but they are probably more effective than psychodynamically oriented psychotherapy, or no treatment at all.

Over a period of ten days to three weeks, *tricyclic* antidepressants gradually block the reuptake of norepinephrine and serotonin. These antidepressants, clinical wisdom suggests, work best with severe depressions where loss of interest in life and somatic symptoms are involved. Their use is limited, however, by the fact that they have a variety of mild side effects, such as dry mouth, as well as moderately serious effects in clients with cardiovascular disease and urinary problems.

Monoamine oxidase (MAO) inhibitors gradually prevent the breakdown of norepinephrine and serotonin, again over ten days to three weeks. They are prescribed less often than the tricyclics because their side effects can be lethal. Taken with cheese, alcohol, or a variety of other medications, MAO inhibitors can actually kill.

Although it is viewed with dread by some people, electroconvulsive shock therapy (ECT) is clearly a quick and effective treatment for severe unipolar depression. Half of the people who do not respond to the tricyclics or the

MAO inhibitors respond favorably to ECT. ECT can be particularly effective with suicidal persons. ECT too, however, has powerful short-term side effects, which include memory loss and motivational changes, and occasional long-term memory loss as well. But these effects are neither as dramatic nor as long-lasting as the public imagines.

The treatment of choice for bipolar depression and for mania itself is lithium. Eighty percent of bipolar depressives either fully or partially remit their symptoms as a result of lithium administration (Depue and Monroe, 1979). Repeated administration with individuals who are predisposed to bipolar depression may prevent the occurrence of that disorder or alleviate its severity. Lithium, however, has serious side effects that can be lethal unless its administration is carefully supervised by a knowledgeable physician throughout the entire course of treatment.

Treatments for Sexual Dysfunction

For the host of problems that generate sexual dysfunction, including fear of sexuality, lack of sexual pleasure, and premature ejaculation, the treatments of choice, as we saw in Chapter 14, are those that are based on the work of Masters and Johnson (1970). Indeed, no psychological treatment program, with the exception of systematic desensitization for phobias, has been quite as successful as the Masters and Johnson therapy regimen. They have reported that better than 80 percent of nearly 800 people who entered their two-week treatment program were greatly improved, and that nearly 75 percent of them maintained that improvement after a five-year follow-up. Similar findings have been reported by other workers who have evaluated these techniques (Hartman and Fithian, 1972; Kaplan, 1974).

Treatments for Addictions

The addictions—alcoholism, obesity, smoking, and drug dependence—are difficult to treat. The solid treatment techniques that are available for phobias, compulsions, depression, and sexual dysfunction are not yet available here. For the soul of addiction is temptation, rather than fear and incompetence, and temptation does not seem to yield to either the rational reasoning of cognitive therapies, the control of behavioral treatments, or the insight of global psychodynamic ones. Most treatment programs, whether conducted by professionals or nonprofessionals (such as Alcoholics Anonymous, Weight Watchers, TOPS, or Daytop Village for drug addicts), experience two overlapping problems: drop out and relapse. Those who drop out of a treatment program almost always fail to change. And those who go through a treatment program but then resume old habits often suffer slights to their sense of hope and efficacy. This corrosion of hope and self-efficacy makes them unavailable for further treatment for a considerable period of time. Thus, in this area, researchers have begun to describe their techniques as "*more* effective" rather than "*very* effective," their typical gains as "*modest* rather than impressive," and their outcomes as "variable rather than consistent" (Mahoney and Mahoney, 1976).

ALCOHOLISM.   The treatment of choice for most of the addictions is abstention. But unfortunately, abstention is more easily recommended than achieved and, as a result, a multiplicity of behavioral and cognitive approaches to the addictive disorders have been suggested. For alcoholism, a program called Individualized Behavior Therapy for Alcoholics (IBTA) seemed especially promising. In contrast to most other programs, the goal of this program was not complete abstinence , but rather *controlled* drinking. Clients were encouraged to select alternative behaviors to drinking, especially for drinking that occurred under stress. Once selected, those alternatives were carefully rehearsed, in the hope that they would become habitual and eventually replace drinking. IBTA recognized that it was probably impossible to eliminate drinking entirely for most alcoholics, and sought rather to control it by reducing intake and ultimately, its effects.

The original results were heartening. Those who were encouraged to control their drinking reported significantly more abstinent days than those for whom the treatment goal was total abstinence (Sobell and Sobell, 1976; 1980). But early on, some writers suggested that the apparent success of the IBTA program might be due to the enthusiasm of its practitioners (Nathan, 1980), an observation that makes sense in light of our earlier observations of the "common ingredients of treatment." Later reports were even more pessimistic, casting serious doubt on the original findings themselves, and suggesting that those findings might have resulted from insufficient follow-up of those who participated in the IBTA program (Pendery, Maltzman, and West, 1982; but see Marlatt, 1983, for a more supportive view).

Treatments that evoke enthusiasm, hope, and commitment from participants are seen again in the help provided by Alcoholics Anonymous (AA). AA describes itself as "a fellowship of men and women who share their experiences, strength and hope with each other that they may solve their common problem and help others to recover from alcoholism." By the time an alcoholic makes first contact with AA, he or she has already acknowledged that alcohol is a problem—an enormous first step. Subsequently, two members of AA meet with the alcoholic and invite him or her to join the group. The group stresses self-help, underscoring that the alcoholic controls the drinking problem, and not vice versa. It offers group support during the struggle to control drinking, and hope—for after all, many of the other members of the group were once alcoholics and are now entirely abstinent. And while receiving support from others enables one to better control the urge to drink, *giving support* to people with similar problems serves much the same purpose. Indeed, in looking back over the AA experience, reformed alcoholics rate altruism and group cohesiveness as two of its most helpful aspects (Emrick, Lassen, and Edwards, 1977). Data on the effectiveness of AA, as well as the drop-out rate, are sparse and hard to come by, but what is available suggests that AA is better than no treatment at all (Emrick, Lassen, and Edwards, 1977).

OBESITY.   Obesity is an even more intractable problem than alcoholism. The simple fact is that it is quite easy to take off weight, but very difficult to keep it off (Schachter and Rodin, 1974). Thus, many reports of diet and treatment "breakthroughs" prove to be premature when clients are followed up.

Modestly successful self-help programs for obese people, such as TOPS and Weight Watchers, have included behavioral techniques to augment their efficacy. Like AA, these programs provide members with information, in this case, about obesity and dieting. A "buddy" system is used for initially controlling temptation, and recognition is given to those members who successfully lose weight. Long-term studies of dieting programs have shown that members who had been trained to self-observe their eating, to control how and where they ate, and to substitute other behaviors for nonnecessary eating were more successful in losing weight and keeping it off. Moreover, such groups suffered less attrition through dropout than did the traditional, non-behavioral groups (Levitz and Stunkard, 1974; Stuart, 1980). The combination of these behavioral techniques in the context of a self-help group has proven more effective than pharmacological treatment (Ost and Gotestam, 1976), ordinary insight psychotherapy (Hall, Hall, DeBoer, and O'Kulitch, 1977), and social pressure (Kingsley and Wilson, 1977), although the superiority of the combined behavioral treatment is most apparent immediately after treatment, and tends to decline over time. Unfortunately, after five years, most people, regardless of treatment, have regained all the weight they had lost (Stunkard and Penick, 1979).

SMOKING.   Smoking is no less a puzzle than obesity and alcoholism. Little is known about why people smoke in the first place or why smoking persists in being so popular (Jarvik, 1977). Unlike eating, it is difficult to know what is reinforcing in smoking behavior. But whatever reinforces smoking, it does so powerfully. The pack-a-day smoker who averages ten puffs to a cigarette will have taken some 70,000 shots of nicotine and tar in a year, a frequency unmatched by any other form of addiction (Russell, 1977). Unhooking the long-term smoker is not an easy matter. The best procedures utilize a broad spectrum of behavioral strategies, including self-monitoring, stimulus control, and self-evaluation. Substituting equally pleasant behaviors for the pleasures of smoking (Best, 1980), as well as aversive procedures (Lichtenstein and Danaher, 1977), have also proven useful here. But once again, relapse turns out to be a serious problem. Within a year, 75 percent of reformed smokers can be expected to be puffing once again (Marlatt and Gordon, 1980).

DRUG ABUSE.   For drug abuse, and especially for heroin addiction, three forms of treatment have shown some modest success. The first pairs aversive stimulation, such as shock, with the client's verbal descriptions of his or her need for the drug and consumption of it. Such direct interference with the pleasures of the drug is often combined with relaxation training and systematic desensitization to reduce the tension that promotes drug taking in the first place. But aversive techniques such as these (which were popularized in Anthony Burgess's novel and film *A Clockwork Orange*) have serious shortcomings. In the first place, they often fail to generalize from the therapist's office to the social world in which the addict lives. Second, while the theory underlying aversive techniques indicates that when shock has been paired with desire, people should feel anxious, in fact they commonly feel merely neutral. Thus, the procedure does not evoke a response that is strong enough to resist the social and personal pressures that lead to drug addiction in the first place. Finally, there are ethical considerations. Often, drug addicts are required by law to undergo treatment. Is it really fair to force them to undergo such harsh treatment?

Some of these concerns have led people to favor a second form of treatment for drug addiction, one that substitutes a different drug, methadone, for the heroin that is being consumed. Methadone is a synthetic narcotic that can be taken orally, does not cloud consciousness, lasts longer than heroin, and partially blocks the "rush" that comes if the addict resumes the heroin habit. Early results of methadone maintenance programs indicated that they reduced incarcerations by 98 percent and criminal activities (which support drug purchases) by 94 percent (Dole and Nyswander, 1965). Moreover, because methadone leaves the addict with a relatively clear consciousness, this study revealed that former addicts found new interest in life and were able to take and retain jobs.

The remarkable success of the early programs, however, was not maintained in later studies. Although present evidence indicates that at least 50 percent of enrolled addicts remain in the program for a year, relapse rates are high. Moreover, methadone itself is an addicting drug, for which a secondary black market now exists. It is also a dangerous drug: an increasing number of deaths from methadone overdose have been reported (Platt and Labate, 1976). In addition, many heroin addicts who live in the ghettos and barrios feel that methadone is "establishment medicine," a palliative for the poverty that often leads people to seek the thrills of heroin, and an addicting way of controlling these people (Senay and Renault, 1972). Finally, the same ethical objection to aversive techniques applies here: Is it fair to require heroin addicts to become addicted to another drug, methadone?

A third kind of treatment consists of self-help, live-in programs conducted by such groups as Odyssey House, Daytop Village, and Synanon. Admission to these therapeutic communities is voluntary and selective. Drugs are prohibited. Addicts are required to avoid former friends and family, to become involved in the social structure of the community, and to "begin at the bottom," performing menial labor at the outset and earning their way up the labor ladder with good performance and drug-free behavior. All residents participate in intensive group therapy, which can be very aggressive and confronting. Finally, therapeutic communities vary in their goals. Some, such as Synanon, require residents to remain within the comunity indefinitely. Others, such as Odyssey House, emphasize returning addicts to the community.

The therapeutic community approach to treatment has, however, serious limitations. Addicts often find the program unappealing, and the drop-out rate is therefore appallingly high. In one study, only 3.7 percent of those who were enrolled completed the program (New York Legislative Commission on Expenditure Review: Narcotics Drug Control, 1971). A more recent study found that residential treatment is about as effective as methadone maintenance for heroin addicts, and both are more effective than no treatment at all, especially for heavy heroin users (Simpson, Savage, and Sells, 1978).

Treatments for the Schizophrenias

Properly diagnosed, the schizophrenias are fundamentally biological disorders that presently respond best to pharmacological treatments. Because the schizophrenias are a diverse collection of disorders, and because the development of psychotropic medications is a burgeoning industry, it is even less useful here than elsewhere, to recommend specific drugs for particular schizophrenic disorders. As discussed in Chapter 17, which drug is prescribed will depend heavily on the particular symptoms that are manifested.

In the treatment of the schizophrenias, it is often necessary to decide whether or not to hospitalize the individual. Such decisions should be made in close consultation with both the client and the therapist. Often enough, brief hospitalizations can be quite useful in that they allow a careful examination of the patient's difficulties, as well as prescription of psychotropic medication. Moreover, such hospitalizations often take the pressure off the patient and his or her family, affording the momentary relief that allows all parties to recoup strength and perspective. Longer periods of hospitalization may prove to be necessary for certain patients, but the longer the hospitalization the greater the probability of merely marginal adjustment after discharge.

If a decision is made to hospitalize, it is important for the patient's well-being that family and close friends establish regular contact with both the patient and the hospital staff. Too often, hospitalized psychiatric patients, especially long-term ones, are "warehoused" out of sight and, without malicious intent, forgotten. Regular contact with loved ones very likely accelerates progress in the hospital and increases the likelihood that post-hospital adjustment will be satisfactory.

Where long-term hospitalization is a prospect, consider first less restrictive alternatives, if they exist within or near the community. Supervised halfway houses are especially attractive as therapeutic alternatives because they minimally disrupt the contact between the patients and their social environment, and because, unlike psychiatric hospitals, they are so patently temporary residences. Day hospitals, which provide daytime care for patients and return them to their families in the evenings, are sometimes also alternatives to full hospitalization.

Specific treatments, where they exist, are the quickest and most effective way of treating specific problems. Unfortunately, however, there continue to be problems for which no specific treatment is really effective. Autism is one such problem, and some forms of schizophrenia are others. Such problems are presently untreatable, but the future holds promise for their treatment. Most of the specific biological and psychological treatments that were described here and in earlier chapters simply did not exist thirty years ago. Progress in this area has been explosive and likely will accelerate further in coming years.

Global Treatments

Besides specific problems, there are also problems that are global and that resist specification. Among these are problems of meaning, where people ask about the purpose of their lives, and problems in loving. The latter, while specific enough, is an affective problem for which, unless it is promoted by fear, no specific treatment remedies exist. For global problems, global treatments may be the only remedy.

Global treatments include those that were discussed in Chapters 4 and 7 and that were reviewed earlier: the psychodynamically oriented therapies, as well as the variety of humanistic and existential ones. These therapies seek to explore, strengthen, and change the *self*—not merely the individual's *image* of self, but the host of traits, abilities, beliefs, attitudes, and broad dispositions that give rise to self. They may even try to help people develop a sense of self, to know who they are, and what they believe. The goals of self-exploration and changing the self in accord with that knowledge are the goals of these global therapies.

The Search for Self

The problems of self—of the meaning of life and work, of loving, and of commitment—are fundamental problems that everyone faces, or avoids, throughout life. In no sense, need these problems be considered abnormal, for we are not put in this world with a script that tells us "what it's all about." Each of us discovers that for himself or herself. This process is often as complicated and painful as it is fascinating, and one simply may want a professional guide to lead one through the forests and around the dead ends.

Traditional vehicles for self-exploration have been Freudian or Jungian psychoanalysis and their many psychodynamic offshoots. These psychodynamic therapies are more than treatments for distress. They are methods of self-examination. In "Psychoanalysis: Terminable or Interminable," Freud (1905/1976) concluded that the process of self-exploration is an interminable one for which psychoanalysis can serve as a useful adjunct throughout life. In fact, the ideal psychoanalytic client is still captured by the acronym YAVIS—young, attractive, verbal, intelligent, and successful—someone who may have some problems but, on the spectrum of these matters, is surely experiencing no real desperation. The YAVIS client benefits fom psychoanalysis to the extent that he or she develops deep understandings of self that, in turn, lead to greater change and self-fulfillment.

The goal of self-understanding—of getting to really know the person you are—is also claimed for a variety of humanistic therapies. For Carl Rogers (1951), it is a fundamental goal of client-centered therapy. The various humanistic and existential group therapies, such as Gestalt, encounter, and psychodrama, can also be described as ways of heightening experience in order to enable clients to better understand themselves (Perls, 1969; Yalom, 1975).

But do they work? The answer to this question is complex. When global treatments are applied to specific problems, they seem to work less well than specific treatments (Kazdin and Wilson, 1978). Even so, however, they are more effective than no treatment at all. But when global treatments are used to facilitate the search for self, questions about effectiveness lose much of their meaning, for here, notions of "cure" and of "symptoms remission" are entirely inappropriate. To the extent that the question has any meaning at all, the answer must be a private one, entirely dependent upon whether the client *believes* it has been meaningful. When asked, close to 90 percent of such clients reported themselves satisfied with the outcomes of such treatment (Strupp, Fox, and Lessler, 1969).

The treatments that have been discussed in this section apply to problems that are full-grown. Such problems already will have taken their toll in human misery, long before they come to the attention of professional therapists. Once they do, moreover, treatment will be expensive and time-consuming, and outcomes will not always be optimistic. Can anything be done to prevent problems from arising in the first place? And if they do arise, can their effects be minimized and contained? Finally, are there alternatives to the kinds of treatment that have been discussed in this section, alternatives that utilize community rather than professional resources? Because, as an old adage tells us, it is the squeaky wheel that gets the oil, clinical psychology and psychiatry have attended mainly to those who are in need of treatment, often desperately in need of it. But plain common sense makes clear that the squeaky wheel principle is wrong. If problems were prevented in the first place, or minimized before they flowered, both human misery and the need for expensive professional treatment would be greatly reduced. In the next section, we turn to efforts to prevent and contain human distress, as well as alternative modes of treatment in the community.

OUTREACH AND PREVENTION: THE HOPES OF COMMUNITY PSYCHOLOGY

Traditional psychological treatment suffers two major liabilities. First, as we have seen, it arrives only *after* a problem has entailed untold misery for the client. And second, there are simply not enough professional therapists to treat all those who are in need. As a result, psychologists and psychiatrists have become increasingly involved in *community* efforts to *prevent* and *contain* psychological disorders. Because they are allied with others, the efforts of psychologists can now influence the psychological well-being of a much larger proportion of the population than is possible through traditional treatment.

These collaborative efforts between psychologists and the community take place on three fronts: prevention, containment, and alternative modes of treatment and rehabilitation. We take these areas up in turn.

Prevention

An ounce of prevention is worth a pound of cure, we are told. And a review of the chapters that deal with anxiety, depression, crime and delinquency, and children's disorders, makes clear that many of the multiple causes of these distresses could well have been prevented. Unfortunately, our society budgets much less for preventive efforts than for treatment, largely because of the squeaky-wheel principle. But it has chosen to invest resources in three areas that are significant for prevention: child-care facilities, preschool preparation, and job training.

Child-Care

Imagine a mother raising three children, all of them under five. Worse yet, imagine her as a single parent, responsible for the economics, as well as the psychological welfare of her brood.

> I had to work at night, while the children slept. If one of them was sick and needed me, and the neighbor's kid wasn't free to baby-sit, I missed work and pay. There was one year when I was fired from four jobs because Julie and Richard were sick a lot and needed me. Finally, I just couldn't take it.

Such mothers are hardly rare in our society. In 1982, it was estimated that more than five million women maintained families while being employed (Monthly Labor Review, 1983). And they were not the only ones who needed child-care facilities. Often, in two-parent families, both adults have to work in order to make ends meet. Either their own needs, or those of their children, and commonly both, are neglected.

Child-care facilities provide a safe and healthy environment for young children, one that parents and children can count on. Not only do they reduce familial pressures, but often they provide children with experiences that simply could not be gotten at home, such as learning to socialize with other children and to respond to adults other than parents. These experiences are likely beneficial for children when they begin school.

Preschool Interventions

The early school years are fertile ground for psychological problems. Once a child falls behind in work, fails to make friends, or becomes disruptive in the classroom or playground, the likelihood is high that these problems will endure and grow. Often, such problems develop because children are ill-prepared for the school experience, either intellectually or socially. Preschool programs, such as Operation Headstart are intended to encourage the development of cognitive and intellectual skills necessary for kindergarten and the early school grades.

Job Training and Retraining

Poverty and unemployment take enormous tolls of psychological distress, and probably spawn more social problems than any other cause. Simple economic need often drives people to crime and violence. Training the unemployed in the host of skills necessary to both finding a job and keeping it goes a long way toward preventing psychological problems.

It is important to note that psychologists do not usually establish or control child-care, preschool, or job-training facilities. Rather, their contribution is made through *consultation* and *collaboration* with members of the community who want to establish these centers in the first place. They often and successfully consult in schools to increase communication between teachers, students, and their families (Sarason, 1974). They may even consult with urban renewal organizations regarding creating new cities that are psychologically stimulating and that encourage neighborliness and conviviality (Lemkau, 1969). And often they consult with legislators, policy-makers, and the courts on such issues as school desegregation and detention of juveniles, issues whose resolution can eventually prevent the development of psychological difficulties. By collaboration with other members of the community, the resources of psychologists can be utilized more broadly and effectively than would be possible in traditional professional roles.

How effective are these efforts at prevention? The evidence with regard to preschool programs such as Operation Headstart suggests that they are not as good as had earlier been hoped, but that they are surely better than no preschool training at all. Child-care facilities and job training, on the other hand, have not yet been evaluated for their impact on psychological distress. Undoubtedly, they are effective, but how effective is not yet clear. The entire

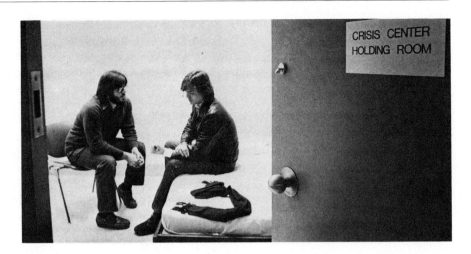

Containment services are designed to limit the consequences of crises. Here a person who has attempted to commit suicide is being counseled. (Photograph by Jeffrey Grosscup)

area of prevention, however, is still in its infancy, still more of a hope than a reality (Cowen, 1977); it may yet be too early to expect full and careful evaluation of these efforts.

CONTAINMENT

Psychological crises often have immediate consequences. A heated argument may result in violence; a painful rejection, in suicide; an overwhelming impulse, in rape, murder, or drunkenness. **Containment services** are designed to limit the consequences of such crises, as they affect the individual, the potential or actual victim, and their families. In the main, these services are characterized by three features. First, treatment is delivered quickly. The potential Friday night suicide, for example, need not wait until Monday morning when the clinics open; by then, it may be too late. He or she can immediately go to a crisis intervention center, or phone a "hot-line" for counseling. Second, services are delivered to a broad range of people, including many who would never seek traditional psychological help. And third, they are located in the community and offered by the community, rather than through hospitals, clinics, or professionally trained therapists. Their very visibility and availability ensures their use.

"Hot-lines"

The telephone **hot-line** is a twenty-four-hour phone service for people who are undergoing deep distress. The first of these hot-lines was established in 1958 by Norman Farberow and Edwin Schneidman as part of the Los Angeles Suicide Prevention Center (Farberow, 1974). Presently, more than 200 communities have developed such centers.

In the main, hot-lines are staffed by carefully trained nonprofessional volunteers. The primary functions of the volunteer are to establish a sympathetic relationship with the caller, to help him clarify his problem, and to formulate a constructive plan that immediately mobilizes the individual's resources as well as those of family, friends, and community. Volunteers will often attempt to assess the suicidal potential of their caller (see Chapter

13), as well as whether the suicide has already been attempted. This kind of work is exceedingly stressful for the volunteers, for they, too, are on the "hot seat." The results of their efforts often determine whether someone will continue to live, yet because callers often hang up without leaving their name or phone number, the volunteers rarely learn to what extent they have helped. As a result, volunteers often become discouraged on this job, and frequently burn out quickly.

Beyond offering instant counseling, hot-lines serve to educate callers about available treatment resources. Often, callers will be referred to a community mental health center, where the causes of the crisis can be explored and treated in greater depth. The emphasis, however, is not on long-term treatment, but on crisis intervention and speedy referral.

Such emergency treatment appears effective in reducing suicide rates. Among 8000 high-risk callers to the Suicide Prevention Center in Los Angeles, Farberow (1970) reports that fewer than 2 percent committed suicide, compared to the estimated 6 percent overall rate of suicide among such persons.

Hot-line services have been extended to people who are experiencing many different kinds of crises. For example, there are child-abuse hot-lines, which seek to cool parental rage before harm is done to children. Other hot-lines exist to defuse impulses to drink, gamble, and engage in violent behavior. Finally, there are yet others that have no particular focus or specialty, but that attempt to provide a listening ear and immediate counsel to whoever calls.

Hot-line users are often ashamed of their behavior and their lack of control. The fact that they are assured of anonymity encourages them to call in the first place; that may be one of the hot-line's greatest strengths. For while hot-line services neither cure nor provide long-term solutions, they diffuse crises and head off serious and immediate losses. That is no small virtue.

Short-Term Treatment

In many cases, distraught individuals may be unable to undertake long-term treatment, but they may be able to go for short-term **crisis treatment.** Such treatment rarely requires more than six sessions. In it, the therapist is extremely active, helping the client to focus on his or her problem, providing support and reassurance, and devising constructive solutions (Golan, 1978). Such crisis intervention often enables a person to resume her life without hospitalization or disruption of employment.

Help for Victims and Their Families

Being the victim of brutality often has enormous psychological consequences that, if left unattended, can be long-lasting. Immediately after being raped, for example, women experience considerable psychological disorganization, including feelings of insecurity and loneliness and rampant fear, and they are subject to heightened influence by others. Depending on their prior experiences and background, these fears and insecurities can develop into stable patterns of avoidance (Burgess and Holmstrom, 1974). Their spouses and families, moreover, often experience changes in these women's

These women and their children are in a shelter for battered women. (Photograph by Ann Chwatsky/Leo de Wys)

attitude and affection that can be directly traced to these traumatic experiences (Bard and Sangrey, 1979). As described in Chapter 10, political hostages, too, have similar reactions to the trauma and humiliation that result from being held against their will (Sank, 1979). Short-term crisis interventions may range from support and counseling, to brief behavioral treatments that are useful in alleviating and containing these symptoms.

Until recently, battered wives and children had no recourse except to "take it," or perhaps to turn to the police and courts. As their numbers have become known, however, concern for these victims has heightened and has led to the establishment of shelters for battered women. Such shelters provide temporary sanctuary for women and their children, enabling them to take some time out to recover from abuse and plan their futures. Staffed almost entirely by nonprofessionals, their central function is protection. Unfortunately, shelters are often dangerous and unhappy places—dangerous because of possible retaliation from still-angry husbands, and unhappy because these women are beset with doubts about themselves and their futures. At present, there are no more than seventy such shelters in the United States, each able to house from ten to fifty women. But wife-battering is a much larger problem than these numbers would suggest. Many more shelters are clearly required, but support from government and social agencies has simply not been generous.

Early Detection of Psychological Difficulties

Several programs have been concerned with detecting behavioral problems in school children. Some programs train teachers to detect the early signs of maladjustment (Zax and Cowen, 1969; Levine and Graziano, 1972), while others use brief tests that can be easily scored (Cowen, 1973). Both types of programs seek to identify early signs of maladjustment so that children can be referred for remediation before their problems become relatively insurmountable.

Here a clinical psychologist is consulting police on how to handle hostage situations. He is providing them with psychological cues for police negotiations and actions in such situations. (Courtesy Dan Cunningham for American Psychological Association)

Consultation

Psychologists and psychiatrists are often consulted by a variety of other professionals and organizations. They may be consulted by teachers on how to increase children's motivation, or about how to handle a particular child's problem in the classroom rather than at the clinic. They will often be consulted by industry about how to make working conditions more pleasant, and how to reduce executive stress.

One ingenious example of consultation has arisen in the training of police who are often called to mediate family quarrels. Family quarrels are a major source of assaults and homicides. They are dangerous, not only for the participants, but also for those who intervene. Many police have been assaulted while attempting to calm family conflicts. In one New York City precinct, police were given extensive training by psychologists on how to intervene in these family quarrels, and then worked as family crisis-intervention teams in that precinct. In contrast to the police in the neighboring precinct, who were not given such training and who both suffered and witnessed the same amount of violence that is usually associated with such calls, the trained police fared much better. In the next 1388 calls to intervene in family crises, trained team members did not suffer an assault, did not witness a family homicide, and were able to markedly reduce the number of assaults on family members (Bard, 1970). The enormous success of this program in New York City has led to its wider adoption. The positive results strongly support the idea of providing psychological consultation for other service agencies.

REHABILITATION

Until quite recently, as we have seen, treatment and rehabilitation of those who were seriously distressed was in the hands of professional psychologists and psychiatrists and was conducted mainly in psychiatric hospitals. But partly because of shortages of fully qualified personnel, and partly because hospitals have serious shortcomings as treatment centers for the psychologically distressed, community psychologists have devised other settings in which such people and problems can be treated. They have trained nonprofessionals to deal with these problems. They have established alternative treatment centers such as halfway houses, residential treatment programs, and day and night hospitals. And they have encouraged patients and former patients to establish self-help groups, designed to find employment for and combat discrimination against, those who suffer or have suffered serious psychological distress.

Training Nonprofessionals

It takes a long time to become a psychologist, psychiatrist, or social worker. Not many people have the time or resources to undertake such training, and as a result, there are far too few trained people to meet current need. Recently, there have been increasing efforts to train paraprofessionals in this area. Whether through on-the-job training, or in undergraduate and junior colleges, these paraprofessionals are trained to take over some of the functions of the professional. Trained paraprofessionals can interview, test, make home visits, and often handle social and vocational rehabilitation under the supervision of psychologists or psychiatrists. They can serve as aides and attendants in psychiatric hospitals. And indeed, some studies have shown that paraprofessionals can be trained to be good therapists (Rioch, 1967). Though their training is narrower than that of fully qualified professionals, and though they can perform fewer tasks, a variety of studies have indicated that what they do, they do quite well (Rioch, 1967; Brown, 1974). Moreover, they vastly increase the number of people who can be treated, enabling professionals to reserve their skills for complicated problems, for consultation and supervision, and for training.

Alternative Treatment Centers

The search for alternatives to the traditional mental hospital is an ongoing one. Long-term patients in such hospitals tend to become habituated to that environment, and subsequently unable to function outside of it. Even short-term patients suffer enormously after discharge; they have difficulty finding adequate employment and establishing satisfying social lives. Alternative treatment centers have tried to overcome these problems by loosening the ties to the hospital, by maintaining patients in the community where they can often retain old friendships and establish new ones, and where they can be trained for job responsibilities.

Day and night hospitals are intended to serve as transition points for fully hospitalized patients, as well as treatment centers for those who were never hospitalized. In day hospitals, patients are treated during the day, and then permitted to join their families at night and over the weekend. Night hospitals are for patients who either have daytime employment, or families with whom they are comfortable and supported. Such patients return to the hospital in the evening to continue their treatment. Participation in day and night treatment is often brief, just long enough to enable the former patient to get his or her feet on the community ground.

Halfway houses or community lodges are also designed as transition experiences between hospital and community. Optimally, these residences house no more than twenty people. With only paraprofessionals in residence, and a psychologist or psychiatrist on call, halfway houses serve to train patients to govern themselves after they have been governed by the hospital. Here patients make decisions about running the house. They often establish small businesses to support themselves, and they receive training both in vocations and in the skills necessary for holding a job. Former patients who have resided in halfway houses before fully entering the community are less likely to be rehospitalized than those who have entered the community directly from the hospital.

Residential treatment centers attempt to avoid the hospital entirely. Here, distressed people are treated in the community, either by families who are willing to take them in (Stein, Test, and Marx, 1975; Polak and Kirby, 1976; Mosher and Menn, 1978), or in residences established for these purposes. Such treatment commonly takes more time than does traditional drug-oriented therapy. But its consequences are commonly more beneficial. People in these settings emerge without a "record" of psychiatric hospitalization, which enables them to find employment more easily and to establish social relationships with greater ease and less stigma. The evidence, moreover, suggests that residential treatment centers cost less to operate than traditional hospitals (Kiesler, 1982).

Self-Help Groups

Funds for treating the psychologically distressed, which never were plentiful, are much less available today than a decade ago. Psychiatric hospitals are being closed. Patients are being discharged, often to "board and care" facilities that provide little more than a bed to sleep in and meals. One would expect that the closing of psychiatric hospitals would free funds for community treatment, but that has not been the case. Rather, patients have been thrown on their own resources—and have done some fairly remarkable things without much help from government and society.

One focus of self-help groups has been to establish a community where patients can associate with and help each other. Because they often reside in the marginal areas of cities, former patients have been plagued by poverty and dislocation in addition to their own psychological difficulties. Self-help groups have established cooperatives where members can obtain food and services at affordable prices. Using their political strength—for they now constitute a sizable voting minority in some neighborhoods—they have been able to locate community facilities in which to meet. Increasingly, they have turned to the law to remedy the abuses of discrimination that they face. Such groups as NAPA (Network Against Psychiatric Assault), moreover, have sought to correct what they perceive to be abuses in patient care. Increasingly, members of such groups are invited to the professional meetings of psychologists and psychiatrists, to "tell their story" and to alert professionals to the difficulties that present and former patients experience.

SUMMARY

1. The kinds of people who offer help for psychological problems, and the kinds of help they offer, are difficult to enumerate, and harder still to catalog properly. Most people are familiar with the names of one or two kinds of traditional therapists: psychologists, psychiatrists, psychiatric social workers, and psychiatric nurses. But the available help for psychological problems extends far beyond those narrow confines and includes friends, teachers, parents, clergy, and self-help groups, to name a few.

2. Psychotherapy, if it is anything, is an active collaborative process in which both therapist and client work to overcome the client's problems. While they clearly depend for their outcome on the competence of the therapist, they depend equally on the hopes and expectations of the client.

3. The therapeutic relationship is facilitated when the therapist shows empathy, warmth, and genuineness. It is also enhanced when the client feels free to question and when treatment goals are specified early in the treatment process.

4. The effectiveness of therapy can be assessed by considering the client's satisfaction with the treatment, by measuring the extent of the client's personality change, and by examining the impact of treatment on target behaviors.

5. After finding a therapist whom one likes, and avoiding poorly trained or simply immature therapists, one is ready to consider the type of treatment that will be most useful. Generally, the more specific the problem, the better the chance that it can be resolved through specific treatments. The less specific the problem, the more likely global treatment will be called upon.

6. There are psychological problems that are quite treatable today that could not be resolved a decade ago. Great strides have been made in behavioral treatment of fears, phobias, and compulsions, in cognitive treatment of depression, and in pharmacological treatment of bipolar depression. But some forms of schizophrenia, and many of the serious childhood disorders, such as autism, are still difficult problems to cope with.

7. Psychologists and psychiatrists have become increasingly involved in community efforts to prevent and contain psychological disorders. Three significant areas in which funds have been invested in an effort to prevent psychological disorders from developing are: child-care facilities, preschool interventions, and job training and retraining. Areas in which containment services have been designed to limit the consequences of psychological crises include hot-lines, short-term crisis treatment centers, and shelters for battered wives.

8. Because some treatments have powerful side effects, and because some treatment settings, such as hospitals, create undesired difficulties for patients, increasing effort has been directed toward finding treatment alternatives. Paraprofessionals are being trained to take on many of the tasks that were once the exclusive province of professionals. Residential treatment centers and halfway houses are increasingly coming to supplement and replace the traditional psychiatric hospital. And former patients are gradually collecting into self-help groups.

The Diagnostic and Statistical Manual of Mental Disorders (DSM-III)

As its name implies, DSM-III is the third, and most recent, version of the *Diagnostic and Statistical Manuals,* the first of which was published in 1952, the second in 1968. DSM-III, which emerged in 1980, differed from its predecessors in many respects (see pp. 174–77). But the main difference was its emphasis on *multi-axial classification.* Earlier versions of the *Diagnostic and Statistical Manual* had concentrated on psychological diagnoses alone. DSM-III, however, enlarged the diagnostic context by insisting that examiners search for "background" physical or psychological disorders that might amplify or otherwise affect diagnosis and treatment. DSM-III also asks examiners to stipulate the environmental stressors that might effect a particular disorder, as well as the individual's highest level of functioning. These considerations emerged on "axes" in the following manner:

Axes I and II: the "traditional" clinical syndromes, personality disorders and developmental disorders.

Axis III: Physical disorders and conditions that might affect psychological functioning and treatment.

Axis IV: The examiner's rating of the severity of psychosocial stressors.

Axis V: The examiner's estimate of the highest level of adaptive functioning that the client attained during the past year.

Axes I and II from DSM-III are reprinted below. These are the traditional psychological nomenclature for such disorders. Axes III, IV, and V, of course, are not classifications, but rather, they deal more generally with the physical and psychosocial stressors that may affect an individual's psychological status.

DSM-III Classification: Axes I and II Categories and Codes*

DISORDERS USUALLY FIRST EVIDENT IN INFANCY, CHILDHOOD OR ADOLESCENCE

MENTAL RETARDATION

(Code in fifth digit: 1 = with other behavioral symptoms [requiring attention or treatment and that are not part of another disorder], 0 = without other behavioral symptoms.)

317.0(x) Mild mental retardation
318.0(x) Moderate mental retardation
318.1(x) Severe mental retardation
318.2(x) Profound mental retardation
319.0(x) Unspecified mental retardation

ATTENTION DEFICIT DISORDER

314.01 with hyperactivity
314.00 without hyperactivity
314.80 residual type

CONDUCT DISORDER

312.00 undersocialized, aggressive
312.10 undersocialized, nonaggressive
312.23 socialized, aggressive
312.21 socialized, nonaggressive
312.90 atypical

ANXIETY DISORDERS OF CHILDHOOD OR ADOLESCENCE

309.21 Separation anxiety disorder
313.21 Avoidant disorder of childhood or adolescence
313.00 Overanxious disorder

OTHER DISORDERS OF INFANCY, CHILDHOOD OR ADOLESCENCE

313.89 Reactive attachment disorder of infancy
313.22 Schizoid disorder of childhood or adolescence
313.23 Elective mutism
313.81 Oppositional disorder
313.82 Identity disorder

EATING DISORDERS

307.10 Anorexia nervosa
307.51 Bulimia
307.52 Pica
307.53 Rumination disorder of infancy
307.50 Atypical eating disorder

STEREOTYPED MOVEMENT DISORDERS

307.21 Transient tic disorder
307.22 Chronic motor tic disorder
307.23 Tourette's disorder
307.20 Atypical tic disorder
307.30 Atypical stereotyped movement disorder

OTHER DISORDERS WITH PHYSICAL MANIFESTATIONS

307.00 Stuttering
307.60 Functional enuresis
307.70 Functional encopresis
307.46 Sleepwalking disorder
307.46 Sleep terror disorder

* Source: The American Psychiatric Association, *Diagnostic and Statistical Manual of Mental Disorders,* Third Edition, 1980. Reprinted by permission of the American Psychiatric Association, Washington, D.C.

PERVASIVE DEVELOPMENTAL DISORDERS

Code in fifth digit: 0 = full syndrome
present, 1 = residual state.

299.0x	Infantile autism
299.9x	Childhood onset pervasive developmental disorder
299.8x	Atypical

SPECIFIC DEVELOPMENTAL DISORDERS
NOTE: THESE ARE CODED ON AXIS II.

315.00	Developmental reading disorder
315.10	Developmental arithmetic disorder
315.31	Developmental language disorder
315.39	Developmental articulation disorder
315.50	Mixed specific developmental disorder
315.90	Atypical specific developmental disorder

ORGANIC MENTAL DISORDERS

Section 1. Organic mental disorders whose etiology or pathophysiological process is listed below (taken from the mental disorders section of ICD-9-CM).

DEMENTIAS ARISING IN THE SENIUM AND PRESENIUM

Primary degenerative dementia, senile onset,

290.30	with delirium
290.20	with delusions
290.21	with depression
290.00	uncomplicated

Code in fifth digit:
1 = with delirium, 2 = with delusions, 3 = with depression, 0 = uncomplicated.

290.1x	Primary degenerative dementia, presenile onset
290.4x	Multi-infarct dementia

SUBSTANCE-INDUCED

Alcohol

303.00	intoxication
291.40	idiosyncratic intoxication
291.80	withdrawal
291.00	withdrawal delirium
291.30	hallucinosis
291.10	amnestic disorder

Code severity of dementia in fifth digit: 1 = mild, 2 = moderate, 3 = severe, 0 = unspecified.

291.2x	Dementia associated with alcoholism

Barbiturate or similarly acting sedative or hypnotic

305.40	intoxication
292.00	withdrawal
292.00	withdrawal delirium
292.83	amnestic disorder

Opioid

305.50	intoxication
292.00	withdrawal

Cocaine

305.60	intoxication

Amphetamine or similarly acting sympathomimetic

305.70	intoxication
292.81	delirium
292.11	delusional disorder
292.00	withdrawal

Phencyclidine (PCP) or similarly acting arylcyclohexylamine

305.90	intoxication
292.81	delirium
292.90	mixed organic mental disorder

Hallucinogen

305.30	hallucinosis
292.11	delusional disorder
292.84	affective disorder

Cannabis

305.20	intoxication
292.11	delusional disorder

Tobacco

292.00	withdrawal

Caffeine

305.90	intoxication

Other or unspecified substance

305.90	intoxication
292.00	withdrawal
292.81	delirium
292.82	dementia
292.83	amnestic disorder
292.11	delusional disorder
292.12	hallucinosis
292.84	affective disorder
292.89	personality disorder
292.90	atypical or mixed organic mental disorder

Section 2. Organic brain syndromes whose etiology or pathophysiological process is either noted as an additional diagnosis from outside the mental disorders section of ICD-9-CM or is unknown.

293.00	Delirium
294.10	Dementia
294.00	Amnestic syndrome
293.81	Organic delusional syndrome
293.82	Organic hallucinosis
293.83	Organic affective syndrome
310.10	Organic personality syndrome
294.80	Atypical or mixed organic brain syndrome

SUBSTANCE USE DISORDERS

Code in fifth digit; 1 = continuous, 2 = episodic, 3 = in remission, 0 = unspecified.

306.0x	Alcohol abuse
303.9x	Alcohol dependence (Alcoholism)
305.4x	Barbiturate or similarly acting sedative or hypnotic abuse
304.1x	Barbiturate or similarly acting sedative or hypnotic dependence
305.5x	Opioid abuse
304.0x	Opioid dependence
305.6x	Cocaine abuse
305.7x	Amphetamine or similarly acting sympathomimetic abuse
304.4x	Amphetamine or similarly acting sympathomimetic dependence
305.9x	Phencyclidine (PCP) or similarly acting arylcyclohexylamine abuse
305.3x	Hallucinogen abuse
305.2x	Cannabis abuse
304.3x	Cannabis dependence
305.1x	Tobacco dependence
305.9x	Other, mixed or unspecified substance abuse
304.6x	Other specified substance dependence
304.9x	Unspecified substance dependence
304.7x	Dependence on combination of opioid and other non-alcoholic substance
304.8x	Dependence on combination of substances, excluding opioids and alcohol

SCHIZOPHRENIC DISORDERS

Code in fifth digit: 1 = subchronic, 2 = chronic, 3 = subchronic with acute exacerbation, 4 = chronic with acute exacerbation, 5 = in remission, 0 = unspecified.

Schizophrenia
295.1x	disorganized
295.2x	catatonic
295.3x	paranoid
295.9x	undifferentiated
295.6x	residual

PARANOID DISORDERS

295.10	Paranoia
297.30	Shared paranoid disorder
298.30	Acute paranoid disorder
297.90	Atypical paranoid disorder

PSYCHOTIC DISORDERS NOT ELSEWHERE CLASSIFIED

295.40	Schizophreniform disorder
298.80	Brief reactive psychosis
295.70	Schizoaffective disorder
298.90	Atypical psychosis

NEUROTIC DISORDERS

These are included in Affective, Anxiety, Somatoform, Dissociative, and Psychosexual Disorders. In order to facilitate the identification of the categories that in DSM-II were grouped together in the class of Neuroses, the DSM-II terms are included separately in parentheses after the corresponding categories. These DSM-II terms are included in ICD-9-CM and therefore are acceptable as alternatives to the recommended DSM-III terms that precede them.

AFFECTIVE DISORDERS

MAJOR AFFECTIVE DISORDERS

Code major depressive episode in fifth digit: 6 = in remission, 4 = with psychotic features (the unofficial non-ICD-9-CM fifth digit 7 may be used instead to indicate that the psychotic features are mood-incongruent), 3 = with melancholia, 2 = without melancholia, 0 = unspecified.

Code manic episode in fifth digit: 6 = in remission, 4 = with psychotic features (the unofficial non-ICD-9-CM fifth digit 7 may be used instead to indicate that the psychotic features are mood-incongruent), 2 = without psychotic features, 0 = unspecified.

Bipolar disorder
296.6x mixed
296.4x manic
296.5x depressed

Major depression
296.2x single episode
296.3x recurrent

OTHER SPECIFIC AFFECTIVE DISORDERS

301.13 Cyclothymic disorder
300.40 Dysthymic disorder (or Depressive neurosis)

ATYPICAL AFFECTIVE DISORDERS

296.70 Atypical bipolar disorder
296.82 Atypical depression

ANXIETY DISORDERS

Phobic disorders (or Phobic neuroses)
300.21 Agoraphobia with panic attacks
300.22 Agoraphobia without panic attacks
300.23 Social phobia
300.29 Simple phobia

Anxiety states (or Anxiety neuroses)
300.01 Panic disorder
300.02 Generalized anxiety disorder
300.30 Obsessive compulsive disorder (or Obsessive compulsive neurosis)

Post-traumatic stress disorder
308.30 acute
309.81 chronic or delayed

300.00 Atypical anxiety disorder

SOMATOFORM DISORDERS

300.81 Somatization disorder
300.11 Conversion disorder (or Hysterical neurosis, conversion type)
307.80 Psychogenic pain disorder
300.70 Hypochondriasis (or Hypochondriacal neurosis)
300.70 Atypical somatoform disorder

DISSOCIATIVE DISORDERS (OR HYSTERICAL NEUROSES, DISSOCIATIVE TYPE)

300.12 Psychogenic amnesia
300.13 Psychogenic fugue
300.14 Multiple personality
300.60 Depersonalization disorder (or Depersonalization neurosis)
300.15 Atypical dissociative disorder

PSYCHOSEXUAL DISORDERS

GENDER IDENTITY DISORDERS

Indicate sexual history in the fifth digit of Transsexualism code: 1 = asexual, 2 = homosexual, 3 = heterosexual, 0 = unspecified.

302.5x Transsexualism
302.60 Gender identity disorder of childhood
302.85 Atypical gender identity disorder

PARAPHILIAS

302.81 Fetishism
302.30 Transvestism
302.10 Zoophilia
302.20 Pedophilia
302.40 Exhibitionism
302.82 Voyeurism
302.83 Sexual masochism
302.84 Sexual sadism
302.90 Atypical paraphilia

PSYCHOSEXUAL DYSFUNCTIONS

302.71 Inhibited sexual desire
302.72 Inhibited sexual excitement
302.73 Inhibited female orgasm
302.74 Inhibited male orgasm

302.75   Premature ejaculation
302.76   Functional dyspareunia
306.51   Functional vaginismus
302.70   Atypical psychosexual dysfunction

OTHER PSYCHOSEXUAL DISORDERS

302.00   Ego-dystonic homosexuality
302.89   Psychosexual disorder not elsewhere
         classified

FACTITIOUS DISORDERS

300.16   Factitious disorder with psychological
         symptoms
301.51   Chronic factitious disorder with physical
         symptoms
300.19   Atypical factitious disorder with physical
         symptoms

DISORDERS OF IMPULSE CONTROL NOT ELSEWHERE CLASSIFIED

312.31   Pathological gambling
312.32   Kleptomania
312.33   Pyromania
312.34   Intermittent explosive disorder
312.35   Isolated explosive disorder
312.39   Atypical impulse control disorder

ADJUSTMENT DISORDER

309.00   with depressed mood
309.24   with anxious mood
309.28   with mixed emotional features
309.30   with disturbance of conduct
309.40   with mixed disturbance of emotions and
         conduct
309.23   with work (or academic) inhibition
309.83   with withdrawal
309.90   with atypical features

PSYCHOLOGICAL FACTORS AFFECTING PHYSICAL CONDITION

Specify physical condition on Axis III.
316.00   Psychological factors affecting physical
         condition

PERSONALITY DISORDERS
Note: These are coded on Axis II.

301.00   Paranoid
301.20   Schizoid
301.22   Schizotypal
301.50   Histrionic
301.81   Narcissistic
301.70   Antisocial
301.83   Borderline
301.82   Avoidant
301.60   Dependent
301.40   Compulsive
301.84   Passive-Aggressive
301.89   Atypical, mixed or other personality
         disorder

V CODES FOR CONDITIONS NOT ATTRIBUTABLE TO A MENTAL DISORDER THAT ARE A FOCUS OF ATTENTION OR TREATMENT

V65.20   Malingering
V62.89   Borderline intellectual functioning
V71.01   Adult antisocial behavior
V71.02   Childhood or adolescent antisocial behavior
V62.30   Academic problem
V62.20   Occupational problem
V62.82   Uncomplicated bereavement
V15.81   Noncompliance with medical treatment
V62.89   Phase of life problem or other life
         circumstance problem
V61.10   Marital problem
V61.20   Parent-child problem
V61.80   Other specified family circumstances
V62.81   Other interpersonal problem

ADDITIONAL CODES

300.90   Unspecified mental disorder (nonpsychotic)
V71.09   No diagnosis or condition on Axis I
799.90   Diagnosis or condition deferred on Axis I

V71.09   No diagnosis on Axis II
799.90   Diagnosis deferred on Axis II

Glossary

addiction Dependence on a drug, resulting in tolerance and withdrawal symptoms when the addict is deprived of the drug. *See also* tolerance and withdrawal.

adrenaline (or *epinephrine*) A hormone secreted by the adrenal glands, which causes increase in blood pressure, release of sugar by the liver, and a number of the other physiological reactions to threat.

adrenergic A descriptive term for the nerve cells that use adrenaline and noradrenaline as chemical transmitters. The sympathetic nervous system is an andrenergic system.

affective disorders A class of mental disorders characterized by a disturbance of mood. Includes unipolar depression, bipolar depression, and mania.

agoraphobia An anxiety disorder characterized by fear of situations in which one might be trapped and unable to acquire help, especially in the event of a panic attack. Agoraphobics will avoid crowds, enclosed spaces (such as elevators and buses), or large open spaces. From the Greek "fear of the marketplace."

alexia Acquired inability to read resulting from brain damage, with vision intact.

altruistic suicide Suicide required by the society (as defined by Durkheim; for example, hari-kari).

Alzheimer's disease Degenerative disease of late middle or old age, in which mental functions deteriorate. An amnesic syndrome is often the major feature of this disorder.

amenorrhea Loss of the menstrual period. A common occurrence in women anorectics.

amnesia (or psychogenic amnesia) A dissociative disorder characterized by loss of memory of happenings during a certain time period, or loss of memory of personal identity. Includes retrograde amnesia, anterograde amnesia, and selective amnesia.

amnesic syndrome A disorder of memory, of organic origin, in which memory for recent events (events occurring after the brain damage) is very poor or completely absent.

amphetamine A stimulant that causes agitation, increase in energy and activity, hyper-responsiveness to the environment, euphoria, and a number of physiological signs of hyperactivation.

anaclitic depression A depression experienced by some infants between the ages of six and eighteen months who have been separated from their mothers for prolonged periods. This disorder is characterized by apathy, listlessness, weight loss, susceptability to illness, and sometimes death.

anal character traits Traits such as orderliness, stinginess, and stubbornness which, according to psychoanalytic theory, result from fixation during the anal stage of psychosexual development.

anal stage The second stage of psychosexual development whose principal foci, according to psychodynamic theorists, are pleasure and the parental control involved in toilet training.

androgen A hormone that is principally responsible for the morphological development of the external genitals of the male.

anomic suicide Suicide precipitated by a shattering break in an individual's relationship to his society (as defined by Durkheim).

anorexia nervosa A disorder in which the individual has an intense fear of becoming fat, eats far too little to sustain herself, and has a distorted body image.

anterograde amnesia The principal feature of the amnesic syndrome: a failure to recall events that occurred since the onset of brain damage or trauma.

anxiety Fear, commonly inferred fear, characterized by the expectation of an unspecified danger, dread, terror, or apprehension, often leading to an emergency reaction and "flight or fight" behavior. As used in psychoanalytic theory, the psychic pain that results from conflicts among the various personality processes.

anxiety disorders A class of mental disorders characterized by chronic and debilitating anxiety. Includes generalized anxiety disorder, panic disorder, phobias, and post-traumatic stress disorder.

aphasia Disorders of language resulting from damage to certain areas of the cerebral cortex.

appraisal Evaluation of short-term mental events, a target of cognitive therapy.

apraxia Disorders of movement, or the organization of movement, resulting from damage to certain areas of the cerebral cortex. The disorders cannot be accounted for by damage to sensory systems or damage to lower levels of motor systems.

arbitrary inference Reaching a conclusion for which there is little or no evidence. According to Beck, depressives are prone to making arbitrary inferences.

archetypes As used by Jung, universal ideas about which we are knowledgeable even at birth.

assimilative projection Attribution to another of beliefs, attitudes, or feelings that we are quite aware of experiencing ourselves.

attention disorder Inability to direct or concentrate attention. It is often found among hyperactive children and in schizophrenics.

attribution An assignment of cause for an event; a short-term mental event, and a target of cognitive therapy.

automatic thoughts Discrete sentences, negative in character, that a person says to himself, quickly and habitually. According to Beck, depressives typically engage in automatic thoughts.

autonomic nervous system The system that regulates the internal environment of the body, including the heart, stomach, adrenals, and intestines. The autonomic nervous system is divided into the sympathetic and parasympathetic nervous systems.

aversion therapy A behavior therapy that seeks to rid a client of undesired behavior by pairing that behavior with aversive consequences.

avoidance-approach conflict A conflict between a desire to approach an object or situation that has some positive value, and a desire to avoid that object or situation because it has been associated with harm. According to traditional learning theory, this conflict is a root of anxiety.

avoidance responding The act of getting out of a situation that has been previously associated with an aversive event, thereby preventing the aversive event. Differs from escape responding, which is getting out of the aversive event itself.

avoidant personality disorder A disorder whose central feature is social withdrawal combined with hypersensitivity to rejection.

Babinski sign A change in the reflex response to scratching of the bottom of the foot that indicates damage to upper levels of the motor system.

barbiturates A class of drugs that depress the central nervous system, decreasing anxiety and blunting sensitivity to the environment. Includes phenobarbital, pentobarbital, secobarbital, and benzodiapines.

behavior therapy A therapy that is rooted in the view that psychological distress results from learned behavior that can be unlearned; the therapy seeks to replace the distressing behavior with more constructive modes of coping and adaptation.

behavioral assessment A record of behaviors and thoughts one wishes to change, including their time of occurrence, duration, and intensity.

behavioral contracting A therapeutic technique in which two people contract with each other to perform some behaviors.

behavioral disorder A disorder in which something behavioral, rather than emotional, is amiss, such as hyperactivity, attentional problems, and aggressive, destructive, and dishonest behaviors.

behavioral school The school of abnormal psychology which claims that behavior is shaped by the environment, and that behavior can be changed by changing the environment. According to the behavioral theorists, the symptomatic behavior of a mental disorder is the disorder, and is that which should be treated.

benzodiazepines A group of mild tranquilizers which result in muscle relaxation, decreased anxiety, and sedation. Includes Librium, Valium, and Dalmane.

biofeedback Therapeutic technique in which the individual is given electronically amplified information on certain (somewhat) controllable physiological systems (such as heart rate and blood pressure) and trained to control that response system.

biomedical school The school of abnormal psychology that claims that mental disorders are illnesses of the body resulting from an underlying physiological pathology such as a virus, disordered biochemistry or genes, or a dysfunctional organ.

bipolar depression (or **manic-depressive disorder**) An affective disorder characterized by alternating periods of depression and mania.

bisexuality Desire for sexual relations with members of both sexes.

borderline personality disorder A broad Axis-II diagnostic category that designates people whose salient characteristic is instability in a variety of personality areas, including interpersonal relationships, behavior, mood, and self-image.

Briquet's syndrome (or **somatization disorder**) A somatoform disorder characterized by the experience of a large number and variety of physical symptoms, for which there are no medical explanations. These symptoms are not under the voluntary control of the individual.

bulimarexia (or **bulimia**) A disorder in which people alternately gorge themselves with enormous quantities of food, and then purge themselves of that food by vomiting, or using laxatives or diuretics.

caffeine A drug that stimulates the central nervous system and the skeletal muscles, lengthening the time it takes to fall asleep, decreasing fatigue, and aiding the individual in doing physical work.

castration anxiety Fear of having one's penis removed or harmed; part of the basis for the Oedipus conflict.

catecholamines Hormones involved in neural transmission in the brain. Includes norepinephrine, epinephrine, and dopamine.

catharsis In psychoanalytic theory, the uncovering and reliving of early traumatic conflicts.

cathexis Charging of a neutral object with psychical energy, either positive or negative. Psychoanalytic basis of acquired fears and lusts.

central nervous system (CNS) That part of the nervous system which coordinates all of the activity of the nervous system. In vertebrates, the CNS is made up of the brain and the spinal cord. All sensory inputs are transmitted to the CNS and all motor impulses are transmitted from the CNS.

cerebral cortex The outermost layer (gray matter) of the cerebral hemispheres.

cerebrospinal fluid A clear fluid, like blood plasma, that accounts for some of the circulation in the brain and spinal cord.

cholinergic A descriptive term for the nerve cells that use acetylcholine as a chemical transmitter. The parasympathetic nervous system is a cholinergic system.

clang associations Associations produced by the rhyme of words. Commonly found in schizophrenics.

clinical case history The record of part of the life of an individual seen in therapy.

clitoris A small organ located forward of the vagina in females. It becomes erect upon sexual arousal and is involved in orgasm.

cocaine The psychoactive agent in the coca plant. Cocaine increases energy, combats fatigue and boredom, and enhances the individual's responsiveness to things in his environment.

cognitions Beliefs, thoughts, attitudes, expectations, and other mental events.

cognitive-behavioral therapy A therapeutic technique in which therapists attempt to alter both the maladaptive thoughts and maladaptive behaviors of a client through restructuring of maladaptive belief systems and re-training behavior.

cognitive restructuring Treatments that are predicated on the assumption that irrational thoughts create irrational behaviors, which can be eliminated by changing the underlying thoughts.

cognitive school The school of abnormal psychology which claims that many disorders result from maladaptive beliefs or thought styles.

cognitive therapy Used primarily in the treatment of depression, this therapy seeks to change the cognitive triad of (a) self-devaluation, (b) a negative view or life experience, and (c) the pessimistic view of the future, as the determining cognitions for depression.

cognitive triad A group of cognitions which, according to Beck, characterizes depressives. These cognitions include (a) negative thoughts about the self, (b) negative thoughts about ongoing experience, and (c) negative thoughts about the future.

collective unconscious As used by Jung, the memory traces of the experience of past generations.

compulsion A repetitive, stereotyped, and unwanted action that can be resisted only with difficulty. It is usually associated with obsessions.

compulsive personality disorder A disorder that is characterized by the long-term inability to express warm emotions, combined with an inappropriate preoccupation with trivial rules and details.

computer-assisted tomography (or **CAT scan**) An X-ray technique, used in neurological diagnosis, for constructing three-dimensional representations of the X-ray density of different areas of the brain.

concordant When both of two twins have a disorder such as schizophrenia, they are called concordant for that disorder. *See also* discordant.

conditioned response (CR) A response that is evoked by a certain stimulus (conditioned stimulus) once that stimulus has become associated with some other stimulus (unconditioned stimulus) that naturally evokes the unconditioned response. *See also* Pavlovian conditioning.

conditioned stimulus (CS) A stimulus that, because of its having been paired with another stimulus (unconditioned stimulus) that naturally provokes an unconditioned response, is eventually able to evoke that response. *See also* Pavlovian conditioning.

conduct disorders A cluster of children's behavioral disorders that consists mainly of aggressive and rule-breaking behaviors.

confound A factor other than the experimentally controlled independent variable that might produce an experimental effect.

consolidation block Failure to establish (consolidate) short-term memories. This is a mechanism proposed as an explanation of the amnesic syndrome.

contiguity Conjunction in time and place.

contingency A conditional relationship between two objects or events, describable by the probability of event A given event B, along with the probability of event A in the absence of event B.

continuous reinforcement Provision of reinforcement every time a subject makes a response. *See also* reinforcement.

control group A group of subjects similar to those in an experimental group, who experience everything the experimental group does, except the independent variable.

conversion *See* hysterical conversion.

coping strategies As used by psychoanalytic theorists, the process by which people alter the meaning and significance of troublesome drives and impulses in order to eliminate anxiety.

corpus callosum The largest tract in the brain, connecting corresponding areas of the two hemispheres.

correlation coefficient A statistic indicating the degree of contingency between two variables.

corticospinal tract A tract of axons from cell bodies in the motor cortex that innervates motor neurons in the spinal cord, and mediates (among other things) voluntary movements of the hands.

co-twin As used in psychological research, one of a pair of twins whose sibling is seen at a psychiatric clinic in order to diagnose a psychological problem.

counterconditioning A therapeutic technique for phobias in which a phobic patient is helped to relax while imagining fear-provoking situations (usually at first the least fear-provoking situation, then gradually more and more fear-provoking situations). The relaxation response to the imagined situation is incompatible with the fear the patient has previously associated with the situation, and the fear is thus extinguished.

counterphobia The pursuit of precisely those activities that are deeply feared.

cross tolerance When tolerance to one drug produces tolerance to other drugs.

defense mechanisms *See* coping strategies.

delayed auditory feedback Used in the treatment of stuttering, this technique involves hearing one's own speech played back over earphones at about a one-second delay.

delirium tremens A dangerous syndrome of withdrawal from alcohol, which is characterized by psychomotor agitation, hyperactivity of the autonomic nervous system, anxiety, loss of appetite, delusions, amnesia, and convulsions.

delusions False beliefs that resist all argument and are sustained in the face of evidence that normally would be sufficient to destroy them.

delusions of control Beliefs that one's thoughts or behaviors are being controlled from without.

delusions of grandeur Unsubstantiable convictions that one is especially important.

delusions of persecution Groundless fears that individuals, groups, or the government have malevolent intentions and are "out to get me."

delusions of reference Incorrect beliefs that the casual remarks or behaviors of others apply to oneself.

demand characteristics Aspects of the experimental setting that induce the subject to invent and act on an hypothesis about how one should behave.

dementia A more or less general deterioration of mental function, found most commonly in old people. Alzheimer's disease is a common form of dementia.

denial As used in psychoanalytic theory, the process by which distressing external facts are eliminated.

dendrites A usually highly branched part of a neuron that is stimulated by neurotransmitters produced by receptors or other neurons.

dependent personality disorder   A disorder wherein people allow others to make major decisions, to initiate important actions, and to assume responsibility for the significant areas of one's life.

dependent variable   The factor that the experimenter expects will be affected by changes in the independent variable.

depersonalization   A dissociative disorder in which the individual feels often cut off from or unsure of his or her identity.

depression   An affective disorder characterized by (a) sad affect and loss of interest in usually satisfying activities, (b) a negative view of the self and hopelessness, (c) passivity, indecisiveness, and suicidal intentions, and (d) loss of appetite, weight loss, sleep disturbances, and other physical symptoms.

dereflection   Used by existential therapists, this technique involves directing the client's attention away from his symptoms and pointing out how much he could be doing and enjoying if he were not so preoccupied with his troubles.

developmental disorders   A cluster of disorders of childhood that may consist of deficits in language comprehension, speech, and responses to others that can result in such serious disorders as infantile autism or childhood schizophrenia.

diathesis   Physical vulnerability or predisposition to a particular disorder.

diathesis-stress model   A general model of disorders which postulates that an individual develops a disorder when he both has some constitutional vulnerability (diathesis) and when he experiences psychological disturbance (stress).

direct sexual therapy   A therapeutic method developed by Masters and Johnson, in which (a) sexual dysfunctions are clearly and simply defined, (b) clients explicitly practice sexual behavior under the systematic guidance of therapists, and (c) clients are treated as couples, not as individuals.

disconnection syndrome   A disorder accounted for by severing of or damage to tracts connecting specific areas of the brain.

discordant   When only one of two twins has a disorder such as schizophrenia, they are called discordant for that disorder. *See also* concordant.

discriminative stimulus   A signal indicating that reinforcement is available if a certain operant response is made.

disinhibition   An increase in some reaction resulting from release of inhibition.

disorganized schizophrenia   A schizophrenic disorder whose most striking behavioral characteristic is apparent silliness and incoherence. Behavior is jovial but quite bizarre and absurd, suggesting extreme sensitivity to internal cues and extreme insensitivity to external ones, but without systematic delusions or hallucinations.

disowning projection   A process whereby feelings and experiences that one personally denies having and that are usually repressed are attributed to others.

displacement   A cognitive alteration of reality that involves replacing the true object of one's emotions with one that is more innocent and less threatening.

dissociative disorders   A group of mental disorders characterized by fragmentation of an individual's identity. Dissociative disorders include amnesia, fugue, multiple personality, and depersonalization disorder.

dizygotic twins   Fraternal twins, or twins who developed from separate eggs, and whose genes are no more alike than are any pair of non-identical-twin siblings.

dopamine   A catecholamine that facilitates neural transmission.

dopamine hypothesis   The theory that schizophrenia results from an excess of the neurotransmitter dopamine.

dose-response relationship   As the amount of drugs one takes increases, one's response to the drug increases, up to a certain ceiling point.

double-blind experiment   An experiment in which both the subject and experimenter are blind as to whether the subject has received an experimental treatment or a placebo.

Down's syndrome (or **mongolism**)   A disorder that results from the fact that an individual has forty-seven rather than the usual forty-six chromosomes in his or her cells.

drug abuse   The mental disorder characterized by (a) a pattern of pathological use of a drug, (b) impairment in social and occupational functioning, and (c) at least one-month's duration of the disturbance.

Durham test   A legal test for insanity which provides that an accused is not criminally responsible if his unlawful act was the product of mental disease or mental defect.

dysfunction   Impairment of functioning.

efficacy expectation   According to Bandura, a person's belief that he can successfully execute the behavior that will produce a desired outcome.

ego   The self.

ego-dystonic homosexuality   Homosexuality that is incongruent with the individual's desire for sexual preference, and which the individual wants to change.

ego strength   The capability of an individual to maintain his or her identity under stress, and to manipulate and modify the environment to meet his or her needs.

ego-syntonic homosexuality   Homosexuality that is congruent with the individual's desire for sexual preference, and which the individual does not want to change.

egoistic suicide   Suicide resulting when the individual has too few ties to his fellow humans (as defined by Durkheim).

ejaculation   The vigorous contraction of the muscles at the base of the penis, which causes sperm to be ejected from the penis *See also* orgasm.

electroconvulsive shock (ECT)   A therapeutic treatment for depression, in which metal electrodes are taped to either side of the patient's head, and the patient is anesthetized. A high current is passed through the brain for a half second, followed by convulsions lasting almost one minute.

electroencephalogram (EEG)   A record of the electrical activity of cells in the brain (primarily the cortex) obtained from wires placed on the skull, and used in neurological diagnosis.

emergency reaction   A reaction to threat in which the sympathetic nervous system mobilizes the body for action. The blood pressure rises, heart rate increases, breathing becomes deeper, perspiration increases, and the liver releases sugar for use by the muscles.

emission   Discharge of semen with contraction of the reproductive organs in the male.

emotional disorders   A cluster of disorders found often among children, in which symptoms of fear, anxiety, inhibition, shyness, and overattachment predominate.

empiricism   The school of philosophy that claims that all that people are and all that they know are the result of experiences.

endogenous depression A depression resulting from disordered biology. From the Greek "arising from within."

enuresis (or bed-wetting) A disorder that is manifested by regular and involuntary voiding of urine.

environmentalism The school of psychology that claims that all organisms, including humans, are shaped by the environment.

epilepsy A disorder of the brain that expresses itself as excessive neuronal discharge (seizure) in some parts of the brain, with appropriate sensory, mental, or motor effects, and frequently some alteration in consciousness.

epinephrine *See* adrenaline.

epiphenomenon A process, which while not causal, reflects the underlying process which is causal.

erectile dysfunction (or impotence) In males, recurrent inability to have or to maintain an erection for intercourse.

erogenous zones Pleasure centers.

erotic arousal Excitement of sexual desire.

escape responding The act of getting out of an ongoing harmful situation. *See also* avoidance responding.

etiology Causal description of the development of a disorder.

exhibitionism A psychosexual disorder in which the individual is sexually aroused primarily by exposing his genitals to unwitting strangers.

existential-humanistic school The school of abnormal psychology that holds that mental disorders result when an individual fails to confront the basic questions of life successfully.

existential therapy A therapy that encourages clients to view their psychological problems as being of their own making.

exogenous depression A depression precipitated by a life stressor. Sometimes called reactive depression. From the Greek "arising from without."

expectations Cognitions that extrapolate the present to the anticipation of future events.

experiment A procedure in which an hypothesized cause (independent variable) is manipulated and the occurrence of an effect (dependent variable) is measured.

experimental artifact Experimental features other than the independent variable, which cause the experimental effect.

experimental effect The change in the dependent variable as a result of the manipulation of the independent variable.

experimental group A group of subjects who are given experience with an independent variable.

experimentalism The behaviorist view that experiments can reveal what aspects of the environment cause behavior.

experimenter bias The exertion of subtle influences by the experimenter on subjects' responses in an experiment.

experiments of nature Studies in which the experimenter observes the effects of an unusual natural event.

expressive aphasia A language disorder that manifests itself primarily as a deficit in speech or the organization of spoken language.

external attribution An assignment of cause for an event to a factor that is outside oneself (i.e., other people or circumstances).

extinction In Pavlovian conditioning, cessation of a previously conditioned response to a conditioned stimulus, due to having learned that the conditioned stimulus no longer signals the onset of an aversive or desirable event. In instrumental learning, cessation of acquired operant responses due to reinforcement being discontinued.

factitious disorder A mental disorder characterized by multiple hospitalizations and operations precipitated by the individual's having self-inflicted signs of illness.

false alarm In experimental analysis, accepting the hypothesis that independent and dependent variables are related, when they really are not. *See also* miss.

feeling substitution A process by which feelings that are stressful are unconsciously replaced by less painful feelings.

fetish A psychosexual disorder characterized by a need to have an inanimate object close by in order to become sexually aroused.

fixation Stagnation of psychological development.

flaccid A flabbiness or lack of firmness in muscles.

flooding A method used by behavioral therapists to treat phobias. The phobic is exposed to the situations or objects most feared for an extended length of time without the opportunity to escape. *See also* response prevention.

free association A psychoanalytic instruction to say whatever comes to mind, regardless of how ridiculous or embarrassing it is, and without attempting to censor.

frequency distribution The number of observations in each given class observed.

frontal lobe A lobe in each cerebral hemisphere that includes control and organization of motor function.

fugue (or psychogenic fugue) A dissociative disorder in which an individual, in an amnesic state, travels away from home and assumes a new identity.

functional analysis A behavioral assessment that is accompanied by a description of the stimuli that are presumed either to increase or decrease the incidence of specified behaviors.

gender identity Awareness of being male or being female.

gender identity disorder A class of mental disorders in which the essential feature is an incongruence between anatomic sex and gender identity. Includes transsexualism.

gender role Public expression of gender identity; what an individual does and says to indicate that he is a man or she is a woman.

general adaptation syndrome According to Selye, a sequence of three stages that ensues when an individual is stressed: (a) the somatic emergency reaction is initiated, (b) the individual engages in defensive behaviors, and (c) eventually the individual's adaptative actions are exhausted.

general paresis A disorder characterized by mental deterioration, paralysis, then death. This disorder is caused by a spirochete involved in syphilis.

generalized anxiety disorder An anxiety disorder characterized by chronic tenseness and vigilance, beliefs that something bad will happen, mild emergency reactions, and feelings of wanting to run away.

genital stage In psychoanalytic theory, the fifth and final stage of psychosexual development during which the adolescent learns to channel sexual energy into love and work.

global attribution An individual's assignment of cause for an event to a factor that will affect a number of different areas of his life.

glove anesthesia   A conversion symptom in which nothing can be felt in the hand and fingers, but sensation is intact from the wrist up.

Gestalt therapy   A therapy that emphasizes taking responsibility for one's life by living in the present.

gray matter   That part of the central nervous system that is composed primarily of neurons and glia cell bodies.

habit disorders   A collection of childhood disorders in which the prominent symptoms include difficulties associated with eating, movement disorders, or tics. These disorders consist of a diverse group of problems with physical manifestations such as bed-wetting, stuttering, sleepwalking and epilepsy.

half-life   The length of time it takes for the level of a drug in the blood to be decreased by 50 percent.

hallucination   A perception that occurs in the absence of an identifiable stimulus.

hallucinogens   Chemicals that cause perceptual disorientation, depersonalization, illusions, hallucinations, and physiological symptoms such as tachycardia, palpitations, and tremors. Includes LSD and PCP.

hemorrhage   Bleeding or loss of blood resulting from rupture or leakage from a blood vessel.

hermaphrodites   People born with ambiguous-looking genitals.

heterosexuality   Preference for sexual partners of the opposite sex.

hierarchy   A form of organization, characteristic of the nervous system, in which narrower "categories" or domains of "control" are subsumed under successively broader "nodes."

homosexuality   Preference for sexual partners of one's own sex.

hormones   Genes that modulate physical growth, bodily differentiation, and psychological growth.

humanistic therapy   A psychological treatment wherein the therapist attempts to see the world through the client's eyes, thereby encouraging clients to value their own experience.

hypomanic personality   A chronic form of mania involving an unbroken two-year-long manic state. *See also* mania.

hyposomnia   Greatly lessened need for sleep.

hyperactivity   A disorder that is marked by developmentally inappropriate impulsiveness, inattentiveness, and excessive motor behavior.

hyperplastic obesity   A form of obesity that results from having more fat cells than is normal.

hypertrophic obesity   A form of obesity that develops in late adolescence and adulthood, which results from having fat cells that are too large.

hypochondriasis   The sustained conviction, in the absence of medical evidence, that one is ill or about to become ill.

hypothalamus   A brain structure that lies under the cortex. The hypothalamus influences eating, drinking, and sexual behavior, and is involved in regulating fundamental bodily processes, including metabolism and water balance.

hysterical conversion   A somatoform disorder characterized by the loss of functioning of some part of the body not due to any physical disorder, but apparently due to psychological conflicts. The loss is not under voluntary control.

id   In psychoanalytic theory, the mental representation of biological drives.

identification   As used by psychoanalytic theorists, the process by which the characteristics of others—their ideas, values, mannerisms, status, and power—are internalized.

incidence   The rate of new cases of a disorder in a given time period.

independent variable   The hypothesized cause of some effect, manipulated by the experimenter in an experiment.

index case   In psychological research, one of a pair of twins who is first seen at a psychiatric clinic.

indoleamines   Hormones involved in neural transmission. Indoleamines include serotonin and histamine.

infantile autism   A childhood disorder whose central feature is the failure to develop the ability to respond to others within the first thirty months of life.

inhibition   An active process through which the excitability of a particular neuron or center (group of neurons) is decreased.

intellectual disorders   Disorders composed of the various levels of mental retardation.

intellectualization   A coping strategy that takes the form of repressing the emotional component of experience, and restating that experience as an abstract intellectual analysis.

instrumental learning (or instrumental conditioning)   a technique in which an organism must learn to perform some voluntary behavior in order to acquire a desired outcome, or to stop an undesirable event.

instrumental response   A response whose probability can be modified by reinforcement; a response that an organism has learned will bring about a desired outcome, or will stop an undesired event. *See also* operant.

intercourse   The sexual act in which the male inserts his penis into the female's vagina and the two move toward ejaculation of semen by the male, and orgasm for the female.

internal attribution   An individual's assignment of cause for an event to a factor that is an aspect of himself.

intromission   Insertion of the penis into the vagina or other orifice.

involutional melancholia   A depressive disorder affecting some forty-five- to sixty-year-old-women, and associated with the endocrine changes of menopause, loss of role when children have grown up, doubts about sexual attractiveness, and taking stock of life.

isolation   A coping strategy in which only the affective component of an unpleasant experience is repressed while the information is retained.

Korsakoff's psychosis   A particular form of the amnesic syndrome caused by alcoholism.

laboratory model   The production, under controlled conditions, or phenomena analogous to naturally occurring mental disorders.

latency stage   In psychoanalytic theory, the third stage of psychosexual development during which sexuality is repressed and attention is directed toward mastering social and cognitive skills.

learned helplessness   A condition characterized by an expectation that bad events will occur, and that there is nothing one can do to prevent their occurrence. Results in passivity, cognitive deficits, and other symptoms that resemble depression.

left visual field   The left half of one's visual world, that is, the part of the world that projects onto the right side of the retina and into the right hemisphere.

lesion   Localized damage to (neural) tissue.

libido   In psychoanalytic theory, psychic energy that can become associated with a host of pleasurable activities.

lower motor neuron   Neurons in the spinal cord whose axons innervate muscles.

LSD (lysergic acid diethylamide)   An hallucinogenic drug which causes changes in body sensations (dizziness, weakness, nausea), perception (distorted time sense), emotion, and cognitive processes.

lycanthropy   A disorder in which people believe they are wolves, and act accordingly.

MAO (monoamine oxidase)   An enzyme that helps to break down catecholamines and indoleamines. MAO inhibitors are used to treat depression.

magnification   Overestimating the impact of a small bad event; error of logic in depression.

malingering   A disorder in which the individual reports somatic symptoms, but these symptoms are under the individual's control, and the individual has an obvious motive for the somatic complaints. *See also* hysterical conversion.

mania   An affective disorder characterized by excessive elation, expansiveness, irritability, talkativeness, inflated self-esteem, and flight of ideas.

marijuana   A psychoactive drug that, when used chronically and heavily, causes impairment of ability to focus on a task, impulsive and compulsive behavior, delusions, sensory-perceptual distortions, and sometimes panic reactions.

masochism   A psychosexual disorder in which the individual prefers to become sexually aroused by having suffering or humiliation inflicted upon him.

masturbation   Self-stimulation of one's genitals for sexual arousal and orgasm.

mean   Average value of a set of values.

mental disorder   In DSM-III, a behavioral or psychological pattern that is genuinely dysfunctional and that either distresses or disables the individual in one or more significant areas of functioning.

methadone   A narcotic used in heroin treatment programs. Methadone acts as a substitute for heroin, and prevents the heroin addict from experiencing withdrawal.

Minnesota Multiphasic Personality Inventory (MMPI)   A widely used personality inventory consisting of 550 test items that inquire into a wide array of behaviors, thoughts, and feelings.

M'Naghten test   A legal test for insanity which provides that a person cannot be found guilty of a crime if, at the time of committing the offense, due to "disease of the mind," the individual did not know the nature and quality of the act or that the act was wrong.

minimization   Downplaying good events; an error of logic in depression.

miss   Rejecting an hypothesis that the independent variable and dependent variable are related, when they really are.

modeling   The observation and gradual imitation of a model who exhibits behavior that the client seeks to adopt in place of an undesirable behavior.

mongolism   *See* Down's syndrome.

moral anxiety   As used by psychoanalytic theorists, anxiety that arises when one anticipates that one's behavior will violate one's personal standards, or when that behavior has in fact violated those standards.

motor cortex   The part of the frontal lobe that directly controls movements. The point of origin of the corticospinal tracts.

multiple personality   A dissociative disorder in which more than one distinct personality exists in the same individual, and each personality is relatively rich, integrated, and stable.

myelin   A fatty substance that surrounds many axons in the peripheral and central nervous system.

narcissistic personality disorder   A personality disorder whose salient characteristics are an outlandish sense of self-importance, continual self-absorption, fantasies of unlimited success, power and/or beauty, and needs for constant admiration.

narcotics   A class of psychoactive drugs that blocks emotional response to pain and produces euphoria, dysphoria, apathy, psychomotor retardation, drowsiness, slurred speech, and maladaptive behavior. Includes opium, morphine, heroin, and methadone.

nature-nurture issue   A major debate in psychology, concerning the relative roles of environment and heredity in the development of personality and behavior.

negative reinforcer   An event that decreases the probability of a response that precedes it; alternatively, an event whose removal increases the probability of a response producing such removal. *See also* punishment.

neuron   A nerve cell.

neurosis   A disorder in which the individual experiences (a) emotionally distressing symptoms, (b) an unwelcome psychological state, (c) reasonably good reality testing, and (d) behavior that is reasonably within social norms. A neurotic disorder is not a transient reaction to stress or the result of organic brain damage.

neurotic anxiety   As used in psychoanalytic theory, anxiety that arises from the possibility that one will be overwhelmed by one's impulses, especially unconscious sexual and aggressive impulses.

neurotic paradox   The phenomenon in which a maladaptive behavior is perpetuated by the person even though this behavior is causing him harm.

neurotransmitter   A chemical that facilitates the transmission of electrical impulses among nerve endings in the brain.

norepinephrine   A hormone involved in neural transmission. Disturbances of the availability of norepinephrine in the brain have been associated with affective disorders.

obsessions   Repetitive thoughts, images, or impulses that invade consciousness, are abhorrent, and are very difficult to dismiss or control; usually associated with compulsions.

obsessive-compulsive disorder   An anxiety disorder in which the individual is plagued with uncontrollable, repulsive thoughts (obsessions) and engages in seemingly senseless rituals (compulsive behaviors).

obsessive personality   A personality characterized by a rigid, methodical, moralistic personality. The individual with an obsessive personality is meticulous in dress and speech, pays much attention to detail, and often has problems making decisions.

occipital lobe   A lobe in each cerebral hemisphere which includes the visual projection area.

Oedipal conflict   The conflict between a boy's desire for his mother, and the fear of punishment by castration for that desire by the father.

operant   A response whose probability can be increased by positive reinforcement, or decreased by negative reinforcement.

operant conditioning   Training the organism to perform some instrumental response in order to escape punishment or gain reward.

operational definition   A set of observable and measurable conditions under which a phenomenon is defined to occur.

opioid   A class of drugs which, when taken, produce euphoria or dysphoria, apathy, psychomotor retardation, pupillary constriction, drowsiness, slurred speech, and impairment in attention and memory.

oral character traits   In psychoanalytic theory, traits such as dependency that result from fixation at the oral stage of psychosexual development and that persist into adulthood.

oral sex   Stimulation of a sexual partner's genitals using the mouth and tongue.

oral stage   In psychoanalytic theory, the earliest psychosexual stage of development during which pleasure arises from feeding.

orgasm   The climax of sexual arousal. In males, orgasm consists of emission and ejaculation. In women, orgasm consists of a series of reflexive contractions of the muscles surrounding the vagina.

outcome expectation   A person's estimate that a given behavior will lead to the desired outcome. *See also* efficacy expectation.

overdetermination   Behaviors that are caused or determined by more than one psychological force and with more than the requisite psychic energy.

overgeneralization   Drawing global conclusions on the basis of a single fact; an error of logic in depression.

panic disorder   An anxiety disorder characterized by severe attacks of panic, in which the person (a) is overwhelmed with intense apprehension, dread, or terror, (b) experiences an acute emergency reaction, (c) thinks he might go crazy or die, and (d) engages in fight or flight behavior.

paradoxical intention   A therapeutic technique that encourages clients to indulge and even exaggerate their symptoms in order to convince them that they really do control those symptoms.

paranoid schizophrenia   A form of schizophrenia in which delusions of persecution or grandeur are systematized and complex.

paraphilias   A group of psychosexual disorders in which bizarre sexual acts or imagery are needed to produce sexual arousal. Includes fetishes, masochism, exhibitionism, voyeurism, transvestism, sadism, zoophilia, and pedophilia.

parasympathetic nervous system (PNS)   That part of the autonomic nervous system which generally works to counteract arousal. *See also* sympathetic nervous system and autonomic nervous system.

parietal lobe   A lobe in each cerebral hemisphere which includes the somatosensory projection areas and is involved with many perceptual functions.

partial reinforcement   Rewarding or punishing only some percentage of instrumental responses.

passive-aggressive personality disorder   A disorder that is characterized by resistance to social and occupational performance demands through procrastination, dawdling, stubbornness, inefficiency, and forgetfulness that seem to border on the intentional.

Pavlovian conditioning (or classical conditioning)   Training in which an organism is exposed to one neutral stimulus (conditioned stimulus) and a stimulus (unconditioned stimulus) that naturally provokes a certain response (unconditioned response). Through the learned association between the conditioned stimulus and the unconditioned stimulus, the conditioned stimulus is able to evoke the conditioned response.

PCP (phencyclidine)   An hallucinogen that causes sensitization to all sensory inputs, depersonalization, diminished awareness of self and the environment, disorientation, muddled thinking, and impaired attention and memory.

pedophilia   A psychosexual disorder in which the individual needs to engage in sexual relations with children below the age of mature consent in order to be sexually aroused.

penile erection   The condition of the penis of being rigid and elevated, as the vessels in the penis fill with blood.

penis envy   In psychoanalytic theory, girls' negative feelings associated with the absence of a penis and possible anger at their mothers for having created them incomplete and inferior.

peptic ulcer   A circumscribed erosion of the mucous membrane of the stomach or of the duodenum, the upper portion of the small intestine. The main symptom of a peptic ulcer is abdominal pain.

perceptual consciousness   As used by Freud, the first of three levels of consciousness that describes the small number of mental events to which the individual is presently attending.

perseveration   A tendency to repeat the same actions, and to have difficulty making transitions from one action (or idea or strategy) to another. Characteristic of frontal lobe damage.

personalization   Incorrectly taking responsibility for bad events; an error of logic in depression.

phallic stage   In psychoanalytic theory, the third stage of psychosexual development during which the libido focuses on phallic pleasures or masturbation.

phenylketonuria (PKU)   A rare metabolic disease that prevents digestion of an essential amino acid called phenylalanine. As a result of this disease, phenopyruvic acid, a derivative of phenylalanine, builds up in and poisons the nervous system, causing irreversible damage.

phobia   An anxiety disorder characterized by (a) persistent fear of a specific situation out of proportion to the reality of the danger, (b) compelling desire to avoid and escape the situation, (c) recognition that the fear is unreasonably excessive, and (d) the fact that it is not due to any other disorder.

physiological   Having to do with the body.

placebo   A neutral stimulus that produces some response because the subject believes it should produce that response.

placebo effect   A positive treatment outcome that results from the administration of placebos.

pleasure principle   As used in psychodynamic theory, biological drives that clamor for immediate gratification.

population   The entire set of potential observations.

positive reinforcer An event that increases the probability of a response when made contingent upon it. *See also* operant, discriminative stimulus, and instrumental learning.

post-traumatic stress disorder An anxiety disorder resulting from experience with a catastrophic event beyond the normal range of human suffering, and characterized by (a) numbness to the world, (b) reliving of the trauma in dreams and memories, and (c) symptoms of anxiety.

pre-conscious As used by Freud, the second of three levels of consciousness, consisting of information and impulses that are not at the center of attention, but that can be retrieved relatively easily.

premature ejaculation The recurrent inability to exert any control over ejaculation, resulting in rapid ejaculation after penetration.

prepared conditioning In learning theory, the concept of the organism as being biologically predisposed to learning about relationships between certain stimuli, and therefore learning the relationship very easily.

prevalence The percentage of a population having a certain disorder at a given time.

primary erectile dysfunction A disorder in which the male has never been able to achieve or maintain an erection sufficient for intercourse.

proband *See* index case.

prognosis Outlook for the future of a disorder.

projection Attributing private understandings and meanings to others; substituting "you" for "I."

psychalgia (or **psychogenic pain disorder**) A somatoform disorder in which the individual experiences pain, not attributable to a physical cause, but to psychological conflict.

psychoactive drugs drugs that affect consciousness, mood, and behavior.

psychoanalysis The psychological theory that claims that disorders are the result of intrapsychic conflicts, usually sexual or aggressive in nature, stemming from childhood fixations. Psychoanalysis is also a therapeutic method in which the therapist helps the patient gain insight into those intrapsychic conflicts behind his or her symptoms.

psychodynamic Dealing with the psychological forces that influence mind and behavior.

psychomotor retardation Slowing down of movement and speech; prominent in severe depression.

psychopharmacology That branch of pharmacology that studies drug actions affecting consciousness, mood, and behavior.

psychosexual Concerning the relationship between the mind and pleasure.

psychosexual disorders A class of mental disorders in which psychological factors impair sexual functioning.

psychosis A mental state characterized by profound disturbances in reality testing, thought, and emotion. *See also* schizophrenia.

psychosomatic disorders A group of disorders in which actual physical illness is caused or influenced by psychological factors. The diagnosis of a psychosomatic disorder requires that the physical symptoms represent a known physical pathology and that psychologically meaningful events preceded and are judged to have contributed to the onset or worsening of the physical disorder.

punishment In psychology experiments, inflicting aversive stimuli on an organism, which reduces the probability of recurrence of certain behaviors by that organism. *See also* negative reinforcement.

Q-sort A personality inventory consisting of a large number of cards, each of which contains a statement such as "is an assertive person," "evades responsibility," or "is sensitive." The person being tested must place each statement in one of nine categories according to whether the statement is more or less characteristic of him. The number of items permitted in each category is ranged in accord with the bell-shaped normal distribution.

random assignment Assigning subjects to groups in an experiment such that each subject has an equal chance of being assigned to each group.

rational-emotive therapy A therapy in which the therapist challenges the irrational beliefs of the client, and encourages the client to engage in behavior that will counteract his irrational beliefs.

rationalization The process of assigning to behavior socially desirable motives, which an impartial analysis would not substantiate.

reaction formation The process of substituting an opposite reaction for a given impulse.

realistic anxiety As used in psychoanalytic theory, the fear that arises from the expectation that real world events may be harmful to the self.

reality principle In psychodynamic theory, the way in which the ego expresses and gratifies the desires of the id in accordance with the requirements of reality.

receptive aphasia An aphasia (disorder of language) where the primary deficit is in the perception of speech.

reinforcement An event which, when made contingent on a response, increases (positive reinforcement) or decreases (negative reinforcement) its probability. A reward or punishment.

relaxation response Physiological response regulated by the parasympathetic nervous system (PNS), which counteracts the emergency reaction to threat. In the relaxation response, the PNS inhibits heart action, constricts respiratory passages, and causes secretion of digestive fluids.

release from inhibition Disinhibition or removal of inhibition.

repeatability The chance that, if an experimental manipulation is repeated, it will produce similar results.

repression A coping strategy by which the individual forces unwanted thoughts or prohibited desires out of consciousness and into the unconscious mind.

reserpine A powerful sedative given to lower high blood pressure. Reserpine occasionally induces depression.

response prevention A therapeutic technique in which a therapist prevents the individual from engaging in a behavior that the therapist wishes to extinguish. *See also* flooding.

retarded ejaculation In men, great difficulty reaching orgasm during sexual intercourse.

retrograde amnesia Loss of memory of events predating some disease or trauma. The loss is often confined to a period seconds or minutes prior to a trauma.

reward In psychology experiments, giving the organism positive stimuli, which increases the probability of recurrence of certain behaviors by the organism. *See also* positive reinforcement.

right visual field   The right half of one's visual world, that is, the part of the world that projects onto the left side of the retina and into the left hemisphere.

role construct repertory test (Rep test)   A personality inventory that examines the constructs that a person uses in interpreting significant events.

Rorschach test   A personality test consisting of ten bilaterally symmetrical "inkblots," some in color, some in black, gray, and white, each on an individual card. The respondent is shown each card separately and asked to name everything the inkblot could resemble. The test is supposed to elicit unconscious conflicts, latent fears, sexual and aggressive impulses, and hidden anxieties.

sadism   A psychosexual disorder in which the individual becomes sexually aroused only by inflicting physical and psychological suffering and humiliation on another human being.

sample   A selection of items or people, from the entire population of similar items or people.

schizoid personality disorder   A disorder that is manifested by the inability to form social relationships, the absence of desire for social involvements, indifference to both praise and criticism, insensitivity to feelings of others, and by lack of social skills.

schizophrenia   A group of disorders characterized by incoherence of speech and thought, hallucinations, delusions, blunted or inappropriate emotion, deterioration in social and occupational functioning, and lack of self-care.

schizophrenogenic families   Families that seem to foster schizophrenia in one or more family members.

school of thought   In abnormal psychology, a theory-driven common focus on specific types of causes, cures, and prevention methods for abnormality. Among these are biomedical, psychoanalytic, humanistic, behavioral, and cognitive schools of thought.

secondary erectile dysfunction   Loss of the ability in a male to achieve or maintain an erection.

selective abstraction   Focusing on one insignificant detail while ignoring the more important features of a situation; an error of logic in depression.

selective amnesia   Loss of memory of all events related to a particular theme.

selective positive reinforcement   Therapeutic technique in which the therapist delivers positive reinforcement contingent on the occurrence of one particular behavior.

selective punishment   Therapeutic technique in which the therapist negatively reinforces a certain target event, causing it to decrease in probability.

sensate focus   A strategy of direct sexual therapy that involves (a) a "pleasuring" phase during which the couple engages in nongenital erotic activity, but restrains from intercourse, then (b) a phase of "genital stimulation" in which the couple engages in genital play, but without intercourse, then (c) the phase of "nondemand intercourse" in which the couple engages in intercourse, but without making demands on each other.

sexual dysfunction   Disorders in which adequate sexual arousal, desire, or orgasm are inhibited.

sexual object choice   The types of persons, parts of the body, and situations that are the objects of sexual fantasies, arousal, and preferences.

sexual unresponsiveness (or frigidity)   In women, lack of sexual desire and impairment of physical excitement in appropriate situations.

shadowing   A technique used in treating stuttering which entails repeating the therapist's words shortly after the latter has spoken them.

single-blind experiment   An experiment in which the subject, but not the experimenter, is blind as to whether the subject has received an experimental treatment or a placebo.

social phobias   Unreasonable fear of and desire to avoid situations in which one might be humiliated in front of other people.

somatic   Having to do with the body.

somatoform disorders   A group of mental disorders characterized by (a) loss or alteration in physical functioning, for which there is no physiological explanation, (b) evidence that psychological factors have caused the physical symptoms, (c) lack of voluntary control over physical symptoms, and (d) indifference by the patient to the physical loss. Includes conversion, Briquet's syndrome, and psychalgia.

spastic   Overactive muscles, more contracted (tense and rigid) than is normal, with increased muscle tone, spasms.

specific attribution   An individual's assignment of cause for an event to a factor that is relevant only to that situation.

specific phobias   There are three classes of specific phobias: animal phobias are unreasonable fears of and desires to avoid or escape specific animals. Illness and injury phobias (nosophobias) are unreasonable fears of and desires to avoid or escape a specific illness or injury. Inanimate objects phobias are unreasonable fears of and desires to avoid certain situations or objects other than social situations, crowds, animals, illness, or injuries.

stable attribution   An individual's assignment of cause for an event to a factor that persists in time.

statistical inferences   Procedures used to decide whether a sample or a set of observations is truly representative of the population.

statistically significant effect   An effect that is highly unlikely (typically less than one time in twenty) to occur solely by chance.

stigmata   Marks on the skin, usually bleeding or bruises, and often of high religious or personal significance, brought on by an emotional state.

stimulants   A class of psychoactive drugs that induces psychomotor agitation, physiological hyperactivity, elation, grandiosity, loquacity and hypervigilance. Includes amphetamines, cocaine, and caffeine.

stroke   Damage to the nervous system caused by loss or severe reduction in the supply of nutrients and oxygen, resulting from damage to blood vessels (e.g., hemorrhage or occlusion by a blood clot).

subject   Participant in an experiment.

subject bias   The influence of a subject's beliefs about what he is expected to do in an experiment on his responses in the experiment.

sublimation   In psychoanalytic theory, the transfer of libidinal energies from relatively narcissistic gratifications to those which gratify others and are highly socialized. More generally, the process of rechanneling psychic energy from socially undesirable goals to constructive and socially desirable ones.

superego   Those psychological processes that are "above the self," i.e., conscience, ideals, and morals.

syllable-timed speech   Used in treating stuttering, this technique requires stutterers to speak in time to a metronome.

sympathetic nervous system (SNS) That part of the autonomic nervous system which mobilizes the body's reaction to stress. *See also* parasympathetic nervous system and autonomic nervous system.

sympathomimetic agents Drugs that induce in the user the same physiological, behavioral, and psychological effects that develop when the sympathetic nervous system is activated. *See also* sympathetic nervous system.

symptom A sign of disorder.

synapse The junction between neurons. Excitation or inhibition is transmitted from one neuron to another by diffusion of neurotransmitters across the synaptic gap.

syndrome A set of symptoms that tend to co-occur.

systematic desensitization A behavior therapy primarily used to treat phobias and specific anxieties. The phobic is first given training in deep muscle relaxation and is then progressively exposed to increasingly anxiety-evoking situations (real or imagined). Because relaxation and fear are mutually exclusive, stimuli that formerly induced panic are now greeted calmly.

tarantism A dancing mania that occurred in Italy and was thought to have been brought on by a tarantula's bite.

tardive dyskinesia A nonreversible neurological side effect of anti-psychotic drug treatment, whose symptoms consist of sucking, lip smacking, and peculiar tongue movements.

temporal lobe A lobe in each cerebral hemisphere that includes the auditory projection area and is particularly involved in memory.

Thematic Apperception Test (TAT) A personality test that consists of a series of pictures that are not as ambiguous as Rorschach cards, but not as clear as photographs either. Respondents look at each picture and make up a story about it. The test is supposed to elicit underlying psychological dynamics.

tolerance The state of drug addiction in which, after repeated use of a drug, the addict needs more and more of the drug to produce the desired reaction, and there is great diminution of the effect of a given dose.

transcendental meditation (TM) A therapeutic technique in which the patient sits in a comfortable position twice a day for twenty minutes with his eyes closed and repeats silently one syllable (mantra).

transsexuality A psychosexual disorder characterized by the belief that one is a woman trapped in the body of a man, or a man trapped in the body of a woman.

transvestism (or transvestitism) A psychosexual disorder in which a man often dresses in the clothes of a woman in order to achieve sexual arousal.

tricyclic antidepressants Antidepressant drugs that block uptake of norepinephrine, thus increasing the availability of norepinephrine.

tumor An abnormal tissue that grows by cell multiplication more rapidly than is normal.

Type A behavior pattern A personality type characterized by (a) an exaggerated sense of time urgency, (b) competitiveness and ambition, and (c) aggressiveness and hostility when thwarted.

unconditioned stimulus (US) A stimulus that will provoke an unconditioned response without training. For example, a loud noise will naturally provoke a startle response in humans.

unconscious In psychoanalytic theory, the third level of consciousness consisting of the large mass of hidden memories, experiences, and impulses.

undifferentiated schizophrenia A category of schizophrenia used to describe disturbed individuals who present evidence of thought disorder, as well as behavioral and affective anomalies, but who are not classifiable under the other subtypes.

unipolar depression A disorder characterized by depression, in the absence of a history of mania.

unstable attribution An individual's assignment of cause for an event to a factor that is transient.

upper motor neurons Motor neurons that innervate lower motor neurons and come from various sites in the brain, including the motor cortex.

vagina The sheathlike female genital canal that leads from the uterus to the external opening.

validity The extent to which a test of something is actually measuring that something.

venereal disease A disease contracted through sexual intercourse.

voyeurism A psychosexual disorder in which the individual habitually gains sexual arousal only by observing the naked body, the disrobing, or the sexual activity of an unsuspecting victim.

white matter Those parts of the central nervous system composed primarily of myelinated axons. The myelin imparts a white color to these areas.

withdrawal A substance-specific syndrome that follows cessation of the intake of a substance that has been regularly used by the individual to induce intoxication.

yoking An experimental procedure in which both experimental and control groups receive exactly the same physical events, but only the experimental group influences these events by its responding.

zoophilia (or bestiality) A psychosexual disorder in which the individual habitually engages in sexual relations with animals in order to be sexually aroused.

References

Abram, H. S., Moore, G. L., & Westervelt, F. B. (1971). Suicidal behavior and chronic dialysis patients. *American Journal of Psychiatry, 127,* 119–21.

Abramowitz, S. I. (1969). Locus of control and self-reported depression among college students. *Psychological Reports, 25,* 149–50.

Abrams, R., Taylor, M., Faber, R., Ts'o, T., Williams, R., & Almy, G. (1983). Bilateral vs. unilateral electroconvulsive therapy: Efficacy and melancholia. *American Journal of Psychiatry, 140,* 463–65.

Abramson, L. Y. (1978). Universal versus personal helplessness. Unpublished doctoral dissertation, University of Pennsylvania.

Abramson, L. Y., Garber, J., Edwards, N., & Seligman, M. E. P. (1978). Expectancy change in depression and schizophrenia. *Journal of Abnormal Psychology, 87,* 165–79.

Abramson, L. Y., & Seligman, M. E. P. (1977). Modeling psychopathology in the laboratory: History and rationale. In J. Maser & M. E. P. Seligman (Eds.), *Psychopathology: Experimental models* (pp. 1–26). San Francisco: Freeman.

Abramson, L. Y., Seligman, M. E. P., & Teasdale, J. (1978). Learned helplessness in humans: Critique and reformulation. *Journal of Abnormal Psychology, 87,* 32–48.

Adams, R. D., & Victor, M. (1981). *Principles of neurology* (2nd ed.). New York: McGraw-Hill.

Addiction Research Foundation. (1981). Report of an ARF/WHO Scientific Meeting on Adverse Health and Behavioral Consequences of *Cannabis* Use. Toronto: Author.

Agras, W. S., Barlow, T. H., Chapin, H. N., Abel, G. G., & Leitenberg, H. (1974). Behavior modification of anorexia nervosa. *Archives of General Psychiatry, 30,* 343–52.

Agras, W. S., & Jacob, R. (1979). Hypertension in Pomerleau. In J. P. Grady (Ed.) *Behavioral medicine theory and practice.* Baltimore: Williams & Wilkins.

Agras, W. S., Sylvester, D., & Oliveau, D. (1969). The epidemiology of common fears and phobias. *Comprehensive Psychiatry, 10* (2), 151–56.

Akhter, S., Wig. N. N., Varma, V. K., Pershard, D., & Verma, S. K. (1975). A phenomenological analysis of symptoms in the obsessive-compulsive neurosis. *British Journal of Psychiatry, 127,* 342–48.

Akiskal, H. S. (1979). A biobehavioral model of depression. In R. A. Depue (Ed.), *The psychobiology of depressive disorders: Implications for the effects of stress.* New York: Academic Press.

Akiskal, H. S., & McKinney, W. T. (1973). Depressive disorders: Toward a unified hypothesis. *Science, 182,* 20–29.

Akiskal, H. S., & McKinney, W. T. (1975). Overview of recent research in depression. *Archives of General Psychiatry, 32,* 285–305.

Aleksandrou, D. (1967). Studies on the epidemiology of hypertension in Poland. In J. Stamler, R. Stamler, & T. N. Pullman (Eds.), *The epidemiology of hypertension.* New York: Grune & Stratton.

Aleksandrowicz, D. R. (1961). Fire and its aftermath on a geriatric ward. *Bulletin of the Menninger Clinic, 25,* 23–32.

Alexander, F. (1950). *Psychosomatic medicine.* New York: Norton.

Alexander, F., French, T. M., & Pollack, G. H. (1968). *Psychosomatic specificity: Experimental study and results.* Chicago: University of Chicago Press.

Allen, M. G. (1976). Twin studies of affective illness. *Archives of General Psychiatry, 33,* 1476–78.

Alloy, L. B., & Abramson, L. Y. (1979). Judgment of contingency in depressed and nondepressed students: Sadder but wiser? *Journal of Experimental Psychology: General, 108,* 441–85.

Allport, G. W. (1937). *Personality: A psychological interpretation.* New York: Henry Holt.

American Psychiatric Association (1980). *Diagnostic and Statistical Manual of Mental Disorders* (DSM-III), Washington, D.C.: Author.

Andersen, B. L. (1983). Primary orgasmic dysfunction: Diagnostic conditions and review of treatment. *Psychological Bulletin, 93,* 105–36.

Anderson, J. R., & Bower, G. H. (1973). *Human associative memory.* Washington, D.C.: Winston.

Angst, J., Baastrup, P., Grof, P., Hippius, H., Poldinger, W., & Weis, P. (1973). The course of monopolar depression and bipolar psychoses. *Psykiotrika, Neurologika and Neurochirurgia, 76,* 489–500.

Anisman, H. (1978). Aversively motivated behavior as a tool in psychopharmacological analysis. In H. Anisman & G. Binami (Eds.), *Psychopharmacology of aversively motivated behavior.* New York: Plenum.

Annau, Z., & Kamin, L. J. (1961). The conditional emotional response as a function of intensity of the U.S. *Journal of Comparative and Physiological Psychology, 54,* 428–32.

Ansbacher, H. L., & Rowena, R. (1956). *The individual psychology of Alfred Adler.* New York: Basic Books.

Anthony, W. A., Buell, G. J., Sharratt, S., & Althoff, M. E. (1972).

Efficacy of psychiatric rehabilitation. *Psychological Bulletin, 78,* 447–56.

Archibald, H. C., & Tuddenham, R. D. (1965). Persistent stress reaction after combat. *Archives of General Psychiatry, 12,* 475–81.

Arendt, H. (1978). *The life of the mind.* New York: Harcourt Brace Jovanovich.

Arieti, S. (1974). *Interpretation of schizophrenia.* New York: Basic Books.

Arieti, S. (1979). New views on psychodynamics of phobias. *American Journal of Psychotherapy, 33,* 82–95.

Arieti, S., & Bemporad, J. (1978). *Severe and mild depression.* New York: Basic Books.

Aronow, E., & Reznikoff, M. (1976). *Rorschach content interpretation.* New York: Grune & Stratton.

Aronow, E., Reznikoff M., & Rauchway, A. (1979). Some old and new directions in Rorschach testing. *Journal of Personality Testing, 43,* 227–34.

Asch, S. E. (1951). Effects of group pressure on the modification and distortion of judgments. In H. Guetzkow (Ed.), *Groups, leadership and men: Research in human relations.* Pittsburgh, Pa.: Carnegie Press.

Ashcroft, G., Crawford, T. B. B., Eccleston, D., Sharman, D. F., MacDougall, E. J., Stanton, J. B., & Binns, J. K. (1966). 5-hydroxylindole compounds in the cerebrospinal fluid of patients with psychiatric or neurological diseases. *Lancet, 2,* 1049–52.

Atkinson, J. W. (1958). *Motives in fantasy, action and society.* Princeton: Van Nostrand.

Auerbach, A. H., & Johnson, M. (1977). Research on the therapist's level of experience. In A. S. Gurman & A. M. Razin (Eds.), *Effective psychotherapy.* New York: Pergamon.

Averill, J. R., & Rosenn, M. (1972). Vigilant and non-vigilant coping strategies and psychophysiological stress reactions during the anticipation of an electric shock. *Journal of Personality and Social Psychology, 23,* 128–41.

Ax, A. F. (1953). The physiological differentiation between fear and anger in humans. *Psychosomatic Medicine, 15,* 433–42.

Ayllon, T., & Michael, J. (1959). The psychiatric nurse as a behavioral engineer. *Journal of the Experimental Analysis of Behavior, 2,* 323–34.

Ayllon, T., & Rosenbaum, M. S. (1977). The behavioral treatment of disruption and hyperactivity in school settings. In B. B. Lahey & A. E. Kazdin (Eds.), *Advances in clinical child psychology* (Vol. 1). New York: Plenum.

Azrin, N. H., Sneed, T. J., & Foxx, R. M. (1974). Dry-bed training: Rapid elimination of childhood enuresis. *Behavior Research and Therapy, 11* (4), 147–56.

Bacon, D. L. (1969). Incompetency to stand trial; commitment to an inclusive test. *Southern California Law Review, 42,* 444.

Baer, D. M., & Guess, D. (1971). Receptive training of adjectival inflections in mental retardates. *Journal of Applied Behavior Analysis, 4,* 129–39.

Baker, T. B., & Cannon, D. S. (1979). Taste aversion therapy with alcoholics: Techniques and evidence of a conditional response. *Behavior Research and Therapy, 17,* 229–42.

Ban, T. A., Choi, S. M., Lamonn, H. E., & Adamo, E. (1966). Conditional reflex studies in depression. *Canadian Psychiatric Association Journal, 11,* 98–105.

Bandura, A. (1969a). *Principles of behavior modification.* New York: Holt, Rinehart & Winston.

Bandura, A. (1969b). Social learning of moral judgments. *Journal of Personality and Social Psychology, 11,* 275–79.

Bandura, A. (1977a). Self efficacy: Toward a unifying theory of behavioral change. *Psychological Review, 84,* 191–215.

Bandura, A. (1977b). *Social learning theory.* Englewood Cliffs, N.J.: Prentice-Hall.

Bandura, A. (1978). The self system in reciprocal determinism. *American Psychologist, 33,* 344–58.

Bandura, A. (1982). Self-efficacy mechanism in human agency. *American Psychologist, 37,* 122–47.

Bandura, A., & Adams, N. E. (1977). Analysis of self-efficacy theory of behavioral changes. *Cognitive Therapy and Research, 1,* 287–310.

Bandura, A., Adams, N. E., & Beyer, J. (1977). Cognitive processes mediating behavioral change. *Journal of Personality and Social Psychology, 35,* 125–39.

Bandura, A., Blanchard, E. B., & Ritter, B. (1969). Relative efficacy of desensitization and modelling approaches for inducing behavioral, affective, and attitudinal change. *Journal of Personality and Social Psychology, 13,* 173–99.

Bandura, A., & Walters, R. H. (1959). *Adolescent aggression.* New York: Ronald Press.

Bandura, A., & Walters, R. H. (1963). *Social learning and personality development.* New York: Holt, Rinehart & Winston.

Barbizet, J. (1970). *Human memory and its pathology.* (D. K. Jardine, Trans.) San Francisco: Freeman.

Bard, M. (1970). *Training police as specialists in family crisis intervention.* Washington, D.C.: U.S. Government Printing Office.

Bard, M. & Sangrey, D. (1979). *The crime victim's book.* New York: Basic Books.

Bardhan, K. D. (1980). Cimetidinea in duodenal ulcer: The present position. In A. Torsoli, P. E. Lucchelli, & R. W. Brimbelcombe (Eds.), *H2 antagonists.* Amsterdam: Excerpta Medica.

Barlow, D. H., Abel, G. G., & Blanchard, E. B. (1979). Gender identity change in transsexuals. *Archives of General Psychiatry, 36,* 1001–1007.

Barrett-Lennard, G. T. (1962). Dimensions of therapist response as causal factors in therapeutic change. *Psychological Monographs, 76,* (43, Whole No. 562).

Bartak, L., & Rutter, M. (1974). Use of personal pronouns by autistic children. *Journal of Autistic Children and Schizophrenia, 4,* 217–22.

Bartlett, D. L., & Steele, J. B. (1979). *Empire: The life, legend, and madness of Howard Hughes.* New York: Norton.

Bass, S. J., & Dole, A. A. (1977). Ethical leader practices in sensitivity training for prospective professional psychologists. *Catalog of Selected Documents in Psychology, 36,* 47–48.

Bateson, G., Jackson, D. D., Haley, J., & Weakland, J. (1956). Toward a theory of schizophrenia. *Behavioral Science, 1,* 251–64.

Baum, M. (1969). Extinction of an avoidance response following response prevention: Some parametric investigations. *Canadian Journal of Psychology, 23,* 1–10.

Baumgold, J. (1977, December 4). Agoraphobia: Life ruled by panic. *New York Times Magazine,* p. 46.

Bazelon, D. (1971). New gods for old: "Efficient" courts in a democratic society. *New York University Law Review, 46,* 653, 658–60.

Beck, A. T. (1967). *Depression: Clinical, experimental, and theoretical aspects.* New York: Hoeber.

Beck, A. T. (1973). *The diagnosis and management of depression.* Philadelphia: University of Pennsylvania Press.

Beck, A. T. (1976). *Cognitive therapy and the emotional disorders.* New York: International Universities Press.

Beck, A. T., & Horvich, M. J. (1959). Psychological correlates of depression. *Psychosomatic Medicine, 21,* 50–55.

Beck, A. T., Kovacs, M., & Weissman, A. (1975). Hopelessness and suicidal behavior: An overview. *Journal of the American Medical Association, 234,* 1146–49.

Beck, A. T., Rush, A. J., Shaw, B. F., & Emery, G. (1979). *Cognitive therapy of depression.* New York: Guilford Press.

Beck, A. T., Ward, C. H., Mendelson, M., Mock, J. E., & Erbaugh, J. K. (1962). Reliability of psychiatric diagnoses II: A study of consistency of clinical judgments and ratings. *American Journal of Psychiatry, 119,* 351–57.

Beck, T. R. (1811). An inaugural dissertation on insanity. Cited in A. Deutsch, *The mentally ill in America.* New York: Columbia University Press, 1949.

Becker, J., & Schuckit, M. A. (1978). The comparative efficacy of cognitive therapy and pharmacotherapy in the treatment of depression. *Cognitive Research and Therapy, 2,* 79–91.

Bee, H. L., Van Egern, L. F., Streissguth, A. P., Nyman, B. A., & Leckie, M. S. (1969). Social class differences in maternal teaching strategies and speech patterns. *Developmental Psychology, 1,* 726–34.

Beech, H. R., & Vaughan, M. (1979). *Behavioural treatment of obsessional states.* Chichester: Wiley.

Beecher, H. K. (1959). *Measurement of subjective responses: Quantitative effects of drugs.* New York: Oxford University Press.

Beecher, H. K. (1961). Surgery as placebo. *Journal of the American Medical Association, 176,* 1102–1107.

Bell, A. P., & Weinberg, M. S. (1978). *Homosexualities: A study of the diversity among men and women.* New York: Simon & Schuster.

Bellisimo, A., & Steffy, R. A. (1972). Redundancy-associated deficit in schizophrenic reaction time performance. *Journal of Abnormal Psychology, 80,* 229–307.

Bellisimo, A., & Steffy, R. A. (1975). Contextual influences on crossover in the reaction time performance of schizophrenics. *Journal of Abnormal Psychology, 84,* 210–220.

Belson, R. (1975). The importance of the second interview in marriage counseling. *Counseling Psychologist, 5*(3), 27–31.

Bemis, K. (1978). Current approaches to the etiology and treatment of anorexia nervosa. *Psychological Bulletin, 85,* 593–617.

Benjamin, H. (1966). *The transsexual phenomenon.* New York: Julian Press.

Benson, H. (1975). *The relaxation response.* New York: Morrow.

Bergin, A. E. (1966). Some implications of psychotherapy research for therapeutic practice. *Journal of Abnormal Psychology, 71,* 235–46.

Bergin, A. E. (1971). The evaluation of therapeutic outcomes. In A. E. Bergin & S. L. Garfield (Eds.), *Handbook of psychotherapy and behavior change* (pp. 217–70). New York: Wiley.

Bergler, E. (1949). *The basic neurosis: Oral regression and psychic masochism.* New York: Grune & Stratton.

Bettelheim, B. (1943). Individual and mass behavior in extreme situations. *Journal of Abnormal and Social Psychology, 38,* 417–52.

Bettelheim, B. (1967). *The empty fortress.* New York: The Free Press.

Bexton, W. H., Heron, W., & Scott, T. H. (1954). Effects of decreased variation in the sensory environment. *Canadian Journal of Psychology, 8,* 70–76.

Bibring, E. (1953). The mechanism of depression. In P. Greenacre (Ed.), *Affective disorders.* New York: International Universities Press.

Binstock, J. (1974). Choosing to die. The decline of aggression and the rise of suicide. *The Luterost, 8,* 68–71.

Biran, M., & Wilson, G. T. (1981). Treatment of phobic disorders using cognitive and exposure methods: A self-efficacy analysis. *Journal of Consulting and Clinical Psychology, 48,* 886–87.

Bird J. (1979). The behavioural treatment of hysteria. *British Journal of Psychiatry, 134,* 129–37.

Birenbaum, A., & Rei, M. A. (1979). Resettling mentally retarded adults in the community—almost 4 years later. *American Journal of Mental Deficiency, 83,* 323–29.

Black, A. (1974). The natural history of obsessional neuroses. In H. R. Beech (Ed.), *Obsessional states.* London: Methuen.

Blair, C. D., & Lanyon, R. I. (1981). Exhibitionism: A critical review of the etiology and treatment. *Psychological Bulletin, 89,* 439–63.

Blakemore, C. (1977). *Mechanics of the mind.* Cambridge, Eng.: Cambridge University Press.

Blanchard, E. B. (1982). Behavioral medicine: Past, present, and future. *Journal of Consulting and Clinical Psychology, 50,* 795–96.

Blanchard, E. B., & Epstein, L. H. (1978). *A biofeedback primer.* Reading, Mass.: Addison-Wesley.

Blashfield, R. K., & Draguns, J. G. (1976). Evaluative criteria for psychiatric classification. *Journal of Abnormal Psychology, 85,* 40–150.

Blessed, G., Tomlinsun, B. E., & Roth, M. (1968). The association between quantitative measures of dementia and of senile change in the cerebral gray matter of elderly subjects. *British Journal of Psychiatry, 114,* 797–811.

Bleuler, E. (1924). *Textbook of psychiatry.* New York: Macmillan.

Bleuler, M. (1974). The offspring of schizophrenics. *Schizophrenia Bulletin, 8,* 93–107.

Bliss, E. L. (1980). Multiple personalities: Report of fourteen cases with implications for schizophrenia and hysteria. *Archives of General Psychiatry, 37,* 1388–97.

Bloch, S., & Reddaway, P. (1977). *Psychiatric terror: How Soviet psychiatry is used to suppress dissent.* New York: Basic Books.

Bootzin, R. R. (1975). *Behavior modification and therapy: An introduction.* Cambridge, Mass.: Winthrop.

Boskind-White, M., & White, W. C. (1983). *Bulimarexia: The binge/purge cycle.* New York: Norton.

Bourne, H. R., Bunney, W. E., Colburn, R. W., Davis, J. M., Davis, J. N., Shaw, D. M., & Loppen, A. J. (1968). Noradrenalin, 5-hydroxytryptamine and 5-hydroxyindoleacidic in hind brains of suicidal patients. *Lancet, 2,* 805–808.

Bowlby, J. (1960). Grief and mourning in infancy and early childhood. *The Psychoanalytic Study of the Child, 15,* 9–52.

Bowlby, J. (1969). *Attachment.* New York: Basic Books.

Brady, J. P. (1958). Ulcers in "executive" monkeys. *Scientific American, 199,* 95–100.

Brady, J. P., & Lind D. L. (1961). Experimental analysis of hysterical blindness: Operant conditioning techniques. *Archives of General Psychiatry, 4,* 331–39.

Brady, J. P., Porter, R. W., Conrad, D. G., & Mason, J. W. (1958). Avoidance behavior and the development of gastroduodenal ulcers. *Journal of Experimental Analysis of Behavior, 1,* 69–73.

Brain, L., & Walton, J. N. (1969). *Brain's diseases of the nervous system* (7th ed.). London: Oxford University Press.

Brask, B. H. (1967). The need for hospital beds for psychotic children: An analysis based on a prevalence investigation in the County of Arthus. *Ugeskrift fur Laeger, 129,* 1559–70.

Bregman E. O. (1934). An attempt to modify the emotional attitudes of infants by the conditioned response technique. *Journal of Genetic Psychology, 45,* 169–98.

Brehm, S. S., & Brehm, J. W. (1981). *Psychological reactance: A theory of freedom and control.* New York: Academic Press.

Brett, C. W., Burling, T. A., & Pavlik, W. B. (1981). Electroconvulsive shock and learned helplessness in rats. *Animal Learning and Behavior, 9,* 38–44.

Broadbent, D. E. (1958). *Perception of communication,* London: Pergamon.

Broadbent, D. E. (1971). *Decision and stress.* New York: Academic Press.

Brodie, H. K. H., & Leff, M. J. (1971). Bipolar depression: A comparative study of patient characteristics. *American Journal of Psychiatry, 127,* 1086–90.

Broen, W. E., Jr. (1968). *Schizophrenia: Research and theory.* New York: Academic Press.

Brooks, A. D. (1974). *Law, psychiatry and the mental health system.* Boston: Little, Brown.

Brooks, L. (1974). Interactive effects of sex and status on self-disclosure. *Journal of Counseling Psychology, 21,* 469–74.

Brown, G. W., & Harris, T. (1978). *Social origins of depression.* London: Tavistock.

Brown, R., & Herrnstein, R. J. (1975). *Psychology.* Boston: Little, Brown.

Brown, W. F. (1974). Effectiveness and paraprofessionals: The evidence. *Personnel and Guidance Journal, 53,* 257–63.

Bruch. H. (1978). *The golden cage: The enigma of anorexia nervosa.* Cambridge, Mass.: Harvard University Press.

Bryan, T. H., & Bryan, J. H. (1975). *Understanding learning disabilities.* New York: Alfred Publishing Co.

Buchwald, A. M., Coyne, J. C., & Cole, C. S. (1978) A critical evaluation of the learned helplessness model of depression. *Journal of Abnormal Psychology, 87,* 180–93.

Budzynski, T. H., Stoyva, J. M., Adler, C. S., & Mullaney, D. M. (1973). EMG biofeedback and tension headache: A controlled outcome study. *Psychosomatic Medicine, 35,* 484–96.

Bunney, W. E., Murphy, D. L., Goodwin, F. K., & Borge, G. L. (1972). The switch process in manic depressive illness. *Archives of General Psychiatry, 27,* 295.

Burgess, A. W., & Holstrom, L. L. (1974). *Rape: Victims of crisis.* Bowie, Md.: Robert J. Brady Co.

Burgess, A., & Holmstrom, L. (1979). Adaptive strategies and recovery from rape. *American Journal of Psychiatry, 136,* 1278–82.

Burgess, E. P. (1968). The modification of depressive behaviors. In R. D. Rubin & C. M. Franks (Eds.), *Advances in behavior therapy.* New York: Academic Press.

Burns, B., & Reyher, J. (1976). Activating posthypnotic conflict: Emergent, uncovering, psychopathology, repression and psychopathology. *Journal of Personality Assessment, 40,* 492–501.

Burns, D., & Mendels, J. (1977). Biogenic amine precursors and affective illness. In W. Fann, I. Karacan, A. Pikorny, & R. Williams (Eds.), *Phenomenology and a treatment of depression.* New York: Spectrum.

Burt, R. A. & Morris, N. (1972). A proposal for the abolition of the incompetency plea. *Chicago Law Review, 40,* 66–80.

Buss, A. H., & Lang, P. J. (1965). Psychological deficit in schizophrenia: Affect reinforcement and concept attainment. *Journal of Abnormal Psychology, 70,* 2–24.

Butcher, J. N. (1969). *MMPI: Research developments and clinical applications.* New York: McGraw-Hill.

Butterfield, E. C. (1964). Locus of control, test anxiety, reaction to frustration, and achievement attitudes. *Journal of Personality, 32,* 298–311.

Cade, J. F. J. (1949). Lithium salts in the treatment of psychotic excitement. *Medical Journal of Australia, 36,* 349–52.

Cameron, N. (1938). Reasoning, regression and communication in schizophrenia. *Psychological Monographs, 50* (Whole No. 221).

Cameron, N. (1947). *The psychology of behavior disorders.* Boston: Houghton Mifflin.

Cannon, W. B. (1942). "Voodoo" death. *American Anthropologist, 44,* 169–81.

Cantor, N., Smith, E., French, R. de S., & Mezzich, J. (1980). Psychiatric diagnosis as prototype categorization. *Journal of Abnormal Psychology, 89,* 181–93.

Cantwell, D. P., Baker, L., & Rutter, M. (1978). Family factors in the syndrome of infantile autism. In M. Rutter & E. Schopler (Eds.), *Autism: A reappraisal of concepts and treatment.* New York: Plenum.

Carkesse, J. (1963). Lucida intetvalla. Quoted in R. Hunter and I. Macalpine, *Three hundred years of psychiatry: 1535–1860.* London: Oxford University Press.

Carlson, G. A., Kotin, J., Davenport, Y. B., & Adland, M. (1974). Followup of 53 bipolar manic depressive patients. *British Journal of Psychiatry, 124,* 134–39.

Carpenter, W. T., Jr., Strauss, J. S., & Bartko, J. J. (1973). Flexible system for the diagnosis of schizophrenia: Report from the WHO International Pilot Study of Schizophrenia. *Science, 182,* 1275–78.

Carpenter, W., Strauss, J., & Bartko, J. (1974). Use of signs and symptoms for the identification of schizophrenic patients. *Schizophrenia Bulletin, 11,* 37–49.

Carrington, R. (1959). *Elephants.* New York: Basic Books.

Carter, A. B. (1949). The prognosis of certain hysterical symptoms. *British Medical Journal, 1,* 1076–80.

Carter, R. B. (1853). *On the pathology and treatment of hysteria.* London: John Churchill.

Cartwright, R. D., & Lerner, B. (1963). Empathy, need to change, and improvement with psychotherapy. *Journal of Consulting Psychology, 27,* 138–44.

Cartwright, R., & Vogel, J. (1960). A comparison of changes in psychoneurotic patients during matched periods of therapy and no therapy. *Journal of Consulting Psychology, 24,* 121–27.

Casey, J. F., Bennett, I. F., Lindley, C. J., Hollister, L. E., Gordon, M. H., & Springer, N. N. (1960). Drug therapy and schizophrenia: A controlled study of the effectiveness of chlorpromazine, promazine, phenobarbitol and placebo. *Archives of General Psychiatry, 2,* 210–20.

Cegelka, W. J., & Tyler, J. L. (1970). The efficacy of special class placement for the mentally retarded in proper perspective. *Training School Bulletin, 67,* 33–68.

Chambers, D. L. (1972). Alternatives to civil commitment of the mentally ill: Practical guides and constitutional imperatives. *Michigan Law Review, 70B,* 1107–1200.

Chambers, W. W., & Reisen, M. F. (1953). Emotional stress and the precipitation of congestive heart failure. *Psychosomatic Medicine, 15,* 38.

Chapman, L. J., & Chapman, D. T. (1969). Illusory correlations as an obstacle to the use of valid psychodiagnostic signs. *Journal of Abnormal Psychology, 74,* 271–80.

Chapman, L. J., & Chapman, J. P. (1973). *Disordered thought in schizophrenia.* New York: Appleton-Century-Crofts.

Chapman, L. J., & Taylor, J. A. (1957). Breadth of deviate concepts used by schizophrenics. *Journal of Abnormal Social Psychology, 54,* 118–23.

Chappell, M. N., & Stevenson, T. I. (1936). Group psychological training in some organic conditions. *Mental Hygiene, 20,* 588–97.

Cherry, C., & Sayers, B. McA. (1956). Experiments upon the total inhibition of stammering by external control and some clinical results. *Journal of Psychosomatic Research, 1,* 233.

Cheseldine, S., & McConkey, R. (1979). Parental speech to young Down's syndrome children: An intervention study. *American Journal of Mental Deficiency, 83,* 612–20.

Chinn, P. C., Drew, C. J., & Logan, D. R. (1979). *Mental retardation: A life cycle approach* (2d. ed.). St. Louis: Mosby.

Chodoff, P. (1963). Late effect of the concentration camp syndrome. *Archives of General Psychiatry, 8,* 323–33.

Chodoff, P. (1973). The depressive personality: A critical review. *International Journal of Psychiatry, 11,* 196–217.

Chodoff, P. (1974). The diagnosis of hysteria: An overview. *American Journal of Psychiatry, 131,* 1073–78.

Chodoff, P. (1982). Hysteria and women. *American Journal of Psychiatry, 139,* 545–51.

Christiansen, K. O. (1977). A review of studies of criminality among twins. In S. A. Mednick & K. O. Christiansen (Eds.), *Biosocial bases of criminal behavior.* New York: Gardner Press.

Christodoulou, G. N., Gergoulas, A., Paploukas, A., Marinopou-lou, A., & Sideris, E. (1977). Primary peptic ulcer in childhood. *Acta Psychiatrica Scandinavia, 56,* 215–22.

Cicero, J. J., Myers, R. D., & Black, W. C. (1968). Increase in volitional ethanol consumption following interference with a learned avoidance response. *Physiology and Behavior, 3,* 657–60.

Claparède, E. (1951). Recognition and "me-ness." In D. Rapaport (Ed.), *Organization and pathology of thought.* New York: Columbia University Press. (Reprinted from Recognition et moiite. *Archives de Psychologie,* 1911, *11,* 79–90).

Clark, R. E. (1948). The relationship of schizophrenia to occupational income and occupational prestige. *American Sociological Review, 13,* 325–30.

Clausen, J. A., & Kohn, M. L. (1959). Relation of schizophrenia to the social structure of a small city. In B. Pasamanick (Ed.), *Epidemiology of mental disorder.* Washington, D.C.: American Association for the Advancement of Science.

Cleckley, H. (1964). *The mask of sanity.* St. Louis: Mosby.

Cobb, S., & Rose, R. M. (1973). Hypertension, peptic ulcer and diabetes and the traffic controllers. *Journal of the American Medical Association, 224,* 489–92.

Cohen, B. M. (1977). Genetics of psychiatric disorders. *McLean Hospital Lecture Series.* Tape recording reproduced by Endo Laboratories, Garden City, N.Y.

Cohen, J. A. (1960). A coefficient of agreement for nominal scales. *Educational and Psychological Measurement, 20,* 37–46.

Cohen, N. B., Baker, G., Cohen, R. A., Fromm-Reichmann, F., & Weigert, E. B. (1954). An intensive study of 12 cases of manic-depressive psychosis. *Psychiatry, 17,* 103–37.

Cohen, N. J., & Squire, L. R. (1981). Retrograde amnesia and remote memory impairment. *Neuropsychologia, 19,* 337–56.

Cohen, S. (1971, December). Statement before the Subcommittee to Investigate Juvenile Delinquency of the U.S. Senate Committee on the Judiciary on Drug Abuse.

Cohen, S. (1980). Coca paste and freebase: New fashions in cocaine use. *Drug Abuse and Alcoholism Newsletter, 9*(3).

Cohn, N.R.C. (1975). *Europe's inner demons: An enquiry inspired by the great witch-hunt.* Chatto, Eng.: Heinemann for Sussex University Press.

Cooke, G., Johnston, N., & Pogany, E. (1973). Factors affecting referral to determine competency to stand trial. *American Journal of Psychiatry, 130*(8), 870.

Cooper, A. F., Garside, R. F., & Kay, D. W. (1976). A comparison of deaf and non-deaf patients with paranoid and affective psychoses. *British Journal of Psychiatry, 129,* 532–38.

Cooper, A. F., & Porter, R. (1976). Visual acuity and ocular pathology in the paranoid and affective psychoses. *British Journal of Psychiatry, 129,* 532–38.

Coppen, A., Prange, A. J., Whybrow, P., & Noguera, R. (1972). Abnormalities of indoleamines and affective disorders. *Archives of General Psychiatry, 26,* 474–78.

Coryell, W., & Norten, S. (1981). Briquet's Syndrome and primary depression: Comparison of background and outcome. *Comprehensive Psychiatry, 22,* 249–56.

Costello, C. G. (1972). Depression: Loss of reinforcers or loss of reinforcer effectiveness. *Behavior Therapy, 3,* 240–47.

Cousins, N. (1979). *Anatomy of an illness: As perceived by the patient.* New York: Norton.

Cowen, E. L. (1973). Social and community interventions. *Annual Review of Psychology, 24,* 423–72.

Cowen, E. L. (1977a). Baby steps toward primary prevention. *American Journal of Community Psychology, 5,* 1–22.

Cowen, E. L. (1977b). Psychologists in primary prevention: Blowing the cover story. An editorial. *American Journal of Community Psychology, 5,* 481–90.

Cowen, E. L., & Zax, M. (1968). Early detection and prevention of emotional disorder: Conceptualizations and programming. In J. W. Carter (Ed.), *Research contributions from psychology to community mental health.* New York: Behavioral Publications.

Cox, P., Hallam, R., O'Connor, K., & Rachman, S. (1983). An experimental analysis of fearlessness and courage. *British Journal of Psychology, 74,* 107–17.

Coyle, J. T., Price, D. L., & DeLong, M. R. (1983). Alzheimer's disease: A disorder of cortical cholinergic innervation. *Science, 219,* 1184–90.

Coyne, J. C. (1976). Depression and the response of others. *Journal of Abnormal Psychology, 85,* 186–93.

Craighead, W. E., Kazdin, A. E., & Mahoney, M. J. (1976). *Behavior modification: Principles, issues and applications.* Boston: Houghton Mifflin.

Creak, M. (1961). Schizophrenia syndrome in childhood: Progress report of a working party. *Cerebral Palsy Bulletin, 3,* 501–504.

Crisp, A. H., Palmer, R. L., & Kalucy, R. S. (1976). How common is anorexia nervosa: A prevalence study. *British Journal of Psychiatry, 128,* 549–54.

Critchley, M. (1966). *The parietal lobes.* New York: Hafner.

Crocetti, G. M., & Lemkau, P. V. (1967). Schizophrenia: II. Epidemiology. In A. M. Freeman & H. I. Kaplan (Eds.), *Comprehensive textbook of psychiatry.* Baltimore: Williams & Wilkins.

Cronbach, L. J., Gleser, G. C., Nanda, H., & Rajaratnam, N. (1972). *The dependability of behavioral measurements: Theory of generalizability for scores and profiles.* New York: Wiley.

Crowe, M. J., Marks, I. M., Agras, W. S., & Leitenberg, H. (1972). Time limited desensitization, implosion and shaping for phobic patients: A crossover study. *Behavior Research & Therapy, 10*(4), 319–28.

Currie, E. P. (1968). Crimes without criminals: Witchcraft and its controls in Renaissance Europe. *Law and Society Review, 3,* 7–32.

Curtis, B. A., Jacobson, S., & Marcus, E. M. (1972). *An introduction to the neurosciences.* Philadelphia: Saunders.

Cushing, H. (1932). Peptic ulcers and the interbrain. *Surgery, Gynecology and Obstetrics, 55,* 1–34.

Cytryn, L., & Lourie, R. D. (1967). Mental retardation. In A. M. Freedman & H. I. Kaplan (Eds.), *Comprehensive textbook of psychiatry.* Baltimore: Williams & Wilkins.

Cytryn, L., & McKnew, D. H. (1972). Proposed classification of childhood depression. *American Journal of Psychiatry, 129,* 149–55.

Dalgard, O. S., & Kringlen, E. (1976). A Norwegian twin study of criminality. *British Journal of Criminality, 16,* 213–32.

Datey, K. K., Deshmuck, S. N., Dalvi, C. P., & Vinekarsl. (1969). "Shavasan": A Yogic exercise in the management of hypertension. *Angiology, 20,* 325–33.

Davenport, H. W. (1972). Why the stomach does not digest itself. *Scientific American, 226,* 86–92.

Davies, J. C. V., & Maliphant, R. (1971). Autonomic responses of male adolescents exhibiting refractory behavior in school. *Journal of Child Psychology and Psychiatry, 12,* 115–27.

Davies, R. (1978). *One half of Robertson Davies.* New York: Penquin.

Davis, J., & Miller, N. (1963). Fear and pain: Their effect on self-injection of ambarbitol sodium by rats. *Science, 141,* 1286–87.

Davis, P. H., & Osherson, A. (1977). The current treatment of a multiple-personality woman and her son. *American Journal of Psychotherapy. 31,* 504–15.

Davison, G. C. (1976). Homosexuality: The ethical challenge. *Journal of Counseling and Clinical Psychology, 44,* 157–62.

Davison, G. C. (1978). Not can but ought: The treatment of homosexuality. *Journal of Consulting and Clinical Psychology, 46,* 170–72.

Davison, G. C., & Wilson, G. T. (1972). Critique of "Desensitization: Social and cognitive factors underlying the effectiveness of Wolpe's procedure." *Psychological Bulletin, 78*(1), 28–31.

Dekker, E., Pelse, H., & Groen, J. (1957). Conditioning as a cause of asthmatic attacks: A laboratory study. *Journal of Psychosomatic Research, 2,* 97–108.

DeMeyer, M. K., Barton, S., Alpern, G. D., Kimberlin, C., Allen, J., Yang, E., & Steel, R. (1974). The measured intelligence of autistic children. *Journal of Autistic Children and Schizophrenia, 4,* 42–60.

Depue, R. (1979). *The psychobiology of the depressive disorders: Implications for the effect of stress.* New York: Academic Press.

Depue, R. A., & Dubkicki, M. D. (1974). Hospitalization and premorbid characteristics in withdrawn and active schizophrenics. *Journal of Consulting and Clinical Psychology, 42,* 629–32.

Depue, R. H., & Monroe, S. (1978). The unipolar-bipolar distinction in depressive disorders. *Psychological Bulletin, 85,* 1001–29.

De Quincey, T. (1823). *Confessions of an English opium-eater.* Cited by LaBarre, Anthropological perspectives on hallucination and hallucinogens. In K. K. Siegel & L. J. West (Eds.), *Hallucinations behavior experience and theory.* New York: Wiley, 1975.

Dershowitz, A. M. (1968). Psychiatry in the legal process: "A knife that cuts both ways." *Trial, 4,* 29.

De Silva, P., Rachman, S., & Seligman, M. E. P. (1977). Prepared phobias and obsessions: Therapeutic outcome. *Behaviour Research and Therapy, 15*(1), 65–77.

Deutsch, A. (1949). *The mentally ill in America.* New York: Columbia University Press.

Devine, P. A., & Fernald, P. S. (1973). Outcome effects of receiving a preferred randomly assigned or nonpreferred therapy. *Journal of Consulting and Clinical Psychology, 41*(1), 104–107.

Diamond, B. L. (1974). Psychiatric prediction of dangerousness. *University of Pennsylvania Law Review, 123,* 439–52.

Diggory, J. C. (1976). United States suicide rates, 1933–1968: An analysis of some trends. In E. S. Shneidman (Ed.), *Suicidology: Contemporary Developments.* New York: Grune & Stratton.

DiPalma, J. R. (1971). Introduction: Brief history. In J. R. DiPalma (Ed.), *Drill's pharmacology in medicine.* New York: McGraw-Hill.

Dohrenwend, B. S., & Dohrenwend, B. P. (Eds.). (1974). *Stressful life events: Their nature and effects.* New York: Wiley.

Dohrenwend, B. S., & Martin, J. L. (1978, February). Personal vs. situational determination of anticipation and control of the occurrence of stressful life events. Paper presented at the annual meeting of AAAS, Washington, D.C.

Dole, V. P., & Nyswander, M. E. (1965). Heroin addiction—a metabolic disease. *Archives of Internal Medicine, 120,* 19–24.

Doleys, D. M. (1979). Assessment and treatment of childhood enuresis. In A. J. Finch, Jr., & P. C. Kendall (Eds.), *Clinical treatment and research in child psychopathology* (pp. 207–33). New York: Spectrum.

Donaldson, D. (1976). *Insanity inside out.* New York: Crown.

Dorsey, M. F., Iwata, B. A., Ong, P., & McSween, T. (1980). Treatment of self-injurious behavior using a water mist: Initial response suppression and generalization. *Journal of Applied Behavior Analysis, 13,* 343–53.

Dorworth, T. R. (1971). The effect of electroconvulsive shock on "helplessness" in dogs. Unpublished doctoral dissertation, University of Minnesota.

Dostoyevsky, D. (1960). *Notes from the underground.* New York: Dell.

Douglas, M. (Ed.). (1970). *Witchcraft: Confessions and accusations.* London: Tavistock.

Doyle, A. C. (1938). The sign of the four. In *The complete Sherlock Holmes.* New York: Garden City Publishing Co.

Dragstedt, L. R. (1956). A concept of the ideology of duodenal ulcer. *American Journal of Roentgenology, 75,* 219–29.

Drossman, D. A. (1982). Patients with psychogenic abdominal pain: Six years' observation in the medical setting. *American Journal of Psychiatry, 139,* 1549–57.

Drummond. (1875). In R. Carrington, *Elephants.* New York: Basic Books, 1959.

Dunbar, H. F. (1943). *Psychosomatic diagnosis.* New York: Hoeber.

Dunbar, H. F., & Arlow, J. (1944). Criteria for therapy in psychosomatic disorders. *Psychosomatic Medicine, 6,* 283–86.

Dunner, D. L., Gershom, E. S., & Goodwin, F. K. (1976). Heritable factors in the severity of affective illness. *Biological Psychiatry, 11,* 31–42.

Early, L. S., & Lisschutz, J. E. (1974). A case of stigmata. *Archives of General Psychiatry, 30,* 197–200.

Eberhard, G. (1968). Personality in peptic ulcer: Preliminary report of a twin study. *Acta Psychiatrica Scandinavia, 203,* 131.

Eidelson, J. I. (1977). Perceived control and psychopathology. Unpublished doctoral dissertation, Duke University.

Eisenberg, L. (1956). The autistic child in adolescence. *American Journal of Psychiatry, 112,* 607–12.

Eisenberg, L. (1977). Psychiatry and society: A sociobiological synthesis. *New England Journal of Medicine. 29,* 903–10.

Ekman, P., & Friesen, W. V. (1975). *Unmasking the face.* Englewood Cliffs, N.J.: Prentice-Hall.

Ekman, P., Friesen, W. V., & Ellsworth, P. (1972). *Emotion in the human face.* New York: Pergamon.

Elashoff, J. D., & Grossman, M. I. (1980). Trends in hospital admissions and death rates for peptic ulcer in the United States from 1970 to 1978. *Gastroenterology, 78,* 280–85.

Ellenberger, H. F. (1970). *The discovery of the unconscious: The history and evolution of dynamic psychiatry.* New York: Basic Books.

Ellis, A. (1962). *Reason and emotion in psychotherapy.* New York: Lyle Stuart.

Ellis, A., & Harper, R. A. (1975). *A new guide to rational living.* Englewood Cliffs, N.J.: Prentice-Hall.

Ellison, G. D. (1977). Animal models of psychopathology. *American Psychologist, 32,* 1036–55.

Ellsworth, P. C., & Carlsmith, M. J. (1968). Effects of eye contact and verbal content on affective response to dyadic interactions. *Journal of Personality and Social Psychology, 10,* 15–20.

Elmhorn, K. (1965). Study in self-reported delinquency among school children. In *Scandinavian studies in criminology.* London: Tavistock.

Emmelkamp, P., & Kuipers, A. (1979). Agoraphobia: a follow-up study four years after treatment. *British Journal of Psychiatry, 134,* 352–55.

Emrick, C. D., Lassen, C. L., & Edwards, M. T. (1977). Nonprofessional peers as therapeutic agents. In A. S. Gurman & A. M. Razin (Eds.), *Effective psychotherapy.* New York: Pergamon Press.

Endicott, J., & Spitzer, R. L. (1978). A diagnostic interview: The schedule for affective disorders and schizophrenia. *Archives of General Psychiatry, 35,* 837–44.

Endler, N. S., Magnusson, D., Ekehammar, B., & Okada, M. O. (1975). The multidimensionality of state and trait anxiety. Reports from the Department of Psychology, University of Stockholm.

Ennis, B. J. (1972). *Prisoners of psychiatry: Mental patients, psychiatrists, and the law.* New York: Harcourt Brace Jovanovich.

Ennis, B. J., & Litwack, T. R. (1974). Psychiatry and the presumption of expertise: Flipping coins in the courtroom. *California Law Review, 62,* 693.

Ennis, B., & Siegel, L. (1973). *The rights of mental patients: The basic ACLU guide to a mental patient's rights.* New York: Discus Books.

Erikson, E. H. (1959). *Identity and the life cycle.* New York: Norton, 1980.

Erikson, K. (1976). *Everything in its path: Destruction of community in the Buffalo Creek flood.* New York: Simon & Schuster.

Exline, R., & Winters, L. C. (1965). Affective relations and mutual glances in dyads. In S. Tomkins & C. E. Izard (Eds.), *Affect, cognition and personality.* New York: Springer.

Exner, J. E. (1974). *The Rorschach: A comprehensive system.* New York: Wiley.

Exner, J. E. (1978). *The Rorschach: A comprehensive system: Vol. 2. Current research and advanced interpretation.* New York: Wiley.

Eysenck, H. J. (1952a). The effects of psychotherapy: An evaluation. *Journal of Consulting Psychology, 16,* 319–24.

Eysenck, H. (1952b). *The scientific study of personality.* New York: Macmillan.

Eysenck, H. J. (1961a). Classification and the problem of diagnosis. In H. J. Eysenck (Ed.), *Handbook of abnormal psychology.* London: Pitman.

Eysenck, H. J. (1961b). The effects of psychotherapy. In H. J. Eysenck (Ed.), *Handbook of abnormal psychology: An experimental approach* (pp. 697–725). New York: Basic Books.

Eysenck, H. J. (1979). The conditioning model of neurosis. *Communications in Behavioral Biology, 2,* 155–99.

Eysenck, H., & Rachman, S. (1965). Causes and cures of neurosis. San Diego, Calif.: Knapp.

Fairweather, G. W., Sanders, D. H., Cressler, D. L., & Maynard, H. (1969). *Community life for the mentally ill.* Chicago: Alpine.

Fancher, R. (1973). *Psychoanalytic psychology: The development of Freud's thought.* New York: Norton.

Farber, L. H. (1966). *The ways of the will: Essays toward a psychology and psychopathology of will.* New York: Basic Books.

Farberow, N. L. (1970). Ten years of suicide prevention—past and future. *Bulletin of Suicidology, 6,* 6–11.

Farberow, N. L. (1974). *Suicide.* Morristown, N.J.: General Learning Press.

Faris, R. E. L., & Dunham, H. W. (1939). *Mental disorders in urban areas.* Chicago: University of Chicago Press.

Farrington, D. P. (1978). The family background of aggressive youths. In L. A. Hersov & D. Shaffer (Eds.), *Aggression and antisocial behavior in childhood and adolescence.* New York: Pergamon.

Fawcett, J., Maas, J., & Dekirmenjian, H. (1972). Depression and MHPG excretion: Response to dextroamphetamine and tricyclic antidepressants. *Archives of General Psychiatry, 26,* 246–51.

Feinberg, I. (1962). A comparison of the visual hallucinations in schizophrenics with those induced by mescaline and LSD. In L. J. West (Ed.), *Hallucinations.* New York: Grune & Stratton.

Feldman, M. P., & MacCulloch, M. J. (1971). *Homosexual behaviour: Theory and assessment.* Oxford: Pergamon.

Fenichel, O. (1945). *The psychoanalytic theory of neurosis.* New York: Norton.

Ferster, C. B. (1961). Positive reinforcement and the behavioral deficits of autistic children. *Child Development, 32,* 437–56.

Ferster, C. B. (1974). Behavioral approaches to depression. In R. J. Friedman & M. M. Katz (Eds.), *The psychology of depression: Contemporary theory and research.* Washington, D.C.: Winston.

Fieve, R. R. (1975). *Mood swing.* New York: Morrow.

Fine, T. H., & Turner, J. W. (1982). The effect of brief restricted environmental stimulation therapy in the treatment of essential hypertension. *Behaviour Research and Therapy, 20,* 567–70.

Fingarette, H., & Hasse, A. (1979). *Mental disabilities and criminal responsibility.* Berkeley: University of California Press.

Fink, M. (1979). *Convulsive therapy: Therapy and practice.* New York: Raven Press.

Fireside, H. (1979). *Soviet psychoprisons.* New York: Norton.

Fisher, J., Epstein, L. J., & Harris, M. R. (1967). Validity of the psychiatric interview: Predicting the effectiveness of the first Peace Corps volunteers in Ghana. *Archives of General Psychiatry, 17,* 744–50.

Fisher, S., & Greenberg, R. P. (1977). *The scientific credibility of Freud's theories and therapy.* New York: Basic Books.

Fiske, D., Cartwright, D., & Kirtner, W. (1964). Are psychotherapeutic changes predictable? *Journal of Abnormal and Social Psychology, 69,* 418–26.

Fiske, D., & Goodman, G. (1965). The post-therapy period. *Journal of Abnormal Psychology, 70,* 169–70.

Fleiss, J. L. (1971). Measuring nominal scale agreement among many raters. *Psychological Bulletin, 76,* 378–82.

Flood, R., & Seager, C. (1968). A retrospective examination of psychiatric case records of patients who subsequently commit suicide. *British Journal of Psychiatry, 114,* 443–50.

Fodor, O., Vestea, S., & Urcan, S. (1968). Hydrochloric acid secretion capacity of the stomach as an inherited factor in the pathogenesis of duodenal ulcer. *American Journal of Digestive Diseases, 13,* 260.

Folstein, S., & Rutter, M. (1978). A twin study of individuals with infantile autism. In M. Rutter & E. Schopler (Eds.), *Autism: A reappraisal of concepts and treatment.* New York: Plenum.

Ford, C. S., & Beach, F. A. (1951). *Pattern of sexual behavior.* New York: Harper.

Forsyth, R. P. (1968). Blood pressure and avoidance conditioning: A study of a 15-day trial on the Rhesus monkey. *Psychosomatic Medicine, 30,* 125–35.

Foucault, M. (1965). *Madness and civilization: A history of insanity in the age of reason.* New York: Random House.

Fowles, D. C., & Gersh, F. (1979). Neurotic depression: The endogenous-neurotic distinction. In R. A. Depue (Ed.), *The psychobiology of the depressive disorders: Implications for the effects of stress.* New York: Academic Press.

Fox, R. (1976). The recent rise of suicide in Britain: The role of the samaritan suicide prevention movement. In E. S. Shneidman (Ed.), *Suicidology: Contemporary developments.* New York: Grune & Stratton.

Frank, J. D. (1978). Expectation and therapeutic outcome—The placebo effect and the role induction interview. In J. D. Frank, R. Hoehn-Saric, S. D. Imber, B. L. Liberman, & A. R. Stone (Eds.), *Effective ingredients of successful psychotherapy.* New York: Brunner/Mazel.

Frankel, B. G., & Whitehead, P. C. (1981). Drinking and damage: Theoretical advances and implications for prevention. *Mono-*

graph of the Rutgers Center of Alcohol Studies, 14. New Brunswick: Rutgers Center of Alcohol Studies.

Frankel, B. L., Patel, D. J., Horwitz, P., Friedewalt, W. T., & Gaarder, K. R. (1978). Treatment of hypertension with biofeedback and relaxation technique. *Psychosomatic Medicine, 4,* 26–213.

Frankl, V. E. (1975). Paradoxical intention and dereflection. *Psychotherapy: Theory, Research and Practice, 12,* 226–37.

Frederick, C. J. (1973). Suicide, homicide and alcoholism among American Indians. (DHEW Publication No. ADM 24–42). Washington, D.C.: U.S. Government Printing Office.

Frederick C. J. (1978). Current trends in suicidal behavior in the United States. *American Journal of Psychotherapy, 32,* 172–200.

Freud, A. (1936). *The ego and mechanisms of defense* (rev. ed.). New York: International Universities Press, 1967.

Freud, S. (1884). Letter to his fiancée. In N. Taylor, *Flight from reality.* New York: Duell, Sloan, & Pearce, 1949.

Freud, S. (1894). The neuro-psychoses of defense. In J. Strachey (Ed. and Trans.), *The complete psychological works* (Vol. 3). New York: Norton, 1976.

Freud, S. (1905). Psychical (or mental) treatment. In J. Strachey (Ed. and Trans.), *The complete psychological works* (Vol. 7). New York: Norton, 1976.

Freud, S. (1909). Some general remarks on hysterical attacks. In J. Strachey (Ed. and Trans.), *The complete psychological works* (Vol. 9). New York: Norton, 1976.

Freud, S. (1909). Notes upon a case of obsessional neurosis. In J. Strachey (Ed. and Trans.), *The complete psychological works* (Vol. 10). New York: Norton, 1976.

Freud, S. (1923). The ego and the id. In J. Strachey (Ed. and Trans.), *The complete psychological works* (Vol. 19). New York: Norton, 1976.

Freud, S. (1933). New introductory lectures on psychoanalysis. In J. Strachey (Ed. and Trans.), *The complete psychological works* (Vol. 22). New York: Norton, 1976.

Freud, S. (1936). A disturbance of memory on the Acropolis. In J. Strachey (Ed. and Trans.), *The complete psychological works* (Vol. 22). New York: Norton, 1976.

Freud, S. (1937). Analysis terminable and interminable. In J. Strachey (Ed. and Trans.), *The complete psychological works* (Vol. 23). New York: Norton, 1976.

Friedman, M., & Rosenman, R. H. (1974). *Type A behavior.* New York: Knopf.

Fromm, E. (1941). *Escape from freedom.* New York: Rinehart.

Frosch, W. A., Robbins, E. S., & Stern, M. (1965). Untoward reactions to lysergic acid diethylamide (LSD) resulting in hospitalization. *New England Journal of Medicine, 273,* 1235–39.

Frumkin, K., Nathan, R., Prout, M., & Cohen, M. (1978). Nonpharmacologic control of essential hypertension in men: A critical review of the experimental literature. *Psychosomatic Medicine, 40,* 294–320.

Fuche, C. Z., & Rehm, L. P. (1977). A self-control behavior therapy program for depression. *Journal of Consulting and Clinical Psychology, 45,* 206–15.

Gagnon, J. H. (1977). *Human sexuality.* Chicago: Scott, Foresman.

Garcia, J., Ervin, F. R., Koelling, R. A. (1967). Toxicity of serum from irradiated donors. *Nature, 213,* 682–83.

Garcia, E., Guess, D., & Brynes, J. (1973). Development of syntax in a retarded girl using procedures of imitation, reinforcement, and modelling. *Journal of Applied Behavior Analysis, 6,* 299–310.

Garcia, J., & Koelling, R. A. (1966). Relation of cue to consequence in avoidance learning. *Psychonomic Science, 4,* 123–24.

Gardner, E. (1975). *Fundamentals of neurology: A psychophysiological approach* (6th ed.). Philadelphia: Saunders.

Garfield, S., & Bergin, S. (Eds.). (1978). *Handbook of psychotherapy and behavior change* (2nd ed.). New York: Wiley.

Garmezy, N. (1966). The prediction of performance in schizophrenia. In I. P. Hoch & J. Zubin (Eds.), *Psychopathology of schizophrenia.* New York: Grune & Stratton.

Garmezy, N. (1971). Vulnerability research and the issue of primary prevention. *American Journal of Orthopsychiatry, 41,* 101–16.

Garmezy, N. (1974). Children at risk: The search for the antecedents of schizophrenia: Part II. Ongoing research programs, issues, and intervention. *Schizophrenia Bulletin, 9,* 55–125.

Garmezy, N. (1977a). DSM III: Never mind the psychologists—Is it good for the children? *The Clinical Psychologist, 31,* 3–4.

Garmezy, N. (1977b). The psychology and psychopathology of Allenhead. *Schizophrenia Bulletin, 3,* 360–69.

Garmezy, N., & Rodnick, E. H. (1959). Premorbid adjustment and performance in schizophrenia. *Journal of Nervous and Mental Diseases, 129,* 450–66.

Gazzaniga, M. (1970). *The bisected brain.* New York: Appleton-Century-Crofts.

Gebhard, P. H., Gagnon, J. H., Pomeroy, W. B., & Christenson, C. V. (1965). *Sex offenders.* New York: Harper & Row.

Gelenberg, A. J., & Klerman, G. L. (1978). Maintenance drug therapy in long-term treatment of depression. In J. P. Brady & H. K. H. Brodie (Eds.), *Controversy in psychiatry.* Philadelphia: Saunders.

Gelfand, D. M. (1978). Social withdrawal and negative emotional states: Behavioral treatment. In B. B. Wolman, J. Egan, & A. O. Ross (Eds.), *Handbook of treatment of mental disorders in childhood and adolescence.* Englewood Cliffs, N.J.: Prentice-Hall.

Gelfand, D. M., Jenson, W. R., & Drew, C. J. (1982). *Understanding child behavior disorders.* New York: Holt, Rinehart & Winston.

Gergen, K. J. (1982). *Toward transformation in social knowledge.* New York: Springer Verlag.

Geschwind, N. (1965). Disconnection syndromes in animals and man. *Brain, 88,* 237–94, 585–640.

Geschwind, N. (1972). Language and the brain. *Scientific American, 226,* 76–83.

Geschwind, N. (1975). The apraxias: Neural mechanisms of disorders of learned movement. *American Scientist, 188,* 188–95.

Geschwind, N. Quadfasel, F. A., & Segarra, J. M. (1968). Isolation of the speech area. *Neuropsychologia, 6,* 327–40.

Ghez, C. (1981). Cortical control of voluntary movement. In E. R. Kandel & J. H. Schwartz (Eds.). *Principles of neural science* (pp. 323–33). New York: Elsevier/North Holland.

Gilberstadt, H., & Duker, J. (1965). A handbook for clinical and actuarial MMPI Interpretations. Philadelphia: Saunders.

Gittelman-Klein, R., Klein, D. F., Abikoff, H., Katz, S., Gloisten, A. C., & Kates, W. (1976). Relative efficacy of methylphenidate and behavior modification in hyperkinetic children: An interim report. *Journal of Abnormal Child Psychology, 4,* 361–79.

Gittleman, M., & Birch, H. G. (1967). Childhood schizophrenia: Intellect, neurologic status, perinatal risk, prognosis and family pathology. *Archives of General Psychiatry, 17,* 16–25.

Gittleson, N. L. (1966). Depressive psychosis in the obsessional neurotic. *British Journal of Psychiatry, 122,* 883–87.

Glazer, H. I., & Weiss, J. M. (1976). Long-term interference effect: An alternative to "learned helplessness." *Journal of Experimental Psychology: Animal Behavior Processes, 2,* 202–13.

Glass, D. C. (1977). *Behavior pattern stress in coronary disease.* Hillsdale, N.J.: Erlbaum.

Gleitman, H. (1981). *Psychology.* New York: Norton.

Gluhbegovic, N., & Williams, T. H. (1980). *The human brain: A photographic guide.* Hagerstown, Md.: Harper & Row.

Golan, N. (1978). *Treatment in crisis situations.* New York: The Free Press.

Goldfried, M. R., & Davison, G. C. (1976). *Clinical behavior therapy.* New York: Holt, Rinehart & Winston.

Goldfried, M. R., Decenteceo, E., & Wineburg, L. (1974). Systematic rational restructuring as a self-control technique. *Behavior Therapy, 3,* 398–416.

Goldfried, M. R., Linehan, M. M., & Smith, J. L. (1978). Reduction of test anxiety through cognitive restructuring. *Journal of Consulting and Clinical Psychology, 46,* 32–39.

Goldstein, K. (1939). *The organism.* New York: American Book Company.

Goodman, L., & Gilman, A. (1941). *The pharmacological basis of therapeutics.* New York: Macmillan.

Goodwin, F., Brodie, H., Murphy, D., et al. (1970). L-dopa, catecholamines and behavior: A clinical and biochemical study in depressed patients. *Biological Psychiatry, 2,* 341–66.

Gorenstein, E. E., & Newman, J. P. (1980). Disinhibitory psychopathology: A new perspective and a model for research. *Psychological Review, 87,* 301–15.

Gottesman, I. I., & Shields, J. (1972). *Schizophrenia and genetics: A twin study vantage point.* New York: Academic Press.

Gould, S. J. (1981). *The mismeasure of man.* New York: Norton.

Gove, W. R. (1975). Labelling and mental illness: A critique. In W. R. Gove (Ed.), *The labelling of deviance: Evaluating a perspective.* New York: Sage.

Grace, W. J., & Graham, D. T. (1952). Relationship of specific attitudes and emotions to certain bodily disease. *Psychosomatic Medicine, 14,* 243–51.

Granville-Grossman, K. L. (1968). The early environment and affective disorder. In A. Coppen & A. Walk (Eds.), *Recent developments in affective disorders. British Journal of Psychiatry.* (Special Publication No. 2).

Gray, B. (Ed.). (1980). Drug abuse from the family perspective: Coping is a family affair (DHHS Publication No. ADM 80–910). Washington, D.C.: U.S. Government Printing Office.

Gray, H. (1973). *Anatomy of the human body* (29th ed.) (C. M. Goss, Ed.). Philadelphia: Lea & Febiger.

Graziano, A. M., DeGiovanni, I. S., & Garcia, K. A. (1979). Behavioral treatment of children's fears: A review. *Psychological Bulletin, 86,* 804–30.

Greenspoon, J. (1955). The reinforcing effect of two spoken sounds on the frequency of two responses. *American Journal of Psychology, 68,* 409–16.

Greer, S. (1964). Study of parental loss in neurotics and sociopaths. *Archives of General Psychiatry, 11,* 177–80.

Gregory, I. (1958). Studies on parental deprivation in psychiatric patients. *American Journal of Psychiatry, 115,* 432–42.

Griffith, J. J., Mednick, S. A., Schulsinger, F., & Diderichsen, B. (1980). Verbal associative disturbances in children at high risk for schizophrenia. *Journal of Abnormal Psychology, 89* (2), 125–31.

Grimshaw, L. (1964). Obsessional disorder and neurological illness. *Journal of Neurology, Neurosurgery and Psychiatry, 27,* 229–31.

Gross, H. J., & Zimmerman, J. (1965). Experimental analysis of hysterical blindness: A follow-up report and new experimental data. *Archives of General Psychiatry, 13,* 255–60.

Grossman, H. J. (Ed.) (1973). Manual on terminology and classification in mental retardation. Washington, D. C.: American Association of Mental Deficiency. (Special Publication Series, No. 2).

Gunderson, J. G., & Mosher, L. R. (1975). The cost of schizophrenia. *American Journal of Psychiatry, 132,* 901–906.

Gurman, A. S. (1973a). Instability of therapeutic conditions in psychotherapy. *Journal of Counseling Psychology, 20,* 16–24.

Gurman, A. S. (1973b). The effects and effectiveness of marital therapy: A review of outcome research. *Family Process, 12,* 145–70.

Gurman, A. S. (1977). Therapist and patient factors influencing the patient's perception of facilitative therapeutic conditions. *Psychiatry, 40,* 218–31.

Guze, S. B., & Robins, E. (1970). Suicide and primary affective disorders. *British Journal of Psychiatry, 17,* 437.

Hackmann, A., & McLean, C. (1975). A comparison of flooding and thought-stopping treatment. *Behavior Research and Therapy, 13,* 263–69.

Haley, J. (1969). *The power tactics of Jesus Christ.* New York: Grossman.

Hall, C. S., & Lindzey, G. (1970). *Theories of personality.* New York: Wiley.

Hall, R. V., Fox, R., Willard, D., Goldsmith, L., Emerson, M., Owen, M., Davis, T., & Porcia, E. The teacher as observer and experimenter in the modification of disputing and talking-out behaviors. *Journal of Applied Behavior Analysis, 4,* 141–49.

Hall, S. M., Hall, R. G., DeBoer, G., & O'Kulitch, P. (1977). Self and external management compared with psychotherapy in the control of obesity. *Behavior Research and Therapy, 15*(1), 89–95.

Halmi, K. A. (1978). Anorexia nervosa: Recent investigations. *Annual Review of Medicine, 29,* 37–149.

Halpern, J. (1977). Projection: A test of the psychoanalytic hypothesis. *Journal of Abnormal Psychology, 86,* 536–42.

Hamilton, J. W. (1973). Voyeurism: Some therapeutic considerations. *International Journal of Psychotherapy, 2,* 77–91.

Hammen, C. L. & Glass, D. R. (1975). Expression, activity, and evaluation of reinforcement. *Journal of Abnormal Psychology, 84,* 718–21.

Hammen, D. L., & Padesky, C. A. (1977). Sex differences in the expression of depressive responses on the Beck Depression Inventory. *Journal of Abnormal Psychology, 86,* 609–14.

Hannum, R. D., Rosellini, R. A., & Seligman, M. E. P. (1976). Retention of learned helplessness and immunization in the rat from weaning to adulthood. *Developmental Psychology, 12,* 449–54.

Harburg, E., Erfurt, J. C., Hauenstein, L. S., Chape, C., Schull, W. J., & Schork, M. A. (1973). Socio-ecological stress, suppressed hostility, skin color, and black-white male blood pressure: Detroit. *Psychosomatic Medicine, 35,* 276.

Hare, R. D. (1965). Temporal gradient of fear arousal in psychopaths. *Journal of Abnormal Psychology, 70,* 442–45.

Hare, R. (1970). *Psychopathy: Theory and research.* New York: Wiley.

Hare, R. D. (1978). Electrodermal and cardiovascular correlates of sociopathy. In R. D. Hare & D. Schalling (Eds.), *Psychopathic behavior: Approaches to research.* New York: Wiley.

Harlow, J. M. (1868). Recovery from the passage of an iron bar through the head. *Publications of the Massachusetts Medical Society, 2,* 327.

Harris, B. (1979). Whatever happened to little Albert? *American Psychologist, 34,* 151–60.

Harrison, R. (1965). Thematic apperceptive methods. In B. B. Wolman (Ed.), *Handbook of clinical psychology.* New York: Wiley.

Hartman, W. E., & Fithian, M. A. (1972). *Treatment of sexual dysfunction.* New York: Jason Aronson.

Hartmann, H. (1958). Ego psychology and the problem of adaptation. New York: International Universities Press.

Hathaway, S. R., & McKinley, J. C. (1943). MMPI manual. New York: Psychological Corporation.

Haynes, S. G., Feinleib, M., & Kannel, W. B. (1980). The relationship of psychosocial factors to coronary heart disease in the Framingham study: III. Eight years incidence in coronary heart disease. *American Journal of Epidemiology, 3,* 37–85.

Heads, T. B. (1978). Ethical and legal considerations in behavior therapy. In D. Margolin (Ed.), *Child behavior therapy.* New York: Gardner Press.

Hecaen, H., & Albert, M. L. (1978). *Human neuropsychology.* New York: Wiley.

Heider, F. (1958). *The psychology of interpersonal relationships.* New York: Wiley.

Heilman, K. M. (1979). The neuropsychological basis of skilled movement in man. In M. Gazzaniga (Ed.), *Handbook of behavioral neurobiology: Vol. 2. Neuropsychology* (pp. 447–61). New York: Plenum.

Heiman, J. R., & LoPiccolo, J. (1983). Clinical outcome of sex therapy. *Archives of General Psychiatry, 40,* 443–49.

Heinicke, C. M. (1973). Parental deprivation in early childhood: A predisposition to later depression. In J. P. Scott & E. C. Senay (Eds.), *Separation and depreciation.* Washington, D.C.: American Association for the Advancement of Science.

Heitler, J. (1973). Preparation of lower class patients for expressive group psychotherapy. *Journal of Consulting and Clinical Psychology, 41,* 260–61.

Hemsley, R., Howlin, P., Berger, M., Hersov, L., Holbrook, D., Rutter, M., & Yule, W. (1978). Treating autistic children in a family context. In M. Rutter & E. Schopler (Eds.), *Autism: A reappraisal of concepts and treatment.* New York: Plenum.

Hendin, H. (1969). Black suicide. *Archives of General Psychiatry, 21,* 407–22.

Henry, J. P., & Cassel, J. C. (1969). Psychosocial factors in essential hypertension. Recent epidemiologic and animal experimental evidence. *American Journal of Epidemiology, 90,* 171.

Henry, J. P., Mehan, J. P., & Stephens, P. M. (1969). The use of psychosocial stimulae to induce prolonged systolic hypertension in mice. *Psychosomatic Medicine, 29,* 408.

Hermelin, B., & O'Connor, N. (1970). *Psychological experiments with autistic children.* Oxford: Pergamon.

Herrnstein, R. (1969). Method and theory in the study of avoidance. *Psychological Review, 76,* 49–69.

Herson, M., Eisler, R. M., Alford, G. S., & Agras, W. S. (1973). Effects of token economy on neurotic depression: An experimental analysis. *Behavior Therapy, 4,* 392–97.

Hersov, L. (1976). Emotional disorders. In M. Rutter & L. Hersov (Eds.), *Child psychiatry: Modern approaches.* Oxford: Blackwell.

Hess, R. D., & Shipman, V. C. (1965). Early experiences and the socialization of cognitive modes in children. *Child Development, 36,* 869–86.

Heston, L. L. (1966). Psychiatric disorders in foster home reared children of schizophrenic mothers. *British Journal of Psychiatry, 112,* 819–25.

Heston, L. L. (1970). The genetics of schizophrenia and schizoid disease. *Science, 167,* 249–56.

Heston, L. L., & Denney, D. (1968). Interactions between early life experience and biological factors in schizophrenia. In D. Rosenthal & S. S. Kety (Eds.), *The transmission of schizophrenia* (pp. 363–76). New York: Pergamon.

Hetherington, E. M., & Martin, B. (1979). Family interaction. In H. C. Quay & J. S. Werry (Eds.), *Psychopathological disorders of childhood.* New York: Wiley.

Hilgard, E. R. (1965). *Hypnotic susceptibility.* New York: Harcourt Brace Jovanovich.

Hilgard, E. R. (1977). *Divided consciousness: Multiple controls in human thought and action.* New York: Wiley.

Hill, P. O. (1972). Latent aggression and drug-abuse: An investigation of adolescent personality factors using an original cartoon-o-graphic aggressive tendencies test. *Dissertation Abstracts International, 33,* 1765.

Hines, E. A., McIlhaney, M. L., & Gage, R. P. (1957). The study of twins with normal blood pressures and with hypertension. *Transactions of the Association of American Physicians, 70,* 282.

Hinsee, L. E., & Campbell, R. J. (1960). *Psychiatric dictionary* (3rd ed.). New York: Oxford University Press.

Hiroto, D. S. (1974). Locus of control and learned helplessness. *Journal of Experimental Psychology, 102,* 187–93.

Hirst, W. (1982). The amnesic syndrome: Descriptions and explanations. *Psychology Bulletin, 91,* 1480–83.

Hodgson, R., Rachman, S., & Marks, I. (1972). The treatment of chronic obsessive-compulsive neurosis. *Behavior Research and Therapy, 10,* 181–89.

Hoehn-Saric, R., Frank, J. D., Imber, S. D., Nash, E. H., Stone, A. R., & Battle, C. C. (1964). Systematic preparation of patients for psychotherapy I. Effects on therapy behavior and outcome. *Journal of Psychiatric Research, 2,* 267–81.

Hoenig, J., & Kenna, J. C. (1974). The nosological position of transsexualism. *Archives of Sexual Behavior, 3,* 273–87.

Hofmann, A. (1968). Psychotomimetic agents. In A. Burger (Ed.), *Drugs affecting the central nervous system* (Vol. 2). New York: Marcel Dekker, Inc.

Hokanson, J. E. (1961). The effects of frustration and anxiety on aggression. *Journal of Abnormal and Social Psychology, 62,* 346.

Hokanson, J. E., & Burgess, M. (1962). The effects of three types of aggression on vascular processes. *Journal of Abnormal and Social Psychology, 65,* 446–49.

Hokanson, J. E., Willers, K. R., & Koropsak, E. (1968). Modification of autonomic responses during aggressive interchange. *Journal of Personality, 36,* 386–404.

Hollingshead, A. B., & Redlich, F. C. (1958). *Social class and mental illness: A community study.* New York: Wiley.

Hollister, L. E. (1962). Drug-induced psychoses and schizophrenic reactions: A critical comparison. *Annals of the New York Academy of Sciences, 96,* 80–89.

Hollister L. E. (1973). *Clinical uses of psychotherapeutic drugs.* Springfield, Ill.: Charles C. Thomas.

Holmes, G. (1935). Treatment of syphilis of the nervous system. *British Medical Journal, 3909,* 1111–14.

Holmes, T. H., & Rahe, R. H. (1967). The social readjustment ratings scale. *Journal of Psychosomatic Research, 11,* 213–18.

Holtzman, W. H. (1961). Inkblot perception and personality: Holtzman Inkblot Technique. Austin: University of Texas Press.

Hope, H., Jonas, J., & Jones, B. (1982). Factitious psychosis: Phenomenology, family history, and long-term outcome of nine patients. *American Journal of Psychiatry, 139,* 1480–83.

Horn, A. S., & Snyder, S. H. (1971). Chlorpromazine and dopamine: Conformational similarities that correlate with the antischizophrenic activity of phenothiazine drugs. *Proceedings of the National Academy of Sciences, 68,* 2325–28.

Horne, R. L., & Picard, R. S. (1979). Psychosocial risk factors for lung cancer. *Psychosomatic Medicine, 41,* 503–14.

Horney, K. (1945). *Our inner conflicts: A constructive theory of neurosis.* New York: Norton.

Horowitz, L. M., Post, D. L., French, R. de S., Wallis, K. D., & Seigelman, E. Y. (1981). The prototype as a construct in abnormal psychology: 2. Clarifying disagreement in psychiatric judgments. *Journal of Abnormal Psychology, 90,* 568–74.

Horowitz, M. (1975). Intrusive and repetitive thoughts after experimental stress. *Archives of General Psychiatry. 32,* 1457–63.

Hugdahl, K., & Ohman, A. (1977). Effects of instruction on acquisition and extinction of electrodermal response to fear-relevant stimuli. *Journal of Experimental Psychology: Human Learning and Memory, 3*(5), 608–18.

Hunt, D. D., & Hampson, J. L. (1980). Transsexualism: A standardized psychosocial rating format for the evaluation of results of sex reassignment surgery. *Archives of Sexual Behavior, 9,* 225–63.

Hunt, J. McV., & Cofer, C. N. (1944). Psychological deficit. In J. McV. Hunt & C. N. Cofer (Eds.), *Personality and the behavior disorders* (Vol. 2) (pp. 971–1032). New York: Ronald.

Hunt, M. (1974). *Sexual behavior in the 1970's.* New York: Dell.

Hunter, R., & McAlpine, I. (1963). *Three hundred years of psychiatry.* London: Hogarth Press.

Huston, P. E., Shakow, D., & Riggs, T. A. (1937). Studies of motor function in schizophrenia: II. Reaction time. *Journal of General Psychology, 16,* 39–82.

Hutchings, B., & Mednick, S. A. (1977). Criminality in adoptees and their adoptive and biological parents: A pilot study. In S. A. Mednick & K. O. Christiansen (Eds.), *Biosocial bases of criminal behavior* (pp. 127–41). New York: Gardner Press.

Hygge, S., & Ohman, A. (1978). Modeling processes in the acquisition of fear: Vicarious electrodermal conditioning to fear-relevant stimuli. *Journal of Personal and Social Psychology, 36* (3), 271–79.

Hyler, S. E., & Spitzer, R. T. (1978). Hysteria split asunder. *American Journal of Psychiatry, 135,* 1500–1504.

Ickes, W. J., & Leyden, M. A. (1978). Attributional styles. In J. H. Harvey, W. J. Ickes, & R. F. Kidd (Eds.), *New directions in attribution research* (Vol. 2). Hillsdale, N.J.: Erlbaum.

Imboden, J. B., Cantor, A., & Cluff, L. E. (1961). Convalescence from influenza: The study of the psychological and clinical determinants. *Archives of Internal Medicine, 108,* 393–99.

Ingham, R. J., Andrews, G., & Winkler, R. (1972). Stuttering: A comparative evaluation of the short-term effectiveness of four treatment techniques. *Journal of Communicative Disorders, 5,* 91–117.

Iverson, S. D, & Iverson, L. L. (1975). *Behavioral pharmacology.* New York: Oxford University Press.

Jacobson, E. (1971). *Depression: Comparative studies of normal, neurotic and psychotic conditions.* International Universities Press.

Jackson, J. H. (1884). Croonian lectures on evolution and dissolution of the nervous system. *British Medical Journal, 1,* 591.

Jahoda, M. (1958). *Current concepts of positive mental health.* New York: Basic Books.

James, W. (1890). *The principles of psychology.* New York: Henry Holt.

Jeffery, D. B. (1977). Introduction: Self control techniques. In J. P. Foreyt, *Behavioral treatments of obesity.* Oxford: Pergamon.

Jenkins, C. D., Rosenman, R. H., & Friedman, M. (1967). Development of an objective psychological test for the determination of the coronary prone behavior pattern in employed men. *Journal of Chronic Disease, 20,* 371–79.

Jenkins, C. D., Zyzanski, S. J., & Rosenman, R. H. (1976). Risk of new myocardial infarction in middle age men with manifest coronary heart disease. *Circulation, 53,* 342–47.

Jenni, M. A., & Wollersheim, J. P. (1979). Cognitive therapy, stress management training, and the Type A behavior pattern. *Cognitive Therapy and Research, 3,* 61–73.

Jens, K. S., & Evans, H. I. (1983, April). The diagnosis and treatment of multiple personality clients. Workshop presented at the Rocky Mountain Psychological Association, Snowbird, Utah.

Jerome, J. (1880). Intern's syndrome. In *Three men in a boat, not to mention the dog.*

Jerome, J. (1979, January 14). Catching them before suicide. *The New York Times Magazine.*

Jourard, S. M. (1974). *Healthy personality: An approach from the viewpoint of humanistic psychology.* New York: Macmillan.

Kahn, M. (1973). Social class and schizophrenia: A critical review and a reformulation. *Schizophrenia Bulletin, 1,* 60–74.

Kahoe, M., & Ironside, W. (1963). Studies on the experimental evocation of depressive responses under hypnosis. II. The influence of depressive responses on the secretion of gastric acid. *Psychosomatic Medicine, 25,* 403.

Kaiko, R. F. et al. (1981). Analgesic and mood effects of heroin and morphine in cancer patients with postoperative pain. *New England Journal of Medicine, 304*(25), 1501.

Kamin, L. J. (1974). *The science and politics of IQ.* Potomac, Md.: Erlbaum.

Kandel, E. R., & Schwartz, J. H. (Eds.). (1981). *Principles of neural science.* New York: Elsevier.

Kanfer, F. H., & Grimm, L. G. (1976). The future of behavior modification. In W. E. Craighead, A. E. Kazdin, & M. J. Mahoney (Eds.), *Behavior modification: Principles, issues and applications.* Boston: Houghton Mifflin.

Kanfer, F. H., & Karoly, P. (1972). Self-control. A behavioristic excursion into the lion's den. *Behavior Therapy, 3,* 398–416.

Kanfer, F. H., & Saslow, G. (1969). Behavioral analysis. In C. M. Franks (Ed.), *Behavior therapy: Appraisal and status.* New York: McGraw-Hill.

Kanner, A. D., Coyne, J. C., Schaefer, C., & Lazarus, R. S. (1981). Comparison of two modes of stress measurement: Minor daily hassles and uplifts vs. major life events. *Journal of Behavioral Medicine, 4,* 1–39.

Kanner, L. (1943). Autistic disturbances of affective contact. *Nervous Child, 2,* 217–50.

Kaplan, H. S. (1974). *The new sex therapy.* New York: Brunner/Mazel.

Kaplan, S. M., Gottschalk, L. A., Magliocco, D., Rohobit, D., & Ross, W. D. (1960). Hostility in hypnotic "dreams" of hypertensive patients. (Comparisons between hypertensive and normotensive groups and within hypertensive individuals.) *Psychosomatic Medicine, 22,* 320.

Karasek, R., Baker, D., Marxer, F., Ahlbom, A., & Theorell, T. (1981). Job decision latitude, job demand, and cardiovascular disease: A prospective study of Swedish men. *American Journal of Public Health, 71,* 694–705.

Karlsson, J. L. (1972). An Icelandic family study of schizophrenia. In A. R. Kaplan (Ed.), *Genetic factors in schizophrenia* (pp. 246–55). Springfield, Ill.: Charles C. Thomas.

Kasl, S. V., & Cob, S. (1979). Blood pressure changes in men undergoing job loss: A preliminary report. *Psychosomatic Medicine, 32,* 19–38.

Kaslow, N. J., Tannenbaum, R. L., Abramson, L. Y., Peterson, C., & Seligman, M. E. P. (1983). Problem solving deficits and depressive symptoms among children. *Journal of Abnormal Child Psychology.*

Kass, F., Spitzer, R. L., & Williams, J. B. W. (1983). An empirical study of the issue of sex bias in the diagnostic criteria of DSM-III axis II personality disorders. *American Psychologist, 38,* 799–801.

Katchadourian, H. A., & Lunde, D. T. (1972). *Fundamentals of human sexuality.* New York: Holt, Rinehart & Winston.

Katz, B. (1952). The nerve impulse. *Scientific American, 187,* 55–64.

Katz, M., Lorr, M., & Rubinstein, E₁ (1958). Remainder patient attributes and their relation to subsequent improvement in psychotherapy. *Journal of Consulting Psychology, 22,* 411–13.

Kaufman, I. C., & Rosenblume, L. A. (1967). Depression in infant monkeys separated from their mothers. *Science, 155,* 1030–31.

Kauffman, J. M., & Hallahan, D. P. (1979). Learning disability and hyperactivity (with comments on minimal brain dysfunction). In B. B. Lahey & A. E. Kazdin (Ed.), *Advances in child clinical psychology* (Vol. 2). New York: Plenum.

Kazdin, A. E. (1979). Nonspecific treatment factors in psychotherapy outcome research. *Journal of Consulting and Clinical Psychology, 47,* 846–51.

Kazdin, A. E. (1980). Acceptability of time out from reinforcement procedures for disruptive child behavior. *Behavior Therapy, 11,* 329–44.

Kazdin, A. E., & Wilcoxon, L. A. (1976). Systematic desensitization and nonspecific treatment effects: A methodological evaluation. *Psychological Bulletin, 83*(5), 729–58.

Kazdin, A. E., & Wilson, G. T. (1978). *Evaluation of behavior therapy: Issues, evidence, and research strategies.* Cambridge, Mass.: Ballinger.

Keefe, J. A., & Magaro, P. A. (1980). Creativity and schizophrenia: An equivalence of cognitive processing. *Journal of Abnormal Psychology, 89,* 390–98.

Keeton, W. T. (1980). *Biological science* (3rd ed.). New York: Norton.

Kehoe, M., & Ironside W. (1963). Studies on the experimental evocation of, depressive responses using hypnosis: II. The influence upon the secretion of gastric acid. *Psychosomatic Medicine, 25,* 403–19.

Keith, S. J., Gunderson, J. G., Reifman, A., Buchsbaum, S., & Mosher, L. R. (1976). Special report: Schizophrenia, 1976. *Schizophrenia Bulletin, 2,* 510–65.

Keith-Spiegel, P. (1977). Violation of ethical principles due to ignorance or poor professional judgment versus willful disregard. *Professional Psychology, 8,* 288–96.

Kelley, H. H. (1967). Attribution theory in social psychology. In D. Levine (Ed.), *Nebraska Symposium on Motivation* (pp. 192–240). Lincoln: Dot Nebraska Press.

Kelly, G. A. (1955). *The psychology of personal constructs* (Vols. 1 & 2). New York: Norton.

Kendall, P., Williams, L., Pechacek, T., Graham, L., Shisslac, C., & Hertzoff, N. (1979). Cognitive, behavioral and patient education interventions in cardiac catheterization procedures: The Palo Alto medical psychology project. *Journal of Consulting and Clinical Psychology, 47,* 49–58.

Kenyon, F. E. (1965). Hypochondriasis: A survey of some historical, clinical and social aspects. *British Journal of Psychiatry, 38,* 117.

Kerr, T. A., Roth, M., Schapira, K., & Gurney, C. (1972). The assessment and prediction of outcome in affective disorders. *British Journal of Psychiatry, 121,* 167.

Kety, J. (1974). Biochemical and neurochemical effects of electroconvulsive shock. In M. Fink, S. Kety, & J. McGough (Eds.), *Psychology of convulsive therapy.* Washington, D.C.: Winston.

Kety, S. S. (1974). From rationalization to reason. *American Journal of Psychiatry, 131,* 957–63.

Kety, S., Rosenthal, D., Wender, P. H., & Schulsinger, F. (1968). The types and prevalence of mental illness in the biological and adoptive families of adopted schizophrenics. In D. Rosenthal & S. S. Kety (Eds.), *The transmission of schizophrenia.* New York: Pergamon Press.

Kiesler, C. A. (1980). Mental health policy as a field of inquiry for psychology. *American Psychologist, 35,* 1066–80.

Kiesler, C. A. (1982). Public and professional myths about mental hospitalization: An empirical reassessment of policy-related beliefs. *American Psychologist, 37,* 1323–39.

Kilburg, R. R., & Siegel, A. W. (1973). Formal operations in reactive and process schizophrenia. *Journal of Consulting and Clinical Psychology, 40,* 371–76.

Kingsley, R. G., & Wilson, G. T. Behavior therapy for obesity: A comparative investigation of long-term efficacy. *Journal of Consulting & Clinical Psychology, 45*(2), 288–98.

Kinsey, A. C., Pomeroy, W. D., & Martin, C. E. (1948). *Sexual behavior in the human male.* Philadelphia: Saunders.

Kinsey, A. C., Pomeroy, W. D., Martin, C. E., & Gebhard, P. H. (1953). *Sexual behavior in the human female.* Philadelphia: Saunders.

Kirigin, K., Wolf, M. M., Braukman, C. J., Fixsen, D. L., & Phillips, E. L. (1979). Achievement Place: A preliminary outcome evaluation. In J. S. Stumphauzer (Ed.), *Progress in behavior therapy with delinquents.* Springfield, Ill.: Charles C. Thomas.

Klein, D. F. (1980). Anxiety reconceptualized. In Klein, D. F. & Rabkin, J. G. (Eds.), *Anxiety revisited.* New York: Raven Press.

Klein, D. F., & Davis, J. M. *Diagnosis and drug treatment of psychiatric disorders.* Baltimore: Williams & Wilkins, 1969.

Klein, D. F., & Gittelman-Klein, R. (1975). Are behavioral and psychometric changes related in methylphenidate treated, hyperactive children? *International Journal of Mental Health, 14*(1–2), 182–98.

Klerman, G. L., Endicott, J., Spitzer, R., & Hirschfeld, R. (1979). Neurotic depressions: A systematic analysis of multiple criteria and meanings. *American Journal of Psychiatry, 136,* 57–61.

Klerman, G. L., Schildkraut, J., & Hassenbush, J. (1963). Clinical experience with dihydroxyphrenylalanine (dopa) in depression. *Journal of Psychiatric Research, 1,* 289–97.

Kobler, J. (1978, July 18). Can blood pressure be self-controlled? *Esquire,* pp. 91–94.

Koh, S. D., & Peterson, R. A. (1974). Perceptual memory for numerousness in "nonpsychotic schizophrenics." *Journal of Abnormal Psychology, 83,* 215–26.

Kohn, M. L. (1973). Social class and schizophrenia: A critical review and a reformulation. *Schizophrenia Bulletin, 7,* 60–79.

Kolata, G. (1983). Incidence of strokes declines. *Science, 591.*

Kolb, B., & Whishaw, I. Q. (1980). *Fundamentals of human neuropsychology.* San Francisco: Freeman.

Kondas, O. (1967). The treatment of stammering in children by the shadowing method. *Behavior Research and Therapy, 5*(4), 325–29.

Korchin, S. J. (1976). *Modern clinical psychology: Principles of intervention in the clinic and the community.* New York: Basic Books.

Korsakoff, S. S. (1889). Etude medicopsychologique sur une forme des maladies de la memoire. *Revue Philosophique, 5,* 501–30.

Kovacs, M., & Beck, A. T. (1977). An empirical-clinical approach towards a definition of childhood depression. In J. G. Schulterbrand & A. Raven (Ed.), *Depression in childhood: Diagnosis, treatment, and conceptual models.* New York: Raven Press.

Kovacs, M., Rush, A. J., Beck, A. T., & Hollon, S. D. (1981). Depressed outpatient treatment with cognitive therapy or pharmaco therapy: A one year follow-up. *Archives of General Psychiatry, 38,* 33–39.

Kraepelin, E. (1919). *Dementia praecox and paraphrenia.* New York: Robert E. Krieger.

Krafft-Ebing, R. von. (1931). *Psychopathia sexualis.* New York: Physicians & Surgeons Book Co.

Kraupl Taylor, F. (1966). *Psychopathology: Its causes and symptoms,* 156–59. London: Butler Wells.

Kringlen, E. (1965). Obsessional neurotics. A long-term follow-up. *British Journal of Psychiatry, 111,* 709–22.

Krystal, H. (1968). *Massive psychic trauma.* New York: International Universities Press.

Kurland, H. D., Yeager, C. T., & Arthur, R. J. (1963). Psychophysiologic aspects of severe behavior disorders. *Archives of General Psychiatry, 8,* 599–604.

Lacey, J. I. (1950). Individual differences in somatic response patterns. *Journal of Comparative and Physiological Psychology, 43,* 338–50.

Lachman, S. J. (1972). *Psychosomatic disorders: Behavioristic interpretations.* New York: Wiley.

Laing, R. D. Mystification, confusion and conflict. (1965a). In I. Boszormeny-Nagy & J. L. Framo (Ed.), *Intensive family therapy.* New York: Hueber Medical Division, Harper & Row.

Laing, R. D. (1965b). *The divided self.* Baltimore: Penguin.

Laing, R. D. (1967). *The politics of experience.* New York: Pantheon Books.

Laing, R. D. (1970). *Knots.* New York: Pantheon Books.

Laing, R. D., & Esterson, A. (1964). *Sanity, madness, and the family.* London: Tavistock.

Lamb, H. R. The new asylums in the community. *Archives of General Psychiatry, 1979, 36,* 129–34.

Lambert, M. J., Bergin, A. E., & Collins, J. L. (1970). Therapist-induced deterioration in psychotherapy. In A. S. Gurman & A. M. Razin (Ed.), *Effective psychotherapy: A handbook of research.* New York: Pergamon.

Lamy, R. E. (1966). Social consequences of mental illness. *Journal of Consulting Psychology, 30,* 450–55.

Lang, P. (1967). Fear reduction and fear behavior. In J. Schlein (Ed.), *Research in psychotherapy.* Washington D.C.: American Psychological Association.

Langer, E. J., & Abelson, R. P. (1974). A patient by any other name . . . : Clinician group difference in labelling bias. *Journal of Consulting and Clinical Psychology, 42,* 4–9.

Langer, E. J., Jannis, I., & Wolfer, J. (1975). Effects of a cognitive coping device and preparatory information on psychological stress in surgical patients. *Journal of Experimental Social Psychology, 11,* 155–65.

Langer, E. J., & Rodin, J. (1976). Effects of choice and enhanced personal responsibility for the aged: A field experiment in an institutional setting. *Journal of Personality and Social Psychology, 34,* 191–99.

LaPouse, R., & Monk, M. (1959). Fears and worries in a representative sample of children. *American Journal of Orthopsychiatry, 29,* 803–18.

Laughlin, H. P. (1967). *The neuroses.* Washington, D.C.: Butterworth.

Lazarus, A. A. (1971). *Behavior therapy and beyond.* New York: McGraw-Hill.

Lazarus, A. A. (1976). *Multimodal behavior therapy.* New York: Springer.

Leff, J. P. (1976). Schizophrenia and sensitivity to the family environment. *Schizophrenia Bulletin, 2,* 566–74.

Leff, M. J., Roatch, J. F., & Bunney, W. E. (1970). Environmental factors preceding the onset of severe depressions. *Psychiatry, 33,* 293–311.

Lehrman, D. (1965). In F. A. Beach (Ed.), *Sex and behavior.* New York: Wiley.

Leiberman, M. A., Yalom, I. D., & Miles, M. B. (1973). *Encounter groups: First facts.* New York: Basic Books.

Leitenberg, H., & Callahan, E. J. (1973). Reinforced practice and reduction of different kinds of fears in adults and children. *Behavior Research & Therapy, 11*(1), 19–30.

Lemkau, P. V. (1969). The planning project for Columbia. In M. F. Shore & F. V. Mannino (Ed.), *Mental health and the community: Problems, programs and strategies.* New York: Behavioral Publications.

Lenneberg, E. H. (1967). *Biological foundations of language.* New York: Wiley.

Leopold, R. L., & Dillon, H. (1963). Psychoanatomy of a disaster: A long-term study of post-traumatic neurosis in survivors of a marine explosion. *American Journal of Psychiatry, 119,* 913–21.

Lester, D. (1977). Multiple personality: A review. *Psychology, 14,* 54–59.

Levenkron, J. C., Cohen, J. D., Mueller, H. S., & Fisher, E. V. (1983). Modifying the Type A coronary-prone behavior pattern. *Journal of Consulting and Clinical Psychology, 51,* 192–204.

Levine, M., & Graziano, A. M. (1971). Intervention programs in elementary schools. In S. E. Golann & C. Eisdorfer (Eds.), *Handbook of community psychology.* New York: Appleton-Century-Crofts.

Levis, D. J., & Carrera, R. (1967). Effects of 10 hours of implosive therapy in the treatment of outpatients. *Journal of Abnormal Psychology, 72,* 504–508.

Levitz, L. S., & Stunkard, A. J. (1974). A therapeutic coalition for obesity: Behavior modification and patient self-help. *American Journal of Psychiatry, 131,* 423–27.

Levy, J. (1972). Lateral specialization of the human brain. Behavioral manifestations and possible evolutionary basis. In J. A. Kiger, Jr. (Ed.), *The biology of behavior* (pp. 159–80). Corvallis, Ore.: Oregon State University Press.

Levy, J. (1980). Cerebral asymmetry and man and the psychology of man. In M. Wittrock (Ed.), *The brain and psychology.* New York: Academic Press.

Lewine, R. R. J. (1981). Sex differences in schizophrenia: Timing or subtypes. *Psychological Bulletin, 90,* 432–44.

Lewinsohn, P. M. (1974). A behavioral approach to depression. In R. J. Friedman & M. M. Katz (Eds.), *The psychology of depression: Contemporary theory and research.* Washington, D.C.: Winston-Wiley.

Lewinsohn, P. M. (1975). Engagement in pleasant activities and depression level. *Journal of Abnormal Psychology, 84,* 718–21.

Lewinsohn, P. M. (1977). The behavioral study and treatment of depression. In M. Hersen, R. M. Eisler, & P. M. Miller (Eds.), *Progress in behavior modification.* New York: Academic Press.

Lewinsohn, P. M., Mischel, W., Chaplin, W., & Barton, R. (1980). Social competence and depression: The role of illusory self-perceptions. *Journal of Abnormal Psychology, 89,* 203–12.

Lewinsohn, P. M., & Shaw, D. W. (1969). Feedback about interpersonal behavior as an agent of behavior change: A case study in the treatment of depression. *Psychotherapy Psychosomatic, 17,* 82–88.

Lewinsohn, P. M., Weinstein, M. S., & Alper, T. (1970). A behavioral approach to the group treatment of depressed persons: A methodological contribution. *Journal of Clinical Psychology, 26,* 525–32.

Lewinsohn, P. M., Weinstein, M. S., & Shaw, D. (1968). Depression: A clinical research approach. In R. D. Rubin & C. M. Franks (Eds.), *Advances in behavior therapy.* New York: Academic Press.

Lewis, J. M., Rodnick, E. H., & Goldstein, M. J. (1981). Interfamilial interactive behavior, parental communication deviance, and risk for schizophrenia. *Journal of Abnormal Psychology, 90,* 448–57.

Liberman, R. (1970). Behavioral approaches to family and couple therapy. *American Journal of Orthopsychiatry, 40,* 106–18.

Liberman, R. P., & Raskin, D. E (1971). Depression: A behavioral formulation. *Archives of General Psychiatry, 24,* 515–23.

Lichtenstein, E. et al. (1973). Comparison of rapid smoking, warm smoky air, and attention placebo in the modification of smoking behavior. *Journal of Consulting and Clinical Psychology, 40,* 92–98.

Lichtenstein, E., & Danaher, B. G. (1977). Modification of smoking behavior: A critical analysis of theory, research, and practice. In M. Hersen, R. M. Eisler, & P. M. Miller (Eds.), *Progress in behavior modification* (Vol. 4). New York: Academic Press.

Lick, J., & Bootzin, R. (1975). Expectancy factors in the treatment of fear: Methodological and theoretical issues. *Psychological Bulletin, 82,* 917–31.

Lidz, T. (1975). *The origin and treatment of schizophrenic disorders.* London: Hutchinson.

Lidz, T., Fleck, S., & Cornelison, A. R. (1965). *Schizophrenia in the family.* New York: International Universities Press.

Liebman, R., Minuchin, S., & Baker, L. (1974). The use of structural family therapy in the treatment of intractable asthma. *American Journal of Psychiatry, 131,* 535–40.

Linden, L. L., & Breed, W. (1976). The demographic epidemiology of suicide. In E. S. Shneidman (Ed.), *Suicidology: Contemporary developments.* New York: Grune & Stratton.

Livermore, J. M., & Meehl, P. E. (1967). The virtues of M'Naghten. *Minnesota Law Review. 51,* 789–856.

Lockyer, L., & Rutter, M. (1969). A five-to fifteen-year follow-up study of infantile psychosis. *British Journal of Psychiatry, 115,* 865–82.

London, P. (1964). *The modes and morals of psychotherapy.* New York: Holt, Rinehart & Winston.

London, P. (1969). *Behavior control.* New York: Harper & Row.

London, P., & Rosenhan, D. L. (1968). Mental health: The promise of behavior science. In P. London & D. L. Rosenhan (Eds.), *Foundations of abnormal psychology* (pp. 599–619). New York: Holt, Rinehart & Winston.

Looney, J. G., Lipp, M. G., & Spitzer R. L. (1978). A new method of classification for psychophysiological disorders. *American Journal of Psychiatry, 135,* 304–308.

Loranger, A., & Levine, P. (1938). Age of onset of bipolar affective illness. *Archives of General Psychiatry, 35,* 1345–48.

Lotter, V. (1966). Epidemiology of autistic conditions in young children: I. Prevalence. *Social Psychiatrist, 1,* 124–37.

Lotter, V. (1978). Follow-up studies. In M. Rutter & E. Schopler (Eds.), *Autism: A reappraisal of concepts and treatment.* New York: Plenum.

Lottman, T. J., & DeWolfe, A. S. (1972). Internal versus external control in reactive and process schizophrenia. *Journal of Consulting and Clinical Psychology, 39,* 344.

Lovaas, O. I. (1966). A program for the establishment of speech in psychotic children. In J. K. Wing (Ed.), *Early childhood autism.* New York: Pergamon.

Lovaas, O. I. (1973). *Behavioral treatment of autistic children.* Morristown, N.J.: General Learning Press.

Lovaas, O. I., & Simmons, J. Q. (1969). Manipulation of self-destruction in three retarded children. *Journal of Applied Behavior Analysis, 2,* 143–57.

Lovibond, S. H., & Coote, M. A. (1970). Enuresis. In C. G. Costello (Ed.), *Symptoms of psychopathology.* New York: Wiley.

Lowinger, P., & Dobie, S. (1969). What makes the placebo work? A study of placebo response rates. *Archives of General Psychiatry, 20,* 84–88.

Luborsky, L. (1972). Another reply to Eysenck. *Psychological Bulletin, 78,* 406–408.

Luborsky, L., Singer, B., & Luborsky, L. (1975). Comparative studies of psychotherapies. *Archives of General Psychiatry, 32,* 995–1008.

Lunde, D. (1975). *Murder and madness.* Stanford: Stanford Alumni Association.

Luria, A. (1970). The functional organization of the brain. *Scientific American, 222,* 66–78.

Luria, A. (1973). *The working brain.* New York: Basic Books.

Lyght, C. E. (Ed.). (1966). *The Merck manual of diagnosis and therapy* (11th ed.). Rahway, N.J.: Merck Sharp and Dohme Research Laboratories.

Lykken, D. T. (1957). A study of anxiety in the sociopathic personality. *Journal of Abnormal and Social Psychology, 55,* 6–10.

MacDonald, M. *Mystical bedlam: Madness and healing in seventeenth-century England.* Unpublished doctoral dissertation, Stanford University.

MacDonald, N. (1960). Living with schizophrenia. *Canadian Medical Association Journal, 82,* 218–21.

MacFarland, J. W., Allen, L., & Honzik, N. P. (1954). *A developmental study of the behavior problems of normal children between 21 months and 14 years.* Berkeley and Los Angeles: University of California Press.

MacMillan, D. L., & Semmel, M. I. (1977). Evaluation of mainstreaming programs. *Focus on Exceptional Children, 6,* 4, 8–14.

MacPhillany, D. J., & Lewinsohn, P. M. (1974). Depression as a function of levels of desired and obtained pleasure. *Journal of Abnormal Psychology, 83,* 651–57.

Magaro, P. A. (1981). The paranoid and the schizophrenic: The case for distinct cognitive style. *Schizophrenia Bulletin, 7,* 632–61.

Maher, B. A. (1966). *Principles of psychopathology: An experimental approach.* New York: McGraw-Hill.

Maher, B. A. (1971). The language of schizophrenia: A review and interpretation. *British Journal of Psychiatry, 120,* 3–17.

Maher, B. A. (1974). Delusional thinking and cognitive disorder. In H. London & R. E. Nisbett (Eds.), *Thought and feeling: Cognitive alteration of feeling states.* Chicago: Aldine.

Mahoney, M. J. (1971). The self-management of covert behavior: A case study. *Behavior Therapy, 2,* 575–78.

Mahoney, M. J. (1974). *Cognition and behavior modification.* Cambridge, Mass.: Ballinger.

Mahoney, M. J., & Mahoney, K. (1976). *Permanent weight control: A total solution to the dieter's dilemma.* New York: Norton.

Mahoney, M. J., & Thoresen, C. E. (1974). *Self-control: Power to the person.* Belmont, Calif.: Brooks/Cole.

Mai, F., & Mersky, H. (1980). Briquet's treatise on hysteria. *Archives of General Psychiatry, 37,* 1401–1405.

Maier, S. F. (1983, May). Colloquium given at University of Pennsylvania.

Maier, S. F., Seligman, M. E. P., & Solomon, R. L. (1969). Pavlovian fear conditioning and learned helplessness: Effects on escape and avoidance behavior of (a) the CS-US contingency and (b) the independence of the US and voluntary responding. In Campbell & Church (Eds.), *Punishment and aversive behavior.* New York: Appleton.

Maletzky, B. M. (1974). "Assisted" covert sensitization in the treatment of exhibitionism. *Journal of Consulting and Clinical Psychology, 42,* 34–40.

Malewsha, H. E., & Muszynski, H. (1970). Children's attitudes to theft. In K. Panziger (Ed.), *Readings in child socialization.* Oxford: Pergamon.

Malitz, S., Wilkens, B., & Escover, H. (1962). A comparison of drug induced hallucinations with those seen in spontaneously occurring psychoses. In L. J. West (Ed.), *Hallucinations.* New York: Grune & Stratton.

Malmo, R. B. & Shagass, C. (1949). Physiological study of symptom mechanism in psychiatric patients under stress. *Psychosomatic Medicine, 11,* 25–29.

Manning, P. (1974). *The witchcraft papers.* London: Routledge & Kegan Paul.

Marchant, R., Howlin, P., Yule, W., & Rutter, M. (1974). Graded change in the treatment of the behavior of autistic children. *Journal of Child Psychology & Psychiatry, 15,* 221–27.

Marin, O. S. M., Saffran, E., & Schwartz, M. (1976). Dissociation of language in aphasia: Implications for normal function. *Annals of the New York Academy of Science, 280,* 868–84.

Marks, I. M. (1969). *Fears and phobias.* New York: Academic Press.

Marks, I. M. (1976). The current status of behavioral psychotherapy: Theory and practice. *American Journal of Psychiatry, 133,* 253–61.

Marks, I. (1977). Phobias and obsessions: Clinical phenomena in search of laboratory models. In J. Maser & M. E. P. Seligman (Eds.), *Psychopathology: Experimental models.* San Francisco: Freeman.

Marks, I. M. (1981). Review of behavioral psychotherapy. II: Sexual disorders. *American Journal of Psychiatry, 138,* 750–56.

Marks, I., Boulougouris, J., & Marset, P. (1971). Flooding versus desensitization in the treatment of phobic patients: A crossover study. *British Journal of Psychiatry, 119,* 353–75.

Marks, I. M., & Gelder, M. G. (1966). Common ground between behavior therapy and psychodynamic methods. *British Journal of Medical Psychology, 39,* 11–23.

Marks, I. M., Gray, S., Cohen, D., Hill, R., Mawson, D., Ramm, E., & Stern, R. S. (1983). Imipramine and brief therapist-aided exposure in agoraphobics having self-exposure homework. *Archives of General Psychiatry, 40,* 153–62.

Marks, I. M., & Rachman, S. J. (1978). Interim report to the Medical Research Council.

Marks, I. M., Rachman, S., & Hodgson, R. (1975). Treatment of chronic obsessive-compulsive neurosis by in-vivo exposure: A two-year follow-up and issues in treatment. *British Journal of Psychiatry, 127,* 349–64.

Marlatt, G. A. (1983). The controlled drinking controversy: A commentary. *American Psychologist, 38,* 1097–1110.

Marlatt, G. A., & Gordon, J. R. (1980). Determinants of relapse: Implications for the maintenance of behavior change. In P. O. Davison & S. M. Davidson (Eds.), *Behavioral medicine: Changing health lifestyles.* New York: Brunner/Mazel.

Marshall, C. D. (1976). The affective consequences of "inadequately explained" physiological arousal. Unpublished doctoral dissertation, Stanford University.

Marshall, E. (1980). Psychotherapy faces test of worth. *Science, 207,* 35–36.

Martin, B. (1977). *Abnormal psychology.* New York: Holt, Rinehart & Winston.

Marx, M. B., Garrady, T. F., & Bowens, F. R. (1975). The influence of recent life experience on the life of college freshmen. *Journal of Psychosomatic Research, 19,* 87–98.

Maslow, A. H. (1954). *Motivation and personality.* New York: Harper & Row.

Maslow, A. H. (1968). *Toward a psychology of being.* New York: Van Nostrand Reinhold.

Maslow, A. H. (1971). *The farther reaches of human nature.* New York: Viking.

Mason, J. W. (1971). A re-evaluation of the concept of "non-specificity" in stress theory. *Journal of Psychiatric Research, 8,* 323–33.

Mason, J. W. (1975). A historical view of the stress field, Part I. *Journal of Human Stress, 1,* 6–12.

Masters, W. H., & Johnson, V. E. (1970). *Human sexual inadequacy.* Boston: Little, Brown.

Mathers, J. A. L., Osborne, R. H., & DeGeorge, F. V. (1961). The studies of blood pressure, heart rate and the electrocardiogram in adult twins. *American Heart Journal, 62,* 634–42.

Matthysse, S. (1973). Antipsychotic drug actions: A clue to the neuropathology of the schizophrenias. *Federation Proceedings, 32,* 200–205.

Matthysse, S. (1977). The role of dopamine in schizophrenia. In E. Usdin, D. A. Homburg, & J. D. Barkus (Eds.), *Neuroregulators and psychiatric disorders* (pp. 3–13). New York: Oxford University Press.

May, R. (1953). *Man's search for himself.* New York: Norton.

May, R. (1969) *Love and will.* New York: Norton.

McCary, J. L. (1978). Human sexuality: Past present and future. *Journal of Marriage and Family Counseling, 4,* 3–12.

McClearn, G. E. (1968). Genetics and motivation of the mouse. In W. J. Arnold (Ed.), *Nebraska Symposium on Motivation.* Lincoln: University of Nebraska Press.

McClelland, D.C. (1979). Inhibited power motivation and high blood pressure in men. *Journal of Abnormal Psychology, 88,* 182–90.

McClelland, D. C., Atkinson, J. W., Clark, R. A., & Lowell, E. L.

(1953). *The achievement motive.* New York: Appleton.

McConaghy, N. (1969). Subjective and penil plethysmograph response following aversion-relief and apomorphine aversion therapy for homosexual impulses. *British Journal of Psychiatry, 115,* 723–30.

McConnell, R. B. (1966). *Genetics of gastro-intestinal disorders.* London: Oxford University Press.

McCord, J. (1979). Some child-rearing antecedents of criminal behavior in adult men. *Journal of Personality and Social Psychology, 37,* 1477–86.

McCord, J. (1980, November 5–8). Myths and realities about criminal sanctions. Paper presented at the annual meetings of the American Society of Criminology, San Francisco, Calif.

McFarlane, A. (1970). *Witchcraft in Tudor and Stuart England; A regional and comparative study.* New York: Harper & Row.

McGarry, A. L., & Bendt, R. H. (1969). Criminal vs. civil commitment of psychotic offenders: A seven year follow-up. *American Journal of Psychiatry, 125,* 1387–94.

McGhie, A. (1969). *Pathology of attention.* London: Penguin.

McGhie, A., & Chapman, J. S. (1961). Disorders of attention and perception in early schizophrenia. *British Journal of Medical Psychology, 34,* 103–16.

McGuire, R. J., Carlisle, J. M., & Young, B. G. (1965). Sexual deviation as conditioned behavior. *Behavior Research and Therapy, 2,* 185–90.

McKinney, W. T., Suomi, S. J., & Harlow, H. F. (1972). Repetitive peer separations of juvenile age Rhesus monkeys. *Archives of General Psychiatry, 27,* 200–203.

McKnew, D. H., Jr., Cytryn, L., & Yahraes, H. (1983). *Why isn't Johnny crying?* New York: Norton.

McLellan, A. T., & Druley, K. A. (1977). Non-random relation between drugs of abuse and psychiatric diagnosis. *Journal of Psychiatric Research, 13,* 179–84.

McLellan, A. T. et al. (1979). Development of psychiatric illness in drug abusers. *New England Journal of Medicine, 301*(24), 1310–14.

McLellan, A. T. et al. (1982). Is treatment for substance abuse effective? *Journal of American Medical Association, 247* (10), 1423–28.

McNeil, T. F. (1971). Prebirth and pastbirth influence on the relationship between creative ability and recorded mental illness. *Journal of Personality, 39,* 391–406.

McNitt, P. C., & Thornton, D. W. (1978). Depression and perceived reinforcement: A consideration. *Journal of Abnormal Psychology, 87,* 137–40.

McReynolds, W. T., Barnes, A. R., Brooks, S., & Rehagen, N. J. (1973). The role of attention-placebo influences in the efficacy of systematic desensitization. *Journal of Consulting and Clinical Psychology, 41,* 86–92.

Medley, E. S. (1978). Peptic ulcer disease in children. *Journal of Family Practice, 7,* 281–84.

Mednick, B. R. (1973). Breakdown in high-risk subjects: Familial and early environmental factors. *Journal of Abnormal Psychology, 82,* 469–75.

Mednick, S. A. (1978). Berkou's fallacy and high risk research. In L. C. Wynne, R. L. Cromwell, & S. Matthysse (Eds.), *The Nature of schizophrenia.* New York: Wiley.

Mednick, S. A., & Schulsinger, F. (1968). Some premorbid characteristics related to breakdown in children with schizophrenic mothers. In D. Rosenthal & S. S. Kety (Eds.), *The transmission of schizophrenia.* Elmsford, N.Y.: Pergamon.

Medvedev, Z. A., & Medvedev, R. A. (1971). *A question of madness.* New York: Knopf.

Meehl, P. E. (1962). Schizotaxia, schizotypy, schizophrenia. *American Psychologist, 17,* 827–38.

Meichenbaum, D. (1977). *Cognitive-behavior modification.* New York: Plenum.

Meichenbaum, D., Gilmore, B., & Fedoravicius, A. (1971). Group insight vs. desensitization in treating speech anxiety. *Journal of Consulting and Clinical Psychology, 36,* 410–21.

Melzack, R. (1973). *The puzzle of pain.* New York: Basic Books.

Mendels, J. (1970). *Concepts of depression.* New York: Wiley.

Mendels, J., & Cochran, C. (1968). The nosology of depression: The endogenous-reactive concept. *American Journal of Psychiatry, 124,* Supplement 1–11.

Mendelsohn, G. A., & Geller, M. H. (1963). Effects of counselor-client similarity on the outcome of counseling. *Journal of Counseling Psychology, 10,* 71–77.

Mendelsohn, G. A., & Geller, M. H. (1967). Similarity, missed sessions, and early termination. *Journal of Counseling Psychology, 14,* 210–15.

Merbaum, M. (1971). Some personality characteristics of soldiers exposed to extreme war stress: A follow-up study of post-hospital adjustment. *Journal of Clinical Psychology, 32,* 558–62.

Merton, R. K. (1957). *Social theory and social structure.* Glencoe, Ill.: Free Press.

Mesulam, M. M. (1981). A cortical network for directed attention and unilateral neglect. *Annals of Neurology, 10,* 309–24.

Meyer, V. (1966). Modification of expectations in cases with obsessional rituals. *Behaviour Research and Therapy, 4,* 273–80.

Meyer, V., & Mair, J. M. M. (1963). A new technique to control stammering: A preliminary report. *Behavior Research Therapy, 1,* 251–54.

Midelfort, H. C. E. (1972). *Witch-hunting in Southwestern Germany, 1562–1684.* Stanford, Calif.: Stanford University Press.

Mill, J. S. (1898). *On liberty: The subjugation of women.* New York: Henry Holt.

Miller, D., & Dawson, W. H. (1965). Effects of stigma on re-employment of ex-mental patients. *Mental Hygiene, 49,* 281–87.

Miller, N. E. (1969). Learning of visceral and glandular responses. *Science, 163,* 434.

Miller, S. M. (1978). Controllability in human stress. In M. E. P. Seligman & J. G. Garber (Eds.), *Human helplessness: Theory and application.* New York: Academic Press.

Miller, W. R., & Seligman, M. E. P. (1975). Depression and learned helplessness in man. *Journal of Abnormal Psychology, 84,* 228–38.

Miller, W. R., & Seligman, M. E. P. (1976). Learned helplessness, depression, and the perception of reinforcement. *Behavior Research and Therapy, 14,* 7–17.

Milner, B. (1964). Some effects of frontal lobectomy in man. In J. M. Warren & K. Akert (Eds.), *The frontal granular cortex and behavior.* New York: McGraw-Hill.

Milner, B. (1970). Memory and the medial temporal regions of the brain. In K. H. Pribram & D. E. Broadbent (Eds.), *Biology of memory.* New York: Academic Press.

Milner, B. (1972). Disorders of learning and memory after temporal lobe lesions in man. *Clinical Neurosurgery, 19,* 421–46.

Mintz, S., & Alpert, M. (1972). Imagery, vividness, reality testing, and schizophrenic hallucinations. *Journal of Abnormal Psychology, 79,* 310–16.

Minuchin, S. (1974). *Families and family therapy.* Cambridge, Mass.: Harvard University Press.

Mirsky, I. A. (1958). Physiologic, psychologic, and social determinants of the etiology of duodenal ulcer. *American Journal of Digestive Diseases, 3,* 285–314.

Mirsky, I. A., Futterman, P., & Kaplan, S. (1952). Blood plasma pepsinogen. II. The activity of the plasma from "normal" subjects, patients with duodenal ulcer and patients with pernicious anemia. *Journal of Laboratory and Clinical Medicine, 40,* 198–99.

Mischel, H. N., & Mischel, W. (1973). *Readings in personality.* New York: Holt, Rinehart & Winston.

Mischel, W. (1968). *Personality and assessment.* New York: Wiley.

Mischel, W. (1973). Toward a cognitive social learning reconceptualization of personality. *Psychological Review, 80,* 252–83.

Mischel, W. (1976). *Introduction to personality* (2nd ed.). New York: Holt, Rinehart & Winston.

Mischel, W., & Baker, N. (1975). Cognitive transformations of reward objects through instructions. *Journal of Personality and Social Psychology, 31,* 254–61.

Mischel, W., & Ebbesen, E. (1970). Attention in delay of gratification. *Journal of Personality and Social Psychology, 16,* 329–37.

Mischel, W., Ebbesen, E., & Zeiss, A. R. (1972). Cognitive and attentional mechanisms in delay of gratification. *Journal of Personality and Social Psychology, 21,* 204–18.

Mischel, W., & Peake, P. K. (1982). Beyond deja vu in the search for cross-situational consistency. *Psychological Review, 89,* 730–55.

Mischler, E. G., & Waxler, N. (1968). *Interaction in families: An experimental study of family processes and schizophrenia.* New York: Wiley.

Mitchell, K. M., Bozarth, J. D., & Krauft, C. C. (1977). A reappraisal of the therapeutic effectiveness of accurate empathy, nonpossessive warmth, and genuineness. In A. S. Gurman & A. M. Razin (Eds.), *Effective psychotherapy: A handbook of research.* New York: Pergamon.

Mittelmann, B., Wolff, H. G., & Scharf, M. (1942). Emotions in gastroduodenal functions. *Psychosomatic Medicine, 4,* 5–61.

Mittler, P., Gillies, S., & Jukes, E. (1966). Prognosis in psychotic children. Report of follow-up study. *Journal of Mental Deficiency Research, 10,* 73–83.

Model Penal Code and Commentaries, Sec. 4.01 (Part I). (1962). Philadelphia, Pa.: American Law Institute, 1980.

Modell, W. (1967). Mass catastrophes and the roles of science and technology. *Science, 156,* 346–51.

Mohler, H., & Okada, T. (1977). Properties of 3H-diazepam binding to benzodiazepine receptors in rat cerebral cortex. *Life Science, 20,* 2101–10.

Monahan, J. (1976). *Community mental health and the criminal justice system.* New York: Pergamon.

Monahan, J., & Wexler, D. (1978). A definite maybe: Proofs and probability in civil commitment. *Law and Human Behavior, 2,* 37–42.

Money, J., & Ambinder, R. (1978). Two-year, real-life diagnostic test: Rehabilitation vs. cure. In J. P. Brady & H. K. H. Brodie (Eds.), *Controversy in psychiatry.* Philadelphia: Saunders.

Money, J., & Ehrhardt, A. A. (1972). *Man and woman, boy and girl.* Baltimore: The John Hopkins University Press.

Money, J., Schwartz, M., & Lewis, V. G. (1983, June). Adult erotosexual status and fetal hormonal masculinization and demasculinization: 46XX congenital virilizing adrenal hyperplasia (CVAH), and 46XY androgen insensitivity syndrome (AIS) compared. Paper presented at the 14th International Congress of the International Society of Psychoneuroendocrinology, New York.

Monthly Labor Review. (1983, July). Washington, D.C.: U.S. Department of Labor, Bureau of Labor Statistics, p. 54.

Moody, R. L. (1946). Bodily changes during abreaction. *The Lancet, 2,* 934–35.

Moore, R. A. (1978). Management of the alcoholic. In J. P. Brady & H. K. H. Brodie (Eds.), *Controversy in psychiatry,* Philadelphia: Saunders.

Morris, R. J., & Suckerman, K. R. (1974a). The importance of the therapeutic relationship to systematic desensitization. *Journal of Consulting and Clinical Psychology, 42,* 142.

Morris, R. J., & Suckerman, K. R. (1974b). Therapist warmth as a factor in automated systematic desensitization. *Journal of Consulting and Clinical Psychology, 42,* 244–50.

Moscovitch, M. (1982). A neuropsychological approach to perception and memory in normal and pathological aging. In

F. I. M. Craik & S. Trehub (Eds.), *Aging and cognitive processes.* New York: Plenum.

Mosher, L. R., Feinsilver, D., Katz, M. M., & Wienckowski, L. A. (1971). *A special report on schizophrenia.* (Publication No. HSM 72-9007). Washington, D.C.: U.S. Government Printing Office.

Mosher, L. R., & Menn, A. Z. (1978). Community residential treatment for schizophrenia: Two year follow-up. *Hospital and Community Psychiatry, 29,* 715-23.

Mosher, L. R., Menn, A., & Matthews, S. (1975). Soteria: evaluation of a home-based treatment for schizophrenia. *American Journal of Orthopsychiatry 45,* 455-67.

Mowrer, O. H. (1948). Learning theory and the neurotic paradox. *American Journal of Orthopsychiatry, 18,* 571-610.

Mowrer, O. H. (1950). *Learning theory and personality dynamics.* New York: Arnold Press.

Mowrer, O. H., & Mowrer, W. M. (1938). Enuresis: A method for its study and treatment. *American Journal of Orthopsychiatry, 8,* 436-59.

Munzinger, H. (1975). The adopted child's IQ: A critical review. *Psychological Bulletin, 80,* 623-29.

Murray, H. A. (1951). Forward. In H. H. Anderson & G. L. Anderson (Eds.), *An introduction to projective techniques.* Englewood Cliffs, N.J.: Prentice-Hall.

Murphy, D., Brodie, K., Goodwin, F., & Bunney, W. E. (1971). Regular induction of hypomania by L-dopa in "bipolar" manic-depressive patients. *Nature, 229,* 135-36.

Murstein, B. I. (1965). New thoughts about ambiguity and the TAT. *Journal of Projective Techniques and Personality Assessment, 29,* 219-25.

Myers, J., & Auld, F. (1955). Some variables related to outcome of psychotherapy. *Journal of Clinical Psychology, 11,* 51-54.

Nash, E. H., Hoehn-Saric, R., Battle, C. C., Stone, A. R., Imber, S. D., & Frank, J. D. (1965). Systematic preparation of patients for short-term psychotherapy. II. Relation to characteristics of patient, therapist and the psychotherapeutic process. *Journal of Nervous and Mental Disorders, 140,* 374-83.

Nathan, P. E. (1980). Ideal mental health services for alcoholics and problem drinkers: An exercise in pragmatics. In P. O. Davidson & S. M. Davidson (Eds.), *Behavioral medicine: Changing health lifestyles* (pp. 279-98). New York: Brunner/Mazel.

National Academy of Sciences, Institute of Medicine. (1982). *Marijuana and health.* Washington, D.C.: National Academy Press.

Nemiah, J. C. (1971). The psychophysiologic management: A treatment of patients with peptic ulcer. *Advances in Psychosomatic Medicine, 6,* 169-85.

Nestel, P. J. (1969). Blood pressure in catecholamine excretion after mental stress in labile hypertension. *Lancet, 1*(2), 692-94.

Neuchterlein, K. H. (1977). Reaction time and attention in schizophrenia: A critical evaluation of the data and theories. *Schizophrenia Bulletin, 3,* 373-428.

New York Legislative Commission on Expenditure Review. (1971). Narcotics Drug Control in New York State, Program Audit Highlights. Albany, N.Y.

Nideffer, R. M., Neale, J. M., Kopfstein, J. T., & Cromwell, R. L. (1971). The effect of previous preparatory intervals upon anticipatory responses in the reaction time of schizophrenic and nonschizophrenic patients. *Journal of Nervous and Mental Disease, 153,* 360-65.

Nisbett, R., & Ross, L. (1980). *Human inference: Strategies and shortcomings of social judgment.* Englewood Cliffs, N.J.: Prentice-Hall.

Odier, C. (1956). *Anxiety and magical thinking.* New York: International Universities Press.

Ohman, A. (1979). Fear relevance, autonomic conditioning and phobias: A laboratory model. In S. Bates, W. K. Dockens, K. G. Blotesharm, L. Melin, & P. O. Sjoden (Eds.), *Trends in behavior therapy.* New York: Academic Press.

Ohman, A., Anders, E., & Olafson, C. (1975). One trial learning and superior resistance to extinction of autonomic responses conditioned to potentially phobic stimuli. *Journal of Comparative and Physiological Psychology, 88* (88), 619-27.

Ohman, A., Fredrikson, M., & Hugdahl, K. (1978). Orienting and defensive responding in the electrodermal system: Palmardorsal differences and recovery rate during conditioning to potentially phobic stimuli. *Psychophysiology, 2,* 93-102.

Ohman, A., Fredrikson, M., Hugdahl, K. & Per-Arne, R. (1974). A dimension of preparedness in human learning: The effect of potentially phobic stimuli as CS's in electro-dermal conditioning. *Biological Psychology, 2,* 85-93.

Ohman, A., Fredrikson, M., Hugdahl, K., & Rimmo, P. (1976). The premise of equipotentiality in human classical conditioning: Conditioned electrodermal responses to potentially phobic stimuli. *Journal of Experimental Psychology-General, 105* (4), 313-37.

Ohwaki, S., & Stayton, S. E. (1978). The relation of length of institutionalization to the intellectual functioning of the profoundly retarded. *Child Development, 49,* 105-109.

Oi, M., Oshida, K., & Sugimura, A. (1959). Location of the gastric ulcer. *Gastroenterology, 36,* 45-56.

O'Leary, M. R., Donovan, D. M., Krueger, K. J., & Cysewski, B. (1978). Depression and the perception of reinforcement: Lack of differences in expectancy change among alcoholics. *Journal of Abnormal Psychology, 87,* 110-12.

O'Leary, S. G., & Pelham, W. E. (1978). Behavior therapy and withdrawal of stimulant medication in hyperactive children. *Pediatrics, 61,* 211-17.

Oltman, J., & Friedman, S. (1967). Parental deprivation in psychiatric conditions. *Diseases of the Nervous System, 28,* 298-303.

Orgel, S. (1958). Effects of psychoanalysis on the course of peptic ulcer. *Psychosomatic Medicine, 20,* 117-23.

Orley, J., & Wing, J. (1979). Psychiatric disorders in two African villages. *Archives of General Psychiatry, 36,* 513-20.

Orne, M. T. (1962). On the social psychology of the psychological experiment: With particular reference to demand characteristics and their implications. *American Psychologist, 17,* 776-83.

Orne, M. T., & Wender, P. H. (1968). Anticipatory socialization for psychotherapy. *American Journal of Psychiatry, 124,* 1202-11.

Ornitz, E. M. (1973). Childhood autism: A review of the clinical and experimental literature. *California Medicine, 117,* 21-47.

Ornitz, E. M. (1978). Biological homogeneity or heterogeneity. In M. Rutter & E. Schopler (Eds.), *Autism: A reappraisal of concepts and treatment.* New York: Plenum.

Osler, W. (1897). *Lectures on angina pectoris and allied states.* New York: D. Appleton and Company.

Osmond, H., & Smythies, J. R. (1952). Schizophrenia: A new approach. *Journal of Mental Science, 98,* 309-15.

Ost, L., & Gotestam, K. (1976). Behavioral and pharmacological treatments for obesity: An experimental comparison. *Addictive Behaviors, 1,* 331-38.

Ost, L. G., & Hugdahl, K. (1981). Acquisition of phobias and anxiety response patterns in clinical patients. *Behaviour Research and Therapy, 19,* 439-48.

Packer, H. (1968). *The limits of the criminal sanction.* Stanford: Stanford University Press.

Paffenbarger, R. S., Wolf, P. A., Natkin, J., & Thorne, M. C. (1966). Chronic disease in former college students. I. Early precursors of fatal coronary heart disease. *American Journal of Epidemiology, 83,* 314–28.

Palmer, R. L. (1980). *Anorexia nervosa.* New York: Penguin.

Parloff, M. B. (1976, February). Shopping for the right therapy. *Saturday Review, 21,* 14–20.

Parloff, M. B. (1979). Can psychotherapy research guide the policymaker? A little knowledge may be a dangerous thing. *American Psychologist, 34,* 296–306.

Parloff, M. B. (1982). Psychotherapy research evidence and reimbursement decisions: Bambi meets Godzilla. *American Journal of Psychiatry, 139,* 718–27.

Parloff, M. B., Waskow, I. E., & Wolfe, B. E. (1978). Research on therapist variables in relation to process and outcome. In S. L. Garfield & A. E. Bergin (Eds.), *Handbook of psychotherapy and behavior change: An empirical analysis* (2nd ed.). New York: Wiley.

Parkes, M. C. (1964). Recent bereavement as a cause of mental illness. *British Journal of Psychiatry, 110,* 194–204.

Parkes, M. C., Benjamin, B., & Fitzgerald, R. G. (1969). Broken heart: A statistical study of increased mortality among widowers. *British Medical Journal, 1,* 740–43.

Patterson, E. M. (1965). Treatment of alcoholic families with nurse home visits. *Family Process, 4,* 75–94.

Patterson, G. R. (1973). Reprogramming the families of aggressive boys. In C. Thoreson (Ed.), *Behavior modification in education: 72nd Year Book, Part I.* Chicago: University of Chicago Press.

Patterson, G. R. (1975). *Families: Applications of social learning theory to family life.* Champaign, Ill.: Research Press.

Patterson, G. R., Weiss, R. L., & Hops, H. (1976). Training of marital skills: Some problems of concepts. In H. Leitenberg (Ed.), *Handbook of behavior modification and behavior therapy.* Englewood Cliffs, N.J.: Prentice-Hall.

Pattie, F. A. (1967). A brief history of hypnotism. In J. E. Gordon (Ed.), *Handbook of clinical and experimental hypnosis.* New York: Macmillan.

Paul, G. L. (1966). Insight vs. desensitization in psychotherapy. Stanford: Stanford University Press.

Paul, G. L. (1967). Insight vs. desensitization in psychotherapy two years after termination. *Journal of Consulting Psychology, 31* (4), 333–48.

Pauly, I. B. (1969). Adult manifestation of male transsexualism. In R. Green & J. Money (Eds.), *Transsexualism and sex reassignment.* Baltimore: The Johns Hopkins Press.

Paykel, E. S. (1973). Life events and acute depression. In J. P. Scott & E. C. Senay (Eds.), *Separation and depression.* AAAS.

Paykel, E. S. (1974a). Recent life events and clinical depression. In E. K. E. Gunderson & R. H. Rahe (Eds.), *Life stress and illness* (pp. 150–51). Springfield, Ill.: Charles C. Thomas.

Paykel, E. S. (1974b). Life stress and psychiatric disorder: Application of the clinical approach. In B. P. Dohrenwend & B. S. Dohrenwend (Eds.), *Stressful life events: Their nature and effects* (pp. 135–49). New York: Wiley.

Paykel, E. S., Meyers, J. K., Dienelt, M. N., Klerman, J. L., Lindenthal, J. J., & Peffer, M. P. (1969). Life events and depression. *Archives of General Psychiatry, 21,* 753–60.

Payne, R. W. (1966). The measurement and significance of overinclusive thinking and retardation in schizophrenic patients. In P. H. Hoch & J. Zubin (Eds.), *Psychopathology of schizophrenia* (pp. 77–79). New York: Grune & Stratton.

Payne, R. W., & Hewlett, J. H. G. (1960). Thought disorder in psychotic patients. In H. J. Eysenck (Ed.), *Experiments in personality* (Vol. 2) (pp. 3–104). London: Routledge & Kegan Paul.

Pendery, M., Maltzman, I., & West, L. J. (1982). Controlled drinking by alcoholics? New findings on a reevaluation of a major affirmative study. *Science, 217,* 169–75.

Perkins, K. A., & Reyher, J. (1971). Repression, psychopathology and drive representation: An experimental hypnotic investigation of impulse inhibition. *American Journal of Clinical Hypnosis, 13,* 249–58.

Perls, F. S. (1969). *Gestalt therapy verbatim.* Lafayette, Calif.: Real People Press.

Perls, F. S. (1970). *Gestalt therapy now.* Palo Alto, Calif.: Science & Behavior Books.

Perly, M. J., & Guze, S. B. (1962). Hysteria: The stability and usefulness of clinical criteria. *New England Journal of Medicine, 266,* 421–26.

Perris, C. The course of depressive psychosis. (1968). *Acta Psychiatrica Scandinavica, 44,* 238–48.

Peterson, C., & Seligman, M. E. P. (1984). Explanatory style and depression: Theory and evidence. *Psychological Review.*

Peterson, D. R. (1968). *The clinical study of social behavior.* New York: Appleton.

Petzel, T. P., & Johnson, J. E. (1972). Time estimation by process and reactive schizophrenics under crowded and uncrowded conditions. *Journal of Clinical Psychology, 28*(3), 345–47.

Phares, E. J. (1976). *Locus of control in personality.* Morristown, N.J.: General Learning Press.

Phares, E. J., Wilson, K. G., & Klyrer, N. W. (1971). Internal-external control and the attribution of blame under neutral and distractive conditions. *Journal of Personality and Social Psychology, 18,* 286–88.

Phillips, L. (1953). Case history data and prognosis in schizophrenia. *Journal of Nervous and Mental Diseases, 117,* 515–25.

Physicians Washington Report. (1980). Cocaine deaths and illness rising. *Physicians Washington Report, 4*(2).

Place, E. J. S., & Gilmore, G. C. (1980). Perceptual organization in schizophrenia. *Journal of Abnormal Psychology, 89,* 409–18.

Platt, J. J., & Labate, C. (1976). *Heroin addiction.* New York: Wiley.

Pokorny, A. D. (1964). Suicide rates and various psychiatric disorders. *Journal of Nervous and Mental Diseases, 139,* 499–506.

Polak, P. R., & Kirby, M. W. (1976). A model to replace psychiatric hospitals. *Journal of Nervous & Mental Diseases, 162,* 13–22.

Pollack, J. M. (1979). Obsessive-compulsive personality: A review. *Psychological Bulletin, 86,* 225–41.

Pollit, J. D. (1960). Natural history studies in mental illness: A discussion based on a pilot study of obsessional states. *Journal of Mental Science, 106,* 93–113.

Pope, H. G. et al. (1981). Drug use and lifestyle among college undergraduates. *Archives of General Psychiatry, 38,* 588.

Pope, H. G., Jonas, J. M., & Jones, B. (1982). Factitious psychosis: Phenomenology, family history, and long-term outcome of nine patients. *American Journal of Psychiatry, 139,* 1480–83.

Porsolt, R. D., Anton, G., Blavet, N., & Jalfre, M. (1978). Behavioral despair in rats: A new model sensitive to antidepressant treatments. *European Journal of Pharmacology, 47,* 379–91.

Post, R., Kotin, J., Goodwin, F. K., & Gordon, E. K. (1973). Psychomotor activity and cerebrospinal fluid amine metabolites in affective illness. *American Journal of Psychiatry, 130,* 67–72.

Prange, A. J., Wilsan, J. C., Knox, A., McClane, T. K., & Lipton, M. A. (1970). Enhancement of imipramine by thyroid stimulating hormone: Clinical and theoretical implications. *American Journal of Psychiatry, 127,* 191–99.

Premack, D. (1959). Toward empirical behavior laws: I. Positive reinforcement. *Psychological Review, 66,* 219–33.

Price, K. P., Tryon, W. W., & Raps, C. S. (1978). Learned helplessness and depression in a clinical population: A test of two behavioral hypotheses. *Journal of Abnormal Psychology, 87,* 113–21.

Prichard, J. C. (1837). *Treatise on insanity and other disorders af-*

fecting the mind. Philadelphia: Haswell, Barrington & Haswell.

Purcell, D., Brady, K., Chai, H., Muser, J., Molk, L., Gordon, N., & Means, J. (1969). The effect of asthma in children during experimental separation from the family. *Psychosomatic Medicine, 31,* 144–64.

Rabavilos, A. D., Boulougouris, J. C., & Stefanis, C. (1976). Duration of flooding session in the treatment of obsessive-compulsive patients. *Behavior Research and Therapy, 14,* 349–55.

Rachman, S. J. (1965). Aversion therapy: Chemical or electrical? *Behaviour Research Therapy, 2,* 289–99.

Rachman, S. J. (1971). *The effects of psychotherapy.* Oxford: Pergamon.

Rachman, S. J. (1976). Therapeutic modeling. In M. Felman & A. Broadhurst (Ed.), *Theoretical and experimental bases of behavior therapy.* Chichester: Wiley.

Rachman, S. J. (1978). *Fear and courage.* New York: Freeman.

Rachman, S. J., Cobb, J., Grey, S., MacDonald, B., Mawson, D., Sartory, G., and Stern, R. (1979). The behavioral treatment of obsessive-compulsive disorders, with and without domipramine. *Behavior Research and Therapy, 17,* 467–78.

Rachman, S. J., & Hodgson, R. J. (1968). Experimentally induced "sexual fetishism": replication and development. *Psychological Records, 18,* 25–27.

Rachman, S. J., & Hodgson, R. J. (1980). *Obsessions and compulsions.* Englewood Cliffs, N.J.: Prentice-Hall.

Rachman, S. J., Hodgson, R., & Marks, I. M. (1971). The treatment of chronic obsessional neurosis. *Behaviour Research and Therapy, 9,* 237–47.

Rachman, S. J., Marks, I., & Hodgson, R. (1973). The treatment of chronic obsessive compulsive neurosis by modelling and flooding in vivo. *Behaviour Research and Therapy, 11,* 463–71.

Rachman, S. J., & Wilson, G. T. (1979). *The effects of psychotherapy.* Oxford: Pergamon.

Rack, P. (1977). Clinical experience in the treatment of obsessional states. *Journal of International Medical Research, 5,* 81–91.

Radloff, L. S. (1975). Sex differences in depression: The effects of occupation and marital status. *Sex Roles, 1,* 249–65.

Radloff, L. S., & Rae, D. S. (1979). Susceptibility and precipitating factors in depression: Sex differences and similarities. *Journal of Abnormal Psychology, 88,* 174–81.

Rado, S. (1928). Psychodynamics of depression from the etiological point of view. In W. Galen (Ed.), *The meaning of despair.* New York: Science House.

Raps, C. S., Peterson, C., Reinhard, K. E., Abramson, L. Y., & Seligman, M. E. P. (1982). Attributional style among depressed patients. *Journal of Abnormal Psychology, 91,* 102–103.

Raskin, A., Crook, T. H., & Herman, K. D. (1975). The psychiatric history and symptom differences in black and white depressed patients. *Journal of Consulting and Clinical Psychology, 43,* 73–80.

Raskind, M. A. (1976). Helping the elderly psychiatric patient in crisis. *Geriatrics, 31,* 51–56.

Rattan, R. B., & Chapman, L. J. (1973). Associative intrusions in schizophrenic verbal behavior. *Journal of Abnormal Psychology, 82,* 169–73.

Rawlings, E. I., & Carter, D. K. (1977). *Psychotherapy for women.* Springfield, Ill.: Charles C. Thomas.

Ray, O. (1983). *Drugs, society, and human behavior* (3rd ed.). St. Louis: Mosby.

Ray, W. J., & Katahn, M. (1968). Relation of anxiety to locus of control. *Psychological Reports, 23,* 1196.

Redmond, D. E., Maas, J. W., Kling, A., & DeKirmenjian, H. (1971). Changes in private school behavior after treatment

with alpha-methyl-para-tyrosine. *Psychosomatic Medicine, 33,* 97–113.

Rehm, L. (1977). A self-control model of depression. *Behavior Therapy, 8,* 787–804.

Rehm, L. P. (1978). Mood pleasant events, and unpleasant events: Two pilot studies. *Journal of Consulting and Clinical Psychology, 46,* 854–59.

Rehyer, J., & Smyth, L. (1971). Suggestibility during the execution of a posthypnotic suggestion. *Journal of Abnormal Psychology, 78,* 258–65.

Reich, L. H., Davies, R. K., & Himmelhoch, J. M. (1974). Excessive alcohol use in manic-depressive illness. *American Journal of Psychiatry, 131*(1), 83–86.

Reisen, M. F., Brust, A. A., & Farris, E. B. (1951). Life situations, emotions and the course of patients with arterial hypertension. *Psychosomatic Medicine, 13,* 133.

Reisenger, J. J. (1972). The treatment of "anxiety-depression" via positive reinforcement and response. *Journal of Applied Behavior Analysis, 5,* 125–30.

Reiss, S., Peterson, R. A., Erron, L. D., & Reiss, N. M. (1977). *Abnormality: Experimental and clinical approaches.* New York: Macmillan.

Rennie, M. A., & Wollensheim, J. P. (1979). Cognitive therapy, stress management training and the type A behavior pattern. *Cognitive Therapy and Research, 3* (1) 61–73.

Rennie, T. A. C., & Srole, L. (1956). Social class prevalence and distribution of psychosomatic conditions in an urban population. *Psychosomatic Medicine, 18,* 449.

Rescorla R. A., & Solomon, R. L. (1967). Two-process learning theory: Relationship between Pavlovian conditioning and instrumental learning. *Psychological Review, 74,* 151–82.

Rescorla, R. A., & Wagner, A. R. (1972). A theory of Pavlovian conditioning: Variations in the effectiveness of reinforcement and nonreinforcement. In A. Black & W. F. Prokasy (Eds.), *Classical conditioning II.* New York: Appleton-Century-Crofts.

Resick, P., & Ellis, E. (1982). Victims of rape: Repeated assessment of depressive symptoms. *Journal of Consulting and Clinical Psychology, 50,* 96–102.

Richardson, S. A. (1970). Age and sex differences in values towards physical handicaps. *Journal of Health and Social Behavior, 11,* 207–14.

Richter, C. P. (1957a). Hormones and rhythms in man and animals. *Recent Progress in Hormone Research, 13.*

Richter, C. P. (1957b). On the phenomenon of sudden death in animals and men. *Psychosomatic Medicine, 19,* 191–98.

Ricks, D. F. (1974). Supershrink: Methods of a therapist judged successful on the basis of adult outcome of adolescent patients. In D. Ricks, M. Roff, & A. Thomas (Eds.), *Life history research in psychopathology* (Vol. 3). Minneapolis: University of Minnesota Press.

Rimland, B. (1964). *Infantile autism.* New York: Appleton-Century-Crofts.

Rimm, D. C., & Masters, J. C. (1974). *Behavior therapy: Techniques and empirical findings.* New York: Academic.

Rioch, M. J. (1967). Pilot projects in training mental health counselors. In E. L. Cowen, E. A. Gardner, & M. Zax (Eds.), *Emerging approaches to mental health problems.* New York: Appleton-Century-Crofts.

Risley, T., & Wolf, M. (1967). Establishing functional speech in echolalic children. *Behavior Research and Therapy, 5,* 73–88.

Rittenhouse, J. D. (1976). Selected themes of discussion. In J. D. Rittenhouse (Ed.), *The epidemiology of heroin and other narcotics.* Menlo Park, Calif.: Stanford Research Institute.

Ritvo, E. R., Rabin, K., Yuwiler, A., Freeman, B. J., & Geller, E. (1978). Biochemical and hematogic studies: A critical review. In M. Rutter & E. Schopler (Eds.), *Autism: A reappraisal of concepts and treatment.* New York: Plenum.

Roberts, M., & Hanaway, J. (1970). *Atlas of the human brain in section.* Philadelphia: Lea & Febiger.

Robins, E., & Guze, S. B. (1972). Classification of affective disorders: The primary-secondary, the endogenous-reactive, and the neurotic-psychotic concepts. In T. A. Williams, M. M. Katz, & J. A. Shields (Eds.), *Recent advances in the psychobiology of the depressive illnesses* (pp. 283–93). Washington, D. C.: U.S. Government Printing Office.

Robins, L. N. (1966). *Deviant children grow up.* Baltimore: Williams & Wilkins.

Robinson, D. S., Davis, J., Nies, A., Ravaris, C., & Sylvester, D. (1971). Relation of sex in aging to monoamine oxidase activity in human brain, plasma, and platelets. *Archives of General Psychiatry, 24,* 536.

Rodin, J. (1977). Bidirectional influences of emotionality, stimulus responsivity and metabolic events in obesity. In J. D. Maser & M. E. P. Seligman (Eds.), *Psychopathology: Experimental models.* San Francisco: Freeman.

Rodin, J. (1983, April). Presidential address given at meeting of Eastern Psychological Association, Philadelphia.

Rodin, J., & Langer, E. J. (1977). Long-term effects of control intervention with the institutionalized patient. *Journal of Personality and Social Psychology, 12,* 897–902.

Rodnick, E., & Shakow, D. (1940). Set in the schizophrenic as measured by a composite reaction time index. *American Journal of Psychiatry, 97,* 214–25.

Rodnight, R. (1978). Biochemical strategies and concepts. In M. Rutter & E. Schopler (Eds.), *Autism: A reappraisal of concepts and treatment.* New York: Plenum.

Roff, J. D., & Knight, R. (1981). Family characteristics, childhood symptoms, and adult outcomes in schizophrenia. *Journal of Abnormal Psychology, 90,* 510–20.

Rogers, C. (1951). *Client-centered therapy.* Boston: Houghton-Mifflin.

Rogers, C. (1961). *On becoming a person.* Boston: Houghton Mifflin.

Rogers, C. R., & Dymond, R. (Eds.). (1954). *Psychotherapy and personality change.* Chicago: University of Chicago Press.

Rogers, C. R., & Truax, C. B. (1967). The therapeutic conditions antecedent to change: A theoretical view. In C. R. Rogers (Ed.), *The therapeutic relationship and its impact: A study of psychotherapy with schizophrenics.* Madison: University of Wisconsin Press.

Rogerson, H. L. (1951). Venerophobia in the male. *British Journal of Venereal Disease, 27,* 158–59.

Rohner, J. J., & Sanford, E. J. (1975). Imipramine toxicity. *Journal of Urology, 114,* 402–03.

Rooth, F. G., & Marks, I. M. (1974). Persistent exhibitionism: Short-term responses to aversion, self-regulation, and relaxation treatment. *Archives of Sexual Behavior, 3,* 227–48.

Roper, G., Rachman, S., & Marks, I. M. (1975). Passive and participant modelling in exposure treatment of obsessive compulsive neurotics. *Behavior Research and Therapy, 13,* 271–79.

Rosellini, R. A., Binik, Y. M., & Seligman, M. E. P. (1976). Sudden death in the laboratory rat. *Psychosomatic Medicine, 38,* 55–58.

Rosenberg, C. M. (1967). Personality and obsessional neurosis. *British Journal of Psychiatry, 133,* 471–77.

Rosenhan, D. L. (1969). Some origins of concern for others. In P. Mussen, J. Langer, & M. Covington (Eds.). *Trends and issues in developmental psychology* (pp. 132–153). New York: Holt, Rinehart & Winston.

Rosenhan, D. L. (1970). The natural socialization of altruistic social autonomy. In J. Macaulay & L. Berkowitz (Eds.), *Altruism and helping behavior* (pp. 251–68). New York: Academic Press.

Rosenhan, D. L. (1973). On being sane in insane places. *Science, 179,* 250–58.

Rosenhan, D. L. (1975). The contextual nature of psychiatric diagnosis. *Journal of Abnormal Psychology, 84,* 462–74.

Rosenhan, D. L. (1983). Psychological abnormality and law. In C. J. Scheirer & B. L. Hammonds (Eds.), *Psychology and the law.* (pp. 89–118). Washington, D.C.: American Psychological Association.

Rosenhan, D. L., Karylowski, J., Salovey, P., & Hargis, K. (1982). Emotion and altruism. In J. P. Rushton & R. M. Sorrentino (Eds.), *Altruism and helping behavior.* Hillsdale, N.J.: Erlbaum.

Rosenhan, D. L., Moore, B. S., & Underwood, W. (1974). Affect moderates altruism and self-gratification. *Journal of Personality and Social Psychology, 30,* 546–52.

Rosenman, R. H., Brand, R. J., Jenkins, C. D., Friedman, M., Straus, R., & Wurm, M. (1975). Coronary heart disease in the western collaborative group study: Final follow-up experience at 8½ years. *Journal of the American Medical Association, 233,* 872–77.

Rosenthal, D. (1970a). Genetic research in the schizophrenic syndrome. In R. Cancro (Ed.), *The schizophrenic reactions* (pp. 245–58). New York: Brunner/Mazel.

Rosenthal, D. (1970b). *Genetic theory and abnormal behavior.* New York: McGraw-Hill.

Rosenthal, D. (1971). *Genetics of psychopathology.* New York: McGraw-Hill.

Rosenthal, D. (1974). Issues in high risk studies of schizophrenia. In D. F. Ricks, A. Thomas, & M. Roff (Eds.), *Life history research in psychopathology* (Vol. 3) (pp. 25–41). Minneapolis: University of Minnesota Press.

Rosenthal, D. (1979). Was Thomas Wolfe a borderline? *Schizophrenia Bulletin, 5,* 87–94.

Rosenthal, D., Lawlor, W. G., Zahn, T. P., & Shakow, D. (1960). The relationship of some aspects of mental set to degree of schizophrenic disorganization. *Journal of Personality, 28,* 26–38.

Rosenthal, R. (1983). Assessing the statistical and social importance of the effects of psychotherapy. *Journal of Consulting and Clinical Psychology, 51,* 4–13.

Rosenthal, T. L., & Bandura, A. (1979). Psychological modeling: Theory and practice. In A. Bergin & S. Garfield (Eds.), *Handbook of psychotherapy and behavior change.* New York: Wiley.

Rosenzweig, S. P., & Forman, R. (1974). Patient and therapist variables affecting premature termination in group psychotherapy. *Psychotherapy: Theory, research and practice, 11,* 76–79.

Roskies, E., Spevack, M., Surkis, A., Cohen, C., & Gilman, S. (1978). Changing the coronary-prone (Type A) behavior pattern in a non-clinical population. *Journal of Behavioral Medicine, 1,* 201–16.

Rosman, B., Minuchin, S., Liebman, R., & Baker, Y. (1976). Input and outcome of family therapy in anorexia nervosa. In J. L. Claghorn (Ed.), *Successful therapy.* New York: Brunner/Mazel.

Ross, A. D. (1976). *Psychological aspects of learning disabilities.* New York: McGraw-Hill.

Ross, L. (1977). The intuitive psychologist and his shortcomings: Distortions in the attribution process. In L. Berkowitz (Ed.), *Advances in experimental social psychology* (Vol. 10). New York: Academic Press.

Ross, L., Greene, D., & House, P. (1977). The false consensus phenomenon: An attributional bias in self perception and social perception processes. *Journal of Experimental Social Psychology, 13,* 279–301.

Rothaus, P., Hanson, P. G., Cleveland, S. E., & Johnson, D. L.

(1963). Describing psychiatric hospitalization: A dilemma. *American Psychologist, 18*, 85–89.

Rothbaum, F., Weisz, J. R., & Snyder, S. S. (1982). Changing the world and changing the self: A two-process model of perceived control. *Journal of Personality and Social Psychology, 42*, 5–37.

Rothman, D. (1971). *The discovery of the asylum.* New York: Harper & Row.

Rotter, J. (1954). *Social learning and clinical psychology.* Englewood Cliffs, N.J.: Prentice-Hall.

Rotter, J. B. (1966). Generalized expectancies for internal versus external control of reinforcement. *Psychological Monographs, 80*(1).

Rotter, J. B., Chance, J. E., & Phares, E. J. (1972). *Applications of a social learning theory of personality.* New York: Holt, Rinehart & Winston.

Rowland, L. P. (1981a). Diseases of the motor unit: The motor neuron, peripheral nerve and muscle. In E. R. Kandel & J. H. Schwartz (Eds.), *Principles of neural science* (pp. 147–54). New York: Elsevier/North Holland.

Rowland, L. P. (1981b). Spinal cord III. In E. R. Kandel & J. H. Schwartz (Eds.), *Principles of neural science* (pp. 305–11). New York: Elsevier/North Holland.

Roy, E. A. (1982). Action and performance. In A. Ellis (Ed.), *Normality and pathology in cognitive function* (pp. 265–98). London: Academic Press.

Rozin, P. (1976). The psychobiological approach to human memory. In M. R. Rosenzweig & E. L. Bennett (Eds.), *Neural mechanisms of learning and memory* (pp. 3–46). Cambridge, Mass.: MIT Press.

Rozin, P. (1978). *Personal communication.* Based on data collected in the introductory course of psychology at the University of Pennsylvania.

Rozin, P., & Kalat, J. (1971). Specific hungers and poison avoidance as adaptive specializations of learning. *Psychological Review, 78*, 459–86.

Rush, H. A., Beck, A. T., Kovacs, M., & Hollon, S. (1977). Comparative efficacy of cognitive therapy and pharmacotherapy in the treatment of depressed outpatients. *Cognitive Research and Therapy, 1*, 17–37.

Ruskin, A., Beard, O. W., & Schaffer, R. L. (1948). "Last hypertension": Elevated arterial pressure in victims of the Texas City disaster. *American Journal of Medicine, 4*, 228.

Russell, M. (1977). Smoking problems: An overview. In M. Jarvik, J. Cullen, E. Gritz, T. Vogt, & L. West (Eds.), *Research on smoking behavior.* (NIDA Research Monograph No. 17). Rockville, Md.: National Institute on Drug Abuse.

Russell, W. R. (1959). *Brain, memory, learning: A neurologist's view.* Oxford, Eng.: Oxford University Press.

Rutter, M. (1968). Concepts of autism: A review of research. *Journal of Child Psychology and Psychiatry, 9*, 1–25.

Rutter, M. (1975). *Helping troubled children.* New York: Plenum.

Ryan, D. V., & Neale, J. M. (1973). Test-taking sets and the performance of schizophrenics on laboratory tasks. *Journal of Abnormal Psychology, 82*, 207–11.

Sackeim, H. A., Nordlie, J. W., & Gur R. C. (1979). A model of hysterical and hypnotic blindness: Cognitions, motivation and awareness. *Journal of Abnormal Psychology, 88*, 474–89.

Safer, D. J., & Allen, R. P. (1976). *Hyperactive children: Diagnosis and management.* Baltimore: University Park Press.

Sakai, T. (1967). Clinico-genetic study on obsessive compulsive neurosis. *Bulletin of Osaka Medical School,* Supplement XII, 323–31.

Salzman, L., & Thaler, F. (1981). Obsessive-compulsive disorders: A review of the literature. *American Journal of Psychiatry, 138*, 286–96.

Sandler, J., & Hazari, A. (1960). The "obsessional": On the psychological classification of obsessional character traits and symptoms. *British Journal of Medical Psychology, 33*, 113–22.

Sank, L. I. (1979). Community disasters: Primary prevention and treatment in a health maintenance organization. *American Psychologist, 34*, 334–38.

Sank, L. (1982, February). Personal communication.

Sappington, W. (1975). Psychometric correlates of defensive style in process and reactive schizophrenics. *Journal of Consulting & Clinical Psychology, 43*(2), 154–56.

Sarason, S. B. (1974). *The psychological sense of community: Prospects for a community psychology.* San Francisco: Jossey-Bass.

Sawrey, W. L., Conger, J. J., & Turrell, E. S. (1956). An experimental investigation of the role of psychological factors in the production of gastric ulcers in rats. *Journal of Comparative and Physiological Psychology, 49*, 457–61.

Sawrey, W. L., & Weiss, J. D. (1956). An experimental method of producing gastric ulcers. *Journal of Comparative and Physiological Psychology, 49*, 269.

Scarr, S. (1975). Genetics and the development of intelligence. In F. D. Horowitz (Ed.), *Child development research* (Vol. 4.) Chicago: University of Chicago Press.

Schachter, J. (1957). Pain, fear and anger in hypertensives and normotensives: A psychophysiologic study. *Psychosomatic Medicine, 19*, 17.

Schachter, S. (1971). Extraordinary facts about obese human beings and rats. *American Psychologist, 26*, 129–44.

Schachter, S. (1982). Recidivism and self-cure of smoking and obesity. *American Psychologist, 37*(4), 436–44.

Schachter, S., & Latane, B. T. (1964). Crime, cognition, and the autonomic nervous system. In D. Levine (Ed.), *Nebraska Symposium on Motivation.* Lincoln: University of Nebraska Press.

Schachter, S., & Rodin, J. (Eds.). (1974). *Obese humans and rats.* Washington, D.C.: Erlbaum.

Schachter, S., Silverstein, B., Kozlowski, L. T., Perlick, D., Herman, C. P., & Liebling, B. (1977). Studies of the interaction of psychological and pharmacological determinants of smoking. *Journal of Experimental Psychology General, 106*, 3–40.

Schachter, S., & Singer, J. E. (1962). Cognitive, social and physiological determinants of emotional state. *Psychological Review, 69*, 379–99.

Schaefer, H., & Martin, P. (1977). *Behavioral therapy* (2nd ed.). New York: McGraw-Hill.

Scheff, T. J. (1966). *Being mentally ill: A sociologicial theory.* Chicago: Aldine.

Scher, M. (1975). Verbal activity, sex counselor experience and success in counseling. *Journal of Counseling Psychology, 22*, 97–101.

Schildkraut, J. J. (1965). The catecholamine hypothesis of affective disorders: A review of supporting evidence. *American Journal of Psychiatry, 122*, 509–22.

Schildkraut, J. J., & Kety, S. S. (1967). Biogenic amines and emotion. *Science, 156*, 21–30.

Schlichting, U. U., Goldberg, S. R., Wuttke, W., & Hoffmeister, F. (1970). D-amphetamine self-administration by Rhesus monkeys with different self-administration histories. *Proceedings of the European Society for the Study of Drug Toxicity, 220*, 62–69.

Schmale, A., & Iker, H. (1966). The psychological setting of uterine cervical cancer. *Annals of the N.Y. Academy of Sciences, 125*, 807–13.

Schmauk, F. J. (1970). Punishment, arousal, and avoidance learning in sociopaths. *Journal of Abnormal Psychology, 76*, 443–53.

Schneider, R. A., & Zangori, V. N. (1951). Variations in clotting time, relative viscosity and other physiochemical properties of the blood accompanying physical and emotional stress in the normotensive and hypertensive subject. *Psychosomatic Medicine, 13,* 289–303.

Schreibman, L. (1975). Effects of within-stimulus and extra-stimulus prompting on discrimination learning in autistic children. *Journal of Applied Behavioral Analysis, 8,* 91–112.

Schreiker, F. R. (1974). *Sybil.* New York: Warner Books.

Schulsinger, F. (1972). Psychopathy, heredity and environment. *International Journal of Mental Health, 1,* 190–206.

Schulsinger, F. (1977). Psychopathy: Heredity and environment. In S. A. Mednick & K. O. Christiansen (Eds.), *Biosocial bases of criminal behavior.* New York: Gardner Press.

Schulterbrand, J. G., & Raven, A. (Eds.). (1977). *Depression in childhood: Diagnosis, treatment, and conceptual models.* New York: Raven Press.

Schuyler, D. (1974). The evaluation of the suicidal patient. In J. R. Novello (Ed.), *Practical handbook of psychiatry.* Springfield, Ill.: Charles C. Thomas.

Schuyler, D., & Katz, M. M. (1973). The depressive illnesses: A major public health problem. Washington, D.C.: U.S. Government Printing Office.

Schwab, J. J., Bialow, M., Holzer, C. E., Brown, J. M., & Stevenson, B. E. (1967). Socio-cultural aspects of depression in medical inpatients. *Archives of General Psychiatry, 17,* 533–43.

Schwartz, B. (1983). *Psychology of learning and behavior* (2nd ed.). New York: Norton.

Schwartz, G. E. (1973). Biofeedback as therapy. Some theoretical and practical issues. *American Psychologist, 29,* 633–73.

Schwartz, G. (1977). Psychosomatic disorders and biofeedback: A psychobiologic model of disregulation. In J. Maser & M. E. P. Seligman (Eds.), *Psychopathology: Experimental models.* San Francisco: Freeman.

Schwartz, G., & Weiss, S. M. (1977). What is behavioral medicine? *Psychosomatic Medicine, 39,* 377–81.

Schwartz, M. (1983). Personal communication.

Scotch, N. A. (1961). Blood pressure measurements of urban Zulu adults. *The American Heart Journal, 61,* 173.

Scovern, A. W., & Killman, P. R. (1980). Status of electroconvulsive therapy: Review of the outcome literature. *Psychological Bulletin, 87,* 260–303.

Scoville, W. B., & Milner, B. (1957). Loss of recent memory after bilateral hippocampal lesions. *Journal of Neurology, Neurosurgery and Psychiatry, 20,* 11–21.

Searles, H. F. (1959). The effort to drive the other person crazy! An element in the aetiology and psychotherapy of schizophrenia. *British Journal of Medical Psychology, 32,* 1–18.

Sears, R. R. (1936). Experimental studies of projection: I. Attribution of traits. *Journal of Social Psychology, 7,* 151–63.

Secunda, S., Katz, M. M., & Friedman, R. (1973). "The depressive disorders in 1973." National Institute of Mental Health. Washington, D.C.: U.S. Government Printing Office.

Seeman, P., Lee, T., Chau-Wong, M., & Wong, K. (1976). Antipsychotic drug doses and neuroleptic/dopamine receptors. *Nature, 261,* 717–19.

Segal, J. (1968). Finding the right therapy for you. *Cosmopolitan, 304,* 262–77.

Seligman, M. E. P. (1968). Chronic fear produced by unpredictable shock. *Journal of Comparative and Physiological Psychology, 66,* 402–11.

Seligman, M. E. P. (1970). On the generality of the laws of learning. *Psychological Review, 77,* 406–18.

Seligman, M. E. P. (1975). *Helplessness: On depression, development, and death.* San Francisco: Freeman.

Seligman, M. E. P. (1978). Comment and integration. *Journal of Abnormal Psychology, 87,* 165–79.

Seligman, M. E. P. (1980). Harris on selected misrepresentation:

The selected misrepresentation of Seligman. *American Psychologist, 35,* 214–15.

Seligman, M. E. P., Abramson, L. Y., Semmel, A., & von Baeyer, C. (1979). Depressive attributional style. *Journal of Abnormal Psychology, 88,* 242–47.

Seligman, M. E. P., & Binik, Y. M. (1977). The safety signal hypothesis. In H. Davis & H. Hurwitz (Eds.), *Pavlovian operant interactions.* Hillsdale, N.J.: Erlbaum.

Seligman, M. E. P., & Hager, J. (Eds.). (1972). *Biological boundaries of learning.* New York: Appleton-Century-Crofts.

Seligman, M. E. P., & Johnston, J. C. (1973). A cognitive theory of avoidance learning. In F. J. McGuigan, & D. B. Lumsden (Eds.), *Contemporary approaches to conditioning and learning.* Washington, D.C.: Winston.

Seligman, M. E. P., Klein, D. C., & Miller, W. R. (1976). Depression. In H. Leitenberg (Ed.), *Handbook of behavior therapy.* New York: Appleton-Century-Crofts.

Selye, H. (1956). *The stress of life.* New York: McGraw-Hill.

Selye, H. (1975). Confusion and controversy in the stress field. *Journal of Human Stress, 1,* 37–44.

Semans, J. H. (1956). Premature ejaculation: A new approach. *Southern Medical Journal, 49,* 353–58.

Senay, E. C., & Renault, P. F. (1972). Treatment methods for heroin addicts. In D. E. Smith, & G. R. Gay (Eds.), *It's so good, don't even try it once.* Englewood Cliffs, N.J.: Prentice-Hall.

Shaffer, D. (1976). Enuresis. In M. Rutter & L. Hersov (Eds.), *Child psychiatry: Modern approaches.* Oxford: Blackwell.

Shakow, D. (1962). Segment set. *Archives of General Psychiatry, 6,* 1–17.

Shakow, D. (1963). Psychological deficit in schizophrenia. *Behavioral Science, 8,* 275–305.

Shapiro, A. K., Struening, E., Shapiro, E., & Barten, H. (1976). Prognostic correlates of psychotherapy in psychiatric outpatients. *American Journal of Psychiatry, 133,* 802–808.

Shapiro, D. (1965). *Neurotic styles.* New York: Basic Books.

Shapiro, D. A., & Shapiro, D. (1982). Meta-analysis of comparative therapy outcome studies: A replication and refinement. *Psychological Bulletin, 92,* 581–604.

Shapiro, D. A., & Shapiro, D. (1983). Comparative therapy outcome research: Methodological implications of meta-analysis. *Journal of Consulting and Clinical Psychology, 51,* 42–53.

Shapiro, R. J. (1974). Therapist attitudes and premature termination in family and individual therapy. *Journal of Nervous and Mental Diseases, 159,* 101–107.

Shaw, B. F. (1977). Comparison of cognitive therapy and behavior therapy in the treatment of depression. *Journal of Consulting and Clinical Psychology, 45,* 543–51.

Shields, J. (1962). *Monozygotic twins brought up apart and brought up together.* Oxford: Oxford University Press.

Shneidman, E. (1976). Suicide among the gifted. In E. S. Shneidman (Ed.), *Suicidology: Contemporary developments.* New York: Grune & Stratton.

Silverman, J. (1964). The problem of attention in research and theory in schizophrenia. *Psychological Review, 71,* 352–79.

Silverman, L. H. (1976). Psychoanalytic theory: The reports of my death are greatly exaggerated. *American Psychologist, 31*(9), 621–37.

Silverstone, J. T., & Salkind, M. R. (1973). Controlled evaluation of intravenous drugs in the specific desensitization of phobias. *Canadian Psychiatric Association Journal, 18*(1), 848–50.

Simpson, D. D., Savage, L. J., & Sells, S. B. (1978). *Data book on drug treatment outcomes.* Fort Worth: Institute of Behavioral Research.

Skinner, B. F. (1971). *Beyond freedom and dignity.* New York: Knopf.

Sklar, L. S., & Anisman, H. (1979). Stress and coping factors influence tumor growth. *Science, 205,* 513–15.

Sloane, R. B., Cristol, A. H., Pepernik, M. C., & Staples, F. R. (1970). Role preparation and expectation of improvement in psychotherapy. *Journal of Nervous and Mental Diseases, 150,* 18–26.

Sloane, R. B., Staples, F. R., Cristol, A. H., Yorkston, N. J., & Whipple, K. (1975). *Psychoanalysis versus behavior therapy.* Cambridge: Harvard University Press.

Smith, J. C., Glass, G. V., & Miller, T. I. (1980). *The benefits of psychotherapy.* Baltimore: The Johns Hopkins Press.

Smith, M. L., & Glass, G. V. (1977). Meta-analysis of psychotherapy outcome studies. *American Psychologist, 32,* 752–60.

Smith, R. E., Sarason, I. G., & Sarason, B. R. (1982). *Psychology: The frontiers of behavior.* New York: Harper & Row.

Smith, R. J. (1978). *The psychopath in society.* New York: Academic Press.

Smith, W. M. (1977). The treatment of mild hypertension: Results of a 10-year intervention trial. *Circulation Research, 40* (Supplement 1), 98–105.

Smolen, R. C. (1978). Expectancies, mood and performance of depressed and nondepressed psychiatric inpatients on chance and skill tasks. *Journal of Abnormal Psychology, 87,* 91–101.

Snapper, K. J., & Ohms, J. S. (1977). *The status of children.* Washington, D.C.: U.S. Government Printing Office.

Snyder, S. H. (1974a). Catecholamines as mediators of drug effects in schizophrenia. In F. O. Schmitt & F. G. Worden (Eds.), *The neurosciences: Third study program.* Cambridge, Mass.: MIT Press.

Snyder, S. H. (1974b). *Madness and the brain.* New York: McGraw-Hill.

Snyder, S. H. (1977). Opiate receptors and internal opiates. *Scientific American, 236,* 44–56.

Snyder, S. H. (1981). Dopamine receptors, neuroleptics and schizophrenia. *American Journal of Psychiatry, 138,* 460–64.

Snyder, S. H., Banerjee, S. P., Yamamura, H. I., & Greenberg, D. (1974). Neurotransmitters and schizophrenia. *Science, 184,* 1243–53.

Sobell, M. B., & Sobell, L. C. (1975). The need for realism, relevance and operational assumptions in the study of substance dependence. In H. D. Cappell & H. E. Le Blanc (Eds.), *Biological and behavioral approaches to drug dependence.* Toronto: Dixon Research Foundation.

Sobell, M. B., & Sobell, L. C. (1976). Second-year treatment outcomes of alcoholics treated by individualized behavior therapy: Results. *Behavior Research and Therapy, 14,* 195–215.

Sobell, M. B., & Sobell, L. C. (1980). *Behavioral treatment of alcohol problems.* New York: Plenum.

Sokolow, M., Werdegar, D., Perloff, D. B., Cowan, R. M., & Bienenstuhl, H. (1970). Preliminary studies relating portably recorded blood pressure to daily life events in patients with essential hypertension. *Bibliotheca Psychiatrica, 144,* 164–89.

Solomon, R. L. (1977). An opponent process theory of acquired motivation: The affective dynamics of addiction. In J. Maser & M. Seligman (Eds.), *Psychopathology: Experimental models,* San Francisco: Freeman.

Solomon, R. L., & Corbit, J. D. (1973). An opponent process theory of motivation: II. Cigarette addiction. *Journal of Abnormal Psychology, 81,* 158–71.

Solomon, R. L., & Corbit, J. D. (1974). An opponent process theory of motivation. *Psychological Reviews, 81*(2), 119–45.

Solomon, R. L., Kamin, L. J., & Wynne, L. C. (1953). Traumatic avoidance learning: The outcomes of several extinction procedures with dogs. *Journal of Abnormal Social Psychology, 48,* 291–302.

Sontag, S. (1978). Disease as political metaphor. *New York Review of Books, 25,* 33.

Sperry, R. W. (1974). Lateral specialization in the surgically separated hemispheres. In F. O. Schmitt & F. G. Worden (Eds.),

The neurosciences: Third study program. Cambridge, Mass.: MIT Press.

Spielberger, C. D., Gorsuch, R. C., & Lushene, R. E. (1970). *Manual for the state-trait anxiety inventory.* Palo Alto, Calif.: Consulting Psychologists Press.

Spitz, R. A. (1946). Anaclitic depression. *The Psychoanalytic Study of the Child, 2,* 313–47.

Spitzer, R. L. (1975). On pseudoscience in science, logic in remission and psychiatric diagnosis: A critique of Rosenhan's "On being sane in insane places." *Journal of Abnormal Psychology, 84,* 442–52.

Spitzer, R. L., & Endicott, J. (1969). Diagno II: Further developments in a computer program for psychiatric diagnosis. *American Journal of Psychiatry, 125,* 12–21.

Spitzer, R. L., Endicott, J., Robins, E., Kuriansky, J., & Gurland, B. (1975). Preliminary report of the reliability of research diagnostic criteria applied to psychiatric case records. In A. Sudilofsky, B. Beer, & S. Gershon (Eds.), *Prediction in psychopharmacology.* New York: Raven Press.

Spitzer, R. L., & Fleiss, J. L. (1974). A reanalysis of the reliability of psychiatric diagnosis. *British Journal of Psychiatry, 125,* 341–47.

Spitzer, R. L., & Wilson, P. T. (1975). Nosology and the official psychiatric nomenclature. In A. Freedman & H. Kaplan (Eds.), *Comprehensive textbook of psychiatry.* New York: Williams & Wilkins.

Sprague, R. L., & Berger, B. D. (1980). Drug effects on learning performance: Relevance of animal research to pediatric psychopharmacology. In R. M. Knights & D. J. Bakker (Eds.), *Treatment of hyperactive and learning disabled children.* Baltimore: University Park Press.

Sprague, R., & Sleator, E. (1973). Effects of psychopharmacologic agents on learning disorders. *Pediatrics clinicians of North America, 20,* 719–35.

Squire, L. R. (1982). The neuropsychology of memory. *Annual Review of Neuroscience, 5,* 241–73.

Srole, L., Langner, T. S. Michael, S. T., Opler, M. K., & Rennie T. A. (1962). *Mental health in the metropolis: The midtown Manhattan study.* New York: McGraw-Hill.

Staats, A. W. (1978). *Child learning intelligence and personality* (rev. ed.) Kalamazoo, Mich.: Behaviordela.

Stampfl, T. G. (1967). Implosive therapy. In S. G. Armitage (Ed.), *Behavior modification techniques in the treatment of emotional disorders.* Battle Creek, Mich.: V.A. Publication.

Stampfl, T. G., & Levis, D. J. (1967). Essentials of implosive therapy: A learning-theory-based psychodynamic behavioral therapy. *Journal of Abnormal Psychology, 72,* 496–503.

Steadman, H. J. (1973). Follow-up on Baxstrom patients returned to hospitals for the criminally insane. *American Journal of Psychiatry, 3,* 317–19.

Steadman, H. J., & Keveles, G. (1972). The community adjustment and criminal activity of the Baxstrom patients: 1966–1970. *American Journal of Psychiatry, 129,* 304–10.

Steadman, H., & Keveles, C. (1978). The community adjustment and criminal activity of Baxstrom patients. *American Journal of Psychiatry, 135,* 1218–20.

Stein, L. (1968). Chemistry of reward and punishment. In D. Efron (Ed.), *Psychopharmacology: Review of progress, 1957–1967* (pp. 105–23). Washington, D.C.: U.S. Government Printing Office.

Stein, L. I., Test, M. A., & Marx, A. J.(1975). Alternative to the hospital: A controlled study. *American Journal of Psychiatry, 132,* 517–21.

Steinmark, W. W., & Borkevic, T. D. (1974). Active and placebo treatment effects on moderate insomnia under counter-demand and positive demand instructions. *Journal of Abnormal Psychology, 83,* 157–63.

Stinnett, J. (1978). Personal communication.

Stoller, R. J. (1969). Parental influences in male transsexualism. In R. Green & J. Money (Eds.), *Transsexualism and sex reassignment.* Baltimore: The Johns Hopkins Press.

Stone, A. A. (1975). *Mental health and law: A system in transition.* Rockville, Md.: National Institute of Mental Health, Center for Studies of Crime and Delinquency.

Storms, M. D. (1981). A theory of erotic orientation development. *Psychological Review, 88,* 340–53.

Strauss, M. E., Foureman, W. C., & Parwatikar, S. D. (1974). Schizophrenics' size estimations of thematic stimuli. *Journal of Abnormal Psychology, 83*(2), 117–23.

Strupp, H. H. (1963). The outcome problem in psychotherapy revisited. *Psychotherapy: Theory, Research and Practice, 1,* 1–13.

Strupp, H. H., & Bloxom, A. (1973). Preparing lower-class patients for group psychotherapy: Development and evaluation of a role induction film. *Journal of Consulting and Clinical Psychology, 41,* 373–84.

Strupp, H. H., Fox, R., & Lessler, K. (1969). *Patients view their psychotherapy.* Baltimore: The Johns Hopkins Press.

Strupp, H. H., Hadley, S. W., & Gomes-Schwartz, B. (1977). *Psychotherapy for better or worse: An analysis of the problem of negative effects.* New York: Jason Aronson.

Strupp, H. H., Wallach, M., & Wogan, M. (1964). Psychotherapy experience in retrospect: Questionnaire survey of former patients and their therapists. *Psychological Monographs, 78* (11, Whole No. 588).

Stuart, R. B. (1969). Operant-interpersonal treatment for marital discord. *Journal of Consulting and Clinical Psychology, 33,* 675–82.

Stuart, R. B. (1980). *Helping couples change: A social learning approach to marital therapy.* New York: Guilford Press.

Stunkard, A. J. (1972). New therapies for eating disorders. *Archives of General Psychiatry, 26,* 391–98.

Stunkard, A. J. (1976). Anorexia nervosa. In J. P. Sanford (Ed.), *The science and practice of clinical medicine* (pp. 361–63). New York: Grune & Stratton.

Stunkard, A. J. (1979). Behavioral medicine and beyond: The example of obesity. In O. F. Pomerleau & J. P. Brady (Eds.), *Behavioral medicine: Theory and practice* (pp. 279–98). Baltimore: Williams & Wilkins.

Stunkard, A. J., & Penick, S. B. (1979). Behavior modification and treatment of obesity. *Archives of General Psychiatry, 36,* 801–11.

Suarez, J. M., & Pittluck, A. T. (1976). Global amnesia: Organic and functional considerations. *Bulletin of the American Academy of Psychiatric Law, 3,* 17–24.

Suedfeld, P., Roy, C., & Landon, P. B. (1982). Restricted environmental stimulation therapy in the treatment of essential hypertension. *Behaviour Research and Therapy, 20,* 553–59.

Suinn, R., & Bloom, L. (1978). Anxiety management training for Pattern A behavior. *Journal of Behavioral Medicine, 1,* 25–35.

Summers, M. (1971). *Witchcraft and black magic.* New York: Grand River Books.

Swanson, D. W. (1968). Adult sexual abuse of children: The man and circumstances. *Diseases of the Nervous System, 29*(10), 677–83.

Swanson, W. C., & Breed, W. (1976). Black suicide in New Orleans. In E. S. Shneidman (Ed.), *Suicidology: Contemporary developments.* New York: Grune & Stratton.

Szasz, T. S. (1961). *The myth of mental illness.* New York: Dell.

Szasz, T. S. (1963). *Law, liberty and psychiatry: An inquiry into the social uses of mental health practices.* New York: Macmillan.

Szasz, T. S. (1970). *The manufacture of madness.* New York: Dell.

Szasz, T. S. (1974). The ethics of suicide. *Bulletin of Suicidology* (Vol. 9). Philadelphia: Charles Press.

Tagiuri, R., Bruner, J. S., & Blake, R. R. (1958). On the relation between feelings and the perception of feelings among members of small groups. In E. E. Maccoby, T. M. Newcomb, & E. L. Hartley (Eds.), *Readings in social psychology* (pp. 110–16). New York: Holt, Rinehart & Winston.

Talland, G. (1965). *Deranged memory.* New York: Academic Press.

Talovic, S. A., Mednick, S. A., Schulsinger, F., & Falloon, I. R. H. (1981). Schizophrenia in high-risk subjects: Prognostic maternal characteristics. *Journal of Abnormal Psychology, 89,* 501–04.

Taube, C. A. (1976). Readmissions to inpatient services of state and county hospitals 1972. Statistical note 110. (DHEW Publications No. ADM 76–308). Rockville, Md: National Institute of Mental Health.

Taubee, E. S., & Wright, H. W. (1971). A psychosocial behavioral model for therapeutic intervention. In C. D. Spielberger (Ed.), *Current topics in clinical and community psychology* (Vol. 3). New York: Academic Press.

Taylor, J. A. (1951). The relationship of anxiety to the conditioned eyelid responses. *Journal of Experimental Psychology, 41,* 81–92.

Taylor, J. A. (1953). A personality scale of manifest anxiety. *Journal of Abnormal and Social Psychology, 48,* 285–90.

Taylor, J. (Ed.). (1958). *Selected writings of John Hughlings Jackson.* New York: Basic Books.

Taylor, N. (1949). *Flight from reality.* New York: Duell, Sloan, & Pearce.

Taylor, W. S., & Martin M. F. (1944). Multiple personality. *Journal of Abnormal and Social Psychology, 39,* 281–300.

Teasdale, J. D., & Rezin, V. (1978). The effect of reducing frequency of negative thoughts on the mood of depressed patients: Test of a cognitive model of depression. *British Journal of Social and Clinical Psychology, 17,* 65–74.

Teitelbaum, P. (1957). Random and food directed activity in hyperphagic and normal rats. *Journal of Comparative and Physiological Psychology, 50,* 486–90.

Teitelbaum, P. (1967). *Physiological psychology.* Englewood Cliffs, N.J.: Prentice-Hall.

Teitelbaum, P. (1977). Levels of integration of the operant. In W. Honig & J. E. R. Staddon (Eds.), *Handbook of operant behavior.* Englewood Cliffs, N.J.: Prentice-Hall.

Temerlin, M. K. (1970). Diagnostic bias in community mental health. *Community Mental Health Journal, 6,* 110–17.

Terenius, L. (1978). Endogenous peptides and analgesia. *Annual Review of Pharmacology and Toxicology, 18,* 189–204.

Terry, R. D., & Davies, P. (1980). Dementia of the Alzheimer type. *Annual Review of Neuroscience, 3,* 77–95.

Teuber, H. L., & Powers, E. (1953). Evaluating therapy in a delinquency prevention program. *Psychiatric Treatment, 21,* 138–47.

Theodor, L. H., & Mandelcorn, M. S. (1978). Hysterical blindness: A case report and study using a modern psychophysical technique. *Journal of Abnormal Psychology, 82,* 552–53.

Theorell, T., & Rahe, R. H. (1971). Psychosocial factors in myocardial infarction. I. An inpatient study in Sweden. *Journal of Psychosomatic Research, 15,* 25–31.

Thigpen C. H., & Cleckley, H. (1954). A case of multiple personality. *Journal of Abnormal and Social Psychology, 49,* 135–51.

Thomas, K. (1971). *Religion and the decline of magic.* New York: Charles Scribner's Sons.

Tizard, J., & Venables, P. H. (1956). Reaction time responses by schizophrenics, mental defectives, and normal adults. *American Journal of Psychiatry, 112,* 803–07.

Tobias, L. L., & MacDonald, M. L. (1974). Withdrawal of maintenance drugs with long-term hospitalized schizophrenics: A critical review. *Psychological Bulletin, 81,* 107–25.

Tonks, C. M., Paykel, E. S., & Klerman, J. L. (1970). Clinical depressions among Negroes. *American Journal of Psychiatry, 127,* 329–35.

Torgersen, S., & Kringlen, E. (1971). Blood pressure and personality. A study of the relationship between intra pain differences and systolic blood pressure and personality in monozygatic twins. *The Journal of Psychosomatic Research, 15,* 183.

Torrey, E. F. (1983). *The roots of treason: Ezra Pound and the secret of St. Elizabeth's.* New York: McGraw-Hill.

Tourney, G. (1967). A history of therapeutic fashions in psychiatry, 1800–1966. *American Journal of Psychiatry, 124,* 784–96.

Trasler, G. (1973). Criminal behavior. In H. J. Eysenck (Ed.), *Handbook of abnormal psychology.* London: Pitman Medical.

Treffert, D. A. (1970). The epidemiology of infantile autism. *Archives of General Psychiatry, 22,* 431–38.

Trevor-Roper, H. (1970). *The European witch-craze of the sixteenth and seventeenth centuries.* New York: Harper & Row.

Truax, C. B., & Carkhuff, R. R. (1967). *Toward effective counseling and psychotherapy: Training and practice.* Chicago: Aldine.

Truax, C. B., & Mitchell, K. M. (1971). Research on certain therapist interpersonal skills in relation to process and outcome. In A. E. Bergin & S. L. Garfield (Eds.), *Handbook of psychotherapy and behavior change.* New York: Wiley.

Truax, C. B., Shapiro, J. G., & Wargo, D. G. (1968). Effects of alternate sessions and vicarious therapy pretraining on group psychotherapy. *International Journal of Group Psychotherapy, 18,* 186–98.

Tryon, W. W. (1976). Models of behavior disorder. *American Psychologist, 31,* 509–18.

Tuke, S. (1813). Description of the Retreat, an institution near York for insane persons of the Society of Friends. Cited in Foucault, M., *Madness and civilization: A history of insanity in the age of reason.* New York: Random House, 1965.

Turner, R. J., & Wagenfeld, M. O. (1967). Occupational mobility and schizophrenia. *American Sociological Review, 32,* 104–13.

Twain, M. (1884). *The adventures of Huckleberry Finn.* New York: Penguin, 1983.

Tyrer, P., Candy, J., & Kelly, D. (1973). A study of the clinical effects of phenelzine and placebo in the treatment of phobic anxiety. *Psychopharmacologin* (Berl.), *32,* 237–54.

Ullman, L. P., & Krasner, L. (1965). *Case studies in behavior modification.* New York: Holt, Rinehart & Winston.

Understedt, V. (1971). Stereotoxic mapping of the monoamine pathways in the rat brain. *Acta Psychiologica Scandinavica, 10,* 1–48.

Upham, Charles W. (1867). Salem witchcraft. Cited in A. Deutsch, *The mentally ill in America.* New York: Columbia University Press, 1949.

U.S. Department of Health and Human Services. (1980). *Angel dust in four American cities* (DHHS Publication ADM 81-1039). Washington, D.C.: U.S. Government Printing Office.

U.S. Department of Health and Human Services, National Institute on Drug Abuse. (1982). *Highlights from student drug use in America 1975–1981.* Washington, D.C.: U.S. Government Printing Office.

Vaillant, G. E. (1977). *Adaptation to life.* Boston: Little, Brown.

Valentine, C. W. (1930). The innate bases of fear. *Journal of Genetic Psychology, 37,* 394–419.

Valins, S., & Nisbett, R. E. (1976). Attribution processes in the development and treatment of emotional disorders. In J. T. Spence, R. C. Carson, & J. W. Thibaut (Eds.), *Behavioral approaches to therapy.* Morristown, N.J.: General Learning Press.

Van Buskirk, S. Review of anorexia nervosa. *Psychological Bulletin, 84,* 529–35.

VandenBos, G. R., & Karon, B. P. (1971). Pathogenesis: A new therapist personality dimension related to therapeutic effectiveness. *Journal of Personality Assessment, 35,* 252–60.

Van Praag, H., Korf, J., & Sheet, D. (1973). Cerebral monoamines and depression: An investigation with the probenecid technique. *Archives of General Psychiatry, 28,* 827–31.

Vaughn, C. E., & Leff, J. P. (1976). The influence of family and social factors on the course of psychiatric illness: A comparison of schizophrenic and depressive-neurotic patients. *British Journal of Psychiatry, 129,* 127–37.

Veith, I. (1965). *Hysteria: The history of a disease.* Chicago: University of Chicago Press.

Venables, P. (1964). Input dysfunction in schizophrenia. In B. A. Maher (Ed.), *Progress in experimental personality research.* New York: Academic Press.

Veterans' Administration Cooperative Study Group (1972). Effects of treatment on morbidity and hypertension. III. Influence of age, diastolic pressure and prior cardiovascular disease. *Circulation, 45,* 991–1004.

Victor, M., Adams, R. D., & Collins, G. H. (1971). *The Wernicke-Korsakoff syndrome. A clinical and pathological study of 245 patients, 82 with post-mortem examinations.* Philadelphia: Davis.

Videnbech, T. (1975). A study of genetic factors, childhood bereavement, and premorbid personality traits in patients with anancastic endogenous depression. *Acta Psychiatrica Scandinavica, 52,* 178–222.

Visintainer, M., Volpicelli, J. R., & Seligman, M. E. P. (1982). Tumor rejection in rats after inescapable or escapable shock. *Science, 216,* 437–39.

Vogel, G. W. (1975). A review of REM sleep deprivation. *Archives of General Psychiatry, 32,* 96–97.

Wagener, J. M., & Hartsough, D. M. (1974). Social competence as a process-reactive dimension with schizophrenics, alcoholics, and normals. *Journal of Abnormal Psychology, 83,* 112–16.

Walker, E., Hoppes, E., Emory, E., Mednick. S., & Schulsinger, F. (1981). Environmental factors related to schizophrenia in psychophysiologically high-risk males. *Journal of Abnormal Psychology, 90*(4), 313–20.

Wallerstein, J. S., & Kelly, J. B. (1980). California children of divorce. *Psychology Today, 13.*

Walinder, J. (1967). *Transsexualism.* Goteburg: Scandinavian University Books.

Ward, C. H., Beck, A. T., Mendelson, M., Mock, J. E., & Erbaugh, J. K. (1962). The psychiatric nomenclature: Reasons for diagnostic disagreement. *Archives of General Psychiatry, 7,* 198–205.

Warheit, G., Holzer, C., & Schwab, J. (1973). An analysis of social class and racial differences in depressive symptom etiology: The community study. *Journal of Health and Social Behavior, 4,* 921–99.

Warrington, E. K., & Weiskrantz, L. (1973). An analysis of short-term and long-term memory defects in man. In J. A. Deutsch (Eds.), *The physiological basis of memory* (pp. 365–96). New York: Academic Press.

Watkins, G. (1960). The incidence of chronic peptic ulcer sounded necropsy: The study of 20,000 examinations performed in Leeds in 1930 to 1949 and in England and Scotland in 1956. *Gut, 1,* 14.

Watson, J. B., & Rayner, R. (1920). Conditioned emotional reactions. *Journal of Experimental Psychology, 3,* 1–14.

Watson, C. G. (1973). Abstract thinking deficit and autism in process and reactive schizophrenics. *Journal of Abnormal Psychology, 82,* 399–403.

Watson, C. G., & Buranen, C. (1979). The frequency of conversion reaction. *Journal of Abnormal Psychology, 88,* 209–11.

Watson, L. S. (1973). *Child behavior modification: A manual for teachers, nurses, and parents.* New York: Pergamon.

Weinberg, M., & Williams, C. J. (1974). *Male homosexuals: Their problems and adaptations in three societies.* New York: Oxford University Press.

Weiner, B. (1972). *Theories of motivation: From mechanism to cognition.* Chicago: Rand McNally.

Weiner, B. (Ed.) (1974). *Achievement motivation and attribution theory.* Morristown, N.J.: General Learning Press.

Weiner, H. M. (1977). *Psychology and human disease.* New York: Elsevier.

Weiner, H., Failer, M., Reiser, M. F., & Mirsky, I. A. (1957). Ideology of duodenal ulcer. I. Rise in specific psychological characteristics to rate of gastric secretion (serum pepsinogen). *Psychosomatic Medicine, 19,* 1.

Weiner, I. (1969). Effectiveness of a suicide prevention program. *Mental Hygiene, 53,* 357.

Weiskrantz, L., Warrington, E. K., Sanders M.D., & Marshall, J. (1974). Visual capacity of the hemianopic field following a restricted occipital ablation. *Brain, 97,* 709–28.

Weisman, A. D. (1956). A study of the psychodynamics of duodenal ulcer exacerbations. *Psychosomatic Medicine, 18,* 2–42.

Weiss, J. M. (1968). Effects of predictable and unpredictable shock on the development of gastrointestinal lesion in rats. *Proceedings of the 76th Annual Convention of the American Psychological Association, 3,* 263–64.

Weiss, J. M. (1970). Somatic effects of predictable and unpredictable shock. *Psychosomatic Medicine, 32,* 397–409.

Weiss, J. M. (1971). Effects of coping behavior in different warning signaled conditions on stress pathology in rats. *Journal of Comparative and Physiological Psychology, 77,* 1–13.

Weiss, J. M., Glazer, H. I., & Pohoresky, L. A. (1976). Coping behavior and neurochemical change in rats: An alternative explanation for the original "learned helplessness" experiments. In G. Serban & A. King (Eds.), *Animal models in human psychobiology.* New York: Plenum.

Weiss, J. M., Pohoresky, L. A., Salman, S., & Gruenthal, M. (1976). Attenuation of gastric lesions by psychological aspects of aggression in rats. *Journal of Comparative Physiological Psychology, 90,* 252–59.

Weiss, J. et al. (1981). Behavioral depression produced by an uncontrollable stressor: Relationship to norepinephrine, dopamine, and serotonin levels in various regions of the rat brain. *Brain Research Reviews, 3,* 167–205.

Weissman, M., & Myers, J. K. (1978). Affective disorders in US urban community. *Archives of General Psychiatry, 35,* 1304–11.

Weissman, M. M., & Paykel, E. S. (1974). *The depressed woman: A study of social relationships.* Evanston: University of Chicago Press.

Welgan, P. R. (1974). Learned control of gastric acid secretions in ulcer patients. *Psychosomatic Medicine, 5,* 411–19.

Werner, E. E., Bierman, J. M., & French, F. E. (1971). *The children of Kauai.* Honolulu: University of Hawaii Press.

Werner, E. E., & Smith, R. S. (1977). *Kauai's children come of age.* Honolulu:University of Hawaii Press.

Wertheimer, M. (1978). Humanistic psychology and the humane and tough-minded psychologist. *American Psychologist, 33,* 631–47.

Wesson, D. R., & Smith, D. E. (1971, December). *Barbiturate use as an intoxicant.* Presented to the Subcommittee to Investigate Juvenile Delinquency of the U.S. Senate Committee on the Judiciary on Drug Abuse.

West, D. J. (1976). Delinquency. In M. Rutter & L. Hersov (Eds.), *Child psychiatry: Modern approaches.* Oxford: Blackwell.

Whalen, C. K., & Henker, B. (1976). Psychostimulants and children: A review and analysis. *Psychological Bulletin, 83,* 1113–30.

White, R. W. (1959). Motivation reconsidered: The concept of competence. *Psychological Review, 66,* 297–333.

White, R. W. (1963). Ego and reality in psychoanalytic theory: A proposal regarding independent ego energies. *Psychological Issues, 3,* 1–210.

Whiting, B. B., & Whiting, J. W. (1974). *Children of six cultures: A psycho-cultural analysis.* Cambridge, Mass.: Harvard University Press.

Wilkins, M. A. (1971). Comparisons of attitudes toward childrearing of parents of certain exceptional and normal children. *Dissertation Abstracts International, 31* (11-A), 5894.

Wilkins, W. (1979). Expectancies in therapy research: Discriminating among heterogeneous nonspecifics. *Journal of Consulting and Clinical Psychology, 47,* 837–45.

Williams, P., & Smith, M. (1980). Interview in "The First Question." London: British Broadcasting System, Sciences and Features Department Film, 1979. Cited in Diamond, M., & Karlen, A. (Eds.), *Sexual decisions.* Boston: Little, Brown.

Willis, M. H., & Blaney, P. H. (1978). Three tests of the learned helplessness model of depression. *Journal of Abnormal Psychology, 87,* 131–36.

Willner, A. G., Brankman, C. J., Kirigan, K. A., & Wolf, M. M. (1978). Achievement Place: A community treatment model for youths in trouble. In D. Marholin (Ed.), *Child behavior therapy.* New York: Gardner Press.

Wilner, A., Reich, T., Robins, I., Fishman, R., & van Doren, T. (1976). Obsessive-compulsive neurosis. *Comprehensive Psychiatry, 17,* 527–39.

Wilson, G. T., & Rachman, S. J. (1983). Meta-analysis and the evaluation of psychotherapy outcome: Limitations and liabilities. *Journal of Consulting and Clinical Psychology, 51,* 54–64.

Wing, J. K., & Hailey, A. M. (Eds.). (1972). *Evaluating a community psychiatric service.* London: Oxford University Press.

Wing, L. (1976). *Diagnosis, clinical description and prognosis.* Oxford: Pergamon.

Winick, M. (1975). *Childhood obesity.* New York: Wiley.

Winkelstein, W., Kantor, S., Ibrahim, M., & Sackett, D. L. (1966). Familial aggregation of blood pressure: Preliminary report. *Journal of the American Medical Association, 195,* 848–50.

Winokur, G. (1972). Family history studies VIII: Secondary depression is alive and well and . . . . *Diseases of the Nervous System, 33,* 94–99.

Winokur, G., & Clayton, P. (1967). Family history studies: I. Two types of affective disorders separated according to genetic and clinical factors. In J. Wartus (Ed.), *Recent advances in biological psychiatry* (Vol. 9). New York: Plenum.

Winokur, G., & Tanna, V. L. (1969). Possible role of X-link dominant factor in manic-depressive disease. *Diseases of the Nervous System, 30,* 89.

Witkin, H. A., Mednick. S. A., Schulsinger, F., Bakkestrom, E., Christiansen, K. O., Goodenough, D. R., Hirschhorn, K., Lundsteen, C., Owen, D. R., Philip, J., Rubin, D. B., & Stocking, M. (1976). Criminality in XYY and XXY men: The elevated crime rate of XYY males is not related to aggression. *Science, 193,* 547–55.

Witkin, M. J. (1981). Provisional patient movement and selective administrative data, state and county mental hospitals, by state: United States, 1977. Mental Health Statistical Note No. 156. United States Department of Health and Human Services, Public Health Service, Alcohol, Drug Abuse and Mental Health Administration, National Institute of Mental Health.

Wittgenstein, L. (1953). *Philosophical investigations.* New York: Macmillan.

Wolf, M. M., Phillips, E. L., & Fixsen, D.C. (1975). *Achievement Place, phase II: Final report.* Kansas: Department of Human Development, University of Kansas.

Wolf, S. W. (1965). *The stomach.* New York: Oxford University Press.

Wolf, S., Cardon, P. V., Shepard, E. M., & Wolff, H. G. (1955). *Life stress and essential hypertension.* Baltimore: Williams & Wilkins.

Wolf, S., & Wolff, H. G. (1947). *Human gastric function.* New York: Oxford University Press.

Wollheim, R. (1974). *Freud: A collection of critical essays.* Garden City, N.Y.: Anchor/Doubleday.

Wolpe, J. (1958). *Psychotherapy by reciprocal inhibition.* Stanford: Stanford University Press.

Wolpe, J. (1969). Basic principles and practices of behavior therapy of neuroses. *American Journal of Psychiatry, 125*(5), 1242–47.

Wolpe, J. (1971). Neurotic depression: Experimental analogue, clinical syndromes and treatment. *American Journal of Psychotherapy, 25,* 362–68.

Wolpe, J., & Lazarus, A. A. (1969). *The practice of behavior therapy.* New York: Pergamon.

Wolpe, J., & Rachman, S. (1960). Psychoanalytic "evidence": A critique based on Freud's case of Little Hans. *Journal of Nervous and Mental Disease, 131,* 135–47.

Wolraich, M., Drummond, T., Salomon, M. K., O'Brien, M. L., & Sivage, C. (1978). Effects of methylphenidate alone and in combination with behavior modification procedures on the behavior and academic performance of hyperactive children. *Journal of Abnormal Child Psychology, 6,* 149–61.

Woodruff, R. A., Clayton, P. J., & Guze, S. B. (1971). Hysteria: Studies of diagnosis, outcome and prevalence. *Journal of the American Medical Association, 215,* 425–28.

Woodruff, R. A., Goodwin, D. W., & Guze, S. B. (1974). *Psychiatric diagnosis.* New York: Oxford University Press.

Woodward, B., & Armstrong, A. (1979). *The brethren: Inside the Supreme Court.* New York: Simon & Schuster.

Wynne, L. C. (1970). Communication disorders and the quest for relatedness in families of schizophrenics. *American Journal of Psychoanalysis, 30,* 100–14.

Wynne, L. C. (1972). *Psychotherapy of schizophrenia.* Amsterdam: Excerpta Medica Foundation.

Wynne, L. C., Rykoff, I. M., Day, J., & Hirsch, S. I. (1958). Pseudo mutuality in the family relations of schizophrenics. *Psychiatry, 21,* 205–20.

Wynne, L. C. Singer, M. T., Bartko, J. J., & Toohey, M. L. (1977). Schizophrenics and their families: Recent research on parental communication. In J. M. Tanner (Ed.), *Developments in psychiatric research.* London: Hodder & Stoughton.

Yalom, I. D. (1975). *The theory and practice of group psychotherapy.* New York: Basic Books.

Yalom, I. D. (1980). *Existential psychotherapy.* New York: Basic Books.

Yalom, I. D., Houts, P. S., Newell, G., & Rand, K. H. (1967). Preparation of patients for group therapy. *Archives of General Psychiatry, 17,* 416–27.

Yates, A. (1966). *Theory and practice in behavior therapy* (2nd ed.). New York: Wiley.

Youkilis, H. D., & DeWolfe, A. S. (1975). The regression hypothesis and scales classification in schizophrenia. *Journal of Abnormal Psychology, 84,* 36–40.

Yule, W. (1973). Differential prognosis of reading backwardness and specific reading retardation. *British Journal of Educational Psychology, 43,* 244–48.

Yule, W. (1978). Behavioural treatment of children and adolescents with conduct disorders. In L. Hersov, M. Berger, & D. Shaffer (Eds.), *Aggression and anti-social behaviour in childhood and adolescence.* Oxford: Pergamon.

Yule, W. (1980). The epidemiology of child psychopathology. In B. B. Lahey & A. E. Kazdin (Eds.), *Advances in child clinical psychology* (Vol. 4) (pp. 1–51). New York: Plenum.

Yule, W., Hersov, L., & Treseder, J. (1980). Behavioral treatments of school refusal. In L. Hersov & I. Berg (Eds.), *Out of school: Modern perspectives in truancy and school refusal.* New York: Wiley.

Yule, W., & Rutter, M. (1976). Epidemiology and social implication of specific reading retardation. In R. M. Knights & D. J. Bakker (Eds.), *The neuropsychology of learning disorders.* Baltimore: University Park Press.

Zahn, T. P., & Rosenthal, D. (1965). Preparatory set in acute schizophrenia. *Journal of Nervous and Mental Disease, 141,* 352–58.

Zangwill, O. L. (1966). The amnesic syndrome. In C. W. M. Whitty & O. L. Zangwill (Eds.), *Amnesia.* London: Butterworth.

Zax, M., & Cowen, E. L. (1969). Research on early detection and prevention of emotional dysfunction in young school children. In C. D. Spielberger (Ed.), *Current topics in clinical and community psychology* (Vol. 1) (pp. 67–108). New York: Academic Press.

Ziegler, F. J., & Imboden, J. B. (1962). Contemporary conversion reactions: II. A conceptual model. *Archives of General Psychiatry, 6,* 279–87.

Ziegler, F. J., Imboden, J. B., & Meyer, E. (1960). Contemporary conversion reactions: A clinical study. *American Journal of Psychiatry, 116,* 901–10.

Ziegler, D. K., & Paul, N. (1954). Hysteria. *Diseases of the Nervous System, 15,* 30.

Zigler, E., & Levine, J. (1981). Age on first hospitalization of schizophrenics: A developmental approach. *Journal of Abnormal Psychology, 90,* 458–67.

Zigler, E., & Phillips, L. (1961). Psychiatric diagnosis and symptomatology. *Journal of Abnormal and Social Psychology, 63,* 69–75.

Zilbergeld, B., & Evans, M. (1980). The inadequacy of Masters and Johnson. *Psychology Today, 14,* 28–43.

Zilboorg, G., & Henry, G. W. (1941). *A history of medical psychology.* New York: Norton.

Zimbardo, P. G. (1977). Shy murderers. *Psychology Today, 148,* 66–76.

Zimbardo, P. G., Andersen, S. M., & Kabat, L. G. (1981). Induced hearing deficit generates experimental paranoia. *Science, 212,* 1529–31.

Zitrin, C. M., Klein, D. F., & Woerner, M. G. (1978). Behavior therapy, supportive psychotherapy, imipramine and phobine. *Archives of General Psychiatry.*

Zitrin, C. M., Klein, D. F., Woerner, M. G., & Ross, D.C. (1983). Treatment of phobias I. Comparison of imipramine hydrochloride and placebo. *Archives of General Psychiatry, 40,* 125–38.

Zubin, J., Eron, L. D., & Schumer, F. (1965). *An experimental approach to projective techniques.* New York: Wiley.

Zubin, J. E., & Spring, B. (1977). Vulnerability: A new view of schizophrenia. *Journal of Abnormal Psychology, 86,* 103–26.

Zuckerman, M., & Lubin, B. (1965). *Manual for the Multiple Affect Adjective Check List.* San Diego, Calif.: Educational and Industrial Testing Service.

Name Index

Subject Index

Acknowledgments

Excerpts

Page 29: From Galen, cited in Veith, I., *Hysteria: The history of a disease.* Chicago: University of Chicago Press, 1963, p. 36. Copyright 1963 by the University of Chicago Press. Reprinted by permission. *Page 33:* From Zilboorg, G., & Henry, G. W., *A history of medical psychology.* New York: W. W. Norton and Company, Inc., 1941. Copyright © 1941 by W. W. Norton and Company. Reprinted by permission. *Page 37:* From Morton, 1897, cited in A. Deutsch, *The mentally ill in America: The history of the care and treatment in colonial times,* 1937. Courtesy of the National Mental Health Association. *Page 41:* From Beck, T. R., 1811, cited in A. Deutsch, *The mentally ill in America: The history of the care and treatment in colonial times,* 1937. Courtesy of the National Mental Health Association. *Pages 109–10:* From Ellis, A., *Reason and emotion in psychotherapy.* Copyright © 1962 by Institute for Rational Living. Published by arrangement with Lyle Stuart. *Pages 136–37:* Personal communication from Dr. James Stinnett, 1977, Hospital of the University of Pennsylvania. *Pages 205–6:* From Laughlin, H. P., *The neuroses,* Woburn: Butterworth Publishers, 1967. Excerpted by permission of the publisher. *Page 227:* From Sank, L. I., Psychology in action: Community disasters. Primary prevention and treatment in a health maintenance organization. *American Psychologist.* Copyright © 1979 by the American Psychological Association. Reprinted by permission of the author. *Page 249:* Personal Communication from Dr. James Stinnett, 1978, Hospital of the University of Pennsylvania. *Pages 261–63:* From Davis, P. H., & Osherson, A., The current treatment of a multiple-personality woman and her son. *American Journal of Psychotherapy.* Copyright 1977, *31,* 304–515. Reprinted by permission of the Association for the Advancement of Psychotherapy. *Page 271:* From Moody, R. L., Bodily changes during abreaction. *The Lancet,* 1946, *2,* 934–35. *Page 327:* From Fancher, R., *Psychoanalytic psychology: The development of Freud's thought.* New York: W. W. Norton & Company, Inc., 1973. Copyright © 1973, by W. W. Norton & Company. Reprinted by permission. *Pages 335–36:* From Beck, A. T., Rush, A. J., Shaw, B. F., & Emery, G., *Cognitive therapy of depression.* New York: Guilford Press, 1979. Reprinted by permission. *Page 391:* From Pauly, I. B., Adult manifestation of male transsexualism. In R. Green & J. Money (Eds.), *Transsexualism and sex reassignment.* Baltimore: The Johns Hopkins University Press. Copyright © 1969, by Johns Hopkins University Press. Reprinted by permission. *Pages 417 and 418:* From Frosch, W. A., Robbins, E. S., & Stearn, M., Untoward reactions to lysergic acid diethylamide (LSD) resulting in hospitalization. *New England Journal of Medicine,* 1965, *273,* 1235–39. Excerpted by permission of the New England Journal of Medicine. *Page 427:* Ray, O., From *Drugs, society, and human behavior,* 3rd ed. St. Louis. C. V. Mosby Co., 1983. *Pages 576 and 577:* From Milner, B., Memory and the medial temporal regions of the brain. In K. H. Pribram & D. E. Broadbent (Eds.), *Biology of memory.* New York: Academic Press, 1970. Reprinted by permission. *Page 617:* Fireside, H., *Soviet psychoprisons.* New York: W. W. Norton and Company, Inc. Copyright © 1979 by W. W. Norton and Company, Inc. Reprinted by permission.

Figures

Figure 5–1: Schwartz, B., *Psychology of learning and behavior,* 2nd ed. New York: W. W. Norton and Company Inc., 1983. Copyright © 1983 by W. W. Norton and Company, Inc. Reprinted by permission. *Figure 5–2:* Blanchard, E. B., & Epstein, L. H., *A biofeedback primer.* Copyright 1978, Addison-Wesley Publishing Inc. Reading, Mass. Reprinted by permission. *Figure 7–1:* Data for the diagram based on hierarchy of needs in "A Theory of Human Motivation" in A. H. Maslow, *Motivation and personality,* 2nd ed. Copyright © 1970 by Abraham H. Maslow. Reprinted by permission of Harper and Row; Publishers, Inc. *Figure 8–2:* Hall, R. V., Fox, R., Williard, D. Goldsmith, L., Emerson, M., Owen, M., Davis, T., & Porcia, E., The teacher as observer and experimenter in the modification of disputing and talking-out behaviors. *Journal of Applied Behavior Analysis,* 1971, *4,* 143. Reprinted by permission by the society for Experimental Analysis of Behavior Inc. *Figure 9–2:* Specimen of the Minnesota Report. Interpretive Scoring Systems, A Division of National Computer Systems, Inc. *Figure 9–3:* Gleitman, H. *Psychology.* New York: W. W. Norton and Company, Inc., 1981. Copyright © 1981 by W. W. Norton and Company, Inc. Reprinted by permission. *Figure 9–4:* Gleitman, H., *Psychology.* New York: W. W. Norton and Company, 1981. Copyright © by W. W. Norton and Company, Inc. Reprinted by permission. *Figure 9–5:* Reprinted from *Insight vs. densensitization in psychotherapy* by Gordon L. Paul with the permission of the publishers, Stanford University Press. © 1966 by the Board of Trustees of the Leland Stanford Junior University. *Figure 10–1:* Ekman, P., & Friesen, W. *Unmasking the face.* Englewood-Cliffs, N.J.: Prentice-Hall, 1975. Reprinted by permission of the author. *Figure 10–3:* Archibald, H. C., & Tuddenham, R. D., Persistent stress reaction after combat. *Archives of General Psychiatry,* 1965, *12,* 475–81. Copyright 1965, American Medical Association. Reprinted by permission. *Figure 12–1:* Moody, R. L., Bodily changes during abreaction. *The Lancet,* 1946, *2,* 934–35. Reprinted by permission. *Figure 12–2:* Oi, M., Oshida K., & Sugimura, A., The location of gastric ulcer. *Gastroenterology,* 1959, *36,* 45–46. Copyright © 1959 The Williams and Wilkins Co. Reprinted by permission. *Figure 12–4:* Selye, H. *The stress of life.* New York: McGraw-Hill, 1956. *Figure 13–3:* Maier, S. F., Seligman, M. E. P., & Solomon, R. L., Pavlovian fear conditioning and learned helplessness: Effects on escape and avoidance behavior of (a) the CS-US contingency and (b) the independence of the US and voluntary responding. *Punishment and Aversive Behavior.* Edited by Campbell and Church, © 1969, p. 328. Reprinted by permission of Prentice-Hall, Inc., Englewood Cliffs, N.J. *Figure 13–4:* Jerome, J., Catching them before suicide. *The New York Times Magazine,* January 11, 1979, Copyright © 1979 by the New York Times Company. Reprinted by permission. *Figure 14–1:* Money, J., & Ehrhardt, A. A. *Man and woman, boy and girl.* Baltimore: The Johns Hopkins University Press, 1972. Reprinted by permission of Johns Hopkins University Press and the authors. *Figure 15–1:* Kaiko, R. F. et al., Analgesic and mood effects of heroin and morphine in cancer patients with postoperative pain. *New England Journal of Medicine, 304,* 1501. Copyright 1981 New England Journal of Medicine. Reprinted by permission. *Figure 17–1:* Rodnick, E., & Shakow, D., Set in the schizophrenic as measured by a composite reaction time index. *American Journal of Psychiatry,* 1940, *97,* 214–25. *Figure 17–3:* Faris, R. E. L., & Dunham, H. W., Mental disorders in urban areas. Chicago: University of Chicago Press, 1937. Reprinted by permission of the authors. *Figure 17–4.* Keith, S. J., Gunderson, J. G., Reifman, A., Buschbaum, S., & Mosher, L. R., Special report: Schizophrenia, 1976. *Schizophrenia Bulletin,* 1976, *2,* 510–65. Reprinted by permission of the National Institute of Mental Health. *Figure 17–5:* Vaughn, C. E., & Leff, J. P., The influence of family and social factors on the course of psychiatric illness: A comparison of schizophrenic and depressive-neurotic patients. *British Journal of Psychiatry,* 1976, *129,* 127–37. *Figure 19–1:* Keeton, W. T., *Biological science,* 3rd ed. New York: W. W. Norton and Company, 1980. Copyright © 1980, 1979, 1972, 1967 by W. W. Norton and Company Inc. *Figure 19–2:* Hecaen, M., & Albert, M. L., *Human neuropsychology.* New York: John Wiley and Sons, Inc. Copyright © 1978 by John Wiley and Sons, Inc. *Figure 19–3A:* Katz, B., The nerve impulse, *Scientific American,* November 1952, *187,* 164–65. Copyright © 1952 by Scientific Ameican Inc. All rights reserved. *Figure 19–3B:* From *Fundamentals of neurology: A psychophysiological approach,* 6th ed., by Ernest Gardner, M. D. Copyright © 1975 by W. B. Saunders Company. Reprinted by permission of Holt, Rinehart and Winston, CBS College Publishing. *Figure 19–5:* Levy, J. Lateral specialization of the human brain. Behavioral Manifestations and Possible Evolutionary Basis, p. 163. In J. A. Kriger, Jr. (Ed.), *The biology of behavior.* Corvallis, Oregon: Oregon State University Press, 1972. Copyright © 1972 by Oregon State University Press. Reprinted by permission. *Figure 19–6:* Gazzaniga, M. *The bisected brain,* New York: Plenum Publishing Corporation, 1970, p. 47. Copyright © 1970 by Plenum Publishing Corporation. Reprinted by permission. *Figure 19–7:* From *Fundamentals of neurology: A psychophysiological approach,* 6th ed., by Ernest Gardner, M.D. Copyright © 1975 by W. B. Saunders Company. Reprinted by permission of Holt, Rinehart and Winston, CBS College Publishing. *Figure 19–9:* Modified from Geschwind, N., The apraxias: Neural mechanisms of disorders of learned movement. *American Scientist,* 1975, *188,* 189. Reprinted by permission. *Figure 19–10:* Modified from *Fundamentals of neurology: A psychophysiological approach,* 6th ed., by Ernest Gardner, M.D. Copyright © 1975 by W. B. Saunders Company. Reprinted by permission of Holt, Rinehart, and Winston, CBS College Publishing. *Figure 19–11:* Modified from Gray, H., *Anatomy of the human body,* 29th ed. Edited by C. M. Goss. Philadelphia: Lea and Febiger. Copyright © 1973 by Lea and Febiger Publisher. Reprinted by permission. *Figure 19–12:* Luria, A., The functional organization of the brain. *Scientific American,* 1970, *222,* 66–78. Copyright © 1970 by Scientific American Inc. Reprinted by permission. All rights reserved. *Figure 19–13:* Blessed, G., Tomlinsun, B. E., & Roth, M. The association between quantitative measures of dementia and of senile change in the cerebral gray matter of elderly subjects. *British Journal of Psychiatry,* 1968, *114,* 797–811. *Figure 19–14A:* Ghuhbegovic, N., & Williams, T. H., *The human brain: A photographic guide.* Hagerstown, Md.: Lippincott/Harper and Row. Copyright © 1980 by Lippincott/Harper and Row. Reprinted by permission. *Figure 19–14B:* Victor, M., Adams R. D., & Collins, G. H. The Wernicke-Korsakoff syndrome. A clinical and pathological study of 245 patients, 82 with post-mortem examinations. Philadelphia: F. A. Davis Company. Copyright © F. A. Davis Company. Reprinted by permission.

Tables

Table 4–1: Valliant, G. E., *Adaptation to life.* Boston: Little, Brown, 1977, p. 88. *Table 6–1:* Abramson, L. T., Seligman, M. E. P., & Teasdale, J., Learned helplessness in humans: Critique and reformulation. *Journal of Abnormal Psychology,* 1978, *87,* 32–48. Copyright © 1978 by the American Psychological Association. Reprinted by permission of the author. *Table 6–2:* Lazarus, A. A., *Multimodal behavior therapy.* New York: Springer, 1976. *Table 9–1:* Butcher, J. N., *MMPI: Research developments and clinical applications.* Copyright © 1969. Used with permission of McGraw-Hill Book Company. *Table 9–2:* Zigler, E., & Phillips, L. Psychiatric diagnosis and symptomatology. *Journal of Abnormal Psychology,* 1961, *63,* 69–75. Copyright © 1961 by the American Psychological Association. Reprinted by permission of the author. *Table 9–3:* Temerlin, M. K., Diagnostic bias in community mental health. *Community Mental Health Journal,* 1970, *6,* 110–17. Copyright © 1970 by the Human Sciences Press, Inc. *Table 10–6:* Sank, L. I. Psychology in action: Community disasters. Primary prevention and treatment in a health maintenance organization. *American Psychologist,* copyright © 1979 by the American Psychological Association. Reprinted by permission of the author. *Table 11–1:* Rachman, S. J., & Hodgson, R. J. *Obsessions and compulsions.* © 1980, pp. 406–7. Adapted by permission of Prentice-Hall Inc., Englewood Cliffs, N.J. *Table 11–2:* Hyler, S. E., & Spitzer, R. T. Hysteria split asunder. *American Journal of Psychiatry,* 1978, *135* (12), 1500–4. Copyright, 1978, the American Psychiatric Association. Reprinted by permission. *Table 12–1:* Weiss, J. M. Effects of coping behavior in different warning signaled conditions on stress pathology in rats. *Journal of Comparative and Physiological Psychology,* 1971, *77,* 1–13. Copyright © 1971 by the American Psychological Association. Reprinted by permission of the author. *Table 12–2:* Reprinted by permission of the publisher from Grace, W. J., & Graham, D. T., Relationship of specific attitudes and emotions to certain bodily disease. *Psychosomatic Medicine, 14,* 243–51. Copyright 1952 by the American Psychosomatic Society, Inc. *Table 12–3:* Holmes, T. H., & Rahe, R. H., The Social Readjustment Ratings Scale. Reprinted with permission from the *Journal of Psychosomatic Research, 11.* Copyright 1967, Pergamon Press, Ltd. *Table 13–2:* Shneidman, E. Suicide among the gifted. In E. S. Shneidman (Ed.), *Suicidology: Contemporary developments.* New York: Grune & Stratton, 1976. Reprinted by permission of Grune & Stratton, Inc., and Edwin Shneidman. *Tables 15–3 and 15–4:* Ray, O., *Drugs, society, and human behavior,* 3rd. ed. St. Louis: C. V. Mosby Co., 1983. *Table 16–1:* Hutchings, B., & Mednick, S. A. Criminality in adoptees and their adoptive and biological parents: A pilot study. In S. A. Mednick & K. O. Christiansen (Eds.), *Biosocial bases of criminal behavior.* New York: Gardner Press, 1977. *Table 17–1:* The American Psychiatric Association, *Diagnostic and Statistical Manual of Mental Disorders,* 3rd ed., Washington, D.C.: American Psychiatric Association, 1980. Reprinted by permission. *Table 17–2.* Mintz, S., & Alpert, M., Imagery, vividness, reality testing, and schizophrenic hallucinations. *Journal of Abnormal Psychology*, 1972, *79*, 310–16. Copyright © 1972 by the American Psychological Association. Reprinted by permission of the author. *Table 17–3:* Adapted and modified from Rosenthal, D., *Genetic theory and abnormal behavior.* New York: McGraw-Hill, 1970. *Table 17–4:* Adapted from Rosenthal, D. *Genetics of psychopathology.* New York: McGraw-Hill. Copyright 1971 by McGraw-Hill. Reprinted with permission. *Table 17–5.* Snyder, S. H., *Madness in the brain.* New York: McGraw-Hill. Copyright 1974 by McGraw-Hill. Reprinted by permission. *Table 19–2.* Hyler, S. E., & Spitzer, R. T., Hysteria split asunder. *American Journal of Psychiatry*, 1978, *135* (12), 1500–4. Copyright, 1978, the American Psychiatric Association. Reprinted by permission.

Boxes
Box 2–1: From Upham, C. *Salem witchcraft,* 1867, cited in A. Deutsch, *The mentally ill in America: The history of the care and treatment in colonial times,* 1937. Courtesy of the National Mental Health Association. *Box 9–1:* The American Psychiatric Association, *Diagnostic and Statistical Manual of Mental Disorders,* 3rd ed. Washington, D.C.: American Psychological Association, 1980. *Box 10–2:* Diagram reprinted by permission of Hawthorne Properties (Elsevier-Dutton Publishing Co., Inc.) from *Bodily changes in pain, hunger, fear and rage* by W. B. Cannon. Copyright © 1929 by Appleton-Century Co.; 1957 by W. B. Cannon. *Box 12–1:* Reprinted by permission of the William Morris Agency, Inc. on behalf of John Kobler, author. Copyright © 1978 by John Kobler (Esquire, July 18, 1978). *Box 12–2:* Drills from Freidman, M., & Rosenman, R. H., *Type A behavior and your heart.* New York: Knopf, 1974, by Alfred A. Knopf, Inc. reprinted by permission of the publisher. *Box 13–1:* Diagram from Alloy, L. B., & Abramson, L. Y., Judgment of contingency in depressed and nondepressed students: Sadder but wiser? *Journal of Experimental Psychology: General,* 1979, *108,* 441–85. Copyright © 1979 by the American Psychological Association. Reprinted by permission of the author. *Box 13–2:* Beck Depression Inventory, from Beck, A. T., Depression: Clinical experimental and theoretical aspects. New York: Hoeber, 1967. Reprinted by permission of the author. *Box 13–4:* Shneidman, E., Suicide among the gifted. In E. S. Shneidman (Ed.), *Suicidology: Contemporary developments.* New York: Grune & Stratton, 1976. Reprinted by permission of Grune & Stratton Inc. and Edwin Shneidman. *Box 18–1:* Robins, L. N., *Deviant children grow up.* Baltimore: Williams & Wilkins, 1966. *Box 18–2:* Reprinted with permission from *Journal of Child Psychology and Psychiatry, 15,* Marchant, R., Howlin, P., Yule, W., & Rutter, M. Graded change in the treatment of the behavior of autistic children. Copyright 1974, Pergamon Press, Ltd. *Box 20–3:* Bazelon, D., New gods for old: "Efficient" courts in a democratic society. *New York University Law Review,* 1971, *46,* 653. Reprinted by permission.

Photos
Page xxiv: Photograph by Arthur Tress. *Page 4:* Photos by permission of the Bethlem Royal Hospital and The Maudsley Hospital Health Authority. *Page 44: Ettore e Andromaca,* painting by Giorgio di Chiciro. *Page 132:* Copyright Sepp Seitz 1982/Woodfin Camp. *Page 154:* From Weiss, J. M., et al., Behavioral depression produced by an uncontrollable stressor: Relationship to norepinephrine, dopamine, and serotonin levels in various regions of the rat brain. *Brain Research Review* 1981, *3,* 167–205. Reprinted by permission of Elsevier Biomedical Press B. V., Amsterdam. *Page 186:* Photograph by Arthur Tress. *Page 304:* © 1983 Stephen Shames/Black Star. *Page 358:* Photograph by Jeffrey Grosscup. *Page 460:* Photograph by Bernard Pierre Wolff/Magnum. *Page 506:* © 1981 Bill Strode/Black Star. *Page 590:* Photograph by G. M. S.